Withdrawn

HISTORICA

1000 YEARS OF OUR LIVES AND TIMES

HISTORICA

1000 YEARS OF OUR LIVES AND TIMES

Chief Consultant Geoffrey Wawro

MILLENNIUM HOUSE

FOR JULIE SILK (1965–2006), WITHOUT WHOM THIS BOOK WOULD NOT HAVE BEEN POSSIBLE

Published in 2006 by Millennium House Pty Ltd
52 Bolwarra Rd, Elanora Heights, NSW, 2101, Australia
Ph: 612 9970 6850
Fax: 612 9970 8136
Email: rightsmanager@millenniumhouse.com.au

ISBN 10: 1-921209-00-3
ISBN 13: 978-1-921209-00-0

Millennium House would like to hear from
photographers interested in supplying photographs

Color separation by Pica Digital Pte Ltd, Singapore

Printed in China

Photo credits appear on page 575

Cover:
Front (l to r): Marilyn Monroe; Mushroom cloud on
horizon; Capitol Building, Washington DC, USA; John
F. Kennedy; Astronaut on moon; Mt Rushmore National
Memorial, South Dakota, USA; Martin Luther King Jr
Back (l to r): Lord Horatio Nelson; The *Hindenburg*;
World War II medal; Unemployed woman, New York
City, USA, 1929; Vietnam War Memorial, Washington
DC, USA; Aftermath of tsunami, Sri Lanka, 2005;
Christopher Columbus

Page 1: Winston Churchill, Franklin D. Roosevelt, and
Joseph Stalin at the Yalta Conference, February, 1945
Pages 2–3: The Temple of Ramses at Abu Simbel, Nile
River, Egypt
Page 4: Pope John Paul II; Temple of Borobodur, Java,
Indonesia
Page 5: Toppling Saddam Hussein's statue, April 9,
2003, central Baghdad, Iraq
Page 7: Martin Luther King Jr at the Lincoln Memorial,
Washington DC, USA, 1963
Page 12: Section from the Bayeux Tapestry, c. 1090
Pages 22–23: The Colosseum, Rome, Italy, built c. 70 CE
Pages 32–33: The *Mir* space station complex, photo-
graphed in 1996

Images used on the cover and preliminary pages from
Getty Images and the Art Archive

Publisher	Gordon Cheers
Associate publisher	Margaret Olds
Project manager	Deborah Nixon
Chief consultant	Geoffrey Wawro
Consultants	Bronwyn Dalley
	Jonathan King
	Nicholas Southey
	G. Bruce Strang

Contributors
Loretta Barnard, Ivan Coates, Neal Drinnan,
Bruce Elder, Linda Evans, Denise Imwold,
James Inglis, Shelley Kenigsberg, Jonathan
King, John S. Major, Simon Roberts, John
Ross, Desney Shoemark, Barry Stone, Anne
Tucker, Tracy Tucker

Mapping
Damien Demaj, John Frith, Glen Vause

Editors
Loretta Barnard, Shelley Barons, Annette
Carter, Belinda Castles, Simone Coupland,
Emma Driver, Kate Etherington, Denise
Imwold, Heather Jackson, Carol Jacobson,
Oliver Laing, Carol Natsis, Deborah Nixon,
Susan Page, Rob Paratore, Janet Parker, Merry
Pearson, Jessica Perini, Marie-Louise Taylor,
Michael Wall

Researchers
Antonia Beattie, Belinda Castles, Gordon
Cheers, Marion Child, Fiona Doig, Alexis
Greenwood, Oliver Laing, Heather McNamara,
Jan Watson

Picture research
Anna Barrett, Anne Cameron, Andrew
Christopher, Denise Imwold, Rebecca Jarvis,
Oliver Laing, Raffaella Morini, Deborah Nixon,
Julie Stanton, Marie-Louise Taylor

Original design concept	Stan Lamond
Cover design	Bob Mitchell
Designers	Warwick Jacobson
	Lena Lowe
Index	Glenda Browne
	Jon Jermey
Typesetting	Susin Chow
Production	Bernard Roberts
Foreign rights	Kanagasabai Suppiah

CONSULTANTS

Chief Consultant

Dr Geoffrey Wawro is General Olinto Mark Barsanti Professor of Military History and Director of the Center for the Study of Military History at the University of North Texas in the Dallas Metroplex. From 2000 to 2005 he was Professor of Strategic Studies at the US Naval War College in Newport, Rhode Island. Dr Wawro's PhD is from Yale University, his BA Magna Cum Laude from Brown University. He was a Fulbright Scholar in Austria from 1989 to 1991, and was Visiting Professor of Strategy and Policy at the Naval War College from 1996 to 1998. From 1992 to 2000, he was Assistant and Associate Professor of History at Oakland University in Rochester, Michigan. He speaks German, French, Spanish, and Italian.

Dr Wawro has written three highly regarded books: *The Franco-Prussian War* (Cambridge, 2003), *Warfare and Society in Europe, 1792–1914* (Routledge, 2000), and *The Austro-Prussian War* (Cambridge, 1996). His fourth book, for Pen-

guin Press in 2007, will be called *Quicksand: America's Pursuit of Power in the Middle East, from the Balfour Declaration to the Bush Doctrine*. He is the North American editor of the *Cambridge Military Histories,* published by Cambridge University Press, and is a member of the *History Book Club* Review Board. Wawro has published articles in *The Journal of Military History, War in History, The International History Review, The Naval War College Review, American Scholar,* and *The European History Quarterly,* among others. He has won several academic prizes. In 2002, he shared the New Orleans Press Club Award for "Best Coverage of a Planned Event" for the live NBC/History Channel coverage of the parade and opening of the D-Day Museum Pacific Wing.

Dr Wawro lectures on military innovation and international security and is the *Naval War College Review's* "special correspondent." He is host of the History Channel programs *Hardcover History, History's Business,* and *History*

versus Hollywood. Married to Cecilia Schilling Wawro, he has two sons, Winslow and Matías, and lives in Dallas, Texas.

Consultants

Bronwyn Dalley is Chief Historian at New Zealand's Ministry for Culture and Heritage. She manages the work of the History Group, which produces histories of government policy (including war history), as well as subjects of national significance, and she also runs a major New Zealand history website. Most recently Dalley co-edited *Frontier of Dreams: The Story of New Zealand* (Hachette Livre, 2005).

Bronwyn's historical interests focus on cultural and social history, especially in the areas of crime, punishment, sexuality, and material culture. She has been a martial artist for 20 years, is a keen runner, amateur chef, and drinks and collects wine. Bronwyn lives in Wellington, New Zealand, with her partner and two cats.

Jonathan King first fell in love with history during the build up to Australia's bicentennial celebrations. A First Fleet descendant, he is a historian who spends his professional life harnessing anniversaries to bring history to life. King re-enacted the London–Sydney voyage of Australia's eleven-ship first convict fleet for the 1988 bicentennial celebrations, covering the voyage for television, radio, newspapers, and publishers. He then retraced Captain William Bligh's *Bounty* voyage, also buying the *Bounty* for Australia; Christopher Columbus's voyage to America; Ernest Shackleton's open boat escape from Antarctica to South Georgia; and Matthew Flinders's circumnavigation of Australia.

On dry land King organized centennial re-enactments of Banjo Paterson's "Waltzing Matilda" and "The Man from Snowy River," as well as Mary and Joseph's biblical journey through the Holy Land from Nazareth to Bethlehem commemorating the turn of the millennium. A father of four daughters who

has also produced 30 historical books and 20 historical documentaries—always with the support of his wife Jane—he now writes history for the *Sydney Morning Herald* for which he also leads battlefield tours.

Nicholas Southey is Senior Lecturer in the History Department of the University of South Africa, Pretoria. He is well respected as a writer and contributor to a number of books, including the *Historical Dictionary of South Africa*. He also writes journal articles on various aspects of South African history. His areas of interest include Cape history, religion and society, and the history of gender.

G. Bruce Strang is Associate Professor and Chair of the Department of History at Lakehead University in Thunder Bay, Ontario, where he lives with his wife Nancy Hennen, his son Sean, and their cat Felix. He writes on twentieth-century international relations, specializing in

the foreign policy of Italy. His first book, *On the Fiery March: Mussolini Prepares for War*, explored Italian expansionism before World War II that led to the Pact of Steel and to Italy's disastrous participation in the conflict that became World War II.

Bruce is currently working on a monograph on Italian post-war economic and political reconstruction, *The Limits of Sovereignty: Italy in the Cold War Era, 1948–1953*. He also has written on British and American foreign policy. Although his research focuses primarily on Europe, he has an abiding passion for Canadian politics, honed in countless discussions around the dinner table, in cafés, and in university halls.

Above
The ancient stone circle of Stonehenge, built between 3000 BCE and 1600 BCE, is now a World Heritage Site.

CONTRIBUTORS

Loretta Barnard is a freelance writer and editor who has worked in the publishing industry for 26 years. She holds a Master of Arts in English Literature, and gives occasional seminars on the writing process. She has contributed to a wide range of publications in a huge variety of fields, including biography, architecture, law, science, psychology, business, botany, nursing, film, and history. Her interests include music, theater, and literature.

Ivan Coates is an academic researching and teaching in the field of American history. A university medallist and winner of the Philippe Erdos Prize in History, he is also a past winner of the James Holt Award from the Australia and New Zealand American Studies Association. He is working on a PhD relating to post-war American cultural history. In the past Ivan has worked as a researcher and editor on diverse projects, including trivia board games, travel books, websites accompanying television shows, and a book on the contemporary Australian music industry.

Neal Drinnan has worked in publishing and journalism for many years and is the author of four novels—*Glove Puppet, Pussy's Bow, Quill,* and *Izzy and Eve*—as well as being a contributor and editor of *The Rough Guide to Australia* series. He has contributed short stories to a number of anthologies. He has written extensively on lifestyle and cultural issues for publishers and journals all over the world. He has a website at www.nealdrinnan.com.

Bruce Elder has been involved in writing over 60 books and he has worked as a print and radio journalist in both London and Sydney. He is an award-winning journalist (Geraldine Pascall Prize for Critical Writing, 1996) who is currently a full-time employee of the *Sydney Morning Herald*, as well as a weekly guest on ABC Radio's Tony Delroy's *Nightlife* program, which is broadcast on over 150 stations around Australia. His books include *Blood on the Wattle* (1988) which, in 2000, was nominated as one of the ten most influential works of non-fiction published in Australia in the twentieth century. Bruce is the Australian editor of *Trivial Pursuit*, and is also involved with various charities.

Linda Evans is a writer/researcher specializing in art, archaeology, and ancient history. For the past 20 years, however, she has worked with her husband, Chris Evans, in the field of animal behavior, studying how animals communicate using vocal and visual signals. This work has taken place in laboratories at Rockefeller University, New York, and the University of California, Davis, in the United States and, most recently, at Macquarie University in Sydney, Australia. She has a Masters degree in Egyptology and has just completed her doctoral dissertation on the representation of animal behavior in ancient Egyptian tomb paintings. She has also published a number of papers on the depiction of animals in the ancient world.

Denise Imwold is a writer and editor, who has also worked for many years as a bookseller. She studied literature and anthropology at Macquarie University, Sydney, where she received a Bachelor of Arts, as well as a Postgraduate Diploma in Editing and Publishing. Denise has contributed to a wide range of publications in fields such as arts and entertainment, travel, sport, gardening, health, and spirituality. Recent titles include *Mythology: Myths, Legends, and Fantasies* (2003); *Cut!—Hollywood Murders, Accidents, and Other Tragedies* (2005); and *501 Must-Read Books* (2006). In her spare time, Denise enjoys reading, walking, swimming, traveling, and animals, and has nearly completed her first novel.

James Inglis specializes in reviews, interviews, and opinion pieces, and has been published in various Australian national and state newspapers and periodicals. His interests include adult learning, workplace training design and presentation, and analysis of language—particularly where it is abused to conceal ulterior motives.

Shelley Kenigsberg has a background in teaching and writing, and has worked in production, editorial, and publishing roles for major educational and trade publishers for the past 24 years. She is active in the professional training of editors, state and national editors' societies, and has coordinated and taught the Macleay College Book Editing and Publishing Diploma for the past 13 years.

John S. Major earned his PhD degree in History and East Asian Languages at Harvard University. He taught East Asian history at Dartmouth College from 1971 to 1984 and later was director of the China Council of the Asia Society. He is currently an independent scholar and editor and also serves as Senior Lecturer at the China Institute, New York. A specialist in the intellectual history of early China, he is the author or editor of many scholarly books and general-interest books on Asia, including *Heaven and Earth in Early Han Thought* (1993); *Defining Chu: Image and Reality in Ancient China* (1999); and *The Asian World, 900–1500* (with Roger V. DesForges, 2005). John has also published extensively in the field of world literature; he is the co-author, with Clifton Fadiman, of *The New Lifetime Reading Plan* (1997) and co-editor, with Katharine Washburn, of *World Poetry: An Anthology of Verse from Antiquity to Our Time* (1998).

Simon Roberts lives in Hobart, Tasmania, Australia. He works with the counter-terrorism unit of Tasmania Police and occasionally contributes to books on subjects such as mythology and history. He worked as an air traffic controller in Melbourne and Brisbane before studying Commerce and Law. Simon traveled widely in Asia, Europe, and the Middle East before settling back in Tasmania. He recently purchased a house—less than 100 meters from the hospital in Hobart in which he was born—and has almost completed renovating it.

Desney Shoemark pursues her combined passions and careers as a writer and book editor in the serene environment of the secluded Macdonald River Valley, just northwest of Sydney, Australia. For the past 30 years or so, she has worked in an editorial and project management capacity for many of major educational and general trade book publishers, as well as being the inaugural teacher and coordinator of the highly regarded Macleay College Diploma in Book Editing and Publishing. These days, she revels in a simple country life and enjoys relaxed time with family and friends.

Barry Stone is a feature writer and photographer and a graduate of the Australian College of Journalism. He currently resides in Sydney where he has been a long time contributor of feature stories to some of Australia's largest daily newspapers including Brisbane's *Sunday Mail,*

the *Sun-Herald* and the *Canberra Times*. His photographic images, usually concerned with the economic and social history of cities and regions, have been exhibited in regional art galleries throughout New South Wales. A recent exhibition, entitled "Smalltown USA," focused on the social and economic trends of rural America over the past 80 years.

Anne Tucker, who was born and raised in Toronto, Ontario, Canada, has vivid childhood memories of Silver Lake on Manitoulin Island (Lake Huron) where she spent her summers. Anne spent her late teens and early twenties in Vancouver, then became interested in Eastern thought, and traveled to India to immerse herself in that rich culture. Returning to Canada in 1987, she graduated from the University of Toronto, and became a Waldorf (Rudolf Steiner) teacher. She taught for three years at the Toronto Waldorf School before moving to Australia in 1999. Anne returned to Canada in 2004 in order to complete an Education Degree in Thunder Bay.

Tracy Tucker has worked in publishing for more than 20 years. She now divides her time between working as a book editor and project manager, counseling people in crisis, and finishing the house she has been building for the past four years. In her spare time she enjoys writing about local issues and delving into history. To borrow the words of historian E. A. Freeman, she believes that "history is past politics, and politics is present history."

Right
Influential physicist Albert Einstein (1879-1955) was one of the greatest minds of modern times.

UBI·NUNTII WILIELMI· DUCIS· VEN

TUROLD

HIC VENIT·NUNTIUS·AD WIL
GELMUM DUCEM

Contents

About This Book

Historica is both a narration and an interpretation of history from the year 1000. It provides a kaleidoscopic view of the major events of the last one thousand years, events that have shaped our history.

The book begins with an introductory "time capsule" summary of the history of the world before the year 999, summarizing the development of humankind, the spread of humans across the planet, and giving a selection of key events leading up to the second millennium.

The main part of *Historica* presents the evolution of people's lives over the last one thousand years, and shows just how dramatically the world has changed in this time. It tells the story of wars, discoveries, inventions, invasions, exploration, and creative endeavors, and the amazing people who played a key part in those events that have brought us to where we are today.

Examining the world from the year 1000 through to the present, *Historica* is divided into sections, or modules, based on periods of time. Within each section there are four streams:

Milestones—politics, rulers, exploration, wars, assassinations, disasters, coronations, abdications

Science and Technology—invention, discovery, physics, chemistry, medicine, mathematics, geology, anthropology, archeology, astronomy

The Arts—painting, literature, music, dance, architecture, theater, film

Lifestyle—fashion, food, entertainment, leisure, sport, education and learning, fads and eccentricities

Up to 1900, there are four pages per stream (Milestones, Science and Technology, The Arts, and Lifestyle); from 1900 to the present, there is one page dedicated to each year for the Milestones, and four pages for the other streams. Generally, events are reported on or around the date they took place, in a journalistic style designed to give a sense of immediacy, as dramatic as today's news stories. Where possible, the place names are given as they would have been at the time (for example, New France, Peking, or Rhodesia).

Historica's user-friendliness is due in no small part to its clear concise design—you can read through a section systematically, or sample little snippets of text at random. Each module contains the main news stories, enhanced by illustrations and photographs, thoughtfully chosen to give a feeling for the period, as well as for their significance and visual appeal. If an image does not relate to an article, a tinted border surrounds it.

The Key Events timeline gives a brief outline of major events in the period and allows a comparison with developments in different parts of the world.

Another interesting inclusion throughout the pages is the Time Out, a quirky and sometimes amusing piece of information or trivia. Informative maps contribute to the understanding of major occurrences such as the Crusades, Boers' Great Trek, or Mao Tse-tung's Long March. Other features include quotes (usually pithy and sometimes provocative) from leading figures of their respective period; and fact files (which highlight artistic, scientific, and sporting achievements, or provide a list of political and religious leaders of the time).

For ready reference, the back of the book includes a summary of the Milestones timelines to give a snapshot of the key events. The extensive index makes it easy to locate subjects of interest.

Historica brings the world's major events and personalities to your fingertips, and is sure to become a key reference book in homes, libraries, and classrooms everywhere for decades to come.

"IF MEN COULD LEARN FROM HISTORY, WHAT LESSONS IT MIGHT TEACH US!"

SAMUEL TAYLOR COLERIDGE (1772–1834), ENGLISH POET

1875–1899

Benjamin Disraeli

Fact files highlight artistic, scientific, and sporting achievements, or provide a list of political and religious leaders of the time.

Quotes amuse, provoke, or inspire, and often reflect the attitudes of the period.

Maps enhance readers' understanding of major occurrences.

1980s

Alfred Hitchcock

"Master of Suspense" Dies of Kidney Failure

Los Angeles, USA, April 29, 1980: One of the world's most prolific and greatly admired directors, the "Master of Suspense" Alfred Hitchcock, has died of kidney failure today, aged 80.

Hitchcock was born and raised in working-class London. Fascinated with motion pictures from his teenage years, he became a title designer at the Famous Players-Lasky Studio in London. His directorial debut was *The Lodger* (1926), and over the next 13 years he made his mark on British cinema with such classics as *The Man Who Knew Too Much* (1934), and *The 39 Steps* (1935).

His first Hollywood film was *Rebecca* (1940), and for several decades he thrilled movie-goers with one great film after another, including *Spellbound* (1945), *Strangers on a Train* (1951), *Rear Window* (1954), *To Catch a Thief* (1955), *Vertigo* (1958), *Psycho* (1960), and *The Birds* (1963).

Hitchcock's final film was *Family Plot* (1976). There are several common threads in Hitchcock movies: the beautiful ice-blonde heroine, the theme of mistaken identity, and the director himself making brief cameo appearances.

Alfred Hitchcock Presents was a popular TV series from 1955 to 1962, best remembered for Hitchcock's rotund silhouette, his witty chats with the audience, and the suitably spooky theme music.

Hitchcock is highly regarded for his innovative editing and camera techniques, and he has influenced a number of directors. He is a recipient of many honors and awards, including Knight Commander of the Order of the British Empire.

"THE BEST ROCK AND ROLL MUSIC ENCAPSULATES A CERTAIN HIGH ENERGY, AN ANGRINESS, WHETHER ON RECORD OR ONSTAGE. ROCK 'N' ROLL IS ONLY ROCK 'N' ROLL IF IT'S NOT SAFE."

MICK JAGGER (b. 1943), ENGLISH SINGER, MEMBER OF THE ROLLING STONES, C. 1981

John Lennon signs an autograph for a fan.

John Lenn[on] Outside H[...]

New York, USA, [...] height of Beatl[...] quoted as sayin[...] off by a loony." [...] almost flippant[...]

car to Rooseve[...] Hospital, but d[...] shortly afterwa[...]

The murder[...] been identified[...] year-old Mark [...] Chapman, wh[...] been stalking Lennon for some ti[...] had even asked him for his autog[...] earlier that day—Lennon had gra[...] obliged. After the shooting, Chap[...] down in front of the building and [...] the novel *The Catcher in the Rye*.

John Winston Lennon was bor[...] Liverpool, England, on October 9[...] After attending Liverpool College[...] he realized his great love was rock[...] and eventually joined forces with [...] Liverpudlians Paul McCartney, R[...] Starr, and George Harrison to for[...] The Beatles. They became a pop-c[...] phenomenon, and in 1966 Lenno[...] a huge stir when he claimed The B[...] were more popular than Jesus Chr[...]

Due to creative and personal d[...] ences, The Beatles split up in 197[...] this time Lennon had married his [...] wife, Japanese artist Yoko Ono, an[...] pair had become famous for their [...] ins for Peace." As a solo artist, Le[...]

260

Key Eve[...]

Los Angeles, USA, April 29, 1980: Alfred Hitchcock dies, aged 80.
Mexico, November 7, 1980: Screen tough guy Steve McQueen, best known for his roles in *The Great Escape* and *Bullitt*, dies aged 50.
USA, November 21, 1980: Soap opera "Dallas" breaks viewing records as the question "Who shot JR?" is answered.
New York, USA, December 8, 1980: John Lennon is shot dead outside his home.

Miami, USA, May 11, 1981: Bob Marley, Jamaican reggae star, dies of cancer, aged 36.
USA, June 12, 1981: *Raiders of the Lost Ark* starring Harrison Ford is released.
USA, August 1, 1981: The first music video shown on MTV is "Video Killed the Radio Star" by The Buggles.
UK, October 12, 1981: *Brideshead Revisited* starring Jeremy Irons and Phoebe Nicholls premières.

New York, USA, February 17, 1982: Jazz pianist Thelonious Monk dies.
Hollywood, USA, March 5, 1982: John Belushi, star of *The Blues Brothers*, dies of a drug overdose.
USA, June 11, 1982: Steven Spielberg's *ET The Extra Terrestrial* is released.
London, England, October 11, 1982: Author Thomas Keneally wins the Booker Prize for *Schindler's Ark*.
Sweden, December 10, 1982: Colombian magic realist author Gabriel García Márquez receives the Nobel Prize for Literature.

464

milestones milestones **1875–1899**

...nged at ... Gaol

...ember 11, 1880: ...n bushranger Ned ... Old Melbourne ...ree policemen at ...ctober 1878. ... the group became ...ks. One of these ...lderie in New ...y captured the ...nade off with ... the bank's vaults. ...gether armor as ...e bullets. They ...l plates together ...tion soon be-

...lled a police ... police traced ...p of Glenrowan, ...that lasted half ...other members ...ly himself was ...tured, and today, ... paid the ultimate ...s years on the run.

...ed by ...on

...ndies, August 27, ...c eruption has ...of Rakata in the ...ava and Sumatra. ...ed the greatest ...story. Massive tidal ...oastal villages ...rakatoa volcano ...death toll esti-...000. ...esi, to the north-... washed out to ...n was uprooted.

Seventy-five percent of the land area of Rakata has disappeared.

Tidal gauges in Aden, Yemen, recorded the wave as reaching the Yemen shoreline in only 12 hours, and the eruption was heard as far away as Rodriguez Island, some 2,800 miles (4,480 km) distant, in the Indian Ocean. It is also being reported that ash from the eruption is falling on Singapore.

There were four distinct explosions, the last of which opened fissures in the walls of the volcano, allowing sea water to flood the subterranean magma chamber. The resultant explosion virtually destroyed the island.

Pyroclastic flows occur when the eruption column, which contains vast amounts of ash, dust, and rock, collapses under its own weight when gases erupting from the volcano can no longer support the column. Traveling at nearly 100 mph (160 kph), these flows raced down the sides of the volcano and, incredibly, had enough heat and momentum to continue across the waters of the Sunda Strait and kill 2,000 people 25 miles (40 km) away in Sumatra.

Shock waves from the eruption at Krakatoa were felt across the world.

French Extend Influence in Indochina

Hue, Vietnam, June 6, 1884: Vietnamese scholar–officials have been forced into signing the Treaty of Hue, confirming the Harmand Convention signed last year. A Treaty of Protectorate signed at the convention established a French protectorate over northern and central Vietnam, formally ending Vietnam's indpendence. The French have been extending their influence in Vietnam since 1858 when their warships first fired on Vietnamese ports.

Borneo
INDONESIA
Java Sea
Jakarta
...NESIA
Java

By June 1862 Emperor Tu Duc had signed a treaty with the French which ceded control of three provinces around Gia Dinh, which was renamed Saigon by the French. Hue fell to French forces last year, not long after the Emperor's death.

It is believed the signing of the Treaty of Hue will enable the French to deal more effectively with continual disruptions by China to French trading arrangements in the country's north.

Indian Resistance Ends at Wounded Knee

South Dakota, USA, January 15, 1891: Largely as a result of the recent massacre at Wounded Knee and the subsequent Indian attack on the 7th Cavalry at White Clay Creek, representatives of the Sioux nation laid down their arms today, which has brought to an end decades of hostility throughout the Great Plains.

The recent rise in Indian militancy resulting from the "Ghost Dance" phenomenon is being seen as heightening tensions, particularly in regard to the Lakota Sioux, and is being viewed as a key ingredient in the lead-up to Wounded Knee. This "Ghost Dance" must be understood if any sense is to be made of this appalling slaughter of the innocents.

A young Paiute mystic named Wovoka, who was born in Nevada in the 1850s and raised by a white rancher, is claimed to have fallen into a trance in 1889.

In his trance he was taken to the spirit world and given a vision of a New Age for the Indian people, where generation after generation of Indians slain in combat would be reborn. It was a world in which buffalo had returned to the plains in their millions, and one where the white man had disappeared.

A ritualistic dance emerged that encompassed these new beliefs—the

Seats of Power

China Qing Dynasty: Tongzhi (reigned 1861–1875); Guangxu (1875–1908).
France Patrice de MacMahon (1873–1879); Jules Grevy (1879–1887); Sadie Carnot (1887–1894); Jean Casimir-Perier (1894–1895); Felix Faure (1895–1899); Emile Loubet (1899–1906).
Japan Modern Japan: Meiji (reigned 1867–1912).
Kingdom of Great Britain Victoria (reigned 1837–1901).
Portugal Brigantine Dynasty: Luis I (reigned 1861–1889); Carlos (1889–1908).
Russia Emperors: Alexander II (reigned 1855–1881); Alexander III (1881–1894); Nicholas II (1894–1917).
Spain Bourbon Dynasty: Alfonso XII (reigned 1874–1885); Alfonso XIII (1886–1931).
Thailand Chakri Dynasty: Rama V (reigned 1868–1910).
Zulu Nation Cetshwayo kaMpande (reigned 1872–1884); Dinizulu kaCetshwayo (1884–1913).

Ghost Dance. It spread throughout the west, particularly among the recently defeated Indians of the Great Plains. The Sioux sent a delegation to visit Wovoka in 1889, and when they returned to their reservations, the dance began to take on militant overtones. Sioux apostles began talking of the day when they would be strong enough to wage all-out war on the white man, and they began fashioning sacred "ghost shirts," which were believed to have the power to stop bullets.

This was the climate of fear and distrust that characterized the months leading up to December 28, 1890.

By November, about 3,000 Indians had assembled on a plateau at the northwest corner of Pine Ridge in an impregnable area known as "the stronghold." Chief Big Foot of the Miniconjou Sioux was on his way there with 350 of his people to persuade the stronghold inhabitants to surrender. On December 28, unaware of this and believing Big Foot to be a Ghost Dancer, 500 men of the 7th Cavalry, under the command of Colonel James Forsyth, surrounded Big Foot. In addition, four cannons capable of rapid fire, called Hotchkiss guns, were set up on the hills around his camp.

The next morning the soldiers entered the camp, demanding that the Sioux hand over their weapons. A medicine man called Yellow Bird objected. He exhorted the others to don their sacred shirts. "The bullets will not hurt you," he was heard to say to the other men.

Another Miniconjou raised his rifle over his head, saying the rifle had cost him a lot of money and he was not prepared to part with it. A shot rang out, and immediately the soldiers began firing into the Indian encampment. An hour later the guns stopped.

Hundreds of Indian men, women, and children lay dead. Twenty-five soldiers were also killed, many by the indiscriminate shelling of their own Hotchkiss guns. Trails of blood trickled along the ground, heading out of camp toward the gulches.

Three days later, a burial party was sent to pull the frozen Indians out from under a blanket of snow. Many of the corpses were naked. Soldiers had stripped the "ghost shirts" from the dead to take home as souvenirs of the encounter.

Colonel Forsyth was relieved of his command at a court of inquiry, although he was later reinstated.

The massacre caused both hostile and friendly Sioux factions to unite, and on December 30, Sioux warriors under Kicking Bear attacked the 7th Cavalry along White Clay Creek. Casualties were minimal, and today Kicking Bear became the last Lakota warrior to surrender to the federal government.

Dreyfus Receives Pardon from French President

Paris, France, September 30, 1899: Earlier this month President Emile Loubet pardoned Alfred Dreyfus following his five-year battle to clear his name of the charge of having been a spy for Germany.

Emile Zola

In 1894 Captain Alfred Dreyfus was sentenced to life imprisonment after being found guilty of the charges. A French spy in the German embassy had discovered a handwritten schedule detailing secret French documents. In the search for the traitor, suspicion fell upon Dreyfus, an Alsatian Jew, who strongly protested his innocence. Tried in-camera by a French court-martial and found guilty, he was deported to the French penal settlement of Devil's Island, off the coast of French Guyana. The French army at this time was influenced heavily

Charged with spying, Alfred Dreyfus stands trial at Rennes.

by monarchists and Catholics—and, it has been suggested, a degree of anti-Semitism as well.

There was a push to reopen the case in 1896, when evidence came to light that the culprit may in fact have been Major Ferdinand Esterhazy, who was deeply in debt. Esterhazy was tried and acquitted in a trial that took only minutes. Emile Zola, a supporter of Dreyfus, wrote an open letter to the president of the French republic claiming that the judges had received orders from the war office to acquit Esterhazy. Zola himself was then tried for libel and sentenced to jail, but he escaped to England. It was then revealed that much of the evidence against Dreyfus had been forged by a Colonel Henry of Army Intelligence.

After a second trial in 1899, Dreyfus was again found guilty "with extenuating circumstances" and sent back to Devil's Island. The recent pardon has made it possible for him to return to Paris.

The so-called "Dreyfus Affair" had a major impact upon France as a nation, pitting radicals, republicans, and socialists against the church and army.

On February 15, 1898, while on a friendly visit to Cuba, the USS *Maine* was destroyed by an explosion.

261

...ion and directed by ...nd Michael Lindsay-... finest-quality produc-...or the small screen. ...was adapted by John ...elyn Waugh's 1945 ... with world-weary ...es Ryder (Jeremy Irons) ...ideshead mansion ...e. He recounts the ...nship with the home, ...o be gradually en-...ed by its owners, the ...nain family: decadent

...rs Jeremy Irons and Diana Quick.

Thomas Keneally Wins Booker Prize

London, England, November 29, 1982: Thomas Keneally has become the first Australian to win the UK's prestigious Booker Prize with his novel, *Schindler's Ark*.

In 1980 Keneally was waiting for his credit card to be approved in a luggage store in Beverly Hills, California. The store owner, Poldek Pfefferberg, told Keneally that he and his wife were among some 1,200 Jews in World War II who were saved from Hitler by one Oskar Schindler.

Keneally tracked down and interviewed some 50 of Schindler's survivors. Schindler died in 1974, but Keneally obtained Schindler's original list of names of Jews who were rescued by him. Keneally calls the book a "documentary novel." It is a well researched, true account which employs some of the storytelling devices of fiction. Most critics agree that it lies somewhere between historical fiction and historical document. Keneally says only the conversations are fictional, and that

USA under the title *Schindler's List*.

Truman Capote Dies

Los Angeles, USA, August 25, 1984: Truman Capote, the author of the bestselling 1966 "non-fiction novel" *In Cold Blood*, has died of phlebitis and liver failure.

time out

The French designer Philippe Starck designed an apartment in the Palais de l'Elysée for Madame Mitterand. He established his first design firm in 1968, specializing in inflatable objects, and in 1969 became the art director of his firm along with Pierre Cardin.

Born on September 30, 1924, in New Orleans, his wandering mother often left him to stay with relatives in Monroeville, Alabama, where he befriended the future author of the classic *To Kill a Mockingbird*, Harper Lee (who later modeled the character of Dill on the young Truman).

At 17, Capote began work as a copy boy at the *New Yorker* magazine. His first published short story, "Miriam," won an O. Henry Award. In 1948, his first novel, *Other Voices, Other Rooms* was published. He reached a wider audience with *Breakfast at Tiffany's* in 1958, subsequently adapted to the much-loved film starring Audrey Hepburn.

The success of *Tiffany's* gave Capote a foot in-to the door of New York society,

victims in Ethiopia after seeing a news report on the BBC. Geldof penned the lyrics, and Midge Ure from Ultravox wrote the music.

On November 25, the supergroup that Geldof dubbed "Band Aid" gathered in a London studio, recording the song in just one day. As well as Geldof and Ure, the group included Phil Collins, Paul Young, George Michael, Sting, David Bowie, Paul McCartney, members of Bananarama, U2, Culture Club, Spandau Ballet, and Duran Duran, among others.

NURSES
OFFICE

Steven Spielberg directs Henry Thomas on the set of the film *ET*.

Key Events

...ew York, USA, February, 1984: Te ...aori exhibition opens to acclaim at ...e Metropolitan Museum of Art.
...s Angeles, USA, April 1, 1984: ...ul singer Marvin Gaye is shot dead ... his father, a priest, after a fight.
...nberra, Australia, April 12, 1984: ...dvance Australia Fair" is restored ... Australia's national anthem.
...s Angeles, USA, August 25, ...84: Truman Capote dies, aged 59.
...K, December 14, 1984: Britain's ...p pop stars record "Do They Know ...s Christmas" to raise funds for ...hiopia.

Saint-Paul, France, March 28, 1985: Marc Chagall, Jewish Belarussian painter often associated with the surrealist movement, dies, aged 97.
London, England, and Philadelphia, USA, July 13, 1985: Bob Geldof has raised $40 million to help the starving in Africa with two *Live Aid* concerts.
USA, October 12, 1985: Orson Wells dies aged 70. This follows Rock Hudson's death from AIDS on October 2 and Yul Brynner from lung cancer, aged 65.

Paris, France, April 14, 1986: Simone de Beauvoir dies, aged 78.
Australia, April 30, 1986: Paul Hogan's *Crocodile Dundee* is a worldwide box office smash, exporting an Aussie larrikin to the world.
UK, August 31, 1986: Modernist sculptor Henry Moore dies, leaving behind a rich (and heavy) body of work.
Stockholm, Sweden, October, 1986: Nigerian Wole Soyinka, poet, dramatist, and author, is awarded the Nobel Prize for Literature, the first African to be honored.

New York, USA, February 22, 1987: The multimedia artist Andy Warhol dies following gall bladder surgery, aged 59.
Rhode Island, USA, August 28, 1987: Actor and film director John Huston dies from emphysema, aged 81. His directorial debut was *The Maltese Falcon*.
New York, USA, November 11, 1987: Vincent Van Gogh's *Irises* sells for $53.9 million at Sotheby's.

Sydney, Australia, February 28, 1988: Author Kylie Tennant dies.
Wembley, England, July 18, 1988: Eric Clapton, Stevie Wonder, and Dire Straits join with others to commemorate the 70th birthday of Nelson Mandela.
UK, September 26, 1988: Penguin publishes Salman Rushdie's *The Satanic Verses*.
UK, October, 1988: *Oscar and Lucinda* by Australian author Peter Carey wins the Booker Prize.

Figueras, Spain, January 23, 1989: Iconic surrealist artist Salvador Dali dies aged 84.
Tehran, Iran, February 14, 1989: A *fatwa* (death sentence) is issued against Salman Rushdie for *The Satanic Verses*.
London, England, May 9, 1989: Pablo Picasso's self portrait sells for $47.9 million at auction.
London, England, July 11, 1989: Sir Laurence Olivier dies, aged 82.
Paris, France, December 22, 1989: Irish playwright, novelist, and poet Samuel Beckett dies, aged 83.

465

Time Out is a quirky and sometimes humorous piece of information or trivia.

Key Events timeline gives a brief summary of major events in the period and allows comparison with developments in different parts of the world.

History: Our Heritage

Right
A German map showing Christopher Columbus's voyages to the New World.

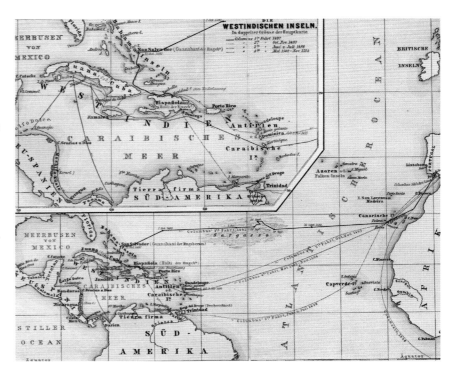

Below
A fifteenth-century painting of Jesus Christ meeting St Peter.

Below
Jacques Marquette was the first European to explore the mighty Mississippi River.

Let's face it! Reading history can be like reading the telephone book. It can be a blizzard of unconnected, unfamiliar names and places that quickly melt into that mental space where we deposit everything else that is perishable. There has to be a better way to transmit and ingrain the beauty, drama, and dash of history. History is, after all is said and done, the lifeblood of society, culture, and human experience. Nations and people are what and who they are because of their historical experience. Why, then, is the study of history so very often classed as "dull," "forgettable," or even "boring?"

Perhaps because it has never been presented quite like this. *Historica* does something remarkable—it narrates and interprets history with the immediacy of today's blog or newspaper. We follow the Great Schism of the Catholic Church in the eleventh century as if it were playing out before our eyes. This is beneficial on a number of counts. First, it is gripping. Second, it forces the historians who have written this book to cast out the assumptions that so often leave general readers in the dark. They must explain everything afresh. Thus, we learn succinctly just *why* the Great Schism occurred. There were five equal Catholic bishops or patriarchs

until the bishop of Rome claimed superior authority because of his descent from St Peter and his seat in the old imperial capital. Predictably, his rivals in Constantinople, Jerusalem, Antioch, and Alexandria rejected that claim with some of their own, and broke away to form an Eastern "Orthodox" church; the bishop of Rome became Pope of a Western "Catholic" church purged of its Eastern patriarchs. Despite their majestic pretensions, popes were mere mortals, and utterly fallible. *Historica* tells us how the Catholic Church decided that priests could not marry. It was because a single, rather sour man—Pope Gregory VII—decided that they couldn't. Certainly the Bible did not support Gregory's view: "It behooves thus a bishop to be blameless, the husband of one wife." But Gregory had a weapon—clerical salaries—and he simply stopped paying married priests.

Historica repeatedly reminds us of another essential truth—that history is made by men and women full of raging passions and prejudices. Bygone monarchs, philosophers, generals, and courtiers were not cleaner, smoother, or nicer because they preceded us in times that we wrongly assume were played by different rules than we play today. No, the men and women of history were as vicious and small-minded or, in some cases, as noble and high-minded as we are today. That is how names were made and the notion of celebrity coined. Peter Paul Rubens became Sir Peter Paul Rubens not just because of his talent for painting, drawing, and sculpture, but also because of his very successful forays

from Green Bay, Wisconsin, to the Gulf of Mexico and back. The star pupil in mathematics discovered (for Europeans, at any rate), paddled, and mapped the Mississippi River. That is how the world was slowly unfolded, like a map. On the other side of the globe, history moved in the opposite direction, leaving cultural imprints that are still visible today. The Japanese soldier-philosopher Yamaga Soko published (in 1685) his principles called *bushido*— "the way of the warrior." Samurai—the "superior men" of the soldier class— would make the transition from mere soldiery to general political and cultural leadership. The Japanese would be trained to obey orders, suppress their fears and individuality, endure privations, and even die for their leaders. Three centuries later, William Whyte published his bestselling *Organization Man,* which warned Americans that they had voluntarily suppressed *their* individuality to become corporate samurai—not charismatic shoguns like *Wall Street's* mythical Gordon Gecko, but cowardly, materialistic, white collar conformists obsessed with "fitting in" above everything else. This is how great

into diplomacy, when he brokered peace treaties between Spain, England, and the Dutch Republic.

William Harvey and Marcello Malpighi shocked the staid seventeenth-century establishment by dissecting animals and corpses and using primitive microscopes to explain how blood circulated from the arteries to the capillaries to the veins. That is how scientific discoveries were implemented. Louis Joliet was a restless, brilliant, French student afflicted with wanderlust. He left his Jesuit school and struck out into the North American wilderness, eventually paddling 2,500 miles (4,000 km)

powers, economies, and empires were constructed, institutionalized, sidetracked, or sometimes set back.

Visit art museums and you are struck by the difference between routine and genius. *Historica* places you on the bridge between the two. Great artists prevailed over stale orthodoxy. Rembrandt shattered the stiff formality of the Amsterdam school. His muscular, twitching, fearsome canvases, picked out with shafts of light and murky shadows that pulled the viewer in for a closer look, enlivened and humanized art forever. We meet Thomas Aquinas—a rare man indeed, in that the

intr duction

Above
The first stone for the Pont Neuf, the oldest standing bridge in Paris, France, was laid in 1578.

Right
One of the greatest composers the world has ever known, the music of Ludwig van Beethoven (1770-1827) remains popular to this day.

thirteenth-century thinker turned down the lucrative Archbishopric of Naples to pursue his unremunerative theological studies. Beethoven's famous Ninth Symphony is a howling thundering rebuke to the sweet arias of Rossini, whom an ageing Beethoven accuses of coating the popular taste in music with sugar, and spoiling it.

History is so often presented in morsels: European history, Asian history, Middle Eastern history, American history, Latin American history. By reading history in this way we lose sight of its essential interconnectedness. *Historica* throws the morsels back into the pot with fascinating results. On a single,

brilliantly illustrated page we see the Turkic Seljuks rampaging across the Middle East to absorb Persia, Syria, Iraq, and Palestine; at the other end of the Mediterranean, El Cid flings the Arabs out of Valencia and Pope Urban II calls for a "crusade" to evict the Seljuks from the Holy Land. The two cultures, Western and Eastern, Christian and Muslim, then collide in what is clearly a clash of great civilizations, made all the more combustible by the addition of Chinese gunpowder.

But readers today will be surprised at the nature of this clash. In the eleventh century the Muslims were renowned for their superior

Braille invents a method for blind people to read and write. This is world history—the sensation of simultaneous crisscrossing developments all over the globe that carve the world into quite different zones of culture, politics, and behavior.

History is something you feel in your skin and under your feet when you travel. But how direly handicapped most travelers are. They look at things and have no ability to place them in context. *Historica* helps here too. We are present at the opening of the Pont Neuf across the Seine in Paris, which was named the "New Bridge" when it was finished in 1606. Wooden arms were projected from the Seine's left and right banks, then paved and bricked over as part of an early modern "beautification" campaign. Were you to board the Orient Express in Paris and ride the rails to Istanbul, you would alight to the shimmering Blue Mosque, which was completed at the same time as the Pont Neuf. Keep going east and you hit another seventeenth-century masterpiece—the "world's most beautiful building." The white marble Taj Mahal, built by the Muslim Mogul, Shah Jahan, involved 20,000 engineers, carvers, artists, and workmen for 22 long years. *Historica* places these marvels beside each other, giving readers the ability to follow and contrast the advances of civilization.

science, art, and culture—astronomy, *al-Jabr* (algebra), medicine, botany, and chemistry—as well as for their religious fervor. Fast forward to the nineteenth century—within a few pages Ned Ludd orders Lancashire textile workers to smash the steam looms and cropping frames that might put them out of work, Goethe's Faust searches for the "meaning of life," Napoleon is defeated at Waterloo, Robert Stuart finds the South Pass through the Rockies in Wyoming (completing the Oregon Trail and opening America to westward expansion), the Turks pitilessly slaughter the entire population of the the Aegean island of Chios, Simón Bolívar struggles through the jungles of Colombia to locate and defeat the Spanish army, Thomas Raffles begins building the speculative little "free port" at Singapore, and Louis

For a Westerner—particularly those from the roistering new countries of America, Australia, and

introduction

Right
The Venus de Milo, one of the Louvre Museum's most famous exhibits, was discovered by a Greek peasant on the island of Melos in 1820.

Above
Singapore's Raffles Hotel retains the colonial charm of the period in which it was first built.

New Zealand—the overall effect can be humbling. When the last stones were being placed in the Taj Mahal, when the Ile de Cité coursed with pedestrians headed for the Pont Neuf, and when hordes of faithful prostrated themselves in the Blue Mosque, John Harvard took his last breath and died, leaving £200 and a roomful of books to the clerics and teachers of an obscure little school in Massachusetts. Or take the case of rich Singapore. It was just a tiny sheltered island at the tip of the Malay Peninsula in 1819 when Sir Thomas Raffles invested in a little free trade port there. The pundits laughed at Raffles: Even with its no-tax policies, the port would never make it. The surrounding Dutch would snuff it out. *Historica* recasts this ancient wager as front-page news: "Raffles is said to have a grand plan to make Singapore one of the biggest ports in the world." Amen to that.

The lessons of history are frequently clouded by "presentism," the instinct to stretch today's virtues and assumptions back to the past. *Historica* remedies that pernicious tendency by recreating events in their broad actual context. Puritans are killjoys, who try to stop King James I from legalizing sports and playing games on Sundays. France's defense of its language and culture is not a spiteful, futile, rearguard action against words like "computer," "internet," and "hamburger," but a rigorous intellectual exercise dating back (at least) to Cardinal Richelieu, his *Académie Française,* and the culture war waged around Pierre Corneille's *Le Cid.*

Similarly, the demand by developing countries for the return of their cultural artifacts must be weighed against the history of the artifacts themselves. The Rosetta

Right
A seventeenth-century depiction of a meeting between England's King James I and the Puritans.

PURITANS BEFORE JAMES I.

Stone, carved by the Greek Ptolemies in 196 BCE, was found in the Egyptian port of Rosetta in 1799 by Captain Pierre Broussard, who forwarded the stone on to the safekeeping of the British Museum, where a French Egyptologist later deciphered it. The Louvre's spectacular Venus de Milo was unearthed in 1820 on the Greek Island of Melos by a peasant named Yorgos, who hid the gorgeously wrought statue—which stood 6 1/2 feet (2 m) tall—in a cave, where it was discovered and confiscated by a meddlesome Turkish official. A French naval officer got wind of the affair, procured the marble statue and sent it on its way to Paris. To whom should the statue belong? Melos, Athens, Istanbul, or Paris? What would have happened to the Venus had the Frenchman not bought her from the Turk, or had Yorgos the Greek fallen from an olive tree and left her secretly interred forever? Who has the soundest claim to the Rosetta Stone? History—not nationalist feelings—must be called in to arbitrate.

Finally, history is good clean fun. It is rife with discoveries that make you sit back and smile. The world's most famous soft drink was invented in 1886 by an accident of Southern Baptist marauding. John Pemberton was forced by the prohibitionist city fathers of Fulton County, Georgia to replace the wine in his only moderately successful "Wine Cola" with Colombian coca leaves. Now there was a pause that refreshed! Drinkers guzzled his "Coca Cola"—they delightedly called it "brain tonic"—and rued the eventual switchover to caffeine and corn syrup. Everyone has heard about Orson Welles's hugely successful 1938 *The War of the Worlds* radio play, which in the United States inspired mass panic and gullibility with its reports of Martian attacks, poison gas clouds, and "death rays" in New Jersey. But what about the many thousands of British BBC viewers who gobbled—hook, line, and sinker—a 1957 April Fool's Day

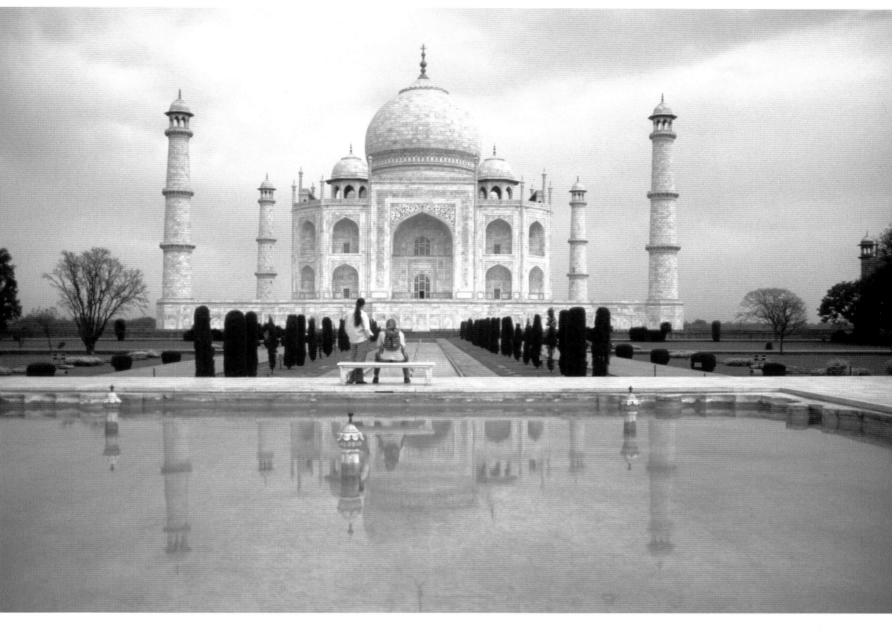

television special about the year's "spaghetti harvest" in southern Europe. The BBC showed images of peasant women picking strands of limp pasta off tree branches,

and viewers phoned in asking where they might purchase their own "spaghetti bushes." That was only in 1957! Spaghetti was plainly still as exotic as sushi, pizza, kebabs, or couscous.

There are many ways in which to imbibe history—in archives "at the source," in scholarly monographs assembled from original documents, in popular narratives keyed for excitement, applause, and the derision of critics, on the web or on television, or in textbooks, which can seem rather pale and insipid. *Historica* is a joy to read because of its kaleidoscopic

coverage and the sheer delight it takes in everyday life, high and low culture, wars, personages, empires, art, sports, business, literature, fashion, finance, architecture, music, and politics. These days, it is fashionable in academic circles to describe everything as complex, and verily most things are. The complexity is eased somewhat by a book like this which places trends, fashions, developments, and unhinging atrocities in a comprehensive, international, multicultural context. There is no politically correct pandering to distort the picture, just a refreshing determination to truly capture and illustrate the pulsing variety of the human spirit—all across the world in every era— at work, leisure, war, and peace.

GEOFFREY WAWRO

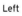

Above
One of the world's most recognizable buildings, India's Taj Mahal was built between 1630 and 1653.

Left
The first glass of Coca-Cola sold for five cents.

Far left
Actor Orson Welles (at right) created mass hysteria when he broadcast *The War of the Worlds* by H. G. Wells (at left) in 1938.

21

From Prehistory to the Year 999

Homer

Before the Second Millennium

It would be difficult to understand the last 1,000 years of human history without reviewing the fundamental events that happened before this relatively recent period. These events included such vital turning points as the migration of *Homo sapiens* out of Africa 100,000 years ago and the Mesopotamian and Egyptian civilizations that started in the Fertile Crescent and then spread along the Nile, nurturing farming, writing, art, religion, and inventions from 4300 BCE. These also include the growth of Buddhism and Hinduism; King David's capture of Jerusalem in 1000 BCE for the Israelites; the first-century CE crucifixion and resurrection of Christ, and seventh-century CE birth of Islam, which help explain religious crusades of the second millennium and perhaps even present conflicts in the Middle East.

Our story really starts about 100,000 years ago with the migration out of Africa by *Homo sapiens*. At first glance this might seem a long time ago until we remember the celebrated dinosaurs died out about 64 million years before our ancestors set off on their great migration, making our human story very recent indeed. The dinosaurs, which had been the dominant terrestrial creature before humans, had survived for a staggering 146 million years from about 210 million years ago to about 64 million years ago, before their extinction. By contrast, modern humans migrated out of Africa, the cradle of humanity, only one tenth of one million years ago.

Yet to date, no earlier evidence of any species related to *Homo sapiens* has been found in Africa any further back than about four million years ago. Bipedal footprints were found at Laetoil in Tanzania indicating hominids lived there 3,600,000 years ago; skeletal evidence of a species of *Australopithecus*

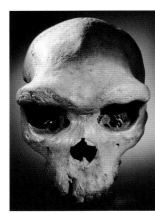
The skull of prehistoric man.

("Lucy") which lived 3,500,000 years ago, was found. That is still about 60 million years after the last dinosaur—so dinosaurs and humans certainly never met.

Homo erectus takes off

The first hominid that is normally seen as human—*Homo habilis* of the Olduvai Gorge in the Rift Valley—and that fashioned simple tools for hunting and eating, did not even appear until 2.4 million years ago, evolving slowly alongside a range of animal species. *Homo habilis* was then displaced by a variation that was much more like us—*Homo erectus*—who sported a brain two-thirds the size of a modern-day human brain but who did not appear till just 1.9 million years ago.

Becoming restless as climatic conditions changed around 1.8 million years ago, some members of *Homo erectus* began to migrate out of Africa, creating a first wave on a journey in search of food that took them to new hunting grounds via the Middle East, through Asia, and to modern China, arriving there about one million years ago.

During the next million years *Homo erectus* did quite well with a brain which was about two-thirds the size of the present-day human brain. *Homo erectus* developed the use of fire (an early breakthrough), hand axes (a quantum leap), and, by 400,000 years ago, spears (for improved hunting methods)—before eventually dying out.

Alongside *Homo erectus*, between 230,000 and 150,000 years ago, yet another species, *Homo neanderthalensis* (Neanderthals), also evolved and these Neanderthals took toolmaking to a new level—before they also died out.

The end of the Cretaceous Period marked the end of the dinosaurs.

Key Events

Earth, 64 million years ago: Dinosaurs become extinct after approximately 146 million years on earth.
Africa, 3.6 million years ago: Early hominids live in East Africa.
Rift Valley, Africa, 2.4 million years ago: *Homo habilis* ("handy man") evolves, and uses primitive tools.
Africa, 1.9 million years ago: *Homo erectus* ("upright man") evolves.
Africa, 1.8 million years ago: *Homo erectus* migrates north from Africa to the Middle East and beyond,
Europe and western Asia, 230,000-150,000 years ago: *Homo neanderthalensis* ("Neanderthal man") arises.

East Africa, 135,000 BCE: *Homo sapiens* ("wise man") emerges in Omro, Ethiopia.
Earth, 115,000 BCE: The last glaciations of the Ice Age begin.
Africa, 100,000 BCE: *Homo sapiens* migrates out of Africa, despite the Ice Age.
Middle East, 90,000 BCE: Modern humans reach the Middle East.
Worldwide, 75,000 BCE: Humans negotiate the encroaching Ice Age, which is freezing over many areas of the northern part of the planet.
Australia, 52,000-40,000 BCE: Aborigines reach Australia.

Europe, 40,000 BCE: Modern humans reach Europe.
Europe, 28,000 BCE: *Homo neanderthalensis* becomes extinct.
Europe, 25,000-22,000 BCE: Artists make "Venus" figurines and fertility dolls with exaggerated sexual features that may have had religious significance.
Earth, 18,000-15,000 BCE: The Ice Age peaks, with sea levels 330-460 feet (100-140 m) lower than today.
Ukraine, 15,000 BCE: People build huts using mammoth bones at Mezhirich.

Siberia, 15,000 BCE: Humans cross from northeastern Siberia to Alaska across the Bering bridge.
France, 15,000 BCE: Artists paint pictures of horses in Lascaux Cave in southwestern France.
Japan, 12,000 BCE: Jomon hunter-gatherers make the first pottery in Japan.
Worldwide, 12,000-9000 BCE: Ice thawing starts, melting polar ice caps and glaciers which create rising seas and increasing flow to rivers like the Nile, Tigris, Euphrates, Ganges, and Yangtze. People begin to settle in the fertile valleys.

Worldwide, 10,000-9000 BCE: Warmer conditions accelerate and reduce the last major glaciations; as the ice retreats from northern land masses, the forests take root and spread along with new plants.
Middle East, 10,000 BCE: In the Fertile Crescent hunter-gatherers harvest wild cereal grasses and farm wild sheep.
Earth, 8000 BCE: Melting of ice creates a sea level rise of 460 feet (140 m) and fertile river valleys. Continents are created. Farming starts as people settle along the fertile rivers.

In spite of the extreme cold, the inhabitants of Tierra del Fuego wore very few clothes.

Confucius

In 1492 when Christopher Columbus discovered the new world, cut off by rising sea levels more than 8,000 years earlier, he perceived Caribbean Indians as aliens, never dreaming that they shared common ancestry. While those on the Eurasian land mass made clothes, those in Tierra del Fuego remained—despite extreme cold—near naked. This is according to eye-witness reports from 1521 from the world's first circumnavigator Ferdinand Magellan. According to Captain James Cook who came to Australia as late as 1770, the Australian Aboriginal people were also near naked.

Homo sapiens did well to survive those migrations 100,000 years ago; for thousands of years large areas were covered by the glaciers of the ice age, which only peaked about 18,000 years ago. But as they were best equipped, *Homo sapiens* did survive, displacing the less well-equipped *Homo erectus* and Neanderthals, both of whom became extinct. These early *Homo sapiens* would become the forefathers of all great historical figures. In the time leading up to the year 1000 these included Menes, Gilgamesh, Abraham, Moses, Tutankhamen, Ramses II, King David, Homer, Buddha, Confucius, Julius Caesar, Cleopatra, Jesus Christ, Alexander the Great, and Mohammed, among others.

Survival of the Fittest

Meanwhile back in Africa, the story of our own ancestors—*Homo sapiens*—takes off with their migration 100,000 years ago on a second but more successful wave to seek their fortunes in the footsteps of earlier hominids. *Homo sapiens,* who had already evolved by 135,000 years ago with anatomically modern physiques, were better equipped and actually reached the four corners of the earth, which were still joined as one great land mass at that time.

If they had been alive back then, the second millennium's eleventh-century Viking navigator Leif Eriksson and fifteenth-century Italian navigator Christopher Columbus could have "discovered" America on foot, by walking across the Bering Strait instead of having to sail across the risky North Atlantic Ocean from Europe.

About 90,000 years ago the first *Homo sapiens* reached the Middle East. Then

time out

In 370 CE, the female mathematician Hypatia was born. She became a professor of mathematics and philosophy at the University of Alexandria in Egypt, specializing in the works of Plato and Aristotle, astronomy, geometry, and algebra.

by 75,000 years ago they had reached China. Those who went further reached far-flung Australia perhaps 52,000 years ago, America (via Alaska) 15,000 years ago and Patagonia, South America, 12,000 years ago. To the best of our knowledge nobody made it to isolated Antarctica, which remained uninhabited.

Those groups that ended up farthest from their African origins—the Indians of North America and Tierra del Fuego, and also the Aborigines of Australia—became the most isolated of all from the great human crossroads of the Middle East and the Fertile Crescent (Mesopotamia) that subsequently developed. But differing racial groups also evolved in different environments including Caucasoids (Caucasians), Mongoloids, and Negroids. These humans developed different physical shapes, facial features, skin colors, and languages, as well as cultural and spiritual ideas.

Ferdinand Magellan was the first explorer to circumnavigate the globe.

Key Events

Middle East and Europe, 8000-6000 BCE: Wheat and barley farming begins in Fertile Crescent. Rudimentary farming also begins in southeast Europe.
China, 6500 BCE: Rice farming begins in China in the Yangtze valley.
Turkey, 6200 BCE: Copper smelting and textile manufacturing begin in settled areas of Turkey.
Egypt, 6000 BCE: The Nile Valley floods delivering fresh silt on a seasonal basis; people living here begin farming of wheat, barley, sheep, and goats.

Middle East, 6000 BCE: Cattle are domesticated in the Middle East.
India, 6000 BCE: Farming begins in India.
China, 5800 BCE: Millet farming begins in China.
Europe, 5400 BCE: Farming begins in central then northern Europe.
Middle East, 5000 BCE: Irrigation agriculture begins on the plains of Mesopotamia.
Southwest Asia, 5000 BCE: People begin to tame horses for riding.
India, 4500 BCE: Farming spreads further along the Ganges plain.

Middle East, 4300 BCE: Fertile Crescent nurtures Mesopotamia's first cities and civilizations.
Middle East, 4200 BCE: Copper is used and smelted in the Middle East.
Middle East, 4000 BCE: People are using copper in Sumeria. Sumerians settle at the site of Babylon.
Middle East, 3800 BCE: First bronze work develops, providing stronger weapons and utensils; first wheeled vehicles are used in Mesopotamia.
Middle East, 3761 BCE: The creation narrative begins in the Jewish tradition.

Middle East, 3700 BCE: High priests run the temples and city-states of Mesopotamia. The people of Uruk, Sumeria, develop the first use of writing, with signs indicating sound of a word rather than a picture of the object or idea it conveyed with cuneiform script. Phonetic elements are used on painted pottery.
Russia, 3650 BCE: A wheeled vehicle is first used in Russia.
Middle East, 3700-3400 BCE: The first cities in Mesopotamia now flourishing at Uruk. Irrigation canals are being used in farming and cattle are pulling ploughs.

Middle East and Europe, 3600-3400 BCE: Religious monuments are built in these regions.
Egypt, 3500-3000 BCE: Walls are constructed around towns. Egyptians develop hieroglyphic script.
Egypt, 3400-3200 BCE: Egyptians base their religion on totemic symbols of nature and sun god Ra.
Middle East, 3400-3200 BCE: Bronze is widely used in the region.
Egypt, 3165-3100 BCE: Menes rules Egypt and unites upper and lower Egypt, setting the precedent of god-king and founding the first dynasty at Memphis.

Constantine the Great

The Ice Age Ends and Civilization Begins

Homo sapiens were fortunate that the glaciers of the Ice Age began melting about 12,000 years ago, thawing out by the end of 8000 BCE. Apart from freeing up hunting grounds and enabling forests and plants to take root, this created rivers full of fresh water and fertile valleys nurturing crops and animals.

This climatic change created a major turning point in history—the birth of agriculture. Now humans could switch from hunting and gathering to farming, enabling them to settle down. Instead of each human requiring a large area in order to survive from hunting, many could now survive together in the one smaller area; and live closer in groups. Conversely, some groups lost contact with others when sea levels rose 460 ft (140 m) cutting off America from Siberia and Australia from New Guinea.

Although humans started harvesting wild cereals from about 10,000 BCE and

> *"HAVING KNOWLEDGE BUT LACKING THE POWER TO EXPRESS IT CLEARLY IS NO BETTER THAN NEVER HAVING ANY IDEAS AT ALL."*
>
> PERICLES
> (495–429 BCE), GREEK
> STATESMAN

domesticating wild sheep from 9000 BCE mainly around the Middle East, it was wheat and barley farming from 8000 BCE to 7000 BCE in the Fertile Crescent that really kick started civilization—that great trading crossroads for humanity where ideas were nurtured and passed between the races. Farming then spread to the great fertile river valleys of the world. From 6000 BCE humans were growing wheat and barley and farming sheep along the Nile, farming in the Indus Valley and growing rice along the Yangtze. But in Mesopotamia by 5000 BCE farmers began irrigating their

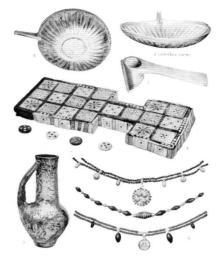
Treasures and artifacts from Ur in Mesopotamia.

crops—using principles their descendants would use for the Hanging Gardens of Babylon in the nearby palace of King Nebuchadnezzar in the year 604 BCE.

Not surprisingly, it was those enjoying benefits of this Fertile Crescent between the Euphrates and Tigris rivers who created the world's first large cities like Uruk and Eridu (in present-day Iraq) which supported thousands of citizens and nurtured our first civilizations in Mesopotamia (Greek for "land between the rivers"). There, between 4300 BCE and 3000 BCE the creative Sumerians in this region achieved the next great breakthroughs impacting on our lives today—pioneering centralized, administrative organization, using bronze, inventing the wheel, writing, and developing a sophisticated belief system complete with high priests, temples, and notions of life after death.

Nearby, the up-and-coming "super power," Egypt, was unified by history's earliest known identifiable figure, Menes, around 3100 BCE. Egypt was hot on the heels of its trading neighbor Mesopotamia. The Egyptians, enjoying their fertile Nile River valley, were both influenced by the Sumerians and also developed their own dynastic, political, economic, and spiritual ideas. They also developed sophisticated art, many technological inventions, and by 2600 BCE, far more enduring structures such as pharaoh Djoser's Step pyramid at Memphis, which still stands today (achieving Djoser's wish to be remembered across a 4600-year divide). Best documented, and lasting for 3,000 continuous years, Egypt was perhaps early history's greatest known civilization.

Moses is found by the daughter of the Egyptian pharaoh. Egypt was the dominant culture for thousands of years.

Key Events

Egypt, 3100 BCE: Egyptians use sails on boats on the Nile.

China, 3000 BCE: Chinese build towns and fortifications; make copper and silk; and use a potter's wheel.

Middle East, 3000 BCE: Phoenicians settle on the coast of Syria.

Egypt, 3000–2800 BCE: Mastaba tombs are constructed for Egyptian notables.

Japan, 3000 BCE: Japanese people cultivate gardens.

South America, 3000 BCE: Alpacas and llamas are domesticated.

Egypt, 2800–2600 BCE: Egyptians invent the first calendar of 365 days.

Middle East, 2800 BCE: Writing becomes more sophisticated in the city of Ur as symbols are invented to represent syllables.

Egypt, 2700 BCE: Egyptians build first pyramid tombs; also papyrus is used for writing.

Americas, 2700 BCE: Mesoamericans are growing maize.

Egypt, 2630 BCE: The Step pyramid—an architectural and construction breakthrough—is erected for Pharaoh Djoser to express the concept of divine kingship and life after death.

Egypt, 2600 BCE: Egyptian priests expand religion to create a total belief system confirming divine kingship and royal authority, claiming the god Horus protected the king. Egyptian people are also baking bread at this time.

Egypt, 2600–2500 BCE: The Great Pyramid for pharaoh Khufu is completed at Giza. It is followed by tombs for pharaohs Khafre and Menkara as the pharaohs' power reaches a zenith consolidated by the belief in the divine right of kings to rule. The Great Sphinx of Giza is also built.

India, 2500 BCE: Hinduism begins.

Middle East, 2500–1700 BCE: Sumerian trade takes development to the Indus Valley.

Middle East, 2400 BCE: Mesopotamia uses four-wheeled war wagons.

Egypt, 2300 BCE: Egypt's first "literature" is written (prayers of pyramid texts).

Americas, 2300 BCE: Maize farming begins in Mexico and permanent farming villages start to flourish. Pottery is first used in Mesoamerica.

Middle East, 2150 BCE: Babylon is flourishing on the lower Euphrates (Mesopotamia) and the first library in the world opens there.

Middle East, 2100 BCE: The Epic of Gilgamesh, the heroic leader of Mesopotamia, has been written. It is claimed to be the world's oldest "book" of clay tablets.

Middle East, 2000 BCE: Abraham is born, perhaps in Ur, Chaldea.

Britain, 2000 BCE: Stonehenge is built, showing the astronomical knowledge of the people of Wessex.

The ruins of the great Step Pyramid which was erected for the pharaoh Djoser.

The Stage is Set: Building on the Past

Those living before 1000 CE set the stage onto which future generations would step by establishing a fixed agenda for their successors. They also wrote the basic scripts for this great drama of humanity, having invented language, writing, literature, drama, and religious beliefs—inspiring succeeding generations to stand on the shoulders of earlier giants.

These earlier players laid religious, political, cultural, and artistic foundations for the ongoing drama by creating precedents to be passed down through collective memories.

They also prepared the way for those who continued representing similar groups—including all the great religions in place by 1000 CE: Hinduism, Judaism, Buddhism, and the more recent Christianity and Islam.

All these faiths had been battling for hearts and minds for many centuries even before the Crusades that would kick start the second millennium CE as religious leaders continued fighting the same religious and territorial conflicts.

King David

Faith and Belief: Ways of Living

As civilizations developed so too did spiritual ideas and the world's most enduring religions.

The earliest ongoing and continuous groups of faith included Hinduism, which was believed to have originated around 2500 BCE, and Judaism, which evolved from the legendary founding father Abraham, who was possibly born in Chaldea around 2000 BCE—about the time people in Britain built Stonehenge for their own spiritual reasons.

The foundations of Judaism consolidated when Moses led the Israelites out of Egypt around 1250 BCE, Joshua captured Jericho, and King David conquered Jerusalem around 1000 BCE establishing their claim to the Holy Land.

Other major belief systems were Buddhism which began when Siddhartha Guatama, born 563 BCE, started a way of living based on his teachings; Christianity which spread after the 30 CE crucifixion and resurrection of Jesus Christ; and Islam which began with Prophet Mohammed's vision in 610 CE, inspiring and underpinning the Arabic conquests and Muslim empire from the late 600s.

So, as humans moved into the second millennium CE the main thing they took with them from this earlier period, was not so much political or built structures of the past, but belief systems which became the seeds of religious conflicts and territorial ambitions.

Shiva, the third god of the Hindu trinity.

Key Events

Middle East, 2000-1900 BCE: It is believed God directs Abraham to Haran in Mesopotamia then Canaan, which God offers to his descendants. Judaism, Christianity, and Islam regard Abraham as a "founding father."
Japan, 2000 BCE: People in Japan start to use bows and arrows.
Americas, 2000 BCE: The people of Peru are now farming extensively.
Russia, 2000 BCE: People on the Russian steppes are domesticating the horse for riding.
China, 1900 BCE: The Chinese are using bronze and have many creative and technological inventions.

Egypt, 1800 BCE: Egyptians are using bronze more extensively.
China, 1700-1600 BCE: China's Shang dynasty is founded by King Tang, creating stability and encouraging the arts.
Greece, 1650 BCE: Mycenaean civilization begins in Greece.
China, 1600 BCE: Pictographic writing begins in China.
Egypt, 1600 BCE: The chariot is now being used in Egypt.
Egypt, 1500 BCE: Egyptians are working with glass, iron, copper, bronze, gold, and silver.

Korea, 1500 BCE: Koreans begin to farm rice.
India, 1500-1200 BCE: The Sanskrit Vedas of India have been written, including *Rigveda*.
Egypt, 1470 BCE: Egypt's Queen Hatshepsut trades with east Africa.
Middle East, 1400 BCE: Hittites use horses in war.
China, 1400 BCE: Chinese have royal burials with human sacrifice; they also build walled cities, use writing, and have wheeled vehicles, bronze vessels, and bamboo strip books.

Egypt, 1348-1340 BCE: Tutankhamen is king of Egypt.
Middle East, 1250 BCE: Moses leads Israelites out of Egypt towards the Promised Land. On Mt Sinai he receives the Ten Commandments.
Egypt, 1250 BCE: The Abu Simbel temple is built in Egypt by the pharaoh Ramses II.
Americas, 1220 BCE: Mayans settle in the Yucatan peninsula.
Middle East, 1200 BCE: The Trojan War takes place.
Greece, 1050 BCE: The Greek alphabet evolves, based on the Phoenician alphabet.

Middle East, 1000 BCE: People are now using iron weapons and tools.
Americas, 1000 BCE: South Americans grow maize. Mayans settle in the Yucatan peninsula.
Middle East, 1000-961 BCE: King David defeats Philistines and makes Jerusalem a political and religious center uniting Jewish tribes.
Middle East, 950 BCE: King Solomon builds the first Temple at Jerusalem with Phoenician craftsmen.
Middle East, 850 BCE: Prophets Elijah and Elisha promote the Jewish faith.

The flight of Mohammed

"Study as if you were to live forever. Live as if you were to die tomorrow."

ISIDORE OF SEVILLE
(ST ISIDORE)
(c. 560–636 ce),
SPANISH HISTORIAN

The Things that Last

Monarchs, empires, and civilizations come and go, but religions seem to go on forever. From its early evolution, religious belief has been passed from century to century and millennium to millennium. These beliefs—which have featured various totemic elements, worship of nature, animals, and divine kings or emperors, promises of life after death, and rules to live by—have played a key inspirational role in human history.

By the start of the third millennium, Hinduism, which began with animistic and totemic forms before 2500 BCE, had more than 900 million followers. Judaism, dating back to Abraham, and then Moses at around 1250 BCE, had 15 million followers. Buddhism, which was first taught by Siddhartha Gautama (563–483 BCE), had more than 500 million followers. Christianity, inspired by the life and resurrection of Christ (06 BCE–30 CE), had the largest number with 2.1 billion, and Islam, spread by Mohammed after his vision in 610 CE, had 1.3 billion.

Leaders understood the power of religion and used it to their own ends. In the fourth century CE Roman emperor Constantine the Great used the fast-growing Christianity to re-bond the crumbling empire together following the decline of Rome—even though fellow Romans had previously hurled some Christians to the lions.

Likewise, after Mohammed's vision in 610 CE, Arab leaders used Islam to inspire and bind their people together in the seventh century as they conquered their neighbors to build their great Muslim empire. Together, the rise of the monotheistic religions of Judaism, Christianity, and Islam have provided the strongest rationale, meaning, ideology, and authority to new power structures enabling enduring civil support and successful military conquests.

Even at the start of the third millennium, the American leader, President George W. Bush—a committed Christian—talked of a "crusade," using language of 1,000 years earlier, after Islamic Fundamentalists attacked and destroyed New York's iconic twin towers of the World Trade Center. Although critics claimed he was just using a religious rationale to justify taking control of Middle Eastern oil, his message still inspired many Americans.

Islam is one of the world's great religions. Here, pilgrims gather at the Grand Mosque in Mecca.

Great Monuments

The list of the Seven Wonders of the Ancient World was compiled around the second century BCE. They are the Great Pyramids of Giza, the Hanging Gardens of Babylon, the Temple of Artemis at Ephesus, the Statue of Zeus at Olympia, the Mausoleum at Halicarnassus, the Colossus of Rhodes, and the Pharos (Lighthouse) of Alexandria.

Apart from the pyramids of Giza built from 2630 BCE (Step) to 2500 BCE (Giza), which have lasted four and half thousand years, all the other wonders of the ancient world have gone.

The Hanging Gardens of Babylon Built on the Euphrates (Iraq) in 604-562 BCE in the palace of Nebuchadnezzar II, about 75 feet (23 m) above the ground on stone arches, watered by a sophisticated irrigation system.

The Mausoleum of Halicarnassus Tomb built for Mausolus of Caria in Greece in 361 BCE by his widow.

The Temple of Artemis On the Ionian coast at Ephesus, built in 356 BCE to celebrate the many breasted fertility goddess Diana of the Ephesians.

The Colossus of Rhodes A 100-foot (31-m) bronze statue of the sun god Helios spanning the entrance to Rhodes Harbor. Built in 280 BCE, it only lasted half a century before an earthquake destroyed it.

The Statue of Zeus at Olympia Built in 430 BCE by the leading Greek sculptor Phidias out of stone (chryselephantine) and covered with jewels. This statue of the supreme king of the gods in the Temple of Zeus at Olympia was 40 feet (12 m) high and lasted until the fifth century CE, nearly 900 years.

The Pharos of Alexandria Egypt This lighthouse stood 440 feet (135 m) high, and was built for Ptolemy II by Sostratus of Knides as a navigational light for sailors in the Mediterranean Sea. Also built in 280 BCE, it lasted the longest of the Seven Wonders, apart from the pyramids—nearly 1,000 years and long enough to have been sighted by the religious crusaders on their voyages to the Holy Land—before it was demolished in the thirteenth century CE.

The Things that Change

Secular leaders are always transitory. Great leaders like Menes, Djoser, Gilgamesh, Khufu, Nebuchadnezzar, Julius Caesar, Alexander the Great, Darius, and Hannibal may strut across the world stage for a brief moment demanding great changes but in an instant they are gone

Key Events

India, 850 BCE: Upanishads set forth the prime Vedic doctrines.
Greece, and Middle East 800 BCE: Greeks colonize Mediterranean and Black Sea to establish their empire. Assyrians use two-wheeled chariots drawn by two horses for hunting lions. Biblical Old Testament narratives are being written.
Greece, 776 BCE: The first Olympic games are held.
Greece, 750 BCE: Homer writes *The Iliad* and *The Odyssey*.
Greece, 650 BCE: Greeks codify law and further develop their city-states.

Egypt, 671 BCE: Assyrians occupy Egypt.
Greece, 670 BCE: Greeks use coins.
Middle East, 604-562 BCE: The Hanging Gardens of Babylon have been built.
China, 604-531 BCE: The life and teachings of Lao-tzu give birth to Taoism in China.
China, 600 BCE: The Chinese begin to use iron.
Americas, 600 BCE: Mayans build pyramid temples at Nakbe and bury mummies in Paracas necropolis.

Middle East, 597-586 BCE: Jerusalem is sacked by Nebuchadnezzar of Babylon and Jews are deported. The Old Testament books are completed.
Northern India/Nepal, 563-483 BCE: Siddhartha Guatama (Buddha) lives and teaches "the middle way."
Middle East, 562 BCE: Nebuchadnezzar dies; Babylon starts to decline.
Middle East, 559 BCE: Persian leader Cyrus begins conquests.
China, 551-479 BCE: Confucius lives and teaches his philosophy.

Middle East, 539-521 BCE: Persians conquer Babylon (539 BCE), Egypt (525 BCE), and in 521 BCE Darius develops the Persian Empire.
Rome, 509 BCE: The Roman Republic is founded.
Greece, 509-400 BCE: Greeks pioneer limited democratic government.
India, 500 BCE: Hinduism is dominant in India.
China, 481-221 BCE: Chinese states go to war with each other.
Greece, 480 BCE: Darius leads his Persian army against Athens.

Greece, 477-432 BCE: The Greeks build the Parthenon.
Greece, 430 BCE: The statue of Zeus is built at Olympia.
Greece, 361 BCE: The Mausoleum of Halicarnassus is completed.
Greece, 356 BCE: The Temple of Artemis at Ephesus is built.
China, 350 BCE: The Chinese invent the crossbow.
Egypt, 332 BCE: Alexander the Great conquers the once mighty Egypt, expanding the Greek empire and founding Alexandria; the city has a new library to foster its growth as a new center of learning.

Of the seven wonders of the ancient world, the pyramids of Egypt are the only ones that still exist.

Nebuchadnezzar

forever, with their great works dismantled and their names a mere memory.

All empires have come and gone, even Egypt's, which lasted longest with 3,000 years of continuous civilization based on divine right of kings. Egypt's astonishing survival certainly put latter-day empires into context, including the relatively long-running empires of Greece or Rome before Christ, let alone the empires that would be established in the second millennium CE by the legendary Genghis Khan, Napoleon Bonaparte, and Adolf Hitler. Gone also are the great civilizations of earlier times: Mesopotamia, Sumeria, Babylon, and Phoenicia.

Even the great "empire" of the sole contemporary superpower in the world, the USA, may fade as both internal and external forces undermine it.

Bronze neck ring, c. 600 BCE.

Progress and Violence: Continuing Traditions?

Just as major faiths have endured and certain cultural foundations have been sustained throughout human history, another continuing tradition is relentless incremental "progress." Past inventions enable new inventions. Humans have developed many breakthroughs either collectively—or simultaneously—sharing ideas. These breakthroughs include weapons, cave art, writing, the wheel, horse riding, copper, bronze, iron, construction techniques, postage, and money. But the breakthroughs from 1000 CE onwards were based on these earlier innovations without which latter-day humans could not have invented steam trains and ships, automobiles, radios, telephones, cameras, jet aircraft, computers, space rockets, mobile phones, or the internet.

Another thread in the human tapestry seems to be a predisposition for violence—often inspired by strong brutal dictators. The propensity for humans in society to fight is endemic whether over territory, religion, or both. This propensity has shaped our world's history more than any other single human characteristic. Power certainly abhors a vacuum, for whenever leaders fall, empires crumble, or religions fail, new leaders, empires, and religions move in to fill the void.

In some ways, such violence seemed necessary for development because as the period before 1000 CE confirms, those societies creating political stability no matter how brutal, normally achieve more that those lacking strong leadership and government. Egypt, which enjoyed a regimented monarchy for 3,000 years, created one of the great civilizations in history manifested through a flourishing economy, surviving pyramids, sculpture, art, and writing. Other disciplined civilizations, including Mesopotamia, Ancient Greece, the Roman Empire, and the Arab empire, also left their indelible marks. Conversely, those societies that suffered internal wars lacked a stable climate for creativity and progress.

Joshua led the Israelite conquest of Canaan.

Key Events

Middle East, 328 BCE: Alexander conquers Persia and north India.

Greece, 322 BCE: Born in 384 BCE, philosopher Aristotle dies.

Greece, 347 BCE: Philospher Plato, born in 427 BCE, dies.

Greece, c. 300 BCE: Greeks write on principles of horsemanship.

Greece, 280 BCE: The Colossus of Rhodes is built.

Alexandria, 280 BCE: The Lighthouse of Alexandria is completed.

Alexandria, 276-194 BCE: Eratosthenes produces an early map of the world.

India, 260 BCE: Buddhism takes off in India once King Ashoka converts.

China, 240 BCE: Taoists adopt Lao-tzu's *Tao te ching* ("The Way and Its Power") as their sacred book.

China, 221-207 BCE: King Zheng of Ch'in unifies China.

Spain, 218 BCE: Carthaginian general Hannibal conquers Spain, crosses the Alps with elephants to defeat Romans in north Italy, but retreats.

China, 214 BCE: The first Great Wall of China is completed.

China, 202 BCE: The Han Dynasty is founded.

Rome, 201 BCE: The Roman empire is in its ascendancy.

Middle East, 201 BCE: Petra, the Nabataeans' capital in Jordan, becomes a great trading center.

Greece, 200-100 BCE: The Old Testament is translated into Greek.

China, 175 BCE: Chinese are using iron weapons and tools.

Greece, 150 BCE: The statue of the Venus de Milo is sculpted.

Americas, 150 BCE: The Mayans establish walled city of El Mirador with temple pyramids and population of 80,000. They develop their writing.

Rome, 149-147 BCE: Rome conquers Carthage and then makes Greece a province.

China, 147 BCE: China invents piston bellows for producing cast iron.

China, 110 BCE: Sima Qian writes a history of China.

Europe/Asia, 100 BCE: The trade route called the "Silk Road" links Rome and China.

Rome, 58-51 BCE: Julius Caesar and the Romans conquer Gaul.

Britain, 55-54 BCE: The Romans invade Britain.

Rome, 45 BCE: The Julian calendar is introduced under Julius Caesar. This established the base year of 365.25 days, which was an advance on the Egyptian calendar. It is only inaccurate by 11 minutes per year.

Rome, 44 BCE: Julius Caesar is assassinated.

Egypt, 30 BCE: The once great Egypt is now a Roman province.

Rome, 27 BCE: Rome becomes an empire, with Octavian becoming Emperor Augustus.

Judas repents

Time: a cultural concept

Our timeline from 64 million years ago to 1000 CE is based on a system of measuring only created in 525 CE by Roman abbott Dionysius Exiguus five hundred years after the birth of Christ. But it was quite arbitrary to start counting from the birth of Christ. Time could also be measured from 135,000 years ago based on the successful emergence of *Homo sapiens*; or 100,000 years ago with the great migration out of Africa; or 8000 BCE when rising seas created today's continents; or the first civilizations of Egypt or Mesopotamia which perfected farming, the wheel, art, and writing around 4300 BCE. There have been many other systems of counting including those of the Mayans and Chinese, and Jews. Time traditionally starts for Jews at 3761 BCE; Buddhists could start counting from 563 BCE when

Buddha was born, and Muslims could start from 610 CE when Mohammed had his vision.

Today's measurement of time has also been adjusted since the Egyptians pioneered the 24-hour day and 365-day calendar, with Julius Caesar modifying time measurement in 46 BCE with the Julian calendar introducing leap years; and with the introduction by Pope Gregory in 1582 of today's measuring system, the Gregorian calendar, to better synchronize the calendar with the astronomical cycles, bringing it into step with seasons.

In this section of the book, dates are approximate due to different calendars used in times gone by, changes to the calendar, different theories of scholars, different dates given, lack of evidence and

> "THE PEOPLE ARE LIKE WATER AND THE RULER A BOAT. WATER CAN SUPPORT A BOAT OR OVERTURN IT."
>
> LI SHIMIM (597–649), CHINESE EMPEROR AMD FOUNDER OF THE T'ANG DYNASTY

time out

In 897 CE, the Cadaver Synod posthumously tried Pope Formosus, who had died nine months earlier, for violating Church law. They dug up his body, dressed him in vestments, and read the charges to his corpse. Found guilty, his body was thrown into the Tiber River.

The Mayan astronomical observatory at Chichen Itza.

also lack of information. Stories of religious leaders such as Abraham, Moses, and Joshua—who is said to have captured Jericho—are derived more from religious mythology than from historical records. The dating of humankind's early history is also approximate, especially milestones like the migration of *Homo sapiens* from Africa around about 100,000 years ago.

A work in progress

At times, historical evidence is unreliable. Those civilizations that recorded activities best are inevitably best represented, such as the Egyptians who preserved their history through hieroglyphic script and artifacts inside the tombs of the pharaohs. They even preserved their people, such as Ramses II who died between the fourth and third millennium BCE. Although had it not been for the chance discovery of the 196 BCE Rosetta stone in 1799 CE, with its Egyptian and Greek script, we would not have known who Ramses II was, nor have understood the sophisticated hieroglyphics and culture of that 3,000-year Egyptian civilization which had died out with the death of the last pharaoh Nectanebo II in 343 BCE.

But of great empires like Mesopotamia, Phoenicia, Babylon, and Persia, we have

The Tulun Mosque in Cairo, Egypt was built by ibn Tulin in 876 CE.

Key Events

Middle East, 06 BCE: Jesus Christ is born in Bethlehem.

Middle East, 06 BCE: Romans conquer Judea (the Holy Land).

Middle East, 30 CE: Crucifixion and resurrection of Jesus Christ inspires new religion: Christianity.

Britain, 62 CE: Occupying Romans defeat Boadicea in Britain.

China, 65 CE: First Buddhist missionaries travel from India to China.

Middle East, 70-100 CE: Four Gospels are being written, forming the basis of the New Testament.

China, 100-200 CE: Chinese are using paper, mirrors, wheelbarrows, and the abacus.

Greece, 150 CE: Astronomer Ptolemy writes *Almagest*.

China, 200-300 CE: Buddhism continues to grow in China.

Rome 200-300 CE: Christianity is a major force in the Roman Empire.

China 200-300 CE: Drinking tea has become very popular in China.

Americas, 200-300 CE: The Mayans build the pyramid of the sun at San Juan Teotihuacán.

Rome, 313 CE: Roman Emperor Constantine adopts Christianity.

Rome, 324 CE: Constantine founds a Christian eastern empire and transfers capital in 330 CE to Constantinople (Byzantium).

Rome, 330 CE: The first church of St Peter is built for Christian worship.

Americas, 330 CE: Mayans develop mathematics including the symbol for zero; Mayan calendars are in use.

Rome, 405 CE: St Jerome translates the Old and New Testament into the Latin "Vulgate" version, to become the first Bible.

Rome, 410 CE: Barbarians (Visigoths) sack Rome, ushering in the "Dark Ages."

Ireland, 432 CE: St Patrick begins converting the Irish to Christianity.

Europe, 452 CE: Attila the Hun's attacks on Gaul and Italy are defeated by Roman/Visigoth alliance.

Rome: 476 CE: The Western Roman Empire starts to decline.

Rome, 525 CE: Dionysius Exiguus, a Roman abbot, selects the birth of Christ as 0 AD.

Rome, 528 CE: Roman law is codified into one body of work.

North America, 550 CE: Indians use the bow and arrow for hunting.

Japan, 552 CE: Buddhism is introduced to Japan.

Middle East, 570 CE: Mohammed, founder of Islam, is born.

Britain, 596 CE: Christian missionaries, including St Augustine, convert people of Britain to Christianity.

Rome, 600 CE: Pope Gregory I codifies plainsong (Gregorian chant).

India, 600-700 CE: Bakhti revival of Hinduism started in India.

Middle East, 610 CE: Mohammed's vision inspires religion of Islam and the growth of a Muslim Arab Empire.

China, 618 CE: The T'ang Dynasty is founded in China.

French king Charlemagne in battle against the Barbarians.

Buddha,
Ladakh, India

subsequently published that may be the Gospel of Judas, and in February 2006 renowned Egyptologist Zarhi Hawass reported a new tomb, in Valley of the Kings, from the age of pharaohs—the first since the 1922 discovery of Tutankhamen's tomb by Howard Carter.

Given that evidence can be unreliable and conflicting, accordingly, the timeline in this section of the book should be seen as an approximate guide to this earlier period of history. It only presents the highlights of those high-impact events that have shaped our world in lasting ways and which have influenced the second millennium CE—the last 1,000 years of history. Our history is very much a work in progress.

No matter how much seems to have happened, it is still only 6,000 years since the first civilizations like the 4000 BCE Mesopotamian cities began having an impact on the planet. Yet in this short time humans have reduced that most fertile "land between the rivers" to a barren and eroded desert.

Given our track record unless we *Homo sapiens* abandon religious bigotry, stop fighting wars, and destroying our fragile environment, it is unlikely we will survive for another 6,000 years.

In which case, this book will never be found by future beings unless preserved in a tomb as safe as Tutankhamen's. It would be better to remind ourselves of our common East African origin and unite to reverse the life-threatening damage that we have inflicted on the planet in just 6,000 years, which compares so badly with the benign impact of the dinosaurs' 146-million-year reign.

The Second Millennium

This timeline now hands over to the next millennium at a suitable moment because it opens the second millennium with turning-point events including the great voyages of the seafaring Norwegian explorers. Erik the Red sailed from Iceland to Greenland establishing the first European colony there while his son Leif Eriksson sailed on to "Vinland" establishing the first settlement in "the new world" in the region of Nova Scotia creating a toehold in a land that would become America—that continent which had been cut off from Siberia by the ice melting back in 8000 BCE. This was the first of many great breakthrough voyages that would soon change the shape of the world during the next 1,000 years.

far less in the hand. Let alone Barbarians who may have sacked the great city of Rome, but left few records.

There is also conflicting evidence. Most accounts are based on secondary sources, often contradictory, with few eye-witness reports and little in writing. Historians have not only used different dates but also definitions, interpretations, and analysis, and all are subjective. Different cultures also sometimes claim the same "first"—like the invention of the wheel or writing. The stories belonging to different religions, based on belief rather than fact, are difficult to verify.

New discoveries provide new evidence, forcing many rewrites. In the twentieth century an Egyptian peasant unearthed an ancient jar containing manuscripts

A page from the illuminated gospel, the Book of Kells.

Key Events

Middle East, 622 CE: Mohammed takes flight from Mecca to Medina.
Middle East, 630 CE: Mohammed conquers Mecca justifying this as a jihad (holy war), establishing Islam.
Middle East, 636-664 CE: Arab conquests create a new Muslim empire beginning with Syria, then Palestine and Mesopotamia; later Iran, Egypt, Armenia, and Afghanistan.
Middle East, 651-656 CE: The Koran achieves its final form.
Middle East, 670 CE: Islamic disputes split Muslims into Sunni, Shi'ite, and Khawarji sects.

China, 700-800 CE: The Chinese invent gunpowder to make fireworks.
Middle East, 711-715 CE: Expanding Muslim Arab empire ends domination of Persian and Roman empires as Arabs capture Spain introducing Arabic language, astronomy, chemistry, and mathematics, among others.
Britain, 735 CE: The Venerable Bede translates some of the scriptures of the Bible into Anglo-Saxon (English).
France, 771-814 CE: Charlemagne unites France, then conquers Italy, northern Spain, Saxony, and Bavaria. In 790 he is crowned as the Holy Roman Emperor.

Spain, 785 CE: Arab conquerors begin constructing the Great Mosque of Cordoba.
Europe, 790 CE: The Irish produce the illustrated Book of Kells.
Britain, 793 CE: Viking raids begin with the sacking of Lindisfarne.
Americas, 800 CE: Indians in North America developing maize farming, irrigation, villages, and towns.
Southeast Asia, 800 CE: Construction of Buddhist temple begins in Java at Borobudur.

Europe, 802-860 CE: Vikings conquer Ireland and raid English, Frankish, and Mediterranean coasts.
Middle East, 867 CE: Basil I leads Byzantium troops against Muslims in Mesopotamia asserting revival of Byzantium against Arab dominance.
Britain, 871-899 CE: Alfred the Great in England negotiates peace with Danish invaders.
900-1000 CE: Cordoba reaches its height as an Arab center for scientific study.
Americas, 900 CE: Mayans establish Chichen Itza as main center.

China, 907 CE: The T'ang Dynasty collapses in China.
Europe, 919 CE: Henry I is first Saxon to rule a unified German people.
Japan, 935 CE: Rise of military class in Japan creates civil strife.
China, 950 CE: Chinese initiate the use of optical lens.
Middle East, 970 CE: Turks convert to Islam.
Europe, 986 CE: Norse leader Erik the Red founds settlement in Greenland.

From the Year 1000 to Today

Ethelred the Unready

Ethelred Flees!

England, December, 1013:
King Ethelred II of England has fled to Normandy, the birthplace of his wife Emma, driven out by the forces of King Sweyn I of Denmark. A consummate politician, Sweyn, often called "Sweyn Forkbeard," has long coveted the throne of England and is known to have hopes of establishing a great empire in the north. He is reported to have responded to pleas for assistance from Danes living in England.

Ethelred came to the throne in 979 after his half-brother, Edward II, was murdered. Rumors have suggested that Ethelred himself played a part in his brother's demise. Long known as "the Unready" because of the seemingly poor advice he is given, Ethelred has not been a popular monarch and many of his subjects feel no particular loyalty to him. Many will recall his brutal 1002 massacre of all Danes in England, which was intended to rid him of the risk of betrayal.

Ethelred's policy of defending the country against Danish attacks through diplomatic means has not been successful, and his "buying off" of attackers with money raised through the Danegeld tax has engendered much local criticism. In 1012 alone, 48,000 lbs (about 21,770 kg) of silver was paid to Danes living near London. Payment of the Danegeld, intended to prevent Danish attacks, has not had the desired effect. Viking raids continued in intensity and Ethelred has paid the price for being unprepared.

Brian Boru Killed in Battle

Ireland, April 23, 1014: Danish rule in Ireland finally came to an end today with the defeat of Danish forces in what is being called the Battle of Clontarf. However, freedom has come at a high

An illustrated list of English kings.

price—Brian Boru, the 87-year-old High King of Ireland, has lost his life.

In the years before the turn of the century, Boru had been victorious over the Vikings in Limerick and had a firm grip on his own province of Munster. He entered an uneasy coalition with High King Malachi Mor in 999, their partnership effectively uniting Ireland. By 1002, however, Boru had ousted Malachi from the throne and taken the position of High King of Ireland for himself, heralding the beginning of a period of peace and stability in the previously fractured country.

Late last year, the Danish king of Dublin, Sitrygg Silkybeard, gathered together friends and allies from many parts of western Europe to take action against Brian Boru in a last-ditch attempt to wrest control of Ireland from the high king's grasp. Sitrygg was joined by the Irish rebel, King Maelmorda of Leinster, brother-in-law of Boru, who brought thousands of men to the battlefield.

Never one to be caught unprepared, Brian Boru assembled the armies of Munster and the neighboring province of Connaught. He was also assisted by armies from Scotland, and even his one-time rival, Malachi Mor, sent men from Meath to join Boru's forces. The battle, which took place on Good Friday, was a bloodbath. An estimated 10,000 men lost their lives.

It is expected that Malachi will succeed to the throne following the death of Brian Boru.

Canute Defeats Edmund Ironside

Ashingdon, October 18, 1016: A ferocious battle was fought today between Edmund Ironside and Canute of the Danes—the prize, the throne of England. Canute, son of renowned warrior Sweyn Forkbeard, had also waged battles against Edmund Ironside's father, Ethelred. Today he finally achieved his goal of devastating the English forces, thereby securing the throne for himself.

Although the deal brokered between the two warriors stipulates that England be partitioned, Edmund is known to be in poor health and it is almost certain that Canute, who has a reputation for doing away with any possible rivals, will become king of all England.

Many believe that it won't be long before Canute takes Ethelred's widow, Emma of Normandy, as his wife, further consolidating his hold on power.

King Canute's brother Harald has held the throne of Denmark since the death of King Sweyn, his father, in 1014.

Brian Boru was killed by Vikings after the main battle.

> "BY THE SPLENDOR OF GOD I HAVE TAKEN POSSESSION OF MY REALM; THE EARTH OF ENGLAND IS IN MY TWO HANDS."
>
> WILLIAM THE CONQUEROR (1027–1087) KING OF ENGLAND, 1066

> "…KINGS AND RULERS SPRANG FROM MEN WHO WERE IGNORANT OF GOD…"
>
> WILLIAM OF MALMESBURY (C. 1080–1143) OF PHILIP I OF FRANCE (1052–1108)

Key Events

North America, 1000: Leif Eriksson reputedly discovers North America.
Norway, 1000: The forces of King Olaf I of Norway are defeated by the Danes at the Battle of Svolder.
Islip, England, 1003: Edward, son of Ethelred II, is born.
Peshawar, India, 1004: Mahmud of Ghazna defeats the armies of a Hindu confederacy. He annexes the Punjab and introduces Islam there.
Jerusalem, 1009: Caliph al-Hakim sacks the Church of the Holy Sepulchre and the tomb believed to be Christ's is hacked down to bedrock.

Hanoi, Vietnam, 1009: Ly Cong Uan founds the Ly Dynasty, and establishes Vietnam as an independent state
Khmer Empire (Cambodia), 1010: Suryavarman I takes the throne, eventually defeating rival claimant Jayaviravarman.
England, 1012: Ethelred II pays 48,000 lbs (about 21,770 kg) of silver to the Danes, after paying 36,000 lbs (about 16,330 kg) two years previously to prevent attacks.
England, December 1013: The Danes overrun England and Ethelred II flees.

Denmark, February, 1014: Harald becomes King of Denmark, upon the death of his father, Sweyn.
Dublin, Ireland, April 23, 1014: Brian Boru, the High King of Ireland, is killed at the Battle of Clontarf.
England, October 18, 1016: Canute's Danish forces defeat the English under Edmund Ironside at the Battle of Ashingdon and Canute becomes king of England.

Java, Indonesia, 1016: Airlangga becomes the founding ruler of the Kingdom of Mataram, greatest of the medieval Southeast Asian island empires.
Denmark, 1019: Harald II, King of Denmark dies, and Canute becomes King of England and Denmark.
Cairo, Egypt, February 13, 1021: Caliph al-Hakim—variously described as compassionate, cruel, or raving mad, depending on the source—mysteriously disappears.

Norway, 1028: Already king of England and Denmark, Canute ousts King Olaf II of Norway.
Stiklestad, Norway, July, 1030: Former king, Olaf II, attempts to regain the throne of Norway, but is defeated in battle.
Ghazna, Afghanistan, April 30, 1030: Emperor Mahmud of Ghazna dies, aged about 59. He is succeeded by his son, Mas'ud.

Brian Boru

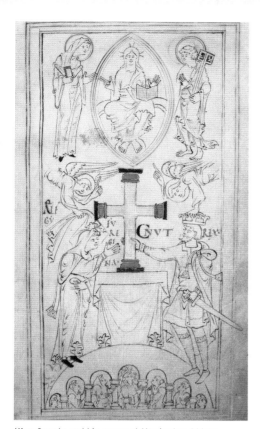

King Canute and his queen at Newington Abbey.

Another Crown for Canute

Norway, 1028: King Canute gained another feather in his cap this month when he added the title of king of Norway to his list of credentials. Canute became king of England in 1016 following his defeat of Edmund Ironside, and in 1019 he took the throne of Denmark after the death of his brother Harald.

It has not been easy to govern two countries, and from 1019 Canute has had to maintain a steady program of expeditions back to Denmark and the Danish colonies in Norway in order to keep a firm grip on his burgeoning empire. Fortunately for Canute, his reign in England is secure and the economy is growing, allowing him to fund his expeditions and thus affirm his power in Scandinavia.

Trouble over Norway has been brewing since 1026, when Canute's brother-in-law Ulf Jarl, the regent of Denmark, rebelliously allied himself with King Anund Jakob of Sweden and King Olaf II of Norway against Canute. Many will remember the bloody battle of the Holy River where Canute's forces lost to the allies. He may have lost that battle, but Canute, a wily politician, managed to turn many Norwegian landowners and businessmen against Olaf.

Olaf II, sometimes known as Olaf the Stout, has been a long-term obstacle to Canute's ambitions. Olaf fought alongside England's King Ethelred against the Danes, something not likely to endear him to the Danish monarch, and it was only a matter of time before Canute made his move.

Gathering a fleet of 50-odd ships, Canute set sail for Norway, where he expelled Olaf and had himself proclaimed king. To strengthen his empire, insiders are predicting that Canute will install his son Harthacanute as king of Denmark and his other son Sweyn as king of Norway, leaving Canute to focus on the bigger issues affecting his empire.

Olaf II ruled Norway from 1015 to 1028.

Marriage Consolidates Mataram Empire

East Indies, 1030: King Airlangga of Mataram has married the daughter of the king of Srivijaya, thus consolidating his hold on his Javanese empire and making the relationship between the two states more cooperative. Born about 30 years ago, Airlangga himself is the son of a Balinese prince and a Javanese princess, and he is mindful of creating strong alliances.

Airlangga has been a popular monarch. One of his great achievements so far has been the promotion of religious tolerance. When faced with tensions between

Mahayana Buddhism and the Vishnu cult of Hinduism, Airlangga refused to nominate one or the other as the state religion. Instead, he declared that both were legitimate faiths and that they should co-exist in Mataram, or Kahuripan as it is sometimes known. By taking the lands of both groups, he was able to avoid the building of power bases that may have undermined his rule. Airlangga has promoted the building of temples of both religions, providing work for artisans across the land.

The king has also vigorously promoted the arts and literature, and many believe that Java's finest works are being produced during his reign. His court poet is currently working on an important epic.

Acutely aware of the importance of agriculture, Airlangga has been instrumental in establishing irrigation systems for farmers in drier regions. He has also constructed a number of aqueducts throughout the kingdom.

Airlangga has brought a new measure of prosperity to the kingdom. May his work continue.

Leif Eriksson is the first European to discover North America.

Shaftesbury, England, November 12, 1035: King Canute dies, aged about 40. He is succeeded by his son Harald.
Wales, 1039: Prince Gruffydd ap Llewelyn of Gwynedd and Powys defeats the English.
Scotland, 1040: King Duncan dies in battle and Macbeth claims the throne.
Pagan, Burma, 1044: Burmese King Anawratha fortifies the capital at Pagan.

Europe, 1054: The Roman Catholic Church and Eastern Orthodox Church go their separate ways.
Lumphanan, Scotland, August 15, 1057: King Macbeth dies, aged about 52. He is succeeded by his stepson, Lulach.
Sicily, 1059: Norman forces, fighting on behalf of the pope, begin their campaign to regain the region from Arab control.
London, England, January 5, 1066: Edward III (Edward the Confessor) dies, aged about 62. He is succeeded by Harold II.

Stamford Bridge, Yorkshire, England, September 25, 1066: Harold II successfully defends his realm, defeating the Norwegians.
Hastings, England, October 14, 1066: The English forces of Harold II are defeated by the Normans under the leadership of William of Normandy. Harold falls in battle.
London, England, December 25, 1066: William the Conqueror is crowned King William I of England.
Isle of Ely, Norfolk, England, 1071: Hereward the Wake leads a rebellion against William I.

Algiers, Africa, 1082: The Almoravids, led by Youssef bin Tachfin, capture the city of Algiers.
Rome, Italy, 1084: Robert Guiscard of Normandy storms the city as he rescues Pope Gregory VII from Holy Roman Emperor Henry IV.
Spain, 1085: The Almoravids begin their quest to control Spain.
Rouen, France, September 9, 1087: William I (William the Conqueror) dies, aged about 59. He is succeeded by his son, William II (William Rufus).

Persia, 1092: Malik Shah, Sultan of the Seljuk Empire, dies, aged 37. He is succeeded by his son, Mahmud I.
Clermont, France, 1095: Pope Urban II appeals to the Christian princes to wrest control of the Holy Land from the grip of the Turks.
Valencia, Spain, July 10, 1099: Rodrigo Diaz de Vivar (El Cid), heroic soldier, dies, aged about 56.
Jerusalem, Middle East, July 15, 1099: The Crusaders seize Jerusalem.

King Macbeth

Church Split

Europe, 1054: The Great Schism has finally been declared official. After hundreds of years of bickering, the Roman Catholic Church and the Eastern Orthodox Church have decided to go their separate ways. In a dramatic move, Pope Leo IX and Patriarch Michael Cerularius of Constantinople have excommunicated one another. This is the culmination of many long-term disputes over papal authority.

The argument between the branches of the Catholic Church has its origins in the early days of the church, when the status, as patriarchs, of three bishops was recognized. In the 450s, the bishops of Rome, Alexandria, and Antioch were joined by the bishops of Constantinople and Jerusalem. Patriarchs were made senior to other bishops in the church hierarchy, and the bishop of Rome was accorded higher status still because he was the successor to Saint Peter and because Rome was the capital of the Roman empire. The bishop of Rome has interpreted this to mean that he has absolute authority over all Christians, which is at odds with the views of the other patriarchs.

Another major stumbling block to church unity is the Roman church's insistence on inserting the *filioque* clause—the phrase "and the Son"—into the

Pope Leo IX and Patriarch Michael Cerularius of Constantinople.

Nicene Creed, allegedly challenging the official doctrine of the Trinity. This is in contravention of the order set by the Council of Ephesus.

The issue of the ecclesiastical calendar and whether to use leavened or unleavened bread for Communion hosts were also bones of contention.

Furthermore, other unresolved issues, including political, geographic, and linguistic disharmony, contributed to the schism. Interestingly, each branch of the church refers to itself as "the one Holy Catholic and Apostolic Church."

Macbeth Dead

Lumphanan, Scotland, August 15, 1057: Macbeth, or to give him his Scots name, Mac Bethad mac Findlàech, was killed today by the forces of Malcolm Canmore. It is a sad day for Scotland—Macbeth, mormaer, or provincial ruler, of Moray, was widely regarded as a good ruler who brought a fair measure of stability and prosperity to the land.

In 1054 Malcolm's allies, among them Edward the Confessor of England, had pressed Malcolm's claim to the Scottish throne. There was a skirmish at Scone, resulting in Macbeth conceding large areas of the southern part of the kingdom to Malcolm.

Malcolm has used these intervening years to his advantage, finally accumulating enough strength to defeat Macbeth's forces and kill their leader.

Macbeth is survived by his widow Gruoch, granddaughter of Kenneth III of Scotland, and her son, Lulach, who is expected to take the throne. Macbeth will be buried on the sacred isle of Iona.

William the Conqueror to Claim his Throne

Hastings, October 14, 1066: In a fierce battle today, King Harold II was mortally wounded by the forces of William of Normandy. William claims that the English throne is his by right, having been bequeathed to him by Edward the Confessor, although the Witan, the council of senior advisers, nominated Harold as king following Edward's death.

William is known as a brilliant military tactician, and he defeated the king of France in 1054 and again in 1057. His forces, who have been promised English lands in return for their allegiance, are experienced infantrymen, cavalry, archers, and crossbowmen, all of whom wear chain mail armor as protection against their enemies.

Harold's army, on the other hand, consists of both professional and casual infantrymen. Harold's one great advantage was that he arranged his forces at the top of Senlac Hill, where they formed an impenetrable wall of interlocked shields. Unfortunately, one group of men broke the formation to give chase to the Breton contingent, a move which proved fatal. It allowed the Normans to infiltrate Harold's ranks and slaughter the Englishmen. Although William had sustained heavy losses, with the shield wall destroyed, Harold's forces were simply and effectively outclassed.

At one point William himself was thought to have been killed. To the cheers of his soldiers, he lifted his helmet to prove he was still alive.

Toward the close of day, William's archers and crossbowmen fired a concentrated volley of shots high into the air, wreaking havoc on the already seriously depleted English forces. Harold's eye was pierced by an arrow and William's men then mutilated his body. When Harold's men heard of his death, many turned tail and ran away.

William is expected to proclaim himself king, possibly on Christmas Day.

Malik Shah Dead

Persia, 1092: Malik Shah, sultan of the Seljuk Empire, has died. He had been a driving force in Persia and the region for

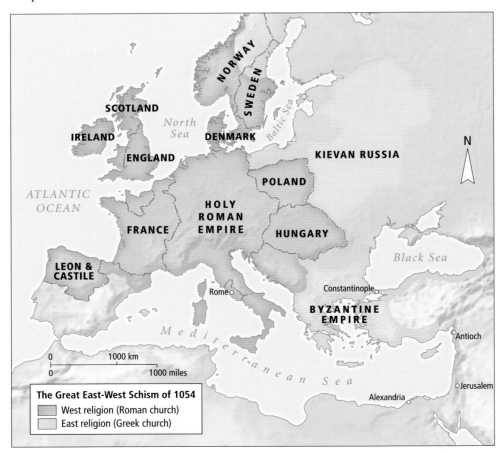

The Great East-West Schism of 1054
- West religion (Roman church)
- East religion (Greek church)

The Seljuk sultans ruled from Isfahan, in Persia.

the last 20 years and many believe that with his passing Seljuk power will decline.

Turkish by birth and a member of the ruling party of Oghuz Turks, Jalal ad-Dawlah Malik Shah continued the work of his predecessor, Alp Arslan, and expanded Seljuk power into Syria, Iraq, and Palestine. He installed client sultans in a number of areas, including Damascus and Aleppo. His goal was to rid Turkey of the Byzantine presence and to make Islam the official religion. He wanted to unite Muslims all over the world. He was successful in this and, in fact, he revived Sunni religious institutions, thus keeping in check the influence of the more radical Shi'ite powerbrokers.

His vizier, Nizam al-Mulk, assisted Malik Shah to govern in the early years of his reign and al-Mulk's influence should not be underestimated. It was he who suggested that armies be made up of men from different nationalities to reduce the risk of coups. This was a wise policy—by 1076, Malik Shah had conquered the Levant, including the holy city of Jerusalem; by 1086, he had been victorious over Suleiman, the sultan of Rum.

Malik Shah promoted the growth of culture and his rule was symbolized by the adoption of many customs from Persia and Arabia. His death has brought speculation over who will inherit the throne, and the empire may be split.

El Cid Dies

Valencia, Spain, July 10, 1099: Valencia is in mourning today following the announcement of the death of its 56-year-old leader, Rodrigo Diaz de Vivar. Popularly known as El Cid Campeador (the Lord Champion), he was renowned for his military prowess and his devotion to his country.

A childhood friend of Sancho of Castile, Rodrigo Diaz served as commander of

Sancho's troops until Sancho was assassinated in 1072. Diaz then allied himself to Sancho's brother, King Alfonso, and in 1074, he married Alfonso's niece Jimena. Later, however, Diaz locked horns with Alfonso, who believed that Diaz was plotting against him. That clash led to his banishment.

Diaz spent 10 years fighting in Muslim lands, having offered his services to al-Mu'tamin, the ruler of Saragossa in northeastern Spain, and his successor, al-Musta'in. Diaz's reputation as a brilliant soldier and inspirational leader was secured during that time.

When eastern Spain was invaded by the Almoravids from North Africa in the 1080s, Alfonso recalled Diaz from exile to enlist his help in fighting the Muslim invaders. Although El Cid did not join the fight at that time, in 1090 he opposed Berber forces and then set about his celebrated siege of Valencia, which he captured from Arab hands. Although Valencia was a predominantly Muslim city, El Cid focused on maintaining the practice of Christianity. Although nominally ruling for King Alfonso, El Cid had complete control of the city due to his superior military strength and local popularity. El Cid will be remembered as a national hero.

Crusaders Seize Jerusalem

Jerusalem, July 15, 1099: Jerusalem was captured today by crusading Christian forces who stormed through the city gates, wielding their swords and killing anyone who got in their way. In what can only be described as outright carnage, thousands of Muslims, Jews, and Orthodox Christians have been slaughtered and synagogues and mosques, including Solomon's Temple, have been razed. Women and children have been cut down while running for shelter, and not even the sacred tomb of Abraham has been spared the Christians' zeal.

In 1071 the Turks invaded Jerusalem. More than 20 years later, the Seljuks attacked the Byzantine Empire, and in 1095, in what has turned out to be possibly his most far-reaching speech, Pope Urban II called for a "crusade" to rescue the Holy Land from Muslim hands. He told the people that they would receive absolution of all their sins if they helped win back the Holy Land, and many—rich and poor alike—took up arms for the cause. Seeking revenge for the deaths of fellow Christians butchered by the Turks, they swore an oath to "do God's will."

However, it must be said that some knights joined the crusades to find wealth rather than redemption.

William the Conqueror

It has been a long campaign for the Christians. In 1097 they took Nicea, and in 1098 they won Antioch. On the way many lost their lives; others abandoned the cause. Yet, today, their efforts have borne fruit—Jerusalem has been taken from the Fatimids of Egypt.

The soldiers of the First Crusade successfully besiege Antioch.

Ibn Sina (Avicenna)

New Super Star in the Firmament

Egypt, May, 1006: Astronomers are marveling at an amazing new star that has been seen in the heavens. Travelers and merchants are reporting that the new super star, which people are referring to as a "supernova," can also be seen in Europe, the Middle East and as far away as China and Japan. The star is yellow and has been in the sky since April. Many see its coming as a sign of imminent disaster; others see it as an omen of prosperity.

Egyptian astronomer Ali bin-Ridwan has written that the star is almost three times the size of the planet Venus and sits low on the southern horizon in the constellation Lupus (the Wolf). He calculates that it is about as bright as a crescent moon, although many say it is much brighter. Scientists will be observing the supernova with continued interest.

Body Piercing for Health and Wellbeing

China, c. 1026: This year has seen great advances in acupuncture, a science

This 1023 astronomical manuscript shows the heavenly sphere.

thought to be based in Daoist traditions that has been practiced in China since ancient times. Acupuncture is the practice of piercing particular parts of the body with fine needles in order to stimulate healing in the patient, or to relieve symptoms. Acupuncture points lie along meridians, which are believed to be energy channels in the body that relate to various physical organs and functions.

Doctor Wang Weiyi has published his *Tongren Shuxue Zhen Jiu Tujing (Illustrated Manual of Points for Acupuncture and Moxibustion on a Bronze Figure with Acupoints)*, having revised the location of certain points and their meridians. The work is expected to revolutionize the practice and teaching of acupuncture.

Wang's use of life-sized bronze statues, crafted with small holes that serve as guides to the body's acupuncture points is highly innovative and effective, and it will go a long way toward standardizing the practice. Never before have medical practitioners had the benefit of 3-dimensional figures. Some 657 holes are drilled into the figures, which have been filled with water and covered over with beeswax. When a student places the needle into the correct acupuncture point, water leaks out.

In moxibustion, a complementary practice to acupuncture, moxa—cylinders of the herb

The application of heat has been used for healing since the third century BCE.

mugwort—are placed on acupuncture points and ignited. Thus heat, rather than a needle, is used to stimulate the energy in the meridians.

Along with the use of medicinal herbs and moxibustion, acupuncture is possibly the most highly respected medical practice in China today. There is talk that Wang's work will be carved on stone stele in medical establishments in Kaifeng so that everyone can learn from it.

Death of Avicenna

Hamadan, Persia, 1037: Physician and philosopher Avicenna, or ibn Sina, has died at the age of 57, reportedly from a gastrointestinal condition. Author of more than 450 books on a wide range of subjects including metaphysics, ethics, and the Arabic language, Avicenna is probably most famous for his work in the field of medicine. The *al-Qanun fi al-Tibb (The Canon of Medicine)* and the *Kitab ash-shifa' (The Book of Healing)* have long been regarded as the best books on medical science to have been published.

The Canon of Medicine, in particular, is a groundbreaking work—in it Avicenna classifies various diseases and postulates reasons for their causes. Knowing the

> "AN IGNORANT DOCTOR IS THE AIDE-DE-CAMP OF DEATH."
>
> IBN SINA (AVICENNA) (980–1037), PHYSICIAN AND PHILOSOPHER

> "GIVEN A LIGHT SOURCE AND A SPHERICAL MIRROR, FIND THE POINT ON THE MIRROR WHERE THE LIGHT WILL BE REFLECTED TO THE EYE OF AN OBSERVER."
>
> ABU AL-HASSAN IBN AL-HAYTHAM (ALHAZEN) (965–1040), IRAQI SCIENTIST AND MATHEMATICIAN, C. 1015

Key Events

World, 1006: History's brightest ever supernova is seen in the sky.

Cairo, Egypt, 1009: Ibn Yunus, famed astronomer, dies. His legacy includes the Hakemite Tables–astrological tables completed during the reign of Caliph al-Hakim, and named in his honor.

Baghdad, Iraq, c. 1010: Ibn Isa (Jesu Haly), physician, dies. His work focused on the field of optics, and he wrote *Tadhkirat al-Kahhalin (Notebook on Ophthamology)*– a comprehensive manual for ophthamologists.

Kaifeng, China, 1012: The Ministry of Agriculture imports some early-yielding rice seeds from Southeast Asia, allowing double-cropping of rice in China.

Spain, 1013: Al-Zahrawi (Albucasis), famed Muslim physician, dies. He introduced a number of surgical techniques and invented several surgical instruments. He wrote *Al-Tasrif (The Method of Medicine)*, a comprehensive encyclopedia of medical knowledge and surgical techniques.

China, c. 1017: Inoculation with infected material from smallpox victims prevents serious cases of the disease in those treated.

China, c. 1026: Physician Wang Weiyi writes *Illustrated Manual of Points for Acupuncture and Moxibustion on a Bronze Figure with Acupoints*.

Baghdad, Iraq, 1029: Al-Karkhi, mathematician, dies. His work includes *al-Kafi*, a book on arithmetic.

Manykheta, India, c. 1030: King Bhoja the Great of the Paramara Dynasty builds extensive irrigation works in west-central India.

Spain, 1035: Ibn al-Saffar, astronomer, dies. He and Maslama ibn Ahmad al-Majriti introduced to Spain the theory of triangulating for surveying.

Hamadan, Persia, before 1037: Ibn Sina (Avicenna), Persian scientist, publishes *al-Qanun fi al-Tibb*, the greatest work of medieval Islamic medicine.

Hamadan, Persia, June, 1037: Ibn Sina (Avicenna), philosopher and great physician, dies, aged 57.

China, 1040: Pi Sheng invents the first movable type using wooden blocks.

Cairo, Egypt, 1040: Al-Haytham (Alhazen), mathematician and physician, dies, aged 57.

China, 1044: For the first time a gunpowder formula is recorded, in a manual on weaponry.

cause helps find the cure. He also advocates good hygiene as a preventative measure for a number of medical conditions.

Avicenna's greatest skills were observation and critical thinking. By carefully observing his patients, he devised new treatments for both common and unusual ailments, and his prowess as a physician has saved many lives. He fostered communication and debate among the medical fraternity, theorizing that the more discussion that took place, the better equipped physicians would be to help their patients. Avicenna encouraged students to come to his lectures and to participate in debate.

A gifted youth, Avicenna attained full status as a physician at only 18 years of age, and he was soon brought to the attention of the Samanid ruler of Bukhara, whom he cured of a debilitating illness. Avicenna was rewarded with the office of vizier. Later he assumed the post of scientific adviser and physician to Abu Ya'fa, the ruler of Isfahan.

At Isfahan and later at Hamadan, Avicenna became interested in astronomy, determining that the planet Venus is closer to the Earth than it is to the Sun. He also worked on theories for calculating the difference in longitude between various cities. He was indeed a great thinker.

Avicenna's medical encyclopedia, *The Canon of Medicine*, is his greatest work.

Physician and Optical Expert Dead

Cairo, Egypt, 1040: Distinguished scientist and mathematician Abu al-Hassan ibn al-Haytham has died in Cairo. Variously called al-Basri (from the city of Basra in Iraq, where he was born in 965), or Alhazen, the Latin version of his name, al-Haytham will probably be best remembered for the advances he made in the field of optics.

His seven-volume *Kitab al-Manazir (Thesaurus Opticus)*, for which he conducted his own experiments rather than relying on ancient theories, is possibly the most important work on optics to have been written to date. Al-Haytham explains that light, whether it comes from sunlight, a fire, or reflections in a mirror, originates in straight lines in all directions. He describes the various parts of the human eye and explains that light is reflected from objects into the eye and that the curvature of the lens in the eye helps us to focus on objects. He continues with a discussion of the conditions needed to see well and explains how and why some visual errors occur. The concept of refraction is also elucidated. His book is the first satisfactory and scientific account of how we see.

Al-Haytham was also the first to realize that light can be broken down into its constituent colors, and he also contemplated the colors associated with sunsets, rainbows, and shadows. In addition, al-Haytham has made important contributions to astronomy and geometry.

time out

The Julius Work Calendar, an illustrated parchment document from around the year 1020, was probably produced at Canterbury Cathedral in England. It lists the holidays and saints' festivals for every month and shows the seasonal tasks.

Explosive News from China

China, 1044: A manual on weaponry and warfare has been published in China. Entitled *A Compendium of Military Technology*, the manual also describes gunpowder and its uses, as well as providing a formula for gunpowder.

The careful combination of 75 percent saltpeter, 15 percent charcoal, and 10 percent sulfur will produce a powder suitable for use in flame-throwers and other incendiary devices. This will be of enormous benefit in battle situations as an enemy will now be able to be assailed from some distance.

Chinese military strategy relies on being smarter than the enemy, and fire and smoke have been effective weapons as they create fear and chaos among opposing armed forces. The addition of gunpowder into arrow shafts has also been a successful method of attack, as when the arrows hit their target they cause damage to more than their immediate target.

Research has been going on for some generations in Daoist temples and, although much of the focus is on unlocking the secrets of eternal life, the scientist–monks have also engaged in more earthly pursuits. About 200 years ago, they warned that certain combinations of substances were dangerous, and many accidental fires were the result.

However, the final part of the puzzle became clear when charcoal was added to saltpeter and sulfur, creating the new material its discoverers called "huoyao," or gunpowder.

While the uses for gunpowder are many, varying from fireworks to smoke screens, the *Compendium* also provides details of a range of other useful tools and stategies for use in military campaigns, thus ensuring the greater glory of the Song Dynasty of China.

Fatimid mural, Egypt

Key Events

Ghazna, Afghanistan, 1048: Al-Biruni, scholar, dies, aged about 75. He was responsible for a number of works on subjects ranging from astronomy and mathematics to geography and culture.
China, 1050: Spinning wheels are widespread throughout China.
China, July, 1054: Chinese astronomers record the creation of the Crab Nebula.

Salerno, Italy, c. 1065: Constantine the African, a Tunisian scholar, visits the school of medicine, and begins translating his books on Islamic medicine into Latin.
Europe, April, 1066: Halley's Comet is observed at the time of the Norman Conquest.
Samarkand, Uzbekistan, 1070: Omar Khayyam writes *Maqalat fi al-Jabr wa al-Muqabila (Treatise on Demonstration of the Problems of Algebra)*.

Baghdad, Iraq, c. 1075: Al-Nasawi, Persian mathematician, dies. He is best known for his translation of Euclid's *Elements* for Arab readers.
Toledo, Spain, 1080: Botanist Ibn Bassal, who is in the employ of the Sultan of Toledo, writes *The Book of Agriculture*.
China, 1086: Shen Kua writes *Dream Pool Essays*, in which he discusses the use of the magnetic compass in navigation.

Toledo, Spain, 1087: Al-Zarqali (Arzachel), renowned instrument maker and astronomer, dies.
Persia, c. 1088: Surgeon Zarrin Dast writes his treatise on ophthalmology, *Nur al-Ayun (The Light of the Eyes)*. This amazing work includes descriptions of a number of groundbreaking treatments for eye problems and gives comprehensive information on surgery of the eye.

Italy, 1091: French-born Walcher observes an eclipse of the moon and uses an astrolabe to determine the exact time of the eclipse.
Kaifeng, China, 1092: Su Sung builds an enormous water-driven clock.
Salerno, Italy, c. 1097: Trotula of Salerno is born.

Wheels Turn Fibers into Thread

King Harold

China, 1050: Spinning wheels—an advanced kind of spindle with a pulley and drive wheel attached—are now in widespread use across the country, revolutionizing the production of threads and yarns. The origin of this marvellous device is not exactly known. Some say it was introduced into China by Persian merchants; others say that it was invented here in China. Whatever its genesis, it is a vast improvement on the simple spindle that has been used for hundreds of years.

The machine is used for both cotton and silk. It can considerably cut down the time spent hand spinning, thus making thread production more economical and less labor-intensive. Another advantage of the device is that it creates a softer thread. The cotton industry in China is growing, and the use of spinning wheels can only improve this situation. Hand spinning of silk takes many laborious hours because of the length of silk threads. The spinning wheel has changed this.

Comet Lights Up Night Sky

Normandy, April, 1066: There has been a mixed reaction to the appearance of a star with a fiery tail, called a comet, in the night skies.

Many people in Europe believe it to be a favorable omen for William of Normandy's rumored incursion into England. For King Harold and the Saxons, the comet is surely a sign of impending doom.

Signs from the heavens have long been considered as precursors to major political upheavals, such as the death of kings, the fall of governments and the invasion of countries. Harold's ascension to the English throne has not been without controversy. Upon the death of his predecessor, Edward the Confessor, in January this year, Duke William claimed that he was the rightful successor to the throne. However, Harold Godwinson, son of Earl Godwin, claimed that Edward had chosen him to rule. It was left to the council to decide who would be king and they chose Harold. Naturally, William was unhappy with this decision and has been said to be planning an invasion to take the land he believes is his by right. It is known that he has also sought the Pope's approval for this course of action.

Observers have calculated that the blazing star is about four times the size of Venus and shines with a light that is approximately one-quarter of that of the Moon. Scholars and theologians are waiting to see whether any misfortune will follow in the comet's wake.

Algebra Made Easy

Samarkand, Uzbekistan, 1070: Omar Khayyam, poet, mathematician and astronomer, has just published a major new work on algebra. In his *Maqalat fi al-Jabr wa al-Muqabila (Treatise on Demonstration on the Problems of Algebra)*, Khayyam has shed new light on some old problems. He has classified many algebraic equations according to their complexity and, relying on a geometric approach and referring to trigonometric tables, has presented solutions for many of them. He has also suggested that there are thirteen different forms of cubic equations.

One outstanding aspect of Khayyam's work is that in it he has shown conclusively that one cubic equation can have more than one solution. This is groundbreaking research and will go a long way to furthering intensive studies in algebra. Cubic equations are polynomial equations where the third power is the highest occurring power of the unknown quantity or "x."

Khayyam has been working on his treatise for some time. He had already considered the issues surrounding quadrants and radii in circles and pondered the properties of the hypotenuse of triangles. This provided the catalyst for him to solve the cubic equation by experimenting with intersecting a parabola and a circle, which led him to discover that the solution to the cubic equation is reliant on conic sections.

Scholars comment that, although Omar Khayyam owes a debt of gratitude to earlier mathematicians, there is no doubt that his work is at the cutting edge of algebra studies today.

Omar Khayyam, or to give him his full name, Ghiyath al-Din Abul Fateh Omar ibn Ibrahim al-Khayyam, is also a well-respected scientist, as he has developed an effective method for accurately determining specific gravity. His poetic works, too, are well regarded.

The Rubaiyat of Omar Khayyam shows another side of this scholar.

Scientific Achievements

Astronomy: Al-Zarqali (Arzachel) invents an astrolabe; Halley's comet is observed.
Botany: Moors introduce many new plant species—including many fruit and vegetables—to Spain.
Chemistry: Arabic knowledge of alchemy is introduced to Spain by Moors.
Geology: Theories on the creation of mountains are put forward by ibn Sina (Avicenna).
Mathematics: Ibn Sina (Avicenna) introduces cubic equations.
Medicine: Al-Zahrawi (Albucasis) writes of current medical techniques.
Physics: Use of the magnetic compass is suggested for navigational purposes.

Observatories
Hamadan Observatory, Hamadan, Persia
Mokattam Observatory, Mokattam, Egypt
Observatory built by Malik Shah, Isfahan, Persia

Universities
University of Bologna, Italy

The appearance of the comet creates quite a stir, with much speculation as to its significance.

New Book Points Way to Better Navigation

China, 1086: Scientist and diplomat Shen Kua has published a remarkable new work entitled *Meng Xi Bi Tan (Dream Pool Essays)*. In it, Shen reveals the amazing fact that compasses do not point to true north, but rather to a magnetic north pole. Having discovered this, Shen deduced that navigation and, by extension, map-making, can be made easier if magnetic compasses are used. A magnetic compass works by providing an immutable reference point, and greater navigational accuracy is achieved because the magnet aligns with the Earth's magnetic field.

Dream Pool Essays also contains dissertations on other subjects, with detailed discussions of aspects of astronomy, geology, music, and mathematics. It includes an interesting theory on fossils, suggesting that they indicate evidence of climate change. Chinese scholars are expected to embrace the new information covered in the book.

Shen Kua came to prominence following the death of his father, Shen Chou, when he took up an administrative position in the bureaucracy. Since 1054, he has been given a number of postings and early on showed a talent for land management. He devised some effective methods for controlling water, which has always been a problem in China. The construction of drains and levees resulted in the reclamation of arable land for farming. Shen went from strength to strength, and in 1069 became part of Wang Anshi's reformist group, which was responsible for more water projects and a restructure of the armed forces.

In 1072, Shen was appointed director of the Bureau of Astronomy, where he engaged in studies of the heavens by plotting the positions of the stars and planets. In 1075, he played a vital part in bringing peace to the north of China by successfully thwarting any possible invasion by tribal groups. A man of many talents, Shen Kua also held the position of finance minister, during which time he formulated techniques for keeping the economy in good order.

The magnetic compass will be used to assist sailors in their travels.

Azarchel's astrolabe was the first that could be used at any latitude.

Arzachel Dies

Toledo, Spain, 1087: Famed mathematician and astronomer Arzachel (Abu Ishaq Ibrahim ibn Yahya al-Zarqali) has died.

The most eminent astronomer of the day, Arzachel, who was born in 1028, will be remembered for creating the Toledan Tables, based on a series of painstakingly accurate astronomical observations he and other astronomers carried out in Toledo. Astronomical tables help scientists to calculate the positions of the planets and make predictions about solar eclipses, the phases of the moon, and, importantly, certain information relating to the different calendars in use around the world today, including the lunar calendar, and the Persian, Coptic, and Roman calendars.

Arzachel's work has also vastly improved the tables by which we measure latitude and longitude. He had a lifelong interest in making astronomical instruments and he is known for his improved "flat" astrolabe, which he called *safiha flatus*, which can be used at any latitude.

Arzachel established that the motion of aphelions of bodies orbiting the sun is relative to the fixed background of the stars, measuring its rate as 12.04 seconds per year. Another of his constructions was a water clock that accurately measures time and the lunar cycles.

Arzachel spent most of his life in Spain, particularly in Toledo and Cordova, where there is a strong Muslim presence.

Saxon ivory seal

Su Sung Builds Water-Driven Clock

Kaifeng, China, 1092: An enormous clock driven by water power has been unveiled in Kaifeng. Standing more than 35 ft (10 m) high, and housed in a pagoda, the mechanism is a testament to Chinese ingenuity. The clock has a number of revolving parts and many gears, and is driven solely by water. Scoops are installed around the rim, and as each scoop is filled with water it becomes heavy enough to fall forward, bringing the next scoop underneath the spout. The uniform pressure created by the constant motion of the wheel provides enough power to drive

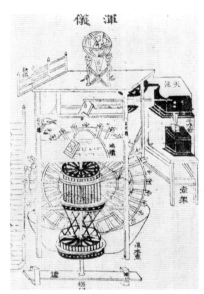

Su Sung's ingenious design for the water clock, the most accurate of the century.

various displays and mechanisms for making important astronomical observations, such as lunar cycles and the movement of the planets. It also tells the time.

Although water clocks have been in use in China for some hundreds of years, this latest clock, the brainchild of scientist and inventor Su Sung, is by far the biggest and most ambitious. Su Sung and his team began construction of his water clock in 1088. The finished clock boasts a bronze celestial globe, a rotating armillary sphere, and other elaborate adornments, and is a thing of beauty as well as an important scientific machine. The water clock is expected to provide more precise information about the solar system.

Su Sung has had an illustrious career in the civil service. He served in the Imperial Library and in 1086 he was appointed minister of justice. This year the emperor appointed him prime minister.

When Alfonso VI of Spain captured the Muslim city of Toledo in 1085, the Christians learned of Arab science.

Epic Tale Committed to Paper

Chola Dynasty bronze

Europe, c. 1000: At last the great epic poem *Beowulf* has been written down. The story has been handed down through the generations, children hearing it at their father's knee. Although no one is sure exactly how old the poem is or who originally composed it, everyone is familiar with the life of the hero Beowulf from youth to old age. The poem is 3,182 lines long, so it has been a feat of endurance to commit the work to paper.

The story begins with an account of the dreaded monster, the Grendel. Each night he came to the Danish king's palace and devoured 15 of his warriors, then swept another 15 into his massive hairy arms and took them back to his lair for later feasting. Hrothgar, the Danish king, was powerless to stop these attacks and they continued for many years.

Beowulf, a Geat who lived across the sea, heard of the monster's nightly rampages and vowed to help his neighbor destroy the Grendel. He managed to wrench an arm right off the monster, hanging his bloody trophy on the wall, but the next night the Grendel's mother entered the hall and seized the arm, taking it back to her swampy lair. Beowulf pursued her to the very depths of the marshes. Locked in battle, Beowulf spied a sword on the ground, an "invincible" blade, grabbed it and killed her. He then saw the Grendel nearby and quickly lopped off his head.

These feats brought lasting fame to Beowulf and he later became the widely loved king of the Geats.

In his old age, a dragon besieged his people and once again Beowulf was forced into battle. His mighty sword made impact, and his kinsman Wiglaf helped Beowulf to strike the death blow to the dragon, but Beowulf had been mortally wounded. His dying words expressed gratitude that he had defeated another scourge, and sorrow that he would be leaving his people.

Japanese Courtier Pens Novel Tale

Japan, c. 1000: Lady Murasaki Shikibu has published a tale of love, life, and relationships called *The Tale of Genji*. The daughter of a scholar and governor, Murasaki has crafted a finely tuned work that is unlike any literature produced before. It is known that her father permitted Murasaki to learn Chinese characters, and while such education for a girl is considered not only unseemly but also unnecessary, it has resulted in a work that people at court are calling a "novel."

Murasaki is currently in the service of Empress Akiko and it is thought that she has used

The first page of *Beowulf*, an epic tale of a warrior.

her experiences at court to inspire her work of fiction.

The Tale of Genji, or *Genji monagatori*, spanning some 75 years, is a story about a boy who is taken under the emperor's wing and brought up at court, where he learns music, poetry, and diplomacy.

In the first part of the book, Genji becomes a handsome young man and enters into many amorous relationships with women. In the second part, in Genji's middle age, focuses on court intrigue as the hero develops a position of power. In the last part of the story, Genji is dead and the hero is Kaoru, said to be Genji's son, although this is disputed by many readers.

The author explores themes such as love, friendship, and loyalty, and she also comments on the position of women in Japanese society. Some parts of the work are considered scandalous, as Genji has love affairs with some women who are not part of the emperor's court. Many readers are fascinated with the character of Genji, which will do much to ensure the success of Murasaki's creation.

Chola Bronze Sculptures in Golden Age

Kanchipuram, India, 1025: King Rajendra Chola, often called Gangaikonda, or "victor of the Ganges," Rajendra built a new capital city, Gangaikonda Cholapuram, to commemorate his triumphs and to announce to the rest of the world the military, economic, social, and cultural supremacy of the Chola kingdom.

The new city's vast stone temples house some of the most magnificent bronze sculptures in the world today, depicting Shiva, Vishnu and other important deities with the highest quality workmanship expressing classic grace.

A picture scroll of *The Tale of Genji* was produced after the publication of the novel.

Key Events

Europe, c. 1000: The epic tale of *Beowulf* is written down; it originated some centuries earlier.
Japan, c. 1000: Lady Sei Shonagon writes *Makura no soshi (Pillow Book)*–a series of tales about Japanese court life.
Kyoto, Japan, 1010: The world's first novel, *Genji monagatori (The Tale of Genji)*, is written by Lady Murasaki Shikibu.

Cairo, Egypt, 1012: The Hakim Mosque is completed by al-Hakim bi-Amr Allah. Its features include a five-aisled prayer hall and two minarets.
Kanchipuram, India, 1014: Bronze and stone sculpture of the Chola Kingdom reaches its zenith during the reign of King Rajendra.
Persia, 1020: Firdausi, poet, dies, aged about 85. He is remembered for his epic tale *Shah Namen (The Book of the Kings)*.

Kaifeng, China, c. 1020: Fan Kuan's *Travelers by Streams and Mountains* defines the ideal of Chinese landscape painting.
Kiev, Ukraine, 1037: Prince Yaroslav the Wise orders the crafting of gold and bejeweled city gates and he orders work to commence on St Sophia's Cathedral.
China, 1037: Su Shih (also known as Su Tung-p'o or Su Dongpo) is born.
Nishapur, Persia, May 18, 1048: Omar Khayyam is born.

Kaifeng, China, 1049: Replacing a wooden structure, the Iron Pagoda is built, by order of the Emperor. Despite its name, the exterior of the thirteen-storied structure is not iron, but is, in fact, clad in glazed tiles that resemble iron in color.
Novgorod, Russia, c. 1050: Inspired by the cathedral of the same name in Kiev, the five-domed structure of St Sophia's Cathedral is completed.
Avellana, near Arezzo, Italy, c. 1050: Guido of Arezzo, musician and teacher, dies, aged about 55.

Reichenau, Germany, September, 1054: Hermannus Contractus, scholar in many disciplines, dies, aged 41.
Tus, Persia, 1058: Al-Ghazali is born.
London, England, 1065: Westminster Abbey is consecrated.
Japan, c. 1065: Lady Sarashina, writer, dies. She wrote *Sarashina nikki (Sarashina Diaries)*–tales of life in eleventh-century Japan.
York, England, 1070: Archbishop of York, Thomas of Bayeux, commissions work to begin on York Cathedral.

Lady Murasaki Shikibu, a lady of the court and author of *The Tale of Genji*.

Yaroslav Builds New Cathedral

Kiev, Ukraine, 1037: Prince Yaroslav the Wise has ordered the construction of a new cathedral in Kiev in honor of Saint Sophia and has himself laid the foundation stone.

The building of the new cathedral will also commemorate his decisive victory last year over the Pechenegs, a nomadic Turkic people whose sights had been set on taking Kiev.

Nomadic tribes had long plagued Yaroslav's extensive domain, causing him to build a long line of fortifications near a number of towns along the Ros, Trubizh, and Sula Rivers and establish manned outposts at various vantage points.

Yaroslav, a staunch patron of art and education, has requested that the new cathedral be built in the Byzantine style. It is named after the spectacular Hagia Sophia in Constantinople and is intended to be more grand, with 13 domes, 5 naves, and 5 apses. There will be a wealth of frescoes and other art within its walls. He intends Saint Sophia to become an important landmark in the city of Kiev.

Yaroslav has also ordered strong new gates for the main entrance to the city. These are to be crafted from the finest gold, precious metals, and gemstones and will be known as the Golden Gates of Kiev. They will be cut into the city walls and will measure approximately 21 ft (6.4 m) high, which will accommodate the prince's military parades.

Musical Innovator Guido Dead

Avellana, near Arezzo, Italy, 1050: Musical scholar, innovator, and member of the Order of St Benedictine, Guido Monaco has died, aged about 55 years.

Author of *Regulae* and *Micrologus*, Guido of Arezzo is well known for having devised a system of musical notation that has revolutionized the learning of choral chants. Now, instead of having to laboriously learn each new hymn, choristers can "sight-sing" by reading the notes from a page that also contains the text. Before this, musicians and choristers had to learn their parts by listening, and many melodies were misheard and thus performed incorrectly.

The *Micrologus de disciplina artis musicae*, which even attracted the attention of Pope John XIX, is now used in many European monasteries. An excellent instruction manual on the use of spaces and lines in sight-singing, it also provides an analysis of today's musical practices, including discussions of polyphony.

Yaroslav the Wise

A devout Hindu, Rajendra has long been known as a patron of the arts, and so far his reign has seen a flourishing in Tamil literature, dance, music, and architecture. When he became king in 1014, he vowed to continue the work of his father Rajaraja and he has done just that. Not only has he achieved many of his father's military goals—completing the occupation of Sri Lanka and annexing Myanmar, Sumatra, Java, the Andaman and Nicobar Islands, and Bengal—but art and literature have continued to blossom under Rajendra's rule.

There is no doubt that Rajendra is leaving a valuable legacy for generations to come and that this period will go down in history as the golden age of the Cholas.

time out

The Toltec, a native American people who dominate much of central Mexico, have developed a range of grand ceremonial architecture in their capital city, Tula. In fact, the name Toltec means "master builders."

The tiles of the Iron Pagoda in Kaifeng, China, are intricately carved.

Key Events

China, 1072: Ou-Yang Hsiu, poet, writer, and historian, dies, aged about 65.

England, c. 1077: The Bayeux Tapestry, one of the most amazing records of the times, is completed.

Constantinople, Turkey, 1078: Michael Psellus, philosopher, diplomat, and scholar, dies, aged about 60. He wrote many works spanning a number of subjects, including a history of the time, *Chronographia*.

Nantes, France, 1079: Peter Abelard is born.

Windsor, England, 1080: The construction of Windsor Castle is completed.

Hangzhou, China, 1080: Su Shi, greatest poet of his age, is exiled to Hangzhou and writes many of his best-known works there.

Bremen, Germany, c. 1081: Adam of Bremen, historian, dies. His works included *Gesta Hammaburgensis ecclesiae pontificum*—a history of the Church of Hamburg.

China, 1086: Wang-Anshi, poet and statesman, dies, aged about 65. Most of his poems were written in the *shi* form.

Najaf, Iraq, 1086: Work commences on the Imam Ali Mosque. The centuries-old mosque had been burnt to the ground, and Seljuk leader Malik Shah orders rebuilding to commence.

China, 1086: Ssu-ma Kuang, Chinese official and historian, dies, aged about 67. He is remembered for his extensive history of China.

London, England, 1087: St Paul's Cathedral is destroyed by fire, and reconstruction begins,

Pagan, Burma, 1089: King Anawrahta commenced the building of the Shwezigon Pagoda during his reign, and his vision for this shrine was continued by his son, Kyanzittha. Completed now, after several decades under construction, this is a stunning example of architecture.

Durham, England, 1093: Construction of Durham Cathedral begins.

Venice, Italy, 1094: The Basilica di San Marco (St Mark's Basilica) is completed. It is built in Byzantine style, with five domes.

Wiltshire, England, c. 1095: William of Malmesbury is born.

London, England, 1098: Some twenty years under construction, the Tower of London—commissioned by William the Conqueror—is finally completed.

Historian Hermannus Contractus Dead

Reichenau, Germany, September 24, 1054:
The death of historian, astronomer, mathematician, and musician Hermannus Contractus, who has made enormous contributions to science and literature, was announced today. He was 41 years old. Born at Altshausen in Swabia, he was the son of Count Wolverad II. Hermannus is possibly best known for his massive history of the world, beginning with the birth of Christ and ending at the present day. It is believed to be the first work of this magnitude in the world. Scholars have praised both its scope and accuracy.

Hermannus spent his life in the Benedictine abbey at Reichenau, a small island in the middle of Lake Constance, under the spiritual guidance of Abbot Berno. Although crippled from childhood (the name Contractus describes his shortened legs), Hermannus was highly intelligent, defying his physical disabilities by applying himself to his studies and becoming one of the country's most gifted scholars.

In addition to his celebrated chronicle, Hermannus was an accomplished musician and poet who will also be remembered for his composition of hymns, including the glorious *Alma Redemptoris Mater (Kindly Mother of the Redeemer)* and *Salve Regina*, both in praise of the Virgin Mary. Hermannus also wrote learned papers on theology and various branches of mathematics, including geometry and arithmetic, and scholars came from across the land to learn from him. He was also a linguist of note, being fluent in Greek, Latin and Arabic. An inventive man and a proficient astronomer, Hermannus constructed various

Edward the Confessor

"EDWARDUS LONGUS SCOTORUM MALLEUS HIC EST."
("HERE IS LONG EDWARD, THE HAMMER OF THE SCOTS.")

INSCRIPTION ON THE TOMB OF EDWARD THE CONFESSOR (D. 1066) IN WESTMINSTER ABBEY

"CAN YOU WALK ON WATER? YOU HAVE DONE NO BETTER THAN A STRAW. CAN YOU FLY IN THE AIR? YOU HAVE DONE NO BETTER THAN A BLUEBOTTLE. CONQUER YOUR HEART; THEN YOU MAY BECOME SOMEBODY."

ABDULLAH ANSARI (1006–1089), SUFI MASTER

Edward the Confessor, the builder of Westminster Abbey, at a banquet with his wife Edith.

astronomical devices, including the astrolabe, one of the newer instruments for studying the heavens.

Westminster Abbey Consecrated

London, England, December 28, 1065: At long last, Westminster Abbey, a true architectural work of art with unparalleled stonework, has been consecrated.

Edward the Confessor ordered the construction of the Abbey, upstream from the city center, back in 1045 and today it is finally open for prayer. When Edward built his royal residence on Thorney Island, on the banks of the Thames in the early1040s, he dreamed of building a magnificent church on the site of a small

Benedictine abbey nearby. It was to be in honor of Saint Peter—a fisherman reported seeing a vision of Saint Peter on that spot in 616.

Edward, the son of Ethelred II and Emma of Normandy, has managed the kingdom well in the last decade or so, and because times are peaceful and there are no major wars to fight, Edward was able to invest public money into a lasting place of worship.

A deeply religious man, Edward is said to have been upset by rumors that the Pope suggested he build an abbey to make amends when he failed to go on a promised pilgrimage. Whatever his reasons for building it, the abbey—or to give it its proper name, the Collegiate Church of Saint Peter, Westminster—will surely go down in history as one of Edward's greatest achievements.

The Abbey will host such important events as coronations and the burials of kings. Unfortunately the king was unable to attend the consecration due to illness.

Tapestry Commemorates Battle of Hastings

England, 1077: An enormous embroidery in colored wools commemorating the victory of William the Conqueror in 1066 has been finished this year. It measures only 20 in (50 cm) high, but is an amazing 230 ft (70 m) long. Many believe it to have been commissioned by Queen Matilda, the wife of King William, but others believe it to be the brainchild of William's brother, Bishop Odo.

The embroidery tells the story of recent history and even includes a panel showing the remarkable passage through the skies of a huge star, later described as

This part of the Bayeux Tapestry shows Edward the Confessor with his successor, Harold, Earl of Wessex.

a comet. Other panels depict William's preparations for war, including boat building and preparing meals for the soldiers. Based in Normandy, William had to wait for favorable winds before setting sail for England and fighting King Harold's forces. The embroiderers have gone into great detail, showing the Normans with the backs of their heads shaved, while Harold's forces wear mustaches. Many aspects of the battle and its aftermath are vividly brought to life.

Not only a work of art, the tapestry is a record of the history of the 1060s, and reminds us of the fashions and customs of the day. Animals figure prominently—202 horses and 55 dogs are shown. More than 620 people are depicted, and the weavers have also created trees, ships, and weapons.

It is expected that the tapestry will be taken to Bayeux in France, to be placed in the cathedral there.

Su Shi Banished

Hangzhou, China, 1080: The poet and civil servant Su Shi has been exiled from the capital and has been sent to Hangzhou. Ideological differences with the ruling faction have been cited as one of the reasons for Su Shi's enforced exile. Others say that his political satire has played a major part— he is quick to condemn the ineptitude and greed of certain government officials, and has often been critical of some government policies.

Born in 1037 in Meishan, he studied hard and in 1057, achieved the prestigious *jinshi* degree, which allowed him to enter the civil service. A natural statesman, Su quickly rose through the ranks and held a number of senior positions in the government.

However, Su Shi is better known to some for his poetry. Also known by his literary name, Su Dongpo, the poet says he will work hard on new forms of poetry while in Hangzhou. He is already an acknowledged master in *shi*, *ci*, and *fu* forms. In *shi*, the poet takes a five-character line and expresses his own feelings; in *ci*, personal desire is usually expressed; and in *fu*, the

Part of the Bayeux Tapestry shows shipbuilding in progress.

poem is often in rhyming verse. *Fu* poetry goes all the way back to the Han Dynasty, which came to an end in 220 BCE. In addition Su Shi established the *haofang* school, which fostered a radical departure from traditional poetic forms.

Possibly Su Shi's most famous work is *Shui diao ge tou*, or *Remembering Su Zhe on the Mid-Autumn Festival*, which was written in honor of his brother. Su Shi is well aware of the importance of this festival to family togetherness. Other works that will no doubt become as well known include his First and Second *Chibifu*, or *The Red Cliffs* and *Nian Nu Jiao: Chibi Huai Gu*, or *Remembering Chibi, sung to the tune of Nian Nu Jiao*.

Su Shi is also an acclaimed painter and calligrapher and is expected to further hone his skills while in exile.

Windsor Castle Completed

Windsor, England, 1080: Another of King William's castles has been completed, this one at Windsor, west of London. As part of his defence policy, William has commissioned the building of a number of fortifications around the greater London area.

It is understood that William leased the site of the new castle in 1070 from the Manor of Clewer. Not long after, he built a motte and bailey castle. This type of castle is popular with William because construction can be done quickly. The motte is an artificial hill, often reinforced with clay, with a keep at the top. The earth for the motte is always taken from the area around it, thus creating a ditch

that provides extra protection. The bailey, or courtyard, is surrounded by a wooden fence. Windsor Castle is expected to be in constant use.

New Tower in London

Tower of London

London, England, 1098: The Tower of London, under construction for 20 years, is finished. Building commenced on the site on the north banks of the River Thames in 1078 under the guidance of Gundulph, the Bishop of Rochester, who may have had some say in its planning and design. Originally commissioned by William the Conqueror, the tower was intended to provide a convenient place from which to keep order in the kingdom and to provide an effective base for the king's forces in London, which has rapidly become the largest city in the country. William has long recognized the importance of keeping London in safe hands. The Tower functions now as a fortress, a barracks and an arsenal.

The Tower is in fact a series of fortified walls, extending some 3,136 ft (956 m) around, with the White Tower dominating the ramparts. Where possible, the old walls built during the Roman occupation have been retained. The finest Norman masons were employed to build the tower and many hundreds of laborers have been kept in work during its construction.

One of the interesting aspects of the Tower of London is the use of ditches on the northern and western sides. As deep as 10 ft (3 m) and up to 25 ft (7.5 m) wide, the ditches render surprise attacks virtually impossible. This fortification is unlike any we have seen in recent times and the tower is expected to become a focal point for the city.

Key Structures

Abbaye aux Hommes and Abbaye aux Dames, Caen, France
Canterbury Cathedral (rebuilt), Canterbury, England
Cathedral of St Sophia, Novgorod, Russia
Chateau Ducal, Caen, France
Church of the Holy Sepulchre (rebuilt), Jerusalem, Middle East
Friday Mosque, Isfahan, Persia
Great Zimbabwe, Zimbabwe
Gunbad-i-Qabus, Gurgan, Persia
Iron Pagoda, Kaifeng, China
Mainz Cathedral, Mainz, Germany
St Sophia's Cathedral, Kiev, Ukraine
Salisbury Cathedral, Salisbury, England
Sun Temple, Modhera, India
The Ancestors' Temple, Foshan, China
Tower of London, London, England
University of Bologna, Bologna, Italy
Wat Ek Temple, Battambang, Cambodia
Winchester Cathedral, Winchester, England
Westminster Abbey, London, England
Windsor Castle, Windsor, England

The Round Tower of Windsor Castle. The Castle is a day's march from London.

Lady Godiva

> *"COFFEE FORTIFIES THE MEMBERS, CLEANS THE SKIN, DRIES UP THE HUMIDITIES, AND GIVES AN EXCELLENT SMELL TO ALL THE BODY"*
>
> IBN SINA (AVICENNA) (980–1037), PHYSICIAN AND PHILOSOPHER, C. 1000

> *"THE MOUNTED KNIGHT IS IRRESISTIBLE; HE WOULD BORE HIS WAY THROUGH THE WALL OF BABYLON."*
>
> ANNA COMNENA, DESCRIBING KNIGHTS OF THE FIRST CRUSADE, 1097

Small is Beautiful for Feet

Kaifeng, China, 1000: It has become common practice in recent years to bind the feet of highborn women at the imperial court. Bound feet are a sign of feminine beauty and culture and more and more parents, even those from the lower classes, are opting to have their daughters' feet bound, thus improving their chances of making a good marriage. Men find these tiny feet very exciting, and images of bound feet have been incorporated into published erotica.

It has been suggested that the practice began when the Empress Taki was born with a club foot. To cover her deformity, her father is said to have ordered that her feet and the feet of all women at court be bound. The practice is now becoming widespread.

The ideal foot size is approximately 3 in (8 cm). In order to achieve perfect feminine feet, it is important to begin binding at the age of about four or five years. The toes must be bent under the foot and the bones broken, so that they will then grow into the desired curved "lotus" shape.

Ibn Sina (Avicenna) treats patients affected with all kinds of disease.

Critics of the practice point to some of the unwanted effects of foot binding, from offensive odors, to excessive pain, to gangrene and possible death. However, the practice is unlikely to cease, as women with smaller feet will do better in society than those with "normal" feet. And for women at court, having unbound feet is simply unthinkable.

Coffee's Health Claims Debated

Middle East, c. 1000: Coffee drinking is becoming more widespread in the Arab world. Persian physician ibn Sina (Avicenna) has advocated the use of the beverage because of its medicinal qualities. Coffee is believed to invigorate the spirit and helps to ward off sleepiness. Islamic scholars and scientists have been debating whether this is in fact a good thing, or whether coffee is a harmful substance.

Islamic theologians are also divided on the merits of the drink. While many agree that it is a good substitute for alcohol, the use of which is forbidden by the *Qu'ran*, others feel that its use is not religiously appropriate. Coffee is sometimes referred to as "gahwa," which means "prevents sleep," and many religious men have seen the advantages of its use in staying awake for prayer and meditation.

Yet while debate is raging, ordinary people are enjoying the taste of the beverage, some sweetening its bitterness with honey or sugar according to their tastes.

Coffee is often said to have been accidentally discovered when a shepherd noticed that his flock became hyperactive when they ate certain berries. Yet coffee beans are believed to have been cultivated for hundreds of years, and there is a reference in Homer's *Odyssey* to an unusual beverage, which many believe is a reference to buchum, or coffee. However, it is only now that it is beginning to gain wider popularity.

Traders first brought coffee beans from Africa and grew the plant for its berries. When mature, the berries are boiled and the resulting beverage is not only delicious but an effective stimulant.

Easy Money

Kaifeng, China, 1024: With the shortage of metal available for minting coins, and the overissue of iron coins, there has been a strong move toward the use of paper money. Originally used as notes of credit, or exchange certificates, paper money was intended to be redeemable within a three-year period, but because it is easier to carry than heavy coins or silver, this restriction has been lifted. Paper money has become very popular because it can now be used in exchange for a wide variety of supplies.

Although China has used paper money in the past, notably in the 900s, it is only now that its use is becoming common and widespread.

Recent advances in the printing process have made the production of paper money easier and more efficient, and merchants in all the major regions have embraced its use.

Another advantage of paper money is that it frees up large amounts of silver, silk and other luxury goods for payment to the Khitan, a northern tribe that has been a thorn in the side of the emperor.

Tiny lotus shoes are sold for women with bound feet.

time out

In 1071, a two-pronged fork was first introduced to Western culture in Venice, Italy. It was brought to Venice by a Byzantine princess who was engaged to be married to the Venetian Doge.

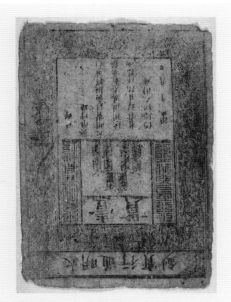

This Chinese banknote is equal to 1000 coins.

Viking brooch

Death of Elder Statesman

Kyoto, Japan, 1027: Japan is in mourning following the announcement of the death of Fujiwara Michinaga, one of the most respected statesmen of our time.

Fujiwara exerted unprecedented influence in Japan, being the father of four empresses and two regents and grandfather to two emperors.

Born in 966, he first came to the imperial court as a teenager. Fujiwara gained the support of Emperor Ichij's mother and sister and was appointed to the position of emperor's secretary. This gave him access to important documents dealing with matters of state, and he soon became one of the most powerful men at court.

A consummate politician, Fujiwara was able to control much of what happened at court and in political circles. Many will recall that he persuaded Ichij to make his daughter Akiko the empress. In 1016, he forced his nephew Emperor Sanjo to abdicate, installing his grandson Go-Ichij as emperor. Although Fujiwara never officially held the position of *kampuku*, or regent, he was the emperor's closest adviser and it has been an open secret that his word was final.

A highly cultivated and educated man, Fujiwara is often said to have been the inspiration for Genji in Murasaki Shikibu's *The Tale of Genji*.

Lady Godiva Rides Naked through Coventry

Coventry, England, 1057: Lady Godiva, or Godgifu, as she is sometimes known, caused a sensation when she rode naked through the streets of Coventry. In doing so she has won a victory for the people, as her bold action has convinced her husband to abolish the current harsh taxation system.

An unassuming and religious woman, Godiva has long been opposed to the very high taxes levied on the townsfolk by her husband, Leofric, Earl of Mercia. Inside sources claim that Leofric and Godiva have argued about the rate of taxation for some time and that Leofric challenged his wife to this ride thinking that she would lack the will to follow it through. But Godiva, although a wealthy woman herself, strongly feels that many poorer people are distinctly disadvantaged by the heavy taxation burden placed upon them by Leofric.

Sources differ on the details of the ride itself. Some say that Lady Godiva requested that the townsfolk remain indoors while she rode through the streets; others say that she rode through the crowded marketplace, from one end to the other. It is said that she wore her hair unbound so that it would provide some cover for her modesty.

Lady Godiva is known as an exceptional horsewoman and a patron of the arts and, apart from this unusual show of wifely rebellion, is a devoted spouse to Leofric. In 1043 the couple established an abbey in Coventry dedicated to Saint Eunice of Saxmundham. Many believe that her husband's insistence on ever heavier taxation in order to fund his public works led to Godiva's fateful ride.

Lady Godiva's courage has made life easier for the people of Coventry; she convinced her husband to lower taxes.

Key Events

England, 1067: Following the Norman conquest of Britain, many French words make their way into English everyday language.

Africa, 1067: Al-Bakri writes of the court of the kingdom of Ghana (now Mali), that "Behind the king stand ten pages holding shields and swords decorated with gold, and on his right are the sons of the (vassal) kings of his country wearing splendid garments and their hair plaited with gold."

Northeast England, 1069-1070: William the Conqueror systematically wipes out the region between the River Humber and Durham in the "Harrying of the North."

Rome, Italy, March, 1074: Pope Gregory VII advocates celibacy for the clergy, and suggests that priests should not be allowed to marry.

Tehran, Persia, 1079: At the Sultan's request, a new, more accurate calendar is implemented this year.

Newcastle-upon-Tyne, England, 1080: Newcastle-upon-Tyne is settled by the conquering Normans when the son of William the Conqueror, Robert Curthose, builds a castle here. The city is strategically located for monitoring the unruly Scots and their warmongering tendencies.

England, c. 1086: William the Conqueror orders that details of his subjects be recorded. Compilation of the information results in the Book of Winchester (the Domesday Book).

Khorasan, Persia, 1090: The Islamic sect known as the Assassins is formed by Hasan ibn Sabbah.

Venice, Italy, 1094: The trademark transport of Venice, the gondola, is mentioned in records for the first time.

France, August, 1096: Peter the Hermit encourages peasants and workers to join the Peasants' Crusade (or People's Crusade) to gain control of Jerusalem.

Citeaux, France, 1098: The first Cistercian monastery is founded by Robert of Molesme with Alberic and Stephen Harding.

Europe, 1099: By the end of this century chimneys and mantled fireplaces are bringing more efficient (and less smoky) heating to the houses of the wealthy.

William the Conqueror

North of England Harried

Northeast England, 1069-70: Thousands of peasants and farmers have died since King William embarked on his "harrying of the north" campaign. In a ruthless bid to enforce his rule and prevent the populace from siding with the Danes under the leadership of Sweyn Estridsen, William has ordered the burning of entire villages and the deaths of those living in them. Animals have been slaughtered and crops and grain houses destroyed so that anyone who escapes the massacre will eventually die of hunger. The devastation spreads from the River Humber to Durham.

Few parts of northern England have not been decimated. William's policy of slaughtering and burning has ensured that his rule is supreme, and there are unlikely to be any insurrections for him to quash.

Unfortunately, thousands of people are now destitute, and where once there were thriving communities, now there are scores of homeless souls who must scavenge for food and shelter to survive, often in competition with wild dogs. Disease is rife, as corpses remain unburied and unshriven. Desperate thieves and pickpockets have no qualms about stealing the little they can.

While it is difficult to determine the number of people who have lost their lives, estimates put the figure at about 150,000.

"THERE WAS SUCH HUNGER THAT MEN ATE THE FLESH OF THEIR OWN KIND, OF HORSES AND DOGS AND CATS."

SIMEON OF DURHAM, DESCRIBING THE "HARRYING OF THE NORTH", 1070

"NOTHING CAN BE WORSE THAN ALLOWING THE DRIVER OF ONE'S OX-CARRIAGE TO BE BADLY DRESSED."

SEI SHONAGON, JAPANESE NOVELIST,

Clifford's Tower in York was built as part of King William's northern campaign.

It will take at least a generation to restore the land and its people to some semblance of productivity and social harmony.

Marriage Out for Priests

Rome, Italy, March, 1074: In a move that is expected to be widely unpopular among the clergy, Pope Gregory VII has called for all priests to be celibate.

Although the idea has been around for some time, the Pope has taken up the cause with great vigor. He has already published a controversial encyclical in which he absolves people for disobedience to those bishops who have permitted married men to become priests. He is expected to go even further and stop any monetary allowances being paid to married men of the cloth.

Pope Gregory VII is already known for his desire to have all differences of opinion about church policy and theological matters mediated in Rome.

Although he has only been on the papal throne since April 1073, the Holy Father is also vehemently opposed to retaining those members of the clergy who have achieved their holy office through payment. He has targeted priests and bishops who have purchased churches or other buildings for themselves, advocating that no one should be allowed to buy or sell any clerical rights.

His penchant for radical reforms has already put him in conflict with many German bishops, who have taken their complaints to Henry IV of Germany. Married German clergy have also expressed their strong condemnation of the new rule of celibacy, saying that the Scriptures do not support such a move. They cite 1 Timothy 3:2 "It behoves thus a bishop to be blameless, the husband of one wife." Pope Gregory VII is unmoved by opposition from within the clergy and intends to implement his reforms as soon as possible.

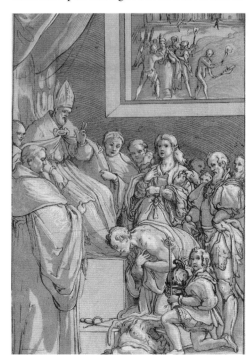

Pope Gregory VII was determined to reform the Church, although he met with much opposition.

New Persian Calendar

Tehran, Persia, March 15, 1079: By order of Sultan Jalal al-Din Malik Shah, a new calendar has come into use today, superseding all other calendars. It will be known as the Jalali calendar in honor of the Sultan.

Five years ago, the Sultan asked well-known astronomer and mathematician Omar Khayyam to join with a group of scientists to more accurately measure the length of the year. By observing the passage of the sun and by beginning the year on the vernal equinox, Khayyam was able to determine that there were 365.24219858156 days in each year. Having such a precise figure led him to suggest that eight "leap" days be inserted into the calendar every 33 years.

Omar Khayyam, who hails from Nishapur, is a very accomplished Persian. In addition to mathematics and astronomy, he is also a philosopher and physician. Many will be familiar with his collection of quatrains, *The Rubaiyat*.

England Surveyed

England, 1086: The Book of Winchester is finished. Last year, King William commissioned the work—a complete survey of his subjects—to be collected in one volume for easy reference. He plans to use the information to better administer his

The Domesday Book helped King William learn about his new realm.

realm and to determine how much tax he can levy. The book contains information on the land and assets of 13,418 settlements in the counties south of the rivers Tees and Ribble.

The information is very detailed, listing the names and assets of landholders and their tenants, as well as the number of people who live on that land, including villagers and even slaves. The assets are broken down into buildings, croplands, numbers of livestock, fisheries, and indeed anything that earns the owner income. William needs to keep money in the state coffers if he is to continue resisting attempted incursions from Scandinavia. The army is costly to run

and William cannot afford to let his defences drop. The survey has given him a basis on which to tax individual land-owners. It has also provided an indication of the country's overall economic position.

William is also mindful of the fact that there are sections of the population who are resentful of his rulership and who are still bitter about the harrying of the north that left thousands impoverished in 1069–70. Interestingly, many of these areas are described as "wasted." William sees that the possession of information about potential threats to his rule is a further benefit of the survey.

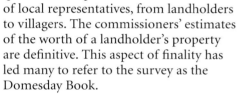

Information has been systematically collected by royal commissioners, who held public meetings at which they asked a series of questions to a panel

Peter the Hermit's preaching inspired many Crusaders.

of local representatives, from landholders to villagers. The commissioners' estimates of the worth of a landholder's property are definitive. This aspect of finality has led many to refer to the survey as the Domesday Book.

Assassins Organized

Khorasan, Persia, 1090: Hasan ibn Sabbah has formed an elite group of freedom fighters, the Hashshashin, or Assassins, made up of men who are willing to die for their beliefs. A secret society, the group is responsible for the deaths of their political enemies, including the Seljuk rulers and Sunni scholars (Hasan ibn Sabbah himself has a personal dislike of Nizam al-Mulk, the Seljuk vizier and a Sunni). The Assassins are highly trained and their weapon of choice is the dagger. They prefer to kill their targets in public places so their message will be relayed to as many as possible.

Two years ago, in 1088, Hasan established a settlement in the mountains at Alamut in northern Persia, and it was not long after that he gathered a small army of followers devoted to his cause, which is the dissemination of Nizari beliefs. The Nizaris are a sect of Ismaili Islam. A fanatical devotee of the cult, Hasan is said to have had his own son executed for consuming alcohol.

Members of the sect refer to themselves as al-da'wa al-jadida, or "the new doctrine," but they are commonly known as Hashshashin. There is some dispute over their name. Some believe that they use hashish to prepare themselves for their missions; others say that the word

simply means "follower of Hasan." Another theory is that the name is derived from al-Assas, which is the base from which operations are carried out.

In any case, the members of this sect are considered outlaws.

Paupers March to Jerusalem

France, August, 1096: The preacher Peter the Hermit, of Amiens has rallied to Pope Urban II's call to make Jerusalem a Christian city. Many thousands of peasants have responded, looking for a way out of their miserable lives. In what is being called the "People's Crusade," men, women, and children have gathered with Peter, who set off from Cologne for Jerusalem via Constantinople. One estimate puts the number of followers at 100,000.

The majority of Peter's followers are peasants and paupers with no fighting experience and no understanding of the ways of foreigners or the rules of conquest. They are undisciplined and disorganized and have joined the Crusade in the hope of improving their lot in life. Many live in appalling squalor, have little to eat, wear threadbare clothing, and suffer high mortality rates. Their weapons are makeshift and they appear unwilling to accept direction, although some are responsive to Peter's leadership.

Along the way, they are pilfering and looting, and engaging in fights damaging to morale. They feel entitled to hospitality

from the cities they pass through, but they are unwilling to accede to local customs. This is causing a great deal of unrest, as skirmishes are constantly breaking out.

In addition to this, anti-Semitic feeling is gaining momentum and the "People's Crusaders" are murdering any Jews they encounter. Some preachers are fomenting hatred by saying that Jews and Muslims are enemies of Jesus Christ and that they deserve to die, unless they can be converted to Christianity. Many in the people's crusade hold the Jews responsible for the death of Christ and are seeking what they see as retribution. They are eager to see Jerusalem in Christian hands.

Whether they achieve their goal remains to be seen, but they have certainly put aside their ordinary lives in this quest for an adventure in God's name.

Peter the Hermit

Religious Leaders

Popes
Sylvester II (999-1003)
John XVII (1003)
John XVIII (1003-09)
Sergius IV (1009-12)
Benedict VIII (1012-24)
John XIX (1024-32)
Benedict IX (1032-45)
Sylvester III (1045)
Gregory VI (1045-46)
Clement II (1046-47)
Benedict IX (1047-48)
Damasus II (1048)
Leo IX (1049-54)
Victor II (1055-57)
Stephen X (1057-58)
Nicholas II (1058-61)
Alexander II (1061-73)
Gregory VII (1073-85)
Victor III (1086-87)
Urban II (1088-99)
Paschal II (1099-1118)

Antipopes
Gregory (1012)
Sylvester III (1044)
Benedict X (1058)
Honorius II (1061-72)
Clement III (1080-1100)

Patriarchs of Constantinople
Michael I Cerularius (1043-1058)
Constantine III Lichudes
(1059-1063)
John VIII Xiphilinus (1064-1075)
Cosmas I (1075-1081)
Eustathius Garidas (1081-1084)
Nicholas III Grammaticus
(1084-1111)

The defeat of the Saxon army at the Battle of Hastings in 1066 gave the English crown to William of Normandy.

49

King William Rufus

King Meets Death

Hampshire, England, August 2, 1100: In a sensational turn of events, William Rufus was killed today while deer hunting with his brother Henry in the New Forest. Reports say that the king was struck in the chest by a stray arrow fired by Walter Tirel, count of Poix, a member of the hunting party.

Few are likely to mourn the loss of William II, especially members of the Church, with whom he had a hostile relationship. Cruel and belligerent, he was renowned for his profane language and blunt manner. Nevertheless, during his short reign he managed to consolidate the kingdom and restore and extend the Norman empire through vigorous campaigns. William also acquired a three-year lease on the duchy of Normandy for 10,000 marks when his older brother, Robert Curthose, mortgaged the lands to pay for his Crusade expenses. The rebellious Robert has disputed both the division of the lands and his brother's succession ever since their father's death.

Henry is now set to seize the throne, as the king had no heir and Robert has not yet returned from the Holy Land. The younger brother's presence at this unfortunate event has caused some to question whether William's death was truly an accident. Indeed, Tirel's close association with supporters of Henry is troubling. However, the dangers of deer hunting are well-known, as both the king's older brother, Richard, and a nephew died in similar circumstances.

Knights to Defend Pilgrims

Jerusalem, Middle East, c. 1118: Thanks to a new military service, pilgrims traveling through the Holy Land to Jerusalem will now receive a greater level of protection during this often perilous journey. Hughes de Payens, a knight from the Champagne region, and his companions have recently formed the Order of the Temple, an organization sworn to defend Jerusalem against the continued Muslim threat.

De Payens and his men are all veterans of the First Crusade, which commenced in 1095 after an impassioned appeal by Pope Urban II for all Christians to liberate the Holy Land from Islamic rule. The pope intended the army to consist largely of knights, but his plea inspired people of all classes, who set off for Jerusalem in their thousands. This first wave of inexperienced crusaders arrived in Constantinople in August 1096, but they were soon decimated when they attempted to take Nicaea and Civetot.

In December, however, several contingents of knights gathered at the Bosphorus. Once they had garnered supplies from the Byzantine emperor, Alexius I, the force marched through Asia Minor, attacking Nicaea and blockading the city of Antioch, before finally winning Jerusalem in 1099 after a lengthy and bloody siege.

The region around the city is still not secure. Christian settlements have been established right through the Levant, but these have come under frequent attack, requiring further military expedi-

This Byzantine gold coin was minted during the rule of Alexius I Comnenus, Emperor of the East (1081-1118).

tions to protect them. Baldwin II, the king of Jerusalem, has gladly welcomed the offer of the Knights Templars to help maintain the vulnerable kingdom.

Song Dynasty Overthrown

Kaifeng, China, 1127: Jurchen barbarians from Manchuria have sacked and torched Kaifeng, the capital of Henan province, marking the end of the great Song Dynasty, which began in 960. Despite superior firepower, the Song army was weak and badly organized and no match for the battle-hardened Jurchen horsemen, who several years ago successfully overthrew the Manchurian Liao Dynasty.

The sacking of Kaifeng comes less than a year after the abdication of Emperor Huizong in favor of his son Qinzong. Father and son have both been stripped of their titles and as commoners will soon be expelled to remote northern Manchuria to live out the rest of their days. Most of the imperial family and many government officials have also been captured.

Reports have emerged, however, that one of the sons of Emperor Huizong has escaped to southern China along with some members of the Song court, and

Culture and the arts flourished during the golden age of the Song Dynasty.

Hampshire, England, August 2, 1100: King William II (William Rufus) dies on a hunting trip, aged about 44. He is succeeded by his brother, Henry I.

Tinchebrai, France, September 28, 1106: The Battle of Tinchebrai is fought between the forces of Henry I of England and his brother, Robert Curthose, Duke of Normandy. Robert is defeated and imprisoned.

Tripoli, Middle East, July 12, 1109: After surviving a number of years under siege, the city of Tripoli finally falls to the Crusaders.

Beirut, Middle East, May, 1110: The city capitulates to the Crusaders.

Sidon, Middle East, December 4, 1110: The Crusaders capture the city of Sidon.

Beijing, China, 1115: Jurchen warriors from Manchuria defeat the Khitan Liao dynasty, and establish the Jin dynasty in northern China.

Jerusalem, Middle East, c. 1118: The religious military order of the Knights Templars is founded by French nobleman Hughes de Payens.

English Channel, November 25, 1120: The heir to the English throne—William the Aethling—drowns after the event known as the "Wreck of the White Ship." Henry I resorts to naming his daughter Mathilda as his heir. This proves unpopular, as the realm is reluctant to accept the possibility of a female monarch.

China, 1127: The Jin army drives the Song dynasty from its capital at Kaifeng. The Southern Song dynasty is later established in southern China.

Guimarães, Portugal, June 24, 1128: The Battle of Sao Mamede is fought out between the forces of Afonso Henriques (the victor, who will go on to become Afonso I of Portugal), and his mother, Teresa.

France, 1131: Louis VII is anointed as successor to his father Louis VI.

Cardiff, Wales, February 10, 1134: Robert Curthose, Duke of Normandy, dies in prison, aged about 80.

China, 1135: Huizong, former Song Dynasty emperor, dies a prisoner, aged 52.

Northallerton, England, August 22, 1138: The Battle of the Standards takes place between local English forces supporting King Stephen and the forces of King David of Scotland.

Tikrit, Iraq, 1138: Birth of Saladin.

Ghazni, Afghanistan, 1140: Ghorid forces of central Afghanistan capture the city of Ghazni.

Uzbekistan, September 8, 1141: The Battle of Samarkand sees Seljuk Sultan Sanjar defeated by the Qara-Khitai forces.

his intention is to gather support and declare a new Song dynasty in the south at Lin'an (Hangzhou). This will be a significant event in Chinese history because it will be the first time the seat of power has moved from the ancestral home-lands along the Huanghe (Yellow River) into the Yangtze valley. Many would say not before time, as for decades people have been abandoning the war-torn north to resettle on the banks of the Yangtze and further south. More than two-thirds of the Chinese population of 110-million is now settled in this region of flourishing ricefields and farmland.

The Song Dynasty will be remembered as a cosmopolitan era, renowned for its efficient bureaucracy and flourishing economy. Technological advancement, especially in the area of firearms, was far ahead of contemporary Europe. Above all, the Northern Song has seen artistic expression flourish with new forms of poetry, painting and ceramics.

Imprisoned Usurper Dies

Cardiff, Wales, February 10, 1134: Robert Curthose, the former Duke of Normandy, died today in Cardiff Castle, the site of his imprisonment for many years. His brother, Henry I, has held Robert captive since 1106, when he was taken prisoner. The brothers' relationship soured when Robert returned from the Crusades to discover his younger sibling had seized the crown, after the untimely death of William Rufus. When his attempted invasion of England failed, Robert finally agreed to recognize Henry as king in the Treaty of Alton. Nevertheless, Henry, in turn, invaded Normandy, first taking the fortified Abbey of Saint-Pierre sur Dives and then besieging the castle of Tinchebrai. Robert endeavored to break the siege, but after a short battle, both he and

time out

In July 1201, a deadly earthquake hit many parts of the eastern Mediterranean, especially Egypt and Syria. An estimated 1.1 million people lost their lives in the devastating natural disaster.

his men were captured. Although usually ruthless with his enemies, Henry condemned his brother to confinement.

King of Khmer Empire Falls

Angkor, Cambodia, 1150: The great ruler of the Khmer Empire, King Suryavarman II, has died. His death occurred during his most recent military campaign against the kingdom of Champa. He came to the throne in 1113, quickly unifying the country after years of unrest. After re-establishing diplo-matic relations with China, he sought to expand his kingdom, eventually push-ing its boundaries west to Burma, south toward the Gulf of Thailand, and east to southern Vietnam. However he embarked upon a series of unsuccessful campaigns

against the kingdom of Dai Viet, during which he fell out with the Chams who had sided with the Vietnamese.

During his reign, Suryavarman took advantage of his nation's extensive irrigation system to build two new cities at Beng Melea and Kompong Svay. He also changed the spiritual lives of his people by choosing Vaisnavism—the worship of Vishnu—as the official religion. Early in his reign, he commissioned a temple to Vishnu at Angkor. Surrounded by a broad moat and an outer enclosure wall, the enormous monument, known as Angkor Wat, consists of three ascending rectangular galleries surrounded by five majestic towers representing the home of the Hindu gods, Mount Meru. Although not yet completed, this exquisite temple stands as a fitting testament to both the highly developed Khmers and their dynamic modernizing king.

Detail, Angkor Wat

Angkor Wat; built during the reign of King Suryavarman II for the worship of the Hindu dieity Vishnu.

Portugal, October 5, 1143: Portugal becomes an independent kingdom.
Europe, 1147: Following the fall of the County of Edessa in 1144, the Second Crusade begins.
Angkor, Cambodia, 1150: Suryavarman II, one of the greatest leaders of the Khmer Empire, dies in battle.
Bordeaux, France, 1152: Henry II marries Eleanor of Aquitaine, consolidating her extensive holdings in France into his realm.

Scotland, May 23, 1153: King David I of Scotland dies, aged about 68. He is succeeded by his grandson, Malcolm IV.
Dover, England, October 25, 1154: King Stephen dies, aged about 57, and is succeeded by Henry II.
Rome, Italy, 1155: Frederick Barbarossa, King of Germany, is proclaimed Holy Roman Emperor.
Oxford, England, September 8, 1157: Birth of Richard I, who will later become better known as Richard the Lionheart.

Lake Baikal, Russia, c. 1167: Birth of Genghis Khan.
Canterbury, England, December 29, 1170: The Archbishop Thomas Becket is murdered in Canterbury Cathedral, aged about 50.
Khandahar, Afghanistan, 1173: Mohammad Ghori becomes the Sultan of Afghanistan and plans the conquest of India.
Angkor, Cambodia, 1181: King Jayavarman VII takes the throne of the Khmer Empire. The empire will expand and be at its most powerful during his reign.

Italy, 1182: Birth of Francis of Assisi.
Dan-no-Ura, Japan, April 25, 1185: Minamoto samurai warriors win the civil war by defeating the Taira clan in a great naval battle.
Tiberias, Middle East, 1187: The Battle of Hattin sees a resounding victory for Saladin's forces over the Crusaders. Over the next few years, the Crusader strongholds will fall to Saladin's forces, with the city of Tyre proving the only exception.
Europe, 1189: In an attempt to regain control of the Holy Land from Saladin, the Third Crusade begins.

France, July 6, 1189: Henry II of England, dies at Chinon, aged about 66. He is succeeded by his son, Richard I (Richard the Lionheart).
Japan, 1192: Minamoto no Yoritomo becomes the first Shogun of the Kamakura dynasty, unifying Japan.
Damascus, Middle East, March 4, 1193: Saladin, Muslim sultan and warrior, dies after a brief illness, aged about 55.
Chalus, France, April 6, 1199: Death of Richard I of England. He is succeeded by his brother, King John.

Henry II Succeeds Stephen

King Henry II

Dover, England, October 25, 1154: King Stephen died today and Henry II, the son of his cousin, Empress Mathilda, shall succeed him. This outcome was inevitable, as Stephen's claim to the throne has always been tenuous.

Born in 1096 to Adela, daughter of William the Conqueror, Stephen was educated at the court of Henry I, his uncle. A lucrative marriage and titles followed, enabling him to become one of the wealthiest barons in the kingdom.

The king's chosen heir was Mathilda, his only surviving legitimate child, but many were unhappy at the prospect of a Queen. With the news of Henry's death in 1135, Stephen rushed to England, where he convinced members of the church and royal administration of his right to the throne.

Mathilda disputed his accession. Her case was helped when he proved to be an inept ruler, alienating both the nobility and the church. After numerous nobles switched allegiance, Mathilda entered England in 1139, precipitating an indecisive Civil war, which raged for a decade until 1148 when she withdrew. In the following years, Stephen's control over his kingdom weakened further when he was unable to reconcile warring barons. When Henry invaded England last year to claim

"OUR KINGDOM AND WHATEVER ANYWHERE IS SUBJECT TO OUR RULE WE PLACE AT YOUR DISPOSAL AND COMMIT TO YOUR POWER ... "

HENRY II (1133–1189) OF ENGLAND, TO EMPEROR FREDERICK I BARBAROSSA, 1157

his inheritance, the nobles finally pressed for peace. Lacking support, Stephen had no choice but to accept Henry as his heir.

New Emperor Crowned

Rome, Italy, 1155: The king of Germany, Frederick I Barbarossa ("Red Beard"), has been crowned Holy Roman emperor. The young king who has ruled for three years, entered into Italy some months ago to fulfil his obligations under the Treaty of Constance, drawn up with Pope Eugenius III in 1153. In that agreement, Frederick promised not to make peace with the Normans in southern Italy and Sicily, nor with the Roman leader, Arnold of Brescia, in return for the imperial crown and all its associated rights.

Although Eugenius has since died, his successor, Adrian IV, honored the treaty by installing Frederick as emperor. For his part, Frederick captured the heretic Arnold, who was executed soon after, but the king has now withdrawn his army of 1800 knights, many of whom are sick with malaria, and abandoned Adrian to the Normans.

Archbishop Killed

Canterbury, England, December 29, 1170: The Archbishop of Canterbury, Thomas Becket, has been murdered. Four knights from Henry II's household entered the church, argued briefly with the cleric, then drew their swords and butchered him.

This assault comes months after the king and Becket were finally reconciled following years of bitter disagreement. The two were inseparable during Becket's time as lord chancellor. Henry found him to be a most agreeable companion—one who not only performed his official duties admirably, but also participated in the more hedonistic activities of court life.

Their friendship ended with Becket's elevation to archbishop. Becket exchanged his former life of decadence for one of piety, taking to his new role immediately. He took seriously his responsibility of protecting the traditional rights of Canterbury, but it was his extreme stand on ecclesiastical immunity that particularly angered the king. Their disagreement soon developed into open hostility, and in the following years both men resorted to a series of underhanded tactics to achieve their objectives. Becket eventually sought exile in

Europe, where both he and Henry endeavored to win support for their case. All attempts at a compromise failed.

In June this year, Henry ensured his lineage, calling on the Archbishop of York to crown his eldest son, an honor usually reserved for Canterbury. Curiously, it was this slight that led them one month later to achieve some measure of civility. Returning to England, Becket excommunicated all those who had supported the prince's coronation. Hearing this news, the king is said to have vented his frustration, exclaiming "Will no-one rid me of this turbulent priest?" His loyal knights appear to have taken his words literally and tonight effected what they believe their master wanted.

Yoritomo is Shogun

Japan, 1192: Emperor Go-Shirakawa has bestowed on Minamoto no Yoritomo the title *seii tai Shogun* (meaning Barbarian-vanquishing General). Japan has changed radically since Yoritomo emerged from exile a decade ago in response to a decree for all Minamoto warriors to rise up against the ruling Taira forces. Undaunted

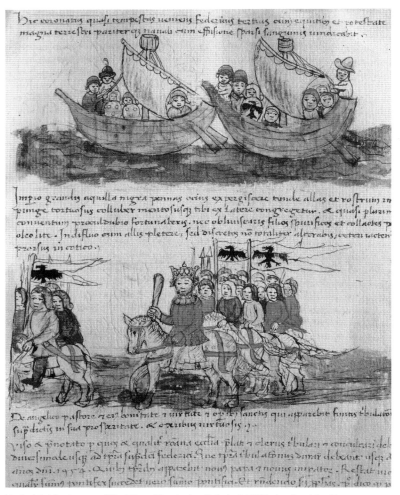

Frederick I Barbarossa ("Red Beard") entering Italy to fulfil his treaty obligations.

Muslim sultan Saladin (1138-1193) and Richard the Lionheart of England (1157-1199) battling for the holy land.

Minamoto no Yoritomo

by an early defeat, he established his headquarters at Kamakura, gathering a force of 200,000 warriors with which he mercilessly crushed the Taira army at the battle of Fujigawa.

Yoritomo chose instead to consolidate his power by improving socioeconomic conditions in his newly acquired territory in eastern Japan and subduing various Minamoto factions. He was then joined by his estranged brothers, Yoshitsune and Noriyori, who were instrumental in later battles at Kyoto and Ichinotani. Although Yoritomo clashed with Yoshitsune, he nevertheless placed his brother in command of the Minamoto forces. Victory was achieved under Yoshitsune's leadership at Yashima and Dannoura.

Since the war ended, Yoritomo has removed all impediments to establishing his warrior government and achieving full control of the country. Yoritomo invaded the north after Yoshitsune rebelled and sought refuge there. The imperial court has been cleared of anti-Minamoto nobles, and new governing institutions, created to meet the demands of military campaigns, have replaced much of the civil administration in Kyoto. With the designation of Shogun, his authority in Japan is now legitimized.

Muslim Leader Dead

Damascus, Middle East, March 4, 1193: Saladin, the courageous Muslim leader, has succumbed to a brief illness. Born in Tikrit in the Middle East, he began his rise to power after joining the army of Nur al-din, the Turkish governor of Syria. Saladin was sent to Egypt, to prevent the ruling Fatimid caliphs from falling to the kingdom of Jerusalem, where he took control as both commander of the Syrian army and as the Fatimid vizier. He then set about strengthening his position, so that when Nur al-din died in 1174, he advanced into Syria, occupying Damascus.

It was clear to the new sultan that Muslim forces would never be successful in their jihad, or holy war, against the Crusaders unless they were united. He thus began a concerted effort to draw together the disparate territories of Syria, Mesopotamia, Palestine, and Egypt using both military domination and diplomatic negotiation. Although the full control of the cities of Aleppo and Mosul remained elusive, by 1187 Saladin had successfully amalgamated his empire and could finally embark upon a major offensive against the Crusader states.

His conquest of the kingdom of Jerusalem was swift and decisive. After annihilating the army of King Guy at Hattin on July 4, he occupied weakly defended garrisons on the coast. On October 2, after a siege of two weeks, Jerusalem surrendered. The forces of the Third Crusade under Philip II and Richard I soon responded to this attack, besieging the port of Acre in 1191, before winning at Arsuf and Jaffa. Subsequent battles against Richard proved indecisive, with his resources now strained after prolonged campaigning, Saladin agreed last year to a limited truce and to recognize the Crusaders' narrow coastal territory. He dies safe in the knowledge that Jerusalem remains in Muslim hands.

The Lionheart Dies

Chalus, France, April 6, 1199: The reign of King Richard the Lionheart has ended with his death today at the castle of Chalus-Chabrol. The king, who shunned the use of armor, died from a crossbow wound he received during a recent siege.

Richard has spent little time in England since he became Duke of Aquitaine in 1172. Rebellious nobles there required a constant show of power, and his desire to expand his holdings in France kept him fighting on the continent until he succeeded his father, Henry II, in 1189.

His stay in England was short-lived, for within nine months of his coronation, Richard left to fight in the Third Crusade. Although he failed to win back Jerusalem, his efforts in battle were heroic and, after achieving a truce with the Muslim leader Saladin, he left for England. However, his return was delayed for a year when, following a shipwreck, he was captured and then sold to Henry IV of Germany.

A ransom finally bought his release in 1194, but while Richard was captive, much of his land in Normandy was lost to Philip of France. Richard's younger brother, John has been widely regarded as the king's likely successor, yet during his brother's absence he set about reinforcing his position by allying with the French king to dismember Richard's continental possessions. Richard forgave his conniving sibling, but has spent the last five years, an untold fortune, and now his life, attempting to recover his lands.

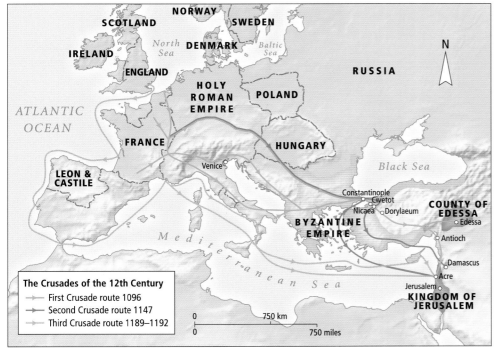

The Crusades of the 12th Century
- First Crusade route 1096
- Second Crusade route 1147
- Third Crusade route 1189–1192

Pope Adrian IV

*"THIS IS HOW
WAR IS BEGUN:
SUCH IS MY
ADVICE. FIRST
DESTROY THE
LAND, DEAL
AFTER WITH
THE FOE."*

PHILIP OF FLANDERS
TO WILLIAM OF
SCOTLAND, 1173

Chinese Develop Explosive New Weapons

China, 1120: The Song Dynasty may have lost Kaifeng to the Manchurian Jurchen, but the battles will also be remembered for the innovative weaponry that was used by the Chinese.

Song weapon-makers have improved upon the catapults of the last century with a new "firing cannon" that launches bombs and grenades over short distances. The barrels of the cannons are made with lengths of bamboo held together by iron rings. The barrels, filled with gunpowder, fire a burning missile at the enemy. The cannons were used to defend the walls of Kaifeng by setting fire to the mobile siege ladders used by the Jurchens.

"Fragmentation bombs" were also used in the battle, exploding like "sky-rending thunder", destroying an area of "more than half a *mu*" (about a tenth of an acre, or 400 sq m). Men, horses, and leather armor were riddled with the barbs contained in the Chinese bomb. Infantry-men were armed with "firespears"— spears with tubes of gunpowder tied to the blades for close combat. Soldiers ignited the tips when in close range of the enemy, throwing the spears to explode on contact with the opposing soldier.

Under the Song dynasty, huge military workshops proliferated to equip its million-strong imperial force. Reports say that output from the workshops this year is in the order of about three million weapons, the bow and crossbow departments separately producing

Invaders overcome Song Dynasty weaponry.

about 16.5 million arrowheads. The bow and arrow remains the most efficient weapon for range and accuracy.

Europe's First Artesian Well Sunk by Monks

Artois, France, 1126-1128: A new type of well—called artesian after the province of Artois— has been sunk in France thanks to the efforts of a group of Carthusian monks. Although this type of well has been used by the Egyptians, they are the first to use it in Europe. European engineering skills have not previously been applied to finding water—perhaps because it has usually been so readily available.

The monks, from Lillers, drilled the initial bore hole, just a few inches in diameter, using a rod with a hard iron cutting edge and a hammer, a so-called percussion drill. The drill punctured an impervious layer of rock allowing the pure water held under pressure beneath to rise to the surface.

A further four wells have been sunk in Artois to a depth of approximately 33 ft (10 m). Observers say the force of the rising water was so strong that a water mill above the bore hole was pushed more than 10 ft (3 m) from the ground.

Death of Jewish Scientist and Translator

Provence, France, 1136: Esteemed Spanish Jewish mathematician, Abraham bar Hiyya—the first man to write scientific works in Hebrew and the first to include the solution to the quadratic equation in a European work—has passed away. Bar Hiyya was a man of encyclopedic knowledge and learning who spent most of his life in Spain, a country that has changed from Muslim to Christian domination during his lifetime.

time out

Pope Celestine III (1191-1198) has charged a tax on windmills, claiming the air they use belongs to the church. Windmills were probably introduced to Europe from the Middle East during the 1100s by returning crusaders.

Scientific knowledge in the Muslim world is much more advanced than in the Christian kingdoms, thanks largely to Arab scholars and scientists who preserved and translated classical Greek texts, developing the ideas found in them. Now western European scholars are hungry to study these works. That some of the texts have now been translated into Latin is because of bar-Hiyya, who worked with Plato of Tivoli in Barcelona.

In his original works, which he wrote in Hebrew, bar-Hiyya often wrote about the aspects of science for which there were practical applications, *Hibbur ha-Meshihah ve-ha-Tishboret (Treatise on Measurement and Calculation)* for example, is a manual on how geometry can be applied to land surveying. *Sefer ha-Ibbur (Book of Intercalation)* written in 1122–1123, is the first Hebrew book entirely about the calendar.

Bar-Hiyya wrote several works in the field of astronomy, including *Heshbon Mahalekhot ha-Kokhavim (Calculation of the Courses of the Stars)*, which describes the movements of the stars and different calendar systems. *Yesodei ha-Tevunah u-Migdal ha-Emunah (The Foundation of Understanding and the Tower of Faith)* covers geometry, arithmetic, optics, and music and is the first encyclopedia written in the Hebrew language.

Ground-breaking Indian Mathematics Text

India, 1150: Indian mathematician and astronomer Bhaskara has completed a landmark work, *Siddhanta Siromani*. Written in four parts, the first volume, *Lilavati*, covers arithmetic and geometry; the second, *Bijaganita*, covers algebra, and the third and fourth volumes, *Grahaganita* and *Goladhyaya*, cover astronomy and mathematics of the planets. The comprehensiveness of the volumes eclipses the

St Bartholomews, London, founded in 1102.

Abbot Suger
of Saint-Denis

detailed calculations and a precisely-crafted timepiece, the exact auspicious moment passed as circumstances conspired against the family. To console his grieving daughter, Bhaskara named the first of the volumes, *Lilivati*, after her.

English Scientific Pioneer, Adelard of Bath, Dies

England, 1150: Adelard of Bath, who will be remembered as England's first scientist and the scholar who brought the work of Islamic scientists to England, has died.

Adelard studied the works of the great Muslim mathematicians and scientists during his travels throughout the Mediterranean and in particular during his time spent in Sicily and possibly Spain, where it is thought he probably learnt the Arabic language. Upon returning to England in about 1130 Adelard was dismayed by the lack of original scientific thought that greeted him, as well as the morals of the time. In response to these issues he wrote *Quaestiones naturales (Natural Questions)*, which contains 76 scientific discussions based on his knowledge of the Arabic sciences.

The book has the unusual format of a dialogue between an uncle and his nephew. Adelard believed in "reason" over "authority." Following on from the Muslim thinkers he greatly admired, he argued against blind faith in God when explanations for certain things were provided for by human knowledge. Adelard addressed such

questions as: "What causes the tides?", "Why do some animals see better at night?", and "How is the globe supported in the middle of the air?"

Following the completion of this work, he translated Euclid's *Elements of Geometry* from Arabic into Latin, the original Greek versions having been lost—and in so doing made available to western Europe a whole segment of Greek learning. He also translated the *Tables* of renowned Arab mathematician al-Khwarizmi, the first time Arabic astronomical tables were translated into Latin. Adelard used Arabic numerals in the translations, a much easier system for calculating with large numbers than the cumbersome Roman numeral system currently used in England. The *Tables* translation also introduced the concept of the number zero.

Adelard's treatise on the abacus and the astrolabe have assisted many in the use of these instruments. A loyal subject of Henry I, Adelard may also have instructed Henry's grandson Henry II in mathematics, along with the preparation of various royal horoscopes.

work done by Bhaskara's predecessors, even the works of Brahmagupta, his inspiration and role model. Bhaskara has described for the first time the process of calculating the volume of a sphere using pyramids, and his work concerning the mathematics of zero is ground-breaking.

Everything from mathematical tables and operations, such as addition and multiplication, to teacher instruction on how to make a model of the solar system has been listed and described. The astronomy volumes also include an exhaustive summation of all contemporary knowledge available on the sun, moon, planets, the orbits, seasonal changes, times of sunrise and sunset at different latitudes and longitudes, astronomical instruments, and eclipses. The text is written in verse, and the author occasionally digresses into pure poetry; for example, in *Goladhyaya*, a chapter completely devoid of calculation, is entirely devoted to a poetic description of the four seasons.

An accomplished astrologer, it is said that Bhaskara brought his computational powers to the fore when trying to effect a happy marriage for his daughter. Despite

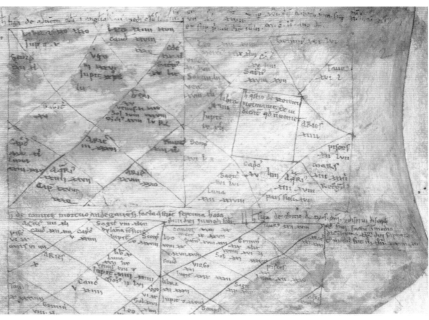

Adelard brought back the knowledge of Islamic scholars to produce this horoscope.

Cutting Edge Hospital Opens in Damascus

Damascus, Middle East, 1156: The doors of al-Nuri Hospital (Bimaristan of Nur al-Din) have opened. the best staffed and best equipped hospital in Damascus—and the first to keep medical records. Physician Abul Majd a Bahilli has been appointed director of the hospital.

The hospital has a fine collection of medical books, thanks to the patronage of Muslim leader Nur al-Din al-Zangi. The collection contains the volume *At-Tasrif (On Surgery)*, records of surgical procedures by the great Spanish surgeon al-Zahrawi, who practiced a century ago.

The eastern hall of the hospital is used for lectures, which are presented daily by the director to physicians, herbalists, pharmacists, and other practitioners. The doctors also go on city rounds, attending ailing dignitaries and noblemen after daily rounds at the hospital.

The hospital is equipped to carry out many procedures, including bloodletting, obstetrics, setting of bones, suturing, treatment of wounds, and the extraction of cataracts. Physicians are also well versed in extracting poison arrows, a procedure needed often during these troubled times. Cauterizing equipment is available for use on more substantial wounds.

Some sources suggest that the hospital exists thanks to a large ransom Nur al-Din claimed for the release of a European hostage, a "high-born warrior." Such hostages would ordinarily face execution, but the ransom money allowed Nur al-Din to improve the health of the citizens of Damascus with this philanthropic act.

Spanish Mathematician Criticized Ptolemy

Seville, Spain, 1160: The mathematician famous for his criticism of Ptolemy's *Almagest*, Jabir ibn Aflah, has died. Ibn Aflah, who lived in Spain, was an influential mathematician during his lifetime because some of his work was translated into Latin, but also because of his questioning of Greek astronomy.

In *Islah al-Majisti (Correction of the Almagest)*, ibn Aflah criticized Ptolemy on numerous astronomical matters, including his rationale for the placement of Mercury and Venus. Ibn Aflah correctly argued that these two planets are positioned between the sun and the earth. He also wrote *Kitab al-Haia (The Book of Astronomy)* and his work on spherical trigonometry has caught the interest of other scholars.

To aid in his observational work, which he often carried out in the Seville Observatory, ibn Aflah designed a portable celestial sphere which allowed him to measure and explain the movements of celestial bodies. It is possible he also invented the torquetum, a complicated instrument for measuring the relative positions of heavenly bodies.

Geographer-Botanist May Be Dead

Sicily, c. 1166: Rumors are circulating that the esteemed geographer, cartographer, and botanist Al-Sharif al-Idrisi al-Qurtubi has died. A direct descendant of the prophet Muhammed, his death is a great loss to the court of King Roger II of Sicily, which al-Idrisi had loyally served for many years. A well-traveled and scholarly man, al-Idrisi was summoned to court by the King to "describe the world." And so he did, compiling a comprehensive and detailed encyclopedia of the seven continents, which he called *Al-Kitab al-Rujari (The Book of Roger)*; this book was also known as *Nuzhat al-Mushtaq fi Ikhtiraq al-Afaq (The amusement of him who desires to journey through the climates)*.

Despite their different faiths (the King a Christian, al-Idrisi a Muslim), the two men shared a mutual quest for knowledge. Using the resources provided him by the King, al-Idrisi combined existing geographic knowledge from sailors, merchants, crusaders, and scholars (mainly Arabic and Greek) with his own knowledge of the world. It took 15 years of meticulous work to complete the atlas, which contains a series of maps with detailed descriptions of climate zones and geographic features.

Many doctors remain in al-Idrisi's debt, as his description of medicinal plants alerted them to the healing properties of many more plants than were previously known about.

Translator Enriched Western Knowledge

Toledo, Spain, 1187: Scholars returning from Toledo have reported the passing of Gerard of Cremona, the greatest translator of our time. Although a native of Italy, Gerard was drawn to the city as a young man due to its reputation as a preeminent center for translation, a status derived from its multicultural history.

Alfonso VI of Castile captured the city from the Arabs in 1085, giving rise to a linguistically mixed population of Christians, Muslims, Jews, and Arabized Christians ("Mozarabs"). Prior to its fall, Toledo had been a focal point of Arabic learning and a repository for manuscripts. These included classical texts, such as the works of Aristotle, translated and studied by Muslim scholars centuries before, as well as original works in the fields of science, medicine, and philosophy. However, access to this priceless corpus by European scholars was hampered by their inability to read Arabic. A practice thus arose in which a Mozarab or Jew acted as an intermediary, translating Arabic texts into the Spanish vernacular from which a Latin translation was then rendered by a Christian scholar.

The Cluniac archbishop, Raymond, encouraged these activities and founded

King Roger II of Sicily

> *"You must accept the truth from whatever source it comes."*
>
> MAIMONIDES (MOSES BEN MAIMON) (1135–1204), JEWISH RABBI AND PHYSICIAN

> *"Large skepticism leads to large understanding. Small skepticism leads to small understanding. No skepticism leads to no understanding."*
>
> XI ZHI (1130–1200), SONG DYNASTY PHILOSOPHER

Patron of geographer and botanist al-Idrisi, Roger II of Sicily entering Palermo.

A map of the Indian Ocean, part of Islamic geographer al-Idrisi's 1182 manuscript atlas.

Alfonso VI of Castile captured Toledo in 1085.

the School of Toledo at the cathedral, of which Gerard was a member. Gerard ultimately translated over 70 texts, on subjects as diverse as mathematics, alchemy, and astronomy, including such seminal works as *The Canon of Medicine*, by the Islamic physician Avicenna. Thanks to these efforts, the advanced knowledge of the Arab world is now enriching that of the Western world.

Neckham publishes *De naturis rerum*

England, 1190: The distinguished English theologian and teacher Alexander Neckham has published *De naturis rerum (On the Nature of Things)*, an encyclopedic work which includes entries on a great many subjects, including natural history, astronomy, and mathematics.

Neckham has described an exciting new navigational instrument, saying, "… sailors use a magnetic needle which swings on a point and shows the direction of the north when the weather is overcast." Such a device has been used in the East for centuries, and possibly among seamen from continental Europe more recently. However, this is the first time that it has been mentioned in a western European text.

Neckham writes about the natural world in great detail, with many entries on birds, marine life, mammals, reptiles, and plants. A list of about 200 plants is included, some of which are not known in England. He also discusses matters of natural phenomena such as the sun, the moon, fire and air, and questions of

general interest, such as "Why no place is a vacuum", and "How it is the sea water is salty." The book begins with a commentary on the six days of creation from the Bible's Book of Genesis.

Humans do not escape Neckham's scrutiny, with entries on the various personality types, such as flatterers, detractors, the ambitious and the wrathful, and conditions such as "the anxiety of the rich and the uncertainty of riches." The book also contains the first mention in Europe of such utilitarian items as the mirror and wheelbarrow.

Neckham was born on the same night as Richard the Lionheart; his mother was the young prince's wet nurse. He studied and taught abroad, as Master of Arts at the University of Paris, and began writing upon his return to England.

Ibn Roschd, Aristotle Commentator, Dead

Marrakesh, Morocco, 1198: The talented ibn Mahommed ibn Roschd (also known as Averroes), variously judge, philosopher, doctor, theologian, and astronomer, has died at the age of 72 years. Thankfully the ban on his work, and the work of other free-thinking philosophers, had been lifted a short time before his death.

In his early life, ibn Roschd was a favorite of the caliph of Morocco and quickly rose to become a judge at the age of 44, first in Seville and then Cordoba. He impressed the caliph's son Abu Ya'qub Yusuf with his ideas, and when the young prince became caliph, he recalled ibn Roschd to Marrakesh as his physician. The caliph also commissioned him to write a series of commentaries on Aristotle.

Over several decades, ibn Roschd wrote on virtually all of Aristotle's works.

Ibn Roschd (Averroes)

Tuhafut al-Tuhafut (The Incoherence of the Incoherence) was his most important work. He was both deeply religious and a free-thinker, so in many of his writings, he dwelt on trying to reconcile religion and philosophy, which he believed could coexist separately if both were properly analysed and understood.

Some years later, a more conservative approach to Islam prevailed in Spain and influential Muslim theologians declared Roschd's ideas heretical. He was banished to a small town near Cordoba. Although his works on medicine, arithmetic, and astronomy were preserved, many works on logic and metaphysics were burnt.

Ibn Roschd wrote more than 80 books in his lifetime, not just on philosophy, but also on medicine, jurisprudence, theology, and astronomy. However, he will be remembered most for the commentaries on Aristotle because they opened people's minds to work that had been banned in the Islamic world and ignored in western Europe for centuries.

Islamic philosopher and theologian ibn Roschd (1126-1198) wrote more than 80 books in his lifetime.

Twelfth-century sculpture of St James

"THE WANTON AND EFFEMINATE SOUND PRODUCED BY CARESSING, CHIMING, AND INTERTWINING MELODIES, A VERITABLE HARMONY OF SIRENS."

JOHN OF SALISBURY (c. 1115–1180), ENGLISH CLERIC AND SCHOLAR, COMPARING POLYPHONY WITH GREGORIAN CHANT

"… A PATRON OF PLAYACTORS AND A FOLLOWER OF HOUNDS TO BECOME A SHEPHERD OF SOULS."

HERBERT OF BOSHAM (FL. 1162–1186), OF THOMAS BECKET, 1162

Rubiayat Author Dead

Nishapur, Persia, 1123: With the death this year of Omar Khayyam, author of the *Rubiayat*, the world has lost an extraordinary polymath, well-versed in both the arts and sciences. Born in Nishapur in 1048, Khayyam lived during a tumultuous period in his country's history, as tribal Seljuk Turks have been slowly taking control of southwestern Asia. After completing his studies in astronomy and geometry, he traveled to Samarkand in Uzbekistan, where he produced books on philosophy and mathematics, as well as a major work entitled, *Treatise on Demonstration of Problems of Algebra*. This work

"A Love"; illustration to Omar Khayyam's *Rubiayat*, c. 1120.

brought him to the attention of the Seljuk sultan, Malikshah, who instructed him in 1074 to build a new observatory at the capital of Esfahan, with the purpose of revising the calendar. The new "Jalali" era, inaugurated on March 16, 1079, is based upon Khayyam's astronomical tables. Yet for all his great scientific achievements, it is his poetry that we most associate with Omar Khayyam, perhaps because its celebration of the pleasures and pains of everyday life reveals the soul of the person himself. Each of the four-line stanzas, or *ruba'i*, that together make up the *Rubiayat* expresses a single thought or observation. Despite their apparent preoccupation with hedonistic matters, many of these hint at Khayyam's personal philosophy, in which he questioned the extent of divine intervention in life—an opinion that has brought criticism from his Islamic contemporaries.

time out

William IX (1071–1126), the Duke of Aquitaine, composed songs about his adventures on his return from the Crusades and was known as "the Troubador." His lyrics led to the genre of writing known as "courtly love."

New History of Kings

England, c. 1137: Rumors are spreading about the newest manuscript by Geoffrey of Monmouth. The Oxford canon has been well-known since his first work, *Prophetiae Merlini (Prophecies of Merlin)*, a collection of predictions by the famed magician, which was copied from an ancient document, according to Monmouth. His new work, *Historia Regnum Britanniae (History of the Kings of Britain)* chronicles the lives of British rulers over a period of 2,000 years. Beginning with Brutus of Troy, the legendary first king of Britain, the book recounts the reigns of subsequent monarchs, including King Lear, King Cole, and treacherous King Vortigern, who invited Saxon mercenaries to the island. The *Historia* concludes with the glorious reign of Arthur, who, after expelling the Saxon invaders and marrying the lady Guinevere, created an order of knights at his newly established court at Caerleon in Wales. With his band of dedicated warriors, Arthur continued to bring victory to Britain until he was eventually betrayed and mortally wounded by his nephew, Mordred.

Monmouth asserts the *Historia* is a translation of a "most ancient book" given to him by Walter, Archdeacon of Oxford. However, many historians doubt its authenticity. Some have suggested that it is a work of fiction drawn largely from Monmouth's own imagination and mixed with legends, folklore, and earlier accounts by Gildas and Bede. Whatever its origins however, no one can dispute the enormous popularity of this romantic saga.

Guide Book for Pilgrims

France, c. 1140: A most useful document has recently been produced for the benefit of travelers, the like of which has never before been seen. Aymeric Picaud, a French monk, has written the *Liber Peregrinationis (Pilgrim's Book)*, which forms the fifth and final volume of the *Liber Sancti Jacobi (Book of St James)*. Picaud has described the *Camino de Santiago*, the principal route taken by pilgrims from France to Santiago de

Detail from an illustrated manuscript of the Kings of England.

Peter Abelard

Compostela in north-western Spain, where St James is reputed to be buried.

The book offers useful information to ease the journey. For example, Picaud has divided the route into 13 stages, each of which can be accomplished in a few days. It also provides the reader with the distances between villages, the location of reliable lodging places, sources of food and water, and rather vivid descriptions of the local inhabitants and their customs.

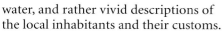
Aymeric Picaud has written a travel guide for pilgrims to Santiago de Compostela.

Heretic Scholar Dies

France, April 21, 1142: The tumultuous life of Peter Abelard ended today. As was revealed in his autobiographical letter, *Historia calamitatum (Story of My Calamities)*, the career of this brilliant scholar was fraught with difficulties. Born in 1079, he attended the Cathedral School in Paris and studied under the leading masters. Abelard revealed his talent at intellectual debate by challenging many of his instructors. Supremely confident, he established his own academy in 1108 and later accepted a position at the Cathedral School, where he was considered a gifted teacher.

His fortunes changed when, in 1118, he embarked upon a love affair with his student, Héloise, niece of canon Fulbert. The pair married after the birth of their son, but, convinced that Héloise had been ruined, Fulbert extracted his revenge by arranging Abelard's castration at the hands of hired thugs. Both Héloise and Abelard then entered monastic life; sadly, their only contact since has been by letter. While teaching at the monastery of Saint-Denis, he produced a number of treatises in which he tackled theological questions by applying logic. These include *Sic et Non (Yes and No)*, a collection of contradictory statements from Scripture, and *Theologia*, which explores the Trinity.

These activities brought Abelard unfavorable attention, for in 1121 he was found guilty of heresy. To avoid imprisonment, he fled to Troyes, where he established the Paraclete, a hermitage that was later bestowed upon Héloise and her nuns. He returned to teaching in Paris in 1136, but his unorthodox writings attracted scrutiny from conservative theologian, Bernard of Clairvaux. Last June, he was again convicted of heresy after a council at Sens, wary of his debating skills, met in his absence. When the pope upheld their decision, Abelard retired to Cluny, where he has remained since. He will be laid to rest at Paraclete.

Alexius's Daughter Pens Byzantine History

Constantinople, Turkey, 1148: Anna Comnena, daughter of the former Byzantine emperor, Alexius I, has recently completed a history of her father's reign entitled the *Alexiad*. It is the result of decades of work, carried out while the princess has been cloistered in the nunnery of Kecharitomene.

Born in 1083, Anna was well-educated, receiving instruction in history, literature, and philosophy. She eventually married Nikephoros Bryennios, a soldier and statesman who had proved invaluable to Alexius in the defence of Constantinople during its occupation by members of the First Crusade. Upon her father's death in 1118, Anna and her mother, the Empress Irene, plotted unsuccessfully to have Bryennios named his successor, an action that resulted in her forced retirement.

The years spent in isolation have allowed her to complete her manuscript. Consisting of 15 chapters, the book builds upon a history of the Comneni line begun earlier by her husband. Although Anna states that her account is impartial, the *Alexiad* is undoubtedly intended primarily to praise her father, often at the expense of his adversaries. It contains descriptions of people and events that marked the emperor's career, such as his confrontations with the Normans and Seljuk Turks, and their impact upon the lives of the Byzantines. She reveals, for example, that the First Crusaders were greedy, violent, and boorish, and although sent to protect Constantinople, they preferred to loot the capital. Despite its personal bias, the *Alexiad* is a remarkable achievement for this female historian.

Lovers Abelard and Héloise entered into monastic life after the revenge of Canon Fulbert.

Key Events

Paris, France, 1163: Construction begins on the new Notre Dame Cathedral, a building deemed to be worthy of the famous city. The original building that stood on the site was demolished three years ago.
Hereford, England, 1167: Robert of Melun, philosopher and theologian, dies, aged about 67. Robert worked as a teacher in France, and his pupils included John of Salisbury and Thomas Becket. He wrote a number of works on theology.

Spain, c. 1167: Ibn Ezra, poet and philosopher, dies, aged 77.
Pisa, Italy, 1173: Work begins on the Tower of Pisa.
Dazu, China, 1179: Monk Zhao Zhifeng begins work on Buddhist cave-sculptures at Baoding Shan.
Bingen, France, 1179: Hildegard of Bingen, writer, visionary, and composer, dies, aged about 81.

Chartres, France, 1180: John of Salisbury, scholar, dies, aged about 65. His works included *Policatricus*, on the subject of court life and the role of the monarchy, and *Metalogicon*, on the school system
France, c. 1183: Chrétien de Troyes, poet, dies, aged about 48. He is remembered for a number of works, mostly based on Arthurian legend.
Angkor, Cambodia, 1186: The temple of Ta Prohm is completed.

Cremona, Italy, 1187: Death of Gerard of Cremona (born 1114). He spent much of his life in Muslim-controlled Spain, and was responsible for the translation of a number of Arabic works into Latin.
Angkor, Cambodia, 1191: King Suryavarman continues his building program, and the temple of Preah Khan is built.
Beijing, China, 1192: Construction of the Lugou Bridge, which spans the Lugou River, is completed.

Wales, 1194: Giraldus Cambrensis, writes *Cambriae description (Description of Wales)*. His collected works offer an insight into the history, geography, customs, culture, and daily life in Ireland and Wales.
Hohenbourg, France, 1196: Herrad of Hohenbourg completes her illustrated *Hortus deliciarum (Garden of Delights)*.
Newburgh, England, 1198: William of Newburgh, historian, dies, aged about 62. He chronicled a history of England from Henry II's reign up to the time of his own death.

From the visions of
Hildegard of Bingen

"I CAME LIKE
WATER, AND
LIKE WIND I
GO."

OMAR KHAYYAM, (1048–
1122) PERSIAN POET
AND ASTRONOMER,
TRANSLATED BY
EDWARD FITZGERALD

"A DEMON
HOLDS A BOOK,
IN WHICH ARE
WRITTEN THE
SINS OF A
PARTICULAR
MAN; AN ANGEL
DROPS ON IT
FROM A PHIAL,
A TEAR WHICH
THE SINNER
HAD SHED IN
DOING A GOOD
ACTION, AND
HIS SINS ARE
WASHED OUT."

ALBERIC OF OSTIA
(1080–1147), FRENCH
MONK, CARDINAL OF
OSTIA

Sanskrit Fables Compiled

Bengal, India, c. 1150: A new collection
of Sanskrit fables has been compiled
by Narayana, under instructions from
King Dhavalacanda. The book, entitled
the *Hitopadesa (Book of Good Counsels),*
offers worldly advice on many aspects
of life through a series of thoughtful
tales in which most of the characters
are animals. The stories deal, in particular, with the very human problem of
getting along with one another.

The *Hitopadesa* is both one story and
many. The saga opens with King Sudarsana
hiring a tutor, Vishnu-Sarman, to teach
his sons the proper ways of conduct so
that they might become wise and effective
rulers. Vishnu-Sarman begins by telling
the princes a humorous story, within
which the animal characters tell a tale.
The book thus progresses with layer upon
layer of connected fables, often amusing
and satirical, each of which is intespersed
with pithy observations delivered in verse.

Narayana claims the *Hitopadesa* is
derived from a much older set of stories,
the *Panchatantra.* Indeed, although the
collection contains 17 new fables, 25
are derived from the earlier work. The
Panchatantra is already known in Europe,
although not by that name. The stories
were translated into Middle Persian in
the sixth century, and later compiled into
the *Fables of Bidpai* by Abdallah ibn al-
Muqaffa. An Arabic version, the *Kalila
wa Dimna,* then appeared which was
subsequently translated into Greek in
the eleventh century, and most recently
into Hebrew. Hopefully the *Hitopadesa*
will arrive a little faster!

Renowned Jewish Man of Letters Dead

Spain, c. 1167: Word has been received of
the death this year of the eminent Jewish
author, mathematician, and astrologer,
Abraham ibn Ezra. Born in Tudela, Spain,
in 1089, he spent the
first half of his life as
a poet. Although he
wrote in Hebrew, his
engaging style was
greatly influenced
by Arabic verse, the
language of his home-
land. In 1140, he left
Spain to spend the
rest of his life as a
traveler, visiting parts
of Italy, France, and
England and possibly
even regions as far-
flung as India.

Despite ibn Ezra's
constant wandering,

most of the works for which he will be
remembered were composed during this
period. These include original treatises
on religious and secular subjects, but also
Hebrew translations of Arabic documents.
During his time in Italy, he wrote a series
of commentaries on the books of the
Bible in which he attempted to determine the literal meaning of the texts
(the *Peshat*) by examining their basic
grammar. He also delved into the principles of Hebrew grammar in his books
Moznayim (The Scales) and *Zahot (Correctness),* as well as translating three
works by Yehuda Hayyuj, the founder
of Hebrew linguistics.

Ibn Ezra's religious writings, as well as
his subsequent books on mathematics,
astronomy, and the calendar all reveal the
influence of his neo-Platonist philosophy
and profound interest in astrology. Indeed,
he is considered one of the greatest astrologers of our time. Through the intellectual endeavors of ibn Ezra, the scholars of
Christian Europe have become acquainted
with both Judaic scholarship and the
scientific achievements of the Arab world.

World Loses Influential Spiritual Visionary

Bingen, Germany, September 17, 1179:
Today marks the loss of a remarkable
woman—the author, composer, physician, and visionary—Hildegard of Bingen.

Born in 1098, Hildegard was sent at
the age of eight to the Benedictine monastery at Disibodenberg, where she received religious instruction and later
became a nun. In 1136, she experienced
a series of visions concerning the meaning of the Scriptures, about which she
was also commanded to write. After
receiving approval from Pope Eugene III,
she completed *Scivias (Know the ways),*
the first of three books describing the
nature of her divine revelations.

Hildegard also produced many other
works, including books on medicine

Creation of the Universe; Hildegard of Bingen.

and natural history,
poems, hymns, and
a musical play, *Ordo
Virtutum.* Sermons
delivered throughout
Europe brought her
to the attention of
kings and religious
leaders, many of
whom subsequently
wrote to her for
advice. Hildegard
will be remembered
for her passion for
humanity, in whom
she believed the
splendor of God's
creation was reflected.

Chrétien de Troyes narrated the deeds of King Arthur and h

Author's Legacy of Courtly Tales

France, c. 1183: The great French author,
Chrétien de Troyes, has died. Two lyric
poems and a handful of lesser works have
been attributed to him, but he is most
famous for his five Arthurian romances,
which were penned between 1170 and
1181. Each of these stories, written in
rhymed couplets, is set around the court
of King Arthur and explores the conflict
between love and the demands of chivalry. In *Erec et Enide,* for example, a be-
sotted knight neglects to perform feats
of prowess after winning his bride. Upon
hearing his wife's complaints, the couple
set off on a difficult quest during which
Enide's love is tested, while Erec must
learn to balance his devotion with his
obligations as a knight. Similar themes
emerge in the stories of *Cligés* and *Yvain.*

Chrétien's most influential works,
however, are *Le Chevalier de la Charrette
(The Knight and the Cart)* and *Le Conte
du Graal (The Story of the Grail).* The
first of these, which was commissioned
by Marie de Champagne, daughter of
Eleanor of Aquitaine, recounts the adulterous love affair between Arthur's queen,
Guinevere, and the knight, Lancelot.
Chrétien did not complete this romantic
work himself, possibly, some say, because
he disapproved of the subject that had
been ordered by his patron.

Chrétien's last work, composed for
Philip d'Alsace, Count of Flanders, is
perhaps his most intriguing. Known

also as *Perceval*, the name of its principal character, *Le Conte du Graal* tells the humorous story of an ignorant squire who, after becoming a knight at the court of King Arthur, causes a crisis throughout the land when he fails to inquire about the mysterious grail as it passes by in a procession. Sadly, the death of Chrétien has left this work unfinished, but he has bequeathed an enduring literary legacy in these tales of courtly love and questing knights.

New Book Chronicles English History

Newburgh, England, 1198: The most accurate history of England currently available is *Historia rerum Anglicarum (History of English Affairs)*, written by the late Augustinian canon, William of Newburgh. Sent as a child to be educated at the priory in Newburgh, Yorkshire, William remained cloistered there until his recent death. Despite his isolation, his history provides an informed overview of the major political events of the last 150 years.

The author took a methodical approach in his work, dividing the manuscript into five books. The first tome recounts the reigns of William the Conqueror and his sons. The second book describes in great detail the reign of Henry II, from 1154 until 1174, while the third covers the period from 1175 until the death of the

king in 1189. The final two books cover the past decade, ending abruptly in May 1198 with William's untimely demise.

Hundreds of different sources were consulted to compile the *Historia* and ensure its authenticity. William makes it clear in the text that works by Henry of Huntingdon and Symeon of Durham supplied material for his first book, while the chronicle of Jordan Fantosme was drawn upon for the political situation of the 1170s. Uniquely, however, the author also provides firsthand accounts of some incidents, supplied by various personal informants. Writing in a clear, unaffected style, he offers a critical, but impartial view of many of the controversial events of our time, such as the quarrel between Thomas Becket and Henry II.

In the prologue, William comments on the works of his predecessors. He praises the work of Gildas and Bede, but denounces *Historia Regnum Britanniae* by Geoffrey of Monmouth for its "impudent fabrications." For an historian such as William, for whom honesty and accuracy were paramount, the errors contained in this popular account were an unforgivable transgression.

Spectacular Bridge Spans Chinese Torrent

Beijing, China, 1192: The people of Beijing are celebrating the opening this year of

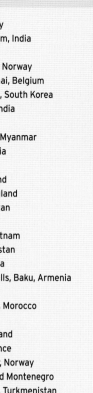

Celadon vessel, Song dynasty

Illustration of the four seasons, from an early twelfth-century manuscript of Bede's *De temporibus liber*.

the Lugou Bridge, which has been constructed 10 miles southeast of the city. The new bridge, built in just four years, spans the notoriously dangerous Lugou River, known locally as the *Wuding*, meaning "lacking stability." Measuring 870 ft long and 26 ft wide (265 m × 8 m), the granite bridge is elegant and strong, and graced by 11 arches, each of which is 52 ft wide and 52 ft high (16 m × 16 m). The front face of its supporting piers are shaped into a point to accommodate the swift and sometimes violent torrent, while the backs are square. Each pier is set deep into a foundation of alluvial sand and gravel that has been reinforced with wooden stakes.

The most striking feature of the bridge, however, is its elegant stone railings which run the length of each side. These are decorated with 250 marble pillars, which hold 485 exquisitely carved lions. Each of these adopts a lifelike pose and, although there are so many, no two are alike. Little wonder, then, that the people of Beijing say that "the lions of the Lugou Bridge are too numerous to count!"

The bridge's fame has spread rapidly throughout China, as the location is renowned for spectacular views of the moon during the mid-autumn festival. Indeed, this beautiful sight has inspired Jin dynasty emperor Zhangzong to label the bridge, *Lugou Xiaoyue*, "The Moon over Lugou at Dawn."

Henry II of England

> "WHEN I WAS
> 42 YEARS AND
> SEVEN
> MONTHS OLD,
> THE HEAVENS
> WERE OPENED
> AND A
> BLINDING
> LIGHT OF
> EXCEPTIONAL
> BRILLIANCE
> FLOWED
> THROUGH MY
> ENTIRE
> BRAIN."
>
> HILDEGARD OF
> BINGEN (1098–1179),
> NUN AND COMPOSER,
> ON UNDERSTANDING
> RELIGIOUS TEXTS,
> 1141

Ash Covers Viking Community

Iceland, 1104: The mighty Vikings have been brought to their knees, not at sea, but on land, about 70 miles (110 km) east of Reykjavik, Iceland, with the violent explosion of Mt Hekla (5000 ft, or 1525 m high). Dormant during the previous 200 years of Viking settlement in Iceland, the snowcapped mountain has spewed forth a shower of volcanic rock and ash from a 3½ mile (5.5 km) long fissure, covering everything within about a 30-mile (50-km) radius of the volcano.

The Thjorsardalur Valley farming community has been annihilated; the wooden frames and turf walls of the Viking longhouses were no match for the towering columns of ash and pulverized rock expelled from the erupting volcano. It is not known how many perished, but at least 11 farms have been buried in volcanic debris and ash. Among the destroyed farms was the settlement of Stong—the stone foundations of the

longhouses will no doubt be all that remains of the once-thriving settlement.

Such was the violence of the eruption, surviving villagers are already starting to speak of the craters of Hekla as the main gateways to Hell.

Moscow on the Rise as Kiev Decays

Kiev, Russia, 1147: The great Kiev, capital of Kievan Rus and once described as the "fairest jewel in all the Greek world," has fallen into a state of decay. For two centuries, this splendid city with no less than 400 churches has been a great trading center where merchants from Byzantium, Hungary, Poland, Germany, Bohemia, Scandinavia, and even the countries of the Orient have traded shoulder to shoulder in the grand marketplaces.

For the past hundred years, Kievan Rus has been governed collectively by royal princes, each with his own principality, the most senior prince claiming the title of Grand Prince of Kiev. Dissatisfied with

Silver filigree funerary jewellery from Bohemia.

the balance of power however, disgruntled princes have been vying for larger pieces of the pie, some with aspirations of taking Kiev. While the princes bicker amongst themselves, the lack of centralized government has undermined the state and left Russia vulnerable to invaders from the Mongolian steppes.

Meanwhile, unconcerned about external invaders, ambitious Prince Yuri Dolgoruki (Vladimirovich) of Sudzal principality has set his sights on the Kiev throne. While waiting to make his move, the prince has continued to consolidate his Sudzal lands, establishing a defence outpost in Moscow, a centuries-old village near the headwaters of the Dvina, Dniepa, and Volga rivers. Moscow is one of a number of small villages to the north and east of Kiev where in recent times the disenchanted peoples of Kiev have migrated in search of safety.

Moscow's situation makes it a suitable site for a fortress and Prince Yuri speaks of building fortress walls around the village to fortify it further. He envisions that Moscow and similar city-fortresses elsewhere in Sudzal, will be economic and administrative centers amid his rural lands. The Prince patronizes the development of stone masonry, especially new and beautiful techniques using local limestone, and plans to build grand churches throughout his lands.

After two centuries of dormancy, Iceland's Mt Hekla has erupted from a fissure 3 miles (5 km) long.

Restaurant Scene Booming in Kaifeng

Kaifeng, China, 1147: Almost 30 years after the world's first restaurant opened in Kaifeng, Henan province, the city has become an exciting culinary center with at least 72 large restaurants, offering sumptuous banquets from the varied and delicious cuisines of China's different regions. Hundreds of small inns, teahouses, noodle shops, and dumpling houses also thrive night and day in this bustling cosmopolitan center.

Bureaucrat and roving critic Meng Yuanlao reports that service standards are high in the best restaurants, with even the slightest slip in etiquette reported back to the restaurateur, who is obliged to dock the waiter's salary—or even dismiss him for more severe breaches of etiquette. In his journals, the critic comments on all aspects of the Kaifeng restaurant scene, including the best seasonal dishes.

For southern Chinese specialties, Meng Yuanlao recommends a walk down Small Sweetwater Alley, while the famed night market is the place for a plate of tripe with blood pasta or chicken tongue soup.

Merchants and visiting officials have driven the gastronomic boom in Kaifeng in their eagerness to sample dishes perfected in earlier dynasties and in other regions. The Song Dynasty has its own sought-after delicacies, including fried purple crisp pork, sea cucumber shaped as lotus flowers, peony and swallow vegetables, hand-stretched noodles, and goose pears. Vegetables, herbs and spices such as eggplant and spinach, nutmeg and saffron brought in by traders on the Silk Road bring new flavors and textures to many of the dishes. Great attention is paid to cooking methods and the beautiful presentation of each dish.

As much as the restaurants flourish, so the teahouses still predominate in Kaifeng's bustling streets. Government officials have been known to sit for hours discussing the different brands of tea; the idle rich and those of an artistic temperament will pay a fortune for a perfectly glazed blue and white teacup.

Amalgamation of Icelandic Farmers

Iceland, 1151: The communities of Iceland have followed the traditions of the Nordic societies from which they emerged and have developed the concept of communal land ownership based on the village communities called Hreppars. These Hreppars are usually comprised of a minimum of 20 farms, each with a five-member commission. They are self-governing and are responsible for, among other things, seeing that orphans and the poor within the area are fed and housed. Taking the Nordic model one step further the Hreppars also act as "property insurance agencies," giving assistance to settlers in case of fire, property damage or losses due to diseased livestock.

Icelanders seem very much at ease with their utopian way of life, based on a network of solidarity, communal life and "mutual insurance"–the notion that personal loss of income or property can be reimbursed by society.

Early Maps of Song Dynasty

China, 1155: In almost every respect the Chinese have been at the forefront in the development of the printed word and illustrations on parchment for hundreds of years.

time out

The Camino de Santiago (Way of St James) in Spain is a popular pilgrimage. By 1122 Pope Calixtus gave special indulgences to pilgrims who completed the journey in any year that St James's Day (July 25) fell on a Sunday.

In 105 CE Ts'ai Lun invented the process for manufacturing paper. By 593 CE the first printing press was invented in China, and the first printed newspaper was available in Beijing in 700 CE. Chinese printer Pi Sheng then invented moveable type in 1041 CE.

The present Song Dynasty has produced many maps detailing the extent of the Empire, believed to be among the first ever produced. Ship-building has reached such a high level with the invention of water-tight bulkheads and vessels even being repaired in what are called "dry docks," that maps are becoming increasingly necessary as aids to navigation for voyages to Korea and the regions beyond.

On land, continuing border disputes with the Khitan and Jurchen people in the northern territories require proof of demarcation lines and borders.

Various Song Dynasty maps have been preserved as historical documents, such as the "Map of China and Beyond" from the late eleventh century. Incised on a stone tablet it is based on a Tang period map. City maps have also been preserved from Suzhou and Guilin.

Japanese emperor Go-Toba

The Qingming Festival by the Riverside, portraying Kaifeng during the Song Dynasty.

Key Events

Kyoto, Japan, 1175: The monk Honen Shonin founds the Pure Land Sect of Buddhism, which becomes popular with the common people.

London, England, 1176: Construction begins on a stone version of London Bridge, under the supervision of Peter de Colechurch, replacing a wooden structure built during the tenth century.

England, c. 1180: Glass windows begin to be used in English houses.

Constantinople, Turkey, 1181-1182: Riots break out as supporters of Maria Porphyrogenita take up arms. Andronicus I Comnenus rises to power, and as he garners public support, the public backlash against Latin members of the population sees them attacked or driven from the city. Andronicus proves to be a ruthless ruler, and in 1185 he is attacked and killed by an angry mob.

Japan, 1181-1182: Japan suffers its worst famine of the century.

France, April, 1182: King Philip Augustus gives notice to French Jews that they have three months to sell their portable goods before being expelled from the country. All their lands and buildings will become the property of the king.

Durham, England, 1183: The Bishop of Durham, Hugh of Pudsey, orders that land and properties in the Durham area be recorded in the Boldon Book, which is often called the "Domesday Book of the North."

England, 1188: Henry II imposes the "Saladin Tithe" to bankroll the Crusades. The tithe demands payment of 10 percent of income and 10 percent of possessions other than land.

London, England, 1188: Henry II commissions the building of the original Newgate Prison.

England, 1189-1190: Anti-Semitism is rife in England, and Jewish communities are in peril as the local population takes up arms against them. The worst massacre takes place at York.

London, England, 1189: Henry Fitz-Ailwyn becomes London's first Lord Mayor.

Kyoto, Japan, 1191: A priest named Eisai brings tea seeds from China. Green tea becomes popular, especially with the nobility, and is touted for its health benefits.

Kamakura, Japan, 1191: Monk Eisai returns from China, and introduces Zen Buddhism, which becomes the dominant religion of the samurai warrior class.

Limerick, Ireland, 1197: By Royal Charter, Limerick is declared a city.

Twelfth-century Chinese artwork

Usury Ban Set to Fall

Genoa, Italy, 1156: Two brothers have entered into a momentous deal when they were loaned 115 Genoese pounds from a Genoese bank, having agreed to reimburse the bank's agents in Constantinople. The terms of the brothers' contract require them to repay the loan in the local currency no later than one month after their arrival in Constantinople.

Not since the fall of the Roman Empire has such a transaction taken place. The Church's ban on usury—the charging of interest on loans—has up until now stalled the development of banking in Europe; however, the impetus of the crusades and the pressing need to finance supplies and equipment for the Crusaders will undoubtedly stimulate a resumption of financial services.

Similar bills of exchange are already in use among Arab traders and Jewish moneylenders for whom usury is not forbidden, but this international contract may well mark a new era of banking controlled by the state.

> "I HAVE LONG SINCE BEEN AWARE THAT YOUR KING IS A MAN OF THE GREATEST HONOR AND BRAVERY, BUT HE IS IMPRUDENT."
>
> SALADIN (1137–1193), SULTAN OF EGYPT AND SYRIA, OF RICHARD I, 1192

> "THE BEGINNING OF WISDOM IS FOUND IN DOUBTING; BY DOUBTING WE COME TO THE QUESTION, AND BY SEEKING WE MAY COME UPON THE TRUTH."
>
> PETER ABELARD (1079–1142), FRENCH PHILOSOPHER

A battle ensued with the Vikings using cables to dislodge the bridge's piers, leading to the collapse of the bridge.

Now 162 years later, Henry II has imposed a tax on the nation's woolen products to raise funds to help pay for the construction of a stone bridge at the same site, under the direction of priest and architect Peter de Colechurch.

Peter de Colechurch was chaplain of St Mary's, Colechurch, and as Thomas Becket was baptized there, the Chapel on the new bridge will be dedicated to the recently martyred saint.

The bridge will be 20 ft (6 m) wide and 300 yds (275 m) long, to be supported by 20 arches in the Gothic style. A wooden drawbridge will allow ships to pass and shall keep invaders at bay.

The course of the Thames will need to be diverted for the digging of massive trenches from Radriffe to Patricksea in order to lay the foundations. Each pier will be formed by driving a ring of elms into the riverbed, filling the area inside with rubble, then laying a floor of oak beams over the result. It is hoped the bridge will serve London for many generations to come.

English Law Transformed

England, 1176: King Henry II has proclaimed the Assize of Northampton, containing a number of procedures for settling disputes about land titles. Heirs of freehold landholders are now granted rights known as *mort d' ancestor* and *novel disseisin* to ensure their rights of possession, and widows are now entitled to a dowry.

Henry has been reforming the legal system for 35 years in an effort to restore royal authority to the English realm, and the legal system has indeed been transformed. Royal judicial courts were established at Westminster and in many counties at least 10 years ago, and increasingly the King or his representatives have heard and determined prosecutions for criminal acts and civil disputes—once the jurisdiction of the county courts, the clergy, and feudal lords.

View of London with London Bridge in the far distance, from a Royal Manuscript.

Replacement London Bridge Erected in Stone

London, 1176: In 1014 and with London in Danish hands, King Ethelred and his Saxons, together with a band of Vikings under King Olaf, hoped to divide the Danes by sailing up the River Thames to destroy a strategic wooden bridge.

The formalization of the legal system started with the Assize of Clarendon, issued in 1166, which declared legal rules and provided for an "accusation jury"—a Grand Assize—a panel of 12 lawful men who were required to state on oath whether a person suspected to be a thief or murderer should go on trial. Trial was by ordeal by water—those who floated were deemed guilty, rejected by waters that had been blessed by a priest. This replaced trial by combat, in which the winner is inevitably the stronger party.

For a time everyone, including the clergy, was accountable in the King's court, although today the clergy has regained some of its authority—a legacy of the unfortunate death of Thomas Becket. Now, a clergyman charged with misconduct is tried in the royal court, but if found guilty is turned over to the

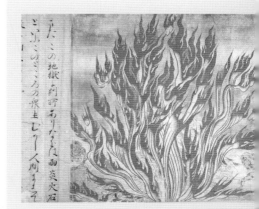

The Buddhist Hells Scroll, from the Kamakura Peri

church for (often lenient) punishment.

While the reforms have not been strictly enforced nor universally accepted—indeed, in matters of little interest to the King, old systems of justice remain—the semblance of a common law for all citizens of England has arrived.

Seal of King Henry II of England from 1176.

Durham Tax Survey Completed

Durham, England, 1183: A century after the completion of the Book of Winchester, which is commonly being referred to as the Domesday Book, the Bishop of Durham has completed a similar economic survey for his county, recording the details of all the church lands under his control. This will mean appropriate land taxes can be collected from those who occupy church land.

Northeast England was not included in the survey area of the Book of Winchester because, after William decimated the northern lands from York to Durham in the so-called Harrying of the North, the counties were of little interest and thought unsafe for the assessors.

People are now referring to the new book as the *Boldon Book* because the taxation system in Boldon, a hamlet near Newcastle, is described in detail in the record and the taxation system in other villages is often described as being similar to that of Boldon's.

The bishop will be well-pleased with the taxes he can collect from his tenants; for example, the book records that the 35 tenants who each occupy an *ox gang* (about 15 acres, or 6 hectares) of land in Quykham must pay 16 pence in rent as well as provide a cow, a hen, 10 eggs, and an additional 9 shillings rent to mill their corn in the bishop's mill. The bishop can also expect three days labor each week from the tenants, who may be obliged to carry the bishop's luggage when he travels or to work in his Tyne fishery.

Jews Slaughtered in York Bloodbath

York, England, March 16, 1190: The Jewish community of York has been wiped out in a brutal massacre at Clifford Tower in the Castle of York. It is the worst act of violence to have been committed against the Jewish people in England.

Yesterday, about 150 Jews led by Joseph of York fled to the royal castle after rioters pelted them with stones and burned down several homes. The incensed mob, led by

Richard Malebys, pursued the terrified Jews and stormed the castle. Trapped and defeated, the majority of those in the tower took their own lives rather than renounce their faith. Those who bargained for their lives were double-crossed and slaughtered on leaving the tower. All evidence of the debts owing to these Jewish people has been destroyed by the angry and unforgiving mob.

Anti-semitic feeling has become rife in England since the coronation of Richard I last year. The hatred has been fueled by Crusaders, Christian clergy, and nobles, like Malebys, who are heavily in debt to Jewish moneylenders. Richard has left England to fight in the Third Crusade. The Crusaders who plan to follow him to defend the Holy Land and further suppress the Muslim "unbelievers" are first crying for the blood of the "killers of Christ" who live among them.

Although King Richard does not condone violence against Jews, he has not acted quickly in their defense, as his predecessor Henry II would have done. The royal court cannot survive without the financial services supplied by the Jewish moneylenders—they have been dependent on Jewish wealth for the past 30 years—so it is likely that Richard will punish the perpetrators and protect Jewish interests upon his return. It is also likely that he will increase the taxes the Royal court receives from every financial transaction that takes place.

Zen Pervades Japanese Life

Kamakura, Japan, 1199: As the century comes to a close, Zen Buddhism has become part of everyday life in Japan. This is thanks to the Japanese monk Eisai, who has been sharing the teachings of Zen since returning from his studies in China in 1191.

Buddhism in some form has been in Japan for perhaps 400 years, but the teachings of Zen

(Ch'an, Ch) and in particular those of Chinese master Lin Chi, called Rinzai Zen in Japan, have struck a chord with the Japanese people.

Lin Chi rejected the philosophical and scholarly approach of the old Buddhist masters. His teachings were about giving up intellectualizing and freeing oneself to pure existence—a state of complete freedom, emptiness and spontaneity. Lin Chi was blunt and straightforward and any lapses by his students into conventional reasoning were met with shouting or a strike with the teacher's stick. Just as Lin Chi's teachings tapped into the warrior spirit in parts of China, Rinzai Zen has flourished amongst the samurai class in Japan.

In addition to the meditations of Buddhism, Rinzai is characterized by *koans*—enigmatic questions without logical answers devised to stop habitual patterns of thinking and bring about sudden awakenings of intuitive understanding. This type of teaching is quite different from other forms of Buddhism, in which freedom of the mind is reached by gradual and repetitive practice.

Along with Zen practice, Buddhist monks have brought powdered green tea from China, and the serving of tea is becoming an important ritual in Japan.

Mid-twelfth century English Bible

A Zen monk in a meditative reverie, with a waterfall in the background.

Fall of Constantinople

Constantinople Falls to Crusaders

Constantinople, Turkey, April 12, 1204: Byzantine power has come to a shocking end with the sacking of Constantinople by the combined forces of Venetians and the Crusaders. Scenes of murder, rape, and pillaging were rife as the Crusaders forced their way into the city, burning and destroying everything in their path. Byzantine forces, under Alexis IV, soon surrendered.

In a sad irony, the invading forces raided Christian churches, wrecking sacred images and reliquaries and plundering treasures. They seized chalices and other holy utensils, ransacked tombs for gold and silver, and even brought mules inside the churches to help carry away their thefts of precious relics. The cathedral of Hagia Sophia, the great church of the city, was looted and altars torn down.

Although they had sworn an oath not to kill or hurt any Orthodox Christians, the Crusaders beat priests and monks. They showed mercy neither for the

"I HAVE TWO HUGE LIONS TEARING AT MY FLANKS, THE SO-CALLED EMPEROR OTTO AND JOHN, KING OF ENGLAND. BOTH TRY WITH ALL THEIR MIGHT TO UPSET THE KINGDOM OF FRANCE. I CANNOT LEAVE THE COUNTRY MYSELF OR DO WITHOUT MY SON HERE."

PHILIP II (1165–1223) KING OF FRANCE, REFUSING THE POPE'S REQUEST THAT HE GO ON CRUSADE, 1209

elderly nor for the very young. They also molested women. Their brutal behavior has left more than a very sour taste in the mouths of right-minded people everywhere. Even the Venetian fleet, which was engaged to transport the Crusaders to Constantinople, was paid with booty snatched from the city's churches.

The Crusades to recapture the Holy Land from the Muslims have been raging for centuries. Pope Innocent III called for this Crusade in 1201, after Jerusalem had fallen to Muslim forces, but all that is likely to be achieved by this Fourth Crusade is lasting resentment between the eastern and western branches of Christianity.

time out

The folk tale of the Children's Crusade tells of a young shepherd who gathered 20,000 young followers, and set off to fight in the Crusades. They never got there, and were supposedly sold into slavery in Africa.

New Sultanate for Northern India

Delhi, India, 1206: Qutb-ud-din Aybak has established a new sultanate in northern India. The former general of Muhammad of Ghor, Qutb-ud-din has proclaimed himself the first Mamluk (or "slave") sultan of Delhi, a reference to his former status as a slave of the Aybak tribe in Turkey.

Qutb-ud-din enjoyed a successful career in Muhammad's army, rising quickly through the ranks to become his right-hand man. Given responsibility for many campaigns in northern India, Qutb-ud-din relished the power that came with victory. When Muhammad died earlier this year, Qutb-ud-din fought off potential rivals and assumed leadership of Muhammad's forces in northern

The Crusaders entering Constantinople, which fell on April 12, 1204.

The Battle of Damme, at the mouth of the Zwyn, Fland[e]

India, Pakistan, and Afghanistan. He has plans to establish a formal administration in the city of Lahore and has promised to build a number of mosques in the country. The new sultan, the first Muslim sultan in India, is expected to move his headquarters to Delhi in the near future.

Genghis Khan Takes China

Central Asia, 1215: Mongol leader Genghis Khan has steadily been expanding his empire and can now add China to his list of conquests. Conflict with China began in earnest in 1211, and by the end of that year, northern China was in Mongol hands. Genghis Khan's army crossed the Great Wall of China in 1213 and by 1214, he had gained control of all lands north of the Yellow River. A short period of peace between the Chinese and the Mongols was broken with renewed outbreaks of fighting and Genghis has stormed the city of Yanjing, forcing the emperor out of the Chinese capital.

A focused, charismatic leader, Temüjin, son of Yesukhei, chief of the Kiyad tribe, used his family connections, political alliances, and his sheer determination to ultimately unite the Central Asian confederations back in 1206, an achievement that led to his acknowledgment as "Khan." He has worked hard to consolidate a Mongol empire and for many years has had his sights set on China, leading

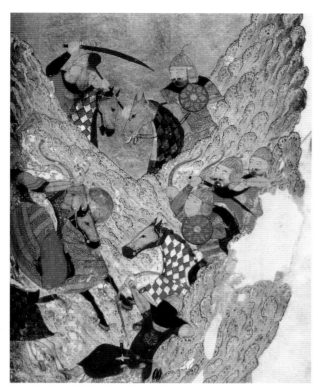

Genghis Khan fighting the Chinese, from an epic poem by Firdausi.

a tightly organized campaign to wrest control from the Jin Dynasty rulers. As well as gaining access to valuable trade routes, Genghis Khan wished to punish the Chinese for their long suppression of the Mongol people.

Often criticized as brutal, Genghis Khan has been dedicated to the establishment of Mongol supremacy in Central Asia, and it is likely that the empire he has founded will continue for many years.

King John Relinquishes Power to Barons

Runnymede, England, June 15, 1215: "It is our wish and command that the English Church will be free and that the men in our kingdom will have and retain these liberties, rights, and concessions, peacefully, fully and entirely for them and their heirs, for us and our heirs…forever." With these words, King John signed off on the

Magna Carta, legally recognizing the rights not only of the country's nobility, but also of ordinary citizens.

There are 63 clauses in the Magna Carta, or the "Great Charter," one of the most important of which is that providing for freedom of religion. The barons insisted that the Church have the right to elect its own officers without royal intervention.

It has been a long campaign for the barons, who have been deeply dissatisfied with many aspects of John's rule. His repeated failures in France caused John to raise taxes to unacceptably high levels without consulting the barons, a breach of feudal law. In addition, his demands for various other financial levies, such as the auxilium which was imposed when an eldest daughter married, were unpopular. The rules of succession have also been contentious, particularly when royal guardianship was involved, with the king had the right to sell widows and daughters into marriage.

The barons demanded that there be systems in place for proper legal redress of any wrongs. It is now possible to have a fair hearing of grievances against anyone in the land, including the king and his officials, many of whom are openly corrupt. This is a major victory for the barons as it means that no-one is now "above the law."

A committee of 25 barons now has the power to overrule the king if his actions are deemed unlawful. In return for the king's relinquishing

King John and the Magna Carta.

of some royal powers, the barons have pledged their allegiance to John and he in turn has promised to be loyal to them.

Batu Khan Takes Russia

Russia, 1242: Batu Khan, grandson of the legendary Genghis Khan, has finally completed his sweep through Russia. The campaign began in 1235, when Batu and his trusted general Subutai led a force of some 125,000 men to invade Europe. By 1236, he had crossed the Volga River, reaching Russia in 1237. He took a number of towns including Moscow before finally sacking Kiev in 1239. Rather than amalgamate Russia with the rest of Central Asia, Batu kept it as a vassal state. Only two cities avoided obliteration, Pskov and Novgorod, both of which agreed to pay tribute to the Mongols in exchange for protection.

Batu Khan now has plans to consolidate his power by invading Poland and Hungary, and ultimately conquer all the lands to the Atlantic coast. One reason for Batu's success in battle has been his use of flags to determine where troops should be placed, a strategy superior to anything in operation by the Europeans.

Batu's plans of European domination did, however, suffer a major setback with the death of Ogedei, the Great Khan, when he, along with other royal princes, was recalled to Mongolia to decide who would be next Great Khan.

Notwithstanding the interruption to his military ambitions, Batu has established the Kipchak Khanate, known in Russia as the "Golden Horde" because of the golden color of his tents. He has settled on Sarai on the lower Volga as the site of his new capital. His Khanate is expected to bring some stability to the region.

King John of England

Russia, 1237: The Mongol forces, under the leadership of Batu Khan, invade Russia.

Karakorum, Mongolia, 1241: Death of Ogedei Khan. He is succeeded by his son, Guyuk.

Liegnitz, Poland, April 5, 1241: The Mongol army overcome the combined forces of the Polish army and the Teutonic knights.

Russia, 1242: Batu Khan establishes the Kipchak Khanate, which is known in Russia as the "Golden Horde."

Middle East, 1248-54: France's Louis IX leads the Seventh Crusade.

Fiorentino, Italy, December 13, 1250: Frederick II, Holy Roman Emperor and King of Germany, dies, aged 55.

New Zealand, c. 1250: Settlers from eastern Polynesia arrive in New Zealand by voyaging canoe.

Venice, Italy, 1254: Marco Polo is born.

Karakorum, Mongolia, May 6, 1260: Kublai Khan becomes ruler of the Mongol Empire.

Evesham, England, August 4, 1265: Simon de Montford dies at the Battle of Evesham.

Middle East, 1270: French king Louis IX leads the Eighth Crusade.

Beijing, China, 1271: Niccolò and Maffeo Polo travel to the court of Kublai Khan, accompanied by Niccolò's son, Marco.

London, England, November 16, 1272: Henry III dies, aged 65. He is succeeded by his son, Edward I.

Germany, 1273: Rudolf I, founder of the Habsburg Dynasty, becomes King of Germany.

Kyushu, Japan, November, 1274: Mongol forces invade Japan but are repelled by samurai aided by a typhoon or *kamikaze* (divine wind).

Beijing, China, 1279: Kublai Khan proclaims himself emperor of China and founds the Yuan Dynasty.

Perpignan, France, October 5, 1285: Philip III dies, aged 40. He is succeeded by his son, Philip IV.

Acre, Middle East, 1291: The Christian-held city of Acre falls to the Mamelukes, who had risen to power in Egypt in 1250.

China, February 12, 1294: Kublai Khan, Mongol leader, dies, aged about 78.

Scotland, 1296: The Battle of Dunbar is won by the English.

Stirling Bridge, Scotland, September 11, 1297: William Wallace is victorious over the English forces.

Falkirk, Scotland, July 22, 1298: Sir William Wallace escapes after defeat of the Scottish forces at the Battle of Falkirk.

Turkey, c. 1299: Osman I establishes the Ottoman Empire.

Osman I

Frederick II Dead

Fiorentino, Italy, December 13, 1250: Frederick II has died, aged 56. A powerful and intelligent man, Frederick was a noted patron of the sciences and literature. He also understood economics and made numerous important social changes, such as legally separating the professions of physician and apothecary.

Following the death of his parents, Pope Innocent III was named Frederick's guardian. He saw the young man as a possible threat to papal interests and gave him scant regard. Frederick often found himself at loggerheads with the papacy, even after becoming king of Germany in 1215 and being crowned Holy Roman Emperor in 1220. His tolerance of Islam and refusal to submit to papal authority made him a thorn in the papal side.

In 1227, following delays in setting off on crusade, Pope Gregory IX saw fit to excommunicate him. When he finally left on crusade in 1228, Frederick was excommunicated once again, this time as punishment for preventing the Church from receiving any credit for his efforts. An expert negotiator, Frederick managed to effect a truce between Christian and Muslim forces, which consequently led to him being proclaimed king of Jerusalem. His victory in Jerusalem gave him unprecedented status and he took on papal authority. Frederick's excommunication was withdrawn in 1230.

Pope Gregory IX (center), who excommunicated Frederick II twice.

In 1245, Pope Innocent IV announced that Frederick was to be deposed as emperor, but he consolidated his forces and continued to challenge papal rule.

Kamikaze Saves Japan

Kyushu, Japan, November, 1274: Mongol forces have been repelled by Japanese warriors assisted by kamikaze (divine wind). A fleet of Kublai Khan's highly disciplined troops arrived at Hakata Bay, forcing the Japanese into retreat. It is almost certain that the Mongol invasion would have been successful but for a severe storm; some 200 Mongolian ships sank and thousands of soldiers perished. The fleet withdrew to Korea.

It was a severe blow to Kublai Khan's plan for military defeat of Japan. For some years now, the khan has been seeking the payment of large tributes, threatening to invade Japan unless such payments were made promptly. But the kamikaze, which many believe to be the result of divine intervention, has put paid to his notions of conquest. He is, however, unlikely to abandon his desire to expand his empire, and the Japanese will need to improve their army and fortifications if they are to remain free of Mongol influence.

Khan, Emperor of China

Peking, China, 1279: With the establishment of what he is calling the Yuan Dynasty, Kublai Khan has become emperor of China, the first foreigner ever to hold this position. Kublai, a grandson of Genghis Khan, succeeded his brother Mongke as khan of the Mongol Empire in 1260, a position he is now expected to hold until his death. Now, after this year's defeat of Song Dynasty forces in the Battle of Yamen, Kublai Khan has become one of the most powerful politicians in the world.

The Yamen naval battle was a resounding victory for Yuan forces. Despite being outnumbered, their superior strategies gave them the advantage, and when young Emperor Bing died after jumping into the sea to avoid capture, the Song Dynasty, in power since 960, came to an end.

An exceptional politician and gifted military tactician, Kublai Khan has put much energy into expanding and uniting his conquests. His choice of "Yuan" as the name for his new government also shows his great political skill—his preference for a Chinese name and his adoption of various Chinese customs into his system of government are making the change of

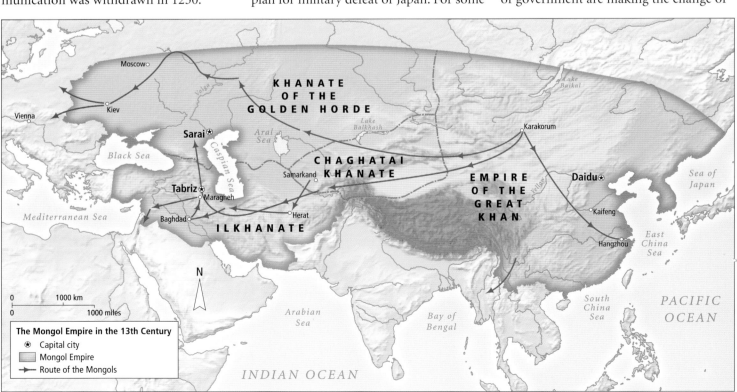

regime easier for the populace. Furthermore, in his quest for a united China, Kublai Khan is expected to embark on a program of rebuilding and promotion of the arts and sciences. Buddhism is likely to be named the state religion. And his endorsement of trade with the west will help to fill state coffers.

Against the advice of some Mongolian counsellors, Kublai Khan has set up his capital in Peking. He has thus lost some support in Mongolia, but his position in China is stronger. Kublai is also building a huge and splendid palace complex, to be known as the Forbidden City.

Tales from China

Venice, Italy, 1295: Explorer, trader, and adventurer Marco Polo has arrived back in Italy from the Far East. One of the first Europeans to travel the Silk Road, Marco Polo spent 24 years traveling through Asia and 17 years in China living in the court of Kublai Khan. Many in Venice are finding his reports of life in China difficult to believe and Polo, resplendent in Tartar costume, has been hosting dinner parties to show off some of his Asian acquisitions, including precious stones and other jewels.

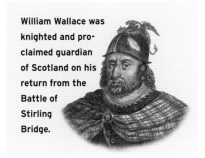

William Wallace was knighted and proclaimed guardian of Scotland on his return from the Battle of Stirling Bridge.

Marco Polo, traveling with his father Niccolò and uncle Maffeo, arrived at Kublai Khan's summer residence in May 1275, where they presented the khan with letters from the Pope. Marco, only 17 at the time, came to the attention of the khan and quickly became his favorite. His skill as a multilinguist led to appointments to various posts in the administration, including missions to Burma, India, and Ceylon.

He was a tax inspector in Yangzhou and also served on the Privy Council. Niccolò and Maffeo also served in Kublai Khan's government. They were well rewarded, but as the khan aged, they became concerned they would not be able to return home. Kublai agreed to let them go home on condition they act as an escort for a Mongol princess on the journey to her Persian betrothed. It took them three years to complete the journey to Venice.

The Polos' accounts of life in China are fascinating. They talk of the khan's great wealth, describing his imperial palace, Xanadu, built of marble and covered in gold and silver, as the most magnificent in the world. They tell of the use of paper money and of fabulous creatures called tigers. Perhaps one day Marco Polo will write of his adventures in the east and the amazing sights he saw.

A Champion Defeated

Falkirk, Scotland, July 22, 1298: Today English forces defeated the army of Sir William Wallace at Falkirk. Although Wallace was the victor in the Battle of Stirling Bridge last year, gaining control of Scotland, the army of Edward Longshanks proved the superior fighting machine in today's decisive encounter. Wallace had devised an ingenious strategy to counter the 3,000-strong English cavalry—he positioned his spearmen into Roman-type phalanxes and stood them in swampy ground in front of thick forest, which protected their rear. These schiltrons, as they are called, were supported by his archers, with his cavalry coming up

behind. However, they were no match for Edward's more experienced forces, and they were greatly outnumbered. Edward is reported to have had some 12,000 foot soldiers in addition to his archers, longbowmen, and horsemen. It wasn't long before the majority of Scots warriors fled the scene, leaving Wallace's forces in disarray. Those who remained were bombarded with arrows. Wallace himself has disappeared. He was last seen riding north toward Callender, and the Scottish hero is now a wanted man.

A long-time resister of English domination in Scotland, Wallace was knighted earlier this year and named "Guardian of Scotland and Leader of Her Armies." A highly popular and respected leader, Wallace had the support of the peasant population who followed him into battle.

Marco Polo

Seats of Power

Byzantine Empire Alexius III Angelus (reigned 1195-1203); Alexius IV Angelus co-emperor with Isaac II Angelus (1203-1204); Alexius V (1204); Theodore I Lascaris (1204-1222); John III Ducas Vatatzes (1222-1254); Theodore II Lascaris (1254-1258); John IV Lascaris (1258-1261); Michael VIII Palaeologus (1259-1282); Andronicus II Palaeologus (1282-1328).

China Emperors of the Song Dynasty: Ningzong (reigned 1194-1224); Lizong (1224-1264); Duzong (1264-1274); Zhao Xian (1274-1276); Duanzong (1276-1278); Zhao Bing (1278-1279). Yuan (Mongol) Dynasty: see Mongol Empire.

England John (reigned 1199-1216); Henry III (1216-1272); Edward I (1272-1307).

France Philip II (1180-1223); Louis VIII (1223-1226); Louis IX (1226-1270); Philip III (1270-1285); Philip IV (1285-1314).

Ghana Empire Diara Kante of the Sosso tribe's Diarisso Dynasty, Kaniaga (1180-1202); Ghana Soumaba Cisse as vassal of Diarisso Dynasty led by Soumaoro (1203-1235); Ghana Soumaba Cisse as allied king to Mali under Sundjata Keita (1235-1240).

Holy Roman Empire Philip (1198-1208); Otto IV (1209-1215); Frederick II (1220-1250); Richard/Alfonso X (rivals 1254-1273); Rudolf I (1273-1291); Adolf (1292-1298); Albert I (1298-1308).

Khmer Empire Jayavarman VII (1181-1219); Indravarman II (1219-1243); Jayavarman VIII (1243-1295); Srindravarman (Indravarman III) (1295-1308).

Mali Empire Sundiata Keita (reigned 1240-1255); Wali Keita (1255-1270); Ouati Keita (1270-1274); Khalifa Keita (1274-1275); Abu Bakr (1275-1285); Sakura (1285-1300).

Mongol Empire Genghis Khan (reigned 1206-1227); Ogedei Khan (1229-1241); Guyuk Khan (1246-1248); Mongke Khan (1251-1259); Kublai Khan (1260-1294); Temur Oljeytu Khan (1294-1307).

Burma (Pagan) Narapatisithu (reigned 1174-1211); Htilominlo (1211-1234); Kyaswa (1234-1250); Uzana (1250-1255); Narathihapati (1255-1287); Kyawswa (Mongol vassal 1287-1298); Sawahnit (1298-1325).

Portugal Sancho I (reigned 1185-1211); Alfonso II (1211-1223); Sancho II (1223-1247); Alfonso III (1247-1279); Dinis (1279-1325).

Scotland William I (reigned 1165-1214); Alexander II (1214-1249); Alexander III (1249-1286); Margaret (1286-1290); First Interregnum (1290-1292); John (1292-1296); Second Interregnum (1296-1306).

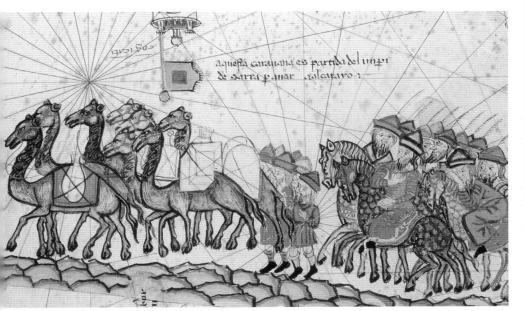

An artist's view of Marco Polo and his traveling caravan making their way along the Silk Road.

Maimonides

"FOR THE THINGS OF THIS WORLD CANNOT BE MADE KNOWN WITHOUT A KNOWLEDGE OF MATHEMATICS.

ROGER BACON, (1214–1294), ENGLISH PHILOSOPHER AND SCHOLAR, 1267

"HAD I BEEN PRESENT AT THE CREATION, I WOULD HAVE GIVEN SOME USEFUL HINTS FOR THE BETTER ORDERING OF THE UNIVERSE."

ALFONSO X (THE WISE) (1221–1284), SPANISH KING

Inventor Publishes New Work

Diyarbakir, Turkey, 1206: An astonishing new engineering work has been written, suggesting that a range of mechanical devices and automata could soon be operational. In *The Book of Knowledge of Ingenious Mechanical Devices*, scholar and inventor ibn Ismail ibn al-Razzaz al-Jazari has come up with some inspired ideas. Al-Jazari has served as the chief engineer at court of Sultan Nasir al-din Mahmoud, a role his father filled before him.

Al-Jazari describes a variety of fascinating labor-saving tools, from locking devices to curious clocks to a blood-letting apparatus. One machine that is attracting a great deal of interest is a water-raising contraption with a wheel that brings a succession of scoops of water from a well to the surface through clever mechanisms along the shaft. His work also discusses fountains and the possibility of having automated scribes.

A mechanism for pumping water, from Al-Jazari's new book.

It will be most interesting to see what this prolific inventor comes up with next.

The Great Wizard is Dead

England, 1234: The great Michael Scott has died. Born in Scotland in 1175, Scott was a master mathematician and astrologer. His deep interest in the occult, sorcery, and alchemy earned him the nickname "The Wizard." In fact, there are those who believe that he possessed magical powers (some said that Scott had an invisible horse upon whose back he rode through the air), and many feared him.

Scott was a learned man who studied philosophy, theology, and astrology at Oxford, Paris, and at the prestigious University of Bologna before he joined the court of the Holy Roman Emperor, Frederick II, in Palermo, Sicily, as an astrologer.

Fluent in the Arabic language, Scott went in 1209 to Toledo in Spain, where he met many Arabic scholars and where he wrote his *Abbreviatio Avicennae*, a dissertation on the works of the eleventh-century philosopher and astrologer, Avicenna. It was in Toledo too that he translated a number of important Arabic astrological and alchemical works into Latin, thus making them accessible to western scholars. He was also interested in the philosophical writings of Averroës and translated many of his works into Latin.

Scott returned to Palermo in 1220 and began to practice medicine. In spite of his interest in the "dark arts," he was offered the Archbishopric of Cashel, in Ireland, but is rumored to have declined it because he did not speak the Irish language.

The cause of Scott's death is uncertain, although some suggest that he was struck on the head by a falling stone.

Inspired by the ancient coins of Rome, this gold coin (or augustalis) was commissioned by Holy Roman Emperor Frederick II and made at the Sicilian mint at Messina.

Complete Set of Buddhist Scriptures

Mt Kaya, Korea, 1237: In the small temple of Haeinsa in Mt Kaya, in southern Korea, Buddhist monks have been very busy. Fearing an invasion by Mongol hordes, the monks have been collecting Buddhist scriptures, and have begun engraving woodblocks containing the most complete collection of sacred Buddhist texts ever seen before. Over 81,000 wooden tablets are being painstakingly engraved in the graceful style of the Chinese master calligrapher Ou-yang Hsun. The monks estimate they will complete this mammoth task within the next 10 years.

Carved on both sides, the wooden blocks, made from the hardwood paktal, measure about 27 in (70 cm) wide and 10 in (25 cm) long; each block contains about 640 characters. When the project is completed, it is estimated there will be over 52 million characters in total, a testament to the monks' dedication and devotion. With characteristic humility, the monks are believed to have prayed after carving every single character, which is said to be the reason for the beautiful uniformity of the calligraphy.

Back in 1231, the Mongols invaded Korea and ruthlessly destroyed all the existing Buddhist prints and blocks that were stored in various monasteries, and this project was intended as a spiritual effort to fend off another incursion and further destruction of Buddhist texts.

Key Events

Italy, 1202: Fibonacci's *Liber abaci (Book of Calculations)* is published.

Chizhou, China, 1203: Shipwright Qin Shifu builds (human-powered) paddlewheel warships with iron plate armor.

Egypt, December 13, 1204: Spanish born philosopher and rabbi, Maimonides (Moshe ben Maimon) , dies, aged about 70.

Diyarbakir, Turkey, 1206: Al-Jazari, the outstanding engineer, writes his *Al-jami bain al-ilm wal-amal al-nafi fi al-hiyal (The Book of Knowledge of Ingenious Mechanical Devices)*. He is also a prolific inventor.

Paris, France, c. 1230: Mathematician and astronomer Sacrobosco writes his book on astronomy—*Tractatus de Sphaera*.

England, 1234: Michael Scott, scholar, dies, aged about 59. His many works covered a range of chiefly scientific subjects, including mathematics, physics, alchemy, astrology, and astronomy.

Mt Kaya, Korea, 1237: Korean monks use 81,258 carved wooden blocks to print a complete edition of Buddhist scriptures in 6,568 volumes.

China, 1247: Ch'in Chui-Shao (Qin Juishao) writes his mathematical treatise *Shushu jiuzhang (Mathematical Treatise in Nine Sections)*.

China, 1248: The first book on forensic science is published. *Hsi duan yu (The Washing Away of Wrongs)* describes how to detect the difference between death by drowning and death by strangulation.

China, 1248: Li Zhi (also known as Li Ye) writes his mathematical work, *Ce yuan hai jing (The Sea Mirror of Circle Measurements)*.

Damascus, Middle East, 1248: Ibn al-Baitar, scientist, dies, aged about 60. His contributions to botany and medicine are remembered in his works *Kitab al-Jami fi al-Adwiya al-Mufrada* on botany, and *Kitab al-Mlughni fi al-Adwiya al-Mufrada*, a work on medicine that incorporated the use of herbal remedies.

England, 1250: Roger Bacon invents the magnifying glass.

Pisa, Italy, 1250: Leonardo of Pisa (Fibonacci), mathematician, dies, aged about 70.

Toledo, Spain, 1252: Commissioned by King Alfonso X and named for him, the Alfonsine Tables are the first European astronomical tables.

Buckinghamshire, England, October 9, 1253: Robert Grosseteste, scholar, dies, aged about 78. His interests included astronomy, mathematics, and optics in particular, and he counted many influential figures among his students, including Roger Bacon.

Maragha, Central Asia, 1259: Persian astronomer Nasir ad-Din al-Tusi builds an observatory for Mongol Great Khan Hulegu.

King Alfonso X the Wise is pictured surrounded by his musicians in this page from a royal manuscript.

quadratorum (The Book of Squares) and *Practica geometriae*, published in 1220, which covered problems in geometry.

First European Astronomical Tables

Toledo, Spain, 1252: New astronomical tables have been drawn up and released this year. Commissioned by Alfonso X, himself a devotee and active supporter of astronomy, the tables are the culmination of a massive project involving about 50 astronomers. Alfonso has been eager to have new tables produced because of the well-known inconsistencies in the Ptolemaic tables that have been used for centuries. The new tables tabulate both the position and the movement of the planets, making it possible for astronomers to divide the year into 365 days, 5 hours, 49 minutes and some 16 seconds.

The Alfonsine Tables, as they are being called, have been named for the king, and are the first astronomical tables of European origin.

Often called "El Sabio" (The Wise), Alfonso encourages scientific inquiry; one of his major contributions has been the establishment of a school of translation. Many works in Arabic, including classical philosophy, astronomy, and other branches of science, have been translated into both Latin and Spanish and this has enabled a more effective exchange of knowledge between European and Near Eastern scholars. Alfonso is also committed to the idea of establishing a stable and reliable justice system, with the aim of creating a harmonious society in which scientists and philosophers will flourish.

There are hopes that the Alfonsine Tables will be published in due course.

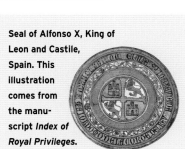

King Alfonso X

Seal of Alfonso X, King of Leon and Castile, Spain. This illustration comes from the manuscript *Index of Royal Privileges*.

Fibonacci's Number is Up

Pisa, Italy, 1250: The death has been announced of acclaimed mathematician Leonardo of Pisa, or Fibonacci, as he is now being called. Fibonacci revolutionized the way we think about mathematical equations when he introduced the use of Hindu-Arabic numerals to Europe. The son of notary and businessman, Guglielmo Bonacci, young Leonardo was brought up in northern Africa, where his father was posted. There, he was exposed to Moorish merchants from an early age. He was always fascinated with their methods of arithmetic and familiarized himself with the Hindu-Arabic numerical system. He learned mathematics in Algeria and furthered his education as he traveled with his father. In 1202, in his *Liber abaci (The Book of Calculations),* he wrote that his father wished him to learn accounting so he could help the family.

With its basis in the algebraic formulas and other arithmetic skills he had picked up during his travels, the *Liber abaci* was well received by the general public. The great benefit of the Hindu-Arabic system for mathematical calculation is its simplicity and its decimal base. It is infinitely easier to calculate Arabic numerals than Roman numerals. Of particular interest is the section for merchants, in which Leonardo explains how to calculate profit and loss, how to calculate weights and measures, and how to convert the different currencies that are in circulation.

However, arguably the most important part of the *Liber abaci* is what is being called the "Fibonacci sequence," in which each number, apart from the first two, is the sum of the previous two numbers— 0, 1, 1, 2, 3, 5, 8, 13, etc. This sequence has since been found to occur in a range of fields of mathematics and even science.

As well as that seminal work, Fibonacci will also be remembered for his other mathematical works, including the *Liber*

In this new permanent form, these sacred scriptures are being referred to as the Tripitaka Koreana.

time out

Theodoric of Luca, a Dominican monk, introduces anesthesia in 1236—he soaks sponges in a mandragora and opium solution, and applies it to the nose of the patients so that they sleep during surgery.

Maragha, Persia, 1262: Al-Tusi, famed Persian scientist, builds the Meraghia Observatory.
Paris, France, August, 1269: Petrus Peregrinus (Petrus de Maricourt) writes his manuscript on magnets, *Epistola de magnete.*
Viterbo, Italy, 1270: Witelo's treatise *Perspectiva (Perspectives)* is published. It outlines his theories on optics.
Baghdad, Persia, June 26, 1274: Al-Tusi, scientist, dies, aged about 73. His interests covered many fields of science and mathematics.

Lombardy, Italy, 1275: William of Saliceto writes Chirugia, a record of his surgery and dissections.
China, 1276: Guo Shoujing, astronomer and engineer, develops instruments to help gather information for the development of the new calendar commissioned by Kublai Khan.
China, 1279: Li Zhi (Li Ye), mathematician, dies, aged about 86. He wrote many works, the most famous being *Ce yuan hai jing (The Sea Mirror of Circle Measurements).*

Beijing, China, 1279: Kublai Khan commissions the building of an observatory in the city to provide Guo Shoujing with more data.
Speyer, Germany, 1280: For the first time, Chinese spinning wheels go on display in Germany.
Cologne, Germany, November 15, 1280: Albertus Magnus, great scholars, dies.
Italy, c. 1284: Eyeglasses are invented. The actual inventor is uncertain, with Alessandro Spina of Florence and Salvino D'Armante of Pisa both credited.

Italy, 1286: William of Moerbeke, scholar, dies, aged about 71. During his lifetime he translated numerous works from Arabic to Latin, bringing the discoveries and theories of Arab scholars in the fields of philosophy, medicine, mathematics, and science to a European audience.
Cairo, Egypt, 1288: Ibn al-Nafis, renowned physician, dies, aged about 75. He was the first to document the workings of the pulmonary circulation of the body, gas exchange in the lungs, and the structure of the lungs.

Oxford, England, 1292: Roger Bacon, scholar, dies, aged about 78. His interests ranged from theology to science, and he was particularly interested in the field of optics.
Viterbo, Italy, 1296: Johannes Campanus (also known as Campanus of Novara) dies, aged about 76. He is known for his works on mathematics and astronomy, including *Theorica planetarum,* which detailed the construction of a planetarium.

Kublai Khan

Magnetic New Work

Paris, France, August, 1269: A fascinating scientific treatise on magnetism has been written by the Frenchman Petrus de Maricourt, or Petrus Peregrinus as he is also known. In his letter *Epistola de magnete*, Petrus describes the laws of magnetism in a clear and logical format, discussing the properties of the lodestone, a stone that can attract iron. He then goes on to explain how he performed a sequence of experiments based on the concept of perpetual motion, proposing that it may be possible to perpetually turn a wheel using a magnet.

Believed to have been written while Petrus was serving in the army of Charles of Anjou at the siege of Luceria, the *Epistola Petri Peregrini de Maricourt ad Sygerum de Foucaucourt, militem de magnete* is a remarkable work which has attracted wide attention. Addressed to his friend, Sygerus of Foucaucourt, Petrus identifies north and south polarity and reveals that strong magnets can cancel out the effects of weaker ones. Another observation made in the *Epistola* is that like, or similar, poles repel one another, while unlike poles attract one another.

Petrus has revealed that he personally performed all of his own experiments on magnetism, rather than relying on current information. He believes many advances can be made with this new knowledge, such as the development of a magnetized needle that pivots in a circle, which may have advantages in the future.

Al-Tusi is Dead

Baghdad, Persia, June 26, 1274: Abu Jafar Muhammad ibn Muhammad ibn al-Hasan Nasir al-Din al-Tusi, or al-Tusi as he was commonly known, died today, aged seventy-three. Scientist, astronomer, philosopher, and mathematician, al-Tusi was a man of many talents who has made major contributions to the sciences in the Arabic world.

A great achievement is his devising of accurate and up-to-date astronomical tables, detailing the movements of the planets and an inventory of all the stars known to humankind. The work, which took 12 years to complete, was published as *Al-zij-Ilkhani (The Ilkhanic Tables)*. It is dedicated to the Halagu Khan, the Mongol conqueror of the region. Al-Tusi also developed a model of circular lunar movement, making a significant deviation from the model proposed by Ptolemy. As chief astronomer of the observatory at Maragha, al-Tusi had access to the latest scientific equipment, and he also invented astronomical instruments himself.

Al-Tusi was also an accomplished mathematician. He established trigonometry, including spherical and plane trigonometry, as a separate branch of mathematics. In his *Treatise on the Quadrilateral*, he listed six basic formulas for right-angled triangles in spherical trigonometry.

Al-Tusi was educated in Nishapur, where he studied the sciences, logic, metaphysics, and philosophy, and he has also left important writings on ethics and Islamic philosophy. One of his hobbies was writing poetry. In spite of the political upheaval of recent years, al-Tusi managed to maintain his professionalism and his lifelong devotion to the sciences. When Mongol forces sacked Baghdad in 1258, al-Tusi chose the course of least resistance and worked with them rather than against them. One consequence was the building of the observatory where he made his famous astronomical calculations. The benefits to science are incalculable.

New Instruments for Imperial Observatory

Peking, China, 1276: The largest observatory in the world, expected to be complete in 1279, already has some new and improved instruments for astronomical study. Engineer, astronomer, and instrument maker Guo Shoujing, who has had

Kublai Khan rewarding his officers for a victory. Kublai is keenly promoting astronomy in China.

"Sea monster found in river by sailors," from *De natura rerum* (*Things of Nature*) by Albertus Magnus.

Roger Bacon

a hand in the observatory's de-sign, has also been involved in research to implement a new calendar. This is seen by Mongol leader Kublai Khan as symbolic of the new administration in China, as well as a move toward improving methods of astronomical observations and determining the movement of the planets.

Born in 1231, Guo displayed a flair for engineering from a young age. In the course of his current research, Guo has built 17 new instruments designed to collect more accurate astronomical data. Thirteen of these are to be housed in the new observatory in the capital. It is believed that the remaining four can be taken to remote locations to verify various findings. The instruments include water clocks and spheres that represent the heavens. Guo has also made significant improvements to the gnomon, that part of a sundial that casts a shadow.

Guo has since been called on to provide advice on water management schemes including flood control. Kublai Khan now fully supports the new observatory.

Mathematician Orders Burning of Own Works

China, 1279: The death of mathematician Li Zhi has been announced. He is known for his *Ce yuan hai jing* (*The Sea Mirror of Circle Measurements*), an important work completed about 1248 while he was living as a recluse in Shansi province. It is rumored that, on his deathbed, Li Zhi (also known as Li Ye) ordered his son to burn all his other works, but it is known that some texts are not in family hands and will be kept for scholastic purposes.

One of Li Zhi's important contributions to the study of mathematics is his coefficient array method, which helps in the construction of equations, and by extension, their solutions. He was intensely interested in the mysteries of numbers and in 1259 published an informative work on computation.

In 1257, his well-known expertise prompted Kublai Khan to ask Li Zhi to advise him on a number of issues,

including the civil service examinations. Three years later, he was invited to take up a position in the government, but declined, citing ill health as the reason.

Albertus Magnus Leaves a Legacy of Knowledge

Cologne, Germany, November 15, 1280: Philosopher, scientist, and theologian Albert of Cologne died today after a short illness. An esteemed scholar in a number of disciplines, Albert has left a great body of work that is sure to prove timeless. His interests encompassed a wide range of subjects, from logic, astronomy, botany, and chemistry, through to philosophy and alchemy. He was known as a "doctor universalis," an acknowledgement of his extraordinary knowledge.

Born in Bavaria perhaps as early as 1193, Albertus Magnus was educated in Padua and soon after joined the Dominican order of monks, studying theology in Bologna. His expert scholarship led to his appointment as lecturer at Regensburg, Cologne, and Strasburg. He received his doctorate in 1245 and taught in Paris. In 1260, Pope Alexander IV made him bishop of Regensburg, but he only held this office for three years, before leaving it to resume his professorship in Cologne. One of his pupils was Thomas Aquinas.

Well-known as an author, Albertus also translated the work of Aristotle, including the notes of his various Arabic commentators, into Latin. Albertus was a great admirer of Aristotle, whose influence can be seen in the approach Albertus takes to his writings, which follow a clear and orderly train of thought. He aimed to present theology in a scientific manner.

Keenly interested in the natural world, Albertus's botanical works include *De vegetabilibus et plantis* and *De animalibus*. His *Mineralium* is considered one of the definitive works on mineralogy. In it, he encourages scholars to do their own investigations and not simply rely on the statements of others. His theological writings, such as *Summa Theologiae* and his commentary on the *Books of the Sentences*

of Peter Lombard, are highly regarded by scholars and churchmen alike. Albertus's great contribution to the sciences and to philosophy cannot be underestimated.

Roger Bacon Dies

Oxford, England, June, 1294: One of the great minds of our time has died. Roger Bacon was the author of a number of important works, among them the *Opus majus*, written in 1267, in which he puts forth his views on theology and philosophy, mathematics, logic, and optics, a field of enormous interest to him.

Scholar, philosopher, and Franciscan monk, Bacon always based his findings on empirical evidence and advocated strict methods of experimentation and reporting. Bacon was educated at Oxford and later taught in Paris, where he lectured on Aristotle, whose works had recently been revived, before returning home to devote himself to research and further study. He was passionate about studying languages, believing that true knowledge of important texts, such as the Bible, comes from being fluent in the language in which it was first written.

Roger Bacon, from an illustrated manuscript.

Bacon has acknowledged the influence of French scholar Petrus Peregrinus in turning him to a contemplation of science and mathematics. He soon realized the relationship between geometry and optics and began experimenting with mirrors and lenses, agreeing with fellow Englishman Robert Grosseteste that using lenses a certain way can make things at a distance appear closer.

Bacon also wrote the *Opus minus*, an encapsulation of the *Opus majus*, and the *Opus tertium* (1268), a guide to understanding his previous works. Bacon was subject to the strict rules enforced by the Franciscans against publishing without permission, although it is said that Pope Clement IV instructed him to disregard this rule and to present his treatises.

Song Dynasty Porcelain Conquers World Market

Ceramic from Jun kiln

Hangzhou, China, 1200: A new export business is thriving in the bustling city of Hangzhou. Since the beginning of the Song Dynasty, much of China's refined culture has thrived, from calligraphy and painting to poetry and other writing. Now the porcelain industry is thriving and visiting western merchants are eagerly buying up pieces for resale in the west and as far away as East Africa.

What makes Song porcelain so desirable is the beauty of the individual pieces. All pieces are given a thick heavy glaze and the colors that are chosen by the potters, ranging from soft greens, aquas, blues, reds, and yellows, are sublime. A number of styles are much admired, and these come from different kilns. The Longquan Yao kiln produces mostly green ceramics. The Jun Yao kiln makes stunning porcelains often with a brown "foot," while ceramics from the Yao Zhou Yao

Song Dynasty vase with phoenix handles.

kiln are known for their beautiful hand-incised designs. The Ge Yao kiln produces simple and delicate porcelains with a distinctive purple fringe, the result of the glazing technique. The Jingdezhen kiln uses cobalt in its glazes to create some startling blue and white porcelain. All chinaware produced is highly sought after.

> "THIS DUMB OX WILL FILL THE WHOLE WORLD WITH HIS BELLOWING."
>
> ALBERTUS MAGNUS (C. 1200–1280), GERMAN BISHOP, OF THOMAS AQUINAS

> "I LOVE THE GAY EASTER-TIDE, WHICH BRINGS FORTH LEAVES AND FLOWERS.... BUT I ALSO LOVE TO SEE... KNIGHTS AND HORSES IN BATTLE ARRAY."
>
> BERTRAND DE BORN, TROUBADOUR, 1210

Reims to Build Gothic-style Cathedral

Reims, France, 1211: Construction has commenced on a cathedral for Reims in Champagne, some 130 miles (209 km) from Paris. Architect Jean d'Orbais has

The nave at Notre-Dame de Reims Cathedral.

drawn up plans for a building of exceptional beauty. The plans include a large nave, some 98 ft (30 m) wide and 125 ft (38 m) high. It is hoped that Notre-Dame de Reims, as it will be known, will be used for important events such as coronations and state funerals.

The new cathedral will be built on the site of a small basilica that burnt down last year. It is the same site where Clovis, king of the Franks, was baptized by the Saint Remi, the bishop of Reims, in 496, so building Notre-Dame here has deep historical and religious significance.

The style and decoration of the cathedral will be gothic, a style in favor since mid-last century, so worshipers can expect to pray in open, elegant surroundings, with wide windows offering plenty of light. There will be three stories and a vaulted ceiling. Highly decorated Corinthian-style columns will support the internal structure and stained glass windows will be

dedicated to the glory of God. A rose window, using the finest stained glass, is planned to go above the main portal.

Notre-Dame de Reims will also feature a central portal dedicated to the Virgin Mary, as well as a number of statues and other sculptures. Building a cathedral of this magnitude is a long-term project, but church officials are hopeful that it will be more or less complete in 50 years.

Competition for University of Bologna

Padua, Italy, 1222: The University of Bologna's academic monopoly has come to an end with the opening of a new university in Padua. The University of Bologna, possibly the oldest European university (established 1088) is renowned for its teachings in law and theology.

However, in recent times, Bologna has been criticized for narrow-mindedness and a somewhat restrictive curriculum. This has been the catalyst for a group of students and professors to found an alternative institution of learning. The University of Padua claims to provide more academic freedom of study. Set up as a self-governing group of students and scholars, the university has also attracted the attention of local authorities and the nobility, who are lending their support to the venture.

So far, only law, including civil law, theology, and canon law, are being taught at Padua, but there are plans to include astronomy, philosophy, medicine, and other disciplines in the syllabus. Its motto is *"Universa universis patavina libertas,"* or "Paduan freedom is complete for everyone."

One innovation of the new university is the creation of separate groups, or *nationes*, of students—the *cismontanes* for Italian students and the *ultramontanes* for foreign students. The *nationes* are

> **time out**
>
> In 1203, German poet Wolfram von Eschenbach writes *Parzival*, a narrative poem about the Holy Grail based on the romantic poem *Le Roman de Perceval ou le Conte du Graal* by Chrétien de Troyes (c. 1175).

Illustration from the *Prose Edda*, the Icelandic saga.

Illustration by
Matthew Paris

assassination. The former president of the Icelandic parliament, Snorri will be best remembered for his writings, in particular the *Heimskringla* and the *Prose Edda*. But today, all thoughts are on his association with the darker side of politics.

A wealthy and very determined man, Snorri, son of the chieftain Sturla Thordsson, often put his own ambitions before his country. Born in Hvammur í Dalir in 1179, he is said to have believed that Iceland's political climate was unstable, causing him to enter into an alliance with Haakon, king of Norway. Many think that he intended to betray his country to Haakon, but it was because he disobeyed Haakon's order to remain in Norway that he was killed in his home in Gut Reykjaholt, on Haakon's orders.

His political motives may not be entirely clear, but it is true to say that Snorri loved Scandinavia's glorious past and he has immortalized this in his literary works. The *Heimskringla*, arguably his greatest work, merges Norse legends with true history. It begins with the founding of civilization by Odin and his pantheon, and continues with tales of the kings and their reigns, ending with the death in battle, in 1177, of Eystein Meyla, son of Norway's King Eystein II. The saga of Olaf Haraldson is the longest part of the work and is often quoted by scholars and the common people alike.

The *Prose Edda*, written in 1220, cosists of three books—the *Gylfaginning,* covering Norse mythology, as well as folk songs and sagas; the *Skáldskaparmál,* which explains poetic language and its use; and the *Háttatal,* a comprehensive list of various verse forms. His writing, of the highest calibre, ensures that Scandinavia's celebrated history will not be forgotten.

St Albans in 1217, and spent most of his life there, applying himself to the study and recording of history, something the monks have long been known for.

Paris penned many works, including a biography of Edward the Confessor and the *Historia Anglorum (History of the English)*, and he was also responsible for a lengthy account of the deeds of the abbots of St Albans. But undoubtedly, Paris's greatest achievement was his *Chronica majora (Great Chronicle)*, a painstakingly detailed and descriptive chronicle of the events of his time.

Although most of Paris's life was occupied with writing, he also had occasion to visit the royal courts, and in 1248 he was sent to Norway to oversee the reorganization of St Benet Holme, the Benedictine monastery at Trondheim. Although he was well acquainted with Henry III, Paris was not necessarily flattering in his observations of the king's policies, and some have questioned whether Paris intended his *Chronica majora* for general distribution. In any case, it is a work that is destined to have long-term value for historians.

governed by two rectors, who will be elected annually from the student body. The students are also responsible for the election of the university's professors and will also determine their salaries. The Paduan administration guarantees to respect the academic freedom of the university and already students are arriving from many parts of Europe.

Poet Murdered

Gut Reykjaholt, Iceland, September 22, 1241: Historian, statesman, and poet Snorri Sturluson is dead, the victim of a political

Great Historian Dies

St Albans, England, 1259: Historian Matthew Paris has died today aged 59. He entered the Benedictine monastery at

Virgin and child by historian Matthew Paris.

World Loses Sufi Poet

Konya, Turkey, December 17, 1273: Persian theologian and poet Jalal al-din Rumi, or to give him his full name, Molana Jalal ad-Din Muhammad ibn Balkhi al-Rumi, has died today, about 66, and will be buried in Konya in the grave of his father.

Rumi is well known for his philosophical writings on *Tawhid*, the Islamic notion of one God, which he expressed mainly in poetic form. His *Mathnawi* is considered one of his finest works. In it he discusses Sufism and its bearing on daily life, and other mystical matters. Many regard it as a spiritual masterpiece, second only to the Koran. Another work for which he will be remembered is *Divan-e Shams-e Tabriz*, a collection of poems with over 40,000 quatrains, odes, and other verses, which he named for his friend, the Sufi mystic Shams Tabriz-i.

Rumi met Shams in 1244 in Konya, an association that changed his life. Before this auspicious meeting, Rumi had spent his days studying and teaching. He received his religious education in Damascus and Aleppo and succeeded his father as head of a religious school. Shams became Rumi's friend and close spiritual adviser, and is credited with inspiring Rumi to the poetic heights for which he is now famous.

Rumi had an interesting life. When he was thirteen years of age, his family left Persia and traveled west. During his travels, Rumi met the celebrated poet Attar who encouraged the boy to begin writing poetry. It it obvious that Rumi took this encouragement to heart.

Thomas Aquinas (center)

> *"Of one Essence is the human race, thus has Creation put the Base; One Limb impacted is sufficient, For all others to feel the Mace."*
>
> SAADI, PERSIAN POET, 1200–1292

> *"Who despises all, displeases all."*
>
> ALBERTANUS OF BRESCIA (c. 1190–1270), ITALIAN SCHOLAR, 1246

Key Structures

Abbey of Mont Saint Michel, Mont Saint Michel, France
Basilica of San Francesco Assisi, Assisi, Italy
Bayon, Angkor, Cambodia
Bourges Cathedral, Bourges, France
Castel del Monte, Abruzzo, Italy
Chartres Cathedral, France
Convent of Christ, Tomar, Portugal
Dover Castle, Dover, England
Durham Cathedral, Durham, England
Geghard Monastery, near Garni, Armenia
Great Mosque, Djenne, Mali
Great Mosque and Hospital of Divrigi, Turkey
Hoysaleswara Temple, Halebid, India
Keshava Temple, Somnathpur, India
La Sainte-Chapelle, Paris, France
Notre-Dame, Amiens, France
Notre Dame Cathedral, Paris, France
Qutb-ud-Din Minaret, Delhi, India
St Etienne Cathedral, Auxerre, France
Salisbury Cathedral, Salisbury, England
Surya Temple, Konarak, India
Tumen Amgalan, Kharkorin, Mongolia
Urquhart Castle, Inverness, Scotland
Wat Chiang Man, Chiang Mai, Thailand
Wat Mahathat, Sukhothai, Thailand
White Monuments of Vladimir and Suzdal, Russia
Winchester Great Hall, Winchester, England

Thomas Aquinas with one of the faithful.

Thomas Aquinas is Dead

Fossanova, Italy, March 7, 1274: Renowned theologian and scholar Thomas Aquinas died today, aged 49. A prolific writer, he will probably be best remembered for his *Summa theologica*. This unfinished seminal work explaining the reasoning behind all aspects of the Catholic faith. It also contains his *"quinquae viae"* (the five streets), being an exposition of five methods by which to prove the existence of God.

At the age of five, Aquinas entered the Benedictine abbey at Montecassino to begin his studies; he later moved to the University of Naples. A natural scholar, Aquinas attended a number of educational institutions, receiving his master's degree and being named a doctor of theology in 1256. He travelled around Italy, France, and even parts of England giving informative lectures on diverse theological questions.

Thomas Aquinas was often called upon to advise the French king about church matters, and the Pope also sought his counsel from time to time. As might be expected, he was a spiritual man and when he wasn't lecturing, he wrote homilies and explanatory works. Although offered the archbishopric of Naples, Aquinas refused, more concerned with getting on with his greatest work, the *Summa theologica*, than being part of the church administration. Interestingly, he stopped work on the *Summa theologica* following a mystical experience in 1273 in which he felt that his writings were inadequate, describing them as "so much straw."

In January of this year, Pope Gregory X sent Aquinas to the Second Council of Lyons to help establish some measure of peace between the Roman and Orthodox churches, but he became ill on the way and stopped at the Cistercian monastery in Fossanova, where he died after some weeks. He was a remarkable intellect and his passing will not go unmarked.

Notre Dame Complete!

Paris, France, 1285: At last, Paris's magnificent new cathedral dedicated to the Virgin Mary is complete. Built on the site of the city's first Christian church, on the Ile de la Cité, the idea for Notre Dame germinated in 1160 when the Bishop of Paris, Maurice de Sully, announced plans for its erection. Work began in 1163, during the reign of Louis VII. Pope Alexander III laid the cornerstone, and steady work over the last seven decades has culminated in the grand cathedral we see today.

Although a number of architectural styles are evident, the overwhelming style is gothic, and the cathedral is sure to become a Paris landmark. The stained glass windows are particularly beautiful. Notre Dame is one of the few churches in

The newly completed Notre Dame Cathedral, Paris.

Europe to use the flying buttress, an arch providing support for some of the walls with large windows. Although complete, many are suggesting that further embellishments will be made in years to come.

Saadi Dead at 92

Shiraz, Persia, December 9, 1292: The famed poet and scholar, Saadi Shirazi, has died today. Many know him through his *Bustan (The Orchard)*, published in 1257, which espouses the traditional Muslim virtues of justice, modesty, and happiness, and *Golistan (The Rose Garden)*, published in 1258, consisting of poetry and prose, and which contains many instructive stories.

Saadi's great knowledge of the human condition and his lyrical skill in conveying

it in words has made him one of the best loved men of letters in Persia. Saadi's lament following the fall of Baghdad to the Mongols is a particularly moving work. What makes Saadi's work so special is his distinction between the physical and the spiritual worlds—he is equally at ease describing the travels of a merchant as he is discussing the finer points of Sufism. His writings appear effortless and they encapsulate a wealth of values important to the Muslim experience.

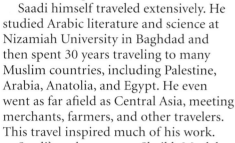

Italian poet Dante Alighieri.

Saadi himself traveled extensively. He studied Arabic literature and science at Nizamiah University in Baghdad and then spent 30 years traveling to many Muslim countries, including Palestine, Arabia, Anatolia, and Egypt. He even went as far afield as Central Asia, meeting merchants, farmers, and other travelers. This travel inspired much of his work.

Saadi's real name was Sheikh Mosleh al-Din. He is reported to have adopted the name Saadi in honor of the ruler of Shiraz, Atabak Abubakr Sa'd ibn Zangy.

Following his travels, Saadi returned to his native Shiraz to live out his days. He was warmly welcomed home and spent the rest of his life penning the wonderful works for which he will be remembered.

"New Life" For Dante

Florence, Italy, 1294: In a newly published work entitled *La vita nuova (The New Life)*, Florentine poet Dante Alighieri has described his deep, lasting, yet platonic, love for a woman he first met when he was only nine years old. This collection of verse comprises poems written over the last decade or so, along with the poet's personal commentaries. These explain Dante's ideas on romantic love and how it can enhance our experience of divine love. The book is dedicated to Dante's friend and fellow poet, Guido Cavalcanti.

What makes *La Vita Nuova* remarkable is its simple style and the fact that the poet has written his work in Italian rather than the traditional Latin, which is sure to give the work wider appeal. Dante describes his first meeting with the woman who unquestionably became the love of his life and later tells of his anguish when he heard of her death only a few years ago. Although he names her only as Beatrice, many are speculating that the woman in question is Beatrice Portinari, the wife of Simone de' Bardi.

Born in Florence in 1265, Dante was a member of the Guelph family. As a young man, he studied philosophy, theology, and grammar. As he was particularly interested in the writings of Aristotle and

Thomas Aquinas, it is not surprising that his account of love verges on the mystical. In 1285, he married Gemma di Manetto Donati and they have four children. Dante is now said to be working on another, more ambitious project.

Marco Polo's Travels Revealed

Genoa, Italy, 1298: Celebrated traveler Marco Polo, who spent many years in the Chinese court of Kublai Khan, has been recounting more stories of his adventures in order to while away the hours he is in prison. Three years ago, Venetians listened in amazement as Polo, his father and uncle regaled them with tales of opulence and excitement in the

Far East. Many of their reports were met with cries of disbelief, but now Marco Polo wants the last word.

Having been captured in a skirmish between Genoa and Venice, Marco Polo has been telling a fellow prisoner, Rustichello da Pisa, about his experiences. Rustichello is a writer himself and there is speculation that Polo's tales are being dictated and will be collected into one volume for publication. A title has even been suggested—*The Description of the World*—although already some are referring to it as *Il milione*—a reference to the many stories contained therein, or perhaps to the fact that there are still those who believe the stories to be a "million lies." Many, for example, do not believe there is a stone, called coal, that can burn as wood does, or that such a thing as the Grand Canal exists in China.

Marco Polo, whose accounts of his travels along the Silk Road to China may soon be published.

Francis of Assisi Sainted

St Francis of Assisi

Rome, Italy, July 17, 1228: The miracles and countless good deeds performed by Francis of Assisi have been recognized by Pope Gregory IX, who canonized Francis yesterday. Today, the pope is laying the first stone in a new church to be built in Assisi in honor of the new saint.

Francis, who died on October 4, 1226, sought the permission of Pope Innocent III to establish a new religious order in 1209. On approval, he named his brotherhood the Franciscan Order, or the Friars Minor. The brothers lead simple lives, having turned their backs on the material world. They wear basic clothing and go barefoot, traveling around the country preaching God's word.

Francis himself felt a deep bond with nature. He is once said to have spoken to a wolf to ask him to stop terrifying local townspeople. Making the sign of the cross, the wolf agreed and both wolf and people lived in harmony from that day. There are many stories of Francis's rapport with animals. Some feel they are symbolic of his closeness to God; others believe in his ability to miraculously transform wild creatures into gentle pets.

The new saint was born into privilege. Son of a prosperous merchant, Francis spent his youth indulging in many pleasures. He loved to sing and party, and always wore the finest clothes. Later, he joined in the fight of the Assisians against the Perugians and was taken prisoner. At about that time he began to take stock of his life, and although he thought of joining the army, it seemed that spiritual matters took precedence.

"EXCEPT BY THE LAWFUL JUDGMENT OF HIS PEERS OR BY THE LAW OF THE LAND. TO NO MAN WILL WE SELL, OR DENY, OR DELAY, RIGHT OR JUSTICE."

MAGNA CARTA, 1215

"THEY ILLUMINATE OUR WHOLE COUNTRY WITH THE BRIGHT LIGHT OF THEIR... TEACHING."

ROBERT GROSSE-TESTE (C. 1175–1253) BISHOP OF LINCOLN, OF THE FRANCISCAN MONKS, 1238

Mourning over the body of Francis of Assisi.

Pope Targets Heretics

Rome, Italy, 1233: In a move likely to impact on many Christians, Pope Gregory IX has established a Papal Inquisition to address the increasing problem of heresy. Dominican monks have already been sent to France to conduct their questioning. At this stage, a month's grace period has been allotted for anyone who wishes to admit to and reject heresy, after which time such people will be brought to trial. Many doubt the fairness of the trials, saying that all verdicts so far have been guilty. The main punishment for heresy is imprisonment. In addition, property of the guilty person can be confiscated.

The Inquisition is partly a result of the failure of the crusades in the Holy Land. Pope Innocent III is known to have encouraged crusaders to take action against other Christians, such as the allegedly heretical Cathars, based in the south of France. Wishing to complete the work begun by his predecessor, Gregory has instructed his inquisitors to target Christian groups that do not submit to papal authority, including the Waldensians, long considered a schismatic group.

Pope Innocent III approves the rule of the Franciscan Order, or the Friars Minor.

Critics of the Inquisition, who understandably remain anonymous, point out that this current campaign has the potential to be much more ruthless than earlier ones, as the inquisitors answer only to the pope. Their paramount authority is open to corruption, and anyone criticizing the inquisitors can be labeled heretics themselves. Many believe this Inquisition will have long-term ramifications for Christians, both rich or poor.

time out

Tofu, or the soybean curd, which has been eaten in China for over 2,000 years, has now been introduced into Japan by traveling merchants; it is quickly becoming a staple food there.

Jewish Talmudic Texts Burned

Paris, France, June 6, 1242: In a dramatic move, papal and royal authorities today ordered the burning of 24 wagonloads of Talmudic texts, which are sacred to Jewish people. The idea for the burning originated two years ago when Nicholas Donin laid charges that the Talmud contains writings blasphemous to Jesus Christ. He held that such texts should not be allowed to circulate

Latvia, 1201: The city of Riga is founded.

Middle East, July, 1201: The worst earthquake in history reverberates throughout Egypt and Syria.

England, 1205: A severe frost lasting for 2 months freezes the Thames and makes tilling of the soil impossible in many areas.

Hangzhou, China, April, 1208: Fire breaks out and destroys more than 58,000 houses over four days.

Italy, 1209: Francis of Assisi founds the Franciscan order of monks.

Japan, 1214: After bringing tea from China to Japan some years earlier, Eisai writes his work on the benefits of tea drinking–*Kissa yojoki (The Medicinal Benefits of Tea Drinking)*.

Russia, 1221: Grand Prince Yuri Vsevolodovich founds the city of Nizhny Novgorod.

Assisi, Italy, October 4, 1226: Francis of Assisi dies, aged about 45.

Germany, c. 1230: The city of Berlin is founded.

Rome, Italy, 1233: Pope Gregory IX establishes the Papal Inquisition to address the problem of heretics.

Japan, 1233: Ohaguro–the practice of blackening the teeth–becomes a popular trend.

London, England, 1235: The English Parliament is established. The first initiative they render is the Statute of Merton–dealing with land ownership.

England, 1237: The Treaty of York is signed by England's King Henry III and Scotland's King Alexander II. The treaty establishes the border between the two countries.

England, 1241: The gruesome execution practice of hanging, drawing, and quartering is introduced as a penalty for treason.

Paris, France, June 6, 1242: Anti-Semitism is still rife–authorities order the burning of 24 wagonloads of Talmudic texts.

London, England, 1247: Bethlem Hospital–or Bedlam as it will become known–is originally built to serve as a priory.

Palermo, Sicily, c . 1249: Frederick II, Holy Roman Emperor and King of Germany writes *De arte venandi cum avibus (The Art of Hunting with Birds)*.

Sweden, c. 1252: The city of Stockholm is founded by Birger Jarl.

England, 1252: The Assize of Arms officially decrees that men should arm themselves with a longbow.

Florence, Italy, 1252: The gold Florentine florin is first minted.

Seville, Spain, May 30, 1252: Ferdiand III of Castille dies.

in a Christian country. A "trial," called the Disputation of Paris, was held at the court of King Louis IX, and resulted in all confiscated copies of the Talmud being incinerated today, by no less a person than the official executioner.

It is not the first time that Jews have watched their texts being destroyed. Only a few years ago, in 1239, Pope Gregory IX ordered that all copies of the Talmud in Italy and France be burned. Today's burning, however, is being mourned by Jews both in France and further afield, as being particularly brutal. They are saying that the move is based solely on anti-Semitic principles.

The Talmud is a central document in the Jewish faith. It consists of the Mishnah and the Gemara, and covers rabbinic law and oral law. Rabbis are claiming that Donin, a former Jew who converted to Christianity, has misinterpreted the scriptures and taken many passages out of context, and that there is no evidence to back up claims of blasphemy. However, the rabbis argued unsuccessfully and the texts have now gone up in flames.

Commentators are now saying that the burning of the Talmud is proof that anti-Semitism in France is on the rise.

King's Guide to Falconry

Palermo, Sicily, c. 1249: Frederick II, King of Germany and Holy Roman Emperor, has added another string to his bow with the release of his manual on ornithology, entitled *De arte venandi cum avibus* (*The Art of Hunting with Birds*). The book contains many of Frederick's own observations and is an excellent guide to the sport of falconry. As well as covering falcon behavior it includes effective training methods. The book's discussion of the anatomy of birds is sure to make it a valuable volume for ornithologists and other scholars.

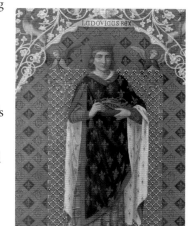

A portrait of King Louis IX.

Frederick is known for his love of animals and birds, and falcons in particular. He has always kept a team of hawkers at court and often acquires birds from foreign lands, including, it is said, Arctic gerfalcons from northern Germany. He even has a zoo that houses numerous exotic animals such as giraffes, elephants, and leopards. A patron of the arts and the sciences, Frederick is interested in a range of subjects and encourages others to better themselves through education.

King Louis IX

Maoris Settle in "Aotearoa"

New Zealand, c. 1250: A group of Polynesians, known as Maoris, from the Cook Islands or Tahiti have settled in a previously uninhabited land they have called Aotearoa. The people claim to have traveled in a great fleet of sea-going canoes from their ancestral homeland Hawaiiki. The names of the seven great fleet canoes are Te Arawa, Tainui, Mataatua, Tokomaru, Kurahaupo, Takitimu, and Aotea.

The name Aotearoa means "Land of the long white cloud," from *ao* (cloud), *tea* (white), and *roa* (long). The first sign of land from a boat is often cloud in the sky above an island. After many days at sea, the daughter of the great chief Kupe exclaimed "He ao! He ao!" ("A cloud! A cloud!"). So the first land sighted was named Aotea (White Cloud). When a larger landmass was found beyond Aotea, it was called Aotea Roa (Long Aotea).

The Polynesians have settled around the north and east coast of Aotearoa, which is comparatively hospitable and temperate in climate. They have introduced animals such as the dog and the small Polynesian rat to the new land. They have also brought food plants with them, including the sweet potato, or kumara.

The Maoris also live off the abundant produce provided by the sea and native birds, including the spectacular flightless bird known as the moa, which can grow up to 12 ft (3.5 m) in height.

King Louis IX gives alms to the poor here, but he has now sanctioned the burning of copies of the Jewish Talmud.

King Edward I

All Men to Bear Arms

England, 1252: King Henry III has decreed that all males between the ages of fifteen and sixty should arm themselves with a longbow, as well as other weapons such as a sword, or a bow and arrow. The longbow is the favored arm as it has a greater degree of accuracy and penetration than other bows. In a decree called the Assize of Arms, not only yeomen and freemen, but also tenants and villeins are obliged to be trained in the use of arms and to carry them with them on all occasions.

The idea behind the new decree is that every man is to become aware of his duties as a citizen, so as well as being armed, all eligible males are expected to keep watch to ensure that communities are kept safe from criminal elements and undesirable behavior. Every man now also has the power to run lawbreakers out of town and to make a citizen's arrest should the need arise.

Yeomen are usually farmers whose lands are worth more than 40 shillings, and who farm the land themselves. Socially they fall well below the knights, but well above both common soldiers and household servants. Villeins, of course, owe allegiance to their lords, but otherwise have a great deal of freedom. Many are predicting that the current social barriers may become blurred with the enactment of the new law, but whether this becomes a reality is yet to be seen.

Bread Standardized

England, 1266: The size, weight, and more importantly, the price, of bread is to become standardized. In a decree called the Assize of Bread and Ale, King Henry III has requested uniformity in the production of this staple food to avoid major price variations and to weed out any dishonest pricing practices.

The Assize was enacted in response to the perceived shortage of grain and wheat. Because farmers only grow wheat in small quantities, prices vary each season. Although there have been cases of unprincipled bakers overcharging for bread in lean times, there have also been some cases where bakers have been mobbed by angry people who believe that bread is being kept from the population.

Filial Piety, one of the many paintings of daily life during the Song Dynasty in China.

The Assize of Bread and Ale is designed to regulate the industry, providing not only bread but fair prices too. Bakers who sell underweight loaves will now be subject to fines or other punishments. Some bakers are now selling 13 loaves at a time to make sure that the total weight complies with the regulations.

Venice Bans Foreign Glass

Venice, Italy, 1271: The Venetian glass industry has been given a cultural and economic boost with the passing of a new law banning all imports of foreign glass. In addition, foreign glassmakers will no longer be allowed to ply their trade in Venice. The ruling is designed to maintain plentiful work for local glassmakers, and to ensure that certain glassmaking skills are kept solely within the Venetian industry.

Venice has long been recognized as the glassmaking center of all of Europe, and at any one time there are estimated to be approximately 8,000 craftsmen working in the industry.

Despite the fact that much of the glassmaking takes place within the city of Venice, there is talk of moving operations to the nearby small island of Murano.

Decorative drinking cups, bottles, vases, and other ornamental objects are

A Venetian glassblower with his hollow pipe.

much prized by Venetians. Molten glass is skilfully gathered onto the end of a hollow pipe, blown into a bubble and then formed into a vessel by blowing, swinging, or rolling the pliable glass on a smooth surface. Their richly colored and ornamental designs are what make Venetian glass so special.

Glassmakers also make panes of glass for new buildings—these can be simple or ornate depending on what is required. Many glassmakers blow only sheet glass.

Public Baths Expanded

Hangzhou, China, 1277: With the installation of more public baths almost complete, this city is set to become one of the most

Religious Leaders

Popes	Patriarchs of Constan
Innocent III (1198-1216)	John X Camaterus (119
Honorius III (1216-1227)	Michael IV Autorianus
Gregory IX (1227-1241)	(1207-1213)
Celestine IV (1241)	Theodore II Irenicus (12
Innocent IV (1243-1254)	Maximus II (1215)
Alexander IV (1254-1261)	Manuel I Sarantenus
Urban IV (1261-1264)	(1215-1222)
Clement IV (1265-1268)	Germanus II (1222-124
Gregory X (1271-1276)	Methodius II (1240)
Innocent V (1276)	Manuel II (1244-1255)
Adrian V (1276)	Arsenius Autorianus
John XXI (1276-1277)	(1255-1269, 1261-12
Nicholas III (1277-1280)	Nicephorus II (1260-12
Martin IV (1281-1285)	Germanus III (1267)
Honorius IV (1285-1287)	Joseph I Galesiotes (12
Nicholas IV (1288-1292)	1282-1283)
Celestine V (1294)	John XI Beccus (1275-
Boniface VIII (1294-1303)	Gregory II Cyprius (128
	Athanasius I (1289-12
	John XII Cosmas (1294

sought after destinations in all of China. One of the country's most urbane cities, Hangzhou has always been a desirable place to live. Situated on the banks of the Jiantang River and surrounded by pristine lakes, the city is a major center for trade, tourism, and entertainment. As the capital city of the Song Dynasty, it is also the seat of government. Today the population is estimated at one million, making Hangzhou the largest city in China, and possibly the largest city in the world.

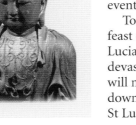

Gilded statue of Buddha, Japan, Kamakura Period. Buddhism was introduced to Japan via China in the sixth century and immediately found favor among the ruling classes. It is now well established.

There have always been a number of bathhouses in the city. It is far too expensive for people to install baths in their own homes and the cost of heating is prohibitive, so public bathhouses have become very well frequented. Visitors can also make use of the hot tubs and steam baths there. Now, in an effort to maintain quality and hygiene, the authorities are introducing an admission fee—ten copper coins—to help maintain the facilities.

The baths are constantly heated with either firewood or coal, and many Chinese like to bathe three or four times a week. This is in marked contrast with Europeans, who bathe much less frequently, often not bothering to bathe at all during the colder months.

Seawalls Collapse

Netherlands, December 14, 1287: A storm, unlike any we have seen in many years, today destroyed the seawalls at Zuider Zee, on the North Sea coast, resulting in a colossal flood that has left an estimated 50,000 people dead. Some are suggesting that many more have perished, putting the number at closer to 75,000 souls. It is unlikely that we will ever know how many people have lost their lives in this catastrophe. All the dikes—the embankments used to hold back the sea—were destroyed and whole villages and communities have been washed away. Many are calling it one of the worst natural disasters in recorded history. It is surely one of the biggest disasters ever seen in the Netherlands.

The area is no stranger to changes in sea level. Until recently, the Zuider Zee, or South Sea, as it is now being referred to, was a shallow inlet, but over the last 100 years or so storms have been steadily eroding the coastal areas, much of it swampy peatland. A serious flood last century completely ruined the seawalls and dramatically widened the mouth of

the once narrow inlet. With this latest storm, much of the land in the north of the Netherlands has now been lost—reclaimed by the sea.

Engineers and many other experts are already talking about the construction of improved dikes along the affected coast to prevent flooding on such a wide scale, but we must wait to see if this eventuates.

Today is the feast day of St Lucia, and this devastating flood will no doubt go down in history as St Lucia's Flood.

All Jews to be Expelled from England

London, England, July 18, 1290: Edward I has issued an edict that expels all Jews from England. Anyone who professes to be of the Jewish faith must leave the country immediately. England is the first country to issue such a decree. Although no accurate records exist, there are believed to be between 4,000 and 15,000 Jews in England at this time. Most of the expelled Jews will probably go to either Germany or France.

Jewish people first arrived in Britain from France about 200 years ago, and they have been mostly involved in the

banking and mercantile industries. They have long been bankers for the ruling classes as they were allowed to lend money and charge interest, something that Christians were not permitted to do. During the reign of Henry III, they in fact provided much of the financial backing for the king and his court.

Yet, during the 1260s, many felt resentful at the economic power that the Jewish banking community was seen to be amassing and anti-Semitic feeling grew. The Jews of England have always worked hard and made handsome profits on their investments and there was a high degree of bitterness about Jewish prosperity. In 1265, the king began dealing with Italian bankers in order to minimize the country's dependence on Jewish fiscal services. Four years later, restrictions were placed on Jewish property rights, and Jewish children could no longer inherit their fathers' estates, any property and assets reverting to government coffers.

The situation worsened in 1275, when Edward I prohibited lending money with interest. Any Jews who disobeyed the Jewish Affairs Bill could be sentenced to death. However, it is believed that, in response, some Jews have opened small pawnbroking businesses, and others have begun trading in wool and grain, in an effort to keep financially afloat.

Jews are now boarding ships to depart the country, although it is also believed that many are now pretending to be Christians in order to remain in England.

Ferdinand III of Castile

The coronation of Theobald I of Navarre (1201-1253), also known as Theobald IV of Champagne.

Frederick III, King of Sicily

War of the Sicilian Vespers Ends

Caltabellota, Sicily, August 31, 1302: A peace treaty has been brokered between the Angevins and the Aragonese, bringing to an end their 20-year war for control of the Kingdom of Sicily. News of the treaty has sparked wild celebrations in the streets of Palermo.

The War of the Sicilian Vespers started with a rebellion in Sicily in 1282 against the rule of the Angevin king, Charles I. The rebellion started when several of the Angevin soldiers, on the pretext of searching for hidden arms, molested a group of noblewomen in front of their families. With the cry "Death to the French!" onlookers set on the soldiers and slaughtered them. Tradition has it that the rebellion started as the church bell rang for vespers—hence the name "War of the Sicilian Vespers."

The peace treaty follows a short period of negotiations between Charles of Valois, acting of behalf of the Angevins, and Frederick of Aragon. The two forces have been in stalemate for at least a year.

time out

In 1315, in Switzerland, the Everlasting League takes on the Hapsburg forces at the Battle of Morgarten. Formed in 1291, the league united the regions of Uri, Schwyz, and Unterwalden. It was the forerunner of the Swiss Confederation.

Under the agreement, Angevin forces will leave Sicily and hostilities will cease. Frederick of Aragon has agreed to take the title of King of Trinacria. He has also agreed to marry Eleanora, the daughter of King Charles II, with the understanding that on his death the kingdom will revert to Angevin control. Both sides have agreed to release all prisoners of war taken during the conflict. Pope Boniface VIII, who has openly supported the Angevins during the conflict, will have no option but to ratify the treaty.

New King for Mali

Mali, West Africa, 1312: Mansa Musa has succeeded to the throne of the formidable empire of Mali in West Africa. Since the death of Mali's founder, the great Sundiata, in 1255 the country has been unsettled, with at least six different rulers. Mansa Musa, who is believed to be Sundiata's grandson, will have the task of forging a nation from many different peoples and tribes.

The new king seeks to enhance Mali's wealth by trading goods such as gold, cotton, kola nuts, ivory, and salt with kingdoms in North Africa and beyond.

Mansa Musa is a devout Muslim. While Mali is already nominally a Muslim empire, the new king will install Islam as the official religion. He will make a pilgrimage to Mecca during his reign (such a pilgrimage is the duty of all Muslims). He also seeks to make Mali one of the world's leading centers of Islamic scholarship.

The killing fields at the Battle of Bannockburn, 1314.

Scottish Rebels Rout English Forces

Bannockburn, Scotland, June 23-24, 1314: Fourteen thousand soldiers lie dead in the fields of Bannockburn tonight following one of the heaviest defeats ever suffered by England on the battlefield.

King Edward II of England led a force of 25,000 men, including several thousand knights, to break the siege of Stirling Castle by Scottish forces. The commander at Stirling, Sir Philip Mowbray, has said that he will have no option but to surrender if the siege is not broken by the end of June.

On Sunday June 23, the English force reached Bannockburn, a few miles south of Stirling, where a Scottish force of 9,000 men was waiting for them under the command of Robert the Bruce.

The main battle took place on June 24. The English forces charged across the stream while the Scots waited for them

English firepower destroys the French fleet at the Battle of Sluys, 1340.

Caltabellota, Sicily, 1302: The Peace Treaty of Caltabellota brokered between the Angevins and the Aragonese ends the 20-year-long War of the Sicilian Vespers.

Kortrijk, Belgium, July 11, 1302: Following the massacre of French residents at Bruges (Brugge Metten), Philip IV of France sends troops to regain the region. However, these crack troops are defeated by the local forces at the Battle of the Golden Spurs.

London, England, August 23, 1305: Sir William Wallace, who had been betrayed and captured earlier in the month, is executed.

Avignon, France, 1305-1378: The pope resides in Avignon, rather than the traditional papal seat of Rome. This is known as the Avignon Papacy, or Babylonian Captivity.

Burgh-by-Sands, England, July 7, 1307: Edward I dies, aged 68. He is succeeded by his son Edward II.

Mali, West Africa, 1312: Mansa Musa becomes king of the formidable Mali Empire.

Avignon, France, March 22, 1312: Pope Clement V issues a papal bull demanding the dissolution of the Knights Templar movement.

Bannockburn, Scotland, June 23-24, 1314: The Scottish forces of Robert I (Robert the Bruce) defeat the English troops of Edward II.

Fontainebleau, France, November 29, 1314: Philip IV dies, aged 46. He is succeeded by his son Louis X.

Vincennes, France, June 5, 1316: Louis X dies, aged 26. His brother Philip becomes regent for Louis' unborn child.

Bursa, Turkey, 1326: Ottoman forces take Bursa, and make it the capital of their empire. The founder of the empire, Osman I, dies, and is succeeded by his son, Orhan.

India, 1326: The Hindu kingdom of Vijayanagara is established in southern India by brothers Harihara and Bukka Sangama.

London, England, January 25, 1327: Edward II is forced to abdicate and is imprisoned. His son, Edward III, claims the throne.

Vincennes, France, February 1, 1328: Charles IV dies, aged about 33. He has no male heirs, and is the last of the Capetian Dynasty. His cousin Philip is finally chosen as successor to the throne, but England's Edward III believes he has a claim to the French throne.

London, England, 1330: Edward III takes full control of the English throne.

Mali Empire, West Africa, 1332: Mansa Musa dies. He is succeeded by his son, Maghan I.

Sultan Osman I, founder of the Ottoman Dynasty.

known as Philippe le Bel (Philip the Fair) because of his light hair and good looks.

His policies greatly increased the royal revenues. He asserted his right to tax the clergy, making permanent a special tax permitted by the popes for the support of crusades. Pope Boniface VIII opposed this measure by the papal bull *Clericis laicos* (1296). In 1301 Philip arrested Bishop Bernard Saisset. The Pope demanded that Saisset be sent to Rome for trial and issued two bulls denouncing Philip.

Threatened with excommunication, Philip had Pope Boniface seized at Anagni. Although freed a short time later, the pope died soon afterward in 1303. Following the brief pontificate of Benedict XI, Philip engineered the election of Clement V as pope. Clement annulled Boniface's bulls and, in 1309, transferred the papal residence to Avignon.

Clement cooperated with Philip in his persecution of the Knights Templar, whose wealth the king appropriated to finance his wars. The Knights Templar are a monastic military order formed to protect Christian pilgrims on their way to the Holy Land. On Friday, October 13, 1307, Philip ordered the arrest of thousands of the knights. After being tortured to extract confessions of wrongdoing, most were eventually executed. Sympathizers of the knights condemned Friday the thirteenth as an evil day. Time has reinforced this belief in "Black Friday."

Other groups persecuted by Philip for their wealth were the Jews and the Lombards (Italian bankers). Philip is succeeded by his son, Louis X.

King Philip of France Dies

Fontainebleau, France, November 29, 1314: The king of France, Philip IV, is dead, aged 46. Philip took the throne in 1285 upon the death of his father, Philip III. His reign will be remembered for his conflict with the papacy, the persecution of Jews and Lombards, and his attack upon the Knights Templar. He was

in *schiltrons* (crouching shoulder-to-shoulder under or behind shields while holding their pikes slanted outward). After disrupting the charge the Scots advanced, still in *schiltrons*, forcing the cavalry back into the English infantry who were trying to join the fray across the stream. Volleys of arrows from the English archers fell on English and Scottish alike. The retreat soon degenerated into a rout. The battle claimed 10,000 English lives, and 4,000 Scotsmen were killed.

Edward II fled early and, after being denied entry to Stirling, escaped by ship back to England.

The victory strengthens Scottish claims for independence, which the Scots lost following the English invasion of 1296.

in deposing his father were his mother Isabella and her lover Roger Mortimer, who have been ruling England for the last three years in Edward III's name.

The rule of Isabella and Mortimer has been precarious and they went to extraordinary lengths to defend it. They imprisoned Edward II at Berkeley Castle in Gloucestershire, and later had him killed by the insertion of a red-hot poker in his anus using a horn. This gruesome method of execution was chosen either because Edward II was a homosexual or because the lack of visible injuries would make it appear that he had died of natural causes.

Edward III was married to Philippa, daughter of the Count of Hainault, at York on January 24, 1328. The birth of his first son, Edward, on June 15 this year seems to have inspired a new confidence and ambition in the young king. He had both Isabella and Mortimer taken prisoner. Despite Isabella's cries of "Fair son, have pity on gentle Mortimer," his mother's lover was executed for treason. Isabella has been retired to Norfolk.

As king, Edward plans to return England to its former glories.

Edward III, King of England

King Edward Takes Control

London, England, October 19, 1330: King Edward III, who succeeded to the throne at the age of 15 when his father Edward II was still alive, has finally seized control of England from his mother and her lover.

Edward's ascension to the throne was of questionable legality. The main players

Edward III's forces storm into Caen in 1346 before sacking the town.

Japan, 1333: Emperor Go-Daigo re-establishes imperial rule as the Kamakura Shogunate comes to an end.

Paterno, Sicily, 1337: Frederick III, king of Aragon and Sicily, dies, aged 64. He is succeeded by his son Peter III, despite the Peace Treaty of Caltabellota.

France, 1338: In his quest for the French throne, which he believes is rightfully his, England's Edward III invades France. This event marks the beginning of the Hundred Years' War.

Bruges, Belgium, June 24, 1340: The English fleet record a solid victory over the French at the Battle of Sluys.

Crécy, France, August 26, 1346: The English longbowmen bring England victory at the Battle of Crécy.

Calais, France, August 4, 1347: After almost 12 months of siege, the city of Calais falls to the English.

Laos, Southeast Asia, 1352: Fa Ngum establishes the Kingdom of Lan Xang (Kingdom of a Million Elephants) and founds his capital of Luang Prabang.

Gallipoli, 1354: The Ottoman Turks capture the peninsula, formerly a Byzantine possession.

Prague, Hungary, 1355: Charles of Luxembourg becomes the Holy Roman Emperor.

Poitiers, France, September, 1356: The English forces, under the leadership of Edward, the Black Prince, score a resounding victory over the French, and capture the French king, John II, his son, and a number of high-ranking nobles.

Turkey, 1361: The Ottoman forces take the city of Adrianople, renaming it Edirne and making it a second capital in the Ottoman Empire.

Nanjing, China, 1368: Rebel Zhu Yuanzhang defeats the Mongols in China and becomes the founding emperor of the Ming Dynasty

London, England, 1377: The acts introduced in the previous year by the "Good Parliament" are rescinded by the "Bad Parliament." This sitting of Parliament introduces unpopular measures such as the poll tax.

France, September 16, 1380: Charles V dies, aged 42. He is succeeded by his son, 11-year-old Charles VI.

Seoul, Korea, 1392: General Yi Songgye overthrows the Koryo Dynasty and establishes the Kingdom of Choson.

Sarai, Asia, 1398: Timur attacks Delhi and brings about the downfall of the Delhi Sultanate.

London, England, 1399: Richard II returns from Ireland, and is forced to abdicate by Henry of Bolingbroke.

Edward of Woodstock,
the Black Prince

Emperor Go-Daigo Retakes the Throne

Japan, 1333: Emperor Go-Daigo has returned to Kyoto to retake the throne from Emperor Kogon. He intends to restore the "old ways" to Japan.

Go-Daigo originally became emperor in 1318, at the age of 29. He immediately began plotting to overthrow the Kamakura Shogunate, the feudal military dictatorship that has been ruled by the shoguns since 1192.

In 1331, Emperor Go-Daigo lost his war with the shogun army and was exiled to Oki Province. The shoguns replaced him with Emperor Kogon.

> *"THE VOICE OF THE PEOPLE, THE VOICE OF GOD."*
>
> WALTER REYNOLDS (D. 1327), ENGLISH ARCHBISHOP OF CANTERBURY, ON THE ASCENSION TO THE THRONE OF EDWARD III

> *"THEY [THE ENGLISH] AMUSE THEMSELVES SADLY AS IN THE CUSTOM OF THEIR COUNTRY."*
>
> JEAN FROISSART (1337–1410), FRENCH HISTORIAN AND POET

Seats of Power

Aztec Empire Acamapichtli (reigned 1376-1396); Huitzilaihuitl (1396-1417).

Byzantine Empire Andronicus II Palaeologus (reigned 1282-1328); Andronicus III Palaeologus (1328-1341); John V Palaeologus (1341-1347); John VI Cantacuzenus (1347-1354); John V Palaeologus (1354-1376); Andronicus IV Palaeologus (1376-1379); John V Palaeologus (1379-1390); John VII Palaeologus (1390); John V Palaeologus (1390-1391); Manuel II Palaeologus (1391-1425); John VII Palaeologus (co-emperor 1399-1402).

China Yuan (Mongol) Dynasty: Temur Oljeytu Khan (reigned 1294-1307); Qayshan Guluk (1308-1311); Ayurparibhadra (1311-1320); Suddhipala Gege'en (1321-1323); Yesun-Temur (1323-1328); Arigaba (1328); Jijaghatu Toq-Temur (1328-1329); Qoshila Qutuqtu (1329); Jijaghatu Toq-Temur (1330-1332); Irinchibal (1332); Toghan-Temur (1333-1370). Ming Dynasty: Hongwu (reigned 1368-1398); Jianwen (1398-1402).

England Edward I (reigned 1272-1307); Edward II (1307-1327); Edward III (1327-1377); Richard II (1377-1399); Henry IV (1399-1413).

France Philip IV (reigned 1285-1314); Louis X (1314-1316); John I (1316); Philip V (1316-1322); Charles IV (1322-1328); Philip VI (1328-1350); John II (1350-1364); Charles V (1364-1380); Charles VI (1380-1422).

Holy Roman Empire Albert I (reigned 1298-1308); Henry VII (1308-1313); Louis IV (1314-1346); Charles IV (1346-1378); Wenceslaus (1378-1400).

Japan Kamakura Period: Go-Fushimi (reigned 1298-1301); Go-Nijo (1301-1308); Hanazono (1308-1318); Go-Daigo (1318-1339). Muromachi Period: Go-Murakami (1339-1368); Chokei (1368-1383); Go-Kameyama (1383-1392); Go-Komatsu (1392-1412).

Mali Empire Sakura (reigned 1285-1300); Gao (1300-1305); Mohammed ibn Gao (1305-1310); Abubakari II (1310-1312); Mansa Kankan Musa I (1312-1337); Maghan (1337-1341); Suleyman (1341-1360); Kassa (1360); Mari Diata II (1360-1374); Musa II (1374-1387); Magha II (1387-1389); Sandaki (1389-1390); Mahmud (1390-1400).

Ottoman Empire Osman I (reigned 1290-1326); Orhan (1326-1359); Murad I (1359-1389); Bayezid I (1389-1402).

Portugal Dinis (reigned 1279-1325); Alfonso IV (1325-1357); Pedro I (1357-1367); Fernando I (1367-1383); Joao I (1385-1433).

Scotland Second Interregnum (1296-1306); Robert I the Bruce (reigned 1306-1329); David II (1329-1371); Robert II (1371-1390); Robert III (1390-1406).

Go-Daigo escaped from the Oki Islands earlier in the year and raised an army in Hoki Province. Ashikaga Takauji, who was sent to destroy Go-Daigo's army, actually sided with Go-Daigo, and together they captured the chiefs of the Kamakura Shogunate in Kyoto. Soon afterward, the army of Go-Daigo's ally, Nitta Yoshisada, destroyed the remnants of the shogunate in the east.

England Defeats French Army at Crécy

Crécy, France, August 26, 1346: Superior weaponry and tactics have won the English army a resounding victory over the French at Crécy. The English army of 12,000 men, led by Edward III, was greatly outnumbered by the French, who had as many as 40,000 soldiers.

The English built a system of ditches to maim and bring down the enemy cavalry. As the heavily armored French knights floundered in these pits, they were cut down by showers of bodkin arrows, delivered en masse by English longbowmen. French crossbowmen, with a firing rate of 3 to 5 arrows a minute, were no match for the English, who could fire 10 to 12 arrows in the same period of time.

During the battle Edward's son, the Black Prince, came under attack, but his father refused to send help, claiming that he wanted his son to "win his spurs." The prince, who is only 16, proved himself to be a great soldier.

While the battle is won, the war continues. It began in 1328 when King Charles IV of France died without a direct male descendant. King Edward III of England, whose mother Isabella was Charles' sister, claimed the French throne. The French nobles, however, asserted that royal succession could not pass through the female line and made Edward's cousin Philip king of France.

Edward declared himself king of France on January 26, 1340, sparking a conflict that may take decades to resolve.

Charles IV Crowned Holy Roman Emperor

Prague, Hungary, 1355: Charles IV of Luxembourg has added another title to his impressive list of honors—that of Holy Roman Emperor.

Charles V of France died in September 1380, and was succeeded by his 11-year-old son, Charles VI. Charles' uncle, Philip the Bold, ruled for him until he assumed the throne in 1388.

Charles was educated at the French Court. He fought with the French against the English at Crécy and became king of Bohemia after his father's death in that battle. Charles is considered to be an excellent diplomat and a generous king. He has protected the lower classes of Bohemia by providing them with courts in which they can sue their overlords.

On Easter Sunday in Rome he was crowned Holy Roman Emperor by the papal legate (Pope Innocent VI is residing at Avignon).

The people, ravaged by the plague, hope that Charles' coronation will end years of conflict between the papacy and the emperors. It is believed that in return for the emperor relinquishing any claims to Italy, the popes will give up the requirement for papal approval and confirmation of emperors in the future. Charles, who changed his name from Wenceslaus at his confirmation, speaks at least five languages fluently and is highly educated. He established his capital at Prague and has concentrated his energies on the economic and intellectual development of Bohemia, founding the Charles University of Prague in 1348 and rebuilding the Cathedral of St Vitus.

The Holy Roman Empire is unique in world history. Ethnically it is mainly Germanic, but many of its most important communities are not German. In addition to Germany, it includes Austria, Switzerland, Liechtenstein,

The Black Prince's forces clash with the French at the Battle of Crécy.

Belgium, the Netherlands, Luxembourg, the Czech Republic, and Slovenia, as well as parts of France, Italy, and Poland. Its territories are ruled by numerous secular and ecclesiastical princes. Although stronger than a confederation, it is not quite a state.

Mongols Ousted, Ming Dynasty Founded

China, 1368: Zhu Yuanzhang, the leader of the peasant rebellion against the Mongols, has now founded the Ming (Bright) Dynasty, with its capital to be located in Nanjing. He has taken the name Hongwu, meaning Immensely Martial, as his title.

Ming Dynasty gray and white vase, 1368-1398.

China has been under the rule of the Mongols since the invasion of Kublai Khan in 1271. Over the last 100 years there has been growing resentment among the Chinese about Mongol influence on art and culture. Most of the Mongol emperors did even not bother to learn the language of the people. The reigns of the later Mongol emperors were short and marked by bitter rivalries. China was torn by famine and crime.

A series of peasant revolts led by Zhu Yuanzhang pushed the foreign invaders back to the Mongolian steppes.

When orphaned in his teenage years, Zhu Yuanzhang entered a Buddhist monastery to avoid starvation. At the age of 25, he joined a gang of rebels and quickly became their leader. Later he came in contact with Confucian scholars, from whom he received an education in state affairs.

Having come from a peasant family himself, Hongwu knows about the suffering of farmers at the hands of the wealthy. He plans to distribute the land to small farmers. Hongwu also plans to reinvigorate the arts, which have been neglected by the Mongols. He has built new ceramics factories in Jingdezhen and seeks to attract the finest artists and artisans from right across China.

Timur Invades Delhi

Delhi, India, 1398: Timur, the great Turkic-Mongol leader, has invaded Delhi. Thousands have been massacred and the city lies in ruins. It is only three years since Timur defeated the Golden Horde (a former Mongol state) and sacked its capital, Sarai. It seems that no army in the region can stop this ruthless conqueror.

The invasion is likely to hasten the end of the Delhi Sultanate (the Muslim dynasties that have ruled in India since the early thirteenth century). The sultanate has been weakened in recent years by a number of civil wars.

On September 24 Timur crossed the Indus River. On December 17 the army of Mahmud Toghluk was defeated, and Timur entered Delhi. Almost all of the inhabitants of the city have been killed or deported as slaves. Some were roasted over open fires. The heads of the dead are stacked in pyramids. It is not clear whether these actions were at Timur's direction or whether his horde simply could not be controlled.

Timur's army is sacking the city. It is reported that 90 captured elephants have been employed merely to carry stones for a mosque that the conqueror plans to erect in his homeland. He is not expected to occupy the city for long because the stench of rotting corpses already hangs heavy in the air.

Timur, which means "iron" in a Turkic dialect, was born in Transoxiana, 50 miles (80 km) south of Samarkand. He traces his genealogical roots to the great Mongol conqueror, Genghis Khan.

King Richard II of England Abdicates

London, England, 1399: Richard II, already imprisoned in the Tower of London, has been forced to abdicate. Henry of Bolingbroke will become King Henry IV. In 1377 Richard became king at the young age of 10. During the early years of his reign his uncle, John of Gaunt, ruled on his behalf.

As Richard began to take control of the court, he marginalized many of the established nobles, including the Earl of Warwick, the Earl of Arundel, the Duke of Gloucester and Gaunt's own son, Henry Bolingbroke. These disaffected nobles formed a group called the Lords Appellant.

In 1397 Richard attempted to destroy the Lords Appellant. He had the Earl of Arundel executed and had Warwick exiled; Gloucester died in captivity. Richard banished Henry Bolingbroke from England for 10 years and then, after Gaunt's death, confiscated Bolingbroke's inheritance, distributing his lands among his own followers.

In 1398 Richard set out on a military campaign in Ireland. Henry Bolingbroke took the opportunity to return to England to reclaim his property, landing in Yorkshire with an army provided by the king of France. By the time Richard finally arrived back on the mainland, Bolingbroke, who was well liked, was being urged to take the crown.

Richard was captured at Conway Castle in Wales and taken to London, where the crowds threw rubbish at him. He was imprisoned in the Tower of London. Thirty-three charges were brought against him, but he was provided with no opportunity to answer them.

Parliament has accepted Henry Bolingbroke as the new king. Richard will be moved from the Tower of London to Pontefract Castle, but he is very emaciated and is not expected to live long.

Richard II of England

The abdication of King Richard II; he hands the crown and scepter to Henry Bolingbroke, who will become King Henry IV.

John Duns Scotus

"GEOMETRY ENLIGHTENS THE INTELLECT AND SETS ONE'S MIND RIGHT ... IT IS HARDLY POSSIBLE FOR ERRORS TO ENTER INTO GEOMETRICAL REASONING, BECAUSE IT IS WELL ARRANGED AND ORDERLY ... IN THIS CONVENIENT WAY, THE PERSON WHO KNOWS GEOMETRY ACQUIRES INTELLIGENCE."

IBN KHALDUN (1332–1406), ARABIC HISTORIAN

Death of the Subtle Doctor Scotus

Cologne, Germany, November 8, 1308: The brilliant philosopher and theologian John Duns Scotus, known as Doctor Subtilis (Subtle Doctor) for his complex and nuanced thought, has died aged 43.

Scotus (a nickname denoting his Scottish origins) was born in the village of Duns in 1265. He began his university studies at Oxford in 1288 and was then ordained as a priest in the Franciscan Order in March 1291.

In 1298 he made his first commentary, the so-called *Opus Oxoniense*, on the four books of *Sentences* of Peter Lombard. By the autumn of 1302 he was lecturing on the *Sentences* in Paris. In 1303 he was expelled from France for siding with Pope Boniface VIII in his dispute against King Philip IV of France, but he was allowed to return in April 1304 and soon after this he completed his lectures on the *Sentences*. In November that year he was appointed regent master in theology in Paris.

In October 1307 Scotus was moved to the Franciscan *studium* (study-house) located in Cologne .

Perhaps he will be best remembered for his work in support of the concept of the Immaculate Conception: that Mary the mother of Jesus was herself conceived without the stain of original sin. Thomas Aquinas had rejected this concept on the basis that Jesus was sent to redeem the whole of humankind—if Mary had in fact been conceived without original sin, then she was not in need of redemption by Jesus.

Scotus devised the following argument to address Aquinas's objection: Mary was in need of redemption like all other human beings, but through the merits of Jesus' crucifixion, given to her in advance, she was therefore conceived without the stain of original sin.

Scotus will be buried in the Church of the Minorites in Cologne.

Renowned Scientist Dies

Tabriz, Persia, 1320: The celebrated Persian mathematician and physicist al-Farisi has died in Tabriz, aged 60.

Al-Farisi made two major contributions to science—one in relation to the field of optics and the other in relation to number theory.

His work on optics was prompted by a question concerning the colors of the rainbow. His teacher, the mathematician and astronomer al-Shirazi (1236–1311), advised him to consult the *Kitab al-manazir (Book of Optics)* by al-Haytham. The study was so comprehensive that it became a separate work entitled *Tanqih al-manazir (Revision of Optics)*.

Al-Haytham had proposed that rainbows were caused by clouds—a theory that did not allow for experimental verification. In his revision, al-Farisi experimented with a glass sphere filled with water, following the beam of light as it refracted upon entering the sphere, reflected once inside, then refracted upon leaving the droplet. By this method he explained both the primary and secondary rainbow, and made the first observation of a tertiary rainbow. Al-Farisi also proposed the wave nature of light.

Al-Farisi's work in number theory relates primarily to amicable numbers and was published as *Tadhkira al-ahbab fi bayan al-tahabb (Memorandum for Friends on the Proof of Amicability)*. Amicable numbers are two numbers for which the sum of the proper divisors of one is equal to the other. Such a pair are 220 and 284. The proper divisors of 220 are 1, 2, 4, 5, 10, 11, 20, 22, 44, 55, and 110, of which the sum is 284. The proper divisors of 284 are 1, 2, 4, 71, and 142, of which the sum is 220. Since antiquity, amicable numbers have been accredited with mystical properties.

Chinese Grand Canal System Completed

Peking, China, 1327: Mongol military engineers have completed the extension and restoration of China's Grand Canal. The canal system now extends more than 1,055 miles (1,700 km) from Hangzhou in the south to the imperial northern capital in Peking.

The Grand Canal system *(Da Yun He)* has been constructed over many centuries. It was begun during the Wu Dynasty

time out

Arabic methods of making paper were introduced to Germany in the early fourteenth century. Paper mills used technologically advanced waterwheels, as well as stamping hammers and one or two vats.

China's Grand Canal links Peking with the southern rural areas.

in 486 BCE and was significantly extended during the Qi Dynasty (479–502 CE).

Emperor Yangdi of the Sui Dynasty made what is perhaps the most important improvement to the canal system during six years of furious construction from 605 to 610 CE. He linked the Yangtze and the Huang He (Yellow River). It took approximately six million laborers to complete this task. It is estimated that three million workers died from exertion and hunger. This was a major contributor to the downfall of the Sui Dynasty.

North of the Yangtze, the canal ascends more than 130 ft (40 m) by means of a system of locks, feeder lakes, and lateral canals. The Chinese are credited with having built the first ever lock as part of the Grand Canal.

The canal now links the imperial capital of Peking in the north of the country with the economic and agricultural centers of central and southern China. It is acknowledged to be a most significant contributor to the economic, social, and political stability of the country.

The Grand Canal first came to the attention of Europe when it was described by Marco Polo after he returned from his travels to the East in 1295.

Theorist Responsible for "Ockham's Razor" Dies

Munich, Germany, 1349: The Black Death has claimed another victim—the theologian and philosopher William of Ockham. He will be remembered for the theory known as "Ockham's razor," which states that one should always opt for a solution in terms of the fewest possible causes, factors, or variables.

Pope John XXII was the second Avignon Pope.

Born in a small village in Surrey, England, in 1285, Ockham wrote many works during his lifetime on the subjects of philosophy, politics, and religion. As a member of the Franciscans, Ockham was devoted to a life of extreme poverty. This support of the concept of apostolic poverty was one of the sources of conflict with the papacy. He was summoned to Avignon in 1324 by Pope John XXII and accused of heresy.

Ockham spent four years there under house arrest while his teaching and writing were investigated, but he fled to Bavaria before any verdict was passed.

He spent the last days of his life in a Franciscan house in Munich.

Black Death Claims the Archbishop of Canterbury

England, August 26, 1349: Thomas Bradwardine, who was confirmed as Archbishop of Canterbury only 40 days ago, has died from the Black Death, aged 59.

Bradwardine acquired a reputation as a profound scholar, mathematician, and theologian at a young age. He was a member of a group of Merton College dons known as the Oxford Calculators, who were devoted to the sciences of astronomy, mathematics, and physics. It was this group that developed the mean speed theorem, which states that the distance traveled by a body moving under constant acceleration is the same as the distance traveled by a body moving at a uniform speed that is equal to half the final speed of the accelerated body.

In 1335 Bradwardine moved to London. He was appointed chancellor of the diocese of London as dean of St Paul's in

1337, and became chaplain and confessor to Edward III. He accompanied the king during his wars in France, including the Battle of Crécy and at the siege of Calais.

In 1349, following the death of Archbishop John Stratford, he was elected Archbishop of Canterbury. He was consecrated as archbishop in Avignon by Pope Clement VI but died at Rochester upon his return to England.

As a theologian he attained great fame. His greatest theological work is entitled *De causa Dei contra Pelagium et de virtute causarum* and relates to the "causes of virtue." The pope awarded him the title of Doctor Profundus (Profound Doctor).

Pope Boniface VIII

Pope Clement VI reigned during the European Black Death pandemic.

John Wycliffe

World's Greatest Surgeon Publishes Surgical Guide

Avignon, France, 1363: The world's most eminent surgeon, Guy de Chauliac, has published a surgical guide that many claim will be used by physicians for centuries to come.

Guy de Chauliac was born in Auvergne, France. He took holy orders and studied at Toulouse, Montpellier, Paris, and Bologna before becoming a physician to the popes in Avignon. In this capacity he attended to popes Clement VI, Innocent VI, and Urban V. Although he contracted the Black Death, he survived. It was this experience that inspired him to record his medical knowledge for future generations.

His manual, *Inventarium sive chirurgia magna* (best known as *Chirurgia magna*) is a guide to surgery and practical medicine. He compiled the information from his own experience and research of historical medical texts. The manual contains over 3,000 references to older medical authorities. It is written in Latin and is more than 450 pages in length.

Chirurgia magna includes a detailed section on anatomy. It also provides information on the treatment of wounds, ulcers, fractures, dislocations, and a variety of other conditions and diseases. Chauliac gives elaborate descriptions of surgical treatments, including the operation for cataracts. In fact, one entire chapter is devoted to ophthalmology.

Guy de Chauliac is already very famous throughout Europe—members of the French and German royal families, including John of Luxembourg (John the Blind), have traveled great distances to be treated by this great surgeon.

Amazing Astronomical Clock Completed

Padua, Italy, 1364: Giovanni de Dondi, working with his father Jacopo, has built a remarkable astronomical timepiece. Both Giovanni and his father are physicians but they share an obsession with astronomy and horology (the science of time measurement).

Giovanni has called the clock an "astrarium." Made out of brass and containing complex internal mechanisms, it calculates the positions of the planets, following the method perfected by Ptolemy in the second century CE and recorded in his influential astronomical treatise *Almagest*.

Giovanni has been working on his astrarium for at least 24 years. It has 107 wheels and pinions, and the outputs are displayed at two levels.

At the upper level, seven dials show the ecliptic longitude (position in the zodiac) of Saturn, Jupiter, Mars, the Sun, Venus, Mercury, and the Moon (in the classic arrangement laid down by Ptolemy).

The lower level includes a 24-hour clock dial, a dial showing the phases of the moon, a calendar giving the date (and the saint associated with that day), and an indicator giving the dates of the Church's significant movable feasts: most importantly, Easter, but also Septuagesima, Quinquagesima, Rogation Sunday, and Whitsun.

People have come from afar to marvel at this remarkable instrument.

Giovanni de Dondi has written a comprehensive account of the design of the astrarium so that others can construct their own version of the clock.

Astronomical clock surrounded by signs of the zodiac.

Indian Astronomer Writes Ground-breaking Work

India, 1370: Mahendra Suri, the head astronomer at the royal court of the Delhi Sultan Firuz Shah Tughluq, has written a pioneering treatise on the astrolabe entitled *Yantraraja*.

The astrolabe is an instrument used by astronomers and astrologers to predict the positions of the Sun, Moon, planets, and stars, allowing the user to determine the local time given the local longitude (or vice-versa).

The astrolabe was developed by Arab astronomers. This is the first work in Sanskrit to describe the construction and use of this instrument.

The Delhi Sultanate was established around 1200, and from that time onward Muslim culture has flourished in this part of India. It is clear from the various references in *Yantraraja* that this work is influenced by Islamic material as well as the traditional Indian works relating to astronomy. Mahendra Suri is a pupil of the great Indian astronomer Madana Suri.

World's Greatest Intellectual Dies

Lisieux, France, July 11, 1382: The world's greatest thinker, Nicolas Oresme—the brilliant economist, mathematician, physicist, astronomer, philosopher, psychologist, musicologist, and theologian, Bishop of Lisieux and counselor to King Charles V of France—has died in Lisieux.

Oresme was awarded the degree of Master of Theology in 1355 and the following year he was appointed grand master of the College of Navarre. It was at this time that Oresme became friendly with the Dauphin, Charles, who went on to become Charles V of France.

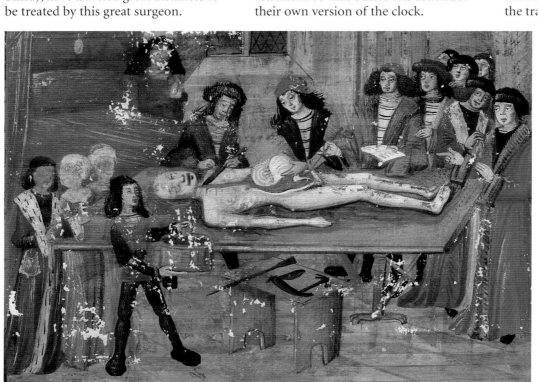

Guy de Chauliac performs a public dissection at the Faculty of Medicine, University of Montpellier.

In 1364 Oresme became dean of the Cathedral of Rouen and, when Charles was crowned king of France on April 8 of the same year, Oresme was appointed as the king's chaplain and counselor.

From 1370 Oresme lived in Paris as adviser to Charles. He translated from Latin to French Aristotle's *Ethics*, *Politics* and *On the Heavens*, as well as *Economics*. As a reward, Charles appointed Oresme Bishop of Lisieux in 1377.

Oresme wrote many works on a wide variety of subjects. In *De configurationibus qualitatum et motuum*, he invented a new type of coordinate geometry (the study of geometry using the principles of algebra). In *De origine, natura, jure et mutationibus monetarum* (*On the Origin, Nature, Juridical Status and Variations of Coinage*), he presented his ideas on economics.

In *Algorismus proportionum* and *De proportionibus proportionum*, he developed the first method of calculation for powers with fractional irrational exponents. In *Livre du ciel et du monde*, Oresme proposed that, rather than being stationary,

John of Gaunt, Duke of Lancaster.

the planet Earth rotates, and in *Questiones super libros Aristotelis de anima*, he discussed the nature and the speed of light.

Oresme's death in Lisieux on July 11 comes only two years after the death of his friend King Charles V.

Death of a "Heretic"

Lutterworth, England, December 31, 1384: The controversial cleric and translator of the Bible into English, John Wycliffe, has died of a stroke. Born in Hipswell, Yorkshire, in 1324, Wycliffe received the degree of Doctor of Theology at Oxford at the relatively advanced age of 48. While at Oxford he also studied the natural sciences. King Edward III appointed him rector of Lutterworth in Leicestershire in 1374.

Wycliffe preached that the right to exercise authority was given to men directly from God—he called this the "dominion founded on grace." A person in a state of mortal sin cannot lawfully act as an official of Church or State, or own property. He argued that the Church had fallen into sin and that it ought to give up its property.

These views were convenient for the king, who had his own reasons for opposing the wealth and power of the clergy. In 1376 Wycliffe moved to London to become clerical adviser to John of Gaunt, who governed England until his nephew, Richard II, was old enough to take the throne. In 1377 Parliament asked Wycliffe's opinion on whether it was lawful to withhold traditional payments from Rome, and he replied that it was.

In the early 1380s he translated the Bible into English and proposed the creation of a new religious order that would preach to the common people from the English Bible.

In 1381 Wycliffe returned to Lutterworth, where he proceeded to publish a series of strong attacks on corruption within the Church.

In 1381 England suffered the Peasants' Revolt, during which many landlords were murdered, lay and clerical alike. It is unlikely that Wycliffe's teachings played any role in the revolt, but the concept of "dominion founded on grace" began to look very dangerous to members of the land-owning class. Wycliffe's movement was bloodily suppressed, along with the revolt. In 1382 his writings were banned.

Wycliffe suffered a stroke early in 1384 and subsequently a second stroke on December 31, which took his life.

New University Founded in Heidelberg

Heidelberg, Germany, 1386: A new university has been founded in the town of Heidelberg in the Rhineland. It provides facilities for the study of philosophy, theology, law, and medicine.

Rupert I, count palatine of the Rhine, established the university after students and teachers from the Rhineland could no longer attend French universities.

After the death of Pope Gregory XI in 1378 two successors were elected: one in Avignon (Pope Clement VII) and the other in Rome (Pope Urban VI). This caused what has become known as the great papal schism. German secular and spiritual leaders, together with those from England, Hungary, Denmark, and Flanders, had supported Pope Urban VI in Rome and, as a result, many of their students and teachers were forced to leave French universities.

Rupert I began talks with the Curia (the papal bureaucracy in Rome), which led to the Papal Bull of Foundation that established the University of Heidelberg.

On October 18, 1386, a ceremonial fair commemorated the opening of the university. The master of the university, Marsilius von Inghen, has chosen *Semper apertus* (The book of learning is always open) as the motto for the new university. He was formerly the master of the Univerity of Paris. The first professors are primarily from Paris and Prague.

The population of the city of Heidelberg, which is only 3,500, will be significantly increased by the influx of students. Almost 600 have enrolled for the university's first year. The first lecture will be held on October 19, 1386.

Duke Rudolf IV of Austria

Richard of Wallingford has invented an astronomical clock.

"Philosopher of Love" Dies of Malaria

Sarzana, Italy, August 27, 1300: The Florentine poet Guido Cavalcanti, best friend and mentor of Dante, has died in Sarzana, aged only 45.

Cavalcanti wrote numerous songs and poems on the philosophy of love, most of which were marked by profound pessimism. His most famous work, "Donna mi prego" ("A lady asks me"), is a stylistically sophisticated example of his view of love as a dark and mysterious force that can often lead to misery and death.

During Cavalcanti's lifetime, Florence was politically divided into the Black Guelphs, who supported the papacy, and the White Guelphs, who opposed papal influence in political affairs. Guido was a militant White Guelph. In 1300 the Florentines, exasperated with the continuing violence between the two factions, exiled the leaders of both parties from Florence.

Ironically, Dante as a *priore* (a sort of governor) of Florence, was one of those responsible for exiling his friend to Sarzana. Guido contracted malaria soon afterwards and died.

Marco Polo

> "THERE IS NO GREATER SORROW THAN TO RECALL A TIME OF HAPPINESS WHEN IN MISERY."
>
> DANTE ALIGHIERI (1265–1321) ITALIAN POET, 1307

> "AND WHAT IS BETTER THAN WISDOM? WOMAN. AND WHAT IS BETTER THAN A GOOD WOMAN? NOTHING."
>
> GEOFFREY CHAUCER (1340–1400), THE CANTERBURY TALES

Reconstruction of the Almudaina Palace Begins

Palma de Mallorca, Spain, 1309: The former home of the Muslim ruler of Mallorca will be converted into a summer palace for King Jaume II. Changes to the original Moorish building will be supervised by architect Pedro Salvá.

Mallorca was conquered by Jaume II's father, King Jaume I of Aragon, who went to war to stop the Moors plundering Catalan ships. After many bloody battles, Jaume I finally annexed the island to the Kingdom of Aragon. The monarch then subdivided his kingdom between his two sons—the younger son, Jaume, was given the Balearic Islands (Mallorca, Ibiza, Menorca, and Formentera).

Under Jaume II Mallorca has enjoyed a golden age. Its economy has flourished and there has been great cultural and intellectual development.

The Moorish building will be transformed into a splendid gothic palace. Situated just outside the city walls, the Almudaina is perched on an escarpment that overlooks Palma Bay. The official residence of the royal court will remain at Perpignan, but Jaume II wants to restore the Almudaina for his summer palace.

Pedro Salvá will modify the original citadel considerably so as to combine the solidity of the original Moorish construction with the luxury required by the Mallorcan court. Four battlemented towers, a portico, and an airy vaulted gallery will be added on the seaward side of the building.

A pennant of an angel by Antonio Campredon will fly over one of the towers so that it can be seen clearly from some distance away.

The palace will be completed with shady gardens and gushing water fountains.

Florentine poet Guido Cavalcanti.

Death of Author of *The Divine Comedy*

Ravenna, Italy, 1321: Having just completed the third and final book of his *The Divine Comedy*, Dante Alighieri has died in Ravenna, aged 56.

Dante was born in Florence in 1265. As a young man he studied rhetoric, philosophy, literature, theology, and medicine. In 1295 Dante commenced his career in government and was quickly promoted, becoming a *priore* (a kind of governor) of Florence in 1300.

Florence was politically divided into two factions—the Black Guelphs, who supported the papacy, and the White Guelphs (including Dante), who opposed papal influence in political affairs. During 1301 Dante headed a delegation that went to Rome to ascertain Pope Boniface VIII's intentions regarding Florence.

While Dante was in Rome, Charles de Valois of France entered Florence with the Black Guelphs. Over the next six days most of the White Guelphs were killed and a new government was installed. Dante was condemned to exile and was fined a large sum of money. If caught by Florentine soldiers, he could have been summarily executed.

Dante was never to return to his beloved Florence again. For the rest of his life he roamed Italian courts under the protection of various noblemen.

Dante and Beatrice in Paradise.

time out

At an event now known as the *Bal des Ardentes* (Ball of the Burning Men), Charles IV of France, and some friends were accidentally set alight with a flaming torch. Four perished; Charles was only saved when the Duchess of Berry smothered him with her flowing skirt.

It was then that he began writing *The Divine Comedy*, a work in 100 cantos, divided into three books of 33 cantos each, with a single introductory canto. *The Divine Comedy* describes Dante's journey through hell, purgatory, and paradise, guided first by the Roman epic poet Virgil, later by his beloved Beatrice.

At a time when all serious scholarly works were written in Latin, Dante wrote *The Divine Comedy* in his regional dialect. By creating such an epic poem in Italian, he helped to establish the Italian language and, simultaneously, established the Tuscan dialect as the standard for Italian.

Prince Guido Novello da Polenta invited Dante to Ravenna in 1318. Dante accepted, finishing the last book of *The Divine Comedy*, "Paradise," there shortly before his death.

Giotto Starts Work on Florence Cathedral

Florence, Italy, 1334: Artist Giotto di Bondone has recently been appointed chief architect for Florence Cathedral. His design includes plans for a bell tower in the Florentine Gothic style.

Born near Florence in 1266 to a poor family, Giotto reputedly spent much of his childhood tending sheep, passing the time by drawing with chalk on rocks. According to the legend, Giotto was about 11 years old when he was discovered by the artist Cimabue. He was so impressed by the boy's talent that he offered to take the boy as an apprentice. Giotto's training then started at Cimabue's workshop.

Giotto has introduced a new naturalism into art—the flat symbolic figures of Byzantine art have, under his influence, given way to three-dimensional figures with real substance.

Giotto has received commissions for many works throughout Italy. When Pope Benedict XI's emissary asked Giotto for a drawing he could submit to the pope to prove Giotto's worth, Giotto smiled and

Italian painter and architect, Giotto di Bondone.

took a sheet of paper, dipped his brush in red paint and with one twist of his wrist drew a perfect circle freehand.

Giotto spent 10 years in Rome and was later employed by the king of Naples.

Giotto's master work is the painting that decorates the interior of the Cappella degli Scrovegni (Arena Chapel) in Padua. Depicting the life of the Virgin and the passion of Christ in a thousand scenes, the painting was finished in 1305.

In 1320 Giotto returned to Florence, where he completed two fresco cycles and a number of altarpieces for the Church of Santa Croce before being appointed chief architect for Florence Cathedral.

Construction Begins on the Ponte Vecchio

Florence, Italy, 1345: The Ponte Vecchio across the river Arno, in Florence, Italy, will be rebuilt according to a design by Taddeo Gaddi. It will be Europe's first segmental arch bridge. The original bridge, made of wood, was destroyed

by a flood in 1333. The new bridge will be built from stone and will consist of three segmental arches. The primary arch has a span of 98 ft (30 m), and the two side arches each span 88 ft (27 m). The rise of the arches is between 11 ft and 15 ft (3.5 m and 4.5 m).

The new bridge has been carefully designed to include space for merchants along its length.

The designer, Taddeo Gaddi, is best known as a painter. He was a favorite pupil and godson of Giotto, whom he assisted with the fresco decoration of the Church of Santa Croce in Florence. Some of Gaddi's experiments with the representation of light have been highly effective, as in his mysteriously radiant *Annunciation to the Shepherds*.

Gaddi decorated the walls of the refectory at Santa Croce with one of the most impressive of his works, a tree of life surrounded by scenes from the life of St Bonaventure who died in 1274.

After Giotto's death in 1337, Taddeo Gaddi became the head of Giotto's art school in Florence.

Francesco Petrarch

Giotto's Gothic-style bell tower, Florence Cathedral.

Boccaccio Completes the *Decameron*

Italy, 1353: The Italian author and poet Giovanni Boccaccio has completed a book called the *Decameron* that is set during the time of the Black Death.

The *Decameron* begins with a vivid description of the horrors of the pestilence before introducing the reader to a company of 10 young characters—7 women and 3 men—who have gathered at a villa outside Naples to escape the epidemic. They spend 10 days at the villa and each day one of the characters tells a story, so that by the end of the book 100 separate stories have been recounted.

The *Decameron* describes a colorful variety of adventures, many types of characters, and depicts myriad shades of emotion. If the characters are based on real people, Boccaccio has taken pains to conceal their identities, although Dioneo may well represent Boccaccio himself.

Little is known about Boccaccio's birth. He is almost certainly illegitimate—there is no record of his mother, but his father was a Florentine banker. He grew up in Florence but moved to Naples in 1327 when his father was appointed to head the bank's branch there. It was in Naples that Boccaccio began to follow his true vocation, poetry.

Boccaccio returned to Florence in early 1341 where he witnessed the terrible effects of the plague, which killed three-quarters of the city's population.

In October 1350 Boccaccio met the great Petrarch, and they have become great friends, Boccaccio calling Petrarch his teacher and *magister* (master).

Giovanni Boccaccio

> "Do as we say, and not as we do."
>
> GIOVANNI BOCCACCIO (c. 1313–1375), ITALIAN LAWYER AND POET, c. 1353

> "Ah! Fredome is a noble thing! … Fredome all solace to man giffio [gives]."
>
> JOHN BARBOUR (c. 1316–1395), SCOTTISH POET, 1375

Leaning Tower of Pisa Finally Completed

Pisa, Italy, 1360: After almost a century of inactivity, Tommaso Pisano has completed construction of the *campanile* (bell tower) of Pisa's cathedral. The distinctive circular structure will be known as the Torre di Pisa (Tower of Pisa).

The identity of the original architect is not known. Many attribute the design to Bonanno Pisano, a twelfth-century resident artist of Pisa famous for his bronze casting, particularly the Portale di San Ranieri (St Ranieri's Gate) to the Piazza del Duomo (Cathedral Square).

The Torre di Pisa has been constructed in three stages. Construction of the white marble bell tower began on August 9, 1173. After the third floor was built in 1178, the tower started to lean as the subsoil was unstable. Construction was stopped for almost 100 years while the Pisans were engaged in battles with Genoa, Lucca, and Florence.

In 1272 construction was resumed by Giovanni di Simone. Another four floors were built at an angle to compensate for the lean of the tower. Construction stopped again in 1284, when the Pisans were defeated by the Genoans in the Battle of Meloria.

Finally, in 1360 the bell chamber was completed by Tommaso di Andrea Pisano and seven bells were installed.

Standing behind the cathedral, the tower is the third structure in Pisa's Campo dei Miracoli (Field of Miracles). The height of the tower is 183 ft (56 m) from the ground on the lowest side and 186 ft (57 m) on the highest side.

Key Structures

Alhambra, Granada, Spain
Almudaina Palace, Mallorca, Spain
Arena Chapel, Padua, Italy
Bastille, Paris, France
Bodnath Stupa, Kathmandu, Nepal
Campanile (Bell Tower), Florence Cathedral, Florence, Italy
Exeter Cathedral, Exeter, England
Khanqah Mosque of Shah Hamdan, Srinagar, India
Kinkakuju (Golden Temple), Kyoto, Japan
Kozha Akhmed Yasaui Mausoleum, Turkistan
Kyongbokkung Palace, Seoul, Korea
Leaning Tower of Pisa, Italy
Mahabuddha Temple, Patan, Nepal
Notre Dame Cathedral, Reims, France
Palace of Husuni Kubwa, Kilwa, Tanganyika
Pisa Cathedral, Pisa, Italy
Ponte Vecchio, Florence, Italy
Pusoksa Temple, Yongju, Korea
Qareh Kalisa Church of St Thaddaeus, Maku, Persia
Salisbury Cathedral, Salisbury, England
Shahr-i-Zindah, Samarkand, Uzbekistan
Siena Cathedral, Siena, Italy
Wat Manolom, Luang Prabang, Laos
Wat Phnom, Phnom Penh, Cambodia
Wat Phra Si Sanphet, Ayuthaya, Siam
Wat Phra Sing, Chiang Mai, Siam

Italian Poet Petrarch Dies

Arquà, Italy, July 19, 1374: The great poet and humanist Francesco Petrarch has died in the village of Arquà a day before his seventieth birthday.

Petrarch was born in Arezzo—his father had been exiled from Florence in 1302 (along with Dante) by the Black Guelphs. Later the whole family moved to Avignon, following Pope Clement V. At the behest of his father, he studied law at Montpellier and Bologna.

When his father died in 1323, Petrarch returned to Avignon and wrote his first large-scale work, *Africa*, an epic in Latin hexameters dealing with the Second Punic War, and particularly the exploits of the great Roman general Scipio Africanus.

On Good Friday 1327, Petrarch first saw Laura, the woman who was to be the inspiration for his most famous work, a collection of poems known as *Il Canzoniere (The Song Book)*.

In January 1337 Petrarch visited Rome for the first time. By the end of the year he had settled in Vaucluse, where he found the peace and the inspiration that resulted in many of his greatest

Sandro Botticelli's painting of *The Story of Nastagio degli Onesti* illustrates one of the stories told in Boccaccio's *Decameron*.

French vellum showing a banquet scene with minstrels playing trumpets from *Poems of Guillaume de Machaut*.

Geoffrey Chaucer

works. On Easter Sunday 1341 he was publicly crowned as a poet in Rome.

Petrarch's career in the Church did not allow him to marry, but he did father at least two children. In 1367 he settled in Padua, where he passed his remaining years in religious contemplation.

Petrarch's fame is largely based on the 366 poems of the *Canzoniere,* dedicated to the love of his life, Laura. Petrarch had little personal contact with Laura and there is little description of her appearance in the *Canzoniere.* She rejected him for the very proper reason that she was already married to another man. Her presence causes him great joy, but his unrequited love creates unendurable despair.

Death of a Great French Composer and Poet

Reims, France, 1377: Guillaume de Machaut, the genius responsible for composing innumerable songs and poems, has died in Reims at the age of 77.

Machaut is the most celebrated and prolific composer of the century. His *Messe de Nostre Dame* (Mass of Our Lady) is acknowledged as the first complete rendition of the Mass Ordinary attributable to a single composer.

In his sixties he wrote the poem *Le Livre du Voir Dit,* which is considered to be his masterpiece. The poem is said by some to recount Machaut's love affair with a girl more than 40 years his junior. Autobiographical or not, the poem tells of the deep sadness of the man separated from his young lover. The narrative is filled with the letters and many poems exchanged by the unhappy couple.

Chaucer Completes *The Canterbury Tales*

England, c. 1386: Geoffrey Chaucer has completed one of the greatest epic works of world literature, *The Canterbury Tales.* Significantly, he chose to write the tales in English rather than Latin or French.

Chaucer has held a number of positions in the king's court, making several journeys abroad on diplomatic missions between 1367 and 1378. It is possible that he met Giovanni Boccaccio and Petrarch in Italy during this period. Chaucer's first narrative poem, *The Book of the Duchess,* was written in September 1369.

In 1380 he was charged with rape, but he paid to have the charge withdrawn, and his guilt or innocence has never been determined. In 1385 he was appointed justice of the peace and, soon after, was elected to Parliament. This was a period of great creativity, during which he produced some of his best poetry, including *Troilus and Criseyde,* based on the love story by Boccaccio.

Chaucer did not begin working on *The Canterbury Tales* until he was in his early forties. The book describes a pilgrimage by 30 people, on a spring day in April, to the shrine of the martyr, St Thomas a Becket. On the way to and from Canterbury they amuse themselves by telling stories. Among the band of pilgrims there are unprivileged people as well as aristocrats—a knight, a physician, a monk, a prioress, a plowman, a miller, a merchant, a clerk, a cook, and a widow from Bath.

Timur Orders Enormous Mosque to be Built

Samarkand, Central Asia, 1398: Timur Leng (Tamerlane) has ordered the construction of a mosque grander than anything he has seen on his campaigns. The building will be known as the Masjid-i Jami' (Bibi Khanum Mosque) and will be the largest built structure in the world.

The mosque will be built using hundreds of slaves, architects, artists, master craftsmen, and masons from all parts of Timur's empire. One hundred elephants, which carried stone for the mosque from India, will also help in the construction of the building.

Some claim that the monumental mosque was started by Timur's wife, Bibi Khanum, as a surprise for her husband when he returned from his campaigns. According to the story, the architect fell madly in love with Bibi Khanum and refused to complete the job unless she agreed to kiss him. When Timur discovered this, he ordered them both to be killed, and decreed that from then on the women of his empire would wear veils in the Arab style so as not to tempt men.

The mosque will push construction techniques to their limits. Many doubt whether the structure will be able to support the enormous weight of stone and suggest that it will collapse.

The mosque will rise to over 115 ft (35 m) with an arch 60 ft (18 m) in diameter and minarets 165 ft (50 m) high. It will include a rectangular court paved with the finest marble, surrounded by a gallery of 400 cupolas supported by marble columns.

Ornamentation will be magnificent—utilizing carved marble and terracotta, glazed mosaics, blue-gold frescoes, and gilt papier-mâché.

Timur's forces attack a walled city in central Asia.

William Tell

Earthquake Damages Pharos Lighthouse

Egypt, 1303: A powerful earthquake has rocked Egypt, causing extensive damage to the famed Lighthouse of Alexandria, the last of the Seven Wonders of the World still surviving.

The lighthouse, on the small island of Pharos just off the coast, was built because of the treacherous sailing conditions in the region. It was conceived and initiated by Ptolemy Soter c. 290 BCE, but was completed after his death, during the reign of his son Ptolemy Philadelphus.

The original height of the building was 384 ft (117 m) and a statue of Poseidon adorned the summit. At the top a mirror reflected sunlight during the day, while fire was the source of the light at night. The internal core was used as a shaft to lift the fuel needed for the fire.

Between 320 and 1303 CE more than 20 earthquakes shook Alexandria, but the lighthouse survived them all. Earthquakes in 796, 950, and 956 caused significant damage and the lighthouse lost its upper tier. In the tenth century, for stability its height was reduced by 72 ft (22 m).

In 1272, the great sultan Salah el-Din (Saladin) undertook extensive restoration work on the lighthouse, but on August 8, 1303, a major earthquake shook the entire eastern Mediterranean, killing many people and damaging the lighthouse beyond repair.

European Weather Finally Returns to Normal

Europe, 1317: The drenching rains and cold weather that have gripped Europe for the last two years have given way to sunny skies as weather patterns return to normal. The rains began in the spring of 1315. The deluge continued through the summer, and the temperature remained cold. Grain crops failed. Hay could not be cured, and there was no fodder for livestock. Wheat more than doubled in price, making bread unaffordable to peasants. People began to harvest wild edible roots, other plants, grasses, nuts, and even bark.

The rain continued all through the spring of 1316. With very little thought for the future, people slaughtered their draft animals and ate their seed grain. There were many incidents of cannibalism.

The tale of Hansel and Gretel originates from this time—in 1316 many children were abandoned because no one could feed them.

Sunny weather may have returned, but much of the seed stock has been eaten and the people are so weakened by diseases such as pneumonia, bronchitis, and tuberculosis that it will be many years before life returns to normal.

The famine was restricted to northern Europe, stretching from Russia in the east to Ireland in the west, and from Scandinavia in the north to the Alps and the Pyrenees in the south. It is estimated that up to a quarter of the population of many cities and towns in this region died as a result of the famine.

Scene from daily life in the fourteenth century, as detailed in this colorful fresco by Lorenzetti.

Mansa Musa Makes Lavish Pilgrimage to Mecca

Mali, West Africa, 1324: Mansa Musa, devoted Muslim and king of the formidable Mali Empire, has made a remarkable pilgrimage (hajj) to Mecca.

Mali is the source of half the world's gold, but many are still astonished at the rate that Musa has been distributing his riches. His lavish entourage includes 60,000 people dressed in fine silk, 12,000 servants, and 80 camels carrying 2 tons (2.03 tonnes) of gold. It has been said that wherever his train finds itself on a Friday, he pays for the erection of a new mosque.

A depiction of everyday life in the Aztec city of Tenochtitlán.

Even Cairo, one of the greatest cities in the world, has rarely witnessed such opulence. Musa has given away so much gold in Egypt that its value may not recover for more than a decade. Other West African rulers have performed a Hajj before Musa, but none has traveled on such a lavish scale. This pilgrimage has opened the eyes of the world to the wealth of Mali.

On his return to Mali, Musa plans to make the cities of his kingdom showpieces of the Islamic world. He will take with him renowned Muslim architect es-Saheli, who will be responsible for building mosques in Gao and Timbuktu, as well as a new royal palace.

New Capital Founded by Aztecs at Lake Texcoco

Mexico, 1325: The Aztecs have established the city of Tenochtitlán as the capital of their empire, on an island in the middle of Lake Texcoco.

The Aztecs are a tribe from Aztlán, in the deserts of northern or western Mexico. They migrated to Lake Texcoco after a legend prophesied that they would find the site for their new city in a place where they would see a mythical vision—an eagle eating a snake while perched on top of a cactus.

The Aztecs eventually witnessed this sight on a small swampy island in Lake Texcoco. Not deterred by the unfavorable terrain, they are constructing artificial islands, on which they produce all the food they require. The small natural island is growing as artificial islands are added to it, and soon Tenochtitlán will become the largest and most powerful city in the region.

Great Plague Decimates Europe

Europe, 1351: A devastating pandemic has killed up to a third of Europe's population, as well as millions across the Middle East and Asia. The outbreak is known as the "Black Death" because of one of its most striking symptoms, acral necrosis, in which a sufferer's skin blackens as a result of subdermal hemorrhages.

It is not known where the pandemic started. The most popular theory locates the first cases in central Asia. In October 1347, a fleet of Genoese trading ships arrived at the port of Messina in Italy with all crew members either infected or dead. From Italy the disease spread northwest across Europe, striking France, Spain, Portugal, Britain, Germany, Scandinavia, and finally Russia.

Contributing to the outbreak was the Great Famine, which struck northern Europe in 1315–1317. Hunger and malnutrition weakened immunity and increased vulnerability to the disease.

It is estimated that between one-third and one-half of the European population died from the Black Death between 1348 and 1350—as many as 25 million people.

Earlier in China an outbreak in the province of Hubei had claimed an initial 5 million lives before spreading to eight other provinces and causing another 25 million deaths—two-thirds of China's population. The number of deaths in the Middle East is not known but may also be in the millions.

Edward II, King of England

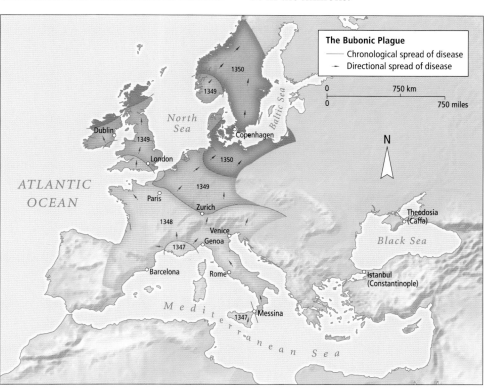

The Bubonic Plague
— Chronological spread of disease
→ Directional spread of disease

0 — 750 km
0 — 750 miles

1350

1349

North Sea

Dublin

1349

London

1350

ATLANTIC OCEAN

Paris

1349

Zurich

1348

Venice

1347

Genoa

Barcelona

Rome

Messina 1347

Mediterranean Sea

Baltic Sea

Copenhagen

N

Theodosia (Caffa)

Black Sea

Istanbul (Constantinople)

Kyoto, Japan, c. 1350: Yoshida Kenkyu writes *Essays in Idleness*, praising a simple Zen-oriented lifestyle.

England, 1351: The economic effects of the Great Plague are far-reaching. A decimated population has resulted in a reduced workforce, and in an effort to avoid escalating wages, Edward III institutes the Statute of Labourers, capping the wages of the workforce. Similar steps are taken by the major powers in Europe in an effort to maintain economic stability.

Ayutthaya, Thailand, 1351: The kingdom of Ayutthaya, with its capital in the city of the same name, is established.

Tangier, Morocco, 1354: Abu Abdallah ibn Battuta publishes his *Travels*, describing his three decades of journeys throughout Asia.

Europe, 1361: Though the continent has barely recovered from the last onslaught of plague, the deadly disease resurfaces.

Europe, 1369: Plague strikes again.

Nanjing, China, 1370: The founding emperor of the Ming Dynasty issues regulations restricting the number of eunuchs in the imperial palace.

England, 1373: Merchants are charged the new taxes of tonnage and poundage.

Europe, 1374–1375: Plague sweeps across the continent once more.

Avignon, France, 1376: Theologian Nicholas Eymeric (1320–1399) publishes his *Directorium inquisitorum*, a manual on torture etiquette and associated methods of extracting confessions from witches.

Florence, Italy, c. 1377: A card game known as *naibbe* becomes popular.

Europe, 1378: Across Europe, loyalties are divided between two papal candidates, causing the Great Western Schism.

London, England, June, 1381: The Peasants' Revolt, which had its beginnings in Essex and Kent, spreads to London.

London, England, June 15, 1381: Wat Tyler, peasant leader, is killed by order of Richard II.

Europe, 1390: Yet again, plague strikes the continent.

China, 1391: The first record of toilet paper appears.

London, England, 1393: Richard (Dick) Whittington becomes Lord Mayor of London. The folk tale of *Dick Whittington and His Cat* is loosely based on his life, though there is little correlation in fact, with the exception of the mayorship.

Florence, Italy, 1397: The influential and wealthy Medici family open their first bank in Florence.

Kingdom of Ayutthaya Established

Ayutthaya, Siam, 1351: The capital of the kingdom of Ayutthaya has been moved 50 miles (80 km) east to an island in the floodplain of the Chao Phraya River. Former Prince U-Thong has adopted the name of King Ramathibodi.

Ayutthaya is made up of a number of self-governing principalities that owe allegiance to Ramathibodi under the mandala system (Asian feudal system). Ramathibodi's task will be to unify this disparate kingdom politically and culturally. He will achieve this by laying the foundations of a common legal system, establishing Buddhism as the official religion, encouraging trade and defending the kingdom against its enemies.

Ramathibodi is maintaining amicable relations with the kingdom of Sukhothai to the north but is waging a continuing campaign against the Khmer kingdom of Angkor to the east.

In relation to trade, Ramathibodi has established his capital as an important international port and is encouraging trade with Persia. In the floodplain of the Chao Phraya, farmers have discovered a new fast-growing type of rice, much of which is being exported to China.

Ramathibodi has composed a common legal code based on traditional law and the Indian Dharmashastra, a volume of Hindu legal texts.

Ramathibodi plans to declare Theravada Buddhism the official religion of Ayutthaya. Members of Buddhist monastic communities in Ceylon will come to

Richard II of England

"START BY DOING WHAT'S NECESSARY; THEN DO WHAT'S POSSIBLE; AND SUDDENLY YOU ARE DOING THE IMPOSSIBLE."

ST FRANCIS OF ASSISI (1182–1226), ITALIAN MONK

"NO MAN SHOULD BE A SERF, NOR DO HOMAGE OR ANY MANNER OF SERVICE TO ANY LORD, BUT SHOULD GIVE FOURPENCE RENT FOR AN ACRE OF LAND, AND THAT NO ONE SHOULD WORK FOR ANY MAN BUT AS HIS OWN WILL, AND ON TERMS OF A REGULAR COVENANT."

WAT TYLER (D. 1381), ENGLISH REBEL, REFERRING TO THE UNFAIR TREATMENT OF WORKERS

Wat Pra Sanpet (king's private temple) in Ayutthaya.

Pope Clement VII, the first antipope of the Great Western Schism, at his coronation in Avignon in 1378.

Ayutthaya in order to establish new religious orders and spread the faith among his subjects.

Ayutthaya is already regarded as one of the strongest nations in the region.

Devastating Plague Strikes Europe Again

Europe, 1374–1375: The Black Death has struck again. This is at least the second recurrence of the plague since the first devastating attack in 1347.

Among the countries most affected by this outbreak are Italy and England. In London a large number of people from the wealthier classes have died of the virulent disease.

In Italy the first-ever quarantine regulations have been enacted by Viscount Bernabo of Reggio. The regulation, dated January 17, 1374, states that every person infected with the plague is to be taken out of the city into the fields and left there to die or recover. Those who attend the patient are not to return to the city for at least 10 days.

The town of Ragusa in Sicily has established a quarantine station where all people arriving from plague-infested regions are kept isolated for a month for "purification by sun and wind."

The Church in Schism

Europe, 1378: The Church is in schism as two popes have been elected—one in Rome and the other in Avignon.

One of the most important decisions of Pope Gregory XI (1370–1378) was to return the papacy from Avignon to Rome. After Gregory died, the Romans rioted to ensure that an Italian was elected to replace him. The cardinals, under duress from the mob, elected Pope Urban VI, who had been a respected administrator in the papal chancery.

However, when he was elected pope he became paranoid and subject to violent outbursts. The cardinals who had elected him soon came to regret their decision and on September 20 they elected another pope, Clement VII, who established a second papal court in Avignon.

The second election has thrown the Church into turmoil. There have been pretenders to the papacy before, but they were appointed by various rival factions. Now, the acknowledged and legitimate leaders of the Church have created two

rival popes. Nations have to choose which pope they will recognize. France, Aragon, Castile and León, Cyprus, Burgundy, Savoy, Naples, and Scotland have chosen to recognize the Avignon claimant. Denmark, England, Flanders, the Holy Roman Empire, Hungary, northern Italy, Ireland, Norway, Poland, and Sweden follow the Roman claimant.

The second election has also caused much consternation among the monasteries, parishes, and religious orders, none of whom know which pope to follow.

Peasants' Revolt Crushed

London, England, June, 1381: Government authorities have regained control in all of the regions that experienced the Peasants' Revolt. The few leaders of the revolt that are still alive will be executed.

In November 1380 Parliament, at the behest of John of Gaunt (de facto ruler of England until King Richard II comes of age), passed the third poll tax in four years at a rate of 1 shilling per person over the age of 15. This was three times higher than the tax of the previous year and, unlike its predecessor, taxed rich and poor at the same rate. It was very unpopular with the peasantry.

The combination of the corruption of tax collectors and the unwillingness or inability of people to pay, has meant the amount of money collected was barely two-thirds of government expectations. As a result, in the spring of 1381 the people of England were taxed again.

The inhabitants of Essex refused to pay and agitation spread quickly to neighboring Kent, where peasants armed with only scythes and very old weapons stormed the castle. The people decided to elect Wat Tyler as their commander.

In June, the Essex and Kentish rebels marched on London where, joined by some of London's poor, they set about attacking political targets in the city, including the home of John of Gaunt.

On June 14, King Richard, who is only 14 years old, met with the Essex peasants. The peasants handed the king a petition that asked for the abolition of serfdom, labor services based on free contracts, and the right to lease land. The king has acceded to all of these demands. Later that same day some peasants entered the Tower of London and took the Archbishop of Canterbury into custody. They then dragged him to Tower Hill and executed him.

The next day, King Richard met the Kentish peasants. They demanded that the Church's estates be confiscated and divided among the wider populace. Again, the king agreed to their demands. However, the rebel leader Wat Tyler addressed Richard with insolence and was killed by one of the king's men.

The crowd prepared to rush the king, but Richard quickly confronted them and convinced them to ally themselves with him. King Richard went on to declare that everyone should be pardoned and should return peacefully to their homes. The revolt was effectively over.

Richard II accedes to the peasants' demands.

Medici Family Establish Bank in Florence

Florence, Italy, 1397: Giovanni di Bicci de' Medici has established the headquarters of his bank in Florence. He plans to add branches in every major European city.

Florence has long been the banking capital of Europe, thanks to its widely recognized and trusted gold coin, the florin, which was first minted in 1252.

In the early 1300s a group of families from northern Italy, known collectively as Lombards, became the principal moneylenders to the rich and powerful. Two families, the Bardi and the Peruzzi, grew immensely wealthy by offering financial services to Europe's rulers. However, in 1345 Edward III of England—who, to finance his wars against the French, had borrowed 600,000 gold florins from the Peruzzi and 900,000 from the Bardi—defaulted on his payments, reducing both houses to bankruptcy.

This has given new families an opportunity to enter the banking industry. The most prominent families among these new bankers are the Pazzi and the Medici. The Medici family has a long history as moneychangers, but the establishment of the Medici bank is a significant step forward for the family.

While the Medici bank extends the usual loans to merchants and royals, it also enjoys the distinction of being the principal banker for the pope.

Cosimo de' Medici

Religious Leaders

Popes	Patriarchs of Constantinople
Boniface VIII (1294-1303)	John XII Cosmas (1294-1303)
Blessed Benedict XI (1303-1304)	Athanasius I (1303-1309)
Clement V (1305-1314)	Nephon I (1310-1314)
John XXII (1316-1334)	John XIII Glycys (1315-1320)
Benedict XII (1334-1342)	Gerasimus I (1320-1321)
Clement VI (1342-1352)	Jesaias (1323-1334)
Innocent VI (1352-1362)	John XIV Calecas (1334-1347)
Blessed Urban V (1362-1370)	Isidore I Bucharis (1347-1350)
Gregory XI (1370-1378)	Callistus I (1350-1354, 1355-1363)
Urban VI (1378-1389)	Philotheus Coccineus (1354-1355, 1364-1376)
Boniface IX (1389-1404)	Macarius (1376-1379, 1390-1391)
	Nilus Cerameus (1379-1388)
Antipopes	Anthony IV (1389-1390, 1391-1397)
Nicholas V (1328-1330)	Callistus II Xanthopulus (1397)
Clement VII (1378-1394)	Matthew I (1397-1410)
Benedict XIII (1394-1423)	

Wat Tyler, the leader of the Peasants' Revolt, is executed by one of King Richard's men for insolence to the king.

Timur, "Butcher of Delhi," Struck Down by Plague

Charles VII

Otrar, Samarkand, February, 1405: The great Timurid military leader Timur (otherwise known as Tamerlane), who was born near Samarkand in 1336, has died in the town of Otrar near the Aral Sea after being infected with fever and plague.

Timur placed a great deal of his early legitimacy on his lineage to the great Mongol emperor Genghis Khan: Timur's father was the head of the Barlas, a nomadic Turkic-speaking tribe. Timur rose to prominence as a military leader and was proclaimed sovereign in 1369 when he mounted the throne at Samarkand, the capital of his dominions.

In 1383, he embarked on the military conquest of Persia, and by 1394 had extended his rule throughout Persia and north through the Black Sea into Georgia and Armenia. His rule has been a brutal one—frequent uprisings were put down ruthlessly, with entire towns massacred and the skulls of the vanquished used to form the masonry for towers, cemented together as a warning to dissenters.

"The whole of the Welsh nation in these parts are concerned in this rebellion."

JOHN FAIRFIELD, RECEIVER OF BRECON, OWEN GLENDOWER'S REBELLION, 1403

"You have gold and I want gold; where is it?"

HENRY IV (1367–1413) KING OF ENGLAND, SEEKING MONEY TO PAY REBELLIOUS TROOPS IN FRANCE, 1407

In 1395, Timur fought a battle with his great rival Tokhtamysh who had been a former refugee at the court of Timur and who had become ruler of the Golden Horde, a region created after the defeat of the Mongol Empire in 1240. When Tokhtamysh turned against his former ally, Timur led an army of over 100,000 men into the harsh and inhospitable region of uninhabited steppes, cornered the enemy army against the Volga River and destroyed it.

Then in 1398 Timur started a campaign against India's Muslim ruler. He crossed the Indus River, capturing towns and villages along the way, and massacring their inhabitants. Prior to the decisive battle for the city of Delhi, he executed some 50,000 captives, before going on to sack the city and reduce it to rubble. Timur remained in Delhi for several months collecting treasure, which he transported to Samarkand on the backs of 120 elephants.

In 1399, Timur mounted campaigns against the sultan of the Ottoman Empire,

The late great Timur.

and in 1401 he defeated a Mameluke army from Egypt, before sacking Damascus.

Later that year, he invaded Baghdad. After the capture of the city, some 20,000 inhabitants were killed, and Timur ordered every soldier to return home with at least two severed heads.

As part of his grand plan to restore the glory of the Mongol Empire, Timur had developed strategies to attack China's powerful Ming Dynasty. However, death intervened in Otrar in 1405.

Timur's body has been embalmed, lain in an ebony coffin, and is being transported to Samarkand where it will be buried in the sumptuous tomb of Gur-e Amir.

Death of Henry V Brings Infant Son to the Throne

Bois de Vincennes, France, August 31, 1422: With all the states of Western Europe brought into his web of diplomacy, having ended the Great Schism by obtaining the election of Pope Martin V, and with all of Christendom finally within his grasp, King Henry V has died of dysentery.

Henry's ascension to the throne was notable for the reactivation of the English claim to the French throne. With the civil war between the Dukes of Burgundy and Orléans leaving France vulnerable, Henry took a small force to France in 1415, capturing the port of Harfleur before encountering a far superior French army at Agincourt.

Completely against the odds, the battle ended in disaster for the French, with Henry capturing key French nobles, including the Duke of Orléans. This victory ensured that he could continue the war, and victories followed at Caen in 1417 and Rouen in 1419, giving Henry control over all of Normandy.

King Charles VI of France negotiated a truce, the Treaty of Troyes, in 1420, which

Henry V's English army defeated Charles d'Albret's French forces at Agincourt, France, in October 1415.

Key Events

Baghdad, Iraq, June, 1401: After his success in taking the city of Damascus earlier in the year, Timur and his forces capture Baghdad.

Northumberland, England, 1402: The Battle of Homildon Hill takes place. Loyal to the English king, the Duke of Northumberland and his son Henry "Hotspur" Percy intercept Scottish rebels during a foray into northern England.

Ankara, Turkey, July 28, 1402: Timur attacks the Ottoman forces at Ankara, conquering the city and capturing the ruler, Bayezid I.

Nanjing, China, 1402: Zhu Di, son of the Ming founder, wins civil war with his nephew and takes the throne as Yongle, the third emperor of the Ming dynasty.

Shrewsbury, England, July 21, 1403: The Battle of Shrewsbury takes place between the forces of King Henry IV and his former ally, Henry "Hotspur" Percy.

Samarkand, Central Asia, February, 1405: Timur, the great Mongol leader, dies, aged about 68. He is succeeded by his son, Shah Rukh.

Domrémy, France, January 6, 1412: Joan of Arc is born.

London, England, March 20, 1413: Henry IV dies, aged 45. He is succeeded by his son, Henry V.

Ottoman Empire, Asia, 1413: Mehmet I eliminates his opposition and takes control of the Ottoman Empire.

Agincourt, France, October 25, 1415: The English troops of Henry V overcome the French at the Battle of Agincourt.

Bohemia, Europe, 1420-1434: The power of the Church is challenged as the Hussite Wars are waged.

Ottoman Empire, Asia, 1421: Mehmet I dies, aged about 32. He is succeeded by his son, Murad II.

Bois de Vincennes, France, August 31, 1422: Henry V of England dies, aged about 35. He is succeeded by his son, Henry VI.

Paris, France, October 21, 1422: Charles VI dies, aged about 35. He is succeeded by his nephew, Henry VI of England, as laid down in the Treaty of Troyes.

Scotland, May, 1424: James I claims the Scottish throne.

Orleans, France, April, 1429: Joan of Arc leads the French troops at Orléans, and the English abandon their siege of the city.

Reims, France, July 17, 1429: Charles VII is crowned King of France.

Rouen, France, May 30, 1431: Joan of Arc, known as the Maid of Orléans, is burned at the stake.

Paris, France, December 16, 1431: The English conduct a French coronation for Henry VI.

saw Henry marry his daughter Catherine, and made him heir to the French throne.

The English throne now has passed to Henry's son, Henry VI, who has not yet celebrated his first birthday.

France's heroine, Joan of Arc, at the taking of Orléans.

James I to Unify Scotland

Perthshire, Scotland, May, 1424: The formal proclamation last week of James I as King of Scotland, establishing him as the first monarch of the Stewart Dynasty, heralds the first shaky steps in restoring law and order to a troubled realm.

When James returned to Scotland, after a ransom was negotiated that ended his 18 years as a hostage of the English, he found a nation that was in a state of near armed insurrection. Murdoch, Duke of Albany, the previous regent, had been grossly corrupt and violent clan warfare in the Highlands had been allowed to continue unabated. Crown taxes were being thieved, and less than 4 percent of taxes were reaching Edinburgh.

In the week since James I's coronation, the Scottish Parliament has declared that

peace would be enforced throughout the realm and "if any man presumes to make war against another he shall suffer the full penalties of the law."

Heroine of France Burns at the Stake

Rouen, France, May 30, 1431: Joan of Arc, who is popularly known as the Maid of Orléans and the French nation's heroine, has been burned at the stake for refusing to renounce wearing male clothing and for believing she was accountable to God rather than the Roman Catholic Church.

Born in Domrémy in the province of Lorraine in 1412, she grew up witnessing the plundering of her people during the Hundred Years War. In 1429 she offered her services to the Dauphin, the future King Charles VII of France, whom she convinced of her divine mission to save France from the English. A board of theologians approved her claims and gave her an army of 10,000 peasants. Marching on Orléans on April 28, 1429, she took the city the following day. One by one, cities held by the English fell to her military genius, their morale devastated by her ability to inspire her troops and her almost supernatural aura.

After Charles was crowned King, she led another campaign against the English at Compiègne without royal assent. She was captured by Burgundian soldiers and given to the English. Charles, realizing she could present a threat to his rule, refused to pay a ransom, and she was in turn given by the English to an ecclesiastical court at Rouen.

Joan of Arc at Reims Cathedral, 1429.

Vlad Tepes (Vlad the Impaler) takes the throne of Wallachia, Romania, for the second time in 1456. He rules for six years, and during that time will live up to his name, committing horrific atrocities in order to maintain control.

After 14 months of interrogation, she was condemned to death, though after she confessed her errors the sentence was commuted to life imprisonment. However, after returning to jail she again began to wear masculine clothes, and was sentenced by a secular court to burn at the stake in the market square of Rouen as a relapsed heretic.

Louis XI

Henry VI Crowned King of France

Paris, France, December 16, 1431: The coronation of Charles VII two years ago, in contravention of the Treaty of Troyes, has served to galvanize the French people while undermining the English claim to the French throne. In an effort to reassert their claim, the English regency council today has conducted a French coronation for Henry VI at the great Notre Dame Cathedral in Paris.

When Henry VI was still a child, he came under the protectorate of his uncles—John of Lancaster, Duke of Bedford, who was regent in France, and Humphrey, Duke of Gloucester, who protected his interests in England— although a great deal of the actual power resided in a regency council dominated by Bishop Henry Beaufort. After the defeat of the English forces in the siege of Orléans at the hands of Joan of Arc, the council decided to shore up English interests in France by crowning Henry King of France. The French people, however, continue to recognize the son of Charles VI as their King Charles VII.

Arboga, Sweden, 1435: A group of nobles from all over the country meet in the nation's first "parliament" as part of the rebellion against King Erik.

Mexico, 1440: The Aztec emperor, Itzcoatl, dies. He is succeeded by his nephew, Montezuma (Moctezuma) I. Itzcoatl first came to power as a member of the Triple Alliance that defeated the Tepanecs.

Ottoman Empire, Asia, 1451: Murad II dies, aged about 46. He is succeeded by his son, Mehmet II.

Constantinople, Turkey, 1453: The fall of Constantinople signals the end of the Byzantine era, and the rise of the Ottoman Empire.

France, 1453: The English have been all but driven from France.

St Albans, England, 1455: The Battle of St Albans between Lancaster and York marks the beginning of the Wars of the Roses.

Belgrade, Hungary, July 14, 1456: The invading Ottomans are defeated by an undermanned but determined Hungarian force under the leadership of János Hunyadi.

England, 1461: York defeats Lancaster at the Battle of Mortimers Cross. King Henry VI is ousted, replaced by Edward IV.

Kyoto, Japan, 1467: Rival daimyo vying for power spark the breakout of the Onin Wars.

South America, 1471: Topa Inca (also known as Tupac Yupanqui) succeeds his father Pachacuti and continues the expansion of the Inca Empire.

London, England, April 9, 1483: Edward IV dies, aged 40, leaving the throne to his son, Edward V, with Richard of Gloucester as regent.

London, England, July 6, 1483: Richard, Duke of Gloucester, is crowned King Richard III.

Bosworth, England, August 22, 1485: The Battle of Bosworth Field sees Richard III killed in battle when his allies switch their allegiance to Henry Tudor. Henry claims the throne as Henry VII.

Stoke, England, June 16, 1487: Victory for Henry VII at the Battle of Stoke Field marks the end of the Wars of the Roses.

Cadiz, Spain, September 25, 1493: Columbus embarks on his second voyage to the New World.

Canada, June 24, 1497: Italian explorer John Cabot (Giovanni Caboto) explores the Atlantic coast of Canada in his English-sponsored search for a northwest passage to India.

Calicut, India, May 22, 1498: Portuguese navigator Vasco da Gama becomes the first European to reach India by sea.

Japan, September 20, 1498: A tsunami kills over 30,000 people.

Henry VII

> "THE BIRD, THE
> BEAST, THE FISH
> EKE IN THE SEA,
> THEY LIVE IN
> FREEDOM
> EVERICH IN HIS
> KIND;
> AND I A MAN,
> AND LACKETH
> LIBERTY."
>
> JAMES I OF SCOTLAND
> (1394–1437), KING OF
> SCOTLAND, IN HIS
> POEM *THE KINGIS
> QUAIR*, 1420

> "IT WOULD BE
> BETTER TO SEE
> THE ROYAL
> TURBAN OF THE
> TURKS IN THE
> MIDST OF
> THE CITY THAN
> THE LATIN
> MITRE."
>
> MICHAEL DUCAS
> (C.1400–C.1470)
> BYZANTINE HISTORIAN,
> OF THE REUNIFICATION
> OF THE ROMAN
> AND ORTHODOX
> CHURCHES, 1452

Reign of Ottoman Sultan Murad II Ends

Adrianople, Anatolia, February 3, 1451:
Murad II, Sultan of the Ottoman Empire since 1421, died today at the age of 47, in the town of Adrianople in north-western Anatolia. Murad's reign has been marked as a period of consolidation and military expansion of the Ottoman Empire, extending throughout Greece, the Balkans, and Asia Minor.

In 1421, Murad II formed an army and marched against the Byzantine Empire. He lay siege to their capital, Constantinople, but was forced to abandon the siege when rebellion broke out in his own lands. After putting down the insurrection, Murad mounted a series of campaigns against Venice, the emirate of Karamanid, Serbia, and Hungary. During the 1430s, he captured extensive territories in the Balkans, annexing Serbia in 1439.

The Ottoman forces fought a series of battles along the Empire's Hungarian border, before Murad decided to go on the offensive and attack Belgrade, the chief fortress. A new crusade against the Ottomans was announced in the wake of Christian coalition forces successfully repelling Murad's assault on Belgrade, with armies led by János Hunyadi winning decisive victories against Murad's forces at Sibiu (Hermannstadt) and at the Battle of Niš, in which the Ottomans were driven from Bulgaria.

The Roman Catholic Church objected to a peace treaty between the two antagonists at the time since the goal of driving Ottoman forces from Europe had not yet been achieved. In 1444, Hunyadi launched another attack against the Ottomans with an army of 30,000 men, consisting mainly of Hungarian and Polish forces. After advancing down the Black Sea coast to Varna, which he captured, Hunyadi was left exposed when promised reinforcements from Constantinople never arrived. When Murad's 120,000-strong army came at Hunyadi's forces from the rear, they never had a chance. More than half of the Christian coalition forces perished, ending any serious attempts to prevent the conquest of Eastern Europe by Ottoman forces.

Forced to abdicate the throne after losing the Battle of Jalowaz toward the end of 1444, Murad regained command in 1446, and two years later he crushed another Christian coalition at the Second Battle of Kosovo.

Hundred Years War Ends: French Society in Ruins

France, 1453: English forces have all but been driven out of northern France, with the exception of Calais, marking the end of the devastating Hundred Years War, which began in 1337 when King Edward III of England declared war on France after the French King Philip VI confiscated Gascony.

By 1428 the English controlled all of northern France, until Joan of Arc broke the siege of Orléans. Her courage and inspiring leadership invigorated the French people, who began pushing England back from the Loire River and off the continent. By 1449 the French had retaken Rouen. The following year French forces used cannons decisively to break up masses of English archers attempting to relieve Caen in the Battle of Formigny, marking one of the final battles in the Hundred Years War.

The war's outcome has ended England's days as a continental power. Victorious French King Charles VII, who has transformed France from a number of independent fiefdoms into a unified, powerful realm, now faces the challenge of rebuilding a country that has been decimated by the war. France's farmlands have been laid waste, and its population almost halved, while marauders, famine, and the Black Death terrorize the countryside. The recent outbreak of a number of civil and local wars has also helped to increase the social disintegration of France.

Clan Warfare in Japan

Japan, 1467–1477: The Onin War, which began as a dispute between the Yamana and Hosokawa clans over succession to the shogunate, has escalated to the point where it threatens to plunge the entire nation into civil war.

Fighting broke out in 1467, when the supporters of each clan organized themselves into opposing factions. In February

Seats of Power

Aztec Empire Huitzilaihuitl (reigned 1396-1417); Chimalpopoca (1417-1427); Itzcoatl (1427-1440); Moctezuma I (1440-1469); Axayacatl (1469-1481); Tizoc (1481-1486); Ahuizotl (1486-1502).

Byzantine Empire Manuel II Palaeologus (reigned 1391-1425); John VII Palaeologus (co-emperor 1399-1402); John VIII Palaeologus (1425-1448); Constantine XI Palaeologus Dragatses (1449-1453).

China Ming Dynasty: Jianwen (1398-1402); Yongle (1402-1424); Hongxi (1424-1425); Xuande (1425-1435); Zhengtong (1436-1449); Jingtai (1449-1457); Zhengtong (1457-1464); Chenghua (1464-1487); Hongzhi (1487-1505).

England Henry IV (reigned 1399-1413), Henry V (1413-1422); Henry VI (1422-1461); Edward IV (1461-1470); Henry VI (1470-1471); Edward IV (1471-1483); Edward V (1483); Richard III (1483-1485); Henry VII (1485-1509).

France Charles VI (reigned 1380-1422); Charles VII (1422-1461); Louis XI (1461-1483); Charles VIII (1483-1498); Louis XII (1498-1515).

Holy Roman Empire Wenceslaus (reigned 1378-1400); Rupert (1400-1410); Sigismund (1410-1437); Albert II (1438-1439); Frederick III (1440-1493); Maximilian I (1493-1519).

Inca Empire Pachacuti (reigned 1438-1471); Topa Inca (1471-1493); Huayna Capac (1493-1527).

Japan Muromachi Period: Go-Komatsu (reigned 1392-1412); Shoko (1412-1428); Go-Hanazono (1428-1464); Go-Tsuchimikado (1464-1500).

Ottoman Bayezid I (reigned 1389-1402); Interregnum (1403-1413); Mehmet I (1413-1421); Murad II (1421-1444); Mehmet II (1444-1446); Murad II (1446-1451); Mehmet II (1451-1481); Bayezid II (1481-1512).

Portugal Joao I (reigned 1385-1433); Duarte (1433-1438); Alfonso V (1438-1481); Joao II (1481-1495); Manuel I (1495-1521).

Scotland Robert III (reigned 1390-1406); James I (1406-1437); James II (1437-1460); James III (1460-1488); James IV (1488-1513).

Songhai Empire Askia Dynasty: Sonni 'Ali (reigned 1464-1492); Mohammed Toure the Great (1493-1528).

A town under siege from cannon and longbows, a scene typical of the Hundred Years War.

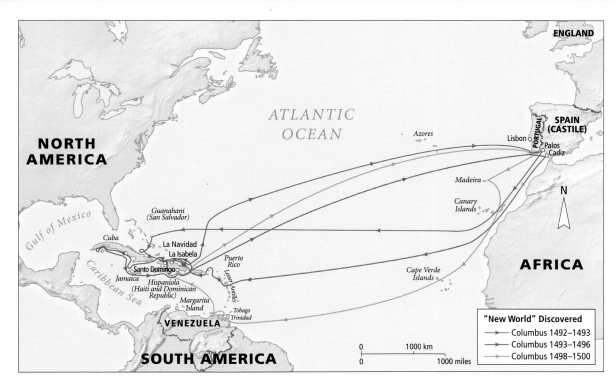

Mehmet II

Lord Stanley looked on as the King's situation steadily worsened, and then joined the fray on the side of Henry, surrounding Richard and his men. Abandoned and isolated, Richard was forced from his horse. Some claim to have then seen the king run through by a Welsh pikeman. With Richard dead and no leader behind whom to unite, the battle ended.

Richard, the last of the Plantagenet kings, today became the just the second English king to die in battle, the first being Harold, killed at Hastings in 1066.

of that year, a house belonging to one of Hosokawa's generals went up in flames. This event triggered looting and pillaging, and by end July much of the north of the city was reduced to rubble. Kyoto's streets were strewn with corpses.

The deaths of the patriarchs of both families in 1473 didn't stop the carnage. By 1477 this once great city has been stripped bare and anarchy rules the streets. The sentiments given full voice in Kyoto are beginning to sweep the country.

The Onin War has effectively brought to an end the system of rule that has characterized the Ashikaga Shogunate. Prior to the Onin War, it was based on a delicate balance among the shugo (officials who oversee a province), who resided mainly in Kyoto. As a result of the war, the shugo have self-destructed, retreating into political insignificance. Power and influence has disappeared from Kyoto and other main cities and is being transferred to various military families in the provinces.

With the decentralization of power from the cities to the countryside, these new provincial warriors (the daimyo) have a firm basis from which to build their power. The concept of "national" politics in Japan has come to an end.

Richard III Dies

Bosworth, England, August 22, 1485: King Richard III has been killed in battle today at Ambion Hill in Bosworth, Leicestershire, fighting a large force of Lancastrians led by Henry Tudor, second Earl of Richmond. It has been reported that Lord Thomas Stanley crowned Henry King of England in the battle's aftermath.

Richard, the protector of the young Edward V, who mysteriously vanished

under Richard's stewardship leaving Richard as King, has fought his last battle against Lancastrian usurpers.

Henry Tudor landed in Pembrokeshire, Wales, on August 7 with 2,000 French mercenaries and a handful of Lancastrian knights. Gathering forces as he marched through Wales then through Shrewsbury, Stafford, and Atherstone, he arrived at Bosworth Field with 5,000 men. Accompanying him were two brilliant military tacticians: Jasper Tudor, the first Earl of Pembroke, and John de Vere, thirteenth Earl of Oxford.

The battle lasted two hours. Although it began well for the King, it appears he missed a critical opportunity to advance on Oxford's troops while they were still deploying and reportedly having trouble lining up on the rough terrain. Richard, forced to come down off a ridge in the face of Lancastrian cannon fire, called for the right wing of his army to join in with fresh troops, but its commander, Lord Northumberland, refused.

It seems though that it was the actions of Lord Stanley, supposedly Richard's ally despite being stepfather to Henry Tudor, which turned the battle irrevocably in Henry's favor. When Richard ordered him to bring fresh troops, he too refused. Long suspicious of Stanley's treachery, Richard's staff advised him to withdraw.

When Richard saw Henry approaching Stanley, apparently to negotiate for his allegiance, Richard made one last attempt at victory. Wearing his battle crown and a robe bearing the royal battle arms over his armor, Richard led his heavily armed household knights in a charge on Henry and his personal guard, killing Henry's standard-bearer and coming within a blade's length of killing Henry himself.

Columbus's "New World"

Palos, Spain, December, 1492: Reports filtering back from explorer Christopher Columbus, an Italian by birth, who was commissioned by the Spanish King Ferdinand and Queen Isabella to set sail in search of the East Indies, claim that he has discovered a "new world."

Columbus set out on his voyage of discovery on August 3 with 90 crewmen and a fleet of three ships: the *Nina*, the *Pinta*, and the *Santa Maria*. After two months at sea, Columbus reports that land was sighted on October 12: an island that they named Guanahani after they went ashore and met the local Indians. They sailed on and landed in Cuba on October 28, before discovering the island of Hispaniola in early December. On Christmas Day, the report reveals that they have suffered the loss of their lead ship, the *Santa Maria*.

Columbus with King Ferdinand and Queen Isabella.

Henry the Navigator

> *"IRON RUSTS FROM DISUSE; STAGNANT WATER LOSES ITS PURITY AND IN COLD WEATHER BECOMES FROZEN; EVEN SO DOES INACTION SAP THE VIGOR OF THE MIND."*
>
> LEONARDO DA VINCI (1452–1519), ITALIAN ARTIST AND INVENTOR

Sketches of Latest Weaponry in *Bellifortis*

Germany, 1405: Military engineer Konrad Keyser has published a significant new work entitled *Bellifortis,* which combines sketches and text covering the many aspects of military warfare and technology, including rockets and gunpowder.

Born in Bavaria in 1366, Keyser was the first engineer to make systematic use of weaponry-related images and sketches. *Bellifortis* contains a visual compendium of classic authors such as Frontinus, and the text devotes considerable attention to firearms that are only now being tested on the battlefield, as well as diagrams for non-military projects such as heated public baths and oil lamps.

China Ends its Golden Age of Discovery

China, 1405–1433: The early part of the fifteenth century witnessed the birth of a remarkable age of exploration in China, with a vast "Treasure Fleet" of over 100 ships and 28,000 men under the command of Admiral Cheng Ho visiting and trading with ports all over the Indian Ocean, including the Persian Gulf and Egypt. It is also likely he reached the northern coastline of *Terra Australis*.

Cheng (later also known as Zheng He) was a 10-year-old peasant boy when taken captive by the Ming Army during its invasion of Yunnan province in 1381, and was raised in the household of the Emperor's fourth son, Zhu Di, who later became Emperor in 1402. The following year Zhu Di ordered Cheng to construct a fleet of ships to explore the vast seas to the east and south of China.

Sixty-two ships comprised the first Treasure Fleet that set out in 1405. The four vessels designated as flagships

Artist's view of Chinese ships on a river. Cheng's magnificent Chinese fleet has explored the vast oceans.

were over 400 ft (121 m) long and 160 ft (49 m) wide, making them among the largest ships ever built. There were ships over 340 ft (103 m) long built to carry horses, water ships filled with fresh water, troop transports, and supply ships laden with Chinese goods to trade. This single fleet was made up of more vessels than all of Europe's fleets combined; the ships were equipped with Chinese inventions such as the rudder and armor plating. Watertight internal compartments ensured they could easily traverse the 10,000 miles (16,000 km) to destinations such as Zanzibar on the southern coastline of Africa. Cheng was astonished by Africa's animals, and he returned to China with giraffes, zebras, and oryx.

time out

In 1420, Prince Henry the Navigator (1394–1460) of Portugal gathered navigators and cartographers to create new navigation technology so he could sail to Africa, India, and lands beyond.

One Chinese historian remarked: "Our ships that sail the southern seas are like houses. When their sails are spread, they are like great clouds in the sky."

Cheng navigated by compass, invented in China during the eleventh century by placing a magnetized needle in a bowl of water to absorb the pitching and yawing of the ocean. He visited over 35 nations, all of whom returned envoys to China to pay homage to the Emperor. He set up diplomatic relations everywhere, opening up vast trading routes and making China the dominant power in the known world.

The demand for Chinese goods was rampant, with foreign kings and princes particularly coveting the famous Ming blue and white porcelain dishes, vases, and cups. Chinese silk and the long-lasting brownish yellow cloth known as Nankeen were also highly prized.

Fujian, China, 1405: Admiral Cheng Ho (Zheng He) leaves on a voyage of exploration to the Indian Ocean.
Germany, 1405: Konrad Keyser publishes his work *Bellifortis,* covering the many aspects of military warfare and technology.
Italy, c. 1406: Ptolemy's *Geography* is translated into Latin, and so becomes available to European scholars and mapmakers.
Leipzig, Germany, 1409: The University of Leipzig is founded, with faculties of Arts, Law, Medicine, and Theology.

Venice, Italy, 1410: Ptolemy's *Geographia,* a comprehensive guide to mapmaking and geography, is translated into Latin.
Venice, Italy, 1410: Benedetto Rinio publishes his herbal (*Liber de simplicibus*), an illustrated guide to more than 400 plants of medicinal use.
Edinburgh, Scotland, 1411: St Andrew's University, the first university in the country, is founded by Henry Wardlaw.

Nanjing, China, October, 1415: Admiral Cheng Ho returns to China from East Africa with a giraffe for the imperial zoo.
Samarkand, Uzbekistan, 1420: Ulugh Beg, Timurid ruler, with a keen interest in both the arts and science, builds an observatory in the city.
Florence, Italy, 1421: Architect Filippo Brunelleschi is given the world's first recorded patent for an invention (a canal barge, with hoists).

Louvain, Belgium, 1425: The University of Louvain is founded.
Samarkand, Uzbekistan, 1427: Al-Kashi publishes his mathemical work, *The Key to Arithmetic.*
Europe, c. 1430: Guns of iron, cast in one piece, are constructed.
Poitiers, France, 1431: The University of Poitiers is founded.
Caen, France, 1432: The University of Caen is founded.
Samarkand, Uzbekistan, 1437: The star catalogue *Zij-I Sultani* is published by Ulugh Beg.

Seoul, Korea, 1438: Astronomers complete the project to re-equip the royal observatory with the world's most up-to-date instruments.
Seoul, Korea, 1443: A royal commission creates a new Korean script (*on'mun*) to improve education and increase the literacy rate.
Mainz, Germany, c. 1450: Johannes Gutenberg invents the printing press, with movable reusable blocks fashioned from metal.
Murano, Italy, 1450: Angelo Barovier invents crystalline glass.

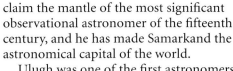

Rather than using the voyages of the Treasure Fleet to conquer and enforce Chinese hegemony over other cultures, Cheng extolled the Ming Dynasty's abstinence from greed and its immunity to the outside world's temptations. Cheng was also sensitive to cultural diversity. During a visit to religiously divided Ceylon, he erected a three-sided monument with sacred carvings in Persian, Tamil, and Chinese, with each side praising the God appropriate for that faith.

Cheng himself died returning to China from India during the seventh and final voyage of the Grand Fleet (1431–1433).

Ulugh Beg dispensing justice.

New Text Published

Samarkand, Uzbekistan, 1427: Growing up in a time of widespread poverty, Jamshid al-Kashi devoted himself to the study of astronomy and mathematics while moving from town to town. After years of study, he has just completed *The Key to Arithmetic*, a major text intended to give students the necessary mathematics for the study of astronomy, surveying, architecture, accounting, and trading. This major work includes the arithmetic of fractions, the measure of plane figures and bodies, and a section on the use of algebra in problem solving.

Samarkand the Center of the Astronomical World

Samarkand, Uzbekistan, 1437: The Timurid ruler Ulugh Beg has attracted some of the world's finest astronomers to his observatory in Samarkand, where he has published *Zij-i Sultani*, the most comprehensive star catalogue to date under his name, though it is undoubtedly a collaborative effort between Ulugh and his esteemed colleagues Jamshid al-Kashi and Qadi Zada. Still, Ulugh can quite rightly claim the mantle of the most significant observational astronomer of the fifteenth century, and he has made Samarkand the astronomical capital of the world.

Ulugh was one of the first astronomers to advocate and to have constructed permanently mounted astronomical instruments. His catalogue of 1018 stars, together with their ecliptic coordinates, is the most ambitious and significant attempt at star mapping since the time of Claudius Ptolemy in 170 CE.

Ulugh's observatory, 55 yards (50 m) in diameter and 50 yards (45 m) high, was built in northern Samarkand in 1428, and there is nothing like it anywhere else in the world. A marble quadrant bisects the building on a north–south axis and it is cut deep into the ground for stability.

News of Ulugh's observatory spread quickly, and 60 or 70 astronomers well versed in mathematics have participated in work at the observatory or attended its seminars.

The largest instrument at the Samarkand Observatory is the Fakhri sextant, a 60° stone arc mounted on the north–south meridian, the largest meridian instrument ever built. It can achieve a resolution of several seconds of arc and is used to determine the transit altitude of stars. Other instruments at Samarkand are designed to determine the angular separations of pairs of stars.

Lenses to Correct Near-sightedness

Germany, 1451: Nicholas of Cusa has invented the first concave lenses designed to correct near-sightedness. A Catholic cardinal, philosopher, and mathematician, he was born Nikolaus Krebs (Latinized as Nicholas of Cusa) in 1401 to a merchant family. He received a doctorate in canon law from the University of Padua in 1423, and was made a cardinal by Pope Nicholas V in 1448. Known for his mystical writings, particularly about the nature of the Holy Trinity, he has avoided any accusations of being heretical.

The earliest eyeglasses may have been invented by Arabian scientists, who are credited with using a type of magnifying lens in the tenth century. Those glasses, however, all had convex lenses to correct far-sightedness. Nicholas of Cusa has discovered the benefits of using concave lenses in the treatment of myopia.

A scientist ahead of his time, he is also credited with the suggestion that the Earth was more or less a spherical shape that orbited the Sun, and that each star is itself a distant sun. As a mathematician, he has also developed the concepts of the infinitesimal and of relative motion.

Fra Luca de Pacioli

A Flemish tapestry depicting the astrolabe (a measuring instrument) and zodiac.

Key Events

Germany, 1451: Nicholas of Cusa invents concave lenses to correct near-sightedness.

Italy, c. 1454: Theodore of Gaza translates botanical works by Theophrastus (a pupil of Aristotle) into Latin.

Mainz, Germany, 1455: Johannes Gutenberg's first book, the Bible, goes into print.

Mainz, Germany, c. 1457: A psalter printed by Fust and Schoffer is the first printed book to use color.

Borgo Sansepolcro, Italy, 1470: Piero della Francesca, acknowledged not only as a great painter but also as a mathematician, publishes *Tratta d'Abaco*, a work on algebra.

Nuremberg, Germany, 1471: Johannes Müller (Regiomontanus) builds an observatory to conduct his studies in astronomy. He also installs his own printing press to enable publication of his findings in the fields of science.

Torun, Poland, February 19, 1473: Nicolaus Copernicus is born.

Westminster, England, 1476: William Caxton sets up the first printing press in England. His first publication is *Dictes and Sayings of the Philosophers*.

Rome, Italy, July 6, 1476: Johannes Müller (Regiomontanus), mathematician and astronomer, dies, aged 40.

Venice, Italy, 1482: Erhard Ratdolt prints a Latin translation of Euclid's *Elements*, a geometry text written in about 300 BCE.

Borgo Sansepolcro, Italy, 1482: Piero della Francesca publishes his *De prospectiva pingendi*, a work on the use of perspective in art.

Lyon, France, 1484: Nicolas Chuquet's *Triparty en la science des nombres* is the first mathematical work to use negative exponents.

Milan, Italy, 1488: Leonardo da Vinci combines his engineering skills with his concept of man taking to the skies when he sketches his famous flying machine.

Leipzig, 1489: Johann Widman writes the first text to use the plus (+) and minus (–) sign to indicate excess and deficiency, making it easier to express mathematics in symbols rather than words.

Nuremberg, Germany, 1492: Martin Behaim is responsible for the first world map on a globe.

Venice, Italy, 1494: Fra Luca de Pacioli publishes his *Summa de arithmetica, geometrica, proportioni et proportionalita*, a synthesis of the mathematical knowledge of his time.

Milan, Italy, 1495: Leonardo da Vinci sketches his design for a parachute.

Leiria, Portugal, 1496: Abraham Zacuto publishes his *Almanach perpetuum*.

Johannes Gutenberg

Gutenberg Prints First Edition of the Bible

Mainz, Germany, 1455: The goldsmith from Mainz who is credited with the invention of movable type, Johannes Gutenberg, has produced a 42-lines per page Bible that has taken him two years to complete. One witness to the process, Enea Silvio Piccolomini, claims that between 158 and 180 copies were produced, with about 135 copies on paper and the remainder on vellum. Gutenberg apparently increased the print run when it appeared that demand for the books would far exceed supply.

Prior to Gutenberg's printing press, books were either copied by hand onto paper or scrolls, or from hand-carved wooden blocks. However, these blocks were very fragile, and the absorption of the ink into the wood meant the blocks had a very limited life.

Gutenberg has used metal molds, made with the use of dies into which he poured hot liquid metal, producing separate letters in the same shape as those written by hand. He then converted a hand-press,

Gutenberg prints the first Bible.

as used in the wine industry, to press the type against the paper, enabling sharp impressions on either side of the paper and many repetitions.

Gutenberg has used carbon to color his ink black, which has a glitter to it owing to the high levels of metal within the carbon. He used hand-made paper imported from Caselle in the Piedmont region of northern Italy. Each sheet contained a watermark, which can be seen when held up to the light.

It is possible that more than one press was used due to the sheer number of pages he needed to print. The type for each line was selected by a typesetter, and then set into a frame, which was then placed on the bed of the press. A moistened sheet of paper was placed over the form and a stout pull by the pressman completed the page.

Gutenberg's movable type has strong vertical and horizontal lines, giving the impression of a woven, textured pattern across the page. Its Gothic style of linked lettering (ligatures) was designed to save space and speed up copying.

Each Bible is sold in folded sheets, and later bound and decorated according to the wishes of its owner.

Gutenberg has revolutionized the distribution of knowledge by making it possible to produce large numbers of books in a relatively short space of time. His contemporaries are referring to it as "the art of multiplying books."

As his reference for this monumental edition of the Bible, Gutenberg used the Latin text (translated from the Hebrew and Greek) of St Jerome.

Noted German Scholar Struck Down by Plague

Rome, Italy, July 6, 1476: The German scholar Johannes Müller, also known as Regiomontanus, died today aged 40. Müller's keen interest in mathematics and astronomy led him to write a number of books, including a translation of Ptolemy's *Almagest* and an important work on trigonometry, *De triangulis omnimodis libri quinque (Five Books on Triangles of All Kinds)*.

Born in Königsberg in 1436, Müller was recognized early as a mathematical prodigy; he entered the University of Leipzig aged 11. He then completed a Masters degree from the University of Vienna. Müller's first major work was at the behest of his astronomical mentor,

Georg Peurbach, who urged him to complete an abridgment of Ptolemy's famous *Syntaxis* into a single work.

In 1470, Müller began looking for a place where he could pursue his life's goal: the determination of the astronomical constants by observation. He chose Nuremberg, at the time the industrial and commercial center of southern Germany.

While in Nuremberg, Müller built an observatory and a workshop to make scientific instruments. His interest in the motion of the moon led him to make the important observation that the method of measuring lunar distances could be used to determine longitude at sea.

By 1472 he had set up a printing press in his home and printed a Prospectus, announcing his plans to publish astronomical, mathematical, and geographical texts.

In 1475, Pope Sixtus IV summoned Müller to Rome to offer his advice on calendar reform. Müller passed away today, the victim of plague brought upon the city of Rome when the Tiber River overflowed its banks last January.

Della Francesca Stresses Geometry in Art

Borgo Sansepolcro, Italy, 1482: Piero della Francesca, a most influential painter of this current period of renaissance, has published a treatise on the mathematics of perspective in art that he calls *De prospectiva pingendi*. In it he attempts to explain a technique for giving the appearance of a third dimension in a two-dimensional painting or sculptured relief.

The work is dedicated to his patron, the Duke of Urbino. The original manuscript

Portrait of Battista Sforza, by Piero della Francesca.

Scientific Achievements

Astronomy: Catalogue of the stars published; solar eclipses viewed and computed.
Botany: Eastern spice trade explored; plants exchanged between Europe and the Americas.
Chemistry: Antimony described.
Ecology: Sailors discover use of seasonal "trade winds"; "Little Ice Age" hits Europe.
Geology: First work published on occupational disease—illness in gold miners studied.
Mathematics: Decimal fraction calculation developed; plus and minus signs, decimal point, and zero introduced.
Medicine: Public dissections of corpses in Italy.

Observatories
Nuremburg, Germany
Oradea, Hungary
Samarkand, Uzbekistan
Machu Picchu, Peru

Universities
University of Barcelona, Spain
University of Basle, Switzerland
University of Bratislava, Slovakia
University of Catania, Italy
University of Copenhagen, Denmark
University of Genoa, Italy
University of Glasgow, Scotland
University of Leipzig, Germany
University of Leuven, Belgium
University of St Andrew, Scotland
University of Uppsala, Sweden

Sketches of a flying machine, by the Italian artist, architect, and engineer, Leonardo da Vinci.

great height without sustaining any injury." The original design for the parachute had been sketched by Leonardo in one of his notebooks in 1483.

The very first attempt at a parachute jump, however, more than likely was in Cordoba, Spain, in 852 CE when a Muslim holy man, Arman Firman, jumped off a tower, trusting that the large cloak he was wearing would billow out and save him. Crashing unceremoniously to the ground, there was enough air in the folds of the cloak to ensure he survived the fall.

Leonardo da Vinci

was handwritten by the artist and contains diagrams on geometric, proportional, and perspective problems. The manual is designed to teach students how to paint in perspective, and the incredibly detailed drawing instructions are mind-numbing in their repetitiousness.

Della Francesca's genius in developing new methods of perspective then employing them in art has seen him create paintings for ecclesiastics, confraternities, and illustrious nobles throughout the Italian peninsula.

In his paintings, perspective and geometry figure prominently. His use of large, plain masses of color gives his paintings an "unfinished" look. There are often large areas of white or near-white in his works, and his skies are big, light, and sunny. Combined with an absence of meticulous clutter, it serves to make his paintings extremely pleasing to the eye.

Caxton Establishes First Printing Press in England

Westminster, England, 1483: After returning from Bruges, where he has printed several books, William Caxton has set up the first printing press in England. His first publication was *The Dictes and Sayengis of the Philosophres*. Among his many other publications is the first edition of Geoffrey Chaucer's *The Canterbury Tales*.

Caxton was probably born in Kent in 1422, though there has always been some conjecture as to the year of his birth. Living through the War of the Roses, Caxton became Governor of the English Merchants at Bruges, where he lived for many years. During this time he learned the art of printing. In 1471, after having been dismissed as Governor of the English Merchants, he moved to Cologne, which had the reputation as Germany's principal city for printing.

Returning to London in 1476, Caxton established himself in the almonry at Westminster Abbey and began printing pamphlets. The first dated book printed in England was Lord River's translation,

revised by Caxton, of *The Dictes and Sayengis of the Philosophres* (1476).

Caxton's first major work in England, however, was to be Chaucer's *The Canterbury Tales*, a canny choice by a man who has a shrewd eye for the market both in choice of books and the style of type. For Chaucer's classic, Caxton decided to use a new style of type based on the handwriting in the luxury manuscripts designed for the Burgundian Court.

Leonardo da Vinci Draws the First "Parachute"

Milan, Italy, 1495: Leonardo da Vinci has sketched a revolutionary design for a parachute, which consists of a section of sealed linen cloth held open by a pyramid of wooden poles, which would, conceivably, allow a person to jump from any height and land safely without injury.

The great inventor explains: "If a man had a tent made of linen, of which all the apertures have been stopped up…he will be able to throw himself down from any

Tables to Predict Eclipses

Leiria, Portugal, 1496: Renowned Iberian astronomer Abraham Zacuto has published the *Almanach perpetuum*, his mathematical and astronomical tables for the years 1497 to 1500. The almanac's highly accurate tables can be used to predict eclipses, as well as the precise hours for the rising of the planets and fixed stars. This potentially life-saving reference, together with Zacuto's new astrolabe made from metal and not wood, as previous models had been, is certain to prove invaluable to ocean-going explorers.

Cast lead medal of the classical scholar and theologian, Desiderius Erasmus of Rotterdam, born in about 1466.

Zacuto was born into a French Jewish exile family in 1452, living in Castile up until the Jewish exile from Spain in 1497. His family was part of the Jewish nobility, and so the young Zacuto was able to acquire an excellent education under the tutelage of Rabbi Isaac Aboab.

English printer William Caxton reading the first proof sheet from his printing press in Westminster Abbey.

Author of *The Canterbury Tales* Dies

Geoffrey Chaucer

London, England, October 25, 1400: Geoffrey Chaucer, author of *The Canterbury Tales*, undoubtedly one of the finest works in English literature, and written at a time when much court poetry was written in Anglo-Norman or Latin, has died.

In 1359, Chaucer went to France with Edward III's army during the Hundred Years War. After being captured in the Ardennes, he was returned to England where it is believed he translated from the French the allegory *Romaunt of the Rose*, his first literary work. He moved to London, became a government official, and was even elected to Parliament.

The Canterbury Tales, his unfinished 17,000-line poem written mostly after 1387, tells the story of a group of pilgrims traveling from London to the shrine of St Thomas à Becket in Canterbury. To pass the time, they begin telling stories, and in the process vividly illuminate medieval customs and attitudes concerning themes such as marriage, religion, and love.

Geoffrey Chaucer, the son of a vintner, has been buried in Westminster Abbey.

"BUT WHERE ARE THE SNOWS OF YESTERYEAR?"

FRANÇOIS VILLON (1431– c. 1475), FRENCH POET AND THIEF, 1461

"THE WORSHIPFUL FATHER AND FIRST FOUNDER AND EMBELLISHER OF ORNATE ELOQUENCE IN OUR ENGLISH, I MEAN MASTER GEOFFREY CHAUCER."

WILLIAM CAXTON (1422–1491), ENGLISH PRINTER, OF CHAUCER (1340–1400)

John Lydgate and pilgrims, illustration for Chaucer's *The Canterbury Tales*.

Forbidden City Completed

Peking, China, 1420: By 1368 the Mongolian influence in China, which commenced with Genghis Khan's occupation of Yan-jing in 1215, had begun to ebb. Ming troops seized Daidu (the City of the Great Khan) in August of that year, and on orders from the Chinese Emperor Zhu Yuan-zhang the capital was moved to Nanjing in the south. Daidu, renamed Beiping, became a mere provincial city.

In 1405, when Emperor Yongle planned the Forbidden City, he decreed it be laid out in accordance with his astrologer's symbolic conception, with wide-open spaces and buildings corresponding to parts of the human body. Its high, sloping, vermilion walls—15 yds (13.7 m) high and 12 yds (11 m) thick at their base—enhance its mystique. The bricks are composed of white lime, glutinous rice, glutinous rice juice, and egg whites, which gives them a thick and strong density and also makes them extremely smooth and impossible to scale.

The site of the city was linked to the position of the Pole Star. Emperor Yongle wanted his new city to be the center of humanity on Earth.

With the addition of more palace buildings in 1417, the project has now finally been completed, and the capital has again been moved from Nanjing to Beiping, which has been renamed Beijing (northern capital), known in the West as Peking.

The Forbidden City is the largest complex in the world with 9,999 rooms, and is surrounded by a deep moat. Its walls are pierced by four large gates that give access to an area of over 2 million sq ft (185,806 sq m). It is

A silk painting of the Forbidden City, by Zhu Bang.

estimated that over a million workers and 100,000 skilled artisans were engaged in its construction.

Its layout is based on a Chinese cosmic diagram of the universe that clearly defines the north–south and east–west axes, and its design is centered on three primary halls of State: the Hall of Supreme Harmony, the Hall of Middle Harmony, and the Hall of Preserving Harmony.

Its outer court is the site for important ceremonies such as the accession of a new emperor, while the inner court serves as the residential area of the Emperor and the imperial household.

New Pinnacle of Realism in Art Achieved in Ghent

Ghent, Belgium, May, 1432: The magnificent altarpiece for Belgium's Ghent Cathedral has finally been completed. While mostly attributed to the painter Jan van Eyck, a Latin inscription on the border of this landmark painting suggests that it may

have been his older brother, Hubert, who started the impressive work of art.

Dedicated on May 6 in the Church of St John, the work has been installed above the altar in a chapel founded by the wealthy patrician Joos Vijdt.

Although the chapel is only open to the public on Sundays and religious holidays, the work is drawing huge crowds to the cathedral.

Painted as a series of individually framed portraits, its astonishing realism rests not only in the fidelity in which figures, plants, and animals are represented in a convincing space, but also in the way it forges a sense of continuity between the pictorial and the real world.

The Adoration of the Lamb is the work's central panel, and this is already being hailed as the most ambitious composition to this point in the world of art. Scores of saints, pilgrims, and dignitaries are set with realism into a complex landscape.

The surrounding tall, thin panels are equally impressive, with all the figures occupying their allotted spaces with complete naturalness and realism.

Van Eyck is one of this century's most famous artists. Born around 1390, he became court painter to Duke Philip the Good of Burgundy. Prior to his work on the Ghent altarpiece, this year he purchased a house in Bruges and signed and dated a number of paintings, all of which were painted in oil and varnished.

Both Hubert and Jan van Eyck see color composition as very important, and they have perfected a type of paint that is a mix of linseed oil, egg yolk, and turpentine, which is responsible for the warm glow from the canvas. *The Adoration of the Lamb* is painted on smooth oak panels, and the impeccable skill displayed allows the viewer to distinguish all the different types of wood and precious metals depicted in the work. Even the

figures' blood vessels and individual drops of water from the fountain are discernible. Is it any wonder that this work is being hailed as the conquest of realism?

time out

Fatih Mehmet II (1432–1481) built the Fatih Mosque in Turkey, wanting a monument more spectacular than the Christian church. When the mosque failed to surpass the height of the church, the sultan cut off the architect's hands.

A True Masterpiece

Siena, Italy, 1445: Giovanni di Paolo has finished his *The Creation and the Expulsion from Paradise*. A masterpiece of Sienese painting, it presents a vision of Paradise reminiscent of Dante's *The Divine Comedy*, with Earth depicted as a celestial globe and God the Father bathed in light as he is held aloft by seraphim.

An influential painter of the Sienese school, di Paolo's works are characterized by vigorous, harsh colors and elongated forms. Typical of the Sienese painters of his era, he has paid scant attention to the artistic innovations being made in nearby Florence, basing his style instead on the Sienese masters of the fourteenth century.

Designer of Florence's Duomo Dies

Florence, Italy, April 16, 1446: Goldsmith and sculptor Filippo Brunelleschi died today, after many years of contributing to Italian culture. He was laid to rest by the citizens of Florence, under the floor of the Cathedral of Florence. He will long be remembered for his design for the magnificent dome, which is to be the crowning glory of Florence's cathedral.

The dome is to consist of two layers—an inner dome spanning the diameter, and a parallel outer shell to protect it from the weather. The dome is to be supported by 24 stone half-arches—7 ft (2 m) thick at the base and tapering to 5 ft (1.5 m)—which will meet at an open stone compression ring at the top.

The structure will be built without formwork, with the circular profiles of the ribs and rings being maintained by a system of measuring wires that will be fixed at the centers of curvature.

Jan van Eyck

"Paradise," detail from *The Last Judgment,* by Sienese master painter Giovanni di Paolo.

Key Events

Kyoto, Japan, c. 1450: Zen artist Bunsei's work initiates a new style of monochrome ink painting.
Vinci, Italy, April 15, 1452: Leonardo da Vinci is born.
Rome, Italy, February 18, 1455: Fra Giovanni da Fiesole (Fra Angelico), painter, dies, aged about 59.
Florence, Italy, December 1, 1455: Lorenzo Ghiberti, sculptor, dies, aged 77. He is remembered for creating the bronze doors of the Florence Baptistry and a number of stunning statues.

Borgo Sansepolcro, Italy, c. 1455: Piero della Francesca paints his *Annunciation*.
Florence, Italy, c. 1455: Paolo Uccello paints *The Rout of San Romano,* in three panels.
Paris, France, c. 1461: Poet François Villon writes *Le testament* (*The Testament*).
Venice, Italy, c. 1465: Giovanni Bellini completes his polyptych *St Vincent Ferrer at the Church of St John and St Paul.*

Tabriz, Iran, 1465: The magnificent Blue Mosque, or Masjed-e-Kabud, with its intricate mosaic decorations and impressive dome, is completed.
Istanbul, Turkey, 1470: The Fatih Mosque is completed for Sultan Mehmet II.
Peru, 1470: The city of Machu Picchu is built for Inca ruler Pachacuti.
Holland, 1471: Jacob Obrecht, composer of sacred music, writes his *Passion According to St Matthew.*
Nuremberg, Germany, 1471: Albrecht Dürer is born.

Caprese, Italy, March 6, 1475: Michelangelo Buonarroti is born.
Florence, Italy, c. 1478: A favorite of the powerful Medici family, Sandro Botticelli is commissioned to paint his famous *Primavera*.
Rome, Italy, c. 1481–1482: Botticelli paints a number of frescoes in the Sistine Chapel.
Florence, Italy, 1485: Botticelli paints *The Birth of Venus.*
Naples, Italy, c. 1485: Jacopo Sannazaro writes *Arcadia,* a pastoral romance in verse and prose.

Nuremberg, Germany, 1493: Hartmann Schedel publishes his *Chronicle of the World.*
England, 1496: Written more than 70 years earlier, Dame Juliana Berner's guide to fly-fishing, *Treatyse of Fysshynge wyth an Angle,* is published.
Milan, Italy, 1498: Leonardo da Vinci paints the fresco of *The Last Supper* at the Convent of Santa Maria delle Grazie.
Rome, Italy, 1499: Michelangelo crafts his magnificent marble sculpture, *Pietà.*

Giuliano de' Medici

Master of Light Completes Latest Masterpiece

Venice, Italy, 1465: Founder of the Venetian school of painting, Giovanni Bellini, who is known for his high degree of realism, new wealth of subject matter, and deep colors, has just finished his latest masterpiece—*The Agony in the Garden*—a work in tempura on canvas.

It depicts Christ praying in the Garden of Gethsemane while his disciples sleep. Judas can be seen with Roman soldiers approaching Christ to arrest him. Bellini has depicted the morning light with great subtlety, softly touching the undersides of the clouds and turning them pink. He has also combined a Flemish-inspired minuteness of brilliantly rendered detail with an Italian understanding of general principles such as no previous artist has been able to achieve.

Bellini's polyptych *St Vincent Ferrer at the Church of St John and St Paul* (1460) was painted for the confraternity of St Vincent Ferrer and is generally regarded to be the artist's first monumental work and first public commission. It comprises nine panels arranged in three parts: above is the Pietà with the Virgin and the Angel of the Annunciation at the side, in the center can be seen St Christopher and St Sebastian, and the predella displays five miracles of St Vincent.

Bellini has made a huge contribution to the world of art with his interesting experimentations in the use of color in oil paintings and has revolutionized Venetian painting, moving it toward a more sensuous and coloristic style.

Blue Mosque Completed in Tabriz

Tabriz, Iran, 1465: The magnificent Blue Mosque (or Masjed-e-Kabud) in Tabriz, Iran, commissioned by Jahanshah at the request of his wife Khatunjan Beygom, has been completed. Sheathed in incomparable blue ceramics, its design follows the Sassanian vaulting tradition, possessing distinctive onion-shaped domes, lofty pointed portals, and magnificent polychrome tiles.

It is, of course, named for its unrivaled tile decoration. Both interior and exterior surfaces are covered in a variety of tile revetment—underglaze-painted and overglaze-painted tiles and luster tiles attest to the richness of the decorative scheme. Patterns are rendered in subtle colors, with extensive use of cobalt blue as a base for inscriptions and arabesque designs in gold and white.

The complex also includes a tomb, a cistern and library, as well as a khanqah or spiritual retreat. Its floor plan is unique in Iran, consisting of a central square chamber covered by a dome and framed on three sides by a continuous arcade of nine domed bays. A domed sanctuary projects from the fourth, and an entrance portal accesses the arcade. It is similar to the covered Ottoman mosques of Bursa, as well as bearing a surprising similarity to Byzantine church architecture.

"Pagan" Masterpiece Unveiled in Florence

Florence, Italy, 1485: Born in 1445 in the Ognissanti parish of Florence, Sandro Botticelli came from an upper middle-class family, serving an apprenticeship with Fra Filippo Lippi, the finest Florentine painter of the time. After becoming a favored painter of the Medici family, Botticelli began painting fresco panels, portraits, and then arguably his two most famous works of art: *The Birth of Venus* and *Spring (Primavera)*.

Botticelli's Venus is so beautiful that the viewer fails to notice the unnatural length of her neck, the way her shoulders fall away or the strange way her left arm hangs from her body. Her anatomy and various secondary details do not display the strict classical realism of Leonardo da Vinci or Raphael. However, such details, whether artistic errors or artistic license, do little to diminish the stunning beauty of the work.

Having access to the artistic circle at the court of Lorenzo de Medici, Botticelli was influenced by its Christian Neoplatonism. This synthesis may indeed explain his depiction of *The Birth of Venus*—Venus emerging from the sea on a shell that is driven to the shore by flying wind-gods amid a shower of roses. The painting is distinctly pagan—a rarity when the vast majority of art of the times depict Roman Catholic themes.

This secular work was painted on canvas, a less expensive surface than the wooden panels used in church and court pictures. A wooden surface would certainly be impractical for a work on such a scale, approximately 9 ft (2.7 m) wide by 6 ft (1.8 m) deep. Canvas is generally thought to be the preferred material for the painting of non-religious and pagan subjects that are occasionally commissioned to decorate country villas in Italy.

History of the World Published in Nuremberg

Nuremberg, Germany, December 23, 1493: Hartmann Schedel has published his *Liber chronicarum* (*Chronicle of the World*, or *The Nuremberg Chronicle* as it is more popularly known). This book on the history of the world is highlighted with exquisite illustrations and many maps.

Schedel was born in Nuremberg in 1440 and studied at Leipzig, where he gained a Master of Arts degree. Despite receiving a doctorate in medicine in 1446, medicine would always remain a poor cousin to the greatest love of his life—books. Schedel amassed the largest privately owned collection of books in all of Europe, and it was the possession of this great library that enabled him to write his *Chronicle of the World*.

The Nuremberg Chronicle was in fact a collaborative effort; among its more well-known contributors are Wilhelm Pleydenwurff, as well as the painter Michael Wolgemut, who has become the first noted book illustrator. The impressive work offers a history of the world from Genesis to the date of printing, and its large-page city views in bold, bright hand-coloring are considered the crowns of city view collections.

Detail of Sandro Botticelli's breathtakingly beautiful painting, *Spring (Primavera)*.

The division of the work into six ages and its point of view are comprehensively medieval. It is a compilation that follows on from earlier chronicles, depending particularly on the *Supplementum chronicarum* which was issued in Venice in 1483 by Brother Jacobus Foresta of Bergamo. In it, the conservative and rigidly orthodox Schedel does not express his own opinions. Undoubtedly, the popularity of the book is due in no small part to the quite marvelous series of woodcut prints of towns, cities, and maps contained within its pages.

First published in Latin on June 12 of this year, Schedel's monumental work has quickly been followed by a German translation, which has just been released. Approximately 1,500 Latin and 1,000 German copies have been produced so far.

Da Vinci Completes his *Last Supper*

Milan, Italy, 1498: Leonardo da Vinci has painted an enormous fresco of *The Last Supper*, measuring 15 ft (4.5 m) by 29 ft (8.8 m), which covers the dining room wall in the Convent of Santa Maria delle Grazie in Milan, Italy.

The technical perspective in *The Last Supper* is undoubtedly one of da Vinci's greatest achievements, with every element of the painting directing the attention of the viewer toward the central character: Jesus Christ. Judas is the only figure in the painting who is leaning away from Christ, and he is the only one in shadow.

The artist painted his mural directly onto the convent's wall without any preparation of the surface, and it is feared that over time dampness may ravage this most exquisite and irreplaceable work of art. Leonardo began the work in 1495.

Michelangelo Creates "Perfect" *Pietà*

Rome, Italy, 1499: The sculptor and painter Michelangelo Buonarroti has crafted a magnificent marble statue of the Virgin Mary cradling the dead body of Jesus after he was lowered from the cross. The artist has named this new work the *Pietà*.

The French Cardinal of Saint-Denis, Jean Bilhères de Lagraulas, wanted a Pietà for his own tomb, which was to be at the ancient Basilica of St Peter. He paid Michelangelo 450 gold papal ducats for its commission.

Up to this time most northern European sculptures were made of wood or terracotta, and looked primitive and awkward when compared to Greek and southern European sculptures. They also showed no consideration for the human form or for weight distribution.

Michelangelo's *Pietà* broke with the tradition of artists before him who always portrayed Mary with the dead Christ in her arms as grief stricken. In this moving rendering she seems almost serene, as though she had already accepted the inevitability of his sacrifice. In her arms, the Savior appears as though he will awaken at any moment from a deep sleep.

Michelangelo has been criticized by some for portraying an exceptionally young looking Virgin, as she would have been between 45 and 50 years old by that time. His response was that the effects of time alone could not mar the face of this most Blessed of women.

There are plans for the statue to be unveiled in St Peter's Basilica next year for the Jubilee of 1500.

Michelangelo had been living in Rome a mere two years and had only completed two sculptures before he received his commission for the *Pietà*.

Apparently, the artist traveled to the marble pits of Carrara and Lucca, which yielded the finest blocks of the brittle

Michelangelo Buonarroti

The stunningly beautiful *Pietà*, by Italian sculptor Michelangelo.

white stone that is so prized by sculptors. In less than two years Michelangelo has sculpted what is surely one of the most magnificent statues ever created.

Leonardo Da Vinci's expansive fresco, *The Last Supper*, which took the artist three years of hard work to produce.

Maximilian I

World's First Brandy Distilled

Armagnac, France, 1411: A new style of drink is being sold commercially throughout southwestern France. Called Armagnac brandy, it has been successfully distilled and produced in the town of Armagnac, located in the province of Gascony, at the foothills of the Pyrénées.

Not only is Armagnac an invigorating beverage, it also can be used to revive the spirits of those suffering from shock and as an antidote during epidemics.

The primary grapes used in the production of Armagnac brandy are Ugni Blanc, Folle Blanche, and Colombard.

Taste testing in a French distillery.

Damp Caves Give Birth to New Style of Cheese

Roquefort-sur-Soulzon, France, 1411: The residents of the town of Roquefort-sur-Soulzon are sporting cheesy grins today. King Charles VI has given them exclusive rights to produce their famous smelly cheese. In an effort to stamp out inferior imitations of the cheese, genuine Roquefort now can only be produced at Roquefort-sur-Soulzon, being aged in the nearby caves that produce the particular mold that is responsible for this unique cheese.

A similar style of cheese has been in existence since Roman times. Mention of it can even be found in the writings of the great Roman historian Pliny. The cheese was a particular favorite of the emperor Charlemagne, and a captivating legend surrounds its discovery.

The story says that a local shepherd once thought he saw a beautiful woman in the distance, and left his sheep to pursue her. He also left his lunch of rye bread and cheese in one of the dank caves of the Grotte du Combalou. When he returned some weeks later, sadly without the young woman, the air currents in the cave, combined with the dampness of the rocks, had caused an odd blue mold to grow in streaks along the surface of his ewe's milk cheese. The shepherd ran down to the village shouting: "It's a miracle, it's a miracle." The people of the town gathered round him, tasted his cheese, and liked it.

Ever since then the limestone caves of Mount Combalou near Roquefort-sur-Soulzon have been used for the production of this famous blue cheese. The cheese makers still use milk from ewes that graze on the Aveyron Plateau. The cheese is white, crumbly, and slightly moist, with the distinctive veins of blue mold that produce a sharp tang. It has no rind, and the exterior of the cheese is edible and slightly salty.

Treading the Grapes, an illustration from *The Playfair Book of Hours*.

Grimaldi Family Become Lords of Monaco

Monaco, 1419: This year the Grimaldi family secured the independence of the tiny enclave of Monaco from Genoa. Since the thirteenth century Monaco has been a province of Genoa, but the Grimaldi family association with Monaco goes back centuries.

Emperor Henry VI gave Monaco to Genoa in 1191, and on June 10, 1215 a group of Genoese Ghibellines under Fulco del Cassello began the construction of a fortress on top of the Rock of Monaco.

In 1297, the Grimaldis, an exiled Genoese family, seized the fortress, lost it in 1317, and regained it in 1335. The principality was established in 1338 by Charles I, who was the son of Rainier I and the father of Rainier II. The family then acquired Menton in 1346 and Roquebrune in 1355, before losing it all in 1401. Rainier II, who never entered Monaco, had a glorious career as a sailor

time out

The distilling process for whiskey has been in practice for some time, but it is not until 1494 in Scotland that the first records of whiskey production, written by monks, appear.

Key Events

Great Zimbabwe, Africa, 1400: The largest center of settlement of the Shona people holds between 10,000 and 20,000 people. Their wealth is based on cattle, trade, and gold.
Canada, 1400: Many native groups live off the land.
London, 1401: Itinerant Lollard preacher William Sawtree is burned at the stake for heresy, the first man in England to be so condemned. He was a follower of John Wycliffe.
France, 1411: The oldest known brandy–Armagnac–is distilled.

France, 1411: Charles VI gives the residents of Roquefort-sur-Soulzon exclusive rights to produce their famous smelly cheese.
St Andrews, Scotland, 1413: Scotland's oldest university, the University of St Andrews, is founded.
Lhasa, Tibet, 1416: Drepung monastery is founded as a center for Buddhist education.
Monaco, 1419: The Grimaldis again possess Monaco and secure independence from Genoa.
Italy, 1422: Federico da Montefeltro is born to a small-time noble family.

Seoul, Korea, 1431: King Sejong orders the publication of *Illustrated Conduct of the Three Bonds* to improve public morals.
England, 1439: The specter of plague is ever-present, and among the measures to prevent the spread of disease is a ban on kissing, instituted by Henry VI.
France, 1440: One of France's wealthiest men of the time, Gilles de Rais, is executed after being found guilty of the murder of more than 100 children.

Eton, England, 1440: Henry VI establishes a college to offer higher education to learned but poor scholars from the lower classes.
Suzhou, China, c. 1450: Favorite retirement city for wealthy officials, Suzhou begins to achieve fame as a center of Chinese garden design.
Mainz, Germany, 1454: Indulgences are printed for Pope Nicholas V to use to reward those who financially supported his crusade against the Turks.

Naples, Italy, December, 1456: Tens of thousands of lives are lost, and many buildings are destroyed or rendered unstable, when an earthquake rocks Naples.
Bucharest, Romania, 1459: The city of Bucharest is founded.
Europe, 1477: When Austrian Archduke Maximilian asks for the hand of Margaret of Burgundy in marriage, he sweetens the proposal with a diamond ring.

in the service of King John the Good and Queen Joan of Naples, and it was his sons, Ambrose, Antoine, and John, who became the Grimaldi Lords of Monaco after a century of struggle with Genoa.

The House of Grimaldi can trace their ancestry to Otto Canella (1070–1143), who was consul of Genoa in 1133. The name Grimaldi is derived from the first name of Canella's youngest son, Grimaldo.

The region has a rich history. The Rock of Monaco served as a shelter for prehistoric civilizations, with its first permanent settlers being the mountain dwelling Ligures from northern Italy.

Monaco derived its name from nearby Monoikos, founded by the Phoenicians in the sixth century BCE, and remained under Roman control until the Western Roman Empire collapsed in 476 CE. After that it came under the influence of the Saracens and various barbarian tribes.

Henry VI Lays Foundation Stone of New School

Eton, England, October 11, 1440: King Henry VI has today laid the foundation stone for a new college at Eton in honor of the Blessed Virgin Mary—the King's College of our Lady of Eton beside Windsor. The charity school will offer free education to 70 scholars who will be educated at the King's expense. The founder's aim is to educate boys into the service of the Church and State.

The college will also serve as a pilgrimage church and an almshouse, with a resident community of secular priests. There are plans to erect a magnificent chapel in the Perpendicular Gothic style.

King Henry has lavished upon this new English college a substantial income from land, and has donated a large number of holy relics. The King has even managed to persuade the Pope to grant a privilege unequalled anywhere in England—the right to grant indulgences to penitents on the Feast of the Assumption.

Insignia of Gilles de Rais, the French scholar turned soldier then rapist, torturer, and mass-murderer. His victims numbered several hundred.

War Hero Executed for Appalling Crimes

Nantes, France, October 26, 1440: One of the wealthiest men in all of France, the serial mass-murderer Gilles de Rais, has been executed after being found guilty of the murder of more than 100 children. It is also suspected he was responsible for the torture and rape of more than 200 young boys and girls.

A commander of a contingent of archers and men-at-arms who fought alongside the heroine Joan of Arc in the Hundred Years War, de Rais became a national hero after helping to free the city of Orléans from the English. He was promoted to Marshal of France by King Charles VII in 1429.

The following year his grandfather died, and de Rais inherited many estates throughout Brittany. Now he was in a position to do what he pleased, and his heroic nature began to give way to a murderous impulse.

Gilles de Rais seemed to have enjoyed killing his victims, mostly young boys, whom he would sodomize before and after decapitating them. Sometimes he would watch as his servants butchered the children. He was able to avoid detection for years due to his noble status.

His fortune dwindled as a result of his keeping a retinue of 200 knights, and his penchant for throwing extravagant parties, even organizing a re-enactment of the Siege of Orléans, with hundreds in small parts and himself in the lead. He was forced to sell the majority of his estates just to stay out of debt.

It wasn't until he assaulted a priest in St Étienne de Mer Morte in May 1440 that de Rais was arrested on charges of murder, sodomy, and heresy.

De Rais voluntarily confessed to the crimes on October 21, thus canceling a court ruling to have him tortured. After tearfully expressing remorse, he was freed from the sentence of excommunication and granted a request to confess to a priest. De Rais and his accomplices were hanged in Nantes on October 26, 1440. His body was placed on a pyre, but his relatives were allowed to remove the body before the flames reached it. De Rais was buried in a nearby Carmelite church.

Guidobaldo Montefeltro

King Henry VI in Parliament. He banned kissing in order to stop the spread of disease.

King Ferdinand

Inquisition to Target Insincere Catholics

Spain, 1483: In 1478, Pope Sixtus IV, in a show of support for King Ferdinand and Queen Isabella of Spain, empowered the sovereigns to establish an "inquisition" in Spain to examine those Jews who, either through coercion or social pressure, had insincerely converted to Christianity. The judges chosen to lead this inquisition were to be at least of 40 years of age, of unimpeachable reputation, to be distinguished in both virtue and wisdom, and to be masters of theology.

This inquisition is proving to be far harsher than the earlier medieval inquisition of the mid-thirteenth century, and it also seems to be becoming involved in adjudging matters far outside its original brief, including crimes of bigamy, seduction, and usury. It is also widening its scrutiny, turning its attention to Muslim converts and those suspected of being Protestants. It appears the concern over Jewish infiltration may have only been a pretext for a more thorough purging of heretical points of view.

One of the most powerful weapons given to these inquisitors is the power to confiscate property, thus adding enormous wealth to the monarchy's coffers and compromising the inquisitors' principles by making it in their interests to pursue every possible conviction. There is also the suspicion that this is all just a clever ploy to help finance a war against the Muslims residing in Grenada.

Pope Sixtus this year bestowed the title of Grand Inquisitor upon one Tomás de Torquemada, a Dominican friar who was prior of the Monastery of Santa Cruz in Segovia and later the young Queen Isabella's confessor. It was Torquemada who advised Isabella to marry King Ferdinand of Aragon in 1469 in order to consolidate their kingdoms and form a power base that he could draw upon for his own purposes.

The Inquisition has published a set of guidelines so that Catholics can inform on those neighbors they suspect of being Jewish and being insincere converts to Catholicism. The guidelines include the following signs: people wearing clean and fancy clothes on Saturdays (the Sabbath); those who clean their houses on Fridays and light candles earlier than usual on that night; those who eat unleavened bread and begin their meal with celery and lettuce during Holy Week; and people who say prayers facing a wall and bowing back and forth.

Scales of punishment continue up until the lighting of the fire. If they recant and kiss the cross, they are mercifully garroted prior to being burnt. If they simply recant,

> "YOU THINK WHEN YOU HAVE SLAIN ME YOU WILL CONQUER FRANCE, BUT THAT YOU WILL NEVER DO. THOUGH THERE WERE A HUNDRED THOUSAND GOD-DAMMEES MORE IN FRANCE THAN THERE ARE, THEY WILL NEVER CONQUER THAT KINGDOM."
>
> JOAN OF ARC
> (c. 1412–1431),
> FRENCH HEROINE

> "IT IS MUCH SAFER TO OBEY THAN TO RULE."
>
> THOMAS À KEMPIS
> (THOMAS HEMMERKEN)
> (c. 1380–1471) GERMAN
> MONK, 1403

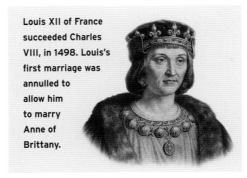

Louis XII of France succeeded Charles VIII, in 1498. Louis's first marriage was annulled to allow him to marry Anne of Brittany.

they are burned using quick-burning, seasoned wood. If they refuse to recant, these suspected criminals are burned using slow-burning green wood.

Methods of torture are equally gruesome. One example often cited is what is known as the "water cure." The accused is roped to a ladder so that their feet are higher than their head. Iron prongs hold the victim's jaw open, while their nostrils are stopped, allowing breathing only through the mouth.

With a piece of linen over the mouth, 2 pints (1 liter) of water is poured down the victim's throat, with the linen closing around the throat and not allowing the person to spit the water out. The overwhelming sensation of drowning forces the person to swallow the water. Up to 2 gallons (8 liters) would be used at any one time. Torquemada, the former friar, wrote the rules of torture himself.

Some prisoners have had a finger cut off for each day spent under torture, as a means of keeping track of how long they had been imprisoned.

Probably the most fiendish torture is the so-called "ordeal by rodents." Rats are placed on the outstretched stomach of the accused and a metal basin placed over

the rodents, trapping them. Hot coals placed on the basin cause the rats to try to escape the heat—the only way for them to go is down into the victim's stomach.

Pope Sixtus IV made a critical error in setting up the Inquisition as a royal court, with all appointments being made by the Spanish monarchy. He has, in effect, ceded all authority from the Vatican to Spain, allowing for the possibility of these awful abuses of power.

New Text Legitimizes Church Torture

Germany, 1486: The publication this year of the book *Malleus maleficarum* (*Witch's Hammer*) has seen it slowly become an influential guide for Inquisitors in the detection and punishment of witches and heretics. This disturbing and controversial witch-hunter's manual was written by two inquisitors of the Dominican order, Heinrich Kramer and Jacob Sprenger, who were empowered by Pope Innocent VIII in 1484 to prosecute witches across northern Germany.

Both men wrote prolifically, and by 1485 Kramer had drafted his comprehensive manual on witchcraft that was to be absorbed into the *Malleus maleficarum*, which draws largely upon the verse in Exodus that says "Thou shalt not suffer a witch to live," as well as from the writings of Thomas Aquinas and Saint Augustine.

During the Dark Ages of the eleventh century, the Catholic Church held that sorcery did not exist since such demoniacal powers would detract from the omnipotence of God, and that those who practiced it were guilty of nothing more than reprehensible superstition. Gaining

The Dominican friar turned Grand Inquisitor, Torquemada, at the Assembly of the Clergy with Pope Sixtus IV.

momentum in the fourteenth century, however, was the view that sorcery and witchcraft were indeed real. In many ways, *Malleus maleficarum* is the theological statement for this resurgent belief within the Church, and it is a crucial text in the legitimization of methods used for detecting and burning those found guilty of practicing the occult.

Sikh Religion Emerges

Punjab, India, 1495: Guru Nanak Dev has founded the new Sikh religion and is considered to be the first of ten "gurus." One morning when he was 28 years old, he went down to the river to bathe and meditate. After three days he returned, filled with the spirit of God, and said: "There is no Hindu and no Muslim." This is one of the pillars of Sikhism. It was then that he began his missionary work, teaching a strict monotheism (as opposed to the many gods of Hinduism) and promoting the brotherhood of humankind.

Columbus's Strange Fruit

Spain, 1496: The Spanish court is buzzing with excitement at their first taste of a succulent new fruit brought back to Europe by Christopher Columbus after his second voyage to the New World.

This exotic fruit has become known as a "pineapple" because it looks just like a large pinecone. It is native to southern Brazil and Paraguay, where it was spread by the Indians northward through South and Central America to the West Indies. Columbus discovered the fruit when he lowered anchor in a cove off the lush

Punjab artwork portraying Guru Nanak Dev, founder of the Sikh religion in India, praying with his followers.

Queen Isabella

volcanic island of Guadeloupe in 1493, and rowed ashore to inspect a deserted Carib village, where he found cultivated plants bearing fruit.

The pineapple has become a "Regal" fruit, an item of celebrity and curiosity for royal gourmets and horticulturalists alike.

Fiery Prophet of Doom Burned at the Stake

Florence, Italy, February 7, 1498: Religious zealot and reformer Girolamo Savonarola was today hanged and burned after having been convicted of treason.

Savonarola, a Dominican monk, was most incensed at the scandalous behavior of Pope Borgia and his numerous illegitimate children. From his pulpit at San Marco, Savonarola regularly denounced the Pope, the ousted Medici family, and the corrupt lives of the Florentines, and the people flocked to see and hear his sermons.

When the influential Medici family was ousted from power in 1493, Savonarola briefly had the city in his power. The population was spellbound by his religious rhetoric, which extolled the virtues of a pious and simple life without the trappings of immoral belongings and behavior. He foretold the death of Innocent VIII and the demise of the Medicis. He believed a great judgment was about to be visited upon the Church: "The Church will be scourged. The Church will be healed. This will happen soon."

In an incident earlier this year that has come to be known as the "Bonfire of the Vanities," Savonarola ordered

that all immoral and ungodly items be handed over to be burned. He organized groups of boys and girls to go throughout Florence, from house to house, begging people to give up their vanities—wigs, perfumes, cosmetics, dice, musical instruments—any worldly things that turn hearts away from Christian living.

People soon began to desert him, and when the new Pope, Alexander VI, excommunicated him and threatened to place an interdict upon Florence that would devastate commerce, the populace arrested him. At his trial, Savonarola was forced to say, under torture, that his many visions were not from God, and he was declared a heretic.

A New Look for the "Wedding Dress"

France, January 8, 1499: France, for a long time associated with the latest trends in fashion, today saw a bold new statement in bridal wear when Anne of Brittany, daughter of Duke Francis II, wore a white bridal gown for her marriage to Louis XII.

Traditionally, a bride's best dress was transformed into the wedding dress by being lavishly embellished with jewelry, embroidery, lacework and knots, tassels and ribbons, and so on. This new white dress, made especially for the wedding day celebration, is a symbol of the bride's purity and innocence—a charming and elegant new idea that seems destined to quickly become popular with many brides across the continent.

Anne of Brittany has started a trend.

Religious Leaders

Popes	Patriarchs of Constantinople
Boniface IX (1389-1404)	Matthew I (1397-1410)
Innocent VII (1404-1406)	Euthymius II (1410-1416)
Gregory XII (1406-1415)	Joseph II (1416-1439)
Martin V (1417-1431)	Metrophanes II (1440-1443)
Eugenius IV (1431-1447)	Gregory III Mammas (1443-1450)
Nicholas V (1447-1455)	Athanasius II (1450-1453)
Callixtus III (1455-1458)	Gennadius II Scholarius (1453-
Pius II (1458-1464)	1456, 1458, 1462-1463, 1464)
Paul II (1464-1471)	Isidore II Xanthopulus
Sixtus IV (1471-1484)	(1456-1457)
Innocent VIII (1484-1492)	Sophronius I Syropulus
Alexander VI (1492-1503)	(1463-1464)
	Ioasaph (1464-1466)
Antipopes	Marcus II Xylokaraves (1466)
Benedict XIII (1394-1423)	Symeon I (1466, 1471-1474,
Alexander V (1409-1410)	1481-1486)
John XXIII (1410-1415)	Dionysius I (1466-1471, 1489-1491)
Clement VIII (1423-1429)	Raphael I (1475-1476)
Benedict XIV (1425-1429,	Maximus III (1476-1481)
1430-1437)	Nephon II (1486-1488,
Felix V (1439-1449)	1497-1498)
	Maximus IV (1491-1497)
	Joachim I (1498-1502)

Montezuma II

*"I SHALL
NEVER BE A
HERETIC. I
MAY ERR IN
DISPUTE; BUT
I DO NOT WISH
TO DECIDE
ANYTHING
FINALLY. ON
THE OTHER
HAND, I AM
NOT BOUND BY
THE OPINIONS
OF MEN."*

MARTIN LUTHER
(1483–1546), GERMAN
RELIGIOUS
REFORMER, 1518

*"LET JUSTICE
BE DONE
THOUGH THE
WORLD
PERISH."*

FERDINAND I (1503–
1564), HOLY ROMAN
EMPEROR, KING OF
BOHEMIA AND
HUNGARY, OF THE
PROTESTANT
SCHMALKALDIC
LEAGUE, C. 1531

Lush New Land Discovered

Brazil, April, 1500: A vast new landmass has recently been discovered to the west of Africa, and claimed for Portugal by naval explorer Pedro Alvares Cabral.

The expedition of 13 ships, on its way to India via the south coast of Africa, had sailed far to the west to escape "the doldrums"—windless weather conditions which becalm ships—when a hitherto unknown territory was spotted. Upon landing, the fleet discovered a lush fertile land, inhabited by naked brown people who use stone tools and bows and arrows.

Two of the ship's carpenters made a wooden crucifix, which was kissed and venerated by the crew to demonstrate their devotion. The natives, while friendly, showed little interest in the religious symbolism, but were most impressed by the iron tools used to make the cross. Cabral named the land Vera Cruz, or True Cross.

Leaving behind several convicts to explore the region, Cabral has now set sail for India.

New Aztec Emperor

Mexico, 1502: Priests have recently appointed Montezuma II the ninth Aztec emperor. Montezuma has inherited from Ahuitzol an empire of six million people stretching across central America, the region recently explored by Italian explorers Christopher Columbus and Amerigo Vespucci.

Educated as a priest, Montezuma is also a successful army commander, and was chosen to ascend to the throne on the basis of his military record and reputation for piety and mercy. However, his first move was to deify himself, and to arrange for the assassination of most of the court officials.

When his supposed ally, Nezahualpilli, the king of adjoining Texcoco, came forward with menacing predictions about the imminent demise of the Aztec Empire, Montezuma was plainly shaken. The ensuing occurrence of other strange omens has only served to intensify his anxiety. Apparitions of men on horses, a smoking comet in the sky, and the destruction of the temple of Huitzilopochtli by fire unsettled him further.

Worst of all was Nezahualpilli's prediction that the creator-god Quetzalcóatl would soon return to rightfully reclaim his kingdom.

The Aztec religion requires the use of large numbers of human sacrifices to appease the gods, tearing out the hearts of their victims, so the Axtecs continually seek new sources of grist for the sacrificial mill by conquering neighboring states.

However, the vast size of the realm makes it difficult to control, and it remains to be seen whether Montezuma's former nonviolent attitude will continue, or whether he will become a pitiless autocrat like his predecessors.

Coronation of the ninth Aztec emperor, Montezuma II.

time out

Denmark's Christian II is deposed in 1523 by the Danish nobility and their allies, after a despotic 10-year reign. He is succeeded by his uncle, the Duke of Holstein who becomes known as Frederick I.

Spanish Discover New Sea

Panama, September, 1513: Spanish explorer Vasco Nuñez de Balboa has become the first European to set eyes upon a vast new ocean which he has named the "South Sea"; he has claimed it in the name of Spanish King Ferdinand II.

Born in 1475 in Jerez-de-los-Caballeros, the conquistador Balboa arrived in the New World in 1501. After failing as a plantation owner in Hispaniola, Balboa stowed away on an expedition to the Gulf of Uraba in 1511.

He took advantage of an insurrection to seize control of the expedition, then established the colony of Darien with himself as governor, and started spreading Spanish influence throughout the region, making allies of the local people.

Hearing tales from them of a large seamass to the west, and the gold treasures of Peru, he led an expedition of 190 Spaniards, about 1,000 Indian slaves, and a pack of bloodhounds across the 45-mile (about 72 km) wide isthmus which separates the two Americas.

Facing almost impenetrable jungle and hostile natives, they hacked their way towards the west for 25 days. Armed with swords, crossbows, and arquebus guns against the natives' bows, arrows, and spears, they fought a series of pitched battles, brutally defeating the natives in the uneven contests.

A witness to the continuing slaughter spoke of how the Spanish swords "hewed from one an arm, another a leg and buttock, and the head from the body at one stroke." On reaching a mountain overlooking the South Sea, Balboa climbed it alone, prayed, then summoned his men to join him.

It is expected that Balboa will be rewarded by the King with a senior position in Spain's Admiralty.

Martin Luther, shown ministering to his congregation.

Martin Luther Excommunicated

Rome, Italy, January, 1521: Pope Leo X has excommunicated reformer Martin Luther following years of acrimony caused by Luther's bitter attacks on papal corruption. Particularly incensed by the auctioning of indulgences (absolution) by Catholic priests, and by the appalling conditions he first encountered on a visit to Rome in 1510–1511, he agitated against the papacy on the grounds that priests should not stand between men and the Bible, and that faith is a gift from God, not the pope. Unlike the humanists, he does not believe faith can be achieved by scholarship.

Born in 1483 in the German town of Eiselben, Luther, son of a miner, studied at the University of Erfurt, spent three years as a monk in the Augustinian convent there, and was ordained as a priest in 1507. He then took up a position as teacher and preacher at the University of Wittenberg, where he attracted some attention for his heretical teachings.

In early October, 1517, he was dismayed to observe the travelling Dominican priest Johannes Tetzel with a Papal Bull on a scarlet velvet cushion, auctioning absolutions in public. Even if the money was to be used in the construction of St Peter's Basilica in Rome, Luther argued that it is immoral and incorrect to suggest that forgiveness of sins can be bought.

On October 31, 1517, Luther gained great notoriety by nailing to the church door in Wittenberg a statement of 95 theses on indulgences, sparked largely by his horror at Tetzel's actions in the name of the pope. Until then, Luther's actions had been largely ignored by the pope, but in 1518 he was summoned to Rome to justify his action and beliefs. Luther's reaction was to attack the papacy even more enthusiastically by way of treatises, lessons, and sermons, giving the pope no option but to excommunicate him.

It is expected that Luther will soon be summoned to Rome to justify himself to Emperor Charles V in the Diet of Worms.

Explorer Meets a Gruesome End

Philippines, April 27, 1521: The gallant Portuguese explorer Ferdinand Magellan, after surviving a tortuous voyage through previously unknown seas, has been killed by natives on the East Indies island of Cebu during a beach skirmish.

Born in 1480, Magellan explored the East Indies from 1509 to 1512. In 1519 he offered his services to Charles V, King of Spain, planning to circumnavigate the world via the East Indies in a westerly direction, a hitherto unaccomplished feat.

He embarked on August 10 with 270 men in five ships, sailing around South America through a wild passage, which he named the Straits of Magellan. He reached a calm ocean (discovered earlier by Vasco Nuñez de Balboa), which he named the Pacific. By this time, one ship had been wrecked, another turned back, and many lives had been lost. In the Pacific he was forced to scuttle a third ship due to lack of available crew members, eventually limping into Cebu.

The chief of Cebu enlisted the help of Magellan and his crew in battle. Magellan was covering the retreat of his crew when he was chopped to death.

Magellan may rightly be regarded as the first man to circumnavigate the world, since he had previously sailed from Europe to the East Indies in an easterly direction.

Martin Luther

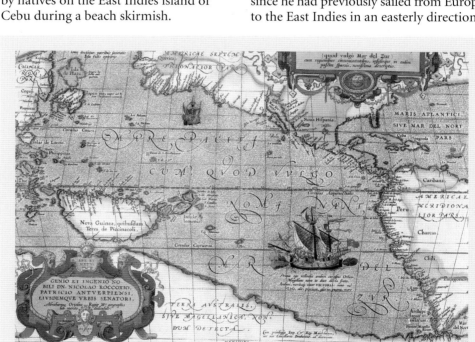

Map of the Pacific Ocean, showing Ferdinand Magellan's ship *Victoria* and the recently discovered lands.

Babur

Moguls Take North India

India, April, 1526: North India has recently capitulated to the Moguls. It took the vastly outnumbered troops of Mogul leader Babur just half a day to vanquish the army of Ibrahim Lodi, the Sultan of Delhi, at Panipat.

Facing a force of 100,000 men and 100 armored elephants, Babur's 12,000 men formed a circle of 700 carts, which they defended with artillery, a weapon not known to the Indians. By noon, the Indian army was so roundly decimated that Babur was able to undertake a classic rearguard action, completing the rout. "That mighty army in half a day was laid to dust," said Babur.

Born Zahir al-Din Muhammad in 1483 in Ferghana, central Asia, the nephew of the Sultan of Samarkand and descendant of Genghis Khan was unable to consolidate power in his homeland due to Uzbek and Persian invasions, so he turned his attention west to Afghanistan, which he conquered in 1504. Babur decided that his best chances for empire-building lay in the south. So, taking advantage of a civil war in the Afghan Lodi Empire in India which started in 1517, he invaded the Punjab in 1525 and set his sights on Delhi and Agra.

After the victory, he sent Humayun, his son, to annexe Agra, central repository of the region's vast riches, and to set up the capital. He returned with a gift—a diamond so huge that its value could provide "two and a half days' food for the whole world." Babur waved it away dismissively with the extravagance of a man who wants for nothing. The stone is called the *Koh-i-Noor* diamond.

Three times king of Ferghana (a tiny portion of the Mogul Empire) and thrice deposed, he has been both emperor and beggar. A Muslim, Babur initiated and has maintained a policy of tolerance toward his non-Muslim subjects.

Renowned Chinese Scholar Dies

China, January 10, 1529: The renowned scholar, philosopher, and soldier Wang Yang-ming has died at the age of 57.

After spending his youth in Nanking and Peking, Wang obtained the "recommended person" degree in 1492, and the "presented scholar" degree in 1499. He then served in several senior government positions, but made many enemies at court, in part because his philosophy of meditation and intuitive knowledge was seen as anti-Confucian. In 1506 he offended the powerful court eunuch Liu Jin and was banished to Kueichow for two years. On the way, he discovered that he was being shadowed by Liu Jin's agents. He escaped after leaving his clothes on a riverbank, tricking them into believing he had drowned.

Between 1510 and 1519, Wang was appointed a judge in Kwangsi, where he built up an impressive record of administration in seven months, served in a range of positions in Peking and Nanking, and suppressed several rebellions in Kwangsi and Fukien. Wang also established schools, rehabilitated numerous bandits, and reconstructed the economy. He was awarded the title Earl of Hsin-chien and promised certain hereditary privileges, but his enemies at court accused him of conspiracy and ostracized him.

From 1521 to 1527 he was in virtual retirement in his native Yueh, studying philosophy. In 1527, he was called to suppress rebellions in Kwangsi, which he achieved successfully. He died while returning to Yueh.

Henry Weds Again

England, 1536: It has been an eventful period in the personal life of Henry VIII. Catherine of Aragon, Queen of England and first wife of Henry, has recently died in exile in Huntingfordshire. Meanwhile, Henry has taken Jane Seymour as his third wife, just 11 days after the beheading of his second, Anne Boleyn, in the Tower of London on May 19.

Catherine, eldest daughter of King Ferdinand and Queen Isabella of Spain, was married to Arthur, son of Henry VII, in 1501. Following his early death, in 1504 she was betrothed to her brother-in-law Henry, then 11 years old. They married in 1509, seven weeks after his accession to the throne. Between 1510 and 1516 she bore him five children, of whom only Mary survived infancy.

Jane Seymour (1536), by Hans Holbein the Younger.

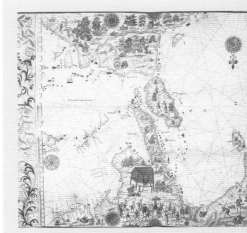

Chart of Southeast Asia (1542), by Jean Rotz.

Thereafter, Catherine's failure to produce a son and Henry's infidelities cruelled the marriage. Henry requested the Vatican for a divorce so that he could marry Anne, his latest favorite, but this was refused. This provoked Henry to break off all relations with the pope, thus drastically altering England's religious landscape forever. In January 1533, Henry married Anne anyway, later obtaining an annulment from the Archbishop of Canterbury, Thomas Cranmer.

Catherine, who had responded to all these machinations with a dignified resistance, was banished to Bedfordshire, where she refused the title of "princess dowager" and retired to lead an ascetic life.

However, Anne also failed to produce a male heir, her only children being Elizabeth (September 1533) and a stillborn son (January 1536). An arrogant woman, Anne often openly mocked Henry, and, after a secret trial, she was executed for treason arising from her alleged infidelity with her brother and four commoners, though many doubt the truth of this claim.

Jane, who was lady-in-waiting to both Catherine and Anne, is now burdened with the task of providing an heir to the English throne.

Incan Conquerer Murdered

Lima, Peru, June 26, 1541: Francisco Pizarro, Spanish conqueror of the Inca empire, has been murdered in his home by followers of his former friend and ally, Diego de Almagro.

Born in Trujillo in 1478, Pizarro served in Italy under di Cordova before traveling to the New World in 1509. He was part of Balboa's expedition which discovered the Pacific Ocean in 1513, and in 1526 he set off for Peru with Almagro. After many delays and misadventures, they reached the port of Tumbes, collecting information about the Inca empire.

In 1529, Charles V appointed Pizarro captain-general and Almagro marshal,

giving them permission to conquer the region. Using a mixture of treachery, extortion, and massacre, they spent several years ransacking the Inca riches and colonizing large tracts of northwestern South America. In 1532 Pizarro, in a brilliant surprise attack, with only 150 soldiers and about 60 horses, took just hours to capture local Inca leader Atahualpa and decimate his force of over 7,000 men. Atahualpa was murdered after paying an enormous ransom.

As Pizarro was busy founding Lima and other coastal centers, and sharing the spoils of conquest among his supporters, Almagro concentrated on plundering and spreading Spanish influence in Chile. Dissension arose between the two as Almagro, dissatisfied with his share of the Inca treasures, besieged and seized the town of Cuzco, then under Pizarro's control.

Almagro imprisoned Pizarro's brother, Hernando, who escaped and murdered Almagro in 1538. Almagro's followers returned the favor, murdering Pizarro three years later in Lima.

Seats of Power

Aztec Empire Ahuitzotl (reigned 1486-1502); Moctezuma II (Montezuma II) (1502-1520); Cuitláhuac (1520); Cuauhtémoc (1520-1521).

China Ming Dynasty: Hongzhi (reigned 1487-1505); Zhengde (1505-1521); Jiajing (1521-1566).

England Henry VII (reigned 1485-1509); Henry VIII (1509-1547); Edward VI (1547-1553).

France Louis XII (reigned 1498-1515); Francis I (1515-1547); Henry II (1547-1559).

Holy Roman Empire Maximilian I (reigned 1493-1519); Charles V (1519-1558).

Inca Empire Huayna Capac (reigned 1493-1527); Ninan Cuyochi (1527); Huáscar (1527-1532); Atahualpa (1532-1533); Tupac Huallpa (1533); Manco Inca Yupanqui (1533-1536; rebelled 1536). Spanish puppets: Paullu Inca (1537-1549); Carlos Inca (1549-1572). Government in exile: Manco Inca Yupanqui (1536-1545); Sayri Tupac Inca (1545-1560).

India Mogul Empire: Babur (reigned 1526-1530); Humayun (1530-1540); Interregnum (1540-1555).

Japan Muromachi Period: Go-Tsuchimikado (reigned 1464-1500); Go- Kashiwabara (1500-1526); Go-Nara (1526-1557).

Korea Choson Dynasty: Yeonsangun (reigned 1494-1506); Jungjong (1506-1544); Injong (1544-1545); Myeongjong (1545-1567).

Ottoman Empire Bayezid II (reigned 1481-1512); Selim I (1512-1520); Suleiman I (1520-1566).

Persia Safavid Shahs: Ismail I (reigned 1501-1524); Tahmasp (1524-1576).

Portugal Manuel I (reigned 1495-1521); Joao III (1521-1557).

Russia Tsars: Ivan IV (reigned 1547-1584).

Scotland James IV (reigned 1488-1513); James V (1513-1542); Mary (1542-1587).

Songhai Empire Askia Dynasty: Mohammed Ture the Great (reigned 1493-1528); Musa (1528-1531); Mohammed Benkan (1531-37); Isma'il (1537-1539); Ishaq I (1539-1549); Dawud (1549-1582).

Spain Habsburg Dynasty: Charles I (reigned 1516-1556).

English Flagship Sinks

Portsmouth, England, July 19, 1545: *Mary Rose*, the pride of the English Fleet, has capsized and sunk in Portsmouth harbor in most embarrassing circumstances. Following the dawn sighting of the French fleet in the Channel by an English fishing boat, the harbor became a frenzy of activity as the recently completed *Mary Rose* was hastily fitted out with new cannons for the encounter.

As the King watched from Spithead, the fleet, led by *Mary Rose*, sailed stylishly down the Solent River with billowing sails as the crews scrambled in preparation to engage the French. But a rogue gust of wind sprang up unexpectedly from the Needles Channel, causing *Mary Rose* to list wildly. Her cannons broke loose, causing such damage to the

Aztecs fight to save Tenochtitlan from Cortés.

lee side of the vessel that the esteemed flagship disappeared beneath the whitecaps in less than a minute.

Conquistador Cortés Dead

Seville, Spain, December 2, 1547: Hernando Cortés, the Spanish conquistador who conquered Mexico, has died in Spain.

Born into a noble family in Medellin in 1485, he accompanied Velazquez on his expedition to conquer Cuba in 1511. Arriving in Vera Cruz on April 21, 1519, he met Aztec envoys who mistook him for the ancient god-king Quetzalcoatl.

Cortés marched west and was at first welcomed by the Aztec ruler Montezuma in Tenochtitlan, the Aztec capital; but Cortés captured him. Uprisings and massacres ensued.

Cortés razed Tenochtitlan and built Mexico City in its place. In 1522 he was appointed captain-general and governor of New Spain.

In May 1528 Cortés returned to Spain. He went back to New Spain in 1530 but with reduced power. Poor and in ill health, he returned to Spain in 1540, and faded into obscurity.

Anne Boleyn

Maritime Exploration of Central and South America
— Columbus 1502–1504
— Cabral 1500
— Balboa 1513
— Magellan 1519–1522
— Pizarro 1526–1533
---► Cortes 1519
---► Cortes 1535

Amerigo Vespucci

> "A MAN WITH
> WINGS LARGE
> ENOUGH
> AND DULY
> ATTACHED
> MIGHT LEARN
> TO OVERCOME
> THE RESIST-
> ANCE OF THE
> AIR, AND
> CONQUERING
> IT SUCCEED IN
> SUBJUGATING
> IT AND RAISE
> HIMSELF UPON
> IT."
>
> LEONARDO DA VINCI
> (1452–1519), 1505

World Map Depicts Unknown Ocean

Saint-Dié, Lorraine, France, 1507: Martin Waldseemüller has recently unveiled a massive world map, made up of 12 sheets, each sized 18 × 24 in (45 × 60 cm). Joined together they create a vast work that covers an entire wall.

The new lands recently discovered by Columbus are named "America," after the Spanish explorer Amerigo Vespucci, who has made several expeditions to the region. Amazingly, the map shows a great oceanic mass to the west of the American continent. No such ocean is known, though its existence has long been speculated on by Columbus, Magellan, and others.

Amazingly too, there is a strait drawn across the narrow isthmus which joins the Americas. During his fourth voyage, Christopher Columbus searched in vain for such a passage to lead him to the unknown ocean. Perhaps such a waterway existed in earlier times.

Should the existence of a western ocean be confirmed, it would appear that sailors in earlier times must have known not only of the existence of a channel between the two oceans, but also of a continent situated between Europe and the East Indies, and they reflected this knowledge on at least one map; a map seen by both Columbus and Waldseemüller. There could be no other possible explanation.

Vespucci was born in Florence, Italy, in 1454, but moved to Spain where he was naturalized in 1505. He sponsored one or two of Columbus' earliest expeditions and surveyed the coast of Venezuela in his own boat in 1499. He states that he landed in the New World in 1497, and he was the first to realize that this was not Asia (as Columbus believed), but a new and separate continent. However, it seems that Columbia is a more suitable name for the newly discovered landmass than America.

Portable Timepiece Invented

Nuremberg, Germany, 1510: A portable timepiece has recently been invented by Nuremberg locksmith Peter Henlein. It is remarkably small, measuring some 4 in (10 cm) across and 3 in (7.5 cm) deep.

Such compactness has beeen made possible by Henlein's earlier invention of the coiled spring, a tiny device which stores power for gradual release. The more the spring is wound, or bent, the more energy it gains and stores. It then passes this energy on to a series of gears and through them on to the hands of the chronometer.

The main problem with the design of the timepiece is the inconsistency in the torque, or force, issued by the spring. When fully wound, the spring exerts more force than at any other time. This presents a crucial difficulty, as the timepiece gradually slows down in between windings.

Henlein and others are now working to overcome this deficiency. Current research is focused on attaching the spring to a conical spindle, whose decreasing diameter would exactly counterbalance the gradual lowering of force in the spring as it unwinds. A system of springs pulling in opposite directions is also being tested.

The first public clock in Europe was constructed in Milan in 1353, while Salisbury cathedral contains England's first example, constructed in 1386. These devices, however, are enormous, and although progressive reductions in size have occurred in the interim, we can thank Henlein for this great advance in miniaturization. Until now, no remotely portable device has existed.

The timepieces, popularly known as "Nuremberg eggs," are now under manufacture, but they are extremely expensive.

Portuguese Take Malacca

Malacca, Malaya, August 24, 1511: Malacca has fallen to the Portuguese, led by the exceptional marine strategist Alfonso d'Albuquerque.

After conquering Goa in India in 1510 and gathering information from passing seamen, Alfonso decided that, "Whoever rules Malacca has the power to throttle Venice." He collected a fleet of 18 ships and 1,400 men, consisting of 800 Portuguese and 600 Malabar Indians, and set sail from Goa, entering Malacca harbor on July 1, 1511.

Stiff resistance was encountered from the Malaccan forces of more than 20,000

time out

The rifle, a firearm where the bullet rotates before leaving the barrel thus allowing greater accuracy, is invented in 1520. There is some debate about who should have the credit—German gunsmith August Kotter, or Austrian gunsmith Gaspard Kollner.

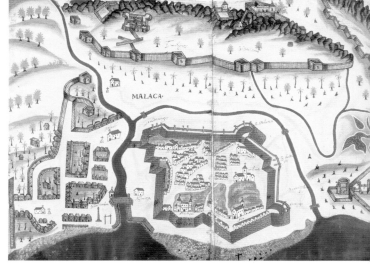

The strategic East Indies trading post of Malacca has fallen to the Portuguese.

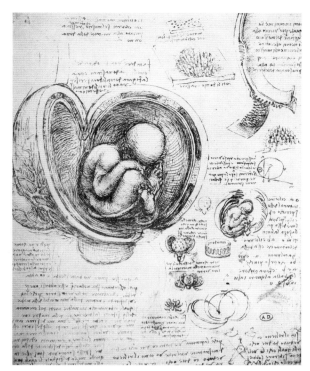

An anatomical drawing from Leonardo da Vinci's private notebooks.

The first ships to return to Portugal are laden with such sought-after spices as cloves, cinnamon, pepper, and nutmeg.

Secret Notebooks Discovered

France, 1519: Secret notebooks kept by Leonardo da Vinci, who died in May, have been discovered and released by his pupil, Francesco Melzi.

All the notes are written in reverse, and may only be viewed easily in a mirror. Some have speculated that this was to deter the prospective snoop, but it is more likely that Leonardo, being unashamedly left-handed, found it easier to write this way.

Among many other things, the books contain a stunning folio of thousands of human drawings, many represented simultaneously in four separate views. Another innovation is the technique of cross-sectional representation, which he uses to display the skull, and systems of veins, arteries, and nerves. The studies are being hailed as more accurate those in current medical books.

Leonardo observed many post-mortem dissections, and performed more than 30 himself. It is apparent that, as in every discipline he practiced, his anatomical studies represent a knowledge that was far in advance of his contemporaries.

Geometry for Making Art

Nuremberg, Germany, 1525: The acclaimed artist Albrecht Dürer has published his *Underweyssung der Messung* (*Treatise on Measurement*), a geometry manual primarily concerned with accurate artistic portrayal of the human form. Dürer has devoted the greater part of his artistic life to depicting the ideal figure, as a means to revealing his deep religious devotion. According to his own testimony, proportion should take first place, other things being attempted "only if God should give me time."

His motivation can be found in his preface to the *Treatise*. He feels that "…many young men of a happy talent for the Art Pictorial…have run riot like an unpruned tree…sane judgment abhors nothing so much as a picture perpetrated with no technical knowledge, although with plenty of care and diligence."

Like Piero della Francesca and other Italian artists, Dürer made many studies of geometrical solids and illustrated how to represent them in correct perspective.

Dürer is sponsored by humanist scholars who feel he can elevate German painting to the level of a truly serious intellectual endeavor; art would become the representational science of nature.

Albeit a brilliant and successful painter, Dürer's metal engravings, copperplates, and woodcuts are regarded as being without equal. His lasting fame is likely to rest primarily on his graphic work.

The foundation of Durer's brilliance is his passion for objective mathematical accuracy and his ability to precisely transfer three-dimensional relationships to two-dimensional surfaces.

Albrecht Dürer

men—most of them Javanese, Persian, and Turkish mercenaries—and 20 war elephants, led by commander Sultan Mahmud Syah. However, their poison arrows, small-bore guns, spears, and blowpipes were no match for the Portuguese artillery, which bombarded the Malaccan defences and overran the city in a frenzy of mass execution.

In little more than a month, the Portuguese have smashed the Malaccan Empire. Europe is now established in the Far East, and Portugal has a continuous string of cities and naval bases running all the way from the Red Sea.

Malacca commands the route between the Indian Ocean and the South China Sea, and, as one Portuguese accountant employed at the newly installed royal factory in Malacca said, "The town is of such importance and profit that it seems to me it has no equal in the world." The path is now clear for Portugal to plunder the region for its bounty.

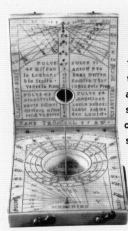

The invention of a portable chronometer by Peter Henlein in 1510 revolutionized timekeeping, but these are expensive. Portable sundials are economical, and have been used since ancient Egyptian times for timekeeping—so long as the sun shines! This ivory pocket sundial is a diptych sundial.

Europe, 1531: A comet, later known as Halley's comet, is observed.
Europe, 1531: The diving bell is invented.
Canada, March, 1536: A native remedy called *annedda* made from brewing the bark of white cedar trees cures Jacques Cartier's crew of scurvy.
Basle, Switzerland, 1536: Paracelsus publishes *Der Grossen Wundertzney* (*The Great Surgery Book*).

Italy, 1539: Olaus Magnus illustrates the first map of Scandinavia, known as the "Carta Marina."
Europe, 1540: German scientist Valerius Cordus creates ethyl ether, a synthetic ether.
Fontenay-le-Comte, France, 1540: François Viète is born.
Pistoia, Italy, 1540: Camillo Vitelli invents the first pistol.
Paris, France, 1542: Jean François Fernel's book on physiology is based on his observations as a physician and anatomist.

Tubingen, Germany, 1542: Leonhart Fuchs writes *De historia stirpium commentarii insignes* (*Notable Commentaries on the History of Plants*).
Poland, March, 1543: Copernicus publishes *Die revolutionibus orbium coelestium* (*On the Revolution of Heavenly Bodies*), which contains his theory on heliocentric motion.
Frombork, Poland, May 24, 1543: Nicolaus Copernicus, astronomer and mathematician, dies, aged 70.

Spain, 1543: The first designs for a steamboat are completed by Blasco de Garay.
Japan, 1543: Portuguese traders introduce first Western-style firearms into Japan.
Basle, Switzerland, 1543: The structure of the human body is the subject matter for *De humani corporis fabrica* (*On the Fabric of the Human Body*), written by Belgian physician Andreas Vesalius.
Germany, 1544: Valerius Cordus, botanist and physician, dies, aged 29.

Italy, 1545: The method for solving cubic and quartic equations is published for the first time in *Ars Magna* (*The Great Art*)—the work of Girolamo Cardano.
Leuven, Belgium, 1546: Gerardus Mercator, famous for his work in mapping, declares that the earth has a magnetic pole.
Knutstorp, Denmark, December 14, 1546: Tycho Brahe is born.
Verona, Italy, 1546: Girolamo Fracastoro publishes his theory of contagion of disease.

Paracelsus

> "THE DROP OF RAIN MAKETH A HOLE IN THE STONE, NOT BY VIOLENCE, BUT BY OFT FALLING."
>
> HUGH LATIMER (1485–1555) ENGLISH CLERIC, 1549

> "SINCE NOTHING STANDS IN THE WAY OF THE MOVABILITY OF THE EARTH, I BELIEVE WE MUST NOW INVESTIGATE WHETHER IT ALSO HAS SEVERAL MOTIONS, SO THAT IT CAN BE CONSIDERED ONE OF THE PLANETS."
>
> NICOLAUS COPERNICUS (1473–1543), POLISH ASTRONOMER, 1543

Firearms Revolutionize Modern Warfare

Europe, 1525: War is becoming increasingly less tactical and more dependent on logistics and technology as the cannon, arquebus (rifle), and pistol are revolutionizing the conduct of warfare.

Armies are being modified and tactics rewritten as the age of armored cavalry comes to an end.

City walls are being rebuilt, with the *trace italienne* (concentric circles of low thick walls) replacing the traditional single high wall. With cities now unconquerable by the usual method of using gunpowder to blast a hole in the wall for soldiers to pour through, new strategies, such as the siege, are being implemented.

In February this year, troops of Holy Roman Emperor Charles V decimated the French army of King Francis at Pavia in Lombardy after an apparently successful winter-long siege that had the Romans on the brink of starvation and surrender. But when the French troops made their final crucial assault, they reckoned without the effect of Spanish arquebusiers, whose weapons carried the day. The French were routed, with 6,000 casualties. King Francis' horse was shot from under him and he surrendered his sword.

Naval warfare is being transformed, too. Grappling, ramming, and boarding vessels, with the winner being decided by hand-to-hand combat, are things of the past as ships can now fire on each other from a distance, using massive cannons fired through openings in the hull.

For 12 years England has been building up a considerable navy of these new gunships. Any seafaring state wishing to have continuing influence must do the same.

Superior weaponry allowed the Romans to capture Francis I, King of France, at the Battle of Pavia in 1525.

Use of Painkilling Drug on the Rise

Europe, 1530: Opium, a rediscovered ancient medicinal plant, is becoming widely used by doctors in Europe. The eminent Swiss physician Paracelsus, experimenting with the medical value of the opium poppy, was so impressed with its analgesic (painkilling) value that he called it "laudanum," from the Latin *laudare*, to praise.

As long ago as 3400 BCE, the Sumerians called it *Hul Gil* (joy plant). The Sumerians' knowledge of poppy cultivation passed to the Assyrians, the Babylonians, and ultimately, the Egyptians. By 1300 BCE, the Egyptians were trading opium all over the Middle

Laudanum contains opium poppy seeds.

East and Europe. Throughout this period, opium's effects were considered magical or mystical. Around 400 BCE, the Greek physician Hippocrates recorded its use in relieving pain. In the first century CE, Dioscorides used opium to treat insomnia, nausea, and diarrhea. In the next century, Galen recognized its potency and used it very sparingly

Around 330 BCE, Alexander the Great introduced opium to Persia and India, where opium poppies were later cultivated on a large scale. By 400 CE, opium was introduced to China by Arab traders. The recent surge in European seafaring, exploring, and trading with the East has reintroduced the drug to Europe.

It is now being widely used for pain management, but some physicians feel the need for a note of caution. It seems that the beneficial effects of laudanum may reduce over time unless the dosage is increased, and it also appears that long-term use may lead to a dangerously debilitating physical addiction.

Book Debunks Medical Beliefs

Basle, Switzerland, 1536: Erudite traveler, physician, chemist, and writer Paracelsus last week released *Der Grossen Wundertzney (The Great Surgery Book);* a summary of his research and conclusions.

In it, he debunks many of medicine's accepted beliefs, in particular the centuries-old tenet that human illness is caused by an internal imbalance in the four body fluids, phlegm, blood, choler (yellow bile), and melancholy (black bile). He argues that the body is really a complex chemical factory, and that "outside agents" cause disease. He proposes that illnesses may be cured by selectively targeting the diseased area with medicines, and, even more contentiously, by administering a tiny dose of whatever originally made the person ill. These and many other assertions in the book have outraged his contemporaries.

Born Theophrastus Bombastus von Hohenheim in Einsieden, Switzerland, in 1493, he later took the name Paracelsus (beyond Celsus—after the first-century Roman physician who compiled an encyclopedia of medicine and other disciplines).

Paracelsus studied alchemy and chemistry at Basle University, then wandered through Europe, Russia, and the Middle East (1510–1524) acquiring great fame and gathering a huge knowledge of metals, minerals, chemistry, anatomy, and medicine, among other things. His research led him to a deep mistrust of traditional medical methods.

Paracelsus advocates the techniques of research, observation, and experimentation to improve knowledge, and he has provided great advances in the fields of pharmacy and therapeutics. His career has been dogged by controversy, with widespread disapproval of his thesis that disease is largely caused by external, rather than internal, factors. The storm of protest may have been magnified by the perception that Paracelsus is arrogant and disrespectful of his peers.

Western Arms to Fuel Japan's Civil War

Japan, 1543: Three Portuguese adventurers, the first known Europeans to set foot in Japan, have introduced shotguns to the shoguns (Japanese heads of state).

Traveling some 2,000 miles (3,200 km) north of Java with the nearby Portuguese fleet, the men disembarked on the southern island of Tanegashima to seek water and explore the new country in search of treasures. They discovered a society armed only with swords, scimitars, and a variety of other exotic manual weapons.

The Japanese, however, were already familiar with gunpowder (invented in, and imported from China), and had been using large, rudimentary Chinese guns and cannon tubes called *tepp* (iron cannon) for about 270 years before the arrival of the Portuguese.

The Portuguese guns, however, are much lighter, are detonated by a matchlock (slow fuse) firing mechanism, and are equipped with sights, making them easy to aim and very accurate.

The Portuguese demonstrated the efficiency of their arquebus gun by shooting and bringing down a flying duck in front of Tokitata, the feudal lord of the Tanegashima district. The shogun was sufficiently impressed to pay a fortune in gold for two of the guns, which he handed to his swordsmith Yatsuita, ordering him to make copies of them.

Yatsuita in turn traded his daughter to the armorer of one of the Portuguese ships in return for lessons in the manufacture of the weapon.

Japanese swordsmiths and ironsmiths are now setting up factories to commence production of the arquebuses and ammunition, which the Tanegashima troops plan to employ in the civil war that is currently ravaging Japan.

Scholar Proves Earth Circles Sun

Frombork, Poland, March, 1543: Nicolaus Copernicus has published a highly controversial treatise *De revolutionibus orbium coelestium (The Revolution of Celestial Spheres)* in which he presents his new, heliocentric view of the world.

Copernicus's model explains the observable motions of the planets—that is, the peculiar asymmetric motions of Mars and other planets—by assuming a central sun around which all planets rotate, with the slower planets having orbits farther from the sun.

It is hard to overestimate the importance of this concept. It challenges our long-held views that celestial bodies revolve around the earth, that the Earth is the center of the universe, and that, by extension, human beings are supreme in the scheme of things. The recognition that we, our planet, and indeed our solar system (and even our galaxy) are quite common in the heavens and replicated by many similar systems provides an unsettling view of the universe. All the reassurances of traditional cosmology are gone and we are left with a new, less secure view of the world.

The idea is hardly new. Aristarchus of Samothrace, the Alexandrian scholar, first proposed c. 200 BCE that the earth revolves around the sun. However, in the lack of firm evidence, and amid great opposition from the church, the notion has gained little currency until now.

Scholars who have examined the evidence are already conceding that Copernicus has proved his point beyond doubt. However, great resistance is expected from various church groups, who believe that his ideas are blasphemous and threatening to the power of God and, by implication, to the clergy.

The book was completed in 1530 and has been seen by a select few scholars. However, anticipating mortal danger in the predictable religious backlash, Copernicus withheld publication until now, when he is apparently on his deathbed.

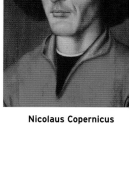

Nicolaus Copernicus

Earth Has Magnetic Pole

Leuven, Belgium, 1546: Gerardus Mercator, famous for his mapmaking, has declared that the earth has a magnetic pole.

In the fourteenth century, it was assumed that, since the compass needle appears to point to the polestar (true north), it received its attraction from the star. However, in the following century, technological advances showed that there was actually a slight deviation from true north (declination). Some attributed this to a large deposit of magnetic rock near the pole, but others disagreed, since many similar deposits are found elsewhere.

Mercator located the magnetic pole by taking precise compass measurements at different points on the earth's surface and determining the intersection point of great circles (meridians) derived from the minute variations in the compass declination at different locations.

He discovered that his great circles intersected at a single point about 300 miles (480 km) from true north, which he named the magnetic pole.

The first meeting of Europeans and Japanese occurs when a Portuguese ship lands three men on Tanegashima.

Donato Bramante

"Master of Notes" Publishes New Motet

France, 1502: The great Flemish composer Josquin des Prez has published his latest motet, the four-part *Victimae Paschali laudes* (*Praise the Paschal Victim*).

Motets are liturgical texts set to music, designed for use in church services. This one lauds the Easter (Paschal) crucifixion and resurrection of Jesus. The magnificent and highly original work expresses Josquin's unique style, with its dense texture, sections without rhythm, occasional dissonance, and exquisitely intricate five-part harmonies, with voices following and imitating each other.

Josquin's works, which include church masses and *chansons* (songs) in French, Italian, and German, are famous throughout Europe. They are regarded as models by many composers, authors, and theorists. He synthesizes two traditions—the polyphony of northern Europe and the more chordal, harmonically orientated structure of Italy.

Josquin is the favorite composer of church reformer Martin Luther, who said: "Josquin alone is the master of notes, which must do as he wishes; other composers do as the notes wish."

Sculpture Wows Crowd

Florence, Italy, September 8, 1504: An astonishing and magnificent marble statue of David, biblical vanquisher of Goliath, has been completed by Michelangelo di Lodovico Buonarroti Simoni and unveiled in Florence.

Amid tumultuous scenes of emotion and acclaim among the huge crowd present in the Piazza della Signoria, much amazement

"WHILE I THOUGHT THAT I WAS LEARNING HOW TO LIVE, I HAVE BEEN LEARNING HOW TO DIE."

LEONARDO DA VINCI
(1452–1519) ITALIAN
ARTIST AND
INVENTOR, 1508

"NATURE MADE HIM, AND THEN BROKE THE MOLD."

LUDOVICO ARIOSTO
(1474–1533), ITALIAN
POET, OF ROLAND,
ONE OF CHARLE-
MAGNE'S PALADINS,
1516

was expressed at the faultless proportions and anatomical correctness of such a huge figure. Many observers reported seeing a movement of David's muscles.

David was sculpted from a flawed and gashed 18-ft (5.5-m) marble block which had been abandoned in 1464. Michelangelo first made a wax sculpture of the figure and, matching it up with the block, calculated that he could use it if he carved the figure on a slight angle. However, that meant a single mistake would mean starting again with a different piece of stone.

He showed neither the wax nor the marble version to anyone until the unveiling of the work.

Michelangelo explained that the proportions of the 13-ft (4-m) figure on a 5-ft (1.5-m) base are designed to appear correct from the viewing height of the observer. In fact, due to perspective—the fact that distant objects appear smaller—he needed to make the feet smaller and the head larger than would be accurate, to counteract the foreshortening effect.

The sculptor also paid tribute to the extensive anatomical knowledge garnered by Leonardo da Vinci in his dissections of corpses.

There was general agreement that the creation of *David* has catapulted Michelangelo to the status of "greatest sculptor who ever lived," surpassing his mentors Donatello, Domenico Ghirlandaio, Bertoldo di Giovanni, etc. The work was originally assigned to the eminent sculptor Agostino di Duccio, then passed on to Michelangelo in 1501.

With the recent completion of Leonardo da Vinci's stunning *Mona Lisa* portrait and Michelangelo's *David*, Florence may lay claim to producing the two greatest artworks in history.

David, by Michelangelo.

Leonardo da Vinci's *La Gioconda (Mona Lisa)*.

Magnificent Plan for St Peter's

Rome, Italy, 1506: The great architect Donato Bramante has commenced work on the rebuilding of St Peter's Basilica in Rome. The design was commissioned by Pope Julius II, who is carrying out his predecessor Nicholas V's deathbed wish that Rome reclaim its standing as the world's greatest city. Accordingly, Pope Julius has also ordered Raphael to decorate his private residences, and Michelangelo to paint frescoes on the ceiling of the Sistine Chapel.

Bramante's work is well known to the pope from the Tempietto of San Pietro in Montorio he designed for him. His magnificent plan for St Peter's includes a dome 138 ft (42 m) in diameter and rising 452 ft (138 m) above the street. The dome is supported internally by four massive columns more than 60 ft (18 m) thick.

While Pope Julius's artistic taste is not questioned, great controversy has arisen over the means he is using to raise the funds for the project. The church's

practice of selling indulgences in return for absolution or other supposed favors, long the subject of attack by Erasmus, Luther, and other church reformers, has escalated significantly.

Papal envoys have been roaming the country, conjuring up the wails of the dead parents of parishioners, and demanding fees in order that their souls may be laid to rest. Critics have labeled this practice "emotional blackmail"—whether or not they have faith in the effectiveness of the exercise, they believe that selling indulgences is a sin.

Even worse, much of the money is being diverted before it reaches Rome. A prime offender is Prince Albert, the Archbishop of Mainz and Magdeburg, who is selling indulgences to repay his huge debt to the German banking company, the Fuggers of Augsburg.

om the Isenheim Altarpiece, by Matthias Grunewald (1475-1528).

Manual for Power and Influence

Florence, Italy, 1513: Niccolò Machiavelli, the prominent Italian diplomat, administrator and author, has published a novel, *Il Principe* (*The Prince*), a work that describes the means by which a prince may gain and maintain his power. The novel has received great acclaim and is regarded by many as his greatest work so far.

Machiavelli has drawn on his experiences to produce a work that has been described as sincere advice, a personal plea for political office, a detached analysis of Italian politics, evidence of early Italian nationalism, or as a political satire on the Medici rule of Florence.

From 1498 to 1512 Machiavelli served on a variety of diplomatic missions and met many important political leaders, including Louis XII of France, Cesare Borgia, Roman Emperor Maximilian I, and Pope Julius II. These experiences supplied the sources from which he drew the events and (thinly veiled) characters that illustrate *The Prince*.

In 1500 he was sent to France to obtain terms from Louis XII for continuing the war against Pisa. In Machiavelli's estimation, the king, in his conduct of affairs in Italy, later committed the five capital errors of statecraft summarized in *The Prince*, and was consequently driven out.

Machiavelli was an envoy at the court of Maximilian in 1507–1508, and attributes his many failures to his secrecy, weakness of character, and neglect of the human agencies necessary to carry out his schemes.

Machiavelli's main contention is that men are the dupes of their simplicity and greed, and in politics there are no perfectly safe courses; prudence consists in choosing the least dangerous.

time out

In 1501, Venetian printer Ottaviano Petrucci (1466-1539) prints the first volumes of sheet music. By the 1530s, music is being printed in Italy, England, France, Germany, and Netherlands.

English Novel Tells of Fantastic Land

England, 1516: Thomas More, the eminent English statesman and scholar, has published the visionary novel *Utopia*. Written in Latin, *Utopia* translates roughly as "no place" in Greek. The book progresses the cause of humanism, a philosophy which is gaining wider currency in Europe as scholars look with new interest at classical Greek and Roman writings, moving towards a more secular, logical, and scientific view of life.

Utopia was inspired by Plato's *Republic* and the accounts of explorers such as Amerigo Vespucci. More, who was under-sheriff of London under Henry VII, has created the fictional world to critique his own society, in particular the corruption of European civil and religious life. The novel is also largely based on the voyages that More has made himself, specifically to the Netherlands.

A mariner tells the story. He says he sailed on three of Vespucci's four voyages, remaining behind with others at a garrison built at the farthest point reached. From there, the mariner discovered a strange land named Utopia.

The first part of the book is a dialogue, with the mariner recounting his own philosophy and the listeners responding to his declarations.

The book's second part is a description of the idealized island kingdom, where religious freedom is total, no one owns anything, and gold and silver are worn only by prisoners (as chains!).

These are radical thoughts, and More may expect a backlash from both religious and secular authorities.

Thomas More

Niccolò Machiavelli

Leonardo da Vinci Dead

Cloux, France, May 2, 1519: The multitalented Leonardo da Vinci has died at the age of 67 in the court of King Francis of France, where he has been an honored guest for the last two years.

Born in 1452 in Vinci, Tuscany, Leonardo was the illegitimate son of Florentine notary, Ser Piero da Vinci, and a peasant girl, Caterina. He received a basic education before taking up an apprenticeship with the renowned sculptor, painter, and engineer Andrea del Verrocchio, who gave up painting when he judged a detail Leonardo had painted in his *Baptism of Christ* to be far superior to his own efforts. During his apprenticeship in Florence Leonardo painted the unfinished altarpiece *Adoration of the Magi*.

In 1582 Leonardo moved to Milan, where he lived until the French invasion of 1499, creating such works as the wall-painting *The Last Supper* and the altarpiece *The Virgin of the Rocks*.

Leonardo's art was barely influenced by past or current styles. His practice was founded on deep study of nature; and his studies of the interplay between light and shade in particular deeply influenced his two greatest contemporaries, Raphael and Michelangelo. He stressed the intellectual aspects of painting and was largely responsible for establishing the idea of the artist as a creative thinker, not merely a skilled craftsman.

Leonardo has left an enormous legacy of drawings, diagrams, and geometric studies, many unfinished. He also created plans for numerous inventions, many requiring vast technological advances before their construction could even be contemplated—for example, various flying machines. His visions for the future, in their number and variety, far surpass those of any of his contemporaries.

> "*MUSIC IS A DISCIPLINE, AND A MISTRESS OF ORDER AND GOOD MANNERS, SHE MAKES THE PEOPLE MILDER AND GENTLER, MORE MORAL AND MORE REASONABLE.*"
>
> MARTIN LUTHER (1483–1546), GERMAN RELIGIOUS REFORMER

Leonardo had a wide knowledge of many arts and sciences, including biology, anatomy, physiology, hydraulics, and aeronautics, making him by far the most widely erudite figure of our time.

Painter to Popes Dies

Rome, Italy, April, 1520: The esteemed artist Raphael (Raffaello Sanzio), believed by many to be the greatest artist who ever lived, has died in Rome.

He was born in Urbino in 1483, son of the humanist painter and writer Giovanni Santi. He studied at Perugia in Umbria with Perugino, but quickly surpassed him and moved to Florence in 1504, where he learned from the woks of Michelangelo, Leonardo da Vinci and Fra Bartolommeo.

In 1508 he was summoned to Rome by Pope Julius II and entrusted with the frescoes in one of the papal apartments in the Vatican, the *Stanza della Segnatura*. On one wall, his tour de force *The School of Athens* shows the ancient philosophers, including Plato and Aristotle, enclosed in a magnificent architectural setting. On the opposite wall is his masterpiece of perspective, *Dispute (The Disputation over the Sacrament)*, showing saints, martyrs, and doctors of the church in a wide outdoor setting. These works had an immediate and profound influence on European art.

Key Structures

Bayazid Mosque, Constantinople, Turkey
Catedral de Santiago, Antigua, Guatemala
Cathedral of St James, Sibenik, Croatia
Château de Chambord, Chambord, France
Château de Chenonceau, Loire Valley, France
Dada Hari Step Well, Ahmedabad, India
Fort St Anthony, Axim, Ghana
Grande Mosque, Niamey, Niger
Hampton Court Palace, London, England
Igreja de Sao Francisco & Capela dos Ossos, Evora, Portugal
Jeongneung Tomb, Seoul, Korea
Kasepuhan Palace, Cirebon, East Indies
King's College Chapel, Cambridge, England
La Fortaleza, San Juan, Puerto Rico
Lodhi Gardens and Tombs, Delhi, India
Mir Castle, Minsk, Belarus
Mosteiro dos Jeronimos, Belem, Portugal
Museo Alcazar de Colon, Santo Domingo, Dominican Republic
Orvietto Cathedral, Orvietto, Italy
Palacio de Cortes, Mexico City, Mexico
Palazzo de Te, Mantua, Italy
Qansuh al-Ghuri, Cairo, Egypt
Regensburg Cathedral, Regensburg, Germany
Revelin Fortress, Dubrovnik, Croatia
Riga Castle, Riga, Latvia
Seville Cathedral, Seville, Spain
Tama-u-dun Royal Tombs, Okinawa, Japan
Tanah Lot, Bali, East Indies
Torre de Belem, Lisbon, Portugal
Varlaam Monastery, Meteora, Greece

Detail from Leonardo's *The Virgin of the Rocks*.

Raphael's fresco, *The Triumph of Galatea*, is one of his fines

By 1514 Raphael was in such demand that many of his commissioned works were being completed, under loose supervision, by his students and other artists. However, the fresco *Galatea* (1512) and altarpiece *Transfiguration* (1520) are works of genius bearing the unmistakable hand of the master.

He was not a solitary genius like his contemporaries Michelangelo and Leonardo, but was renowned for his personable and compassionate nature, and commitment to humanist ideals and practice. This attitude is notably reflected in his religious paintings. His holy figures display glowing human health, serenity, and a sense of deep inner integrity, compared with Leonardo's more intellectual characterizations and Michelangelo's powerful and more symbolic depictions.

While in Rome Raphael also produced numerous portraits, worked as an architect, and undertook an archeological survey of ancient Rome.

In 1514 he succeeded Donato Bramante as the architect of St Peter's Basilica. Pope Leo X is reported to have "wept bitterly when he died."

Machiavelli Pens Guide to War

Florence, Italy, 1521: Niccolò Machiavelli's latest work, *Dell' Arte della Guerra (The Art of War)*, has recently been published. The book echoes and expands upon many of the themes and ideas from his widely-read works, *The Prince* and *The Discourses*, and outlines procedures for acquiring, protecting, and using a military force.

The book takes the form of a series of dialogues between Cosimo Rucellai, a friend of Machiavelli who died young, and citizens and captains of the Florentine republic, including Lord Fabrizio Colonna (a transparent disguise for Machiavelli himself). The book's purpose, declared by Fabrizio at the outset, is: "To honor and reward virtue, not to have contempt for poverty, to esteem the modes and orders of military discipline, to constrain citizens to love one another, to live without factions, to esteem less the private than the public good."

Machiavelli considers war to be the most significant aspect of statecraft, and regards this as his foremost work.

New Palace Shows Multicultural Influences

Cirebon, Java, East Indies, 1529: A magnificent and unique palace combining several architectural traditions has been built for local ruler Sultan Syamsuddin in the Javanese city of Cirebon.

Islam has recently taken root in Java, and Kasepuhan Palace incorporates Muslim as well as European influences, while retaining some characteristics of the local Hindu–Buddhist tradition.

Following the basic mosque design found throughout the Middle East, it features a Hindu-style split gate and pavilion. The interior includes the use of blue and crimson delft—a very fine glazed and decorated earthenware made in the Netherlands—in the floor and wall tiling. Its circular outer enclosure and immense gates and pillar bases show an affinity with the region's palaces of the pre-Islamic Majapahit kings.

Constructed alongside the town square, which is used for public gatherings and traditional ceremonies, Kasepuhan Palace faces north and has a large square field with a road surrounding it, in the customary Javanese fashion.

Illustration (1535) for Firdausi's *Shahnameh*.

Cirebon occupies a crucial position at the center of many trade routes, and over the centuries has been subjected to numerous influences from traders, explorers, expansionist forces, and missionaries. This awe-inspiring palace represents a marvellous compromise between the various influences at play in the region.

Erasmus Dead

Basle, Switzerland, July 12, 1536: Desiderius Erasmus has died. Loved by both Catholics and Protestants, he believed that mankind could learn to be good by means of diligent study of the Scriptures.

His most influential works include *Encomium moriae (In Praise of Folly)*, a satirical religious and social critique; and *Colloquia familiara*, an audacious commentary and exposé of church abuses.

His crowning achievement was the publication, in 1517, of Greek and Latin editions of the New Testament, which greatly facilitated the progress of religious and social thought in Europe.

Born Gerrit Gerritszoon in Rotterdam in 1466, the illegitimate son of a priest began life in poverty-stricken obscurity. In 1492, after six years in an Augustinian monastery, he became a priest, and private secretary to the Bishop of Cambrai. He then taught in Paris and other great cultural centers before becoming professor of both Divinity and Greek at Cambridge, where he wrote and published *In Praise of Folly* in 1509. He traveled extensively around Europe writing, teaching and meeting many of Europe's top intellectuals, including Thomas More.

Erasmus was the very model of the cultivated and dedicated scholar. The publication of *Colloquia* in 1518 inspired and helped pave the way for Martin Luther and the Reformation, though Erasmus opposed much of the dogma of the Reformers. He enjoyed great respect and fame in Basle, where he spent his last years.

Masterful Design for New Louvre

Paris, France, 1546: Work has started on the rebuilding of the Louvre, France's traditional repository of royal treasures. King Francis I has commissioned Parisian Pierre Lescot, possibly France's greatest classical architect, to design and oversee the massive revamp.

Built by Philip Augustus as a castle fortress and arsenal in 1190, the original Louvre held the royal treasures of jewels, armor, weapons, illuminated manuscripts, and other artworks. It was enlarged and beautified in the mid-1300s by Charles V (1337–1380), and used as a residence for royal visitors by his successor, Charles VI (1368–1422).

Over the last 20 years, Francis I has demolished almost all of the existing buildings and appointed Lescot to build a new palace of four wings around a square court, roughly the same size and in the same position as the original castle.

The vision is for the new Louvre to serve as the museum for France's great works of art, sculpture, and invention, and to epitomize the nation's history and culture in its grandeur and beauty.

Lescot appears to have succeeded in this—his colossal and exquisite design is widely regarded as a masterpiece. He is already renowned for such classic works as the screen of St Germain L'Auxerrois, the Fontaine des Innocents and the Hotel de Ligneris. Lescot is expected to oversee construction of the entire Louvre project, which will take many years to complete.

François Rabelais

The rebuilding of the Louvre in Paris is progressing under the direction of architect Pierre Lescot.

Machine Fights Fires

Baldassare Castiglione

Augsburg, Germany, 1518: A mobile machine for extinguishing fires has recently been invented by German goldsmith Anthony Blatner.

It is called "instrument for fires" or "water syringe" and consists of a wheeled carriage with a lever-operated water pump connected to an inbuilt tank. The carriage is pulled to the site of the fire, where firemen pump the lever to create pressure in the water tank, which in turn directs a stream of water through a movable nozzle.

Since the progressive introduction of building regulations in the last 70 years, the rate of fire damage in European cities has been falling. Augsburg's first fire-restriction law was passed in 1447. In 1466, straw and thatched roofs were prohibited in Frankfurt, followed in 1474 by a ban on the use of wooden shingles. Similar regulations have been instituted in many other European cities.

This valuable machine will further reduce the incidence of death and damage caused by fires in cities.

"THE DIVINE DRINK, WHICH BUILDS UP RESISTANCE AND FIGHTS FATIGUE…"

MONTEZUMA II (c. 1480–1520) AZTEC EMPEROR, ON COCOA, c. 1520

"I SPEAK SPANISH TO GOD, ITALIAN TO WOMEN, FRENCH TO MEN, AND GERMAN TO MY HORSE."

CHARLES V (1500–1558) HOLY ROMAN EMPEROR, 1530

Taste Sensation Arrives from New World

Europe, 1520: Chocolate, a food and drink made from the cocoa bean recently brought back from the New World, has appeared in Spain.

Chocolate soon became popular with Spanish people.

The conquistador Hernando Cortés was introduced to the creation by Montezuma, the vanquished and murdered emperor of the Aztecs.

Cortés reports that Montezuma "took no other beverage than the *chocolatl*, a potation of chocolate, flavored with vanilla and spices, and so prepared as to be reduced to a froth of the consistency of honey, which gradually dissolved in the mouth and was taken cold." The fact that Montezuma drank his *chocolatl* in golden goblets before entering his harem led Cortés to believe that the substance has aphrodisiac qualities.

The superstitious Aztecs have many gods and believe that their world is under constant threat. One god, Quetzalcoatl, creator-god and protector of agriculture, is principally associated with cocoa beans. Great temples were built to honor him.

The cocoa bean was originally brought to Spain in 1504 by Christopher Columbus after his fourth voyage to the Americas. However, the bitter beans were overlooked among the massive variety of other treasures in his cache.

Their importance was also unrecognized by English and Dutch sailors, who found cocoa beans in Spanish ships captured as they returned from the New World laden with rich plunder. In one instance, the precious beans were thrown overboard by angry sailors who thought they were sheep's droppings.

The versatile chocolate is being consumed as a hot or cold drink, a solid confection, and a seasoning for a range of sweet and savory dishes.

time out

Spanish explorer Gonzalo Jimenez de Quesada (1499–1579), conquistador of Colombia, discovers the potato in the Andes and brings it back to Europe in 1530, where it soon becomes a cheap staple food.

Innovative Agricultural Manual Published

England, 1523: *The Boke of Husbandrie*, a brilliant new treatise on agriculture, has been published by king's sergeant, eminent judge, and horsebreeder, Sir Anthony Fitzherbert of Derbyshire.

A highly detailed and practical work, its topics include the fertilization and rotation of crops, design of farms and gardens, care and breeding of animals, upkeep of buildings, legal issues, division of labor, and relations between owners, tenants, and manual workers.

Fitzherbert was knighted last year on becoming a justice of the common pleas, but his legal duties have not curbed his literary output. This year he has also published a definitive legal treatise, *Diversité de courtz et leur jurisdictions (On Courts and their jurisdictions)*, and also one on law and agriculture combined, the *Boke of Surveyinge and Improvements*, covering relations between landlord and tenant and methods of developing an estate.

Quetzalcoatl is believed to have brought cocoa as a gift from paradise.

Key Events

Europe, 1503: The pocket handkerchief becomes the smart accessory of the upper classes.

Spain, 1504: Columbus returns from the New World, bringing cocoa to Spain.

East Africa, 1505: Portuguese slave traders establish trading posts.

West Indies, 1506: The Spanish conquerors begin growing sugar cane.

Riga, Latvia, 1510: A tree is decorated and then burned in a combined Christmas and winter solstice ceremony.

England, 1511: Although he enjoys the game himself, Henry VIII confirms earlier bans on bowls for the common people.

Augsburg, Germany, 1518: Goldsmith Anthony Blatner builds the first fire engine.

England, 1518: Wine from the Champagne region is sent to England for the first time.

Mexico, 1519: Hernando Cortés uses the Aztec belief in a white god called Quetzalcoatl to help him defeat their forces.

Europe, 1520: Chocolate is brought back from Mexico.

Spain, 1521: The first "running of the bulls" takes place in Pamplona.

Mexico, 1522: The Spanish forces take grape vines to the New World.

England, 1523: A manual on agriculture is published—*The Boke of Husbandrie*, written by Anthony Fitzherbert.

Cuba, 1523: Sugar cane plantations are established in Cuba. Puerto Rico gets its first sugar processing plant.

Europe, 1523: Maize is brought back from South America.

England, 1524: Members of the English court taste turkey for the first time.

Worms, Germany, 1526: William Tyndale translates the New Testament from Latin into English, making the work accessible to a wider audience.

Agra, India, 1526: Mogul Dynasty founder Babur, emphasizing his Islamic cultural heritage, orders Persian-style gardens built in Agra.

Spain, 1528: After the conquest of Mexico, Cortés returns from New Spain bearing more than golden treasure. He introduces tomatoes, avocados, papaya, and vanilla to the Spanish palate.

Italy, 1528: No self-respecting courtier should be without a copy of Baldassare Castiglione's *Il Libro del Cortegiano (The Book of the Courtier)*—a manual on etiquette.

France, 1528: Paris officially becomes the nation's capital once more.

William Tyndale

These books expand upon the themes he developed in *La Graunde Abridgement* (1514), his summary and interpretation of the legal yearbooks, which was the first systematic attempt to provide a summary of English law; and in his edition of *Magna charta cum diversis aliis statutis* (1519).

Renowned for his integrity and ability, Fitzherbert is the sixth son of Ralph Fitzherbert of Norbury, Derbyshire, and Elizabeth Marshall. His brothers all dying young, he is expected to succeed his father as lord of the manor of Norbury, an estate granted to the family in 1125. *The Boke of Husbandrie* supersedes Walter of Henley's gardening manual, and could become England's definitive agricultural text.

Illustration from St Matthew's Gospel in Tyndale's New Testament.

English New Testament Published

Worms, Germany, 1526: The first English edition of the New Testament has been produced and published by William Tyndale. The Bristol tutor commenced the controversial work in 1522, inspired by the ignorance and corruption of local priests and the church hierarchy. He believed that "it was impossible to establish the lay people in any truth except when the Scripture were plainly laid before their eyes in their mother tongue, that they might see…the meaning of the text."

Tyndale moved from Bristol to London in 1523 to further his research, but following Bishop Tunstall's refusal to sponsor or support his translation, and amidst court intrigues and wariness about his support for the New Learning, he fled to Germany in 1524. He found a more congenial environment and encouragement to complete his work there.

Tyndale, influenced by the views of Martin Luther and drawing upon Erasmus' 1516 Greek translation, shares their ideas about the need to reform church structures—in particular, to reduce the status of local priests' "interpretations" of the Scriptures, which often lead to direct cash payments from parishioners to obtain absolution. The papal court and English bishopric have already expressed misgivings about many aspects of Tyndale's work, especially his claim that he has eliminated many fraudulent "embellishments" and laid bare the original text.

Bishop Tunstall has recently ordered the burning of hundreds of copies of the work, but many survive. Against such powerful opposition, and with the growing popularity and influence of his work, Tyndale may rightly hold concerns for his safety.

Indigo Ban Protects Jobs

France, 1528: The import and cultivation of the blue-dye plant, indigo, has been banned in Europe.

Blue dye—very costly and highly prized by the royal courts and upper classes—comes chiefly from two sources, woad and indigo. Indigo was originally cultivated in India, where it is referred to in manuscripts dating from the fourth century BCE. The Venetian explorer Marco Polo described the Indian indigo industry, and by the eleventh century, Arab traders had introduced it to the Mediterranean region, where it became a higher quality, less expensive source of blue dye.

Woad, the highest quality local source of blue dye, is indigenous to England and its use has spread throughout Europe. However, its dye is not as bright, clear, colorfast, or cheap to manufacture as that of indigo.

The process of extracting the dye from the plant is extremely long, complicated, and labor intensive, providing employment for large numbers. It is also very smelly, as it requires many weeks of fermenting in manure, which must be stirred constantly. Queen Elizabeth of England has outlawed the processing of woad within five miles of any royal estates because she loathes the stench.

The growing European trade in indigo is threatening the woad industry in England, France, and Germany, so the importation of indigo is now forbidden in these countries.

The ban is seen as a victory for the working classes, but it remains to be seen how long the ban will last in the face of demand from the upper classes for a higher quality blue dye.

Dyeing with indigo gives cloth a clearer, brighter blue.

Catherine of Aragon

> "WHO LOVES
> NOT WINE,
> WOMAN, AND
> SONG, REMAINS
> A FOOL HIS
> WHOLE LIFE
> LONG."
>
> MARTIN LUTHER (1483–1546) GERMAN RELIGIOUS REFORMER, 1530

> "APPETITE
> COMES WITH
> EATING…
> THIRST GOES
> WITH
> DRINKING."
>
> FRANÇOIS RABELAIS (c. 1494–1553), FRENCH WRITER, 1534

Spain Adopts Exotic New World Plants

Spain, 1528: Hernando Cortés, the great conquistador is back in Spain after completing his conquest of the Aztec empire and other parts of the Americas. Along with further hoards of gold, silver, and other precious minerals, this time he has delivered a treasure trove of exotic foods and other plants.

Among the most sensational are the sweet but pungent spices known as clove, cinnamon, nutmeg, and pimento.

These related plants are being added to various sweet and savory dishes, imparting a wonderful warming flavor. They have the added beneficial effect of preventing fermentation, making them efficient food preservatives and useful medicines in a variety of gastric complaints.

The tomato, a close relative of belladonna, deadly nightshade, and other poisonous plants, has been domesticated by the Americans. It is a bright red, sweet, acidic, and juicy fruit which is finding a wide variety of culinary uses, whether raw or cooked.

The orange-colored papaya is a large, very sweet, and delicious fruit, while the green avocado is a smaller, rather bland and oily fruit used mainly as a cosmetic.

Cortés also procured a wide variety of beautiful colorful flowers from the New World, including the sunflower, petunia, black-eyed Susan, dahlia, and marigold.

He also brought back an apparatus for making a chocolate drink from the cocoa beans he acquired on his 1520 expedition. Cortés blended the beverage with sugar (unknown in America) to create a fascinating and seductive drink

that is now very fashionable among the nobility. The beans are also mixed with the new flavorings now available—vanilla (a large sweet bean), nutmeg, cloves, and cinnamon.

King Charles V is particularly enamored of the chocolate infusion, which is reputed to be an aphrodisiac. He received Cortés very cordially, and made him a marquis.

Cortés and other members of the nobility have set up large plantations to propagate the new plants, which are well-suited to the Spanish climate.

Papaya, from the New World.

Hooped Fashion Spreads

England, 1530: The Spanish farthingale is now all the rage in Europe. Reputedly introduced to the English court by Catherine of Aragon (and soon copied by the French), its popularity is now spreading among the upper classes of all Europe.

One of the great advantages of the farthingale (a wide billowing hooped underskirt or "petticoat") is its ability to conceal the ample posterior of the lady who may have overindulged in the fine provender served in the courts and parlors.

Another attractive attribute is that it emphasizes the desirably slim waist of the wearer—an effect accentuated even further by the corset and bumroll, other accessories in forming an elegant silhouette.

In the finest farthingales, the hoops are made of whalebone, while the more popular and affordable versions are made from hemp rope. Ladies glide gracefully around the salons, resembling a sea of swaying birthday cakes, each bearing a single tiara candle.

Portuguese Missionary Converting Goans

Goa, India, 1542: Francis Xavier (Francisco do Yasu y Javier), Basque, Jesuit, and first Christian missionary in Asia, has arrived in India and is carrying out his mission to spread the gospel.

Last year, Francis sailed with two companions from Portugal, arriving at the recently conquered west coast colony of Goa in May 1542 after a very dangerous voyage. He proceeded to rapidly learn the local language, and wrote a catechism for the instruction of converts.

He visits prisons and hospitals, performs worship services for lepers, and walks the streets ringing a bell to call children for religious instruction. A talented tunesmith, his chief method of instructing the people is to write musical

verses in their own language setting forth the truths of the Christian faith.

The songs are written in a simple, popular style, and his doggerel directives are extremely well liked and sung everywhere. He is well loved and preaches tirelessly, to the native peoples and to the resident Europeans.

However, Francis has found to his chagrin that the Portuguese settlers and the soldiers of the protectorate are ruthless in their treatment of the local population. He has written to the King of Portugal to express his objection: "It is possible that when our Lord God calls your Highness to his Judgement that your Highness may hear angry words from him: 'Why did you not punish those who were your subjects and owned your authority, and were enemies to me in India?'"

Spanish Explorers Find "Black Gold"

North America, 1543: A new mineral treasure has recently been discovered in North America. It has been named "oil" or "black gold" by Spanish explorer Luis de Moscoso Alvarado, who led a Spanish expedition that was forced ashore on the south coast of North America and found the unusual substance floating on the surface of the water.

Alvarado had been part of Spanish conquistador Hernando de Soto's gold- and treasure-seeking expedition of 570 men and women which arrived in North America in May 1539, many hundreds of miles to the east of the find. His party became the first Europeans to penetrate

Religious Leaders

Popes
Alexander VI (1492-1503)
Pius III (1503)
Julius II (1503-1513)
Leo X (1513-1521)
Adrian VI (Hadrian) (1522-1523)
Clement VII (1523-1534)
Paul III (1534-1549)

Archbishops of Canterbury
Thomas Cranmer (1533-1556)

Patriarchs of Constantinople
Joachim I (1498-1502)
Nephon II (1502)
Pachomius I (1503-1504, 1504-1513)
Maximus IV (1504)
Theoleptus I (1513-1522)
Jeremias I (1522-1545)
Joannicus I (1546)
Dionysius II (1546-1555)

Catherine of Aragon and her ladies wear the new style.

Hernando de Soto leads an expedition in search of gold.

the southeast of North America during a long and eventful trek westwards.

In May 1541, the group arrived at a large river, which de Soto named the Rio Grande de la Florida. They followed the river downstream for another year, during which more than half of the force died from various causes. De Soto himself fell ill and died on May 21, 1542.

Led by Alvarado, the 322 remaining Spaniards continued the journey down the Rio Grande de la Florida. They reached the mouth after 17 days of constant harassment by the native Americans. They followed the coastline and discovered the oil floating in a cove. Ashore they found large oozing pits of it, which they called "seeps." They used the substance to caulk their boats and waterproof their boots.

Natives in the area use the tar-like substance found at the surface to treat a variety of ailments and to waterproof their canoes and tepees.

The viscous substance found deeper down is an excellent lubricant which could enable rapid advances in technology by increasing the efficiency and lifespan of machines with moving parts.

It is also readily combustible and has the potential to provide a cheap source of light and heat if plentiful reserves can be unearthed.

Educational Garden Established

Padua, Italy, 1544: The world's first garden devoted to the study of medicinal plants has been created at Italy's famous 322-year-old University of Padua. Designed by Andreas Moroni, it is called a "physic garden," or "botanic garden," and hopes are high that its plants will flourish.

Since medieval times, monasteries have contained dedicated herb gardens for the purpose of medicine and cuisine. The new garden, while retaining these aims, is also to be used by teachers and students for scientific and educational research. It reflects the growing influence of the experimental method that is gradually beginning to dominate scientific study.

Virtually all of the traditional esthetic and decorative garden elements, such as statues, grottoes, mazes, and fountains, are excluded. The garden does contain many exotic and hitherto unknown plant species, such as the tomato, vanilla, sunflower, and papaya, all from recently discovered parts of the world.

Other universities in Europe are in the process of setting up similar gardens.

Anti-Prayer Book Rebellion Quelled

England, 1549: The violent rebellion against the Act of Uniformity now in force in southern England has finally ended, resulting in at least 4,000 deaths.

The Act, passed by Parliament earlier this year, requires the clergy to use, from Whitsunday onwards, *The Booke of the Common Prayer*. This reformed handbook of worship is largely the work of the Archbishop of Canterbury, Thomas Cranmer. It is to meant to provide common prayer in two senses of the word: The worship of the Church of England, hitherto almost entirely in Latin, is to be in the common tongue, and usage of the book must be common to every diocese throughout the whole of the kingdom, where previously there have been several different uses.

The protest against the book has several causes. There is widespread Catholic resentment against the recent institution of the Church of England as the sole religious authority. Further, many inhabitants of southern England believe that they do not receive sufficient value for the taxes they pay to the Crown, nor from the indulgences charged by many clergymen in return for absolution and other favors. Prices of essential items have also been rising. Importantly, most of the residents of south England do not speak English, so church services have traditionally been held in Latin or local languages such as Cornish, and this is no longer allowed.

The rebellion started on Whitmonday after protesting parishioners at Samford Courtenay in Devon ran a pitchfork through a proponent of the change (a William Hellyons) on the church steps.

The rebellion spread like wildfire until King Edward VI ordered Lord John Russell to take an army, composed mainly of German and Italian mercenary gunmen, to impose a military solution.

The rebels were largely farmers armed with little more than pitchforks, and the mercenaries killed more than a thousand rebels in the first major battle at Crediton, Devon. Over the ensuing months, the protests and massacres continued and spread to Cornwall.

Another three thousand rebels were killed before the bloodshed finally ceased.

Hernando Cortés

Ruffs of various shapes and sizes are becoming very popular. Lace is used as a border or as the main material.

Elizabeth I

Ottoman Forces Take Tripoli

Libya, Africa, 1551: Ottoman forces led by Muslim admiral Sinan have conquered the Mediterranean port of Tripoli.

The occupation of the Libyan city will be of great assistance to the Ottomans in their continuing wars against Christian maritime powers in the Mediterranean. Situated on a large oasis, Tripoli has a very unsettled history, its crucial strategic position attracting a series of invaders.

Founded by the Phoenicians around 600 BCE, the city was ruled by Roman conquerors from 74 BCE until the Vandals took possession in 455 CE. In 647 CE Muslim Arabs took over, using Tripoli as a terminus for vital trans-Saharan caravan routes, and retaining domination until the conquest in 1146 by Sicilian Normans.

In 1510 Tripoli was taken for Spain by Don Pedro Navarro, who in 1523 assigned it to the Knights of St John, recently expelled by the Ottomans from their stronghold on the island of Rhodes. The Knights kept control, with some difficulty, until their recent surrender to Sinan.

This is yet another great victory to the forces of Ottoman Sultan Suleiman I.

Teen Rules Moguls

India, 1556: After the death of his father, Humayun, thirteen-year-old Akbar has become the ruler of the Mogul Empire.

Akbar was born in Umerkot, Sindh, when Humayun (the son of Emperor Babur) and his wife were fugitives, escaping toward Iran following an uprising. It is said that Humayun prophesied a bright future for his son, and thus named him Akbar, meaning "the Great."

Akbar was raised in the harsh mountain country of Afghanistan on the northern fringe of the Mogul empire, rather than in the splendor of the Delhi court. He spent his youth learning to hunt and fight, with little time for academic pursuits. He is the only illiterate Mogul ruler so far, but despite this, he shows a great desire for education on many topics. He has books read out to him by his courtiers,

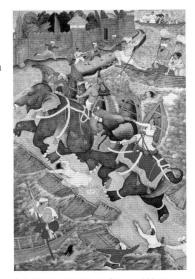

Outside the Red Fort of Agra, Akbar bravely restrains a runaway elephant.

and shows he values learning in every way.

Akbar is fortunate to have an exceptionally capable and loyal guardian in Bahram Khan, who recently led a much smaller army to an unlikely victory over Hemu, a Hindu opportunist, in Panipat, northern India.

Hemu appeared to have the upper hand when he was struck in the eye by an arrow. His army, seeing him slumped over his renowned war-elephant Hamai, fled. The unconscious Hemu was hauled before Akbar and Bahram and decapitated, possibly by Akbar himself.

Akbar's prospects as leader depend largely on the support and good advice that Bahram Khan may be able to give him, until he can rule unassisted.

New Queen for England

London, England, November 17, 1558: England has a new queen. Elizabeth, the only surviving child of Henry VIII and Anne Boleyn, has ascended the throne upon the death of her half-sister Mary.

After a life fraught with danger, religious intrigue, and a series of spurned suitors, Protestant Elizabeth is carrying England's hopes of an end to half a century of sectarian violence.

Henry had hoped that Anne would bear him a male heir, but on September 7, 1533, she gave birth to Elizabeth instead. Henry had his marriage to Anne dissolved. Anne was beheaded in 1536 on trumped-up charges of incest and promiscuity, and baby Elizabeth was banished from Court. She received a good education from her governess, Katherine Champernowne, and was an excellent student.

Tripoli has been an important trading center since it was founded by the Phoenicians in the seventh century BCE.

Key Events

Libya, Africa, 1551: Ottoman forces invade and conquer Tripoli.

Devon, England, 1552: Walter Raleigh is born.

London, England, July, 1553: Edward VI dies, and 4 days later Lady Jane Grey takes the throne. She reigns for just 9 days before being ousted.

London, England, July 19, 1553: Mary I, daughter of Henry VIII and Catherine Aragon, takes the throne and sets about re-establishing the Catholic religion into English life.

Arctic region, 1554: Hugh Willoughby, the British explorer who discovered Novaya Zemlya, perishes in the Arctic weather.

London, England, July 25, 1554: Mary I of England marries Prince Philip of Spain, but the British Parliament do not recognize him as king.

India, 1556: Humayun, Mogul of India, dies, aged 48. He is succeeded by his son Akbar.

Macau, China, 1557: Portuguese traders found the port city of Macau, the first European trading enclave in China.

France, 1558: The French retake the port of Calais, formerly an English possession.

London, England, November 17, 1558: Elizabeth I succeeds to the English throne, following the death of her half-sister, Mary I.

Amboise, France, 1560: The Huguenots fail in their attempt to capture Charles IX. This act sparks fresh religious fighting.

Spain, 1560: Madrid becomes the Spanish capital.

Spain, 1561: Philip II ends colonizing activities in Florida in the New World after a number of failed attempts.

England, 1563: Witchcraft is declared an offence punishable by death.

Manila, Philippines, 1565: First Manila galleon laden with Mexican silver arrives in the Philippines from Acapulco, inaugurating Spanish trans-Pacific trade.

Edinburgh, Scotland, June 19, 1566: James VI of Scotland is born.

Constantinople, Turkey, September, 1566: Suleiman I, Ottoman leader, dies, aged about 71. He is succeeded by his son, Selim II.

Edinburgh, Scotland, May 1567: Mary, Queen of Scots marries the Earl of Bothwell at the Palace of Holyroodhouse. Bothwell had been implicated in the murder of her second husband, Lord Darnley.

Carberry Hill, Edinburgh, Scotland, June 15, 1567: The forces of Mary, Queen of Scots, are defeated by the Protestant lords.

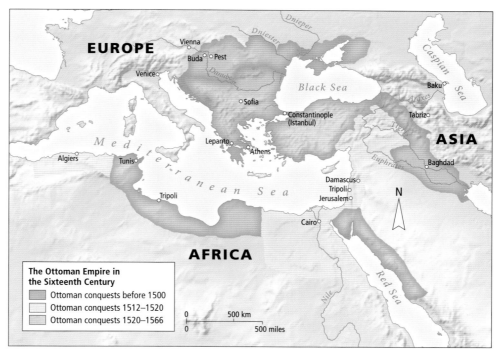

Suleiman I

Henry's next wife, Jane Seymour, did provide him with an heir—Edward, later King Edward VI. During Edward's reign, the ambitious Lord-Admiral Thomas Seymour asked for Elizabeth's hand in marriage, which she refused. Thomas and Elizabeth were suspected of plotting against the king. Elizabeth was questioned, but never charged. Seymour, however, was eventually executed for treason.

When King Edward died in 1553, the incoming Queen Mary soon married the Catholic Prince Philip of Spain and set about burning bishops and other influential Anglicans at the stake. The persecuted Protestants saw Elizabeth as their savior, since she was seen as an icon of "the new faith." Because of this, several rebellions and uprisings were made in her name, although she probably had little or no knowledge of them.

Elizabeth ascended the throne after Mary died this morning of an ovarian disease. The strong, beautiful, and highly educated Elizabeth will surely attract many new suitors.

Ottoman Leader Dead

Hungary, September, 1566: Suleiman, the revered and fearless Ottoman leader, has died while on campaign.

During his 46-year-long reign as the tenth Ottoman ruler, Suleiman's empire has become a great world power, and he was one of the pre-eminent rulers of Europe.

He personally led Ottoman armies to conquer an area stretching from the Balkan provinces to North Africa, including most of the Middle East. He achieved naval dominance in the Mediterranean Sea, the Red Sea, and the Gulf of Persia.

In Jerusalem, Suleiman introduced religious peace and freedom for Jew, Christian, and Muslim alike; the city is now open to all religions, and one may find, for the first time, a synagogue, church, and mosque in the same street.

Suleiman was known as a fair ruler and an opponent of corruption. He was a great patron of philosophy and the arts and is considered one of the greatest Islamic poets.

All other potential heirs having been murdered in various intrigues, Suleiman is succeeded by his dissolute and inept son Selim. Many observers have predicted the imminent decline of the Ottoman Empire in the absence of Suleiman's guiding hand.

time out

Charles V (1500–1558), King of Spain and Holy Roman Emperor, dies of indigestion after eating an eel pie. He had abdicated in 1556, spending the last years of his life in the monastery at Yuste.

Northwest Passage Still Eludes Explorer

London, England, 1576: British explorer Martin Frobisher has returned from the frozen lands of North America believing he is close to discovering the long-sought north-west passage to Cathay.

Frobisher's expedition consisted of two small ships, the *Gabriel* and the *Michael*, and set sail on June 7. The *Michael* had to be abandoned in a storm, but on July 28 the *Gabriel* sighted the coast of Labrador.

Some days later they reached a cove, which Frobisher named after himself. Because ice and wind prevented further travel north, Frobisher sailed westward, and the *Gabriel* reached Butcher's Island on August 18, encountering some Inuit people and swapping gifts. Five of Frobisher's men were captured there, and never seen again.

Frobisher headed home, arriving in London on October 9 with a sample of black rock flecked with gold.

Frobisher is now planning another expedition to seek mineral riches, and the elusive north-west passage.

The Inuit people were wary of strangers.

Scots' Queen Executed

Mary, Queen of Scots

Fotheringhay, England, February 8, 1587:
After almost 20 years of captivity, Mary, Queen of Scots, has been executed, on the orders of Queen Elizabeth of England.

The imprisoned daughter of King James V of Scotland and great-grand-daughter of King Henry VII of England was found guilty of treason after her correspondence, apparently advocating Elizabeth's murder, was intercepted.

Born at Linlithgow Palace, West Lothian, Scotland, in 1542, she was one week old when she became queen upon her father's death. King Henry VIII of England promptly betrothed her to his son, Prince Edward, in order to gain control of her and Scotland. However, this was annulled by the Scottish Parliament, triggering war between the two countries.

After Scotland's defeat in 1547, Mary was sent to France, where she was educated in the glittering French court of Henry II, excelling in dancing, hunting, and sports of all sorts. In 1558 she married the Dauphin, later Francis II, but was widowed two years later.

She married her English cousin, Lord Darnley, in 1565 in an attempt to gain succession to the English throne. However, his debauchery disgusted her, and he died in a mysterious explosion at Kirk o' Field in 1567. Only three months later she married Darnley's probable murderer, the Earl of Bothwell.

This fatal error of judgment led her army to desert her, whereupon in 1568 she fled to England and threw herself on the mercy of Queen Elizabeth, who promptly imprisoned her for life. As a Catholic and possible heir to the throne of England, her very presence caused much unease, and there are whispers that she was executed on trumped-up charges.

The indisputably beautiful Mary spoke six languages, played numerous musical instruments, sang well, and built a superb library which included a large collection of French and Italian poetry. She died bravely, after pardoning her executioner.

> "ENGLAND IS NOT ALL THE WORLD."
>
> MARY, QUEEN OF SCOTS (1542–1587), SAID AT HER TRIAL, 1586

> "IT IS CRUELTY TO BE HUMANE TO REBELS, AND HUMANITY IS CRUELTY."
>
> CHARLES IX (1550–1574), KING OF FRANCE, ON POWER

While the ships of the Spanish Armada anchored, waiting to take on extra soldiers, the English fleet attacked.

Spanish Armada Routed

English Channel, 1588: The English have inflicted the greatest defeat in maritime history upon the Armada of King Philip II of Spain. With approval and sponsorship from the Pope, Philip intended to invade England, end the Protestant Reformation, and recover Catholic lands and property stolen by Henry VIII.

On July 20, the 130-ship-strong Armada arrived in the English Channel and the skirmishing began. After a week of hit-and-run battles off the south coast of Devon, the English ambushed the re-grouping Spanish fleet at midnight off Calais, France. Using explosives, burning pitch, and firewood, they ignited and sunk many galleons in the ensuing firestorm.

The Spanish galleons were cumbersome ocean-going vessels with large holds designed for carrying supplies, and their purpose-built land-cannon proved very slow to reload. The English ships, on the other hand, were fast and maneuverable, having been designed to defend their coastal waters. Gun crews were able to reload their trolley-mounted portable cannons rapidly. The English were able to fire once per hour, while the Spanish struggled to get off more than one shot per day, and that of much lesser range.

The battle raged all the next day, and was not conclusive. However, the Spaniards, unaware that the English had run out of food and ammunition, retreated northward in the face of a howling south-westerly gale, which took a toll of the remaining fleet as it limped homeward.

The Spanish lost 65 ships and more than 10,000 men; the British less than 100 men and not a single ship.

Commoner Rules Japan

Japan, 1590: A common soldier's son is now master of all Japan. After centuries of warring between states, Japan is finally united under Toyotomi Hideyoshi—who is unique among all Japanese shoguns in being of humble birth.

Hideyoshi's noble predecessor Oda Nobunaga, ruler of Kyoto since his successful takeover in 1568, went about the work of conquering neighboring districts and islands as Hideyoshi rose to become his finest general. They frequently overpowered armies of much greater number with brilliant, ruthless tactics (and the use of the newly imported, mass-produced arquebus guns).

By the time of Nobunaga's murder in 1582, he controlled, directly or through vassals, 32 of the 60 Japanese provinces. In the ensuing power vacuum, as Nobunaga's sons squabbled fratricidally, Hideyoshi rose above his rivals to succeed his former lord. He conquered Shikoku, then Kyushu, finally uniting Japan by defeating the Hojo clan in the recent siege and conquest of Odawara.

A superb soldier and strategist, the new ruler is also a brilliant politician and administrator. While directing several simultaneous wars, Hideyoshi found time to decree a land survey, revise the land tax, and develop a code of maritime law. He promotes and sponsors the arts, and also encourages foreign trade. He sent delegations to the Vatican, and at first he received Jesuit missionaries cordially. However, in 1587, believing them to be a political danger because of their proselytizing zeal, he issued a decree expelling all Christian missionaries.

The Spanish Armada's first battle was off Plymouth.

Philip II

With Japan now united, Hideyoshi is believed to have set his sights on the conquest of neighboring Korea and China.

Drake Buried at Sea

Panama, January 28, 1596: The great seafarer, Sir Francis Drake, has died in the West Indies. The first Englishman to circumnavigate the earth has succumbed to dysentery off the Portobello coast, his body consigned to the depths in a lead coffin.

Drake was born in 1540 in Crowndale, Devon, to Protestant farmers who were later driven from their home by a Catholic uprising. He learned his trade in the coastal industry from age 13, and by 1565 was leading piracy expeditions to the West Indies on behalf of Queen Elizabeth.

In 1567 he led an unsuccessful raid on the Spanish fleet in Mexico, which left many English dead and saw the capture of the slave cargo and one of Elizabeth's

Sir Francis Drake, explorer.

ships. Fired by revenge, Drake went on to become England's most successful pirate, relentlessly pursuing and seizing Spanish cargoes of spice, slaves, and gold.

At the end of 1577, he became the first Englishman to sail around the world. He raided Spanish harbors in the Caribbean, traveled down the coast of South America and through the Straits of Magellan, and was the first Englishman to see the Pacific Ocean.

Drake claimed the west coast of North America for England, then sailed on to the Moluccas, where he arranged for England to run the clove trade before heading home in 1581.

He returned with enough treasure to pay off the national debt, whereupon Elizabeth knighted him. His finest hour came in 1588 when Drake, as vice-admiral of the English fleet, played a large part in the English navy's defeat of the mighty Spanish Armada.

In 1595, after a disastrous attempt to sack Lisbon, Portugal, Drake and his large flotilla sailed to the Caribbean to capture the Spanish treasure fleet. However, they were vanquished by the well-prepared Spaniards, and struck down by deadly diseases. The remnants of Drake's crew consigned his body to the water, and are now limping back to England.

Edict Quells French Religious Strife

Nantes, France, April, 1598: A shaky peace has taken hold in France, after four million deaths in almost four decades of bloody and complicated religious war.

In a diplomatic masterstroke, King Henry IV has issued the Edict of Nantes, allowing equal rights and religious freedom to both Catholics and Huguenots.

In effect, the edict creates a "state within a state" in southern France where Protestant Huguenots are now guaranteed unprecedented freedom of religion and employment in 100 towns, with full access to land, commerce, and legal systems.

Church reformation in France, as in most of Europe, has been proceeding rapidly. By 1561 there were over 2,000 French Huguenot churches, their growing influence being seen as a threat by the central Catholic administration and much of the population.

Catholic discontent erupted in a succession of popular uprisings, the most terrible being the St Bartholomew's Day massacre of 1572. Without warning, Catholic soldiers in Paris launched a strike against Protestant residential areas,

slaughtering men, women, and children indiscriminately. The attack sparked a general bloodlust that spread throughout Paris and the rest of the country like wildfire, resulting in about 100,000 deaths in the first week.

The River Seine was so polluted by corpses that for many months no fish were eaten. In the valley of the Loire, packs of wolves came down from the hills to feed upon the decomposing bodies.

Other countries were drawn into the sectarian strife, with Spain and England supporting the Catholics and Huguenots respectively. Henry, a Huguenot when he ascended the throne in 1584, converted to Catholicism in 1593. He has now negotiated one of the most far-reaching decrees of religious tolerance in history.

Many Catholics are displeased at the "perpetual and irrevocable" edict, and some areas of central France are still afflicted by skirmishing factions, but such is the war-weariness of the population that general agreement is expected.

Spanish King Dead

Madrid, Spain, September 13, 1598: Covered in ulcerous boils, King Philip II of Spain has passed away.

Philip was born at Valladolid, Spain, on May 21, 1526, the only legitimate son of Roman Emperor Charles V and Isabella, daughter of King Manuel I of Portugal. His four wives included Queen Mary I of England and Elisabeth, daughter of Henry II of France.

In 1556 Prince Philip was proclaimed king of Spain.

Under Philip's reign, Spain became the predominant European power, conquering southern Italy, Portugal, the Netherlands, much of northern Africa, and the Philippines, which were named for him.

Philip established a colony in Florida, and initiated trade across the Pacific between Asia and America in 1565. However, his star began to wane after the defeat of his armada by the British in 1588.

He was a champion of the Roman Catholic faith and sponsored the ruthless measures of the Spanish Inquisition.

Anatomy of the Inner Ear Revealed

Tycho Brahe

"YOU CANNOT TEACH A MAN ANYTHING. YOU CAN ONLY HELP HIM DISCOVER IT WITHIN HIMSELF."

GALILEO GALILEI (1564–1642), ITALIAN ASTRONOMER AND PHYSICIST

Rome, Italy, 1552: An inner ear organ has been discovered by Italian anatomist and physician Bartolommeo Eustachio (also known as Eustachius).

Dubbed the Eustachian tube, the organ connects the middle ear to the pharynx, which in turn connects the mouth and air tubes to the esophagus, or food passage.

The Eustachian tube has the effect of equalizing the pressure on either side of the eardrum, an important consideration when pressure in the ear becomes unbalanced by either a change in atmospheric pressure or by an internal malady such as inflammation of the sinus.

Eustachio has also discovered three small bones—the malleus, stapes, and stapedius—in the tympanal, or middle-ear, cavity, and revealed the complicated spiral structure of the inner-ear cochlea.

Eustachius is also the first to study accurately the anatomy of the teeth, including the phenomenon whereby the milk teeth fall out and are replaced.

He has recently completed his *Tabulae anatomicae (Anatomical Engravings)*, a series of plates that illustrates the complex internal structures of the ear, teeth, heart, brain, spinal cord, nerves, muscles, and organs of the chest and abdomen.

He dissected and investigated the detailed structure of numerous organs in great detail. He inspected features too small for unaided vision with a magnifying glass. Structures which could not be comprehended in their raw state, he treated by marination in various fluids, or rendering their details more distinct by dehydration or by injection with various solvents and dyes.

Eustachius, with his contemporary Vesalius, is credited with inventing the new science of human biology, or anatomy.

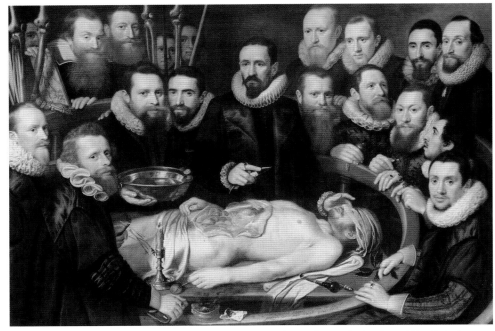

In some parts of Europe anatomy lessons feature human dissection, to the great advantage of the students.

English Lift Ban on Dissection

London, England, 1565: After years of lobbying, the Royal College of Physicians has finally been granted permission to perform dissections on human corpses, a practice that has been going on for at least the last 2,000 years.

The first recorded human dissection was in Greece in the sixth century BCE.

By 275 BCE, Herophilus in Alexandria, Greece, had founded the first school of anatomy, where he oversaw the practice of cadaver dissection. He was the first to describe the duodenum, liver, spleen, circulatory system, eye, brain tissue, and genitals, and the first to distinguish between the nerves of the sensory and motor nervous systems.

There were rumors of dismemberment and vivisection of living criminals in Alexandria during the reigns of Ptolemy II and III (285–221 BCE).

The Roman encyclopedist and physician Celsus published a famous collection of Greek medical writings around 30 CE in which he suggested that "opening the bodies of the dead…is essential to learners," even though such practices were strictly forbidden.

In 180 CE, the Greek physician Galen published several great works on anatomy, primarily from knowledge gained while performing two secret dissections.

After centuries of frequently ignored papal bans, the recognition of the value of dissection made a major resurgence around 1500, probably due largely to Leonardo da Vinci's thousands of highly detailed drawings, the results of his own observations of dissections.

Now that the Reformation has freed Protestants from Catholic rule, Parliament has passed a law allowing members of the Royal College of Physicians to dissect executed criminals, and others where surviving kin have given permission.

time out

Trigonometry tables are published in 1596 by Austrian mathematician Georg Joachim Rheticus. These are the best trigonometric tables to date, containing values for sines, tangents, and secants and their functions.

New Map is World First

Duisburg, Germany, 1569: The eminent Dutch cartographer Gerardus Mercator has published an unusual comprehensive map of the world, in 18 pages.

He has incorporated a brilliant new solution to the old problem of representing the curved surface of the earth on a flat plane. His cylindrical projection radiates out from the equator and shows, for the first time, the true positioning of east–west and north–south lines.

He produced his first map, of Palestine, in 1537, followed by a map of the world in 1538. The latter is notable for being the first to represent both the northern and southern regions of America, and for giving North America its name.

Mercator has long planned to produce a world map by combining individual maps. As part of this project he set to work mapping Europe in 1540. There were many problems with a world map, however, since the rapid increase in information coming from exploration meant that maps rapidly became outdated.

Another problem was that contemporary maps were incorrect because sailors wrongly assumed that following a particular compass course would lead them in a straight line. Mercator realized that they would follow a curve called a rhumb line.

In 1544, Mercator was charged with heresy, partly because he traveled so widely—a suspect activity—to obtain data for his maps. He was released six months later due to lack of evidence.

Further maps followed, including one of the British Isles in 1564, which was commissioned for political ends—for use by Catholics against Queen Elizabeth. Around that time he also began to perfect his pioneering new projection.

Thanks to Mercator's projection, navigators will now be able to plot their bearings as straight lines. Great advances are also expected in the fields of surveying, cartography, and astronomy.

Mercator's projection is soon adopted by mapmakers.

New Camera Turns the World on Its Head

Italy, 1570: Italian scientist and writer Giambattista della Porta has invented an improved version of the pinhole camera, or "camera obscura."

Pinhole cameras are not new; around 1460 the Italian painter and architect Leon Battista Alberti made a rudimentary version with a hole in one side and a screen opposite.

Around 1500, Leonardo da Vinci produced drawings of light rays as they enter the pinhole of a box. He demonstrated, and explained how, if objects reflect rays of light in all directions, then images can be formed "at any place" by the passage of reflected light rays through a small hole onto a screen, forming "on the opposite wall an inverted image of whatever lies outside."

For his first demonstration, della Porta made a huge "camera"— a room, in effect—in which he seated his guests, having arranged for a group of actors to perform outside. The visitors observed the images projected through a lens in the "pinhole" onto the wall of the camera.

However, the sight of upside down performers

Brahe's observatory, a center of excellence.

was too much for the viewers, who panicked and fled. Della Porta, who has long been interested in the occult, has been charged with sorcery.

Many artists are believed to be already using the camera to assist them in drawing. However, either because of the connection with the occult, or because they consider that in some way their creativity is lessened, few admit to it.

The camera obscura is certain to revolutionize the use of perspective in art, and rapidly attain use around the world.

Gerardus Mercator

New Swiss Clock Measures Minutes

Switzerland, 1577: The world's first timepiece with a separate hand for measuring minutes has been invented by Swiss mathematician Jost Bürgi. He has added the smaller minute hand into a clock made for the eminent Danish astronomer Tycho Brahe, who is in the process of mapping the movements of the heavens.

Brahe has recently set up the Castle of the Heavens observatory on the island of Hven, Denmark, and has discovered some serious inaccuracies in the existing astronomical tables.

The ability to measure movements of heavenly bodies by the minute, rather than rough fractions of an hour, will provide a quantum leap in accuracy and discovery for Brahe and other astronomers.

Mechanical clocks, using mainsprings and balance wheels, have been made in Europe for more than 100 years, but Bürgi's creation of a series of gear-wheels of sufficient precision to divide the hour into 60 identical sections marks a great advance in timekeeping.

Ambroise Paré

Jesuit Maps China

Macau, China, 1584: Matteo Ricci, the multi-talented Italian Jesuit, has produced the first European-style map of the world in Chinese. His *Great Map of Ten Thousand Countries* is a remarkable achievement, showing for the first time China's geographical position in the world, particularly in relation to oceans and landmasses.

After being educated at home by his parents, Ricci went to Rome in 1568 to study law, but was attracted to the Jesuit religious order, which he joined in 1571. He then studied mathematics, painting, and astronomy. He set out on sea voyages in 1577, arriving first in Portugal.

In 1578, he sailed to Portuguese Goa on the west coast of India, where he studied for the priesthood, becoming ordained in 1580. He then sailed to China, arriving in Portuguese Macau on the east coast in 1582. He set about studying Chinese language and culture, including the works of Confucius. Known as Li Matou, he is fully accepted in the Chinese court, dressing in the style of a mandarin scholar.

Ricci is teaching Chinese scholars the mathematical ideas he learnt in Rome—the first time that European and Chinese mathematics have interacted. He and other Jesuits are also showing the Chinese that the West possesses superior knowledge in such vital areas such as cartography and astronomy, translating accounts of western ideas and Christian doctrine into Chinese.

Ricci's radical map is regarded as being more accurate than any contemporary map of Europe, and may be expected to profoundly influence western cartography. It shows that China is only three-quarters of the breadth that was assumed by western geographers.

Although eastern Asia—China in particular—is represented clearly and with scientific precision, several of China's own cartographers, writing independently of the court, have criticized the layout as an insult to China's centrality.

Scientist Promotes Decimal System

Antwerp, Belgium, 1585: The eminent mathematician and scientist Simon Stevin has published a 29-page booklet in which he presents an elementary and thorough account of decimal fractions, *La Thiende (The Tenth)*. He says it was written for the benefit of "stargazers, surveyors, carpet-makers, wine-gaugers, mint-masters, and all kind of merchants."

Although he did not invent decimals (the Arabs and Chinese have been using them for the extraction of square roots for some five centuries), Stevin has introduced their use to mathematics in Europe, and advocates many original and practical applications for them.

He maintains that the decimal system is much more useful and practical than the current system of counting by twelves, and declares that the universal introduction of decimal coinage, measures, and weights is only a matter of time.

The eclectic Stevin has also written on many other subjects, including optics, geography, astronomy, hydrophysics, geometry, and philosophy.

Youngster Claims Invention of Microscope

Netherlands, 1590: The pioneering Dutch lens-maker Zacharias Janssen claims to have invented the radical new compound microscope that is now being produced for the scientific market. However, many are saying that, due to Zacharia's extreme youth (his exact age is unknown, but the word is that he couldn't be more than about 13 years old), it is likely that his father Hans is the true inventor.

In any case, the compound, double-lens microscope is a great advance on the single-lens version (or "magnifying glass") in use up to now.

The traditional simple microscope consists of a single, bi-convex lens (bulging outward on both sides), mounted on a plate, with an apparatus to hold firm the specimen under observation. It can magnify by up to four times.

The Janssen microscope is a cylinder with two lenses, one at each end. It comprises two tubes that slide, one within the other, and is focused by sliding the tubes. The lens in the eyepiece is bi-convex, while the lens at the far end—the objective lens—is plano-convex (flat on one side and bulging outward on the other).

The microscope also incorporates a holding mechanism and a light, and can magnify objects by three to nine times.

The invention has been welcomed by doctors, botanists, anatomists, and scientific researchers of all persuasions.

Pioneering Surgeon Dead

Paris, France, December 20, 1590: Ambroise Paré, the brilliant, compassionate, and much-loved surgeon known as the "father of modern surgery," has died.

Ambroise Paré did much to advance medical treatment.

Born near Laval, France, Paré went to Paris in 1533, where he became an apprentice barber–surgeon at the Hôtel-Dieu. He learned anatomy and surgery, and in 1537 was employed as an army surgeon.

At the time, surgeons cauterized gunshot wounds and amputations with boiling oil or a red-hot poker. On one occasion, Paré's supply of oil ran out, so he treated the wounds with a mixture of egg yolk, rose oil, and turpentine. He found

This map of the heavens by Copernicus illustrates his theory of the earth and planets circling the sun.

William Lee

astronomy, including (among many other subjects) descriptions of astronomical instruments and their use, reflections upon the theories of Regiomontanus, and much useful information for navigators and geographers.

Rheticus, one of the first scientists to adopt Copernicus' heliocentric theory, also wrote significant works on mapmaking and navigational instruments.

New Measuring Device Does It All

Padua, Italy, 1597: Scientific genius Galileo Galilei has invented the proportional compass, a multipurpose measuring tool.

The device combines two separate instruments; one for making observations, the other for solving problems in proportion, trigonometry, multiplication, and division. It also calculates various functions such as squares and cube roots. Its several scales permit simple and highly accurate reckonings by comparing the sides and angles of similar triangles.

Throughout the Renaissance, many attempts have been made to develop a universal instrument to perform arithmetical calculation and geometric operations easily—especially in the military field, where the technology of firearms requires precise mathematical data.

To satisfy these requirements, the first rudimentary proportional compasses were developed in the second half of this century. Now Galileo's geometric and military compass has incorporated and improved on these designs, resulting in an instrument of greater simplicity yet with far more wide-ranging application. It arises from Galileo's teaching and research activities in the Accademia Delia, recently founded in Padua to provide mathematical instruction for young noblemen training for a military career.

Galileo envisages a number of potential uses for his latest invention, such as for determining the distance of a star above the horizon, calculating the inclination of walled structures; and it can also be employed in battle to determine the trajectory of a cannon.

The knowledge provided by this remarkable instrument will greatly facilitate advances in the fields of astronomy, engineering, architecture, navigation, surveying, and warfare. It may be expected to open up entirely new fields of scientific research.

that this alternative treatment was much more successful. He also introduced the use of linen ligatures to stem bleeding.

In 1545 he published his findings in *The Method of Treating Wounds Made by Arquebuses and Other Guns*, which became so popular that it was translated from French into German, Spanish, English, Dutch, Italian, and Japanese. He also wrote several other pioneering medical texts.

By 1552 he had gained such popularity that he became surgeon to the king of France, eventually serving four French monarchs: Henry II, Francis II, Charles IX, and Henry III.

Paré was a pioneer of the use of prosthetics, inventing artificial hands and feet. He made "Le Petit Lorrain," a hand which is operated by springs and catches, for a French Army captain. He also invented an above-knee prosthesis, with a kneeling peg leg, artificial foot, adjustable harness, knee lock control, and other features.

His groundbreaking achievements were numerous. Unlike most surgeons, Paré resorted to surgery only when he found it absolutely necessary. He was one of the first surgeons to discard the practice of castrating patients who required surgery for a hernia. He also invented many scientific instruments, and introduced the implantation of teeth, and artificial eyes made of gold and silver.

Definitive Text Published Posthumously

Prague, Hungary, 1596: A groundbreaking mathematical work has been published

20 years after the death of its author, Georg Joachim Rheticus. His *Opus palatinum de triangulis (The Palatine Work on Triangles)*, completed in 1533 and hitherto known only to scholars, is a comprehensive treatise on trigonometric tables, combining and advancing current knowledge.

It is the first time that all six trigonometric functions (sine, cosine, tangent, secant, cosecant, cotangent) are linked and appear together for the first time. Its publication will greatly advance the fields of cartography and navigation, among other things.

Rheticus studied the works of mathematician Regiomontanus, who in 1464 published the first comprehensive treatise on trigonometry, *De triangulis omnimodis libri quinque (Of triangles of every kind in five books)*.

He later became a student of the brilliant astronomer Copernicus, influencing his well-known 1543 work *De revolutionibus orbium coelestium (On the Rotation of Planets)*, which Copernicus was still composing when Rheticus gave him a copy of *Opus* in 1539.

A second, very rare edition was published in 1541 with an appendix by Georg Peurbach, and including the complete tables by Regiomontanus. In 1561, the current third edition was completed. It contains detailed and extensive treatises on

Galileo Galilei explains his new theories.

Prophet Claims Divine Inspiration

Nostradamus

Salon, France, 1555: French doctor and self-styled prophet Michel de Nostredame, known as Nostradamus, has released a book of prophecies called *Les Prophéties (The Centuries)*.

The book maps out the earth's future in 353 quatrains (four-line verses), which are arranged non-chronologically in "centuries" of 100 verses. It makes numerous predictions, culminating 6,000 years hence in a final battle with the Antichrist and the overthrowing of Babylon, leading to a new age of peace and the Last Judgment.

Because his Jewish parents converted to Catholicism in his youth, Nostradamus was exposed to both the occult wisdom of the Kabala and the prophecies of the Bible. At home, he was educated in Hebrew, Latin, and Greek, as well as astronomy and other sciences. At the age of 19, he was sent to study medicine at the University of Montpellier, where he also studied classical Chaldean and Assyrian magic, astrology, and the writings of the Sufis.

After becoming a doctor of medicine he worked for some time as a professor, losing his wife and two children to the plague in 1534. He spent the next decade wandering Europe.

Critics have condemned his work as heretical, but Nostradamus stresses his belief in God and states that his work "has been accomplished through divine power and inspiration."

He used the power of "scrying" (divination by concentration), using a bowl of water on a tripod to focus his attention. Some claim that he also used narcotic herbs to stimulate his clairvoyant powers.

> *"ANCORA IMPARO." ("I AM STILL LEARNING.")*
>
> MICHELANGELO BUONAROTTI (1475–1564), ITALIAN ARTIST

> *"THREE BLIND MICE, SEE HOW THEY RUN!"*
>
> NURSERY RHYME, SAID TO BE ABOUT ARCHBISHOP CRANMER, BISHOP RIDLEY, AND BISHOP LATIMER, EXECUTED FOR HERESY DURING THE REIGN OF MARY I (THE "FARMER'S WIFE"), 1556

Painting Captures Failed Flight

Antwerp, Belgium, 1558: Pieter Brueghel, unquestionably the greatest Flemish painter and draftsman, has completed

The Tower of Babel by Pieter Breughel.

a marvelous artwork titled *Landscape with the Fall of Icarus*. The painting shows the vain Icarus falling into the sea after flying too close to the sun, while various ordinary people unconcernedly go about their everyday productive activities, like plowing, herding animals, and fishing.

A pictorial rendition of the classical myth of the flight of Daedalus and Icarus as told by Ovid in *The Metamorphoses*, the masterwork displays Brueghel's brilliant craftsmanship, and unsurpassed empathy and human understanding.

World Loses Beloved Sculptor

Rome, Italy, February, 1564: Michelangelo is dead. The funeral of the world's greatest all-round artist will be held in Rome, where he spent much of his life and the last 30 years.

Sculptor, architect, poet, and painter, Michelangelo Buonarroti was born on March 6, 1475, in Caprese, Italy. At the age of 13, while he was apprenticed to the artist Domenico Ghirlandaio in Florence, Michelangelo learned the art of fresco.

Michelangelo left Florence in 1494, spending the next 40 years traveling between

Michelangelo's Drunken Bacchus.

Bologna, Rome, Venice, and Florence, depending on his commissions, as well as trying to evade numerous religious and military intrigues.

All agree that Michelangelo's marble carving of *David* is the finest sculpture ever created, for its perfection of form, and its symbolic expression of the self-confident poise of the new Italian Republic. However, the painting of his frescoes on the Sistine Chapel ceiling in Rome is possibly his most praiseworthy achievement, not only for its excellence as a work of art, but also in terms of the endurance he showed in completing such a vast and uncomfortable task so quickly.

His finest sculptures also include *Bacchus* (1496–1497); the tragically expressive and yet beautiful and harmonious *Pietà (Pity)* (1499), and several representations of the Madonna.

Also a brilliant architect, the finest example of his numerous triumphs is St Peter's Basilica in Rome.

Michelangelo's frescoes, paintings, and murals also form an unrivaled catalog, but he always thought of himself first and foremost as a sculptor. He once said to the biographer Vasari, "What good I have, comes… because I sucked in chisels and hammers with my mother's milk."

Michelangelo's career was one of the major causes of the far-reaching improvement in public esteem and social rating of artists and the visual arts, for he epitomized the inspired genius— antisocial and completely engrossed in his work.

Treated with awe by his contemporaries, and loved and revered by all, it is doubtful we will ever see his likes again.

Florence, Italy, May, 1550: Giorgio Vasari's *Vita de' pui eccelenti architetti, pittori, et scultori Italiani (The Lives of the Most Excellent Italian Architects, Painters and Sculptors)* is published.

Paris, France, April 9, 1553: François Rabelais, writer, dies. His works included his 5-book series *Gargantua and Pantagruel*.

Florence, Italy, c. 1554: Benvenuto Cellini completes his bronze statue of *Perseus and Medusa*.

Salon, France, 1555: Nostradamus publishes his *Book of Prophecies*.

Antwerp, Belgium, 1558: Pieter Brueghel completes his amazing artwork *The Fall of Icarus*.

Canterbury, England, February, 1564: Christopher Marlowe is born.

Stratford-upon-Avon, England, April, 1564: William Shakespeare is born.

Rome, Italy, February, 1564: Michelangelo (Michelangelo di Lodovico Buonarroti Simoni), painter, sculptor, and architect, dies, aged 88.

Paris, France, 1565: Poet Pierre de Ronsard, one of the Pléiade group of writers, publishes *Abrégé de l'Art Poétique Français*, on literary theory.

Edirne, Turkey, 1569: Work commences on the construction of the Selim Mosque. Selim dies a year before the mosque is completed in 1595. The work is carried out by the great architect Sinan, who had previously worked on the Suleiman Mosque in Constantinople.

Venice, Italy, 1570: The architect Palladio publishes *I Quattro Libri dell' Architettura*, a series of four books on architecture.

Antwerp, Belgium, 1570: The first atlas, *Theatrum orbus terrarum (Theater of the World)* by Abraham Ortelius, is published.

London, England, 1573: The first English atlas, containing detailed maps of England and Wales—the work of Christopher Saxton—is published.

Venice, Italy, August, 1576: Tiziano Vecellio (Titian), painter, dies, aged about 88.

Azuchi, Japan, 1576: Painter Kano Eitoku pioneers new style of interior decoration for castles based on gold-leaf painted screens.

Antwerp, Belgium, June, 1577: Peter Paul Rubens is born.

France, 1580: Michel de Montaigne publishes his *Essays*.

Vicenza, Italy, August, 1580: Andrea Palladio, architect, dies, aged 72.

New Atlas Details the Whole World

Belgium, 1570: Flemish scholar and geographer Abraham Ortelius has published a revolutionary new map book (or "atlas"), *Theatrum orbus terrarum (Theater of the World)* in Antwerp.

The beautifully-bound collection of 70 map sheets, each measuring 22½ by 16¾ in (57.2 × 42.5 cm), is logically organized to represent continents, groups of regions, and nation-states, and includes relevant information and further references on each sheet's back.

It is an encyclopedic summary of cartography up to now, and, as well as Ortelius' own maps, contains many based on other sources. Some of those sources no longer exist; others are extremely rare.

The single most crucial source is last year's revolutionary 1569 world map by Gerardus Mercator, from which at least eight plates are directly derived.

Unusually, Ortelius has appended a unique list *(Catalogus Auctorum)* identifying the names of his cartographic sources, some of whom would otherwise have remained obscure. He pays special homage to Mercator, whom he had befriended as a young man in the early 1550s, and who encouraged and assisted the production of this remarkable atlas.

Ortelius is a respected student of classical history and collector of books and old coins, but has hitherto found only moderate acclamation for his map-making skills. However, he has made a living as a professional illuminator since 1554, illustrating hundreds of maps and making at least six maps of his own between 1564 and today.

Recently, European map production has been shifting from Italy to Antwerp, Ortelius's home town.

time out

In 1565, Italian composer Giovanni Pierluigi da Palestrina composes his masterpiece, *Missa Papae Marcelli,* a mass in honor of Pope Marcellus II, reportedly to persuade church authorities not to ban polyphonic music.

Painter Celebrated Color and Light

Venice, Italy, August, 1576: Titian, Venice's greatest painter, is dead.

Born Tiziano Vecellio in the small northern Italian alpine village of Pieve di Cadore, he started art training in Venice in about 1498, at the age of nine or ten. He soon fell under the influence of legendary painters Bellini and Giorgione.

Upon Bellini's death in 1516, Titian became official painter to the Republic. He was commissioned to paint a new work for the altar in the Church of Santa Maria Gloriosa dei Frari in Venice, the *Assumption of the Virgin (Assunta),* completed in 1518. Its robust colors, golden light, and enormous, gesticulating figures caused a sensation. It was immediately recognized as the highlight of Venetian art and made Titian the most celebrated painter in Venice, a status he maintained until his death.

Over the next 20 years, Titian received many prestigious commissions, including the masterpieces *The Death of St Peter Martyr,* and *The Worship of Venus.*

In 1538, he completed the amazing *Venus of Urbino,* one of numerous female

Another superb religious painting from Titian.

nudes depicting Titian's ideal of female beauty. Based on Giorgione's *Sleeping Venus,* it substitutes an immediate sensual appeal for Giorgione's heavenly aloofness.

By 1560, Titian had evolved from the precise contours and finish of his early portraits to a much bolder, freer style.

Titian was supreme in every sphere of painting, his accomplishments so diverse that he has inspired artists of very different character, and no doubt will continue to do so.

Titian

Father of Modern Italian Architecture Dead

Vicenza, Italy, August, 1580: Palladio, the renowned Italian architect, has died.

Palladio transformed modern Italian architecture, shunning Gothic ornamentation and introducing a style based on the classical Roman principles of symmetry, regularity, and correctness of detail.

Born Andrea di Pietro della Gondola in 1508 in Padua, he was apprenticed to a stonecutter when he was 13 years old. However, he broke his contract after only 18 months and fled to nearby Vicenza, where he became a superb stonemason.

In 1537, he was engaged by Trissino, one of the period's leading scholars, to assist with additions for his villa. Trissino introduced him to the principles of classical architecture, and bestowed upon Andrea the name Palladio, after Pallas Athene, the Greek goddess of wisdom.

By the 1540s, Palladio was designing country villas and urban palaces for the nobility of Vicenza, where he also designed the Basilica. In the 1560s he began working in Venice, where San Francesco della Vigna, San Giorgio Maggiore, and Il Redentore are among his finest works.

Palladio published several books, including in 1570, his masterwork, *I Quattro Libri dell' Architettura (The Four Books of Architecture),* setting out his architectural principles and enshrining his place in architectural history.

England, 1580: A printed copy of the popular folksong "Greensleeves" is now available.

England, 1582: Christopher Marlowe's play *Tambourlaine the Great* is published.

Florence, Italy, 1583: Sculptor Giovanni da Bologna completes *Rape of the Sabines* in marble.

Fatehpur Sikri, India, 1585: The city of Fatehpur Sikri is completed as the new capital for the Mogul Empire; it is soon abandoned, possibly because of inadequate water supply.

Toledo, Spain, c. 1586: The success of *The Burial of Count Orgaz* brings Domenicos Theotocopoulos (El Greco) more commissions.

Japan, 1586: Kabuki theater gains popularity in Japan.

London, England, c. 1589: Playwright Thomas Kyd writes *The Spanish Tragedy.*

England, 1591: *Astrophel and Stella,* a sonnet cycle by Sir Philip Sidney, is published posthumously. It is the first of the Elizabethan sonnets.

Venice, Italy, 1591: Work is completed on the Rialto Bridge, replacing the previous wooden structure with stone.

China, c. 1592: The novel *Xiyou ji (Journey to the West)* is published anonymously, although most believe it is the work of Wu Cheng-en.

Deptford, England, May 30, 1593: Christopher Marlowe, playwright, dies, aged 29.

Venice, Italy, 1594: Jacopo Robusti (Tintoretto) completes his painting of *Paradise,* a work on enormous scale for the Doge's Palace.

Songjiang, China, c. 1595: Painter and calligrapher Dong Qichang emerges as the leading theorist of Ming Dynasty art.

Cremona, Italy, 1596: Nicolò Amati is born.

London, England, 1596: The second half of *The Faerie Queen,* by Edmund Spenser, is published.

Isfahan, Persia, 1598: Shah Abbas I names Isfahan his capital, and makes it a showplace of Persian Islamic architecture.

London, England, 1599: The Globe Theatre opens for business.

Stratford-upon-Avon, England, 1599: William Shakespeare's output for the decade includes *Henry VI, Parts I, II, III* (in 1590); *Comedy of Errors* (in 1592); *Titus Andronicus, The Taming of the Shrew* (in 1593); *The Two Gentlemen of Verona, Love's Labour's Lost, Romeo and Juliet* (in 1594); *Richard II, A Midsummer's Night Dream* (in 1595); *King John, The Merchant of Venice* (in 1596); *Henry IV, Part I* (in 1597); *Henry IV, Part II* (in 1598); *Julius Caesar, Much Ado About Nothing, As You Like It* (in 1599).

Akbar Abandons City of Victory

India, 1585: The newly completed capital of the Mogul Empire, Fatehpur Sikri (City of Victory), has been left eerily deserted with the departure of Emperor Akbar and his armies to Lahore in the north.

Akbar commissioned the fabulous new city to celebrate his triumph in finally uniting North India under his control, and to honor the birth of his three sons (Salim, Murad, and Daniyal). Construction on the site, 23 miles (37 km) from Agra in Uttar Pradesh, commenced in 1571 and was completed earlier this year.

This magnificent palace complex, the crowning achievement of Mogul architecture, comprises two separate complexes, both of red sandstone. The royal enclosure of numerous palaces includes formal courtyards, reflecting pools, harems, tombs, and official buildings such as army barracks, audience halls, and the treasury. Alongside this impressive structure is an enormous mosque (one of the largest in the country), framed by a superb gateway. The mosque is dedicated to the Sufi saint Sheikh Salim Chishti.

The distinct architectural style blends two styles—the precise geometric Islamic approach and the more florid Hindu and Buddhist style, echoing Akbar's famous religious tolerance and encouragement of science, commerce, and the arts.

There are rumors that the city was abandoned due to an inadequate water supply, but it is difficult to believe that Akbar's architects would have overlooked such a basic necessity.

However, it seems more probable that Akbar, who has headed north with his army to deal with threats to the Mogul Empire and perhaps make new conquests, simply decided that resting on their laurels in the luxurious city would be military suicide.

Andrea Palladio

> "BOOKS MUST FOLLOW SCIENCES, AND NOT SCIENCES BOOKS."
>
> FRANCIS BACON (1561–1626), ENGLISH ESSAYIST

> "THEY ARE NEVER ALONE WHO ARE ACCOMPANIED BY NOBLE THOUGHTS."
>
> PHILIP SIDNEY (1554–1586), ENGLISH POET

Akbar astride an elephant, symbol of status and wealth.

Before the show, kabuki performers prepare for their audience with makeup and costumes.

Japanese Act Out the Forbidden

Japan, 1586: A new form of theater known as "kabuki" has appeared in Japan, and is rapidly gaining in popularity.

Kabuki directs itself at common people rather than the noble class, so the plays are passionate, lurid, sometimes violent, and often scandalous. Because the plays deal primarily with topics forbidden in the highly formalized Japanese society, the playwrights cleverly write history plays, using historical incidents—most of which are familiar to the audience—to discuss contemporary politics and scandals.

They bravely battle censors, producing plays on taboo topics in a forum where social and cultural anxieties can be worked out. It is strident lower-class entertainment that includes spectacular and gory formal fight scenes and dances.

The actors' movements are exaggerated, formal, and conventionalized. They speak in a rhythmic musical style with musical accompaniment from a hidden orchestra. Each time an actor moves, a member of the *geza* orchestra beats time on a wooden block.

Costumes are elaborate and extravagant, as the play itself is full of spectacle and special effects. Lightning-fast costume changes are performed onstage.

The plays don't really have scripts; the playwright writes out a set of basic situations, leaving the actors to ad-lib most of the actions and speeches.

Even though actors are considered the lowest form of human life in Japan (classed among animals in some censuses), audiences are nonetheless enamored and enthralled by their skills. Enthusiasts may even join a fan group for their favorite kabuki actor or troupe.

Controversial Bridge Completed

Venice, Italy, 1591: A controversial new bridge across the Grand Canal in Venice, *Ponte di Rialto*, has been completed.

It is remarkably similar to the wooden bridge it succeeded, featuring two inclined ramps with rows of shops on either side leading up to a central porch. The original

Key Structures

Azuchi Castle, Lake Biwa, Japan
Casa de Azulejos, Mexico City, Mexico
Cathedral of San Ildefonso, Merida, Mexico
Cathedral of St Basil, Moscow, Russia
Fatehpur Sikri, near Agra, India
Fort Jesus, Mombasa, Kenya
Fort St Elmo, Valletta, Malta
Ghent Cathedral, Ghent, Belgium
Globe Theatre, London, England
Gwanwangmyo Shrine, Andong, Korea
Japanese Covered Bridge, Hoi An, Vietnam
Kronborg Castle, Elsinore, Denmark
Library of St Walburga, Zutphen, Netherlands
Litomysl Castle, Czech Republic
Mausoleum of Humayun, Delhi, India
Olavinlinna Castle, Savonlinna, Finland
Palace of Charles V, Granada, Spain
Palazzo Chiericati, Vicenza, Italy
Pha That Luang, Vientiane, Laos
Rialto Bridge, Venice, Italy
San Pedro de Andahuaylillas, Andahuaylillas, Peru
Santa Catalina Monastery, Arequipa, Peru
Segovia Cathedral, Segovia, Spain
Selim Mosque, Edirne, Turkey
Simsujong Pavilion, Yangdong, Korea
Stari Most, Mostar, Bosnia
Suleiman Mosque, Constantinople, Turkey
Taleju Temple, Kathmandu, Nepal
Teatro Olimpico, Vicenza, Italy
The Escorial, near Madrid, Spain
Villa Farnese, near Viterbo, Italy
Wat Xieng Thong, Luang Prabang, Laos
Woolaton Hall, Nottinghamshire, England

pontoon bridge, built in 1181, was replaced around 1250 by a wooden bridge, with a movable central section that could be raised to allow the passage of tall ships. It was partly burnt in a revolt in 1310, and collapsed in 1444 and 1524 under the weight of crowds watching boat parades.

In 1551 Venetian authorities requested proposals to rebuild the bridge. Plans were tendered by several famous architects, but most involved a classical approach with several arches, and these were judged to be inappropriate to the situation.

Instead, radical architect Antonio da Ponte's austere unadorned single-span design was chosen. The engineering of the bridge is considered so audaciously simple, that several eminent architects are predicting its imminent collapse.

Hints of Intrigue at Playwright's Death

Deptford, England, May 30, 1593: Brilliant and promising dramatist Christopher Marlowe has died in Kent, at the age of 29. Mystery surrounds the circumstances of his passing, with several different theories doing the rounds. In the official version of events, he became involved in a brawl at the Bull's Tavern in Deptford, where he was meeting with three men, possibly secret agents. During the fracas, Marlowe received a stab to the right eye, dying instantly. However, there are few, if any, reliable witnesses to this.

Some have speculated that Marlowe faked his death, and fled to Italy to avoid various dangers, and that he plans to secretly publish his plays under Shakespeare's name. He had certainly attracted

attention for his very public espousal of atheist views, with rumors that agents of the Court were planning to murder him.

His life was in many ways dissolute; he was fond of mingling with commonfolk in public houses, and is known to have made many enemies. In 1589, his friend, the sonneteer Thomas Watson, killed a man in a street fight after coming to Marlowe's assistance.

Born in Canterbury in 1564, he studied at the King's School and Cambridge, graduating as Master of Arts in 1587.

His dark, sometimes violent lifestyle is reflected in his seven plays, which include *The Jew of Malta*, *The Massacre at Paris*, and *Dr Faustus*.

Marlowe moved away from the tradition of writing on religious topics, basing his themes on

A model of the Globe Theater in London.

individuals and their motives, using well-known historical events or classical legends as the setting. He published several other snippets and translations, ranging from the ordinary to the superb.

Recently William Shakespeare has written several brilliant tragedies, which clearly give a nod to the Marlowe influence—in fact, there is speculation that the two collaborated on the recently published and highly popular *Henry VI* and *Titus Andronicus*.

Christopher Marlowe's elegant and spare style has set a new standard for the emerging "blank verse" fashion, making

his dramatic predecessors appear mundane and wooden by comparison.

Shakespeare Unveils Two New Plays

London, England, 1594: The darling of England's theater set has produced two new plays, *Titus Andronicus* and *The Taming of the Shrew*.

The brilliant actor, poet, and playwright William Shakespeare has recently returned to London from an acting tour of the provinces with his "Strange's Men" troupe, featuring these plays, along with his *Romeo and Juliet*.

Titus Andronicus, inspired by Thomas Kyd's *The Spanish Tragedy*, is a gruesome tragedy with several appallingly violent scenes. Through the leading female character, Lavinia, Shakespeare examines various aspects of a woman's sexual status, first as virgin daughter, then chaste wife, and finally maimed widow. The play includes mutilation, dismemberment, tongue-ripping, and rape, and is wildly popular with audiences.

It is widely believed that Shakespeare collaborated with the recently deceased Christopher Marlowe on *Titus*, and also on the recent three-part historical drama *Henry VI*, but Shakespeare will not be drawn on this speculation.

The Taming of the Shrew is a lively comic satire, dealing with the ever-changing relationships between several courting couples. Full of action, intrigue, and deception, the numerous plots and sub-plots revolve around the age-old "battle of the sexes." It mixes English comedy with French farce and the new Italian comedy heavily influenced by *Commedia dell'arte*.

These two new plays, along with the romantic tragedy *Romeo and Juliet*, show the emerging young playwright to be a master of diverse styles.

An unpublished folio of several dozen brilliant sonnets by Shakespeare is being circulated in London. He has also recently produced two narrative poems; *Venus and Adonis* and *The Rape of Lucrece*. The first of these, with its "unpolished lines," is dedicated to his noble patron, the Earl of Southampton.

Life in the professional theater can be risky, especially as Parliament is soon expected to order the indefinite closing of all English theaters as a result of the latest plague which is ravaging London.

William Shakespeare

A view of the Rialto Bridge in Venice—built in only three years, it provides a secure walkway across the Grand Canal.

John Calvin

"UNLESS A MAN FEELS HE HAS A GOOD ENOUGH MEMORY, HE SHOULD NEVER VENTURE TO LIE."

MICHEL DE MONTAIGNE (1533–1592) FRENCH ESSAYIST, 1580

"FOOTEBALL... CAUSETH FIGHTING, BRAWLING, CONTENTION, QUARREL PICKING, MURDER, HOMICIDE AND GREAT EFFUSION OF BLOODE..."

PHILIP STUBBS (FL. 1583–1591) ENGLISH PURITAN, 1583

Introduced Species Changing American Life

North America, 1550: The domestic animals imported by the Spanish to North America are proving a mixed blessing for both the Spaniards and the local Indian people.

Every Spanish expedition to the New World since Columbus's second journey has included livestock of various sorts, and these have spread rapidly throughout the continent and nearby islands, many becoming wild.

The first animals imported were horses (to assist in the conquest), pigs, poultry (for rapid breeding), and cattle, while subsequent journeys transported sheep, goats, and pigeons.

Many of these were let loose on La Española and other occupied islands in the Caribbean, where they bred rapidly with abundant food and without the diseases found in Europe. They are now being imported to the mainland for the benefit of the colonial forces.

In the unfenced agricultural areas of Indian cultivation, the unrestricted trampling and foraging of cattle, sheep,

The gardens of the Indian town of Secota, Virginia.

and goats has caused severe damage to local crops, to the growers' dismay.

On the other hand, the rapidly proliferating herds of wild cattle spreading through the grasslands provide a much more abundant food supply than the meager forms of game and plant life on which the Indians have traditionally subsisted. Indeed, they are now in control of some of the feral horses that roam through the region, and have gained greater mobility than their forefathers had. The Indians are now posing a military threat, giving the Spanish some of the most serious opposition they have encountered anywhere in the New World.

Strict Bans Issued by Straightlaced Reformer

Geneva, Switzerland, 1552: Dancing, along with other pastimes seen as irreligious, has been banned by Protestant reformer, John Calvin. He has spent the last 11 years in Geneva, successfully reorganizing the church and state, putting into place the principles contained in his *Ecclesiastical Ordinances* amid widespread opposition.

The brilliant, though uncompromising Calvin has encountered opposition before. In 1533, while preaching his Reformist doctrine in Paris, he was forced to leave by followers of Catholic King Francis I.

He fled to Basle, Switzerland, where he learned Hebrew and issued his influential *Christianae religionis institutio (Institutes of the Christian Religion)* with a scathing preface addressed to King Francis.

In 1536, he was invited to Geneva to assist with the Reformation. He issued his *Protestant Confession of Faith*, an ethical and religious primer in which moral rigor takes the place of immoderation.

In the face of a backlash from libertine and other forces, who resented the drastic changes he was instituting, he retired to

Strasbourg in 1538, where he studied the New Testament, marrying in 1539.

However, he was recalled to Geneva in 1541, and commissioned with the task of reducing decadent influences on civic and religious life. That year, he issued his *Ecclesiastical Ordinances*, which clearly lay down what is right and wrong, and demand strict moral order along with unswerving religious conformity in order to improve the spiritual health of the local citizenry.

Despite strong opposition from many sides—not least, the entrenched, rigorous theocracy—Calvin's ordinances are now entrenched in law, and are accepted as the basis of management of church and state in Geneva. They regulate funerals, weddings, and so on, but also restrict many everyday activities, including the wearing of slashed breeches; the use of traditional folk remedies; and many popular games and pastimes, such as dancing, which is seen as inflaming the baser passions.

time out

The first running with the bulls occurs in 1591, when a group of men runs in front of the bulls that are being taken from the corral to the bullring, through the streets of Pamplona, Spain.

Windswept Golf Course is World's Best

Scotland, 1552: The finest golf course in the world has opened on a windswept clifftop at St Andrews, Scotland.

Archbishop Hamilton recently released a charter in which the people of Fife are reserved the right to use the venue "for golff, futball, shuteing and all gamis" (golf, football, shooting, and all games). Permission has also been granted for a local gentleman to set up a rabbit warren on the site.

However, golf has not always enjoyed such official approval. In 1457, James II banned "futball and ye golff" because their popularity was interfering with his subjects' compulsory archery practice and preparations for war against England.

Key Events

England, 1550: The first record of the game of cricket appears.

North America, 1550: The Spanish take cattle and livestock to North America.

Constantinople, Turkey, 1550: The first coffee shop opens.

Europe, 1550: The treadle-operated spinning wheel comes into use.

England, 1552: Legislation to regulate alehouses is enacted, introducing liquor licencing.

Geneva, Switzerland, 1552: John Calvin bans dancing.

Scotland, 1552: Laws forbidding golf are relaxed, and the course at St Andrews is established.

Delhi, India, 1555: Emperor Akbar abolishes all religious tests for citizenship in the Mogul Empire, and proclaims religious toleration.

Spain, 1555: The Spanish bring back tobacco from the New World.

China, January 23, 1556: An earthquake rocks Shaanxi Province; more than 800,000 people are killed.

Rome, Italy, July 31, 1556: Ignatius of Loyola, founder of the Society of Jesus (the Jesuits), dies, aged about 64.

England, March 21, 1556: Under Mary I's policy of burning Protestants, Thomas Cramner is burned alive at Oxford, where Bishop Latimer and Bishop Ridley were burned in 1555.

France, 1560: Broccoli appears in France. It is believed to have been introduced to the French court by Catherine de' Medici, the bride-to-be of Henry II of France.

Spain, 1561: Priest Ruy Lopez writes a book on chess, focusing on opening gambits (a word he introduced).

Europe, 1562: Tulips are introduced from Turkey.

London, England, 1563: John Foxe's *Book of Martyrs* is published in English, four years after its first Latin edition.

London, England, 1563: Elizabeth I establishes the Church of England, including some Catholic and some Protestant ideas.

Europe, 1563: Plague sweeps through the continent, and in London alone more than 20,000 people die as a result.

England, 1565: John Hawkins introduces tobacco to England, a year after bringing in the sweet potato.

Canada, 1565: Basque people (from Spain) continue to fish for cod and whale off the coast of Newfoundland.

Brazil, 1565: The city of São Sebastião do Rio de Janeiro is founded.

Golf's popularity in Scotland continued undiminished throughout the years the game was banned.

The ban was never entirely successful, with the game continuing to be played on clandestine courses in remote areas.

The ban was confirmed by Parliament in 1470 and 1491, and golf remained illegal until 1502, when King James IV signed the Treaty of Glasgow, ending the wars between England and Scotland.

It probably helped that James, who approved and authorized the 1491 ban, became a keen player—though the game's illegal status restricted him to the royal grounds. He didn't dilly-dally; Treasury records in 1502 show that just after the ban was lifted, he paid 14 shillings for some clubs, while other entries show bills for balls. It is also recorded that he lost a 14-shilling wager, on a game with the Earl of Bothwell.

Though the game's exact origins are unknown, it is believed that the game was being played in St Andrews well before the foundation of the university in 1411.

Tobacco Use Spreads to England

England, 1565: A new plant, "tobacco," has been introduced by seafarer and slave trader John Hawkins following his recent visit to the New World.

The leafy plant—described variously as a narcotic and a panacea—is dried, shredded, rolled in a paper or tobacco tube, then ignited and the fumes inhaled. It may also be burned in a "pipe"—a small bowl attached to a stem for inhaling,

or unshredded plugs of the plant are placed beneath the tongue, allowing the drug to dissolve in saliva. Some users grind the plant into powder and sniff it through the nose.

Tobacco is said to aid concentration and digestion, and also to induce feelings of euphoria, while scientists and physicians believe it may be useful in treating lung and heart diseases.

A pirate and opportunist, Hawkins has been prowling the Atlantic Ocean between Europe, Africa, and the Indies, kidnapping slaves from the mainland, and hijacking them from Spanish and Portuguese ships. His exploits have caused the Spanish to ban all English ships from trading in their West Indies colonies.

Undeterred, Hawkins last year rented from Queen Elizabeth a huge old 770-ton (782-tonne) ship *Jesus of Lubeck* and set forth on his second voyage to the Caribbean, returning with slaves and bales of the dried tobacco plant, along with a new vegetable, the potato.

Tobacco, already becoming widespread in mainland Europe, is now being used by sailors, including those employed by Sir Francis Drake.

Explosive Discovery for Brewers

London, England, 1568: Bottling factories in England are preparing to add beer to their inventory, following a discovery by Alexander Nowell, the beer-drinking

Dean of London's St Paul's Cathedral, who inadvertently left a corked bottle of beer by the river while on a fishing outing earlier in the year.

Reports indicate when he returned on July 13 and opened the well-sealed bottle, to his surprise he found "no bottle, but a gun, so great was the sound."

He discovered that the bottle's contents, far from being spoiled, were actually improved in flavor and potency, apparently as the result of the occurrence of secondary fermentation in the bottle.

The impending mechanization of brewing is expected to result in the further exclusion of women from the industrial workforce, as working with bottling machines is men's work rather than that of women.

However, the news that beer is now portable is bound to cheer up English army officers, who have long complained about the lack of good beer in France.

Sir John Hawkins

May Day festivities are held in many parts of Europe.

England, 1565: The lead pencil, invented by Swiss scientist Konrad von Gesner, comes into use.

Salon, France, July, 1566: Michel de Nostredame (Nostradamus), physician and astrologer, dies, aged 62. His mysterious prophecies were published progressively during his life.

London, England, 1568: Bottled beer is invented by Alexander Nowell.

Kyoto, Japan, 1570: Buddhist priest Sen no Rikyu establishes rules of etiquette for the Tea Ceremony.

Yangzhou, China, 1570: Scholar Chen Yao writes that clothing styles "change without warning–it's what they call fashion."

London, England, 1571: The Royal Exchange is opened by Queen Elizabeth I.

Italy, 1575: Italian craftsmen attempt to reproduce the delicate Chinese porcelain.

Kokonor, Tibet, 1577: Sonam Gyatso is installed as the first Dalai Lama.

Canada, 1581: Fur trade begins in the St Lawrence River.

England, 1581: More advice on correct behavior is available for the upper classes with the English translation of Italian Stefano Guazzo's *Civil Conversations*.

Europe, 1582: The Gregorian calendar is implemented in some Catholic countries, including Italy, Portugal, and Spain.

Antwerp, Belgium, 1585: Once the undisputed commercial center of the world, Antwerp relinquishes some of its stronghold as Rotterdam and Amsterdam become the favored ports.

Roanoke, North America, August 15, 1587: Virginia Dare is born, the first child born to English parents in America.

Momoyama Castle, Japan, 1587: Shogun Hideyoshi issues an edict prohibiting peasants from owning swords or other weapons.

England, 1587: Billiards becomes a popular sport among the upper classes.

Italy, 1589: Giambattista della Porta's book *Magiae naturalis* (*Natural Magic*) is published, covering a diverse range of topics.

France, 1589: Thoinot Arbeau publishes *Orchésographie*, a detailed how-to-dance manual.

Europe, 1595: Flat-soled styles are given the boot—stylish members of society favor shoes with heels.

England, 1595: Tomatoes finally make their way to English tables.

England, 1596: Jewelry and adornment are popular and the well-to-do are bejewelled from head to toe.

Spain, 1599: The failing economy is made worse by the death toll from the plague devastating the country.

Pope Gregory XIII

Italian Porcelain Still No Match for China

Italy, 1575: Potters in Italy are producing beautiful examples of porcelain pottery, but are so far unable to match the fine quality of Chinese porcelain (also known as "china" or "chinaware").

The Chinese say that porcelain was first made in the Han period (206 BCE–220 CE), when traditional clay pottery became more refined in body, form, and decoration. They made vitreous (glass-like) products (known as "protoporcelain") before they developed the white vitreous ware ("true" porcelain), now so widely appreciated and imitated in Europe.

True porcelain appeared in Europe during the thirteenth century, when the first European merchants returned from China with vases and kitchenware made of the mysterious material. Increasingly large quantities of porcelain have been brought back since 1497, when Vasco da Gama established the first sea trade route between Europe and China.

Artisans in many European courts have since tried to discover the secret of chinaware, but the formula remains elusive. Francesco de' Medici, grand duke of Tuscany, is producing the most impressive examples in his Florence workshop, but even he cannot match the Chinese samples he is using as models.

The Italian wares are invariably translucent and lead glazed, produced from a composition of ground glass and other ingredients, including the finest white kaolin clay, and fired at a low temperature.

It is believed that the more transparent Chinese pottery also uses kaolin, and is probably fired at a higher temperature, but that there must be another "mystery ingredient" which gives the Chinese porcelain its superiority.

Despite many requests, the Chinese potters have so far shown no inclination to reveal their secret.

Year to Lose 10 Days with Pope's New Calendar

Europe, 1582: A new calendar has been introduced in Europe. On February 24, Pope Gregory XIII issued a Papal Bull, *Inter Gravissimas*, which outlines reforms designed to correct the inaccuracies in Julius Caesar's calendar, which has been in place since 46 BCE.

The Julian calendar, which consists of 11 months of 30 or 31 days and a 28-day February (extended to 29 days every fourth year), is actually quite accurate. Since a year contains only 365.242199 days (slightly less than 365.25 days), it differs from the real solar calendar by the margin of 11½ minutes a year.

Over the centuries, though, this small inaccuracy has caused the Julian calendar to lag behind the solar calendar by 10 days. This is especially troubling to the Catholic Church because it affects the determination of the date of Easter, which is well on the way to slipping into summer.

To compensate for this error, Pope Gregory decreed that the 10 days between October 5, 1582, and October 14, 1582, will be taken from the calendar.

The rule for leap years has also been changed. In the Julian calendar a year is a leap year if it is divisible by four. In the new Gregorian calendar, a year ending in 00 is not a leap year unless the first two numbers are divisible by four. Thus the years 1600 and 2000 are leap years, but 1700, 1800, 1900, and 2100 are not.

The Catholic countries France, Spain, Portugal, and Italy have already agreed to observe the correction. The Germanic countries, Belgium, the Netherlands, and Switzerland are expected to follow suit shortly, while England, currently involved in bitter struggles with the Vatican, has no intention of adopting the Gregorian calendar in the near future.

The switchover is bitterly opposed by much of the general population, who fear that losing 10 days will lead to an attempt by landlords to cheat them out of a week and a half's rent.

Medici porcelain plate, made in Italy.

English Take Up New Ball Game

England, 1587: Billiards, a ball game played on a table and popular in France, has appeared in England. It is played in the courts of the Duke of Norfolk and the Earl of Leicester and its popularity is spreading through the upper classes.

A descendant of ground billiards (which also spawned croquet), the game was adapted to be played indoors during the long and inclement winters. It is played on a table with holes in each corner into which balls are propelled with a stick. The table is covered in green cloth, an echo of the lawn from which the game was taken.

The earliest mention of billiards played on a table was in 1470 in a list of items bought by King Louis XI of France which included "billiard balls and billiard table for pleasure and amusement."

Even Mary, Queen of Scots, who is imprisoned in England awaiting execution for treason, has a billiard table in her prison cell. She is renowned for her love of culture and sport.

Author Sums Up Popular Science

Italy, 1589: Multitalented Italian scholar Giambattista della Porta has published an extraordinary and wide-ranging book, *Magiae naturalis (Natural Magic)*.

The 20-volume series, which is already a best-seller, covers many popular science topics, including cosmology, geology, optics, plant products, medicines, poisons, and cooking as well.

There are books on transmutation of the metals (not only the elusive alchemical pursuits, but chemical changes generally); distillation; gunpowders; the

Pope Gregory XIII presided over the commission for calendar reform, with Christopher Clavius giving expert advice.

magnet and its properties; known remedies for numerous ailments; cosmetics; fires; and invisible writing.

Della Porta includes statements of the ancients from the time of Aristotle and Theophrastis, as well as the latest contemporary knowledge. The volume on imitation gems is of interest, including the coloring of glass by metallic compounds (burned copper for aquamarine, manganese for amethyst, cobalt for sapphire, copper and iron for emerald, etc.). The making of enamels and their coloring for pottery are also described here, the art of ceramics being further advanced in Italy than anywhere else except China.

The author has claimed that he was only 15 years old in 1558, when the first four-volume version of the book was published. However, many believe that della Porta was born in 1535, making him at least 22 in 1558. We may suspect that in his youth he unduly emphasized his maturity, but in later years retrospectively overstated his splendid precocity.

Nonetheless, the information in *Magiae naturalis* is specific and practical, presenting the reader with a clear impartial view of the beliefs, observations, and achievements of a host of historically significant scientists and philosophers.

Inigo Jones

Hardwick Hall in Derbyshire, designed by Robert Smythson, a leading proponent, with Inigo Jones, of the new style.

English Tastes Warm to Tomatoes

England, 1595: The tomato, a fruit regarded with suspicion until recently in England, is finally making its way from the ornamental garden to the dining table.

A plant native to the coastal highlands of western South America, the tomato first emigrated to Central America and then to Mexico, where the indigenous peoples first crossbred and cultivated them, naming them *tomatl*.

Imported to Europe from the New World by Spanish conquistadors early this century, the tomato initially suffered from a case of mistaken identity. European botanists recognized it as a member of the Solanaceae family, whose only local relatives are the delirients, mandrake and deadly nightshade, leading to the inference that the fruit of the tomato must also be poisonous.

In fact, the Solanaceae family also includes such useful and decorative plants as tobacco, chili, sweet pepper, eggplant, potato, and petunia—all previously unknown in Europe but now achieving widespread use.

In his 1544 book, Italian herbalist Matthiolus documents the existence of tomatoes in local gardens and reports

Tomato fruits are now known to be harmless.

that Italians ate them. It will be interesting to see how they are used in Italian cuisine.

The popular English herbalist John Gerard wrote that, while Spaniards and Italians ate tomatoes, the plant was nevertheless "of ranke and stinking savour."

It has already achieved a variety of nicknames. The Dutch botanist Dodoens labelled it "amorous apple," observing that tomatoes "be of two sortes, one red and the other yellowe, but in all other poyntes they be lyke."

In Italy it is called "Moor's apple," *pomo dei mori*, and another name with a similar sound, *poma amoris*, or "love apple." The French use the same term, *pomme d'amour*.

The English call it "stinking golden apple," and routinely throw it at mediocre actors and other performers as a sign of displeasure.

Architecture Embracing Neoclassical Forms

England, 1598: A new form of architecture is taking hold in England. The new "Elizabethan" style is strongly influenced by the no-frills elegance which has been in vogue in Italy since the turn of the century and uses the simple classical lines of ancient Greek and Roman architecture.

This use of neoclassical symmetry reflects the ideal Elizabethan expression of order and harmony, with the emphasis on domestic comfort and practicality, rather than the ostentatious ornamentation that has been so popular.

Traditional intricate flying buttresses, alcoves, and columns are being replaced with simple arches, triangular gables over porches, and flat, rather than recessed

exteriors. Recent advances in engineering have allowed the manufacture of much larger windows, resulting in an airier and lighter interior space.

Brick and stone exteriors are giving way to exposed wood framing, the spaces between the timber being filled with plaster, brick, or stone.

Small farmhouse complexes are yielding to great single-purpose houses which often feature wide carved oak staircases, rather than gloomy circular stairwells. Interiors, while simpler in plan, still maintain some ornate features. Ceilings and fireplaces are often extremely elaborate, and walls, which once featured displays of art, are now art forms in themselves.

Gardens are also becoming an important feature, with flowers, herbs, topiary, and walkways being arranged in formal artistic layouts.

Key Religious Leaders

Popes
Julius III (1550-1555)
Marcellus II (1555)
Paul IV (1555-1559)
Pius IV (1559-1565)
Pius V (1566-1572)
Gregory XIII (1572-1585)
Sixtus V (1585-1590)
Urban VII (1590)
Gregory XIV (1590-1591)
Innocent IX (1591)
Clement VIII (1592-1605)

Archbishops of Canterbury
Thomas Cranmer (1533-1556)
Reginald Pole (1557-1558) (last Roman Catholic Archbishop of Canterbury)
Matthew Parker (1559-1575)
Edmund Grindal (1575-1583)
John Whitgift (1583-1604)

Dalai Lama of Tibet
Sonam Gyatso (1578-1588)

Patriarchs of Constantinople
Dyonisius II (1546-1555)
Joasaph II (1555-1565)
Metrophanes III (1565-1572, 1579-1580)
Jeremias II Tranos (1572-1579, 1580-1584, 1587-1595)
Pachomius II (1584-1585)
Theoleptus II (1585-1586)
Matthew II (1596, 1598-1602)
Gabriel I (1596)
Theophanes I Karykes (1597)
Meletius I Pegas (coadjutor) (1597-1598)

Pocahontas
(Rebecca Rolfe)

> "*I KNOW I HAVE THE BODY OF A WEAK AND FEEBLE WOMAN, BUT I HAVE THE HEART AND STOMACH OF A KING.*"
>
> ELIZABETH I (1533–1603), QUEEN OF ENGLAND

> "*MAGNA CHARTA IS SUCH A FELLOW, THAT HE WILL HAVE NO SOVEREIGN.*"
>
> EDWARD COKE (1552–1634) ENGLISH POLITICIAN, 1628

Ieyasu's Troops Rout Forces Loyal to Hideyoshi

Japan, October 21, 1600: Military genius Tokugawa Ieyasu has seized power in Japan after a short, brutal battle near the village of Sekigahara. His forces routed the army of the late Toyotomi Hideyoshi.

The battle followed months of skirmishing and intrigues, during which Ieyasu has been gathering together the armies of various regional warlords to make a final assault on the ailing and unpopular Hideyoshi regime.

The armies, about 80,000 on each side, have been massing in the area for months, and Ieyasu has been sending secret inducements to opposing generals, promising to give them power and riches, and also emphasizing his military superiority.

This morning the armies faced each other in heavy fog, engaging in hand-to-hand combat with machetes, swords, and rifles. When the fog cleared, it became apparent that Hideyoshi's troops held the superior tactical position, surrounding the challenging army, and also holding the high ground.

But many of Hideyoshi's troops hesitated to follow orders to attack. Ieyasu secured their active collaboration when he ordered his troops to open fire only upon the army of Kobukawa, one of the opposing generals. Realizing his position was hopeless, Kobukawa then ordered his troops to attack Hideyoshi, which in turn led to a mass desertion by most of the remaining generals.

The battle was over by four o'clock, with casualties estimated at 10,000. Many of the vanquished generals fled, many ritually disembowelling themselves. Ieyasu has already sent his troops in pursuit of his remaining enemies, who are now so decimated that they have little chance of mounting any real resistance. They can expect to be tortured and murdered.

Hideyoshi, whose army was defeated by Ieyasu.

James of Scotland Succeeds Elizabeth

Richmond, Surrey, England, March 24, 1603: The Virgin Queen is dead. England's Queen Elizabeth—daughter of Henry VIII and his second wife, Anne Boleyn—has been succeeded by James VI of Scotland, now known as James I of England.

When her 44-year reign began in 1558, the Protestant Elizabeth inherited a monarchy and dominion riven by religious warfare and bankruptcy—the legacy of her Catholic predecessor, Queen Mary Tudor. She faced a raging war with France, murderous court intrigues, and a huge debt to European banks.

Elizabeth's accession was greeted with partly justified optimism. Her reign featured less sectarian violence, no new civil wars, and many successes at home and overseas. However, the exchequer coffers are still empty, drained by the English sponsorship of the Protestant uprising in Spain.

Elizabeth attracted many suitors, but rejected them for various reasons. There is no doubt that her refusal to marry enabled her to shrewdly avoid "taking sides" in the numerous intrigues that confronted her. She cannily led on potential suitors (and usurpers), leading them to treat her with a deference borne of hope for her favors. However, there are strong whispers that she enjoyed affairs with several courtiers, including the Earls of Essex and Leicester.

Elizabeth always denied that women are inferior, famously saying before decimating the Spanish Armada in 1588: "…I have the heart and stomach of a king…and think foul scorn that any prince of Europe should dare invade the borders of my realm."

Elizabeth's enjoyment of a few beers, and her penchant for spitting and swearing, did not alienate her subjects. On the contrary, she has been England's most-loved monarch in centuries.

The accession of Protestant James marks the end of the Tudor Dynasty, the start of the Stuarts, and the uniting of the English and Scottish thrones.

time out

In 1612, a group of English colonists, originally bound for Virginia, establishes a colony on the island of Bermuda, claimed by Britain in 1609, and begins building the town of St George. Tobacco is a major cash crop.

Emperor Brought Peace and Tolerance to Moguls

Agra, India, October 17, 1605: The Mogul emperor Akbar (the Great) has died after a rule of almost 50 years. He has presided over an empire encompassing most of India and Afghanistan during a period of unprecedented peace and progress.

Akbar was born in Umerkot, Sindh, on November 23, 1542, and was raised in the harsh mountain country of Afghanistan. He ascended to the throne at the age of 13 after the death of his father Humayun,

---

Key Events

Sekigahara, Japan, October 21, 1600: Tokugawa Ieyasu defeats forces loyal to Toyotomi Hideyoshi, and establishes the Tokugawa (Edo) Shogunate.

London, England, 1600: The British East India Company is founded.

Fife, Scotland, November 19, 1600: Charles, son of James I of Scotland, is born.

Netherlands, 1602: The Dutch East India Company is founded.

Turkey, 1603: Mehmet III, Ottoman ruler, dies, aged about 36. He is succeeded by his son, Ahmed I.

Richmond, Surrey, England, March 24, 1603: Elizabeth I dies, aged 69. She is succeeded by James VI of Scotland, who becomes James I of England.

Agra, India, October 17, 1605: Akbar the Great, Mogul ruler, dies, aged about 63. He is succeeded by his son, Jahangir.

North America, 1610: After several previous voyages, Henry Hudson once more sails for an English trading company, and discovers the bay and the strait that will bear his name.

Paris, France, May 14, 1610: The assassination of Henry IV, aged 57, cuts short a peaceful reign. He is succeeded by his son, Louis XIII.

Northern Europe, 1611-1613: Disputed seafaring trade routes see Denmark and Sweden engage in the Kalmar War.

Russia, 1613: Mikhail Romanov comes to the Russian throne, ending the "Time of Troubles."

Jamestown, North America, April 5, 1614: Pocahontas, an Algonquin princess, marries John Rolfe, English tobacco farmer.

Canada, 1616: William Baffin, English maritime explorer, arrives at the bay named for him–Baffin Bay.

Constantinople, Turkey, November 22, 1617: Ahmed I, Ottoman ruler, dies, aged 27. He is succeeded by his brother Mustafa I.

Prague, Eastern Europe, 1618: The Bohemian nobility oppose the Austrian (Habsburg) overlords, beginning with an incident known as "the Defenestration at Prague."

London, England, 1618: Sir Walter Raleigh, adventurer, courtier, and poet, is beheaded, aged about 64.

Europe, 1619: Ferdinand II becomes the Holy Roman Emperor.

Provincetown, North America, November 21, 1620: A group of English Puritans known as the Pilgrims land in North America after a 65-day voyage from Portsmouth, England in the *Mayflower*.

Netherlands, 1621: The Dutch West India Company is founded.

New Plymouth, Massachusetts, North America, 1621: After the death of their first elected Governor, John Carver, William Bradford is elected Governor of the Pilgrims' colony.

Algonquin Princess Weds Colonial Farmer

Jamestown, North America, April 5, 1614: The 19-year-old Algonquin princess Pocahontas is now known as Rebecca Rolfe, following her morning baptism—and afternoon marriage—to English tobacco farmer John Rolfe.

Her life has been beset by abductions and other intrigues, as the princess with a foot in both camps was used by the warring Indians and English as a pawn in their negotiations.

In December 1607, English captain John Smith was captured by Pocahontas's father, Chief Powhatan. According to Smith, his life was saved after a dramatic and romantic intervention by Pocahontas, but many say he was merely participating in an Indian ritual of initiation and welcome which he failed to understand.

Pocahontas recently converted to Christianity while living as a guest with governor Sir Thomas Dale. Rolfe, who made his riches after developing a particularly sweet strain of tobacco, asked both Dale and Powhatan for Pocahontas's hand in marriage. They agreed, but Powhatan refused his wedding invitation.

Peregrine White, was born two days ago as the ship lay at anchor a few miles north. King James has granted territory to the colonists in Jamestown, to the south, but navigational problems and storms caused them to sail further north than intended.

Before disembarking, the passengers met in the cabin of the *Mayflower* and elected John Carver—who had organized the ship's charter—as their first governor. They also drew up and signed a "plantation covenant," known as the Mayflower Compact, in which they agreed to set up a "Civil Body Politic" (temporary government), and to be bound by its laws.

This is a very significant step in the annals of governance. The ancient concept of democracy—government of the people by the people—receives little more than lip service in Europe these days (and even less than that everywhere else).

It remains to be seen whether the small steps outlined in the Mayflower Compact will take hold and spread throughout the New World.

The Pilgrims will spend some time exploring the region before deciding upon whether to settle here or set sail southward in search of a more promising location to set up their colony.

Queen Elizabeth I

Turkish dancers entertain the court of Akbar the Great.

and received wise guidance and education from his adviser Bahran Khan until 1562, when he became ruler in his own right.

Akbar, a Muslim, will be remembered as a tolerant leader. He studied Hinduism, Christianity, Jainism, and other beliefs represented in his dominion, and started a new faith, Din-i-Ilahi, an attempt to blend them with Islam. He appointed Hindus to important military and civil positions, and married a Hindu princess. His attitude towards neighboring states was based on cooperation and trade.

Akbar set up an world-class administrative system, *Mansabdari*, as the basis for the efficient governance of his civil and military structures that is becoming widely imitated in Europe. A key feature of his administration has been the fair distribution of taxes, a policy that has ensured widespread acceptance of his rule.

Akbar had been very ill recently, amid whispers that he may have been poisoned. He is succeeded by his oldest son Jahangir, who is now 36 years old.

Colonists Set Up Democratic Rule

Provincetown, North America, November 21, 1620: The 180-ton *Mayflower* arrived in Provincetown this morning after a 65-day voyage from Portsmouth, England. On board were 37 Puritans escaping persecution, and an assortment of other settlers aiming to start a new life in the New World.

Two of the 102 passengers died en route, while a boy, Oceanus Hopkins, was born at sea, and another,

In 1609, Henry Hudson discovered the mouth of the Hudson River.

K e y   E v e n t s

Paris, France, 1624: Cardinal Richelieu becomes the Prime Minister of France.

London, England, March 27, 1625: James I dies, aged 58. He is succeeded by his son, Charles I.

Agra, India, 1628: Jahangir, Mogul ruler, dies, aged 59. He is succeeded by his son, Shah Jahan.

Persia, 1629: Shah Abbas I (known as Abbas the Great), Safavid ruler, dies, aged about 72. He is succeeded by his son Safi I.

London, England, 1629: Constant conflict sees Charles I dissolve the Houses of Parliament.

Asia, 1634: Ligdan Khan, the last great Mongol ruler, dies, after a reign of 30 years.

Quebec, Canada, 1635: Samuel de Champlain, explorer, dies, aged about 68.

Shimabara, Japan, 1636: The rebellion of Christians ends in the slaughter of over 30,000 rebels.

Japan, 1638: Japan embarks on a period of isolation from the rest of the world.

Ireland, 1641: Dissatisfied with years of English control, the Irish nobility band together and launch a rebellion to regain control of the country and oust the English administration.

England, 1642: England is plunged into civil war, as the parliamentarian "Roundhead" forces and the royal "Cavalier" forces engage in battle.

Tasmania, Australia, 1642: Dutch explorer Abel Tasman discovers Van Diemen's Land (Tasmania).

New Zealand, 1642: Abel Tasman sights New Zealand.

Persia, 1642: Shah Safi, Safavid ruler, dies. He is succeeded by his son, Shah Abbas II.

Paris, France, May 14, 1643: Louis XIII dies aged 41. He is succeeded by his four-year-old son, Louis XIV, with his wife, Anne of Austria, taking on the role of regent.

Peking, China, April 25, 1644: Zhu Youjan, the last Ming emperor, hangs himself as Manchu forces enter the Forbidden City.

Tainan, Taiwan, 1645: Pirate-patriot Zheng Chenggong establishes the Ming loyalist regime on Taiwan, and resists the newly-established Qing (Manchu) Dynasty.

Europe, 1648: The Peace of Westphalia brings about the end of the Thirty Years War.

London, England, 1649: Charles I of England is found guilty of treason and executed on January 30. His son and heir, Charles, is forced into exile in Europe. Oliver Cromwell becomes Lord Protector of England.

New Plymouth Pilgrims Making Progress

New Plymouth, Massachusetts, North America, Spring, 1621: Hard times have befallen the Pilgrims in New Plymouth. Nearly half have died of starvation and disease since they arrived from England last year, but there is light on the horizon.

After landing last January, the first settlers inadvertently disturbed some local Wampanoag Indian graves, attracting an attack which they successfully warded off with gunfire. This, however, meant facing winter without the benefit of local knowledge, not to mention crop seeds.

The Pilgrims divided into 19 family groups. The single men were assigned to different households, and each family was given a plot of land to build a home. However, the first two timber-framed, thatched-roof homes had to be converted into a hospital and a communal area.

They tried to survive by catching fish and foraging for grains and vegetables, but met with little success. With no agricultural skills or medicine, the cold winter and lack of food was devastating for the settlers, already weakened by their two-month voyage. They buried their dead on nearby Cole's Hill and sowed grain over the graves. Their numbers are down from about 100 to 50.

In March, the Pilgrims signed a peace treaty with Wampanoag chief Massasoit, and later welcomed Samoset, chief of the neighboring Monhegan Tribe, to New Plymouth for two days of peace ceremonies and feasting. The Indians have shared valuable food cultivation tips, and, even more importantly, seeds.

The entire surviving male workforce—21 men and 6 boys—are now cultivating 20 acres of Indian corn; 6 acres of wheat, rye and barley; and several home vegetable gardens. They have also begun breeding a delicious local bird, the turkey.

While working in the fields recently, the elected governor John Carver succumbed to sunstroke and died. The settlers have elected William Bradford,

Charles I of England

> "IF YOU GIVE ME SIX LINES WRITTEN BY THE HAND OF THE MOST HONEST OF MEN, I WILL FIND SOMETHING IN THEM WHICH WILL HANG HIM."

CARDINAL RICHELIEU (1585–1642), PRIME MINISTER OF FRANCE

> "PUT YOUR TRUST IN GOD, AND KEEP YOUR POWDER DRY."

OLIVER CROMWELL (1599–1658), ENGLISH STATESMAN, BEFORE THE BATTLE OF NASEBY, 1645

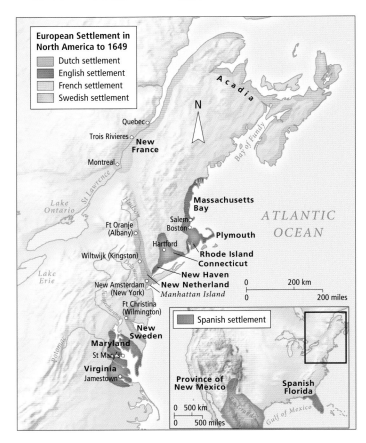

European Settlement in North America to 1649
- Dutch settlement
- English settlement
- French settlement
- Swedish settlement

Acadia

Quebec
Trois Rivieres
New France
Montreal
Lake Ontario
Lake Erie
Ft Oranje (Albany)
Wiltwijk (Kingston)
New Amsterdam (New York)
Manhattan Island
Ft Christina (Wilmington)
New Sweden
Maryland
St Mary's
Virginia
Jamestown

Massachusetts Bay
Salem
Boston
Plymouth
Hartford
Rhode Island
Connecticut
New Haven
New Netherland

Bay of Fundy

ATLANTIC OCEAN

0   200 km
0   200 miles

Spanish settlement

Province of New Mexico
Spanish Florida
Gulf of Mexico

0   500 km
0   500 miles

whose wife drowned last year as they were coming ashore, as his replacement.

Shah Jahan Seizes Power in Mogul Bloodbath

Agra, India, 1628: Shah Jahan has seized control of the Mogul empire. Following the death of his father Jahangir last year, he has resolved the ensuing power vacuum in the usual Mogul manner—by defeating his brother in a brutal war.

Jahangir's 23-year term as emperor took Mogul culture to its highest point. His rule was largely peaceful, and he showed little interest in expanding the Mogul empire, apart from conquering Bengal in eastern India.

He was a student and patron of the arts, with a keen interest in the various philosophies and religions in his dominion. He commissioned many superb buildings, and sponsored numerous painters, architects, and writers. He continued his father Akbar's tradition of tolerance and negotiation in dealing with his subjects and neighboring states.

War ensued after Jahangir's death when Shah Jahan and his brother, Shahryar, were unable to agree on a succession arrangement. Their mother, Nur Jehan, supported Shahryar, so the victorious Jahan killed them both.

Japanese Ban Foreigners

Japan, 1641: Foreigners have now all been banned from mainland Japan. Shogun Emperor Iemitsu believes that alien influences are having a destructive effect on Japanese society and he has blamed them for several recent peasant uprisings.

Over recent decades, Japan has been trading with several European countries, including France and England, but all relations have now been terminated. Only the Dutch are permitted to continue trading, but even they have been banished to the artificial island of Dejima in Nagasaki harbor, built for the Portuguese before they were banished to Macau two years ago. The Dutch mainland trading port at Hirado was demolished recently.

The Portuguese were the first Europeans to be accepted into Japan, and experienced initial success in introducing Western ideas and technology, and setting up trade and friendly relations. Their Jesuit missionaries were also granted relative freedom to spread the word.

Recently, however, Japan has been progressively introducing trade freezes against European countries, and last year a Portuguese delegation from Macau went to Nagasaki to request the lifting of their ban. The members of the delegation no doubt held reasonable hopes that their previously cordial and mutually beneficial associations would persuade the Japanese to withdraw the embargo.

However, Iemitsu held the Portuguese responsible for a Christian uprising at Shimabara two years ago, and decided to make an example of them. He ordered the public beheading of 61 Portuguese, sparing only 13, who were permitted to return to Macau with the grim news.

Persian tile panel showing the great Safavid ruler Shah Abbas I (1587–1629) with members of his court.

Roundheads Threaten King Charles's Reign

England, 1642: Tensions between King Charles's Cavalier forces and Parliament's Roundhead forces have spilled over, plunging England into civil war.

King Charles has been quarreling with Parliament recently, amid local insurrections, a Scottish-led rebellion against the new prayer book, and continuing hostilities against Ireland. Parliament refused to allocate any more resources for wars until he addressed their concerns, so Charles ordered his sergeant-at-arms to arrest several parliamentary ringleaders.

Parliament refused to authorize the arrests, and so in November, 1640, Charles turned up at Parliament with hundreds of troops to arrest all and sundry. Forewarned, the members had taken sanctuary in the City of London, where they set up a "Long Parliament" which has been in bitter dispute with Charles ever since.

Warfare erupted last week at Nottingham when Charles raised the royal standard against the parliamentary forces, both armies numbering about 13,000. Cavalier support comes mainly from

Seats of Power

China Ming Dynasty: Wanli (reigned 1572-1620); Taichang (1620); Tianqi (1620-1627); Chongzhen (1627-1644). Qing Dynasty: Shunzhi (reigned 1644-1661).
England Elizabeth I (reigned 1558-1603); James I (1603-1625); Charles I (1625-1649). The Commonwealth: Oliver Cromwell (1649-1658).
France Henry IV (reigned 1589-1610); Louis XIII (1610-1643); Louis XIV (1643-1715).
Holy Roman Empire Rudolf II (reigned 1576-1612); Matthias (1612-1619); Ferdinand II (1619-1637); Ferdinand III (1637-1657).
India Mogul Empire: Akbar (reigned 1556-1605); Jahangir (1605-1627); Shah Jahan (1628-1658).
Japan Muromachi Period: Go-Yozei (reigned 1586-1611). Edo Period: Go-Mizunoo (1611-1629); Empress Meisho (1629-1643); Go-Komyo (1643-1654).
Korea Choson Dynasty: Seonjo (reigned 1567-1608); Gwanghaegun (1608-1623); Injo (1623-1649); Hyojong (1649-1659).
Ottoman Empire Mehmed III (reigned 1595-1603); Ahmed I (1603-1617); Mustafa I (1617-1618); Osman II (1618-1622); Mustafa I (1622-1623); Murad IV (1623-1640); Ibrahim I (1640-1648); Mehmed IV (1648-1687).
Persia Safavid Shahs: Abbas I (reigned 1587-1629); Safi (1629-1642); Abbas II (1642-1666).
Portugal Spanish Rule (1580-1640). Brigantine Dynasty: Joao IV (reigned 1640-1656).
Russia Tsars: Boris Godunov (reigned 1598-1605); Feodor II (1605); Dmitri I (1605-1606); Vasili IV (1606-1610); Interregnum (1610-1613); Michael I (1613-1645); Aleksey I (1645-1676).
Scotland James VI (reigned 1587-1625) (Union of the Crowns with Kingdom of England from 1603); Charles I (1625-1649); Charles II (1649-1685).
Spain Habsburg Dynasty: Philip III (reigned 1598-1621); Philip IV (1621-1665).

the nobility and peasantry in England's north and west, while the emerging middle class and tradesmen to the south and east support the Roundheads. The words "Cavalier" and "Roundhead" were originally used as insults to describe the enemy. The Roundheads favor short hair and plain dress, while the Cavaliers wear elaborate costumes, with long flowing ringlets under feathered hats.

The Roundheads are confident they have enough support (and military strength) to defeat Charles and seize control on behalf of the people. Since Parliament controls the purse strings, many predict that Charles will eventually run out of resources and be defeated.

Four-year-old Ascends the French Throne

Paris, France, May 14, 1643: King Louis XIII has died, leaving the throne to his four-year-old son, Louis XIV.

Born in Fontainebleau in 1601, the eldest son of Marie de Medicis and Henry IV, Louis ascended the throne at the age of nine, marrying Anne of Austria in 1615. Marie withheld power from him until 1617. Louis had her exiled to Blois in 1619 and appointed the brilliant strategist Cardinal Richelieu as his chief minister. The two reconciled in 1622.

Richelieu, who died last December, played a central role in Louis's administration, effectively shaping France's destiny. With his help, Louis defeated the Habsburgs after decades of war, kept the nobility firmly in line despite numerous religious and political intrigues, and retracted the special privileges granted to the Protestant Huguenots by his father.

The port of Le Havre was modernized, and the navy strengthened. In foreign affairs, Louis organized the administration and development of New France, expanding the settlement of Quebec westward along the St Lawrence River.

Louis's widow, Anne, will act as regent for the incoming four-year-old king.

King Charles Publicly Beheaded

London, England, January 30, 1649: After seven years of civil war, England's King Charles is dead. At two o'clock this afternoon in Whitehall, Charles was beheaded in front of a large crowd.

Charles, second son of King James I, was born in Dunfermline, Scotland, in 1600. In 1623 he failed in a bid to marry the Infanta Maria of Spain, eventually marrying the Catholic French Princess Henrietta Maria in 1625, the first of many actions which caused consternation among the general populace.

Oliver Cromwell

Upon ascending the throne the same year, Charles set about reducing the power of Parliament. He dissolved three Parliaments in the next four years, then decided to rule without one. He introduced a series of unpopular taxes to fund wars with France, Spain, and Scotland.

He restored Parliament in 1640 in an attempt to regain respect, but Parliament refused to supply any resources until he changed his tax and other policies. A series of civil wars between the Royalist "Cavaliers" and Oliver Cromwell's Parliamentarian "Roundheads" ensued, culminating in Charles's defeat at Naseby in 1645. He unsuccessfully sought assistance from the Irish, promising favors if they helped the Pope to restore his monarchy.

Queen Anne of France with her son, the Dauphin Louis XIV.

He was jailed by Parliament in 1646, but escaped and surrendered to the Scots at Newark. Because Charles promised the Scots that he would restore Presbyterianism, he expected to find sanctuary. However, the Scots, mistrustful of his many past double-dealings, refused to believe in his change of heart and handed him back to Cromwell.

The Parliament set up a High Court to condemn Charles as "a tyrant, traitor, murderer and enemy of the people."

The crowd was divided as the executioner's ax came down upon Charles's neck, some shouting "Justice! Justice!" and others "God save the King!"

Cromwell has been installed as Lord Protector of England, and has announced immediate plans to crush the remaining Royalist strongholds in Ireland and Scotland which had aligned themselves with Charles.

Book Explains Magnets and Electricity

Sir Francis Bacon

England, 1600: The eminent physician William Gilbert has published *De Magnete (On Magnets)*, the first major English science work. The book describes a magnetic field surrounding the Earth, and introduces the term "electricity" to describe the phenomenon of an electric charge traveling along a sympathetic medium, called a "conductor."

Gilbert reveals that electricity and magnetism are closely linked, and divides substances into electrics (glass, amber and metals such as iron) and nonelectrics.

He has also discovered various methods for producing and strengthening magnets. For example, when a steel rod is stroked by a natural magnet, the rod itself becomes a magnet; and an iron bar aligned to Earth's magnetic field for a long period gradually develops magnetic properties of its own.

He also observes that the magnetism of a piece of material is destroyed when the material is sufficiently heated.

Gilbert, who is known as "the father of magnetism," is likely to be appointed as royal physician to Queen Elizabeth in the near future.

> "LOOK SOMEWHERE ELSE FOR SOMEONE WHO CAN FOLLOW YOU IN YOUR RESEARCHES ABOUT NUMBERS. I CONFESS THAT THEY ARE FAR BEYOND ME, AND I AM COMPETENT ONLY TO ADMIRE THEM."
>
> BLAISE PASCAL (1623–1662), FRENCH MATHEMATICIAN

Tycho Brahe's subterranean Stjerneborg observatory on Hven Island.

Valves are Secret to Blood Flow in Legs

Padua, Italy, 1603: Hieronymus Fabricius, the much-loved and multitalented Italian anatomist, has discovered why gravity does not cause blood to form pools in our feet and legs. His findings are published in his latest work *De venarum ostiolis (On Veins in the Leg)*.

When we are standing, trapdoor-like valves in the veins close totally at periodic intervals to prevent the backflow of blood, closing in sympathy and rhythm with the beating of the heart. When we are at rest, however, the valves are not needed and remain open, allowing the free flow of blood to the heart.

If the valves fail to work efficiently, the high pressure in the large internal veins is transmitted to the much weaker, unsupported surface veins. These veins become swollen and twisted, leading to such maladies as varicose veins, edema, pigmentation, eczema, and leg ulcers. *De venarum* is the latest in Fabricius' series of anatomical observations, and follows his 1600 publication of *De visione, voce, auditu (On sight, speech, hearing)*.

Fabrici is a very wealthy man, thanks to his practice as a surgeon and physician, and his academic appointments. He treats the poor for free, and often does not even charge his very wealthy patients, including the dukes of Mantua and Urbino, who are rumored to have rewarded him handsomely nonetheless. Although he is a brilliant surgeon, Fabricius has devoted most of his life to teaching, research, and patient care. However, he plans to spend more time on writing, and on developing new surgical instruments and orthopedic devices.

time out

Science hastened Francis Bacon's death. An advocate of proving scientific facts, Bacon tried to find out the preservation qualities of freezing, by stuffing a chicken with snow. Exposure to cold conditions led to pneumonia, and ultimately his death.

Intellectual Life in the Spotlight

London, England, 1605: Sir Francis Bacon has just released *The Proficience and Advancement of Learning*, perhaps the most important philosophical work ever published in English. In it, the lawyer, statesman, essayist, historian, intellectual reformer, philosopher, and champion of modern science summarizes, as he sees it, the current state of English knowledge.

Bacon claims that, owing mainly to an undue reverence for the past, as well as an unwarranted fascination with trivial cultural conceits, English and European intellectual life has reached the point of stagnation. However, he states that this may be overcome if, equipped with new methods and insights, people simply open their eyes and minds to the world around them.

The author proposes the notion that humans possess internal obstacles to learning and understanding, which must be eradicated before further progress is possible. To take the place of the established tradition (a mishmash of scholasticism, religion, humanism, and natural magic), he proposes an entirely new system based on empirical and inductive principles, and the development of new arts and inventions for "the use and benefit of men."

Logicians have traditionally practiced induction by simple enumeration—that is, drawing general conclusions from particular data. Bacon's method, however,

---

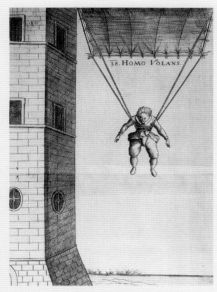

An early design for a rigid-framed parachute.

consists in drawing inferences from a body of scientific knowledge to create a theory that is then tested against known facts. This fundamental innovation will add significantly to the improvement of scientific hypotheses.

Bacon's philosophy emphasizes his belief that people are the servants and interpreters of nature; that truth is not derived from authority or tradition; and that knowledge is the fruit of experience, rather than of belief or faith.

Four Moons Shown to Circle Jupiter

Rome, Italy, March, 1610: The great astronomer and teacher Galileo Galilei has published *Sidereus Nuncius (The Sidereal Messenger)*, which contains astronomical observations of the surface of Earth's moon, and indicates the existence of four moons orbiting the planet Jupiter.

Using a homemade telescope, which magnifies by 32 times—far superior to any previous version of the instrument—he is now able to observe the heavens

with much greater clarity and detail than was hitherto possible.

He has ascertained that the moon is covered in mountain ranges, craters and seas (with or without water). He also observed that Saturn is surrounded by a mysterious circle of what he calls "ears."

Galileo first observed Jupiter's moons last January 7. He originally thought that he had seen three stars, strung out in a line across the planet. The next evening, these stars seemed to have moved in the wrong direction, and all appeared to the west of Jupiter. On January 11, he noted a fourth star had appeared.

After a week, Galileo noted that the four stars never left the vicinity of Jupiter and appeared to be carried along with the planet, and that they changed their position in relation to each other, and to Jupiter. He therefore decided that what he was observing were not stars, but planetary bodies that actually were in orbit around Jupiter. This discovery provides evidence in support of the Copernican system, which holds that everything does not revolve around the Earth.

Galileo writes: "I therefore concluded, and decided unhesitatingly, that there are four stars in the heavens moving about Jupiter, as Venus and Mercury around the Sun; which was at length established as clear as daylight by numerous other subsequent observations."

The news is bound to upset the Catholic Church, which holds that the stars, sun, and planets revolve around the Earth, which is the center of the universe. Galileo is a favorite of the Pope, but it remains to be seen whether he will tolerate Galileo's heretical observations and statements.

Galileo with Torricelli and Viviani studying gravity.

Mechanical Device Does Arithmetic Calculations

Tübingen, Germany, 1623: An extraordinary arithmetical device has been invented by German theologian, professor, and mathematician Wilhelm Schickard.

The box-shaped machine, known as the "calculating clock," can perform all calculations up to 999,999. It features internally and externally sprocketed gear wheels, dials, buttons, levers and revolving cylinders. It even includes a bell to warn the operator that a calculation exceeds the six-figure maximum.

Schickard has ordered a copy of the device to be made for eminent astronomer and star-mapper Johannes Kepler, who is sure to find it invaluable in his quest to accurately record the past, present and future positions of all the planets. He recently wrote to Kepler, giving details of the machine's functioning and offering advice on how to apply it to his ephemera project. As he explained:

"What you have done by calculation I have just tried to do by way of mechanics. I have conceived a machine consisting of eleven complete and six incomplete sprocket wheels; it calculates instantaneously and automatically from given numbers, as it adds, subtracts, multiplies and divides. You would enjoy to see how the machine accumulates and transports spontaneously a ten or a hundred to the left and, vice-versa, how it does the opposite if it is subtracting…"

Schickard, a professor of Hebrew at the University of Tübingen, has also made advances in the fields of cartography, surveying and physics.

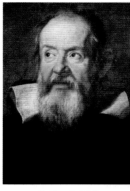

Galileo Galilei

Star Catalog Expands Astronomical Knowledge

Ulm, Germany, 1627: The pre-eminent mathematician and astronomer Johannes Kepler has unveiled his latest magnum opus, *Tabulae Rudolphinae (Rudolphine Tables)*, the most wide-ranging work on astronomy ever published.

The book contains updated planetary tables and a star catalog, based initially on the observations of seminal stargazer Tycho Brahe, and is accurate to an unprecedented few minutes of arc. It shows the position of 1,005 stars (an increase on Brahe's 777), and provides directions for locating the planets at any time in the past, present or future.

It is the first catalog to take account of corrective factors for atmospheric refraction, and also incorporates other vital information, such as a map of the world, and tables of eight-figure logarithms—including, for the first time, proof of how and why they work.

The planet tables use Tycho's observations, but modify and improve them by incorporating Kepler's first two laws of motion: that the planets travel in elliptical orbits, and that they sweep out equal areas of their orbits in equal times.

Kepler had studied in Prague under Brahe, who he found arrogant and demanding, for a short time before his death in 1601. Brahe's dying wish to Kepler was that he complete *Tabulae*.

Kepler was excommunicated from the Church in 1612 for his heliocentric Copernican views. This causes him much anguish, but, despite his distinguished social standing as imperial mathematician to Holy Roman Emperor Rudolph, has not succeeded in having the ban lifted.

Like most people, Kepler accepts the principle of astrology—that heavenly bodies influence what happens on Earth—for example, the Sun causes the seasons, and the Moon the tides. But as a Copernican, he does not believe in the physical

Johannes Kepler

> *"EPPUR SI MUOVE." ("YET IT MOVES.")*
>
> GALILEO GALILEI (1564–1642), ITALIAN ASTRONOMER AND PHYSICIST, OF THE EARTH, HAVING RECANTED ON HIS BELIEF IN THE COPERNICAN MODEL OF ASTRONOMY, 1632

> *"IT IS NOT ENOUGH TO HAVE A GOOD MIND. THE MAIN THING IS TO USE IT WELL."*
>
> RENÉ DESCARTES (1596–1650), FRENCH PHILOSOPHER, FROM *DISCOURSE ON THE METHOD*, 1637

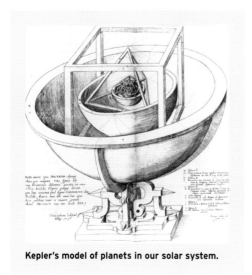

Kepler's model of planets in our solar system.

Galileo is summoned to defend his "heretical" heliocentric ideas before the Inquisition in Rome in 1633.

reality of the constellations, and his astrology is based only on the angles between the positions of heavenly bodies.

He expresses disdain for the complicated systems of conventional astrology.

Scientist Claims That Heart Pumps Blood

London, England, 1628: Pioneering scientist William Harvey has published new controversial findings on the operation of the human circulatory system in *De Motu Cordis et Sanguinis in Animalibus (On the Motion of the Heart and Blood in Animals)*.

Harvey proposes that the heart propels blood on a circular course through the body, leaving through arteries and returning through veins. He notes that blood squirts from a cut artery in rhythm with the heart's muscular contractions, and that clamping a vein causes it to swell with blood on the side further from the heart.

Common wisdom holds that blood is consumed by the organs, and that venous blood originates in the liver and arterial blood in the heart.

As always in the solution of his biological problems, in *De Motu* Harvey uses the scientific method, ignoring traditional physical and religious dogma which, he says, hinders the search for truth.

Many will refute his radical conclusions, but it remains to be seen whether they can debunk them scientifically.

Galileo Jailed for Holding Heretical Views

Florence, Rome, 1633: The great scientist Galileo has been imprisoned for life by Pope Urban. The sentence, which is

expected to be commuted to house arrest, follows last year's publication of his work *Dialogo sopra i due massimi sistemi del mondo, Tolemaico e Copernicano (Dialogue Concerning the Two Chief World Systems, Ptolemaic and Copernican)* in which Galileo declares his support for the banned Copernican system.

The book is written in the form of a conversation between three friends about the relative merits of the Copernican and Ptolemaic systems. Salivati puts forward the case for the heliocentric Copernican system, and Simplicio puts forward the Ptolemaic (Aristotelian) view, which states that the Earth is the center of the universe. Sagrado is the layman who asks questions of the other two, but always agrees with Salivati in the end.

Their discussions and conclusions about the motion of the moon, stars, planets, falling bodies and sunspots are inconsistent with a stationary, central Earth. Indeed, Galileo's numerous astronomical discoveries all indicate that the Earth and planets revolve around the Sun. This idea is regarded as heretical by the Church, which has imprisoned or killed many of its proponents.

The Pope had given permission for Galileo to give a balanced discussion of the two theories, but *Dialogo* was seen as a barely disguised attempt to debunk the Aristotelian system.

Accordingly, Galileo was summoned to Rome last year to appear before the Inquisition. After interrogation and a long trial, he was made to renounce his Copernican beliefs, which he did in a carefully worded statement.

Galileo has fallen foul of the Church before. In 1616, he was officially ordered to

stop supporting Copernicanism and to cease his advocacy of rational scientific thinking in opposition to established belief, superstition, and religious authority.

As a result, Galileo became more circumspect in his writings, but *Dialogo* leaves little doubt as to his true viewpoint. Three members of the judgment panel of cardinals refused to sign Galileo's sentence.

Expansive Technology Resource from China

Jiangxi, China, 1637: The remarkable, multi-volume encyclopedia of technology, *Tiangong Kaiwu (Exploitation of Resources)*, has been published by Chinese scholar Song Yingxing. It summarizes the state of Chinese technology and covers an exceptionally diverse range of topics, including descriptions of techniques and tools unknown in the West.

The first volume, "On Crop Growing," describes radical methods of breeding new strains of rice—and new species of silkworm—by artificial hybridization.

"On Weaving" introduces tools and technology of weaving, and indicates that China's cotton fluffer is the most advanced

in the world. "On Forging" lists metal processing techniques, such as quenching (cooling a hot substance in cold water), and tempering (alternate heating and cooling of metal or glass). Piston bellows, the most advanced blast devices in the world, are used in the smelting industry.

"On Dyeing" provides recipes for pigments for silk and textile coloring, while "On Potting" will be welcomed by Western practitioners, who are unable to match the excellence of Chinese ceramics.

The astonishingly wide-ranging series of books also contains sections devoted to sugar refining, shipbuilding, navigation, papermaking, chemical engineering, mining, weaponry, and other topics. It includes bibliographies, a glossary, and appendices on Chinese measurements, dynasties, and communication of methods to the West.

Song praises Nature for its power and ingenuity to create all things in the world. He writes that: "Only with due respect to the work of nature and the proper application of work by people, can humankind explore nature and benefit from it."

Prime Numbers Figure in Mersenne's Paris Salon

Paris, France, 1644: French theologian Marin Mersenne has published *Cogitata Physico-Mathematica*, his latest book on mathematical physics. It is a treatise on prime numbers, which are numbers that can only be divided by themselves or by the number one.

The work is being discussed by the eminent mathematicians and scientists who make up Mersenne's Paris salon, including Fermat, Pascal and Galileo. Many eminent scholars meet regularly at Mersenne's home to disseminate and discuss their latest discoveries and ideas. His respected learning in a wide variety of areas makes Mersenne the perfect conduit. He is greatly appreciated for the comments and insights he offers, often advising on the next step to take in research.

Cogitata follows Mersenne's *Traite de mouvements (Treatise on Motion)* (1633), and *Les Mécaniques de Galilée* (1634), a translation and explanation of Galileo's lectures on mechanics. Mersenne has also translated parts of Galileo's *Dialogo* into French, and in 1639 published a translation of Galileo's *Discorsi*. It is through Mersenne that Galileo's work has become known outside Italy.

Up to 1630, Mersenne had listed Galileo among those whose views should be rejected. Since then, however, he has been one of Galileo's strongest supporters.

It is a mark of Mersenne's eminent reputation that so far he has avoided Papal censure for his heretical views,

in particular the Copernican belief that the Earth orbits the Sun. Many have been burned at the stake for less.

Descartes Sums Up His Philosophical Principles

Amsterdam, Netherlands, 1644: René Descartes, the philosopher, mathematician, and scientist, has recently published his most comprehensive work, *Principia Philosophiae (Principles of Philosophy)*, a compilation of his physics and metaphysics. It comprises four parts: *The Principles*

René Descartes

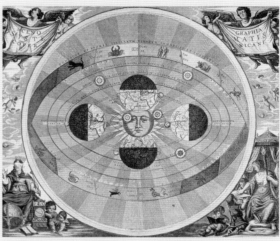

A 1660 depiction of the heliocentric Copernican system.

of Human Knowledge; *Of Material Things*; *Of the Visible World*, and *Of the Earth*.

Descartes says that a human being is a union of body and mind, two dissimilar substances that interact in the pineal gland. He contends that each action on a person's sense organs causes subtle matter to move through tubular nerves to the pineal gland, causing vibrations, which inspire emotions and passions, and also cause the body to act. Thus action is the final result of a reflex that originates with external stimuli, then involves an internal response—for example, when one sees a wild animal, feels fear, then flees.

Most importantly, the mind can change the pineal vibrations from those that cause fear, to those that cause courage.

The 48-year-old Descartes is called "the father of modern philosophy" for good reason. He has always systematically mistrusted knowledge based on faith, the senses, and reason. He found what many call the first indubitable truth in his intuition that when he is thinking, he exists. He expressed this in his famous statement "*cogito ergo sum*" ("I think, therefore I am").

Descartes' spiritual system is intuitionist, and derived by reason from instinctive ideas, but his scientific ideas, which are solely based on sensory knowledge, are mechanical and experiential.

Scientific Achievements

Astronomy: Telescope invented; works published on laws of planetary motion and observations of lunar surface; Orion nebula discovered.
Botany: Tea imported to Europe; Dutch begin growing tulips as a cash crop.
Chemistry: Barium sulphide discovered.
Ecology: Book published on fishing and conservation.
Geology: Francis Bacon notices how coasts of South America and Africa fit together.
Mathematics: Works on geometry and prime numbers published.
Medicine: Circulatory system and function of heart published; study on perspiration and metabolism published.
Physics: Works on magnets and law of refraction published; barometer invented.

Botanic Gardens
Amsterdam, Netherlands
Copenhagen, Denmark
Oxford, England
Paris, France

Observatories
Copenhagen, Denmark
Danzig/Gdansk, Poland
Leiden, Netherlands
Prague, eastern Europe

Universities
University of Amsterdam, Netherlands
University of Cambridge, North America
University of Cordoba, Argentina
University of Helsinki, Finland
University of Salzburg, Austria
University of Tartu, Estonia
University of Trnava, eastern Europe
University of Utrecht, Netherlands

New Bridge Spans Seine

Paris, France, c. 1606: After 28 years, a revolutionary new bridge across the River Seine has been completed. At 92 ft wide and 1,083 ft long (28 m × 330 m), it is the widest bridge in Paris and the first without houses lining the edges to obscure the view of the river.

Parisians have dubbed it Pont Neuf (New Bridge) and are already using it as a thoroughfare, meeting point, and promenade venue—especially during evening twilight and on weekends. Comedy and theatre acts perform against the stunning backdrop of the Seine—including a unique mid-river vista of the Louvre gallery, which, as usual, is undergoing reconstruction.

The bridge comprises two sections, a "long arm" of seven arches from the right bank of the Seine to the western end of the Ile de la Cité (City Island) and a "short arm" of five arches from the island to the left bank. The wooden supports were constructed separately and joined together by stone paving and walls.

The decision to build the bridge, designed by the royal architects Baptiste du Cerceau and Pierre des Illes, was taken by King Henri IV, who laid the first stone himself in 1578.

The bridge is part of a flurry of construction commissioned by King Henri III, and continued under Henri IV, which also includes the Tuileries, a new town hall, and the transformation of the city and Saint-Germain districts.

Enigmatic Painter Reported Dead

Rome, Italy, 1610: Caravaggio, master of the chiaroscuro (light and shadows) style of painting, and the world's most influential painter in his short career of 10 years, has died in dubious circumstances. Born the son of a mason in Lombardy in 1571, he burst upon the Rome art scene in 1600 with his *Calling of St Matthew* and *Martyrdom of St Matthew*.

He never lacked patrons, yet handled his success atrociously. It is said that Caravaggio "put the *oscuro* (shadows) into chiaroscuro," darkening the shadows and transfixing his subject in a dazzling beam of light. His dramatic, theatrical approach and his acute depiction of physical and psychological reality created both his immense popularity and his frequent problems with religious commissions.

In 1606, he fled Rome after murdering the pimp Ranuccio Tomassoni. Some say this followed a row over a tennis match, but a Vatican source claims that it was a botched attempt by Caravaggio to cut off Tomassoni's testicles after a dispute over a female prostitute Fillide Melandroni, whose services both men had sought.

Caravaggio fled to Naples, then Malta, where he received patronage from the Order of the Knights of Malta, producing a huge *Beheading of Saint John the Baptist* and *Portrait of Alof de Wignacourt and his Page*. But in August, 1608, he was arrested and imprisoned after yet another brawl, during which the door of a house was battered down and a knight wounded.

On July 28, an anonymous *avviso* (private newsletter) from Rome to the ducal court of Urbino reported that Caravaggio was dead. Three days later another *avviso* said that he had died of fever. His body has not been found.

Novel Finally Reaches the Last Chapter

Spain, 1615: Miguel de Cervantes has published the long-awaited second instalment of his highly popular novel *Don Quixote*.

It is not as wildly hilarious as part one, published 10 years ago, but it retains its narrative power and mastery of dialogue, while showing more human insight, a clearer and more concise style, and more realism in action. Cervantes has certainly upheld his aim to express himself "in simple, honest, and well-measured words."

Marie de' Medici, wife of Henri IV of France

> "NO MAN IS AN ISLAND, ENTIRE OF ITSELF; EVERY MAN IS A PIECE OF THE CONTINENT, A PART OF THE MAIN… THEREFORE NEVER SEND TO KNOW FOR WHOM THE BELL TOLLS; IT TOLLS FOR THEE."
>
> JOHN DONNE, (1572–1631), ENGLISH POET, 1624

time out

April 23, 1616 is the date of death for writers Cervantes and Shakespeare, but they actually died 10 days apart–Spain had adopted the Gregorian calendar while England was still using the Julian calendar, which ran 10 days behind the Gregorian.

Bustling traffic on the Pont Neuf in Paris, from a seventeenth-century engraving by Nicolas Guérard.

The author always intended to write a follow-up to volume one, and was goaded into action by the recent publication of a very poor sequel by an unknown writer who was undoubtedly trying to cash in on *Don Quixote*'s popularity.

Cervantes has not been idle since the publication of the first volume, producing various works of mixed quality. The most popular is his 1613 publication *Novelas Ejemplares (Exemplary Tales)*, a collection of superbly crafted short

Tile painting of Don Quixote and Sancho Panza tilting at windmills.

stories about love, idealism, the gypsy life, lunatics, and talking dogs.

Cervantes has always said that, as much as he loves writing in verse, he realizes he is deficient in poetic gifts. Undeterred, last year he published *Viaje del Parnaso*, a series of affectionate verse critiques of some of his fellow writers. That provoked the general reaction that as a poet, Cervantes makes a great prose writer.

Opulent "Blue Mosque" Truly a Place to Worship

Constantinople, Turkey, 1616: The skyline of Constantinople is now dominated by a magnificent newly completed mosque.

It was commissioned seven years ago by the great Mogul leader Sultan Ahmed, who told his architect Sedefhar Mehmet

Aga to spare no expense in creating the most magnificent and beautiful place of Islamic worship in the world. There is no doubt he has succeeded.

The floor measures 210 ft × 236 ft (64 m × 72 m) and is topped by an ascending system of opulent domes and semi-domes, culminating in the central dome, which is 108 ft (33 m) in diameter and 141 ft (43 m) high at its central point.

Pure gold calligraphy adorns the walls, while the upper levels are covered in intricate carvings and painted murals. More than 200 stained glass windows with elaborate designs admit natural light.

Locals have dubbed it "the Blue Mosque" due to the ethereal blue light imparted by the 21,043 handmade tiles lining the interior.

Prodigious English Playwright Dead

Stratford-upon-Avon, England, April 23, 1616: The Bard is dead. William Shakespeare, Stratford-on-Avon's most famous son and England's greatest playwright, passed away today on his 52nd birthday.

Born the eldest son of alderman John Shakespeare and Mary Arden, he was educated at Stratford Grammar. In 1582, aged just 18, he married Anne Hathaway, seven years his senior, who presented him with a daughter, Susannah, six months later.

The family moved to London, where William joined several acting companies as actor and playwright, often touring the provinces. Twins followed in 1585, a son Hamnet and daughter Judith. Hamnet died in 1596.

Shakespeare emerged in the theater scene as a playwright about 1590 with plays such as *Romeo and Juliet, King Henry IV,* and *Taming of the Shrew,* and maintained a prodigious output for the rest of his life. His later works include the superb tragedies *Julius Caesar, Hamlet, King Lear,* and *Macbeth.*

Speculation abounds as to the identity of the male and female muses in Shakespeare's 1609 *Sonnets,* and whether the poems are, in fact, autobiographical. Shakespeare himself was always silent on this topic, but all readers agree that the poems surpass all before them in their astonishing conciseness, emotion, beauty, and linguistic brilliance.

Few can argue that Shakespeare, who is universally admired for his honesty, wit, and generosity, has produced the greatest body of literature in English. His mastery of poetry and diverse dramatic styles—romantic comedy and tragedy, historical drama, farce, fantasy, and satire—is without equal.

Miguel de Cervantes

Chart of the Constantinople skyline, showing the Hagia Sophia, the Blue Mosque, and Topkapi Palace.

London, England, 1619: Nicholas Hilliard, painter, dies, aged about 72. He is remembered for his exquisite miniature portraits.

London, England, 1622: Inigo Jones, one of England's most influential architects, completes the Banqueting Hall at Whitehall.

Essex, England, July 4, 1623: William Byrd, composer, dies, aged about 80. He is remembered for his many ecclesiastical compositions.

Haarlem, Netherlands, 1624: Franz Hals paints *The Laughing Cavalier.*

Paris, France, 1629: Architect Jacques Lemercier oversees the construction of the Palais Cardinal (now the Palais Royal), built for Cardinal Richelieu.

India, c. 1630: Shah Jahan commissions the writing of an illustrated history of his reign, *Padshahnama (King of the World).*

London, England, 1632: After spending time in a number of European locations, Dutch painter Anthony van Dyck becomes court painter to Charles I.

Agra, India, 1632: Shah Jahan orders the building of Taj Mahal as a memorial to his wife, Mumtaz Mahal.

Amsterdam, Netherlands, 1632: Rembrandt's latest work, *The Anatomy Lesson of Dr Tulp,* offers an insight into surgical techniques.

England, 1633: John Ford publishes *'Tis Pity She's a Whore* and *Love's Sacrifice.*

Spain, 1635: Court painter Diego Velázquez completes his painting *The Surrender of Breda.*

Ireland, c. 1636: Combining many accounts, a history of Ireland is produced by four authors, headed by Michael O'Clery, known as the *Annals of the Four Masters.*

London, England, 1637: Ben Jonson, writer, dies, aged about 65. He is remembered for his numerous plays such as *Volpone, Bartholomew Fair,* and *The Alchemist.*

Japan, 1637: Hon'ami Koetsu, calligrapher, potter and lacquer artist, dies, aged about 79. He became famous for his tea ceremony, bowls of Raku, and lacquer.

Antwerp, Belgium, May 30, 1640: Peter Paul Rubens, painter, dies, aged 62. He is remembered for his many paintings incorporating religious or mythological themes.

Europe, c. 1642: John Suckling, poet, dies, aged about 33.

Amsterdam, Netherlands, 1642: Rembrandt paints his famous masterpiece *The Night Watch.*

London, England, 1643: Roger Williams publishes *Key into the Languages of America.*

Agra, India, 1648: Work is completed on the Taj Mahal.

England Mourns Loss of Revered Composer

Essex, England, July 4, 1623: William Byrd, now recognized as the "father of English music," has died at the age of 80. The multitalented Byrd was a fine organist and a virtuoso performer on the virginal (a small harpsichord), for which he wrote numerous pieces, including fantasias, dances and variations.

He also excelled in chamber music of many kinds—sacred and secular songs for domestic use, and a wide variety of forms and styles ranging from theater music to lullabies.

The London-born son of a musician studied music principally under the renowned composer Thomas Tallis, and became organist at Lincoln Cathedral in 1563. He was appointed to the prestigious position of organist of the Chapel Royal in 1575, and later founded the English Madrigal School.

By 1577, Byrd and his family had attracted attention for being too "papist," and a period of constant danger and harassment by English Church authorities followed. The persecution continued until 1591, until it was, remarkably, ended by a royal decree of Queen Elizabeth.

It is a mark of his esteemed status that, although an unreformed and steadfast Catholic, Byrd escaped the heretic's usual punishments of imprisonment, torture or death. It no doubt helped that, uniquely, he composed pieces for both Catholic and Protestant liturgies, although most of the former were confined to private performances for like-minded friends.

Byrd's *Psalms, Sonnets and Songs*, graduals, and sacred songs are among his most loved and widely-performed works.

Byrd equaled the highest accomplishments of his European contemporaries, and his pupil Thomas Morley was entirely justified in stating that Byrd should "never without reverence be named among the musicians."

Peter Paul Rubens

"Be not afraid of greatness: some are born great, some achieve greatness, and some have greatness thrust upon them."

WILLIAM SHAKESPEARE (1564–1616), ENGLISH DRAMATIST, FROM *TWELFTH NIGHT*, 1601

"Stone walls do not a prison make, Nor iron bars a cage."

RICHARD LOVELACE (1618–1658) ENGLISH POET, 1642

The Laughing Cavalier **is one of the world's most famous portraits.**

Hals' Portrait Captures Subject's Infectious Smile

Haarlem, Netherlands, 1624: Frans Hals, the Netherlands' most famous painter, has just completed *The Laughing Cavalier*, an oil painting hailed instantly as a masterpiece.

The strikingly handsome, 26-year-old subject looks out at the viewer, apparently sharing a joke with the artist, leaving one charmed yet slightly disconcerted—is it we who are being laughed at? His upward-pointing moustache, pointy beard, shiny nose, pink cheeks and hat give him an air of almost insufferable verve.

In reality the cavalier is not laughing at all, but smiling in a rather self-satisfied, provocative, and disdainful fashion. One itches to wipe that smile away—yet it is irresistible, almost infectious. The brush-strokes in the work are spontaneous and freely handled, and appear to have been painted rapidly, giving the sense of a frozen moment in the midst of life.

The painting has confirmed Hals' reputation as one of the most brilliant of all portraitists.

Artistic Triumph by Dutch Painter

Amsterdam, Netherlands, 1632: The up-and-coming Dutch painter Rembrandt has established himself as a portrait painter *par excellence* with the unveiling of a startling new work, *The Anatomy Lesson of Dr Tulp*.

Rembrandt began working as a professional portraitist only last year, with his competent yet unremarkable depictions of merchant Nicolaes Ruts and scholar Maarten Looten. This new study, of Amsterdam's leading surgeon, Dr Nicolaes Tulp, performing a public dissection, shows how quickly Rembrandt has transcended the smooth, stiff formality of the Amsterdam school.

This is not the traditional static, descriptive representation, but an action-packed and vibrant lesson in practical anatomy. The corpse—that of Aris Kindt, who was hanged for armed robbery on January 16—is the focus of the composition. It is illuminated by an intense beam of light that, contrasted with the scene's gloomy, indistinct background, brings to mind Caravaggio's chiaroscuro technique. Our eye is then led to the less luminous heads of the spectators—five wealthy friends of Tulp and two physicians—and to Tulp's face and hands. With his forceps, Tulp grasps the muscles and tendons of the forearm that control the movement of the corpse's left hand, while the bent fingers of Tulp's left hand accurately reveal its intricate mechanism.

The composition of the painting and the arrangement of the spectators conveys a great sense of movement. We sense the onlookers' wonder at what is being demonstrated, as they concentrate intently on the cadaver's arm. The observers look anxious, their faces showing both a keen interest and a deep disquiet.

The strong chiaroscuro and sculptural quality of the forms convey the excitement of the moment, and create the feeling of an extraordinary psychological event.

Potential clients and patrons will be impressed by the innovative vitality and pictorial richness that Rembrandt displays in this awe-inspiring work, and we may look forward with great enthusiasm to his future creations.

Ben Jonson Dies

London, England, August 6, 1637: The brilliant playwright, poet and unsurpassed writer of masques, Ben Jonson, has died.

Born the posthumous son of a clergyman in Westminster around June 11, 1572, Jonson was educated at Westminster School and then worked briefly as a bricklayer. Unsatisfied with that, he joined the army, serving in Flanders.

He returned to England in about 1592 and married Anne Lewis on November

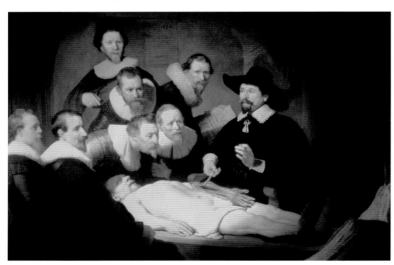

Dr Nicolaes Tulp explains the musculature of the arm to spectators.

14, 1594. In 1597, he began working in London as an actor and playwright.

In 1598, Jonson was tried for killing another actor in a duel but escaped execution by claiming "right of clergy" (meaning he could read and write). In that year he also produced his first important play, *Every Man in His Humour*, with William Shakespeare in the cast. In 1599, he produced the sequel, *Every Man out of His Humour*.

Jonson's great period began in 1606 with the production of *Volpone (The Fox)*. That was followed by the comic master-pieces *Epicoene* (1609), *The Alchemist* (1610), and *Bartholomew Fair* (1614).

Jonson also wrote many excellent masques for the court of James I, and is acknowledged as the master of the form. Masques are a magnificent and highly popular dramatic spectacle, performed by masked players representing mythological or allegorical figures. They feature verse, music and dance, and are presented in public theaters and royal courts. Jonson's later productions were relative failures, and with the accession of Charles I in 1625 his stocks fell at the royal court.

Nonetheless, the high-spirited enthu-siasm of Jonson's plays and the all-around brilliance of his language have secured his reputation as one of England's greatest playwrights.

Key Structures

Ali Qapu Palace, Isfahan, Persia
Amber Palace, Jaipur, India
Baghdad Koshk, Constantinople, Turkey
Banqueting Hall, London, England
Bukjijangsa Temple, Daegu, Korea
Blue Mosque, Constantinople, Turkey
Dalada Maligawa (Temple of the Tooth Relic),
  Kandy, Ceylon
Eman Mosque, Isfahan, Persia
Emperor Fasilada's Castle, Gonder, Ethiopia
Golden Temple, Amritsar, India
Himeji Castle, Himeji, Japan
Imperial Villa Katsura, Kyoto, Japan
Khass Mahal, Delhi, India
Krishna Mandir Temple, Patan, Nepal
La Catedral, Lima, Peru
Lyabi Hauz, Bukhara, Uzbekistan
Nijo Castle, Kyoto, Japan
Nizwa Fort, Oman
Palais Royal, Paris, France
Pont Neuf Bridge, Paris, France
Pura Taman Ayun, Bali, East Indies
Red Fort, Delhi, India
Royal Palais, Abomey, Benin
St Peter's Basilica, Rome, Italy
St Agatha's Tower, Mellieha, Malta
Santa Clara Church, Bogota, Colombia
Sheikh Lotfollah Mosque, Isfahan
Shir-Dar-Madrassa, Samarkand, Uzbekistan
Taj Mahal, Agra, India
Taman Ayun Temple, Bali, East Indies
Terem Palace, Moscow, Russia
The Queen's House, Greenwich, England
Wazir Khan Mosque, Lahore, Indian subcontinent

Painter's Work Was Imbued with Exuberance

Antwerp, Belgium, May 30, 1640: Sir Peter Paul Rubens, the most renowned north-ern European artist of our time, has died.

His fusing of the realistic baroque Flemish tradition with the inventive freedom and classical stylized themes of the new Italian painting revitalized European painting.

Rubens was born in 1577 in Siegen, Germany, and completed his apprentice-ship in Antwerp. By the age of 21, he had become a master painter whose esthetic and religious outlook led him to Italy to complete his education.

While assimilating the lessons of the Italian masters, Rubens fell under the in-fluence of Titian. He spent time in Venice and Rome, where he painted altarpieces for the churches of Santa Croce di Gerusa-lemme and Chiesa Nuova (1607), his first widely acknowledged masterpieces.

In 1608, his reputation established, Rubens returned to Antwerp and quickly became the dominant artistic figure in the Spanish Netherlands.

Rubens either executed personally or supervised the execution of an enormous body of works that spanned all areas of painting and drawing. His many religious and mythological paintings resonate with the lusty exuberance, frenetic energy and often violent emotional overtones of the Counter-Reformation.

His mastery of monumental forms and dynamic effects is readily apparent in the vast decorative schemes he executed in the 1620s, including the famous 21-painting cycle chronicling the life of Marie de' Medici, the wife of Henry IV of France.

In 1625, Rubens conducted negotia-tions to end the war between the Spanish Netherlands and the Dutch Republic, and, in 1630, finalized a peace treaty be-tween England and Spain. Charles I of England was so impressed with his efforts that he knighted him.

"World's Most Beautiful Building" Completed

Agra, India, 1648: The superlative Taj Mahal (Crown Palace), the world's finest example of Mogul architecture, has recently been completed in Agra.

Made entirely of white marble, the structure was commissioned by Emperor Shah Jahan, and designed by renowned Islamic architect Ustad Isa. It serves as a mausoleum to honor the memory of Mumtaz Mahal, the Shah's second and favorite wife, who died in 1631.

Some 20,000 engineers, carvers, artists, calligraphers, architects, craftsmen of all sorts, and common laborers spent 17 years constructing the glistening monument.

All who view it agree that its over-whelming architectural beauty is beyond adequate description, particularly at dawn and sunset. It glows brightly in the light of the full moon, while on a foggy morning, when viewed from the other side of the nearby Jamuna River, it appears to float in mid-air.

The Taj Mahal stands on a raised square platform (186 × 186 ft; 57 × 57 m) with the four corners truncated, forming an unequal octagon. It uses the "interlock-ing arabesque" design, in which each element stands on its own, while reflecting and integrating with the main structure.

Its central dome is 58 ft (17.5 m) in diameter and 213 ft (65 m) high, and flanked by four subsidiary domed chambers. The four elegant slender minarets are $162\frac{1}{2}$ ft (49.5 m) high.

The entire mausoleum (inside and out) is decorated with inlaid designs of flowers and calligraphy using precious gems such as agate and jasper. The main archways, chiseled with passages from the Koran, lead to the central and adjoining chambers, whose walls are also covered in intricate Islamic decorations.

Many well-traveled observers consider the Taj Mahal to be the most beautiful building in the world.

Sir Walter Raleigh

Appearing to float in mid-air, the Taj Mahal is the pre-eminent expression of a man's love for his wife.

Louis XIII of France

Plot to Blow Up Parliament Foiled

London, England, November 5, 1605: Guy Fawkes, a Catholic Yorkshireman, has been caught red-handed in the cellars of Parliament with more than two tons of gunpowder. Under torture, he confessed his plot to blow up the House of Lords, where the king and queen and members of both houses were due to assemble for the opening of Parliament. He also revealed his authorship of the plot, and the names of co-conspirators.

The scheme was uncovered when Lord Monteagle—a Catholic peer nonetheless loyal to the king—recently received an anonymous warning to stay away from Parliament today because "God and man" would strike "a terrible blow."

The warning was probably provided by a Catholic conspirator concerned about his fellow Catholics who would have been present at Parliament. However, Monteagle passed the letter on to Lord Salisbury, the king's chief minister, who ordered the searching of Parliament. This led to the discovery of Fawkes, 20 barrels of explosives, and nine other conspirators, four of whom died resisting arrest.

Recently, England has been swaying back and forth on a theological pendulum, and Fawkes is most dissatisfied with the current Protestant ascendancy. With the recent death of Queen Elizabeth, he saw the opportunity to strike a blow against the court and its representatives.

Fawkes and his fellow traitors planned to throw the whole country into turmoil, out of which they would advance a new monarch sympathetic to their cause and return England to its Catholic past.

The surviving conspirators are expected to be tortured, then hung, drawn and quartered.

"THE WORLD ITSELF IS BUT A LARGE PRISON, OUT OF WHICH SOME ARE DAILY LED TO EXECUTION."

SIR WALTER RALEIGH (1554–1618) ENGLISH EXPLORER, FOLLOWING HIS TRIAL FOR TREASON, 1603

"NEITHER DO THOU LUST AFTER THAT TAWNEY WEED TOBACCO."

BEN JONSON (1573–1637) ENGLISH DRAMATIST, 1614

time out

King Louis XIII (1601-1643) of France was the instigator of the fashion of men wearing wigs. Apparently he took up wearing a wig to hide his hair loss from both the court and the French public.

Guy Fawkes is arrested attempting to blow up the Houses of Parliament.

Jesuit Took Christ to the Chinese

Peking, China, 1609: Matteo Ricci, the Italian Jesuit priest who introduced Christianity to China and heightened Euro-pean awareness of Chinese culture and science, has died of unknown causes.

After quitting legal studies in Rome, and joining the Society of Jesus, Ricci accepted missionary undertakings in Goa, India. He then learned to speak and write Chinese fluently in Macau, before moving to mainland China in 1583.

Believing that Christianity would have to adapt to local customs in order to be accepted, he adopted mandarin clothing and took the name Li-Mateo. He excited immediate curiosity and interest with his knowledge of mathematics, astronomy, and cartography, and with his clocks, globes, maps, and books of European engravings. In 1584, he caused a sensation with his produc-

Jesuit missionary Matteo Ricci with a Chinese official.

tion of the first European-style map of the world in Chinese, with many objecting that China did not occupy a sufficiently prominent position.

He translated many Christian texts into Chinese, including the Lord's Prayer and the Ten Commandments, and later published *True Meaning of the Lord in Heaven*, a brilliant and well-received explanation of Christianity.

Ricci went on to write, edit, or translate various works on theology, geography, astronomy, geometry, and arithmetic for both Chinese and Western readers.

He became a convert to Confucianism before trying to convert the Chinese, believing that such Confucian principles as filial piousness, reciprocity, and personal merit could and should be accommodated in the Christian Church.

New Authorized King James Bible Released

London, England, 1611: A new, officially approved translation of the Bible has been published by Robert Barker, the king's printer.

Peking, China, 1601: Jesuit priest Matteo Ricci becomes the first Christian missionary to be allowed to preach in China's capital.
Russia, 1601-1603: Successive crop failures see famine strike Russia, resulting in the deaths of hundreds of thousands of people.
London, England, 1602: John Willis introduces a shorthand system based on phonetics in *The Art of Stenographie.*
India, c. 1603: Mogul ruler Akbar grants his subjects the freedom of religion.

Japan, 1603: Tokugawa Ieyasu makes Edo (Tokyo) his capital. He establishes his headquarters at the newly completed Nijo Castle.
London, England, November 5, 1605: Guy Fawkes and his band attempt to blow up the Houses of Parliament in the Gunpowder Plot.
Virginia, North America, 1607: An English settlement is established, and named Jamestown.
North America, 1608: French geographer and explorer Samuel de Champlain founds the city of New France (Quebec).

Peking, China, 1609: Matteo Ricci, Italian missionary, dies, aged 56.
Europe, 1610: Tea is introduced into Europe from China.
London, England, 1611: Approved by King James I, an official translation of the Bible is published.
Japan, 1614: Shogun Tokugawa Ieyasu bans Christianity and expels Christian missionaries.
Venice, Italy, 1615: Coffee is imported into Europe for the first time by Venetian traders.

England, 1618: James I issues a country-wide declaration "Concerning lawful sports" which allows certain sports to be played on Sundays, despite Puritan opposition.
Virginia, North America, 1619: Settlers at Berkeley Plantation enjoy a dinner of thanksgiving—though whether it is the first Thanksgiving is a matter of dispute. Also in this year, the first African slaves are transported here.
Philippapolis, Turkey, 1620: The merry-go-round is first recorded.

Japan, 1620: Will Adams, English trader and adviser to Ieyasu, dies, aged about 46.
Plymouth, Massachusetts, North America, October, 1621: Following a successful harvest, the Pilgrims enjoy a dinner in celebration.
North America, 1625: The city of New Amsterdam (New York) is founded by the Dutch.
Naples, Italy, 1626: An earthquake causes more than 70,000 deaths.

Authorized and sponsored by King James, the black-type edition features an exquisitely engraved title page signed by the artist Cornelius Boel. It replaces the unpopular 1568 Bishops' Bible and the Geneva Bible currently favored by most clergy and laypeople.

King James, who believes that the Geneva version contains seditious and blasphemous comments, commissioned a new version at the 1604 Hampton Court conference of bishops.

It is the work of at least 45 scholars based at Westminster, Oxford, and Cambridge, and is based primarily on original Hebrew and Greek translations, with reference to Syrian, Latin, Spanish, French, Italian, and Dutch editions.

The translators were organized into six working groups. Ten at Westminster were assigned Genesis through Kings; seven had Romans through Jude. At Cambridge, eight worked on Chronicles through Ecclesiastes, while seven dealt with the Apocrypha. Oxford engaged seven scholars to translate Isaiah through Malachi, with eight covering the Gospels, Acts, and Revelations.

Their efforts were reviewed and edited by a committee of twelve, before fine-tuning by the king's representatives, Thomas Bilson and Myles Smith, who wrote the preface.

Despite the piecemeal nature of the book's creation, critics have lauded its uniformity of style, and the splendor and melody of the tempo of the language.

The King James Bible is being hailed as an accurate depiction of the word of God, and also as a superb work of literature.

Pioneer in Japan Dead

Japan, 1620: Will Adams, the first Englishman to reach Japan and the first European to be granted the title shogun, has died.

Born William Adams in 1564 in Gillingham, Kent, he was apprenticed at the age of 12 to a shipyard owner. He spent the next 12 years learning shipbuilding, astronomy and navigation. He entered employment as a navigator with the Dutch navy in 1598.

Upon arriving in Japan in 1600, Adams was imprisoned almost immediately after having been framed by jealous Portuguese traders. However, his design and construction of two excellent sailing ships for Japan's ruler, Tokugawa Ieyasu, led to his release.

Ieyasu took a liking to Adams and appointed him as diplomatic and trade adviser. Against all odds, Adams succeeded in negotiating separate trade deals between Japan and the warring European states of England, Portugal, the Netherlands, and Spain.

In time, Adams became Ieyasu's personal adviser on all things pertaining to the West, was promoted to the rank of shogun, and showered with riches.

Musical gatherings were a feature of seventeenth-century culture.

Dutch Buy Island from North American Natives

Manhattan, North America, 1626: Last August 10, the island of Manhattan in the colony of New Amsterdam was purchased from local Canarsee Indians.

Governor Peter Minuit arrived in the colony last May, with instructions from the Dutch West India Company (which is financing construction), saying: "In case any Indian should be living on the aforesaid land or make any claim upon it or any other places that are of use to us,

James I of England

Peter Minuit purchases Manhattan from the Canarsee.

they must not be driven away by force or threat, but by good words be persuaded to leave, or be given something therefor to their satisfaction…"

When the *Arms of Amsterdam*, returned to Amsterdam from North America on November 4, Peter Schagen, a member of the governing board of the Dutch West India Company, interviewed the passengers and crew. In a letter to the board, he said: "They report that our people are in good heart and live in peace there; the women have also borne some children there. They have purchased the Island Manhattes from the Indians for the value of 60 guilders; 'tis 11,000 morgens [about 22 sq miles, 57 sq km] in size."

It is not yet known what form the payment took. There are rumors that the Indians refused offers of silver and gold, instead preferring beads and trinkets.

Key Events

Manhattan, North America, 1626: The Dutch West India Company, buys the island of Manhattan from the local Native Americans for 60 guilders (around $24).

Massachusetts, North America, 1630: The city of Boston is founded.

Paris, France, 1630: Parisians are the first to enjoy the new thirst-quenching lemonade.

Boston, North America, 1630: Boston Latin School—America's first school—is established.

Italy, 1631: Mt Vesuvius erupts, causing the deaths of more than 3,000 people.

Canada, 1634: Jesuit missionaries, (Jean de Brébeuf, Antoine Daniel, and Ambroise Davost) continue attempts to convert native people to Christianity.

Amsterdam, Netherlands, 1634: Tulips have been gaining in popularity, attracting enthusiasts and investors.

France, 1635: Tobacco is only available for sale to those with a doctor's prescription.

Paris, France, 1635: Cardinal Richelieu establishes the Académie Française as a watchdog authority to guard against words from other languages entering everyday use.

Charlestown, Massachusetts, North America, September 14, 1638: English settler John Harvard bequeaths a substantial amount to the local college along with his extensive library of books.

Deshima, Japan, 1641: Dutch merchants are granted a monopoly on European trade with Japan under strict government supervision.

Canada, 1642: The French establish the city of Montreal.

New Zealand, December, 1642: The first known contact between Maori and Europeans occurs when Maori canoes approach the ships of Dutch explorer Abel Tasman. A day later one Maori and four Europeans are killed in a conflict at sea.

Peking, China, 1645: Rulers of the newly established Qing Dynasty decree that all Chinese men must wear their hair in a Manchu-style queue or face execution.

Canada, 1646: Smallpox continues to take the lives of the native people. Father Isaac Jogues is killed by Iroquois who believe he is spreading the disease.

Canada, March, 1649: Jesuit priests Jean de Brébeuf and Gabriel Lalemant are tortured to death by the Iroquois.

Asia, 1649: The city of Urga (Ulan Bator) is founded.

Edo (Tokyo), Japan, 1649: The Tokugawa Government issues laws prohibiting non-samurai from wearing gold or silver ornaments.

Cardinal Richelieu

Missionary's Memoirs Reveal Japanese Culture

Macau, 1633: Papers uncovered since the recent death of the Portuguese Jesuit João Rodrigues in Macau contain observations about Japanese geography, climate, agriculture, astronomy, and etiquette.

Rodrigues arrived in Japan in 1577 and spent more than 30 years there as a missionary, diplomat, linguist and one-time adviser to two Japanese emperors. However, he was forced to flee in 1610 when the Japanese implemented a policy of torturing and murdering Christians. He spent the last 23 years of his life writing in exile in Macau.

Four chapters of Rodrigues's fascinating memoirs are devoted to the Japanese tea ceremony, a widespread ritual that is performed in seats of government and private houses alike.

The ceremony had its origins in China hundreds of years ago, and was brought by monks to Japan, where it first found favor among the upper classes. It is based on a set of precise and formalized procedures that govern the preparation of the tea, the method of service, rules of conversation, and etiquette of the participants.

The ceremonial structure and underlying Buddhist philosophy are designed to create a serene atmosphere that leads the

> *"Do not eat garlic or onions; for their smell will reveal that you are a peasant."*
>
> MIGUEL DE CERVANTES SAAVEDRA (1547–1616), SPANISH NOVELIST, 1614

> *"Humpty Dumpty sat on a wall, Humpty Dumpty had a great fall. All the king's horses, And all the king's men, Couldn't put Humpty together again."*
>
> NURSERY RHYME BASED ON AN INCIDENT IN THE ENGLISH CIVIL WAR, WHEN CHARLES I UNSUCCESSFULLY USED A MACHINE TO CROSS A RIVER, 1643

Religious Leaders

Popes
Clement VIII (1592-1605)
Leo XI (1605)
Paul V (1605-1621)
Gregory XV (1621-1623)
Urban VIII (1623-1644)
Innocent X (1644-1655)

Archbishops of Canterbury
John Whitgift (1583-1604)
Richard Bancroft (1604-1610)
George Abbot (1611-1633)
William Laud (1633-1645)
Vacant (1645-1660)

Dalai Lamas of Tibet
Yonten Gyatso (1601-1616)
Ngawang Lobsang Gyatso (1642-1682)

Patriarchs of Constantinople
Matthew II (1598-1602, 1603)
Meletius I Pegas (coadjutor) (1601)
Neophytus II (1602-1603, 1607-1612)
Raphael II (1603-1607)
Timotheus II (1612-1620)
Cyril I Lucaris (1612, 1620-1635, 1637-1638)
Gregory IV of Amasea (1623)
Anthimus II (1623)
Cyril II Kontares (1633, 1635-1636, 1638-1639)
Athanasius III Patelaros (1634)
Neophytus III of Nicea (1636-1637)
Parthenius I (1639-1644)
Parthenius II (1644-1646, 1648-1651)
Joannicus II (1646-1648)

By the seventeenth century, coffee had made its way to Europe and was becoming popular across the continent.

partakers to a sense of inner peace. Approved activities while enjoying tea include reading poetry, writing calligraphy, painting, and discussing philosophy.

The tea ceremony is now becoming popular in all levels of society.

Tulipomania Toppled

Amsterdam, Netherlands, February, 1637: The bottom has suddenly fallen out of the Dutch tulip market, leaving most speculators bankrupt. The price of a bulb has dropped by over 99 percent in a week as owners scramble to offload their ridiculously overpriced stock.

The madness of "tulipomania" has gripped the Netherlands in recent years, with investors fanatically trading the bulbs of the once-lowly flower.

Conrad Guestner imported the first tulip bulb into Holland from Constantinople in 1593. Within a few years, tulips became a status symbol for the rich. Later, some tulips contracted a non-harmful virus called mosaic, producing blooms with beautiful streaks of color on their petals. This unique effect further increased the value of the highly exclusive tulip bulb.

The rapidly rising price attracted speculators, with the bulbs being traded on local exchanges. By 1630, tulipomania had spread to the Dutch middle class, with everyone seeking a quick fortune. Most buyers had no intention of even planting the bulbs.

Two years ago, prices escalated even further when a futures market in bulbs

French dramatist Pierre Corneille.

was established. This enabled people to buy non-existent bulbs, with money they did not have, in the hope that when the bulbs became available they could be sold for a profit. In less than a month, the price of bulbs went up 2,000 percent. Last week, when no more foolish buyers could be found for the ever-increasing supplies, the market collapsed.

An investor recently paid for a single bulb: four tons of wheat, eight tons of rye, one bed, four oxen, eight pigs, 12 sheep, one suit of clothes, two casks of wine, four tons of beer, two tons of butter, 1,000 pounds of cheese, and a silver drinking cup. Today that bulb is almost worthless.

New Academy to "Purify" French Language

Paris, France, 1637: A new watchdog to oversee the French language has been established by Cardinal Richelieu who is the chief minister of France. The role of the Académie Francaise is to standardize and "purify" the language by setting out rules governing the use of grammar, spelling, orthography, and rhetoric.

The mission of the Académie is to create standards that will enable the language to be understood by everyone without ambiguity, and to replace the dozens of "vulgar" vernaculars currently spoken throughout the country with a single, pure, authorized form.

The Académie's origins lie in an informal group of writers, scholars, and

philosophers that has been meeting in Paris for some years to discuss language and literature. Richelieu took the body under his wing and, in anticipation of the formal creation of the Académie, last year appointed several members.

On February 22, 1635, at Richelieu's urging, King Louis XIII granted "letters patent," formally establishing the body. The patent was registered at the Parlement de Paris last July.

The first notable act of the society has been to attack the play *Cid*, by master tragedian Pierre Corneille, and produced earlier this year. Based on a Spanish play, the masterpiece took Paris by storm, and "beautiful as the *Cid*" has become a popular phrase. But Académie member Jean Chapelain composed a paper that attacked the play as plagiaristic and faulty in composition. Corneille has agreed to stick to classical rules in his future writing.

The Académie has just started work on a definitive dictionary, a project expected to take several decades.

Fledgling College Renamed for Benefactor

Charlestown, Massachusetts, North America, 1639: The Massachusetts General Court has decreed that Newtowne College shall be renamed Harvard College in honor of its benefactor, John Harvard, who died last year. The cleric and teacher left half his estate to the fledgling three-year-old college, thus securing its future.

Harvard was born in 1607, the son of a butcher in Stratford-on-Avon, England. The plague killed his father and most of his brothers and sisters in 1625. His mother remarried, and John was sent by his mother and stepfather to Emmanuel College, Cambridge, in 1627. He graduated in 1631 and then received his masters degree in 1635.

Upon the death of his mother in 1637, Harvard inherited considerable property in England, which he sold before marrying Ann Sadler and departing for the New World. During the period between selling and sailing, Harvard also acquired many of the books he brought with him to his new home, probably realizing the importance of education in a growing colony. It has been estimated that Harvard spent £200 on his superb library, which he has also bequeathed to the school that will forever bear his name.

On November 2, 1637, John Harvard became a freeman of Charlestown, Massachusetts Bay Colony. He was soon recognized as a learned and virtuous man, and served as assistant pastor of the First Church of Charlestown. However, less than a year after arriving in Charlestown, he died of tuberculosis.

Tasman Finds New Lands

South Pacific Ocean, 1643: Dutch maritime explorer Abel Janszoon Tasman has recently discovered two new lands in the South Pacific. The Dutch East India captain is on a voyage to map the large landmass known as New Holland.

Traveling further south than previous explorers, he made landfall on a rugged coast, which he named Van Diemen's Land after the governor-general of Batavia. It is not known if it is joined to New Holland.

Sailing east for five days, he discovered another unknown land, which may also be part of New Holland, or perhaps of South America. He named it Staten Landt. After nightfall, five of his crew were killed by native Maoris, possibly because he mistook their conch-shell challenges for a welcome, and instructed his bugler to return their melodies note for note. Tasman named the area Murderers' Bay and set sail northward.

Time will tell if these new lands contain similar riches to the Americas and Indies.

Ming to Qing as Manchus Take Control of China

Peking, China, 1645: The 276-year Ming Dynasty has finally been overthrown by semi-nomadic Manchu forces, who have taken advantage of the political instability and popular rebellions convulsing China to establish the Qing Dynasty.

Last year the Mings were torn apart by an internal coup when the ambitious army general Li Tzu-ch'eng led a mutiny against the demoralized, starving forces of Emperor Ch'ung-chen. One general has reported that, "When you whip one soldier, he stands up; but at the same time another is lying down."

The royal granaries and treasury were also empty after years of war against the Manchus and the many other insurgent groups who have been rebelling against high taxes, corruption, poverty, and the breakdown of government.

Li's massed forces stormed the city after the treacherous eunuch Cao Huajun opened the city gates. This resulted in the suicide of the emperor, who hanged himself in the pavilion of the Imperial Hat and Girdle department of the palace complex. Unsurprisingly, many government troops defected to Li.

The highly organized military forces of the Manchus were well placed to take advantage of the strife and confusion. They recently swept into Peking, massacred all those who opposed them and quickly established rule.

The Manchus' first act was to ban traditional dress, and introduce the "cut the hair or cut the head" rule. The Chinese, under threat of decapitation, are now required to adopt the Manchu "queue" hairstyle, in which all the hair is shaved from the front of the skull, with the remaining hair trained into a "pigtail."

The law is designed to emphasize the reality of the Manchu's physical domination, while at the same time inflicting a humiliating psychological blow on the defeated populace.

In an act that confirms the end of the Mings, Manchu general Dorgan has installed Fu-Lin as Qing Emperor.

Abel Janszoon Tasman

The popularity of pipe smoking increased during the Thirty Years War, as illustrated by this group of smokers.

Oliver Cromwell

Aurangzeb Seizes Control of Mogul Empire

Agra, India, 1658: Aurangzeb, the favorite son of Emperor Shah Jahan, has placed his father under house arrest in his own harem, and has seized control of the northern Indian Mogul Empire. Shah Jahan, who became seriously ill last year, had once described Aurangzeb as more "worthy and saintly" than his other three sons, Dara, Shuja, and Murad.

Shah Jahan presided over a period of unprecedented peace and prosperity, but has been overthrown in the palace revolution, which also saw Aurangzeb eliminate his brothers, fellow contenders to the throne. The succession was blood-thirsty and violent, in typical Mogul fashion, as the sons launched into a series of bloody wars against each other.

When Jahan first became sick, Dara—the most honorable of the brothers—took power, but Shuja, the debauched alcoholic Governor of Bengal, routed his army at the Battle of Samugarh near Delhi. But Dara managed to muster another army and defeat Shuja, who fled the country.

Emperor Aurangzeb with the women of his harem.

Aurangzeb in turn routed Dara's forces, and tricked Murad, Governor of Gujarat, into an alliance by promising a share of the spoils in return for assistance in overthrowing their father. Murad is now missing, believed murdered.

During the later stages of Shah Jahan's rule, the Mogul Empire has been virtually bankrupt, largely as a result of Jahan's building program, which saw the construction of the Taj Mahal and many other superb edifices.

Charles II Restored to English Throne

London, England, May 29, 1660: The English monarchy, vacant since the execution of Charles I in 1649, has been restored. Charles II, exiled in Scotland for the past 11 years, today returned triumphantly to London, and will soon be crowned King.

England has been torn apart by civil wars since Charles I's beheading. Oliver Cromwell seized power in the name of the people in 1653, dissolving Parliament, and installing himself as "Lord Protector." But his self-righteous, Puritan govern-ment continued to lose popularity.

After Oliver Cromwell's death in September 1658, his son, Richard, was installed as Lord Protector. However, he proved unable to carry on his father's policies, lacking the confidence of the populace, and—more importantly—the Army. After seven months in office, the Army removed him, and on May 6 last year it reinstated Parliament.

Charles Fleetwood, the former com-mander-in-chief of Ireland, was nomi-nated Lord-General of the Army, but his power was undermined by Parlia-ment, which chose to disregard the army's authority in a similar fashion to the pre-civil war Parliament.

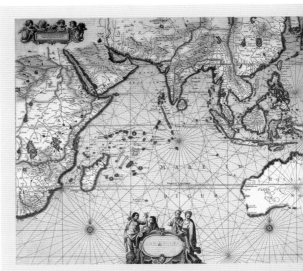

Jan Jansson's 1659 map of the Indian Ocean and surrounding count*

It was into this fraught atmosphere that George Monck, Governor of Scot-land under the Cromwells, marched south with his army. The rudderless and disillusioned English Army, yearning for the stability they believed only the King could provide, refused to oppose him and deserted. Fleetwood was stripped of his command, and ordered to appear before Parliament to answer for his conduct.

Last April 4, Charles II made known the conditions of his acceptance of the crown of England. Monck organized the Conven-tion Parliament, which met for the first time on April 25. On May 8 it proclaimed that King Charles II had been the lawful monarch since the execution of his father.

Charles II, shrewdly waiting until the power vacuum was complete, arrived in Dover three days ago, and made a proud return to London in front of cheering crowds this morning, on his 30th birthday.

Kangxi Becomes the Third Qing Emperor

China, February, 1661: Kangxi has ascended the Manchu (Qing) throne of China, following the death of his father, Shunzhi,

Cardinal Jules Mazarin

who has ruled the empire since the overthrow of the Ming Dynasty in 1644.

Shunzhi became Emperor of China at the age of six, and ruled the country when he turned fourteen. The young Emperor disliked the ruling Chief Regent, his uncle Prince Dorgon, and stripped him of his titles following his death in 1650, though Shunzhi was only twelve at the time. He quelled the remnants of the Ming Army, and put down a series of peasant uprisings initiated by local warlords intent on benefiting from the post-Ming power vacuum.

Renowned for his tolerant outlook, Shunzhi allocated positions of power to members of all ethnic groups. He also had a Jesuit adviser, Adam Schall Von Bell, who opened China's first Catholic mission. Shunzhi's death, from smallpox, comes four months after the death of his favorite concubine.

Until Kangxi comes of age, China's regent will be his grandmother, the Empress Dowager Xiaozhuang.

Full State Funeral for Cardinal Mazarin

Paris, France, March 9, 1661: Cardinal Jules Mazarin, the de facto ruler of France for the past 18 years, has died in Paris. King Louis XIV has ordered full mourning for the priest who, along with his mother, Anne of Austria, took control of France in 1643, when the five-year-old Louis ascended the throne upon the death of his father, Louis XIII.

Born on July 14, 1602, in central Italy, Mazarin had an action-packed boyhood and youth. He accompanied the future Cardinal Colonna to war in Madrid, and he was a captain of papal troops in the Valtelline War (1624) and the Mantuan War of Succession (1628–1630).

In 1630, he negotiated a truce between France and Spain, which won him the

esteem of Cardinal Richelieu, Louis XIII's confidant and adviser. On his deathbed in 1642, Richelieu commended Mazarin to the King as his replacement.

The exact character of Mazarin's relations with Queen Anne of an enigma, but there have been persistent whisperings that they secretly married. In any case, Mazarin's humble appearance and kind manner, and his gentle and kindly ways, contributed to his elevation, and Anne's affection for him was the best guarantee of his continuation in office.

He held the title of Bishop of Metz from 1653 to 1658, and effectively kept the disenfranchised Protestant Huguenots distracted with empty promises and many calculated delays. For six years they believed themselves to be on the verge of recovering their privileges, but in the end obtained nothing.

time out

More than 200,000 people die in Amsterdam, the Netherlands, as a result of the spread of the Black Plague during the early 1660s. The plague soon spreads to Belgium and Britain.

Deadly Bubonic Plague Devastates London

London, England, December, 1665: A terrible pestilence has swept through London, wiping out almost one third of its residents. The "bubonic plague"—or "Black Death"—started last spring and spread rapidly; and in some parishes so many corpses littered the streets that nobody was left to bury them.

The ghastly disease causes victims' skin to turn black, and inflames glands or "buboes" in the groin, accompanied by compulsive vomiting, a

swollen tongue, and splitting headaches. Incubation takes a mere four to six days, and authorities have been forced to take strict measures when symptoms of the plague appeared in a household, sealing off the house and condemning the whole family to death.

Diseased houses were identified by a red cross painted on the door, alongside the words, "Lord have mercy on us." At night, corpses were brought out to the streets in answer to the cry "Bring out your dead," before being placed in a cart and hauled away to enormous burial pits.

The plague originated in the East, possibly in China, and is spread by rats and fleas. In London it was first reported in the poor, overcrowded parish of St Giles-in-the-Field. It started slowly at first, but 43 people had died by May, followed by 6,137 deaths in June, 17,036 deaths in July, and 31,159 deaths at its peak in August.

King Charles II and his retinue left London and fled to Oxford. Those who could sent their families out of London, though the poor had no recourse but to stay. The epidemic appears to have been contained for the moment, as the onset of winter has helped kill off the fleas that spread the disease.

During the Great Plague in London, a bellringer calls for people to bring out their dead.

Key Events

Europe, 1672-1674: The Third Anglo-Dutch War takes place as the maritime rivals take up the contest again for control of the high seas, and trade.

North America, 1673: Louis Joliet and Father Marquette travel down the Mississippi by canoe to determine the river's path and the opportunities it may offer.

Carolina, North America, 1677: John Culpepper and George Durant lead a rebellion against the British restriction of the colonies' trade.

Louisiana, North America, April 9, 1682: René-Robert Cavelier, Sieur de la Salle, claims the Mississippi area for France, naming the area Louisiana in honor of the king.

Russia, 1682: Brothers Ivan IV and Peter I take the Russian throne after the death of Fyodor III, with Peter's half-sister Sofia as regent.

Pescadores Islands, China, 1683: The Qing Dynasty fleet defeats Ming loyalist forces based on the island of Taiwan; Taiwan surrenders three months later.

Africa, 1684: Changamire Dombo resists the Portuguese traders and starts to establish his Rozvi Empire.

Bombay (Mumbai), India, 1685: British forces take Bombay, which becomes a base for expansion of East India Company control.

Australia, 1688: Englishman William Dampier and other crew members land on the west coast.

London, England, February, 1689: William III and Mary II accept the throne as co-rulers, after James II has been forced into exile following the "Glorious Revolution."

Scotland, July 27, 1689: Supporters of James VII of Scotland (former James II of England) take on the English forces of the new royals at the Battle of Killiecrankie. Among the Jacobite force is Rob Roy.

Ireland, July 1, 1690: Ousted English King James II is defeated by the English and Dutch forces of the Parliament-appointed William III.

Scotland, February 13, 1692: The Massacre at Glencoe sees clan leader Maclain and his kinfolk murdered in their homes by their guests.

Sweden, October 13, 1694: German historian, Baron Samuel von Pufendorf, dies aged 62.

Quebec, North America, 1694: The intrepid Louis Joliet sets off to explore the Labrador region.

Australia, 1698: William Dampier, a former English pirate, sails to the west coast of Australia to investigate the region.

Eastern Europe, 1699: Defeat at the Battle of Zenta brings an end to the Great Turkish War, made official with the signing of the Treaty of Karlowitz by the Ottomans.

Charles II of England

London Reduced to Ash

London, England, September 7, 1666: Most of inner London lies in smoldering ruins, as the great fire that started five days ago finally appears to have burned itself out. The fire started in Pudding Lane, at the house of Thomas Farynor, King Charles II's baker. Farynor apparently forgot to douse his oven, and embers ignited the nearby firewood stack.

By 1 a.m., three hours after the household had retired to bed, the house and shop were aflame. Farynor's assistant awoke to find the house full of smoke and raised the alarm. Farynor, his wife and daughter, and one servant escaped through an upstairs window and along the rooftops, but the maid was too afraid to follow them, becoming the first victim of the terrible fire.

As strong winds fanned the flames, the blaze spread with staggering speed through London's pitch-covered timber buildings, most with thatched roofs. The whirling sparks set fire to the Star Inn, St Margaret's Church and Thames Street. The inferno raged through the wharf areas, incinerating warehouses packed with oil, spirits, tallow, hemp, straw, coal, and other combustibles.

At that stage the fire was far too fierce to be fought, and by 8 a.m. the flames had reached halfway across Old London Bridge. Only the gap left by a previous fire in 1633 prevented the flames from crossing the bridge and igniting Southwark, on the south bank of the Thames.

The fire raged uncontrollably until last night, laying waste to an area of 2 square miles (5 square kilometers). A total of 87 churches, including St Paul's Cathedral, and more than 13,000 houses were destroyed. Amazingly, only six people are known to have died, but it seems certain the actual toll will be much higher.

If there is the smallest ray of hope among the ashes, it is that, by destroying the crowded, unsanitary slums, the fire may have finally put an end to the Great Plague that started last year.

> "DO NOT HACK ME AS YOU DID MY LORD RUSSELL."
>
> DUKE OF MONMOUTH (1649–1685), ILLEGITIMATE SON OF CHARLES II, TO HIS EXECUTIONER, 1685

> "LET THE PEOPLE THINK THEY GOVERN AND THEY WILL BE GOVERNED."
>
> WILLIAM PENN (1644–1718), AMERICAN STATESMAN, FOUNDER OF PENNSYLVANIA, 1693

In the Battle of Texel, 1673, a Dutch fleet opposes the landing of troops by a combined Anglo-French fleet.

East India Company Gains Stronghold in Bombay

Bombay, India, 1670: King Charles II has empowered the East India Company to govern itself, granting it the rights to mint currency, command forts and soldiers, form alliances, make war and peace, and exercise legal jurisdiction over acquired regions.

In 1668 the East India Company established a stronghold in Bombay in southwestern India, giving them yet another trade and military base in the country. It followed the installation of British strongholds in Bengal (1610), northwestern Surat (1615), and Madras in the far south of the country (1639).

The Company has steadily increased its power and profitability ever since it gained its first toehold in India, despite being surrounded by trading competitors, other imperial powers, and hostile native rulers. It is now undertaking a rapid military recruitment program.

James II Defeated at Battle of the Boyne

Ireland, July 1, 1690: James II, the deposed King of England, has suffered a major military defeat in Ireland at the hands of English Parliamentary troops. The Catholic king was crowned on April 23, 1685, and for a while enjoyed popular support. Many conservative Protestants even supported him, and the new Parliament, which assembled in May 1685, granted him a large income.

Soon after this, however, James was defeated in the Monmouth Rebellion, led by his predecessor Charles II's illegitimate son, James Scott, who declared himself King on June 20, 1685. But James defeated Scott's forces at the Battle of Sedgemoor on July 6, and had him executed at the Tower of London.

To protect himself from any further rebellions, James established a large army. By putting Roman Catholics in charge of several regiments, the King was drawn into conflict with Parliament, which was dissolved in November 1685, never to sit again during James' reign.

When the French Prince of Orange attacked on November 5, 1688, the King's Protestant army defected, and James fled across to France. James's daughter Mary was declared Queen, to rule jointly with her husband, the Prince of Orange, now William III. Scotland agreed, and terminated his reign as James VII, which he had been serving simultaneously.

The Irish Parliament did not follow their example, declaring that James remained King. In March 1689, James arrived in Ireland with a French army, bent on revenge against William. How-

Seats of Power

China Qing Dynasty: Shunzhi (reigned 1644-1661); Kangxi (1661-1722).
England The Commonwealth: Oliver Cromwell (1649-1658); Richard Cromwell (1658-1659) (monarchy restored) Charles II (reigned 1660-1685); James II (1685-1688); William III, Mary II (1689-1702).
France Louis XIV (1643-1715).
Holy Roman Empire Ferdinand III (reigned 1637-1657); Leopold I (1658-1705).
India Mogul Empire: Shah Jahan (reigned 1627-1658); Aurangzeb (1658-1707).
Japan Edo Period: Go-Komyo (reigned 1643-1654); Go-Sai (1655-1663); Reigen (1663-1687); Higashiyama (1687-1709).
Korea Choson Dynasty: Hyojong (reigned 1649-1659); Hyeonjong (1659-1674); Sukjong (1674-1720).
Ottoman Empire Mehmed IV (reigned 1648-1687); Suleiman II (1687-1691); Ahmed II (1691-1695); Mustafa II (1695-1703).
Persia Safavid Shahs: Abbas II (reigned 1642-1666); Suleiman I (1666-1694); Sultan Hoseyn I (1694-1722).
Portugal Brigantine Dynasty: Joao IV (reigned 1640-1656); Afonso VI (1656-1667); Pedro II (1667-1706).
Russia Tsars: Aleksey I (reigned 1645-1676); Feodor III (1676-1682); Ivan V (co-ruler with Peter I from 1682-1696); Peter I (1682-1721).
Scotland Charles II (reigned 1649-1685); James VII (1685-1689); Mary II (co-monarch 1689-1694); William II (1689-1702: co-monarch until 1694).
Spain Habsburg Dynasty: Philip IV (reigned 1621-1665); Charles II (1665-1700).

People flee in boats to escape the Great Fire of London in 1666.

ever, he was crushed by English troops at the Battle of the Boyne on July 1, 1690.

James returned to exile in France, leaving Ireland at England's mercy. His cowardice lost him much of his support in Ireland, and earned him the nickname *Séamus á Chaca* ("James the Turd").

Joliet Explores Wilderness

Quebec, North America, 1694: Louis Joliet, the American Indian explorer, is about to embark upon an expedition to the wilderness of Labrador, north of Quebec.

The son of a wagon-maker, Joliet was born in Quebec on September 21, 1645. He attended the Jesuit school in Quebec, showing enormous promise as a student, especially in mathematics, and graduated in 1663. But, caught up in the adventurous spirit of the times, he soon abandoned his studies and became a rambler in the Canadian wilderness, and a trader with the Indians. He searched for a copper mine on the borders of Lake Superior in 1669, and planted France's flag at Sault Sainte Marie in 1671.

In 1672, he was sent by Governor Frontenac to explore the *grand riviére* (great river) beyond the Lakes, which Indians had told him flowed into a great southern sea. In May 1673, Joliet and his compatriots set off down the Wisconsin River, and on June 17 drifted into the Mississippi. For a month they paddled south, confirming that the great river did indeed empty into the Gulf of Mexico. They turned around, returning to Green Bay in September, after paddling a distance of 2,500 miles (4,000 km).

Joliet then married Claire-Francoise Bissot, and continued to explore the region on the government's behalf. In 1680, he was granted the Island of

Anticosti, where he erected a fort that was captured by the English in 1690, and his wife was taken prisoner. In 1693, he was appointed royal hydrographer, and last year was granted the seigneury of Joliet, south of Quebec.

But Joliet's wanderlust remains undimmed, and the wild, unknown country of Labrador beckons.

German Theologian Dies

Sweden, October 13, 1694: Baron Samuel von Pufendorf, the eminent German historian and legal philosopher, has died aged 62. Born near Chemnitz in 1632, Pufendorf studied at the universities of Leipzig and Jena, and then became tutor to the sons of the Swedish ambassador in Copenhagen, before his appointment in 1661 as professor of international law at the University of Heidelberg.

Pufendorf's 1672 masterwork, *De Jure Naturae et Gentium (On the Law and Nature of People)*, contends that natural law does not extend beyond the limits of this life. He disputes English philosopher Thomas Hobbes' contention that the natural state of mankind and nature is antagonistic and selfish, and states that humans are social beings with natural rights. The function of governments is to uphold these rights, and to organize society so that citizens are free to express their inherent peaceful impulses.

But, he says, this peace is feeble and insecure, and unless it is assisted and regulated, can do very little to benefit mankind. Pufendorf personifies public law as a moral being, and teaches that the will of the State is but the sum of the individual wills that constitute it, and that the law should be based on a social contract of cooperation.

Controversially, he contends that morality is not the exclusive preserve of Christendom, but constitutes a common bond between all nations, which are bound by a mutual humane spirit. He also argues for the formation of a United Protestant Church from the Reformed and Lutheran churches.

Ottomans Sign the Treaty of Karlowitz

Eastern Europe, January 26, 1699: The Ottoman Empire has suffered an enormous blow with the recent signing of the Treaty of Karlowitz in Montenegro. The Turkish Ottomans have been fighting a series of wars against various European powers since 1683, but have finally overreached their ability, suffering a resounding defeat at the Battle of Zenta.

The Habsburg-Ottoman War started first, after Habsburg and Venetian *agents*

Robert (Rob Roy) MacGregor

The Doge of Venice's fleet pursues the Turkish fleet in 1689.

provocateurs persuaded the Christian population in Hungary and the Balkan Peninsula to rebel against the Muslim rule of the Ottomans. The Ottomans were soon forced to defend opportunist uprisings in Poland and Venice, resulting in the fatal situation where they were fighting major wars on three fronts.

During the course of the wars, the Ottoman forces adopted European-style military uniforms, and hired Prussian advisers. They even embraced military music by Donizetti, but to no avail. The conflicts gradually drained the Ottoman treasury, while the European powers were steadily growing ever more prosperous in the wake of the Industrial Revolution. They were able to mass-produce military equipment and large quantities of cheap goods to sell around the world. The Turks were simply unable to supply enough troops to win any of these conflicts.

Under the terms of the Treaty, Turkey has been forced to cede most of Hungary, Slavonia, and Transylvania to Austria, while Podolia passes to Poland. Most of Dalmatia has been handed over to Venice, along with the Peloponnesus Peninsula.

The Treaty of Limerick in 1691 ended the bitter war between the Jacobites and William of Orange's troops.

Christopher Wren

> "ALL EXCEL-
> LENT THINGS
> ARE AS
> DIFFICULT AS
> THEY ARE
> RARE."
>
> BENEDICT DE
> SPINOZA (1632–1677),
> DUTCH PHILOSO-
> PHER

> "SCIENCE IS
> THE KNOW-
> LEDGE OF
> CONSE-
> QUENCES, AND
> DEPENDENCE
> OF ONE FACE
> UPON
> ANOTHER."
>
> THOMAS HOBBES
> (1588–1679), ENGLISH
> PHILOSOPHER, 1651

Royal Society of Fellows Founded in London

London, England, December, 1660: King Charles II has pledged his support to a group of scientists and philosophers who have been meeting recently in London. Known as the Royal Society, the institution is dedicated to the acquisition of knowledge by experimental investigation, rather than faith or traditional wisdom.

The Society's beginnings came about in 1645, when a group of scientists began to hold regular discussions. The founding members included Christopher Wren, Robert Moray, Robert Boyle, John Wilkins, and John Wallis.

Originally known as the Invisible College or Philosophical College, Boyle wrote in 1646 that members discussed: "...natural philosophy, the mechanics and husbandry according to the principles of the Philo-sophical College, that values no knowledge but that it has a tendency to use."

The group met regularly until 1658, when they had to disband as the military took over their meeting rooms, and London underwent a period of terror. In May this year, after a period of exile, King Charles II returned to London, order was restored, and the meetings resumed.

At the inaugural meeting of the 12 founding members on November 28, they decided to invite 40 more members, 35 of whom accepted the invitation. Of these, 19 were scientists. The remaining 16 members were statesmen, soldiers, historians, administrators, and literary men.

King Charles II has indicated that he wishes to become a Fellow of the new Society, and has promised to provide funding.

time out

Dutch physicist and mathematician Christiaan Huygens (1629-1695) modernizes clockmaking with the invention of a new clock regulated by a pendulum that provides the most accurate time-keeping to date. He patents it in 1656.

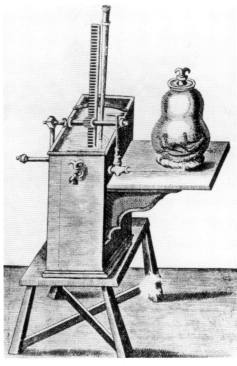

Apparatus used by Boyle in his experiments on gases.

Christopher Wren discusses plans to rebuild St Paul's Cathedral.

Malpighi Identifies Capillary System

Bologna, Italy, 1661: Italian anatomist and botanist Marcello Malpighi, the pre-eminent pioneer in the use of the recently invented microscope, has located tiny blood vessels that carry blood from the arteries to the veins and skin. Malpighi has published his findings, *De Pulmonibus*, in the form of letters to his friend and mentor, the mathematician and naturalist Giovanni Borelli.

The brilliant English scientist William Harvey, who died four years ago, correctly inferred the existence of this network of blood vessels, which he named the "capillary system," but without a microscope was unable to prove his theories. Malpighi made his discoveries by dissecting dead and live animals, and human corpses. His views are evoking much controversy and dissent, partly because many of his discoveries fly in the face of traditional wisdom.

Boyle Proposes Radical New Scientific Law

London, England, 1662: Innovative English scientist Robert Boyle has made a radical discovery, already being hailed as "Boyle's Law." It states that the product of the volume and pressure of a fixed quantity of a gas is constant, given constant temperature. Expressed mathematically, the formula for Boyle's law is: $V \times P = k$, where V is the volume of the gas, P is the pressure of the gas, and k is a constant.

Boyle is now regarded as one of England's foremost scientists after last year's publication of *The Sceptical Chymist*. Written in the form of a dialogue, the

Bologna, Italy, 1651: Giovanni Riccioli publishes his *Almagestum novum*, including a map of the moon (drawn by Francesco Grimaldi), which names many of the craters after scientists.

Copenhagen, Denmark, 1652: Thomas Bartholin discovers the lymphatic system.

London, England, 1654: Irish churchman and religious scholar James Ussher uses his biblical knowledge to determine the date of creation of the world as 4004 BCE.

The Hague, Netherlands, c. 1656: Christiaan Huygens invents the pendulum clock.

England, November 8, 1656: Edmond Halley is born.

London, England, 1660: The Royal Society is founded, formalizing the meetings of several scientists of the time. The Society gains the approval of King Charles II.

Paris, France, February, 1661: Melchisedech Thevenot is credited with the invention of the spirit level.

Bologna, Italy, 1661: Marcello Malpighi becomes the first to view the capillary system and writes an article on his discovery.

London, England, 1662: Robert Boyle advocates the use of experimentation to provide proof of scientific theories in *The Sceptical Chymist*.

Paris, France, August 19, 1662: Blaise Pascal, mathematician and religious philosopher, dies, aged 39.

Cambridge, England, 1664: Thomas Willis publishes his work on the anatomy of the brain and nervous system–*Cerebri Anatome*.

Castres, France, January, 1665: Pierre de Fermat, mathematician, dies, aged about 63.

London, England, 1665: Robert Hooke publishes a book on microscopes–*Micrographia*.

Amsterdam, Netherlands, 1665: Athanasius Kircher publishes *Mundus subterraneus*, describing the geology and biology of the underground world.

Bologna, Italy, 1666: Giovanni Domenico Cassini discovers a polar ice cap on Mars.

France, June, 1667: The first recorded blood transfusion is carried out by Jean-Baptiste Denys. He uses blood from a lamb to save the life of a young boy.

Seoul, Korea, 1669: Song Lyong and Yi Minch'ol construct a clockwork-driven armillary sphere modeling movements of heavenly bodies.

Europe, 1671: Though a number of calculators had been invented in previous years, Gottfried Wilhelm von Leibnitz improved the design with his Step Reckoner.

book presents Boyle's theory that matter consists of atoms and clusters of atoms in motion, and that every event is the result of collisions of moving particles. He urges chemists to experiment, and asserts that research should not be limited to the traditional four elements: earth, water, fire, and air.

He also declares that chemistry should not be subservient to medicine or alchemy, but should grow to the status of a science.

The book contains flashes of humor. For example, Boyle compares alchemists with "the Navigators of Solomon's Tarshish Fleet, who brought home…not only Gold, and Silver, and Ivory, but Apes and Peacocks too," since their theories "either like Peacock's feathers make a great shew, but are neither solid nor useful; or else, like Apes, if they have some appearance of being rational, are blemish'd with some absurdity or other which makes them appear ridiculous."

The book also presents many ground-breaking chemical facts, shows the chemist how to employ empirical terms in chemical explanation, and contains the results of numerous chemical experiments.

Boyle has already been dubbed "the Father of Chemistry."

Untimely Death of a Mathematical Genius

Paris, France, August 19, 1662: Blaise Pascal, the influential French mathematical genius who devoted his later years to religious contemplation, has died in Paris at the age of 39.

Born at Clermont-Ferrand on June 19, 1623, Pascal was a child prodigy who was educated by his father, a judge and scientist of some note. Pascal mastered calculus when he was nine years old, and

Blaise Pascal in contemplative mode.

his earliest work was in the field of natural and applied sciences.

He was a mathematician of the highest rank, who helped to create several major new areas of research, writing a significant treatise on conic sections and projective geometry at the age of 16. He corresponded with physicist Pierre de Fermat on probability theory, managing to prove the validity of several of Fermat's theories. Pascal's discoveries are already finding some application in the fields of economics and the social sciences.

Pascal made significant contributions to the study of fluids, and in 1641 he constructed a prototype mechanical calculator. He shed new light on our understanding of pressure and vacuums, building on the work of Evangelista Torricelli. He invented the barometer, the syringe, and the hydraulic press.

Following a mystical experience in late 1654, Pascal converted to Jansenism and abandoned his scientific pursuits, devoting himself to reflection, and writing about philosophy and theology. He produced two brilliant works, *Lettres Provinciales* and the so far unpublished *Pensées*. However, he was dogged by ill health throughout his life, and his newfound religious interests were cut short by his untimely death, two months after his 39th birthday.

Willis Unlocks the Secrets of the Brain

Cambridge, England, 1664: Thomas Willis, the Sedleian Professor of Natural Philosophy at Oxford University, has published *Cerebri Anatome (Anatomy of the Brain)*, an anatomical and philosophical work that sheds new light on the workings of

the brain and nervous system. The 29-chapter treatise argues that a vital soul, the *flamma vitalis*, acts within the blood and rises to the soul through cerebral arteries that supply the brain. They are responsible for basic biological functions such as sensation, motion, knowledge, and simple reasoning.

Willis dissected bodies of human and animal corpses, and repeatedly refers to the similarity in structure between man and animals, and also to the differences, as evidence of an immaterial, God-given human soul. He surmises that the network of arteries at the base of the human—but not animal—brain is the seat of the soul.

In his introduction to the work, Willis states that the study of anatomy can "unlock the secret places of Man's Mind and…look into the living and breathing Chapel of the Deity."

Robert Boyle

An armillary sphere used to demonstrate celestial orbits.

Delft, Netherlands, 1672: Regnier de Graaf publishes his findings on the human reproductive system and describes the ovarian follicles–named Graafian follicles in his honor.
Paris, France, 1673: Christiaan Huygens, Dutch astronomer, mathematician, and physicist, writes *Horologium Oscillatorium*.
Peking, China, 1673: Jesuit astronomer Ferdinand Verbiest re-equips the Imperial Observatory with European-style instruments.

Hamburg, Germany, 1674: Alchemist Hennig Brand discovers the chemical element phosphorus.
Greenwich, England, 1675: King Charles II founds the Royal Greenwich Observatory.
Paris, France, 1675: Danish astronomer Ole Romer uses his observations of Jupiter's moons to estimate the speed of light.
Delft, Netherlands, 1676: With no formal training or education in the sciences, Anton van Leeuwenhoek becomes the first to view bacteria through his own self-built lens.

Peking, China, 1678: Li Shizhen compiles the *Bencao Gangmu (Compendium of Essential Herbs)*, a massive encyclopedia of traditional Chinese medicine.
London, England, 1678: While working with springs, Robert Hooke comes up with the formula that states the forces applied to a spring and its subsequent extension are in direct proportion.
London, England, 1682: Edmond Halley follows the progress of a passing comet and calculates the date of its recurrence.

Edo (Tokyo), Japan, 1684: The threshing-comb, which improves effiency of processing of harvested rice, is described in the anonymous *Peasants' Chronicle*.
England, 1686: Following his earlier volume on plant classification *Methodus Plantarum Novum*, John Ray classifies around 18,000 British plants in his great work, *Historia Plantarum*.
London, England, 1687: Isaac Newton publishes a work on his law of universal gravitation and several laws of motion.

Marburg, Germany, 1690: Exiled Frenchman Denis Papin invents a pump with a piston driven by steam.
Ulm, Germany, 1696: Eberhard Gockel discovers that the lead in wine sweetening causes a serious colic epidemic.
England, 1698: Thomas Savery patents his design for a pump to extract water from mine shafts.
Lucca, Italy, 1699: In an attempt to stop the spread of the disease, the body and possessions of anyone dying of consumption (tuberculosis) are burned, by government order.

Huygens Pioneering Work on Pendulums

Christiaan Huygens

Paris, France, 1673: Christiaan Huygens, the famous Dutch astronomer, mathematician, and physicist, has just published *Horologium Oscillatorium Sive de Motu Pendulorum*. This pioneering work deals with the movement of pendulums, and sets down laws relating to centrifugal forces in revolving bodies.

Huygens proves that the time taken by a swinging pendulum to return to its starting point is always identical, independent of the distance traveled. He clearly describes the descent of bodies in a vacuum, either vertically or along curves. He defines the evolutes and involutes of curves, and maps the evolutes of the cycloid (the path defined by a point on the circumference of a circle traveling across a flat surface), and of the parabola.

Another interesting aspect of the *Horologium* is that Huygens attempts, for the first time, to study the dynamics of complete bodies, rather than just their constituent particles.

In 1656, Huygens patented the first pendulum clock, accurate to five minutes per day, marking a great improvement in the accuracy of time measurement.

Huygens's work on the pendulum was linked to other mathematical work that he had been doing on the cycloid, following a challenge by fellow mathematician Blaise Pascal.

Mathematician Blaise Pascal was a child prodigy.

Huygens believed that a pendulum swinging in a large arc would be more useful at sea, and invented the cycloidal pendulum with this in mind. He built several pendulum clocks designed to determine longitude, and they underwent sea trials in 1662.

Tutored at home by private teachers until he was 16 years old, Christiaan learned geometry, how to make mechanical models, as well as social and artistic skills such as playing the lute. His mathematical education was influenced by family friend René Descartes, who was a frequent visitor to the Huygens's home.

Huygens recently became a founding member of the French Academy of Sciences, whose royal funding will greatly assist his future researches.

New Royal Observatory Will Make Navigation Safer

Greenwich, England, 1675: A new celestial observatory has recently been completed in Greenwich. The brilliant astronomer John Flamsteed—along with Isaac Newton, Edmond Halley, and others—has long argued that British sailors need more accurate and reliable information for navigational purposes, and King Charles II eventually agreed.

Charles has now appointed Flamsteed to the new position of Royal Observator, and his primary task is to "apply himself with the most exact care and diligence to the rectifying of the tables of the motions of the heavens, and the places of the fixed stars, so as to find out the so much desired longitude of places for the perfecting of the art of navigation."

King Charles also authorized the construction of "a small observatory within our royal park at Greenwich," but has committed only minimal resources for the project. A demolished gatehouse from the Tower of London provided iron, wood, and lead, while bricks were supplied from nearby Tilbury Fort.

Situated on a hill overlooking the River Thames, the new observatory is Britain's first ever purpose-built scientific research facility. The site was chosen by Christopher Wren, who also designed the two-story building, which will double as the Royal Observator's residence.

Flamsteed paid for most of the equipment—including telescopes, sextants, and a quadrant—out of his own pocket, and has been forced to take on private pupils to supplement his income.

Trade with the British Empire, particularly in the New World and India, is becoming ever more important to Great Britain. The current, outdated navigational methods being used are resulting in the loss of many ships. The observatory is long overdue.

Hooke Discovers Physical Law of Elasticity

London, England, 1678: Eminent English physicist, chemist, and architect Robert Hooke, Secretary of the Royal Society of England, and Professor of Physics at London's Gresham College, has discovered the mathematical relationship between the force applied to a spring and the length of its extension.

Expressed in mathematical terms: if a spring is elongated by some distance, x, the restoring force exerted by the spring, F, is proportional to x by a constant factor, k. That is, $F = -kx$.

For example, if a spring is stretched one inch by a force of two, it will be stretched two inches by a force of four, and so on. But when the spring reaches its elastic limit, the law ceases to apply; increases in weight will result in a lesser extension, until the spring breaks.

In 1665 Hooke published *Micrographia*, which revealed his invention of the microscope and the Gregorian telescope. It includes details of his microscopic research into botany and

The Royal Observatory at Greenwich was built to improve navigation at sea and accurately determine longitude.

chemistry, his discovery of a fifth star in the constellation Orion, and the rotation of Jupiter. He has also drawn up designs for a steam-powered engine.

Clockmakers have hailed Hooke's latest discovery. By using two springs that pull in opposite directions, they will be able to overcome the problem of clocks slowing down as the tension in the main spring decreases. Hooke initially published his discovery as the anagram ceiiinosssttuv, which he later revealed to mean *ut tensio sic vis*, or "as the extension, the force."

Halley Formulates Theory on Comet's Periodic Orbit

London, England, 1682: English astronomer Edmond Halley claims that the spectacular comet that is currently passing across the night skies is not taking a straight path, but is actually in a solar orbit of some 76 years. Halley has deduced that this comet is the same object as the comet of 1531 and 1607.

Already an expert astronomer at 17, Halley published three papers—on planetary orbits, on sunspots, and on the occultation of Mars—while still an undergraduate at Queen's College, Oxford. He was subsequently introduced to John Flamsteed, the Astronomer Royal, and in 1676, influenced by Flamsteed's project to compile a catalog of northern stars, he traveled to the island of St Helena to compile a similar, southern star chart.

He recorded the latitudes and longitudes of 341 stars, and observed the transit of Mercury across the sun. His *Catalogus Stellarium Australium*, published in 1679, was the first to contain telescopically determined locations of southern stars, and resulted in Halley being elected as a Fellow of the Royal Society.

Isaac Newton's reflecting microscope was a major breakthrough in the field of optics.

Along with other Society members—microscopist Robert Hooke, architect and mathematician Sir Christopher Wren, and physicist Isaac Newton—Halley has been attempting to develop a mechanical explanation for the motion of heavenly objects. Although some progress had been made, they have so far been unable to deduce a predictable orbit that matches observable planetary motions.

Newton, it is reported, is closer than anyone else to producing a mathematical formula to explain not only planetary, but also earthly motions. The Royal Society has charged Halley with assisting Newton in the completion of his work in progress, *Principia Mathematica*.

While some scientists tentatively agree with Halley's speculation on the orbit of this comet, his theory will not gain widespread acceptance unless the comet reappears in December 1758.

Newton Explains Physical Universe in Radical Work

London, England, July, 1687: Isaac Newton, the brilliant physicist and mathematician, has published a revolutionary and wide-ranging new book, *Philosophiae Naturalis Principia Mathematica (The Mathematical Principles of Natural Philosophy)*.

Two years in the writing, the work has been acclaimed as a masterpiece by those intellects who can understand it.

In the book, Newton explains the motion of heavenly bodies as a function of the gravitational force that all bodies exert on each other, from the largest star to the smallest particle. He states that an

object will travel in a straight line (or will stay at rest) unless an external force acts upon it, and he produces mathematical proof that the orbits of planets, with their differing speeds and masses, conform to this law.

Newton states that any change in the direction or velocity of an object is directly related to its mass, and to the force applied to it. In other words, the acceleration of a body depends upon the force and the mass of the object. For example, a fully laden carriage requires a greater force to operate than an empty one.

Sir Isaac Newton

Newton further explains that every action produces an equal and opposite reaction, as demonstrated by the fact that the harder we hit a wall, the harder it hits back—despite being immobile.

For the first time in world history, the entire structure of the universe has been empirically explained, and all the mechanical phenomena in Heaven and Earth are now reduced to a series of predictable and provable mathematical rules.

Savery Patents Steam-Powered Water Pump

England, July 2, 1698: English inventor Thomas Savery has patented an "engine to raise water by fire," otherwise known as a steam pump. It uses pressurized steam to force water upwards through a pipe, and is used to extract water from wells and mineshafts. The unit has two boilers connected by a pipe with a series of valves to create and then reduce pressure, drawing the groundwater to the surface.

Savery has written: "My engine at 60, 70, or 80 feet raises a full bore of water with much ease." In fact, it turns out that the effective distance of the machine is only about 25 feet (7.6 m).

Greater pressure does increase the functioning distance, but some dreadful explosions have occurred when overzealous mine operators have located the pump at greater depths, thus increasing the pressure required to draw the water to the surface.

Other teething problems are being experienced due to the technical difficulties of placing a boiler with a raging fire in a deep well.

Savery has widely advertised his invention and it has aroused much interest among mine owners.

Jean de la Fontaine

Velázquez Creates his Magnum Opus

Madrid, Spain, 1656: Diego Velázquez, the Spanish master artist hailed as "the painter's painter" and the "painter of truth," has produced an extraordinary and unconventional masterpiece, *Las Meninas (The Maids of Honor)*, which many critics have already acclaimed as the world's greatest painting.

It is a puzzling work, featuring two dwarfs, a dog, a self-portrait, and various members of the nobility reduced to subordinate background positions. It represents the artist's humanist sympathies, and is seen by many as taking a sly dig at the pretensions of the upper classes, in the same allegorical fashion as Miguel de Cervantes' *Don Quixote*.

Measuring 10 ft 6 in × 9 ft (3.18 m × 2.76 m), the oil painting displays marvelous color values and draftsmanship, and unrivaled skill in merging color, radiance, space, and mass in such a way that all have equal value.

Velázquez has turned the social scale upside down by giving more prominence to Princess Margarita and her ladies in waiting than to the royal couple in the dim background, and, more audaciously, even greater importance to the dwarfs and the dog by placing them in the foreground. His large, prominent self-portrait also leaves us in no doubt as to his opinion on the rightful status of the artist in society.

The painting contrasts the decadent, debauched court of King Philip IV and the aristocracy with the great suffering of the Spanish people. Because of the oppressive power of the Church, Velázquez was forced to discreetly obscure his message through the use of artistic metaphor.

> "MUSIC HATH CHARMS TO SOOTHE THE SAVAGE BREAST, TO SOFTEN ROCKS, OR BEND A KNOTTED OAK."
>
> WILLIAM CONGREVE (1670–1729), ENGLISH DRAMATIST, 1697

> "PEACE HATH HER VICTORIES NO LESS RENOWNED THAN WAR."
>
> JOHN MILTON (1608–1674) ENGLISH POET, OF CROMWELL, 1652

Velázquez turns the social scale upside down in *Las Meninas*.

De Bergerac's Comic History Published

Paris, France, 1662: Humanitarian author Cyrano de Bergerac's "latest" satirical work, *L'histoire des États et Empires du Soleil (History of the States and Empires of the Sun)* has been published in Paris. It is a hilarious companion to his *History of the States and Empires of the Moon*, published in 1656, the year after his death.

The books use imaginary visits to the moon and the sun to lampoon aspects of contemporary religion, philosophy, and politics. On the sun he hears about a woman who claims that her husband has killed her child twice. He did not fulfill his conjugal duty, and by refusing to let the child "come into existence, he caused him not to be, which was the first murder, but subsequently he caused him never to be able to be, which was the second. A common murderer knows that the man whose days he cuts short is no more, but none of them could cause a man never to have been."

Vermeer's *A Young Woman Seated at a Virginal*.

De Bergerac opposed Descartes' description of animals as soulless automatons unable to feel pain, and argued that they are fellow creatures worthy of respect and compassion. For this—in an odd twist that must have appealed to his sense of the ridiculous—the Church condemned *him* as a dangerous heretic.

After acquiring fame as a dashing dueler and bohemian, de Bergerac enlisted in the army at the age of 20. However, being a libertarian individualist who opposed war and the death penalty, he quit the army after barely a year. He could not suffer fools, phonies, or bad writers, and succeeded in irritating almost everyone, reserving special contempt for establishment lapdogs.

He died in Paris on July 28, 1655, after a plank dropped on his head.

Vermeer's Latest Work Hailed as a Masterpiece

Delft, The Netherlands, c. 1665: Critics have acclaimed the latest in Dutch master painter Jan Vermeer's "pearl" series, *Girl with a Pearl Earring*, as his finest yet. It features the head of a hauntingly beautiful young woman, gazing at the viewer

Molière

over her left shoulder while showing off an outrageously large ovoid pearl earring.

Its form and substance are defined by a thick white speckle of glowing impasto that transmits the same rays of light that cross the girl's face and blue turban, and by the soft reflection that has collected the light cast off by her intensely white collar. It is likely that a pearl of such dimension and form does not exist, and that Vermeer has either represented an artificial one or has deliberately exaggerated its dimensions for artistic effect.

Pearls are a metaphor not only for vanity, but also virginity.

time out

Italian instrument maker Antonio Stradivari (1644-1737) creates the first Stradivarius violin, improving the original design by Amati, by carefully determining the thickness of the wood, altering the scroll, and using a strongly colored varnish.

Dutch Master Leaves Lasting Legacy

Amsterdam, The Netherlands, October 4, 1669: The incomparable Dutch master Rembrandt, indisputably the greatest northern European artist, has died today in Amsterdam.

Rembrandt Harmenszoon van Rijn was born in Leiden in 1606, the son of a miller, Harmen Gerritszoon. He was educated at Leiden Latin School, and then went to Leiden University. However, he soon dropped out to pursue his real passions—painting and drawing.

In 1623, he moved to Amsterdam, where he was apprenticed to Pieter Lastman, who trained him in Caravaggio's modern historical and religious painting style. He soon mastered etching, and in 1627 he returned to Leiden to explore emotions and psychology through self-portraiture in drawing, etching, and painting. He also produced highly regarded historical studies that fetched large sums of money.

In 1631, already esteemed as the greatest Dutch portraitist, he returned to Amsterdam, opened a studio, and took on numerous students. In 1634 he married Saskia van Uylenburgh, the rich cousin of a successful art dealer, and made her the subject of many of his works. The union enhanced his career, bringing him into contact with many wealthy patrons who eagerly commissioned portraits.

Saskia died in 1642, shortly after the birth of their fourth and only surviving child, and Rembrandt completed his masterpiece, *The Night Watch*, a dramatic and dynamic portrayal of a local militia group. In 1649 Rembrandt took on a mistress, Hendrickje Stoffels, who was the model for his stunning nude *Bathsheba*, a triumph of composition, compassion, and sensitive emotional complexity. He continued to paint prolifically, though blighted by financial woes and various personal

Self-portrait as a young man shows Rembrandt at the age of 18.

tragedies. Rembrandt lives on through more than 650 oil paintings, 1,400 drawings and studies, and 300 etchings. But his pioneering, psychological self-portraits are widely admired as his greatest achievements.

Last Act for Comic Dramatist Molière

Paris, France, February 17, 1673: Molière, the much-loved paragon of French drama, died last night in Paris in classically theatrical fashion. He collapsed on stage during the fourth performance of his latest comedic masterpiece, *La Malade Imaginaire (The Imaginary Invalid)*, and passed away at home at about 10 p.m. He had been battling lung disease for several years.

Born Jean Baptiste Poquelin in Paris on January 15, 1622, he studied at the Jesuit Collège de Clermont. In 1643, adopting the pseudonym Molière, he founded the Illustré Théâtre, which attracted the patronage of Philippe d'Orléans and toured the provinces.

In 1658, he performed before King Louis XIV, who helped him organize a regular theater in Paris. After a difficult start, Molière's plays soon enjoyed popularity. Producing at least one play per year, he created a dazzling array of despicable hypocrites, who are nonetheless portrayed sympathetically.

French audiences have grown to love such rogues as Argan, the hypochondriac; Harpagon, the miser; Alceste, the misanthrope; Tartuffe, the hypocrite, and a veritable gallery of cuckolds, impostors, charlatans, and lapdogs.

Molière attempted to conceal his criticisms of the Church and State behind humor, song, and dance, but his comic farce *Tartuffe* managed to arouse the wrath of the Jansenists, and was banned.

Molière's most-loved works include *The School for Wives* (1662), *Don Juan* (1665), *The Misanthrope* (1666), and *The Learned Ladies* (1672).

Key Events

London, England, 1674: Work begins on the rebuilding of the Theatre Royal under the direction of architect Christopher Wren, who has recently been knighted.

England, November 8, 1674: John Milton, poet, dies, aged 65. He is best remembered for *Paradise Lost*.

London, England, 1675: Work begins on the rebuilding of St Paul's Cathedral, which had been destroyed in the Great Fire.

London, England, 1678: The first part of John Bunyan's *The Pilgrim's Progress* is published.

Edo (Tokyo), Japan, 1680: Ihara Saikaku, satirical humorist, publishes *The Life of an Amorous Woman*.

Rome, Italy, 1680: Giovanni Lorenzo Bernini, architect, sculptor, and painter, dies, aged about 82.

Paris, France, 1682: Versailles becomes the official residence of Louis XIV. No expense has been spared on the construction.

Jingdezhen, China, 1683: Cang Yingxuan revitalizes the imperial porcelain kilns, creating new glazes and decorative styles.

Osaka, Japan, 1686: Ihara Saikaku, writes another of his works on human relationships—*The Great Mirror of Male Love*.

Athens, Greece, 1687: The Parthenon, a 2,000 year-old temple, is damaged in the conflict between the Turkish occupiers and the Venetian forces.

London, England, c. 1689: Henry Purcell's opera *Dido and Aeneas* is performed for the first time, to an appreciative audience.

Kyoto, Japan, 1689: Matsuo Basho, writes his masterpiece travel diary *The Narrow Road to the Deep North*.

Peking, China, 1690: Kong Shangren's drama *The Peach Blossom Fan* marks symbolic acceptance by Ming loyalist intellectuals of the Qing Dynasty.

Nuremberg, Germany, c. 1690: Johann Cristoph Denner (1655-1707) invents the clarinet.

London, England, 1692: Inspired by William Shakespeare's *A Midsummer Night's Dream*, Henry Purcell writes *The Fairy Queen*.

Osaka, Japan, 1694: Matsuo Basho, haiku poet and writer, dies, aged about 50.

London, England, 1697: With a number of successes already under his belt, which have made him the darling of the English audience and earned him the respect of his peers, William Congreve writes *The Mourning Bride*.

London, England, 1697: William Dampier publishes *A New Voyage Around the World*, detailing his adventures at sea.

Paradise Awaits Eminent Poet John Milton

Rembrandt Harmenszoon van Rijn

Buckinghamshire, England, November 8, 1674: John Milton, the celebrated English poet, has died today at the age of 65. Milton was born in London on December 9, 1608, the son of a wealthy notary and musical composer. He was educated at St Paul's School, London, later receiving a Bachelor of Arts (1629) and a Master of Arts (1632) at Christ's College, Cambridge.

He wrote poetry in English, Greek and Latin, and in 1637 published his great pastoral elegy *Lycidas*, universally hailed as one of the greatest examples of the form. It reveals the great Christian faith that lays at the heart of Milton the poet. The end of *Lycidas* resounds with a powerful expression of faith in resurrection and redemption.

In 1638, Milton undertook a European tour, where he met many of the major thinkers of the day, especially in Italy. On his return to civil war-torn England, Milton became a Puritan, and an opponent of both the Catholics and King Charles I's Stuarts. He became Oliver Cromwell's foreign language secretary and chief propagandist. In 1652, he became completely blind, and all his subsequent works were dictated to his family.

Key Structures

Badshahi Mosque, Lahore, Pakistan
Cape Coast Castle, Cape Coast, Ghana
Castillo de San Pedro del Morro, Santiago de Cuba, Cuba
Catedral Basilica, Salvador, Brazil
Chapelle Notre-Dame du Bonsecour, Montreal, Canada
Church and Capilla Domestica, Cordoba, Argentina
Churches of Peace in Jawor and Swidnica, Poland
Erdene Zuu, near Ulaan Batur, Mongolia
Grand Place, Brussels, Belgium
Hotel de Beauvais, Paris, France
Jabrain Castle, Oman
Jama Masjid, Delhi, India
Kastellet, Copenhagen, Denmark
Katsura Imperial Villa, Kyoto, Japan
Khwajir Bridge, Isfahan
La Catedral, Cuzco, Peru
Monastery of Horezu, Romania
New Lutheran Church, Amsterdam, The Netherlands
Palace of Versailles, Versailles, France
Piazza of St Peter's, Vatican City
Potala Palace, Lhasa, Tibet
Registan, Samarkand, Uzbekistan
St Ivo della Sapienza, Rome, Italy
St Louis des Invalides, Paris, France
St-Sulpice Seminary, Montreal, Canada
San Francisco Church and Monastery, Lima, Peru
San Lorenzo, Turin, Italy
Santo Domingo Church and Convent, Cuzco, Peru
Schonbrunn Palace, Vienna, Austria
Sri Meenakshi Temple, Madurai, India
Taj Mahal, Agra, India
Theatre Royal, London, England
The Lion Gate, Bhaktapur, Nepal
White Dagoba (Bai Ta), Beijing, China

The open space before St Peter's Basilica was redesigned by Giovanni Lorenzo Bernini in 1656.

In 1667, he published his masterpiece *Paradise Lost*, which begins just after the revolt of Satan against God. It follows Satan's actions against Adam and Eve, leading to the Fall. Its sequel, *Paradise Regained* (1671), is an optimistic work that deals with Christ's temptation in the wilderness. Milton argues that, while the earthly paradise was lost because of Adam and Eve's failure to resist temptation, it was regained through Christ's successful resistance against Satan's misdeeds.

Milton died peacefully today at his home in Buckinghamshire.

St Paul's Cathedral Rises from the Ashes

London, England, 1675: Work has finally commenced at Ludgate Hill on the rebuilding of St Paul's Cathedral, destroyed by the Great Fire in 1666.

The site has always attracted fire. In the early seventh century, the original Saxon temple was dedicated to St Paul by King Ethelbert of Kent. It was destroyed by fire in 1087, and was replaced by a Norman structure, which was completed in 1240. In 1561 it was struck by lightning. Major rebuilding was not undertaken until 1628, when Royal Surveyor-General Inigo Jones, who also designed Covent Garden, was commissioned to restore it to its former grace.

The proposed magnificent new building was designed by the recently knighted founding member of the Royal Society, Christopher Wren. His first design, to build a replacement on the foundations of the old cathedral, was refused by King Charles II in 1669. His second, in the shape of a Greek cross, was rejected in 1672 as being too radical.

Wren's latest design was inspired by St Peter's Basilica in Rome, a fact that is causing consternation in some Protestant circles, not least because its dome will be smaller than St Peter's. Wren has signed up the brilliant Dutch sculptor and woodcarver Grinling Gibbons to carve the choir stalls. When completed, St Paul's Cathedral will be the largest Protestant church in England.

Wren also designed the new, 2,000-seat Theatre Royal, which opened last year. It replaced the original 1663 theater, which burnt down in 1672, and was the venue for star actress Nell Gwyn's stage debut. King Charles II took Nell as his mistress after falling in love with her at first sight during a performance in 1665.

Wren has recently been commissioned to design 51 new churches in London, to replace 87 churches that were destroyed by the Great Fire.

Dryden Publishes His Tribute to the Bard

Poet John Dryden dominated the literary life of Restoration England.

London, England, 1678: English Poet Laureate John Dryden has published his latest play, *All for Love, or The World Well Lost*. It is an admitted adaptation of Shakespeare's *Antony and Cleopatra*, and has been immediately hailed as a masterpiece and his greatest work yet. It focuses on the last hours of the lives of its hero and heroine, and does not suffer by comparison with the Bard's version.

A tragedy written in blank verse, it is another step in Dryden's quest to reinvigorate serious drama, which has suffered

recently—partly due to the closing down of all London theaters in 1666 following the plague that swept the city in the wake of the Great Fire. The play combines features of neo-classical and Shakespearean drama in its rather elaborate, formal structure. Dryden employs prose and dialogue for debate, and wit and satire to demonstrate inconsistencies between Church and State.

After his highly acclaimed *Annus Mirabilis* (1667), which celebrates the English Navy's victory over the Dutch, Dryden retired to the country during the plague threat, but continued to write. *An Essay of Dramatic Poesy* was published in 1668. In that same year, Dryden entered into a contract to produce three plays a year for the King's Theatre Company; the Archbishop of Canterbury awarded him a Master of Arts; and King Charles II selected him as Poet Laureate.

All for Love demonstrates Dryden's mastery of the art of comparative criticism, and illustrates why people say we are living in "the age of Dryden."

French Royal Court Moves to Versailles

Paris, France, May 6, 1682: The French royal court and government of King Louis XIV was today transferred to the opulent, recently renovated Palace of Versailles.

Louis fell in love with the original castle upon his first visit in 1651, and commissioned architect Louis Le Vau with the task of transforming the hunting lodge into Europe's foremost palace.

In 1663, master landscape gardener André Le Nôtre began to landscape new gardens. The first task was to drain the swamps and level the land, during which thousands of laborers died from fever and pneumonia. An elaborate underground network of reservoirs and aqueducts supplies hundreds of fountains and waterfalls throughout the grounds.

Le Vau built an orangerie and a menagerie, while esteemed artists, including sculptor François Girardon and painter Charles Le Brun, have produced hundreds of works for the grounds and interior.

The fortified palace is designed to protect Louis from uprisings by the Parisian mob, and to distract visiting noblemen from meddling in affairs of state by drowning them in luxuriant decadence.

The Man Who Spent His Life in Love

Osaka, Japan, 1686: *The Great Mirror of Male Love*, the latest work of popular erotic Japanese writer and performance artist Ihara Saikaku, has been published in Osaka. It is a collection of short stories about love between samurai men and boys, monks and boys, and kabuki theater prostitutes with just about anyone.

Saikaku's first novel, *A Man Who Loved Love*, published only four years ago, tells the story of a man who roamed the countryside seducing men, women, and children. He followed it with other steamy stories, such as *Five Women Who Loved Love*, *The Life of an Amorous Man*, and *The Woman Who Spent Her Life in Love*.

Saikaku frequents back alleys and slums, gay theaters, and teahouse brothels. He flouts the caste system by consorting with beggars, peddlers, and prostitutes, and later entertains royalty and rich merchants with his salacious tales. His work captures the cosmopolitan air of Osaka, and the developing *chinindo* (way of the townspeople), which is gradually replacing *bushido* (way of the warrior).

His work represents a new genre of writing, *ukiyo-zoshi* (tales of the "floating world" of pleasure), which may be seen as a companion to *ukiyo-e* (collections of pornographic pictures), which are all the rage in Japan.

Death of a *Haiku* Master

Osaka, Japan, 1694: Matsuo Basho, Japan's greatest *haiku* poet and travel diarist, has died at the age of 50. Born in 1644 in Iga Province, about 30 miles (48 km) southeast of Kyoto, Basho's father was a samurai who farmed when he was not fighting.

As a youngster, Basho entered the service of a youthful master, Todo Yoshitada, a relative of the feudal lord of Iga. He wrote his first *haiku* (a three-line poem of five, seven, and five syllables) in 1662.

In the summer of 1666, following Yoshitada's sudden and premature death, Basho left home and embarked on a life of wandering and writing. He wrote many superb *haiku* during his journeys, and the resulting journal, *The Narrow Road to the Deep North* (*Oku no Hosomichi*), is regarded as Japan's greatest poetic diary.

Basho's numerous poems and journals reflect his Zen Buddhist philosophy, that one's petty ego must be absorbed into the limitless, marvelous universe.

John Milton

A sweeping perspective of the gardens and Palace of Versailles, seat of King Louis XIV's court and government.

Vincent de Paul

First European Settlement Established at Cape Town

Cape Town, South Africa, April 6, 1652: A Dutch expedition arrived this morning at the south cape of Africa. It was led by seafaring merchant Jan van Riebeeck, on a commission from the Dutch East India Company. The force put down anchor in a picturesque bay at the foot of a beautiful flat-topped mountain.

The Company wishes to establish a settlement as a halfway point between Europe and the East Indies. Riebeeck's commission is to plant fruit and vegetables, and farm local animals in order to supply passing ships with fresh food and thus prevent scurvy and other diseases that cause many deaths on long sea voyages.

Riebeeck has had a checkered past. He joined the Dutch East India Company in 1639, where he served in a number of posts, including that of assistant surgeon in the East Indian port of Batavia.

Jan van Riebeeck established a Dutch colony at Cape Town.

He then visited Japan, and later served as the head of the Dutch trading post in Tonkin, Vietnam. However, Riebeeck was recalled when it was discovered that he was conducting trade under the counter for his own profit.

Riebeeck's first tasks will be to build a fort, improve the natural anchorage in the bay, and obtain livestock from the indigenous Khoikhoi people.

In March 1647, the Dutch ship *Nieuwe Haarlem* was wrecked here. The survivors built a fort, which they named the "Sand Fort of the Cape of Good Hope." They were rescued a year later, and recommended the site for future settlement.

"Ring-a-ring o'roses, A pocket full of posies, A-tishoo! A-tishoo! We all fall down."

NURSERY RHYME REFERRING TO THE PLAGUE; RING-A-ROSES REPRESENTED THE APPEARANCE OF AFFECTED SKIN, 1665

Stuyvesant Imposes Law on New Amsterdam

New Amsterdam, North America, 1653: Peter Stuyvesant, the Governor of New Amsterdam, has instituted a series of new laws on Manhattan Island in an attempt to quell what he sees as excessive debauchery. Since he became governor in 1647, Stuyvesant's autocratic style has aroused much resentment, and so a municipal government was recently installed.

Despite the change, Stuyvesant maintains tight control—which is not surprising, since he appointed all the officials. As a result of the new laws, bars are forced to close at 9 P.M., a prohibition has been imposed on Sunday drinking, and knife-fighting is illegal. Stuyvesant deemed that men have been driving their wagons and carts too fast, and so a speed limit has been imposed on all streets except for Broadway. As a result, all horses and wagons must now be led by hand.

Sexual promiscuity has been banned, especially between European men and native women. Anyone caught having sexual relations with "heathen women and girls" will have to pay "a fine of 25 guilders," or 50 if she becomes pregnant, and 100 if she gives birth.

Stuyvesant is also overseeing many basic improvements in New Amsterdam. Cobblestone streets are replacing dirt roads, the city has introduced fire protection and police patrols, and the first hospital is under construction. The government recently ordered the construction of a 9 ft (2.75 m) high wall on Manhattan Island, to protect the colony from threatened attacks by British forces in New England.

time out

Aqua Toffana, a face powder made from arsenic, was sold by its creator, Signora Toffana, to wealthy women who wished to rid themselves of their husbands. The powder was applied to the cheeks and ingested when a man kissed his wife!

Saintly Man Dies

Paris, France, September 27, 1660: Vincent de Paul, the revered theologian and philanthropist, has died. Born in Pouy, Gascony, in about 1580, of peasant stock, Vincent was ordained into the Catholic Church at the age of twenty, and at thirty accepted a post as chaplain and tutor in the household of Philippe de Gondi, Count of Joigny.

In 1625, Vincent established the Congregation of the Mission, a community of priests who undertook to renounce all ecclesiastical advancement and devote themselves to work in small towns around

Court ladies offering their jewels to Vincent de Paul for charity.

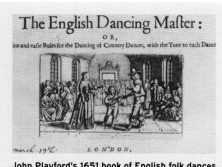
John Playford's 1651 book of English folk dances.

William Penn

France. He instructed his missionaries that Protestants were to be treated as brothers, with respect and love.

Many wealthy parishioners sought him out, and so he organized them into a Confraternity of Charity, and set them to work caring for the poor and sick. Out of his Confraternity arose an order called the Sisters of Charity, devoted to nursing the sick and poor.

He established an orphanage, and rescued abandoned babies in the Paris slums. He once complained to the King that ecclesiastical posts were distributed simply as political favors. The King responded by creating a Council of Conscience to oversee nominations to such posts, with Vincent at the head.

In another story illustrative of Vincent's Christian virtue, a noblewoman, infuriated with Vincent because he would not nominate her son as a bishop, once threw a stool at him. With blood pouring from his forehead, he said to a bystander: "Is it not wonderful how strong a mother's love for her son can be?"

Explorer Discovers Terrifying Waterfall

Niagara Falls, North America, 1678: Louis Hennepin, the Belgian explorer and Franciscan missionary, claims he has discovered a gigantic waterfall in northern America. He writes: "Betwixt the Lakes Ontario and Erié is a vast and prodigious cadence of water which falls down after a surprizing and astonishing manner, insomuch that the universe does not afford its parallel."

He refers to "wild beasts while endeavoring to pass it to feed on the other side, they not being able to withstand the force of its current, which inevitably casts them down headlong above six hundred foot."

He claims that the waterfall makes "an outrageous noise, more terrible than that of thunder; for when the wind blows from off the south, their dismal roaring may be heard above fifteen leagues off." But many do not credit the possibility of a 600 ft (180 m) waterfall that can be heard 45 miles (70 km) away, their suspicions heightened because Hennepin is claimed to be a notorious liar and self-promoter.

Quakers Found Pennsylvania

Pennsylvania, North America, October, 1682: The Quaker William Penn has established a community in North America dedicated to justice, equality, and religious freedom. Penn has been a leading defender of religious tolerance in England, and was jailed six times for speaking out against persecution. He successfully challenged oppressive government policies in court, and helped secure the right to trial by jury. He used his legal skills and family connections to free large numbers of Quakers from jail, saving many from the gallows.

In Europe, Protestants persecute Catholics, Catholics persecute Protestants, and everyone persecutes Quakers, Jews, and gypsies. Convinced that religious tolerance was unachievable in England, Penn's vision is to establish a fair and equal sanctuary in America, to be known as Pennsylvania.

Last year he asked King Charles II for a charter enabling him to establish an American colony. The King agreed, and granted him a large tract of land as payment for a £16,000 debt owed to his deceased father, Admiral Penn.

William Penn arrived here a few days ago on the 300-ton sailing ship *Welcome*, bearing Quaker refugees. He has written a constitution that limits the power of government, provides a humane penal code, and guarantees a number of fundamental liberties. It enshrines equal rights for men and women, and forbids the theft of land from the Indians.

Penn's *First Frame of Government*, states: "…Men being born with a title to

William Penn negotiates the Great Treaty with local Indian tribes in 1682.

perfect freedom and uncontrolled enjoyment of all the rights and privileges of the law of nature…no one can be put out of his estate and subjected to the political view of another, without his consent…"

Where the English penal code specifies the death penalty for around 200 offences, Penn reserves it for just two—murder and treason.

England, September 1685: Judge George Jeffries presides over the "Bloody Assizes" of those accused of treason for their participation in the earlier Monmouth Rebellion, and sentences many defendants to be executed.

France, October 22, 1685: The Edict of Nantes, which granted religious freedom in 1598, is revoked by King Louis XIV.

Edo (Tokyo), Japan, 1685: Yamaga Soko formulates the principles of *bushido*, the "way of the warrior," ideology of Japan's samurai class.

Texas, North America, 1685: French explorer René-Robert Cavelier, Sieur de la Salle, establishes a settlement at Fort St Louis.

London, England, November, 1687: Eleanor (Nell) Gwyn, the popular actress and mistress of Charles II, dies, aged 37.

Osaka, Japan, 1688: The "Townsman culture" of Japan's newly wealthy mercantile cities begins to reach its peak of brilliance.

Smyrna, Turkey, 1688: The ancient city of Smyrna is almost destroyed by an earthquake.

London, England, 1689: The *Bill of Rights* is issued to cap the excesses and power of the monarchy and the *Toleration Act* promotes tolerance of religious beliefs, although Roman Catholics are excluded from the throne.

Calcutta, India, 1690: Representatives of the British East India Company establish a trading base at Calcutta.

Jamaica, Caribbean, June 7, 1692: An earthquake rocks Jamaica. Several thousand lives are lost, and much of the major town of Port Royal is destroyed.

Salem, Massachusetts, North America, 1692: Accusations of witchcraft abound in the community of Salem, and trials are held.

France, 1693: Benedictine monk Dom Pérignon is credited with the invention of champagne.

Languedoc, France, 1694: Pierre Paul Riquet's dream of a waterway connecting the Mediterranean and the Atlantic is realized with the completion of the Canal du Midi. Despite being involved in much of its construction, Riquet did not live to see his vision become a reality.

England, 1694: The Bank of England is founded.

Scotland, July 17, 1695: The Bank of Scotland is founded.

England, 1695: The English glass industry is shattered when a Window Tax is imposed by Parliament—yet another in a procession of equally unpopular taxes, such as the 1663 Hearth Tax, which taxed every hearth in a household.

Louisiana, North America, 1699: The expedition led by Pierre Le Moyne, Sieur d'Iberville, claims the region of Louisiana for France.

Edict of Nantes Revoked

King Louis XIV of France

France, October 22, 1685: King Louis XIV of France, who has been determined to stamp out Protestantism, today revoked the Edict of Nantes, causing much rejoicing among Catholics.

The edict was issued at the end of last century, when France was warring with Spain and undergoing internal struggles between Catholics and Huguenots. Protestant King Henry IV suffered the wrath of the influential Catholic League, but when he converted to Catholicism in 1593, he bore the animosity of Protestants instead of Catholics.

This so bothered Henry that, after making peace with Spain in 1598, he issued the Edict of Nantes, guaranteeing freedom of religion as well as employment to the Protestant Huguenot minority, and granting them a share in the administration of justice and public office.

Now Louis has done more than merely reverse the edict; he has ordered that all Protestant pastors be exiled, while forbidding laypeople from emigrating.

"MEN ARE NOT HANGED FOR STEALING HORSES, BUT THAT HORSES MAY NOT BE STOLEN."

GEORGE SAVILLE HALIFAX (1633–1695) ENGLISH STATESMAN, 1685

"GOD IS ALWAYS ON THE SIDE OF THE BIG BATTALIONS."

HENRI DE LA TOUR D'AUVERGNE, VICOMTE DE TURENNE (1611–1675) FRENCH MARSHAL, 1675

Protestants are banned from employment and industry, and all their churches will be destroyed. This has raised eyebrows, even in the French court, with many of Louis' advisers predicting an acceleration in the Huguenot exodus to England, Germany, and the Netherlands.

These countries are welcoming the many rich merchants and skilled artisans who have been flooding across their borders in the face of Louis' increasingly strident anti-Huguenot pronouncements.

France is already suffering the consequences of the resulting loss of wealth and talent, and many are predicting that Louis' bigotry will lead France into calamity.

The Edict of Nantes did not eliminate the simmering resentments between Catholics and Huguenots, but at least it has kept a lid on them for the past 87 years. One wonders how the Protestants will react, now that they are not allowed to worship or earn a legal living.

Religious Leaders

Popes
Innocent X (1644-1655)
Alexander VII (1655-1667)
Clement IX (1667-1669)
Clement X (1670-1676)
Innocent XI (1676-1689)
Alexander VIII (1689-1691)
Innocent XII (1691-1700)

Archbishops of Canterbury
William Juxon (1660-1663)
Gilbert Sheldon (1663-1667)
William Sancroft (1678-1691)
John Tillotson (1691-1694)
Thomas Tenison (1694-1715)

Dalai Lamas of Tibet
Ngawang Lobsang Gyatso (1642-1682)
Tsangyang Gyatso (1697-1706)

Patriarchs of Constantinople
Parthenius II (1648-1651)
Joannicus II (1651-1656)
Cyril III (1652-1654)
Paisius I (1652-1655)
Parthenius III (1656-57)
Gabriel II (1657)
Parthenius IV (1657-1662, 1665-1667, 1671, 1675-1676, 1684-1685)
Theophanes II (1659)
Dionysius III (1662-1665)
Clement (1667)
Methodius III (1668-1671)
Dioysius IV Muselimes (1671-1673, 1676-1679, 1682-1684, 1686-1687, 1693-1694)
Gerasimus II (1673-1674)
Athanasius IV (1679)
James (1679-82, 1685-16 88)
Callinicus II (1688-1702)
Neophytus IV (1688)

Bushido and the Warrior Arts of the Samurai

Edo (Tokyo), Japan, 1685: The Japanese philosopher and military strategist Yamaga Soko has formulated a set of principles called *bushido*, or "way of the warrior."

Yamaga has applied the Confucian idea of the "superior man" to the samurai, or soldier class, and has formulated a code of conduct based on self-defense and respect for the enemy. He emphasizes that the arts, letters, and history are essential to the academic discipline of the samurai, and encourages the study of Western ideas, military tactics and technology, as introduced into Japan by the Portuguese and the Dutch. These views are very unpopular among Japan's isolationist ruling class, and are rare even among intellectuals.

Japan has been relatively peaceful under the present Tokugawa rule, and Yamaga is concerned that, without practice, the samurai will forget the skills necessary to overcome future threats. Bushido provides a set of precepts that are designed to be relevant to the entire population, so that, in effect, all citizens may become warriors.

Yamaga advocates the transformation of the samurai from a purely military aristocracy to one with a more general political and cultural leadership. He says that samurai should serve as a model for the rest of society; it is not enough to merely understand moral behavior, one must put it into action.

In particular, one must embody devotion to duty *(giri)* and unwavering loyalty. The moral life centers on the responsibilities that the samurai has agreed to—self-control, selflessness, discipline, and fearlessness in the face of death.

Samurai warriors practise their martial skills.

New Base at Calcutta for East India Company

Calcutta, India, 1690: Job Charnock has established another British East India Company trade center at Calcutta in Bengal, northern India. The British first gained a foothold in Bengal in 1633, when a factory was established at Hariharpur on the Mahanadi delta. Mogul Emperor Shah Jahan granted the Company permission to pursue tax-free trade and commerce for an annual fee of 3,000 rupees. In 1668, a British factory was opened in Dhaka, Bengal's capital.

But these centers are not on the coast, and so Calcutta has long been coveted for its excellent strategic position. It is protected by the Hooghly River to the west, a creek to the north, and by salt lakes to the east. There is also direct access to the mighty river Ganges, which will open up large areas of northern India for trade and conquest.

Charnock, the chief agent of the East India Company since 1686, has been in India since 1655. He was stationed first at Cossimbazar, north of Calcutta, and then at inland Patna, where the Mogul viceroy recently threatened to kill him.

Frequently at odds with Indian leaders—and his superiors—Charnock has been guilty of mismanagement, theft, brutality to Indian prisoners, and questionable morality. He was once recommended for dismissal, but has survived because he is a brilliant tactician, and consistently delivers profits. He lives with an Indian widow who he rescued, and has fathered several of her children.

Witchcraft Hysteria Grips Town of Salem

Salem, Massachusetts, 1692: A wave of hysteria, blamed on witchcraft and on religious fervor, has swept through Salem Village. More than 20 people have been executed, and hundreds imprisoned.

Last February, nine-year-old Betty Parris, the small daughter of Salem's parish priest Reverend Samuel Parris, and her cousin, eleven-year-old Abigail Williams, became strangely ill.

They raced about aimlessly, hid under furniture, and complained of fevers and hallucinations. They contorted into grotesque poses, fell down motionless, uttered strange sounds, and complained of biting and pinching sensations.

The Witch Trials of Salem saw neighbors accuse each other of witchcraft.

When his medicines failed to effect a cure, Doctor William Griggs suggested that the girls' problems might have a supernatural origin.

Suspicion began to focus on Tituba, the Reverend Parris' Indian slave, who had been known to tell tales of omens, voodoo, and witchcraft, from her native folklore. After first adamantly denying any guilt, afraid of being made a scapegoat, Tituba eventually admitted that she was a witch, and that she had often been approached by a tall, horned man from Boston, who sometimes appeared as a dog or a pig. She named four others, who had flown through the air on magic sticks with her.

Magistrates Jonathan Corwin and John Hathorne interrogated the suspects, who named others, who were in turn questioned and charged with doing Satan's work. One, Giles Corey, aged over 80, pleaded not guilty and refused to stand trial. However, his examiners subjected him to interrogation and torture, placing heavy stone weights on his body. Corey survived for two days before dying.

Many villagers, perhaps hoping to avoid suspicion, came forward to offer stories, such as cheese and butter mysteriously going bad, or animals born with deformities, after visits from one of the suspects.

As the number of accusations grew, including many pious and respected members of the community, some citizens grew concerned about possible miscarriages of justice.

In October the madness ended as suddenly as it began.

Window Tax is Proving Highly Unpopular

England, 1695: After the withdrawal of the dismally unsuccessful Hearth Tax in 1689, the British Government has recently introduced a tax on windows.

The Hearth Tax was highly unpopular, not least because it required inspectors to enter houses and workplaces. It failed because many people bricked up their fireplaces well before the twice-yearly inspections—on Lady Day and Michaelmas Day—and because many of the collectors stole a larger cut than their due.

The new tax was supposed to be more efficient, as windows are visible from the street. But many are dodging payment by bricking in windows, camouflaging them, or even building dummy windows to bamboozle inspectors. Others block up windows, only to unblock them as soon as the collector has gone.

The outraged masses are saying that the Window Tax is actually a tax on air and light, while glassmakers are predicting that their industry will soon be shattered.

Le Moyne Establishes Colony of Louisiana

Louisiana, North America, 1699: Pierre Le Moyne, Sieur d'Iberville, has claimed the North American region of Louisiana for France, and has started building the first settlement in the area.

This follows a previous unsuccessful attempt by René-Robert Cavalier, Lord of La Salle, who explored the Illinois River and the Mississippi from the mouth of the Illinois to the Gulf of Mexico, in search of a water route across North America.

On April 9, 1682, La Salle claimed Louisiana in the name of His Majesty Louis XIV. Already in control of Quebec, King Louis wanted to colonize Louisiana in order to restrict England to the area between the Atlantic Ocean and the Appalachian Mountains.

La Salle returned to France for supplies to set up a French colony, but upon his return two years later, he failed to find the Mississippi again, and was forced instead to set up a base, Fort Saint Louis, on the coast much further to the west. That settlement foundered after La Salle was murdered on the Trinity River by his own men on March 19, 1687.

There had been rumors of Frenchmen on the Mississippi at an earlier date, but it is certain that, in the summer of 1673, Louis Joliet, the Indian son of a Quebec wagon-maker, and Jacques Marquette, a Jesuit priest, reached the Gulf of Mexico after drifting down the great river from the mouth of the Wisconsin.

Last March, Le Moyne managed to rediscover the Mississippi River, and is now constructing a fort 54 miles (87 km) upstream of the delta.

Titus Oates

Explorer René-Robert Cavalier claims the territory of Louisiana for King Louis XIV of France in 1682.

Louis XIV of France

"I HAVE NOT TIME TO SAY MORE, BUT TO BEG YOU WILL GIVE MY DUTY TO THE QUEEN, AND LET HER KNOW HER ARMY HAS HAD A GLORIOUS VICTORY. MONSIEUR TALLARD AND TWO OTHER GENERALS ARE IN MY COACH, AND I AM FOLLOWING THE REST."

DUKE OF MARL-BOROUGH (1650–1722) BRITISH MILITARY COMMANDER, OF THE BATTLE OF BLENHEIM, 1704

One Parliament for Wales, England, and Scotland

Great Britain, May 1, 1707: In a hard-won landmark victory, the Parliament of England and Wales and the Parliament of Scotland have today individually and jointly signed historic Acts of Union.

Both parliaments will now be dissolved and the new Parliament of the Kingdom of Great Britain—to be housed in the Palace of Westminster on the banks of the River Thames—will be formed.

As one of its final acts, the Parliament of Scotland has imposed martial law, in anticipation of widespread public rioting. The vast majority of the Scottish population strongly disapprove of the union, and many petitions were presented to the Scottish Parliament in the build-up to the signing of the Acts.

Nevertheless, there are many political, religious, social, and economic benefits for both countries.

The Acts of Union ensure that British royal succession will be strictly Protestant, with Roman Catholics banned from ever taking the throne, and also guarantee the

The Parliament of Great Britain will meet at the Palace of Westminster.

continuation of the Presbyterian Church of Scotland. England and Scotland will both enjoy the union's economic and trade advantages, while retaining their own legal and educational systems.

Mass Casualties from Surprise Indian Raids

North Carolina, North America, September 22, 1711: Violent dawn raids by hostile Indians have today devastated the peaceful settlement of New Bern on the Neuse River, as well as other settlements along the Pamlico, Trent, and Roanoke Rivers, leaving mass death and ruin in their wake. In a shocking turn of events, peaceful relations between the local Tuscarora tribes and the European settlers have been irrevocably shattered.

Details are still sketchy, but it appears that Chief Hancock and his southern Tuscarora tribe may have joined forces with Indians from other nearby tribes in a wild, murderous frenzy, although the northern Tuscarora peoples do not seem to be involved. Early reports indicate that British, Dutch, and German settlers and planters, who began moving into this district in 1653, have been slaughtered.

Since these settlers and the Indians are renowned for getting along peacefully together, officials are unsure of the motivation behind the surprise attacks. It has been rumored, however, that Chief Hancock has become increasingly frustrated and angered by raids on the women and children of his villages, who are apparently being sold into slavery.

Both northern and southern Tuscarora populations have been hit hard by diseases introduced by the European settlers, as have all the Native American peoples. On top of that, Indian lands are being taken over to provide homes and plantations for the new arrivals, squeezing the Native Americans into increasingly small and unviable areas. Unfortunately, the stage seems set for further bloodshed as the surviving settlers gear up to retaliate.

The Treaty of Utrecht ended French expansion.

Brilliant Reign of the Sun King Comes to an End

Versailles, France, September 1, 1715: The entire French nation is reeling today following the announcement of the king's death from gangrene. King Louis XIV, also known as the Sun King, or Louis the Great, would have been 77 next week. His 72-year reign has dominated Europe for most of the seventeenth century and has lasted longer than that of any other European monarch.

Louis XIV's birth on September 5, 1638, at Saint-Germain-en-Laye to Louis XIII and his wife, Anne of Austria, was seen as a miracle, as the royal couple had been childless for 23 years. The young prince was named Louis-Dieudonne

Key Events

London, England, March 19, 1702: William III of Orange dies, aged 51. Anne, his wife's sister, succeeds the throne.

Turkey, August 22, 1703: Sultan Mustafa II is deposed.

Blenheim, Bavaria, August 13, 1705: The Battle of Blenheim is won by English, Austrian and Dutch forces.

Ahmadnagar, India, March 3, 1707: Aurangzeb Alamgir, Mogul emperor, dies aged 88.

Great Britain, May 1, 1707: England and Scotland unite under one ruler and one Parliament.

Poltava, Russia, July 8, 1709: Charles XII of Sweden is defeated by Peter I of Russia at the Battle of Poltava.

Malplaquet, France, September 11, 1709: Great Britain, Netherlands and Austria defeat France, with enormous loss of life on both sides.

London, England, 1710: The *Post Office Act* is passed, regulating the passage of mail between England and North America.

Pruth River, Ukraine, July 21, 1711: The Treaty of Pruth is signed by Russia and Turkey, restoring lost territory to the Turks.

North Carolina, North America, September 22, 1711: The Tuscarora Indians attack, killing settlers and destroying farms.

Utrecht, Netherlands, 1713: The War of the Spanish Succession is ended by the Treaty of Utrecht. Philip V remains King of Spain, but Spanish territories in other parts of Europe are given up. The American colonies see fighting too (known as Queen Anne's War).

Hanover, Germany, June 8, 1714: Sophia, Electress of Hanover and heir to Great Britain, dies, aged 84.

London, England, March, 1715: William Dampier, English explorer and privateer dies, aged about 63.

Versailles, France, September 1, 1715: Louis XIV dies of gangrene, aged 76.

Belgrade, Serbia, August 22, 1717: Prince Eugene of Savoy defeats the Turks at the Battle of Belgrade.

Fredriksten, Norway, November 30, 1718: Charles XII, King of Sweden, dies, aged 36.

Louisiana, North America, 1718: French rulers establish a trading post named New Orleans.

Liechtenstein, September 23, 1719: The newly-established principality declares its independence.

Delhi, India, 1720: Mohammed Ibrahim, Mogul emperor, dies after a short reign, the fourth emperor in two years.

Easter Island, South Pacific, April 5, 1722: Discovered by Dutch explorer Jacob Roggeveen.

Berkshire, England, June 16, 1722: John Churchill, Duke of Marlborough, dies, aged 72.

Peking, China, December 20, 1722: Emperor Kangxi dies, aged 68.

(God-given). On the death of his father in 1643, young Louis succeeded to the throne under his mother's guidance, finally assuming control in 1661.

In his rich and eventful life, the king knew much love, pain, and war. He experienced the untimely loss of seven of his eight legitimate children, but also exercised great power. In his campaign to extend France's influence throughout Europe, Louis fought wars and built lavish palaces. One of his most enduring legacies is sure to be the stunning Palace of Versailles, a magnificent complex that has housed his court of 10,000 people.

Although the common people might not agree, France is now in a position to exert great influence throughout much of Europe, with French the commonly accepted language of commerce, culture, and cuisine. It is believed Louis XIV will be succeeded by his young great-grandson, Louis XV, under the guardianship of the Duc du Maine.

Louisiana's Capital Named

Louisiana, North America, 1718: The American colony of Louisiana, so named in 1682 by French explorer René-Robert Cavelier de la Salle, to honor France's King Louis XIV, now has an official trading post and capital: New Orleans.

Ironically, Louisiana's governor Jean Baptiste le Moyne, Sieur de Bienville, has named the town after Philippe II, Duke of Orléans—the younger brother of Louis XIV and current ruler of France. It seems Philippe, always kept in Louis's shadow and prevented by Louis and their parents from taking the French throne in his own right, is set to make a permanent impression on the booming new colony.

The influence of the French in this part of the country continues to grow, as New Orleans is well situated on the banks of

the Mississippi River about 100 miles (160 km) north of where the river flows into the Gulf of Mexico. Already, wealthy French plantation owners are setting about construction of elegant mansions along the curving banks of the mighty river, seemingly in defiance of its low-lying flood-prone terrain.

time out

In 1739, shipmaster Robert Jenkins shows the British House of Commons his ear-amputated by Spanish coastguards–resulting in a declaration of war against Spain. The incident becomes known as "The War of Jenkins's Ear."

There is an air of excitement and prosperity, with plans for cafés and restaurants where French cuisine and culture are expected to flourish. The original inhabitants of the area—the Chickasaw, Choctaw, and Natchez Indians—are no longer in evidence.

With such excellent shipping access, the French trade in furs and other goods is likely to boom, and there appears to be little concern about other colonizing nations accessing the town via the river.

Death of Military Genius

Berkshire, England, June 16, 1722: The outstanding military leader John Churchill, first Duke of Marlborough, who has been suffering from paralysis, died today at Blen-heim Palace. He was 72 years old. As a mark of respect, he will be buried at Westminster Abbey.

Churchill was born in Devonshire to Elizabeth and Sir Winston Churchill, and developed an early fascination with military strategy. At 17, he took up a position in the household of the Duke of York and joined the British Navy shortly afterwards, seeing active service in a number of arenas before settling down to married life with Sarah Jennings.

By the time the Duke of York succeeded to the throne as King James II of England in 1685, Churchill was again active in the military, albeit awkwardly as major-general of the loyalist forces rebelling against James. In 1689, with James II exiled in France, and William

on the throne, Churchill was created Earl of Marlborough in recognition of his contribution to the overthrow.

Following William's death in 1702, Marlborough's close association—via his wife, Sarah—with Queen Anne, saw him rise rapidly through the ranks to become Captain-General Lord Marlborough, the commander-in-chief of the Allied armies. He will be remembered for his outstanding victories in the War of the Spanish Succession (1701–1714). In the Battle of Blenheim on August 13, 1704, leading the Allied forces, Marlborough defeated the French and Bavarians, thus saving Vienna and driving the French out of Germany. In 1709, in the bloodiest battle of this long war, he again led the Allied forces to victory, although they suffered heavy losses and were unable to conquer Paris. Despite numerous ups and downs in his career, Marlborough will go down in history as a military genius.

Charles XII of Sweden

William Dampier was the first Englishman to land in Australia.

Peking, China, 1723: Prince Yin-zhen, outwitting his brothers and executing or imprisoning some of them, takes the throne as Emperor Yongzheng.

England, November, 1724: Henry Kelsey, Canadian explorer, dies, aged 57.

Madrid, Spain, August, 1724: King Philip V returns to the throne, after the death of his son Louis I.

St Petersburg, Russia, February 8, 1725: Peter the Great dies, aged 52.

Montevideo, South America, 1726: The city of Montevideo (later the capital of Uruguay) is founded.

Kiakhta, Russia, 1727: The Treaty of Kiakhta defines the boundary between the Chinese and the Russian empires.

St Petersburg, Russia, May 17, 1727: Catherine I, Empress of Russia, dies, aged 43.

Hanover, Germany, October 11, 1727: George I, King of Great Britain, dies, aged 67. He is succeeded by his son, George II.

Bering Strait, August 13, 1728: Vitus Bering discovers the passage between Russia and Alaska.

Dublin, Ireland, 1728: Irish Catholics lose the right to vote.

Moscow, January 29, 1730: Peter II, Emperor of Russia, dies of smallpox, aged 14.

Turkey, September, 1730: Ottoman Sultan Ahmed III is deposed by janissaries, as was his predecessor.

Tupelo, Mississippi, North America, May 26, 1736: The French governor of Louisiana attacks the Chickasaw Indian town of Ackia in an attempt to control traffic along the Mississippi.

Peking, China, 1736: Emperor Qianlong ascends the throne, inaugurating the golden age of the Qing Dynasty.

Kandahar, Afghanistan, 1738: The Persian army of Nadir Shah takes Kandahar, making way for invasion of India in the following year.

Vienna, Austria, October 20, 1740: Charles VI of Austria, Holy Roman Emperor, dies, aged 55, leaving no male heirs. This sparks the War of the Austrian Succession.

Russia, October 28, 1740: Empress Anna Ivanova dies, aged 47.

St Petersburg, Russia, September 25, 1741: The reign of the one-year-old Ivan VI, with his mother as regent, is overthrown.

Russia, May 2, 1742: Russian explorer Semyon Chelyuskin reaches the most northern point in Eurasia.

North America, February, 1743: Louis and François La Vérendrye, reach the base of the Rocky Mountains.

Culloden, Scotland, April 16, 1746: The British Army defeat Scottish Highlander clansmen at the Battle of Culloden.

Fathabad, Persia, June, 1747: Nadir Shah is assassinated, aged 58.

Aachen, Germany, October 18, 1748: The Treaty of Aix-la-Chapelle ends the War of the Austrian Succession.

**Maria Theresa
of Austria**

"Now indeed with God's help the final stone has been laid in the foundation of St Petersburg."

PETER THE GREAT
(1672–1725), TSAR OF
RUSSIA, ON HIS
VICTORY AT THE
BATTLE OF POLTAVA,
1709

"…There are fifty thousand men slain this year in Europe, and not one Englishman."

ROBERT WALPOLE
(1676–1745), BRITISH
STATESMAN,
DEFENDING HIS
DECISION NOT TO SEND
BRITISH FORCES TO
FIGHT IN THE WAR OF
POLISH SUCCESSION,
1734

Peter the Great Succumbs to Lingering Illness

St Petersburg, Russia, February 8, 1725:
The tsar is dead. At the age of 52, Tsar Peter I—Peter the Great, Emperor of all the Russias—has died. Never one to shirk physical activity, late last year the tsar dived into the frigid waters of the northern ocean to assist in a ship rescue, and soon after developed the illness that led to his demise.

Peter Alexeyevich Romanov, who was born in Moscow on June 9, 1672, to Tsar Alexei Mikhailovich and his second wife, Nataliya Kyrillovna Naryshkina, was the youngest son of Alexei. After years spent in the shadow of his half-siblings, Sophia and Ivan V, Peter finally became the sole ruler of Russia in 1696.

An exceedingly tall, striking man, Peter always exuded restless energy, and loved ships and working with his hands. He will long be remembered as the tsar who swept Russia from insignificant isolation to its current position as a major force in Europe. As a young man, Peter's interest in military and naval matters brought him into contact with many other Europeans and he embarked on sweeping reforms, which have modernized and in many ways "westernized" Russia.

Frequently at war with his neighbors, Peter has extended the area of Russia's dominance to include parts of Karelia, and all of Ingria, Estonia, and Livonia.

His legacies are many—reform of the Orthodox Church, the stunningly beautiful new capital city of St Petersburg, implementation of the Julian calendar, adoption of many "western" customs, expansion of local industry and foreign trade, and development of modern educational and cultural institutions. All this has come at a cost—those who opposed

Peter's reforms have been dealt with very harshly. Tsar Peter will be succeeded by his widow, the Empress Catherine, who has ruled by his side for many years.

Bering Confirms Northern Passage

Bering Strait, August 13, 1728: The shape of the known world has changed forever. A Russian expedition aboard the vessel *St Gabriel* today rounded the northeastern corner of Asia and sailed far enough north to establish that there is no landmass linking Siberia to Alaska.

Although thick fog prohibited sighting of the Alaskan coast, expedition leader Vitus Jonassen Bering is convinced that he has proven the existence of a northern passage. The well-known Danish-born seaman and explorer, who has demonstrated his seamanship skills in service to the Russian Navy, was chosen by Peter the Great (Tsar Peter I of Russia) in early 1725 to explore the extent of Russia's unknown lands and territories.

Bering, born in Horsens, Denmark in 1681, joined the newly formed Russian Navy in 1703, and has settled in Russia with his Russian-born wife and children. His journey cannot have been easy. Departing from St Petersburg in late February 1725, his party took two years to traverse the rugged Siberian terrain and arrive finally in Okhotsk. Here, they built a boat and sailed across to the Kamchatka Peninsula, where they built the *St Gabriel*.

With fog and poor weather obscuring vision, Bering and his expedition are set to make the arduous journey home to St Petersburg. However, given the passion of both the late tsar and Bering to further map Russia's boundaries, it is highly likely that another expedition will be mounted in the near future.

"Mountains of Bright Stones" Discovered

North America, February, 1743: Adventurous French fur traders have reported an extraordinary discovery—a massive snow-capped mountain range, which they describe as the "the mountains of bright stones" (the Rocky Mountains).

Brothers Louis-Joseph and François La Vérendrye last year headed west from the Great Lakes with their father, Pierre, in search of a western ocean and intent upon setting up trading posts along the way. When Pierre became ill and turned back, his sons pushed on, accompanied by a large party of local Bow Indians to protect them from possible attack by hostile Shoshones. In their journal, they report that on the morning of January 1 they awoke to see the outlines of huge

The spectacular grandeur of the Rocky Mountains.

mountains on the horizon. Twelve days of hiking westwards brought them to the foot of the mountains, which they report as being "well wooded and very high."

Bonnie Prince Charlie's Jacobite Army Routed

Culloden, Scotland, April 16, 1746: The Scottish highland city of Inverness is again witnessing the aftermath of battle. Flushed with victory after the gory hourlong Battle of Culloden, the Duke of Cumberland—Prince William Augustus of Great Britain—has today ridden through the streets with bloody sword brandished, leaving the highlanders in no doubt as to his punitive intentions.

Bonnie Prince Charlie and the demoralized remnants of his starving, rag-tag highlander army are on the run. The prince's attempt to regain the Scottish throne for his exiled father, Prince James Francis Edward Stuart (often called the Old Pretender), has failed dismally, and Scotland remains firmly under the control of the British Government.

It is a day of bitter disappointment for the Jacobites, who have been trying to

Founded by Tsar Peter in 1710, the Alexander Nevsky Monastery in St Petersburg houses relics of the great saint.

Defeat at the Battle of Culloden in 1746 brought an end to Bonnie Prince Charlie's attempt to reclaim the throne.

restore Stuarts to the Scottish throne ever since Charles's grandfather, King James VII of Scotland (King James II of England and Ireland), was deposed in 1688. At the heart of the often violent dissension lies religion—the Stuarts are Catholic, while the British rulers are Protestant—and fierce adherence to the Scottish highland clan system (with Catholics in the majority).

Seats of Power

China Qing Dynasty: Kangxi (reigned 1661-1722); Yongzheng (1722-1735); Qianlong (1735-1796).

England (Replaced by the Kingdom of Great Britain in 1707) William III, Mary II (reigned 1689-1702); Anne (1702-1714); George I (1714-1727); George II (1727-1760).

France Louis XIV (reigned 1643-1715); Louis XV (1715-1774).

Holy Roman Empire Leopold I (reigned 1658-1705); Joseph I (1705-1711); Charles VI (1711-1740); Interregnum (1740-1742); Charles VII (1742-1745); Francis I (1745-1765).

India Mogul Empire: Aurangzeb (reigned 1658-1707); Shah Alam I (1707-1712); Jahandar Shah (1712-1713); Furrukhsiyar (1713-1719); Rafi Ul-Darjat (1719); Rafi Ud-Daulat (1719); Nikusiyar (1719); Mohammed Shah (1719-1720); Mohammed Ibrahim (1720); Mohammed Shah (1720-1748); Ahmad Shah Bahadur (1748-1754).

Japan Edo Period: Higashiyama (reigned 1687-1709); Nakamikado (1709-1735); Sakuramachi (1735-1747); Momozono (1747-1762).

Ottoman Empire Mustafa II (reigned 1695-1703); Ahmed III (1703-1730); Mahmud I (1730-1754).

Persia Safavid Shahs: Sultan Hoseyn I (reigned 1694-1722); Tahmasp II (1722-1732); Abbas III (1732-1736); Nazir Shah (military leader 1736-1747); Suleiman II (1749-1750).

Portugal Brigantine Dynasty: Pedro II (reigned 1667-1706); Joao V (1706-1750).

Russia Tsars: Peter I (Peter the Great) (reigned 1682-1721). Emperors: Peter I (reigned 1721-25); Catherine I (1725-1727); Peter II (1727-1730); Anna (1730-1740); Ivan VI (1740-1741); Elizabeth (1741-1762).

Spain Habsburg Dynasty: Charles II (reigned 1665-1700). Bourbon Dynasty: Philip V (1700-1724); Louis I (1724); Philip V (1724-1746). Ferdinand VI (1746-1759).

Zulu Nation Mageba kaPhunga (1727-1745); Ndaba kaMageba (1745-1763).

Bonnie Prince Charlie—who brought 5,000 men with him to this battle—is now likely to return to France. Ill-prepared, disorganized and half-starved, his army did not stand a chance. An early count indicates that 1,250 Jacobites have died, almost as many are injured, and 560 have been taken prisoner. Cumberland, on the other hand, has lost only about 50 men, with another 250 reported wounded.

Ruthless Conqueror Nadir Shah Assassinated

Fathabad, Persia, June, 1747: Nadir Shah, ruler of Persia (Iran) since 1736 and founder of the Afsharid Dynasty, has been assassinated by officers of his own guard, who killed him with a sword blow to the head after rousing him from sleep. This powerful military genius, born Nadir Qoli Beg on October 22, 1688, in Kohban, Persia, has expanded the reach of the Persian empire as far as the Indus River to the west, the Caucasus Mountains to the north, and India to the east, acquiring enormous wealth in the process. His paranoia in recent years is perhaps not surprising, given his ruthlessness and his pillaging of neighboring territories.

Nadir was born into a poor peasant family and lost both parents when he was very young. In order to survive, he joined a group of bandits, and rose to become their leader. By 1719, Nadir—leading a force of 5,000 fighting men—was supporting the usurped Safavid Iranian ruler, Shah Tahmasp II, against Afghan invader, Mahmud Gilzai. In 1729, he defeated the Afghans and by 1730 had driven them out of Persia.

Nadir's loyalty, however, was short-lived. Soon after, he deposed Tahmasp, placed his infant son Abbas III on the throne and named himself regent. With the death of Abbas in 1736, Nadir took the throne and declared himself shah.

Nadir Shah's rule was characterized by vicious campaigns against neighbors, including the ransacking and taking of Delhi in India. He returned with such wealth from this victory that he was able to suspend taxes in Persia for the following three years. He also brought back such treasures as the stunning Peacock Throne and the Koh-i-Noor diamond.

Treaty Ends Eight Years of Relentless Conflict

Aachen, Germany, October 18, 1748: Today's historic signing of the Treaty of Aix-la-Chapelle has brought to an end the War of the Austrian Succession. For eight long years, Maria Theresa has fought off all comers in her courageous efforts to retain the territory previously ruled by her late father, Charles VI, sovereign of Austria and Holy Roman Emperor. Allegiances have formed and dissolved across Europe since Frederick II of Prussia first invaded Silesia in 1740.

The treaty—negotiated primarily by Britain and France—has resulted in a return to the *status quo ante bellum*, literally "as things were before the war." Maria Theresa retains Austria, Bohemia, and Hungary, while agreeing to sacrifice most of Silesia to Frederick, thereby cleverly separating him from his allies.

Since the war has flowed well beyond Europe into India and North America, peace will be welcomed in those countries too. Madras in India will now revert to British rule, while the conflict known as King George's War gives back to France and Great Britain the territories each of them held in North America before the conflict. Notably, Louisburg—captured by the British in a daring raid in 1745—will be returned to France.

Unease and discontent persist, however, as the treaty does nothing to further the cause of commercial harmony between France and England in the West Indies, Africa, and India.

Tsar Peter I of Russia

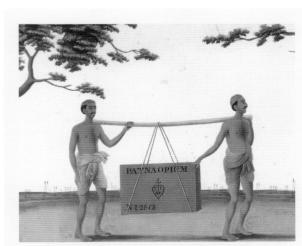

The Qing Dynasty tried to suppress the emerging opium trade.

Seed-Planting Machine Being Field-Tested

Edmund Halley

Wallingford, Oxfordshire, England, 1701: British farmers are waiting with considerable interest, as well as some skepticism, to see the results of a new horse-drawn, mechanized seed-planting drill. A young Wallingford farmer, Jethro Tull, frustrated by what he considers to be wastage, inefficient work practices, and inconsistent yields, has devised the new machine and is using it on his farm this season instead of having laborers scatter seed by hand.

Tull, born to Jethro and Dorothy Tull on March 30, 1674, at Basildon in Berkshire, seemed set for a political career after studying law at Oxford and Gray's Inn, London. However, poor health and a lack of funds have seen him married and back on the land.

Although others have for some time been experimenting with mechanical seed drills, Tull's machine is unique in that it plants three even rows of seeds simultaneously, with all the seeds planted at the same depth, thus minimizing waste and allowing ease of access between the rows for crop cultivation. Tull says he gained inspiration for the ingenious design by studying the workings of his local church organ. At the center of the drill is a rotating cylinder, into which grooves have been cut. Hoppers filled with seed sit

above the cylinder, and the seeds pass down through the grooves into funnels, which direct them into three shallow trenches dug by a plow at the front of the machine. A harrow attached to the rear covers the sown seeds with soil.

Brilliant Mathematician Bernoulli Passes Away

Basle, Switzerland, August 16, 1705: The highly respected professor of mathematics at the University of Basle Jacob Bernoulli (also known as Jakob, James, or Jacques) has died. He has requested that the logarithmic spiral, with which he has long been fascinated, be carved on his tombstone. It is believed that his younger brother and academic archrival, Johann, will take up the chair of mathematics.

Born on January 6, 1655 into an eminent Basle family, Jacob Bernoulli graduated from the University of Basel in 1671 with a master's degree in philosophy, and in 1676 with a licentiate in theology. (Bernoulli had also been studying mathematics and astronomy secretly.) In 1676, he took up a tutoring job in Geneva, and began traveling throughout Europe, meeting and studying with influential teachers, including Malebranche, a follower of mechanical philosopher Descartes.

In 1681, Bernoulli met many mathematicians in the Netherlands before traveling to England, where he studied with the likes of Boyle, Hooke, Wallis, and Barrow (who triggered his interest in infinitesimal geometry). He began publishing in the journal *Acta Eruditorum* in 1682

and, although he returned to teach mathematics at the University of Basle in 1683, he maintained a lifelong correspondence with many of the mathematicians he had met during his travels.

Appointed to the chair of mathematics in 1687, Bernoulli will be most remembered for his work on algebra, infinitesimal calculus, the calculus of variations, mechanics, the theory of series, and the theory of probability. He is survived by his wife, Judith, and their two children.

Coke-Fired Furnace Cuts Cost of Iron

Coalbrookdale, England, 1709: Abraham Darby, the newly-arrived ironmaster, is experimenting with a revolutionary technique that looks set to save the forests of England from further devastation.

For centuries now, charcoal has been used for heating iron ore to facilitate the extraction of iron. Because charcoal is produced by the burning of wood, ironworks have traditionally moved from area to area as the local forests become depleted. Darby, who served his apprenticeship with a malt-mill maker in Birmingham before joining the Baptist Mills Brass Works in Bristol, has received funds from fellow Quakers to establish his coke-fired blast furnace.

Darby gained his inspiration from the malt-drying industry, which has found a way of creating coke from coal without any undesirable gaseous by-products, and without emitting billowing clouds of smoke. Low-sulfur bituminous coal is plentiful in Shropshire, and Darby is using it to make the coke with which he fires his new blast furnace.

Until now, iron has been produced in small batches by putting iron ore into pans, covering it with burning sheets of charcoal, and firing the mix with the aid

time out

In 1743, Thomas Boulsover (1705–1788), an English cutler, bonds together heavy copper sheets with thin sheets of silver, inventing silverplate. He names it "Sheffield silver" in honor of the city in which he was born.

Jethro Tull's mechanized seed drill promises greater efficiency in agriculture.

Eighteenth-century engraving of University College and Queen's College, Oxford University.

Jethro Tull

scientist seems to have been aware of his mortality in recent years, having had numerous portraits painted and generously distributing his wealth among fellow scientists and his younger relatives.

Always reclusive, generally modest, and increasingly paranoid of late, Sir Isaac would no doubt prefer his passing to go more or less unnoticed. So great is his contribution to the realms of human understanding, however, that his published works and recorded discoveries and inventions are likely to be remembered for decades, if not centuries.

Isaac Newton was born in Woolsthorpe on January 4, 1643, and spent most of his childhood in the care of his grandparents, following the early death of his father, and his mother's remarriage. A loner, he was considered odd for inventing mechanical devices such as mouse-powered windmills and other strange but useful gadgetry.

In 1661, Newton entered Trinity College, Cambridge, where he studied mechanical philosophy and developed a fascination with the nature of matter, cosmic order, light, colors, and sensations. By 1666, he had arrived at many of the realizations that inform much of his subsequent work—the theory of universal gravitation (in simple terms, explaining how the universe is held together by the force of gravity); the true nature of light and color; and a new approach to mathematics known as calculus.

Newton's reflective telescope (as opposed to the refractive telescopes that are commonly in use) is a legacy appreciated by astronomers. His work on gravitation and the laws of motion can be studied in the *Philosophiae Naturalis Principia Mathematica*, while *Opticks* explains his discoveries regarding the nature of light and color.

of bellows. The labor and wood required to produce such small quantities means that iron is very expensive. Using coke instead of charcoal, however, Darby is able to stack large amounts of iron ore and coke into a huge furnace, thus producing greater quantities of iron at vastly reduced cost. From this iron, he is manufacturing reasonably priced pots and other cast-iron items.

Stars Move, Says Halley

Greenwich, England, 1718: Edmund Halley, the controversial astronomer and mathematician, has established beyond a doubt that stars, which have been thought to be "fixed" in the sky, must have a slight motion of their own. Having mapped numerous stars throughout his career to date, he has now detected proper motion in at least three stars.

Born in Haggerston near London on October 29, 1656, to wealthy parents, Halley is currently Savilian Professor of Geometry at Oxford University.

He is well known for his theory of periodic cometary orbits published in *Astronomy of Comets* (1705), as well as for his financial and academic support for Isaac Newton's *Philosophiae Naturalis Principia Mathematica* (a publication providing a mechanical explanation for planetary motion), his mapping of the southern skies *(Catalogus Stellarum Australium*, 1678*)*, his development of a deep-sea diving bell, and his analysis of age-at-death demographic records, published in an article on life annuities.

Isaac Newton's reflective telescope.

Newton Leaves Great Legacy to Humanity

London, England, March 31, 1727: After a series of debilitating illnesses, Sir Isaac Newton, master of the London Mint and president of the Royal Society, has died, aged 84. The great mathematician, astronomer, and

Greenwich, England, 1725: John Flamsteed's star catalog, *Historia Coelestis Britannica*, is published posthumously.
London, England, March 31, 1727: Isaac Newton dies, aged 84.
London, England, 1728: James Bradley's star observations lead him to calculate the speed of light to be 183,000 miles (295,000 kilometers) per second.
Paris, France, 1728: Pierre Fauchard publishes *The Surgeon Dentist*, the first dental textbook, and invents the term "dentist."

Jaipur, India, 1728: A new royal observatory is completed. Contains one of the world's largest sundials.
London, England, 1729: Stephen Gray shows that electricity can travel along some materials and not others.
London, England, 1731: John Hadley invents the reflecting quadrant (the basis of the sextant). American Thomas Godfrey independently invents the same instrument.
Bury, Lancashire, England, 1733: John Kay invents the flying shuttle, speeding up the weaving process.

Teddington, Middlesex, England, 1733: Stephen Hales publishes studies of blood pressure measurements.
Greenock, Scotland, 19 January 1736: James Watt, inventor, born.
Paris, France, 1737: Philippe Buache uses contour lines to show elevation on maps.
London, England, 1738: Instrument maker Benjamin Martin creates his first Universal microscope, a new type of portable microscope.

Switzerland, 1738: Daniel Bernoulli publishes *Hydrodynamica*, including Bernoulli's Principle, that as the speed of a fluid increases the pressure it exerts decreases.
St Petersburg, Russia, June 7, 1742: Mathematician Christian Goldbach conjectures that every number greater than 2 is a sum of 3 primes, in a letter to Leonhard Euler.
Sweden, 1742: Anders Celsius proposes that a temperature scale of 0 to 100 (based on the boiling and melting points of water) be adopted for all scientific measurements.

Sheffield, England, 1743: Thomas Boulsover creates Sheffield plate.
Philadelphia, North America, 1746: Benjamin Franklin's kite experiment proves that lightning is a form of electricity.
Bazentinele-le-Petit, Picardy, Erfurt, Germany, 1745-1746: Scottish monk Andreas Gordon describes a device that can be used to store electricity. Musschenbroek and Cunaeus build this "Leyden jar."
Plymouth, England, June 16, 1747: James Lind's experiments with scurvy show citrus fruits to be the cure.

Benjamin Franklin

New Device Speeds up the Production of Cloth

Bury, England, 1733: British weavers are up in arms, while textile manufacturers are quietly excited at an invention that will radically speed up the weaving process. Local mill manager John Kay has patented a device he calls the flying shuttle, which will allow one person to operate a loom that previously required two operators. It also means that looms will be able to produce much wider cloth. The traditional handloom weaving process has, for centuries, been carried out by single operators, often working at home. With warp threads fixed vertically to a wooden loom, a weaver would wind the weft thread onto a slim wooden shuttle that he or she "throws" back and forth across the loom, from hand to hand. This means that the fabric width is limited to the reach of the weaver, unless the loom is operated by two people—thus considerably increasing the cost of the operation.

With the flying shuttle, however, there is a box at either end of the loom, joined by a long connecting board called a shuttle race. A single weaver can use one hand to pull a cord that knocks a peg back and forth across the loom from one shuttle box to the other, and the other hand to comb and compact the cloth.

With Kay's revolutionary invention, manufacturers will be needing more cotton yarn to keep up with the increased production capacity, while weavers are anxious that jobs might be lost.

In 1730, Kay patented a machine that can twist and cord mohair and worsted.

Force of Blood Measured

Teddington, England, 1733: Inventor, chemist, physiologist, and clergyman Stephen Hales has published a fascinating work that helps to explain the mysterious workings of the blood and how it flows throughout the bodies not only of humans but also of animals.

In his new work, *Haemastaticks*, he reveals the results of his experiments on horses, sheep, deer, and dogs over recent years, explaining that he has found a way to measure blood pressure. After cutting through the animal's skin, he inserted and bound into place a 9 ft (2.7 m) long glass tube (attached to the flexible windpipe of a goose) in one of its arteries. By measuring the rise and fall of the column of blood in the tube, he has charted the "force of the blood," its rate of flow, and the capacity of different blood vessels. He reports, for example, that the blood from the carotid artery rises to a height of 8 ft (2.4 m), while the blood from the jugular vein rises less than 1 ft (30 cm).

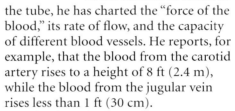

John Kay revolutionized weaving.

Hales, born in September 1677 at Bekesbourne in Kent, is the perpetual curate of Teddington, a Fellow of the Royal Society, and a member of the committee for establishing a colony in Georgia, America. He is already well known for his first publication, *Vegetable Staticks*, in which he details numerous experiments in plant physiology to do with loss of water by evaporation, the growth rate of shoots and leaves, and variations in root pressure at different times of the day.

Silver Look at Lower Cost

Sheffield, England, 1743: While repairing a silver and copper knife handle at his workshop on the corner of Tudor Street and Surrey Street, cutler Thomas Boulsover has made a delightful and extraordinary discovery. He has found that by heating these two metals to a very high temperature, he can cause them to melt and flow together.

Apparently, the silver adheres to the copper in a thin coating, so that the cooled item combines all the strength and usefulness of a copper object with the beautiful appearance of silver. The cost is also considerably less than that of a pure silver item.

Boulsover, working with his business partner Joseph Williams, plans to use the discovery to create desirable "silver" items such as buttons, buckles, knife handles, spurs, snuff boxes, and the like. He calls the new material Sheffield plate.

Midwifery Courses Promise Safer Births

Glasgow, Scotland, 1745: William Smellie, practicing London midwife and former Scottish country doctor and apothecary, has been granted his medical doctorate by the University of Glasgow. Some people are calling Smellie "the master of British midwifery," while others—mainly older, traditional, female midwives—are treating him with hostility and suspicion.

John Kay's flying shuttle is one of a number of inventions that has helped to propel Britain to become the dominant industrial power of the eighteenth century.

With over 20 years of general medical practice behind him, as well as formal midwifery training gained during his time in Paris, Smellie has been teaching courses in obstetrics and midwifery in London since 1741. These courses attract large numbers of midwives and medical students, as Doctor Smellie is the first to offer this training on a scientific basis.

Part of the training relates to the safe and effective use of forceps to deliver babies during breech births, as well as in births where the mother's pelvis does not allow for a safe delivery. One student describes Smellie's classes as "distinct, mechanical, and unreserved." While forceps are not a new invention, having been developed almost a century ago by a Huguenot immigrant family, the Chamberlens, they have remained a very well-kept secret until recent times.

William Smellie's distress at what he considers unnecessary maternal deaths during childbirth is his motivation for devising more streamlined, leather-clad forceps and teaching their safe and

Scientific Achievements

Astronomy: Halley proposes comets travel in elliptical orbits and determines return date for Halley's comet.
Botany: Plant hybridization begins.
Chemistry: Fahrenheit invents the mercury thermometer; cobalt, platinum discovered.
Ecology: Hundreds lose lives in India trying to protect trees; soil conservation promoted; attempts made to control air and water pollution.
Geology: Theory forwarded using salinity and evaporation to work out the age of Earth; geological map of southeast England and mineralogical map of France produced.
Mathematics: Theory forwarded that every number greater than 2 is a sum of three prime numbers.
Medicine: First smallpox inoculations given; counting the rate of pulse beats introduced; discovery that scurvy can be prevented by eating citrus fruits.
Physics: Theory forwarded that atmospheric pressures determine boiling point of water; centigrade thermometer invented by Celsius.

Botanic Gardens
Philadelphia, North America
Savannah, North America

Observatories
Berlin, Germany
Chennai, India
Delhi, India
Jaipur, India
Lund, Sweden
Mathura, India
Ujjain, India
Uppsala, Sweden
Varanasi, India

Universities
University of Caracas, Venezuela
University of Connecticut, North America
University of Havana, Cuba
University of St Petersburg, Russia

Citrus fruit was found to be a simple cure for scurvy.

scientific use. By delivering poor women free of charge, as long as his students are allowed to watch and learn, he has established new standards of safety and a trend toward the attendance of medically trained staff at births.

Physician Discovers Citrus Cure for Scurvy

Plymouth, England, June 16, 1747: HMS *Salisbury* has docked today after a ten-week stint with the Channel Fleet. Scottish physician James Lind, currently serving as a naval surgeon on board the *Salisbury*, is keen to report on his apparent successes during this voyage.

So concerned was Lind at the incidence of scurvy among the sailors on board—80 of the 350 men were suffering from the disease—that on May 20 he undertook a controlled experiment. The symptoms of scurvy are painful and debilitating (bleeding gums, loosened teeth, swollen and sore limbs, bruising, general weakness), and render the sailors incapable of doing any useful work.

Doctor Lind says that he chose 12 of the worst-affected men, accommodated in the "sick bay" of the ship, and fed them all the same basic healthy diet of sugar-sweetened gruel, fresh mutton broth, barley, raisins, rice, currants, sago, and so on. In addition, each pair in the group received a different course of daily treatment, with the results carefully noted. Two men drank apple cider; two were given a strong elixir; two took seawater; two consumed a mix of garlic, mustard, and horseradish; two were dosed on vinegar; and two ate two oranges and one lemon each.

While ten of the men have shown but little improvement, the two sailors on the citrus fruit supplement recovered dramatically. Lind is so heartened by these results that he intends to publish them in a document. Meanwhile, the *Salisbury*'s

commander has agreed to stock up on oranges and lemons for future voyages.

Benjamin Franklin Retires to Pursue Other Interests

Philadelphia, North America, 1748: At the age of 42, Benjamin Franklin—printer, writer, publisher, and philanthropist—has retired from printing in order to take up further investigative studies and to diversify into other areas of business. He retains a 50 percent silent partnership with his foreman, David Hill, who has now taken over the running the operation.

One of many areas of fascination Franklin intends to explore further is that of electricity. He suggests that "vitreous" and "resinous" electricity are not different types of "electrical fluid" but the same electrical fluid under different pressures. He has labeled these as positive and negative respectively, and is experimenting with the idea that the electrical charge might be able to be conserved.

Born in Boston, Massachusetts, on January 17, 1706, he is the youngest son of chandler Josiah Franklin and his second wife, Abiah. With little formal education, Franklin has nevertheless excelled in many areas of public life and business, and is renowned for his contributions to the improvement of postal and civic systems, and conditions in Philadelphia.

Franklin's newspaper, the *Pennsylvania Gazette*, which he established in 1730, has provided him with an excellent forum for airing his social and political views, as well as his suggestions for visionary reforms, while his extremely popular *Poor Richard's Almanac* has been entertaining the American people since 1733.

Generous in sharing the findings of his exploratory work and also in promoting scientific experimentation, in 1743 Franklin founded the American Philosophical Society—a forum that allows scientists to share and discuss their discoveries. It is believed he will now focus on furthering his investigations into the nature and workings of electricity.

Anders Celsius

Poor Richard's Almanac is a popular bestseller in the American colonies.

Samuel Pepys

"MUSIC WASHES AWAY FROM THE SOUL THE DUST OF EVERYDAY LIFE."

JOHANN SEBASTIAN BACH (1685–1750), GERMAN COMPOSER

"NOTHING IS CAPABLE OF BEING WELL SET TO MUSIC THAT IS NOT NONSENSE."

JOSEPH ADDISON (1672–1719) BRITISH ESSAYIST, 1711

Dryden to Be Buried at Westminster Abbey

London, England, May 12, 1700: Former Poet Laureate and Royal Historiographer—and arguably the most gifted playwright, poet, translator of classics, and literary critic of our times—John Dryden died today and is to be buried at Westminster Abbey. He is survived by his sons and his wife, Lady Elizabeth (Howard).

Dryden—the eldest of Erasmus and Mary Dryden's 14 children—was born on August 9, 1631, at his grandfather's rectory in Aldwinkle, Northamptonshire. His landowning Puritan parents were loyal to the parliament of the time, and Dryden has maintained a keen interest and involvement in politics and religion throughout his life.

Educated at Westminster School and Trinity College, Cambridge, Dryden graduated top of his year in 1654 with a Bachelor of Arts degree. He moved to London in the late 1650s and began writing poetry there, moving on to plays, critiques, and translations in order to earn a living. By 1668, his large body of work—panegyrics, poems, plays (both tragic and comic)—had earned him the

Westminster Abbey, resting place of poet John Dryden.

role of Poet Laureate, and in 1670 he was appointed Royal Historiographer. Both positions were stripped from him when King James II was deposed in 1688.

Among Dryden's most famous plays are *All for Love* (1677), *The Conquest of Granada* (1670, 1671), and the comedy, *Marriage à la Mode* (1672). His poems are too numerous to list, but include the satires "Absalom and Achitophel" (1681), "The Medal" (1682), and "MacFlecknoe" (1682), as well as works focused on religion—"Religio Laici" (1682) and "The Hind and the Panther" (1687).

Pepys Leaves Extensive Personal Library

London, England, May 26, 1703: Retired influential civil servant, diarist, and naval administrator, Samuel Pepys, has died at his home in Clapham at the age of 70, leaving a detailed will in which he bequeaths his estate to his nephew, John Jackson. He has also made specific provisions for care and storage of his excellent library of more than 3,000 books, which includes bound copies of his personal diaries.

Written largely in Thomas Shelton's form of shorthand (tachygraphy), with only people's names written in longhand, Pepys's diaries cover the period from 1660 to 1669. It is likely that they include some fascinating reading, such as accounts of Pepys's relationships with Charles II and James II, and his observations regarding the Great Plague of London and the Great Fire of London, as well as the ins and outs of the politics of the times. No doubt there are also mentions of his contemporaries, Sir Christopher Wren, Sir Isaac Newton, and John Dryden.

Samuel Pepys was born in London on February 23, 1633, the son of tailor John Pepys and his wife, Margaret, the sister of a Whitechapel butcher. His father's first cousin, Richard Pepys, was well connected, and Samuel received a good education,

Italian composer and violinist Arcangelo Corelli.

graduating with a Bachelor of Arts degree from Magdalene College, Cambridge in 1654. In 1655, he married his 15-year-old sweetheart, Elisabeth Marchant de St Michel, with whom he had a passionate relationship until her death in 1669.

During his career, Pepys has served as secretary of the Admiralty, introducing reforms to the appointment of naval officers, the maintenance of dockyards, and many other key areas of operations. He has also served as a member of Parliament several times and was president of the Royal Society in 1684 and 1685.

Wren's St Paul's Cathedral Finally Finished

London, England, 1710: Thirty-five years since building work began, the magnificent new St Paul's Cathedral—the seat of the bishop of London—is complete. Its architect, Sir Christopher Wren, has designed and supervised the building of more than 50 other churches, but St Paul's is surely his masterpiece.

Following the devastation of Old St Paul's in the Great Fire of 1666, King Charles II commissioned Wren to design the new cathedral in a modern style, and construction started on Ludgate Hill in June 1675. The cathedral is built of Portland stone in Renaissance style. It features a strikingly elegant central dome that rises 365 ft (111 m) above the main space of the cathedral, and is said to have been inspired by St Peter's Basilica in Rome. The dome supports three galleries. The Stone Gallery and the Golden Gallery are both external, while the internal Whispering Gallery—so named because of its fascinating acoustics—is high inside the dome, 259 steps up from ground level.

Born on October 20, 1632, in Wiltshire, Wren was a scientist and academic of note before devoting himself to architectural works. He served formerly as the Savilian Professor of Astronomy at Oxford University, and is a founding member and past president of the Royal Society. His earlier architectural works include the Sheldonian Theatre at Oxford, and Pembroke and Emmanuel Colleges at Cambridge. He was knighted in 1673 and has served two terms as a member of Parliament.

Palladio's Major Work Now Available in English

London, England, 1715: Recently arrived Italian exponent of Palladian architecture, Giacomo Leoni, has published the first English edition of Andrea Palladio's famous and highly influential work, *I Quattro Libri dell'Architettura (The Four Books of Architecture)*. While Palladio's designs, ideas, and theories have long been a major influence on British architecture, most notably in the works of Inigo Jones (1573–1652), they will from this time onward be more readily accessible to our promising young architects.

Leoni, aged 29, produces fresh, stylish, uncluttered designs, showcasing Andrea Palladio's distinctive style. The English edition of Palladio's *Four Books*, well-organized and clearly illustrated by Leoni, lays out all his key principles of design and theory. Book I deals with basic issues and problems of construction; Book II offers designs for domestic buildings; Book III provides designs for public buildings and advice on town planning; and Book IV is devoted to designs for temples and churches.

time out

On Easter Sunday 1708, composer Arcangelo Corelli conducts a performance of Handel's "La Resurrezione" in Rome. The next day, the soprano is replaced by a castrato, in deference to the papal decree that women should not perform on stage.

Revered Japanese "Shakespeare" Dies

Osaka, Japan, 1725: With the death of Chikamatsu Monzaemon (originally Sugimori Nobumori) at the age of 72, Japan has lost its greatest playwright. His legacy of well over 100 plays for puppet theater and kabuki (live drama) has so impressed the world that Monzaemon is called by some "the Japanese Shakespeare."

Born in 1653 into a samurai (military nobility) family, Monzaemon was a prolific writer who is said to have worked at unbelievable speed, apparently writing a play in a night when the mood took him. Unlike his father and brother, who had both been medical doctors, Chikamatsu began his involvement with theater and drama around the age of 20 while he was studying at Gon-shoji Temple. At about this time he met Osaka playwright Takemoto Gidayu, with whom he was to work many years later in Naniwa.

Monzaemon's dramatic masterpieces enthralled audiences with their poetic quality and their capacity to present simple characters such as shop clerks, prostitutes, merchants, and geishas as tragic figures starring in extraordinary dramas—which frequently end in double suicides. His works combine comedy and tragedy, poetry and prose, with gripping plots that vividly present love, passion, combat, torture, childbirth, and death.

Sir Christopher Wren

Actor with puppets performing to women, from *Ukiyo-e (Pictures of the Floating World)*.

Key Events

Osaka, Japan, 1725: Chikamatsu Monzaemon dies, aged 72.

Venice, Italy, 1725: Antonio Vivaldi's *Four Seasons* (four violin concertos) are published.

London, England, 1726: Jonathan Swift anonymously publishes his political satire *Gulliver's Travels*.

London, England, January, 1728: *The Beggar's Opera* by John Gay, a satirical musical, premières at Lincoln's Inn Fields Theatre.

Venice, Italy 1728: Canaletto (Giovanni Antonio Canale) completes *The Stonemason's Yard*.

London, England, 1728: Ephraim Chambers publishes his *Cyclopaedia; or an Universal Dictionary of Arts and Sciences*, the model for future encyclopedias.

London, England, January 19, 1729: William Congreve dies, aged 58.

London, England, April 26, 1731: Daniel Defoe dies, aged about 70.

Philadelphia, North America, December 28, 1732: Benjamin Franklin publishes the first *Poor Richard's Almanac* under the nom-de-plume Richard Saunders.

London, England, June 25, 1735: William Hogarth publishes his engravings with the protection of an Engraver's Copyright Act, passed the same day.

Cremona, Italy, December 18, 1737: Master luthier Antonio Stradivari dies, aged about 93.

Madrid, Spain, 1737: Carlo Broschi (Farinelli), the greatest of the castrato singers, ends his public career to join the court of King Philip V.

St Petersburg, Russia, 1738: Her Majesty's Dancing School is established, with Jean Baptiste Lande as balletmaster.

Vienna, Austria, July 28, 1741: Antonio Vivaldi, composer, dies, aged 63.

Germany, 1741: Johann Sebastian Bach publishes the *Keyboard Exercises (Goldberg Variations)*.

Dublin, Ireland, April 13, 1742: George Frideric Handel's oratorio *Messiah* premières.

Japan, 1743: Ando Kaigetsudo, painter, dies, aged about 72.

Delhi, India, c. 1745: Mir Taqi Mir pioneers composition of Urdu lyric poetry in Persian *ghazal* style.

Venice, Italy, 1747: Giambattista Tiepolo completes frescoes featuring Antony and Cleopatra in the ballroom of the Palazzo Labia.

Geneva, Switzerland, 1748: *The Spirit of the Laws*, written by influential philosopher Montesquieu (Charles de Secondat), is published anonymously.

London, England, February 28, 1749: Henry Fielding's novel, *The Adventures of Tom Jones*, is published.

William Hogarth

Congreve Dies in Accident

London, England, January 19, 1729: A recent coach accident has claimed the life of one of our best Restoration poets and playwrights, William Congreve, whose health and eyesight have been deteriorating for some years. Although he never married, Congreve has settled an amount on his illegitimate daughter, Mary (born in 1723 to Henrietta, Lady Godolphin), and will be sorely missed by his many friends and admirers. His wish is to be interred in the Poet's Corner of Westminster Abbey.

Congreve, born near Leeds on January 24, 1670, is well-known for his witty comedies. He is probably most famous, however, for his one tragedy, *The Mourning Bride* (1697), which gives us such wonderful lines as "Heaven has no rage like love to hatred turned, Nor hell a fury like a woman scorned," and "Music hath charms to soothe a savage breast."

While at school in Dublin, Congreve formed a lifelong friendship with author Jonathan Swift, and after graduating from Trinity College, Dublin, became a devotee and friend of John Dryden. According to these and other friends such as Frances Porter, Alexander Pope, and Henrietta, Duchess of Marlborough, he was a genial and generous man who lived up to his own words: "A clear wit, sound judgment and a merciful disposition."

Sadly, because of severe gout and possibly also because of harsh criticism from Jeremy Collier, Congreve's body of work is limited to five plays (all of which were written before 1700), a libretto for *The Judgment of Paris*, a handful of poems, and *The Works of Mr William Congreve* (a collaboration with Dryden, published in 1710). Congreve's leading female roles—including Angelica in *Love for Love* (1695) and Mrs Millamant in *The Way of the World* (1700)—were written for popular actress Anne Bracegirdle, whom some say may have been Congreve's mistress.

Robinson Crusoe's Prolific Creator Passes Away

London, England, April 26, 1731: Merchant trader, pamphleteer, journalist, novelist, double agent, sometime political prisoner, high-profile writer and social commentator Daniel Defoe died today at his lodgings in Ropemaker's Alley, Moorfields, in southeast London.

Born Daniel Foe, son of strict Nonconformist parents, in 1660 in Stoke Newington, Daniel was groomed by his father for the religious ministry.

As a young man, though, he traveled widely, took on the name Defoe, and began to write prolifically. He also set up trading businesses, which accrued major debts and landed him briefly in prison. In 1684, he married Mary Tuffley, a cooper's daughter, who bore him seven children, five of whom survived.

By 1702, Defoe, himself a political dissenter, was writing political pamphlets and carrying out intelligence work for the Whig Government while ostensibly supporting the Tory cause, which resulted in his imprisonment again. His mock ode, "Hymn to the Pillory," won him such public sympathy that in the pillory he was showered with flowers rather than the usual putrid waste.

While Defoe's political writings have been prolific throughout his life, it is his novels that have had the most striking impact. *Robinson Crusoe*, published in 1719, tells a captivating tale (based on a true story) of an island castaway made good. It was followed by *Moll Flanders*, *A Journal of the Plague Year*, *Colonel Jack*, and—in 1724—*Roxanna*.

Defoe's body of work broke new literary ground by using simple, captivating prose to tell the stories of believable characters in real-life situations, while also exploring grand themes.

"A libertine's destiny," from *The Rake's Progress*.

Engraved Images Will Be Protected by New Law

London, England, June 25, 1735: Painter, engraver, cartoonist, and art critic William Hogarth has taken advantage of a new act of Parliament to publish more engravings. Having learned from his experiences with an earlier work of his, *The Harlot's Progress*, that opportunists can all too easily reproduce and capitalize on engraved images, Hogarth arranged for an Engraver's Copyright Bill to be put before the House of Commons. It has passed into law today, and subscribers will now receive their copies of Hogarth's latest work, for which they have paid a guinea and a half a set.

Hogarth's eight paintings—now reproduced as engravings and entitled *The Rake's Progress*—illustrate the mannerisms, failings, and absurd behaviors of real human beings. In particular, they follow the reckless life of Tom Rakewell, the son of a rich merchant, who wastes all his money on luxurious living, whoring, and gambling, and ultimately finishes his life in Bedlam (London's infamous hospital for the insane).

Bach's Exquisite *Keyboard Exercises* Published

Germany, 1741: Baroque composer for the royal court of Poland and the electoral court of Saxony, Johann Sebastian Bach, has had a series of works called *Keyboard*

Defoe based his narrative for *Robinson Crusoe* on the real-life story of the Scottish castaway Alexander Selkirk.

Exercises formally published by Nuremberg publisher Balthasar Schmidt. The fourth in a series of harpsichord works for skilled and discerning amateurs, the *Exercises* have been commissioned by former Russian ambassador to Saxony, Count Kaiserling, who often travels to Bach's home town of Leipzig with his talented young harpsichordist, Johann Gottlieb Goldberg. So frequently does Goldberg play the *Exercises* to soothe his insomniac employer that already the music is being referred to as the "Goldberg Variations."

Bach, who was born in Eisensach, Germany, in 1685, is an organist and an extraordinarily prolific, talented composer, although only a small number of his compositions have been published. A devout Lutheran, Bach believes that religion is an integral part of life and work, and often inscribes *I.N.J.* (In the Name of Jesus) on his manuscripts.

His range of works is rich and diverse, encompassing cantatas, liturgies, sonatas, chorales, concertos, and suites for both solo instruments and orchestra. The style and nature of his work has shifted as he has matured, and is generally grouped into several periods. From the first period (1703–1708), the cantata *Gottes Zeit*—a funeral piece—is strong and expressive. His second period (1708–1717) produced many brilliant works including *Toccata and Fugue in D Minor*. In the third period (1717–1723), he produced a great many works, including the six *Brandenburg Concertos*. The "Goldberg Variations" fall within his fourth period of work.

Antonio Stradivari crafting one of his fine creations.

Master Craftsman of Cremona's Final Bow

Cremona, Italy, December 18, 1742: "Antonius Stradivarius Cremonensis Faciebat Anno [date]"—the Latin inscription indicating that an instrument has been handcrafted in Cremona by master luthier Antonio Stradivari, will be inscribed no more. At the ripe old age of 93, Stradivari has died.

A wealthy and highly respected man, his superbly crafted violins, violas, cellos, guitars—and one harp—bring joy to all those who play or hear them.

A member of the renowned Cremona instrument-making community, and in his early years a student of Nicolo Amati, Stradivari has long been acknowledged as the craftsman who has brought violins to their present state of near perfection. Within a short time of setting up shop in the Piazza San Domenico in 1680, he began to display originality, improving on Amati's design in subtle but important ways. The violins he crafted in the years between 1698 and 1725 are particularly fine, with everything designed to perfection—wood rich and selected with great care; gentle, regular curves; superbly carved scrolls; fine, supple varnish; precision workmanship evident in the beautifully finished and adjusted interiors.

Stradivari fathered 11 children—six by his first wife, Francesca (who died in 1698), and five by his second, Antonia. For a man whose origins are not entirely clear, other than that he was born to Alessandro Stradivari and Anna Moroni in a village somewhere near Cremona, Antonio Stradivari lived an extraordinary life, one that has brought joy to him, to his family, and to countless music lovers.

Handel's New Choral Work Is a Resounding Success

Dublin, Ireland, April 13, 1742: A thrilling new oratorio, *Messiah*, by George Frideric Handel, has finally premièred today in St Patrick's Cathedral in Dublin, after production difficulties and last-minute rearrangements of the score.

Handel himself led the performance from the harpsichord, while Irish violinist and composer Matthew Dubourg conducted the orchestra. The cathedral choir of 26 boys and five men did great justice to the stunning choruses, which showcase Handel's capacity for evoking atmosphere, along with his very considerable technical expertise and acumen.

In a break from Handel's operas and his 1739 oratorio *Saul*, *Messiah* contains no dramatic action, but is based on quotations compiled by Charles Jennens (a friend of Handel's) from the King James Bible. The text traces the foundations of Christianity, beginning with the prophecy of the coming of Christ, and progressing then through His birth, life, death, and triumphant resurrection.

The thrilling "Hallelujah" chorus provides an outstanding demonstration of Handel's talent, while the dance-like quality of "And the glory of the Lord" evokes joy and lightness. Taking us through a wide range of emotions, "And He shall purify" is exquisite, with its four voice parts. "O thou that tellest good tidings" takes us back to earlier times with its cheerful melody. "Surely He hath borne our grief" is dense with solemn rhythms and fine harmonies.

Although Handel was born in Halle, Germany, in 1685 and spent his childhood in Europe, he moved permanently to England in 1712 and became a English citizen in 1726. He is said to have written *Messiah* in just 24 days, sitting at his desk at home—25 Brook Street, London. Handel's reputation as a composer is already well established. He has penned more than 40 operas, including *Julius Caesar* (1724), *Orlando* (1733), and *Alcina* (1735), as well as the stunning orchestral suite, *Water Music* (c. 1717).

The Music Hall in Dublin was the venue for an early performance of the *Messiah*.

Johann Sebastian Bach

Key Structures

Amarbayasgalant Khiid, Mongolia
Basilica de Nuestra Senora de Pilar, Buenos Aires, Argentina
Blenheim Palace, Woodstock, England
Bolghatty Palace, Kochi, India
Buckingham Palace, London, England
Eglesia de Betlem, Barcelona, Spain
Einsiedeln Abbey, Einsiedeln, Switzerland
Fortress of Suomenlinna, Suomenlinna, Finland
Giac Lam Pagoda, Ho Chi Minh City, Vietnam
Hall of Arhats, Azure Clouds Temple, Peking, China
Iglesia de Los Dolores, Tegucigalpa, Honduras
Iglesia y Convento de La Recoleccion, Antigua, Guatemala
Iglesia y Convento de Santa Clara, Antigua, Guatemala
Kadriog Palace, Tallinn, eastern Europe
Kampong Hulu Mosque, Melaka, Malaya
Koopmans de Wet House, Cape Town, South Africa
La Merced, Quito, Ecuador
Madraseh-ye Madar-e Shah, Esfahan, Persia
Metropolitan Cathedral, Sucre, Bolivia
Nosso Senor do Bonfim, Salvador, Brazil
Nyatapola Temple, Bhaktapur, Nepal
Palamidi Fortress, Nafplio, Greece
Piazza di Spagna, Rome, Italy
Pilgrimage Church of St John of Nipomuk, Zdar, eastern Europe
Royal Covent Garden Theatre, London, England
Schloss Charlottenburg, Berlin, Germany
Schonbrunn Palace, Vienna, Austria
St Paul's Cathedral, London, England

Captain Edward Teach (Blackbeard)

> "AND OF ALL
> PLAGUES WITH
> WHICH
> MANKIND ARE
> CURSED,
> ECCLESIASTIC
> TYRANNY'S
> THE WORST."
>
> DANIEL DEFOE (1660–
> 1731) BRITISH WRITER,
> 1701

> "GOD SAVE
> OUR GRA-
> CIOUS KING,
> LONG LIVE
> OUR NOBLE
> KING, GOD
> SAVE THE
> KING. SEND
> HIM VICTORI-
> OUS, HAPPY
> AND GLORI-
> OUS."
>
> HENRY CAREY
> (C. 1690–1743) ENGLISH
> POET AND
> COMPOSER, 1740

Nun's Prayers Answered

Montreal, Canada, January 12, 1700: In a truly remarkable demonstration of the power of prayer, Sister Marguerite Bourgeoys, aged 79, of the Congregation of Notre Dame (CND), has passed away, 12 days after offering herself to God as a replacement for a young sister who had been critically ill and dying. The young sister who was ill is now completely well.

Grace, compassion, and service have typified the life of this wonderful woman, who some claim is likely to be canonized as Canada's first female saint. Marguerite Bourgeoys was born the sixth of 12 children in a middle-class, Christian family in Troyes, France, on Good Friday, April 17, 1620, and was baptized that same day. When she was 19, her mother died, and the following year, during a religious ceremony, Marguerite was inspired to consecrate herself to the service of God. She immediately joined a religious association of young girls dedicated to charitable work.

In 1653, after some years of teaching the poor in Troyes, she accepted an invitation to migrate to the new settlement of Ville Marie in Canada, where, with nurse, Jeanne Mance, and designer, Monsieur de Maisonneuve, she helped found Montreal. Her establishment of an education system and social services led her to be revered as "mother of the colony." In 1671, she founded the uncloistered community of CND, thus ensuring that her work will be carried on. Sister Marguerite has provided an exemplary role model for a life of prayer, heroic poverty, and untiring devotion to the service of others.

Samurai Avenge Their Master's Wrongful Death

Edo (Tokyo), Japan, December 14, 1702: Forty-seven *ronin* (masterless samurai) of Ako have today raided the heavily guarded residence of Lord Kira Yoshinaka and assassinated him, in order to avenge what they consider to be the wrongful death of their lord. The revenge had been more than a year in the planning, and it presents the shogunate with a dilemma.

What happened is this: Asano Naganori (1664–1701), the late Lord of Ako, had been asked to represent the shogun of Edo in receiving envoys bearing New Year's greetings from the imperial court in Kyoto. The shogun's chief of protocol was Kira, who apparently treated Asano with disdain and did not advise him properly on unfamiliar points of protocol.

So enraged was Asano by Kira's arrogance that on the third day he attacked Kira in the shogun's castle, wounding him on the forehead with his dagger. Since drawing a weapon in Edo Castle is a grave offense, Asano was then given the order to commit *seppuku* (ritual suicide)—an act that left his samurai without a master, yet obliged to remain loyal to their late master, Asano.

Now Kira is dead, and Asano's passing has been avenged. However, by resorting to violence as a group, the 47 (or actually, the 46 who eventually took part in the assassination) have knowingly and willingly committed an illegal act by defying the authority of the shogun, who had expressly forbidden any acts of revenge or retaliation. It is therefore highly likely that the 46 *ronin*—led by Oishi Yoshio and ranging in age from 15 to 77—will, like their master, be ordered to commit *seppuku*.

Site Selected for New Russian Capital

Russia, May 27, 1703: In line with his vision of expanding, modernizing, and "westernizing" Russia, Tsar Peter the Great has laid the foundations for a new capital city, which he has named St Petersburg, after his patron saint. Tsar Peter has chosen as its location the delta of the river Neva at the eastern end of the Gulf of Finland on the Baltic Sea—territory that he has only recently reclaimed in Russia's continuing war against Sweden.

Despite the swampy conditions, Peter believes the new city will be well located as a naval base, and also for trade, providing a "window to the West." The extreme northern location of the city means it will have very short periods of daylight during winter, and several weeks of "white nights" during summer.

A team of invited German engineers is supervising the immediate building of a fortress on the Island of Enisaari, using local timbers and clay for the walls. It will be named the Peter and Paul Fortress. A wooden cabin for Tsar Peter himself will be constructed nearby, although he has plans for grand winter and summer palaces a little further down the river.

Samurai warrior with three swords (Kano School).

A cartoon symbolizing the South Sea Bubble and the financial ruin faced by many of the company's investors.

Dick Turpin

Work on the fortress is progressing at a phenomenal rate, despite the primitive conditions, as soldiers and peasants toil from dawn to dusk with little sustenance. There have reportedly been many thousands of deaths, but because of the war, the need for the fortress is considered urgent.

Petty Criminals to Be Transported to Colonies

London, England, 1718: British criminals now face a deterrent that some will consider a fate worse than death—transportation to the new colonies in North America.

Since the War of Spanish Succession ended in 1714, authorities have become increasingly concerned about the rise in civil disorder and crime in Britain. In an attempt to curb this trend, the British Parliament has passed the *Transportation Act*, which allows courts to sentence felons to seven years' transportation to America.

Furthermore, it establishes that to return from transportation before the prison term has elapsed is a capital offense. It is intended that a sentence of transportation can be imposed for lesser felonies, and as a possible commutation of the death penalty, available via royal intervention. Up until now, many of those tried at the Old Bailey have been subject to the "bloody code"—a death sentence—for crimes as petty as stealing a handkerchief or a sheep, although judicial procedures have often been used to mitigate these sentences if the crime is considered to be relatively minor.

In the past, juries have frequently used partial verdicts, benefit of clergy, and pardons to reduce sentences to branding or imprisonment, but they now have the option of transmuting a sentence to transportation. Benefit of clergy spares the lives of first offenders whose crimes are not too heinous. Branding a letter on the thumb of these prisoners—"T" for theft, "F" for felony, "M" for murder—ensures that this device can be applied only once.

It is hoped that transportation will reduce overcrowding in British prisons, act as a deterrent for those considering embarking on a life of crime, and make Britain safer. Understandably, there is strong opposition from many of those pioneers and settlers seeking to begin life afresh in the American colonies.

Thomas Guy Dead, but Good Works Continue

England, December 17, 1724: Bookseller, publisher, and philanthropist, Thomas Guy, who never married, has died, leaving a will that ensures his generosity and good works will benefit England's sick and underprivileged for generations to come. Already, Guy's Hospital in London—founded by Thomas in 1721 as an adjunct to St Thomas's Hospital—and additional St Thomas wards attest to the man's extraordinary benevolence, determination, and vision.

Yet Guy was born into humble circumstances, the eldest son of a Southwark coalmonger, who died when Thomas was still a child. After completing his education in Tamworth, Staffordshire, young Thomas served an apprenticeship as a bookseller in London and went on to build a highly successful bookselling and publishing business of his own. Always frugal, Guy saved hard and made a fortune by selling out his South Sea Company shares just before the bubble burst in 1720.

A reception at a Freemasons' lodge in Vienna.

Canton, China, c. 1725: New crops from Americas, such as sweet potatoes and maize, help fuel steep rise in Chinese population.

Edinburgh, Scotland, 1726: Bookseller Allan Ramsey establishes Britain's first circulating library.

Spain, 1726: Francisco Romero of Ronda introduces the sword and small cape to bullfighting on foot.

Brazil, 1727: Coffee is first planted in Brazil.

China, 1729: Emperor Yung Chang issues an edict prohibiting opium smoking in China.

Amsterdam, Netherlands, May, 1730: Zacharias Wilsma's confession of sodomy leads to executions throughout the country.

Oxford, England, 1730: Brothers John and Charles Wesley found the Methodists.

Philadelphia, North America, July 1, 1731: Benjamin Franklin establishes the Library Company.

Bologna, Italy, 1732: Laura Brassi is the first woman appointed to the staff of a European university (the University of Bologna).

New York, North America, 1732: A bowling green is established for playing ninepins.

Devonshire, England, 1733: William Kent invents the baby carriage.

England, 1734: George Sale translates the Koran into English.

Japan, 1735: Kitamura Enkin publishes *Tsukiyama Teizoden* (*Creating Landscape Gardens*).

Calcutta, India, October, 1737: A cyclone (sometimes reported as an earthquake) causes great devastation to the city and local shipping, and much loss of life.

Raynham, England, June 21, 1738: Viscount Charles "Turnip" Townshend dies, aged 63.

York, England, April 10, 1739: Dick Turpin is executed for horse stealing.

Versailles, France, 1743: King Louis XV uses a counterweighted elevator in his private rooms.

London, England, August 16, 1743: English boxing champion Jack Broughton codifies a set of rules for boxing bouts, known as "Broughton's Rules."

London, England, 1744: The rules of cricket are first formulated, by the players using the Artillery Grounds.

Peru, October 28, 1746: A tsunami hits the central coast. Callao and Lima are destroyed, and 4,000–5,000 lives are lost.

London, England, 1746: The *Disarming Act* prohibits Scottish Highland rebels from bearing arms and from wearing tartan.

Pompeii, Italy, 1748: The buried city is excavated.

Yangzhou, China, c. 1749: Wu Jingzi finishes his novel *Rulin Waishi (The Scholars)*, satirizing the scholar-official class.

Louis XV of France

New Trend in Bullfighting

Ronda, Spain, 1726: The age-old Spanish tradition of bullfighting, which some say dates back as far as the Moors, or even the Romans, has taken an exciting and daring turn. Typically, picadors (bullfighters on horseback) have come from among the ranks of the nobility, although recent opposition from royalty and Church leaders has discouraged their involvement in this "barbarous and appalling" pastime. In spite of—or even because of—this opposition, bullfights continue to occur, and men of less aristocratic background have become involved.

One such humble working-class man is Francisco Romero, aged in his mid-20s, who is currently revolutionizing the sport (or art form, as some call it). Romero, a matador committed to fighting the bull on foot, has devised a short red cape—a *muleta*—which he uses to obscure his sword, swishing it back and forth to entice and infuriate the bull, before thrusting the sword between the bull's shoulders.

A matador holds his sword aloft after killing his bull.

"Methodist" Spiritual Group Formed at Oxford

Oxford, England, 1730: Many students at Oxford University are sniggering behind their hands at a newly formed religious group, the "Holy Club" or "Bible Moths," often referred to as "Methodists" because of their noticeably methodical approach to life and spiritual practice.

The instigator of the group gatherings, Charles Wesley, has been joined in these endeavors by his older brother, John, recently ordained (1728) as a priest in the Church of England.

These Methodists focus on mutually supportive spiritual observances (such as prayer, meditative study of the scriptures, and Holy Communion); faith in the supreme love of God revealed in one's personal life; and the practical application of Christian teachings in society (caring for the poor and under-privileged, the sick, and those who are in prison).

The Wesley brothers were born fifteenth and eighteenth respectively out of the 19 children to Susanna Wesley and her husband, Samuel (an Anglican minister). They have been raised—by their mother, in particular—as devout, practicing Christians.

When John was 6 years old, and Charles a mere 15 months, their family home—the rectory at Epworth—was burnt to the ground. This seems to have been a formative experience for each of the young men. John still refers to himself as a child of Providence, a "brand plucked from the burning," while Charles was rescued from the flames by a maid.

It seems that the brothers spent little time together during their childhood years, but have recently reconnected at Oxford. John, with his theological training and religious commitment, is a spiritual mentor to his younger brother Charles, who in 1728 experienced a return to spirituality after some years pursuing frivolous activities. They appear united in their dedication to the Methodist groups and the program of prison-visiting that constitutes a key part of their pastoral work.

New Library Seeks Book-Lovers as Subscribers

Philadelphia, North America, July 1, 1731: Benjamin Franklin, well-known printer, philosopher, and publisher of the *Pennsylvania Gazette*, must be feeling satisfied today, after signing—with a number of his book-loving friends—an "instrument of association" to found the non-profit Library Company of Philadelphia.

Franklin has always been a devoted reader and lover of books, so it is only natural that he has gathered around him a group of like-minded friends. For some years, the Junto group—most of them young men of artisan backgrounds—has met in Philadelphia to discuss issues of a social, economic, philosophical, intellectual, and political nature.

Since reference books are scarce in the colonies, they tried pooling their personal libraries a year or so ago, but the experiment foundered when books became lost or damaged. Undeterred, Franklin came

John Wesley preaches while standing on his father's tombstone.

up with the idea of the subscription library, which today has become a reality.

He has appointed 10 directors, plus a treasurer and a secretary, but in future, these positions will be open to annual elections by the subscribers. The initial goal is to attract 50 subscribers, each of whom will pay a joining fee of 40 shillings, plus an annual subscription fee of 10 shillings. Donations of cash and books are also being invited.

Franklin has designed a seal, to be engraved by silversmith Philip Syng with a Latin motto meaning "To pour forth benefits for the common good is divine." The board of directors, under Franklin's guidance, is actively seeking library subscribers who are "lovers of reading."

The *Qur'an* Translated Direct from Arabic

London, England, 1734: Kent orientalist and lawyer George Sale has published an English translation of the Islamic holy book, the *Qur'an*, under the title *The Alcoran of Mohammed*.

Printed by C. Ackers for publisher J. Wilcox, the work is being hailed as the first of its kind to have been translated directly from the Arabic language. Certainly, Alexander Ross's 1649 attempt, translated from Sieur du Ryer's French translation, is known to contain both its own inaccuracies and inaccuracies carried over from the French.

It is not entirely clear how Sale has come to be proficient in Arabic. By 1726, however, his grasp of the Arabic language was sufficient for him to be a corrector for the *Arabic New Testament*, which is published by the Society for Promoting Christian Knowledge (SPCK).

Sale's *Alcoran* is a stylish quarto volume of over 500 pages, bound in red morocco leather with gold lettering on the spine. The title page is printed in red and black, and there are five plates, displaying a map of Arabia, genealogical tables, and other illustrations.

It is widely believed that Sale has been influenced in his work by Ludovico Maracci's Arabic and Latin edition (Padua, 1698). Nevertheless, the opinions expressed in his preface, notes, and preliminary discourse indicate both his Christian evangelical leanings and a level of admiration for the teachings of Mohammed. He writes, for example, "For how criminal soever Mohammed may have been in imposing a fake religion on mankind, the praises due to his real virtues ought not to be denied him."

Death of Aristocratic Experimental Farmer

Raynham, England, June 21, 1738: The man who has encouraged revolutionary agricultural practices in England, and been ridiculed by some for doing so, has died of a stroke. Charles "Turnip" Townshend, Second Viscount of Raynham, aged 63, ended his days experimenting with farming techniques on his family estate in Norfolk.

Townshend succeeded to the peerage at the age of 12, in 1687, and completed his education at Eton and Cambridge. During his early years in the House of Lords, his Tory tendencies shifted, and he became increasingly supportive of Whig politics. After serving as an ambassador in the Netherlands for several years, he returned to England in 1711 and was appointed Secretary of State under King George I, a position that he lost and regained before policy and personality differences caused him to retire in 1730.

The medieval manorial system of farming communally owned land is giving way to a system of enclosure, where larger, privately owned fields can be farmed at the owner's discretion. During his time in the Netherlands, Viscount Townshend became aware of the benefits of planting turnips as fodder

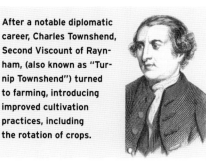

After a notable diplomatic career, Charles Townshend, Second Viscount of Raynham, (also known as "Turnip Townshend") turned to farming, introducing improved cultivation practices, including the rotation of crops.

crops for feeding cattle in winter. Instead of rotating two or three crops, and leaving one field fallow, Townshend has introduced the system of rotating four crops—the traditional barley and wheat, plus turnips, and clover to nitrogenize the soil. So passionate has he been about the benefits of this system that he is likely to go down in history by his nickname, "Turnip" Townshend.

Excavations May Unearth Ancient City of Pompeii

Italy, 1748: Spurred on by archeological discoveries at Herculaneum in 1738, the young Bourbon king Charles III of Spain (Charles VII of Two Sicilies—formerly Naples and Sicily) has instructed former military engineer Roque Joachim de Alcubierre to begin excavations at the site known as "Civita" near the Sarno River at the base of Mt Vesuvius. There is speculation that this might be the site of the long-buried ancient city of Pompeii, and that excavations are highly likely to unearth valuable items of jewelry, art, statues, frescoes, and so on.

Although he has no formal archeological training, Alcubierre is finding the excavation process remarkably easy, because the ruins are covered in layers of ash and pumice that are light and uncompacted. His main concern is the risk to himself and his 22 workers—either of being poisoned when they

release long-sealed pockets of toxic gases, or of being crushed under slippages of the light, unstable debris.

The site has been undisturbed for more than 1,500 years following the volcanic eruption of Mt Vesuvius in 79 CE. Eyewitness accounts preserved in the writings of Pliny the Younger provide graphic details of the events leading up to that fateful day—of the eruption itself and of the devastation to life and property. Although it appears that many residents escaped, there were probably thousands who were not able to do so. Speculation is rife that Pompeii would have been a prosperous city with a thriving cultural life. In a letter to a friend, some years after the event, Pliny wrote, "You could hear the shrieks of women, the wailing of infants, and the shouting of men… I admit that I derived some poor consolation in my mortal lot from the belief that the whole world was dying with me and I with it."

Charles Wesley

Religious Leaders

Popes
Innocent XII (1691-1700)
Clement XI (1700-1721)
Innocent XIII (1721-1724)
Benedict XIII (1724-1730)
Clement XII (1730-1740)
Benedict XIV (1740-1758)

Archbishops of Canterbury
Thomas Tenison (1694-1715)
William Wake (1716-1737)
John Potter (1737-1747)
Thomas Herring (1747-1757)

Dalai Lamas of Tibet
Tsangyang Gyatso (1697-1706)
Kelsang Gyatso (1720-1757)

Patriarchs of Constantinople
Callinicus II (1694-1702)
Gabriel III (1702-1707)
Neophytus V (1707)
Cyprianus I (1707-1709, 1713-1714)
Athanasius V (1709-1711)
Cyril IV (1711-1713)
Cosmas III (1714-1716)
Jeremias III (1716-1726, 1732-1733)
Paisius II (1726-1732, 1740-1748)
Serapheim I (1733-1734)
Neophytus VI (1734-1740, 1743-1744)
Cyril V (1748-1751)

When Mt Vesuvius erupted some 1,500 years ago, the people of Pompeii fled for their lives.

Captain James Cook

Major Powers to Exchange Territories

Paris, France, February 10, 1763: After seven years of wars between France, Spain, and Britain, a treaty has been signed in Paris to end hostilities. It involves colonial territories being exchanged in Europe, North America, and Asia.

The seeds of war were sown in 1753, when France began building forts along the Ohio River in North America—a region also claimed by the British colony of Virginia. This was part of an overall French strategy to destabilize the American frontier and tie up British forces in America.

The conflict spread to Europe on May 15, 1756, when Britain declared war on France, and to India, the Caribbean isles, the Philippines, and Africa. Spain, which owned Florida and Martinique, declared war on Britain on January 4, 1761. Austria and Prussia were drawn into the conflict, not wishing to miss out on the spoils.

Under the settlement France cedes India and Senegal to Britain, while Cuba and the Philippines go to Spain. France and Spain return Minorca to Britain, while France withdraws from Germany and Prussia. France cedes New France (Canada) and its territories east of the Mississippi to Britain, and Louisiana to Spain in compensation for Florida, which Spain yields to Great Britain. France retains the islands of St Pierre and Miquelon, and recovers the Caribbean islands of Guadeloupe and Martinique from Britain, while ceding Grenada.

Some eyebrows have been raised over Britain's choice to take the barren New France over Guadeloupe and Martinique. However, others hail this as a shrewd move, expecting the overall terms of the settlement will lead to Britain's future colonial and maritime supremacy.

British Control of Bengal is Official

Benares, India, August 12, 1765: King Shah Alam, emperor of the crumbling Mogul Empire, signed the Treaty of Allahabad with Britain today, ceding control of Bengal to the East India Company. Alam had little choice, since the treaty merely recognizes the control of northeast India that Britain has gained in a recent series of wars.

The treaty was co-signed by Robert Clive, administrator of the East India Company.

In 1756 local Mogul warlord Siraj-ud-Daula gained infamy when he captured Calcutta from the British, and crammed 123 British soldiers into the "Black Hole of Calcutta," a room so small and hot that many of the men died.

Clive's forces then defeated Mogul ally France, as well as a number of Indian princes who were attacking the British and the Moguls in a bid to capture spoils. In 1760 Clive completely routed Siraj's army and killed him, installing the puppet ruler Mir Jafar in his place.

Two years ago, however, Jafar was overthrown by his son-in-law, Mir Kasim, who hates the British for bleeding Bengal dry. Mir Kasim then foolishly launched five unsuccessful wars against the British, which left his troops in tatters.

Many expect the treaty will lead to even more extortion, lawlessness, and racketeering. However, Clive is no doubt excited at the prospect of greater British control of India, and the opportunity this gives him to feather his own nest.

Captain Cook Claims South Land for Britain

New Holland (Australia), August 22, 1770: After spending the last four months traveling northward up the east coast of New Holland, Captain James Cook today claimed the continent on behalf of the king of Great Britain.

HMS *Endeavour* set off from Plymouth on August 26, 1768, for the South Pacific island of Otaheite, charged by the Royal Society with observing the June 1769 transit of Venus across the sun. On board were various scientists, including eminent botanist Joseph Banks.

After observing the transit, Cook sailed southwest to confirm the existence of a "Great South Land." In April 1769 the *Endeavour* reached the island of Tahiti, spending three months there.

Sailing southward, Cook reached New Zealand in September 1769, and mapped its two islands. The expedition then headed west in search of Van Diemen's Land (Tasmania), but prevailing winds forced them further north.

On April 19, 1770, they reached a bay that yielded so many botanical specimens that it was named "Botany Bay." Cook decided to recommend the place for future colonization.

time out

As Mahmud I, Sultan of the Ottoman Empire, gets off his horse after a journey in 1754, he drops dead of a suspected heart attack. He is succeeded by his brother, who becomes known as Osman III.

Captain Cook was killed in Hawaii in 1779.

Paris, France, 1751: Charles-Marie de la Condamine publishes the journal of his voyage down the Amazon River.
Europe and Africa, November 1, 1755: An earthquake shakes Italy, Switzerland, France, North Africa, and Portugal. Lisbon is destroyed.
London, England, May 15, 1756: Great Britain declares war on France, formalizing the existing conflict in the American colonies and starting the Seven Years' War.

Calcutta, India, June 20, 1756: Indian troops confine British prisoners to a room so small and hot that many deaths occur. It is later dubbed the "Black Hole of Calcutta."
Plassey, India, June 22, 1757: Robert Clive's victory over French forces ensures British domination of India.
Quebec, Canada, September 13, 1759: James Wolfe and the British and American forces defeat Louis-Joseph, Marquis de Montcalm, and the French and Canadian forces. Wolfe dies in the battle and Montcalm is fatally wounded.

St Petersburg, Russia, January 5, 1762: Elisabeth, Empress of Russia, dies, aged 52.
Moscow, Russia, September 22, 1762: Catherine II is crowned Empress of All Russia.
Paris, France, February 10, 1763: The Treaty of Paris ends wars in both Europe and North America.
Great Lakes, North America, 1763: Chief Pontiac, Ottawa tribal leader, organizes a series of raids against British forts to reclaim tribal lands.
Brazil, 1763: Rio de Janeiro replaces Salvador as the nation's capital.

Benares, India, August 12, 1765: The Treaty of Allahabad gives the East India Company control of much of India.
North America, 1765: Great Britain imposes the unpopular *Stamp Act* on the American colonies. The tax covers just about everything produced by the Americans, which leads to civil unrest.
Kathmandu, Nepal, September 25, 1768: Gorkha King Prithvi Narayan Shah becomes first king of Nepal.
New Zealand, October, 1769: The *Endeavour*'s crew become the first Europeans to land on New Zealand.

New Holland (Australia), August 22, 1770: Captain James Cook claims the east coast for Great Britain.
Java, Dutch East Indies, August 12, 1772: An avalanche caused by the eruption of Papandayan volcano destroys about 40 villages and leads to almost 3,000 deaths.
Afghanistan, April, 1773: Ahmad Shah Durrani dies, aged about 50.
Boston, North America, December 16, 1773: Chests of tea are thrown overboard by local colonists disguised as Indians.

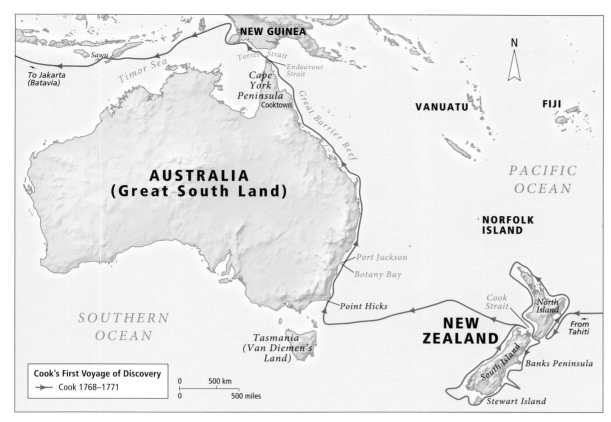

NEW GUINEA

To Jakarta (Batavia)

Timor Sea

Sawu

Torres Strait

Cape York Peninsula
Cooktown

Endeavour Strait

Great Barrier Reef

N

VANUATU

FIJI

PACIFIC OCEAN

AUSTRALIA (Great South Land)

NORFOLK ISLAND

Port Jackson

Botany Bay

Point Hicks

Cook Strait

North Island

From Tahiti

NEW ZEALAND

SOUTHERN OCEAN

Tasmania (Van Diemen's Land)

South Island

Banks Peninsula

Stewart Island

Cook's First Voyage of Discovery
→ Cook 1768–1771

0   500 km
0   500 miles

Catherine II of Russia

boarded three British ships and heaved hundreds of chests of British tea into the harbor. Disguised as Indians and armed with axes, patriots in their hundreds ran from the Old South Meeting House and boarded the *Dartmouth*, the *Eleanor*, and the *Beaver*, all of which were carrying tea imported under preferential tariffs.

Britain's East India Company is on the verge of bankruptcy, sitting on large stocks of tea that it cannot sell in England, so the British government recently passed the Tea Act, permitting the company to export its goods to the colonies without paying taxes. The company is now underselling American merchants and monopolizing the tea trade, frustrating colonists who have recently protested in a number of ways.

The rebels are hoping that their deeds will spur others into action, and eventually lead to an uprising against the exploitative actions of the British.

Cook then headed north, mapping the coastline and confirming that he had, indeed, found a new continent. Yesterday, on reaching latitude 12 degrees south, he wrote, "the Northern Promontory of this country I have named York Cape in honour of His late Royal Highness the Duke of York." This morning Cook went ashore on an island and claimed the land for King George III.

Afghanistan's Founder Dies

Afghanistan, April, 1773: Ahmad Shah Durrani, the "Father of Afghanistan," has died, aged about 50. He was the second son of Muhammad Zaman Khan, chief of the Abdali tribe.

As a young man in 1738, Ahmad entered into the service of Nadir Shah, Persian ruler and conqueror of Afghanistan, where he quickly rose to the rank

of cavalry commander. In the power vacuum that followed the assassination of Nadir in June 1747, the Abdalis proceeded to take control of Afghanistan, electing Ahmad as leader.

Despite his youth, Ahmad had several factors in his favor. He was an intelligent charismatic leader and a seasoned warrior who had at his disposal a trained mobile force of several thousand cavalrymen. He also owned much of Nadir Shah's treasury.

Ahmad had adopted the title Durr-i-Durrani ("pearl of pearls"). He will be remembered as a bold energetic leader who quelled tribal hostilities and created and managed a large unified empire.

British Tea Steeped

Boston, North America, December 16, 1773: In a revolt against taxation without representation, Boston colonists tonight

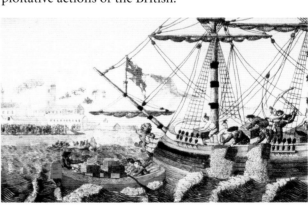

The colonists' symbolic action became known as the Boston Tea Party.

Marie Antionette

America Declares Independence from Britain

Philadelphia, North America, July 4, 1776: The Continental Congress this morning passed a revolutionary piece of legislation, the "Declaration of Independence."

America has long sought freedom from British rule, and has been warring since April 18 last year, when Boston engraver and dentist Paul Revere got wind of a British attack planned for the next morning against the colonial arsenal at Lexington Green, Massachusetts.

That night, Revere and William Dawes rode 20 miles (32 km) from Boston in order to warn the colonial patriots, who were waiting at dawn when the British advance guard arrived. About 70 armed green-jacketed Massachusetts militiamen faced some 700 British troops in an uneasy silence, until someone—no one seems to know who—fired a shot, causing all hell to break loose. A volley of British rifle fire, followed by a bayonet charge, left 8 Americans dead and 10 wounded.

The British next headed for the depot in Concord, destroying the colonists' weapons and supplies, and suffering 14 casualties. Then they began the long retreat back to Boston, but were attacked by farmers and rebels, suffering 250 casualties.

News of the events spread throughout the colonies, and bitter all-out war ensued.

Seats of Power

China Qing Dynasty: Qianlong (reigned 1735-1796); Jiaqing (1796-1820).
France Louis XV (reigned 1715-1774); Louis XVI (1774-1792). First Republic: National Convention (1792-1795); Directory (1795-1799); Consulate (1799-1804).
Holy Roman Empire Francis I (reigned 1745-1765); Joseph II (1765-1790); Leopold II (1790-1792); Francis II (1792-1806).
India Mughal Empire: Ahmad Shah Bahadur (reigned 1748-1754); Alamgir II (1754-1759); Shah Jalan III (1759); Shah Alam II (1759-1806).
Japan Edo Period: Momozono (reigned 1747-1762); Go-Sakuramachi (1762-1771); Go-Momozono (1771-1779); Kokaku (1780-1817).
Kingdom of Great Britain George II (reigned 1727-1760); George III (1760-1820).
Ottoman Empire Mahmud I (reigned 1730-1754); Osman III (1754-1757); Mustafa III (1757-1774); Abd-ul-Hamid I (1774-1789); Selim III (1789-1807).
Persia Safavid Shahs: Suleiman II (reigned 1749-1750); Ismail III (1750-1760).
Portugal Brigantine Dynasty: Joao V (reigned 1706-1750); Jose I (1750-1777); Maria I and Pedro III (1777-1816).
Russia Emperors: Elisabeth (reigned 1741-1762); Peter III (1762); Catherine II (the Great) (1762-1796); Paul I (1796-1801).
Spain Bourbon Dynasty: Ferdinand VI (reigned 1746-1759); Charles III (1759-1788); Charles IV (1788-1808).
Zulu Nation Ndaba kaMageba (reigned 1745-1763); Jama kaNdaba (1763-1781); Senzangakhona kaJama (1781-1816).

The Congress has offered King George III several olive branches, all of which have been contemptuously rejected.

The independence legislation was prepared by a committee that included Benjamin Franklin and John Adams. The first draft, written by Virginian delegate Thomas Jefferson, condemns King George, saying he is "unfit to be the ruler of a free people," and lists many tyrannies inflicted by the British upon the American people.

The declaration includes the words, "We hold these truths to be self-evident, that all men are created equal, that they are endowed by their creator with certain unalienable rights, that among these are life, liberty, and the pursuit of happiness."

African War Ends in Uneasy Peace

Cape Colony, southern Africa, 1781: The bitter war in southern Africa between Dutch settlers and Xhosa tribal people has ended.

Both groups are recent arrivals to the district. The Bantu-speaking Xhosa were recently displaced by war from their traditional homelands to the east, while the Dutch are fleeing war in Europe and seeking to establish a colonial empire.

The needs of both the Xhosa and Dutch settlers are essentially agricultural, and for a while they coexisted peacefully enough. It seemed there was enough land for all, but conflicting attitudes toward land and property ownership, and intolerance of each other's spiritual beliefs, led to festering discontent that finally erupted into open fighting.

In 1779, after a series of skirmishes, the two sides reached agreement that the territorial boundary would run along the fertile Great Fish River—with the Dutch to the west and the Xhosa to the east. Despite this agreement, the Dutch began raiding Xhosa settlements to steal cattle and other supplies, and the Xhosa set up several hidden settlements on the west side of the Fish. Under the cover of night, the Xhosa emerged from the thick forests to reclaim their property, and the situation eventually escalated into bloody war.

The harsh terrain and dense bush, which is ideal for guerrilla warfare, made things difficult for the Dutch soldiers. Their distinctive uniforms—tightly buttoned, brightly colored jackets and white trousers—were not only absurdly impractical, but made them easy targets for the poisoned spears of the Xhosa, masters of camouflage and concealment.

Nonetheless, Dutch military superiority, as well as a series of massacres, eventually forced the Xhosa to retreat back across the Great Fish River.

The war has ended, but the peace, it seems, may turn out to be short-lived.

A truce has been declared between the Dutch and the Xhosa

New King and New Capital for Siam

Bangkok, Siam, 1782: Siam's new king, the popular poet and warrior Jao Phraya Chakri, has assumed the name Rama. He was crowned after illness put an end to the rule of his predecessor and friend, King Taaksin.

Rama has spent most of his life fighting off invasions from Burma, trying to keep control of Siamese territories in Cambodia and Laos, and quelling local tribal insurrections. He has now invited previously exiled scholars, merchants, and traders to return to Siam, and has dispatched an envoy to the Portuguese governor of Macau, inviting his Christian missionaries to return, saying he looks forward to renewing friendship and trade with Portugal and other European countries.

Rama has shifted Siam's capital—and royal seat—across the river from Thonburi to the more secure site of Bangkok, and ordered the construction of a Grand Palace, a magnificent complex of buildings that will house the superlative Emerald Buddha he recently captured in Laos.

New British Penal Colony

Port Jackson (Sydney), New South Wales, January 26, 1788: A new British penal colony has been established in New South Wales, Australia. A fleet of 11 ships under the command of Captain Arthur Phillip has ended its long voyage from Portsmouth, making landfall at Port Jackson on the east coast.

With the industrial revolution, and the resulting population explosion in cities, crime in Britain has increased markedly,

"Bonnie Prince Charlie"

but transportation of convicts to America has not been possible since that country gained independence in 1781. To combat overcrowding in gaols, the British government decided to establish a new penal outpost in the southern land discovered by Captain James Cook in 1770.

The government hired nine ships, contracted two naval vessels, and provided enough rations to supply the 759 convicts, their guards (some with families), and a few civil officers, until they are able to become self-sufficient.

The fleet left England on May 13, 1787, restocking at Tenerife, Rio de Janeiro, and Cape Town. It arrived at Botany Bay, the location recommended by Cook, last week. On closer inspection, the site was deemed unsuitable, lacking water and a protected harbor, so the fleet headed north, arriving at Port Jackson this morning. Second-in-command John Hunter says that the verdant land resembles a deer park, while Phillip calls the port "one of the finest harbours in the world."

This morning the new arrivals raised the Union Jack at a protected inlet half a mile (800 m) deep and quarter of a mile (400 m) across, naming it Sydney Cove.

Louis of France Executed

Paris, France, January 21, 1793: The troubled reign of King Louis XVI ended at 10.30 this morning, when he was guillotined in the Place de la Révolution in front of a cheering crowd. Louis's last words were: "I die innocent of all the crimes charged to me, I pardon those who caused my death, and I pray to God that the blood you are about to spill may never be visited upon France." He appeared calm before the blade fell upon his neck.

His rule appeared doomed from the start. When he ascended the French throne in 1774, he inherited an empty treasury, a huge debt—mostly resulting from unpopular wars—and a demoralized populace crushed by a huge tax burden. There was high unemployment, bread was unaffordable to most people, religious intolerance

was rampant, and the court and aristocracy were deemed out of touch and degenerate.

In 1789, these grievances, and Louis's failure to redress them, led to the storming of Bastille prison, and the start of the revolution that now rages across France.

Louis tried to flee to Austria 18 months ago, but was recognized while shopping in Varennes. He was apprehended, returned to Paris, and put under house arrest. It is said that the store clerk who informed the authorities recognized his face from the image on coinage.

Last August, Louis was stripped of the monarchy, then on September 21 the National Assembly declared France to be a republic. On January 21, 1793, the Legislative Assembly convicted Louis of high treason and sentenced him to death.

Louis's wife, Marie Antoinette, is likely to meet the same fate. Always unpopular, she has been even more despised since her comment, on being told that most people cannot afford bread, "Let them eat cake!"

King Louis is nominally succeeded by his second son, Charles Louis; however, he is in prison and not expected to be released soon.

First US President Is Dead at 67

Virginia, USA, December 14, 1799: George Washington, the United States' first president, has died of a throat infection.

The much-loved leader was born in 1732 in Bridges Creek, Virginia, of British stock.

Despite an interrupted education, he showed a flair for surveying, and traveled widely in the employ of Lord Fairfax.

In 1752 George Washington inherited a property in Mt. Vernon, Virginia, became a farmer and social activist, and joined the British army to fight in Britain's war against France. He had mixed fortunes as a soldier, but gained a reputation for bravery and impeccable morality. He rose to the rank of commander-in-chief of the Virginian forces. In 1758, Washington resigned his commission and wed Martha Dandridge Custis.

Washington represented Virginia in the first Continental Congress in 1774, and the following year was appointed

Upon hearing of the death of George Washington (pictured above), his former enemy, Britain, fired a 20-gun salute in his honor.

commander of the colonial forces in the War of Independence against the British. A brilliant tactician, his strategy was to retreat slowly, then strike unexpectedly. In 1781, in an inspired military move, he persuaded the French to join the war, and forced the surrender of British leader Charles Cornwallis at Yorktown, thus achieving American independence.

Washington was a key instigator of the Constitutional Convention of 1787, and when the new Constitution was ratified, the Electoral College unanimously elected him president. He was re-elected in 1793.

He insisted upon neutrality when the French Revolution led to another war between France and England, and warned against making any long-term alliances with any power.

Disillusioned by congressional bickering and personal attacks, George Washington left the presidency in 1797 and retired to Mt Vernon to manage his estate.

The prison ship HMS *York* in Portsmouth harbor, England.

Carl Linnaeus

"NATURE DOES NOT MAKE JUMPS."

CARL LINNAEUS, (1707–1778), SWEDISH SCIENTIST AND TAXONOMIST, 1751

"MAN IS A TOOL-MAKING ANIMAL."

BENJAMIN FRANKLIN (1706–1790), AMERICAN SCIENTIST AND STATESMAN, 1778

Plant Classification Published

Uppsala, Sweden, 1753: The pre-eminent Swedish botanist, doctor, and professor Carl Linné, better known as Linnaeus, has published *System plantarum*, in which plants are categorized and named in an ordered system for the first time. His system is based solely on the number and arrangement of a plant's reproductive organs: that is, a plant's class is determined by its stamens (male organs), and its order by its pistils (female organs).

Linnaeus draws some vivid parallels between plant sexuality and human love. In 1729, as a medical student, he wrote, "The flower's leaves…serve as bridal beds which the Creator has so gloriously arranged, adorned with such noble bed curtains, and perfumed with so many soft scents that the bridegroom with his bride might there celebrate their nuptials with so much the greater solemnity."

As botany professor at Uppsala University since 1741, he has restored the university's botanical garden, arranging the plants according to his system. He has also made plant-collecting expeditions to various parts of Sweden. An inspiration to his students, he has arranged to send many on worldwide trade and exploration voyages.

He continues to revise and expand on his ideas, as more and more plant and animal specimens are sent to him from every corner of the globe.

The sexual basis of Linnaeus's classification is raising eyebrows, with some critics attacking it for its explicit nature. Fellow botanist Johann Siegesbeck, has called it "loathsome harlotry." Linnaeus has retaliated by naming a small, useless European weed *Siegesbeckia*.

Uproar at New Theory of Embryo Development

Halle, Germany, 1759: German physician Kaspar Wolff has proposed the radical theory—known as epigenesis—that embryos develop gradually from clusters of similar cells, and not by the simple expansion of miniature babies. Wolff's dissertation, published as *Theoria generationis*, is his doctoral thesis from the University of Halle, and consists of three parts—development of plants, development of animals, and theoretical considerations. It suggests that organs are formed in differentiated layers from undifferentiated cells.

Although this idea has been floated by Aristotle and others, traditional and current wisdom holds that animal organisms are already formed in the seed at conception (the theory of pre-formation), and that in human beings, a homunculus (fully formed dwarf) is already sitting in the sperm, ready to grow.

Wolff's ideas have created a storm of controversy, with the eminent anatomist and magistrate Albrecht von Haller—among others—trying to have Wolff expelled from Halle University.

Helianthus, as classified by Linnaeus.

Faster Weaving with Jenny

Lancashire, England, 1769: An illiterate English carpenter and weaver, James Hargreaves, has invented a most efficient thread-weaving device known as the "spinning jenny." He has been working on the device since 1764, when he created a spinning wheel that uses eight spindles instead of the single one found on traditional spinning wheels. The jenny's wheel controls the eight spindles, enabling it to create a simultaneous weave of eight threads, or "rovings."

Hargreaves attempted to patent his original device, but the courts rejected his application because he had already made and sold several of the machines.

One of the drawbacks of the jenny is that the machine currently produces thread that is too coarse to be used for warp threads (yarns that extend lengthwise in the weaving frame) and can only produce weft (crosswise) threads. Hargreaves is now working to address this problem, and is hoping to patent his latest, 16-spindle model soon. It is believed he has also drawn up plans for a jenny with up to 120 spindles.

Despite the undoubted efficiency of the devices, they have aroused opposition in some quarters. Last year a group of spinners broke into Hargreaves's house and destroyed all his machines, fearing that jobs will be lost if the new machines are introduced. Mill owners, however, have hailed the appliance, which is certain to revolutionize the textile industry.

One story tells us that Hargreaves's daughter Jenny knocked over a spinning

time out

In 1794, French chemist and scientist, Antoine Lavoisier is guillotined as a traitor during the so-called Reign of Terror following the French Revolution. The judge at his trial is reported to have said, "The Republic has no need of scientists."

Hargreaves's "spinning jenny" with an upright wheel.

Stockholm, Sweden, 1751: Axel Frederik Cronstedt discovers nickel.

London, England, 1752: Great Scottish obstetrician William Smellie publishes *A Treatise on the Theory and Practice of Midwifery*.

Uppsala, Sweden, 1753: Carl von Linné (Linnaeus) publishes *System plantarum*.

Halle, Germany, 1754: Dorothea Erxleben is the first woman awarded a medical degree in Germany.

Edinburgh, Scotland, 1754: Joseph Black discovers carbon dioxide, which he calls "fixed air."

Cape of Good Hope, South Africa, 1754: French astronomer Nicolas Louis de Lacaille and his assistants complete their study of the southern sky, identifying about 10,000 stars.

Prohlis, Germany, December, 1758: Johann Georg Palitzsch observes the return of Edmund Halley's comet.

Halle, Germany, 1759: Kaspar Wolff publishes his dissertation *Theoria generationis* on embryos.

Peking, China, 1760: First explanation of the Copernican system in Chinese presented to Emperor Qianlong by Jesuit priest Michel Benoist.

Lyons, France, 1762: Claude Bourgelat establishes the world's first veterinary school.

Lancashire, England, 1764: James Hargreaves invents the original spinning jenny with eight spindles.

Moscow, Russia, November 20, 1764: Christian Goldbach, mathematician, dies, aged 74.

London, England, 1766: Henry Cavendish discovers the gas known as "inflammable air"; it is later named hydrogen.

Eaglesfield, Cumberland, England, September 6, 1766: John Dalton, scientist, born.

Derbyshire, England, 1768: Richard Arkwright invents the spinning frame, which makes very strong thread. The invention makes spinning a factory process rather than a cottage industry.

Glasgow, Scotland, January 5, 1769: James Watt patents an improvement to the steam engine.

London, England, 1771: Joseph Banks returns from his Pacific expedition with many new plant specimens.

London, England, June, 1773: John Harrison is finally paid in full the prize for his marine chronometer.

Edo (Tokyo), Japan, 1774: Sugita Gempaku produces first Japanese translation of a European textbook on anatomy and medicine.

Leeds, England, 1774: Joseph Priestley experiments with air in sealed containers and isolates "dephlogisticated" air, later known as oxygen.

Lyons, France, January 20, 1775: André Ampère, physicist, is born.

Shropshire, England, 1779: The world's first cast iron bridge is built across the River Severn near Telford by Abraham Darby III.

James Watt's efficient new steam engine.

James Watt

wheel, and as Hargreaves watched the spindle roll across the floor, the idea for the spinning jenny came to him. Others say that he named the invention after his wife, whose name is also Jenny.

Watt's Revolutionary Steam Engine

Glasgow, Scotland, January 5, 1769: Scottish inventor James Watt was today granted a patent on his groundbreaking invention, the condenser steam engine. It marks a great improvement in efficiency over the current engine—used primarily to pump water from mines—patented by English blacksmith Thomas Newcomen in 1712.

Steam engines use atmospheric pressure to do the work. Steam is first pumped from a boiler into a cylinder then condensed by cold water, creating a vacuum on the inside of the cylinder. The resulting pressure operates a piston.

Watt obtained a broken Newcomen machine, repaired it, and through experimentation soon realized that it wasted energy in several ways. Heat dissipated through the cylinder, which is made of brass—both a good conductor and a good radiator. So heat was lost because it was necessary to cool down the cylinder at

every stroke. Power was then lost because of the pressure of vapor beneath the piston.

Watt determined that the engine's inefficiencies could be overcome by separating the condenser from the heat source. He made a small prototype model by converting a 10 in (25 cm) long surgeon's syringe into a cylinder. At each end was a pipe carrying steam from the boiler, and fitted with a valve. A pipe led from the top of the cylinder to the condenser, the syringe and the piston rod hanging downward for convenience. The condenser was made of two 10 in (25 cm) long vertical tin pipes connected at the top by a larger pipe fitted with a "snifting valve." The whole unit was set in a cistern of cold water. This little model worked so well that it lifted a remarkable weight of 18 lb (8 kg), so Watt constructed an equally successful larger model.

Watt's engine, due to its much greater efficiency and safety, is certain to lead to great improvements—and new applications—in the manufacturing industries.

Inventor of Longitude Chronometer Rewarded

London, England, June, 1773: Eighty-year-old John Harrison, English inventor and horologist, has finally received the prize offered by the British Board of Longitude in 1714, for the first marine clock capable of accurately determining longitude.

The reward was offered to the inventor of a clock capable of measuring longitude to within 30 miles (48 km). Harrison set himself to the task, and by 1762 had created a clock that maritime tests proved to be accurate to an amazing 18 miles

(29 km), but red tape has delayed payment of the impressive £20,000 prize until now.

Latitude, or distance from the equator, is simple to determine by measuring the angle of the sun at noon and other times, but longitude is much harder, since measurement of celestial bodies depends on knowing the precise time of day.

Until Harrison's chronometer, the motion of the sea, and the fact that temperature and latitude cause metals to expand and contract at different rates, rendered marine clocks so inaccurate as to be virtually useless for navigation purposes. Ships at sea were effectively lost, often traveling hundreds of miles further east or west than intended.

To overcome the problem of different rates of expansion and contraction of metals, Harrison composed a grid frame with alternate bars of steel and of brass, arranged so those that expanded the most were counteracted by those that expanded the least. He also replaced the pendulum with a spring and compensating balance.

A fanciful depiction of botanist Joseph Banks.

Thomas Malthus

Hot-Air Balloons Aloft!

France, November, 1783: Aerial balloons are creating great excitement in the skies over France. The first hot-air balloon flight took place on June 4. Brothers Joseph Michel and Étienne Jacques Montgolfier, paper-mill owners, built a large paper-lined silk balloon and demonstrated it in front of a sizable crowd at the market-place at Annonay. Their contraption, which they call a Montgolfière, ascended to the amazing height of 6,562 ft (about 2,000 m) after they filled it with hot gas by burning a cauldron of damp hay under an opening in the base of the balloon.

The brothers discovered one limitation of hot-air balloons: that when the air in the balloon cools, the balloon descends. Also, if the fire is kept burning to warm the air, sparks are likely to reach the bag and ignite it. However, a solution was at hand. On August 27, physicist Jacques Charles filled a balloon with hydrogen gas. The silk-covered and rubber-lined vessel rose to a height of about 3,000 ft (914 m) above the Tuileries Gardens, in front of an audience estimated at around 400,000—half the population of Paris!

Not to be outdone, on September 19 the Montgolfiers launched another air balloon containing the world's first air travelers (aviators)—a rooster, a duck, and a sheep. The flight was successful, but the rooster's skull was crushed when the balloon landed. However, the duck survived the flight and the sheep is now a member of Marie Antoinette's menagerie.

On October 15, Pilatre de Rozier and the Marquis d'Arlandes made history by becoming the first human aviators, flying in a Montgolfière.

The Montgolfiers assert that they have invented a new lighter-than-air gas.

> *"The art of medicine consists of amusing the patient while Nature cures the disease."*
>
> VOLTAIRE (FRANÇOIS-MARIE AROUET) (1694–1778) FRENCH PHILOSOPHER, 1788

> *"The perpetual struggle for room and food."*
>
> THOMAS ROBERT MALTHUS (1766–1834) BRITISH CLERIC, ON THE GROWING POPULATION, 1798

The Montgolfier brothers' hot air balloon, the Montgolfière, in 1783.

Plant Remedy for Dropsy

Birmingham, England, 1785: English physician and herbalist, William Withering, has applied scientific research to an ancient herbal remedy, and published his findings that *Digitalis purpurea*, or the foxglove plant, is highly effective in curing dropsy—the often-fatal accumulation of fluid caused by congestive heart disease.

Ten years ago Withering was asked his opinion of a folk medicine cocktail which "had long been kept a secret by an old woman in Shropshire who had some-times made cures after more regular practitioners had failed." The botanically trained Withering detected only one ingredient in her mixture that he considered potentially "active"—foxglove.

An artist's impression of Benjamin Franklin using a kite in his lightning experiment.

Since then Withering has been applying varying doses of the active ingredient digitalis to numerous gravely ill patients, achieving some successes but also causing some painful deaths.

In *An Account of the Foxglove and Some of Its Medical Uses; with Practical Remarks on Dropsy and Other Diseases*, he details his research, most notable for its discovery that very small repeated doses of digitalis are effective in curing dropsy, even when other treatments have failed.

Prominent US Scientist-Statesman Dead at 84

Philadelphia, USA, April 17, 1790: Benjamin Franklin, the brilliant scientist and political figure, has died.

He was born in Boston on January 17, 1706, the tenth son of soap maker, Josiah Franklin. Benjamin was apprenticed to his printer brother James at the age of twelve, as his parents could not afford to educate him. James was imprisoned for his outspoken views, so Benjamin took over their newspaper, the *New England Courant*.

After the brothers fell out, Benjamin worked as a printer in London from 1724 to 1726. Upon returning to Philadelphia he purchased the *Pennsylvania Gazette* in 1729 and the following year he married Deborah Read, by whom he had a son, who died young, and a daughter, Sally. He also fathered an illegitimate son, William. In 1732 he started publishing (and writing for) the satirical news magazine *Poor Richard's Almanac*, which became enormously popular.

Franklin made numerous scientific discoveries, including finding proof that lightning and electricity are identical, which he verified, so it is said, with an experiment involving a kite in the early 1750s. He was also a keen inventor, creating objects as varied as a flexible urinary catheter, the lightning rod, the Franklin stove, and bifocal spectacles.

For the 20 years following his retirement from publishing in 1748, he served in several government positions, and in 1754 was appointed deputy postmaster-general for the colonies. In 1757 he was posted to London for five years to negotiate (successfully) the right of the American colonies to tax landowners to pay for the cost of defending it from the French and Indians. During this time he was granted honorary degrees from Oxford and Edinburgh University.

He was sent to England again in 1764 to contest the Parliament's right to tax the American colonies without representation. The British would have none of this, so he returned to America, where he played an active role in the lead-up to the Declaration of Independence on July 4, 1776.

In 1778 Benjamin Franklin enlisted the aid of France in the War of Independence against the British, resulting in the defeat of the British on September 3, 1783. He was US minister in Paris until 1785, and then returned to the United States, where

cast iron bridge, across the Severn River in England.

Eli Whitney

he was three times elected president of Pennsylvania. He actively participated in framing the US constitution before retiring from public life two years ago.

New Cotton Gin Increases Daily Fiber Yield

Georgia, USA, March 14, 1794: The Georgia Court has granted Yale graduate Eli Whitney a patent for his recent invention of the cotton gin, a machine that automatically separates cottonseed from fiber.

Simple, manually operated cotton-cleaning devices have been around for centuries, but are slow and very labor-intensive. Until now in the United States, cottonseed has been removed by slaves, without whose free labor cotton farmers could not run a profitable operation.

Whitney's apparatus consists of spiked teeth mounted on a boxed revolving cylinder which, when turned by a crank, pulls the cotton fiber through small slotted openings and separates the seeds from the lint. A rotating brush, operated by a belt and pulleys, then removes the fibrous lint from the projecting spikes. The gin enables a single operator to generate up to 50 lb (23 kg) of cleaned cotton daily, a vast improvement on traditional methods.

However, since the gin was unveiled last year problems have arisen for Whitney and his business partner Phineas Miller. Other manufacturers have already begun selling counterfeit gins, and are now claiming that a loophole in the Patent Act allows them to continue production.

Whitney and Miller have meanwhile appealed to the court, and are manufacturing as many gins as possible, installing them throughout Georgia at no cost, instead charging farmers 40 percent of their cotton yield as payment.

Along with the recent inventions of the spinning jenny, spinning frame, and flying shuttle, the cotton gin looks set to transform the southern American textile industry into a much more lucrative, streamlined operation.

Food Can't Keep Pace with Population, Warns Malthus

London, England, June 7, 1798: Economist and demographer Reverend Thomas Robert Malthus has published an essay on the dangers of overpopulation.

In his "Essay on the Principle of Population, as it affects the Future Improvement of Society with remarks on the Speculations of Mr. Godwin, M. Condorcet, and Other Writers," he contends that future population growth will outstrip the food supply unless certain steps are taken. He claims that all human, animal, and plant populations, if unchecked, increase at a geometric rate (that is, 2, 4, 8, 16, 32, etc.), whereas the food supply only grows at an arithmetic rate (that is, 1, 2, 3, 4, 5, etc.).

Malthus makes the following points about overpopulation: (1) Population levels are limited by available nutrition. (2) When nutrition increases, population always increases accordingly. (3) Population pressures encourage increases in productivity. (4) Increases in productivity in turn lead to further population growth. (5) As this productivity cannot keep up with population growth, checks must be imposed on population growth to keep it in line with available nutrition. (6) Population and production can be expanded or contracted through cost/benefit decisions regarding sex, work, and children. (7) Positive checks must be introduced as population exceeds subsistence level. (8) These checks will have beneficial effects on misery, vice, poverty, and similar social ills.

Malthus supports his thesis with examples, including the rapid growth of new colonies such as the United States, and the current population explosion in Europe.

William Godwin and the Marquis of Condorcet, mentioned in the essay's title, are philosophers who have recently published utopian essays. Malthus debunks many of their views, but remains optimistic that we can prevent potential disaster if we take several appropriate steps, which his essay outlines.

Stone Holds Key to Ancient Egyptian Scripts

Rosetta, Egypt, July, 1799: French soldiers from Napoleon's army have unearthed an intriguing ancient stone near the town of Rosetta on Egypt's Nile delta. The black basalt slab contains inscriptions written in three scripts—Egyptian hieroglyphic, demotic (a cursive, popular version of hieroglyphic), and ancient Greek.

Scholars soon realized that all three inscriptions contain the same text and, since the Greek on the stone is similar to modern Greek, that they could use it as a key to deciphering the Egyptian. This is a momentous discovery, as Egyptian scripts have, until now, been indecipherable.

The stone is dated March, 196 BCE, the ninth year of the rule of Ptolemy V, who was part of a Greek family that had been ruling Egypt since the fall of Alexander the Great's empire, and had maintained their Greek lifestyle and language.

The stone's inscription begins with praise of Ptolemy, then gives an account of the siege of nearby Lycopolis. It eulogizes Ptolemy's many good deeds, and lists a series of compulsory devotional rules.

It appears that the stone's purpose was to reinforce the legitimacy of Ptolemy V in the eyes of the Egyptian elite, by commemorating a coronation ceremony in the nearby city of Memphis.

Scholars are thrilled by the discovery, as they will now be able to make sense of the large trove of hitherto impenetrable inscriptions on ancient Egyptian artefacts that have been unearthed over the ages.

Scientific Achievements

Astronomy: Galaxies and shape of Milky Way discussed; Uranus discovered.

Botany: Discovery that plants convert carbon dioxide into oxygen.

Chemistry: Nickel, bismuth, magnesium, hydrogen, nitrogen, oxygen, chlorine, manganese, molybdenum, tellurium, tungsten, uranium, zirconium, strontium, yttrium, titanium, chromium, and beryllium discovered.

Ecology: US naturalist publishes book on wildlife and wilderness areas.

Geology: Theory of earthquakes as wave motions inside Earth forwarded; age of the Earth discussed; ideas that some rocks are formed from molten lava.

Mathematics: France adopts metric system for weights and measures.

Medicine: First successful appendectomy is performed; homeopathy founded.

Physics: Benjamin Franklin invents a lightning conductor, shows lightning is electricity; discovery that water is composed of oxygen and hydrogen, air of oxygen and nitrogen; book published on the electrical nature of nerve impulses.

Zoology: Zoos established in Vienna, Madrid, and Paris; *Systema entomologiae*, a classification of insects, is published; the first veterinary school established.

Botanic Gardens
Coimbra, Portugal
Glasnevin, Ireland
Kew, England
Kingstown, St Vincent
Kolkata, India
Palermo, Italy
Stockhom, Sweden
Vienna, Austria

Observatories
Armagh, Ireland
Eger, Hungary
Florence, Italy
Palermo, Sicily
Stockholm, Sweden
Vilnius, Lithuania

Universities
University of Antigua, Guatemala
University of Manhattan, North America
University of Moscow, Russia
University of New Brunswick, Canada
University of Valletta, Malta
University of Williamsburg, North America

Jean Jacques Rousseau

> *"To put one's thoughts into action is the most difficult thing in the world."*
>
> JOHANN WOLFGANG VON GOETHE (1740–1832), GERMAN POET AND NOVELIST

> *"There can hardly be a stranger commodity in the world than books."*
>
> GEORG CHRISTOPH LICHTENBERG (1742–1799) GERMAN PHYSICIST, 1764

Prolific German Composer Dies

Leipzig, Germany, July 28, 1750: Following a recent stroke and high fever, the composer Johannes Sebastian Bach has died. Often regarded as the greatest of all German composers, his major accomplishments are considered to be his six Brandenburg concertos (1708–20), his Mass in B Minor (1724), and The Art of Fugue (1740s).

Born into a family of musicians, Bach was taught violin and music theory by his father, who died when he was ten. At the age of fifteen he spent two years at the choir school of St Michael's Church in Luneberg and sang in the choir. In 1708 he was appointed organist and chamber musician to the Duke of Saxe-Weimar, and in 1717 he became Kapellmeister (director of music) at Cöthen, where he focused on instrumental composition. It was here that he wrote his famous Brandenburg concertos as well as many sonatas, suites, and keyboard works.

In 1723 he became the cantor at Leipzig's St Thomas's School, where he

The late J. S. Bach and his home town of Leipzig.

remained for the rest of his life, composing for the weekly liturgy and feast days. His compositions during that time included five cantata cycles, the Magnificat, and the St John and St Matthew Passions.

He held classes in music, gave private singing lessons, and even taught Latin. Gradually losing his eyesight in his final years, he was totally blind for the last year of his life.

Cabinet-maker Displays His Wares

London, England, 1754: Furniture maker Thomas Chippendale has published a catalogue of his designs entitled *Gentlemen and Cabinet-Maker's Director*. An elegant work, it contains 160 plates of furniture drawings and sketches, each accompanied by a brief text, and covers three principal themes: gothic, Chinese, and modern.

His gothic style is largely confined to ornamental forms on chair backs, such as cusped arches and piercings that imitate gothic tracery.

Chinese designs have become hugely popular, and Chippendale has catered to this growing market with pagoda roof forms, and elaborate frets and railings. Chippendale's extensive use of japanning and painting, an oriental technique that often resembles lacquering, has become the last word in style.

By "modern" Chippendale of course means rococo, which is the late baroque style popularized in France. The rococo style is the driving force behind the majority of drawings in this sumptuously presented catalogue.

Chippendale's preferred timber is mahogany, particularly Cuban mahogany—a dense, heavy wood with a close grain, which is imported from the West Indies. His pieces are characterized by meticulous fitting and joinery work as well as deep sharp carvings.

time out

Around 1792, Japanese artist Ito Jakuchu (1716–1800) paints *Yasai Nehan (Vegetable Parinirvana)*, portraying the Buddha as a radish surrounded by other vegetables. His intention is to show that Buddha's message applies to all living things.

Chippendale has become particularly known for his desks and secretaries (desks that incorporate bookshelves), and is the first to design what he calls a "Pembroke table"—a drop-leaf table that has an oblong or rectangular fixed centerpiece with a drawer beneath it and two narrow drop leaves, either square or shaped.

However, his masterpieces are clearly his side chairs and armchairs. A rare versatility distinguishes the backs, including pierced splats carved to produce distinctly gothic impressions and others carved so intricately that they almost resemble lacework.

Arriving in London from Yorkshire in 1727, Thomas Chippendale, the son of a carpenter, was well established by 1749 in Long Acre and moved to more spacious premises in the fashionable paved thoroughfare of St Martin's Lane in 1753. Although not trained in foreign fashions like William Kent, he is a genius at adapting foreign ideas and designs.

Creator of the *Messiah* Laid to Rest

London, England, April 20, 1759: George Frideric Handel was buried in Westminster Abbey today. Regarded by many as the greatest composer of our times, his wide range of musical expression comes through not only in his operas with their rich and diverse arias, but also in the English oratorio, which he created.

In 1741 he composed, in a mere 21 days, his masterpiece the *Messiah*, an oratorio that is epic in its scope and depth, encompassing the essential beliefs of Christianity from Old Testament prophets through to the crucifixion of Christ and the final victory over sin, death, and decay. Handel's vivid sense of the dramatic and his originality of composition place him

---

Catherine II will enjoy the new Winter Palace.

Designed in ornate rococo style, which became popular during the final stages of the baroque period, the three-story palace occupies no less than an entire city block. It is an extravagant mix of typical rococo features such as lavish arches, statuary, pediments, and columns.

When viewed from different angles the building produces quite different impressions, an effect that is due to the varied compositions of its facades. Although sharing a common symmetry, they are at different scales and have varying degrees of decoration. The whimsical nature of the window and door frames, the splendid Corinthian capitals of the columns, sophisticated cornices, and the abundance of statues on the roof of the palace, not to mention the festive colors of its walls—all exude the sumptuousness that is characteristic of baroque architecture.

Unfortunately Empress Elisabeth died before the building was completed, and it is Empress Catherine II who will enjoy the splendid interiors of Elisabeth's home.

Rastrelli arrived in Russia with his father from Italy in 1715, bringing with him an ambition to combine the latest Italian architectural fashions with the traditions of the Muscovite baroque style. His first important commission came in 1721 when he was asked to build a palace for Prince Cantemir, the former ruler of Moldavia. He was appointed senior court architect in 1730, retaining that post until the recent death of Empress Elisabeth.

disseminate texts, particularly Buddhist scriptures. The color prints now being produced frequently depict seductive courtesans and kabuki actors, and employ a new single-sheet method of printing that involves a large range of colors.

Prints are designed on paper before being pasted onto wooden blocks, one for each color. A carver chisels and cuts the design into the wood to create an original in negative, with lines and areas to be colored raised in relief. Ink is applied to the woodblock's surface, a piece of paper is laid on top of the inked board, and then a round pad is rubbed over the back of the paper to transfer the design to the paper. The process is repeated for each color, taking care to align each color accurately to produce the final polychrome print.

George Frideric Handel

alongside Johannes Sebastian Bach—they are both undoubtedly supreme masters of the baroque style of music.

Russian Winter Palace Completed

St Petersburg, Russia, 1762: At the heart of the Russian city of St Petersburg a distinctly European-style building has been completed after eight years of construction. The Winter Palace, built for Empress Elisabeth, daughter of Peter the Great, as an official royal residence, has 1,057 rooms, 1,945 windows, and 1,987 doors.

Located between the bank of the River Neva and Palace Square, the palace was designed by Elisabeth's favorite architect, Bartolomeo Rastrelli, who said that it was built "solely for the glory of Russia." It is one of the many Rastrelli-created architectural masterpieces in St Petersburg.

New Art Form in Japan

Edo (Tokyo), 1766: The celebrated artist Suzuki Harunobu has played a leading role in the development of the multicolored woodblock prints that have become so popular. He has taken the art to new heights with his stylish color prints, which are sought after for their delicate and graceful lines.

Black and white woodblock prints were initially used in eighth-century Japan to

The Walk, a colored woodblock print by Suzuki Harunobu.

Edo (Tokyo), Japan, c. 1775: Printmaker Kitagawa Utamaru introduces a new fashion for woodblock prints featuring actors and courtesans.
Nanking, China, 1776: Yuan Mei gains recognition as the foremost Chinese poet of his time.
Edinburgh, Scotland, August 25, 1776: David Hume, writer and philosopher, dies, aged 65.
Cologne, Germany, March 26, 1778: Child musical prodigy Ludwig van Beethoven makes his first public appearance, aged 7.

Paris, France, May 30, 1778: François Marie Arouet (Voltaire), writer and philosopher, dies, aged 83.
Ermenonville, France, July 2, 1778: Jean Jacques Rousseau, writer and philosopher, dies, aged 56.
London, England, December, 1784: Samuel Johnson dies, aged 75.
Kyoto, Japan, 1785: Reigen Eto, Japanese Zen painter and chief priest, dies, aged about 64.
London, England, 1785: The East India Company publishes Charles Wilkins's translation of the *Bhagavad-Gita* from the Sanskrit.

Vienna, Austria, May 1, 1786: Mozart's comic opera *The Marriage of Figaro* premières at the Burgtheatre.
Konigsberg, East Prussia (Kaliningrad, Russia), 1788: Immanuel Kant's *Critique of Practical Reason* is published.
London, England, 1789: *The Interesting Narrative of the Life of Olaudah Equiano*, one of the first slave narratives, is published.
Bordeaux, France, 1789: Choreographer and dancer Jean Dauberval presents the ballet later known as *La Fille mal Gardée*.

London, England, 1789: William Blake publishes his series of verses entitled *Songs of Innocence*.
Edinburgh, Scotland, July 17, 1790: Adam Smith, writer, economist, and moral philosopher, dies, aged 67.
Vienna, Austria, December 5, 1791: Wolfgang Amadeus Mozart dies, aged 35.
Seoul, Korea, 1791: Kang Se-hwang, literati painter, dies, aged about 78.
Peking, China, 1791: The first complete version of *Dream of the Red Chamber* by Cao Xueqin is published.

London, England, 1792: Mary Wollstonecraft publishes *A Vindication on the Rights of Women*.
Paris, France, 1793: The former royal art collection is displayed at the Louvre.
Edinburgh, Scotland, July 21, 1796: Robert Burns poet, writer, and pioneer of the Romantic movement dies, aged 37.
London, England, 1798: *Lyrical Ballads* is published.
Germany, 1798: Alois Senefelder invents the printing technique of lithography.

Royal Academy Shows Gainsborough Painting

William Blake

London, England, 1770: *The Blue Boy*, one of Thomas Gainsborough's best-known portraits, is currently exhibiting at the Royal Academy of Arts in London.

Thomas Gainsborough is the most inventive and original English painter this century has seen, and is the only significant portrait artist who also devotes much of his time to landscapes. He composes in chalk, pen and wash, and water-color, sometimes varnishing the works and always looking for new papers and new techniques.

The Blue Boy portrays Jonathan Buttall, the son of a successful hardware merchant. The blue costume dates from the early 1600s and is familiar from the portraits by the well-known Flemish painter Anthony van Dyck.

Two years ago Gainsborough was elected a founding member of the Royal Academy of Arts.

> "NO MAN BUT A BLOCKHEAD EVER WROTE, EXCEPT FOR MONEY."
>
> SAMUEL JOHNSON (1709–1784) BRITISH WRITER AND LEXICOGRAPHER, 1776

> "POETRY IS THE SPONTANEOUS OVERFLOW OF POWERFUL FEELINGS: IT TAKES ITS ORIGIN FROM EMOTION RECOLLECTED IN TRAN-QUILLITY."
>
> WILLIAM WORDS-WORTH (1770–1850) ENGLISH POET, 1798

"Man of Letters," Samuel Johnson, is Dead

London, England, December 13, 1784: Doctor Samuel Johnson, the renowned English writer, has died, at the age of seventy-five. Essayist, critic, conversationalist, and poet, Johnson is considered to be one this century's outstanding literary figures.

In 1748 he began working on a monumental task that alone would have assured him a place in history—his *Dictionary of the English Language*, which took him until 1755 to complete.

In 1612 the Italian academy produced a dictionary of the Italian language that had taken 20 years to compile. A French dictionary, published in 1718, took French scholars 55 years to prepare and another 18 to revise. When it was agreed that England, too, should have a first-rate dictionary, it was Samuel Johnson who undertook the task.

Paid the sum of 1,575 pounds, he singlehandedly wrote over 40,000 definitions, with six clerks to copy out quotations as his only assistance. The literary quotations, of which there are around 140,000, are used to illustrate the meanings of words and are an impor-tant innovation.

The late Dr Samuel Johnson.

Shakespeare, Milton, and Dryden, for example, are often quoted. Unlike most previous lexicographers, Johnson some-times introduced humor or prejudice into the definitions—for example, "Excise: A hateful tax levied upon commodities."

Although highly acclaimed and very influential, the dictionary failed to turn a profit for Johnson, due to the fact that he was the one who had to bear the expense of its lengthy compilation.

In his early years, Johnson waged a constant fight against poverty, as the son of a poor bookseller in the country town of Lichfield in Staffordshire. Dissatisfied with his job as a schoolteacher, Johnson traveled 100 miles (about 160 km) to London and found a job writing for Edward Cave's *Gentlemen's Magazine*. Although initially unsuccessful at selling his writing, he slowly began to gain recognition. His poem "London," pub-lished anonymously in 1738, was praised by the well-known poet Alexander Pope and this gained him entry into London's literary circles.

In the years after the publication of his dictionary, he co-founded the Literary Club of London and was its leading light. In 1773 he toured the New Hebrides and in 1775 wrote an account of the trip, *A Journey to the Western Islands of Scotland*.

Samuel Johnson's last major work was a collection of biographical essays on English poets published in 1781 as *The Lives of the Poets*. He spent the summer of 1784 visiting Lichfield and Oxford, returning to London depressed. He is to be buried in Westminster Abbey.

The Blue Boy, a portrait by Thomas Gainsborough.

Engraver-Poet Produces Book of Poems

London, England, 1789: A poet from the streets of London's Soho, William Blake, has self-published a series of verses entitled *Songs of Innocence*. He engraved the text and illustrations himself.

Blake started writing poetry at the age of twelve, and when he was twenty-six friends paid for the first collection of his verses to be published. Despite Blake's obvious talents as a poet, his profession has remained engraving: He completed a six-year apprenticeship with the engraver James Basire in 1778.

In *Songs of Innocence*, the poems and artwork were reproduced by Blake himself, using the technique of copper-plate engraving colored with washes by hand. Blake engraved the plates separately, varying the order of presentation so that no two editions of the work are the same. Two poems may be printed side-by-side in one edition and far apart in another.

Blake's poems contrast the stages of innocence and experience through which we all must pass, and are very similar to the current established genre of children's

Key Structures

Annaglee, Cootehill, Ireland
Babulnath Temple, Bombay, India
Brandenburg Gate, Berlin, Germany
Catedral de San Cristobal de la Habana, Havana, Cuba
Christ Church, Melaka, Malaya
Colegio de San Jeronimo, Antigua, Guatemala
Convento de San Felipe Neri, Sucre, Bolivia
Dar Al-Hajar, Sana'a, Yemen
Emin Minaret, Turpan, China
Eo Myeong-gi House, Daei-ri, Korea
Fuerte San Cristobal, San Juan, Puerto Rico
Golden Gate and 55 Window Palace, Bhaktapur, Nepal
Hermitage Winter Palace, St Petersburg, Russia
Igreja de Sao Francisco de Assis, Sao Joao del Rei, Brazil
Ketchaoua Mosque, Algiers, Algeria
Kraton of Yogya, Yokyakarta, East Indies
Lak Muang, Bangkok, Siam
Laleli Camii, Istanbul, Turkey
La Maison des Esclaves, Dakar, Senegal
La Scala, Milan, Italy
Lazienki Palace, Warsaw, Poland
Monticello, Charlottesville, North America
Norbulinka Palace, Lhasa, Tibet
Old East, Chapel Hill, North America
Palace of the Winds, Jaipur, India
Pantheon, Paris, France
Petajavesi Old Church, Petajavesi, Finland
Qing Dynasty Summer Palace, Chengde, China
Regent's Mosque, Shiraz, Persia
Royal Salt Works, Arc-et-Senans, France
St Andrew's and St George's Church, Edinburgh, Scotland
San Felipe de Barajas, Cartagena, Colombia
Somerset House, London, England
Udaipur City Palace, Udaipur, India
Wat Mai Suwannaphumaham, Luang Prabang, Laos
Wat Pho, Bangkok, Siam

Scene from a production of *The Magic Flute*, an opera by the late Wolfgang Amadeus Mozart.

Cao wrote *Dream of the Red Chamber* during his years in poverty. Describing the life and declining fortunes of a large feudal family, it was intended to be an account of his childhood, but it is unclear whether the novel's heroic central character, Bao-yu, is meant to represent Cao.

Dream of the Red Chamber is regarded as a masterpiece of Chinese literature. Although a tragic love story lies at the heart of the novel, Cao goes beyond any superficiality, tapping into the social origins of the tragedy by probing deep into the minds of the characters and their complex relationships. The author depicts a broad swathe of society through his description of conflicts and struggles, ultimately predicting the doomed nature of China's feudal system, denouncing its corrupt politics, its cruelty, and its inherent inhumanity.

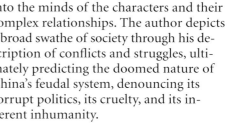

Mary Wollstonecraft

poetry. They are deliberately simplistic in order to present the moral dilemmas of our time in a form that can be understood. In the words of its author, the work "shows the two contrary states of the human soul."

Mozart Buried in Pauper's Grave

Vienna, Austria, 1791: Wolfgang Amadeus Mozart, the musical genius of the century, has died, probably of rheumatic inflammatory fever. He was 35 years old.

Born in Salzburg, Austria, in 1756, he soon learned to play the harpsichord and violin. He began composing minuets at age five and in 1763 his father took him and his sister Maria Anna on an extended concert tour of western Europe, not returning to Salzburg until 1766. It was during this time that Mozart composed his first symphony and published his first sonatas. At twelve he wrote his first opera, *La Finta Semplice (The Pretended Simpleton)*. After several tours through Italy in the early 1770s, he returned to Salzburg to the position of honorary Konzertmeister (concert master) at the Salzburg court.

In 1777 he took leave from this post and traveled with his mother throughout Germany, seeking a better position but finding nothing. The next year he and his mother went to Paris where he wrote the Paris Symphony. His mother fell ill and died shortly after the work's Paris debut.

Against the advice of his father, he wed Constance Weber in 1782. The couple had six children, but only two survived. Mozart's most productive years were from 1782 to 1787 in Vienna, when he was Emperor Joseph II's chamber composer, and include the operas *The Marriage of Figaro* (1786) and *Don Giovanni* (1787), as well as numerous piano concertos.

Mozart's beloved father died in 1787, and his world was filled with despair. Deep in debt and frequently ill, he began another series of tours in 1789.

Returning home to Vienna for the last time, Mozart was approached by Emanuel Schikaneder, actor and theatrical manager, with a libretto he had written for an opera based on an oriental fairy tale and entitled *The Magic Flute*. Mozart completed its final notes on September 29, and it then premièred in Vienna the very next day.

Collapsing from exhaustion after the première, Mozart's illness worsened. A stranger approached him during his final days and commissioned him to compose a requiem mass. Mozart, in his deteriorating state, came to believe the stranger was a messenger from heaven, and that the mass was to be his own.

Wolfgang Amadeus Mozart has been buried in a suburban churchyard, St Marx cemetery, in an unmarked grave.

Landmark Chinese Novel Published

Peking, China, 1791: China's greatest novel, *Dream of the Red Chamber*, has finally been published in its entirety, some 28 years after the death of its author Cao Xueqin (Tsao Hsueh-chin), and despite the ambiguity surrounding the authorship of the last 40 chapters of this mammoth 120-chapter saga.

Little is known of Cao's early years—he was discovered living in poverty in the western suburbs of Peking in 1742. His grandfather Cao Yin had been the textile commissioner in Jiangning (Nanking) and greatly favored by Emperor Kangxi. In the early 1730s the family had been very influential; however, later political misfortunes diminished its power.

Poetic Norms Overturned in Experimental Work

London, England, 1798: A collection of poems entitled *Lyrical Ballads* has been published anonymously. Actually written by William Wordsworth and Samuel Taylor Coleridge, the poets omitted their names from the title page for fear readers might find the poems too experimental.

Illustration to Wordsworth's "Tintern Abbey," from *Lyrical Ballads*.

Lyrical Ballads attempts to combine two different poetic traditions, lyric and ballad. Lyric is the term used to describe any short poem where personal emotions are expressed, while a ballad tells a story in the popular language of the day. In other words, the aim was to use the real, earthy language of ordinary people. Both Wordsworth and Coleridge hope to overturn what they consider to be the priggish, learned, and highly sculpted forms of present-day English poetry.

It is agreed that Wordsworth's "Tintern Abbey" and Coleridge's "Rime of the Ancient Mariner" are two of the most striking poems in the collection.

Golf Club at St Andrews

Father Junípero Serra

St Andrews, Scotland, May 14, 1754: There is a new golf club in St Andrews. Twenty-two nobles and gentlemen have donated a silver golf club, which is to be the prize in an annual competition at the local links. As well as enjoying the game and the conviviality that follows, they hope that an annual contest for a significant trophy will help to revive the reputation of St Andrews as the home of golf and stimulate a return to the glory days when royalty and religious leaders were regular visitors.

Golf has been a popular pastime in St Andrews since Scotland's first university was founded there in 1413. The city is also the country's religious capital and the resting place of the relics of St Andrew, but the Reformation destroyed much of its religious significance. The underfunded university is now in danger of being moved to Perth, and the huge cathedral—once attended by Robert the Bruce—lies in ruins.

The annual golf challenge follows the example established 10 years earlier by the group of gentlemen golfers at Leith, who are generally recognized to have formed the world's first golf club.

Some historians believe that golf is descended from a Roman game known as *paganica*, which was played in the streets with a bent stick and a leather ball stuffed with feathers. Others trace it back to a Dutch game called *het kolven*, a French and Belgian game known as *chole*, or an English game called *cambuca*. Most believe, however, that it was in Scotland that golf developed into the game as we know it today.

> "MAN WAS BORN FREE AND EVERY-WHERE HE IS IN CHAINS."
>
> JEAN JACQUES ROUSSEAU (1712–1778) FRENCH PHILOSOPHER, 1762

> "LAWS GRIND THE POOR, AND RICH MEN RULE THE LAW."
>
> OLIVER GOLDSMITH (1728–1774) IRISH DRAMATIST, 1764

The game of golf has been revived with the establishment of a new golf club in St Andrews, Scotland.

King's Mistress Dies at 42

Versailles, France, April 15, 1764: Madame de Pompadour, the brains behind King Louis XV of France, has died. She was born Jeanne-Antoinette Poisson in 1721. Shortly after her marriage to the unfortunate Le Normant d'Étoiles in 1741, Louis installed her as his mistress and ennobled her as the Marquise de Pompadour.

Madame de Pompadour has effectively ruled France from behind the scenes for the last 20 years or so, using a combination of charm, intelligence, and cunning. It was thanks to her that France's amicable policy toward Prussia was reversed, because Frederick II lampooned her. All public offices and ministerial positions were filled by her friends. Accomplished and witty, she was a generous patron of the arts. She also influenced all of France's domestic and foreign policies, most of them universally regarded as disastrous.

At first, she kept the weak and pliable Louis under her thumb by relieving him of all public duties—and pleasuring him in private. In more recent years she kept him content by ensuring a supply of attractive young girls to keep him company.

time out

Frederick the Great of Prussia's sexual dalliances with men were an open secret. Had he been a "warm brother," as Prussia's homosexuals were called, he could have been executed. Yet he never repealed the law against sodomy.

Monk to Produce Wine in California

California, North America, 1769: The pioneering Franciscan monk, Father Junípero Serra, has planted the first wine grapes in America's west. Serra recently traveled to California to help establish the first European settlements there, and is setting up a series of missions. Serra was born on the island of Majorca, Spain, in 1713. At the age of 16 he joined the Order of St Francis, substituting Junípero for his baptismal name of Miguel José. After entering the order, he undertook training as a priest, and was appointed lecturer in philosophy even before he had received his doctorate. He became an eminent preacher and was often invited to speak in Majorca's larger towns.

Key Events

London, England, 1750: Edmund Hoyle publishes a collection of his works on the rules of various games, including chess and backgammon.
London, England, September, 1752: Great Britain and her colonies adopt the Gregorian calendar; 11 days are deleted between September 2 and 14.
Europe, 1752: The first of the China roses, "Old Blush," reaches Europe.
London, England, June 7, 1753: The British Museum Act is given royal assent by King George III; Sir Hans Sloane's collection thus forms the basis of the British Museum.

New York, North America, 1754: The King's College (later Columbia University) holds its first classes.
St Andrews, Scotland, 1754: The Society of St Andrews Golfers is founded.
London, England, May 5, 1760: Laurence Shirley, the 4th Earl Ferrers, is hanged for murder, aged 39, becoming the last member of the English aristocracy to die by hanging.
Medzeboz, Ukraine, May 23, 1760: Baal Shem Tov (Rabbi Yisrael Ben Eliezer), the founder of Hasidism, dies, aged about 61.

Canton, China, 1760: Imperial regulations restrict trade between China and the West; they confine trade to the port of Canton.
Fort Pitt, Pennsylvania, North America, 1763: Indians besieging the fort are infected with smallpox by British forces.
Versailles, France, April 15, 1764: The Marquise de Pompadour dies, aged 42.
London, England, 1768: Philip Astley performs "feats of horsemanship," in the first circus.

Brescia, Italy, August, 1769: A lightning bolt causes a gunpowder explosion that devastates the city and kills thousands.
Dublin, Ireland, 1769: Brewer Arthur Guinness sends his popular darker beer, known at first as porter, to England.
California, North America, 1769: Father Junípero Serra plants wine grapes at Mission San Diego.
Bengal, India, 1770: Millions die during a famine in southern India.

Moscow, Russia, September 27, 1771: Grigory Orlov heads a commission to help fight the bubonic plague and restore order to the riot-torn city.
Edinburgh, Scotland, 1771: The first edition of the *Encyclopaedia Britannica* is published in book form in three volumes.
London, England, June 22, 1772: Baron Mansfield rules that escaped slave James Somerset may not be forcibly taken away from England.

In 1749 he journeyed to America with some other Franciscan monks, several of whom later went with him to California. He taught briefly in Mexico City, where he encountered local grapes and wine for the first time. However, he was soon posted as a missionary to the Indians in the Sierra Madré area.

Two years ago, he was appointed to establish missions in lower California. He reached San Diego earlier this year, taking with him cuttings from Mexican vines, which had originally been imported from Spain in the mid-1500s.

Fr Serra's Carmel Mission, California.

The grape strain, which Serra has named Mission, shares many traits with the Spanish varieties Monica and Criolla, and the South American Criolla del Vino and Pais.

A teetotaller, Serra plans to use the wine for sacramental purposes, as well as for the culinary and table needs of the missions. He has no shortage of willing and able workers to assist with the planting and propagation of the vines.

New Style Reference Work Published

Edinburgh, Scotland, 1771: A remarkable new three-volume reference work, *Encyclopaedia Britannica*, has been published in Edinburgh. It marks a great improvement on existing reference dictionaries, the most popular to date being John Harris's 1704 *Lexicon Technicum* and Ephraim Chambers's 1729 *Cyclopaedia*.

Encyclopaedia Britannica is the brain-child of Scottish bookseller and printer Colin Macfarquhar and engraver Andrew Bell, who published the work under the pseudonym "A Society of Gentlemen." It was edited by 28-year-old scholar William Smellie, who was paid 200 pounds to produce the three volumes in 100 parts.

The first installment appeared back in December 1768, priced sixpence. The complete edition consists of 2,391 pages and 160 superbly engraved illustrations. It comprises three equally sized volumes covering A–B, C–L, and M–Z. Three thousand copies have been printed.

The title-page states that a new plan has been followed in compiling the work. The different arts and sciences are "digested into distinct treatises or systems," of which there are 45 with cross-headings (titles printed across the page) and about 30 other articles more than three pages in length.

The compilers continue: "The various technical terms etc. are explained as they occur in the order of the alphabet… Instead of dismembering the sciences, by attempting to treat them intelligibly under a multitude of technical terms, they have digested the principles of every science in the form of systems or distinct treatises, and explained the terms as they occur in the order of the alphabet, with references to the sciences to which they belong." This arrangement, as the compilers point out, differs markedly from that of all previous dictionaries of arts and sciences.

British Ship Opium to China

Canton, China, 1773: The British East India Company has delivered its first shipment of opium from Bengal to China, after obtaining the monopoly on the export of Benares and Patna opium, the favorites of China's millions of addicts.

Chinese tea is in demand in Europe, and for the last 50 years private British and Portuguese merchants have been trading Indian opium for tea, while the East India Company has been trading cotton. Britain has been manufacturing large amounts of opium in India for 40 years, learning the art from the Moghuls, who have been trading in opium for 200 years. When the British conquered Bengal in 1764, they saw the potential profit in the opium trade (previously dominated by the Dutch in Batavia). Poppies grow almost anywhere and profits are around 400 percent. America also gains from the opium trade.

British exports of opium skyrocketed from an estimated 15 tons (15.3 tonnes) in 1730 to 75 tons (76.5 tonnes) last year. The opium is shipped in chests, each containing 140 lb (74 kg) of the drug.

As importation of opium into China is illegal (the Chinese manufacture enough opium for their own medicinal purposes), the East India Company buys tea in Canton on credit, carrying no opium, but instead sells opium at auction in Calcutta on the condition it is smuggled to China.

The Chinese government is making half-hearted efforts to curb the opium trade, and the emperor has appointed Lin Tse-hsu imperial commissioner in charge of an anti-opium publicity campaign.

Madame de Pompadour

Weighing opium. British opium traders learnt from Indian Moguls.

London, England, 1772: Chemist Joseph Priestley publishes *Impregnating Water with Fixed Air*, in which he demonstrates his invention of carbonated water.

London, England, 1773: Stockbrokers group together to form "The Stock Exchange."

Canton, China, 1773: Opium is shipped from India to China.

Moscow, Russia, March 28, 1776: Catherine II gives Petr Urusov permission to establish a theater and ballet company, later known as the Bolshoi Ballet.

Philadelphia, USA, July 4, 1777: Congress is adjourned for the celebration of the anniversary of the signing of the Declaration of Independence with fireworks.

Paris, France, February, 1778: Franz Anton Mesmer campaigns to have his theory of animal magnetism accepted as a valid healing process.

London, England, 1778: Joseph Bramah patents his modern water closet.

Sandwich Islands (Hawaii), March, 1779: Lieutenant James King, aboard the *Discovery*, describes the sport of surfing.

Clerkenwald, England, 1780: William Addis establishes a company to first mass produce toothbrushes.

London, England, February 6, 1783: "Capability" Brown dies, aged about 67.

Spain, 1783: More anti-Gypsy laws are passed, continuing the persecution occurring all over Europe this century.

Paris, France, April 26, 1784: Benjamin Franklin proposes daylight saving in a letter to the *Paris Journal*.

New York, USA, September, 1784: Ann Lee, founder of the Shakers, dies, aged 48.

Mont Blanc, France, August 8, 1786: Jacques Balmat and Michel-Gabriel Paccard become the first to reach the summit of Mont Blanc, the highest mountain in western Europe.

Edo (Tokyo), Japan, 1787: Japan has been in the grip of famine for several years. More than a million people have died.

France, November 29, 1787: Louis XVI ends decades of persecution of Protestants with an edict of tolerance.

Paris, France, April 25, 1792: Highwayman Nicolas-Jacques Pelletier becomes the first French criminal to be guillotined.

London, England, April 30, 1792: John Montagu dies, aged 73.

Posen, Poland, 1793: The last burning of a witch in Europe takes place.

London, England, December, 1798: A new tax is introduced to fund the war against Napoleon.

London, England, 1799: British Parliament passes the *Combination Act* to prevent workers joining together to improve conditions.

Unique English Garden Style is Brown's Legacy

"Capability" Brown

London, England, February 6, 1783: The landscape gardener who revolutionized English garden design, "Capability" Brown, has died, aged about sixty-seven.

Lancelot Brown was born in 1716 into a farming family in Kirkhale, Northumberland, and educated at Cambo School. He began work as a gardener's boy in the service of Sir William Loraine and later of Lord Cobham at Stowe, Buckinghamshire, where he served under William Kent, one of the originators of a new English style of landscape gardening. While at Stowe, Brown married a local girl, Bridget Wayet, who bore him four children.

As Brown's reputation grew, he was sought after by the landed gentry. In 1751 Horace Walpole wrote of Brown's work at Warwick Castle, "The castle is enchanting; the view pleased me more than I can express, the river Avon tumbles down a cascade at the foot of it. It is well laid out by one Brown…"

Brown's distinctive style of smooth, undulating grass with strips and clumps of greenery, scatterings of trees, artifices, and meandering lakes has created a unique new English style. His judicious manipulation of components—adding a tree here or a concealed head of water there—graces the formal potential of ground, water, trees, and plants.

The problem with this style is that less competent imitators and less refined spectators do not see nature perfected, but simply see what they call nature. Indeed, one obituarist has written, "Such, however, was the effect of his genius that when he was the happiest man, he will be least remembered; so closely did he copy nature that his works will be mistaken."

Brown was responsible for more than 170 gardens surrounding the finest country houses and estates in England, including Blenheim Palace, Kew Gardens, and Milton Abbey. He always refused offers to work in Ireland because he said he had not yet finished England. He got his nickname from telling customers their gardens had "capabilities" for improvement.

Franklin Urges Daylight Saving

Paris, France, April 26, 1784: Benjamin Franklin, has written a whimsical letter to the *Paris Journal* proposing that clocks be set forward in order to utilize daylight hours more efficiently. The letter appears under the heading "An Economical Project," and is a discourse on the thrift of natural lighting versus artificial lighting.

Franklin begins by noting that much discussion had followed the demonstration of an oil lamp the previous evening, regarding the quantity of oil used for the amount of light produced. He parodies himself, his love of thrift, his scientific papers, and his passion for playing chess until the wee hours of the morning, then sleeping until midday. He then recommends several humorous regulations that Paris might adopt, including that a tax should be laid on every window built with shutters to keep out the light of the sun; that candles should be rationed to 1 lb (500 g) per family per week, and the regulation enforced by the constabulary; that guards should be posted to stop the passage of all coaches and carriages upon the streets after sunset, except those of physicians, surgeons, and midwives; and that every morning as soon as the sun rises church bells—and cannons—should tell people of the advent of light and "awaken the sluggards effectually and make them open their eyes to see their true interests."

Franklin, a brilliant negotiator, has been living in Paris since 1776, when the

A woman in typical Quaker dress.

American Congress posted him to France to secure its assistance in the ultimately victorious War of Independence against Great Britain. He has been in ill health recently, and is virtually confined to his house in the Paris suburb of Passey. To amuse himself and others, he pens satirical and comical pieces, but many are saying that much good sense lies in this latest example of Franklin's wit.

Shaker Founder Dead at 48

New York, USA, September, 1784: Ann Lee, the illiterate English-born mystic who founded the American Order of the Shakers, has died.

Born the daughter of a blacksmith in 1736 in Toad Lane, Manchester, Lee worked in the cotton mills before becoming a cook. In 1762 she married Abraham Stanley, also a blacksmith.

In 1758 Ann Lee joined the Shakers or Shaking Quakers, a Christian community otherwise known as the United Society of Believers in Christ's Second Appearing who believe in separation from the outside world, equality of the sexes, common ownership of property, and devotion to hard work. They tremble violently when taken by the Lord's spirit.

In 1770, Lee claimed revelation in a vision that the second coming of Christ was fulfilled in her. She soon became the Shakers' accepted leader and was known as "Ann the Word" or "Mother Ann." She claimed the gift of being able to channel the direct word of God, the ability to release that word to the world by speaking in tongues, and the facility to discern spirits and work miracles. She was also a staunch advocate for celibacy in the quest for true holiness.

She sailed to America in 1774 with a band of eight disciples in the *Mariah*. Two years later, at Niskayuna, near Albany in New York state, she set up America's first Shaker settlement.

Mother Ann's status as a prophet and chief was denounced by most. She triggered intense resistance and was accused of spying for the British. The Shakers advocate pacifism, and Lee was gaoled as a traitor during the Revolutionary War for publicly preaching her views as a conscientious objector. She and her credulous followers remained unbowed in their fervent commitment, although lately she

Religious Leaders

Popes
Benedict XIV (1740-1758)
Clement XIII (1758-1769)
Clement XIV (1769-1774)
Pius VI (1775-1799)

Archbishops of Canterbury
Thomas Herring (1747-1757)
Matthew Hutton (1757-1758)
Thomas Secker (1758-1768)
Frederick Cornwallis (1768-1783)
John Moore (1783-1805)

Dalai Lamas of Tibet
Kelsang Gyatso (1720-1757)
Jamphel Gyatso (1762-1804)

Patriarchs of Constantinople
Cyril V (1748-1751, 1752-1757)
Calinicus III (1757)
Serapheim II (1757-1761)
Joannicus III (1761-1763)
Samuel I Chatzeres (1763-1768, 1773-1774)
Meletius II (1769)
Theodosius II (1769-1773)
Sophronius II (1774-1780)
Gabriel IV (1780-1785)
Procopius I (1785-1789)
Neophytus VII (1789-1794, 1798-1801)
Gerasimus III (1794-1797)
Gregory V (1797-1798)

had been forced to move from one friend's home to another in fear for her life.

In the Shakers' eyes, Manchester's Toad Lane is now as hallowed as Bethlehem.

Japanese Famine Causes Mayhem

Edo (Tokyo), Japan, 1787: Over a million people have starved to death in Japan, which after five years is still in the grip of a terrible famine. It began in 1782 following two unseasonably cold winters and dry summers, and is now causing food riots around the country, with poverty-stricken citizens looting rice shops and trashing government offices.

This calamity is pitting borough against borough in a desperate race to survive, while the government attempts to stay afloat by continually raising taxes. Brutal crackdowns against the rioting populace are the order of the day, as the government, caught up in its own economic misfortunes, greets the riots with what can only be called a lofty indifference.

The crisis is the latest in a series of recent natural disasters to strike Japan. Drought in the Ou district to the north, floods in Kyushu and Kyoto, the destruction of most of Edo by fire, a volcanic eruption in Kagoshima, and a plague that claimed over half a million lives were a prelude to this latest disaster.

Death of a Bungling Peer

London, England, April 30, 1792: John Montagu, the fourth Earl of Sandwich, has died, aged 73.

Born in 1718, Montagu succeeded his grandfather to the earldom in 1729, and served as first lord of the Admiralty from 1748–51, and 1771–82. Renowned for being corrupt and militarily incompetent, he displayed great ineptness in the American War of Independence, contributing to several comprehensive naval defeats. He administered the Royal Navy so badly, in fact, that the United States may, ironically,

The Sandwich Islands, named to honor John Montagu.

thank Montagu for his not insubstantial contribution to its independence.

The late earl was a member of the Knights of St Francis of Wycombe, a group led by bungling spendthrift, chancellor of the exchequer, and postmaster-general Francis Dashwood. The group was more widely known as "the mad monks of Medmenham Abbey" and "the hell-fire club" because of their wild, naked orgies in the cathedral ruins.

Montagu participated in the persecution of his former friend and fellow "mad monk" John Wilkes, the parliamentary champion of free speech who was imprisoned—then banned from Parliament on his release 22 months later—for writing the supposedly obscene "Essay on Women."

The war against Napoleon (pictured left) has become an enormous financial burden for Britain.

John Montagu leaves a two-fold legacy. In 1778 Captain James Cook discovered an island group in the northern Pacific Ocean and named it the Sandwich Isles in the earl's honor. When he was at the gambling table, the earl often requested that a piece of meat between two slices of bread be delivered to him, so as not to interrupt his betting. This gave rise to the term "sandwich," although in fact such a snack is well-known in many other cultures around the world.

Graduated Income Tax Introduced to Fund War

London, England, December, 1798: The British prime minister William Pitt has introduced yet another tax to fund the war against Napoleon. As a result, he is continually threatened by angry mobs of people, and is under constant protection by armed guards.

When France declared war on Britain on February 1, 1793, it sparked many changes to British domestic and foreign policy. In May of the same year, Pitt suspended habeas corpus, designed to prevent unlawful imprisonment, and anyone advocating parliamentary reform was charged with sedition and jailed.

The prime minister decided to form a European coalition against France, and concluded alliances with Spain, Portugal, Russia, Prussia, Austria, and several German principalities. These tactics were successful for a while, but in 1794 the Allies suffered a series of defeats.

At the opening of Parliament in October 1795, King George III was pelted with missiles and greeted with cries of

William Pitt

"Bread!," "Peace!," and "No Pitt!" Pitt responded by passing a new sedition bill that redefined the law of treason. He also increased all taxes and raised a loan of £18 million. The recent series of bad harvests, however, have made the situation worse than ever.

Britain's financial woes convinced Pitt to seek peace with France in May 1796, but his proposals were rejected, so he introduced new taxes on horses, tobacco, tea, sugar, and spirits. Even so, by last year Britain had a budget deficit of £22 million. Newspapers declared the prime minister insane. Pitt responded by passing laws to suppress and regulate them.

Britain's problems are now so grave that the current budget has introduced a new graduated income tax. It starts with a 5 percent tax on incomes of £60, and rises by degrees until it reaches 10 percent on incomes of over £200. Pitt claims this tax will raise £10 million.

Napoleon Bonaparte

Congress Meets in New Capital

Washington DC, USA, November 17, 1800: Today the Sixth Congress met for the first time in Washington, now the nation's capital. Though the Capitol building is not yet complete, today it has welcomed the Senate, the House of Representatives, the Supreme Court, the Library of Congress, and the district courts. The American flag flies atop the building. Work on the Capitol began in 1793, but construction and labor costs have exceeded the budgeted amount, and the building is unlikely to be finished for some time. Criticisms of the quality of the workmanship have not stopped the business of government from continuing.

The First Congress of the United States was held in New York in March 1789, after which the seat of government moved to Philadelphia, where it stayed for the next ten years before moving to the new capital.

In a few days' time, on November 22, President John Adams is expected to make an appearance before both houses, which will be sitting in joint session in the Senate chamber. Vice-President Thomas Jefferson will preside over the Senate, and the Honorable Theodore Sedgwick, from Massachusetts, will be Speaker of the House of Representatives.

With the move to Washington, another change is in the air. Rumor has it that the Senate's "closed door" practice will cease, and that henceforth the chamber—like the House of Representatives—will be open to the general public.

Louisiana Sold!

Paris, France, April 30, 1803: The United States of America today purchased almost 828,000 sq miles, or 2,100,000 sq km, of land—extending from the Mississippi

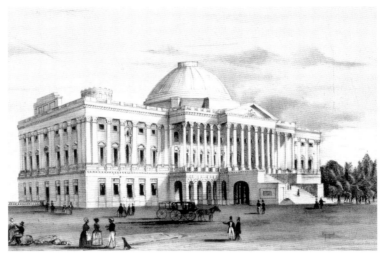

The Capitol building in Washington DC. The House wing was completed in 1811.

River to the Rocky Mountains—from the government of France. The area, known as the Louisiana Territory, had an asking price of 60 million francs, or $15 million. The Louisiana Purchase Treaty was signed by James Monroe and Robert Livingston on behalf of President Thomas Jefferson, and the Marquess de Barbé Marbois on behalf of Napoleon Bonaparte.

The area has had an interesting history. In 1762, France ceded it to Spain, but the secret 1800 Treaty of Ildefonso resulted in the area remaining in French hands. It is believed that Napoleon wished the area to be at the heart of a vast French empire. His plans centered on gaining control of Hispaniola, where Haitian slaves were staging a rebellion.

Unfortunately, however, thousands of French troops succumbed to disease, so they were unsuccessful in quelling the unrest there. Napoleon decided to cut his losses, and abandoned the scheme. No longer of strategic value, Napoleon decided to offer Louisiana for sale to the United States. The sale has provided the French government with much-needed funds to continue its various military campaigns in Europe.

President Jefferson is said to be pleased with the purchase, as it expands the total area of the United States, as well as opening up the Mississippi for trade purposes. There is some opposition to the purchase within the United States—the so-called Federalists are calling it unconstitutional. However, the Senate is expected to approve the purchase and ratify the Treaty.

Explorers Triumph

St Louis, Missouri, USA, September 23, 1806: After a gruelling three-year overland expedition, explorers Captain Meriwether Lewis and Captain William Clark have finally returned to Missouri. The expedition came about following the Louisiana Purchase of 1803. President Jefferson was eager for western expansion and engaged Lewis and Clark and their team, known as the Corps of Discovery, to undertake exploration of the west to the Pacific coast. As well as determining whether trade routes could easily be established, the men were also to study the indigenous people, and the flora and fauna in the region.

The main part of the contingent left Camp Dubois, Illinois, on May 14, 1804,

Horse thief "Hell Fire Jack" was hanged in 1805.

United Kingdom, January 1, 1801: The Act of Union between Ireland and Great Britain comes into effect.
Washington DC, USA, March 4, 1801: Thomas Jefferson becomes the new president.
St Petersburg, Russia, March 23, 1801: Paul I, Tzar of Russia, is assassinated and succeeded by his son Alexander.
London, England, 1802: The *Health and Morals of Apprentices Act* limits the working hours of children in textile mills to 12 hours a day.

Hue, Vietnam, 1802: The country is reunited after about 30 years of internal conflict.
Paris, France, April 30, 1803: The French government sells its Louisiana Territory to the USA.
Haiti, January 1, 1804: Jean-Jacques Dessalines declares Haiti a free republic after slaves mount a successful revolution against France.
Paris, France, December 2, 1804: Napoleon Bonaparte crowns himself Emperor of France at Notre Dame Cathedral.

Cape Trafalgar, Spain, October 21, 1805: Admiral Horatio Nelson leads the British Royal Navy to victory against France and Spain at the Battle of Trafalgar. He is fatally wounded.
Liechtenstein, July, 1806: The tiny nation joins the Rhine Confederation as an independent sovereign state.
London, England, March 25, 1807: The Abolition of the Slave Trade Act is passed, outlawing the transport of slaves by British ships.
USA, January 1, 1808: Congress bans the importation of slaves.

South America, 1810: South American Wars of Independence begin. Columbia and Mexico gain independence.
Paris, France, 1810: The Napoleonic Code prohibits abortion unless the mother's life is at risk.
London, England, February 5, 1811: The Prince of Wales takes office as regent for King George III after his father becomes insane.
Batavia, Dutch East Indies, August 6, 1811: The British fleet captures Batavia, and wrests control of Java from the Dutch.

England, 1811–1812: Textile workers destroy new machines.
Mississippi Valley, USA, February 7, 1812: The country's most powerful earthquake strikes.
Fort William, Canada, 1812: English-born David Thompson, explorer for the North West Company, retires, after mapping much of Canada.
Wyoming, USA, 1812: Robert Stuart and his party find an easy crossing through the Rocky Mountains.
Washington DC, USA, 1812: America declares war on British North America.

and joined up with Captain Lewis in St Charles, Missouri, from where they traveled westward. On their journey, they met some Sioux tribesmen who gave them advice about other more aggressive tribes further west. Luckily, Lewis and Clark managed to avoid any violent confrontations with the Native Americans. The team doggedly traveled on, through freezing winters, hot summers, and coping with harsh unknown landscapes until finally, in December 1805, they reached the Pacific Ocean.

In July 1806, Lewis and Clark split into two teams, Lewis setting off to explore the Marias River, where a group of Blackfeet Indians attempted to steal their guns. A scuffle ensued and Lewis's team beat a hasty retreat. Meanwhile, Crow Indians had stolen some of Clark's horses. In August, at the junction of the Missouri and Yellowstone Rivers, Lewis and Clark met up again to complete their journey.

Their return is indeed a triumph. They have gathered important information about the geography of the United States and new maps will be drawn up in the wake of their discoveries. In addition, the expedition team has collected many botanical samples, and after they have examined them, scientists are hopeful of naming a large number of new species.

Luddites Smash Machinery

Nottingham, England, 1812: Angry textile workers have been rampaging around the Midlands and the north of England, destroying any machinery that has been installed in textile factories and wool

and cotton mills. Stocking-frames, steam looms, and cropping frames have been smashed by disgruntled workers who are complaining that the new labor-saving equipment will cost them their jobs. A cotton mill in Lancashire was recently burnt to the ground, and many factory owners are now employing armed security guards to protect their property.

The Luddites, who are named after their leader Ned Ludd, are critical of wage reductions and the increasing use of unskilled labor, and they are reacting with violence. In one incident, sacked workers tried to demolish the cloth-finishing machinery in a mill in Yorkshire. In the ensuing clash with the mill's guards, two of the Luddites were killed.

There are conflicting reports about the organization of the attacks. Some assert that the Luddites train at night in fields outside industrial towns. Others maintain that there is little, if any, real organization behind the attacks, and that workers are reacting to the steady

decline in their standard of living. The slow economy is another reason for worker dissatisfaction. The new technology has limited employment opportunities and many are facing severe economic hardship as a result.

In response to this civil unrest, the government has enacted the Frame Breaking Act, which prescribes the death penalty for anyone found guilty of wilfully breaking machinery. Less serious offenders risk transportation to a penal colony. Already, eight men have received the death sentence and another seven men have been transported.

Earthquake Changes Course of Mississippi

Mississippi Valley, USA, February 7, 1812: A massive earthquake in the Mississippi Valley, the third in as many months, has permanently altered the course of the Mississippi River. In the early hours of the morning, the people of New Madrid awoke to the now eerily familiar sounds of the earth splitting apart. Houses fell to the ground; some say tremors are being felt as far away as Washington DC.

The area is joined to the New Madrid seismic zone, and experts are calling these quakes the largest in United States history. The currents have caused the Mississippi to change its course. Small islands have been submerged, and other islands created. Experienced river men are calling it a new river. The trail of destruction also extends along the Ohio and Arkansas Rivers.

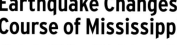

time out

Mortally wounded in a battle against a British frigate in June 1813, Captain James Lawrence, commander of the US ship *Chesapeake*, utters the phrase, "Don't give up the ship," words that become the catch-cry of the US Navy.

James Monroe

Map

Expedition of Lewis and Clark
— Lewis & Clark journey
····▶ Return detour for Lewis
····▶ Return detour for Clark
• Camp site

ROCKY
Cape Disappointment
Travelers' Rest
Camp Disappointment
Fort Clatsop
Mt Hood
The Dalles
Great Falls
Fort Mandan
Camp Fortunate
Lemhi Pass 7,373 ft (2,247 m)
GREAT PLAINS
MOUNTAINS
PACIFIC OCEAN
Columbia
Marias
Yellowstone
Missouri
Snake
Mississippi
Lake Superior
Lake Huron
Lake Michigan
Lake Erie
Camp Dubois, St Louis
Kansas
La Charette
St Charles
Mississippi
N

0 — 500 km
0 — 500 miles

**Sir Thomas
Stamford Raffles**

Going West Just Got Easier

Wyoming, USA, July 1812: At last an overland route has been mapped that effectively opens up the western United States. Explorer Robert Stuart and his team have discovered a passage, wide enough to accommodate wagons, through the Rocky Mountains in southwest Wyoming. The passage has been named the South Pass. Although Native Americans are said to be familiar with the pass, this is the first time white people have come across it.

The discovery of this natural route through the mountains is significant—not only will it make moving west quicker and easier for ordinary settlers, who may wish to make a new life and seek their fortune in the west, it will also facilitate trade, hunting, and further exploration.

But how did Robert Stuart come to discover the South Pass? Stuart has been part of a team of men who set up an outpost at the mouth of the Columbia River, working for fur trader John Joseph Astor. Given the job of informing Astor of the progress of the Pacific Fur Company in the region, Stuart led a smaller team and headed back to St Louis from Oregon. Interestingly, Stuart traveled from west to east—earlier explorers have moved from east to west.

Already, the route is being referred to as the Oregon Trail and it is expected that thousands of people will make use of the new route to move west.

Napoleon Defeated at Waterloo

Waterloo, Belgium, June 18, 1815: Napoleon Bonaparte has fought his last battle. At Waterloo today, the Duke of Wellington and Field Marshall Gebhard von Blücher defeated the beleaguered French army. Victory, however, came at a high cost—Wellington, whose forces are made up of British, German, Belgian, Dutch, Prussian, and Austrian soldiers, lost approximately 15,000 men to death or serious injury. The Prussians lost more than 7,000 men, and an estimated 25,000 French forces are said to have died in battle, with thousands more taken prisoner.

This conflict is the seventh time that an alliance of European countries has been pitted against France. In March this year, Napoleon was declared an outlaw by the Congress of Vienna, and steps were taken to bring his rule to an end.

Despite having more troops and guns than the allied forces, Napoleon's Grande Armée lost the Battle of Waterloo.

Ever the tactician, Napoleon hoped to win the advantage by attacking the Allied armies first, anticipating that by dividing forces he stood a better chance of success. By positioning his men strategically, he was able to prevent Allied forces assisting the Prussians. But he was unable to see the plan through when his generals misinterpreted his orders, and Prussian forces had time to regroup in Wavre.

He then ordered Marshall Grouchy to head north to intercept Blücher's army to stop it combining forces with Wellington. Grouchy did not succeed in this mission and missed the major conflict. This left Napoleon with 30,000 fewer men when they were most needed.

The definitive battle started in the morning, but Napoleon delayed his attack until the rain-soaked ground had dried enough to support the weight of his

The Governor's 1816 Proclamation to Aborigines.

cannon. Unfortunately for him, the soft ground meant that the impact of cannon-fire was significantly lessened. By early evening the Prussians had linked themselves with Wellington's men, and French forces were forced into retreat. Napoleon's time has finally come to an end.

East India Company Has a New Port

Singapore, February 1819: English businessman Sir Thomas Stamford Raffles has established a free trade port in Singapore, which sits at the southern tip of the Malay Peninsula, for the British East India Company. By extending Britain's foreign influence through trade, the East India Company has long acted as a de facto government trading company. Its original charter was to extend trade benefits to India; however, since its inception in 1600, the company has expanded its trading territories and has effectively taken on many of the tasks of colonial government.

The case of Singapore is seen by some as rather daring, as it sits within an area long considered to be under Dutch influence—but Raffles has always been a man of action. He first spent time in Asia when he was a young man, working as the secretary for the company in Penang, and it was then that he recognized the importance of the British having a strong presence in the area, for both strategic and commercial advantage. He also served as the Lieutenant-Governor of Java for five years from 1811 to 1816. Raffles is known to have had his eye on Singapore for some time before he finally came to an agreement with the Sultan of Jahore, whereby he bought the island of Singapore for the British East India Company.

Raffles's no-tax policy in Singapore is already attracting many hundreds of traders to the port, and he is said to have in mind a grand plan to make Singapore one of the biggest ports in the world.

Singapore, destined to become one of the largest ports in the world.

Eleven Killed in Manchester Riot

Manchester, England, August 16, 1819: What was to have been a peaceful demonstration in favor of parliamentary reform, instead turned into a savage riot resulting in the deaths of eleven people and the wounding of many more.

At St Peter's Field today, an estimated crowd of 50,000 gathered to hear speakers from the Manchester Patriotic Union Society, which has been advocating universal suffrage and a repeal of the corn laws. They argue that the corn laws benefit rich landowners rather than ordinary farmers.

Apparently, local magistrates feared that the presence of so many people would lead to riots, and dispatched four squadrons of cavalry, a few hundred infantrymen, and 400 special constables to police the meeting. This was uncalled for, in the opinion of those who came to hear the speakers. One man said that if trouble had been intended, they would hardly have brought their wives and children along.

Wanting the meeting to end, at about 1.30 p.m., the authorities had the Riot Act read out to the crowd, and then had the leaders arrested. Cries of outrage from the people led to them being attacked by armed men, who charged into the crowd brandishing their sabres. In the ensuing fracas, which soon became a bloodbath, eleven people were killed including a woman and child, and about 400 people were injured, many of them women.

The atrocity is expected to receive wide press coverage, as a number of eminent newspapermen were at the meeting. Shocked Manchester residents are now calling the scene of carnage the "Peterloo Massacre," a reference to Wellington's defeat of Napoleon a few years ago.

Massacre in Chios

Chios, Greece, April 2, 1822: The island of Chios in the Aegean Sea has today been almost totally destroyed by Turkish forces working on orders to suppress the independence movement throughout Greece. Countless thousands of people have lost their lives in the massacre. In a particularly brutal attack, Ottoman forces swept across the island, slaughtering anyone in their path. They showed no mercy to women, children, or the elderly. Some 300 people who had sought refuge in the monastery of Agios Minas near Nechori were also ruthlessly killed. Chios is devastated.

The struggle for independence from the Ottoman Empire had its origins in central Greece last year, and the movement has spread quickly throughout the country. Ottoman authorities, however, are unsympathetic to the cause and have been systematically and fiercely suppressing any Greek uprisings. Though fighting has been escalating steadily, Greek leaders are confident that independence will be achieved in the end. Sadly, it will come too late for the island of Chios.

The Liberator Victorious

Lima, Peru, February 10, 1824: Simón Bolívar—the Liberator—has today been named as dictator of Peru. It is the culmination of a long struggle by South American countries for independence from Spain. Bolívar has been leading the struggle for independence for 14 years, having first participated in the 1810 junta that expelled the Spanish governor of Venezuela. When Venezuela's independence was revoked in 1812, Bolívar committed himself to liberating the entire area of New Granada from Spanish rule.

It has been a hard road for Bolívar and his supporters. After a sustained campaign against the Spanish, he reclaimed Venezuela in 1813 and became dictator there. He pushed on to Bogotá, which he took from the Spanish, though they took it back soon after. In 1819, in a tactical inspiration, Bolívar attacked Bogotá from the direction of the Orinoco River and achieved the surrender of the Spanish army. Victorious, Bolívar proclaimed the republic of Gran Colombia.

Though Spanish forces still occupied vast areas of land, Bolívar's persistence resulted in success over Spain in Carabobo, Caracas (Bolívar's home town), Pichincha, and Quito by 1822. Simón Bolívar then set his sights on Peru, which had already been partly liberated through the efforts of independence fighter, General José de San Martin, the "Protector of Peru."

San Martin wanted to secure Peru for himself, and although he shared the same goals as Bolívar, namely liberation from Spain, it is clear that Peru was not big enough for both men. San Martin knew Bolívar's forces were superior to his own and retreated, leaving the way clear for Bolívar to become dictator of the newly proclaimed republic. To the cheers of the people of Lima, Bolívar has promised to make Peru a "free and sovereign" state.

Simón Bolívar

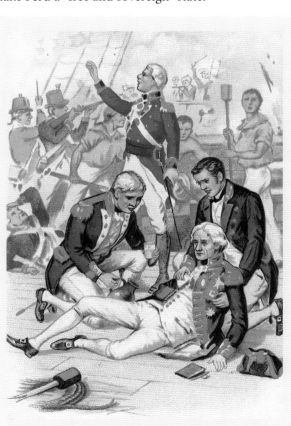

Lord Nelson was fatally wounded at the 1805 Battle of Trafalgar.

Seats of Power

China Qing Dynasty: Jiaqing (reigned 1796–1820); Daoguang (1820–1850).

France First Republic: Consulate (1799–1804) (Napoleon Bonaparte First Consul 1802–1804). First Empire: Napoleon I (1804–1815). Bourbon Restoration: Louis XVIII (reigned 1814–1824); Charles X (1824–1830).

India Mughal Empire: Shah Alam II (reigned 1759–1806); Akbar Shah II (1806–1837).

Japan Edo Period: Kokaku (reigned 1780–1817); Ninko (1817–1846).

Kingdom of Great Britain George III (reigned 1760–1820); George IV (1820–1830).

Ottoman Empire Selim III (reigned 1789–1807); Mustafa IV (1807–1808); Mahmud II (1808–1839).

Portugal Brigantine Dynasty: Maria I and Pedro III (reigned 1777–1816); Joao VI (1816–1826).

Russia Emperors: Paul I (reigned 1796–1801); Alexander I (1801–1825).

Spain Bourbon Dynasty: Charles IV (reigned 1788–1808); Ferdinand VII (1808). French Rule: Joseph Bonaparte (1808–1813). Bourbon Dynasty: Ferdinand VII (reigned 1814–1833).

Thailand Chakri Dynasty: Rama I (reigned 1782–1809); Rama II (1809–1824); Rama III (1824–1851).

Zulu Nation Senzangakhona kaJama (1781–1816); Shaka kaSenzangakhona (1816–1828).

Alessandro Volta

An Electric Invention

Pavia, Italy, March 20, 1800: Physicist and inventor Alessandro Volta has written to Sir Joseph Banks, the President of the Royal Society in London, to inform him of his latest invention—an electric "pile," a battery that produces a steady stream of electricity. A battery is a device that stores up energy until such time that it is needed, so this invention promises to revolutionize both science and society.

Volta has explained that he soaked pieces of cardboard in a salt solution and placed them between alternating circles of copper and zinc. When he attached a wire to both the bottom and top of the "pile," he produced an electric current.

Volta's fascination with electricity is well-known, and in his younger days he was deeply interested in the work of Luigi Galvani, who discovered, in his experiments on frogs, that when two dissimilar metals come into contact with muscles, a contraction of the muscle occurs. Galvani believed that electricity had its source in animals, but Volta disagreed, realizing that an electric current is produced when dissimilar metals come into contact with one another, and that the muscles did not play a role at all. The invention of his electric "pile" has put an end to Galvani's theories and has ensured Volta a lasting place in scientific history.

Alessandro Volta is professor of physics at the University of Pavia, a position that he has held since 1778.

Atomic Theory Proposed

London, England, October 1803: Chemist and physicist John Dalton has proposed a fascinating theory on atoms. Born in Cumberland County, Dalton has found that all matter is made up of tiny indivisible particles called atoms, and that these cannot be destroyed. During his study of the properties of Earth's atmosphere and certain other gases, Dalton came to

The Italian physicist and inventor, Alessandro Volta, demonstrates his new battery for Napoleon Bonaparte.

the conclusion that all the atoms of one element are identical and have the same mass, and that they differ from the atoms of any other element.

He goes on to suggest that when two or more elements are combined, a compound is formed. Dalton uses the example of the combination of oxygen and carbon, where two separate compounds are formed, namely carbon monoxide and carbon dioxide. The final statement in his atomic theory is that when atoms are rearranged, a chemical reaction takes place.

It is well-known in scientific circles that Dalton has been keeping meteorological records for many years, and it is believed that many of his observations in this field provided him with the idea for his atomic theory. For example, while conducting experiments in meteorology, he came to the conclusion that when water evaporates it still exists in the air as a gas. So how, he questioned, could water

and air be in the same place simultaneously, when solid things cannot? This was the catalyst for him to further investigate the properties of gases and he soon came up with the idea that each element must be completely individual.

Of course, Dalton is by no means the first person to "discover" atoms. Since ancient Greek times, scientists have been contemplating the nature of atoms, but it is John Dalton who has made the appropriate investigations. Many scientists are already praising the theory, seeing in it many possible practical uses; others, however, are more sceptical. Dalton's intriguing findings are expected to be published in the near future.

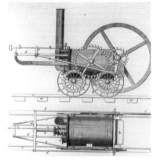

Richard Trevithick's locomotive.

The Power of Steam

Merthyr Tydfil, Wales, February 21, 1804: Engineer Richard Trevithick is a happy man. Today, his steam-powered locomotive has commenced operating out of

Merthyr Tydfil. Trevithick, 33, an inventor of some note, has already developed a high-pressure engine that has been used for raising ore and equipment from mines. He has been working on steam engines for a number of years, and has had a great deal of success using a one-piece boiler and engine.

This new locomotive has been made possible partially through sponsorship. The son of a mining engineer, Trevithick had demonstrated some of his ideas in London last year, and this led to the owner of the Penydarren Ironworks in Merthyr Tydfil, Samuel Homfray, to offer the young inventor some financial backing to help develop his design. The resulting locomotive harnesses the power of high-pressure steam to propel the piston. The steam is then forced up through a chimney, causing the wagons to move.

The maiden run was not completely problem-free: at one point, the locomotive was forced to stop while rocks were moved off the track. However, Trevithick estimates that the locomotive traveled at a speed of 5 miles (8 km) per hour. This will prove of enormous benefit to the ironworks as more than 10 tons of iron and about 80 men can be transported to the canal for unloading. The new technology is safe and effective and is sure to have positive commercial significance.

There are concerns, however, that the locomotive may well prove to be too heavy for the rails, which were designed for the passage of horse-drawn vehicles.

Taking the Steamboat

New York, USA, August 1807: Taking a trip from New York to Albany has never been easier. This month a new commercial steamboat, the *Clermont*, begins operating from New York, traveling up the Hudson River the 150 miles (240 km) to Albany at a speed of about 4½ miles (6.7 km) per hour. The trip takes 32 hours to complete, which includes an overnight stop.

The brainchild of Robert Fulton, the steamboat was constructed in a shipyard on the East River. The boat is 142 ft (43 m) long and 62 ft (19 m) high, and the paddlewheels at the sides are 4 ft (1.2 m) wide with a diameter of 15 ft (4.5 m). The engine, purchased from the British firm of Watt and Boulton, has been specially adapted for the steamboat.

Along with other inventors and engineers, Fulton has been experimenting with steam for some years now. In 1803, with his colleague Robert Livingston, Fulton constructed a steamboat for the Seine River in France, but with limited success. From that time, Fulton was determined to build a successful steamboat that was suitable for passengers and that would be able to complete the trip in record time.

Fulton is delighted with the success of the first trip, saying it "gives me great hopes that such boats may be rendered of great importance to my country." The trip up the Hudson River is sure to become popular, as Fulton and Livingston intend to make passenger comfort a priority. The cabins are roomy and the meals are said to be of first-class standard.

Food Can Now Last Longer

London, England, 1810: Preserving food has always been difficult, but all that is about to change. The introduction of tin-plated containers, or tin cans, specially designed to preserve food for long periods, is bound to change the way we think about food. The merchant Peter Durand has patented a method of packing food in sealed, airtight, tin-plated cans. The cover is soldered on and is best removed with a hammer and chisel.

Durand is said to have based his tin-can method on the work of Frenchman Nicolas Appert, who has been developing ways to keep food fresh in glass containers. It is the airtight factor that has made this idea such a success. Food does not spoil when kept in this airtight environment.

One advantage of the new technology is that soldiers will have a ready supply of good food when they go off to fight in foreign lands. Durand is rumored to be considering selling his patent to willing and able entrepreneurs who can establish a factory to make tin cans.

time out

In 1802, British army officer Henry Shrapnel (1761–1842) develops an explosive apparatus consisting of a hollowed-out cannonball filled with shot. The device becomes known as the "shrapnel shell."

Robert Fulton

Robert Fulton's new commercial steamboat, the *Clermont*.

John MacAdam

> "MACHINES
> ARE THE
> PRODUCE OF
> THE MIND
> OF MAN;
> AND THEIR
> EXISTENCE
> DISTINGUISHES
> THE CIVILIZED
> MAN FROM
> THE SAVAGE."
>
> WILLIAM COBBETT
> (1763–1835), BRITISH
> WRITER, OF THE
> LUDDITES OF
> ENGLAND, 1816

> "THAT
> KNOWLEDGE
> IS NOT
> HAPPINESS,
> AND SCIENCE
> BUT AN
> EXCHANGE OF
> IGNORANCE
> FOR THAT
> WHICH IS
> ANOTHER KIND
> OF IGNORANCE."
>
> GEORGE GORDON,
> LORD BYRON
> (1788–1824), ENGLISH
> POET, 1817

Stephenson's Engine on Track

Killingworth, England, July 25, 1814: The improvements in rail travel are happening at a great pace. Today, a steam railway engine that uses flanged wheels running on the rails, with traction dependent on the contact between the wheel and the rail, has set off for the first time from Killingworth Colliery. In a new take on engine design, the cylinder rods on this new locomotive are connected directly to the wheel disks.

George Stephenson, an enginewright at the Killingworth Colliery, has built this new locomotive, and it promises to change the way we think about railways. The locomotive has been christened the *Blucher*, after the Prussian general Blücher, who helped Wellington defeat Napoleon's forces at Waterloo. This powerful locomotive can pull 30 tons of coal, loaded into eight wagons, at a speed of 4 miles (6.5 km) per hour—a speed it maintains even when ascending slopes.

Stephenson is an enterprising young man. When he heard that enginewrights in other collieries were developing locomotives, he approached the manager of Killingworth Colliery and asked that he be permitted to develop a steam-powered engine of his own—one specifically for hauling coal.

Born in 1781 near Newcastle-upon-Tyne in the north of England, Stephenson has been interested in engines and other mechanical devices since boyhood. He taught himself to read and write, and as a teenager he started work in a local colliery. By the time he was 20 he was an engineman. His penchant for taking engines apart and reconstructing them taught him a great deal about engines and

he eventually became an enginewright. That Stephenson is good at his work is an understatement—the *Blucher* is the most successful railway engine seen in Britain to date. Certainly not one to rest on this success, Stephenson is already talking about making further improvements to his locomotive.

Better Roads from MacAdam

Bristol, England, 1817: The Scottish engineer John MacAdam has developed a brand new process for building roads, making them smoother and harder, and thus more efficient. As an estate owner, MacAdam has found today's roads quite insufficient for their purpose and he set himself the task of improving the system of road building. He has already published an article concerning roads—in 1816, he wrote *Remarks on the Present System of Road Making*. Following his appointment last year to the position of surveyor to the Bristol Turnpike Trust, MacAdam began remaking the roads using his new method.

MacAdam believes that roads need to be higher than the surrounding ground, and made from layers of rocks, crushed stones, and gravel. The largest stones are placed at the bottom, topped by a layer of smaller stones, and finished off with gravel on the surface. A cast-iron roller is then rolled over the road to make it smooth and to compress the layers.

By digging ditches along the sides of the road, MacAdam also ensures that any excess rainwater will drain away from the road, so the underlying foundations will not be disturbed.

John MacAdam was born in 1756 in Ayr. While in his teens, he moved to New York, where he lived and worked for many years. He returned to Scotland in 1783, when he bought his estate at Sauchrie. There is much interest in his new road-building method, which is expected to be called "macadamization."

The late James Watt, best known for his work on steam engines.

Inventor James Watt Dead at 83

Heathfield, England, August 19, 1819: The Scottish inventor and engineer James Watt died today, aged 83. He will probably be best remembered for his radical improvements to steam engine technology and his establishment of a steam engine factory, this in partnership with Matthew Boulton. His early engines were mainly used by collieries to pump water from the mines; however, his later engines were more sophisticated, had a greater number of applications, and soon found their way into factories and mines all around the country.

Watt began his illustrious career as an instrument-maker, setting himself up in business in Glasgow in the 1750s. His interests soon turned to steam and the power it can produce: when he was fixing a model engine designed by Thomas Newcomen in the 1760s, he realized that he had ideas for improving it. Observing that most of the heat of the steam was used for heating the cylinder, he designed an engine that consisted of a separate condensing chamber that stopped that steam being lost. This increased steam pressure and resulted in a stronger and more efficient engine.

Over the years Watt made further improvements on the steam engine, and in 1774 he entered into a very successful business partnership with Matthew Boulton. Based in Birmingham, their factory produced reliable, economically viable engines that in no time made the pair quite wealthy.

Among Watt's other inventions were an apparatus for copying letters and a new way of measuring distances using

Crowds inspect George Stephenson's new locomotive. Advances in rail travel are steaming ahead.

a telescope. Watt's work has been instrumental in changing the face of industry in Britain and overseas.

Rosetta Stone Deciphered

Grenoble, France, 1822: The mysteries of the Rosetta Stone have been solved. Egyptologist Jean-François Champollion has been working industriously on deciphering the stone's messages for a number of years, continuing the work begun by Englishman Thomas Young.

The stone itself was found by Captain Pierre Boussard in 1799, in the Egyptian port of Rosetta, and was brought to the Institut de l'Egypte in Cairo; in 1802, it was taken to the British Museum in London. Its significance was quickly recognized and scholars and linguists have been working ever since to unlock its meaning. The stone is made of granite and contains text in demotic Egyptian, Greek, and hieroglyphics. It didn't take long for Egyptologists to recognize that the Greek text was actually a translation of the hieroglyphs.

Using the Greek text as the starting point, and determining that the demotic Egyptian script was used primarily for secular records, Champollion was able to translate the hieroglyphics and hence decipher the code.

The Rosetta Stone is now dated March 196 BCE, the ninth year of the reign of Ptolemy V. It contains a list of honors conferred on the pharaoh and details the siege of Lycopolis, as well as the great benefits that Ptolemy had provided for the temples. The main part of the text concerns the establishment of a cult to the pharaoh.

But why the three texts? The Ptolemies were of Greek origin and although they had held power in Egypt for over one hundred years, they still regarded themselves as Greek, and Greek was the official language. Demotic Egyptian is a later form of early Egyptian using Greek characters. And hieroglyphs were used for formal writing. Interestingly, the stone itself instructs that the text should be set in stone in the three scripts.

The work of Jean-François Champollion's will now act as a foundation for further understanding of the ancient Egyptian language.

The Egyptologist, Jean-François Champollion.

Morphine comes from the opium poppy.

Waterproof!

Glasgow, Scotland, 1823: A new waterproof garment, ideal for walking in the rain, has just been patented, the invention of a young chemist, Charles Macintosh. He has been experimenting with naphtha, a by-product of coal-tar distillation, and he found that he could join a thin sheet of India rubber over a woollen fabric by dissolving the rubber in the naphtha, thus creating a waterproof cloth.

He came about this remarkable process while he was attempting to find uses for the waste products of Glasgow's gasworks. One of the other waste products, ammonia, he used to produce cudbear, a purple dye obtained from lichen. This allows the coloring of a range of fabrics.

There are still a few teething problems with the garment, as careless sewing can allow rain to get into the cloth, but it looks as if the "raincoat" or "macintosh" will become a part of everyone's wardrobe.

The Blind Can See!

Paris, France, 1824: A young inventor, Louis Braille, only 15 years old, has devised a groundbreaking method that allows blind and partially blind people to read and write by using just six raised embossed dots that correspond to letters of the alphabet. It is a vast improvement on the raised dots method taught at his school, the Royal Institution for Blind Youth, and a clever modification of a system employed by the military in which twelve raised dots are used as a "night" language—soldiers can read information without having to speak. In addition, although the blind have been able to read some texts using the earlier methods, they have not been able to write. Braille's raised dots allow them to do this.

Blind since the age of four, as the result of an infection following an accident in his father's workshop, Braille has avoided feeling sorry for himself. He is determined not to miss out on the world of intellectual pursuit simply because he cannot see. Over the last couple of years, he painstakingly created his reading method for the blind using a stitching awl, ironically the very tool that caused him to go blind. Braille is hoping to publish his system to make it available to as many people as possible.

So how does it work? Each letter is represented by a dot or a number of dots placed in a certain position. Once the positions have been learned, reading and writing is possible, even without eyes.

George Stephenson

Scientific Achievements

Astronomy: Asteroids Ceres and Pallas discovered; irregularities in the orbit of Uranus noted.
Botany: Rubber used to create waterproof fabrics.
Ecology: World population grows to 1 billion.
Geology: First geological survey of eastern USA completed.
Mathematics: Bases of differential geometry laid.
Medicine: Anesthetic properties of nitrous oxide detected; stethoscope invented; discovery that hemophilia is restricted to males but passed on by unaffected females.
Physics: Infrared and ultraviolet radiations discovered; wave nature of light presented.

Botanic Gardens
Bogor, Dutch East Indies
Glasgow, Scotland
Nikitsky, Ukraine
Oslo, Norway
Port of Spain, Trinidad
Sydney, Australia

Observatories
Cambridge, England

Universities
University of Bonn, Germany
University of Ljubljana, eastern Europe
University of Montreal, Canada
University of Oslo, Norway
University of Warsaw, Poland

Johann Wolfgang
von Goethe

Napoleon's Arch of Triumph

Paris, France, 1806: At the height of his military career, Napoleon Bonaparte has commissioned the construction of an impressive arch to commemorate his victory at Austerlitz, to honor his army, and also to serve as a rallying point for Parisians. It is to be built in the center of Paris, at the top of the Avenue Champs Elysées. Napoleon, an admirer of Roman architecture, has ordered that the arch be styled on classical models and has asked the architect Jean François Chalgrin to draw up plans for its erection.

Napoleon has made it quite clear that he wants the Arc de Triomphe, as he is calling it, to be the largest triumphal arch in the world. It is to be an amazing 165 ft (50 m) high and 148 ft (45 m) wide, which will surely guarantee the arch's place as a future city landmark. When it is finished, the Arc de Triomphe will feature striking sculptured reliefs depicting magnificent scenes of French military glory.

Compendious Dictionary Published

New Haven, Connecticut, USA, 1806: Lexicographer and journalist Noah Webster has this year published *The Compendious Dictionary of the English Language* to wide acclaim. Webster is a strong advocate for American books for American people, and the dictionary is a natural follow-up to his three-volume *A Grammatical Institute of the English Language*, consisting of a speller, a grammar, and reader, which were published in the 1780s and aimed primarily at American school children.

Until now, the only dictionaries published in the United States have had English authors. This new dictionary is the first dictionary with an American emphasis. It is being hailed by linguists and scholars for a number of reasons, one of which is Webster's revised spelling and pronunciation to accommodate American usage. He avoids using British spelling where he feels that the American version is easier and more logical; so, for example, Webster defines "center" not "centre," and "harbor" not "harbour." For the first time, the letters "I" and "J" have separate entries, as do the letters "V" and "U."

Another innovation that is evident in this new dictionary is the inclusion of various technical terms relating to science and technology. This is a genuine shift away from the choice of words based purely on their appearance in literary contexts.

A further striking feature of this new dictionary is that it contains approximately 5,000 more words than appear in Samuel Johnson's ground-breaking English dictionary published in 1755.

A respected journalist, Noah Webster founded the first daily newspaper in New York—*American Minerva*—back in 1793, and has been involved in other current affairs publications since that time. Not one to rest on his laurels, Webster has already started work on a second dictionary, which he intends to be even more comprehensive than *The Compendious Dictionary of the English Language* and to more fully document American usages.

Devil of a Story

Weimar, Germany, 1808: There is a new star in Germany's literary firmament—Johann Wolfgang von Goethe has just published *Faust: der tragödie erster teil (Faust: A Tragedy)*, a fresh retelling of the story of the legendary Faust and his unnatural pact with the forces of darkness, represented by the menacing figure of Mephistopheles.

Goethe himself is a versatile poet, dramatist, and novelist, and he has plans to write a second part to this epic work over the next few years.

Commissioned by Napoleon in 1806, the magnificent Arc de Triomphe was completed almost 30 years later.

Key Events

Faust begins with the prologue in Heaven which brings to mind the Book of Job, where the Lord, as part of a challenge, gives the Devil permission to test the honesty and morality of Faust. Giving Faust his youth back, and setting him on a path of pleasure, Mephistopheles makes a deal with the elderly Faust—if he experiences pure happiness and contentment, he must forfeit his soul. Along the way, he betrays the love of an innocent girl and causes her death. Faust then seeks more intellectual pursuits and although he encounters Helen of Troy, he still does not achieve contentment.

Grown old once more, Faust attempts to reclaim land from the sea, an enterprise that gives him no return except for the benefits it confers on the local people. It is then that Faust finds true happiness and redemption. And so Mephistopheles is cheated of Faust's soul.

Goethe's work is a rich commentary on the search for meaning in life, and his poetic expression and superior storytelling will grant this book lasting appeal.

Byron's Brain-Childe

London, England, 1812: Fans of poet Lord Byron are in for a treat. His new work *Childe Harold's Pilgrimage* is being praised by critics and readers alike. Byron evokes strong images of exotic places in this epic poem that follows the travels and musings of the world-weary young Harold. His vivid descriptions of bullfights in Spain, of Muslim minarets, and of snow-capped mountains are just the remedy for readers looking for adventure without having to leave their armchairs. This is particularly relevant these days, as various conflicts with the French have made it rather more difficult for the English to travel abroad.

The English poet Lord Byron.

Those who know Byron recognize some biographical elements to the poem, something that Byron himself has not denied. He has traveled extensively throughout the Mediterranean and other parts of Europe and he uses his experiences to add a rich flavor to his poem.

Byron has chosen to write *Childe Harold's Pilgrimage* in Spenserian stanzas, which follow a strict rhyme pattern, and consist of eight iambic pentameters, and one alexandrine (a 12-syllable iambic). So far the poet has published two of an expected four cantos. Byron further acknowledges his debt to Spenser by the use of a number of archaic words, such as "whilome," which, readers will know, appears in the first line of Spenser's classic *Faerie Queen*.

One unexpected outcome of the poem's publication is that Byron, who is 24, has become a sensation—he is now the darling of high society.

Rossini's *Barber* Opens

Rome, Italy, February 20, 1816: Gioacchino Rossini's new opera, *The Barber of Seville*, premièred tonight at the Argentine Theater, with the composer himself conducting the orchestra. Based on the 1775 play by Frenchman Pierre Beaumarchais, and with a fine libretto by Cesare Sterbini, this comic opera promises to be a hit, although opening night was not without its problems!

When Rossini came onstage, he was booed by hecklers: The tenor's aria had not finished and instead he sang a Spanish folk song; the baritone playing Basilio fell and was left with a bleeding nose; later a cat walked onstage, causing further mayhem.

The young composer, who was born in 1792 in Pesaro, already has a string of operas to his credit and he is said to have written the entire score for tonight's production in three weeks! In spite of the speed with which he wrote the opera, the individual arias are very polished, although it appears that he has occasionally borrowed themes from some of his earlier work. Even the overture, with its energetic rhythms, owes something to the composer's earlier operas.

The story concerns the barber, Figaro, and his efforts to help his former boss Count Almaviva win the heart of Rosina from her strict guardian Bartolo, who wishes to marry her himself so he can claim her fortune. There are disguises and various comic maneuvers put into effect before the story reaches its comic climax.

Gioacchino Rossini

An illustration for the Brothers Grimm story, "Sleeping Beauty."

Franz Schubert

> "WHENEVER
> BOOKS ARE
> BURNED MEN
> ALSO IN THE
> END ARE
> BURNED."
>
> HEINRICH HEINE
> (1797–1856), GERMAN
> POET, 1821

> "LANGUAGE IS
> NOT AN
> ABSTRACT
> CONSTRUCTION
> OF THE
> LEARNED, OR
> OF DICTIONARY
> MAKERS, BUT
> IS SOMETHING
> ARISING OUT
> OF THE WORK,
> NEEDS, TIES,
> JOYS, AFFEC-
> TIONS, TASTES,
> OF LONG
> GENERATIONS
> OF HUMANITY,
> AND HAS ITS
> BASES BROAD
> AND LOW,
> CLOSE TO
> THE GROUND."
>
> NOAH WEBSTER
> (1758–1843), AMERICAN
> WRITER AND
> LEXICOGRAPHER

Austen Novels Published Posthumously

England, 1818: Only months after the death of the novelist Jane Austen, two new books have been published by her brother Henry Austen. Interestingly, it is only now, after her death, that the authorship of her novels has been revealed. Readers may be surprised to learn that *Sense and Sensibility*, *Emma*, *Mansfield Park*, and *Pride and Prejudice* are all the works of this most remarkable woman.

The first of these new novels is *Northanger Abbey*, which is a satire on the Gothic romances that were popular in England around the turn of the century, when Austen penned this work. She apparently sold it to a bookseller in Bath, who did nothing to promote it and sold it back to Henry Austen upon his request. *Persuasion* is the last novel Jane Austen completed before her death at the age of just forty-one years.

Northanger Abbey is set in Bath, where Austen herself lived for a few years, and is the story of a young woman by the name of Catherine Morland, who loves to socialize. At one gathering she meets Henry Tilney, who invites her to stay at his medieval home, Northanger Abbey. There she lets her imagination run away with her, fancying that the abbey is full of mystery, which is far from the truth. It is an engaging book, made all the more pleasing by Austen's wonderful characterizations.

Persuasion is also set in Bath, and tells the story of one Anne Elliot who allows herself to be persuaded to give up the man she loves. It takes eight long years for the couple to become reconciled. This final book, which is shorter than any of the other novels, is notable for its beautiful descriptive passages.

Austen's novels are quite different from other books currently being published. She illustrates—in intricate detail—the various aspects of ordinary everyday life, and employs humorous turns of phrase. The result is most enjoyable and it is likely that the number of Austen's fans will increase with the passage of time.

Ancient Aphrodite Statue Found by Peasant

Melos, Greece, 1820: An ancient marble statue of the goddess Aphrodite has been discovered on the Greek island of Melos.

It stands well over 6½ ft (2 m) high, and is striking because the arms have long since vanished. Its grace and elegant beauty have led experts to speculate that the statue is the work of the famous Greek sculptor Praxiteles, although this has yet to be confirmed.

The tale of the discovery of the marble Aphrodite, or Venus, is as romantic as the goddess herself. A peasant named Yorgos on the Aegean island of Melos discovered the statue in an underground cave, hoping to keep his find secret. But almost immediately it was confiscated by Turkish authorities. A French naval officer then quickly arranged for it to be transported to Paris.

The *Venus de Milo*, which has been found on the Greek island of Melos.

Art specialists and ordinary people alike are hypothesizing as to what aspect of the goddess the statue represents. Classical scholars are suggesting that Aphrodite was originally holding an apple. This is symbolic because Paris presented her with an apple before he abducted Helen, which was the catalyst for the Trojan War, and also because the island's name, Melos, happens to mean "apple" in Greek.

Already, this priceless work of art is being referred to as the "Venus de Milo," and there are rumors that it will be housed in the Louvre Museum in Paris.

Who is Geoffrey Crayon?

England, February 1820: *The Sketch Book of Geoffrey Crayon* contains a number of wonderful short stories, including two that have caused something of a sensation in literary circles. The first story, "Rip Van Winkle," which was published last year, is set in the Catskill Mountains, New York, and tells the tale of a man who, in order to get away from his nagging wife, takes himself up to the mountains. Following some fascinating adventures, he takes a nap under a tree, only to wake up 20 years later. The story is humorous and whimsical, yet instructive—when Rip awakens he has no idea that the Revolutionary War has even taken place.

"The Legend of Sleepy Hollow" also features a memorable hero—Ichabod Crane, who has much to contend with in the pursuit of love. He woos a local girl, Katrina, but is forced to run away in fear as he is chased by the Headless Horseman. It is a story with plenty of action and forms the last piece in the final instalment of the *Sketch Book*.

But who is Geoffrey Crayon? Many clues lie in the writing itself. The author clearly has a deep interest in the Revolutionary War and his descriptions of the American countryside suggest his roots are, in fact, American. Indeed, there are some who believe that Geoffrey Crayon is Washington Irving, who is not only a writer, but a diplomat. Irving left the United States in May 1815 to travel and work in England and Europe. He was the attaché to the American Legation in Madrid, and is reportedly keen to take up a similar position in London. Irving was born in New York in 1783, and trained as a lawyer before setting off on his travels.

Royal Pavilion Completed after Seven Years

Brighton, England, 1822: The architect John Nash has at last finished his rebuilding of the Royal Pavilion, or Brighton Pavilion, as it is known. The pavilion was originally

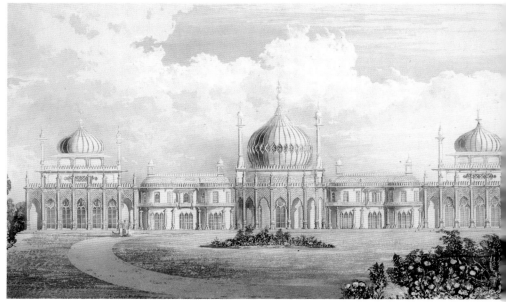

Brighton Pavilion was rebuilt for King George IV, who first visited the seaside town for health reasons.

Percy Bysshe Shelley drowned on July 8, 1822.

a large villa, and King George IV commissioned Nash to convert it into a palace. The king intends for it to be his seaside retreat, although there are rumors that he will also be entertaining his wife, Mrs Fitzherbert, there. The king's marriage is considered void due to the fact that his wife is a Catholic.

Using many and varied elements from India and the Far East in his design, Nash has created a truly impressive structure that is sure to enhance his reputation. The most striking feature about the palace is its exterior, which conjures up images of India and other exotic locales.

Nash has been engaged on the project since 1815. He has made other significant contributions to English architecture, including Marylebone Park.

Schubert Publishes Song Cycle, or "Lieder"

Vienna, Austria, 1824: Composer Franz Schubert has published a haunting and lyrical song cycle based on the poems of Wilhelm Müller. Entitled *Die schöne Müllerin (The Beautiful Millmaid)*, the work is performed by a pianist and a solo male singer, in this case a tenor. A song cycle, or "lieder," as it is known in German, is a group of romantic songs with the same theme—they are intended to be sung in sequence and should be performed as one work, rather than being broken up into individual songs.

This has been a very productive year for Schubert. He has also published a beautiful string quartet called *Der tod und das mädchen (Death and the Maiden)* and his Octet in F, which has been most favorably received by the public.

Born in 1797, Franz Schubert has been a driving force in German music since he was a young man. Unfortunately, however, the composer has contracted

syphilis, a very debilitating disease that causes him to spend long periods of time resting in bed.

Die schöne Müllerin is Schubert's first song cycle, and if this is any indication of what is to come, fans no doubt will be eagerly waiting for more.

A Joyous New Symphony

Vienna, Austria, May 8, 1824: Acclaimed German composer Ludwig von Beethoven, aged 54, conducted his new symphony at a concert last night at the Kärntnerthor Theater in Vienna. His ninth symphony, it is a significant departure for Beethoven, as he is using a full choir, as well as soloists, for the finale, which is based on the poem *"An Die Freude"* ("Ode to Joy") by the poet Friedrich von Schiller. The première is a real coup for Vienna—the composer had wanted it to debut in Berlin, but he is reported to have been disillusioned by what he perceived as a lack of interest in his work in Germany. He blames the popularity of Rossini's music for the decline in enthusiasm for his own work in his own country.

Music critics are aware that the new symphony is in D Minor and that it is dedicated to King Friedrich Wilhelm III of Prussia. The final movement is not only spectacular, but wonderfully uplifting. It is the first time voices have been put on the same footing as the instruments in the orchestra. Musicologists are praising Beethoven's symphonic innovations. He has moved away from the strict order that defines the symphonies of Haydn and Mozart, and given the genre more freedom, and this was undoubtedly evident in last night's musical offering.

Unfortunately, over the years the composer himself has suffered a steady loss in hearing, and is now totally deaf. In a moving moment on stage last night, one of the singers had to turn Beethoven around so that he faced the audience—although he was not able to hear their applause, at least he could see it.

Beethoven is also in poor health, suffering, among other things, severe stomach cramps. The composer's deafness, however, has not impaired his creativity or his compositional faculties, as is witnessed by some of the notable works he has composed since the onset

Key Structures

Acheen St Mosque, Georgetown, Malaya
Cadman's Cottage, Sydney, Australia
Char Minar, Bukhara, Uzbekistan
Citadel, Hue, Vietnam
City Walls, Acre, Israel
Dulwich Gallery, London, England
Grande Mosquee, Mopti, Mali
Hunting Lodge, Antonin, Germany
Hyde Park Barracks, Sydney, Australia
La Moneda, Santiago, Chile
Lamu Fort, Lamu, Kenya
Malacanang Palace, Manila, Philippines
Masjid Kapitan Keling, Penang, Malaya
Milan Cathedral, Milan, Italy
Notre-Dame Basilica, Montreal, Canada
Phung Son Pagoda, Ho Chi Minh City, Vietnam
Royal (Brighton) Pavilion, Brighton, England
St Anne's Church, Vilnius, Lithuania
San Francisco de Asis, Rancho de Taos, USA
Sans Souci Palace, Milot, Haiti
Schauspielhaus, Berlin, Germany
Siddhivinayak Temple, Mumbai, India
Thai Hoa Palace, Hue, Vietnam
The Citadelle, Cap-Haitien, Haiti
Twelve Prophets, Congonhas, Brazil
Wat Si Saket, Vientiane, Laos
Wat That Luang, Luang Prabang, Laos
White House, Washington DC, USA

Jane Austen

of deafness. His Symphony No. 7 is a masterpiece, as are his piano sonatas, piano concertos, and string quartets.

This latest work by Beethoven, Symphony No. 9, or "The Chorale" as many are already calling it, is expected to be performed in London next year.

Beethoven, who published his first symphony in 1800, at the age of 30.

John Jay

Extra! Extra! New Paper Published

New York, USA, November 16, 1801: A brand new newspaper has hit the stands today. The *New York Evening Post* promises in-depth analysis of all the latest current affairs, as well as informed commentary on the important happenings in government and industry. Births, deaths, and marriages will also be reported.

Founded by two local men, Alexander Hamilton and John Jay, the paper will also espouse federalist views, which favor strong representation both by the people and of the people. John Jay is a politician and jurist, and a former chief justice of New York. He co-wrote the *Federalist Papers* with Alexander Hamilton, who is also a politician, writer, and lawyer. In that publication, which consists of a series of separate articles, the authors wrote strongly in favor of ratifying the Constitution of the United States.

The inaugural editor of the *New York Evening Post*, which will come out daily, is Boston-born William Coleman, 35, an experienced journalist who practiced as a lawyer for some years before turning his hand to journalism. Coleman is also a believer in the federalist cause. He is known for his even-handedness and as such is an excellent choice as editor.

It will be interesting to see whether the new daily newspaper will effect any lasting social change on the city.

Military Academy Opens its Doors

New York, USA, July 4, 1802: The United States Military Academy opened today at West Point on the Hudson River with a great deal of fanfare. Situated approximately 50 miles (80 km) from the city of New York, the new military academy

West Point, location of the United States Military Academy.

promises to become the country's premier training institution for the armed forces.

The academy has already had a long history, the location having been chosen by George Washington during the Revolutionary War. He felt it was of prime strategic importance, given its vantage points over the river, and had fortifications built there. He also ordered the laying of a chain across the river between Constitution Island and West Point to obstruct any British ships coming up the Hudson. Although this was never needed, it showed great foresight. West Point soon became the permanent stronghold of Washington's forces.

Washington was keen to establish a military academy on the site, first lobbying for it back in 1783, but his efforts to make it a reality were blocked by the then Secretary of State, Thomas Jefferson, who believed such an establishment went against the principles of democracy. Ironically, when Jefferson took on the presidency in 1800, he agreed to the founding of the academy, and Congress passed an Act establishing the United States Military Academy in March of this year.

As well as providing training to cadets for entry into the cavalry and the infantry, and also officer training, West Point is offering military engineering and science courses. In fact, West Point is the first engineering school in the United States. Military experts believe that a sound knowledge of engineering and the "useful sciences" is absolutely critical for an effective army. Already, both politicians and academics are predicting that the United States Military Academy will soon achieve a solid reputation for engineering studies.

Woman Competes in Horse Race

York, England, August 25, 1804: In a first in racing history, a woman rode a horse in the four-mile course in York today. Alicia Meynell, sometimes called the "Norwich Nymph," sat sidesaddle on Vingarillo, a horse from Colonel Thornton's stable. She looked splendid, wearing a leopard ensemble, complete with racing cap.

In an exciting race, Meynell competed against Captain William Flint and she was leading most of the way. It was only in the last mile of the race that Captain Fleet

Until now, only men have competed in horse races in England.

Washington DC, USA, November 1, 1800: President John Adams moves into the almost-completed White House.

Philadelphia, USA, 1800: William Young designs shoes specifically for left and right feet.

Cane Ridge, Kentucky, USA, August, 1801: Presbyterian pastor Reverend Barton Stone hosts a revival meeting attended by about 20,000 people.

West Point, New York, USA, July 4, 1802: The United States Military Academy opens.

Gloucester, England, 1802: Robert Raikes retires as editor of the *Gloucester Journal*, the family paper in which he publicized Sunday schools.

Hue, Vietnam, 1802: Newly enthroned Emperor Gia Long gives free rein to French Catholic missionaries to preach in Vietnam.

Sydney, Australia, March 5, 1803: The first issue of *The Sydney Gazette and New South Wales Advertiser*, Australia's first newspaper, is published.

York, England, August 25, 1804: Alicia Meynell becomes the first woman to compete in a horse race.

London, England, 1804: The British and Foreign Bible Society is founded.

Champagne, France, October 1805: Champagne maker François Clicquot dies. His widow takes over the family business.

France, January, 1806: The Gregorian calendar comes back into effect, replacing the French Revolutionary calendar.

London, England, January 28, 1807: Pall Mall becomes the first street to have gas lighting.

London, England, February 23, 1807: About 40,000 people watch the hanging of murderers John Holloway, Owen Haggerty, and Elizabeth Godfrey. Several people are trampled to death.

Wales, March 25, 1807: The first regular passenger service in the world is established by the Swansea and Mumbles Railway.

Philadelphia, USA, 1807: Townsend Speakman mixes fruit flavoring with carbonated water and sells the new soft drink in his drugstore.

Macau, China, 1807: Robert Morrison, the first Protestant missionary in China, and translator of the Bible into Chinese, arrives in Macau.

New Jersey, USA, 1807: A Bill rescinds the right of women and black men to vote.

Paris, France, July 20, 1808: Napoleon decrees that all French Jews must take permanent family surnames.

Devon, England, 1809: Dartmoor Prison begins operation as a prisoner of war facility.

A copper foundry at Swansea, the starting point for the new railway service.

John Adams

managed to get the better of her and went on to take line honors. Meynell is said to have taken this rather badly indeed, and has accused the captain of discourtesy.

Alicia Meynell is reported to be the long-time mistress of Colonel Thornton, who placed a very large wager on the race. Sources put the figure at 1,000 guineas, but this has not been confirmed.

Meynell's appearance in the saddle has raised a few eyebrows, so it will be very interesting to see whether more female jockeys will now enter race meetings.

Regular Passenger Service Established

Swansea, Wales, March 25, 1807: Rail travel has taken on a whole new meaning today with the first regular train service to carry passengers from Swansea to Mumbles, a village near Oystermouth in the south of the country. The service is being hailed as the first railway passenger service in the world—a grand claim, yet true!

The railway line between Swansea and Oystermouth began in 1804. It was then that the government recognized the need for such a line to transport supplies such as coal and iron ore, there being no roads linking the two towns. The first tracks consisted of lengths of iron about 3 ft (0.9 m) long, set into granite blocks. By spring of last year, horse-drawn cars were making the journey between Swansea and Mumbles.

The railway line has been operating for a year or so now, but the beginning of the passenger service heralds a whole new era for Great Britain. The person who came up with the exciting notion of creating a regular passenger service along the line is one Benjamin French, who paid the Oystermouth Railway Company the amount of 20 pounds for the rights to convey passengers. There are sure to be great social and commercial changes associated with the new service.

The Swansea and Mumbles Railway, as it is being called, is attracting a great deal of attention both at home and abroad. Social commentators are already predicting that it won't be long before "I'm taking the Mumbles train" becomes a local catchphrase.

The Sûreté: A New Force for Law and Order

Paris, France, 1811: A new police force dedicated entirely to detective work has just been established in Paris. Called the Brigade de la Sûreté (the "Security Brigade"), it is headed by Eugène François Vidocq, who is eminently qualified for the role. Vidocq is a former criminal, having spent the better part of his youth living on the wrong side of the law—as a thief, a highwayman, and forger, among other things. He has served time in prison and it was during one of these periods that he decided to work for the law rather than against it. He was engaged by the police as a spy, and later began regular police work. Vidocq soon became so adept at catching wrongdoers that he was the first choice to head the Sûreté.

Vidocq's firsthand knowledge of the criminal mind undoubtedly gives him an edge over other investigating police officers, and he is also reported to have employed a number of ex-convicts for his force, reasoning that their experiences and knowledge of the criminal underworld make them better equipped to hunt down law breakers. The new chief prefers his officers to wear civilian clothes in order that they appear less conspicuous. Vidocq, a master of disguise himself, believes that surveillance is more effective when it is not obvious, and few can argue with that logic. He also has other radical ideas, including taking the fingerprints of suspected criminals.

Inside sources reveal that Vidocq, who is 36, insists on accurate record-keeping, and has an interest in inks and papers. Criminologists will be watching Vidocq and the new Sûreté with interest.

Emma Hamilton died penniless ten years after Lord Nelson's death.

Key Events

London, England, May 21, 1810: Charles Chevalier d'Éon de Beaumont, French spy and transvestite, dies, aged 81.

Musselburgh, Scotland, December 14, 1810: Musselburgh Golf Club promises a prize for the best female golfer, the first recorded women's golf competition.

Paris, France, 1811: Eugène François Vidocq is appointed as the first head of the Sûreté of Paris.

Canton, China, 1811: Annual imports of opium into China from India reach 5,000 chests.

Thistleton Gap, England, 1811: The bare-knuckle boxer Tom Cribb defeats freed slave Tom Molineaux in the British heavyweight championship bout.

Moscow, Russia, September, 1812: The city is almost destroyed by fires.

York, England, January, 1813: A judicial commission sentences 17 Luddites to death by hanging, others to be deported to prison in Australia.

Liverpool, England, July 9, 1813: The *Liverpool Mercury* becomes the first newspaper to publish a chess column.

London, England, February, 1814: The last Frost Fair is held on ice over the River Thames. Stalls sell food and drink, and dancing and donkey rides are offered.

Bay of Islands, New Zealand, December 25, 1814: Samuel Marsden conducts the first Christian service.

Calais, France, January 15, 1815: Emma Hamilton, mistress of Lord Horatio Nelson, dies, aged about 50.

London, England, July 1816: The waltz is introduced to the English court. *The Times* warns parents against "so fatal a contagion."

New Orleans, USA, 1819: Dentist Levi Spear Parmly publishes *A Practical Guide to the Management of the Teeth*, recommending flossing.

Virginia, USA, 1819: Slaves banned from learning to read and write.

Vienna, Austria, 1819: In a book, Johann Wilhelm Klein suggests training guide dogs for blind people.

Adams, Massachusetts, USA, February 15, 1820: Susan Anthony, women's rights activist, is born.

France, 1822: Louis Bernard Rabaut develops a coffee machine that uses steam pressure.

Vermont, USA, 1823: Alexander Lucius Twilight is the first African-American to graduate from college.

Palmyra, New York, USA, 1823: Joseph Smith tells his father the angel Moroni appeared to him.

London, England, June 16, 1824: The Society for the Prevention of Cruelty to Animals is formed, with Arthur Broome as the first secretary.

Canton, China, 1824: Ruan Yuan founds the *Xuehaitang* (Sea of Learning) Academy, a school that focuses on classical studies.

Moscow Burns!

Moscow, September 17, 1812: The city of Moscow has been ablaze for days now—fires have destroyed almost two-thirds of the city. As most of the buildings here are made of wood, there is little hope that anything much will remain standing. The fire has been spreading quickly and those who have remained in the city are finding it a truly horrendous sight. Churches, cathedrals, and fine homes have all been consumed by the relentless blaze.

Reliable reports say that patriotic Russians were responsible for the fires—they refuse to relinquish their city into the hands of the enemy and want to make it impossible for Napoleon Bonaparte's forces to find shelter in the ravaged city. It has been a planned strategy. The city's governor, Fyodor Rostopchin, has ordered that Muscovites evacuate the city—current estimates suggest that only about 25,000 people, or 10 percent of the city's population, are still in Moscow.

When Napoleon entered Moscow on September 14, he was surprised to find it empty. Many of his soldiers, however, took this as a cue for widespread looting, and discipline has been dificult to restore. One consequence of the burning is that there is little for the French to steal. Muscovites would rather their capital city be demolished than become a French conquest.

It has been a very long campaign for Napoleon, who began the invasion in June of this year by marching into Poland. By the time of the Battle of Borodino earlier this month, it was clear that French forces were superior and the Russian army was forced to retreat, leaving the way clear for Napoleon to march into Moscow and take over. But the French had not counted on Russian national fervor, and reinforcements joined the army in large numbers.

Napoleon Bonaparte

> "THE INTEREST OF THE LAND-LORD IS ALWAYS OPPOSED TO THE INTERESTS OF EVERY OTHER CLASS IN THE COMMUNITY."
>
> DAVID RICARDO
> (1772–1823),
> ENGLISH POLITICAL
> ECONOMIST, 1817

> "TRUTH HAS ALWAYS BEEN FOUND TO PROMOTE THE BEST INTERESTS OF MANKIND."
>
> PERCY BYSSHE SHELLEY
> (1792–1822),
> ENGLISH POET

Pope Pius VII, who died on August 20, 1823.

The evacuation and burning of Moscow has proved to be the decisive point in the war against the French. It is now thought that Napoleon will return to Paris.

Marquis de Sade Dead

Charenton, France, December 2, 1814: Today the death was announced of the notorious writer Donatien Alphonse François de Sade, the Marquis de Sade, at the age of 74 years. The son of a count, de Sade will be remembered for his outrageous erotic writings, some of which contain lurid descriptions of brutal torture.

A well-known libertine, de Sade is said to have had affairs with both men and women. He was eventually imprisoned on charges of sodomy and poisoning and it was there that he began to write his infamous books, which were published anonymously. He spent from 1770 until 1790 in a number of prisons, and was finally released following the Revolution.

It was the publication of *Juliette, or Vice Amply Rewarded* that brought him to the attention of Napoleon, who, in 1801, ordered his imprisonment without trial. The novel that so incensed Napoleon concerns a young girl, Juliette, who lives a debauched lifestyle, wantonly engaging in sexual misconduct, torture, and even murder. The novel attacks religious ideals and morality, these virtues falling by the wayside in the pursuit of pleasure.

This is by no means de Sade's most offensive book. He also penned *Philosophy in the Bedroom*, *The 120 Days of Sodom*, and *Dialogue Between a Priest and a Dying Man*. His works describe various perverse sexual practices in great detail, and they often reiterate his atheistic views. Though denounced by authorities and the Church, de Sade's books have garnered a following among the general population.

The Marquis de Sade died today in a lunatic asylum at Charenton, where he had been incarcerated since 1803.

Foreign Dance Furor

London, England, July 1816: A new dance craze, the waltz, is starting to become popular all over the country, but there are many who are more dismayed than delighted, calling the dance "indecent." What makes this dance so much more risqué than other dances is that the man must hold his partner in a very close embrace as they make their way across the dance floor. This is deemed inappropriate, particularly for young girls and unmarried women. And because it is a moderately fast dance, the women must hold up the ends of their gowns, in order

Religious Leaders

Popes
Pius VII (1800-1823)
Leo XII (1823-1829)

Archbishops of Canterbury
John Moore (1783-1805)
Charles Manners-Sutton (1805-1828)

Dalai Lamas of Tibet
Jamphel Gyatso (1762-1804)
Lungtok Gyatso (1808-1815)
Tsultrim Gyatso (1822-1837)

Patriarchs of Constantinople
Neophytus VII (1798-1801)
Callinicus IV (1801-1806, 1808-1809)
Gregory V (1806-1808, 1818-1821)
Jeremias IV (1809-1813)
Cyril VI (1813-1818)
Eugenius II (1821-1822)
Anthimus III (1822-1824)
Chrysanthus I (1824-1826)

After the burning of Moscow, Napoleon's soldiers were forced to retreat from the city.

The waltz is bound to become popular among younger members of English society.

Marquis de Sade

that they will not be trodden on. This, critics argue, brings the dancing couple even more closely together, setting the scene for possible moral compromise.

The Church has also condemned the dance as sinful and obscene; and *The Times* has published a stern editorial, labeling the waltz as an "indecent foreign dance" that "is far removed from the modest reserve which has hitherto been considered distinctive of English females."

The waltz, a dance in 3/4 time, has been in favor in Europe for some years now, especially in Germany where it has its origins. The name comes from the word "walzen" meaning to glide, or turn.

Black Man Graduates from College

Vermont, USA, 1823: Alexander Lucius Twilight has become the first African-American man in the United States to graduate with a degree from an American college. Twilight was awarded his baccalaureate degree by Middlebury College in Vermont, and is now expected to take up a teaching post.

Twilight attended the highly regarded Randolph Academy before enrolling at Middlebury College in 1821. His was an unusual case, as he was granted advanced standing from his junior years there.

Twilight is also interested in theology and has expressed a desire to become a preacher in the Presbyterian Church. This young man, just 28 years old, is certain to have a brilliant career.

Boy Meets Angel

Palmyra, New York, USA, September 1823: Seventeen-year-old Joseph Smith has today reported receiving several visits from the angel Moroni. The visits, which have been kept secret until now, portend something of deep religious significance. Smith is a devout youth, and those who

know him attest to his search for the "true religion." Three years ago, Smith claims to have been visited by divine beings, who advised him not to join any existing church.

With the angel's permission, Smith has reported to his father that on the night of the first visit, before he slept, he had prayed for his sins to be forgiven, and for guidance. Suddenly a bright light appeared in his room and "a personage" dressed in white, appeared at his bedside. The personage, who introduced himself as Moroni, quoted the scriptures and told Smith about an ancient record, written on gold plates, that provided an account of the former inhabitants of the continent and their origins. He said that the location of these plates would soon be disclosed. The angel returned to repeat what he had said and to remind Smith that he must reject material wealth if he is to find the record and establish a church.

It was not until young Joseph Smith collapsed at work in the fields a few days later that he told his father what had happened. His father agreed that God's hand was apparent and that Moroni's instructions should be obeyed. Apparently, Moroni has promised that when the time is right, Smith will find the ancient record and make its words available to all.

Joseph Smith is being hailed by many as a prophet, and many believe he will do everything in his power to find and translate this so-called "Book of Mormon."

"Sea of Learning" Opens

Canton, China, 1824: Scholar and senior government official Ruan Yuan has founded a new academy in the city of Guangzhou (Canton). Called the *Xuechaitang*, or Sea of Learning, the academy will focus on classical studies. Its location on top of a hill is to remind people that learning should be looked up to, respected, and admired. At present teaching is taking place in the existing buildings, but there are plans to build new blocks for the students and scholars.

Ruan Yuan, who was born in 1764, received his master's degree in 1786, and was appointed to the prestigious Hanlin Imperial Academy in 1789. He has held the position of minister in the education department of a number of provinces and was appointed governor of Zhejiang province in 1800. Ruan is widely respected for his biographical work on famous Chinese astronomers and mathematicians. In that work, *Chouren zhuan*, Ruan suggested that western science owes much to the Chinese. Now he wants to ensure that new students are exposed to the ancient studies—the sciences and arts that have given China such cultural wealth.

Ruan is an advocate of Han Learning, believing that Chinese academics and students need to examine the classic texts and the ancient commentaries on them if they are to gain a deep understanding of Chinese culture, the sciences, and the arts.

At least eight printing presses were set up at the 1814 Frost Fair, to make commemorative cards of the enchanting event.

**Tsar Nicholas I
of Russia**

Attempted Revolt Defeated

St Petersburg, Russia, December 14, 1825: In Senate Square today, the troops of newly inaugurated Tsar Nicholas I, under the command of Prince Sergei Trubetskoy, opened fire on Russian military officers and a loyal band of approximately 3,000, killing and wounding hundreds. The rebel officers and men had assembled to publicly refuse to swear allegiance to the new tsar and to demand that his older brother, Constantine (Alexander's rightful heir), be installed. They demanded, too, that Constantine put in place a Russian constitution.

These soldiers, most of them aristcrats, are part of the Northern Society, who, like their fellow Southern Society, broke away from the 1816 organization—Union of Salvation—in 1821. Though they have different primary aims, each group is dedicated to reform: basic human rights, mass democracy, and an end to serfdom are among their goals. Exposed to the politics and social systems of many western European nations during the Russian defeat of Napoleon in 1812, they dream of a Russia where monarchical power is limited and prosperity is more evenly distributed across the population. The groups have been planning some form of action to promote their aims for several months.

The unexpected death of Tsar Alexander last month forced their hand. Today, the officers marched to the Square. It is understood that they were expecting to gain support from other troops stationed in St Petersburg, but this failed to eventuate and the men were overwhelmed by the tsar's artillery. The hundreds wounded or killed spell the end of this dramatic attempt at revolution.

Russia, France, and Britain Unite

Greece, October 20, 1827: The Bay of Navarino, in the west Peloponnese, was the site of a decisive victory today by joint British, French, and Russian naval forces, under Admiral Sir Edward Codrington, against the Turkish–Egyptian fleets, led by Tahir Pasha. This battle in the war for Greek independence from Turkish rule comes after significant gains since 1821–24. However, the Turkish–Egyptian fleet reconquered Crete mid-1825. On July 6 this year, Allied forces signed the Treaty of London in an effort to force the Turks to free Greece. When the Turkish–Egyptian fleet left Alexandria on August 5 and arrived at the Bay of Navarino in western Greece five weeks later, the Allies realized their hopes of peaceful resolution were unattainable. Now, after failed attempts at an armistice, the naval forces are at war. Allied casualties are 177 killed and 515 wounded to date. Few ships have been damaged. Ottoman–Egyptian casualties are high, with an estimated 5,000 dead and 72 ships sunk.

Battle of Navarino, Greek War of Independence, October 1827.

Zulu Leader Murdered by His Half-brothers

Southern Africa, September, 1828: Shaka Zulu, aged almost 40, has been murdered in a raid by two half-brothers, one of whom, Dingane, immediately claimed the title of king.

Shaka had been a sad and troubled young boy who went on to became ruler of the powerful Zulu nation. His mother, Nandi, was a chief's daughter and his father, Senzangakhona, was chief of the Zulus, who were at that time a small clan in the Mtetwa confederation. When the relationship failed, Shaka and his mother found refuge with the Mtetwas. The tormented young boy vowed revenge on his father.

By the age of 23, Shaka was a soldier under the Mtetwa chief, Dingiswayo, whom he impressed with his knowledge of efficient new military strategies and weapons, and rose steadily through the ranks. When Senzangakhona died in 1816, Dingiswayo sent Shaka to lead the Zulus (then fewer than 1,500). Shaka's leadership marked the beginning of the Zulus' greatness as warriors.

Shaka demanded total loyalty from his Zulu regiments. Opposition spelled instant death. They trained barefoot over thorns to harden their feet for battle and used short thrusting spears, which forced them to fight at close quarters. When they went on raids, their tactics were to kill almost all of the opposing tribe and then to assimilate the remainder, thereby amassing an invincible army. Shaka led by example, forgoing the chief's trappings and living with his men.

In 1827, Shaka heard that his mother was dying. Inconsolable, he slipped into

South America, 1825: Bolivia declares separation from Peru, and Uruguay from Brazil.

Istanbul, Turkey, June 14, 1825: The Janissaries' revolt fails with the Sipahis (Ottoman cavalry) killing thousands.

Southeast Asia, 1825: Indonesians revolt against the Dutch colonists in the Java War.

Yandaboo, Burma, February 24, 1826: Following British victory in the First Anglo-Burmese War, the Treaty of Yandaboo secures British control of Assam.

USA, July 4, 1826: Thomas Jefferson dies, aged 83, on the 50th anniversary of the Declaration of Independence.

Mediterranean, October 20, 1827: Russia, France, and Britain unite to destroy the Turkish and Egyptian armada at the Battle of Navarino.

South Africa, 1828: Shaka, founder and dictator of the Zulu empire is murdered by his half-brothers.

Italy, March 31, 1829: Pius VIII becomes pope.

Australia, 1829: Western Australia becomes a free colony.

Paris, France, July, 1830: Charles X abdicates and flees to England. His cousin Louis Philippe is crowned the "citizen king."

Algeria, July, 1830: France invades after Algeria threatens to withdraw French trading rights.

Europe, 1830: Revolutionary unrest in France, Italy, Germany, and Poland.

Belgium, October 3, 1830: Belgium wins independence from the Netherlands.

Colombia, December 17, 1830: Simón Bolívar, national hero and liberator, dies, aged 47.

Anatolia, 1832: Egyptian viceroy Mehemet Ali defeats the Ottomans at the Battle of Konya.

Falklands, 1832: Britain occupies the Falklands.

India, 1833: Hindu social reformer Ram Mohan Roy dies, aged 60.

1835: Haley's Comet reappears.

Southern Africa, 1835: More than 10,000 Boers leave Cape Colony to found the republics of Natal, Transvaal, and Orange Free State. This mass migration becomes known as "The Great Trek."

USA, 1836: Texas gains independence from Mexico.

UK, 1837: Victoria becomes Queen of the United Kingdom of Great Britain and Ireland.

Canada, 1837: Constitutional revolts occur in upper and lower Canada.

New York, USA, May 10, 1837: Inflated land values and paper speculation cause financial panic; banks stop payment in gold and silver coinage.

Quetta, Afghanistan, 1838: The first Anglo-Afghan War erupts when the British governor of India attacks.

madness, ordering almost 7,000 Zulus to be executed and thousands more to fast.

The madness affected his warriors too, who started to weaken and could not defend him against his enemies.

Simón Bolívar Dies In Exile

Santa Marta, Colombia, December 17, 1830: Simón Bolívar, "The Liberator," has died from tuberculosis, aged 47. Born in Venezuela in 1783, Bolívar became the region's most important revolutionary soldier and statesman. An earnest child who was orphaned at the age of nine, Bolívar loved ideas and travel, going to Spain at the age of 16. After a brief visit to Venezuela, he returned to Europe in 1804, where, immersed in the ideas of philosophers such as Rousseau, Locke, and Voltaire, he dreamed of an independent Hispanic America. Back in Venezuela in 1807, he joined other patriots in resisting Spanish occupation. By 1810, the independence movement was launched.

In 1813 he began his "Admirable Campaign," invading Venezuela and fighting against the Spanish army. Victories in this campaign were interspersed with defeats. In 1815, Bolívar fled to Jamaica after a number of bitter disputes with the government.

In 1819, Bolívar's daring Battle of Boyacá in New Granada turned the tide. He led the congress that declared the Republic of Grand Colombia (including Ecuador, Colombia, Panama, and Venezuela), and was named president in 1821.

Within four years Upper Peru became a brand new nation—Bolivia—with Bolívar as its dictator.

By 1826, internal divisions in Grand Colombia erupted, and by 1829 Venezuela and Ecuador had left the coalition. Bolívar, now physically weakened, grew more disheartened by these threats to his dream for South America. In May 1830 he resigned his presidency and left his beloved Venezuela for exile in Santa Marta, Colombia.

Boers on "Great Trek"

Southern Africa, December, 1835: Earlier this year hundreds of Boer families began a mass migration from Eastern Cape frontier towns, notably Grahamstown, Uitenhage, and Graaff-Reinet. With no hope of fresh pasturelands near the

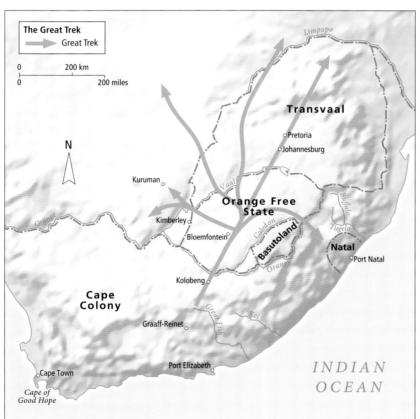

Eastern Cape frontier towns, the families are traveling north to the highveld and northeast to the coast. This is in response to increasing pressures on Boer communities, who claim that since the British took over the Cape Colony administration in 1806 their lives have worsened.

Since 1828, when the Cape government abolished the Dutch-made Hottentot Codes and declared all free citizens (including blacks) equal in the eyes of the law, the political situation has changed. These staunch Calvinist Boers see Britain's *Abolition of Slavery Act* of 1833 and its application to British dominions as a threat to social order. Equal rights before the law threaten white dominance, which is not only the basis of Boer social order but considered God's will. Fearing that emancipation would undermine their commitment to racial separation, the Voortrekkers say that the only solution is for them to leave the colony.

Reports from scouts sent north speak of fertile land, abundant in wild animals, beyond the Orange and Vaal rivers, and have inspired thousands of families to pack their worldly possessions into ox-wagons and make their move.

Louis Trichardt and Hans van Rensburg lead the first wagonload. They are likely to be soon followed by Piet Retief and Andries Pretorius as the communities search for political, economic, and religious autonomy. The number of people undertaking the trek has grown rapidly. Estimates suggest as many as 12,000 people are planning to join this Great Trek.

Simón Bolívar

USA, 1838-1839: Cherokee Native Americans are forced to relocate; they move westward on the brutal "Trail of Tears."

Canton, China, November, 1839: Imperial commissioner Lin Zexu seizes opium from British warehouses.

Spain, 1839: The Carlist War, ends with the Convention of Vergara.

Bay of Islands, New Zealand, February 6, 1840: The Treaty of Waitangi is signed between Maori chiefs and Captain William Hobson, granting British sovereignty.

London, England, 1840: Queen Victoria marries a German, Prince Albert.

Canada, 1840: Act of Union unites upper and lower Canada.

London, England, July 13, 1841: The Straits Convention is signed by Britain, France, Russia, Austria, and Prussia.

Nanking, China, August 29, 1842: Treaty of Nanking signed, signalling China's defeat in First Opium War. British demands such as opening of ports, monetary compensation, fixed tariffs, ceding of Hong Kong granted.

USA, 1842: The border dispute between America and Canada is settled with the signing of the Webster-Ashburton Treaty.

Tahiti, 1842: The French begin their occupation of Tahiti.

Sindh, India (Pakistan), 1843: British troops conquer the Sindh region.

New Zealand, 1843: The Maoris revolt against the British.

Morocco, 1844: The Treaty of Tangiers, recognizing French sovereignty over Algeria, ends the conflict.

Ireland, 1845-1850: Potato blight causes famine, and begins mass migration to Britain and the USA.

Sabraon, India, 1845: The Sikhs are defeated by the British, resulting in the signing of the Treaty of Lahore, giving Jalandhar and Kashmir to the British.

UK, 1846: The Corn Laws are repealed to move toward complete free trade.

Poland, 1846: The Poles revolt against Russian rule.

Mexico, 1846: The USA declares war on Mexico.

Canada, 1847: British naval officer Sir John Franklin and all crew die in their ice-bound ship only miles short of completing their voyage through the Northwest Passage.

London, England, 1848: Karl Marx and Freidrich Engels publish the *Communist Manifesto*, attacking capitalism.

Europe, 1848: Revolutions are staged in Italy, France, Hungary, Austria, Germany, Switzerland, and Denmark.

Germany, March 28, 1849: The first German *Reichsverfassung* (Constitution) is passed.

Queen Victoria

Cherokees Forced West on the "Trail of Tears"

Oklahoma, USA, February, 1839: The depleted and displaced Cherokee nation has arrived at its destination after the journey along the brutal "Trail of Tears."

The May 1838 deadline for forced removal of the Cherokee American Indians from the states of Georgia, Tennessee, North Carolina, and Alabama to lands west of the Mississippi River caused deep distress and protest among many American Indians and whites alike. General John Wool, who was responsible for enforcing the Treaty of New Echota's arrangements for the removal, resigned in protest last year.

Writer Ralph Waldo Emerson urged the president not to inflict "so vast an outrage." Wool's replacement, General Winfield Scott, brought 7,000 soldiers to round up the Cherokees. Approximately 17,000 (and some 2,000 slaves) were forced at gunpoint—some elderly and ill—to leave their homes. Families were separated, and many were given only moments to collect their possessions. The forced march, known as the "Trail of Tears," was a journey of more than 1,200 miles (1,920 km) on foot, horse, wagon, and boat and has been marked by un-bearable hardship, illness, and the deaths of an estimated 4,000 Cherokees.

> "I KNOW YOU DO NOT MAKE THE LAWS BUT I ALSO KNOW THAT YOU ARE THE WIVES AND MOTHERS, THE SISTERS AND DAUGHTERS OF THOSE WHO DO…"
>
> ANGELINA GRIMKE (1805–1879), AMERICAN WRITER, ON THE EVILS OF SLAVERY, 1836

> "HISTORY IS THE ESSENCE OF INNUMERABLE BIOGRAPHIES."
>
> THOMAS CARLYLE (1795–1881), SCOTTISH HISTORIAN AND WRITER, 1838

Maori Chiefs Sign Treaty

Waitangi, Bay of Islands, New Zealand, February 6, 1840: Today, 43 northern Maori chiefs signed the historic Treaty of Waitangi, which recognizes the Maori's prior occupation of New Zealand, enables the peaceful acquisition of land by the Crown, and establishes British law in New Zealand while also guaranteeing Maori authority over Maori lands and culture.

The treaty was presented yesterday to an assembled audience of 500 Maori,

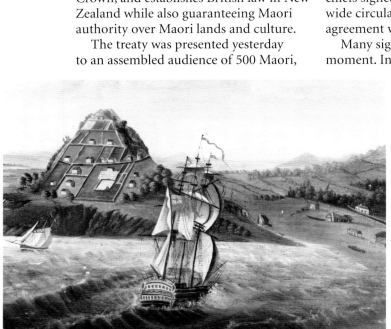

A missionary settlement has been established on the Bay of Islands.

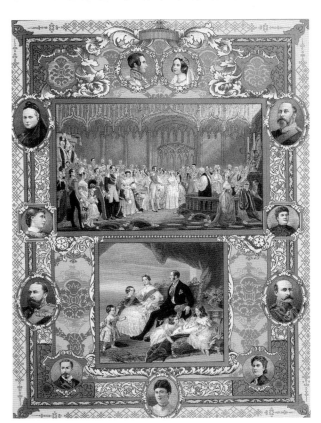

The glorious wedding of Victoria and Albert at St James Chapel.

British government, and church representatives, and public guests. Drafted by lieutenant-governor Captain William Hobson and James Busby, the British Resident—and translated by Henry Williams of the Church Missionary Society, and his son, Edward—the treaty was read aloud in English and Maori. Maori leaders Waka Nene, Hone Heke, and Patuone commended it, and the crowd began their vigorous debate, lasting late into the night.

Captain Hobson was first to sign, followed by Hone Heke, *rangatira* (chieftain) of the Ngapuhi. Today more chiefs signed, and it is hoped that after wide circulation further marks of agreement will be added.

Many significant events led to this moment. In 1833, the British appointed Busby to protect British trading interests and to counter the growing lawlessness among traders and settlers.

By 1835, with the French looking to buy land, the British drafted a Declaration of Independence with 34 northern Maori chiefs, declaring New Zealand to be an independent state under British rule and stating that "no claim could be made on New Zealand without Maori agreement."

By late 1839, lawlessness throughout the land had escalated. Arriving on January 29 this year to take up his post, Captain Hobson immediately joined his colleague Busby to draft this important covenant.

Queen Victoria Marries Albert

London, England, February 10, 1840: Today, the Queen of England, splendid in bridal satin trimmed with orange blossom, married her cousin Prince Albert of Saxe-Coburg Gotha, impressive in British field-marshal uniform, in St James's Chapel in London.

Since their birth the British and German royal houses have conspired to link the cousins in marriage. Victoria, born Alexandrina Victoria, on 24 May 1819, is the daughter of Edward, Duke of Kent, and Victoria of Saxe-Coburg. Albert's father is the brother of Victoria's mother.

The young "Drina" was tutored at home and has grown into a strong-willed girl, who is artistic and intelligent. At the age of 10 when she learned that she was heiress-apparent of the British Crown she wrote in her diary, "I will be good."

When her uncle William IV died in 1837, Victoria was declared Queen. She was 18. Albert wrote: "Felicitations…in your hand lies the happiness of millions." She liked his warmth; her earlier impression of Albert had not been favorable.

Seats of Power

China Qing Dynasty: Daoguang (reigned 1820–1850).
France Charles X (reigned 1824–1830); Louis Philippe (1830–1848). Second Republic: Louis Napoleon Bonaparte (president 1848–1852).
India Mughal Empire: Akbar Shah II (1806–1837); Bahadur Shah II (1837–1857).
Japan Edo Period: Ninko (reigned 1817–1846); Komei (1846–1867).
Kingdom of Great Britain George IV (reigned 1820–1830); William IV (1830–1837); Victoria (1837–1901).
Korea Choson Dynasty: Sunjo (reigned 1800–1834); Heonjong (1834–1849); Cheoljong (1849–1864).
Ottoman Empire Mahmud II (reigned 1808–1839); Abd-ul-Mejid (1839–1861); Abd-ul-Aziz (1861–1876).
Portugal Brigantine Dynasty: Joao VI (reigned 1816–1826); Pedro IV (1826); Maria II (1826–1828); Miguel I (1828–1834); Maria II and Fernando II (1834–1853, Fernando II regent 1853–1855).
Russia Emperors: Alexander I (reigned 1801–1825); Nicholas I (1825–1855).
Spain Bourbon Dynasty: Ferdinand VII (reigned 1814–1833); Isabella II (1833–1868).
Thailand Chakri Dynasty: Rama III (reigned 1824–1851).
Zulu Nation Shaka kaSenzangakhona (1816–1828); Dingane kaSenzangakhona (1828–1840); Mpande kaSenzangakhona (1840–1872).

An exodus of people flee a troubled Europe seeking a better life across the seas.

Italian nationalist
Giuseppe Mazzini

Victoria has put considerable energy into governing, and did not seem to be interested in marrying, but her advisers stressed to her how important this is. Last October, Albert visited. Her diary records: "Albert is excessively handsome, such beautiful eyes…my heart is quite *going*." Well-educated and interested in science, young Albert was thrilled when Victoria proposed; he accepted immediately.

Treaty Defines Border Between USA and Canada

Washington DC, USA, August 9, 1840: Diplomacy triumphed today as the US Secretary of State, Daniel Webster, and the British envoy in Washington, Alexander Baring, Lord of Ashburton, signed a treaty of mutual cooperation. The Webster–Ashburton Treaty defines the location of the Maine–New Brunswick border between the United States and Canada; the border (at the 49th parallel) on the westward frontier up to the Rocky Mountains; and the shared use of the Great Lakes, including the St Johns River, now open to free navigation by both countries. This treaty signals the end of the unofficial fighting along the Maine–New Brunswick border over the last two years (known as the Lumberjack's or Aroostook war).

As well as determining the borders and dividing disputed territories, the treaty calls for cooperation in suppressing the slave trade and provides a solid basis for resolving the question of mutual extradition of criminals between the countries.

The new borders place 7,015 sq. miles (18,169 sq. km) under the control of the United States and 5,102 sq. miles (13,214 sq. km) under Britain's control.

With the exception of the Oregon line, most of the frontier between Canada and the United States has now been determined by this agreement, which therefore represents a significant achievement for international relations.

Treaty of Nanking Signed

Nanking Harbor, China, August 29, 1842: The signing of the Treaty of Nanking on board HMS *Cornwallis* today signals the end of the "Opium Wars," waged between China and Britain since 1839.

The historic agreement was negotiated between British envoy, Henry Pottinger, and a representative of the Chinese government, who is a member of the imperial family of the Qing dynasty.

The treaty cedes the island of Hong Kong to Britain, and grants Britain extensive trading and commercial rights and a payment of 21 million ounces (59,400 kg) of silver. It also ends the complex *cohong* trade system, under which foreign traders had no direct access to Chinese merchants and had to negotiate with assigned representatives of guilds *(cohongs)*. Britain has also gained "most favored nation" status, and fixed tariffs; British citizens have been granted extraterritoriality on Chinese soil; and for the first time British missionaries will be allowed into the interior of China.

Britain involved itself in the opium trade as a strategy to correct the chronic trade imbalance caused by increasing European demand for Chinese teas, silks, and porcelain without a corresponding Chinese demand for European goods. When the Chinese government took action in 1839, concerned about the

Chinese war junks are no match for *Nemesis*, pride of the British Navy.

serious social and economic disruption caused by opium addiction, this set off a chain of events leading to war. This year, the British blockaded Chinese ports, occupied Shanghai, and took control of Canton. With no effective equipment to counter or repel the powerful British navy, the Qing Dynasty has admitted defeat. The signing of the treaty today in no way legalizes the opium trade, but effectively halts Chinese efforts to stop it.

Revolution Sweeps Europe

Europe, 1848: The revolutions sweeping Europe will not surprise many. Recent political and economic changes are the most dramatic the world has seen since Europe's national borders were effectively set at the Vienna Congress in 1815, after the Napoleonic Wars. Boundaries have been relatively stable in the past few decades, but the Congress preserved the old monarchical regimes and the past few years have brought much upheaval.

While industrial modernization has delivered significant progress, not every European has benefited. New freedoms of the press may lead to greater political awareness, and social debate has liberalized. But the past few years have also seen the worst food and financial crises in Europe's recent history. Many farmers have left the land for cities, which are unable to cope with the resulting growth and huge unemployment. In the worst-hit countries revolts have been ignited.

The first signs came from France with Louis Blanc overthrowing King Louis Philippe and declaring the Second Republic on February 24. Then in March, Milan's citizens armed and expelled the Austrian forces, spurred on by news of an insurrection in Vienna in which 61 Italians were killed by local forces for failing to support the Austrian treasury's tobacco and lottery sales. Revolutions in other parts of Italy have caused Pope Pius IX to flee, but have given the radical Giuseppe Mazzini a chance at unification.

Heightened nationalism among the German, Hungarian, Czech, and Danish populations has led to riots. Metternich and the Hapsburg emperor Ferdinand I have been ousted and a constituent assembly formed in Vienna. The Frankfurt Assembly of May saw the German parliament attempting to create a united German state with a national parliament. Within weeks, Croats and Romanians demanded autonomy.

Magnetic North Pole Discovered

North Pole, June 1, 1831: Today, 31-year-old James Clark Ross has successfully located the magnetic north pole while on an expedition with his uncle, Captain John Ross. James Clark Ross joined the British navy in 1812 at the age of 11, and this is not his first trip to the Arctic regions. He and his uncle set out in 1829, with James as second-in-command. Their mission was to find the Northwest Passage and the magnetic north pole. Today, James Clark Ross placed the British flag at 70° 05.3' N, 96° 46' W at Cape Adelaide, on the west coast of Boothia Peninsula (named in honor of Mr Felix Booth of the British gin-distilling family, who sponsored this current expedition).

Ross writes: "It almost seemed as if we had accomplished everything that we had come so far to see and to do; as if our voyage and all its labors were at an end and that nothing now remained for us but to return home and be happy."

James Clark Ross

"The loco-motive Monster, carrying eighty tons of goods, and navi-gated by a tail of smoke and sulphur, coming thro' every man's grounds between Manchester and Liver-pool."

THOMAS CREEVEY
(1768–1838), BRITISH
POLITICIAN, 1835

The expedition sailed into dramatic seas, and in May the ship became stuck in the ice. Though the ship was ice-bound, the crew managed to explore unknown regions of west and north Canada with the help of local Eskimos. While exploring, James Clark Ross made his discovery—the magnetic north pole, the exact point where Earth's geomagnetic field points downward at 90°.

This is a significant achievement for science and will benefit sailors worldwide, who will now be able to fix their position more accurately than ever before.

Faraday Discovers Electromagnetic Induction

London, England, August 29, 1831: Michael Faraday, a member of London's Royal Society, today astounded his colleagues and the public with his demonstration of

time out

English pharmacist John Walker invents the first friction match in 1827. The "Lucifer," as it becomes known, is made of a mixture of potash, gum arabic, and sugar, and must be drawn through a piece of sandpaper to light.

the principle of electromagnetic induction, a major contribution to scientific thinking that may signify the birth of a powerful new technology. A prolific experimenter, Faraday became convinced that since an electric current could create a magnetic field, a magnetic field should be able to produce an electric current, and has shown that the induced electromagnetic field is equal to the rate of change of magnetic flux.

Born in Surrey, Faraday became apprentice to a bookbinder. "Whilst an apprentice," he has said, "I loved to read the scientific books which were under my hands." His interest in electricity led to experiments.

At the age of 20, Faraday attended the Royal Society to hear the chemistry lectures of president Sir Humphry Davy, an eminent physicist and chemist. The young enthusiast took his notes and presented them to Davy after the lecture. The professor was impressed enough to offer Faraday a position as a laboratory assistant the following year, in 1813.

Faraday has worked in chemistry (discovering benzene, a common carbon compound), but his particular interest is in energy (specifically, force) and magnetism. In 1820, he accompanied Sir Humphry on a tour of France and met many prominent scientists, among them Hans Oersted and André Ampère. That same year, Faraday repeated Oersted's experiments on electric currents and magnetic fields and discovered the force exerted by magnets on wire carrying electric current.

By 1821, Faraday had discovered electromagnetic rotation and invented the dynamo (a device capable of converting electricity to motion). In 1824, he was elected a Fellow of the Royal Society.

Today, nearly 10 years to the day after discovering electromagnetic rotation, 40-year-old Michael Faraday brings his new and exciting discovery to the public.

Michael Faraday, discoverer of electromagnetic induction, hard at work in his well-equipped laboratory.

Key Events

Denmark, 1825: Hans Christian Oersted, physician and chemist, successfully produces aluminum.
England, 1825: William Sturgess invents the electromagnet.
England, 1825: Michael Faraday isolates and describes benzine.
England, 1825-1826: Marc Brunel invents a tunneling shield, and starts building the first subaqueous tunnel, under the Thames.
Germany, 1826: Georg Simon Ohm formulates the relationship between voltage, current and resistance (Ohm's Law).

USA, 1829: W. A. Burt patents his typographer.
Sydney, New South Wales, Australia, 1831: A paddlesteamer called *Surprise*, the first steamship to be built in Australia, is launched at Neutral Bay.
England, 1831: Michael Faraday discovers electromagnetic induction, making possible the electric transformer and generator.
USA, 1831: Joseph Henry discovers the principals of the electric telegraph.

Canada, 1831: James Clark Ross discovers magnetic North Pole.
Germany, France, USA, 1831: German chemist Justus von Liebig, French pharmacologist Eugène Soubeiran, and American chemist Samuel Guthrie independently discover chloroform.
USA, 1834: Henry Blair patents a corn planter, becoming the second black person in the USA to do so.
England, 1834: Charles Babbage conceives a design proposal for the Analytical Engine, which possesses the logical features of the modern computer.

USA, 1834-1835: Blacksmith Thomas Davenport invents the electric motor and makes a small electric railway.
England, 1835: Henry F. Talbot invents calotype photography.
USA, 1835: The wrench is patented by Solymon Merrick.
Germany, 1836: Johann Nikolaus von Dreyse designs the needle gun, capable of breech loading.
USA, 1836: Samuel Colt patents the first revolver.
England, 1836: Isambard Kingdom Brunel begins construction of the Clifton Suspension Bridge.

Germany, 1836: Wilhelm Beer and Johann von Madler publish the first exact map of the moon, entitled *Mappa Selenographica*.
Edo (Tokyo), Japan, 1837: Udagawa Yoan begins translation of chemical works of Antoine-Laurent Lavoisier into Japanese.
London, England, 1837: J. F. Royle's *Antiquity of Hindoo Medicine* introduces Indian Ayurvedic medicine to the western world.
England, 1837: Charles Wheatstone and William Cooke patent the electric telegraph.

Colt's pistol, with its revolving cylinder, greatly increases firepower.

Colt Patents a Revolving Pistol

Paterson, New Jersey, USA, 1836: The US Patents Office has recognized Samuel Colt's amazing invention of a "revolver," a pistol that allows several shots to be fired in succession without reloading. This represents a dramatic advance on current pistols, which fire only a single shot and take 20 seconds to reload.

The new "Colt" comes equipped with a unique cocking device and an innovative automatic revolving chamber that holds five or six bullets. Colt applied for a patent for the weapon in England and France last year.

Colt left Hartford, Connecticut, at the age of 15 as an apprentice sailor. It was during a long voyage to India that he carved a wooden model for his revolver. Was he inspired by observing the ship's wheel, or the workings of the

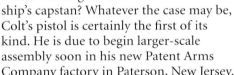
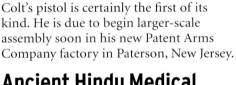

Samuel Colt and his revolver.

ship's capstan? Whatever the case may be, Colt's pistol is certainly the first of its kind. He is due to begin larger-scale assembly soon in his new Patent Arms Company factory in Paterson, New Jersey.

Ancient Hindu Medical Systems Revealed

London, England, 1837: British scholars' medical knowledge is now significantly richer thanks to distinguished botanist J. F. Royle. Royle recently returned from India and has presented lectures to King's College, Cambridge, in which he has introduced his fellow scholars to ancient Hindu medical systems (some of which date back to the fifth century). Royle describes the Unani, Siddha, and Ayurveda systems, as well as folk medicines of different kinds, which challenge the traditional Western system in many ways. The Ayurvedic approach, in particular, is based on the creation of a balance between the processes of the human body and the factors influencing these processes from outside. According to the Ayurvedic doctrine, there are five elements based on three "humors" (*tridoshas*) that make up all the body's processes and are also the source of all diseases. Ayurvedic cures require a delicate combination of diet, the use of plants as medicine, physical exercise, and contemplation, and it was the plants that first fascinated Royle.

Royle's lectures, published as *An Essay on the Antiquity of the Hindoo Medicine*, have stimulated a deep interest in these systems. Drawn to the rich and very diverse field of *materia medica* in the original Sanskrit manuscripts, many English scholars are now eager to learn Sanskrit, and are keen to meet and interview local Indian practitioners (*kabirajas*)—usually high-caste Hindus, who are well-versed in Sanskrit. The healers are generally the only people entitled to make medicinal preparations. Attaining and maintaining good health, in Ayurveda, is a result of equilibrium or harmony, while imbalance makes for disease. If you correct the balance, then you are set to live a long and very healthy life.

Morse's New Electric Telegraph

New York, USA, June, 1838: One man's inspiration on a trans-Atlantic journey has produced a spectacular advancement in communication. Traveling on the *Sully* in 1832 on his return to America from his art studies in England, Samuel Finley Breese Morse met Charles Jackson, physics professor at Boston University, and was inspired by new research about electromagnetics. Having some knowledge of electricity, Morse realized that pulses of electrical current could convey information over wires. By the time the ship had docked, he had developed his ideas for an electric telegraph.

By 1835, Morse had made a model of an electric telegraph from a battery he made himself and clockwork gears—to drive an electromagnetic pendulum carrying a pencil in constant contact with moving paper.

In June last year, Cooke and Wheatstone of England patented their electrical telegraph. With his new partners, Leonard Gale, a science professor, Alfred Vail, a wealthy industrialist, and United States congressman F. O. J. Smith, Morse has now also applied for a patent.

Samuel F. B. Morse

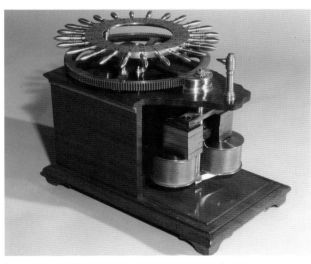

The telegraph transmitter can send 10 words per minute!

Isambard Kingdom Brunel

"This world, after all our science and sciences, is still a miracle; wonderful, inscrutable, magical and more, to whosoever will think of it."

THOMAS CARLYLE (1795–1881), SCOTTISH WRITER, 1841

"What God hath wrought."

SAMUEL MORSE (1791– 1872), AMERICAN INVENTOR, QUOTING THE BIBLE AND SENDING THE FIRST TELEGRAPHED MESSAGE, 1844

Mechanization on the Docks

Buffalo, New York, USA, 1842: Manual labor on the docks is about to be replaced by mechanization, and the longshoremen are happy. The Dart Elevator, an impressive 50 ft by 100 ft (15 m by 30 m), has been erected at the junction of Buffalo Harbor and the Evans Ship Canal. This invention represents a major step forward for the grain and shipping industries. It has been named for the brilliant team of entrepreneur Joseph Dart and his Scottish mechanical engineer, Robert Dunbar (known for his recent success with the Black Rock water-powered flour-mill).

With the huge increase in river traffic since the Erie Canal opened in 1825, Buffalo is the ideal location for this new elevator. The ingenuity and acumen of these two men will revolutionize the storage and transport of bulk grain.

No longer will longshoremen break their backs carrying barrels. With Dart's steam-powered bucket elevator, the grain can be scooped up by legs lowered into the hulls via steam-powered mechanisms and drawn into bins (with a capacity of

Scientific Achievements

Astronomy: Nebula with spiral shape discovered; Neptune and Triton discovered.
Botany: Invention of wood-grinding machine promoted use of wood pulp for papermaking.
Chemistry: Theory presented that all living organisms are composed of cells.
Ecology: US Dept of Interior established to manage land, natural resources, and wildlife conservation.
Geology: Glaciation studies suggest Earth has experienced an Ice Age.
Mathematics: Potential theory used to solve partial differential equations.
Medicine: First administration of anesthesia for a surgical operation.
Physics: Laws of electrical resistance and induction put forward.
Zoology: London Zoo established.

Botanic Gardens
Belfast, Northern Ireland
Birmingham, England
Cambridge, England
Melbourne, Australia
Ooty, India
Sheffield, England

Observatories
Cambridge, USA
Markree, Ireland
Williamstown, USA
Washington, USA

Universities
University of Belfast, Northern Ireland
University of Brussels, Belgium
University of Cape Town, South Africa
University of Kiev, Ukraine
University of Virginia, USA

55,000 bushels [1.9 megaliters]) to be weighed and stored. This transfer can be done quickly. Something that used to take a week may take only a few hours.

Once the grain is sold, for milling or export, it will be another swift transfer as the grain is poured from the storage bins onto waiting canal boats heading eastward for the 363-mile (580-km) journey to Albany. From there, the shipments will board vessels for the 150-mile (240-km) journey down the Hudson to New York City—and from there, perhaps, to Europe and the world.

Doppler Makes Waves

Prague, Austrian Empire, May 25, 1842: At tonight's meeting of the Royal Bohemian Society, the crowd was entranced by a presentation from Christian Doppler "On the colored light of binary stars and certain other stars of the heaven." Doppler seeks to explain these striking phenomena by considering the properties of light and sound as longitudinal waves. His hypothesis is that the frequency of sound waves (and therefore the pitch of the sound) is dependent on how fast the source and the observer are moving in relation to each other. A typical demonstration is the change in sound of a train approaching and then disappearing: the frequency appears to decrease as the distance increases and to increase as the distance decreases.

The young professor of practical geometry and elementary mathematics at Prague's State Technical Academy is an associate member of the society. Interestingly, Doppler considered emigrating to America some seven years ago but was persuaded to remain in Europe.

Doppler began his scientific studies as assistant to Professor Adam von Burg at the University of Vienna's department of higher mathematics and mechanics in 1829. The first of his scientific papers, "A Contribution to the Theory of Parallels," was published while he was working with Professor von Burg.

Since Doppler arrived in Prague in 1835, he has met and collaborated with many other eminent men of science, among them the notable philosopher and mathematician Bernard Bolzano, current secretary of the Royal Bohemian Society of Sciences.

World's Largest Steamship Launched

Bristol, England, July 19, 1843: Direct from its purpose-built dry dock in Bristol Harbor, SS *Great Britain* was launched today in the presence of His Excellency, Prince Albert.

Mrs Miles, the wife of Mr J. Miles, a principal director of the Great Western Steamship Company, the ship's owners, unfortunately missed the bow when she swung the launch bottle. The Prince, standing close by, gallantly grabbed a spare bottle and, smashing it against the ship's side, launched the world's first iron-hulled, screw-propeller-driven, steam-powered passenger liner.

The ship's design team includes Thomas Guppy, Christopher Claxton, William Patterson, and Isambard Kingdom Brunel—the last a man who enjoys ambitious projects. A gifted engineer, Brunel has the design and construction of many projects to his credit, including railway bridges and the Great Western Railway linking Bristol to London.

SS *Great Britain* is yet another in a long line of feats by gifted engineer, Isambard Kingdom Brunel.

Brunel worked with his father, Marc, in planning and constructing the Thames tunnel from Rotherhithe to Wapping—the world's first pedestrian tunnel under a river—which was successfully completed this year.

SS *Great Britain* is 322 feet (98 m) long and is estimated to weigh 3,000 tons (3,060 tonnes). Designed for the transatlantic luxury passenger trade, she can carry up to 252 first- and second-class passengers, with 26 in single first-class cabins. In addition there is accommodation for 130 officers and crew. Her design sets new standards in engineering, reliability, and speed and represents a bold attempt to enter the transatlantic passenger trade. With a vessel such as this, the company is bound to succeed.

Thames Tunnel workers were protected by Marc Brunel's new tunneling shield.

Christian Doppler

of submarine telegraphy depends on a strong connection as well as effective insulation of the electric wire. S. W. Silver & Co. has now successfully extruded gutta percha (a thermoplastic substance that molds when warm) to be used as casing for the electric cable, so the insulating material is now available.

The technical challenges notwithstanding, for the two brothers from Bristol the dream of "instant" communication across the world is now many steps closer.

Carriage Travel Revolutionized

London, England, December 10, 1845: Scottish engineer Robert Thomson today registered his patent for the "aerial wheel," or pneumatic tire. Aged just 23, Thomson has taken a superb idea—the wheel—and made it even better. Thomson's tire comprises a flexible leather casing over an impermeable lining filled with compressed air. Packed within the leather cover are a number of thin inflated tubes, ensuring that pressures can be varied according to conditions and, more importantly, that one puncture is not disastrous. The casing is firmly bolted to the wheels, which form "a cushion of air to the ground, rail or track on which they run," says Thomson, proud of his contribution to the comfort and safety of public and private travelers. Reduced vibration also means that the tire can withstand the abrasion of surface contact longer.

Thomson's study of chemistry, electricity, and astronomy has served him well. He designed and built a ribbon saw, and completed the first working model of his elliptic rotary steam engine. After completing his engineering apprenticeship in Aberdeen and Dundee, he moved to Edinburgh. Here he invented a detonation method for explosives using electricity, a technique that has helped save countless lives in the mining industry.

Thomson's latest invention has been rigorously tested. A set of the new tires has run for 1,200 miles (1,920 km) on an English brougham and remains in good repair. While Thomson has also invented solid-rubber tires, he is very proud of the aerials, convinced that their compressed air cushions will provide increased comfort, traction on all surfaces, and,

very likely, a decrease in noise from the carriage wheels. Most carriages today have wooden wheels and steel tires, and which wear well, but produce a jolting, vibrating ride and are known to skid. With Thomson's tire, carriage travel will become a comfortable, even silent, ride.

Communicating Across The Channel

England, 1849: The world of communication is seeing a great leap forward in this decade, particularly in the field of electric telegraphy. On May 24, 1844, Samuel Morse sent the message "What God hath wrought?" via electric telegraph from the Supreme Court Room in Washington DC. The words, which were recorded onto paper tape as raised dots and dashes, were decoded minutes later 40 miles (64 km) away at the B & O Railroad depot in Baltimore, Maryland.

With rapid communication over land now easier, it appears that the continental divides are the next challenge—a challenge taken up by the Anglo-French Telegraph Company, owned by Jacob and John Watkins Brett. The company is planning on laying an underwater cable from England to France, across the English Channel.

Having "inherited" a project commenced by William Cooke (who, with Charles Wheatstone, patented the working needle telegraph in 1839) but abandoned through lack of funds, the Bretts' company plans to lay electric cable on the seabed, covering the 20 miles (32 km) from Dover to Cape Gris Nez in France. The success

Monier Invents "Reinforced Concrete"

Paris, France, 1849: Joseph Monier, a commercial gardener and manufacturer of garden tools in Paris, was searching for something more durable than wooden tubs for small trees. In the process, he has invented a new form of concrete. By embedding metal (steel bars or iron netting) in his sand and cement aggregate, thereby making an iron network, and enveloping the network in concrete, he has constructed a strong, durable tub capable of withstanding significant loads, and with superior tensile strength. He claims that his invention, called "reinforced concrete," will, in time, come to be used for many forms of construction, including arches and bridges, railway ties, pipes, and floors.

Monier's concrete is an advance on the 1824 invention by Joseph Aspdin, whose Portland cement (ground limestone and clay) has, until now, been the favored medium for building construction.

HMS *Widgeon* escorts PS *Goliath* as it lays underwater/submarine telegraphic cable in 1850.

Felix Mendelssohn Bartholdy

Mendelssohn Completes Opus 21

Berlin, Germany, 1826: This year's latest offering from the prodigiously talented, 17-year-old Felix Mendelssohn-Bartholdy is *A Midsummer Night's Dream, Overture in E Major*, his Opus 21. It is sure to bring a new dimension of richness and joy to audiences' enjoyment of Shakespeare's much-loved play. Based on the Schlegel translation, Mendelssohn's light-hearted incidental music is perfectly suited to the tone of this romantic comedy. He and his siblings—particularly his sister Fanny (also a very talented pianist)—know the play intimately, having often performed it at family events hosted by their grandfather, philosopher Moses Mendelssohn.

The Mendelssohn family converted from Judaism to Christianity in 1816. Felix is already displaying a firm grasp of form, harmony, and composition. He has so far produced sonatas, a piano trio, a cantata, and two operettas, and only last year he completed his Opus 20, *String Octet in E-flat Major*.

Mendelssohn has been most fortunate in having had his works performed at home by a private orchestra before an audience of Berlin's intellectual elite—associates of his wealthy family. He has also developed a strong friendship with artist, scientist, and philosopher Johann Wolfgang von Goethe, whom he met through Karl Zelter, his harmony teacher and himself a composer. Though Felix was only 12 when he met Goethe (then 72), the two have developed and continue a close and generous association.

Mendelssohn is also a talented painter and fluent in many languages. He will be entering Berlin University this year.

William Blake Dies

London, England, August 12, 1827: The poet, painter, and engraver, William Blake, was buried today at Bunhill Fields cemetery in the London suburb of Islington. Born in 1757, Blake displayed great imagination at an early age. At the age of 9, he told of seeing "a tree filled with angels;" he was at art school by 10, writing poetry

Baptism of Christ by the late William Blake.

and working as an apprentice engraver by 12, and a journeyman by 19 years.

In 1782, Blake married Catherine Boucher, and in 1784 he began a publishing partnership with James Parker. By the early 1790s, the partnership was over, but Blake made a living from commissions from fellow artists and writers.

Blake was a gifted and prolific poet. Many considered his poetry naive and fantastical, yet even they know his lines from "Auguries of Innocence:"

To see a world in a grain of sand
And a heaven in a wild flower,
Hold infinity in the palm of your hand
And eternity in an hour

He published *Songs of Innocence* in 1789, and five years later, *Songs of Experience*. Inspired by the harsh experiences of adult life and the terror the universe holds, the latter collection includes the poem "The Tyger," with the famous line "Tyger, tyger, burning bright."

In 1800, the Blakes moved to Felpham, the home of patron William Hayley. Here, over a couple of years, William Blake developed *Milton: A Poem In Two Books, To Justify The Ways Of God To Men*, and wrote "Jerusalem," Blake's condemnation of England's Industrial Revolution, in

Mendelssohn's overture to Shakespeare's *A Midsummer Night's Dream* heralds a great career for the composer.

Brussels, Belgium, December 29, 1825: Jacques-Louis David, neo-classical painter and official artist of the revolutionary government, dies, aged 76.
Russia, 1825: Aleksandr Pushkin writes *Boris Godunov*.
England, 1826: James Fenimore Cooper, American novelist, publishes *The Last of the Mohicans*.
Berlin, Germany, 1826: At 17, Felix Mendelssohn composes *A Midsummer Night's Dream Overture*, based on William Shakespeare's comedic play.

England, 1826: Romantic painter Samuel Palmer moves to Shoreham and founds the "Ancients," a group of artists with a passion for the Medieval world.
France, 1827: Eugène Delacroix, leader of the Romantic movement and renowned for his use of colour, paints *The Death of Sardanapalus*.
England, August 12, 1827: Poet, painter and engraver, William Blake dies, aged 69.
Germany, 1827: Heinrich Heine's collection of early poetry *Buch der Leider* (*Book of Songs*) is published.

Skien, Norway, March 20, 1828: Henrik Ibsen, dramatist, is born.
Peking, China, 1828: Painter Gai Qi dies, aged about 55. His paintings of beautiful women are much sought after by Chinese connoisseurs.
France, 1828: Spanish master painter Francisco de Goya dies, aged about 82. His works span 60 years and he is considered the "Father of Modern Art."
Edo (Tokyo), Japan, 1830: Printmaker Hokusai Katsuhika publishes *36 Views of Mt Fuji*.

Paris, France, December 5, 1830: Hector Berlioz's *Symphony Fantastique* premières, dealing with melody in a radical and revolutionary manner.
France, 1831: Victor Hugo publishes *The Hunchback of Notre Dame*.
Russia, 1831: Aleksandr Pushkin completes *Eugin Onegin* a verse novel.
England, 1832: Scottish essayist Thomas Carlyle writes his spiritual autobiography *Sartor Resartus*.
Moscow, Russia, 1832: Ballerina Marie Taglioni dances *La Sylphide* at the Bolshoi Theater.

Germany, 1832: Poet Johann Wolfgang Goethe completes *Faust* and dies, aged 82, shortly after. During his lifetime he was a student of science, pioneered Romanticism and wrote a book on the theory of colour.
Edo (Tokyo), Japan, 1833-1834: Printmaker Ando Hiroshige publishes *The Fifty-three Stages of the Tokaido*.
London, England, 1835: Canton School artist Guan Qiaochang, known as Lamqua, exhibits work at the Royal Academy.

which he calls for a New Jerusalem "in England's green and pleasant land."

By 1804, the Blakes had moved back to London, and Blake had no major commercial success from 1808 to 1818. In 1818, however, John Linnell, provided him with creative projects. Blake was still working on one of these, Dante's *Divine Comedy*, at the time of his death.

In his final years Blake suffered bouts of an unknown disease. He died at the age of 69, surrounded by devoted family and friends, and is survived by his wife, Catherine. The Blakes have no children.

Spanish Painter Goya Dies

Bordeaux, France, April 16, 1828: Francisco José de Goya, once Spain's court painter, died today, aged 82, in his adopted home France, with a few friends by his bedside.

The life of this brilliant, independent painter and printmaker encompassed more than 60 years of change in Spain's political and cultural life. Born in 1746 in Saragossa, he was fascinated by art from an early age. Keen to develop his skills, he traveled to Madrid and Italy. In 1763, he met Francisco Bayeu, who was working at court in Madrid. This led, years later, to an introduction to Bayeu's sister, Josefa, who would become Goya's much-loved wife in 1773.

Goya's *The Fates*. Of the three Fates, Clotho, Lachesis, and Atropos, it is Atropos who cuts the thread of life.

In 1789 Goya was appointed court painter to Charles IV. By 1792, however, he resented the repressive atmosphere at court and went to Andalusia to reinvigorate himself. Instead, aged just 42, he was struck by a disease that left him permanently deaf and raging "with ill humor." By 1799 he had recuperated and produced 80 aquatinted etchings entitled *Los Caprichos*. He claimed they were made "to occupy an imagination mortified by the contemplation of my sufferings." In 1808, his pessimism about the future of Spain deepened, and he produced two powerful anti-war paintings: *2nd of May, 1808* and *3rd of May, 1808*.

Josefa died in 1812, and in 1819, aged 72, Goya moved into "Deaf man's villa," where he produced the *Black Paintings*—among them *Saturn Devouring One of His Sons*.

By 1824 Goya had fled Spain for France, where he spent his final years.

Victor Hugo Publishes New Work

Paris, France, 1831: Though just 29, Victor-Marie Hugo is already recognized as a talented writer and poet. His latest title,

The Hunchback of Notre Dame, is sure to increase the esteem in which he is held. A redemptive tale of love and beauty set in fifteenth-century Paris, it tells of the deformed, deaf bellringer Quasimodo, whose outward form belies his inner beauty, and the love he shows in rescuing young Esmeralda from the clutches of a jealous and evil priest.

Hugo, a passionate romanticist, weaves political and philosophical questions into his poems and novels that examine France's status and challenges after the upheaval of the revolution.

Author of *Faust* Mourned

Weimar, Germany, March 22, 1832: Johann Wolfgang von Goethe, the German painter, novelist, poet, scientist, dramatist, and philosopher, who for 10 years was chief minister of state at Weimar, has died, aged 83.

Goethe's epic, *Faust*, a tragedy about a man's pact with the Devil, and written in two parts, is believed to be based on the life of a German alchemist, Dr Johann Georg Faust. *Part One* was published in 1808, to immediate acclaim, even inspiring an operatic version by Spohr in 1814. But Goethe only wanted *Part Two* to be published after his death. Now, those who have had to wait decades can read the work in its entirety. But far from being a total tragedy, *Faust Part Two* ends with Faust saved and a character (Gretchen) interceding for him in the kind of heaven Goethe did not believe existed.

A dominant figure in German literature, Goethe's influence is not confined to the arts. An accomplished scientist, he wrote the *Theory of Colors*, which he considered his most important work.

Goethe's influence extends far, and the achievements of this German polymath will be remembered for a long time.

Johann Wolfgang von Goethe

England, 1835: J. W. M. Turner paints *The Burning of the Houses of Parliament*, a depiction of the scene watched by thousands in 1834.

Denmark, 1835: Author Hans Christian Andersen publishes his *Fairy Tales*.

Paris, France, 1835: Frenchman Alexis de Tocqueville publishes *De la Démocratie en Amérique*, a study of American politics and people.

USA, 1836: Ralph Waldo Emerson writes his essay on "Nature" and helps to found the Transcendental Club.

England, 1837: Thomas Carlyle publishes *The French Revolution, A History*.

Russia, 1837: The writer and poet Aleksandr Pushkin dies, aged 37, from wounds received in a duel whilst defending the honor of his wife.

England, 1837: Artist John Constable, factual painter of rural landscapes, dies, aged 60.

England, 1838: Sir Charles Wheatstone's stereoscope, which shows pictures in 3D, is patented.

England, 1838: *Oliver Twist*, by Charles Dickens, is published in monthly instalments.

Spain, 1839: Frederyk Chopin completes his composition of 24 Preludes.

USA, 1840: Austrian Romantic ballerina Fanny Elssler begins tour.

Paris, France, 1841: *Giselle*, the first great Romantic ballet, premières.

England, 1841: Poet Robert Browning writes his dramatic piece and poem *Pippa Passes*, with the lines: "God's in His heaven—All's right with the world."

USA, 1841: Edgar Allen Poe writes *The Murders in the Rue Morgue*.

England, 1843: Alfred Lord Tennyson publishes *Poems*.

Germany, 1843: Richard Wagner's fourth opera *Der Fliegende Holländer (The Flying Dutchman)* premières.

Venice, Italy, 1843: Artist J. M. W. Turner paints *Approach to Venice*.

England, 1843: *A Christmas Carol*, by Charles Dickens, is published.

Keeseville, New York, USA, April 4, 1843: William H. Jackson, painter, photographer, and explorer, is born.

England, 1843: Fox Talbot publishes *The Pencil of Nature*, the first photographic book.

USA, 1845: Benjamin Disraeli writes *Sybil*.

France, 1844-1845: Alexandre Dumas publishes *The Count of Monte Christo* and *The Three Musketeers*.

England, 1847: Charlotte Brontë publishes *Jane Eyre* and her sister Emily publishes *Wuthering Heights*.

Italy, 1849: British painter, John William Waterhouse, is born.

England, 1849: Charles Dickens publishes *David Copperfield*.

French View of *Democracy in America*

Paris, France, January 23, 1835: Alexis de Tocqueville has published volume 1 of his *De la Démocratie en Amérique* (*Democracy in America*). Since coming to the United States five years ago, this aristocratic 30-year-old Frenchman has made a far-reaching study of American society, covering religion, the press, money, class structure, and more. Of the nation's racial problems, he observes, "Although the law may abolish slavery, God alone can obliterate the traces of its existence."

A champion of liberty and democracy, Tocqueville is concerned with improving citizens' lives (without government intrusion). Democracy, he says, requires a balance of liberty and equality, of concern for the individual and concern for the community. When people come together for a common purpose, they form a "civil society" bound to an idea of nation larger than selfish desires.

One day, he predicts, democracy will eventually extend its rights and privileges to women, Native Americans, and slaves.

Ralph Waldo Emerson

"To be great is to be misunderstood."

RALPH WALDO EMERSON (1803–1882), AMERICAN POET AND WRITER, 1841

"Wuthering Heights—all the faults of Jane Eyre are magnified a thousandfold, and the only consolation which we have in reflecting upon it is that it will never be generally read."

JAMES LORIMER, ENGLISH CRITIC, OF ENGLISH NOVELIST EMILY BRONTË (1818–1848), 1849

Transcendental Club Founded

Boston, USA, September 9, 1836: His deep, unbounded enthusiasm enraptured the crowd when Ralph Waldo Emerson today delivered his essay "Nature" at Harvard University's bicentennial celebrations. With ideas that go beyond the usual descriptions of nature as an all-encompassing divine entity, Emerson's essay is a rallying cry to his fellow intellectuals. Emerson is already considered a radical thinker, also by other prominent thinkers and artists, including William Wordsworth, Samuel Taylor Coleridge, John Stuart Mill, and Thomas Carlyle.

Yesterday, some university colleagues (Henry Hedge, James Freeman Clarke, Amos Bronson Alcott, and even Emerson himself) met at Willard's Hotel in Cambridge. Disappointed at the lack of discussion of the deeper issues in their universities, these men want to organize a symposium, as "a protest"—as a way to engage with these issues and find solutions. They are inspired, they say, to make "a better world." The name? The Transcendental Club.

Polish composer, Frederyck Chopin.

J. M. W. Turner's *The Fighting Temeraire* shows the Battle of Trafalgar champion being tugged to her final berth in 18

They will no doubt be joined by others, and though their practical aims differ (some are committed to a utopian view, others more attuned to socialism), all are passionate about change.

They were inspired by Emerson's provocative call at the end of his essay: "So shall we come to look at the world with new eyes. It shall answer the endless inquiry of the intellect—what is truth, and of the affections—What is good?"

English Artist Turner Paints *Approach to Venice*

Venice, Italy, 1843: J. M. W. Turner's atmospheric use of color (often at the expense of form) is the hallmark of his huge body of painting. His latest work, *Approach to Venice*, inspired by his recent visit here, surpasses all his previous efforts. Turner's seemingly effortless use of oils for his increasingly impressionistic compositions belies his enormous skill, honed through thousands of exploratory works in watercolor.

A talented boy, by the age of 14 he had joined the Royal Academy. By 1804 he had produced enough works to open a gallery at his home; sales of his works and the drawings he did for illustrated books provided financial independence. In 1807, he was appointed professor of perspective at the Royal Academy.

Turner's paintings have grown increasingly abstract as he strives to portray light, space, and the elemental forces of nature. His fascination with color has deepened through his study of Goethe's theory of color. He is so drawn to creative experiences that he is reported to have tied himself to a ship's mast as it sailed through a violent storm so he could fully experience the elements.

Turner's regular trips to Europe's great cities have supplanted his English travels: Rome, Paris, and Venice have become his particular favorites.

Key Structures

Acacia Cottage, Auckland, New Zealand
Altes Museum, Berlin, Germany
Arc de Triomphe, Paris, France
Beit-al-Sahel, Stone Town, Zanzibar
Bom Jesus do Monte, Braga, Portugal
Brest Fortress, Brest, Belarus
Catedral Metropolitana, Buenos Aires, Argentina
Duyen Thi Duong, Hue, Vietnam
Eglise de La Madeleine, Paris, France
Grand Kremlin Palace, Moscow, Russia
Grande Mosquee et Palais du Sultan, Agadez, Niger
Groote Kerk, Cape Town, South Africa
La Citadelle, Quebec, Canada
Man Mo Temple, Hong Kong, China
Mohammed Ali Complex, Cairo, Egypt
Old Melbourne Gaol, Melbourne, Australia
Msikiti wa Balnara (Malindi Mosque), Stone Town, Zanzibar
Palace of Princess Ljubice, Belgrade, Serbia
Port Arthur, Australia
Salamanca Place, Hobart, Australia
Sinaia Monastery, Sinaia, Romania
St George's Cathedral, Cape Town, South Africa
Tian Hock Keng Temple, Singapore
Thien Mu Pagoda, Hue, Vietnam
Tomb of Minh Mang, Hue, Vietnam
Tua Pek Kong Temple, Kuching, Malaya
US Capitol, Washington DC, USA
US Mint, New Orleans, USA

Turner's ideas and work are influential, and though he has his detractors, many—philosopher John Ruskin among them—champion his genius. Ruskin wrote: "Who is there who can do this as Turner will?…the uncertainty, the palpitating, perpetual change…the unity of action with infinity of agent."

Jane Eyre and Wuthering Heights Published

Haworth, Yorkshire, England, 1847: Location is a major force in the novels recently published by sisters Charlotte and Emily Brontë. Emily (writing as Ellis Bell) uses the lonely moors (located near her father's rectory) for her story of love and revenge, *Wuthering Heights*. In *Jane Eyre: An Autobiography*, Emily's older sister, Charlotte (Currer Bell), has based Lowood School on the Clergy Daughters' School she attended at Cowan Bridge, Lancashire.

Haworth, where their father, a clergyman, has been posted, is the center of the sisters' lives. Their mother died in 1821, and all the Brontë children were schooled at home, their lives revolving around the small rectory and their father's well-stocked bookshelves, which offered the Bible, Homer, Virgil, Shakespeare, Milton, Byron, Scott, and access to contemporary intellectual and current affairs journals.

Whether out of loneliness or fervid imagination, or many things besides, the Brontë children are a creative force: Emily and Anne created Gondal, a fictional land and the setting for many of their poems; Charlotte and her brother Branwell, recorded stories about Angria, a magic kingdom; as a teenager, Charlotte wrote 23 complete "novels."

In 1845, Charlotte discovered Emily's poems, and last year the sisters published a book of poems at their own expense under pseudonyms starting with the first letter of each of their names. They sold only two copies of *Poems by Currer, Ellis, and Acton Bell*, but each sister already had further writing plans.

Charlotte writes in her preface to *Jane Eyre*: "Conventionality is not morality. Self-righteousness is not religion. To attack the first is not to assail the last." This message may be an attempt to preempt criticism of her family's unconventional approach to writing, and to life.

The Pre-Raphaelite Brotherhood Founded

London, England, September, 1848: Recently the painter John Everett Millais hosted a meeting to discuss the formation of a secret association. Millais and his companions—writer Dante Gabriel Rossetti and painter William Holman Hunt—are dedicated to reforming what they see as the current stultifying and mechanistic approach to art. They are opposed to the "sloppy and formulaic form of academic Mannerism" of Joshua Reynolds, founder of the Royal Academy of the Arts.

They are inspired by the possibilities of art students—painters, sculptors, writers, others—throwing away the "rules" and regaining the depth of color, abundance of detail, and complexity of composition that was present in art before the over-elegant, classical styles of Raphael and Michelangelo came into favor. They are calling themselves the Pre-Raphaelite Brotherhood, and will sign their works "PRB," as a coded message to supporters.

The Brotherhood is keen to reinstate art's links with Romanticism. The newly formed "Pre-Raphaelites" want artists "to have genuine ideas to express; to study nature attentively…to sympathise with what is direct and serious and heartfelt in previous art, to the exclusion of what is conventional and self-parading and learned by rote; and…to produce thoroughly good pictures and statues."

Charles Dickens Publishes David Copperfield

London, England, 1849: In his latest literary offering, the author Charles Dickens, who has long enthralled us with his astutely observed characters, his impeccable ear for conversation, and his cheeky, well-honed sense of humor—cleverly mixed with his solid dedication to exposing hypocrisy, social injustice, and hardships—presents us with a charming new character, the aspiring novelist David Copperfield. Dickens's fans will be delighted.

Dickens is a man attuned to the subtleties and sensitivities of human relationships. Mostly self-educated, by the age of 18 he had a reader's ticket at the British Museum, which gave him access to Shakespeare and a great deal of non-fiction. He worked as a law office clerk and as a shorthand reporter in the civil courts at Doctors Commons, in the 1830s; he could transcribe speech verbatim. As the "fastest and most accurate man" in the journalists' gallery, he honed the skills critical to writing accurately and drawing believable, fascinating characters. His journalism

Charlotte Brontë

Mr Micawber and young David, from Dickens's *David Copperfield*.

in *The Evening Chronicle* in 1833 and his editorship of *Bentley's Miscellany* (1836–39) led him to fiction writing. "A Dinner at Poplar Walk" was serialized in *Monthly Magazine* in December of that year; *Sketches by Boz*, in book form in 1836–1837. *The Posthumous Papers of the Pickwick Club* was published in monthly parts from April 1836 to November 1837 to wide appeal. This led to a new prosperity for Dickens—very different circumstances from those of the young boy of 12 who was forced to leave school to work at a boot-blacking factory (for just 6 shillings a week) when his father was sent to the debtors' prison.

Perhaps that is when young Dickens not only learned the value and discipline of hard work but was also introduced to the often wicked consequences of child labor and the burgeoning Industrial Revolution. These insights have inspired Dickens's good, bad, and comic characters, such as the cruel miser Scrooge from *A Christmas Carol* (his most recent book, published in 1843); the trusting and innocent Mr Pickwick from *Pickwick Papers*; and his latest creation, the idealistic David Copperfield.

Holman Hunt's depiction of Rienzi vowing justice for his brother's death.

George Stephenson

World's First Passenger Steam Railway Opens

Stockton, England, September 27, 1825:
Scores of rapt onlookers today witnessed the arrival of *Locomotion*, the world's first goods and passenger locomotive, as it traveled the 9-mile (14-km) track from Darlington, in northeast England, to the terminus at Stockton port. In just under two hours, the *Locomotion* hauled the 80-ton (82-tonne) load of the first-ever purpose-built passenger car, *Experiment*, plus 20 more cars with 450 dignitaries and others, and 6 wagons loaded with coal and flour. At the controls was George Stephenson, of Robert Stephenson & Company, Forth Street, Newcastle-upon-Tyne, the world's first locomotive builder.

Barely four years ago, on April 19, 1821, an Act of parliament was passed authorizing Stockton & Darlington Railway (S&DR) to build a horse-drawn railway from Darlington to Stockton, linking collieries in the Darlington area to the port at the River Tees, Stockton.

Luckily for British engineering and transport, S&DR director Edward Pease met George Stephenson, now chief engineer at S&DR, when Stephenson designed the innovative *Blutcher*, the first successful flanged-wheel adhesion

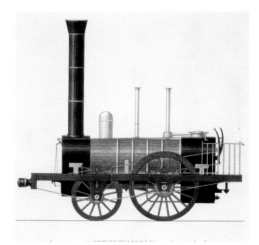

The *Rocket* reached the speed of 18 mph (29 km/h).

History in the making with the grand opening of the Stockton to Darlington railroad.

locomotive, built by Killingworth Colliery. So impressed was Pease that he re-surveyed the Stockton route, working part of it by steam. Foresight and ingenuity met: history was in the making.

Pease lobbied for a new law that would allow "locomotive or moveable engines" to come into use. The Act also provided passenger transport.

So today, for the first time in history, a steam locomotive has transported passengers on a public railway. British transport has been raised to a new height. Congratulations are due to those responsible for this achievement.

Unfortunately Edward Pease was unable to attend the opening celebrations today owing to the untimely death last night of his son Isaac.

New Cocoa Powder Process

Amsterdam, Netherlands, 1828: The Mayan civilization cultivated it in the Yucatan Peninsula as early as 600 CE and drank it with chili. Hernando Cortez introduced it to Spain in 1528, and for almost 100 years the Spanish guarded it as a secret. It has been used as a currency, as precious as gold, and though in France many people

considered it a "barbarous product and noxious drug," there were others who considered it an aphrodisiac.

What is it? It's cacao—and its beans are roasted and ground to produce cocoa powder.

Cacao trees are native to tropical America. The French, Dutch, and English all cultivate it in their colonies, and so cacao has started to reach a wider audience, though it has so far been relatively expensive to produce.

That is, until this year. Dutch chemist Coenraad van Houten has invented an effective method of extracting the cocoa oil and leaving a cake to be ground into powder. His innovative and inexpensive process uses a hydraulic press to extract much of the cocoa butter from the center of the beans. The residue is then mixed together with alkaline salts, which ensure that the cocoa powder can be easily mixed with water or milk. (The alkali neutralizes the acidic chocolate.) This new process is being called dutching or Dutch processing.

No longer reserved for the aristocracy and the upper classes, cocoa powder is now set to become a firm favorite with people everywhere.

time out

American Presbyterian minister, Sylvester Graham, in his "Lectures on the Science of Life" (1839) encourages Americans to become vegetarians in order to avoid digestive complaints. Instead of bread, he suggests people eat his graham crackers.

England, September 27, 1825: The first passenger steam railway in the world opens, with George Stephenson at the controls of *Locomotion*, pulling 36 wagons.
France, 1825–1826: Chemist Joseph Nicéphore Niépce produces the first permanent camera photography image by using a process he names heliography.
England, 1826: Inventor James Sharp patents and manufactures the first practical gas stove to be sold.
England, 1826: J. A. Paris sells the "Thaumatrope," a spinning animated toy.

Amsterdam, Netherlands, 1828: Coenraad Johannes van Houten invents the process that turns roasted cacao beans into cocoa powder.
Henley-on-Thames, England, June 10, 1829: The first Oxford and Cambridge Boat Race is won by Oxford.
France, 1829: Louis Braille publishes the first Braille book for the visually impaired.
Calcutta, India, December 4, 1829: British authorities prohibit the practice of *suttee* or widow-burning.

Southern Africa, April 9, 1830: The Dutch-Afrikaans newspaper *De Zuid Afrikaan* is issued in the Cape Colony.
England, September 15, 1830: The first fatal railway accident occurs when William Ruskin misjudges the speed of the oncoming locomotive, *Rocket*, on the inaugural run of the Liverpool to Manchester railway.
USA, July, 1831: The mechanical reaper is invented by Cyrus Hall McCormick, a step forward in grain harvesting.
Sydney, Australia, 1831: *Sydney Morning Herald* is first published.

England, 1833: The Slavery Abolition Act is passed by Parliament, which grants all slaves in the British Empire their freedom.
USA, 1833: The *New York Sun*, a popular penny daily, is founded.
England, 1833: Parliament passes Factory Act to improve the working conditions of children in factories.
Vermont, USA, June 14, 1834: Isaac Fischer Jr. patents sandpaper.
London, England, July 25, 1834: Society for the Promotion of Female Education in China, India and the East is founded by missionary, David Abeel.

Canton (Guangzhou), China, c. 1835: A dramatic population increase and economic downturn lead to widespread peasant unrest.
USA, 1835: Horseshoe manufacturing machine is patented by Henry Burden.
London, England, June 16, 1836: The Working Men's Association is formed.
England, 1837: Sir Isaac Pitman invents shorthand.
Germany, 1837: Educator Friedrich Froebel opens the first kindergarten.
Canada, 1837: Black people are given the right to vote.

Braille Invents Book for Visually Impaired

A captain of the French Chasseurs à Pied in 1841.

Paris, France, 1829: Persistence and ingenuity have led young Louis Braille, blinded by an accident at the age of four, to be the first publisher of books for the visually impaired. Louis lost his sight when he pierced his eye with an awl in his father's workshop. Within days, infection spread and he was blind.

In 1819, aged 10, this talented, determined boy won a scholarship to the Royal Institution for Blind Youth in Paris, where he met Charles Barbier, who was visiting the school to demonstrate his "night writing" code of 12 raised dots and dashes, devised for soldiers to share information in silence on the battlefield. Louis perfected the complex system, using six small dots in differing configurations, placed close enough together to allow many words to fit on each line. This new system was named after him, and this year 20-year-old Louis Braille has published the first Braille book. Six dots. Six bumps. Many miracles.

Widow-burning Prohibited in India

Calcutta, India, December 4, 1829: The governor-general, Lord William Bentinck, has formally banned *suttee*, the practice of burning widows on their husbands' funeral pyres, in the Bengal Presidency lands. Though Bentinck has been responsible for a number of significant administrative and social reforms in India (including reforming financial administrative systems, opening up judicial posts to Indians, and banning *thuggee*, or ritual murder by robber gangs), this ban is perhaps the most poignant. *Suttee* is prevalent among parts of Indian society, who deem it an honor for widows to die on their husbands' funeral pyres. This may be voluntary, but many widows are forcibly burnt alive. This act signifies her as a virtuous woman who will go to heaven and redeem her ancestors' sins.

Attempts have previously been made to limit or ban the practice. The first formal British ban was in 1798, but it only covered Calcutta. The practice continued in other regions, though many are opposed to it, among them English missionary William Carey and parliamentarian William Wilberforce, anti-slavery campaigner. Their efforts have been boosted by those of the tireless social reformer Ram Mohan Roy of Bengal, whose Hindu reformist sect, the Society of Brahma (which melded Unitarian and other liberal Christian elements into its beliefs) ran its own campaign against the practice. (Roy had witnessed his own sister-in-law commit *suttee*.)

John Deere Invents Steel Plow

Grand Detour, Illinois, USA, 1837: John Deere, a 32-year-old blacksmith, has only recently arrived in Grand Detour from Vermont, but he has already made a huge difference to the lives of Illinois farmers. Plowing the fields will never be as hard again, thanks to Deere's invention of a steel "self-polishing" plow.

In talking with locals, Deere heard stories of the difficulties farmers faced in plowing the moist, sticky soils of the Midwest—the soil some call the "rich black gumbo." Farmers using wrought iron plows spend a lot of time stopping to scrape the sticky soil off the blades to ensure they are clean enough to cut. This slows them down and is hard work.

Deere he was determined to help. He was convinced that the soil would shed itself from a plow if the moldboard and share were of exactly the right shape and highly polished. Using a discarded steel saw blade found at the Andrus sawmill, he fashioned bits of steel into the new plow that scours itself as it turns the furrow slice. This invention has farmers in the area rejoicing. Deere's claim is: "I will never put my name on a product that does not have in it the best that is in me."

The horrifying practice of *suttee*, whether voluntary or involuntary, has finally been banned.

UK, 1837: The Act of Parliament Birth, Death, Marriage Registration 1837 comes into effect.

England, 1838: John Lea and William Perrins perfect Worcester Sauce, using a recipe brought back from India by Lord Marcus Sandys.

Massachusetts, USA, 1839: Charles Goodyear invents vulcanised rubber.

England, 1839: First Official Aintree Grand National is run, with "Lottery" the winning horse.

England, 1839: Kirkpatrick Macmillan develops a pedal bicycle, which he calls a velocipede.

UK, 1840: Post office issues the Penny Black, the first pre-paid postage stamp.

England, 1841: Thomas Cook starts a travel agency and creates the package tour.

France, 1841: Tailor Barthelemy Thimonnier uses 80 of his machines to make uniforms for the French army. Fearing for their livelihood, a mob of tailors destroys his factory by fire.

England, 1842–1843: A detective branch with plainclothes officers is established at Scotland Yard.

England, December, 1843: Henry Cole commissions illustrator John Callcott Horsley to design a Christmas card that he can send to his friends by post. Cole prints 1,000 and sells them for an exorbitant price: 1 shilling each.

USA, 1844: The first international cricket match is played between the USA and Canada.

Sweden, 1844: The safety match is developed by Gustave E. Pasch.

London, England, March 17, 1845: Stephen Perry patents the rubber band.

Massachusetts, USA, October 16, 1845: William Morton uses anesthetic for a tooth extraction.

USA, 1846: William Howe patents a lockstitch sewing machine.

Paris, France, 1846: Belgian Adolphe Sax patents a woodwind instrument, the saxophone.

Hungary, 1847: Physician Ignaz Semmelweis pioneers a policy of handwashing, with antiseptic chloride solution, by medical staff, before treating patients.

Hartford, Connecticut, USA, 1847: Yung Wing, pioneer Chinese student, begins his education in America.

England, 1847: Scottish obstetrician James Young uses diethyl ether to alleviate labor pain during childbirth.

New York, USA, April 10, 1849: Mechanic Walter Hunt patents the safety pin.

England, 1849: London hatters make the bowler hat, as occupational wear for hunters and gamekeepers.

USA, 1849: Gail Borden Jr. develops a commercial method of condensing milk.

The World's First Prepaid Stamp

The Penny Black stamp

> "WHAT A BLESSING THIS SMOKING IS! PERHAPS THE GREATEST THAT WE OWE TO THE DISCOVERY OF AMERICA."
>
> ARTHUR HELPS (1813–1875), BRITISH HISTORIAN, 1847

> "UNDER A GOVERNMENT WHICH IMPRIS-ONS ANY UNJUSTLY, THE TRUE PLACE FOR A JUST MAN IS ALSO A PRISON."
>
> HENRY DAVID THOREAU (1817–1862), AMERICAN WRITER, ON CIVIL DISOBEDIENCE, 1849

Bath, England, May 6, 1840: From today, the British Post Office takes a great leap forward, becoming the world's first postal system to release a prepaid adhesive postage stamp. Until now, postage fees were calculated according to weight and distance, and (typically) fees were paid by the addressee. With the new "Penny Black," issued today, any letter weighing up to half an ounce (14 g) can be sent anywhere within Great Britain for one penny. The prepaid stamp eliminates the complexity of calculating postage by weight and distance, and transfers the cost to the sender.

Last year, the parliament passed the Penny Postage Act, supporting postmaster general Rowland Hill in his attempts to reform the postal service. In 1837, he had trialed the ideas of prepaid envelopes and (for those using their own stationery) adhesive postage stamps. The envelopes failed to gain interest, but the stamps were an immediate success: a one-penny design in black and—for letters weighing more than half an ounce (14 g)—a two-penny design in blue. The two-penny stamp will be issued on May 8.

The competition for the design of the stamp attracted many entries. The winning entry featured an engraved profile of Queen Victoria (by Charles and Fredrick Heath from a sketch by Henry Cole). The stamps have the words "Postage" at the top and "One Penny" or "Two Pennies" at the bottom—but nowhere are the words "Great Britain" to signify the country that has led the world in this communications triumph.

Baptist Minister Invents "Package Tour"

Leicester, England, July 5, 1841: Watching the local trains pass by one day as he walked to work, Baptist minister Thomas Cook dreamed of how glorious it would be if the newly developed power of the railway and locomotives could be made subservient to a cause dear to his heart: the cause of temperance.

Seizing the opportunity presented by an upcoming church meeting in the neighboring town of Loughborough, Cook arranged to hire a train, and today it took 570 passengers on the 22-mile (35-km) round trip from Leicester to Loughborough at a cost of one shilling per passenger.

Cook printed flyers and sold tickets for what is believed to be the first publicly advertised excursion train ever run in England. Cook has since received many more requests to organize more such trips.

The man behind this enterprising idea is known locally for his conscientiousness and hard work. His father died when he was young, and Cook left school at the age of 10, in 1818. A Bible reader, by the age of 20 he was a Baptist homeland missionary and had also saved enough to start his own printing business in Leicester. Four years later he married, and in 1836 he became a total abstainer. He is fervent in his support of the temperance movement, and produces temperance literature at his own expense. Last year he published the *Children's Temperance Magazine*, the first of its kind in England.

Henry Cole Invents "Christmas Card"

London, England, December, 1843: To send greetings to family and friends at Christmastime, many people are accustomed to writing a note and delivering it in person. Now, in an exercise that he has called "the union of fine-art with manufacture," artist and art critic Henry Cole has changed all that. Earlier this year Cole commissioned the illustrator John Callcott Horsley to illustrate and print a card that families can post, saving themselves much time and effort.

Perhaps he was inspired by the French, who send illustrated postcards when on vacation, or by the cards schoolchildren illustrate and send to friends (displaying their writing skills in the process). Either way, Cole asked Horsley to use religious symbolism in the illustrations and to include the message: "Merry Christmas and A Happy New Year to You."

The first mass-produced Christmas greeting card.

Horsley's card is a triptych, with garlands of ivy and holly surrounding the images on each panel. The side images show acts of charity—the naked being clothed and the hungry being fed—a message that Cole wants to spread, particularly at this time of year. The middle panel, depicting a family scene, has come under criticism, however. It shows a large, happy family sipping wine and enjoying the festivities, and temperance groups are outraged, claiming the image is blatantly "fostering the moral corruption of children."

Cole hopes that this will not discourage everyone from buying his cards. He has published 1,000, under the label Felix Summerly Art-Manufacturers, and hopes to sell them for one shilling each.

First International Cricket Match

Bloomingdale Park, New York, USA, September 24–25, 1844: Some 20,000 people have watched St George's Cricket Club of New York play a two-day match against the Toronto Cricket Club. The Canadians' win, by 23 wickets, with scores of 82 and 63 against the USA's 64 and 58, makes them eligible for the $1,000 stake.

The introduction of the "Penny Post" will make the Royal Mail run much more efficiently.

The New York Cricket Club was beaten on their home ground by the Canadian team.

Ironically, this important match—being hailed as the first ever international cricket fixture—is the result of a hoax. Four years ago, a mystery man, "Mr. Phillpotts," invited the St George's Cricket Club to Canada for a friendly game. But Toronto Cricket Club knew nothing of the proposed match, though they hastily called a team together.

The United States won by 10 wickets, and according to reports both sides had such a marvelous time at the gala dinner celebrations that night that they have built up a very strong rapport that has continued ever since.

Anesthetic Relieves Labor Pains

London, England, January 19, 1847: James Young Simpson, the brilliant young doctor at the forefront of researching

Women will benefit from anesthetic in childbirth.

pain relief for women in childbirth, has demonstrated the use of the anesthetic diethyl ether to alleviate labor pains. While this has the potential to benefit expectant mothers everywhere, it has brought opposition and disapproval from powerful conservatives in medical and religious fields across the country.

Simpson has had an outstanding career to this point, combining brilliance with compassion. In 1839, at the age of 28, he was named professor of medicine and midwifery at the University of Edinburgh, and this year, at the age of 36, he was appointed one of the Queen's physicians in Scotland. Simpson's talents are legendary: he improved the design of obstetrical forceps and, like Semmelweis, has worked to reduce the spread of infections such as puerperal fever.

However, perhaps his greatest contribution to medicine is in the realm of anesthetics. Distraught after witnessing surgery without anesthetics, Simpson wrote of his commitment to "…the exercise of any power by which we can mitigate and alleviate that suffering." He has been heartened by news of successes in the use of anesthetics across the Atlantic, in dentistry and general surgery.

Nonetheless, he faces strong opposition from medical and religious groups to its use in obstetrics. In spite of recognizing, at least in principle, the desirability of alleviating the agony of childbirth, some people claim the practice to be against nature and against God's will (with some even referring to "unnatural painlessness in delivery" as "an invention of the Devil"). Simpson states his belief simply: "All pain…is destructive and ultimately fatal in its nature and effects."

Born the seventh son and eighth child of a baker, this remarkable man has made a contribution that will go on to help many thousands around the world.

Mechanic Patents New Safety Pin

New York, USA, April 10, 1849: It took a small piece of wire, a massive imagination, and a little time—three hours to be exact—and the result? A new, improved version of the safety pin, from New York mechanic and inventor Walter Hunt, who was granted his patent today.

A form of "safety pin" has long been in use as an effective means of attaching pieces of cloth. It was invented by the ancient Greeks, and records show the "fibula" was in use as early as 1050 BCE. But Hunt, working with a rigid but bendable wire (a combination of copper, iron, aluminum, gold, silver, and platinum) has vastly improved the design, making it easier and safer to use. Hunt's version includes a safety clasp into which the sharp needle tip is slotted to close the pin, and a spring to provide tension, helping to keep the pin firmly in place.

Walter Hunt is an original thinker but not, it would seem, an astute businessman. Fifteen years ago, this creator of—among other things—a successful flax spinner, a knife sharpener, a streetcar bell, a stove that burns hard coal, road-sweeping machinery, and improved the sewing machine by inventing the world's first sewing machine with an eye-pointed needle. He was so concerned that it would cause unemployment that he neglected to take out a patent.

Henry Cole

Religious Leaders

Popes
Leo XII (1823-1829)
Pius VIII (1829-1830)
Gregory XVI (1831-1846)
Pius IX (1846-1878)

Archbishops of Canterbury
Charles Manners-Sutton (1805-1828)
William Howley (1828-1848)
John Bird Sumner (1848-1862)

Dalai Lamas of Tibet
Tsultrim Gyatso (1822-1837)

Patriarchs of Constantinople
Chrysanthus I (1824-1826)
Agathangelus I (1826-1830)
Constantius I (1830-1834)
Constantius II (1834-1835)
Gregory VI (1835-1840)
Anthimus IV 1840-1841, 1848-1852)
Anthimus V (1841-1842)
Germanus IV 1842-1845)
Meletius III (1845)
Anthimus VI (1845-1848)

Florence Nightingale

Gold Discovered in Australia

Australia, June 29, 1851: James Esmond has discovered gold near Clunes, north of Ballarat in Victoria. Esmond took up the challenge issued by the Gold Discovery Committee, offering substantial rewards to anyone who found gold within 200 miles (320 km) of Melbourne. The business community and the Victorian Government (which received autonomy from the colony of New South Wales last year) were concerned because so many of their men went to the goldfields near Bathurst; they hoped a Victorian strike would stimulate their flagging economy.

The gold rush had begun several months earlier when adventurer Edward Hargraves, having recently returned from a fruitless prospecting trip to California, found a small amount of gold near Bathurst, 124 miles (200 km) to the west of Sydney. Hargraves enlisted the help of John Lister and James Tom, and when the news of further finds had spread, thousands of diggers arrived in the area to seek their fortunes.

Diggers in their thousands flock to the Australian goldfields.

Great Exhibition Held at Crystal Palace

London, England, October 15, 1851: The Great Exhibition of the Works of Industry of All Nations closed its doors today, having entertained and informed six million visitors since it opened on May 1 this year.

The idea of an Exhibition was originally conceived by Prince Albert, who, along with a specially appointed Royal Commission, brought the concept to fruition. The Prince Consort attended the French Industrial Exposition of 1844, and desired "to illustrate the point of the industrial development at which the whole of mankind has now arrived." He also wanted the Exhibition to be a monument to Great Britain's industrial, technological, and economic leadership.

As well as highlighting the achievements of the British Empire, the Exhibition showcased displays from many other countries, including the United States and China. Design and manufacturing exhibits included such items as musical instruments, textiles and furnishings, agricultural equipment, tools, and appliances. In addition, the Exhibition housed displays of flora and fauna, and provided such varied amusements as dog and cat shows, circuses, and concerts.

A major attraction in its own right was the Exhibition building itself, the Crystal Palace in Hyde Park. Designed by glasshouse expert Joseph Paxton, the Crystal Place is an architectural marvel. Built with cast iron and glass, the total area comprises some 19 acres (7.7 ha)—six times greater than St Paul's Cathedral. Amazingly, the edifice took only nine months to complete.

The Exhibition has been a financial success, with takings estimated at £500,000.

Treaty of Kanagawa Ends Japanese Isolation

Japan, March 31, 1854: Representatives from Japan and the United States today signed the Treaty of Kanagawa (Empire of Japan Treaty), marking the end of 250 years of Japanese isolation from the rest of the world. Since the early seventeenth century, no outsiders were allowed into Japan (except the Dutch), and Japanese citizens were forbidden to travel abroad. Japan's policy was a reaction to European military threats, as well as fear of cultural infiltration by western countries.

The United States saw Japan as a potential trading partner, and also desired entry into Japanese waters so their ships could refuel en route to other locations. So early in 1853, President Millard Fillmore sent Commodore Matthew C. Perry on a diplomatic mission to Japan. Later that year, Perry led a squadron of four warships into Edo Bay with a list of requests, which were refused.

In February 1854, Perry returned to Japan with a larger fleet, and persuaded the Japanese Government to agree in part to their demands. The Treaty encourages "permanent friendship" between the two nations. It guarantees that survivors of shipwrecks in Japanese waters would not be imprisoned or killed, and it agrees to

Six million people visited London's Great Exhibition.

the provision of fueling ports for American ships. In addition, the United States would be allowed to set up a consulate on Japanese soil. A trade agreement is planned for the not-too-distant future.

Treaty Concludes Crimean War

Paris, France, March 30, 1856: The Treaty of Paris was signed today, ending the war between Russia and the alliance of the Ottoman Empire, Great Britain, France, and Sardinia.

Russia wanted to acquire territories in Eastern Europe. When the Sultan gave the French permission to protect Christian holy sites in Jerusalem, Russia precipitated a conflict, firing shots against the Ottomans in October 1853. The war began in earnest on November 30 when Russia attacked the Ottoman fleet at Sinope on the Black Sea. Britain and France joined in March 1854, after Russia refused to evacuate Walachia and Moldavia. Sardinia joined a few months later.

The Crimean War has been mainly a naval war, with fighting taking place on the Crimean Peninsula, the Baltic Sea, and the Black Sea. As well as Sinope, other major battles included Alma, Balaclava, Inkerman, Sebastapol, and Kars. In many respects it was a shameful war, marked by ineptitude and negligence on both sides. The Battle of Balaclava ("The Charge of the Light Brigade"), in which over a third of the men were injured or killed, was a glaring example of poor military leadership. Even more disgraceful was the lack of supplies, equipment, and proper medical care. More men died from typhus, cholera, malaria, and dysentery than died in battle, and if it were not for the efforts of crusading British nurses Florence Nightingale and Mary Seacole from Jamaica, the death rate would have been much higher.

time out

American President Zachary Taylor (1784-1850) dies in office from severe gastroenteritis, reportedly brought on by eating an excess of iced cherries during Independence Day celebrations.

The Russian defeat at Sebastapol on September 8, 1855, marked the end of the war. The Treaty of Paris closes the Black Sea to all naval vessels, opens the Danube to free navigation, and grants independence to Moldavia and Walachia. Russia has also agreed to return southern Bessarabia to the Ottomans.

Mutiny Ends with British Control

India, August 2, 1858: Britain has taken over direct rule of India, after the dissolution of the East India Company. This is the result of a 13-month conflict, known as the Indian Mutiny or the Sepoy Rebellion.

The Sepoys (*sipahi*), native soldiers employed by the East India Company, refused to use the Lee-Enfield rifle, because to load it required soldiers to bite the ends of the cartridges, which they believed to be oiled with animal fat—prohibited for Hindus and Muslims. This was the catalyst, but the rebellion was actually the last straw in a long-standing unrest caused by British expansionism, taxation, and cultural, economic, and religious imperialism. The mutiny began at Meerut on May 9, 1857, after some officers refused to load the cartridge. The insurrection swept across the Ganges Basin to Delhi, and the Mughal emperor, Bahadur Shah II, was reinstated as ruler.

At first, the Indians outnumbered the British by six to one, and held their own. However, British forces, under Sir Colin Campbell, were more experienced. When the British received reinforcements of troops of Nepalese Gurkhas and Crimean War veterans, the tide turned. The war ended on July 8, 1858.

Matthew Perry

The Indian Mutiny has left many dead and wounded, and both sides are guilty of shameful atrocities.

Key Events

USA, 1861-1865: American Civil War.
Prussia (Germany), 1862: Otto von Bismark becomes Minister-President of Prussia.
Williams Creek, British Columbia, Canada, 1862: Gold miners hit vast deposits of gold.
USA, April 9, 1863: President Abraham Lincoln issues his *Emancipation Proclamation*, declaring that all slavery must end.
USA, April 14, 1865: President Abraham Lincoln is assassinated.
USA, 1865: An estimated 4 million slaves are freed upon defeat of the south in the American Civil War.

China, 1866: Sun Yixian, considered founder of modern China, is born.
England, 1866: First petition for women's suffrage is presented to parliament.
Sitka, Alaska, October 18, 1867: Russia sells Alaska to USA for $7.2 million.
Canada, 1867: The Dominion of Canada is created by the British North America Act.
Kimberley, South Africa, 1867: Diamonds are discovered.
Spain, 1868: The Spanish Revolution begins.

Kyoto, Japan, 1868: Emperor Meiji assumes full governmental powers, ending military rule and ushering in Japan's modern era.
Egypt, 1869: Suez Canal opens.
USA, 1869: Fifteenth Amendment is passed, which requires all Southern States to allow Negroes to vote.
India, 1869: Mohandas Karamchand Ghandi, statesman and religious leader, is born.
Paraguay, 1870: Fighting ends bringing the War of the Triple Alliance to a close.

France, 1870: Emperor Napoleon III is deposed and Third Republic is declared.
Russia, 1870: Vladimir Ilyich Lenin, statesman, is born.
France, 1870: Franco-Prussian War begins.
USA, 1871: The National Rifle Association is granted a charter by the State of New York.
UK, 1871: The Trade Union Act legalizes the trade union movement.
Germany, 1871: Wilhelm I becomes kaiser.

Paris, France, 1871: The Paris Commune uprising begins.
Germany, 1871: Proclamation of German Empire.
UK, 1872: The Ballot Act is passed, which allows for secret ballots at elections.
Spain, February, 1873: The First Spanish Republic is proclaimed when Cortes deposes King Amadeus.
Hanoi, Vietnam, 1874: French occupation.
West Africa, March 14, 1874: The Anglo-Ashanti War is ended with the signing of the Treaty of Fomena.

Giuseppe Garibaldi

> "ALL WE ASK IS
> TO BE LET
> ALONE."

JEFFERSON DAVIS (1808–
1889), PRESIDENT OF
THE CONFEDERATE
STATES OF AMERICA,
1861

> "I OFFER
> NEITHER PAY,
> NOR QUARTERS,
> NOR FOOD; I
> OFFER ONLY
> HUNGER,
> THIRST, FORCED
> MARCHES,
> BATTLES, AND
> DEATH. LET HIM
> WHO LOVES HIS
> COUNTRY WITH
> HIS HEART, AND
> NOT MERELY
> WITH HIS LIPS,
> FOLLOW ME."

GUISEPPE GARIBALDI
(1807–1882), ITALIAN
PATRIOT AND SOLDIER

Garibaldi Drives Francis II From Naples

Naples, Italy, September 7, 1860: Giuseppe Garibaldi was given a hero's welcome after he drove the Bourbon King Francis II out of Naples. With the arrival of Garibaldi and his army of only 4,000 men, the king retired to Capua. The conquest was another triumph for the Italian nationalist leader. His crusade to unify the country began in 1834 when, as a member of Mazzini's "Young Italy" movement, he was sentenced to death for his involvement in the siege of Genoa. He was pardoned and fled to South America, where he learned guerrilla warfare. Upon his return to Europe, he distinguished himself as a major general in the 1859 Austro–Sardinian War.

Earlier this year, Garibaldi again came to Mazzini's aid in an attempt to free the Kingdom of the Two Sicilies from the control of Naples. His 1,000-strong army of volunteers are known as the Red Shirts. On May 6 they sailed with two steamers from Genoa, landing a week later on the Sicilian west coast, near Marsala. The army soon quadrupled its size, but was no match for the 25,000-strong Neapolitan forces. Garibaldi nominated himself dictator of Sicily under the auspices of King Victor Emmanuel II of Italy. On May 25, the Red Shirts took Palermo, Sicily, and by the end of July Messina also fell. Garibaldi is being acclaimed by freedom fighters everywhere.

End of Anglo–French War in China

Peking, China, October 18, 1860: The Convention of Peking was signed today, ending a four-year conflict that became known as the Second Opium War. The war dealt with issues left over from the First Opium War (1839–1842), namely, British trading rights in general, and the importation of opium, in particular. The conflict was also called the *Arrow* War, because the inciting incident happened on October 8, 1856 when some Chinese officials boarded a British-registered ship, the *Arrow*, pulling down its flag. The French became involved after a missionaries was murdered in central China.

After nearly two years of war, the allies presented the Chinese with the Treaty of Tientsin in June 1858. Its major demands were the establishment of American, British, French, and Russian embassies in Peking; the opening of more Chinese ports for foreign trade; and permission for missionaries to travel in China.

The Chinese then refused to ratify the Treaty, and resumed hostilities. Anglo–French forces retaliated, and after the burning of the emperor's Summer Palace in Peking, the Chinese surrendered.

The Convention of Peking included the terms of the 1858 Treaty of Tientsin. In addition, the opium trade was legalized, and Christian missionaries were permitted to own property. The Convention also ceded the Kowloon Peninsula, across from Hong Kong Island, to the British. (The British had previously acquired Hong Kong as a result of the Treaty of Nanking in 1842.)

General Robert E. Lee Surrenders

Virginia, USA, April 9, 1865: At Appomattox Court House today, Confederate General Robert E. Lee surrendered to Union General Ulysses S. Grant, thus marking the end of the American Civil War.

Although the war officially began in 1861, the conflict had been brewing for

decades. The question of slavery, along with the related issue of states' rights, had long polarized the North and South. The southern agricultural economy was dependent on slave labor, whereas the more populous northern industrial states had abolished slavery as early as 1819.

By the late 1850s, the conflict between the North and the South had come to a head. In October 1859, anti-slavery campaigner John Brown caused a furor when he attacked the armory in Harper's Ferry, Virginia. In 1860, Abraham Lincoln became President. The election of Lincoln, who in 1858 had said "this government cannot endure permanently half slave and half free," was another blow to the southern states—the days of slavery were numbered unless drastic measures were taken. So South Carolina became the first state to secede from the Union in December 1860, and with Mississippi, Florida, Alabama, Georgia, Louisiana, and Texas formed the Confederate States of America.

On April 12, 1861, Confederate forces attacked federal troops at Fort Sumter, South Carolina. Lincoln summoned 75,000 volunteers to retaliate. As a result, Virginia, Tennessee, Arkansas, and North Carolina joined the Confederacy.

The war that the Union thought would be over in months dragged on for four years, with the total death toll estimated at more than 600,000. Despite the Union's obvious advantages, the first two years of the war were dominated by the Confederacy, with major victories at Bull Run and Fredericksburg. Although they won

The defeat of Francis II's army at Palermo made the conquest of Naples a relatively easy affair.

the Battle of Antietam in 1862, the Union suffered huge losses.

In an attempt to prevent Britain from allying itself with the South, Lincoln issued the Emancipation Proclamation on January 1, 1863; this proclamation freed 4 million slaves in the Confederate states. Six months later at Gettysburg, Pennsylvania, Lee's army was decimated. The Union had virtually won the war, but it wasn't until General Sherman captured the cities of Atlanta and Savannah, and Grant took Richmond, that the Confederates finally surrendered.

President Lincoln meets General Grant.

Dominion of Canada Established

London, England, July 1, 1867: The British Parliament today has passed the British North America Act, creating a nation to be known as the Dominion of Canada. The new Dominion consists of the provinces of Quebec (formerly Lower Canada), Ontario (formerly Upper Canada), Nova Scotia, and New Brunswick. There is provision for other colonies to become part of the federation in the future.

Ottawa (which was the capital of the United Province of Canada) has been named capital of the Dominion. John Alexander Macdonald, leader of the Conservative Party of Upper Canada and one of the major advocates of self-government, is the first Prime Minister. The Dominion will have its own Constitution and be self-governing, except for matters of foreign policy.

The *Canada Gazette* has declared this day to be a "day of rejoicing," and large number of Canadians will agree. There have been several motivating factors in the creation of the new Dominion, not the least of which is a growing feeling of nationalism, as well as fear of encroachment by the United States.

Suez Canal Opens

Egypt, November 17, 1869: Amid fireworks and fanfare, the Suez Canal was opened today by Empress Eugenie of France. The canal, which is about 100 miles (160 km) long, connects Port Said on the Mediterranean Sea with Suez on the Red Sea—enabling ships to sail between Asia and Europe without going around Africa. It

is open to the ships of all nations.

Late last century, Napoleon envisaged such a waterway, mainly to gain trade advantages over the British. The idea did not eventuate, and the project was taken up again by retired French diplomat Ferdinand de Lesseps. With the permission of Egypt's Prince Said, the Compagnie Universelle du Canal Maritime de Suez was formed in December 1858.

It took 11 years and 20,000 laborers, working under extremely harsh conditions, to complete the canal, at a cost of more than twice the original budget. The first vessel to enter the canal was the Imperial yacht *Aigle*, followed by the P&O liner *Delta*.

Wilhelm is Emperor of Unified Germany

Versailles, France, January 18, 1871: In the Hall of Mirrors at Versailles, King Wilhelm of Prussia was today proclaimed Emperor Wilhelm I of the Second German Empire (Second Reich). Otto von Bismarck, the major force behind German unity and Chancellor of Prussia from 1862 to 1870, has been appointed Imperial Chancellor.

The unification of Germany is the culmination of many years of negotiation and conflict. In the middle of the nineteenth century, Germany was a confederation of small states, dominated by Austria. Prussia was a second-rate power,

but gaining in strength. There had been a growing intellectual and political movement toward a united Germany, and to that end a conference was held in Frankfurt in 1849, drafting a constitution for a unified country. Plans were rejected, and put on hold for over a decade.

When Otto von Bismarck became Chancellor in 1862, nationalist feeling was running high. In 1864, Prussia and Austria came together to fight to reclaim the Duchies of Schleswig and Holstein from Denmark. The Danes were defeated, and agreed that Austria would govern Holstein and that Prussia would manage Schleswig. Two years later, in 1866, the Austrian–Prussian War was fought over the administration of the duchies. Prussia was victorious, asserting her dominance over Austria and proving to be a mighty military power. In 1867, von Bismarck formed the North German Confederation, in which the German states that are north of the River Main came under Prussian control.

Then, on July 19, 1870, Napoleon III of France declared war on Prussia over the possibility of a Prussian Hohenzollern becoming the King of Spain. Field-Marshall Helmuth von Moltke (who had led the Prussians to victory against Denmark and Austria) was placed in command of the Prussian troops. They now had the backing of the North German Confederation as well as the southern German states.

The Franco–Prussian War has clearly demonstrated the superiority of the German military. After the capture of Napoleon III on September 2, 1870, and the subsequent Siege of Paris, the war is now all but over. A German victory should ensure the acquisition of Alsace.

Robert E. Lee

The opening of the Suez Canal was celebrated in Port Said at a ball attended by 6,000 guests, including royalty.

Isaac Singer

Singer's Continuous Sewing Machine Patented

USA, August 12, 1851: Isaac Merritt Singer has patented his improvement to the sewing machine. Sewing machines of varying degrees of functionality have been around since the eighteenth century, but it is thought that Singer's practical machine, which is capable of continuous stitching, should be of great benefit in both the home and the factory.

The child of German immigrants, Singer was born in Pittstown, New York, in 1811. At 19 he became a machinist's apprentice, also worked as an actor and mechanic. Singer obtained his first patent in 1839 for a mechanical excavator, which he sold for $2,000, a sum that enabled him to set up a theater troupe called the Merritt Players.

Singer's next invention was a type-casting machine for book printing, which he patented in 1849. It was displayed in a Boston machine shop owned by Orson Phelps. As it happened, Phelps manufactured and sold Lerow and Blodgett sewing machines, and he asked for Singer's help with the machines, which were rather clumsy and impractical. Singer thought that the machine would be vastly improved if the shuttle moved back and forth in a straight line rather than going around in a circle. The Lerow and Blodgett machine possessed a curved needle that moved horizontally; Singer suggested a straight needle that moved up and down.

Phelps firmly believes that Singer will be more successful with the sewing machine than with the type-casting machine, and has become his partner in the new venture.

Quinine Saves Lives on Nigerian Expedition

Nigeria, 1854: Long-term prophylactic treatment for malaria was effected for the first time during Dr William Balfour Baikie's exploration of the Niger River. It has long been known that the bark of the South American cinchona tree is effective in treating fevers, but it was not until 1820 that the alkaloid quinine was isolated as the active agent.

During an 1841 Nigerian expedition, almost every European died of malaria. When physician and naturalist Dr Baikie became commander of the 1854 expedition on the *Pleiad*, he ordered everyone on the *Pleiad* to take quinine as a prophylactic. By the time the expedition reached the mouth of the Niger River after 118 days, no-one had died of the disease.

Cinchona bark produces quinine.

Aluminum Economically Viable At Last

Paris, France, 1854: Henri-Etienne Sainte-Claire Deville, Professor of Chemistry at Paris's Ecole Normale Supérieure, has devised a system for extracting aluminum from its compounds, thereby making it possible for aluminum to become a commercial metal. Deville's process treats the aluminum with sodium. This is an improvement on the process devised by German chemist Friedrick Wöhler in 1827, which used potassium, a much more expensive substance.

This latest invention is yet another achievement in Deville's illustrious scientific career. The son of a French diplomat, Deville was born in 1818 in St Thomas, Danish Virgin Islands. He and his older brother, Charles, a geologist, were educated at the Collège Rollin in Paris. Deville received degrees in both medicine and chemistry in 1844. As an undergraduate, he had written and published a paper on his research on turpentine. From 1845 to 1851, Deville served as Dean of Science and Professor of Chemistry at the University of Besançon, before being appointed to his present position at the Ecole Normale Supérieure. Along with his teaching and administrative duties, he has continued to carry on his research, specializing in thermal and inorganic chemistry.

Exposition Universelle Held at Palais d'Industrie

Paris, France, November 15, 1855: The Exposition Universelle (World Exposition) has ended today. Since its opening on May 15, the exposition has played

In 1851 Léon Foucault uses a pendulum to prove the Earth spins anti-clockwis

England, 1850: Robert Bunsen perfects the gas burner.

Berlin, Germany, 1850: Rudolph Clausius states the 2nd law of thermodynamics.

USA, 1851: Isaac Singer devises and patents a continuous stitching sewing machine.

Germany, 1851: Franz Neumann formulates the laws of electromagnetic induction.

England, 1852: Herbert Spencer, biologist, writes *The Developmental Hypothesis*, first using the word "evolution."

France, 1852: Henri Giffard's airship, driven by steam, takes flight.

Bombay, India, April 16, 1853: Service begins on India's first railway, a 21-mile (33-km) route from Thane to Bombay.

London, England, 1853: Samuel Colt, American manufacturer, opens a small arms (weapons) factory.

Nigeria, Africa, 1854: For the first time quinine is administered successfully to treat malaria.

France, 1854: Scientist Henri Sainte-Claire Deville synthesizes aluminum to create the first commercial process.

England, 1854: George Boole publishes *An Investigation into the Laws of Thought*, on which are founded the Mathematical Theories of Logic and Probabilities.

London, England, 1854: John Tyndall demonstrates the principles of fiber optics to the Royal Society.

USA, 1855: David E. Hughes invents the printing telegraph, allowing messages to be sent as text.

France, 1855: Paris hosts the Exposition Universelle (World Exposition).

England, 1856: Henry Bessemer invents his Bessemer Converter, a new method of working steel.

England, 1856: W. H. Perkin produces the first brightly colored cottons, including mauve, obtained by analine (coal tar) dyes.

New York, USA, 1857: Elisha G. Otis's first passenger safety elevator is installed in a department store.

Germany, 1858: Physicist Julius Plucker identifies cathode rays (electrons) and discovers that they are deflected by a magnetic field.

England, 1859: Charles Darwin publishes *On the Origin of Species by Means of Natural Selection*.

France, 1859: Scientist Gaston Plante develops lead-acid battery.

Pennsylvania, USA, 1859: Edwin Drake strikes oil.

Paris, France, 1860: Belgian Jean Joseph Etienne Lenoir patents the first internal-combustion engine.

Shanghai, China, 1861: The first modern, mechanized silk-reeling mill in China begins production.

France, 1862: Léon Foucault determines the speed of light.

A striking building, the Palais d'Industrie is regarded by many as ugly and insufferably hot in summer.

First Passenger Safety Elevator is Installed

New York, USA, March 23, 1857: Elisha Graves Otis's first passenger-safe, steam-powered elevator was installed today in the E. V. Haughwout and Company Department Store, a five-story building on the corner of Broome Street and Broadway. Haughwout purchased the elevator, which travels at a speed of 40 ft (12 m) per minute, for a cost of $300.00.

Elisha Otis was born in 1811 on a farm in Halifax, Vermont. From his boyhood, he enjoyed tinkering with machinery. From 1838 to 1845 he worked in Brattleboro, Vermont, for a wagon and carriage-manufacturing company. In 1845, he was hired as master mechanic at O. Tingley & Company's bedstead factory in Albany, New York, where he invented a railway safety brake and other devices.

In 1852, Otis invented the "safety hoist" for the purpose of moving heavy items between floors within the factory. The invention was an elevator equipped with a device that would keep it from falling if the rope or chain broke. A toothed guiderail on both sides of the elevator shaft would lock the car in position if the cable failed. When Maize and Burns went bankrupt, Otis began his own business, Union Elevator Works, in 1853.

In May 1854 Otis demonstrated the automatic safety elevator at the first New York World's Fair—the Crystal Palace Exhibition, amazing the spectators, and Otis sold seven elevators in 1854 and 15 the following year.

Now that the passenger elevator is safely housed in Haughwout's New York store, Otis hopes to see it installed in hotels, factories, hospitals, and other buildings in the foreseeable future.

Louis-Napoleon Bonaparte III

Elisha Graves Otis

host to over five million visitors, along with 24,000 exhibitors from 34 countries around the globe.

After Napoleon III attended the Great Exhibition in London in 1851, he decided to hold an even bigger and better one in France, as part of his plan to restore his country to its former grandeur. To rival London's Crystal Palace, the Palais d'Industrie (Palace of Industry) was built between the Seine and the Champs-Elysées. The Palais was designed by architects Jean-Marie-Victor Viel and Alexandre Barrault, and despite its massive proportions—850 ft (260 m) long by 350 ft (105 m) wide—it still wasn't large enough to house all the displays, so two smaller buildings were erected. The exposition was a celebration of science and industry, so the trees in front of the building were tightly pruned, and planted in boxes, to symbolize the triumph of technology over nature.

time out

American Ezra Warner invented an effective can opener in 1858, as thinner steel cans came into use. The first can openers were used only in grocery stores—the grocer had to open the can before it left the shop.

Like the British exhibition, the Exposition Universelle was a showcase for imperialism, and featured displays from the French colonies of Senegal, Réunion, Gabon, Madagascar, the Antilles, and Algeria. Many world leaders and dignitaries attended, including Queen Victoria and Abd el-Kader, former ruler of Algeria.

The displays were organized into eight categories: raw materials (including mining and agriculture); mechanical engineering (including shipbuilding and railroads); physical or chemical agents; learned professions (including medicine and pharmacy); manufacture of mineral products (including steel and jewelry); fabric manufacture; decorative arts, printing, and music; and fine arts.

Unfortunately, the World Exposition in Paris has not been a financial success—the organizers have estimated that the total deficit will come very close to 8 million francs.

Key Events

Indiana, USA, 1862: Richard Gatling patents the Gatling Gun, the first rapid repeating firearm.

France, 1863: Siemen-Martin improve upon Bessemer process of 1856 to mass produce steel, enabling the building of skyscrapers.

England, 1863: Thomas Huxley publishes *Evidence on Man's Place in Nature*, making the first claim to imply evolution directly to the human race.

Atlantic Ocean, 1865: A transatlantic telegraph cable is successfully laid.

England, 1866: Robert Whitehead invents the underwater torpedo.

Canada, 1867: Emily Stowe, the first female doctor in Canada, practices medicine illegally after being declined permission to write the Canadian exams required for foreign practitioners.

Stockholm, Sweden, 1867: Alfred Nobel, chemist and industrialist, patents dynamite.

St Petersburg, Russia, 1869: Dmitry Ivanovitch Mendelyeev publishes his periodic table of the chemical properties of the elements.

USA, 1872: George Westinghouse patents a triple valve air brake, which will revolutionize the railroad industry.

Tokyo, Japan, October 14, 1872: Official inauguration of Japan's first railway, an 18.6-mile (30-km) line from Shimbashi Station (Tokyo) to Yokohama.

England, December 21, 1872: HMS *Challenger* sails from Portsmouth on a three-year voyage of exploration. Chemists, physicists and biologists will collaborate with navigators to map the sea.

England, 1873: James Clerk Maxwell, eminent Scottish physicist, publishes his *Treatise on Electricity and Magnetism*, expounding his ideas on field theory and magnetism.

USA, 1873: Christopher Sholes develops the first practical typewriter, manufactured by Remington.

Germany, 1873: Graduate student Othmar Zeidler synthesises DDT when working in a laboratory at the University of Strasbourg.

Vienna, Austria, 1873: The International Meteorological Society is formed.

England, 1874: George Stoney estimates the unit of charge in electrochemistry and calls it the electron.

France, 1874: Engineer Emile Baudot introduces a binary code system, the Baudot printing telegraph. This will allow up to six operators to send messages on the same communications line.

USA, 1874: Thomas Edison invents the perfected quadruplex telegraph, a method to transmit four messages simultaneously, two in each direction.

Darwin's *The Origin of Species* Released

Charles Darwin

London, England, November 22, 1859: The first 1,250 copies of Charles Darwin's scientific abstract *On the Origin of Species by Means of Natural Selection* all but sold out when the book was released today. There has been a huge interest in Darwin's work since he presented his ideas on "natural selection" presented at the Linnaean Society last year.

Darwin proposes that organisms are changeable, and that species are descended—in a modified way—from previous forms. Influenced by the theories of Thomas Malthus, Darwin believes that organisms produce more offspring than their habitat can sustain, and thus have to compete with each other for survival. He concludes his abstract by stating, "… whilst this planet has gone circling on according to the fixed law of gravity, from so simple a beginning endless forms most beautiful and most wonderful have been, and are being, evolved."

While Darwin's thoughts are by no means original (some of them have been around since Aristotle's time), they are the culmination of over 20 years of painstaking research and study.

Darwin's interest in the natural world began in his youth. The son of a physician in Shrewsbury, England, Darwin entered the University of Edinburgh to study medicine. He wasn't suited for surgery, and transferred to Christ's College, Cambridge, to train as a clergyman.

As a result of a recommendation by Reverend John Henslow, his botany professor, Darwin was to embark on a journey that would completely change his direction. On December 27, 1831, he sailed from Devonport on the HMS *Beagle* as naturalist and gentleman companion to Captain Robert FitzRoy. On the expedition, which lasted for five years, Darwin traveled to South America, the Galapagos Islands, New Zealand, Australia, and Tahiti, all the while gathering specimens, collecting data, and formulating ideas that would influence his work for the next two decades.

> "I ALMOST THINK IT IS THE ULTIMATE DESTINY OF SCIENCE TO EXTERMINATE THE HUMAN RACE."
>
> THOMAS LOVE PEACOCK (1785–1866), ENGLISH WRITER, 1860

> "AND IN CONCLUSION, I WOULD LIKE TO ASK THE GENTLEMAN… WHETHER THE APE FROM WHICH HE IS DESCENDED WAS ON HIS GRANDMOTHER'S OR GRANDFATHER'S SIDE OF THE FAMILY."
>
> SAMUEL WILBERFORCE (1805–1873), ENGLISH CLERIC, ON DARWIN'S THEORY OF EVOLUTION, 1860

HMS *Beagle* arriving at Sydney, Australia, on Charles Darwin's second survey expedition.

Gatling Gun is Patented

Indianapolis, USA, May, 1862: Richard Jordan Gatling has patented his invention, the Gatling gun, and established the Gatling Gun Company. After hearing of the carnage in the American Civil War, Gatling invented an efficient weapon that eliminated the need for large armies.

The Gatling gun is a mechanical, rapid-repeating, six-barreled gun that is capable of firing .58-caliber cartridges at 200 rounds per minute. It uses percussion caps, has reloadable steel chambers, and can be mounted.

Born in North Carolina, Gatling inherited his ingenuity from his father, a farmer and inventor. When he was only 21, Gatling invented a screw propeller for steamboats, which had been recently patented by someone else. He worked in a variety of occupations, and while self-employed as a shopkeeper in 1839, he patented a rice-sowing machine, which he later adapted for use as a wheat drill. Over the next few years, Gatling received many accolades and reaped the financial rewards from these inventions.

Ever versatile, Gatling decided to become a doctor after he suffered from smallpox in 1845. In 1850 he received a degree from Ohio Medical College, but he never practiced medicine, and instead turned his attentions back to farm machinery. In 1857, Gatling invented a new steam-driven plow, which was not as successful as his previous agricultural inventions.

Alfred Nobel's Explosive Invention Is Dynamite

Stockholm, Sweden, 1867: Alfred Nobel, a 34-year-old Swedish chemist and engineer, has patented an explosive device that he has named "dynamite" (from the Greek word *dynamis*, meaning *power*). Nobel had been interested in

Inventor and philanthropist Alfred Nobel.

explosives since the age of 17, when he studied chemistry in the Paris laboratory of Théophile Jules Pelouze. There he met Ascanio Sobrero, an Italian chemist who had invented nitroglycerin in 1846.

At the end of the Crimean War in 1856, Nobel's father, Immanuel, went bankrupt. The Russian armed forces no longer needed the military equipment supplied by his St Petersburg engineering company. However, the Nobels could see a market for explosives, to facilitate the construction of roads, railway tunnels, bridges, and buildings in Europe's cities.

In 1860, Nobel began to experiment with nitroglycerin, and two years later set up a small family-run factory outside Stockholm to produce the substance and devise ways to harness its volatility. Nobel received a patent on nitroglycerine ("blasting oil") for industrial purposes in 1863, and invented a detonator that triggered the substance's explosive properties. The following year, 1864, Nobel's brother Emil and several others were killed by a nitroglycerin explosion, a tragedy that made Nobel even more determined to find a way to make nitroglycerin safer and easier to control. In 1865, Nobel improved on his detonator and renamed it a "blasting cap."

Finally, in a serendipitous discovery, Alfred Nobel added the porous organic material known as *kieselguhr* (diatomaceous earth) to nitroglycerin, which rendered it more stable and pliable, thereby creating dynamite.

Mendelyeev Presents Periodic Table of Elements

St Petersburg, Russia, March 6, 1869:
Professor Dmitri Ivanovich Mendelyeev today presented his paper entitled *The Dependence between the Properties of the Atomic Weights of the Elements*. The crux of Mendelyeev's paper is his periodic table—a simple chart that arranges the 63 known elements in a logical order according to atomic weight, along horizontal and vertical axes.

Mendelyeev's interest in chemistry began during his childhood in Tobolsk, Siberia, when he would visit his mother's glass factory. At age 15, he entered the Main Pedagogical Institute in St Petersburg, and later received his doctorate in

chemistry from the University of St Petersburg. He also studied with Robert Bunsen in Heidelberg. He taught at the St Petersburg Technological Institute, where he taught until his appointment at the University of St Petersburg in 1867.

This year, Mendelyeev co-founded the Russian Chemical Society, and is writing a textbook, *The Principles of Chemistry*.

Treatise on Electricity and Magnetism Published

England, 1873: Scottish physicist James Clerk Maxwell has published his *Treatise on Electricity and Magnetism*, expounding his ideas on field theory and magnetism. Maxwell was influenced by Michael Faraday's "Lines of Force." But Faraday was not a mathematician, and Maxwell extended and applied mathematical formulae to Faraday's ideas, proving the quantitative relationship between electromagnetism and light. His treatise is a culmination of over a decade's work.

Born in Edinburgh, Scotland, in 1831, Maxwell was a quiet child, considered by some to be intellectually backward. He proved himself otherwise when he was accepted at age 16 into Edinburgh University, and later distinguished himself at Trinity College, Cambridge, where his interest in electricity and magnetism began. Maxwell held the chair of the Natural Philosophy at Marischal College, Aberdeen, from 1856 to 1860, was Professor of Physics and Astronomy at King's College from 1860 to 1868, and is currently Professor of Experimental Physics at Cambridge.

As well as electromagnetism, Maxwell has led the field in the study of color and color-blindness, and has devised instruments to use in this branch of research. He has also experimented with color photography. In 1859, he won the prestigious Adams Prize for his paper *On the Stability*

of *Saturn's Rings*, proving that the rings are comprised of small particles. Maxwell published *Illustrations of the Dynamical Theory of Gases* in 1860, and in 1861 became a member of the Royal Society.

Thomas Edison Invents Quadruplex Telegraph

Newark, New Jersey, USA, 1874: Inventor and former telegraph operator, 27-year-old Thomas Alva Edison, has devised the quadruplex system, capable of transmitting four messages simultaneously, two in each direction. This is a cost-efficient boon to the telegraph industry, as more messages can be sent using fewer wires. The Western Union Telegraph Company has offered Edison $40,000 for the system.

Edison's invention is an improvement on the systems devised by Julius Gintl of Austria in 1853, and J. B. Stearns of Massachusetts in 1871.

Born in 1847, Edison became partially deaf as a result of his frequent boyhood illnesses. At 12, he was selling newspapers on the railroad between Port Huron and Detroit. A keen inventor even then, he created a moving laboratory in one of the train's baggage cars. When he was 16, he saved the life of the stationmaster's child, and the stationmaster gave Edison the opportunity to become a railroad telegrapher, a lucrative profession. He became proficient in this relatively new technology, and honed his mechanical and engineering skills as he traveled around the country with the railway.

In 1868, at the age of 21, Edison patented his first invention in Boston—an electrical vote recorder. However, there was not much interest in his machine. A few years later he moved to New York, where he devised an improved ticker for the stock market. Shortly thereafter, he set up his own laboratory and workshop in Newark, New Jersey.

Thomas Edison

Scientific Achievements

Anthropology: Ideas on "natural selection" proposed.
Astronomy: *General Catalogue* of nebulae and star clusters published.
Botany: Darwin publishes *On the Origin of Species by Means of Natural Selection*.
Ecology: Yellowstone National Park established, first in the world.
Chemistry: Pasteurization invented.
Geology: Attempts made to calculate the age of Earth.
Mathematics: Mathematical theories of logic and probability published.
Medicine: Germ theory of disease confirmed.
Physics: Theories on blue sky and sunsets stated.
Zoology: Zoos established in USA at Philadelphia and Lincoln Park.

Botanic Gardens
Adelaide, Australia
Belgrade, eastern Europe
Brisbane, Australia
Bucharest, eastern Europe
Darwin, Australia
Frankfurt, Germany
Hong Kong
Kalmthout, Belgium
St Louis, USA
Singapore, Singapore
Washington DC, USA

Observatories
Copenhagen, Denmark
Melbourne, Australia
Neuchatel, Switzerland
New York, USA
Sydney, Australia
Utrecht, Netherlands

Universities
University of Athens, Greece
University of Beirut, Lebanon
University of Bucharest, eastern Europe
University of Colombo, Ceylon
University of Dublin, Ireland
University of Kolkata, India
University of Long Beach, USA
University of Melbourne, Australia
University of Sydney, Australia
University of Tehran, Iran
University of Venice, Italy

Amidst much celebration, Japan's first railway is opened between Tokyo and Yokohama in 1872.

Harriet Beecher Stowe

Wordsworth's Magnum Opus is Published

England, July, 1850: *The Prelude*, an autobiographical poem by William Wordsworth, has been published three months after the poet's death. The untitled poem was actually completed in 1805, and Wordsworth continued to make revisions throughout his life. His wife, Mary, named the previously untitled work *The Prelude*, and arranged for its publication. *The Prelude* is composed of 14 "books," and deals with the familiar Wordsworthian themes of imagination, memory, and nature.

Wordsworth was born on April 7, 1770, in the Lake District of Northern England. He found solace and inspiration in the landscape of the district, where he lived for most of his life. In 1787, his first poem was published in *The European* magazine, and in that year he entered St John's College, Cambridge.

After completing his education in 1791, Wordsworth lived for a year in France, where he was caught up by the revolutionary ideals of liberty and equality. He also fathered a child to a French girl, Annette Vallon, but left mother and daughter in France and returned to England. Following a period of inner turmoil, Wordsworth met fellow Romantic poet Samuel Taylor Coleridge, and their long and sometimes turbulent friendship had a profound effect on both of them, personally and poetically.

Wordsworth produced his best and most innovative work between the years 1797–1807. *Lyrical Ballads, with a Few Other Poems* was published in 1798, and included Wordsworth's "Tintern Abbey" and Coleridge's "The Rime of the Ancient Mariner." The moving pastoral poem "Michael" was published in 1800, and

William Wordsworth, the poet.

"Ode: Intimations of Immortality from Recollections of Early Childhood" in 1807. During this period he married Mary Hutchinson, who, with his sister, Dorothy, would be a significant influence on his life and work. Between the years of 1805 and 1812, he endured the tragic deaths of his brother and two of his children.

As he grew older, Wordsworth lost his romantic vision and became more conservative—religiously, politically, and artistically. In 1843 Wordsworth succeeded Robert Southey as the Poet Laureate, and died at 80 years of age.

Anti-slavery Novel a Smash Hit

Boston, USA, March, 1852: Harriet Beecher Stowe's anti-slavery novel, *Uncle Tom's Cabin: or, Life among the Lowly*, has sold 10,000 copies in the first week of release. Published by J. P. Jewett of Boston, the

novel was originally serialized in 40 episodes in the abolitionist journal *The National Era*, reaching a wide readership.

Stowe was born Harriet Beecher in Litchfield, Connecticut, in 1811. Her father, Lyman, was a Congregational minister, and both parents were devoted to the causes of education and social justice. She moved with her family to Cincinnati, Ohio, working as a schoolteacher until her marriage to Calvin Stowe, a theology professor. The couple had seven children, and Stowe wrote articles and stories to augment the family income. A collection of stories entitled *The Mayflower* was published in 1834.

Uncle Tom's Cabin is entertaining as well as edifying, and is destined to become an American classic. It was motivated, in part, by Stowe's reaction to the 1850 *Fugitive Slave Law*, which made it a criminal offense to give aid or shelter to escaped slaves. The book was also inspired by personal tragedy. In 1849, Stowe's 18-month-old son, Samuel Charles, died of cholera. In writing the novel, she was able to exorcise her own grief, and at the same time call attention

In *Uncle Tom's Cabin*, Harriet Beecher Stowe entreats her fellow Northerners to shelter escaped slaves.

to the plight of the slaves, who are so often wrenched away from their families.

Verdi's Opera *La Traviata* Premières

Venice, Italy, March 6, 1853: *La Traviata*, Giuseppe Verdi's operatic adaptation of Alexandre Dumas *fils'* novel and play *La Dame aux Camélias (The Lady of the Camellias)*, opened tonight at the Teatro La Fenice. Both critics and audience gave it a hostile reception, complaining that the male lead tenor, Lodovico Graziani, was in poor voice, and that plump soprano Fanny Salvini-Donatelli was unconvincing as Violetta Valery, a consumptive prostitute. The fact that the producers placed the opera in the year 1700, rather than giving it a contemporary setting, also did not sit well with either Verdi or the audience. Some critics complained that the subject matter was immoral. It was a great disappointment for Verdi, whose recent successes, *Rigoletto* (1851) and *Il Trovatore* (1853), were well received by both the musical elite and popular audiences.

Verdi was born on October 10, 1813, in the tiny Italian village of Le Roncole. He was refused admission to the Milan Conservatory of Music, and began private music studies with Vincenzo Lavigna. He composed his first opera, *Oberto*, in 1839, but resolved to give up music forever after the deaths of his wife and two children. However, he was inspired by the nationalist movement for a free and united Italy, and his next opera, *Nabucco* (1842), reflected his political sentiments; it was a resounding success when it opened at Milan's La Scala. One of the songs from *Nabucco* ("Oh, my country so beautiful and lost!") became an anthem for the unification of Italy movement.

Emma Bovary: misguided dreamer or wicked adultress?

Flaubert Acquitted on Morals Charge

Paris, France, April 12, 1857: Writer Gustave Flaubert has gratefully dedicated the new edition of his novel *Madame Bovary* to his defence lawyer, Marie-Antoine-Jules Senard, stating "for it is to you, above all, that I owe its publication."

Two months earlier, Flaubert and the *Revue de Paris* (in which the novel was serialized in 1856) were charged by the French Government for crimes against decency and morality. Both author and publisher were acquitted on the grounds that the offending passages comprised just a small percentage of the book.

It took Flaubert six years to complete his controversial work. It tells the story of Emma Bovary, a young wife who regrets her marriage to a dull country doctor and finds adventure and passion in two extramarital affairs. It

time out

Two years before his death from syphilis, German composer Robert Schumann (1810-1856) attempts suicide while in a depressed state. He flings himself into the Rhine River, is rescued by boatmen, and spends the rest of his life in an asylum.

is thought that Flaubert drew on his own experiences as inspiration; his first love affair at age 15 was with a 25-year-old married woman, and he enjoyed a sporadic eight-year liaison with married poet Louise Colet. The romantic, yet highly realistic novel is considered to be fresh, original, and well-crafted.

Flaubert was born in 1821 in Rouen, and began writing when he was a boy. After completing his education in Rouen, he went to Paris to study law, but abandoned his legal studies when he was diagnosed with a nervous condition (possibly epilepsy). Living on an inheritance, he traveled throughout Europe and the Middle East. His first novel, *The Temptation of St Anthony* (1842), was poorly received.

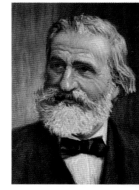
Giuseppe Verdi

Barbizon Artist Millet Paints *The Gleaners*

Barbizon, France, 1857: Jean-François Millet has completed his painting *The Gleaners*, depicting three rustic women working in a field. It is a gentle vignette, painted in golden autumn tones.

Millet was born in 1814 at Gruchy in northwest France. After studying art in Cherbourg, Millet won a scholarship with Paul Delaroche in Paris.

Millet's early work consisted mainly of stylized scenes from mythology, as was the fashion at the time. In 1849, an outbreak of cholera in Paris, forced Millet to take his family to live in Barbizon, near the Forest of Fontainebleau. It was there he met Théodore Rousseau, who with Jean-Baptiste Camille Corot, Charles-Francois Daubigny and others formed the Barbizon school, which fostered the trend toward naturalism in art. His earlier works from the Barbizon period include *Haymakers* (1850) and *Harvesters* (1853).

Key Events

Paris, France, January 15, 1863: The Salon des Refuses opens.
Paris, France, 1863: Edouard Manet's painting *Le Déjeuner sur L'Herbe* is exhibited at the Salon des Refuses.
Paris, France, 1863: Jean Auguste Dominique Ingres' sensuous masterpiece *The Turkish Bath* is exhibited in the Louvre.
France, 1863: Artist Eugène Delacroix, once considered leader of the Romantic movement, dies.
USA, November 26, 1865: Lewis Carroll publishes *Alice's Adventures in Wonderland*.

Russia, 1866: Novelist Fyodor (Mikhaylovich) Dostoevsky's novel *Crime and Punishment* is serialized in *Russkii Vestnik (The Russian Messenger)*.
Germany, 1867: Karl Marx publishes *Das Kapital*, a critical analysis of capitalism.
France, 1867: Emile Zola publishes his novel, *Therese Raquin*.
England, 1867: Edward Lear, artist, illustrator and writer of nonsense poetry and limericks, publishes *The Owl and the Pussycat*.

France, 1867: Jean Auguste Dominique Ingres dies. During his lifetime he was acclaimed as the leader of the Neoclassic movement.
USA, 1868: *Little Women*, a novel about life in New England, by Louisa May Alcott, is published.
Russia, 1868: Maxim Gorky, influential writer, is born.
Moscow, Russia, December 26, 1869: *Don Quixote* the ballet, premières.
Russia, 1869: Publication of Leo Tolstoy's *War and Peace*, is complete; writing of this classic novel has taken six years.

Australia, 1869: Swiss born artist Louis Buvelot paints *Water Pool at Coleraine*, painting "en plein air" (on location), capturing the unique Australian light.
Paris, France, 1869: Café Guerbois, in the Batignolles quarter, has become the favorite meeting place for artists and writers.
Algeria, 1870: The artist Frédéric Bazille, best known for his fine examples of outdoor figural work, such as *Family Reunion*, is killed in action.

Paris, France, 1873: Artist Gustave Courbet flees to Switzerland to avoid massive fines for complicity in the destruction of the Napoleon Column in Place Vendôme. He has already served six months in jail.
Paris, France, 1874: In a group exhibition Claude Monet exhibits a painting entitled *Impression: Sunrise*. Received unfavourably by newspaper critics, the artists in the group are labelled Impressionists, implying that they have lost touch with reality and are producing half finished works.

Morris, Marshall, Faulkner Opens in Red Lion Square

Karl Marx

London, England, April, 1861: Artist and poet William Morris, along with businessman Charles Faulkner, surveyor P. P. Marshall, architect Philip Webb, and artists Dante Gabriel Rossetti, Edward Burne-Jones, and Ford Madox Brown, has opened an art and design company with premises at 8 Red Lion Square, London.

The company came into being, in part, as a reaction against the plethora of mass-produced goods. The company offers design services for churches, homes, and public buildings. The range of modalities includes stained glass, wall paintings, sculpture, woodcarving, furniture, furnishings, embroidery, carpet, and jewelry—all individually designed and crafted by the artisan.

William Morris's prodigious energy and eclectic interests make him well suited to head up such an enterprise. He was educated at Marlborough College and Exeter College, Oxford, where he became friends with Edward Burne-Jones, a fellow divinity student. After a trip to France in 1855, they both gave up their plans to enter the church, hoping to devote their lives to art. Morris had a short-lived apprenticeship in an architectural firm, and Burne-Jones became the protégé of leading Pre-Raphaelite artist Dante Gabriel Rossetti.

The Pre-Raphaelite Brotherhood is a group of painters influenced by the esthetic ideals of the artist and philosopher John Ruskin, "to trust nature and forsake all else." They scorn modern sensibilities, drawing inspiration from the medieval (particularly Arthurian) world and the romantic visions of Shakespeare, Keats, and Shelley.

Morris discovered his true calling when he and his wife, Jane, furnished and decorated their South London home "Red House," which was designed by architect Philip Webb. Morris created the stained-glass windows, textiles, and tapestries with a distinctly medieval theme.

Great Expectations by Dickens is Published

London, England, October, 1861: *Great Expectations*, the thirteenth novel by leading British author Charles Dickens, has just been published in book form. The story had previously appeared in weekly installments in *All the Year Round*, a magazine owned and edited by Dickens. The novel, which began serialization in 1860, was written to boost the magazine's falling readership, and has proven to be a financial, literary, and popular success.

English author Charles Dickens.

Although not as autobiographical as *David Copperfield*, *Great Expectations* does borrow considerably from the author's own life. It takes place from 1810 to 1830, the time of Dickens's own childhood and young adulthood, and it is set in Kent, where the Dickens family once lived.

Because his previous book, *A Tale of Two Cities* (1859), was criticized for being too serious, Dickens said "he has made the opening, I hope, in its general effect exceedingly droll." The story tells of the adventures of Pip, a young orphan who becomes a gentleman due to the generosity of a mysterious benefactor. As in the best of Dickens's works—*Pickwick Papers* (1836), *Oliver Twist* (1837), *Nicholas Nickleby* (1838), *A Christmas Carol* (1843), and *David Copperfield* (1850)— the novel has an exciting dramatic plot and is full of colorful characters. While *Great Expectations* is often light and funny, it also deals with serious themes such as the nature of class, injustice, and the importance of love and friendship over wealth and privilege.

As well as being a prolific author, magazine publisher, and public speaker, Dickens devotes much of his time to campaigning for social reform.

Das Kapital by Karl Marx is Published

Hamburg, Germany, October, 1867: The first volume of *Das Kapital (Capital)*, a philosophical and economic treatise by Karl Marx, has been published. A critique of the capitalist system, the work is the culmination of over 10 years of research.

In *Das Kapital*, Marx proposes many thought-provoking ideas: for example, unemployment is a construct of capitalism, created to keep workers in a state of fear. He believes that capitalism is inherently unstable, and predicts that the workers will one day band together to overthrow the capitalist system.

Marx was born in Trier, Germany, in 1818, the son of a Jewish lawyer (who later converted to Christianity). At university, Marx became fascinated with the philosophies of Bruno Bauer and G. W. F. Hegel, and Immanuel Kant and Jean-Jacques Rousseau. He began his career as writer and editor for *Rheinische Zeitung (Rhenish Gazette)*, and was later forced to resign because of his extremist viewpoints.

In Paris in 1844, Marx met Friedrich Engels, who had recently published *The Condition of the Working Class in England*. They joined forces in 1848 to produce *The Communist Manifesto*, based on an unfinished draft by Engels entitled *The Principles of Communism*.

At various times throughout his career, Karl Marx had been deported from Germany, France, and Belgium because of the controversial nature of his works. *Das Kapital* is sure to disturb many people. The Russian Government is not censoring it as they feel that most people will find it incomprehensible.

Key Structures

Abdin Palace, Cairo, Egypt
Adare Manor, Limerick, Ireland
Astors' Beechwood, Newport, USA
Balai Seni Rupa, Jakarta, Dutch East Indies
Belle Meade Plantation, Nashville, USA
Crystal Palace, London, England
Imperial Palace, Kyoto, Japan
Istana, Kuching, Malaya
Maha Uma Devi Temple, Bangkok, Siam
Majidjiyyeh Mosque, Beirut, Lebanon
Masmak Fortress, Riyadh, Saudi Arabia
Old Clock Tower, Rhodes, Greece
Old St Paul's Church, Wellington, New Zealand
Paris Opera, Paris, France
Semmering Railway, Austria
St Andrew's Cathedral, Singapore
St Florin Parish Cathedral, Vaduz, Liechtenstein
St Patrick's Basilica, Ottawa, Canada
Sveta Nedelya Cathedral, Sofia, eastern Europe
The Grand Serail, Beirut, Lebanon
Tomb of Tu Doc, Hue, Vietnam
Vimanmek Teak Mansion, Bangkok, Siam
Westminster Palace, London, England
Yasukuni Shrine, Tokyo, Japan

Wallpaper design from Morris, Marshall, Faulkner & Co.

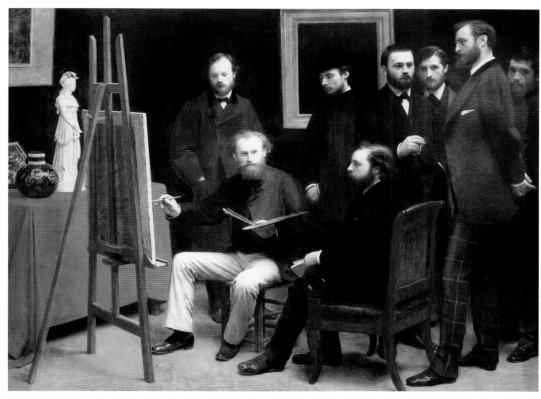

L'Atelier des Batignolles, by Henri Fantin-Latour (1870), shows Parisian artists, including Manet (painting), Renoir, and Monet.

Artists Fail to Make an Impression

Paris, France, May 15, 1874: An art exhibition, held at the former studio of photographer Felix Nadar at 35 Boulevard des Capucines in Paris, ended today after a month-long season. The exhibition was organized by a group of experimental artists known as the Artists' Cooperative Society of Painters, Sculptors, Engravers, etc. as a clear reaction to being rejected or dismissed by the prestigious, conservative Paris Salon.

A total of 165 works were displayed, including paintings by Pierre August Renoir, Alfred Sisley, Camille Pissarro, Berthe Morisot, Paul Cézanne, Armand Guillamin, and others.

While the artists differ from each other in many respects, they share a number of common themes and techniques. Rather than using historical or mythological figures as their subjects, they focus on ordinary people in both rural and urban settings. They prefer to paint outdoors (*en plein air*) rather than in a studio, and are influenced by non-European (particularly Japanese) art forms. They paint on a white ground, and eliminate earth tones and blacks from their palettes. Rather than blending their colors before painting, they apply them straight onto the canvas. In addition, their brushstrokes are broken and choppy.

To some, the effect is fresh and luminous, but many critics have come away baffled and unconvinced. One of the most vitriolic detractors was Louis Leroy, in *Le Charivari*. In his critique of Monet's *Impression, Sunrise,* he says: "Impression…since I was impressed, there had to be some impression in it…Wallpaper in its embryonic state is more finished than that seascape." Since this review, the artists have become known as "Impressionists." Another disparaging comment was made about Pissarro by Albert Wolff in *Le Figaro*: "…it is startling to see how far astray human vanity can go, even to the point of total madness."

Not all the reviews of the exhibition have been negative, and although the exhibition was not a financial success, more have been planned for the future.

Paul Cézanne

Leo Tolstoy's *War and Peace* Published at Last

Russia, 1869: After six years, the publication of Leo Tolstoy's novel *War and Peace* is finally completed. The author has described his book as an "epic in prose," and indeed, at 1,500 pages, 365 chapters, and 580 characters (including Napoleon Bonaparte and Alexander I), the word "novel" simply doesn't do it justice.

Set against the backdrop of Napoleon's invasion of Russia in 1812, *War and Peace* centers on the members of four noble families, and how their lives are affected by the historical events taking place around them. It explores the themes of free will and predestination, proposing that man cannot live unless he believes that he has some control of his destiny.

Tolstoy was born into an aristocratic family in 1828. He failed to complete university, and for a time led a dissolute existence in St Petersburg. In 1851, he entered the Russian Army and served in the Crimean War. Tolstoy's first attempts at writing were a trilogy of thinly disguised autobiographical novels: *Childhood* (1852), *Boyhood* (1854), and *Youth* (1856). His war experiences inspired *Sevastapol Sketches* (1856).

After completing his military service, Tolstoy traveled to Germany, Switzerland, and France. When he returned home, he established a school for peasant children and also studied educational theory. Tolstoy married Sonya Andreyevna Behrs in 1862. His next novel, *The Cossacks* (1863), was originally called *Young Manhood* and is a sequel to *Youth*.

Tolstoy is an avid reader of fiction, and is influenced by the works of renowned British novelists Charles Dickens, George Eliot, and Laurence Sterne.

Duel at the Café Guerbois

Paris, France, February, 1870: At the Café Guerbois, 11 Grande rue des Batignolles, a duel took place between painters Edouard Manet and Louis Edmond Duranty. Manet shot Duranty over an artistic difference of opinion; Duranty was wounded, but not seriously.

For several years now, the café has been a stimulating gathering place for the *Bohèmes*, a group of artists, writers, and hangers-on. It is a place where people eat, drink coffee and wine, and, most importantly, share ideas about life and art.

Manet, whose studio is in the neighborhood of the café, is the unofficial leader of the group. The circle also includes his fellow artists Claude Monet, Henri Fantin-Latour, Edgar Degas, Pierre-Auguste Renoir, Alfred Sisley, Paul Cézanne, Camille Pissarro, photographer and cartoonist Felix Nadar, poets Charles Baudelaire and Stéphane Mallarmé, and novelist Emile Zola.

Manet's 1869 sketch, *Au Café Guerbois*, captures the lively atmosphere of what is sometimes referred to by the artistic community as "The Batignolles School."

Berthe Morisot by Edouard Manet.

Isabella Beeton

America Wins Prestigious Regatta

Isle of Wight, England, August 22, 1851: Sporting history was made today when the US schooner *America* outraced 14 British vessels to win the Hundred Guineas Cup. Her Majesty Queen Victoria was one of the honored guests to witness the event. The 101 ft 3 in (30.85 m) craft, representing the New York Yacht Club, was skippered by John Cox Stevens. By the time she finished the 58-mile (93-km) race around the Isle of Wight in 10½ hours, *America* was in front of her closest competitor, *Aurora*, by some 20 minutes.

The Isle of Wight race is a big feature of the Royal Yacht Squadron of Great Britain's summer regatta, but to coincide with the Great Exhibition, the Squadron extended an invitation to the USA to participate. They accepted, commissioning New York boat modeler George Steers to come up with a suitable craft. Designed to resemble a clipper ship, the $30,000 black schooner has a reversed bow; the hull was made a mix of cedar, chestnut, locust wood, and white oak. *America* was launched in May this year, and sailed first to France where she was fitted with her racing sails before traveling to England.

> "WEALTH IS LIKE SEA-WATER; THE MORE WE DRINK, THE THIRSTIER WE BECOME; AND THE SAME IS TRUE OF FAME."
>
> ARTHUR SCHOPENHAUER (1788–1860), GERMAN PHILOSOPHER, 1851

> "I DO NOT ASK FOR MY RIGHTS. I HAVE NO RIGHTS; I HAVE ONLY WRONGS."
>
> CAROLINE NORTON (1808–1877), ENGLISH POET AND ADVOCATE OF WOMEN'S RIGHTS, 1853

The trophy that the Americans will take home is a solid silver pitcher created in 1848 by Royal Jeweler, Robert Garrard. The inscription on the cup reads: "100 Guineas Cup Won August 22nd, 1851 at Cowes, England by Yacht *America* at the Royal Yacht Squadron Regatta."

Johan Lundström's Safety Match is Patented

Sweden, 1855: Swedish scientist Johan Edvard Lundström has invented and patented a safety match made from red phosphorus. The match is ignited by the friction caused when the chemicals on the match-head are struck against the paper attached to the matchbox, which contains the red phosphorus.

This invention could be a real breakthrough, as up until now, matches have been made from toxic white phosphorus. People who come into contact with white phosphorus, especially employees in the match factories, are likely to develop a fatal condition known as "phossy jaw." The disease begins as a toothache or swelling in the jaw. As the phosphorus eats into the jawbone, the jawbone rots, causing severe pain, abscess, and offensive-smelling discharge. Eventually, the disease spreads to the internal organs. The jawbone can be surgically removed, but this is not always successful, and the operation causes severe disfigurement.

New Divorce Law Passed

London, England, 1857: The Divorce and Matrimonial Causes Act of 1857 has been passed, which makes secular divorce

Women gain some rights under the new divorce laws.

possible in England for a greater number of people. Up until now, divorce was only possible through the Parliamentary permission, and as this was so expensive, only the wealthy could afford it. In fact, only a few couples were divorced under the old Parliamentary system. Ecclesiastical divorces have also been available in extreme cases, but the divorcing parties were not allowed to remarry.

Under the terms of the new Act, the divorce court could order a husband to pay maintenance to his former wife. In addition, a divorced wife would be allowed to inherit property, enter into contractual arrangements, or be a party in lawsuits. The Act also states that a husband can divorce his wife on the grounds of adultery only; however, if a woman is to divorce her husband, in addition to adultery, she has to prove that she has been deserted for two years, or that her husband had also committed acts of extreme cruelty, bigamy, incest, sodomy, or rape.

The Divorce and Matrimonial Causes Act of 1857 follows the Custody of Infants Act of 1839, which permitted divorced women of "unblemished character" (i.e. not adulterous), to apply for custody of children under the age of seven. Up until now, the father had always been granted custody regardless of his character.

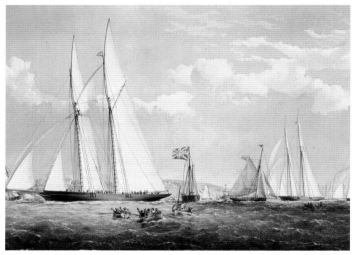

Sailing around the Isle of Wight tests the skill of skippers and crew alike.

Key Events

Birmingham, England, 1850: The world's first purpose-built exhibition hall opens.

UK, March 30, 1851: A population census is taken.

Massachusetts, USA, 1851: Adoption Law is passed to set legal precedents.

Isle of Wight, England, August 22, 1851: The yacht *America* wins the first Hundred Guineas Cup.

London, England, 1851: Reuters News Service is founded.

UK, 1851: Doctor John Gorrie invents a working refrigeration unit.

Winchester, England, 1851: First free public library is opened.

London, England, February 11, 1852: First public toilet for women opens.

England, 1852: Samuel Fox invents and manufactures the steel rimmed umbrella.

USA, 1853: Chef George Crum invents thin potato chips by chance when trying to please an angry customer.

USA, 1855: The rotary washing machine is invented by Hamilton Smith, consisting of a wooden drum and hand-cranked wringer.

France, 1855: Dry cleaning introduced by Jean-Baptiste Jolly.

London, England, 1855: Sewers are modernized after the fourth outbreak of cholera.

Sweden, 1855: Johan Lundström patents the red phosphorous safety match. Previously, poisonous white phosphorus was used.

USA, 1857: Toilet paper is invented.

UK, 1857: Divorce and Matrimonial Causes Act makes divorce without parliamentary approval legal.

USA, 1857: Hollywood is founded.

Australia, 1858: Tom Wills devises Australian rules football as an attempt to maintain cricketers' fitness.

England, 1858: *The Wedding March* by Felix Mendelssohn becomes popular when played at Queen Victoria's wedding.

Simla, India, July 28, 1859: Bishop Cotton School, a private Western-style boarding schools in Asia, is founded.

London, England, 1860: The first professional school of nursing is opened in St Thomas's Hospital.

England, 1860: The first open championship of golf is played.

Toronto, Canada, 1860: The Queens Plate for thoroughbred horse racing is inaugurated.

New York, USA, 1860s: German immigrants begin using pushcarts on the streets to sell frankfurters in buns, with sauerkraut relish.

London, England, 1861: Horse-drawn trams are introduced.

England, 1861: Mrs Beeton publishes *Book of Household Management*.

Australia, 1861: The first Melbourne Cup race is won by "Archer."

Many people believe that more improvements need to be made to the marriage laws. For example, at the time of writing, a woman's body is still legally considered to be the property of her husband, and a man is entitled to have his wife sent to prison if she refuses him conjugal rights.

School of Nursing Opens at St Thomas's Hospital

London, England, July 9, 1860: The first probationers have arrived today at St Thomas's Hospital's first professional school of nursing in London. The school owes its existence to nursing pioneer and social activist, Florence Nightingale.

Nightingale first heard the call to help the sick and wounded at the age of 17, despite the fact that nursing was considered an unseemly occupation for respectable women. In 1851, at the age of 31, she trained for several months at an innovative hospital at Kaiserwerth, Germany, run by Catholic nuns. Two years later, Nightingale became superintendent of the Institute for the Care of Sick Gentle-women in London. She abandoned her post in 1854 when she and 38 volunteers traveled to Scutari in Turkey to provide nursing services for the injured soldiers of the Crimean War. The standards of the military hospital there were appalling, but within six months, under Nightingale's management, the mortality rate dropped from 40 percent to 2 percent.

In recognition of Nightingale's work in the Crimea, a group of influential people in London set up the Nightingale Fund, and £45,000 was raised to set up the Nightingale Training School at St Thomas's. The year-long program will train girls in midwifery, clinical, and surgical nursing, and the basic text will be the 136-page book that Nightingale penned herself, *Notes on Nursing*.

While most people believe that the nursing school is a great medical and social advance, a few senior surgeons have voiced their opposition, claiming that nurses need little or no training.

time out

Bavarian-born American businessman Levi Strauss (1829-1902) arrives in the Californian goldfields in the 1850s. Hearing of the miners' need for sturdy, durable pants, he creates "bibless overalls," made first of canvas and later of denim, held together by copper rivets.

Mrs Beeton's Hints on Managing Households

London, England, October, 1861: After appearing in 24 monthly parts in *The Englishwoman's Domestic Magazine* (which is owned and operated by her husband, Samuel Beeton), Isabella Beeton's advice on all things domestic has at last been published in one volume.

It is hard to believe that this book was written by someone still in her twenties, containing, as it does, such a wealth of knowledge. Everything about it is big: the extent is 1,112 pages—900 of which feature a total of 2,000 recipes—and even the full title is enormous: *The Book of Household Management Comprising Information for the Mistress, Housekeeper, Cook, Kitchen-maid, Butler, Footman, Coachman, Valet, Upper and under housemaids, Lady's-maid, Maid-of-all-work, Laundry-maid, Nurse and nurse-maid, Monthly, wet, and sick nurses, etc. etc.—also, sanitary, medical, & legal memoranda; with a history of the origin, properties, and uses of all things connected with home life and comfort.*

While *The Book of Household Management* deals with a variety of topics, the focus is primarily on food because, according to Mrs Beeton, "there is no more fruitful source of family discontent than a housewife's badly cooked dinners and untidy ways." The wholesome recipes in the book have detailed instructions and are very easy to follow.

The book is aimed at a particular type of woman—one of the new city-dwelling "middle classes" who has risen from a humbler station and has never been taught the finer things in life, or how to delegate responsibility to servants. As this class is continually growing, it is likely that Mrs Beeton's *Book of Household Management* will find a wide readership.

Florence Nightingale's work in Scutari, Turkey, earned her the respect and admiration of soldiers.

Key Events

France, 1861: Pierre Michaux invents a practical bicycle.

Australia, March, 1862: The English cricket team tours for the first time.

England, 1863: The world's first underground metropolitan railway opens.

USA, 1863: Alanson Crane patents the fire extinguisher.

England, 1863: Football Association is formed.

Geneva, Switzerland, 1864: The International Red Cross is formed.

Whitechapel, London, July 2, 1865: William Booth forms Salvation Army.

UK, July 5, 1865: First speed limits introduced of 2 mph (3.2 kmh) in town and 4 mph (6.4 kmh) in the country.

Tennessee, USA, 1865: The Ku Klux Klan is formed.

England, 1866: Barnardo's founded when Doctor Thomas Barnardo begins working with destitute children.

USA, 1866: The Metric Act authorizes use of metric system.

England, 1866: Amateur Athletics Club hosts National Championships.

England, 1867: Marquess of Queensbury boxing rules set.

Shanghai, China, February, 1867: Geographer Xu Jiyu is appointed director of newly established Interpreters' College.

Bangkok, Siam (Thailand), 1868: Newly enthroned King Rama V embarks upon an ambitious program of western modernization.

USA, 1868: The first parade in USA to have floats is held at Mardi Gras in New Orleans.

New Zealand, November 2, 1868: Nationally observed standard time is officially adopted.

USA, 1869: Heinz Foods established.

Italy, 1869: The Roman Catholic Church prohibits abortion at any stage of pregnancy.

USA, 1869: The Cincinnati Red Stockings, baseballs first all-professional team, is founded.

New York, USA, February 28, 1870: The first pneumatic subway opens.

New Zealand, May 14, 1870: The first rugby match is played.

USA, June 26, 1870: Christmas Day is declared a public holiday by Congress.

Sydney, Australia, 1870: The first Australian rules football match is played.

London, England, 1871: The Royal Albert Hall is opened by Queen Victoria.

USA, 1871: The first professional baseball league is established.

England, 1872: The first international Association football game is played.

USA, March 1, 1872: Yellowstone National Park is declared the world's first national park.

New York, USA, March 1, 1873: Remington start manufacturing their first commercial typewriter.

Pennsylvania, USA, 1874: First public zoo in USA is opened.

Thomas Barnardo

International Red Cross is Formed

Geneva, Switzerland, August 22, 1864: The Geneva Convention for the Amelioration of the Condition of the Wounded and Sick of Armies in the Field was adopted of 1864 by 12 countries today. It stipulates that the medical personnel of the armed forces shall be politically neutral, civilian volunteers shall be neutral, and those wounded in war shall be treated in a humane manner. The convention also decided that an international emblem should be adopted, and be placed on uniforms, ambulances etc., so that their neutrality would be recognized. A red cross on a white background—the Swiss flag with colors reversed—was chosen, in honor of Jean Henri Dunant of Switzerland, whose vision brought this organization into being.

Clara Barton, founder of the American Red Cross.

In June of 1859, Dunant was traveling through northern Italy when he saw the devastation caused by the Battle of Solferino, in which the Austrians were defeated by Franco–Sardinian troops in the cause of Italian unification. Inspired by the work of Florence Nightingale in the Crimean War, he gathered a team of helpers to attend to the needs of the sick and injured, giving them basic nursing care, supplies, and moral support. When he returned home, he wrote a book entitled *A Memory of Solferino*, which was published at his own expense in 1862. The book described Dunant's dream of a network of "relief societies whose object would be to have the wounded cared for in time of war by enthusiastic, devoted volunteers."

Dunant's book came to the attention of Gustave Moynier, the chairman of the Geneva Public Welfare Society. Moynier invited Dunant to join a new committee, which became known as the International Committee of the Red Cross, and convened on February 17, 1863. This committee led to the convention in Geneva.

The fundamental principles of the Red Cross are humanity, impartiality, neutrality, independence, voluntary service, unity, and universality.

H. J. Heinz Establishes Food-processing Company

Sharpsburg, USA, 1869: In partnership with L. Clarence Noble, 25-year-old Henry John Heinz has set up a food-processing company in Sharpsburg, Pennsylvania.

Heinz was born in Pittsburgh in 1844, a year after his parents John and Anna emigrated from Germany. The Heinz family moved to Sharpsburg when John established a brick-making factory there.

Henry enjoyed helping his mother in her vegetable patch, and when he was only eight years old he was selling his produce around the neighborhood. A few years later he had his own garden of close to 1 acre (0.4 ha) and needed a wheelbarrow for his deliveries. By the age of 12, Heinz's garden had expanded to $3\frac{1}{2}$ acres (1.4 ha), and he was using a horse and cart for his deliveries to grocery stores in the Pittsburgh area.

One of Heinz's major crops was horseradish. When grated and mixed with vinegar or cream, it is a tasty sauce for beef, sausages, or smoked fish. At 15, Heinz bottled horseradish according to his mother's German recipe, and sold it along with his produce. He wisely used clear bottles to show that his horseradish was not adulterated with fillers such as turnip or wood fiber. By the age of 17, he was earning over $2,000 a year.

Heinz & Noble will concentrate on the production and sale of bottled horseradish, and in the next few years hope to expand their lines to include other condiments such as pickles, sauerkraut, and vinegar.

Red Stockings End First Professional Season

Cincinnati, USA, November 6, 1869: The first fully professional baseball team, the Cincinnati Red Stockings, played their final official game of the season today at their home field, Union Grounds. They beat the Mutuals of New York 17–8, ending an impressive season of 57 wins, 0 losses, and 1 tie.

Up until this year, the National Association of Base Ball strictly forbade paying salaries to the players, although they had allowed the charging of admission to the games.

The Red Stockings were formed as an amateur team in 1866; their original name was the Resolutes, which was then changed to the Cincinnati Base Ball Club. In 1868, they sported a new uniform—white cap, white knickerbockers, white flannel shirt, and red stockings—and the nickname "Red Stockings" became their official title.

In 1869, the club president, with the winning name of Aaron B. Champion, decided that the team would become completely professional and that all the players would go on contract and receive a salary. He appointed British-born centerfielder Harry Wright, the son of a cricket player, as player-manager at a salary of $1,200. His brother George Wright, who is shortstop, was paid $1,400, pitcher Asa Brainard and third baseman Fred Waterman were both paid $1,000, and the rest of the team were paid $800 each. Substitute Richard Hurley received $600.

It is thought that Cincinnati will now replace New York as the baseball capital of the world. Ironically, only one of the Red Stockings is from Cincinnati—the rest of the players hail from New York.

The Red Stockings, led by Harry Wright, have had an amazingly successful touring season (1869).

Ulysses S. Grant

Christmas Day a Holiday

Washington DC, USA, June 28, 1870: Illinois member of the House of Representatives, Burton Chauncey Cook, introduced a bill to establish Christmas Day and other important dates as legal holidays. The bill was approved today by the Senate, and signed by President Ulysses S. Grant today.

The bill before the House reads: "Be it enacted by the Senate and House of Representatives of the United States of America in Congress assembled, that the following days, to wit: the first day of January, commonly called New Year's day, the fourth day of July, the twenty-fifth day of December, commonly called Christmas day, and any day appointed or recommended by the President of the United States as a day of public fast or thanksgiving, shall be holidays within the District of Columbia…"

When the Puritans colonized America, the celebration of Christmas was seen as decadent, with pagan associations. It was even banned in Boston from 1659 until 1681. In recent years, there has been a revived interest, possibly due to the influx of German immigrants.

Holiday celebrations in Washington.

Yellowstone: World's First National Park

Washington DC, USA, March 1, 1872: President Ulysses S. Grant today signed a bill that will "withdraw from settlement, occupancy, or sale, under the laws of the United States, a tract of land 55 by 65 miles [approximately 88 × 105 km], about the sources of the Yellowstone and Missouri Rivers, and dedicates… as a great national park or pleasure-ground for the benefit and enjoyment of the people." Nathaniel Langford has been named as the first park superintendent.

The park, which straddles the territories of Wyoming, Montana, and Idaho, is named Yellowstone National Park because of the yellow rock cliffs along the river banks. The name originated with the Minnetaree Indian expression *Mi tsi a-da-zi*, which translates to "Yellow Rock" or "Yellow Stone." As well as these geological formations, the other most distinctive features are the geysers and hot springs that can be found throughout the park.

There has been interest in this region since early in the century, when John Colter, after returning from the Lewis and Clark Expedition, told of a place of "fire and brimstone." Some 50 years later, the frontiersman Jim Bridger described the incredible sights he saw in the area of the park. This inspired the geologist Ferdinand V. Hayden to undertake an expedition with army surveyor W. F. Raynolds. From 1860 to 1870, several more investigative expeditions took place.

In 1871, Hayden received a $40,000 grant from the US Government in order to explore the Yellowstone territory. Assisted by a team of scientists, artists, and photographers, Hayden compiled a 500-page report, which included spectacular paintings and photographs. This report was highly instrumental in convincing the government to preserve the Yellowstone Basin for posterity.

Yellowstone National Park is abundant in trees such as Lodgepole pine, spruce, aspen, and fir. Some of the animal species that have been sighted in the park include bison, black bear, grizzly bear, moose, elk, and mountain lion.

Religious Leaders

Popes
Pius IX (1846-1878)

Archbishops of Canterbury
John Bird Sumner (1848-1862)
Charles Thomas Longley (1862-1868)
Archibald Campbell Tait (1868-1882)

Dalai Lamas of Tibet
Khendrup Gyatso (1855-1856)
Trinley Gyatso (1860-1875)

Patriarchs of Constantinople
Anthimus IV (1848-1852)
Germanus IV (1852-1853)
Anthimus VI (1853-1855, 1871-1873)
Cyril VII (1855-1860)
Joachim II (1860-1863, 1873-1878)
Sophronius III (1863-1866)
Gregory VI (1867-1871)

Scotland Loses First International Football Game

Scotland, November 30, 1872: As well as celebrating the feast of their patron saint, St Andrew, the Scots are rejoicing today in the sterling performance of their Queens Park team against the English football club, in what marks the first international football game. Thousands of spectators attended the exciting match at Partick, near Glasgow. It ended in a 0–0 draw, with the Scottish team demonstrating its remarkable skill in the unorthodox "short pass."

Scotland's uniform consisted of blue shirt, white knickerbockers, and blue and white socks; the English side wore white shirts, but their knickerbockers and socks were the colors of their individual members' public schools.

It is believed that English football was first played as far back as 800 CE. During the Middle Ages, rival villages were pitted against each other in fierce competitions marked by extreme physical violence. Although both Edward III and Elizabeth I tried to outlaw the game, their efforts proved to be fruitless.

The natural wonders of Yellowstone National Park are now preserved for all time.

In 1815, Eton College drew up rules that were later standardized and developed into the Cambridge Rules; these were accepted in 1848 by most of England's centers of learning.

Football was becoming polarized. Some institutions preferred to follow rules established by Rugby School, which allowed carrying the ball, kicking, and tripping; the Cambridge Rules did not permit these tactics. In October 1863, representatives of 11 London clubs met in the Freemason's Tavern to formulate a single set of basic rules. The Football Association was born out of this meeting. Six years later, Rugby football and Association football finally parted ways.

Porfirio Díaz

Custer's 7th Cavalry Slaughtered

Little Big Horn, Dakota, USA, June 28, 1876:
On May 17 this year an expeditionary force set out from Fort Abraham Lincoln in the Dakota territory under the command of Brigadier General Alfred H. Terry. It was under orders from President Ulysses S. Grant to locate the encampment of renegade chief Sitting Bull and to force his followers back into the reservations. The United States had earlier ordered the Sioux to return to their reservation by January 31, 1876.

The deadline passed with no response. The Lakota Sioux leaders Sitting Bull and Crazy Horse were not signatories to the treaty of 1868 under which many Sioux leaders agreed to move to the Great Sioux Reservation in South Dakota. They feared becoming dependent upon the government and preferred to remain on the plains, where they had always lived, far from the nearest reservation.

Several days ago Terry received a report of a large Indian encampment from his Crow Indian scouts. Lieutenant Colonel George Armstrong Custer paid no heed to Terry's request for him and his 7th Cavalry to await the arrival of Colonel Gibbon and his Gatling Gun Division, instead heading directly for the valley of the Little Big Horn, making forced marches late into the night and starting again before dawn.

Custer's initial plan was to use the Wolf Mountains, 15 miles (24 km) east of the Little Big Horn River, as cover and to launch a surprise attack at dawn on June 26. However, when his troops were seen by a Lakota scout, Custer ordered his men to advance immediately.

Believing his 7th Cavalry to be invincible, Custer divided his troops into three separate commands. Captain Benteen and his 125 men were to move toward the foothills and engage any Indians they found. A battalion under Major Marcus Reno was sent in to engage the Indians in the village across the Little

> *"No man has a right to fix the boundary of the march of a nation; no man has a right to say ... thus far shalt thou go and no further."*
>
> CHARLES PARNELL
> (1846–1891), IRISH
> STATESMAN, 1885

> *"The prolonged slavery of women is the darkest page in human history."*
>
> ELIZABETH STANTON
> (1815–1902), AMERICAN
> SUFFRAGETTE, C. 1890

time out

Alfonso XII (1857–1885), King of Spain and son of Isabella II, dies of tuberculosis. In his short life, he has escaped two assassination attempts.

Big Horn. Custer with his battalion was to provide whatever support was needed.

Hundreds of warriors rode out of the encampment, assaulting Reno's command and forcing him into a chaotic retreat. The Sioux and Cheyenne later compared this phase of the battle with "a good buffalo hunt."

Custer rode northward along a bluff to a place called Medicine Tail Coulee, where his companies were systematically slaughtered. Companies C and L offered stubborn resistance before being cut down, while Company I perished on the eastern side of the ridge.

It appears that Company E attempted to drive the warriors out of the deep ravines on the western side of the ridge but were overwhelmed by smoke. Custer was with Company F—80 men surrounded by over 2,000 Lakota warriors. Not a single member of the 7th Cavalry survived.

The lifeless body of George Armstrong Custer was found on the pinnacle of the hill where he and the remnants of his shattered 7th Cavalry had made their "last stand," with the flag of the 7th Cavalry flying over him.

New Age of Reform in Mexico

Mexico City, Mexico, November 29, 1876:
Porfirio Díaz, a hero in the war against the French occupation of Mexico, has appointed himself president after overthrowing the government of Sebastián Lerdo de Tejada.

Defeated by Benito Juárez in the elections of 1871, Porfirio Díaz claimed the elections to be fraudulent and led a revolt against the government, which was eventually suppressed. When Juárez died in office, his foreign minister, Sebastián Lerdo de Tejada, was appointed as the provisional president.

Angered by repeated incursions into their lands, the Sioux and Cheyenne take on the might of the US Cavalry.

Key Events

Washington DC, USA, March 1, 1875: The Civil Rights Act implements equal rights in public accommodations regardless of race.
Little Big Horn, Dakota, USA, June 25, 1876: The 7th Cavalry, commanded by General George Custer is obliterated; 265 troopers face 3,500 Indian warriors led by chiefs Sitting Bull and Crazy Horse.
Mexico City, Mexico, November 29, 1876: Porfirio Díaz, war hero, appoints himself president after overthrowing the government of Sebastián Lerdo de Tejada.

Transvaal, South Africa, April 12, 1877: Britain annexes Boer Republics.
Russia, April 24, 1877: Russia declares war on the Ottoman Empire in order to liberate the Balkans.
Chicago, USA, July 25, 1877: Nineteen striking railwaymen are killed when police open fire.
Kumamoto, Japan, September 24, 1877: Satsuma Rebellion of samurai is quashed by government troops.
New Zealand, November 29, 1877: Education Act provides free and secular primary education, compulsory for ages 7-13.

Berlin, Germany, July 13, 1878: The Treaty of Berlin divides the Balkans, following the Russo-Turkish War.
Isandhlwana, southern Africa, January 22, 1879: Zulu warriors slaughter around 1,600 British imperial troops, in response to British demands for cultural change.
Afghanistan, May 26, 1879: The Treaty of Gandamak is signed between the Afghans and British, ceding the strategic Khyber Pass to the British.
China, 1879: Millions die in the north as famine and drought stretch into a third year.

Melbourne, Australia, November 11, 1880: The colony's most notorious bushranger Edward (Ned) Kelly is hanged, aged 25.
St Petersburg, Russia, March 13, 1881: Reforming tsar, Alexander II is assassinated by the People's Will (a revolutionary organization).
Transvaal, South Africa, March 23, 1881: The Boers are given self-government following numerous victories in bloody battles.
Vienna, Austria, May 20, 1882: Italy enters into the triple alliance treaty with Germany and Austria-Hungary.

London, England, March 13, 1883: Karl Marx, co-author of the *Communist Manifesto*, dies aged 64.
Sunda Strait, Dutch East Indies, August 27, 1883: The Krakatoa volcano erupts, destroying two-thirds of the island and killing 36,000 people.
Hue, Vietnam, June 6, 1884: Treaty of Hue gives France effective control of Vietnam.
Berlin, Germany, February 26, 1885: Three months of negotiations by 15 nations divides Africa among the colonial powers.

Earlier this month, when congress gave its consent to Lerdo's continuing in office, Díaz came out of self-imposed retirement to lead a successful insurgency, triumphantly entering Mexico City five days ago as the nation's provisional president.

Díaz promises to take Mexico—a country that has had 52 dictators in the past 59 years—down the path of strict economic and political reform. His promises include settling all national debt and bringing together Mexico's more than 150 distinct ethnic tribes.

Samurais Crushed in Failed Rebellion

Kumamoto, Japan, September 24, 1877: The Satsuma Rebellion of samurai led by Saigo Takamori has been quashed by government troops. After leading 30,000 disaffected samurai against the army and being injured in the final battle, Takamori took his own life on the battlefield.

Twice exiled for his political views, in 1864 Takamori returned from exile to assist in the Meiji restoration. He was a key figure in toppling the Tokugawa shogunate and became an adviser in the emperor Meiji's new government. When his request to be appointed as an envoy to Korea was rejected, he left the government and returned to his homeland, to establish an academy to train samurai in frugality, honesty, and courage.

However, the Meiji government's attempts to abandon Japan's old feudal structures also meant the abolition of the samurais' social status, and with a long tradition of opposition to central authority behind them, samurais began what has become known as the Satsuma Rebellion, with Takamori at its head.

Though the samurai were armed with some modern weaponry, Takamori's tactics were traditional and antiquated. With 30,000 warriors, he led an attack on the government stronghold of Kumamoto. The government responded

Samurai were bound together by a strict code of honor.

with a 300,000-strong counterattack, and after a six-week battle, which ended today—with Takamori's surviving samurais numbering only in the hundreds and retreating to Kagoshima—Takamori asked a fellow samurai to cut off his head before he was captured.

The siege of Kagoshima marks both the end of the Satsuma Rebellion, and the demise of Japan's samurai class.

British Soldiers Massacred in Zululand

Isandhlwana, southern Africa, January 22, 1879: In one of the most humiliating defeats ever suffered by a British army, six entire companies of the 24th Foot Regiment have been wiped out, including 52 officers—more than at the Battle of Waterloo—in a fierce battle with 10,000 Zulu warriors at Mount Isandhlwana, southern Africa.

British commander Lord Chelmsford split his forces and left his Number III column at Mount Isandhlwana while he set off with 2,500 troops to investigate Zulu presence elsewhere.

With the British line spread too thin, it took the Zulus only four hours to completely overrun the regiment. Of the 915 soldiers left behind at Isandhlwana, only 55 survived, by escaping on horseback. Two thousand Zulus were killed.

Afghans Forced to Cede Khyber Pass to British

Afghanistan, May 26, 1879: London has long seen Afghanistan as a "buffer state" between its interests in the subcontinent and Russian encroachment to the north. So when Russia sent an uninvited diplomatic mission to the Afghan capital, Kabul, last July, the British insisted that the Amir receive a corresponding British mission. When it was denied entry into Afghanistan, the British government in India ordered the Amir to apologize for the "insult." No apology was forthcoming, and so on November 19 Britain declared war on Afghanistan. British forces occupied the Korram Valley, the Paywar Pass, the Khyber Pass, and Quetta toward Jalalabad and Kandahar. With British troops occupying much of the country, the Afghan government signed the Treaty of Gandamak to prevent further invasion.

The treaty gives Britain jurisdiction over the strategic Khyber and Paywar Passes and the Korram and Pishin Valleys, and a British mission in Kabul.

Chief Sitting Bull

Afghan soldiers on the lookout at the Khyber Pass.

Bombay, India, December, 1885: The Indian National Congress forms after lobbying by British civil servant Allan Hume.

London, England, June 8, 1886: The Irish Home Rule Bill, tabled by William Ewart Gladstone, leading his third cabinet, is defeated and an election is called.

London, England, June 21, 1887: Queen Victoria celebrates 50 years on the throne with lavish golden jubilee celebrations attended by 50 heads of state.

Potsdam, Germany, June 15, 1888: Emperor Frederick III dies after a 3-month reign; his son, Wilhelm II ascends to power.

Brazil, November 16, 1889: A republic is proclaimed after a coup. Pedro II abolished slavery in 1888, despite resistance from plantation owners; thus signing the monarchy's death warrant.

Salisbury, Mashonaland, southern Africa, September 12, 1890: British South Africa Company founds Fort Salisbury.

Wounded Knee, South Dakota, December 29, 1890: The cavalry massacres hundreds of Sioux.

London, England, August 3, 1892: Independent MP James Kier proposes to form a Labour party.

Ontario, Canada, 1892: Women permitted to study and practice law.

Paris, France, June, 1893: Investors lose over 1 billion francs in the Panama Canal scandal.

Onehunga, New Zealand, November 29, 1893: Elizabeth Yates is elected mayor; she is the first woman mayor in the British Empire.

Paris, France, December 22, 1894: Captain Alfred Dreyfus is sentenced to life imprisonment. Found guilty of spying for Germany, his case has been extremely divisive, splitting France into factions.

Shimonoseki, Japan, April 17, 1895: Japan defeats China in the Sino-Japanese War. Japan now controls Taiwan and Korea.

Adwa, Ethiopia, March 2, 1896: The Ethiopian army routs Italian troops bent on a foreign conquest.

Turkey, August 29, 1896: More than 3,000 Armenians are massacred by Ottoman authorities, three days after Armenians seized an Ottoman bank in Istanbul.

Paris, France, December 10, 1898: Spain cedes Cuba, Puerto Rico, Guam, and the Philippines to the USA for $20 million.

Peking, China, 1899: Boxer Uprising rebels besiege foreign legations in Peking for 100 days before being defeated.

Benjamin Disraeli

Bushranger Hanged at Old Melbourne Gaol

Melbourne, Australia, November 11, 1880: The notorious Victorian bushranger Ned Kelly was hanged at the Old Melbourne Gaol today for killing three policemen at Stringybark Creek in October 1878.

The "Kelly Gang," as the group became known, robbed two banks. One of these was a daring raid at Jerilderie in New South Wales, where they captured the town's policeman and made off with more than £2,000 from the bank's vaults.

Last year they put together armor as protection against police bullets. They roughly fashioned metal plates together over hot fires; the invention soon became their trademark.

In June 1880, they killed a police informer, and when the police traced the gang to the township of Glenrowan, a gun battle took place that lasted half a day and left the three other members of Ned's gang dead. Kelly himself was wounded and easily captured, and today, at the age of just 25, he paid the ultimate price for his murderous years on the run.

Island Destroyed by Massive Eruption

Sunda Strait, Dutch East Indies, August 27, 1883: A massive volcanic eruption has occurred on the island of Rakata in the Sunda Strait, between Java and Sumatra.

It's already being called the greatest volcanic eruption in history. Massive tidal waves swept over 165 coastal villages when the flank of the Krakatoa volcano fell into the sea, with a death toll estimated at more than 30,000.

On the island of Sebesi, to the northeast, 3,000 people were washed out to sea and all the vegetation was uprooted.

> *"Don't cheer, boys; those poor devils are dying."*
>
> JOHN W. PHILIP (1840–1900), AMERICAN MILITARY COMMANDER, AFTER THE BATTLE OF SANTIAGO, 1898

> *"I thought he was a young man of promise; but it appears he was a young man of promises."*
>
> ARTHUR BALFOUR (1848–1930), BRITISH STATESMAN, OF THE ENTRY OF WINSTON CHURCHILL INTO POLITICS, 1899

Seventy-five percent of the land area of Rakata has disappeared.

Tidal gauges in Aden, Yemen, recorded the wave as reaching the Yemen shoreline in only 12 hours, and the eruption was heard as far away as Rodriguez Island, some 2,800 miles (4,480 km) distant, in the Indian Ocean. It is also being reported that ash from the eruption is falling on Singapore.

There were four distinct explosions, the last of which opened fissures in the walls of the volcano, allowing sea water to flood the subterranean magma chamber. The resultant explosion virtually destroyed the island.

Pyroclastic flows occur when the eruption column, which contains vast amounts of ash, dust, and rock, collapses under its own weight when gases erupting from the volcano can no longer support the column. Traveling at nearly 100 mph (160 kph), these flows raced down the sides of the volcano and, incredibly, had enough heat and momentum to continue across the waters of the Sunda Strait and kill 2,000 people 25 miles (40 km) away in Sumatra.

French Extend Influence in Indochina

Hue, Vietnam, June 6, 1884: Vietnamese scholar–officials have been forced into signing the Treaty of Hue, confirming the Harmand Convention signed last year. A Treaty of Protectorate signed at the convention established a French protectorate over northern and central Vietnam, formally ending Vietnam's indpendence. The French have been extending their influence in Vietnam since 1858 when their warships first fired on Vietnamese ports.

By June 1862 Emperor Tu Duc had signed a treaty with the French which ceded control of three provinces around Gia Dinh, which was renamed Saigon by the French. Hue fell to French forces last year, not long after the Emperor's death.

Shock waves from the eruption at Krakatoa were felt across the world.

It is believed the signing of the Treaty of Hue will enable the French to deal more effectively with continual disruptions by China to French trading arrangements in the country's north.

Indian Resistance Ends at Wounded Knee

South Dakota, USA, January 15, 1891: Largely as a result of the recent massacre at Wounded Knee and the subsequent Indian attack on the 7th Cavalry at White Clay Creek, representatives of the Sioux nation laid down their arms today, which has brought to an end decades of hostility throughout the Great Plains.

The recent rise in Indian militancy resulting from the "Ghost Dance" phenomenon is being seen as heightening tensions, particularly in regard to the Lakota Sioux, and is being viewed as a key ingredient in the lead-up to Wounded Knee. This "Ghost Dance" must be understood if any sense is to be made of this appalling slaughter of the innocents.

A young Paiute mystic named Wovoka, who was born in Nevada in the 1850s and raised by a white rancher, is claimed to have fallen into a trance in 1889.

In his trance he was taken to the spirit world and given a vision of a New Age for the Indian people, where generation after generation of Indians slain in combat would be reborn. It was a world in which buffalo had returned to the plains in their millions, and one where the white man had disappeared.

A ritualistic dance emerged that encompassed these new beliefs—the

Sumatra

Borneo

INDONESIA

Java Sea

Java

Anak Krakatoa

Sertang · Panjang

Krakatoa volcano 1883 ▲ Rakata

Sunda Strait

Jakarta

INDIAN OCEAN

I N D O N E S I A

Java

N

0   30 km
0   30 miles

Krakatoa Eruption 1883
◼ Area flooded by Krakatoa volcano, 1883

Seats of Power

China Qing Dynasty: Tongzhi (reigned 1861-1875); Guangxu (1875-1908).
France Patrice de MacMahon (1873-1879); Jules Grevy (1879-1887); Sadie Carnot (1887-1894); Jean Casimir-Perier (1894-1895); Felix Faure (1895-1899); Emile Loubet (1899-1906).
Japan Modern Japan: Meiji (reigned 1867-1912).
Kingdom of Great Britain Victoria (reigned 1837-1901).
Portugal Brigantine Dynasty: Luis I (reigned 1861-1889); Carlos (1889-1908).
Russia Emperors: Alexander II (reigned 1855-1881); Alexander III (1881-1894); Nicholas II (1894-1917).
Spain Bourbon Dynasty: Alfonso XII (reigned 1874-1885); Alfonso XIII (1886-1931).
Thailand Chakri Dynasty: Rama V (reigned 1868-1910).
Zulu Nation Cetshwayo kaMpande (reigned 1872-1884); Dinizulu kaCetshwayo (1884-1913).

Ghost Dance. It spread throughout the west, particularly among the recently defeated Indians of the Great Plains. The Sioux sent a delegation to visit Wovoka in 1889, and when they returned to their reservations, the dance began to take on militant overtones. Sioux apostles began talking of the day when they would be strong enough to wage all-out war on the white man, and they began fashioning sacred "ghost shirts," which were believed to have the power to stop bullets.

This was the climate of fear and distrust that characterized the months leading up to December 28, 1890.

By November, about 3,000 Indians had assembled on a plateau at the northwest corner of Pine Ridge in an impregnable area known as "the stronghold." Chief Big Foot of the Miniconjou Sioux was on his way there with 350 of his people to persuade the stronghold inhabitants to surrender. On December 28, unaware of this and believing Big Foot to be a Ghost Dancer, 500 men of the 7th Cavalry, under the command of Colonel James Forsyth, surrounded Big Foot. In addition, four

cannons capable of rapid fire, called Hotchkiss guns, were set up on the hills around his camp.

The next morning the soldiers entered the camp, demanding that the Sioux hand over their weapons. A medicine man called Yellow Bird objected. He exhorted the others to don their sacred shirts. "The bullets will not hurt you," he was heard to say to the other men.

Another Miniconjou raised his rifle over his head, saying the rifle had cost him a lot of money and he was not prepared to part with it. A shot rang out, and immediately the soldiers began firing into the Indian encampment. An hour later the guns stopped.

Hundreds of Indian men, women, and children lay dead. Twenty-five soldiers were also killed, many by the indiscriminate shelling of their own Hotchkiss guns. Trails of blood trickled along the ground, heading out of camp toward the gulches.

Three days later, a burial party was sent to pull the frozen Indians out from under a blanket of snow. Many of the corpses were naked. Soldiers had stripped the "ghost shirts" from the dead to take home as souvenirs of the encounter.

Colonel Forsyth was relieved of his command at a court of inquiry, although he was later reinstated.

The massacre caused both hostile and friendly Sioux factions to unite, and on December 30, Sioux warriors under Kicking Bear attacked the 7th Cavalry along White Clay Creek. Casualties were minimal, and today Kicking Bear became the last Lakota warrior to surrender to the federal government.

Dreyfus Receives Pardon from French President

Paris, France, September 30, 1899: Earlier this month President Emile Loubet pardoned Alfred Dreyfus following his

five-year battle to clear his name of the charge of having been a spy for Germany.

In 1894 Captain Alfred Dreyfus was sentenced to life imprisonment after being found guilty of the charges. A French spy in the German embassy had discovered a handwritten schedule detailing secret French documents. In the search for the traitor, suspicion fell upon Dreyfus, an Alsatian Jew, who strongly protested his innocence. Tried in-camera by a French court-martial and found guilty, he was deported to the French penal settlement of Devil's Island, off the coast of French Guyana. The French army at this time was influenced heavily

Emile Zola

Charged with spying, Alfred Dreyfus stands trial at Rennes.

by monarchists and Catholics—and, it has been suggested, a degree of anti-Semitism as well.

There was a push to reopen the case in 1896, when evidence came to light that the culprit may in fact have been Major Ferdinand Esterhazy, who was deeply in debt. Esterhazy was tried and acquitted in a trial that took only minutes. Emile Zola, a supporter of Dreyfus, wrote an open letter to the president of the French republic claiming that the judges had received orders from the war office to acquit Esterhazy. Zola himself was then tried for libel and sentenced to jail, but he escaped to England. It was then revealed that much of the evidence against Dreyfus had been forged by a Colonel Henry of Army Intelligence.

After a second trial in 1899, Dreyfus was again found guilty "with extenuating circumstances" and sent back to Devil's Island. The recent pardon has made it possible for him to return to Paris.

The so-called "Dreyfus Affair" had a major impact upon France as a nation, pitting radicals, republicans, and socialists against the church and army.

On February 15, 1898, while on a friendly visit to Cuba, the USS *Maine* was destroyed by an explosion.

Robert Koch

Bell Wins Race to Patent His "Telephone"

Philadelphia, USA, March 10, 1876: Born in Scotland and educated in England, Alexander Graham Bell moved to America in 1870. For two generations his family have been leading authorities on elocution and speech. As a teenager, Alexander observed that a chord struck on a piano in one room is echoed by a piano in another room. He realized that chords are transmitted through the air, vibrating at a distance at the same pitch.

Settling in Boston, he opened his own school for the training of teachers of the deaf, and later became professor of vocal physiology and elocution at Boston University. He soon began to consider the feasibility of converting human speech into electrical oscillations and then sending those oscillations through wires and converting them back into speech at the other end. For five years he worked in league with his assistant, Thomas Watson, a gifted electrician and model-maker, to develop an apparatus for electrically transmitting the spoken word. They experimented with many machines, but continued with their goal. They captured sounds, but the sounds were indistinct.

By June of last year the two men had proved that different tones vary the strength of an electric current in a wire. All that was then required was to build a transmitter capable of varying electric currents, as well as a receiver that would reproduce these variations at audible frequencies. And while experimenting with a technique called "harmonic telegraph," Bell discovered that he could hear the sound of a ticking clock over a wire.

Today, in the middle of an experiment, Bell inadvertently knocked over a jar of acid and spoke the words: "Mr Watson,

Alexander Graham Bell demonstrating his telephone.

come here. I need you." Watson heard the words coming from one of their machines, racing to Bell's side, shouting: "I can hear you! I can hear the words!"

Also today, in probably the closest "patent race" of all time, an inventor in Highland Park, Illinois—a Quaker named Elisha Gray—has similarly invented what he calls a device for "transmitting vocal sounds telegraphically." Both inventors raced to their respective patent offices to have their invention registered. In Boston, Bell's entry was the fifth of the day. In Chicago, Gray's was the 39th. The US Patent Office has therefore awarded Bell the patent, number 174,465. Bell is just 25 years old.

time out

In 1887, American Dorr Felt (1862-1930) patents a design for the comptometer, a mechanical device designed to perform arithmetical calculations, particularly addition and subtraction, purely by pressing the keys on the device.

Edison Publicly Unveils Electric Lighting System

Menlo Park, New Jersey, USA, December 31, 1879: In 1875, in Toronto, Canada, Henry Woodward and Matthew Evans patented a light bulb. Unfortunately, the two inventors were not able to secure the necessary finance to commercialize it, and the enterprising American Thomas

Edison, who had also been working on the idea, bought the rights to their patent.

Over the next few years, Edison refined their work, using a lower current, a small carbonized filament, and an improved vacuum inside the globe.

The first public demonstration of Edison's incandescent lighting system was held at his electrically lit Menlo Park laboratory complex earlier today Pennsylvania Rail ran special trains to Menlo Park and over 3,000 people traveled there to witness the demonstration.

Warren De la Rue made the first known attempt to produce an incandescent light bulb, in 1820. He enclosed a platinum coil in an evacuated tube and passed an electrical current through it. Having a high melting point, platinum could operate at high temperatures. It was an efficient design, but the high cost of platinum made it impractical for commercial purposes.

In 1860, the English physicist Sir Joseph Wilson Swan produced his first experimental light bulb, using carbonized paper as a filament. Unfortunately, Swan didn't have a strong enough vacuum or batteries of sufficient power, and his prototype failed to achieve incandescence.

In 1875, with the aid of a better vacuum and using a carbonized thread as a filament, Swan successfully demonstrated a true incandescent bulb, receiving a British patent for his device in 1878, a year before Edison.

What Thomas Edison alone has achieved is to invent an electrical lighting system that provides all the elements necessary to make the incandescent light practical, safe, and economical.

Edison's incandescent light

New Zealand, February 18, 1876: Completed submarine cable enables virtually instantaneous communication between Australia and the UK.
Philadelphia, USA, March 10, 1876: Scottish-American inventor Alexander Graham Bell transmits his voice via the first phone, saying "Mr Watson, come here. I need you."
Grays, Essex, England, May, 1876: Alfred Wallace publishes *The Geographical Distribution of Animals*, which divides the world into six fauna regions and introduces the concept of biogeography.

Menlo Park, New Jersey, USA, December 24, 1877: Thomas Edison applies for a patent for his latest invention, the phonograph.
Tokyo, Japan, March 25, 1878: Japan's first electric light bulb is turned on.
Menlo Park, New Jersey, USA, October 21, 1879: Thomas Edison develops the incandescent electric light bulb. In England, Joseph Swan has a similar breakthrough.
Calcutta, India, January 28, 1882: Central telephone exchanges open in Calcutta, Madras, and Bombay, inaugurating telephone service in India.

Berlin, Germany, March 24, 1882: Robert Koch presents his discovery of the bacterium that causes tuberculosis.
Rochester, New York, USA, October 14, 1884: George Eastman patents flexible, paper-based photographic film. This supersedes the large and cumbersome glass plates that are widely used.
Paris, France, November 17, 1884: Count Hilaire de Chardonnet produces artificial silk from cellulose, the first man-made fabric, later known as rayon.

London, England, 1884: American inventor Hiram Maxim builds the first effective machine gun. It can fire 666 rounds per minute.
Paris, France, July 6, 1885: Dr Louis Pasteur's rabies vaccine is used on humans for the first time. Nine-year-old Joseph Meister makes a miraculous recovery after being bitten by a rabid dog.
Mannheim, Germany, January 29, 1886: Karl Benz patents the Tri-car, the world's first automobile, fuelled by a gas combustion engine.

Stuttgart, Germany, March 8, 1886: Inventors of the "Grandfather clock" internal combustion engine, Daimler and Maybach, install one in a stagecoach, creating an automobile.
Karlsruhe, Germany, 1887: Heinrich Hertz begins his experiments to produce Maxwellian electromagnetic waves, the first radio waves.
Rochester, New York, USA, September 4, 1888: George Eastman's camera, the Kodak, is patented. The Kodak slogan "you press the button, we do the rest" becomes a well-known phrase.

Tuberculosis Bacillus Isolated

Berlin, Germany, March 24, 1882: Scientist and researcher Robert Koch has today announced his discovery of the bacterium that causes tuberculosis to the Physiological Society of Berlin.

Koch was appointed to the Imperial Health Bureau in Berlin in 1880, and his work there has greatly advanced our knowledge of how diseases are transmitted. One of his major contributions to this developing area of study is to have devised a method by which "pure cultures" of bacteria (germs) can be grown outside the body. This consists in mixing organisms in melted gelatin and then, after the gelatin has solidified and the organisms have grown, placing portions of the pure colonies into different tubes of broth or other substances in which they can grow.

Following this success, he concentrated his efforts on finding the cause of tuberculosis. Thanks to an improved method of "staining" he has developed (a technique that makes organisms more visible on a glass slide under a microscope), he has been able to identify the bacillus that causes this disease.

Pasteur Cures Rabies in 9-Year-Old Boy

Paris, France, July 6, 1885: Dr Louis Pasteur's rabies vaccine has been used on humans for the first time. Nine-year-old Joseph Meister has made a miraculous recovery after being bitten by a rabid dog.

Pasteur, the world-renowned French chemist and biologist who founded the science of microbiology, experimented with the saliva of animals suffering from the disease and concluded that the disease rested in the animals' nerve centers. When an extract from the spinal column of a rabid dog was injected into healthy animals, those animals developed the symptoms of rabies.

Pasteur developed an attenuated form of the virus that could be used for the purpose of inoculation. The treatment of Joseph Meister lasted for 10 days. When his mother brought him to Pasteur's laboratory, the boy was so badly mauled that he could barely walk. By the end of the treatment he was being inoculated with the most potent rabies virus known, yet he remained healthy and recovered.

Chemist and biologist Louis Pasteur in his laboratory. It was here that he developed the first successful treatment for rabies.

German Physicist Discovers Radio Waves

Karlsruhe, Germany, December, 1888: James Clerk Maxwell predicted the existence of radio waves mathematically in 1864, but it wasn't until earlier this year, when the German physicist Heinrich Hertz successfully applied Maxwell's theories to the production and reception of radio waves, that Maxwell's theory could be proved. In his physics classroom at Karlsruhe Polytechnic in Berlin, Hertz has generated electric waves using an electric circuit and proved that they are transmitted through the air by detecting them with a similar circuit some distance away. By measuring their wavelength and velocity, he has also proved that radio waves travel at the speed of light but have a much longer wavelength than light waves.

Hertz has also noted that electrical conductors reflect the radio waves, while non-conductors allow them to pass through. He has conclusively proved the existence of radio waves, confirming Maxwell's prediction that electromagnetic waves exist in the form of both light and radio waves.

Alexander Graham Bell

First Edition of Magazine Published

Washington DC, USA, October, 1888: On January 13 last, 33 men met at the Cosmos Club to "discuss the advisability of organizing a society for the increase and diffusion of geographical knowledge." The National Geographic Society was founded two weeks later. Nine months later, the first edition of its *National Geographic* magazine has been published and dispatched to the society's 200 charter members across the country.

The society's first president is lawyer Gardiner Greene Hubbard, who declared that this magazine will be a magazine for the people, not simply for academia: " […] the membership of our Society will not be confined to professional geographers, but will include [those who] desire to promote special researches by others, and to diffuse the knowledge so gained...so that we may all know more of the world."

The new magazine's enlightening articles take the reader into uncharted waters, allowing us all a glimpse into the wonders of the great unknown.

Key Events

Washington DC, USA, October, 1888: The first edition of *National Geographic* magazine is released. The National Geographic Society was founded in January by 33 influential Americans seeking to advance geographical knowledge.

Cambridge, England, July, 1890: The first volume of Alfred Marshall's *Principles of Economics* is published, establishing economics as a science.

England, December 18, 1890: The first deep-level electric railway is opened. It goes from the City of London under the Thames to Stockwell.

Baltimore, USA, October, 1891: William Osler completes the manuscript for *The Principles and Practice of Medicine*, a text that codified medical practice.

West Orange, New Jersey, USA, February 1, 1893: Thomas Edison's Black Maria film studio is completed. The first motion picture studio, it is built on tracks so it can rotate to capture the sunlight throughout the day, necessary for quality pictures.

Augsburg, Germany, August 10, 1893: Rudolf Diesel's pressure-ignited heat engine runs on its own power.

Chicago, USA, August 29, 1893: Whitcomb L. Judson invents the zipper, which he calls a "clasp locker." It is not popular during his lifetime.

Scotland, August 4, 1894: Chemists William Ramsey and Lord Rayleigh discover the inert element argon.

Bologna, Italy, August, 1895: Guglielmo Marconi transmits radio waves over a distance of about 1.3 miles (2 km). He embarked on study of the works of Heinrich Hertz last year, experimenting with the wireless transmission of messages using Hertzian waves.

Würtzberg, Germany, December 28, 1895: Physics professor Wilhelm Röntgen presents a paper outlining his discovery of x-rays. On November 8, he produced the first of this new type of ray and had spent the next eight weeks repeating his experiments.

Berlin, Germany, August 10, 1896: Aviator Otto Lilenthal dies after crashing his experimental glider.

Vienna, Austria, 1896: Sigmund Freud coins the term psychoanalysis or "free association," referring to the investigation of the psychological causes of mental disorders.

Stockholm, Sweden, 1897: Physicist Vilhelm Bjerknes develops the circulation theorems bringing together hydrodynamics and thermodynamics. His work leads to the development of weather forecasting.

Paris, France, July, 1898: Marie and Pierre Curie coin the term radioactivity after they discover the elements polonium and radium.

Calcutta, India, 1898: After eight years of research, Scottish physician Ronald Ross determines that the disease is transmitted by mosquitoes.

Marie Curie

First Gasoline Engine Installed in Carriage

Stuttgart, Germany, October 31, 1889: Earlier this year, engineers Gottlieb Daimler and Wilhelm Maybach successfully placed their new petroleum-fueled engine into a carriage usually pulled by a horse. They then began working on a new vehicle designed to be the world's first automobile. The engine, which runs on gasoline, is equipped with a surface carburetor that vaporizes the gasoline and mixes it with air. The new automobile was displayed this month at the Paris World Exhibition which closed today.

Daimler was born in Stuttgart in 1834 and became an engineer after training as a gunsmith. Maybach was born in Heilbronn and orphaned after his family moved to Stuttgart. He was raised by a charitable organization, which sent him to a special factory called a *Brüderhaus* in Reutlinger, where he studied industrial design. Here, in 1865, he met Daimler. The two men soon began developing an internal combustion engine for propelling road vehicles.

After moving to the Deutz factory in Cologne in 1882, where they worked on gas engines, Daimler and Maybach had a dispute with their employer, Nikolaus Otto, and decided to set up their own company. The lightweight, high-speed engine they have now developed achieves a speed of 900 revolutions, compared with the 130 revolutions achieved at Deutz—although the Daimler/Maybach engine is based on a design of Otto's. Back in 1876, Otto had built a four-stroke gas engine in which the fuel/air mixture was compressed prior to ignition.

Alfred Marshall Produces Classic Economics Text

Cambridge, England, July, 1890: In 1842, Alfred Marshall was born in the London suburb of Bermondsey. His father was a stern evangelical, and for a time it seemed Alfred was destined for the ministry. He declined to pursue a classical education at Oxford, instead entering St John's College, Cambridge, in 1862.

Marshall read for Cambridge University's most prestigious degree, the Mathematical Tripos, emerging in the exalted position of "second wrangler."

In 1868 he became a college lecturer in moral sciences at St John's, specializing in political economy, and by 1870 he had committed himself to transforming the subject into a new science of economics.

His first work was *The Economics of Industry* (1879), which contains a general statement of his economic theories. It was written in collaboration with his wife, Mary, an early student of his at Newnham Hall (later Newnham College), where he was professor of political economy. With the death of W. S. Jevons in 1881, *The Economics of Industry* saw Marshall become Britain's leading advocate of the new scientific school of economics.

What separates Marshall from other economists is his interest in philosophy, and his concern with poverty and other social inequalities stemming from England's rapid industrial growth.

Marshall has stayed out of the long debate on supply-side versus demand-side theories, finally commenting rather disparagingly that the argument is an empty one, akin to arguing which blade of a pair of scissors actually cuts the cloth.

In 1875 he visited the United States to refine his economic ideas. However, prior to the publication of his *Principles of Economics*, conceived in 1877, his publications were meager—a book on international trade and protectionism in the mid-1870s and a collection of short essays on various theoretical concepts.

Marshall's *Principles of Economics* is a summation of his concepts developed over many years, such as competitive equilibria, internal and external economies of scale, and consumer surplus. It is set to become the most influential treatise of our era. Finding time to write has proved difficult amid the competing demands of teaching and administrative work. Marshall did much of his writing during long vacations in England and Austria. The book is set to eventually become a two-volume work.

Scientific Achievements

Astronomy: *Carte du Ciel* proposed to photographically map entire sky to fourteenth magnitude.
Botany: Proven that eating brown rice as opposed to white prevents beriberi.
Chemistry: Theory proven that fertilized eggs are composed of both female and male nuclei.
Ecology: Some fish species return to Thames after massive sewage clean-up.
Geology: Use of radioactive decay in rocks to date the Earth.
Mathematics: Modern geometry founded.
Medicine: Vaccines for anthrax, rabies, tetanus, and diphtheria developed.
Physics: Radio waves and x-rays discovered.

Botanic Gardens
Boston, USA
Entebbe, Uganda
Ness, England
New York, USA

Observatories
Boswell, USA
Denver, USA
Flagstaff, USA
Hong Kong
Greencastle, USA
Madison, USA
Omaha, USA
Ondrejov, Czech Republic
Palani, India
Paris, France
Providence, USA
San Jose, USA
Toulouse, France

Universities
University of Auckland, New Zealand
University of Peking, China
University of Cagliari, Italy
University of Dundee, Scotland
University of Gothenburg, Sweden
University of Johannesburg, South Africa
University of Santiago, Chile
University of Sofia, Bulgaria
University of Stellenbosch, South Africa
University of Washington, USA

Thomas Edison's motion picture machine, the Vitascope, opened in New York in April 1896.

Definitive Text on Patient Care

Baltimore, USA, October, 1891: William Osler, diagnostician and clinician, has completed his work, *The Principles and Practice of Medicine*, an authoritative text that has codified medical practice

Baltimore, Maryland, USA, home of Johns Hopkins University.

and is likely to become one of the most prestigious medical texts ever written.

Born in Ontario, Canada, Osler is one of the most famous physicians of our day. Intrigued by the nature of disease—its pathology, origins, and progression—he traveled the cities of Europe and then returned to Canada to lecture at McGill University. In 1888 he moved to Baltimore, Maryland, where as physician-in-chief he has helped shape the new Johns Hopkins University's medical program.

He teaches all medical students at the patient's bedside, believing students learn best by doing and that clinical instruction should begin and end with the patient.

All medical students are also expected to work in the bacteriology laboratory. He introduced the German postgraduate training system, instituting one year of general internship which is followed by several years of residency with increased clinical responsibility.

Osler's skill in diagnosing illness is based on his vast knowledge of the science and pathology of disease. When students and teachers fall ill, it is Osler whom they want as their physician.

His new work supports this imaginative new curriculum, and meticulously takes account of all the advances in medical science made over the past 50 years. Osler has often been quoted as saying: "He who studies medicine without books sails an uncharted sea, but he who studies medicine without patients does not go to sea at all."

Freud Announces New Psychoanalytic Approach

Vienna, Austria, December, 1896: The psychologist Sigmund Freud earlier this year coined the term "free association" or "psychoanalysis" in his paper "On the Etiology of Hysteria," in reference to the psychological causes of mental disorders. Freud states that this technique will replace hypnosis as his primary tool for exploring his patients' neurotic antecedents.

The radical new technique involves asking patients to relate any memory at all that comes into their mind, regardless of how irrelevant, unimportant, or potentially embarrassing that memory may be. It assumes that all memories are arranged in a single associative network, and that at some point in the process the subject will stumble across the crucial memory—although Freud does not discount the possibility that some memories may be so deeply repressed that it is not possible for them to be accessed at all.

Nevertheless, Sigmund Freud has found what is known as the "talking cure" effective in uncovering the unconscious roots of hysteria, phobias, anxiety states, obsessive compulsive disorders, and numerous panic disorders.

Mosquitoes Now Known to Spread Malaria

Calcutta, India, 1898: Eight years of research into the cause of malaria have come to fruition for Scottish physician Ronald Ross, who has finally proved that the disease is transmitted by mosquitoes.

Dr Ross's father had been a soldier in the British Indian army, and the young Ross had lived in India until he was eight years old, before being sent off to boarding school in Southampton, England.

In 1874 he became a medical student at St Bartholomew's Hospital, London, where he just managed to pass his Royal College of Surgeons examination. In 1881 he joined the British Indian army medical services, and 11 years later began his investigations into the transmission and control of malaria.

At that time, malaria was taking an estimated one million lives a year in India. It was known to be caused by a microscopic parasite called *Plasmodium*, but no one was sure how the parasite was being transmitted.

In field hospitals in India, Dr Ross noticed that soldiers in open wards—that is, without netting over their beds—were more likely to contract malaria than those in wards with closed windows or screens, leading him to suspect that a mosquito called *Anopheles* was spreading the horrible disease from those who had malaria to those who did not.

On investigation, last year he found parasites in the blood of mosquitoes that had fed on the blood of malaria patients. Carefully dissecting each mosquito's stomach, he found mosquitoes that fed on malaria patients contained living malaria parasites.

However, when he gathered newly hatched mosquitoes that had not yet eaten, and then fed them blood from people who did not have malaria, he found no malaria parasites.

Ross has demonstrated, by a process of careful dissection, that the parasites spread through the mosquito's body to its salivary glands, and are then passed in the mosquito's saliva to anyone that it happens to bite.

Sigmund Freud

A British military station in India. It was in Calcutta that physician Ronald Ross made his discoveries about malaria.

Fyodor Dostoyevsky

Composer Bizet Dies of Heart Attack

Bougival, France, June 3, 1875: Acclaimed composer Georges Bizet has died from a heart attack at the age of 36, three months after the première of his opera *Carmen*.

Although many critics are hailing this new opera as a masterpiece, speculation is rife that the composer's death is due to despondency over the perceived failure of *Carmen*, but Bizet has long suffered from many throat ailments. The official cause of death is heart failure.

Bizet was well known as a composer (his works also included the operas *The Pearl Fishers* and *The Fair Maid of Perth*, and his incidental music *L'Arlésienne* and *Children's Games*), but he was also recognized as a great pianist by such a practitioner as Franz Liszt himself.

Horses' Hooves Proved to Leave the Ground

Palo Alto, California, USA, June 15, 1878: California governor Leland Stanford, whose passion is racehorses and horse-racing, has asked the photographer Eadweard Muybridge to prove or disprove the common assertion that a horse always has at least one hoof on the ground when cantering or galloping.

Muybridge placed 12 cameras, each 22 in (55 cm) apart, to record the entire stride of a single horse. As the horse ran across specially installed trip-wires, past a massive screen painted white to provide the appropriate contrast, pins were dislodged, which triggered the camera's shutter and took a picture.

Muybridge has indeed proved, once and for all, that all four hooves do leave the ground. This exciting series of photos is known as *The Horse in Motion*.

Dostoyevsky, Author and Prophet, Dies

St Petersburg, Russia, February 9, 1881: Fyodor Dostoyevsky, author of *Crime and Punishment* and *The Idiot*, died in St Petersburg today of a lung hemorrhage caused by emphysema and epilepsy. He was 60 years of age.

Dostoyevsky was recognized throughout Russia as one of the country's greatest writers. His novels embodied a public voice during a period of intense crisis, and the writer himself was seen as something of a prophet. His major concern was with the spiritual transformation of the individual rather than social revolution. The great existentialist Friedrich Nietzsche said of him: "He is the only psychologist from whom I have anything to learn."

In 1864, Dostoyevsky lost both his brother and his wife. Burdened by grief and his brother's debt, his predilection to gambling worsened. It was during this time that he wrote perhaps his greatest novel, *Crime and Punishment*.

In 1867, he married his stenographer, Anna Snitkin, and they traveled abroad and settled for some time in Dresden. The couple returned to Russia in 1873. During this period his popularity reached its zenith and he completed yet another masterpiece, *The Brothers Karamazov*, published in 1879.

It is estimated that some 40,000 people will attend his funeral—Russia's first state funeral in honor of a writer. Dostoyevsky will be buried in the beautiful Alexander Nevsky Monastery in St Petersburg.

time out

English poet and painter Dante Gabriel Rossetti dies on April 10, 1882, after unsuccessfully trying to shake his addiction to the drug chloral hydrate. Rossetti was one of the founders of the Pre-Raphaelite movement.

Manet's New Work Flouts Convention

Paris, France, 1882: When Edouard Manet began painting in Paris in the 1850s, it was a city without the broad tree-lined streets we see today, and the life of the city did not particularly interest French artists. A young artist's only route to success was through the Paris Salon, the official exhibition of the Académie des Beaux-Arts. Manet's revolutionary *Absinthe Drinker*, submitted to the Salon in 1859, was rejected by the jury despite the protestations of the great romantic painter Eugene Delacroix.

Success was to follow, however, with *The Guitarist* (1861) being accepted by the Paris Salon. *Dejeuner sûr l'herbe* (*Luncheon on the Grass*, or *The Picnic*, 1863) was rejected by the Paris Salon and later exhibited by the *Salon des Refusés*, which displayed works rejected by the Paris Salon. *Dejeuner sûr l'herbe* made a great impression on Claude Monet and led the great novelist Emile Zola to publish a series of articles on Manet in 1866, in which he prophesied a place in the Louvre for the aspiring young artist.

Detail of fruit from Edouard Manet's *Luncheon on the Grass*.

Bougival, France, June 3, 1875: Georges Bizet dies from a heart attack, aged 36, shortly after the première of his opera *Carmen*.

Hartford, Connecticut, USA, May, 1876: Samuel Langhorne Clemens, under the pen name of Mark Twain, writes *The Adventures of Tom Sawyer*.

Bayreuth, Bavaria, August 13-17, 1876: Richard Wagner's *Der Ring des Nibelungen* premières.

Moscow, Russia, February 20, 1877: Pyotr Ilyich Tchaikovsky's ballet *Swan Lake* premières at the Bolshoi.

England, November 24, 1877: *Black Beauty*, Anna Sewell's only book, is published.

Palo Alto, California, USA, June 15, 1878: Englishman Eadweard Muybridge uses photography to explore movement. He freeze frames images of a horse proving all hooves are off the ground at some point.

Sydney, Australia, August 21, 1878: Conrad Martens, the colony's most prolific landscape artist, dies at 77.

Calcutta, India, 1878: Bengali poet Rabindranath Tagore publishes *Kabi Kahini* (Tale of a Poet).

London, England, November, 1878: Art critic John Ruskin's attack on American artist J. M. Whistler's *Nocturne in Black and Gold* results in a libel case in which the artist is awarded damages of one farthing.

Copenhagen, Denmark, December 21, 1879: Henrik Ibsen's *A Doll's House* premières. Critical of Victorian marriage mores, the play courts controversy.

Paris, France, December, 1880: This year, Auguste Rodin models *The Thinker* as part of the monument, *The Gates of Hell*.

St Petersburg, Russia, February 9, 1881: Fyodor Dostoyevsky, author of *Crime and Punishment*, dies at 60.

Braemar, Scotland, January, 1882: Scottish author Robert Louis Stevenson writes *Treasure Island*; it is serialized in *Young Folks* magazine.

Paris, France, 1882: Edouard Manet paints his last great work, *The Bar at Folies-Bergere*, a depiction of the mirrored bar in his favorite haunt.

London, England, May, 1884: George Bernard Shaw, playwright, joins the Fabians, a middle class political socialist group.

Calcutta, India, 1884: Lal Deen Dayal is appointed court photographer to Viceroy Lord Curzon.

Paris, France, May 22, 1885: The funeral of Victor Hugo is attended by two million people.

Paris, France, May, 1886: Neo-Impressionist painter Georges Seurat, exhibits *Sunday Afternoon on the Island of Grande Jatte* at the last Impressionist exhibition.

Bayreuth, Bavaria, July 31, 1886: Virtuoso pianist and composer, Franz Liszt, contracts pneumonia and dies, aged 74.

Impression: Sunrise by the impressionist painter Claude Monet. Monet was a supporter of painter Edouard Manet.

Victor Hugo

Manet's unconventional treatment of traditional subjects represents a turning point in contemporary painting. Manet considers the subject matter to be less important than the processes by which the subject is painted. Despite maintaining close contacts with the emerging impressionists, his liking for strong black and white contrasts has kept him outside the mainstream of impressionism.

Manet's latest work, *A Bar at the Folies-Bergère* (1882), depicts a scene in the well-known Paris nightclub. Details of the perspective in this artwork have been criticized by the French press, yet it could be assumed that Manet is playing with the concept that artists can do more than simply paint what is before them—do more than merely imitate life.

Victor Hugo's Funeral Draws Two Million Mourners

Paris, France, May 22, 1885: Today, in Paris, an estimated two million people have filled the streets for the funeral of the nation's most famous poet and novelist.

It took 10,000 police to control the crowds. After lying in state under the Arc de Triomphe, Victor Hugo was finally laid to rest in the Pantheon in a pauper's coffin, alongside Rousseau and Voltaire.

His literary abilities first surfaced at the Académie Française, where his early poems won a number of awards. By the 1820s he was firmly established as one of the leading figures of the Romantic movement. For the next 12 years, a torrent of great literature flowed from his pen, and in 1841 he was elected to the Académie Française, whereupon he promptly turned his attention to politics.

Elected to the Legislative Assembly following the 1848 revolution, Hugo denounced Louis Napoleon's excessive policies. When Napoleon declared himself king of France, Hugo remarked: "We have had Napoleon the Great, now we must have Napoleon the Small." He left for Belgium in December, 1851, to avoid arrest after an abortive coup, and traveled to Guernsey in the Channel Islands, where he remained for 19 years.

Though legally able to return to France in 1859, he chose to remain on Guernsey, where he wrote many of the works for which he is best remembered, including *Les Contemplations* (1856), *Les Chansons des Rues et des Bois* (1865), and *Quatre-Vingt-Treize* (1874). It was the publication of *Les Misérables* in 1862, however, that caused the greatest sensation.

Hugo's critics were quick to condemn him for what they saw as his profiting from the misery of France's underclass, although the poor bought the novel in unprecedented numbers. It was a book about the people and for the people that demanded a change in the way society judged its citizens—a vindication of the poor forced by poverty and starvation to commit crimes just to survive.

Hugo left Guernsey and returned to France in 1870 after the fall of Louis Napoleon, and was again elected to the Legislative Assembly.

In a land where children have been shot in the streets and governments are violently overthrown every 20 years, his presence has been a blend of true courage, genius, and kindness. His humanity will etch him forever into our history.

Cosette, heroine of *Les Misérables*, is said to be based on Hugo's wife.

Key Events

Vincent van Gogh

Van Gogh Takes His Own Life in Auvers

Auvers, France, July 29, 1890: The Dutch painter Vincent van Gogh died today in the town of Auvers after shooting himself two days ago with a revolver. His brother, Theo, raced to Auvers from nearby Paris, where he found Vincent still conscious and being cared for at the Ravoux Inn, where he lived, by a Dr Gachet and the innkeeper's daughter, Adeline Ravoux.

The prolific yet tormented artist left his easel by a haystack at dusk and wandered into the surrounding fields to end his life. The bullet missed his heart, and he managed to make his way home, but infection set in and he died with his brother by his side two days later.

The tranquility that van Gogh sought in Auvers, where he took up residence in 1890, proved rather elusive. The pervasive melancholy of his youth persisted well into his adulthood.

When he became an artist at the age of 27, van Gogh thought he had finally found a remedy for his depression. Yet, the more than 650 letters he wrote to his brother over many years bear testimony to the fact that his work did not provide a solution his sadness. Vincent van Gogh's works—more than 800 canvases and 1,000 drawings—were produced over a frenzied 10-year period that ended today.

He had gradually become engrossed in art in a search for ultimate truth, and said that art was "greater and higher than our own adroitness or accomplishments or knowledge." This belief gave him a great modesty, and he often signed his paintings simply "Vincent."

After living with his brother in 1887, he left Paris for Arles, in Provence, hoping to found an artists' colony there. Gauguin arrived in October 1888, but soon began to move in opposite artistic directions. When Gauguin decided to leave, Vincent had become so dependent on him that on December 23 he attacked Gauguin with an open razor, stopping short of harming him. Van Gogh returned to his home, where he cut off a portion of his left ear.

After spending a lonely year at a clinic in Saint-Rémy, in the south of France, he traveled to Paris to again visit Theo, then to Auvers, having just sold the one and only painting he would sell in his life-time, *The Red Vineyard*, for 400 francs. In Auvers, he painted more than 80 pictures during the last weeks of his life, including his masterpiece *The Church in Auvers*.

"I can't change the fact that my paintings don't sell," he once said. "But the time will come when people will recognize that they are worth more than the value of the paints used in them."

America's Favorite Poet Is Dead

Camden, New Jersey, USA, March 26, 1892: Acclaimed poet, journalist, and essayist Walt Whitman died today, aged 73.

Born the son of a Quaker carpenter in 1819, Whitman's wavelike verse and fresh use of imaginative language helped to liberate American poetry. It was his firm belief that a poet's style should be simple and natural, without the use of orthodox meter and rhyme.

In 1855, Whitman published, at his own expense, a volume of 12 poems entitled *Leaves of Grass*. Ralph Waldo Emerson wrote him a famous letter of congratulation, and critics generally realized that a powerful new force in poetry had well and truly emerged.

Whitman was a quiet, circumspect, and gentle man who will have an incalculable effect on all poets to come.

Cholera Claims Tchaikovsky at 53

St Petersburg, Russia, November 6, 1893: Pyotr Tchaikovsky, composer of *Swan Lake* and *The Nutcracker*, has died today, nine days after the première of his Sixth Symphony, known as the *Pathétique*.

Born into a close-knit family of seven on May 7, 1840 in Votkinsk, Tchaikovsky began piano lessons at the age of five. In 1863, he entered the new St Petersburg Conservatory for private tuition.

He composed his First Symphony in 1866 and it was warmly received in Moscow on its first performance there in 1868. Acclaim was to follow for his Second Symphony and his First Piano Concerto. *Swan Lake* and the tone poem *Francesca da Rimini* followed.

Constantly struggling with his homosexuality, in 1877, two weeks after a hasty and ill-considered marriage, he made a failed attempt at suicide by walking into the cold Moska River. However, in late 1876 he was contacted by Nadezhda von Meck, a wealthy widow who admired his music. She gave him several commissions

A painting by Vincent van Gogh of the hospital at St Remy, where he spent some time.

and became his sponsor for the next 14 years. It was in this period that he composed some of his greatest works, including the Violin Concerto (1878) and his Fourth Symphony.

According to first-hand accounts, he contracted cholera after drinking a glass of unboiled water and died today.

Pioneering Female Impressionist Dies

Paris, France, March 2, 1895: One of the few female artists to have exhibited with both the Paris Salon and the highly innovative and influential Impressionists, Berthe Morisot, has died today, aged 81.

She first exhibited at the Paris Salon in 1864, at the age of 23. Ten years later she was asked by Edgar Degas to join a fledgling group of painters that included Renoir, Monet, and Pissarro. They have become known as the Impressionists.

The art world of France for most of this century has, of course, been dominated by the Académie des Beaux-Arts, which selected the juries that judged the works exhibited at the Paris Salon. These jurors were mostly academics, who rarely viewed the work of the Impressionists favorably. Morisot's works, however, were generally very well received by the Salon. Her most famous work, *The Cradle*, was a painting of her sister Edme gazing at her newborn daughter, Jeanne. It electrified the Salon judges in 1872.

Morisot exhibited with the Impressionists every year until their last exhibition in 1886 (which she organized)—with the exception of 1878, the year her daughter, Julie, was born. The Impressionists saw that her pictorial technique, with her loose brushstrokes, unfinished

The Cradle, one of Berthe Morisot's best known works.

backgrounds, and dreamy, light-infused color, exemplified their esthetic aims.

In perhaps her most famous painting, *Summer's Day* (1879), two middle-class ladies are captured in a moment of quiet reflection in a boat on a lake in the Bois de Boulogne, a wooded area on the outskirts of Paris.

She often painted with quick zigzag brushstrokes, giving a streaky texture to her work that the critics sometimes mistook for sloppiness. One early reviewer of her work complained: "Why, with her great talent, does she not take the time to finish?" But most of the critics raved about her lovely pearly-soft color harmonies.

During Morisot's lifetime her paintings often fetched higher prices than those of her male counterparts, but she remained modest. "I only want to capture something of what goes by…the smallest thing. A smile, a flower, the branch of a tree, any of these things would be enough for me."

New Novelist Travels Through Time

London, England, December, 1895: Author Herbert George Wells has made his debut as a novelist this year with a futuristic novel called *The Time Machine*.

The novel arose out of a commission to Wells from the famous editor W. E. Henley, who had already published some tales by Wells in the *National Observer*.

Wells was born in Kent, England, in 1866, the son of domestic servants who went on to own their own crockery shop. As a child, he was always imagining far-off places. Friends recall that he used to build little Martian cities from pieces of broken crockery he found in the yard behind his parents' shop.

The Time Machine is Wells's first novel. The central character, an inventor known as the Time Traveler, believes that time is the fourth dimension and builds a device that takes him to the year 802,701.

It is being described as a "scientific romance" and has a natural appeal in its attempt to fathom what will ultimately become of the human race. The author explores many themes throughout the book, including social inequality, evolution, and the relationship between science and society.

Stoker's *Dracula* Hailed a Classic

London, England, May 26, 1897: The Irish author and former civil servant Abraham (Bram) Stoker's *Dracula*, a thrilling tale

Bram Stoker, author of *Dracula*.

about a vampire, has been published today after seven long years of research.

Bram Stoker was born near Dublin, Ireland. His father was in the civil service and his mother was a charity worker and writer. Stoker was a sickly child, virtually bedridden, and he himself says that he was unable to stand upright until he was seven. To keep him entertained, his mother used to tell him ghost stories.

Stoker studied mathematics at Trinity College in Dublin, where he also became president of the Philosophical Society and the Historical Society before making the decision to follow in his father's footsteps and become a civil servant, working at Dublin Castle. He maintained his contacts at Trinity College and developed an interest in the Romantic poets, establishing a productive correspondence with respected American poet Walt Whitman.

In 1878, he wrote *The Duties of Clerks of Petty Sessions in Ireland*, drawing on his experiences as a civil servant.

Dracula is an epistolary novel—the story is told mostly through the characters' diaries and letters, as well as from fabricated newspaper clippings.

Pyotr Tchaikovsky

Key Structures

Balai Besar, Alor Setar, Malaya
Beit-al-Ajaib, Stone Town, Tanganyika
Buchan House, Scotland
Casa Vicens, Barcelona, Spain
Chateau Lake Louise, Lake Louise, Canada
Chwigajeong Pavilion, Damyang, Korea
Cologne Cathedral, Cologne, Germany
Eiffel Tower, Paris, France
Fort Margherita, Kuching, Malaya
Grande Mosquee, Bobo-Dioulasso, Burkina Faso
Indian Museum, Kolkata, India
Kabaka's Palace, Kampala, Uganda
Majolika Haus, Vienna, Austria
Neuschwanstein Castle, Bavaria, Germany
Palacio Nacional da Pena, Sintra, Portugal
Parliament Buildings, Quebec, Canada
Queen Victoria Markets, Melbourne, Australia
Raadsaal, Pretoria, South Africa
Raffles Hotel, Singapore
Silver Pagoda, Phnom Penh, Cambodia
Statue of Liberty, New York, USA
St Joseph's Cathedral, Stone Town, Tanganyika
St Mary's Cathedral, Sydney, Australia
Tassel House, Brussels, Belgium
Teatro Amazonas, Manaus, Brazil
Teatro de Cristbal Colon, Bogota, Colombia
Teatro Nacional, San Jose, Costa Rica
The Louvre, Paris, France
Tower Bridge, London, England
Vajdahunyad Castle, Budapest, Hungary
Vanderbilt Marble House, Newport, USA
Wat Benchamabophiy, Bangkok, Siam

First Cricket Test at MCG Won by "Colonials"

Henry Stanley

Melbourne, Australia, March 19, 1877: The first Test match between England and Australia has been played at the Melbourne Cricket Ground. Australia has won the contest by 45 runs.

The Australian team, a combined Sydney and Melbourne XI, included four Englishmen. They faced England's touring cricket team captained by James Lillywhite.

The Australian batsman Charles Bannerman faced the first ball and went on to score an unbeaten 165 runs.

As the English team is made up entirely of professionals, the great cricketer of the present era, W. G. Grace, was not playing. In first-class cricket he is averaging between 60 and 70 runs per match. He and his two brothers, "EM" and "GF," have turned Gloucestershire into a first-class county in only one season. It is assumed that he would have swung the match in England's favor had he played.

Nevertheless, euphoria is sweeping the nation. It is the first time "Mother Country" England has been defeated by the "colonial" Australians in an even contest. The *Daily News of Sydney* commented: "In this distant land, a generation has arisen which can play the best bowlers of the time."

The history of the game remains shrouded in mystery. The word cricket may derive from the French *criquet*, a kind of club or goal post. The earliest known reference is from the Borough of Guildford, which records a game of "creckett" played between pupils of the Royal Grammar School in Surrey in about 1550, and references to the game

"POVERTY IS AN ANOMALY TO RICH PEOPLE. IT IS VERY DIFFICULT TO MAKE OUT WHY PEOPLE WHO WANT DINNER DO NOT RING THE BELL."

SAMUEL BUTLER (1835–1902), BRITISH NOVELIST, 1879

"WHEN A DOG BITES A MAN THAT IS NOT NEWS, BUT WHEN A MAN BITES A DOG THAT IS NEWS."

CHARLES A. DANA (1819–1897), AMERICAN JOURNALIST, 1882

are found increasingly throughout the 1600s. The logbook of HMS *Assistance* (part of a British fleet on the Levantine coast) records some of her crew playing cricket at Antioch on May 6, 1676.

The Australian XI defeated England at the Melbourne Cricket Ground.

World's First Skyscraper Rises in Chicago

Chicago, USA, 1885: Partly in response to rising land values within the city of Chicago, William Le Baron Jenney has this year completed what is being called the world's first "skyscraper," the Home Insurance Building.

Rising to a height of 138 ft (42 m), it comprises nine stories and is built with a load-carrying structural frame. Jenney used metal columns and beams instead of stone and brick to support the building's higher levels. On learning that its weight is one-third of that of a comparable stone structure, city officials were so concerned that they halted its construction while they investigated the safety issues involved.

Jenney is a civil engineer and architect who studied architecture in Paris. He

constructed a railroad in Panama prior to serving in that country's civil war as an engineering officer. Having left the Panamanian army with the rank of major, he has been practicing architecture in Chicago since 1868.

"Coca-Cola" Sells for 5 Cents a Glass

Athens, Georgia, USA, May 8, 1886: Following on from recent "soda water" drinks such as Hires Root Beer and Dr Pepper, a pharmacist named Dr John Pemberton has produced a new syrup that, when squirted into a glass and combined with cold carbonated water from a soda fountain, tastes "quite satisfactory" according to those who have tried it.

Owing to Fulton County going "dry" last year, Dr Pemberton was no longer able to use wine as the base for his French Wine Coca and started experimenting with coca and other additives.

It is currently selling for 5 cents a glass in Jacob's Pharmacy at 2 Peachtree Street in Atlanta, and has apparently been given the name "Coca-Cola" by Frank Robinson, Pemberton's bookkeeper.

Its name is derived from the drink's ingredients of coca leaves and kola nuts, and it is being sold as a "brain tonic" and a temperance drink.

time out

In 1878, US President Rutherford B. Hayes invited children to roll their Easter eggs on the White House lawn. He gave each participating child a wooden spoon as a memento.

Rescue Mission Finds Pasha Alive

Lake Albert, Central Africa, April 27, 1888: Famous explorer Henry Stanley has led a rescue expedition from the mouth of the Congo River to Lake Albert in Central Africa to relieve Emin Pasha, the governor of Equatorial Egyptian Sudan. Over half of Stanley's expedition are said to have perished en route.

Pasha, a German convert to Islam, has been cut off from the outside world since

Calais, France, August 25, 1875: Matthew Webb becomes the first person to swim the English Channel. It takes him 21 hours 45 minutes.
Pittsburgh, USA, May, 1876: Henry John Heinz produces ketchup, bringing the popular condiment into millions of homes.
London, England, July 9–16, 1877: W. Spencer Gore beats 21 men to win the inaugural Wimbledon tennis Championships.
London, England, May, 1878: The Christian Mission becomes The Salvation Army.

London, England, September, 1878: Cleopatra's Needle (a granite obelisk commemorating the defeat of Napoleon), is placed on the Thames embankment.
Cévennes, France, September 22– October 3, 1878: Robert Louis Stevenson travels solo through southern France, and writes *Travels with a Donkey in the Cévennes*; he is one of the first to present hiking and camping as recreational activities, and is credited with the first use of the sleeping bag.

Kansas, USA, November, 1880: Kansas becomes the first US state to legislate against the consumption of alcohol, introducing prohibition following a referendum.
Athens, Georgia, USA, May 8, 1886: Doctor John Pemberton develops Coca Cola, a cola-based health tonic and offers it for sale at Jacob's pharmacy in Athens, with limited success.
New York, USA, October 28, 1886: President Cleveland dedicates the Statue of Liberty, a gift from France signifying the friendship between the two countries.

Albany, New York, USA, January 5, 1887: Melvil Dewey, the inventor of the decimal system of library cataloguing in 1872, founds the State Library School.
Lake Albert, Central Africa, December 13, 1887: Explorer Henry Stanley leads a rescue expedition from the Congo River to Lake Albert to relieve Emin Pasha, governor of Equatorial Egyptian Sudan. Over half of the expedition perish en route.
England, September 8, 1888: The first season of the Football League commences. Twelve clubs participate.

Greenland, October, 1888: Fridtjof Nansen completes the first crossing of the ice cap of Greenland. Travelling from east to west with no support, this crossing takes two months to complete.
Paris, France, June 10, 1889: Gustave Eiffel opens the Eiffel Tower, built for the World's Fair. The world's tallest man-made structure is meant to be only a temporary erection.
New York, USA, January 25, 1890: Nellie Bly, a pioneering investigative journalist completes an around the world trip in 72 days, 6 hours, and 11 minutes, a world record.

the outbreak of a Muslim revolt six years ago, in which the Sudanese under the Mahdi rose up against Egyptian rule.

Stanley split his force of 1,500 men into two groups, leading the advance column up the Congo and Aruwimi rivers. After fighting his way through the Ituri, one of the densest jungles on Earth, he finally reached Pasha on April 27.

Nansen First to Cross Greenland's Ice Fields

Greenland, October, 1888: The Norwegian explorer and author Fridtjof Nansen has completed the first crossing of Greenland's ice cap, traveling from east to west over two months with no support.

All previous attempts at the crossing had been made from west to east, and had failed miserably.

Nansen and five others sailed to Greenland's deserted east coast, leaving their ship there and trekking for 37 days westward. Landing 200 miles (320 km) further south than intended owing to

Nansen at the North Pole with his dogs and sleds.

shifting ice packs, they traveled north before finally setting out on their westward crossing on August 15, during which they endured temperatures as low as minus 79°F (minus 26°C) and scaled to 8,920 ft (2,720 m).

They reached the west coast on September 26, where they made boats of willow branches and sail cloth, and then sailed on to Godthaab, the country's Danish capital. Owing to their later than expected arrival, they missed the last ship back to Europe and will see out the Greenland winter before returning home.

On a previous voyage to the Arctic, in 1882, Nansen kept meticulous records of winds, ice movements, and animal life. Intrigued by the behavior of ocean currents, he decided to cross Greenland's ice cap to study the movement and structure of continental glaciers.

Nansen's observations are expected to confirm that these glaciers are thick enough and heavy enough to depress the Earth's crust beneath them, supporting the theory of isostatic rebound—that the Earth's crust is capable of sinking under massive weight.

Tallest Man-made Structure Opens in Paris

Paris, France, June 10, 1889: Back in 1882, Maurice Koechlin, the chief of the Eiffel Company's research unit, and his colleague Emile Nouguier conceived the idea of a metal tower for the 1889 World Fair to be held in Paris, submitting their first draft on June 6, 1884.

Gustav Eiffel, the engineer who was made famous by the construction of the viaduc de Garabit in 1868, which allowed

The Eiffel Tower, a new landmark.

the railway from Béziers to Clermont-Ferrand to cross the Truyère Gorge, did not initially want to be involved with it, and allowed two of his engineers to develop plans for the tower. It was not until September of that year that Eiffel joined the project, buying the patent from the engineers. Today Eiffel opened his tower to the public.

Built for the Paris Exposition in May, the Eiffel Tower stands 985 ft (300 m) high, making it the world's tallest man-made structure.

Its design has been harshly criticized, and described as "useless" and "monstrous." The concept that iron on its own, without an outer skin, could be beautiful flies in the face of contemporary architectural mores—to leave it exposed is considered by many to be in poor taste.

A mathematician even told the press that the tower would collapse when it achieved a height of 700 ft (214 m).

The tower weighs a massive 8,000 tons (8,160 tonnes) and measures 412 sq ft (105 sq m) at its base. Over 18,000 pieces of iron feature in the lattice-style structure, which was pieced together by more than 300 ironworkers over a 26-month period. An estimated 50 tons (51 tonnes) of paint will be required every seven years to keep it in its current pristine condition.

The tower is built of puddled iron, a very pure structural iron. The four pillars supporting the tower are aligned to the four points of the compass, and can be used as a reference point in finding one's way through the city.

Eiffel's design was chosen from over 700 submitted drawings. He has been nicknamed "the magician of iron."

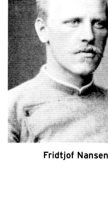

Fridtjof Nansen

St Louis, USA, 1891: The world's first skyscraper is completed. Designed by Louis Sullivan, the 10-story building has been constructed out of steel girders.

North America, 1893: It is estimated that around 1,000 bison are left after hundreds of years of unchecked exploitation. Seventy million bison are thought to have roamed North America around 1600.

New Zealand, September 19, 1893: New Zealand becomes the first country to grant suffrage for women.

Chicago, Illinois, USA, May 1–October 30, 1893: The World's Fair Grand Colombian Carnival celebrates the 400th anniversary of the discovery of America. George Ferris' 250 ft (76.2 m) high "Ferris wheel" is designed for the extravaganza.

Paris, France, July 22, 1894: The world's first automobile race takes place between Paris and Rouen.

Pullman, Illinois, USA, July, 1894: Some 50,000 railway workers strike over wages and conditions, led by Eugene Debs, who is eventually jailed to end the strike.

Stanwell Park, New South Wales, Australia, November 12, 1894: Aviator Lawrence Hargrave is lifted from the ground on an experimental box kite.

Cape Adare, Antarctica, January 24, 1895: The first confirmed landing on the Antarctic mainland is achieved by a Norwegian expedition.

London, England, May 25, 1895: Oscar Wilde is found guilty of sodomy and sentenced to jail.

Rhode Island, USA, October 4, 1895: Englishman Horace Rawlins wins the first US Open Golf Championship.

Shanghai, China, 1895: Anti-footbinding movement gains momentum under leadership of Western missionaries and Chinese social reformers.

Athens, Greece, April 6–15, 1896: After a hiatus of 1,500 years the first modern Olympic Games are attended by 14 nations. Greek shepherd Spyridon Louis wins the marathon in front of 100,000 spectators.

London, England, October 3, 1896: William Morris, designer, writer, and socialist dies, aged 62. His firm produced fabrics and wallpaper.

Elberfeld, Germany, August 10, 1897: Dr Felix Hoffman creates a chemically pure form of acetylsalicylic acid, later known as aspirin.

Basle, Switzerland, August 29, 1897: Over 200 Jewish leaders meet at the World Zionist Conference. Spearheaded by Theodor Herzel its goal is to create a homeland for the Jewish people in the Middle East.

Seoul, Korea, September 9, 1898: *Chanyang Hoe (Group to Promote Growth)* issues manifesto calling for the establishment of schools for women.

William Booth

New Zealand Suffragettes Win Right to Vote

New Zealand, September 19, 1893: New Zealand has become the world's first self-governing nation to grant women, including indigenous Maori women, the right to vote.

The suffragettes' struggle can be traced back to the pro-suffrage literature of Mary Muller in the late 1860s. In 1885, a representative of the Women's Christian Temperance Union (WCTU) of the United States, Mary Leavitt, toured New Zealand and in the process founded 15 branches of the association, which soon ranged far beyond issues of temperance, developing distinctly feminist overtones. Many of New Zealand's socially active and prominent women began to join the new movement, and in 1887 Kate Sheppard of Christchurch became its national franchise superintendent. A well-educated immigrant from Great Britain, she led the WCTU in campaigns for equality in the nation's divorce laws, the raising of the age of consent, and the provision of preschool education and night shelters. She traveled around the country speaking at many public functions, persuading sympathetic men to join the cause, and wrote prolifically on the issues, keeping the debate very much in the public domain.

Although the suffrage movement began in the United States around the middle of the century, the debate has spread quickly throughout British colonies. New Zealand had long given women opportunities in education they are denied elsewhere. Secondary schools for girls have been in existence since the 1870s, at which time women were even admitted to universities.

Cleopatra's Needle on London's River Thames.

The 1893 World's Fair in Chicago featured the debut of a thrilling new ride—the Ferris Wheel.

Kate Edger became the first woman in the British Empire to gain a bachelor of arts degree, graduating from the University of New Zealand in 1877. She went on to teach at Christchurch Girls High School and gained a master of arts in 1882 from Canterbury College.

Women throughout New Zealand began entering the workforce as they became better educated. By the late 1880s, more than 700 working women, who were denied the vote, were employing men, who had the vote.

The first Suffrage Bill, presented to the New Zealand parliament in 1887, was defeated. Two more unsuccessful petitions were presented in 1891 and 1892.

The 1891 Bill actually passed through the Lower House but was voted down in the Legislative Council. But it was the so-called "monster petition" of 1893 that provided the catalyst for today's historic decision. More than 30,000 signatures from women over the age of 21 were collected from across the country and sent to Christchurch, where Kate Shepperd pasted the sheets together end-on-end and rolled the resulting document around a section of broom handle.

It was presented in parliament by the suffrage supporter John Hall, who rather dramatically unrolled it down the central aisle of the debating chamber until it hit the wall with a thud.

The ruling Liberal Party passed the measure, and today it was signed into law by Governor Glasgow.

Despite efforts by some council members to dissuade the governor from signing the Bill, the suffragettes maintained pressure to the last, dispatching telegrams and—in a gesture designed to publicize those who stood in their way—white camellias to every member of parliament who supported the vote and red camellias to all their opponents.

Kate Sheppard, defiant as ever, wryly remarked after the Bill's signing: "It does not seem a great thing to be thankful for, that the gentlemen who confirm the laws which render women liable to taxation and penal servitude have declared us to be 'persons.'"

New Amusement Park Ride Captivates

Chicago, USA, May 1–October 30, 1893: At the Chicago World's Fair Grand Columbian Carnival, celebrating the 400th anniversary of the discovery of America, a Mr George Ferris, a bridge-builder from Pittsburgh, has unveiled his 250-ft (76-m) high amusement ride which he has dubbed the "Ferris wheel."

Two 140-ft (43-m) tall steel towers support a 250-ft (76-m) wheel with a circumference of 825 ft (252 m), to which 36 wooden cars are attached. The wheel rotates with the help of two 1,000-hp reversible engines and lifts its 60 passengers into the heavens for the princely sum of 50 cents.

Englishman Wins Inaugural US Golf Open

Newport, Rhode Island, USA, October 4, 1895: The United States Golf Association (USGA) has held its first US Open Championship at Newport Golf and Country Club in Rhode Island, New York. Played on a 9-hole course, the 36-hole competition was completed in one day.

Horace Rawlins, a professional from England aged just 21, is the championship's inaugural winner, receiving a cash prize of $150 as well as a $50 golf medal and the Open Championship Cup, which will go to his club.

The USGA Open has been played on the same course and in the same week as the much higher fancied US Amateur Championship.

Movement Against Foot-Binding Gathers Strength

Shanghai, China, December, 1895: This year missionaries in China have been advocating that the practise of footbinding be discontinued. Footbinding began late in the T'ang Dynasty (618–906 CE) and involves wrapping a 10-ft (3-m) length of bandage around the feet of a young girl, usually aged 4 to 7 years, in such a way as to bend the arch and force the four small toes under the sole. The bandages are progressively tightened over a two-year period until the feet become shorter and narrower. The young bones, mostly composed of pre-bone cartilage, are easily molded, and the "ideal feminine foot" eventually fits into a shoe that measures only 3 to 4 inches (5 to 10 cm) in length.

Though the precise reasons for the emergence of this practice can now only be guessed at, it is accepted that Confucian teachings stressed the dominance of the man over the woman as a basic element of social order. It began as a luxury among the rich and evolved into becoming almost a prerequisite for making a good marriage, particularly among the upper classes.

Bound feet have to be properly washed and manicured on a daily basis. Poorly manicured toenails can lead to serious

Chinese women with bound feet find it difficult to walk.

infections, and if the bindings are too tight the feet can become gangrenous.

Recently, missionaries have been demanding that all girls entering their schools unbind their feet, and various Natural Foot Societies organized by Chinese citizens are attempting to put an end to the practice.

German Chemist Creates Pain-relieving Tablet

Elberfeld, Germany, August 10, 1897: In the 1850s a little-known French chemist, Charles Frederick Gerhardt, created the compound acetylsalicylic acid. Unfortunately, at the time he possessed neither the will nor the means to manufacture and market his invention.

In 1894, a young graduate chemist from the University of Munich, Dr Felix Hoffman, joined the German company Bayer as a research chemist and began to search for a pain reliever to help ease his

father's debilitating rheumatism. On August 10, 1897, Hoffman produced a less toxic variant of salicylic acid, much as Gerhardt had done 40 years earlier. With the backing of Bayer Pharmaceuticals, Hoffman's acetylsalicylic acid, or ASA, is to be marketed as "Aspirin" to be sold as a powder supplied in glass bottles.

Salicylic acid is the active ingredient in salves and teas made from willow bark and certain other plants. Extracts of willow bark were used in folk medicine as early as 400 BCE, when the Greek physician Hippocrates is recorded as recommending a brew made from willow leaves to treat labor pains.

In 1763, an English clergyman, the Reverend Edward Stone, carried out the first scientific study of the herbal medicine when he described the benefits he observed after giving ground-up willow bark to more than 50 of his parishioners suffering the effects of rheumatic fever.

Salicylic acid was isolated in the 1850s, and in 1859 Herman Kolbe determined its chemical structure and synthesized it. However, it had unwanted side-effects, including nausea and gastric pain. The less toxic variant created by Hoffman was tested first on animals, then on patients in a hospital in Hall an der Salle.

The pharmacologist responsible for verifying these results was skeptical at first, but by the time several large-scale studies had been completed, it had become clear that Hoffman had discovered a pain-relieving, fever-reducing, anti-inflammatory substance.

The name trade name "Aspirin" is derived from "A" for acetyl and "spirin," which comes from the genus name for the shrubs that are an alternative source of acetylsalicylic acid.

Robert Louis Stevenson

Religious Leaders

Popes
Pius IX (1846-1878)
Leo XIII (1878-1903)

Archbishops of Canterbury
Archibald Campbell Tate (1868-1882)
Edward White Benson (1882-1896)
Frederick Temple (1896-1902)

Dalai Lamas of Tibet
Trinley Gyatso (1860-1875)
Thupten Gyatso (1895-1933)

Patriarchs of Constantinople
Joachim II (1873-1878)
Joachim III (1878-1884)
Joachim IV (1884-1887)
Dionysius V (1887-1891)
Neophytus VIII (1891-1894)
Anthimus VII (1895-1896)
Constantine V (1897-1901)

Englishman Matthew Webb swam the English Channel on August 24 and 25, 1875, in 21 hours and 45 minutes.

Queen Victoria

World Expo Showcases French Capital

Paris, France, April 14: The World Exposition has opened in Paris. More opulent than any previous world's fair, monumental exhibits cover a large area of the French capital. Including technology as well as the arts and sciences, the events organizers have unfolded a panorama dedicated to the progress made over the past few years.

The entire city seems to have become a giant stage. From Paulin's water palace has sprung a waterfall flowing against the backdrop of a lavishly ornamented reinforced concrete facade. Plastic animals and human figures populate the city's parks and grottos. Brightly illuminated at night, the Palais de l'Électricité is crowned by an impressive iron structure of stars spreading out to all sides, which, together with the illuminated

"THE ADMIRAL OF THE ATLANTIC SALUTES THE ADMIRAL OF THE PACIFIC."

WILHELM II (1859–1941), EMPEROR OF GERMANY AND KING OF PRUSSIA, TO TSAR NICHOLAS II

"SO LITTLE DONE, SO MUCH TO DO."

CECIL RHODES (1853–1902), ENGLISH ENTREPRENEUR AND COLONIZER OF RHODESIA (LATER ZIMBABWE)

water effects, has transformed the Champs de Mars into an atmospheric sea of light.

The Expo site covers approximately 295 acres (120 hectares) in Paris and an additional 110 acres (45 hectares) in nearby Vincennes. There are over 83,000 exhibits from 43 participating nations.

It is estimated that more than 50 million visitors will attend this year's Expo over the next 212 days. The exhibition will end on November 12.

Siege at Peking Ends after 55 Days

Peking, China, August 14: The Boxers, a disparate group of the military Chinese angry at the continuing presence of foreigners on Chinese soil, have had their siege of the legations in Peking abruptly ended today when 20,000 US marines along with Russian and British troops stormed their barricades.

In 1898 the Boxers led a rebellion to drive out foreigners. The ruling Manchu court, at first ambivalent, had by early this year given the Boxers their blessing.

By early June, the Boxers were destroying foreign property and killing foreign nationals. The foreign legations were all located within a semi-walled area, close to the Forbidden City, which was connected by telegraph to Shanghai. When the telegraph lines were cut and the siege began, the legations worked together to hastily enclose the remainder of the perimeter. It was to be a further eight weeks until the arrival of the rescue force.

Converts to Catholicism being executed during the Boxer rebellion.

Over 6,000 Perish in Texas Tidal Wave

Galveston, USA, September 8: The island city of Galveston, Texas, has been devastated by a category 4 hurricane in what observers are saying is the worst natural disaster ever to hit the United States. It is estimated that over 6,000 men, women, and children have perished in the disaster. The city is now in a state of chaos. The storm did not hit without warning. In the days leading up to the disaster, telegraph reports were being received detailing the havoc the storm was causing in the Caribbean.

Anemometers in Galveston measured the storm's wind strength at 100 mph (160 km/h) before they were themselves blown away. A huge 16 ft (5 m) tidal surge swept the across the city, which had never constructed a sea wall, and all of Galveston was under water by 3 p.m.

At St Mary's Orphanage, home to 93 children and 10 Catholic nuns, only three boys who managed to cling to an uprooted tree survived.

Rich and poor alike huddled together in ornate mansions such as Bishop's Palace, whose strong walls provided shelter for over 200 people.

Galveston was a wealthy port, with a population of 30,000 people. It had become the hub of the booming cotton trade because it had the only deep-water port in Texas. There was more money here than in Newport, Rhode Island. The Strand in the city's downtown was known as "the Wall Street of the southwest."

This morning Galveston's city streets were lined with imposing Italianate, Greek Revival, and Romanesque mansions. Streetcars ran along the beach.

Tonight, three-quarters of this once beautiful city has simply ceased to exist.

London, England, February 27: Various socialist organizations and trade unions unite as the Labour Representation Committee, hoping to elect candidates to Westminster.
Ladysmith, South Africa, February 28: Ending a four-month siege by Boer forces, General Sir Redvers Buller liberates Ladysmith in a decisive victory for the British.
India, March 27: Famine is affecting at least five million people throughout the subcontinent as Viceroy Lord Curzon pledges 8.5 million pounds in famine relief.

Brussels, Belgium, April 4: The Prince of Wales (Albert Edward) survives an assassination attempt by a 16 year-old anarchist in retaliation for the British role in the Boer War.
Coomassie, Gold Coast, April 6: West African Ashanti tribesmen, incensed by British imperial demands to hand over important icons, attack British troops.
Paris, France, April 14: The World Exposition opens in Paris. More opulent than any previous World's Fair, monumental exhibits cover a large area of the French capital.

Mafeking, South Africa, May 20: British troops are relieved after a seven-month siege, causing ecstatic celebrations throughout the Empire.
China, May 31: The Boxer Rebellion begins. Known as I-ho ch'uan, the Boxers are a secret nationalistic society hostile to foreign interests.
Berlin, Germany, June 12: The Reichstag passes legislation continuing Germany's naval expansion. It is projected that 38 battleships will be built in the next 20 years.

Australia, July 9: The British parliament and Queen Victoria accept the Commonwealth of Australia Act, uniting the colonies under a federal government.
Monza, Italy, July 20: An anarchist assassinates Umberto I, aged 56.
Peking, China, August 14: Allied troops break the Boxers' siege.
Gulf of Mexico, September 8: Cyclonic winds cause a massive tidal wave, inundating Galveston—over 6,000 perish; $10 million damage results on the Gulf Coast.

Philippines, October: The Philippine Insurrection descends into bloody guerrilla warfare as nationalists battle US troops. The USA has colonized the country following Spain's withdrawal in 1898.
USA, November 6: Republican William McKinley wins a second term with Theodore Roosevelt as his running mate.
Italy and France, December 16: A Franco-Italian agreement allows France free reign in Morocco and Italy likewise in Libya.

Edward VII

Queen Victoria Is Dead

Cowes, England, January 22: After a reign of 64 years that has seen the British Empire reach its greatest extent, Queen Victoria has died at her home on the Isle of Wight at the age of 82. Her son Edward VII will ascend to the throne.

On January 14 after an interview with Lord Roberts—who had just returned victorious from South Africa a few days before—she suffered a collapse. On January 15 her medical entourage realized her condition was hopeless, yet over the following two days her indomitable spirit fought on as she continued to discharge the duties of the queen of England. With all of her family present around her, she passed away today, ending the longest reign in the history of the English monarchy.

President McKinley is shot by a deranged assailant.

McKinley Shot: Roosevelt Sworn In

Buffalo, USA, September 14: Eight days ago, while visiting the Pan-American Exposition in Buffalo, New York, President William McKinley was shot twice with a .32-caliber hand gun by a deranged assailant—Leon Czolgosz, a 28-year-old factory worker from Cleveland. The first bullet caused only a flesh wound, but the second tore into the president's stomach.

As McKinley was still alive, the first physicians to arrive at the scene of the shooting decided to remove the bullet. As the president was seemingly on the road to recovery, Vice-President Roosevelt was even convinced to take a short vacation in the Adirondack Mountains.

Yesterday morning, however, the president's condition began to worsen and he passed away in the early hours of this morning. Theodore Roosevelt has now been sworn in as president.

McKinley was a Civil War veteran who signed up as a private in the 23rd Regiment, Ohio Volunteer Infantry, seeing action at Antietam, Fisher's Hill, and Cedar Creek. He was elected to Congress in 1890.

He became governor of Ohio in 1892 and Republican presidential candidate in 1896, and thence the nation's 25th president.

One of the key events of McKinley's administration was the war with Spain, which resulted in the destruction of the Spanish fleet and the United States' acquisition of the Philippines, Guam, and Puerto Rico.

McKinley embodied the political and social conservatism of the Republican party. A long-time ally of big business, he made his name by sponsoring protective tariffs. In 1896 he campaigned for president from his front porch, while his challenger, Democrat William Bryan, stormed all over the country. In McKinley's first term an economic boom boosted profits and the Spanish-American War gave the nation new imperial possessions. In 1900 he became the first president in 28 years to win a consecutive term.

Marconi Transmits First Wireless Message

UK and Canada, December 12: The Italian inventor Guglielmo Marconi has received transmitted wireless telegraphic signals from Cornwall in England sent to his "shack" at Signal Hill, Newfoundland, Canada—2,232 miles (3,593 km) apart.

Marconi and his assistant George Kemp today heard the faint clicks of Morse code for the letter "S."

Despite strong gale-force winds that were interfering with reception balloons and carried off the first one sent up, the second balloon stayed aloft long enough for the two men to hear the Morse code signals through a telephone earpiece connected to the receiver.

Marconi transmitting messages with his wireless apparatus.

On April 26 last year Marconi took out Patent 7777, which documented a system for tuned coupled circuits and allowed simultaneous transmissions to take place on different frequencies. Adjacent stations would be able to operate without interfering with one another, and ranges would be increased.

He has today proven that wireless waves are not affected by Earth's curvature, as has been the prevailing opinion of scientists and engineers.

Marconi made the first wireless transmission across water on May 13, 1897, from Lavernock Point in south Wales to Flat Holm Island. Today's trans-atlantic signal was received at Signal Hill in the Canadian province of Newfoundland, using a 500 ft (150 m) balloon-supported antenna for reception.

Cecil Rhodes

"PERHAPS IT
IS GOD'S WILL
TO LEAD THE
PEOPLE OF
SOUTH AFRICA
THROUGH
DEFEAT AND
HUMILIATION
TO A BETTER
FUTURE AND
A BRIGHTER
DAY."

JAN SMUTS (1870–
1950), SOUTH
AFRICAN STATESMAN
AND MILITARY
LEADER, AT A PEACE
CONFERENCE THAT
ENDED THE BOER
WAR, 1902

Texas's Sea of Oil to Fuel US Economy

Texas, USA, April 7: The Texas Company (Texaco) has been founded today, three months after discoveries at Spindletop, a salt-dome formation south of Beaumont.

Three unsuccessful shallow attempts had been made to drill here previously using cable-tool drilling equipment. Anthony Lucas, the leading US specialist on salt domes, took a lease with the Gladys City Company to drill the area in 1899. He drilled to a depth of 575 ft (175 m) before running out of money, never losing his conviction there was oil there. After securing more financial backing, he brought in an experienced drilling team and switched to using a heavier rotary type drill bit. From October to Janu-ary 1901 the team struggled to overcome the difficult oil sands that had hampered previous efforts.

Then, on January 10, mud began bubbling from the hole. The startled drilling team fled as tons of 4 in (10 cm) drilling pipe shot out of the ground. The mud turned to gas, and the gas to oil. The Lucas geyser was found at a depth of 1,139 ft (347 m) and blew a stream of oil 100 ft (30 m) high until it was capped nine days later. One hundred thousand barrels a day was soon being pumped from the geyser. In a single day it is likely that more oil will flow from the wells at Spindletop than from the wells of the rest of the world combined. Wild speculation has led to rocketing land values. One man who has been trying to sell a parcel of land for three years for $150 has now sold it for $20,000.

time out

Doctor Eugène-Louis Doyen of Paris successfully separated a pair of Siamese twins of the Barnum and Bailey Circus. A pioneer of the filming of medical procedures, Doyen recorded the operation and presented the film as *La Séparation de Doodica-Radica.*

Island Paradise Turns to Hell

Saint-Pierre, Martinique, May 8: In January Mt Pelée on the Caribbean island of Martinique began to show an abrupt increase in fumarole activity, but the public and officials showed little concern.

Today the volcano erupted with a deafening roar, sending a large black cloud of superheated gas, ash, and rock down the south flank of the mountain at 100 mph (160 km/h) straight into the once-picturesque town of Sainte-Pierre, population 20,000 people.

It took less than one minute to hit with the force of a hurricane. The heat cloud spread over the town and out into the harbor, where it destroyed at least 20 ships anchored offshore. Only three inhabitants of Sainte-Pierre, the "Paris of the West Indies," have been found alive.

Boer War Ends

Pretoria, South Africa, May 31: The Treaty of Vereeniging was signed today between the British government and the Boers, with Britain gaining sovereignty over South Africa, ending the bloodiest war ever fought on South African soil. Britain has agreed to pay £3 million for rebuilding farms and homes destroyed in the war.

The British position was delivered to the Boer commanders in the veld, who then had to choose representatives for the meeting at Vereeniging on May 15. That meeting then selected five members to negotiate in Pretoria. The Boer commission returned to Vereeniging with the conditions for peace on May 27. The Boers voted 54 to 6 to accept these conditions.

The two former Boer republics were incorporated into the British Empire as crown colonies, with the Boers agreeing to surrender their independence in return for the repatriation of prisoners of war, limited protection of the Dutch language, the maintenance of property rights, and honoring of the republican war debt.

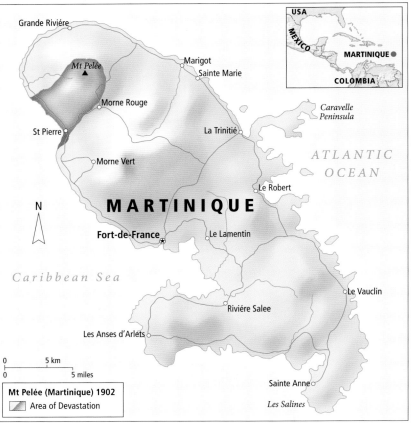

Mt Pelée (Martinique) 1902
Area of Devastation

UK and Japan, January 30: Interests in China and Korea are safeguarded with the signing of the Anglo-Japanese Treaty. Japan has been resolutely isolationist prior to this treaty.

Russia, February 4: Thirty thousand students strike in response to laws aimed at controlling student organizations.

Barcelona, Spain, February 20: Five hundred strikers die as tensions rise between industrialists and workers. A state of siege is declared and 80,000 workers stop work.

Cape Town, South Africa, March 26: Cecil Rhodes, former prime minister of the Cape Colony, founder of the DeBeers Mining Company and in honor of whom Rhodesia was named, dies, aged 48.

Texas, USA, April 7: The Texas Company (Texaco) is founded after discoveries at Spindletop and other Texan oil fields.

Russia and China, April 8: The Sino-Russian conflict over Manchuria comes to an end with the signing of a treaty committing to the withdrawal of Russian troops.

Dublin, Ireland, April 20: Twenty thousand people gather to protest draconian British laws aimed at stifling dissent among nationalists.

Saint-Pierre, Martinique, May 8: Mt Pelée, a volcano in the French West Indies, erupts destroying the town of Saint-Pierre. Only three people survive out of 30,000.

Pretoria, South Africa, May 31: The Treaty of Vereeniging is signed.

New Zealand, June 4: Lieutenant Robert McKeich is the last New Zealander to be killed in the Boer War, after the treaty was signed.

Madrid, Spain, May 31: Alphonso XIII suspends the Cortes (parliament) and imposes martial law following widespread strikes.

Australia, July: A restrictive immigration policy is established aiming to keep the number of non-white immigrants low. This follows similar legislation in the USA, where the Chinese Exclusion Act was passed in April.

Russia, July 3: The Tsar agrees to talk to 200 citizens following riots among peasants who are suffering from starvation and unemployment.

Agram, Croatia, September 1: The Austro-Hungarian rulers impose martial law as violence erupts between Croats and Serbs.

Finland, September 22: Tsar Nicholas II of Russia abolishes Finnish autonomy.

Aswan, Egypt, December 10: The first dam to tame the Nile River is completed.

Venezuela, December 19: The government agrees to honor its debts after Britain, Germany, and France blockade five ports and seize the Venezuelan fleet of four boats.

Second Longest Pontificate Ends

The Vatican, Italy, July 20: Pope Leo XIII died today after a 25-year pontificate that has seen him work untiringly to unify Christendom. Profoundly interested in the advancement of learning, he opened the doors of the Vatican archives to all scholars and reminded Catholic historians that nothing but the truth should be found in their historical papers.

Pope Leo XIII's death is announced to the cardinals.

He encouraged Bible study, and sponsored a number of faculties and universities, including the Catholic University in Washington DC. For sheer productivity Pope Leo XIII has surpassed all his pre-decessors in modern times.

Long-standing Border Dispute Settled

Alaska, October 16: The land boundary between Alaska and Canada is 1,538 miles (2,476 km) long. In 1867 its exact location was unknown when the US Secretary of State William Seward offered Russia two cents an acre for the purchase of Russian America. The land was then renamed

Alaska. The Anglo-Russian treaty of 1825 gave the 141st meridian as the boundary between Canada and Russia but much of the area was unsurveyed and the line was uncertain. The border was described as following a range of mountains in the southeast; where there was no mountain range, the border was to run parallel to the coast. The line is sometimes obvious, but in other places it is not.

During the Klondike gold rush of the late 1880s and 1890s, border relations between the USA and Canada became difficult. Canadian officials wanted ownership of certain areas to allow them access to the gold fields without having to travel across American soil.

To finally settle the dispute, Britain and the United States agreed to appoint a committee to meet this year. The committee consisted of three Americans, two Canadians, and England's chief justice, Lord Richard Alverstone. Alverstone's decision unexpectedly came down on the side of the United States, thereby rejecting the Canadian claims.

With a boundary now agreed upon, the next job will be to survey and mark it.

Powered Flight a Reality at Kitty Hawk

Kitty Hawk, USA, December 17: The first heavier-than-air powered flight was today achieved by the Wright brothers, Orville and Wilbur, at Kitty Hawk, on North Carolina's outer banks.

In the 1890s the brothers owned a profitable bicycle repair shop in their home town of Dayton, Ohio.

They chose Kitty Hawk as the location for their experiments, despite it having no electricity, no running water, and no phone lines. There were no cars, and all the roads were sand tracks. There wasn't even a doctor to service the 250 residents, who were split into two communities known simply as "up the road" and "down the road."

But what Kitty Hawk did possess, 600 miles (966 km) from the Wright brothers' home in Ohio, was steady winds.

They began with a glider in 1900 and redesigned it in 1901, changing the curvature of the wings. However, the lift they expected to see from the new glider design just was not there.

In 1902 another glider, designed from data collected in a crude wind tunnel they had constructed, flew better. In 1903 they began experimenting with a four-cylinder engine. Engineering problems with the propeller beset them, as there were no existing data to start with.

The Wright brothers' biplane glider had grown in size with each passing year, and the addition of an engine gave it a weight of 605 lb (275 kg) and a 40 ft (12 m) wingspan.

This morning it dawned clear, and the toss of a coin meant that it was Orville's turn to fly. He flew 120 ft (36 m) in 12 seconds. Wilbur then made a second flight, covering 175 ft (53 m) in 15 seconds. On the last flight of the day Wilbur flew 852 ft (260 m) in 59 seconds.

The world's first powered aircraft lifted itself off the ground, traversed a section of the sky under the full control of the operator and then landed, ready to fly again. This momentous event was witnessed by just four people.

Kaiser Wilhelm II of Germany

The Wright Brothers' biplane, which they called "the Flyer."

Key Events

Delhi, India, January 1: At a vast ceremony unattended by the primary participant, Edward VII is proclaimed Emperor of India.

Cuba, February 23: The government accepts the Platt Amendment at the insistence of the USA. Cuba agrees to US intervention if deemed necessary and leases two naval bases.

Washington DC, USA, March 3: An anti-immigration law is ratified, seeking to keep out "undesirables," a significant change from the "open door" policy of last century.

Kishinev, Russia, April 16: Peasants' anti-Semitic feelings are encouraged by officials under Tsar Nicholas II. A bloody pogrom results in the deaths of hundreds of Jews.

France, April 29: Nine years of conflict between church and state leads to the government of President Combes closing monasteries.

Belgrade, Serbia, June 11: Serbian Army officers assassinate King Alexander and Queen Draga. The army installs Prince Karageorgevitch as leader.

The Vatican, July 20: Pope Leo XIII dies, aged 93, after a 25-year pontificate that has seen him work toward unifying Christendom.

Paris, France, August 10: A fire started by an electrical fault in the Paris Metro leaves 84 dead.

Bogotá, Colombia, August 12: The Colombian government fails to ratify the Hay-Herran Treaty on US construction of a canal in Panama.

Basle, Switzerland, August 19: At the sixth Zionist Conference, Theodor Herzl declares Palestine the best site for a Jewish state.

Monastir, Bulgaria, September 8: Turkish troops massacre 50,000 Bulgarians after Macedonian revolutionaries urge uprising.

Vienna, Austro-Hungarian Empire, September 16: Facing widespread dissatisfaction from Hungarian Magyars, Emperor Franz Josef declares his intention to maintain a unified and common army and empire.

Alaska, USA, October 16: Conflict between the USA and Canada over the southeastern Alaskan border is resolved in favor of the USA.

London, England, November 17: Russian Social Democratic Party splits into Mensheviks (minority party), led by Martov, and Bolsheviks (extremists, majority party), led by Lenin.

Panama, November 18: Following Panama's secession from Colombia, the USA signs a treaty with the new state, which opens the way to a canal being built under US control.

Kitty Hawk, USA, December 17: The first heavier-than-air powered flight is achieved by the Wright Brothers.

Theodore Roosevelt

> "YOU CANNOT
> FEED THE
> HUNGRY ON
> STATISTICS."
>
> DAVID LLOYD
> GEORGE (1863–1945),
> BRITISH STATESMAN
> AND PRIME
> MINISTER, ON TARIFF
> REFORM, 1904

> "ONE STEP
> FORWARD,
> TWO STEPS
> BACK…IT
> HAPPENS IN
> THE LIVES OF
> INDIVIDUALS,
> AND IT
> HAPPENS IN
> THE HISTORY
> OF NATIONS
> AND IN THE
> DEVELOPMENT
> OF PARTIES."
>
> VLADIMIR LENIN
> (1870–1924), RUSSIAN
> REVOLUTIONARY
> LEADER, 1904

Over 1,000 Perish in Ferry Sinking

New York, USA, June 15: Today the passenger steamer *General Slocum* caught fire in the waters off New York City. A church group of mostly German immigrants had chartered the vessel for a day of recreation and picnicking. Because it was the middle of the week, the passengers were largely women and children who were unable to swim.

As the ship passed East 90th Street smoke began to billow from a forward storage room. Crewmen who had never conducted a fire drill used hoses that split from the pressure of the water. The flames, accelerated due to the application of a fresh coat of highly flammable paint, soon enveloped the ship, and passengers began jumping overboard.

Old life-preservers that had rotted and filled with disintegrated cork had long ago lost their buoyancy. Lifeboats were wired in place and couldn't be dislodged. Fearful of starting a blaze in the city the captain, rather than docking at a city pier and risking the fire spreading to the city, sailed a mile (1.6 km) upriver to North Brother Island. It was a fateful decision.

By the time the ferry reached the island it was completely engulfed in fire.

The island's workers caught children being thrown overboard by distraught parents. Rescue workers openly wept as the corpses piled up. The death toll now stands at 1,021 people.

British Trawlers Under Attack

North Sea, October 22: Warships from Russia's Baltic fleet under the command of Admiral Zinovy Petrovich Rozhestvensky have attacked a number of British fishing trawlers from the Hull fishing fleet at Dogger Bank in the North Sea. The Russian vessels were on their way to the Far East to take part in the Russo-

The Dalai Lama flees from Lhasa, Tibet, to evade the British forces.

Japanese War, and it is understood that they attacked under the mistaken impression that the British trawlers were Japanese warships.

The Russian officers on duty sighted the vessels, interpreted their signals incorrectly, and opened fire. The British trawler *Crane* was sunk and two British fishermen lost their lives. On the other trawlers six fishermen were wounded. In the chaos, the Russian ships even managed to shoot at each other. When the Russian armored cruiser *Aurora* approached, she was bombarded and slightly damaged. At least one Russian sailor was killed and another wounded.

New Yorkers Go Underground

New York, USA, October 27: New York City's promise and potential has for too long been constrained by the absence of an effective mass transit system. Thirty years ago an intriguing idea was put forward for an "under-street railway," unaffected by weather and able to operate independent of the traffic above.

New York, of course, has had an elevated system since 1870, stretching from Manhattan to the Bronx and Brooklyn, but it has proved incapable of providing for the city's burgeoning growth.

In 1898 a number of counties, including Westchester and Queens, were incorporated into the City of New York, and since then the demand has grown for an infrastructure and services capable of providing for these outlying areas.

The City of New York decided to issue rapid transit bonds outside of its regular bonded debt limit and build the subways itself. It contracted the Interborough Rapid Transit Company (IRT) to equip and operate the subways, sharing the profits with the City and guaranteeing a fixed 5-cent fare.

Today New York's first official subway system opened in Manhattan, just seven years after the Rapid Transit Commission first presented its subway plan to City Hall. The IRT will be operating this subway, which is 9 miles (14 km) long. The subway services 28 stations from City Hall north to 145th Street and Broadway. Mayor McClellan was at the controls for part of the inaugural run, which departed at 7 p.m.

A total of 30,000 workers, mostly of Italian and Irish backgrounds, worked on the project, and it is estimated that over 100,000 people will use the subway on this, its first day.

Okahandja, southwest Africa, January 11: Over 100 German settlers are massacred by Herero warriors in retaliation for a lack of compensation for dispossessed tribesmen.

Havana, Cuba, February 5: US troops withdraw from the Caribbean island. Tomas Palma is the first prime minister of the new republic.

Port Arthur, Manchuria, February 8: The beginning of the Russo-Japanese War. Japan launches a surprise attack on the Russian fleet stationed at Port Arthur.

Tibet, March 31: British forces kill over 300 of the Dalai Lama's men on a mission in central Asia.

Aceh, Dutch East Indies, April 3: Dutch colonial forces kill over 500 Achinese in 30-year Sumatran War.

UK and France, April 8: An Anglo-French treaty, "Entente Cordiale," is signed between the two colonial powers, settling a number of disputes.

Port Arthur, Manchuria, April 13: Russian forces suffer a major blow in the Russo-Japanese War, losing a battleship with 600 men.

New York, USA, June 15: Over 1000 people perish as the steamer *General Slocum* catches fire on the East River.

London, England, July 12: The British government pledges to resolve disputes with Germany through arbitration. The border dispute between Brazil and the UK over British Guiana was resolved in June in a similar manner.

The Vatican, July 29: The French Ambassador to the Holy See is recalled as tension between church and state in France escalates.

Lhasa, Tibet, September 7: A treaty is reached between the UK and the Dalai Lama, giving the British trading posts.

Belgium, September 15: King Leopold agrees to investigate claims of atrocities in the Congo.

North Sea, October 22: The Russian Navy sinks British fishing trawlers at Dogger Bank, mistaking them for Japanese warships.

New York, USA, October 27: The New York subway opens, and some 100,000 citizens take a ride on the new convenience.

St Louis, USA, October 28: St Louis Police Department try a new investigation method—fingerprints.

Panama, November 16: The USA buys the concession for building the waterway from French interests.

Washington DC, USA, December 6: Theodore Roosevelt's corollary to the Monroe Doctrine, invoked to force the Dominican Republic to pay its debts, sees the USA take on the role of international police.

Moscow, Russia, December 26: The Tsar promises reforms in an effort to quell peasant unrest.

Russian Baltic Fleet Crushed

Tsushima Strait, Sea of Japan, May 27–29: The Battle of Tsushima has been fought over the past two days in the Tsushima Strait between the naval forces of Japan and Russia and has resulted in a crushing defeat for the Russian navy.

The Russian fleet had spent the entire summer fitting out for the battle, sailing from Liepaja on October 15. The fleet, under the command of Admiral Rozhestvensky was a formidable armada, but many of the ships were old and unserviceable and their crews poorly trained for combat.

Admiral Togo's Japanese fleet was lying in wait near the Korean port city of Pusan for the Russians to make their way toward Vladivostok via the Tsushima Strait.

The Japanese ships are superior in both speed and armament, and during the course of the two-day battle two-thirds of the Russian fleet has been sunk and six ships captured. Only four ships made it through to Vladivostok, with six taking refuge in neutral ports.

After a seven-month voyage and almost within sight of its destination, Russia's Baltic fleet has been devastated.

Russian Sailors Mutiny: Odessa in Flames

Odessa, Russia, June 27: After the humiliating defeat of Russia's Baltic fleet at the hands of the Japanese navy last month, military forces at home became demoralized. In addition, a worsening economic situation and widespread unrest among factory workers and intellectuals has led to strikes that have been felt as far away as Odessa on the shores of the Black Sea.

On June 27, while en route to Tendra, the crew of the battleship Potemkin refused to eat maggot-infested meat. The ship's second-in-command chose 12 sailors at random to be executed, which led Torpedo Quartermaster Afanasy Matushenko, a Social Democrat agitator, to shout to the firing squad, "Don't kill your own shipmates." This was followed by shouts to seize the ship. Within half an hour seven officers had been killed and thrown overboard. Matushenko ordered the ship to return to Odessa.

Tsar Nicholas declared a "state of war" to exist with the mutineers. That night demonstrators in Odessa were caught between two detachments of Cossacks and the city was engulfed in riots, with as many as 6,000 people killed. The *Potemkin* eventually sailed to Romania for refuge, where the majority of her crew were awarded Romanian citizenship.

Map

Russo-Japanese War 1904–1905
→ Japanese advances
→ Russian naval advance

MONGOLIA

MANCHURIA

Battle of Mukden
Feb 21–Mar 10, 1905

Battle of Liaoyang
Aug 25–Sept 3, 1904

Vladivostok

Battle of Nanshan
May 25–26, 1904

Mukden
Liaoyang

Battle of Yalu River
May 1, 1904

Siege of Port Arthur
Aug 1904–Jan 1905

Port Arthur

Sea of Japan

Chemulpo Seoul
KOREA

Tokyo
JAPAN

Japanese naval attack
on Port Arthur
Feb 8, 1904

Huang He

Yellow Sea

CHINA

Naval Battle of Tsushima
May 27, 1905

Japanese naval attack
on Chemulpo
Feb 9, 1904

PACIFIC OCEAN

Yangtze

0   500 km
0   500 miles

Birth of Sinn Fein Movement

Dublin, Ireland, November 28: Sinn Fein (Gaelic for "we ourselves"), a loose collection of nationalists whose goal is to unite Ireland, has formed. Journalist Arthur Griffith has outlined the political ideals and objectives of the pacifist group. Born in Dublin in 1872, Griffith founded the *Weekly United Irishman* in 1899, and wrote eloquent editorials that urged the Irish to work toward self-government and the Irish members of Parliament to organize their own assembly and withdraw from Westminster.

Sinn Fein had its origins in the Irish cultural revival of the late nineteenth century and the growing disenchantment with Home Rule.

The fundamental principles under which Sinn Fein was to operate were outlined in a book published in 1904 by Griffith entitled *Resurrection of Hunger*, in which he compared Ireland to Hungary in 1867. At that time, Hungary went from being a part of the Austrian Empire to a separate co-equal kingdom in Austria-Hungary. Griffith also advocated a protected Irish economy, which would allow native Irish industry to grow, and a dual monarchy in which the British monarch would be crowned in Dublin as the king or queen of the Kingdom of Ireland.

Official policies of Sinn Fein include passive resistance to the British, the withholding of taxes, and the establishment of an Irish ruling council and independent courts. Sinn Fein is also seeking a revival of Irish Gaelic.

Arthur Griffith

time out

A fire starting in a neckwear factory in the industrial and commercial area of Toronto burned for nine hours, destroying 104 buildings. The fire caused over $10 million in damage and put 5,000 of the city's 200,000 inhabitants out of work.

Emmeline Pankhurst

British Census Confirms Growth of Empire

England, March 8: The results of the Census of the British Empire taken in 1901 were released today by the government. Four hundred million people live on 12 million sq miles (31 million sq km) of land under British rule. The white population of the empire is 53 million, or one-eighth of its entire population. The European portion of the empire amounts to 125,095 sq miles (323,995 sq km), an inconsiderable fraction of the total area under British rule.

Since the time of the last census of the empire in 1861, the aggregate area of the British colonies has increased some 40 percent, amounting to more than one-fifth of the land surface on the globe. This substantial augmentation in the size of the British Empire has mostly occurred since 1881, with annexations in the sub-continent, Africa, and Asia.

San Francisco Destroyed by Massive Earthquake

San Francisco, USA, April 18: An estimated 1,000 people have been killed by a powerful earthquake that has devastated the city of San Francisco and a narrow band of towns stretching to the city's northwest and southeast this morning.

Fires have broken out all over the city and are being fed by ruptured gas lines as chimneys collapse, electrical wires fall, and stoves are overturned. Severed water mains across the city have made fighting the fires all but impossible.

Along the San Andreas rift, the earth has fractured for more than 250 miles (400 km). Thirty miles (48 km) north of San Francisco the displacement of the land has been measured in excess of 21 ft (6 m). Geologists have been confounded by the large horizontal displacements and the great length of the fracture zone. The shaking lasted from 45 to 60 seconds and was felt from southern Oregon to the

Residents of San Francisco inspect earthquake damage.

south of Los Angeles and as far eastward as the deserts of central Nevada.

The fire that followed did more damage than the earthquake, destroying over 28,000 buildings. An estimated 225,000 people have been made homeless out of a population of 400,000. Four hundred and ninety city blocks have been wiped out and streets have been left twisted and cracked. Virtually all of San Francisco's landmark buildings have been lost, including City Hall, the new post office, the 20 story high "Call" building, Stanford University at Palo Alto, the Grand Opera House, and St Ignatius's church.

Police and state troopers attempted to create fire breaks around the burning city by detonating blocks of buildings. The black powder they used, however, often just set the ruins on fire.

Exclusively Muslim Political Party Formed

Dacca, India, December 31: Aga Khan III has been elected president of the All-India Muslim League, set up to champion the cause of Muslims in Indian society, which is dominated by Hindus. The main objectives of the organization are to instill among Muslims a feeling of loyalty to the

government, to advance their political rights, and to prevent ill will between Muslims and other denominations.

In October a delegation of Muslim nobles, legal professionals, and other elites gathered in Simla under the leadership of the Aga Khan to present an address to Lord Minto. They demanded proportional representation of Muslims in government jobs, appointment of Muslim members in the viceroy's council, and Muslim judges to the High Courts. Despite the failure of the Simla deputation to obtain any commitment from the viceroy, it was a catalyst for change.

The formation of the All-India Muslim League is a turning-point, representing the initial formal entry of a centrally organized political party exclusively for the often marginalized Muslims.

Food hand-outs for the poor during the Russian winter.

> "LENIN'S METHOD ... THE PARTY ORGANIZATION AT FIRST SUBSTITUTES ITSELF FOR THE PARTY AS A WHOLE. THEN THE CENTRAL COMMITTEE SUBSTITUTES ITSELF FOR THE PARTY ORGANIZATION, AND FINALLY A SINGLE DICTATOR SUBSTITUTES HIMSELF FOR THE CENTRAL COMMITTEE."
>
> LEON TROTSKY (1879–1940), RUSSIAN REVOLUTIONARY LEADER, 1906

London, England, January 31: Suffragette leader Emmeline Pankhurst warns that women are impatient with waiting for the right to vote and are prepared to take radical action to advance their cause.

England, February 7: The Liberals are swept to power in a landslide victory over the Conservatives after 10 years in opposition. The Labour Party increased its representation significantly.

Tahiti, February 8: A fierce typhoon inundates the Pacific kingdom, killing 10,000 people.

England, March 8: The "Census of the British Empire" of 1901 is released.

San Francisco, USA, April 19: Over 1,000 people are killed and the city is devastated in the aftermath of an earthquake.

Lhasa, Tibet, April 27: China reluctantly cedes control of Tibet to Britain. In an attempt to forestall Russian ambitions, no foreign power may occupy Tibetan territory without British permission.

St Petersburg, Russia, May 10: The Tsar inaugurates the Duma, elected by universal suffrage.

Chicago, USA, May 10: At a government commission into unfair practices, the Standard Oil Company is charged with stifling competition.

Switzerland and Italy, May 19: The Simplon Tunnel is opened to traffic. It is the longest tunnel in the world, at 12.3 miles (20 km).

Auckland, New Zealand, June 12: Longest-serving prime minister Richard Seddon dies, aged 61.

Central America, July 20: Guatemala signs peace treaty with El Salvador and Honduras after war breaks out in May.

Tehran, Persia, August 5: Mozafaredin Shah is forced to decree a constitution and create a parliament (the majlis), limiting royal power after revolutionary agitation.

Valparaiso, Chile, August 18: A massive earthquake, measuring 8.6 on the Richter scale, kills 5,000 people and destroys the port.

Cuba, September 28: US War Secretary William Taft is installed as provisional governor. President Palma resigned after fierce fighting between liberal forces and government troops.

Russia, November 2: Bolshevik Leon Trotsky is exiled to Siberia for revolutionary activities. Anti-Tsarist feelings are running high after Nicholas II suspended the Duma in July.

Transvaal, Southern Africa, December 12: Limited autonomy is granted, with white males gaining the right to vote.

Dacca, India, December 31: Aga Khan is elected president of the All-India Muslim League, set up to advance the cause of Muslims in the Hindu-dominated society.

US Targets Malaria in Panama

Washington DC, USA, February 26: President Roosevelt has today put the US Army Corps of Engineers in charge of the construction of the Panama Canal, lead by Colonel George Washington Goethals, with Colonel William Crawford Gorgas in charge of sanitation.

An earlier attempt by France to build the canal ended in disaster with 25,000 dead, mostly from malaria and yellow fever. Smallpox, typhoid, and dysentery are also common to the region, but it is the mosquito-borne malaria and yellow fever that present the greatest danger. When US canal builders arrived in Panama to begin this enormous task, Panama City and Colon were both small, squalid towns, connected by a single railway left over from the earlier French attempts at construction. Gorgas realized that if the United States were to succeed where the French had failed, the specter of malaria and yellow fever had to be overcome.

So-called "Gorgas's Gangs" have begun digging ditches to drain standing water and have been spraying puddles with films of oil. Buildings have been fumigated and a pure water supply has been constructed as well as a modern system for the disposal of sewage.

The most challenging aspects of the canal's construction are expected to be cutting through the mountain ridge at Culebra, building a dam at Gatun to trap the Rio Chagras and form an artificial lake, and the building of three double sets of locks—Gatun Locks, Pedro Miguel Locks, and Miraflores Locks—to raise the ships to the lake, almost 78 ft (28 m) above sea level, and then to lower them again.

US President Roosevelt, the champion of the Panama Canal.

Sun Yat-sen Wants End to Manchu Dynasty

China, September 8: Sun Yat-sen has established the Kuomintang party, which is built upon his notions of nationalism, democracy, and livelihood. Known as "The Three Principles of the People," Sun developed these ideas into a comprehensive plan for restoring economic and social strength to his country, first by expelling the Manchus, then by curbing the influence of foreign powers.

He also hopes to free China from the graver forms of social exploitation by building a central government that will counter the rampant forces of capitalism in industry, and of powerful landlords in the countryside.

Kuomintang encompasses several political parties, all with the common goal of overthrowing the Manchu dynasty and establishing a parliamentary democracy and moderate socialism.

Also known as the Revolutionary National People's party, it is the sole inspiration of Sun, who is heavily influenced by the west but is also a student of Karl Marx. Although Sun believes China should initially be controlled by a rigorously structured central party, ultimately he believes that after a period of "tutelage," the Chinese people can be introduced to the principles and practices of representative government.

Tsar Nicholas II

Conference Fails to Deliver Arms Cuts

The Hague, Netherlands, October 11: The Second International Peace Conference has closed with a commitment to the establishment of an International Court of Justice. The conventions of war have also been extended.

The initiative for this second conference came in 1903 from the American Peace Society in Boston. The conference petitioned the Massachusetts legislature to pass a resolution requesting Congress authorize President Theodore Roosevelt to invite the governments of the world to establish a regular international congress to discuss matters of common interest.

The conference was convened on June 15 by Tsar Nicholas of Russia. He proposed an agenda restricted to improvements in arbitration and humanitarian law, while the United States suggested discussing the limitation of armaments and the application of force in the collection of debts.

This second conference, like the International Peace Conference of 1899, has not succeeded in effecting a reduction in armaments, but it has established conventions respecting the rights of neutral shipping during times of war and the protection of non-combatants.

time out

United States Senator Nathan B. Stott of West Virginia, vacationing in Mexico City, rescued two prominent local women from a runaway horse. The 65-year-old jumped from the sidewalk and seized the horse's reins, bringing it under control after a violent struggle.

Kingston, Jamaica, January 14: Kingston is devastated by an earthquake followed by a fire.

Dutch East Indies, January 22: 1,500 people die when a tsunami hits the East Indies.

London, England, February 13: Police repel suffragettes attempting to storm Westminster. Sixty women are arrested in fierce struggles.

Washington DC, USA, February 26: President Roosevelt puts the US Army in charge of the construction of the Panama Canal.

Transvaal, Southern Africa, March 22: The Indian population of the newly independent state, led by Mohandas Gandhi, vows a campaign of passive resistance if restrictive racial legislation is introduced.

Manchuria, April 15: Russian and Japanese troops complete their withdrawal, ceding the territory to China, under the terms of the Treaty of Portsmouth, negotiated to end the Russo-Japanese War.

Russia, April 20: Up to 20 million people are starving in the worst famine ever experienced in Russia.

Boise, Idaho, USA, May 9: Labor relations are strained as angry workers march in support of union leader Bill Haywood, who is on trial for commissioning a 1905 murder.

Cartagena, Spain, May 16: The UK, France and Spain sign the Pact of Cartagena in an effort to quell German expansionist aspirations in the Mediterranean.

St Petersburg, Russia, June 16: Tsar Nicholas II dissolves the second Duma (parliament), charging that socialists have been plotting against the monarchy.

Korea, July 25: Emperor Kojong abdicates as the country is placed under Japanese control.

Philippines, July 30: The first parliament is elected and victorious nationalists press for independence from the USA.

Casablanca, Morocco, August 4: French troops enter Casablanca after two days of intense shelling leaves the town devastated.

China, September 8: Sun Yat-sen founds the Kuomintang Party.

New Zealand, September 26: The colony is granted dominion status.

India, October 11: A nationwide ban on public meetings is imposed. Rioting has been rife since May—not helped by the British government's stance that under no circumstances would they withdraw.

The Hague, Netherlands, October 18: The Second Peace Conference closes with a commitment to the establishment of an International Court of Justice. The Conventions of War have been extended.

Russia, December 31: Of the 169 delegates from the first Duma, 167 are found guilty of treason.

Henry Ford

Automobile Production Now Mechanized

Detroit, USA, August 12: The Ford Motor Company's first Model T rolled off Henry Ford's new production line today, "large enough for the family, but small enough for the individual to run and care for."

American engineer and industrialist Henry Ford is the first person to use a conveyor belt-based assembly line, revolutionizing factory production at his plant located at Highland Park, Michigan.

After early work as a machinist, Ford built a gasoline engine in 1893. In 1896 he built a "horseless carriage," which he called the "quadricycle," meaning "cycle with four wheels." In 1899 he formed the Detroit Automobile Company.

The Model T automobile was designed by Henry Ford, Childe Harold Wills, and two Hungarian immigrants—Joseph Galamb and Eugene Farkas. The concept of the assembly line came from William Klann who, after returning from a trip to a Chicago slaughterhouse where a conveyor system for transporting carcasses was in operation, then put the idea to Ford.

Henry Ford has comprehensively reformed the methods for the large-scale manufacture of cars, as well as for the management of a large workforce, whom he pays above-award wages. The Ford Motor Company was launched from a converted wagon factory with $28,000 cash secured from 12 investors. During its formative years it produced just a few cars a day at its factory on Mack Avenue, Detroit. Groups of two or three men worked on each automobile from components made to order by other companies.

Cholera Grips St Petersburg

Russia, September: St Petersburg is being devastated by the worst cholera outbreak since 1892, more than 7,000 people are estimated to have died.

Little has been learnt since the last outbreak, as the city remains a repository of filth and disease. Many factories are permitted to discharge their waste into its rivers and canals. With a cholera outbreak on average once every three years, St Petersburg's death rate is the highest of any European city. Water must be fetched in buckets and boiled before it is safe, but thirsty workers are giving scant attention to this. London has eradicated similar problems by constructing an efficient new sewerage system, but nothing like that has even been attempted here.

Built below sea level at the edge of the Baltic, St Petersburg has always been an insalubrious city. Thousands of slave laborers died of disease and hunger to realize Peter the Great's grand design of a window on the West. It was Gogol's city of shadows and phantoms. The poverty and squalor of the streets and squares still remain much as in Dostoyevsky's nightmarish vision.

Southern Italy Rocked by Quake

Sicily, December 28: Over 100,000 people have died in what many are calling the deadliest earthquake in European history. Centered on the Straits of Messina, which separate Sicily from Calabria, it generated a massive tsunami with 40 ft (12 m) waves that has had a devastating impact on dozens of coastal towns and villages. The shaking continued for around 30 seconds, toppling buildings and burying their inhabitants. Of the population of some 150,000 that inhabited the region of Messina and Reggio Calabria, only a few hundred are believed to have survived.

The majority of Sicily's towns have lost upward of half their residents.

Sicily and Calabria are known as *la terra ballerina* (the dancing land) due to the frequent seismic activity that plagues the region. In 1693, 60,000 people were killed in an earthquake in southern Sicily, and in 1783 most of the Tyrrhenian coast of Calabria was hit by a massive quake that killed an estimated 50,000.

Veteran sailors have spoken of their difficulty in recognizing parts of the coast— long stretches of coastline have slipped several feet into the sea.

Three thoroughly modern ladies enjoying a drive in the first production Model T Ford.

Key Events

Transvaal, Southern Africa, January 30: Mohandas Gandhi is released from jail, after a two-month sentence for refusing to register under the "Asiatic Law."

Lisbon, Portugal, February 3: Following the assassination of King Carlos and the Crown Prince on February 1, dictator Premier Franco and his cabinet resign. Prince Manuel is proclaimed King.

London, England, April 12: Liberal Herbert Asquith takes over as prime minister from Campbell-Bannerman, who has been ill for some time.

Muzaffarpur, India, April 30: Colonial forces crack down on extremist nationalists after a bomb meant for a British magistrate kills two English women by mistake.

Washington DC, USA, May 22: The Wright brothers apply for a patent for their "flying machine."

Baltic Sea, Russia, June 9: Britain's monarch Edward VII and Tsar Nicholas II meet, signalling closer relations.

London, England, June 21: Over 200,000 turn out for a demonstration in support of women's suffrage.

Tehran, Persia, June 26: Shah Muhammad Ali leads a successful counter-revolution, ousting the government and abolishing the liberal constitution.

Ottoman Empire, July 24: The Young Turk movement, supported by the army, forces the Sultan to reinstall the constitution of 1876.

Detroit, USA, August 12: The Model T Ford begins production.

The Congo, August 20: Belgium officially annexes the Congo, formally the fiefdom of King Leopold, who ruthlessly exploited it.

St Petersburg, Russia, September: The city suffers the most devastating cholera outbreak since 1892; over 7,000 die.

Lucerne, Switzerland, September 29: The International Conference for the Protection of Labor legislates against night time work for children. In the USA, some 1.75 million children under 16 work in factories.

Bosnia and Herzegovina, October 6: Widespread condemnation greets Austria-Hungary's annexation of the Balkan provinces. Russia, Turkey, Serbia and Montenegro all had similar designs and protest.

North Island, New Zealand, November 9: The first scheduled passenger trains run between Wellington and Auckland. The trip takes two days.

Peking, China, December 2: Three year-old Pu Yi is crowned Emperor of China. Dowager Empress Tsu-Hsi, who wielded true power, died last month, one day after Emperor Kuang-Hsu.

Sicily, Italy, December 28: Over 100,000 people die in a massive earthquake centered on the Straits of Messina.

Louis Blériot

Turks Throw off Ottoman Yoke

Constantinople, Turkey, April: Sultan Abdul Hamid II has been ousted, as Parliament votes to end his rule. An Islamic modernizer and friend of the United States, he emphasized the role of Islam within the Ottoman Empire and emerged as a protector of Muslims around the world. Abdul Hamid pressed for a new railway to the holy places of Mecca and Medina and sent emissaries to distant countries to preach Islam.

His principal opponents were young Turks who portrayed him as a despot. An uncompromising reactionary, he attempted but generally failed in his reforms in such areas of Turkish society as education, finance, and central government administration, although he was instrumental in founding the nation's first archeological museum, faculty of medicine, and public library.

His rule, however, was forever sullied by his association with the massacre of 30,000 Armenians, while financial mismanagement forced him to consent to foreign control over the national debt.

Abdul Hamid's attempts to marry Islam with modernity were cut short by the counter-revolution of April 13, when an uprising by soldiers backed by a conservative public upheaval in the capital overthrew the Cabinet. The government, restored by soldiers from Salonica (Thessaloniki), then decided on Abdul Hamid's deposition.

Blériot First to Cross English Channel

Dover, England, July 25: French aviator Louis Blériot has crossed the English Channel in his X1 monoplane, winning a £2,500 prize. Blériot made his fortune manufacturing acetylene lamps for automobiles, spending nearly all of it on various aviation adventures.

Sultan Abdul Hamid grants a constitution to the Turks.

Blériot fervently believed he would be the first person to cross the English Channel, despite financial woes and a injury that at the time of the flight saw him walk to the plane with the aid of crutches. He took off at 4.37 a.m. and, guided by smoke from a French destroyer, he soon spotted St Margaret's Bay. Turning toward Dover, he was caught by the wind and made a crash landing at Northfall Meadow, damaging his undercarriage and propeller. The flight took him just 20 minutes.

Former Prime Minister Assassinated

Harbin, Manchuria, October 26: The former prime minister of Japan, Prince Ito, has been assassinated by a Korean nationalist, Ahn Jung-geun, on a railway platform in Harbin, Manchuria.

Ito served as a junior councilor in a number of different ministries after the Meiji Restoration, a chain of events that led to a maturing in Japan's political and social structure. In 1878 , he became home minister and gained control of the government. As prime minister in 1901 he tried to negotiate a settlement with Russia before being forced from office by more militaristic politicians.

In June 1907, in an effort to break free from Japanese control, the Korean emperor, Ko-Jong secretly sent an emissary to the Hague Peace Conference to expose to the world Japan's aggressive policy of occupation. When Ito found out, he forced Ko-Jong to abdicate on July 19, 1907, and the Japanese officially took over the government of Korea.

Russia was becoming increasingly nervous at the level of Japanese activity in the northern Korean area and Japan's obvious imperialistic aspirations toward Manchuria. To calm the Russians fears, Ito agreed to meet for diplomatic discussions at Harbin over Japanese intentions to invade Manchuria and possibly China.

When Ito arrived at the railway station, Ahn Jung-geun was waiting for his opportunity, shooting Ito after he stepped off the train. The assassin had previously mutilated several of his fingers and used his blood to write "Korean independence" on the Korean national flag.

Louis Blériot's historic flight across the Channel.

USA, February: The temperance movement is gaining momentum throughout the country with individual states and counties adopting laws banning the sale of alcohol.

Morocco, February 8: A new Franco-German agreement is reached recognizing France's preeminent position and Germany's interests in North Africa.

London, England, March 12: Britain's Naval fleet is to be strengthened, as parliament legislates to regain naval pre-eminence over Germany.

Serbia, March 31: The war crisis in the Balkans is resolved with Serbia agreeing to recognize the Austrian annexation of Bosnia and Herzegovina.

Constantinople, Turkey , April 26: Sultan Abdul Hamid II is deposed, as parliament votes to end his rule.

Sofia, Bulgaria, April 27: Austria-Hungary, Germany, and Italy recognize the Black Sea country, after it declared independence from the Ottoman Empire the previous year.

Georgia, USA, May 17: In protest at the hiring of African-American workers, white firemen strike. Racial tensions rise as African-Americans strive to achieve equal rights.

India, May 25: The Indian Councils Act (Morley-Minto Reforms) is introduced to end nationalist terrorism. The Act allows Indians to be elected to the legislative councils.

Paris, France, July 21: The Clemenceau cabinet resigns after a violent altercation concerning the navy's capability. Aristide Briand succeeds as premier.

Dover, England, July 25: French aviator Louis Blériot crosses the English Channel, flying a monoplane.

Crete, August 8: Forty years of ethnic tension is resolved as Greece seeks to acquire the Mediterranean island.

Pittsburgh, USA, August 22: Striking for better conditions, five steelworkers are killed in a violent confrontation with police.

Catalonia, Spain, September 26: Alfonso XIII brutally suppresses a Catalan uprising over military service.

Harbin, Manchuria, October 26: First Prime Minister of Japan, Prince Ito, is assassinated by a Korean nationalist.

South Africa, December 7: By royal decree, the Union of South Africa is formed from the colonies of the Cape of Good Hope, Natal, Transvaal and Orange River.

Nicaragua, December 17: A two-month civil war ends as anti-US President Zelaya resigns under pressure from US Marines. José Madriz replaces him.

Lighter-than-air Craft Flies for 17 Minutes

Friedrichshafen, Germany, July 2, 1900: At its first trial today the LZ-1, a dirigible balloon developed by Ferdinand Graf von Zeppelin, flew at an altitude of 1,300 ft (400 m) for a distance of 3.7 miles (6 km) in 17 minutes, carrying five passengers.

Von Zeppelin was born into a wealthy family in 1838, on the shores of Lake Constance (Bodensee). He joined the military and distinguished himself in the Franco-Prussian War. At age 52, however, his views on the Prussian leadership lost him his commission. Made a "general in retirement", he vowed to regain his honor by designing a war-winning weapon.

In 1891 he committed his vast personal fortune to the design, construction, and flight of airships. On an official visit to the United States during the American Civil War he witnessed the use of tethered balloons to gather information on enemy movements.

In 1884 the French had developed an electric-powered dirigible that could be steered, the first aircraft to fly and return to where it had taken off. Von Zeppelin could not allow Germany's traditional foe to maintain such an advantage.

Von Zeppelin has spent nearly a decade on the LZ-1. It has a rigid frame with the interior consisting of a row of 17 gas cells each covered in rubberized cloth, all confined in a cylindrical framework covered with cotton cloth. It is around 420 ft (130 m) in length and 38 ft (12 m) in diameter and is propelled by 400,000 cu ft (11,330 cu m) of highly volatile hydrogen gas.

In 1894 von Zeppelin had presented his ideas to an expert committee, which had not been impressed, leaving him to realize his dream alone. Lacking the technical expertise, von Zeppelin enlisted the aid of engineer Professor Müller-Breslau, who revised turned Zepellin's proposals into practical propositions.

Construction began in 1899 in a floating assembly hall on Lake Constance. The assembly hall was designed so it could be aligned to take advantage of prevailing winds. Two 15-horsepower (11 kW) Daimler engines drive the craft, which is steered by rudders forward and aft. Two aluminum gondolas below carry the passengers and crew.

$1 Camera on Sale Today

Trenton, New Jersey, USA, October 24, 1900: With a simple slogan, "You push the button, we do the rest," George Eastman of the Eastman Kodak Company has begun marketing the Box Brownie camera, made from jute board and wood. The camera sells for $1 and film is 15 cents a roll for 100 exposures. At last, taking pictures is within anyone's reach.

Once the film is used, the camera and the film need to be returned to Kodak, where the film will be developed and new film put back in. The camera has a meniscus lens that takes $2\frac{1}{4}$ sq in (14.5 sq cm) pictures.

Eastman chose the name Brownie to draw on the popularity of characters created by a Canadian author, Palmer Cox, who writes children's stories about pixies, elves, and brownies.

Inventor, manufacturer, and philanthropist, George Eastman was born in Waterville, New York, in 1854. At 14, he left school to help support his widowed mother. While working as a bookkeeper he developed a process for making dry plates in his photographic studio. In 1880 he established The Eastman Dry Plate Company with partner Henry Strong.

During the next decade George Eastman transformed photography from a laborious and costly art into an easy, inexpensive hobby that could be enjoyed by millions. In 1883 Eastman announced the invention of photographic film in rolls, and Kodak the company was born in 1888 when the first Kodak camera entered the market.

New Light Shed on Physical Universe

Berlin, Germany, December 14, 1900: As a youngster in Germany, Max Planck was told there was nothing left to discover in physics. Today he unveiled a theory that turns this statement on its head.

Max Planck

> "SCIENCE CANNOT SOLVE THE ULTIMATE MYSTERY OF NATURE… BECAUSE, IN THE LAST ANALYSIS, WE OURSELVES ARE A PART OF THE MYSTERY THAT WE ARE TRYING TO SOLVE."
>
> MAX PLANCK (1858–1947), GERMAN PHYSICIST

> "THE AIRPLANE STAYS UP BECAUSE IT DOESN'T HAVE THE TIME TO FALL."
>
> ORVILLE WRIGHT (1871–1948), AMERICAN AVIATOR

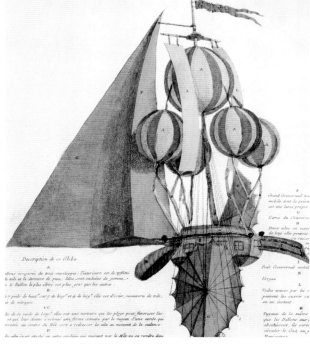

Early concept of dirigible from the eighteenth century.

Kodak advertisement.

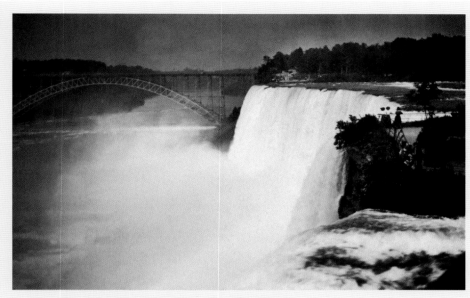
The power of Niagara Falls has now been harnessed for electricity.

George Eastman

Until today, light was considered to be a continuous electromagnetic wave. Planck's new "quantum theory" claims that light must be emitted and absorbed in discreet amounts if it is to describe observed phenomena. To put it more simply, energy does not flow in a steady continuum, but is delivered in discreet particles, or "quanta" (from the Latin "how many?"). The theory seeks to explain why, when a body heats up, the light given off is orange, then yellow, and eventually bluish. The wavelength emitted is a function of the energy times a constant.

A Car for the People

Lansing, Michigan, USA, April, 1901: The Curved Dash Oldsmobile is the first automobile to be mass-produced in the United States, built by Ransom Eli Olds.

Olds began making steam and gasoline engines years before with his father in Lansing, Michigan in 1885 and designed his first steam-powered car in 1887. In 1899 Ransom, armed with his growing knowledge of gasoline engines, moved to Detroit to start the Olds Motor Works. Sadly, before production could begin the factory burnt down and only one prototype, a single cylinder buggy, survived.

Olds's latest automobile is proving extremely popular with the public thanks to its low price of $625, and he is currently producing them on what has been called a "production line" at the astonishing rate of 10 a week.

time out

Days after establishing a world record for an airplane flight with a passenger, Wilbur Wright set a new record of 64 minutes, fulfilling conditions set by a business syndicate that paid $100,000 for the plane's French patent rights.

6,000-Mile Railway Unites Russia

Russia, July 31, 1904: A rail line stretching nearly 6,000 miles (9,660 km) to the capital Moscow was completed today, 13 years after construction began with a ceremony in the area of Kuperovskaya in the eastern city of Vladivostok.

Given the title Trans-Siberian Railway, it was the dream of railway administrator Count Sergei Yulyevich Witte, later to be minister of communications and then minister of finance under Tsar Nicholas II.

In a similar approach to the US Transcontinental Railroad, Russian workers began building the line at both ends, working toward the center. From Vladivostok the line was laid north along the right bank of the Ussuri River to Khabarovsk. In the west, other links connected Moscow to Kuenga. Convicts and Russian soldiers were drafted into service to build the railway, almost literally by hand.

Originally the plan called for an all-Russian road, but a treaty with China in 1896 enabled the Russians to construct an 800-mile (1,290 km) line through Manchuria, thus shortening the distance to Vladivostok. After Manchuria passed into Japanese hands following the recent Russo-Japanese War, the Russians proceeded with a longer railway entirely on their own territory.

In 1898 the first train reached Irkutsk on the shore of Lake Baikal, which due to its size presented a formidable natural barrier. As it ices over for much of the year, a special icebreaker ferryboat was purchased from England to span the lake.

The new rail line will undoubtedly revolutionize travel throughout Russia. Before its completion, travel time from Moscow to Vladivostok was nearly a year.

The 6,000 mile Trans-Siberian railway is a mammoth undertaking.

Key Events

France, April 31, 1905: Psychologist Alfred Binet develops the Intelligence Quotient (IQ) test, finding a method by which to measure the ability to think and reason.
London, England, November, 1905: Electrification of the London Underground is completed.
Bern, Switzerland, December, 1905: Albert Einstein publishes four papers—including articles on special relativity, Brownian motion and the photoelectric effect—providing the foundations of modern physics.

Portsmouth, England, February 10, 1906: HMS *Dreadnought* is launched. Built in only four months, it is the fastest warship in the water.
Germany, May 10, 1906: Microbiologist August von Wasserman devises a test for syphilis.
Norfolk, Virginia, USA, September 8, 1906: Robert Turner invents the automatic return typewriter.
USA, December 24, 1906: Canadian Reginald Fessenden, discoverer of AM radio waves, broadcasts over 100 miles (160 km).

Lyon, France, June 10, 1907: The Lumière brothers, developers of the Cinematograph in 1895, start marketing a practical method for color photography, invented in 1903.
New York, November, 1907: The Cunard ocean liner *Mauretania* crosses the Atlantic in a new record, besting the record set by its sister ship *Lusitania* in September.
Stockholm, Sweden, December 10, 1907: Alphonse Laveran wins the Nobel Prize in Physiology for his discovery of the role of protozoa in causing malaria and leishmaniasis.

USA, February 11, 1908: Thomas Edison, inventor of the motion picture projector, gains a virtual monopoly, winning a ruling that others have been infringing his patent, issued in 1891.
Salzburg, Austria, April 27, 1908: The inaugural International Congress of Psychoanalysis opens.
Manchester, England, December, 1908: Hans Geiger and Ernest Rutherford develop a device for measuring radioactivity, the Geiger counter. Rutherford is also awarded the Nobel Prize in Chemistry.

New York, USA, January 29, 1909: The world's tallest building, the 50-story Metropolitan Life Insurance building, is completed in Manhattan.
Denmark, March, 1909: Biochemist Soren Sorensen invents the pH scale of acidity.
New York, USA, December 7, 1909: Leo Baekeland patents Bakelite, or phenolic resin, the first plastic to solidify with heat.
Stockholm, Sweden, December 10, 1909: Guglielmo Marconi and Karl Braun share the Nobel Prize in Physics.

Ernest Rutherford

Human Reasoning Is Put to the Test

France, April 31, 1905: Psychologist Alfred Binet has developed what he calls an "intelligence quotient" (IQ) test—a method by which to measure our ability to think and reason.

Binet often asks his daughters questions and queries how they solve them. This has led him to an understanding of individual differences in mental performance and, most importantly, to conclude that not all thought processes follow the same course. His extensive observations and experimental studies of his daughters have allowed him to develop several theories about cognitive development. Binet believes that the purpose of cognitive development is to allow children to adapt to the physical and social demands of their environment, emphasizing the fact that children learn by assimilating new experiences into their existing ways of thinking.

Since 1894 Binet has been director of the psychology laboratory at the Sorbonne in Paris, where he and colleague Theodore Simon have devised a series of tests that, with revisions, have come into wide use in schools, industries, and the army. These tests have evolved into what has become known as the Simon-Binet Scale. In the IQ test children perform tasks such as following commands, copying patterns, naming objects, and putting things in order or arranging them properly. Binet has given the test to Paris schoolchildren and created a standard based on his data. For instance, if 70 percent of 8-year-old children can pass a particular test, then success on the test represents an 8-year-old's level of intelligence. Binet believes that a lower IQ score merely indicates the need for more teaching, rather than an inability to learn.

Born in Nice in 1857, Binet entered college in order to study for a medical degree but dropped out when he became interested in psychology.

The Universe Explained

Bern, Switzerland, December, 1905: *Annalen der Physik* have published four papers on Brownian motion, special relativity, and the photoelectric effect, submitted to the journal by the physicist Albert Einstein.

In March Einstein expanded upon Max Planck's observations in 1900 that light exists as tiny packets or particles called "photons." Alongside Planck, Einstein is proposing that we live in a "quantum universe," one built out of tiny, discreet chunks of energy and matter.

In April and May Einstein published two papers. In one he invented a new method of counting atoms or molecules in a given space and determining their size, and in the other he explains the phenomenon of Brownian motion. The net result constitutes proof that atoms do actually exist, and puts an an end to the old debate on the fundamental nature of the chemical elements.

Then last June Einstein completed his paper on special relativity, in which he considers light to be a continuous field of waves. This at first seemed to contradict his March paper that light is a particle. Einstein, though, is claiming that light is both a particle *and* a wave.

A few months later has come his addendum to special relativity, the equation $E = mc^2$ (the energy content of a body is equal to the mass of the body multiplied by the speed of light squared). Albert Einstein is 26 years old.

HMS *Dreadnought* Launched Today

Portsmouth, England, February 10, 1906: The British Navy today launched the revolutionary battleship HMS *Dreadnought*. So completely has it changed battleship design that already everything that preceded it is being called a "pre-dreadnought."

While all previous battleships had a mixture of light, medium, and heavy guns, HMS *Dreadnought* has done away with medium-caliber guns in favor of a greater number of heavy guns, although some 12 lb (5.5 kg) guns were added for torpedo defense. Larger guns that are able to fire at enemy ships from greater distances became more desirable in the face of the threat from the torpedo.

HMS *Dreadnought* took only four months to build, having being laid down on October 2 last year and launched on February 9. Despite the emphasis on heavy armament, however, it is really her propulsion system that makes her so revolutionary.

The *Dreadnought* runs on steam turbine engines, which are smoother and more reliable than the older reciprocating steam engines used in other ships, the

The HMS *Dreadnought*, which took only four months to build, is designed to carry heavy artillery.

The *Mauretania* is the world's largest, fastest, and most luxurious liner.

Albert Einstein

huge rods and pistons of which cause tremendous vibration. The Parsons steam turbines give HMS *Dreadnought* a top speed of 21 knots, at least 3 knots faster than her contemporaries. Maintenance time is reduced, and with less vibration by virtue of her smoother running, accurate range finding at much greater distances is possible.

The speed of her construction has been a deliberate attempt by the Royal Navy to clearly demonstrate its design and construction capabilities to other would-be naval powers.

Mauretania Claims New Atlantic Record

New York, USA, November, 1907: The Cunard ocean liner *Mauretania* has set a new record for crossing the Atlantic, beating the previous best time set by her sister ship *Lusitania* in September.

Today the *Mauretania* arrived back in Liverpool, England, after leaving New York harbor and making the eastward crossing in under five days at an average speed of 23.69 knots.

This great ship was built to regain the Blue Riband award from the German liners. In 1897 the German ship *Kaiser Wilhelm der Grosse* shocked Britain by winning the Blue Riband with a passage of 5 days, 22 hours, and 30 minutes at a speed of 21.39 knots.

The *Mauretania*'s turbines produce 70,000 horsepower (53 MW). On her trials she attained speeds of 27 knots. She has 11 watertight bulkheads and six decks. The doors between the bulkheads can be closed from the bridge where the captain stands 100 ft (30 m) above sea level. Four million steel rivets were used in her hull. Each of her three anchors weighs 10 tons. There are even two electric elevators for passengers.

She is nearly 800 ft (240 m) long and weighs over 30,000 tons (30,480 tonnes). (Previously the largest vessel was White Star's *Oceanic*, at just over 700 ft (213 m)

long and a mere 17,000 tons [17,272 tonnes] in weight.) The turbine engines that helped propel the *Mauretania* to the record were manufactured by Wallsend Slipway and Engineering Co. Ltd., bringing their power to four huge, three-bladed propelers.

Making the Invisible Visible

Manchester, England, December, 1908: Hans Geiger and Ernest Rutherford have developed a device for measuring radioactivity—the Geiger counter. Rutherford has also been awarded the Nobel Prize in Chemistry for his work on the structure of the atom. The prize recognizes his achievement in "investigations into the disintegration of the elements, and the chemistry of radioactive substances."

Born in 1882 Geiger studied physics at the University of Munich and then moved to England to work at the University of Manchester with the renowned New Zealand scientist Ernest Rutherford. With Rutherford, Geiger conducted research related to radioactivity that would prove critical to the field's advance.

Geiger and his colleague J. M. Nuttall developed the Geiger-Nuttall rule, which states that a linear relationship exists between the logarithm of the range of alpha-particles and the radioactive time constant, which is involved in the rate of decay of emitting nuclei. In 1908 Geiger created a measuring device that could count the number of alpha-particles and amounts of other ionizing radiation being emitted. He called the device a "Geiger counter." It uses a sealed, gas-filled metal tube, which acts as an electrode. A voltage is then applied to the device so a current can almost pass through the gas from one electrode to the other.

When the counter nears a radioactive substance the gas becomes ionized, and the ionized gas particles can carry the current in a complete circuit from one end to the other. When this occurs, the device measures each passing particle via an electronic mechanism set up to produce audible "clicks" for each ionized particle by amplifying the current.

Geiger counters may also be used to detect cosmic rays and locate radioactive minerals. The instrument has a number of scientific and medical applications, and even allows you to check for radioactive materials in the home, for instance if you suspect that radon is present in your basement.

World's Tallest Building Rises over New York

New York, USA, January 29, 1909: In 1907 the president of the Metropolitan Life Insurance Company commissioned the firm of Napoleon LeBrun to design a tower for the expansion of the company headquarters. Construction began that year and today that building opened in Manhattan above Madison Avenue at 23rd Street. It is the world's tallest building, and confirms Metropolitan Life Insurance as the world's leading insurer.

With its slender shaft and high-pitched roof and lantern, the building is evocative of the famous bell tower of St Mark's in Venice. Climbing to 700 ft (213 m) in height, the structure is sheathed in white Tuckahoe marble, which is a brilliant white dolomite that is extremely hard and almost devoid of impurities. At night the "light that never fails", as it is known, glows from its lantern, flashing each hour and quarter hour.

The tower is graced with four enormous clocks on each of its four sides, inlaid with blue and white mosaics, each circled with Italian Renaissance motifs of wreaths and flowers. Its traditional appearance belies the state-of-the-art technology found within, such as Otis high-speed elevators, which can travel 600 ft (180 m) in 60 seconds.

The Metropolitan Life Building dominates the New York skyline.

Joseph Pulitzer

Brilliant Playwright Dies Penniless

Paris, France, November 30, 1900: Notorious wit, dramatist, and aesthete Oscar Wilde, author of *The Importance of Being Earnest*, has died penniless in a cheap Paris hotel. He was 46.

The son of an eminent Dublin surgeon, he studied at Trinity College in Dublin and then at Magdalen College in Oxford, where he founded the Aesthetic Movement, advocating "art for art's sake."

In London in 1892 Wilde burst upon the theatrical world with a series of brilliant domestic comedies—among them *Lady Windermere's Fan* (1892) and *A Woman of No Importance* (1893). Their combination of polished social drama and witty dialogue was repeated in 1895 in two hits that played simultaneously on the London stage—*An Ideal Husband* and *The Importance of Being Earnest*.

Known for his flamboyant and extrovert style, Wilde would sometimes hire a cab simply to cross the street. However, his years of triumph ended dramatically. Despite being married with two children, his personal life was open to scandal due to his close association with Alfred Douglas, son of the Marquess of Queensbury.

Two weeks after the première of *The Importance of Being Earnest*, Queensbury confronted Wilde at his club and left the famous misspelled note accusing him of posing as a "somdomite." After a sensational trial he was sentenced to two years hard labor and sent to Wandsworth Prison in 1895, later being transferred to Reading Jail. Bankrupt and ruined in health, Wilde left prison in 1897 and settled, a

Oscar Wilde at the peak of his career.

bitter and broken man, in Paris, where he lived out the remainder of his life under the pseudonym Sebastian Melmoth.

Alcohol Finally Claims Parisian Painter

Paris, France, September 9, 1901: Best known for the posters he produced for the Moulin Rouge, Henri de Toulouse-Lautrec has died at the age of 36.

Painter, lithographer, and illustrator, he almost single-handedly documented the bohemian nightlife of Paris in the late nineteenth century.

Born into an aristocratic family, he began to draw and paint at the age of 10. He broke his left leg at 12 and his right leg at 14. Due to a genetic disorder both failed to heal properly and his legs stopped growing, so that he reached young adulthood with a normal torso but abnormally short legs. He was only 4 ft 6 in (1.40 m) in height.

Seemingly deprived of what many would call a normal life, he lived only for his art. He settled in the Montmartre district of Paris surrounded by cabarets, dance halls, and nightclubs, and began to record it all in sketches and paintings of striking originality and power.

Toulouse-Lautrec is best known for his depictions of the Moulin Rouge, literally translated as the "Red Mill," which is exactly what it is—a large windmill painted red that has become a landmark of Paris and a symbol of its *joie de vivre*.

He began to drink heavily in the 1890s and was confined to a sanatorium and to his mother's care at home, but he could not stay away from alcohol. It is believed severe alcoholic consumption brought

Toulouse-Lautrec captured the spirit of Parisian life.

on a paralytic stroke, to which he succumbed at Malromé, one of his family's many estates.

Gauguin Dead in the Marquesas

Marquesas Islands, French Polynesia, May 8, 1903: Post-impressionist Paul Gauguin has died, at the age of 55, in his shack in the Marquesas Islands near Tahiti. Heavily in debt, his paintings have been almost universally derided. His death may be attributed to his dependence upon morphine, which he took for the syphilis sores found on his legs.

Raised among distant cousins in Peru, Gauguin returned to France for a formal education before roaming the world as a merchant seaman. At 25 he married and worked at the stock exchange, but after the crash of 1882 he threw it all in and became an artist. In 1891, frustrated in his efforts to establish himself as a leader of the French avant-garde movement, he abandoned his wife and children and

"*His absurd cacophony will not be music even in the thirtieth century.*"

CESAR CUI (1835–1918), RUSSIAN MUSIC CRITIC, OF GERMAN COMPOSER RICHARD STRAUSS (1864–1949), 1904

"*There is no such thing on earth as an uninteresting subject; the only thing that can exist is an uninteresting person.*"

G. K. CHESTERTON (1874–1936), ENGLISH WRITER, 1905

Rome, Italy, January 14, 1900: Giacomo Puccini's opera *Tosca* premières at the Costanzi Theater.

Weimar, Germany, August 25, 1900: Philosopher Friedrich Nietzsche, author of *Thus Spoke Zarathustra* and *Beyond Good and Evil*, dies. He had been confined to an asylum for the last 10 years.

Paris, France, November 30, 1900: Oscar Wilde dies, destitute, aged 46.

France, December, 1900: Monet paints *Water Lilies*, Renoir *Nude in the Sun* and Toulouse-Lautrec *La Modiste*.

Paris, France, April 21, 1901: Auguste Rodin unveils his latest sculpture, of author Victor Hugo. His semi-nude representation causes a stir.

Paris, France, April 24, 1901: Spanish artist Pablo Picasso, 19, exhibits his work for the first time.

Paris, France, September 9, 1901: Best known for his posters for the Moulin Rouge, Toulouse-Lautrec dies, aged 36.

USA, December, 1901: Scott Joplin's *The Easy Winners* exposes ragtime jazz to a wider audience.

Madrid, Spain, January, 1902: Greek artist of the Spanish school, El Greco (1541-1614), has works exhibited for the first time in 300 years.

Paris, France, September 1, 1902: Georges Méliès's film *Le Voyage dans la Lune (A Trip to the Moon)* premières. His interpretation of a space voyage captivates audiences.

Notable Books, 1902: Beatrix Potter's *The Tale of Peter Rabbit*, Rudyard Kipling's *Just So Stories*, and Joseph Conrad's *The Heart of Darkness* are published.

Marquesas Islands, French Polynesia, May 8, 1903: Post-impressionist Paul Gauguin dies, aged 55.

New York, USA, August 15, 1903: Publisher Joseph Pulitzer gives Colombia University $2 million to establish a school of journalism.

USA, October, 1903: *Kit Carson*, the first Western movie, premières.

Letchworth, England, December, 1903: Work starts on Letchworth Garden City, based upon the principals of Ebenezer Howard outlined in *Garden Cities of Tomorrow*.

New York, USA, February 1, 1904: The Italian tenor Enrico Caruso cuts his first recording for the American public, on the Victor label.

Milan, Italy, February 18, 1904: Puccini's new opera, *Madame Butterfly*, premières amid uproarious scenes encouraged by his rivals.

Badenweiler, Germany, July 15, 1904: Russian dramatist and short story writer Anton Chekhov dies of tuberculosis, aged 44.

London, England, December 27, 1904: *Peter Pan* by J. M. Barrie debuts as a play.

Paul Gauguin's later paintings are set in a lush tropical paradise.

Anton Chekhov

Chekhov enrolled in the Moscow University Medical School in 1879, where he first began to publish hundreds of comic short stories to support his family.

After graduating Chekhov practiced medicine until 1892, and also became a regular contributor to the St Petersburg daily *Novoe Vremya*. It was during this time that he developed a dispassionate non-judgmental style, an absence of critical social commentary that gained him some detractors, but also some admirers, such as Leo Tolstoy and Nikolai Leskov.

In 1888 he was awarded the Pushkin Prize (for literary excellence). In 1892 he purchased an estate in the country village of Melikhove to devote himself full-time to writing. What followed were some of his most memorable works, including the short stories *Ward Number 6* (1892), *The Black Monk* (1894), *Murder* (1895), and *Ariadne* (1895).

Chekhov's final play was *The Cherry Orchard*, which had its première this year at the Moscow Art Theater in January. Terminally ill by this time, Chekhov's appearance shocked the play's company when he appeared at the theater on opening night after a protracted self-imposed "exile" at his home in Yalta. Some present likened it to seeing "a living corpse."

Serious health issues such as tuberculosis had plagued Chekhov since early adulthood. In 1901 he was diagnosed with "irreversible necrosis" of the lungs, as well as severe pulmonary damage and chronic colitis.

Early this morning at the Badenweiler health resort in Germany, his heart gave out. After a sip of champagne—a German medical convention that dictates that "a doctor at a deathbed, when all hope is gone, should offer champagne"—Chekhov remarked, "I haven't had champagne for a long time." He then laid down on his side and died.

sailed to Tahiti, where he remained for the rest of his relatively short life.

Journalism School to Be Established at Columbia

New York, USA, August 15, 1903: Publisher Joseph Pulitzer today bequeathed Columbia University $2 million to establish a school of journalism to encourage "public service, public morals, American literature and the advancement of education."

Pulitzer took over the *New York World* in 1883, and announced in the first issue of the newspaper that it would be "truly democratic, dedicated to the cause of the people rather than that of the purse potentates." He turned the mediocre daily into one of the city's premier papers, the changes in style and content he introduced increasing the paper's circulation tenfold, from 15,000 to over 150,000 in just five years.

In the summer of 1902 at his expansive estate in Bar Harbor, Maine, Pulitzer dictated a rough plan for endowing a school of journalism to Columbia University. His outline also included a provision for "annual prizes to particular journalists or writers for various accomplishments, achievements, and forms of excellence."

Russia Loses Talented Writer

Badenweiler, Germany, July 15, 1904: Russian dramatist and short-story writer Anton Chekhov has died of tuberculosis at the age of 44.

Born in 1860 in the tiny seaport of Taganrog in southern Russia, the son of a grocer and grandson of a slave, he taught himself to read and write. After the family moved to Moscow,

time out

My Brilliant Career by Miles Franklin was published in Edinburgh. It tells the story of 16-year old Sybylla Melvyn, a passionate, headstrong girl, trapped on her parents' remote farm and yearning for culture. Her life is transformed when she goes to live with her grandmother.

Amiens, France, March 24, 1905: Jules Verne, author of *A Journey to the Center of the Earth*, dies, aged 77.

Paris, France, October 1, 1905: An art critic, likening the colorful work of Matisse and others to wild beasts, names the movement Fauvism.

Dresden, Germany, December 9, 1905: Richard Strauss's opera *Salome*, inspired by Oscar Wilde, causes a sensation.

Buffalo, USA, December, 1905: Frank Lloyd Wright's Larkin office building is completed.

Berlin, Germany, January 4, 1906: American dancer Isadora Duncan is forbidden to dance when police label her work obscene.

Christiana, Norway, May 23, 1906: Poet and playwright Henrik Ibsen dies, aged 78.

Aix-en-Provence, France, October 22, 1906: Only receiving widespread acclaim for his art in the last two years, Paul Cézanne dies, aged 67.

Melbourne, Australia, December 26, 1906: The world's first feature film, *The Story of the Kelly Gang*, is released.

Paris, France, March 14, 1907: Picasso unveils *Les Demoiselles d'Avignon*, abandoning conventional concepts of perspective.

Melbourne, Australia, May 17, 1907: Artist Frederick McCubbin departs to exhibit in Europe, following Roberts and Streeton.

Dublin, Ireland, July 10, 1907: Rioting breaks out at the Irish première of J.M. Synge's play *The Playboy of the Western World*.

Bergen, Norway, September 4, 1906: Edvard Greig, composer of *Peer Gynt*, dies, aged 64.

Pasadena, USA, March, 1908: Construction begins on the Gamble House, designed by Greene & Greene in the Arts and Crafts style.

Paris, France, May 15, 1908: Extremely critical of his own work, Claude Monet destroys canvases valued at $100,000.

St Petersburg, Russia, June 21, 1908: Rimsky-Korsakov, composer of *Scheherazade*, dies, aged 64.

London, England, December, 1908: Kenneth Grahame's *The Wind in the Willows* is released. "Clean of the clash of sex," according to Grahame.

Paris, France, February 20, 1909: Filippo Marinetti publishes the *Futurist Manifesto* in *Le Figaro*, claiming that the essential elements of poetry shall be courage, audacity and revolt.

Paris, France, May 18, 1909: The *Ballets Russes* of Sergei Diaghilev, starring Nijinsky and Pavlova, causes a sensation upon debut.

Glasgow, Scotland, December, 1909: The Glasgow School of Art building, designed by Charles Rennie Mackintosh, a graduate of the school, is completed.

Beatrix Potter

New "Aggressive" Style of Painting Recognized

Paris, France, October 1, 1905: The term "fauvism" was coined today at the annual Salon d'Automne exhibition by the art critic Louis Vauxcelles, who has likened some of the exhibited works of Matisse, Derain, and de Vlaminck to wild beasts because of their strong use of pure brilliant colors applied straight from their paint tubes in an aggressive and direct manner.

Matisse is the group's leading exponent. After critically analyzing the works of a number of post-impressionists, such as van Gogh, Matisse seems to have come to reject tradi- tional renderings of three-dimensional space and now seeks to define images through the movement of color.

André Derain alters every tone in his landscapes into pure color, while Vlam- inck's works are characterized by agitated swirls of intense color in a style reminis- cent of van Gogh.

Fauvism, as this style is now known, has also drawn in other artists such as Othon Friesz, who finds the emotional connotations of the bold colors a relief from mediocre impressionism.

Gustave Moreau is the movement's inspirational teacher, and a professor at the Ecole des Beaux-Arts in Paris, who pushes his students to think freely, outside the lines of formality, and to follow their instincts.

The fauvist movement represents the first break with the artistic traditions of the past. Its emphasis on formal values and expressive use of color, lines, and

brushwork has liberated painting from the representational expectations that have dominated Western art since the Renaissance.

Doll's House Creator Dead

Christiana, Norway, May 23, 1906: Henrik Ibsen, the Norwegian playwright and poet famous for *A Doll's House* and *Ghosts*, has

A 1904 caricature of Henrik Ibsen.

died today at the age of 78, after suffering a series of strokes and being unable to write for the last few years of his life.

Born in Skien, Norway, into a sea- faring family, he was perceived as an un- sociable child with a sense of isolation that intensified as a teenager when his father's business had to be sold in order to pay off creditors.

At 16 he left his family and went to live in the small isolated town of Grimstad, and it was here that he began to write. Inspired by the revolutions that were spreading throughout Europe in 1848, he wrote satirical and elegant poetry. He moved to Oslo and there wrote his first play, *Cataline*.

From 1864 he spent 27 years living in Italy and Germany. During this extensive period Ibsen penned a number of suc- cessful works, including *Brand* (1866) and *Peer Gynt* (1867).

However, it was not until he moved to Munich that he wrote his groundbreaking play, *A Doll's House*, for the next 10 years pursuing his interest in realistic drama and earning international acclaim.

In his final period, embittered by the lack of public enthusiasm for some of his

plays, he wrote *The Master Builder*. This is a moving portrait of an ageing architect who, having abandoned his dreams of building great monuments and churches with towers reaching up to the heavens, contents himself with building everyday houses for people to live in. When the architect realizes the public does not even appreciate his sacrifices, he returns to the mythical structures of his youth.

Recently Acclaimed Artist Dies

Aix-en-Provence, France, October 22, 1906: After having received widespread acclaim for his vivid canvases only in the last two years, Paul Cézanne has died, aged 67.

Born in Aix-en-Provence in 1839, he studied law there from 1859 to 1861, at the same time attending drawing classes. Moving to Paris in 1861 he met Camille Pissarro and others in the impressionist group, with whom he exhibited in 1874 and 1877. Although he submitted his work to the official Paris Salon, he consistently saw it rejected.

Through a continuing association with Pissarro he painted at Auvers out- side Paris, assimilating the impressionist principles of color and lighting, and loosening up his brushwork.

The late 1870s saw his work dominated by groupings of parallel hatched brush- strokes in formations that had the effect of building up a sense of mass.

***The Thames and the Houses of Parliament*, by André Derain (1905).**

Late in his career, Cezanne painted many still lifes.

A still later phase saw a concentration on still lifes and studies of bathers. Finally there were the landscapes of his final years that have a transparent unfinished look, influenced no doubt by his contemporaries' use of watercolors.

New Larkin Building Breaks with Tradition

Buffalo, New York, USA, December, 1906: Architect Frank Lloyd Wright's Larkin office building in Buffalo, New York, has been completed. The world's first entirely air-conditioned office building is block-like in design with very little ornamentation, a dramatic departure from the beaux arts fashion followed by the vast majority of US architects.

Constructed from a dark red brick using pink-tinted mortar, it stands five stories high and cost $4 million to construct. The entrances to the building are flanked by two waterfall-like fountains. Above them are bas-reliefs by Richard W. Bock, who also designed the globes on the tops of the central exterior piers of the building.

The interior contains a five-story central court with a glazed roof that provides daylight to the inner spaces, even though the building has electric lighting throughout. The upper level has kitchens, dining rooms, a roof garden, and even a branch of the Buffalo Public Library. Its large windows have unusually high sills 5 ft (1.5 m) above floor level, with no sun protection, in distinction from most of the buildings being built today.

The use of a material called magnesite is interesting. It is usually employed to line the inside of steel-making furnaces, but Wright has mixed it with cement and used it for the building's floors.

Air-conditioned buildings are a new concept in America. The Larkin building's ventilation system provides heating and cooling by around 5°F (3°C) of full fresh air per hour treated in the basement's air handling plant. It is also the first building ever constructed that incorporates all the infrastructure required for air conditioning, such as service ducts.

Children's Story of River Animals

London, England, December, 1908: A children's book written by Bank of England official Kenneth Grahame, *The Wind in the Willows*, has been released this month.

The book is based on stories that its author started to tell his son Alistair from his fourth birthday. It is "clean of the clash of sex," according to its author. Its principal characters are animals that live around "the river"— Mole, Rat, Badger, and Toad. Although these characters all have their faults, they are idealized in many ways. Virtues are epitomized to the extent that they become themes. The book is replete with examples of forgiveness, hospitality, compassion, and humility.

At first Grahame had trouble placing *The Wind In The Willows* with a publisher. It was rejected both by his English editor and by *Everybody's*, the American periodical that initially solicited it. Finally it was picked up early this year by Methuen.

This is Grahame's fourth book of fiction. He is already well-known for *The Golden Age* and its sequel *Dream Days*. The work will very likely establish Grahame's international reputation as a writer of children's stories.

Arts and Crafts House Hailed as Masterpiece

Pasadena, USA, March, 1909: Construction has been completed on the Gamble House, designed by Charles and Henry Greene in the Arts and Crafts style and commissioned by Proctor and Gamble heir David Gamble.

A symphony in wood, this 8,100 sq ft (750 sq m) house hums with hand-rubbed maple, mahogany, cedar, oak, and Burmese teak. On the exteriors, broad eaves cap cascades of hand-split redwood. It melds the exotic influences of a Swiss chalet and a Japanese temple. Sophisticated yet casual, it has captured the Californian spirit.

Drawings for the house were completed in February 1908 and the first ground was broken in March. Ten months later the house was finished, and is already being hailed internationally as a masterpiece of the current Arts and Crafts style of architecture. Wide terraces and open sleeping porches facilitate indoor–outdoor living, with careful siting and cross-ventilation capturing the cool breezes of the nearby Arroyo.

Everything in the building's interior has been custom-designed by the architects—furniture, built-in cabinetry, wood carvings, rugs, lighting, leaded stained glass and landscaping. Everything—every peg, oak wedge, downspout, air vent, and switchplate—has been designed to be harmonious with its environment and contribute to the single design concept.

Emil Lange, a German-born stained-glass artisan from Iowa, was responsible for executing the leaded art glass, including the magnificent entry doors. The aim of connecting the house with its environment while at the same time maintaining its privacy is achieved by means of low-walled terraces and a sunken driveway.

The Arts and Crafts movement began in England in the 1880s as a search for an authentic and meaningful style and as a reaction to the historicism of the Victorian era. When you walk into a Craftsman home such as the Gamble House, the sense of space and openness of the rooms together with the rustic, bold-square styling feels a world apart from the many Victorian-style homes still being built today.

Ignacy Paderewski

Actress Gabrielle Ray, said to be England's most beautiful woman.

Maurice Garin

"I MARRIED
BENEATH
ME—ALL
WOMEN DO."

NANCY ASTOR (1879–
1964), AMERICAN-
BORN BRITISH
POLITICIAN, FIRST
WOMAN TO SERVE IN
THE BRITISH HOUSE
OF COMMONS, 1900

"WE ARE
THINKING
BEINGS, AND
WE CANNOT
EXCLUDE THE
INTELLECT
FROM PARTICI-
PATING IN ANY
OF OUR
FUNCTIONS."

WILLIAM JAMES
(1842–1910),
AMERICAN
PHILOSOPHER AND
PSYCHOLOGIST, 1902

Olympics and Exposition Make Paris World Capital

Paris, France, May 14–October 28, 1900:
The second modern Olympic Games are
being held in Paris, coinciding with the
Exposition Universelle Internationale, the
World's Fair. It must be said, however,
that the Olympics are a disappointment.

With the World Expo being held
concurrently, there are few spectators
at many of the Olympic events, and the
Games risk becoming a sideshow to the
more popular Expo.

Numerous internal rivalries in French
sport have left many sports without experienced officials or adequate venues.
Because they are presented as part of the
Expo, the Olympic Games are running
from May to October—an incredibly
long period of time.

Press coverage of many events has been
nearly non-existent, and there is often
confusion over the names and nationalities of medalists. On a positive note,
women have been allowed to participate
for the first time, although there were
only 11 of them.

In one incident in the rowing, a French
boy was drafted at the last minute to cox
the Dutch pair. They won, but the boy
disappeared unrewarded—the youngest
gold medalist in Olympic history.

The athletics, the major draw-
card, has managed to attract
only some 3,000 spectators
a day compared to the estimated 48 million people who
have attended the exhibition,
a daily average of 300,000.

Swimming events were
conducted in the murky
waters of the river Seine. Some
events were even staged for non-
amateurs by the organizers themselves, and the winners were rewarded
with 250 French francs.

However, despite the organizational
farces and distinct lack of public interest,
there have been some notable
performances and innovations by
the athletes. The Swedish gymnas-
tic team have shown new styles
and techniques, and the US athlete
Alvin Kraenzlein introduced the
leg-extended style in hurling.

New "Hamburger" Snack Created

**New Haven, Connecticut, USA,
December, 1900:** A small lunch
wagon that sells steak sandwiches
to local factory workers in tiny
New Haven, Connecticut, has
served what they are calling a
"hamburger," which was hastily
made for a man who dashed in off
the street asking for a quick meal
that he could eat on the run.
According to the diner's owner,
the "snack" consisted of a hur-
riedly broiled beef patty thrown
between two slices of bread. "I
don't like to waste the excess beef
from the daily lunch rush, so I ground it
up, grilled it, and served it in a sandwich."
The chef preferred not to be identified.

New Endowment to Honor Excellence

time out

Sport the elephant, at Bostock
Zoo, Baltimore, Maryland, had to be
put to death by hanging. An enormous freight derrick was used. Sport
was given large quantities of ether
beforehand. He had been injured
by falling from a freight train
and had suffered partial
paralysis.

**Stockholm, Sweden, December,
1901:** Nobel prizes for literature, physics, chemistry,
medicine, and peace have
been awarded for the first
time this year.

Alfred Nobel was the
inventor of dynamite,
the holder of over 355
patents, including synthetic
rubber and artificial silk, and
a man whose dream it was to be
of service to humanity. After passing
away five years ago it was learned he had
left the bulk of his considerable estate
to a fund, the interest from which was
to be awarded annually to the persons
whose work has been of the greatest
benefit to humanity.

Nobel died in San Remo, Italy, on
December 10, 1896. Despite his last will
and testament clearly stating that much
of his fortune was to be used to establish
the Nobel Foundation, not everybody
was pleased with this. His will was opposed by his relatives and questioned by
authorities in various countries. It took
four years for his executors to convince
all parties to follow his wishes. The
statutes of the foundation that are to
administer the fund, the Nobel Foundation, were adopted on June 29, 1900.

The recipients of this year's Nobel
prizes are as follows.

Chemistry—Jacobus H. van't Hoff, "in
recognition of the extraordinary services
he has rendered by the discovery of the
laws of chemical dynamics and osmotic
pressure in solutions."

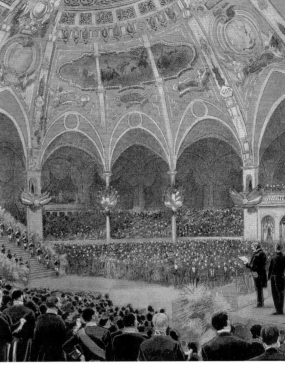

The World Expo attracted more people than the Paris Olympics.

Bluff, New Zealand, May 2, 1900:
Borchgrevink's Antarctic expedition
returns from a winter on the frozen
continent, having attained the
farthest south point ever.
**Paris, France, May 14–October 28,
1900:** The second Olympic Games
of the modern era are held.
Victoria, Canada, July 25, 1900:
The first influx of Japanese
immigrants arrive in the country.
New Haven, USA, December, 1900:
Louis's Lunch Diner serves the first
hamburger, consisting of ground
beef between sliced bread.

Stuttgart, Germany, March, 1901:
Gottlieb Daimler's car company
produces the first Mercedes.
New York, USA, August 26, 1901:
Robert Walthour sets a new world
record for 1 mile on a bicycle.
**Niagara Falls, Canada, October 24,
1901:** Annie Taylor, a retired teacher,
is the first person to go over the Falls
in a barrel. She survives.
Boston, USA, December 2, 1901:
King C. Gillette begins manufacturing the safety razor.
**Stockholm, Sweden, December 10,
1901:** The first Nobel Prizes are
awarded.

Paris, France, April 20, 1902: Art
Nouveau, characterized by works
such as Guimard's cast metal
entrances to the Parisian Metro, is
exhibited at La Société Nationale
des Beaux-Arts.
Venice, Italy, July 14, 1902: The bell
tower of St Mark's Basilica, dating
back to 902, collapses while being
inspected by engineers.
Brooklyn, USA, November 18, 1902:
Morris Michtom makes a soft toy
bear and names it "Teddy's Bear,"
after US President Theodore
Roosevelt.

Antarctica, March 28, 1903: After a
fierce polar winter, news is received
from the Scott expedition; on
December 30, 1902, Scott, Wilson
and Shackleton reached the farthest
ever south position of 82°15′ S.
Paris, France, July 19, 1903:
Maurice Garin wins the inaugural
Tour de France.
Detroit, USA, July 23, 1903: The
first Model A Ford, designed by
Henry Ford, is produced.
**Manchester, England, October 10,
1903:** Emmeline Pankhurst starts
a women's suffrage organization.

London, England, May 9, 1904:
African explorer Sir Henry Stanley
dies, aged 63. He was best known
for his 1871 trek to rescue Doctor
Livingstone.
**St Louis, USA, July 1–November 23,
1904:** The third Olympic Games
introduces gold, silver, and bronze
medals. US gymnast George Eyser
wins six gold medals despite having
a wooden leg.
France, August, 1904: The
International Miners Congress calls
for the establishment of a minimum
wage and an 8-hour working day.

Physics—Wilhelm Conrad von Röntgen, "in recognition of the extraordinary services he has rendered by the discovery of the remarkable rays subsequently named after him."

Literature—Sully Prudhomme, "in special recognition of his poetic composition, which gives evidence of lofty idealism, artistic perfection, and a rare combination of the qualities of both heart and intellect."

Medicine—Emil Adolf von Behring, "for his work on serum therapy, especially its application against diphtheria, by which he has opened a new road in the domain of medical science and thereby placed in the hands of the physician a victorious weapon against illness and death."

St Mark's Bell Tower Collapses

Venice, Italy, July 14, 1902: The bell tower of St Mark's Basilica in Venice, dating to the year 902 CE, collapsed today while it was being inspected by engineers. An eyewitness described the event: "On

Monday the Campanile was resplendent in the sunshine…Suddenly I saw it slowly sink directly downward behind a line of rooftops, and a dense gray dust rose in clouds…On arrival, the sight was pitiful. Of that splendid shaft all that remained was a mound of white dust, spreading to the walls of St Mark's Cathedral."

Remarkably, no one was killed. It has been decided to rebuild the tower exactly as it was, with some internal reinforcement to prevent a further collapse.

Teddy Bear's Striking Likeness

"Teddy Bear" is a huge hit.

Brooklyn, New York, USA, November 18, 1902: Two Russian-Jewish immigrants now living in Brooklyn, Rose and Morris Michtom, have made a soft bear toy and named it "Teddy's Bear" after US President Theodore "Teddy" Roosevelt, who refused to shoot a tethered bear earlier this month.

Earlier this year a boundary dispute in one of the nation's least developed areas between the states of Louisiana and Mississippi saw the governors of both states invite the president down in order to arbitrate. An avid hunter, he decided to combine the trip with a five-day black bear hunt. On the final day of the hunt and without having sighted a single bear, a companion of Roosevelt's tied a young bear cub to a tree with an invitation to shoot it. The president refused, saying he could only shoot at something that had a chance to defend itself.

This act endeared him to the nation. That night, Rose cut and stuffed a piece of plush velvet into the shape of a bear, sewed on shoe-button eyes and placed it in the window of the Michtom's modest candy store. They labeled it "Teddy's Bear," and it is proving immensely popular amongst the residents of Brooklyn.

Alfred Nobel

Inaugural Tour de France Is Huge Success

Paris, France, July 19, 1903: Maurice Garin has won the inaugural Tour de France bicycle race, ahead of Lucien Pothier and Fernand Augereau, both Frenchmen, in a time of 94 hours 33 minutes.

The first 50 riders were given 5 francs a day for expenses. The prize money was 20,000 francs. When Garin entered Paris, a crowd of 20,000 paying spectators were there to greet him.

In part, inspired by a novel by G. Bruno entitled *Tour de France par Deux Enfants*, about two boys who cycle their way around France, the race was composed of six individual "stages" with a total distance of 1508 miles (2,428 km), the longest stage being the 290 miles (467 km) from Paris to Lyons.

St Mark's Square in Venice draws large crowds at carnival time.

Monte Verità, Italy, January 1, 1905: Belgian Henri Oedenkoven founds the world's first vegetarian organization.

London, England, June 29, 1905: The Automobile Association (AA) is formed to help motorists avoid police speed traps.

London, England, July 8, 1905: May Sutton (USA) becomes the first non-Briton to win at Wimbledon.

London, England, September 19, 1905: Doctor Thomas Barnardo, founder of institutions for deprived children, dies, aged 60.

London, England, January 27, 1906: Oil pollution on the River Thames causes a fire upon the river.

Italy and Switzerland, May 19, 1906: The Simplon tunnel, started in 1898, is completed. At 12 miles (19.3 km), it is the longest tunnel in the world.

Le Mans, France, June 26, 1906: The first Grand Prix is won by Hungarian Ferenc Szisz.

Washington DC, USA, June 30, 1906: The Pure Food and Drug Act is introduced to prohibit the tampering with and mislabeling of foodstuffs.

Helsinki, Finland, March 15, 1907: Finland is the first European country to give women the right to vote.

Dunedin, New Zealand, May 14, 1907: The Plunket Society, promoting of the health of women and children, holds its first meeting.

Brownsea Island, Poole, England, July 29, 1907: Sir Robert Baden-Powell starts the Scouting movement.

Paris, France, August 10, 1907: Italian Prince Borghese wins the Peking-Paris auto race in 62 days, driving his car across 8,000 miles (12,875 km) of rugged terrain.

New York, USA, January 22, 1908: Miss Mulcahey is the first woman to be arrested for smoking in public following the introduction of the Sullivan Smoking Act.

London, England, April 27-October 31, 1908: The fourth Olympic Games sees 22 nations competing in 110 events. In a dramatic conclusion to the marathon, Italian Dorando Pietri collapses and is assisted across the finish line, but is later disqualified.

London, England, June 22, 1908: At 37, Charlotte Sterry becomes the oldest Wimbledon singles title winner.

Antarctica, January 9, 1909: Shackleton's party is forced to turn back 97 miles (156 km) from the South Pole, as food supplies are low.

USA, April 1, 1909: The Opium Exclusion Act, prohibiting the importation of smoking opium, sees the start of national drug prohibition.

North Pole, April 6, 1909: Robert Peary and Matthew Henson (USA) arrive after a 36-day trek.

Boston, USA, October 22, 1909: Harvard Law School excludes Inez Mulholland, who is seeking support from other suffragettes.

Dr Thomas Barnardo

Californian Teenager Wins Wimbledon

London, England, July 8, 1905: May Godfrey Sutton of the United States has become the first non-Briton to win the Wimbledon tennis title. Only 18 years of age, she defeated Dorothea Douglass of Great Britain, the Ladies Singles Champion in 1903 and 1904.

A previous winner of the US National Singles Title, the American had learned how to play on a court built by her father on the family's ranch near Pasadena, California, after moving there from Plymouth, England, where she was born on September 25, 1886.

Shocking the British public by rolling up her sleeves on the court and baring her elbows, she also wore a skirt that showed her ankles.

Dorothea Douglass lost Wimbledon crown.

Father to London's Displaced Children Dies

London, England, September 19, 1905: Dr Thomas Barnardo, the philanthropic founder of institutions for deprived children, died today aged 60.

A strong evangelical Christian, he displayed a commitment to social work from a young age. While studying medicine at London Hospital, he began to become involved in homes for disadvantaged children and started to open hostels. In 1873 he married Syrie Louise Elmslie, who shared his commitment to evangelism and philanthropic work. They went to live at Mossford Lodge, and in October 1873 12 girls came to live in a converted coach house next to the lodge.

In 1874 Dr Barnardo established a photographic department in his Boys' Home in Stepney. Over the next 30 years all children who entered one of Barnardo's homes had their picture taken when they first arrived, then again when they left, after having recovered from their experience of living on the streets. These "before and after" cards were sold in packs of 20 for 5 shillings. This enabled Barnardo to publicize his work and also to raise money for his growing list of charitable causes.

By 1880 the Village Home for Girls was opened, with space for 1,000 girls. Dr Barnardo also began setting up homes for the mentally ill and for children and young people with disabilities.

Thomas Barnardo died in London today of angina pectoris, a condition characterized by a lack of oxygen to the heart muscle, caused by an obstruction or spasm of the coronary arteries.

European Tunnel Opens

Italy and Switzerland, May 19, 1906: Today the magnificent feat of engineering that is the Simplon Tunnel, joining Brig in Switzerland and the Italian town of Iselle under the Lepontine Alps, has finally been completed.

At 12½ miles (20 km), it is the longest tunnel in the world, consisting of a single-line railway, rising to a elevation of 2,313 ft (706 m). The Simplon Pass has been a significant trade route between northern and southern Europe since the thirteenth century.

There were unique engineering difficulties to overcome in constructing the approach lines to the two tunnel portals at Iselle and Brig. The bore needed to drive through the range between the Rhone and the Diviera valleys at a tangent, with curves at each entrance.

The tunnel has a height of 18 ft (6 m) and is 16 ft (5 m) across at its widest point. A smaller parallel shaft was also constructed so that supplies and materials for the workmen on the main tunnel could be brought in quickly—this tunnel was also used to efficiently remove the rock dislodged by the blasting process.

Work began on August 13, 1898, but quickly ran into difficulties. An unexpected "heat zone" inside the mountain was encountered on the Swiss side, with temperatures soaring to 127°F (53°C). A powerful ventilation system had to be installed, but even this proved insufficient. Finally the walls of the tunnel were sprayed with icy water brought from a nearby stream and the work was able to continue.

Workers on the southern approach had their problems too. Torrents of hot and cold water burst through fissures caused by blasting, rendering parts of the tunnel unworkable until a method was devised to divert the water and close the fissures.

It was not until February 24 that the last barrier of rock yielded to blasting.

Greatest Sporting Event in History

London, England, April 27–October 31, 1908: Rome was to have hosted this year's Olympic Games, but an eruption of Mt Vesuvius in 1906 created chaos, causing the Italian government to divert its priorities and finances to rebuilding the area shattered by the explosion. The International Olympic Committee asked the British Olympic Association if it could step into the breach.

With less than a year to get organized, the British Olympic Association was fortunate that it was able to share a site acquired in Shepherd's Bush northeast of London for the upcoming Franco-British Exhibition. In January 1907 work began on the former Wood Lane farmland and was completed early this year.

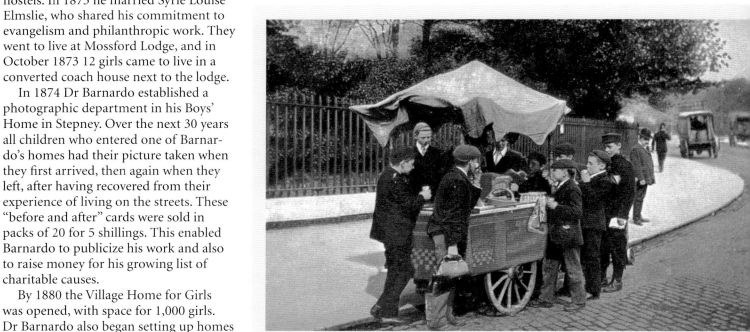

Ice-cream vendors are a familiar sight during the summer months, selling their confection from colorful carts.

Dorando Pietri crossed the finish line with help, and was later disqualified.

Ernest Shackleton

England is ideally placed to host these games. Many of the events are being held at the new White City Stadium, which has room for 70,000 spectators. Twenty-two countries are competing, the same number as in 1900, but the numbers of athletes participating has increased considerably, from 1,330 to 2,035, competing in a total of 110 events.

The opening ceremony took place on July 13. Cambridge and Oxford Blues and an Eton Eight member led the British team into the stadium.

Controversy has not been far away, however. These are the first Olympic Games of the modern era where athletes have marched into the stadium behind the flags of their respective countries, and this has been the cause of some moments of high drama. The Finnish team were told they would have to parade under the flag of the Soviet Union rather than that of Finland. In the end they chose to march without any flag at all. Similarly, Irish athletes who wanted to march for their country had to enter under the auspices of Great Britain.

The marathon also ended in controversy when Dorando Pietri of Italy collapsed after entering the stadium ahead of the other runners. *The Times* described the scene: "A tired man, dazed, bewildered, hardly conscious, in red shorts and white vest, his hair white with dust, staggers onto the track. He looks about him, hardly knowing where he is. Just the knowledge that somehow, by some desperate resolve of determination, he must get round the 200 yards (182 m) to the tape of the finish line." After collapsing, doctors and officials assisted him across the line. Pietri was declared the winner ahead of American runner John Hayes. However, the Americans protested and the race, after a long determination, was given to Hayes.

Britain won all the gold medals in boxing, football, hockey, men's and women's lawn tennis, rowing, polo, water polo, and racquets—a total of 56 gold medals and 145 medals overall. Britain's gold medal-winning foot-ball team included professionals. A figure skating event was held for the first time at the Prince's Skating Rink.

These events would have to be called the greatest sporting meet in history. There have been many advances in officiating, judging, and scoring. Unfortunately, disaster struck the White City on August 14. A hydrogen-filled silk balloon, which was due to fly over the Franco-British Exhibition being held to celebrate four years of the Entente Cordiale, exploded, killing three people.

Shackleton: So Close Yet So Far

Antarctica, January 9, 1909: Sir Ernest Shackleton's second Antarctic expedition has been forced to turn back as food supplies begin to run dangerously low.

The supply ship Nimrod deposited the party alongside the ice foot at Hut Point Peninsula and began its return journey to New Zealand on February 3. Shackleton's party spent the next seven months planning their assault on the pole and set out in late September. Three weeks later, Shackleton was complaining in his diary about the size of the rations.

On November 21 they shot one of the ponies for meat. On November 26 they passed the previous "farthest south" point, reached by Robert Scott in 1902. On December 11 they were still 250 miles (400 km) from the pole, with only three weeks' supply of biscuits left.

On December 27 they reached the Polar Plateau at 10,200 ft (3,100 m). Weak from lack of food, and with their feet and hands constantly on the verge of frostbite, they stoically fought their way through a terrible blizzard from January 4 that lasted until January 8.

Acknowledging the inevitable, their "farthest south" point was reached at 9 a.m. on January 9, at 88° 23′ south, longitude 162°—no more than 97 miles (156 km) from the South Pole.

US Flag Flies on Top of the World

North Pole, April 6, 1909: Robert Peary and Matthew Henson reached the North Pole after a 36-day trek from Ellesmere Island.

Peary's meticulous preparation involved observing Eskimo ways and learning all he could about dogs, sleds, furs, and igloos. It was decided that Ellesmere Island was the best starting point, and that it was preferable to make the journey in winter, as progress over the ice was easier when it was firmer.

They departed on March 1 with an entourage of 23 men, 133 dogs, and 19 sleds. As they traveled north, they progressively lightened their load and reduced the size of their party. When they arrived at the North Pole, only six men remained to witness the planting of the American flag—Peary, Henson, and four Eskimos.

Sporting Achievements

Baseball World Series: 1903 Boston (American League); 1904 no series; 1905 New York (National League); 1906 Chicago (AL); 1907 Chicago (NL); 1908 Chicago (NL); 1909 Pittsburgh (NL).

Cycling Tour de France: 1903 M. Garin; 1904 H. Cornet; 1905 L. Trousselier; 1906 R. Pottier; 1907-1908 L. Petit-Breton; 1909 F. Faber.

Horse Racing Epsom Derby: 1900 Diamond Jubilee; 1901 Volodyovski; 1902 Ard Patrick; 1903 Rock Sand; 1904 St Amant; 1905 Cicero; 1906 Spearmint; 1907 Orby; 1908 Signorinetta; 1909 Minoru. Kentucky Derby: 1900 Lieut. Gibson; 1901 His Eminence; 1902 Alan-A-Dale; 1903 Judge Himes; 1904 Elwood; 1905 Agile; 1906 Sir Huon; 1907 Pink Star; 1908 Stone Street; 1909 Wintergreen. Melbourne Cup: 1900 Clean Sweep; 1901 Revenue; 1902 The Victory; 1903 Lord Cardigan; 1904 Acrasia; 1905 Blue Spec; 1906 Poseidon; 1907 Apologue; 1908 Lord Nolan; 1909 Price Foote.

Ice Hockey Stanley Cup: 1900 Montreal; 1901 Winnipeg; 1902 Winnipeg/Montreal; 1903 Montreal/Ottawa; 1904 Ottawa; 1905 Ottawa; 1906 Ottawa/Montreal; 1907 Kennora/Montreal; 1908 Montreal; 1909 Ottawa.

Marathon Boston: Men 1900 J. Caffery; 1901 J. Caffery; 1902 S. Mellor; 1903 J. Lorden; 1904 M. Spring; 1905 F. Lorz; 1906 T. Ford; 1907 T. Longboat; 1908 T. Morrissey; 1909 H. Renaud.

Sailing America's Cup: 1901 *Columbia*; 1903 *Reliance*.

Tennis Australasian Championships: Men's Singles 1905 R. Heath; 1906 A. Wilding; 1907 H. Rice; 1908 F. Alexander; 1909 A. Wilding.

French Championships, Men's Singles: 1900 P. Ayme; 1901 A. Vacherot; 1902 M. Vacherot; 1903-1904 M. Decugis; 1905-1906 M. Germot; 1907-1909 M. Decugis. Women's Singles: 1900 Y. Prevost; 1901 P. Girod; 1902-1903 A. Masson; 1904-1906 K. Gillou-Fenwick; 1907 D. Kermel; 1908 K. Gillou-Fenwick; 1909 J. Matthey.

US National Championship, Men's Singles: 1900 M. Whitman; 1901-1902 W. Larned; 1903 H. Doherty; 1904 H. Ward; 1905 B. Wright; 1906-1909 W. Larned. Women's Singles: 1900 M. McAteer; 1901 E. Moore; 1902 M. Jones; 1903 E. Moore; 1904 M. Sutton; 1905 E. Moore; 1906 H. Homans; 1907 E. Sears; 1908 M. Barger-Wallach; 1909 H. Hotchkiss Wightman. Wimbledon, Gentlemen's Singles: 1900 R. Doherty; 1901 A. Gore; 1902-1906 L. Doherty; 1907 N. Brookes; 1908-1909 A. Gore. Wimbledon, Ladies' Singles: 1900 B. Hillyard; 1901 C. Sterry; 1902 M. Robb; 1903-1904 D. Douglass; 1905 M. Sutton; 1906 D. Douglass; 1907 M. Sutton; 1908 C. Sterry; 1909 D. Boothby.

Queen Alexandra

Britons Farewell Their Beloved King

London, England, May 20: Over half a million Britons gathered for the funeral of King Edward VII, who died of pneumonia two weeks ago. King George V led the ceremony, which was attended by kings of nine European countries.

The eldest son of Queen Victoria and Prince Consort Albert, Edward married Princess Alexandra of Denmark in 1863. He succeeded his mother at the age of 59, after having been heir apparent longer than any other prince in British history.

Fluent in French and German, he made a number of trips abroad during his brief reign, making him an ideal ambassador for his country. He was also related to nearly every royal house in Europe, which not only earned him the nickname of "Uncle of Europe," but allowed him to play a useful part in foreign policy negotiations.

"Everything great in the world is done by neurotics; they alone founded our religions and created our master-pieces."

MARCEL PROUST (1871–1922), FRENCH NOVELIST, ON THE STATE OF THE WORLD, 1910

Johnson Retains Boxing Title

Reno, USA, July 4: What has been billed as the "Fight of the Century" took place today in Reno, Nevada. African-American boxer Jack Johnson easily beat former heavyweight champion Jim Jeffries in a brutal encounter that has sparked race riots and has led the Texas Legislature to announce a ban on all films of Johnson's victories over his white opponents.

Johnson was born in Galveston, Texas, in 1878. He was the son of a former slave. Johnson quit school after he had completed the fifth grade and eventually found a job as a janitor at a local gymnasium, where he developed an interest in boxing.

In 1897 he turned professional. Johnson left Galveston in 1901 after having

Boxers Jack Johnson and Jim Jeffries have it out in the "Fight of the Century."

been arrested and jailed for boxing, which at that time was illegal in Texas.

A victory over "Denver Ed" Morton in 1903 gave him the unofficial title of black heavyweight champion. Jim Jeffries, the white heavyweight champion, refused to fight Johnson because of his color.

On December 26, 1908, however, Johnson defeated the then heavyweight champ Tommy Burns at a match in Sydney, Australia. This spurred Jeffries to come out of retirement to fight Johnson as America's "Great White Hope" and to "restore boxing's natural racial hierarchy."

time out

Surgeons had prepared a boy in Pittsburgh for an appendectomy, but just as incision was about to begin, he suffered a coughing fit, which appeared to cure him. He had coughed up a needle, which was believed to have been the cause of his pain.

Author of *War and Peace* Is Dead

Astapovo, Russia, November 10: The famous Russian novelist and writer Leo Tolstoy was found dead today, having died of pneumonia at 82 years of age.

He was born in 1828 into a noble land-owning family, but his parents died when he was a young child and he was raised by relatives. As a young man he became

bored managing his parents' country estate, and moved to Moscow and St Petersburg, in 1852 joining the army in search of adventure.

After leaving the army in 1856, he traveled through Europe, developed an interest in education, and began a school for peasant children.

In 1862 he met and married Sonya (Sofia) Bers, who bore him 13 children over the next 15 years. It was during this time, while also managing his estate, that Tolstoy wrote his two most celebrated and well-known novels.

War and Peace took him seven years to write. This novel is considered to be one of the greatest literary masterpieces of all time. *Anna Karenina* is a dark, pessimistic account of upper-class Russian society in the 1860s.

After finishing *Anna Karenina*, Tolstoy entered a period of spiritual crisis. He began to read the Bible and developed his own moral system, writing about it in *A Confession* (1882). In 1883 he began to publish *The Mediator*, distributing his ideas through tracts and fiction. The secret police followed him for some time and his book *What I Believe* (1884) was removed from the printer.

During his last years Tolstoy enjoyed fame and a large income, yet this time was also his unhappiest. His marriage had deteriorated and he yearned for the monastic life, free of possessions and devoted to the service of humanity. No doubt he was in search of such a life when he left home a few days ago. He was found dead today at the remote railway junction of Astapovo in Ryazan Province.

Paris, France, January: Floods inundate Paris; the Seine threatens the art collections at the Louvre.
India, February 4: A new press censorship bill restricts nationalist sentiment. In January, five provinces banned "seditious" gatherings in a bid to quell unrest.
UK, February 14: The general election results in a tie between the Liberals and the Conservatives.
Egypt, February 21: Prime Minister Butros Ghali is assassinated, leading to severe repression of nationalists by the British administration.

Lhasa, Tibet, February 23: The Dalai Lama flees, as Lhasa is occupied by Chinese troops.
London, England, May 20: Over half a million gather for the funeral of Edward VII, who died of bronchitis, aged 68. His successor, George V, leads the ceremony, attended by kings from nine European countries.
Kiev, Russia, May: Around 12,000 Jews flee Kiev as anti-Semitism, encouraged by the Tsar, leads police to conduct searches. The USA is unwilling to grant sanctuary to large numbers of these refugees.

South Africa, July 1: The Union of South Africa becomes a British dominion. Boer War hero Louis Botha is prime minister. Perceived by many Boers as too pro-British, Botha faces challengers already.
USA, July 4: Race riots break out throughout the country as African-American boxer Jack Johnson wins his world title defense against Jim Jeffries.
Canada, July 31: Doctor Crippen, suspected of murdering his wife in London, is apprehended on a ship off the east coast of Canada.

Korea, August 24: Japan announces that it will annexe Korea, formalizing a situation that began in 1904.
Lancashire, England, October 2: As 700 mills close, 150,000 mill workers lose their jobs. In September, 50,000 dockworkers were sacked after striking for better pay and improved conditions.
Portugal, October 3-7: Soldiers of the Portuguese Royal Army revolt. King Manuel II flees to England. The monarchy is abolished and all nuns and monks are expelled.

Greece, October 18: Eleftherios Venizelos becomes prime minister of Greece, implementing a program of constitutional, administrative, and financial reform.
Astopovo, Russia, November 20: Leo Tolstoy, author of *War and Peace* and *Anna Karenina* dies, aged 82. Born into nobility, he abandoned his possessions and turned ascetic in his later years.
Palestine, December 14: Turkish troops are sent to Palestine to suppress an uprising of 200,000 Bedouin Arabs.

Dictator Diaz Flees Mexico

Mexico City, Mexico, May 25: Ending 35 years of rule, Porfirio Diaz today resigned as president of Mexico. He has now departed for exile in France.

Of humble origins, Diaz pursued an illustrious military career, eventually taking control of Mexico by force in 1877, when he became president. Establishing a strong, centralized government he maintained tight control over the country.

When Diaz announced his intention to campaign for re-election in 1910 rather than retire, the democratic reformer Francisco Madero attempted to run against him but was arrested on the eve of the election. Released from jail in July 1910, Madero fled to San Antonio, Texas, but then returned to Mexico in November with 60,000 followers to lead a rebellion against Diaz. The capital Juarez fell to Madero on May 10.

Madero is refusing to take office until he is officially elected and in the meantime Vice President La Barra has been installed as interim president.

Long Live the King!

London, England, June 22: The coronation of King George V took place today in sumptuous style in London's Westminster

Abbey, with heads of state from around the British Empire attending the event.

After George became heir to the throne upon the death of his elder brother, the Duke of Clarence, in 1897, he visited many parts of the empire and developed a keen interest in imperial affairs, which it is hoped will stand him in good stead in the years to come.

Roald Amundsen proudly photographs the Norwegian flag.

Amundsen Beats Scott to South Pole

South Pole, December 14: Norwegian adventurer and explorer Roald Amundsen has reached the South Pole. Both poles have been conquered in the last three years.

Born in 1872, the young Amundsen insisted on sleeping with his bedroom windows open, even during the frigid Norwegian winters, to condition himself for a life of polar exploration.

When Shackleton failed to reach the South Pole by a mere 97 miles (156 km), Amundsen studied Shackleton's attempt and began planning his own expedition. Amundsen reached the Ross Ice Shelf aboard the *Fram* on January 14. He chose the Bay of Whales as his headquarters because it was a degree further south, or 60 miles (97 km) closer

to the pole, than McMurdo Sound where Robert Scott's British expedition was based.

After setting up a base camp, which was dubbed Framheim, Amundsen's men took on specific chores over the winter to prepare for the coming assault. Olav Bjaaland reduced sled weights; Oscar Wisting spent the winter sewing new tents complete with floors; and Adolf Lindstrom, the chef, prepared buckwheat cakes for breakfast, frozen seal meat for lunch, and seal steak for dinner, with bread and whortleberry jam. Brandy was served on Saturday evenings.

After abandoning an attempted start a month earlier, Amundsen set out for the pole on October 19 from Framheim with four men and four sleds pulled by 52 dogs. Crucial to Amundsen's success in reaching the South Pole was his careful selection of sled dogs. He used to refer to them as "our children" and would often say, "These dogs are the most important thing for us. The whole outcome of the expedition depends upon them."

Robert Scott, dependent upon Siberian ponies rather than dogs, had begun his trek three weeks earlier.

Amundsen split the expedition into two groups, sending the second to explore King Edward VII land so that Norway would still have a "first" to celebrate if Amundsen's team failed to reach the pole.

On December 8 Amundsen's team passed Shackleton's "farthest south" point at 88 degrees 23 minutes, and were only 95 miles (153 km) from the pole. On December 14 at 3 a.m. they halted when their sled meters registered that they had at last reached their goal. Hands grasped the Norwegian flag, planting it at the geographical South Pole. Amundsen named the plain King Haakon VII's Plateau. At midnight, observations put them at 89 degrees 56 minutes south. Their objective had been attained.

Leo Tolstoy

Commemorative picture of King George V and Queen Mary.

London, England, January 3: Winston Churchill joins police at the siege of Sidney Street. Three anarchists holed up in a house keep 1,000 police at bay for 10 hours. Fire in the building ends the drama; two suspects die.

Mexico, April 15: USA troops fight rebels led by Francisco Madero, on the Mexican frontier.

Fez, Morocco, April 23: French troops arrive to end a revolt at the Sultan's request. Germany objects, citing that the Algeciras Agreement of 1906 has been breached.

Canada, May 11: The introduction of section 49A of the Indian Act further diminishes Native rights.

Mexico City, Mexico, May 25: Ending a 35-year rule, Porfirio Diaz departs for France, after the revolution instigated by Madero achieves its aims.

Washington DC, USA, June 12: The Senate amends the Constitution to provide election of representatives by popular vote.

London, England, June 22: The coronation of George V is held at Westminster Abbey.

Agadir, Morocco, July 2: Germany sends a warship to southern Morocco in a show of force.

Machu Picchu, Peru, July 24: American explorer Hiram Bingham re-discovers the ancient Inca city.

London, England, August 10: The House of Lords agrees to surrender its veto power. Asquith had threatened to force the bill through by creating hundreds of peers to vote for it.

Lisbon, Portugal, August 24: Manuel de Arriaga is elected first president and adopts a liberal constitution.

China, September: Up to 100,000 people perish in flooding on the Yangtze River. Plague and famine kill thousands more.

Kiev, Russia, September 14: Premier Piotr Stolypin is shot while attending the opera.

Tripoli, Libya, September 30: Italy declares war on the Turkish Empire after entry into Tripoli by Italians is rejected.

China, October 30: Revolution comes to China, as boy Emperor Pu Yi of the Manchu dynasty is forced to grant a constitution.

Morocco, November 4: France and Germany sign a treaty recognizing France's right to establish a protectorate in Morocco. France cedes land in the French Congo to Germany.

South Pole, December 14: Norwegian Roald Amundsen reaches the South Pole. Both poles have been conquered in just three years.

Nanking, China, December 30: Leader of the revolutionary forces, Sun Yat-sen, is elected president of a provisional government.

Captain John Smith of the *Titanic*

Unsinkable *Titanic* Is Lost—1,500 Dead

Atlantic Ocean near Newfoundland, April 15: The pride of the White Star Line, the *Titanic*, has been lost at sea after colliding with a rogue iceberg in the freezing waters of the North Atlantic. More than 1,500 people have lost their lives.

In calm waters under a full moon, following the standard Great Circle Route to New York, the "unsinkable" liner sailed into a vast sea of ice, striking the iceberg on her starboard side below the water line. Observations from other ships in the area showed a vast ice field stretching for 75 miles (121 km), from 46 degrees north to 31 degrees south, with the *Titanic*'s course of 42 degrees taking her right through the middle of it.

Using 24 of her 29 boilers, the *Titanic* had been traveling at an impressive 22 knots. Scheduled boat drills had apparently not been carried out, and it seems from eyewitness accounts that an air of complacency existed among the crew. Reports of an ice field from the Greek steamer *Athinai* took over five hours to be posted on the bridge. An iceberg watch

Watercolor of "unsinkable" *Titanic*, by C. A. Wilkinson.

was ordered as darkness descended, but apparently there were no binoculars available in the crow's nest.

At around 11 p.m. an iceberg was sighted and the *Titanic* turned hard to port, but too late to prevent the iceberg scraping and piercing the ship's starboard bow.

No. 1, no. 2 and no. 3 cargo holds were the first to flood, spilling over into no. 5 and no. 6 boiler rooms. Water flooded a total of five compartments and then washed over bulkheads that failed to go to the ceiling and into other compartments. The *Titanic* was designed to withstand flooding to only four compartments.

All lifeboats under davits were then ordered to be lowered, and distress messages were sent out. Although the liner *Carpathia* was the nearest vessel, it was some 58 miles (93 km) away. *Carpathia* immediately set course for the stricken liner. Witnesses said the iceberg looked like the Rock of Gibraltar.

Initially refusing to believe the ship was in danger, some passengers are said to have stayed inside to avoid the chilly night air. Just after midnight, however, the order was given to swing out the lifeboats. Revolvers were reportedly given to crew members to enforce the "women and children first" policy.

At 2.15 a.m., with 1,500 people still aboard, the *Titanic* began to go under. Six survivors were picked up by lifeboats. Many of the lifeboats were reluctant to row toward the survivors for fear their boats might be overturned.

The *Carpathia* has reportedly rescued 711 people. She is now en route to New York and is expected to arrive tonight.

Volcano Erupts over Wilderness

Alaskan Peninsula, USA, June 6-8: Over the past three days the Alaskan volcano Novarupta has transformed 40 sq miles (104 sq km) of the world's most pristine bear country into a desolate wasteland, burying nearby valleys in 500 ft (152 m) of ash and volcanic rock. Miraculously, no fatalities have been recorded.

The volcano's plume reached a height of 20 miles (32 km) and the eruption removed the top of Mt Katmai. Around 4 cu miles (16 cu km) of ash was ejected with a foot (30 cm) of ash falling on the town of Kodiak, 100 miles (160 km) away.

Forty-two volcanoes have erupted in Alaska since observations began in 1767.

Qemal Proclaims Albanian Independence

Albania, November 28: Albania has today declared its independence from Ottoman rule. The League of Prizren, the Albanian nationalist organization established in 1878, promoted the idea of an Albanian nation-state and established the modern Albanian alphabet. A series of revolts over the last three years have demanded unification and autonomy for Albania.

In October, however, a coalition of Balkan states declared war on the Ottoman Empire, with one of their goals being to divide up Albania between them. As hostilities came to an end, a group of Albanian nationalists led by Ismail Qemal met at Vlore (Valona) and moved swiftly to issue a proclamation of independence.

Key Events

Peking, China, February 15: The Manchu dynasty ends as Emperor Pu Yi abdicates. Yat-sen resigns and Yuan Shikai is elected president.
Berlin, Germany, March 8: Anglo-German discussions on naval power end abruptly when the Reichstag passes a bill enlarging the navy.
Belfast, Ireland, April 11: The Asquith government introduces the Third Home Rule Bill. Thousands of Protestants in Ulster protest against the bill, which they believe is against their interests.

Atlantic Ocean, near Newfoundland, April 15: The White Star liner *Titanic*, on its maiden voyage, strikes an iceberg and sinks. Almost 1,600 people perish.
Dardenelles, Turkey, April 18-May 4: In the Tripolitan War, attempting to wrest control of Libya from the Ottomans, Italian ships bomb the Dardanelles and Beirut. The Turks close the straits, blockading Russian trade.
Havana, Cuba, May 31: US Marines land in Cuba in order to protect US interests.

Alaskan Peninsula, USA, June 6-8: The Novarupta volcano forms, rising to 2,759 feet (841 m), in the largest eruption since Krakatoa in 1883.
London, England, June 22: Lord of the Admiralty, Winston Churchill, recalls the British Navy's Malta fleet and redeploys it to the North Sea to combat the growing threat from the strengthened German Navy.
Tokyo, Japan, July 30: Emperor Mutsuhito, known also as Meiji, who oversaw the modernization of Japan, dies, aged 60. His son Yoshihito succeeds him.

Chicago, USA, August 5: The Progressive or "Bull Moose" Party formed by Theodore Roosevelt meets, nominating Roosevelt as its candidate in the forthcoming election.
Morocco, August 11: Sultan Mulai Abd al-Hafiz abdicates, as internal dissent follows the signing of the Treaty of Fez, making the country a French protectorate.
Ulster, Ireland, September 28: Unionists and loyalists are both opposing Home Rule for Ulster, although for different reasons.

The Balkans, October 18: Following Montenegro's lead, Bulgaria, Serbia and Greece declare war on Turkey.
Lausanne, Switzerland, October 18: Italy and Turkey sign a treaty, bringing the Tripolitan War to a close.
USA, November 5: Democrat Woodrow Wilson wins the presidency with a minority vote.
Albania, November 28: Albania declares independence from the Ottoman Empire, after 500 years of external rule.

Foundation Stones of New Capital Are Laid

Canberra, Australia, March 12: Three foundation stones were laid at the base of the commencement column for the new Australian capital today.

For over 21,000 years the bushland region has been home to the Ngunnawal Aboriginal people. Europeans began to settle here in the 1820s, and the settlement became known as Canberry, a name derived from an Aboriginal word meaning "meeting place" that eventually evolved to Canberra.

Following Federation in 1901, after much debate, in 1909 Canberra was ratified as the site for the country's new capital city. The New South Wales government surveyor Charles Scrivener envisaged the flood plain of the Molonglo River as an ornamental lake in the center of the new city. On January 1, 1911, the Australian Capital Territory came into being with a mere 1,714 residents.

An international competition was launched to choose a design for the new capital, and out of 137 entries US architect Walter Burley Griffin's plan was awarded first prize.

Suffragette Trampled at Epsom

Epsom, England, June 4: With the flags of the Women's Social and Political Union pinned to her jacket, Emily Davison threw herself under "Anmer," King George V's horse, on the racetrack at the Epsom Derby today. The incident happened in full view of the king.

The horse went over and the jockey, Herbert Jones, came off. The impact lifted Davison clear off the ground.

She has been a long-time campaigner for the suffragettes. During the week leading up to today's tragic events, Davison has been observed stopping horses to

Feminist Emily Davison is a martyr to the cause of women's suffrage.

place a suffragette rosette on their bridles. Davison is not expected to survive.

Mona Lisa Returned Home

Paris, France, December 31: Today, some 27 months after its disappearance from the Louvre Museum in Paris, the world's most famous painting, the *Mona Lisa* by Leonardo da Vinci, has been returned.

In August 1911, the museum staff noticed the *Mona Lisa* wasn't hanging in its usual spot, but they didn't think it particularly odd. They had assumed that an official museum photographer who had been working there had taken it to his studio to photograph it.

A day later the painting still hadn't been returned. Police were notified, but all that was found was the heavy picture frame that had surrounded it, left in a museum staircase leading to a cloakroom.

It appears that an Italian, Vincenzo Perugia, had tried to sell the work to the Uffizi Gallery in Florence, Italy, for $100,000. The directors of the Uffizi Gallery, at first skeptical, agreed to meet Perugia, and to their great surprise he removed the rolled-up painting from inside the false bottom of an old trunk. The Uffizi's directors then said they had to check the authenticity of the painting before they could buy it. Perugia gave them

permission to take the painting for verification while he waited patiently in his hotel room. After the painting was authenticated, Perugia was arrested.

Allegedly an Argentinian con-artist named Eduardo de Valfierno had commissioned the French forger Yves Chaudron to make copies of the famous painting, which de Valfierno then intended to sell as the missing original.

During his interrogation Perugia told police how he had spent the Sunday night in the Louvre, hiding in an obscure room. On the Monday morning, while the museum was closed, he had unhooked the painting from the wall, and walked out the door.

Interestingly, ten months before the painting was stolen, the Louvre decided to have all its masterpieces put under glass. Perugia was one of four men assigned to the job.

Initial reaction in Paris to the disappearance in 1911 was one of denial. Many believed it to be a bad joke. However, when the Louvre re-opened a week later, Parisians filed past the room where the painting had hung, like mourners at a funeral.

Emperor Mutsohito

The Battle of Tripolitania was a victory for Italy.

Istanbul, Turkey, January 23: The Young Turks overthrow the Ottoman government in a coup.

Antarctica, February 12: News of the discovery of the remains of the Scott polar expedition reaches the world. The three remaining men perished in a blizzard in March 1912.

Mexico City, Mexico, February 23: Deposed President Madero is shot dead. A coup led by General Huerta on February 9 overthrew Madero, who had come to power in a similar fashion in 1910.

Auburn, New York, USA, March 10: Harriet Tubman dies, aged 93. She led more than 300 slaves into freedom from the South on the Underground Railroad in the 1860s.

Canberra, Australia, March 12: The foundation stone for the new Australian capital is laid.

Salonika, Greece, March 18: George I is assassinated. Born a Danish prince, he was elected monarch of Greece in 1863.

Peking, China, April 8: Chinese parliament convenes for the first time.

London, England, May 30: Turkey signs a treaty with the Balkan League members, ending the eight-month war. Turkey is compelled to cede large amounts of territory in the Balkan Peninsula.

Epsom, England, June 4: Emily Davison is struck by a horse when she runs onto the Derby track to gain publicity for the suffragette cause.

Salonika, Greece, June 30: Greek and Serbian troops rout Bulgarian forces as the Second Balkan War begins, with dispute over Macedonia.

Bucharest, Romania, August 10: A peace treaty is signed by Bulgaria and the Balkan states, ending one theater of the Second Balkan War.

Michigan, USA, October 7: Henry Ford establishes an assembly line at his automobile plant. Production time for a Model T Ford is scheduled to decrease from 14 hours to two.

Panama, October 10: After a construction phase of 10 years, the link between the Pacific and Atlantic oceans is completed.

New Zealand, November: Much of the country is brought to a standstill in a major waterfront strike.

Juarez, Mexico, November 15: Rebel leader "Pancho" Villa captures Juarez, with plans to move on Mexico City and oust dictator Huerta's troops.

Natal, South Africa, November 25: Widespread rioting follows the jailing of Mohandas Ghandi.

Paris, France, December 31: The *Mona Lisa* is returned to the Louvre. It was discovered in Florence two years after Vincenzo Perugia stole it.

US Marines Storm Mexican Port City

Victoriano Huerta

Vera Cruz, Mexico, April 21: One thousand US marines today seized the Mexican Gulf port of Vera Cruz in retaliation to the detention by Mexican soldiers of a small group of US sailors in the eastern oil port of Tampico.

US and European warships had been gathering in Tampico to safeguard their nationals after General Victoriano Huerta murdered Mexico's first revolutionary president, Francisco Madero, and established a new government.

This morning, 41 battleships of the Atlantic Fleet began a bombardment of Vera Cruz, and by 11.30 a.m. US marines had begun landing operations, prompting the retreat of Mexican forces under General Gustavo Mass to avoid bloodshed.

Late this afternoon it was reported that US troops had captured and secured the central town square.

"I DON'T MIND YOUR BEING KILLED, BUT I OBJECT TO YOUR BEING TAKEN PRISONER."

LORD HORATIO KITCHENER (1850–1916), BRITISH MILITARY LEADER, TO THE PRINCE OF WALES, 1914

War Spreads in Europe

Europe, August 3–4: Germany has declared war on France, German forces have invaded Belgium, and as a result Great Britain has declared war on Germany. These events are the latest in a complicated series that were set in motion by the assassination, on June 28, 1914, of Archduke Ferdinand of Austria and his wife in the Bosnian capital Sarajevo by Gavrilo Princip of the Serbian Black Hand Gang.

In the years leading up to the archduke's murder, however, other forces had long been at work. The competition for "colonies" was becoming a source of antagonism. All the major powers were building up huge armies and navies, creating a class of professional and powerful military officers who were beginning to dominate civil authorities.

Assassination of Archduke Ferdinand and his wife.

Strong feelings of nationalism had also been feeding the fires of hatred in Europe, turning Frenchman against German and Russian against Austrian.

What is more, since the end of the Franco-Prussian War in 1871, a system of secret alliances has been developing in Europe that has virtually split the continent into two opposing camps. Because so many powers have become involved in mutual defense pacts, this war is likely to involve virtually every nation on the continent.

Austria-Hungary held Serbia responsible for Ferdinand's assassination, and Germany promised Austria-Hungary its support in any action against Serbia. Austria-Hungary declared war on Serbia on July 28. On July 30 Austria-Hungary and Russia, supporting Serbia, mobilized their armies against each other, and on August 1 Germany, allied to Austria-Hungary, declared war on Russia.

Germany then occupied Luxembourg as a preliminary to invading France. The Belgians denied Germany free passage through their territory to invade France,

time out

US President Woodrow Wilson designated the second Sunday in May the first national Mother's Day. The announcement was the result of a six-year campaign by Mrs Ana Jarvis of West Virginia, who began the movement by organizing a church memorial to her own mother.

so Germany declared war on France on August 3, and invaded Belgium on August 4. This violation of Belgium's neutrality has given Britain the reason it needs to declare war on Germany as, along with Prussia and France, Britain is committed to defending Belgium.

Germany Abandons Ypres Offensive

Ypres, Belgium, November 22: The battle of Ypres, also called the battle of Flanders, has come to a halt with the onset of winter. Meanwhile, German and Allied troops are facing each other in trenches all along on the Western Front, which stretches from the English Channel to the Alps. Ypres was taken by Germany at the beginning of the war, but by October the town had been recaptured by the British Expeditionary Forces (BEF). An attempt by German forces to re-take the town began on October 15, but the British held their positions.

With the arrival of French reinforcements and a deterioration in weather conditions, the German army today decided to abandon the Ypres offensive and their push toward the sea ports of Dunkirk and Calais.

It is estimated the offensive has cost Germany 135,000 killed or wounded, with BEF casualties amounting to 75,000.

Trenches stretch from the Alps to the English Channel.

South Africa, January 28: Following a month of intense unrest, with miners striking over poor conditions and pay, the government exiles 10 strike leaders to England.
Ulster, Ireland, February 25: The Ulster Volunteer Force, set up in opposition to Home Rule for Ireland as a whole, has over 100,000 men prepared for a civil war.
Europe, March 17: An arms race fuels fears of a war. The UK unveils a massive new navy budget, while Germany's and Russia's largest expenditure is on the military.

Vera Cruz, Mexico, April 21: US Marines seize the Gulf port in retaliation for the arrest of Marines at Tampico, as the Mexican revolution continues.
London, England, June 26: A black South African delegation visits the Colonial Secretary to protest the Native Titles Act, which gave all but 7 percent of land to whites the previous year.
Sarajevo, Bosnia, June 28: The heir to the Austrian throne, Archduke Franz Ferdinand, is assassinated by a 19 year-old Serbian nationalist.

Belgrade, Serbia, July 29: Following a month of increasing tensions, Austria-Hungary declares war on Serbia and bombs Belgrade.
Germany, August 1: In support of Austria-Hungary, Germany declares war on Russia as Russian troops mobilize to protect Serbia.
Europe, August 2: Germany invades France, Switzerland, and Luxembourg as Russia pushes into Germany, capturing Eydtkuhnen.
London, England, August 3–4: Britain declares war on Germany as German troops invade Belgium.

Togoland, Africa, August 26: Four days after Japan declares war on Germany and begins capturing German interests in the Far East, British colonial troops capture the first of Germany's colonies.
Samoa, August 29: New Zealand military administration takes over Samoa, ousting previous German administration without conflict.
East Prussia, Germany, August/September: At the battles of Tannenberg and Masurian Lakes, 225,000 Russian troops are captured as Russia's advance is halted.

France, September 8-12: German advance across Western Europe is halted 30 miles (48 km) from Paris, as Allied troops hold their ground at the Battle of the Marne.
Turkey, November 5: England, France and Russia declare war on supposedly neutral Turkey, after German ships were allowed through the Dardanelles, then bombarded Russian Black Sea ports.
Ypres, Belgium, November 22: The Battle of Ypres bogs down at the onset of winter; German and Allied troops face off in the trenches.

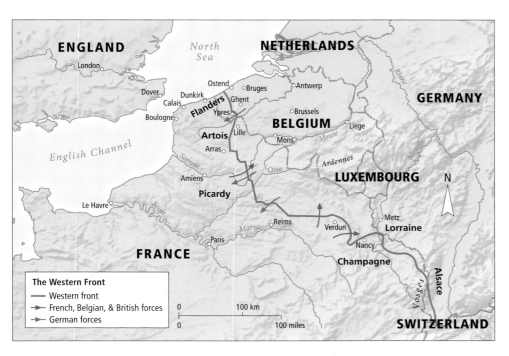

The Western Front
- Western front
- French, Belgian, & British forces
- German forces

0 — 100 km
0 — 100 miles

(Map labels: ENGLAND, London, North Sea, NETHERLANDS, GERMANY, Ostend, Bruges, Antwerp, Dover, Dunkirk, Ghent, Calais, Flanders, Ypres, Brussels, BELGIUM, Liege, Boulogne, Lille, Mons, Meuse, Artois, Arras, English Channel, Amiens, Somme, Oise, Ardennes, LUXEMBOURG, N, Picardy, Le Havre, Marne, Reims, Verdun, Metz, Lorraine, Paris, Nancy, Champagne, FRANCE, Alsace, Vosges, Rhine, Moselle, SWITZERLAND)

Field Marshall von Bulow

Lusitania Sunk by U-Boat

Atlantic Ocean, May 7: German U-boats have torpedoed and sunk the passenger liner *Lusitania* 14 miles (22 km) off the coast of southern Ireland at Old Head of Kinsale, with the loss of 1,198 lives.

Within 18 minutes of being hit, the *Lusitania,* captained by William Thomas Turner, had sunk.

Even though there were more than enough lifeboats for everyone on board, the severe listing of the ship prevented most of them from being launched.

The torpedo from *U-20* hit the starboard side of the *Lusitania*. At first many people thought that the U-boat had fired two torpedoes, but it appears the second explosion heard by many was the igniting of the vessel's coal dust. Whatever it was, it was this second explosion that caused the *Lusitania* to sink. Her 201st Atlantic crossing was to be her last.

Of the passengers who perished, 128 were American citizens. This incident pushes the United States ever closer to entering the war on the side of the Allies.

Italy Opens Second Front

Italy, May 23: After quitting the Triple Alliance with Germany and Austria earlier this month, Italy has joined the war in Europe on the side of the Allies. A second front has opened up against Austria in the disputed Trentino region, where Italian troops have headed off an offensive by Austro-Hungarian forces.

The Triple Alliance was originally formed in 1882. In 1902 Italy reached a secret agreement with France to remain neutral should either be attacked, an agreement contrary to Italy's obligations to Germany and Austria. Even though Italy later renewed the Triple Alliance twice, it finally decided to enter the war in opposition to Germany and Austria.

Allies Successfully Withdraw from Gallipoli

Gallipoli Peninsula, Turkey, December 20: Allied troops have withdrawn from Gallipoli after failing to take the Turkish positions and in the face of government indifference in London. The evacuation was carried out under the noses of the Turks with minimal losses.

It was planned as a staged withdrawal of 136,000 men, 17,000 horses, and 400 heavy guns. The operation was carefully orchestrated so that the Ottoman army would have no idea if what was happening until all Allied troops and equipment were clear of the beach and safely offshore in their transport ships.

Before the decision to withdraw, as winter had set in, the flies and sunstroke of the summer were replaced by frostbite and extreme cold. At Suvla there were over 12,000 cases of frostbite and exposure. Heavy seas made supplies hard to land, and some officers argued in favor of staying because losses during a withdrawal could be as high as 30 percent.

In the days leading up to the withdrawal, the supply of fresh meat and bread had ceased. All inward mail had stopped and the postal organization had been disbanded. Men undergoing field punishment were released and returned to their units. The supply of firewood stopped, and with it collective cooking. A casualty clearing station for 1,200 patients was established in case of heavy fighting during the final stages of re-embarkation.

Anzac Cove and Suvla Bay were evacuated over the nights of December 11–16, with selected units of the 1st and 2nd Australian Divisions, the New Zealand and Australian Division, and the Indian Mounted Brigades being the first to go. A number of strategies were designed to conceal the evacuation, including keeping campfires burning, and pre-setting rifles to fire at various intervals using devices activated by water-weights.

In the four days up to December 16, the Allied strength at Anzac was reduced from 45,000 to 20,000 men, who held the line against 170,000 Turks. By 8 p.m. on December 19, the numbers had been reduced to 5,000. By December 20, all had been successfully evacuated.

Avezzano, Italy, January 13: A massive earthquake, measuring 6.8, completely obliterates the city, leaving over 30,000 dead.

Norfolk, England, January 19: German Zeppelins bomb Great Yarmouth and King's Lynn, killing 20.

Dogger Bank, North Sea, January 24: The British navy sinks the German battleship *Blucher*.

North Sea, February 4: Germany declares blockade; U-boats attack Allied and neutral shipping. Britain retaliates with the seizure of all goods bound for Germany.

Gallipoli Peninsula, Turkey, February 19: Churchill orders a bombardment of Turkish positions in an effort to divert the Turks from Caucasian objectives. Russia is uneasy as capture of Constantinople (Istanbul) is its prerogative.

East Prussia, Germany, February 21: In the second Battle of Masurian Lakes, begun in a blizzard, Russia suffers heavy losses–over 50,000 casualties and 100,000 captured.

Ypres, Belgium, April 22: Poison gas is used by Germany in desperate trench warfare on the Western Front.

Gallipoli Peninsula, Turkey, April 25: Allied troops land at Gallipoli.

Atlantic Ocean, May 7: German U-boats torpedo the *Lusitania*.

Peking, China, May 8: President Yuan Shikai acquiesces to 21 restrictive Japanese demands that threaten Chinese sovereignty.

Italy, May 23: Italy joins the Allies, having quit the Triple Alliance.

Turkey, June: The Turkish Government murders and displaces thousands of Armenians, using the pretext of the war to carry out domestic objectives.

Warsaw, Poland, August 4: The Polish capital falls to Germany as Russian troops withdraw on the Eastern Front.

Gallipoli, Turkey, August 8: The Wellington Battalion seizes the summit of Chunuk Gair in a campaign which cost the lives of over 2,500 New Zealand soldiers.

Western Front, France, September 28: Allied troops make initial gains at Loos and Artois in the major Allied offensive of 1915, but no significant result is achieved.

Serbia, October: Germany-Austria and Bulgaria overrun Serbia. Allied forces landing at Salonika in Greece render little assistance.

London, England, November 12: First Lord of the Admiralty Winston Churchill resigns as dissent within the Asquith government grows.

Gallipoli Peninsula, Turkey, December 20: Allied troops withdraw from Gallipoli in the wake of the failure to take Turkish positions and indifference from London. The evacuation is carried out with minimal losses.

Grigory Rasputin

Huge Losses in Fierce Sea Battle

Jutland, North Sea, May 31: The battle of Jutland, already being called the largest naval battle in history in terms of the number of ships involved, has been fought between the German High Seas Fleet and the Royal Navy. The German fleet drew the British into their path and through the course of the evening more than 250 ships were engaged in a fierce battle.

Fourteen British and 11 German ships were sunk, with great loss of life. Under cover of darkness, the German ships then cut across the wake of the British fleet and returned to port. Both sides claimed victory in this battle.

Bloody Conflict Yields No Advantage

Verdun, France, July: In what has been the costliest and bloodiest engagement of the war so far, the French are finally taking the offensive at Verdun. Germany has been obliged to divert troops away from this area to the offensive at the river Somme, where the Allies began an advance on German forces on July 1. Hundreds of thousands of casualties on both sides have been suffered for little or no territorial advantage.

In February, Germany switched its war effort from the Eastern to the Western Front, massing artillery to the north and east of the medieval town of Verdun. The town had been a Gallic fortress before Roman times, and more recently was a key asset in the French wars against Prussia. It is the northernmost town in a long, continuous line of sunken fortifications beginning at the Swiss border, a line the French hoped would prevent

A German U-boat attacks a merchant ship; U-boats are causing great damage at sea.

any German advance. Germany's General Erich von Falkenhayn knew that the French would throw thousands of troops into the defense of this line.

Von Falkenhayn started his bombardment of the town on the morning of February 25. In the early months of the battle, the German forces succeeded in capturing several French forts, including Fort Douaumont in February and Fort Malancourt in March. Throughout the months of March and April the hills and ridges to the north of Verdun changed hands several times. The area was always under heavy bombardment and casualty rates were appallingly high on both sides. The Verdun battlefield has the highest density of dead per square yard of any battlefield so far in this war.

German forces also took the French forts of Thiaumont and Vaux last month, and on June 23 almost reached Belleville heights, the last stronghold before Verdun itself. The French General Henri Pétain was preparing to evacuate the east bank

of the Meuse River when pressure on French forces was diminished as German troops were moved to the Somme region.

"Mad Monk" Rasputin Murdered

Petrograd, Russia, December 30: Grigory Rasputin, the self-styled Russian mystic, has been murdered by nobles eager to end his influence over the Russian royal family.

Born in 1872 in Pokrovskye, a small village in Siberia, he became a hermit and a holy man, endearing himself to the Russian Orthodox Church and to peasants with his charisma and reputed ability to heal the sick. Introduced to the royal family in 1905 he impressed both Tsar Nicholas II and Tsarina Alexandra, especially when he healed their hemophiliac son. By 1911 he had been appointed the tsar's chief advisor, against the advice of the tsar's court officials, who were particularly critical of Rasputin's very public lechery and drunkenness.

Worried that Rasputin was unduly influencing Alexandra and in turn affecting affairs of state, Prince Feliks Yusupov (husband of the tsar's niece), Vladimir Purishkevich (a member of the Duma, the lower house of parliament) and the Grand Duke Pavlovich (the tsar's cousin) invited Rasputin to the Yusupov's palace today for dinner and the chance to meet the tsar's beautiful niece.

When poisoned wine and tea cakes failed to kill Rasputin, he was shot and his body thrown into the Neva River.

time out

Dutch count Ferdinand von Zeppelin, aviation pioneer, died at the age of 78. He was reportedly disappointed at the failure of his airships to end the war quickly and that his name would be linked to the first air raids on civilian targets.

"WHAT SHOULD I DO? I THINK THE BEST THING IS TO ORDER A NEW STAMP TO BE MADE WITH MY FACE ON IT."

CHARLES OF AUSTRIA (1887–1922), EMPEROR OF AUSTRIA AND KING OF HUNGARY, ON HIS ACCESSION TO THE AUSTRIAN THRONE, 1916

"THIS WAR, LIKE THE NEXT WAR, IS THE WAR TO END WAR."

DAVID LLOYD GEORGE (1863–1945), BRITISH STATESMAN AND PRIME MINISTER, ON THE VIEW THAT WORLD WAR I WOULD BE THE LAST MAJOR WAR, 1916

London, England, January 6: Compulsory military service is introduced as voluntary conscripts are falling short of the number of men required on the frontline.
Netherlands, January 14: Extensive flooding, caused by a storm surge, leads to reappraisal of plans to reclaim the Zuyderzee.
Verdun, France, February 21: Germany switches its focus from the Eastern to the Western Front, launching into battle at Verdun. One million German troops are pitted against 200,000 French defenders.

Haiti, February 28: Following the murder of President Guilliaume Sam and the subsequent occupation by US Marines, Haiti becomes a US protectorate.
Guerrero, Mexico, March 31: US troops attack Pancho Villa's rebels.
Maungapohatu, New Zealand, April 2: The violent arrest of Maori leader Rua Kenana confirms the end of no-go areas for law enforcement.
Kut-al-Amara, Persia, April 29: After a siege lasting 196 days, 8,000 sick and emaciated Anglo-Indian troops surrender to Turkish forces.

Dublin, Ireland, May 1: The Easter Uprising of republicans is put down by British forces. An Irish Republic is declared.
North Sea, May 31: The Battle of Jutland is fought between Germany's High Seas Fleet and the Royal Navy. Both sides suffer great losses, but the British have a strategic victory as their dominance of the North Sea is assured.
Hejaz, Arabia, June 5: Grand sheriff of Mecca, Hussein, leads an Arab revolt against the Turkish with the assistance of the British.

The Somme, France, July 1: Over 58,000 British casualties are sustained, one-third fatalities, in the first day of the new Western Front offensive.
London, England, July 7: Lloyd George becomes Secretary of State for War one month after Lord Kitchener's death aboard HMS Hampshire, exploded by a mine.
Berlin, Germany, August 27: General von Falkenhayn is replaced by Field Marshall von Hindenburg as Chief of Staff.
Transylvania, August 27: Romania enters the war on the side of the Allies.

Philippines, August 29: The USA announces its intention to withdraw sovereignty from the Philippines.
Ontario, Canada, September 1: The city of Berlin changes its name to Kitchener due to anti-German sentiment.
Vienna, Austria, November 21: After a 68-year reign, Austrian Emperor Franz Josef dies, aged 86.
London, England, December 7: David Lloyd George replaces Herbert Asquith as Prime Minister.
Petrograd, Russia, December 30: "Mad monk" Rasputin is murdered.

USA Declares War on Germany

Washington DC, USA, April 6: President Woodrow Wilson has today reluctantly brought the United States into the war against Germany in order to make the world "safe for democracy."

Isolationist feelings have dwindled in the face of persistent attacks by German submarines on US merchant ships trading with Great Britain. Isolationism also took another blow when the contents of a note from the Germany foreign minister Dr Arthur Zimmerman to his ambassador in Mexico were revealed.

The note stated that Germany would re-commence unrestricted submarine warfare, and that an alliance between Germany and Mexico would be proposed if America entered the war. If Mexico agreed, its land in New Mexico, Texas, and Arizona that had been lost to the United States would somehow be returned. The ambassador was also asked to approach the Mexican president to propose an alliance with Japan, then on the Allied side. These alliances would have created a new Pacific and Central American front, intended to shift US focus away from Europe.

The release of the details of the telegram ignited a public furor in the United States, pushing the country closer to war. In fact it was British Intelligence that first intercepted the "Zimmerman Note," as it has come to be known, and then leaked it to the United States, no doubt in the hope that it would bring America into the war and alleviate the pressure on Great Britain and her allies.

President Wilson realized war was inevitable but agonized over what it might do to the spirit of the nation. "Once lead these people into war," he said, "and they'll forget there ever was such a thing as tolerance…the spirit of ruthless brutality will enter into the very fiber of our national life."

The battles of Ypres were fought under the most difficult conditions.

AEF Lands on French Soil

France, June 27: US soldiers, under the command of General Pershing, have landed in France to a rapturous reception from the beleaguered populace.

The men of the American Expeditionary Force (AEF) are viewed as saviors by many at a time when 837,000 tons (853,740 tonnes) of shipping in the Atlantic has been sunk by German U-boats. This also follows the failure of the French Nivelle offensive, which saw widespread mutinies in the French army.

The German spring offensive convinced Pershing that the intervention of the AEF was required immediately. In June it was agreed that US troops would go to France without space-occupying equipment, which would be provided by Britain (mortars) and France (heavy guns) once they arrived.

In June and July more than 584,000 American troops were dispatched.

Guns Fall Silent at Ypres

Passchendaele, Belgium, November 6: Sir Douglas Haig has called off the third battle of Ypres as Canadian and British forces captured Passchendaele village after three months of fighting in the mud. It is now estimated that upward of 300,000 British troops have died in Haig's remorseless offensive, which has already been the subject of bitter controversy.

General John Pershing

The British objective was to break through to the Flemish coast and capture the German naval bases at Zeebrugge and Ostend.

On July 18 the initial bombardment saw over four million shells fired at the German lines, smashing them into oblivion but also destroying the drainage system in this low-lying area. Incessant rain also began that same day, filling the craters and failing to drain away. This turned the local landscape into a sea of mud.

The offensive continued through August and September, with Haig insisting on capturing the village of Passchendaele, which is set on a low ridge between Ypres and Roulers. Throughout October he fed his men into a virtual meat-grinder—craters filled with fetid mud and slime were taken, lost and recaptured. Disinterred bodies were strewn everywhere.

Passchendaele was captured today. The battle is over, and it is hoped the effect on German public opinion will be such as to end this war before another Ypres is deemed necessary.

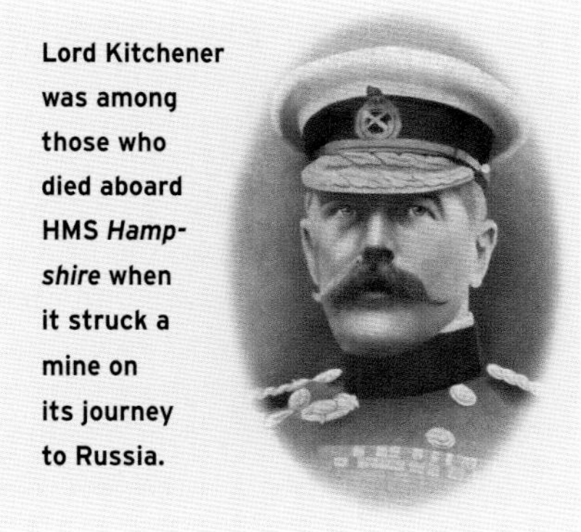

Lord Kitchener was among those who died aboard HMS *Hampshire* when it struck a mine on its journey to Russia.

Key Events

USA, February 3: The USA severs diplomatic ties with Germany in response to Germany's resumption of unrestricted submarine warfare.
Mexico, February 5: A new constitution is adopted, the most progressive socialist constitution in the world to date. It provides for universal suffrage, separation of church and state, and a bill of rights.
Puerto Rico, March 2: Puerto Rico becomes a US protectorate, with all citizens awarded American citizenship.
Russia, March 16: A provisional government is formed as months of turmoil force Nicholas II to abdicate.
Victoria, Canada, April 5: Women in British Columbia win provincial voting rights. The Prairie Provinces were granted similar rights last year.
Washington DC, USA, April 6: The USA declares war against Germany. The discovery of the "Zimmerman Note," outlining German designs on the Americas, was a deciding factor.
Petrograd, Russia, April 10: Vladimir Ilyich Lenin arrives in Russia after 11 years in exile.
France, April 20: The Nivelle Offensive, including the second Battle of Aisne and third Battle of Champagne, is unsuccessful. Germany inflicts massive losses on the infantry, resulting in widespread disillusionment in the French troops.
Athens, Greece, June 12: Pro-German King Constantine abdicates under pressure from the Allies.
France, June 27: US soldiers, under the command of General Pershing, land in France to a rapturous reception from the beleaguered populace.
Moscow, Russia, July 20: Aleksandr Kerensky, Minister of War, assumes the leadership of the provisional government after a failed Eastern Front offensive and an attempt to seize power by the Bolsheviks.
Corfu, Greece, July 20: Croatian, Montenegrin, Serbian, and Slovenian politicians sign the Corfu Declaration, providing for the establishment of a new nation, Yugoslavia, at the end of the war.
Verdun, France, August 20: The Allies gain several key positions at the second Battle of Verdun.
Vincennes, France, October 15: Dutch exotic dancer Mata Hari is executed by the French for spying.
Passchendaele, Belgium, November 6: Sir Douglas Haig calls off the third Battle of Ypres as Allied forces capture Passchendaele.
Petrograd, Russia, November 7: Lenin's Bolsheviks revolt, seizing power in the year's second coup.
Jerusalem, Palestine, December 9: British troops capture Jerusalem from the Turks. Britain announced its support of a Zionist homeland with the Balfour Declaration.

"Red Baron" Killed in Combat

Vaux-sur-Somme, France, April 21: The elusive German flying ace credited with more than 80 kills, known as the "Red Baron," has himself been shot down and killed today in a barrage of ground fire. The Australian troops who controlled the area immediately recovered the plane and identified the body as that of Manfred von Richthofen. Various people have claimed responsibility for shooting down the "Red Baron", but it is uncertain just who is responsible.

Since becoming a fighter pilot in September 1916, Richthofen had been in command of a fighter group whose red, fancifully decorated planes earned the group the nickname of "Richthofen's Flying Circus."

**Baron Manfred
von Richthofen**

"MY CENTER IS GIVING WAY, MY RIGHT IS IN RETREAT; SITUATION EXCELLENT. I SHALL ATTACK."

FERDINAND FOCH (1851–1929), FRENCH MILITARY COMMANDER, ON THE SECOND BATTLE OF THE MARNE, 1918

"COME ON, YOU SONS OF BITCHES! DO YOU WANT TO LIVE FOR EVER?"

DAN DALY (D. 1937), SERGEANT IN THE US MARINES, RALLYING HIS MEN AT BELLEAU WOOD, JUNE 1918

Millions Dead in Flu Pandemic

Worldwide, September: In the spring of this year large numbers of soldiers fighting in the trenches in France became ill. Their symptoms included sore throat, loss of appetite, and headaches. Despite the disease being highly infectious, those who were affected recovered quickly. Doctors referred to the unknown illness as "the three-day fever."

By the summer, symptoms had become much more severe, with a fifth of the victims developing bronchial pneumonia or septicemic blood poisoning. Many of them died. This second wave of epidemic spread quickly. By the end of summer it had reached the German army, and then spread to German civilians, 400,000 of whom have since died of the disease.

The origins of the illness are uncertain, although it is thought to have come from China in a rare genetic shift of the influenza virus. It is also likely that the mass movement of soldiers around the globe at the close of the Great War has helped spread the virus.

The illness develops very quickly, turning into a form of pneumonia that can kill within hours of the first symptoms appearing. Extreme chills and fatigue are accompanied by a build-up of fluid in the lungs. One doctor remarked of his patients, "Their faces wear a bluish cast. A cough brings up the blood-stained sputum. In the morning the bodies are stacked around the morgue like cordwood."

As the lungs of the stricken continue to fill with fluid, their faces turn brown or purple, and their feet go black. The lucky ones simply drown in their own lung fluid. The unlucky ones develop bacterial pneumonia as an agonizing secondary infection.

Outbreaks of the epidemic have swept through every continent of the world, with the highest mortality rate in India—a staggering 50 per 1,000 cases. Half of all US military casualties in Europe are dying from influenza, and not in combat.

This current outbreak is seeing up to 10,000 deaths per week in large US cities with possibly as much as 50 percent of the population being infected. Morgues have been overwhelmed, with the dead buried in simple pine boxes. Spitting in the street has been declared a crime in the United States. Corpses are everywhere. In Philadelphia they were piled three deep in the streets and rotting in the open air. In Alaska many have been buried in mass graves under the tundra.

time out

The Eighteenth Amendment to the US Constitution prohibited the sale, manufacture, or transportation of liquor, formalizing "prohibition." Mississippi was the first state to ratify the amendment, though 26 of 48 states already had legal prohibition in place.

In Britain some factories have changed their "no smoking" rules, in the belief that smoke can hinder the spread of the virus. Others maintain that eating porridge can give you immunity.

The good news, if there is any, is that the virus peaks within two to three weeks of showing up in any given city, then disappears as quickly as it comes.

Influenza is an ancient disease, first described by the ancient Greek physician Hippocrates in 412 BCE. In 1580 a disease originating from Asia and thought to be influenza spread through Europe, Africa, and the Americas along the trade routes.

Armistice Signed– Great War Is Over

Rethondes, France, November 11: The "War to End All Wars" is finally over. It came to an end at 11.01 a.m. today, after an armistice was formally signed at 5 a.m. by Allied Supreme Commander Ferdinand Foch and German politician Matthias Erzberger on behalf of Germany in Foch's railway carriage on the Western Front.

On November 8, a German delegation had met with Foch in the forest of Compiegne, 50 miles (80 km) northeast of Paris, to finalize arrangements for the surrender of all German armed forces.

French, British, and German representatives sign Armistice.

Key Events

Washington DC, USA, January 8: President Wilson presents his 14-point plan for a post-war settlement. Disarmament, reparations, and a League of Nations are key facets.
Finland, January 28: Following its declaration of independence, Finland descends into a bloody civil war between the socialist Reds, who control the south, and the Whites, supported by the new senate.
Brest-Litovsk, Belarus, March 3: Hostilities on the Eastern Front cease with the signing of the Treaty of Brest-Litovsk.

Moscow, Russia, March 7: The Bolsheviks are renamed the Russian Communist Party. Moscow becomes the permanent seat of power.
Western Front, March 31: A new German offensive gains 40 miles (64 km) of territory in 10 days, the most dramatic advance on this front.
New Zealand, April 10: National prohibition is avoided due to strong opposition from servicemen abroad.
The Somme, France, April 21: German flying ace, Baron von Richthofen, "The Red Baron," is shot down and killed, aged 26.

Ireland, May 17: Eamon de Valera, leader of Sinn Féin, and 500 nationalists are imprisoned on grounds of colluding with Germany.
Canada, May 24: All female citizens of Canada over the age of 21 are allowed to vote in federal elections.
Russia, May: Peace is short lived, as the Czechoslovak Corps, followed by the White Russians, rebel against the Red Guard, launching civil war.
Ekaterinburg, Russia, July 16: The Romanov dynasty is eliminated with the execution of Tsar Nicholas and his family by Bolsheviks.

Amiens, France, August 8: In a black day for Germany, Allied forces push German troops back to the Hindenburg Line. Both sides sustain heavy losses.
Europe, September: The Central powers are on the back foot, with the Hindenburg Line breached, the British offensive in Palestine taking its toll and Bulgaria's surrender.
Western Front, October 4: Successful military campaigns at Ypres and Argonne by the Allies force the German government to begin negotiations for an armistice.

Worldwide, October: The "Spanish Flu" virus is spreading rapidly, killing more people worldwide than the war.
Vienna, Austria, October 31: Revolution breaks out in Austria and Hungary after Emperor proclaims reorganization of the monarchy. The Habsburg dynasty comes to an end.
Worldwide, November 11: The Great War comes to an end at 11:01 a.m. as Germany surrenders.
Iceland, December 1: Iceland proclaims independence from, but retains ties with, Denmark.

Lloyd George (UK), Vittorio Orlando (Italy), Georges Clemenceau (France), and Woodrow Wilson (US) at the Paris Peace Conference.

International Peace Organization Established

Paris, France, February 14: At the Paris Peace Conference, 27 nations voted for the establishment of the League of Nations, which will act as an international peacekeeper and mediator. Its goals are to include disarmament, preventing wars through collective security, settling disputes through negotiation and diplomacy, and improving global welfare.

The organization was proposed directly by President Woodrow Wilson of the United States who, in his "Fourteen Points" address of January 8, 1918, stated, "A general association of nations must be formed under specific covenants for the purpose of affording mutual guarantees of political independence and territorial integrity to great and small states alike."

The principal executive organs of the league are to be the assembly and the council. Each state will have one vote, all decisions must be unanimous, and at least one session is to be held each year. The League of Nations has no armed forces at its disposal, instead relying on boycotts and sanctions to control or influence member states.

The Paris Peace Conference was attended by the leaders of 32 nations, representing 75 percent of the world's population. Before the League of Nations was formed, the only means of facilitating discussion between nations was the congress system; European nations would hold occasional summit meetings to discuss issues they felt to be pressing.

At the end of the Great War, the major powers would have preferred to have gone no further than strengthening the congress system. However, in the aftermath of war the prevailing spirit of the times, personified by the crusading Woodrow Wilson, made inevitable the creation of a global organization where even the smallest nation would have a voice.

The League of Nations is to have its base in Geneva, Switzerland, a nation that has long held a policy of strict neutrality, and where the International Red Cross already has its headquarters.

German Fleet Scuttled: 51 Sunk

Orkney Islands, Scotland, June: Today the entire German Fleet, interned at Scapa Flow at the end of the war, has been scuttled. Scapa Flow is a stretch of water that lies, atoll-like, within the Orkney Islands to the north of Scotland. It forms one of the largest harbors in the world and has been a haven for shipping for over a thousand years.

The German naval commander Admiral von Reuter became involved in a misunderstanding about the progress of peace talks, apparently coming to the belief that the war was about to resume. To stop the fleet falling into British hands, he waited until the British fleet left on exercises and then ordered some 74 battleships and other warships to be scuttled, 51 of them sinking. The ships cocks were opened and the mechanisms for closing them were disconnected and damaged. They began slowly and quietly to take on water until they sank.

Nine sailors were killed during the scuttling, as fights with British sailors broke out when they realized what was happening. These were the last recorded deaths of the Great War.

First Woman Elected to House of Commons

London, England, November 28: US-born Lady Astor was the first woman to become a member of Parliament after winning the seat of Plymouth for the Conservative party.

She was born Nancy Langhorne in Danville, Virginia, on May 19, 1879, of a well-to-do family, her father having made

Emiliano Zapata

MP Lady Astor, with her six children.

a fortune in railway development. In 1904 she moved to England and married the immensely wealthy Waldorf Astor. Astor was a member of the Conservative party and represented the Sutton division of Plymouth. When his father passed away, he became a member of the House of Lords, enabling his wife Nancy to become the party's candidate for the House of Commons in the following by-election.

Berlin, Germany, January 15: Communist Spartacists revolt against the government; the army quells the insurrection, killing hundreds. Spartacist leaders Karl Liebknecht and Rosa Luxemburg are murdered while in custody.
Dublin, Ireland, January 21: The first unofficial Dáil Éireann (Irish parliament) is convened. Sinn Féin MPs refuse to attend Westminster.
Weimar, Germany, February 6: The first session of the new German parliament is held, electing Friedrich Ebert president of the new republic.

Paris, France, February 14: At the Paris Peace Conference, 27 nations vote for the establishment of a League of Nations. The brainchild of US President Wilson, the league is to be formed as an international peacekeeper and mediator.
Moscow, Russia, March 4: Lenin convenes The Third International, with the goal of international communist revolution.
Chinameca, Mexico, April 10: Rebel leader Emiliano Zapata is killed in an ambush set up as a meeting.

Amritsar, India, April 13: At the Jallianwala Bagh, British troops open fire on a peaceful gathering, killing at least 379 and injuring thousands.
Korea, April: Occupied by Japan since 1910, rioting and open rebellion breaks out. Japan agrees to install a civil government and introduce self-rule in an effort to quash the unrest.
Kelut, Java, Dutch East Indies, May 19: A massive volcanic eruption claims up to 16,000 lives.

Scapa Flow, Orkney Islands, Scotland, June 21: Interned at the end of the war, 51 German ships are scuttled to prevent them falling into the possession of the Allies.
Versailles, France, June 28: Germany signs the Treaty of Versailles, officially ending the war. German officials are resentful at the terms of the treaty and the manner in which they are treated.
Budapest, Hungary, August 4: Romanian troops enter the Hungarian capital, ending the short rule of Bela Kun's communist party.

Rawalpindi, India, August 8: The end of the third Anglo-Afghan War is negotiated. The war was sparked by Afghan nationalist Amanullah Khan's attack on British forces.
South Africa, August 31: General Jan Smuts becomes prime minister after the death of Louis Botha.
London, England, November 28: US-born Lady Astor becomes the first woman in parliament.
Russia, November: The advantage has been gained by Trotsky's Red Army in the Russian Civil War; the White Army now seems worn out.

Marie Curie

Neon Light Makes Its Debut

Paris, France, December 11, 1910: Professor Georges Claude, French engineer, inventor, and chemist, displayed the first neon lamp to the French public at the Grand Palais in Paris today.

In 1898 in England William Ramsey and M. W. Travers discovered neon gas, thus accelerating the development of gas-charged tubing. At the same time Professor Claude in France was working on a method of isolating oxygen for medical and welding applications. In 1902 he applied an electrical discharge to a sealed tube containing neon gas. When the electric current passed through the inert gas, it caused the gas to glow very brightly. The glow is visible even in daylight, which means that the neon lamp has tremendous potential for outdoor advertising.

Georges Claude's neon lamp is demonstrated at the Grand Palais, Paris.

Lost City of the Incas Discovered

Machu Picchu, Peru, July 24, 1911: A Yale University expedition in the Peruvian Andes led by American archeologist Professor Hiram Bingham has rediscovered the lost Inca city of Machu Picchu.

The original objective of the expedition had been to locate the legendary last refuge of the Incas from the Spanish, Vilcabamba. Instead, a chance meeting in the Urubamba River canyon with peasant farmer Melchor Arteaga led the team to Machu Picchu. Arteaga guided Bingham and his team along the Urubamba River and up to the summit of a mountain where a city had lain undisturbed for approximately 400 years.

The group approached the ruins through a network of extensive terraces, and found themselves entangled in thick forest that hid superb constructions from a bygone age, built without mortar with granite blocks cut with bronze or stone tools. The joints were so tight that not even a knife blade could penetrate them. Sculptures were carved into rock, water flowed through cisterns and stone channels, and temples clung onto steep precipices. Bingham knew he had stumbled across an awesome find.

Machu Picchu is situated 43 miles (69 km) northwest of the Peruvian city of Cuzco, on a ridge that obscures it from the Urubamba gorge below. It lies between the immense Huaynac Picchu and an adjacent highland.

Machu Picchu was forgotten by the time the Spanish arrived in 1532. Around 1527 about 50 percent of the Inca population in the area had died of smallpox and the Inca Empire had disintegrated into civil war. Machu Picchu was probably abandoned by the Incas at this time.

Most likely a royal estate and religious retreat, it was built between 1460 and 1470 CE and is at an altitude of 8,000 ft (2,439 m), high above the Urubamba

The name Machu Picchu means, simply, "Old Peak."

canyon cloud forest, or rainforest. Its 200 buildings include storage structures, temples, public edifices, and residences, and would have supported a population of some 1,200 people, mostly women, children, and priests.

Like most Inca sites, it would have been constantly undergoing construction and would have had a resident population of builders, attendants, and planters. The houses were in groups of 10, each group built either around a communal courtyard, or aligned on narrow terraces and connected by alleyways. Potatoes and maize were grown there, using complex terracing and irrigation to reduce erosion and increase the area under cultivation.

An astonished Bingham is believed to have written in his diary, "Would anyone believe what I have found?"

Marie Curie Wins Second Nobel Prize

Stockholm, Sweden, December 10, 1911: Physicist Marie Curie has been awarded the Nobel Prize for Chemistry for her work on radiation. Unprecedented in the history of the prize, this is the second time she has received the award. In 1903

Bouy, France, January 8, 1910: Hubert Latham sets a new altitude record of 3,300 feet (1 km) in his monoplane. Fellow aviator, Leon Delagrange, died in a flying accident four days ago.

New York, USA, February 27, 1910: In a world first, an X-ray machine is used to guide doctors in removing a nail from a child's lung.

Paris, France, December, 1910: In an attempt to develop an inexpensive method by which to produce pure oxygen, Georges Claude invents the neon light.

New York, USA, 1911: Thomas Hunt Morgan, studying the cross-breeding of fruit flies, proves that genes are carried on chromosomes.

Dayton, USA, July 1, 1911: Charles Kettering invents the self-starter for automobiles, eliminating the need to crank start the engine.

Stockholm, Sweden, December 10, 1911: Marie Curie is the recipient of an unprecedented second Nobel Prize in Chemistry for her work on radium. Despite this honor, the Académie des Sciences refuses to admit her, as she is a woman.

Kent, England, February 10, 1912: Surgeon Joseph Lister, inventor of antiseptic surgery, dies, aged 85.

St Louis, USA, March 1, 1912: Albert Berry makes the first successful parachute jump from a moving aircraft.

New York, USA, September, 1912: Carl Jung delivers the lectures that shall form the basis of his *Theory of Psychoanalysis*.

Russia, December, 1912: Polish biochemist Casimir Funk coins the term "vitamine" following his isolation of vitamin B1.

Sheffield, England, August 13, 1913: Harry Bradley invents stainless steel while trying to develop a steel that is resistant to erosion, not corrosion.

English Channel, September 29, 1913: Inventor of the diesel engine, Rudolf Diesel, disappears on an overnight passage from Antwerp to Harwich.

Cambridge, England, December, 1913: The third volume of Russell and Whitehead's *Principia Mathematica* is published. Its defense of logicism is greatly influential.

Munsterlingen, Switzerland, February 13, 1914: French criminologist, Alphonse Bertillon, inventor of scientific identification of criminals, dies, aged 61.

London, England, December, 1914: Ernest Rutherford, 1908 recipient of the Nobel Prize for Chemistry for his work on the atom, is knighted. His current work is on detection of submarines by radio monitoring.

Strasbourg, Germany, December, 1914: Seismologist Beno Guttenberg discovers the discontinuity between the earth's mantle and the core.

she and her husband Pierre were awarded the Nobel Prize for Physics for the discovery of spontaneous radioactivity.

Born Maria Skiodowski in Warsaw, Poland, in 1867, she moved to Paris in her teens to live with her sister, who invited her to study at the Sorbonne. Changing her name to Marie, she studied physics and mathematics, receiving a master's degree in both subjects.

After graduating she met her husband, Pierre Curie. They began work together, comparing the radioactivity of uranium ores with that of metallic uranium. They observed that ores were more radioactive than might be expected from their uranium content. Marie Curie began to look for substances other than uranium that would account for this increased radioactivity, and discovered radium, a compound that is two million times more radioactive than uranium.

Lister, Inventor of Antiseptics, Passes On

Kent, England, February 10, 1912: The noted surgeon Sir Joseph Lister, responsible for introducing antiseptic procedures that have saved thousands of lives following surgery, has died, aged 85.

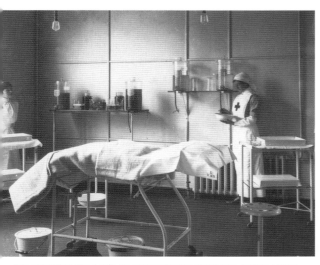

The operating theater is cleaner and safer, thanks to Joseph Lister.

Born in Essex in 1827, Lister studied at the University College in London before moving to Scotland, where he then spent most of his life.

After reading a paper by Louis Pasteur about the "germ theory" of disease, he reasoned that disease was caused by microbes, and that the best way to combat it was to kill the microbes before they reached the open wound. He wrote of his experiments with carbolic acid: "The material which I have employed is carbolic or phenic acid, which appears to exercise a peculiar destructive influence upon low forms of life."

His emphasis on a clean environment was in marked contrast to the practices of the times. Doctors were held in such low regard that they were often expected to use the servant's door when entering a house. Surgeons operated without facial masks or gloves. Rarely would a doctor wash his hands before operating, often arriving at his next appointment in street clothes or even in a smock that still bore dried blood from a previous operation. Often a doctor would begin his day with an autopsy, and then proceed to operate on the living. Nearly half of all surgical patients died.

In his hospital routines, Lister always washed his hands before operating, and cleaned instruments and dressings. As a result postoperative fatalities were significantly reduced. He was also a pioneer in the establishment of early theories of antiseptic surgery as well as in the introduction of the drainage tube and improved types of ligatures.

Eventually he realized the most effective approach to controlling infection was a

combination of "antisepsis"—killing infective agents inside the wound, and "asepsis"—preventing infectious bacteria from getting into the wound.

Criminology Pioneer Is Dead

Münsterlingen, Switzerland, February 13, 1914: French criminologist and anthropologist Alphonse Bertillon died today. The inventor of the first scientific method of identifying criminals, he has inspired a greater confidence in the police's ability to bring criminals to justice.

Born in Paris in 1853, he went to work as a records clerk in the police department. His obsessive love of order led him to reject the imperfect methods then used to identify suspects, and in 1882 he developed his own system. Bertillon identified a person by head and body measurements, as well as by individual markings such as tattoos, scars, and birthmarks, and by individual psychological characteristics. At that time it was easy for criminals to give a false name and thus divorce themselves from their criminal past. The only way suspected wrongdoers were identified was by eyewitness accounts, which are notoriously unreliable.

In 1883 the Paris police adopted Bertillon's system, called "bertillonage." The measurements were put on a card that also included photographic front and side views of the offender. This method quickly identified many offenders, and it was soon adopted by the police forces of Great Britain, Europe, and the Americas.

The system eventually fell into disrepute because the data collected were not constant. Officers would measure people differently, and measurements also changed as a criminal aged. Eventually police forces began to abandon bertillonage in favor of fingerprint identification.

Joseph Lister

time out

The American Garrett Morgan used his invention, the gas mask, to rescue two men trapped in a tunnel full of natural gas. The incident was widely reported and he received orders from police, firemen, and military all over the world.

Key Events

Berlin, Germany, November 25, 1915: Einstein's General Theory of Relativity is published.

Germany, December 18, 1915: Engineer Hugo Junkers designs the world's first all metal aircraft. Also in Germany, meteorologist Alfred Wegner publishes his controversial theory of continental drift and the super-continent of Pangaea in *The Origins of Continents and Oceans*.

France, December, 1915: This year physicist Paul Langevin invents the first active sonar-type device for detecting submarines.

The Somme, France, September 15, 1916: Tanks are introduced into action for the first time as the British attempt to gain the upper hand in this protracted battle.

London, England, November 24, 1916: Sir Hiram Maxim, inventor of the fully automatic machine gun in 1884, dies, aged 76.

USA, December, 1916: Frederick Kolster develops the radio direction finder, allowing ships to take bearings out of sight of land. The US Navy realized the importance of this and continued work on it.

Berlin, Germany, September, 1917: Einstein adds a cosmological constant to the General Theory of Relativity, in order to describe a universe that conforms to theoretical expectations.

Australia, October 17, 1917: The trans-Australian railway is complete with one straight stretch of track reaching almost 300 miles (478 km).

Switzerland and Austria-Hungary, December, 1917: This year Sigmund Freud releases *Introductory Lectures in Psychoanalysis* and Carl Jung, *The Psychology of the Unconscious*.

Paris, France, March 21, 1918: Paris is bombarded from a distance of 81 miles (131 km) by Germany's massive Paris Gun, the shells of which are capable of reaching Earth's stratosphere.

Stockholm, Sweden, June 1, 1918: German physicist Max Planck is awarded the Nobel Prize in Physics for his work on the establishment of the theory of elementary quanta.

New York, USA, December, 1918: The first three-color traffic lights are installed in New York. Two-color lights had been used since 1914.

Manchester, England, January 3, 1919: Ernest Rutherford successfully splits an atom.

London, England, February 9, 1919: The first commercial flight between London and Paris is completed in 3 hours 30 minutes.

Principe, Gulf of Guinea, West Africa, May 29, 1919: Arthur Eddington photographs changes in the stars' positioning that confirm Einstein's theory of relativity.

Ireland, June 14-15, 1919: Alcock and Whitten Brown are first to fly non-stop across the Atlantic.

Theory of "Continental Drift" Ridiculed

Germany, December, 1915: In a work entitled *The Origin of Continents and Oceans*, the German physicist and meteorologist Alfred Wegner has advanced the astounding theory that the continents originated from a single supercontinent and later drifted apart. According to Wegner the supercontinent, which he calls Pangaea (Greek for "all the Earth"), broke up long ago. Ever since then, its pieces—the continents—have been moving imperceptibly across Earth's surface until they reached their present positions.

In 1911 Wegner was browsing through literature in the University of Marburg's library when he found a scientific paper listing fossils of identical plants and animals found on opposite sides of the Atlantic. While orthodox science explained this by saying that land bridges once connected the continents but had been eroded, Wegner instead began to look closely at the geological features of opposing coastlines and realized how perfectly they seemed to fit together. He found that the Appalachian mountains of North America were an uncanny match with the Scottish Highlands, and that the rock strata of the Karroo system of South Africa was identical to the Santa Catarina system in Brazil, and so on.

Sir Hiram Maxim

"I LIKE MATHEMATICS BECAUSE IT IS NOT HUMAN AND HAS NOTHING PARTICULAR TO DO WITH THIS PLANET OR WITH THE WHOLE ACCIDENTAL UNIVERSE—BECAUSE, LIKE SPINOZA'S GOD, IT WON'T LOVE US IN RETURN."

BERTRAND RUSSELL (1872–1970), BRITISH PHILOSOPHER AND MATHEMATICIAN, 1912

"MY PACIFISM IS NOT BASED ON ANY INTELLECTUAL THEORY BUT ON A DEEP ANTIPATHY TO EVERY FORM OF CRUELTY AND HATRED."

ALBERT EINSTEIN (1879–1955), GERMAN PHYSICIST AND NOBEL PRIZE WINNER, ON THE OUTBREAK OF WORLD WAR I, 1914

Scientific Achievements

Astronomy: Stars near the sun photographed during an eclipse.
Botany: Chlorophyll and other plant pigments researched.
Chemistry: Rutherford artificially splits an atom of nitrogen.
Ecology: National Park Service established in USA.
Geology: Radioactivity used to date rocks.
Mathematics: Third volume of *Principia Mathematica* published.
Medicine: Jung proposed the personality types "introvert" and "extrovert."
Physics: Einstein presents his general theory of relativity.
Zoology: New kinds of birds and mammals discovered in northwest America.

Botanic Gardens
Pyin U Lwin, Burma
Cape Town, South Africa

Observatories
Canberra, Australia
Cleveland, USA
Poznan, Poland

Universities
University of Lima, Peru
University of Manila, Philippines
University of Reykjavik, Iceland
University of Tallinn, Estonia
University of Vancouver, Canada

Reaction to Wegner's theory has been hostile and scathing. Opponents wonder how the continents can plow through miles of thick oceanic crust, and Wegner himself acknowledges that at this stage he cannot explain their movement by any known mechanism.

Freud and Jung Publish Landmark Papers

Switzerland and Austria-Hungary, December, 1917: This year two very different studies of the unconscious have been published—Austrian neurologist Sigmund Freud's *Introductory Lectures in Psychoanalysis* and eminent Swiss psychologist Carl Jung's *The Psychology of the Unconscious.*

Freud was born in 1856, moving to Vienna when he was four years old. In 1873 he entered the University of Vienna Medical School but he hoped to go into neurophysiological research—the idea of becoming a doctor was repugnant to him. Eventually he went into private practice specializing in neurology.

Jung was born in Kesswil, Switzerland, in 1875. A solitary and introverted child, he had always wanted to study archeology. However, his family was too poor to send him further afield than the University of Basle, where archeology was not taught, so he studied medicine instead. Jung later worked in the Burghölzli, a psychiatric hospital in Zürich.

In his series of lectures, Freud points to the interplay of the unconscious and conscious forces within the individual psyche. In reasoned progression he outlines core psychoanalytic concepts such as repression, free association, and libido.

These remarkable lectures, which were originally given in Vienna, provide an excellent insight into Freud's most important psychological breakthroughs, and go a long way toward summarizing his views on issues he has studied all his life, including the subjects of hysteria, dementia praecox, dream interpretation, narcissism, fetishism, civilization, society, religion, and female sexuality.

The lectures also tell us something about the man himself, the development of his ideas, and his arguments with other scholars, particularly his notorious falling-out with Carl Jung. In 1906 Jung had published *The Psychology of Dementia Praecox*, sending a copy to Freud, and a close six-year friendship had followed between the two men. At first

Dr Sigmund Freud and his daughter Anna on vacation.

Jung and Freud held a common understanding of the profound role of the unconscious. Largely through Freud's efforts, Jung was appointed permanent president of the Association of Psychoanalysis in 1910. Later, however, their views began to diverge, leading to an irreconcilable break between the two in 1913.

From 1913 to 1917 Jung was largely ostracized from the psychoanalytic community, and it during this period that he embarked on a deep self-analysis. He emerged from this with having developed the structures for his theories on the "collective unconscious."

Jung and Freud had very different concepts of the unconscious. To Jung, Freud's theory was needlessly negative, with the unconscious being only the storehouse of repressed emotions and desires. Jung's unconscious had a more creative role, with the collective unconscious being an essential part of society and culture.

Massive Cannon Bombards Paris

Paris, France, August, 1918: For five months, the French capital has been bombarded from the Forest of Coucy 75 miles (121 km) away by Germany's massive "Paris Gun." Its barrel measures about 112 ft (34 m) and it weighs 138 tons (141 tonnes). The shells take 3 minutes to reach their target, ascending to a maximum height of 24 miles (39 km) during their trajectory.

German cannon, made by Krupp.

Ernest Rutherford attends an international physics conference, which was held in Brussels in 1911.

Carl Gustav Jung

Known in Germany as the Kaiser Wilhelm Geschutz, the gun was manufactured by the German engineering firm Krupp to the design of Professor Rausenberger, who was the firm's ballistic expert. It was built solely for the purpose of shelling Paris. Since March this year it has fired almost 400 shells upon the city.

Each shell weighs 264 lb (120 kg) and requires 400 lb (180 kg) of gunpowder to propel it out of the barrel. The gun, which has an 8 in (210 mm) bore and was created by modifying a 15 in (380 mm) naval gun, has to be transported on railway tracks to its firing position.

It is estimated that deaths from the shelling have totaled over 250, with more than 600 people wounded. The effect on morale in Paris has been considerable. As a military weapon however, the gun has been a failure. The payload is minuscule, the barrel needs replacing after 65 firings, and accuracy is virtually non-existent.

Rutherford Unlocks the Atom

Manchester, England, January 3, 1919: Ernest Rutherford has transmuted atoms of nitrogen into oxygen. The New Zealand physicist, already well-known for his nuclear theory of the atom, is the first to carry out a transmutation reaction.

Ernest Rutherford was born in New Zealand. One of 12 children and an excellent student, he won a scholarship to study at Cambridge University in England. A long career in atomic physics followed, with Rutherford coining new terms such as gamma rays, proton, neutron and half-life, to name a few.

In 1910 his research into the scattering of alpha rays and the inner structure of the atom led him to postulate the existence of a "nucleus." This was his greatest contribution to physics and it led to a revolutionary conception of the atom

as a miniature universe in which the mass is concentrated in the nucleus, which is itself surrounded by electrons.

In 1913 he bombarded atoms with cathode rays, thus revealing how an atom's inner structures correspond with a group of lines that characterize the elements. The elements could then be assigned an atomic number, so that the properties of each element could be identified and defined by this number.

Rutherford has stated publicly that he hopes that humanity will never discover how to extract the energy from the nucleus until all nations were living at peace with their neighbors.

Vickers Biplane Conquers Atlantic in 16 Hours

Clifden, Ireland, June 14–15, 1919: In an aviation first, Captain John Alcock and Arthur Brown have flown an aircraft non-stop across the Atlantic Ocean, taking off from St Johns in Newfoundland yesterday and arriving today at Clifden in County Galway on the west coast of Ireland. The flight took a little over 16 hours and covered a distance of 1,890 miles (3043 km). Alcock piloted the Vickers-Vimy biplane and Brown was the navigator. The aircraft, specially fitted out with long-range fuel tanks, was powered by a Rolls Royce engine.

Passing through fog and sleet storms, the flight was a difficult one, and the two aviators had only coffee, beer, sandwiches, and chocolates to sustain them. Visibility was so poor that at one stage they were flying as low as just 10 ft (3 m) above the Atlantic Ocean. Nonetheless Alcock and Brown touched down near the Clifden wireless station, a mere 10 miles

(16 km) away from their intended course, and some 50 miles (80 km) from Galway, their intended destination.

John William Alcock was born in Manchester in 1892 and joined the Royal Naval Air Service at the outbreak of the Great War. After the war he became a test pilot for Vickers Aircraft. Arthur Whitten Brown was born in Glasgow in 1886 and was an engineer before becoming a pilot for the Royal Air Force.

Eclipse Confirms Einstein's Theory

Principe Island, West Africa, March 29, 1919: British astrophysicist Arthur Eddington has today proved Einstein's theory of general relativity—a geometric theory postulating that the presence of matter (for example, a planet) can curve space–time and affect the passage of free particles to the point of even being able to "bend" light.

Einstein's theory solved some serious problems that astronomers of his day were having in understanding the orbit of Mercury. Many scientists believed an unseen planet, which they called Vulcan, was affecting the orbit of the sun's closest neighbor. The problems surrounding Mercury's orbit, however, went away when the theory of general relativity was applied.

To confirm the theory, Eddington traveled to Principe Island off the west coast of Africa to photograph a starfield near the sun during a total solar eclipse. This is the only time that the bending of light can be observed, as normally the sun's brightness makes it impossible to see the stars. Comparing the photos to the same starfield when the sun was not present, Eddington found that the stars appeared to have shifted, just as Einstein's theory predicted they would. Their light had been slightly curved by the sun's gravitational field.

Ross and Keith Smith make the first England-Australia flight in 1919.

Popular Novelist Mark Twain Dies

August Strindberg

Danbury, Connecticut, USA, April 21, 1910: Following "greatly exaggerated" reports of his death seven years ago, popular US humorist and author Mark Twain has died aged 74, a commendable age for someone who smoked 40 cigars a day.

Born Samuel Clemens in 1835 in Florida, Missouri, he grew up in Hannibal on the west bank of the great Mississippi, eventually getting a job piloting steamboats on the river. He started writing under the pseudonym Mark Twain in 1863, taking the name from a riverman's term that meant "two fathoms deep."

His most popular books are those that center on life in and around the river—*Tom Sawyer* (1876), *Life on the Mississippi* (1883), and *Huckleberry Finn* (1883)—books that also contain much of the political and social satire typical of his earlier writings. Twain later turned to historical fiction with *A Connecticut Yankee in King Arthur's Court* (1889).

In 1891 financial difficulties forced him to leave his home town of Hartford, Connecticut, to live in Europe, where he embarked on a worldwide lecture tour in 1895 to restore his finances. He traveled to New Zealand, Australia, India, and South Africa, describing the tour in *Following the Equator* (1897).

His later life was overshadowed by the deaths of his two daughters, and of his wife in 1904. Twain's literary reputation, however, rests on *The Adventures of Huckleberry Finn*, in which he created one of the most memorable characters in fiction. His use of vernacular speech in the book has revolutionized the language of American fiction and will no doubt exert a great influence on many American writers.

> *"I MUST SAY I HATE MONEY BUT IT'S THE LACK OF IT I HATE THE MOST."*
>
> KATHERINE MANSFIELD (1888–1923), NEW ZEALAND WRITER, C. 1910

> *"I LIKE TO WRITE WHEN I FEEL SPITEFUL; IT'S LIKE HAVING A GOOD SNEEZE."*
>
> D. H. LAWRENCE (1885–1930), ENGLISH NOVELIST, 1913

Art Challenged by New Guard

Munich, Germany, December, 1911: The Russian abstract artist Vassily Kandinsky and the German expressionist Franz Marc have joined forces to form a new art movement called *Der Blaue Reiter* (The Blue Rider), the name being a fusion of Kandinsky's love of the color blue and Marc's love of horses. Together they have broken away from the New Artists' Society. Earlier this month the Blue Rider group, which is one of two Expressionist groups in Germany, held their first exhibition in Munich.

Kandinsky studied law before traveling to Germany from Russia, and was the intellectual leader of what was by most standards in the art world a small and unstructured group. Born in Munich, Marc attended the local art academy, his favorite subject being animals in their natural environment.

Seeking to liberate art from its conventional task of minutely copying nature, those in the Blue Rider school are seeking a language of self-expression that is made up not of words but of abstract combinations of lines, colors, and shapes. They are attempting, as Kandinsky explains, to "uncover the expressive language of painting that has lain dormant in the medium from the Renaissance to the present."

Through the use of distorted forms and startling color, their art ranges from the pure abstraction of Kandinsky to the romantic imagery of Marc. The members of the group, which includes Paul Klee and August Macke, share a philosophical spirit, an intellectual approach to technique, and great lyrical spontaneity.

The Dream, by Franz Marc, expresses his love of horses.

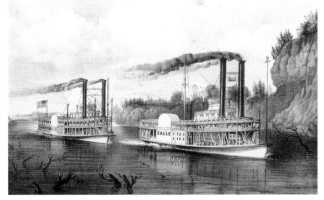

Mark Twain's best works were inspired by the Mississippi River.

Troubled Swedish Playwright Dead at 63

Stockholm, Sweden, May 14, 1912: Swedish playwright and novelist August Strindberg has died from stomach cancer, at the house he called the Blue Tower, where he has lived in isolation since 1908.

Born in 1849, Strindberg was an unwanted fourth child. Raised in poverty, he was forced to leave college without a degree, taking various jobs as a tutor, journalist, and librarian.

New York, USA, January 1, 1910: Enrico Caruso sings for the first radio broadcast transmitted live.

Hollywood, USA, March 10, 1910: *In Old California*, directed by D. W. Griffith, is the first movie to be made in Hollywood.

Danbury, Connecticut, USA, April 21, 1910: Following reports of his death being greatly exaggerated seven years ago, humorist and author Mark Twain dies, aged 74.

Paris, France, June 25, 1910: Stravinsky's *The Firebird*, written for the Ballet Russes, debuts.

Helsinki, Finland, April 3, 1911: Sibelius's *4th Symphony in A minor* debuts to a bemused crowd.

London, England, April 7, 1911: The Copyright Bill passes into law, providing protection of literature and music for 50 years after the creator's death, ending unchecked plagiarism.

Paris, France, August 22, 1911: The *Mona Lisa* is stolen from the Louvre; the theft is unnoticed for a day.

Munich, Germany, December, 1911: *Der Blaue Reiter* art movement is founded by Kandinsky and Marc.

Stockholm, Sweden, May 14, 1912: Swedish playwright and novelist August Strindberg dies, aged 63. His best known works include *Miss Julie* and *The Ghost Sonata*.

New York, USA, June 8, 1912: Bavarian immigrant Carl Laemmle founds the Universal Film Manufacturing Company.

Germany, December, 1912: Thomas Mann's *Death in Venice* is published. It is a striking work on the nature of beauty and spirituality, with homosexual overtones.

New York, USA, February 17, 1913: The "Armory Show" opens, exhibiting 16,000 works by European artists. The innovations of Kandinsky, Rodin, and Duchamp shock American art lovers.

Paris, France, May 29, 1913: Stravinsky's *The Rites of Spring* premières. With wild dissonances and tumultuous rhythms, the audience reaction is extreme.

Stockholm, Sweden, December 10, 1913: Bengali poet Rabindranath Tagore wins the Nobel Prize in Literature for his work *Gitanjali*.

London, England, April 12, 1914: George Bernard Shaw's *Pygmalion* premières.

London, England, July, 1914: Following the founding of the American Society of Composers, Authors & Publishers (ASCAP) in January, the Performing Rights Society is set up by music publishers who want to safeguard their music.

Vienna, Austria, December, 1914: Disciple of Gustav Klimt, Egon Schiele's star continues to rise with his first solo exhibition in Paris showcasing his expressionist art.

In his first major work, *Master Olof* (1872), his extensive use of prose was unprecedented for dramatic tragedy and the play was rejected by the Royal Theater. His first novel, *The Red Room* (1879), brought him to public attention with its satire of hypocrisy and injustice in Swedish life, which had never before attempted in Swedish fiction.

In 1891 the first of his three disastrous marriages ended in divorce. This precipitated what he called his "inferno crisis." During this personal crisis, he even experienced the delusion that creatures from another world were following him around.

After years of painful struggle and almost universal rejection of his plays *Miss Julie* and *The Father* by his countrymen, in 1894 Strindberg suffered an emotional collapse. The specter of mental illness continued to haunt him until his death. His last years were spent in isolation, although he continued to write masterful plays such as *The Ghost Sonata*, which finally brought him the recognition he deserved.

During his career, Strindberg wrote more than 70 plays, as well as novels, short stories, and studies in Swedish history.

Mann's Masterpiece Unveiled

Germany, December, 1912: Thomas Mann's recently published *Der Tod in Venedig* (*Death in Venice*) is already being hailed as one of the great novels of this century. It tells the story of Gustav von Aschenbach, an aging writer whose wanderlust leads him to a Venice that is in the grip of an unnamed epidemic. A search for spiritual fulfillment becomes instead an obsession for a young Polish boy named Tadzio, an obsession that leads von Aschenbach to his erotic doom.

Despite an encroaching epidemic he chooses to stay in the city for the immediate experience of beauty, as seen in the boy. After exchanging just one significant look with the boy on the day of Tadzio's departure, Aschenbach dies of cholera.

Thomas Mann was born in Lübeck, Germany, in 1875. His father died in 1891 and the family moved to Munich, where Mann was educated at the Lübeck high school. His first novel was published in 1898 in the magazine *Simplicissimus*.

In the following years he became drawn to the writings of the philosopher Friedrich Nietzsche and the music of Wagner. In *Buddenbrooks*, his early masterpiece, Mann starts off by focusing on a single individual and then over the course of the novel he expands its scope so that it becomes the saga of a wealthy Hanseatic family which declines from strength to decadence.

time out

The five-member Original Dixieland Jass Band of New Orleans is formed, billed as "the creators of Jazz." The band members had played in the Papa Jack Laine bands for parades, dances, and promotional events. They were known by their initials: the O.D.J.B.

Riots Greet Stravinsky's Rite of Spring

Paris, France, May 29, 1913: Today in Paris, Les Ballets Russes staged the first performance of composer Igor Stravinsky's *The Rite of Spring*, with choreography by Vaslav Nijinsky. Listening to its wild dissonances and tumultuous rhythms, shocked audiences who are more accustomed to the demure conventions of classical ballet greeted it with catcalls and whistles. Satirical requests for a doctor were heard. As the complex score led to violent dance steps depicting fertility rites, fights broke out in the aisles and eventually a riot ensued.

The choreography, set design, and storyline are no doubt confronting, the music jarring, dissonant, and difficult. In Part One the curtain rises to reveal young men and women in different groups. Their surroundings are primitive, the

forces dark. Men take possession of women and take them offstage as the music gathers intensity.

In Part Two a woman is sacrificed to Earth. Standing alone in the middle of the stage after a mystic dance, she is surrounded by members of the tribe, who dance around her in a crescendo of brutal excitement. The dancing grows more and more violent until the chosen maiden collapses exhausted and dies.

By the intermission, the Paris police had arrived, but were able to restore only limited order. Nijinsky and Stravinsky are reportedly despondent at the public's reaction, with Stravinsky seen storming out of the concert hall in a fury. However, Sergei Diaghilev, the director of Les Ballets Russes, was overheard to have said, "This is just what I wanted."

Samuel Clemens (Mark Twain)

Ballet Russes star and choreographer, Vaslav Nijinsky.

USA, April 11, 1915: Charlie Chaplin stars in *The Tramp*, creating his role with the twirling cane, side-footed walk, and baggy trousers.

Lemnos, Greece, April 23, 1915: British poet Rupert Brooke, best known for his *War Sonnets*, dies of septicemia on his way to Gallipoli, aged 28.

London, England, August 12, 1915: W. Somerset Maugham's semi-autobiographical novel *Of Human Bondage* is published.

Paris, France, November, 1915: Pablo Picasso paints *The Harlequin*.

Zurich, Switzerland, February 5, 1916: Switzerland becomes a refuge for artists from the war. Poets Hugo Ball and Tristan Tzara begin Cabaret Voltaire, the birthplace of Dada arts.

Rye, England, February 28, 1916: Henry James, US-born author of *The Portrait of a Lady* and *The Turn of the Screw* dies, aged 73.

USA, May 20, 1916: Norman Rockwell's first cover for the *Saturday Evening Post* is a success.

Glen Ellen, California, USA, November 22, 1916: Novelist and adventurer Jack London dies, aged 40.

USA, February 26, 1917: The Victor Talking Machine Company releases the first jazz record by the Original Dixieland Jass Band.

Edinburgh, Scotland, August 17, 1917: Wilfred Owen and Siegfried Sassoon meet while recuperating in hospital; Owen shows the elder Sassoon his poetry.

France, November 17, 1917: Sculptor of *The Thinker* and *The Kiss*, August Rodin dies, aged 77.

Netherlands, December, 1917: This year, Piet Mondrian founds the de Stijl group of artists.

USA, January 27, 1918: *Tarzan of the Apes* is released.

Vienna, Austria, February 6, 1918: Artist Gustav Klimt dies of a stroke, aged 55. His work, including *The Kiss*, had an eroticism that shocked contemporary sensibilities.

New York, USA, February 14, 1918: George Gershwin's song "Swanee," sung by Al Jolson in the musical *Sinbad*, is a great hit.

Vienna, Austria, December, 1918: Arnold Schoenberg founds the Society for Private Musical Performances.

Hollywood, USA, April 17, 1919: D. W. Griffith, Mary Pickford, Douglas Fairbanks, and Charlie Chaplin found United Artists to produce their own motion pictures.

Weimar, Germany, April 25, 1919: Walter Gropius founds the Bauhaus movement of art and design.

Cagnes, France, December 3, 1919: Impressionist master Pierre-Auguste Renoir dies, aged 78.

Germany, December, 1919: Robert Wiene directs *The Cabinet of Doctor Caligari*, bringing expressionism to the cinema.

Henry James

Prolific US Writer Dead

Rye, England, February 28, 1916: Henry James, US-born author of *Portrait of a Lady* and *The Turn of the Screw*, has died, aged 72. In all James wrote 20 novels, 112 stories, 12 plays, and a number of works of literary criticism. He was the acknowledged master of the psychological novel and was one of the most distinctive prose stylists in the English language.

From 1866 to 1869 and from 1871 to 1872 while in America, he was a contributor to *Nation and Atlantic Monthly*. James' early pieces were written mainly for periodicals, but it was when he finally decided to settle in Europe that he produced some of his best work, such as *The American* (1877) and *Portrait of a Lady* (1881). *Daisy Miller* (1879) is often cited as one of his true masterpieces, in which, as a young and innocent American, Daisy finds herself in conflict with conservative European sophistication.

The Bostonians (1886), an ambitious novel with a substantial set of characters, portrays what James saw as the conflicting commercial and idealistic strains of American society after the Civil War. His focus was on the lives of American women—on the movement to grant women the vote, and on the supposed decline of gender differences and sexual attraction. Writing with insight, condescension, and hostility, in this novel James set forth a conservative, biting critique of democratic culture.

A series of critical prefaces that he wrote for reprints of his novels also won him a reputation as a superb technician.

At the outbreak of the Great War in 1914 he became involved in the war effort, devoting much time and energy to supporting the troops. Disturbed by the United States' reluctance to enter the war, he became a British citizen in 1915.

In 1899 he purchased Lamb House, a 1723 Georgian house in Sussex, for £2,000, and most of his last 18 years were spent there. It was at this house in 1726 that the modest Lamb family had hosted King George I for three days after he had been driven ashore by a storm. It was here that James wrote *The Wings of the Dove* (1902), *The Ambassadors* (1903), and *The Golden Bowl* (1904), his last and perhaps his greatest novels. In these, he reached his highest level of literary expression in the portrayal of the intricate subtleties of character and in the use of a complex, convoluted style to express delicate nuances of thought.

Jack London Dies at 40

Glen Ellen, California, USA, November 22, 1916: Novelist and adventurer Jack London, author of the outstanding wilderness novels *The Call of the Wild* and *White Fang*, has died, aged 40. Considered by many to be America's finest author, he was born in San Francisco in 1876, spending most of his youth on the waterfront in Oakland, California. With little formal schooling, he educated himself at public libraries. An avid reader, he went on to become the state's first poet laureate.

In the late 1890s London prospected for gold in the Klondike gold rush, and then joined the Hearst Press, writing about the Russo-Japanese War in 1904 and about the Mexican Revolution for Colliers in 1914. His first novel, *Son of the Wolf*, appeared in 1910 and was widely read.

In 1902 he traveled to England, where he studied living conditions in London's East End and other working class areas of the British capital. His subsequent report about the economic degradation of the poor—*The People of the Abyss*—was a surprising success in the United States, although it was criticized in England. His Alaskan stories—*The Call of the Wild* (1903) and *White Fang* (1906)—gained a large following.

In 1910 he purchased a large tract of land near Glen Ellen in Sonoma County, California, and devoted much time and money to developing it with additional land purchases. In 1913 his Beauty Ranch burned to the ground, and his doctor told him his kidneys were failing.

Debts, alcoholism, and illness clouded London's final years and he died today of gastrointestinal uremia.

Rodin's controversial sculpture, *The Thinker*.

Artist Rodin Passes Away

Paris, France, November 17, 1917: Auguste Rodin, one of the most prolific sculptors of the nineteenth and twentieth centuries, and the creator of the famous bronzes *The Kiss* and *The Thinker* has died today, aged 77.

Rodin was born in Paris in 1840, and at the age of 13 he started to attend a school for drawing and modeling. After failing three times to gain entrance to the prestigious Ecole des Beaux-Arts, he studied to become a decorative stone mason.

Devastated by the sudden death of his sister in 1862 he joined the Order of the Holy Sacrament. However, he quickly realized the monastic life was not for him, and he returned to Paris in 1863 to follow his dream of being a sculptor.

Forest Acclivity in Unterach at the Attersee Lake, by Gustav Klimt.

Achievements in the Arts

Key Structures
Adziogol Lighthouse, Chersson, Ukraine
Breslau Office Building, Breslau, Germany
Casa Mila, Barcelona, Spain
Chick House, Berkeley, USA
Colonia Guell, Barcelona, Spain
Fagus Shoe Factory, Alfred an der Leine, Germany
Hotel Guimard, Paris, France
Koshoji Temple, Kyoto, Japan
Palais Royal du Sultan Bamoun, Foumban, Cameroon
Post Office Savings Bank, Vienna, Austria
Presidential Palace, Taipai, Taiwan
Stoclet Palace, Brussels, Belgium
Teatro Nacional, San Salvador, El Salvador
The Salutation, Sandwich, England
Union Buildings, Pretoria, South Africa
Villa Roma, Asmara, Eritrea
Werkbund Theater, Cologne, Germany
Woolworth Building, New York, USA

Nobel Prize for Literature
1910 Paul Heyse; 1911 Count Maurice Maeterlinck; 1912 Gerhart Hauptmann; 1913 Rabindranath Tagore; 1914 no award; 1915 Romain Rolland; 1916 Verner von Heidenstam; 1917 Karl Adolph Gjellerup/Henrik Pontoppidan; 1918 no award; 1919 Carl Spitteler.

In 1880 the French government commissioned him to create a bronze door for the planned Museum of Decorative Arts. The project was called *La Porte de l'Enfer* (*The Gates of Hell*), and was inspired by "The Inferno," the first chapter of Dante's *Divine Comedy*.

Of all the sculptor's works, his most famous is unquestioningly *The Thinker*, which was modeled in 1880–1882 for the *Gates of Hell* sculpture and first exhibited in its original size (28 in/71.5 cm) in 1888 in Copenhagen. Enlarged in 1902, it was shown at the Salon in Paris in 1904, where it attracted strong reactions from the press. It was also the first work by Rodin to be erected in a public place, inaugurated in front of the Pantheon on April 21, 1906, amid a political and social crisis, a fact that gave the sculpture symbolic significance.

By 1910 Rodin was so popular that he was given his own pavilion at the Paris World Exposition, where he displayed 150 of his works in bronze, plaster, and marble. Museums and collectors from around the world sought out his pieces, bringing him fame and fortune.

In 1908 he moved his studio into the ground floor of the Biron Hotel, previously home to a religious community. In 1912 the hotel was scheduled for demolition and its residents were forced to leave. Rodin was able to successfully negotiate with state officials to allow him to stay there by offering to bequeath his entire estate to the French government if the hotel were instead converted into a museum for his work after his death.

Hollywood's "Big Four" Create New Studio

Hollywood, USA, April 17, 1919: D. W. Griffith, Mary Pickford, Douglas Fairbanks, and Charlie Chaplin have today founded their own motion picture distribution company, fulfilling an often-discussed goal of having greater control over their work and their careers. The new company, which is called United Artists, will release pictures made by independent filmmakers.

The company's founders are four of the most influential people in Hollywood today. Chaplin has an unparalleled degree of control over his movies, having built the Charlie Chaplin Film Studio in 1917. Actress Mary Pickford almost single-handedly made Paramount Pictures Hollywood's number one film company,

Charlie Chaplin is now a movie mogul.

while Broadway star Douglas Fairbanks heads up his own film producing company. D. W. Griffith is the pre-eminent director who directed the 1915 blockbuster *The Birth of a Nation*, a film about the American Civil War.

When Richard Rowland, head of Metro Pictures, learned of the new company, he was overheard to have said, "Well, the inmates are taking over the asylum."

Gershwin's "Swanee" a Hit for Jolson

New York, USA, 1919: Composer George Gershwin's song "Swanee" has become the stand-out hit of Al Jolson's musical *Sinbad*, and it regularly drives the audience to frenzied applause.

George Gershwin was born in Brooklyn in 1898. It wasn't until he was about 12 years old that George showed any musical aptitude. When his family bought a secondhand piano for his older brother Ira, George began playing songs on it by ear. This prompted his parents to look for a piano teacher for him.

He earned $15 a week as a teenage songwriter on Tin Pan Alley (New York's music industry district). By the time he was 20 he had been signed as a composer for $35 a week, plus a modest royalty.

This past summer Gershwin wrote a song with lyricist Irving Caesar, composing most of it on the top of a bus en route from T. B. Harmes Publishing Company to Gershwin's apartment. Within a few hours the hit song "Swanee" was born. Not an immediate hit, it may have fallen into obscurity had not Al Jolson heard it and incorporated it into his show *Sinbad*, his smash musical playing at New York's Wintergarden Theater.

Master Impressionist Renoir Is Dead

Scagnes, France, December 3, 1919: Master impressionist painter Pierre-Auguste Renoir has died, aged 78.

Born in Limoges in 1841 into a family of artisans, Renoir's artistic talent was quickly recognized by his parents, who sent him to work in a porcelain factory from the age of 13. Later he studied at the School of Fine Arts in Paris and took painting lessons at an artist's studio.

Renoir was hugely prolific, producing more than 6,000 paintings. He was a master of color and figure painting, and one of the early exponents of the Impressionist style. His focus was always on Parisian men and women, dappled in sunlight, simply and elegantly enjoying life.

Jack London

Renoir painted *Oarsmen at Chatou* in 1879, at the height of his creativity.

Jim Thorpe

Nothing to Fear from Halley's Comet

Worldwide, May 20, 1910: Halley's comet today passed within 13 million miles (21 million km) of Earth. The comet's approach has been awaited with much apprehension since it was revealed that its tail contains poisonous gases, including cyanide. News from astronomers that Earth will be passing through this poisonous tail has led to much concern. Pills to alleviate comet sickness are being sold by peddlers on the streets of New York, San Francisco, and London. Some concerned citizens have been seen moving their belongings underground.

The comet's 1066 appearance was recorded on the Bayeux Tapestry. It is named for the English astronomer and mathematician, Edmond Halley, who calculated its orbit. Halley's famous *Catalogus Stellarum Australium*, which was published in 1678, was the first to contain telescopically determined locations of the southern stars. In 1705 Halley published a paper describing the orbits of 24 comets observed from 1337 to 1698, demonstrating that the characteristics of three comets seen in 1531, 1607, and 1682 were so similar that all three must actually have been successive returns of the same comet. Halley accurately predicted the comet's return in 1758, an event that he did not live to witness, passing away in 1742.

The Lady with the Lamp Is Dead

London, England, 1910: Pioneering nurse Florence Nightingale passed away today in Park Lane, at the age of 90, and will be buried in the family plot at East Wellow in Hampshire. A memorial service is to take place in St Paul's Cathedral.

Born into a world of wealth and privilege, Florence Nightingale taught herself the art of nursing, by the age of 30 becoming England's preeminent expert on nursing and hospitals. She later showed that the mortality rate for patients in London's hospitals was 90 percent, whilst the death rate for patients who did not go to hospital was around 60 percent.

In March of 1854 the Crimean War broke out, with subsequent reports of the suffering of English troops in the camps precipitating intense anger at home. Nightingale embarked for the Crimea on October 21, accompanied by 38 nurses, arriving in Scutari on November 4. Her full title was "Superintendent of the Female Nurses in the Hospitals in the East," but she was known more colloquially as simply "The Lady-in-Chief."

In the barracks hospital there were no vessels for water, no soap, no towels, and no hospital clothes. Sick and injured soldiers were lying in their uniforms covered in filth. There was no milk, the bread was sour, and the Irish butter was in a state of decomposition.

By the end of the year, Nightingale and her nurses had transformed the hospital at Scutari, establishing a vast kitchen and laundry, and in December 46 more nurses arrived. The only nurse allowed in the wards after 8 p.m. each night, Nightingale soon became known as "The Lady with the Lamp."

In 1855 the Nightingale Fund was established to set up a training school for nurses. In retirement Nightingale wrote papers on the causes of famine, the need for irrigation, and the poverty of the people in India. Her book *Notes on Nursing* was published in 1860 and has been reprinted many times since.

Swedish Games Free of Controversy

Stockholm, Sweden, May 5–July 27, 1912: The Fifth Olympic Games have just concluded in Stockholm, where innovations

time out

In a major overhaul of conditions at his automobile plant, Henry Ford promised to give $10 million in bonuses to staff, to set a minimum wage of $5 a day, and provide protection against cases of unfair dismissal.

Impressive Swedish gymnasts march past the Royal Family at the Stockholm Olympics.

Worldwide, May 20, 1910: Halley's comet passes within 13 million miles (20 million km) of Earth. In France and Russia, the comet's passing is thought to be responsible for the poor weather this year.
New York, USA, July 1, 1910: The Tango, an energetic dance imported from South America, causes a stir on the dance floors of the USA and in Europe.
London, England, August 13, 1910: Florence Nightingale, first woman recipient of the Order of Merit for her nursing work, dies, aged 90.

Indianapolis, USA, May 30, 1911: Champion driver Ray Harroum comes out of retirement to win the first Indianapolis 500 car race.
Calais, France, September 7, 1911: On his thirteenth attempt, Thomas Burgess becomes the second person to swim the English Channel, 36 years after Matthew Webb.
Stockholm, Sweden, December 10, 1911: The Nobel Peace Prize is shared by Tobias Asser, organizer of the international law conferences at The Hague, and Alfred Fried, publisher of *Der Freidenswarte*.

Stockholm, Sweden, May 5–July 27, 1912: The fifth Olympic Games introduces electronic timing devices and a public address system.
Paris, France and London, England, August 1, 1912: An airmail service opens between the two cities.
London, England, August 12, 1912: Reverend William Booth, founder of the Salvation Army dies, aged 83. He renamed the Christian Mission Church in 1873.
Philadelphia, USA, May 29, 1912: Fifteen women are fired for dancing the Turkey Trot in their lunch break.

USA, January 27, 1913: Olympic champion Jim Thorpe is stripped of two gold medals, as the IOC rigidly interprets their professionalism ruling. He received payment from a minor league baseball team in 1910.
New York, USA, February 2, 1913: Grand Central Station opens.
USA, June, 1913: Over one million immigrants have arrived in the USA in the past year.
Bizerta, Tunisia, September 23, 1913: French aviator Roland Garros crosses the Mediterranean, the longest flight over water to date.

Detroit, USA, January 5, 1914: Henry Ford announces sweeping reforms in his factories. Workers shall be paid a minimum of $5 per day for an eight-hour shift.
Paris, France, July 26, 1914: Philippe Thys of Belgium wins his second Tour de France.
Europe, August 14, 1914: European stock exchanges close as the war breaks out; the convertibility of many currencies is suspended. A run on the Bank of England for armament purposes saw gold reserves decrease by £10 billion.

included electric timing devices and a public address system. Free of controversy or protest, they have been the most successful games to date and are already being dubbed the "Swedish Masterpiece."

Twenty-eight nations sent 2,547 athletes, including 57 women. There was a total of 102 events in 14 sports. Gymnastics came of age as a sport at these games, attracting a field of some 1,275 competitors from 13 countries.

The new Grand Central Station is an impressive New York landmark.

"New" Grand Central Opens for Business

New York, USA, February 2,1913: Grand Central Terminal, the world's largest railway station, designed in the beauxarts style, has opened in New York.

In 1903 a select group of architects were approached to submit designs for the new Grand Central Terminal. The architectural firm of Reed and Stem was to produce the overall design, while another firm—Warren and Wetmore—were made responsible for the architectural details and the beaux-arts style.

It is not, of course, the first building on this site. Grand Central Depot was built here in 1869. When the New York Central railroad moved to the new station in 1871, the old station at 27th Street was bought by P. T. Barnum and turned into Madison Square Garden.

Built at a cost of $4 million, Grand Central Depot was inadequate from the very day it was completed, because of the congestion and smoke belching from the steam engines. A massive track fire in 1902 caused by the collision of two trains prompted the decision to electrify the train lines.

The Grand Central Corporation was founded to oversee the new plan, envisioning the project as a "terminal city," a

multi-lot development linking the station with apartment blocks, hotels, and office buildings running along 42nd Street and up Park Avenue. The directions also called for the station to be linked with the new subway system (1904), with distinct departure areas for commuter and long-distance trains, a main circulation concourse, subsidiary ticketing spaces, and well-appointed waiting rooms. The station was to provide for the changing requirements of the booming metropolis in a new and innovative way.

Reed and Stem's station efficiently links the city's streets, and boulevards, trains, subways, elevated railways, and adjacent buildings with a viaduct encircling the station, while suburban and longhaul trains are isolated from each other on two separate levels of tracks.

The solution to recouping some of the project's massive $80 million cost was to cover over the tracks from 45th to 49th streets and allow real estate developers to erect buildings over the concealed tracks, for which privilege they would pay a premium to New York Central Railroad.

Construction lasted 10 years. Modeled after the Roman Imperial Baths, Warren and Wetmore's beaux-arts design is merely an extravagant window dressing for Reed and Stem's masterful circulation plan. The monumental main concourse, all 75,000 sq ft (6,944 sq m) of it, has a

majestic vaulted sky ceiling depicting constellations and a series of Roman-inspired ramps designed to keep pedestrians on the move from the street to their trains. Sixty-foot-high (18 m) arched windows bathe the massive interior of this beaux-arts juggernaut in dappled sunlight. The building has already become an American landmark.

French Aviator Crosses Mediterranean

Florence Nightingale

Bizerta, Tunisia, September 23, 1913: French aviator Roland Garros has arrived in Bizerta today after flying across the Mediterranean from a beach southwest of Cannes in the south of France, a distance of 453 miles (729 km).

Garros had been studying to become a concert pianist when his attention turned to aviation. He eventually convinced the Brazilian flyer Alberto Santos-Dumont to teach him to fly. The lessons took place in a Santos-Dumont-built monoplane that is only 5 yards (4.5 m) long and has its tail supported on a slender bamboo pole.

In 1911 Garros finished second in both the Paris–Rome and Circuit of Europe races. He made today's epic flight in a Morane Saulnier model H aircraft powered by a 60 horsepower (45 kW) Gnome engine. He arrived with only enough fuel for a further seven minutes of flying time.

Former pianist Roland Garros has traded the keyboard for the cockpit.

UK, March 18, 1915: The government appeals for women to take up jobs in industry, especially armament factories, as men depart for the frontline.

London, England, April 8, 1915: George V pledges to abstain from alcohol in an effort to convince armament workers to cut down on heavy drinking.

Neuve Chapelle, France, May 9, 1915: Wimbledon champion Anthony Wilding is killed in action. The Tour de France and Wimbledon are postponed. The 1916 Olympic Games in Berlin were cancelled.

Elephant Island, Antarctic Peninsula, August 30, 1916: Ernest Shackleton rescues the crew of the *Endurance* after three previous attempts were thwarted by sea ice. He and four others reached South Georgia to find help on May 21.

Detroit, USA, August 31, 1916: The Ford Motor Company announces a roll back in prices of automobiles in order to increase their market share.

Brooklyn, USA, October 10, 1916: Public health nurse Margaret Sanger founds the first birth control clinic in the USA.

New Zealand, January, 1917: Six o'clock closing in hotels introduced.

Denver, USA, January 10, 1917: William Cody, better known as "Buffalo Bill," dies, aged 71.

Washington DC, USA, January 29, 1917: US Congress passes a bill requiring all immigrants to know 30-80 English words upon arrival. Asian immigration, with the exception of Japan, is banned.

London, England, June 26, 1917: George V orders his family to lose Germanic titles; Saxe-Coburg becomes Windsor.

Russia, January 31, 1918: The Gregorian calendar is adopted to bring Russia in line with the majority of western countries. In the changeover, 13 days are lost.

London, England, March 23, 1918: Chung Ling Soo (stage name of US magician William Robinson) is killed when the bullet catch trick he is performing goes horribly wrong.

Beaulieu, France, May 14, 1918: American newspaper publisher James Gordon Bennett Jr dies, aged 77. He made the *New York Herald* an international paper.

Boston, USA, January 19, 1919: A 50-foot (15-meter) high storage tank fails, sending a gigantic wave of molasses through the downtown area, killing 21 and injuring 150.

Australia and New Zealand, April 25, 1919: The ANZAC troops' contribution to the Great War is commemorated by celebrations on ANZAC Day.

London, England, July, 1919: Wimbledon resumes after the war. Suzanne Lenglen, offending sensibilities with her exposed arms and ankles, wins the women's title.

Shackleton Rescues Antarctic Crew

King George V

> "IT'S OFTEN
> SAFER TO BE IN
> CHAINS THAN
> TO BE FREE."
>
> FRANZ KAFKA (1883–
> 1924), CZECH NOVELIST,
> 1914

> "THE WHOLE OF
> NATURE IS A
> CONJUGATION
> OF THE VERB TO
> EAT, IN THE
> ACTIVE AND
> THE PASSIVE."
>
> DEAN INGE (1860–1954),
> BRITISH CLERIC, 1919

Elephant Island, Antarctic Peninsula, August 30, 1916: Ernest Shackleton has rescued the crew of the *Endurance* after three previous attempts were thwarted by sea ice.

After Amundsen was the first to reach the South Pole in 1911, Shackleton decided to attempt the first crossing of the Antarctic from the Weddell to the Ross Sea. That crossing, a 2,000-mile (3,220 km) odyssey involving 28 men and 68 dogs, was a spectacular failure, with the expedition's ship, *Endurance*, becoming trapped and crushed by ice in the Weddell Sea.

Resigned to spending an indefinite period ice-bound, Shackleton ordered his

Inhospitable Elephant Island was home for the crew of the *Endurance*.

men onto the ice, where they established the makeshift Ocean Camp. After four months floating away from the Antarctic continent on their "iceberg," they landed on Elephant Island on April 15, 1916. Shackleton realized their only hope of rescue was to reach the whaling stations on the east side of South Georgia Island, 800 miles (1,288 km) away.

In one of the greatest small boat journeys ever made, he and five men from the 28-strong party crossed one of the roughest seas in the world in their 22 ft (7 m) boat, *James Caird*.

Using only a sextant for navigation, the superb New Zealand navigator, Frank Worsley, was held steady in the tiny boat by two of the crew as it pitched and yawed. He managed only four sightings of the sun through the clouds, yet after 17 days guided them safely to South Georgia, arriving there on May 10.

It wasn't until today that Shackleton and a rescue team was able to return to Elephant Island and rescue the men he had left behind, who all survived.

First Birth-control Clinic Opens in Brooklyn

Brooklyn, USA, October 16, 1916: Today, in the marginalized Brownsville section of Brooklyn, New York, the first birth-control clinic in the United States has been opened by Margaret Sanger, together with her sister Ethel Higgins and Fania Mindell, all three women are registered nurses. The clinic will provide birth-control information, counseling, and supplies to dozens of women in the area.

Margaret Sanger was born on September 14, 1879, in Corning, New York, the sixth of 11 children. Margaret's

father was a rebel who imbued in his daughter the need to stand up for what she believed in. When, at the age of 50, Margaret's mother died from tuberculosis after 18 pregnancies and 11 live births, the young Margaret decided she would join the nursing profession and specialize in caring for pregnant women.

With her father active in the causes of labor reform and social equality, Margaret grew up in a household that was a frequent meeting point for radical social reformers—so much so that the townspeople referred to Margaret and her siblings as "children of the devil." Surprisingly, she rather enjoyed living amongst the controversy, an attribute that would stand her in good stead in life.

Attending to her gravely ill mother through tuberculosis inspired her to enroll in a nursing program at White Plains Hospital. Just before finishing her studies, she married the architect William Sanger in 1902 and they moved to Hastings, a small suburb of New York City.

It was while working in some of the city's poorest districts that she was called upon to deliver babies and to nurse desperately weak mothers back to health. At a time when the majority of wealthy women could access illegal birth control methods as well as have relatively safe illegal abortions, the poor had no option but to continue to risk death with unsafe and illicit abortion practices.

In 1912 Margaret gave up nursing and began writing a column for the *New York Call* entitled "What Every Girl Should Know," dealing forthrightly with sex education and women's health. She also challenged the ruling of the 1873 federal Comstock law, which prevented the "importing or distribution of any device, medicine, or information designed to prevent conception or induce abortion."

Fleeing to England to avoid prosecution, she met Havelock Ellis, a psychologist who argued that a woman should be

Sporting Achievements

Baseball *World Series* 1910 Philadelphia (American League); 1911 Philadelphia (AL); 1912 Boston (AL); 1913 Philadelphia (AL); 1914 Boston (National League); 1915 Boston (AL); 1916 Boston (AL); 1917 Chicago (AL); 1918 Boston (AL); 1919 Cincinnati (NL).
Cycling *Tour de France* 1910 O. Lapize; 1911 G. Garrigou; 1912 O. Defraye; 1913-1914 P. Thys; 1915-1918 no competition; 1919 F. Lambot.
Horse Racing *Epsom Derby* 1910 Lemberg; 1911 Sunstar; 1912 Tagalie; 1913 Aboyeur; 1914 Durbar II; 1915 Pommern; 1916 Fifinella; 1917 Gay Crusader; 1918 Gainsborough; 1919 Grand Parade. *Kentucky Derby* 1910 Donau; 1911 Meridian; 1912 Worth; 1913 Donerail; 1914 Old Rosebud; 1915 Regret; 1916 George Smith; 1917 Omar Khayyam; 1918 Exterminator; 1919 Sir Barton. *Melbourne Cup* 1910 Comedy King; 1911 The Parisian; 1912 Piastre; 1913 Posinatus; 1914 Kingsburgh; 1915 Patrobas; 1916 Sasanof; 1917 Westcourt; 1918 Night Watch; 1919 Artilleryman.
Ice Hockey *Stanley Cup* 1910 Montreal; 1911 Ottawa; 1912 Quebec; 1913 Quebec; 1914 Toronto; 1915 Vancouver; 1916 Montreal; 1917 Seattle; 1918 Toronto; 1919 not awarded.
Marathon *Boston, Men's* 1910 F. Cameron; 1911 C. DeMar; 1912 M. Ryan; 1913 F. Carlson; 1914 J. Duffy; 1915 E. Fabre; 1916 A. Roth; 1917 B. Kennedy; 1918 no race; 1919 C. Linder.
Tennis *Australasian Championships, Men's Singles* 1910 R. Heath; 1911 N. Brookes; 1912 C. Parke; 1913 E. Parker; 1914 A. O'Hara Wood; 1915 F. Lowe; 1916-1918 no competition; 1919 A. Kingscote. *French Championships, Men's Singles* 1910 M. Germot; 1911 A. Gobert; 1912-1914 M. Decugis; 1915-1919 no competition; *Women's Singles* 1910-1912 J. Matthey; 1913-1914 M. Broquedis; 1915-1919; no competition. *US National Championship, Men's Singles* 1910-1911 W. Larned; 1912-1913 M. McLoughlin; 1914 R. Williams; 1915 W. Johnston; 1916 R. Williams; 1917-1918 L. Murray; 1919 W. Johnston; *Women's Singles* 1910-1911 H. Hotchkiss Wightman; 1912-1914 M. Browne; 1915-1918 M. Bjurstedt; 1919 H. Hotchkiss Wightman. *Wimbledon, Gentlemen's Singles* 1910-1913 A. Wilding; 1914 N. Brookes; 1915-1918 no competition; 1919 G. Patterson; *Ladies' Singles* 1910-1911 D. Lambert-Chambers; 1912 E. Larcombe; 1913-1914 D. Lambert-Chambers; 1915-1918 no competition; 1919 S. Lenglen.

HMS *Queen Elizabeth* in the Aegean Sea off Gallipoli Peninsula, April 25, 1915.

Buffalo Bill's Wild West spectacular entertained the crowds at Queen Victoria's Jubilee celebrations.

Newspaper Magnate and Playboy Dies

Beaulieu, France, May 14, 1918: The American newspaper publisher James Gordon Bennett Junior died today in the town of Beaulieu, in the Alpes-Maritimes region in the south of France.

His father, James Gordon Bennett was the founder of the *New York Herald* and co-founder of the Associated Press. Bennett Junior was born in 1841 and educated in Europe, serving as a naval officer in the American Civil War before taking over the *Herald* from his father.

After 1877, James Gordon Bennett Junior spent most of his time running his newspaper from his 300 ft (91 m) yacht moored off the coast of Europe in virtual exile from the United States, after disgracing himself by urinating into a fireplace at his fiancée's father's New Year's Eve party. The engagement was, needless to say, broken off. Sadly, the newspaper's fortunes gradually declined over the years, due to his prolonged absence.

Best known for his contribution to sports, he is credited with introducing polo to the United States, and organizing the world's first major automobile race, the Gordon Bennett Motor Car Racing Trials (1910–1905), although he never drove a car himself.

Margaret Sanger

able to enjoy sex without the worry of becoming pregnant. When she returned to the United States, she founded the National Birth Control League, lecturing across the nation and gathering funds to support her cause.

At her Brownsville clinic today it is reported that hundreds of women have been lining up for blocks. Inside, the nurses have been conducting general checkups and recording details of each woman's economic status and number of children. These case histories will be used to prove the benefits of birth control on the physical, emotional, and economic well-being of women and their families.

Buffalo Bill Crosses the Last Frontier

Denver, USA, January 10, 1917: William Cody, known to America and the world as Buffalo Bill, the embodiment of the rugged western frontiersman and showman, has died today in Denver aged 71.

Born in Iowa in 1846, he started out as a messenger boy, progressed to riding for the Pony Express, the cross-continent fast mail delivery service, and then enlisted in the Seventh Kansas Cavalry in 1864, during the American Civil War. He saw action in Tennessee, Mississippi, and Missouri, serving a total of 19 months, including a year of active duty.

After his discharge he was hired to kill buffalo for track workers by the Kansas Pacific Railroad, and it was there that he received the nickname that would stay with him for ever.

Receiving massive publicity in 1872 when he was chosen to act as a guide for the Grand Duke Alexis of Russia on a hunting trip, Cody was awarded the Medal of Honor later that year for action

against the Pawnee Indians at the South Fork of the Loup River in Nebraska.

His first stage appearance was in 1883 and he continued to appear in various "wild west" shows for decades afterward.

He became interested in developing the Big Horn Basin in Wyoming in the 1890s, and the Cody Canal was built in 1895 as part of the Shoshone Land and Irrigation Project. This project eventually led to the building of the Shoshone Dam, which was completed in 1910.

Buffalo Bill made a fortune from his show-business successes, but lost it all to mismanagement and a weakness for dubious investment schemes. In the end, even the wild-west show was lost to creditors. Buffalo Bill Cody will be buried in a tomb to be blasted from solid rock at the summit of Lookout Mountain not far from Denver, Colorado.

Russia Loses 13 Days in Calendar Changeover

Russia, January 31, 1918: Russians went to sleep on January 31 last night, and woke up this morning on February 13. Bowing to the inevitable, Russian leader Vladimir Lenin yesterday finally decreed the adoption of the Gregorian calendar.

Russia has been following the Julian calendar since it was first printed there in 1709, even though the more accurate Gregorian calendar has been in use throughout Europe for more than 125 years. Unsuccessful attempts were made in the first half of last century to move Russia to the Gregorian standard.

Because the Julian calendar lags 13 days behind the Gregorian, the changeover has meant that for all Russians 13 days has simply disappeared in the leap to join Western Europe.

Seven-time Winner Defeated at Wimbledon

Wimbledon, England, July, 1919: The Wimbledon tennis championships, which have resumed this year after an enforced hiatus for the duration of the Great War, have a new ladies singles champion, Suzanne Lenglen of France. Lenglen has defeated seven-time British-American champion Dorothea Douglass Chambers 10–8, 4–6, 9–7.

The contrasting attire of the two women is the main talking point, with Dorothea Chambers swathed in a high-necked shirt, petticoats, and a long skirt that swept the court. The challenger by contrast shocked the British public in a dress that revealed her ankles and forearms.

Born in Paris in 1899, Lenglen plays an excellent all-court game, moving with rare grace unencum-

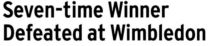

Suzanne Lenglen and Bunny Ryan.

bered by the traditional stifling attire. It is said that her father used to place a handkerchief on the tennis court and gave her five francs every time she hit it.

Warren Harding

"Communism is Soviet power plus the electrification of the whole country."

LENIN (VLADIMIR ILICH ULYANOV) (1870–1924), RUSSIAN REVOLUTIONARY LEADER, PROMOTING ELECTRICITY, 1920

"Russia will certainly inherit the future. What we already call the greatness of Russia is only her prenatal struggling."

D.H. LAWRENCE (1885–1930), ENGLISH NOVELIST, 1920

Sign Here for Peace

New York, USA, January 10: The League of Nations, the most ambitious coalition of peace-seeking countries the world has yet witnessed, was formally ratified today. Its formation has come as a direct response to the carnage and devastation wreaked during the Great War. The League of Nations' charter is to replace the old order of diplomatic secrecy between power-wielding nations with open discussion of the issues.

The larger nations within Europe previously have been signatories to the Congress System and have been less than keen on the establishment of such an organization. However, the governing President of the USA, Woodrow Wilson, has called for a more comprehensive global system of diplomatic moderation—one that would give voice to even the world's smallest nations. The USA, however, has so far declined to be a signatory to the League.

The signatories are: Argentina, Australia, Belgium, Bolivia, Brazil, Canada, Chile, China, Colombia, Cuba, Czechoslovakia, Denmark, El Salvador, France, Greece, Guatemala, Haiti, Honduras, India, Italy, Japan, Liberia, Netherlands, New Zealand, Nicaragua, Norway, Panama, Paraguay, Persia, Peru, Poland, Portugal, Romania, Siam, South Africa, Spain, Sweden, Switzerland, United Kingdom, Uruguay, Venezuela, and Yugoslavia.

Lips That Touch Liquor Shall Not Touch Ours!

USA, January 16: Following last year's joint resolution, the USA's official ban on the sale and consumption of alcoholic beverages has come into effect. Today the entire nation prepares to follow the 25 states that had previously banned the substance under Section 18 of the legislation, which was ratified one year ago as follows: "After one year from the ratification of this article the manufacture, sale, or transportation of intoxicating liquors within, the importation thereof into, or the exportation thereof from the United States and all territory subject to the jurisdiction thereof for beverage purposes is hereby prohibited."

While this move has been seen as a victory for members of the temperance movement, there is already plenty of evidence from the existing prohibition states to support fears that the illegal manufacturing of alcohol will become the nation's leading source of criminal activity fueled by the public demand for alcoholic beverages.

The last week has seen customers lining up for blocks to purchase legal liquor for the last time, while California's 700 wineries are preparing to either close down, produce sacramental wines for Christian and Kosher services, or begin growing other varieties of fruit for non-alcoholic grape juices and fruit.

The first session of the League of Nations in the Salle de Reforme in Geneva.

The passing of "John Barleycorn" is mourned.

All US Women to Vote!

USA, August 26, 1920: Today, the nineteenth amendment to the Constitution of the United States has granted women the right to vote. The amendment was signed into law by the Secretary of State, Bainbridge Colby, on August 18, 1920, and today it takes effect.

Amendment XIX states: "The right of citizens of the United States to vote shall not be denied or abridged by the United States or by any State on account of sex."

The struggle for women's suffrage in the USA has lasted one hundred years since it was begun by Fanny Wright in 1820, and the success of the movement has already been seen by those states in which women already enjoy democratic liberty, beginning with Colorado (1893), and followed by Utah (1896), Idaho (1896), Washington (1910), California (1911), Arizona (1912), Kansas (1912), Oregon (1912), Illinois (1913), Nevada (1914), and Montana (1914).

Canada, January: Native people are given the right to vote, but must give up their Indian status to do so.

USA, January 16: The 18th Amendment officially bans beer, wine, and liquor.

London, England, February 11: The first session of the League of Nations is held. Delegates from Britain, France, Belgium, Japan, Spain, Greece, Italy, and Brazil attend.

Russia, February 22: Ninety thousand Allied troops are on the verge of defeat against Bolshevik forces.

Germany, March 19: The country is beset by socialist unrest. Strikes bring industry to a standstill. A monarchist coup led by Doctor Kapp in Berlin failed a week ago.

Frankfurt, Germany, April 7: French troops occupy the Ruhr region following German forces violating the Treaty of Versailles. Colonial troops open fire on German civilians, killing seven.

San Remo, Italy, April 25: The League of Nations gives the British mandate over Mesopotamia and Palestine.

Ireland, May 14: Tensions run high as 94 police stations are attacked. The British government released 40 Irish hunger strikers from jail in London last week.

Versailles, France, June 4: The Treaty of Trianon redefines Hungary's borders. The German, Austrian, Russian, and Turkish empires have all been radically redrawn since the end of the war.

Northern Mexico, July 28: Pancho Villa, one of the leaders of the Mexican Revolution, surrenders to the government.

Warsaw, Poland, August 23: The Polish Army bravely turns back the Bolsheviks from the capital's gates.

USA, August 26: American women gain the right to vote.

India, September 10: The Indian Congress adopts Gandhi's proposals for self-determination (Hind Swaraj) including non-cooperation.

New York, USA, September 16: A bomb explodes in Wall Street, killing 39 and injuring 300. The bomb was detonated from a horse-drawn carriage outside the J. P. Morgan building.

UK, October 18: Over a million miners strike in support of a pay rise. A demonstration in London turns violent when police restrain 5,000 miners.

USA, November 2: Republicans sweep to victory in the general election. Warren Harding is elected president with Calvin Coolidge as vice-president.

Ireland, December 14: The British government partitions Ireland into two separate territories, following Bloody Sunday (November 21), when 26 people are killed.

Colombia, You May Pass

Panama, April 20: The US Senate today brought a long-awaited closure to a territorial dispute in Colombian Panama with the ratification of the Thomson–Urrutia Treaty. The treaty provides $25 million dollars in compensation for the land used to create the canal and grants Colombia free access to the facility. The state of Panama was originally seized by the USA in 1903 in order that the Panama Canal could be constructed, which joins the Atlantic and Pacific Oceans via the narrow neck of land separating the two continents.

The treaty, originally devised by Thaddeus A. Thomson, a US lawyer and diplomat, was completed in 1914 at the ten-year conclusion of the canal's construction. The blatant US seizure of the region in order to construct the canal, and the ongoing civil unrest within the region by those in favor of the riches that the canal would bring to the area, have finally found resolution with this move.

Germany's Costly War

Berlin, Germany, May 11: The German Government has today accepted the Allies' claims for war reparations. The reparations agreement, which was originally signed by the defeated German nation at Versailles after the conclusion of the Great War, required Germany to take entire responsibility for causing the conflict. In Article 231, the "war guilt clause" called for the establishment of a reparations commission in order to determine the amount of damages to be paid. The final tally was prepared in April of this year and totaled US$33 billion or 133 billion gold marks. Payments are to be made in cash or by commodities such as steel or coal, with the first payment of $250 million being due in September of this year.

Many commentators have grave fears that these exorbitant reparations have been devised with an international vengefulness that will plunge Germany into poverty for the foreseeable future.

time out

Reformers attempted to have the boxer Jack Dempsey arrested for assault and battery after knocking out Georges Carpentier in the ring. They claimed that the fight was a prizefight, to be decided by knockout, rather than a boxing exhibition fought on points.

Other central powers involved in the conflict that are also required to pay reparations under the terms of their individual peace agreements are Austria, Hungary, Bulgaria, and Turkey.

Freedom for Ireland's South

Ireland, December 6: After Sinn Féin's overwhelming victory in the parliamentary elections of Southern Ireland, the controlling British Government has agreed to allow 26 of the 32 counties of

David Lloyd George

The Irish delegation at the signing of the Irish Free State Treaty.

Ireland to form the Irish Free State (or *Saorstát Éireann* in Gaelic). This state will no longer be considered part of "the United Kingdom of Great Britain and Ireland;" instead, under the Anglo–Irish Treaty that was signed by British and Irish Republic representatives in London today, it will replace the two coexisting but nominally rival states that had previously existed. The British Government had partitioned Ireland into two states called Southern Ireland and Northern Ireland under the terms of the Government of Ireland Act 1920. The Irish Free State will have the status of "Dominion within the British Empire," while the six remaining counties will form the Province of Ulster, or Northern Ireland, and will continue to be considered part of the United Kingdom.

The Panama Canal, with its locks to raise and lower ships, is an impressive engineering feat.

Paris, France, January 24: The Allies, without German input, have decreed a figure of $56 billion in war reparations that Germany shall be paying over the next 42 years.

Ireland, February 18: Eamon de Valera, leader of the Irish independence movement, heads a violent rebellion against British troops.

Germany, March 8: Allied troops occupy Dusseldorf, Mulheim, and other cities in response to Germany's rejection of reparation demands.

Russia, March 12: In an attempt to win over peasants, Lenin announces that state planning of the economy is to be ended.

Mongolia, March 13: With the help of White Russian troops, Mongolia expels the Chinese after 200 years.

Panama, April 20: Colombian treaty grants Colombia free access to the Panama Canal and $25 million in exchange for US possession of the strategic waterway.

Berlin, Germany, May 11: The German government finally agrees to war reparations.

Tulsa, Oklahoma, USA, June 1: In the worst race riots ever seen in America, 85 people are killed, hundreds are injured and thousands made homeless.

Shanghai, China, June 30: The Chinese Communist Party holds its first meeting.

London, England, July 22: Peace talks are held between British Prime Minister David Lloyd George and Eamon de Valera, the Irish Republican leader. A truce is declared.

Russia, August 4: Lenin appeals to the West for aid to combat a famine that is sweeping the country. Over 18 million people are thought to be suffering a shortage of food.

Rif, Northern Morocco, September 19: Abd el-Krim, leader of the Rif tribes, declares the Rif Republic. His forces have had a number of military victories over the Spanish colonial troops this year.

Ludwigshafen, Germany, September 21: An explosion at the BASF factory kills 574 workers and injures over 1,000.

Budapest, Hungary, October 21: The former leader of Austria, Emperor Charles, marches on Budapest with 12,000 troops. After making initial gains, they are routed by the Allied armies.

Milan, Italy, November 7: Benito Mussolini, head of the National Fascist Party, names himself *Il Duce*, or leader of the party.

Ireland, December 6: Southern Ireland becomes a free state under the dominion of Britain. The eight counties forming Ulster in the North shall remain part of the United Kingdom.

Mahatma Gandhi Imprisoned

Michael Collins

Ahmedabad, India, March 18: Mahatma Gandhi, the leader of the Indian National Congress (the country's most powerful spearhead for independence), has today been sentenced to six years' imprisonment for "...bringing or attempting to excite disaffection towards His Majesty's Government established by law in British India." While always a staunch advocate for peaceful resolutions of conflict, the Mahatma saw it as his duty to shoulder responsibility for various actions of violent insurrection that had taken place in the country. He pleaded guilty, and in an unforgettable speech that called the judges to consider the justice of British domination in India, demanded for himself the most severe sentence:

> "AMERICA HAS ALL THAT RUSSIA HAS NOT. RUSSIA HAS THINGS AMERICA HAS NOT. WHY WILL AMERICANS NOT REACH OUT A HAND TO RUSSIA, AS I HAVE GIVEN MY HAND?"
>
> ISADORA DUNCAN (1878–1927), AMERICAN DANCER, ON THE AFTERMATH OF THE 1917 REVOLUTION IN RUSSIA, 1922

Mahatma Gandhi with his wife, shortly before his arrest.

"...I am here, therefore, to invite and submit cheerfully to the highest penalty that can be inflicted upon me for what in law is deliberate crime, and what appears to me to be the highest duty of a citizen. The only course open to you, the Judge and the assessors, is either to resign your posts and thus dissociate yourselves from evil, if you feel that the law you are called upon to administer is an evil, and that in reality I am innocent, or to inflict on me the severest penalty, if you believe that the system and the law you are assisting to administer are good for the people of this country, and that my activity is, therefore, injurious to the common weal."

One Strike Ends as Others Continue

USA, September 13: A national rail strike has ended after the National Guard was called out in several US states to control striking coalminers, as unions and workers reach boiling point. The coalminers have been striking for nearly six months to protest about wage cuts. The strike, which was one of several organized by the United Mine Workers of America since 1919, has crippled the coal-mining industry.

One of the most shocking and outrageous displays of pro-union violence ever witnessed took place in Herrin, Illinois, on June 21–22, when 22 strikebreakers were brutally murdered by union supporters.

The horrific events that occurred at what has become known as The Herrin Massacre have come to symbolize the appalling lengths that coalminers will go to in order to protect union rights and demands.

A Tomb to Excite the Whole World

Valley of the Kings, Egypt, November 5: Howard Carter, a dedicated British archeologist and Egyptologist whose work in the Valley of the Kings has been funded by the enthusiastic amateur, Lord George Carnarvon, yesterday discovered the tomb of Tutankhamen. It is a discovery that is sure to capture the world's imagination. The tomb is by far the best preserved and most intact pharaonic tomb ever found in the Valley of the Kings.

Funerary mask of Tutankhamen.

Carter wrote in his diary: "Though I was satisfied that I was on the verge of perhaps a magnificent find, probably one of the missing tombs that I had been seeking for many years, I was much puzzled by the smallness of the opening in comparison with those of other royal tombs in the valley. Its design was certainly of the XVIIIth Dyn. Could it be the tomb of a noble, buried there by royal consent? Or was it a royal cache? As far as my investigations had gone there was absolutely nothing to tell me. Had I known that by digging a few inches deeper I would have exposed seal impressions showing Tut.ankh.Amen's insignia distinctly I would have fervently worked on, and set my mind at rest, but as it was, it was getting late, the night had fast set in, the full moon had risen high in the eastern heavens, I refilled the excavation for protection, and with my men selected for the occasion—they, like myself, delighted beyond all expectation—I returned home and cabled to Lord Carnarvon (then in England) the following message: 'At last have made wonderful discovery in Valley a magnificent tomb with seals intact recovered same for your arrival congratulations.'"

Residents and workers inspect the devastating earthquake damage in central Tokyo.

The Earth Moves and Terror Follows

Tokyo, Japan, September 1: Tokyo and its surrounding areas have been devastated by what has been named as the Great Kanto Earthquake, one of the worst earthquakes the world has yet seen. The devastating quake has killed 150,000 people, destroyed 570,000 homes, and has left 2.5 million people homeless. The damage has already been estimated at approximately US$1 billion.

The earthquake occurred at lunchtime when many people were using open flames to cook with, and the consequent fires that broke out in numerous areas amplified the number of casualties. Due to a typhoon in the north of the country, some fires developed into firestorms that swept across heavily populated areas in one instance, killing 30,000 victims who were gathered together in an open space at Rikugun Honjo Hifukusho.

Many homes have been buried or swept away in mountainous areas, and the entire village of Nebukawa, along with a train carrying 100 passengers, and the village station, were plunged into the sea. Tsunamis reaching heights of up to 32 ft (10 m) were recorded within just a few minutes of the quake's occurence in several coastal areas.

A New Free Turkish Republic

Angora, Turkey, October 29: The leader of the nationalist movement who brought an end to the Ottoman Empire, Mustafa Kemal, has been unanimously elected president of the new Turkish Republic. Kemal emerged as a hero at the Battle of Gallipoli in 1915, and has become a charismatic leader throughout Turkey's ongoing struggle for liberation. In recent years, he has emerged as a triumphant commander who has crushed those attempting to invade his lands. Turkey can now boast full independence and the end to six centuries of the Ottoman dynasty's domination.

Buckets of Money, but Nothing to Buy

Germany, November 15, 1923: The costs of Germany's defeat in the Great War continue to extract a terrible price from the pockets of the beleaguered nation as hyperinflation drastically reduces the value of the mark. One US dollar is now worth four trillion marks, and an entire nation remains utterly perplexed at how such a state of affairs has been able to occur. There are several reasons but no absolute answers.

Germany abandoned its gold-backed currency in 1914, and the huge reparation costs extracted from the defeated nation have left an enormous debt upon the shoulders of all Germans, and yet workers continue demanding higher wages. The assassination of the moderate Foreign Minister, Walter Rathenau, by right-wing fanatics last June has also resulted in a destabilizing effect on the treasury, and inflation has galloped since.

Prices doubled in the first half of 1922, with milk going from 7 marks per liter to 16, but so rampant is it now that students are advised by waiters to order two cups of coffee at once so that the price doesn't increase by 20 percent in the time it takes them to drink one. Teachers who are paid at 11 a.m. have their families come to collect their wages so that they can buy goods while the money still has some value, and factory workers dutifully line up as the bundles of notes that constitute their weekly pay are offloaded from trucks. Wealthier citizens have been putting all their money into diamonds, pianos, artworks, gold, and real estate, while a huge black market in goods and foreign currencies has emerged as a second economy. Many individual cities and regions have even begun to produce their own currencies.

Mustafa Kemal (Atatürk)

time out

American silent film comedian Roscoe "Fatty" Arbuckle was acquitted of the murder of actress Virginia Rappe by a San Francisco jury in his third murder trial following two hung juries. He received a written apology from the jury for his ordeal.

Ruhr region, Germany, January 11: French and Belgium troops occupy the Ruhr district as Germany defaults on war reparations. Civilians are encouraged to passively resist occupying forces.
Moscow, USSR, March 9: Ill health forces Vladimir Lenin to step down following his third stroke.
Kabul, Afghanistan, April 9: A new constitution aimed at modernizing the country is enacted.
Sofia, Bulgaria, June 9: A bloodless coup overthrows the regime of Stambuliski.

Germany, June 22: The decline of the Deutsch mark is becoming increasingly desperate, losing more than half its value in the last month. The war contributed to the present crisis, which is being exacerbated by the French occupation of the Ruhr.
USA, June 30: Membership of the Ku Klux Klan passes one million. Their anti-minority stance has proven popular throughout the USA.
Lausanne, Switzerland, July 24: The Near East Treaty establishes peace between Greece and Turkey.

Washington DC, USA, August 3: Calvin Coolidge is sworn in as President after the sudden death of President Harding from a stroke, aged 58.
Tokyo, Japan, September 1: The Great Kanto Earthquake (magnitude 8.3 on the Richter scale) levels Tokyo and Yokohama, killing 150,000 and leaving 2.5 million people homeless.
Southern Rhodesia, September 1: The British Crown takes control of the southern African colony from the British South Africa Company.

Madrid, Spain, September 13: Miguel Primo de Rivera leads a coup with the blessing of the King. The parliament is abolished and there is no guarantee of civil liberties.
India, September 25: The Swaraj Party, advocates of self-determination, win control of the Indian National Congress.
Persia, October 28: Reza Khan, commander-in-chief since 1921, becomes premier. The Shah of Persia, in response to a near-dictatorship, goes into exile.

Angora (Ankara), Turkey, October 29: Leader of the nationalist movement that brought an end to the Ottoman Empire, Mustafa Kemal has been elected President of the new Turkish republic.
Munich, Germany, November 12: Disaffection and conflict throughout Germany is exploited by Adolf Hitler to gain popular support in Bavaria. The Beer Hall Putsch fails and Hitler and other key figures are arrested.
Germany, November 15: Chronic inflation has devalued the mark. One US dollar is now worth 4 trillion marks.

Frank Hurley

Russia Mourns Death of Leader

Moscow, USSR, January 21: Russia's leader, Vladimir Lenin, has died at the relatively young age of 53. The leader has suffered a series of strokes since 1922, and his declining health has led him to try to change what are believed by some to be the excesses of his regime. He had hoped that Leon Trotsky, not Joseph Stalin, would succeed him. In this he has not been successful. His final stroke caused paralysis and rendered him speechless. The official cause of death was given as arteriosclerosis. However, some doubts have been raised about the accuracy of these claims, and several of the doctors who treated him at the time suggested it was in fact syphilis that killed him.

"TODAY, 23 YEARS AGO DEAR GRAND-MAMA DIED. I WONDER WHAT SHE WOULD HAVE THOUGHT OF A LABOUR GOVERN-MENT."

KING GEORGE V
(1865–1936), ON THE
FORMATION OF THE
FIRST LABOUR
GOVERNMENT IN THE
UNITED KINGDOM

Vladimir Lenin, with the Kremlin in the background.

Throughout Lenin's confinement, Stalin has taken full advantage of his growing autonomy as the General Secretary of the Communist Party, and has expelled many people who he believes to be "unsatisfactory" party members, including a great many of rival Leon Trotsky's supporters. Some political analysts believe that Stalin's new government appointments are set to ensure that Trotsky will no longer be his rival for leadership in the future.

Britain's New Rule

London, England, November 6: Following the Conservative Party's landslide victory in the October general election (419 seats to 151), Stanley Baldwin has replaced the Labor Prime Minister and nominated Mr Winston Churchill as Chancellor of the Exchequer, the second highest post in the British Government. The new chancellor was reported as commenting: "This fulfills my ambition. I still have my father's robe as Chancellor. I shall be proud to serve you in this splendid Office."

Churchill's appointment, however, has been greeted with considerable resistance and criticism from within the party and by *The Times*. Austin Chamberlain, the leader of the Conservative Party, has made his feelings clear on the matter, "I am alarmed at the news that you have made Winston Chancellor, not because I do not wish Winston well, but because I fear that this particular appointment will be a great shock to the party."

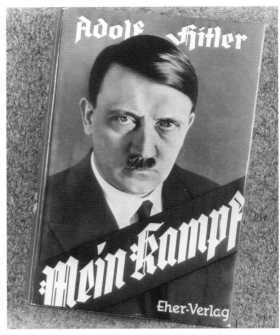

Adolf Hitler on the cover of his autobiography *Mein Kampf*.

Hitler's New Struggle

Munich, Germany, December 20: Adolf Hitler has been freed after only eight months in Landsberg Prison, where he was serving a sentence for High Treason after a failed attempt at a coup with Erich Ludendorff and other sympathetic members of the police and military last year. The coup had been modeled on Mussolini's "March on Rome," and Hitler had hoped to make his own "march on Berlin," but several important factions withdrew their support at the last hour.

Hitler's imprisonment was turned into something of a publicity stunt by the ambitious leader of the Nazi Party. His original sentence was for five years, but after having found favor with the judiciary, prison guards, and other influential supporters, it was cut short. Adolf Hitler's time in prison was predominantly spent in dictating his book *Mein Kampf (My Struggle)* to his deputy Rudolf Hess. The book is both an autobiography and a political manifesto.

Gorky, USSR, January 21: Vladimir Ilyich Lenin, the architect of the Russian revolution, dies following a fourth stroke, aged 54.

London, England, January 23: Ramsey MacDonald becomes the first Labour Prime Minister, forming a minority government.

Bombay, India, February 4: Mohandas Ghandi's deteriorating health lead authorities to release him from jail unconditionally.

Luxor, Egypt, February 12: Howard Carter opens King Tutankhamen's sarcophagus.

Ankara, Turkey, March 3: President Kemal Ataturk declares a new constitution. In an effort to modernize the country, the caliphate (Islamic spiritual leadership) is abolished and a secular state is established.

Greece, March 25: In a peaceful uprising, George II abdicates in favor of a civilian government.

Munich, Germany, April 1: Adolf Hitler is sentenced to five years jail for his role in the 'beer hall' putsch. He shall be eligible for parole in six months.

India, April: Plague decimates the Punjab region, claiming over 25,000 lives.

Moscow, USSR, May 26: Joseph Stalin is elected General Secretary of the Communist Party. He survives an attempted censure by Lenin in his testament, recommending Leon Trotsky for the top job.

Rome, Italy, June 10: Socialist leader Giacomo Matteotti is kidnapped and murdered by fascists. Mussolini's party was swept to power in elections in April, gaining 64 percent of the vote.

Germany, August 30: In an effort to stabilize the economy, the Reichsbank is made independent. This follows on from the Dawes plan for war reparations, including a loan for eight million reichsmarks.

Geneva, Switzerland, October 2: The Geneva protocol is put forward at the League of Nations, providing for compulsory arbitration of disputes.

Shanghai, China, October 13: The northern factions' headquarters is captured after three years of civil war. Their leader flees to Japan.

USA, November 4: Republican Calvin Coolidge wins a second term in office in a decisive victory over Democratic hopeful John W. Davis.

London, England, November 6: A conservative government under Prime Minister Stanley Baldwin replaces the Labour leadership, in power for just 11 months. Winston Churchill has been promoted to Chancellor of the Exchequer.

Munich, Germany, December 20: Hitler is freed after eight months in prison. He completed his book *Mein Kampf* during his incarceration.

The Death of a Father

Peking, China, March 12: Sun Yat-sen, the founding father of the Republic of China, died of cancer in Peking today aged 58. Sun came to be known as the "Father of the Republic" after several periods of political exile and a life-long quest to abolish the monarchy, to open the road to socialism, and to modernize his country and bring it into line with the west. With help from Soviet advisers in 1924, he was able to implement his political philosophy of the Three Principles of the People (nationalism, democracy, and the people's livelihood), to reorganize the Kuomintang along the lines of military forces in communist Russia, and to establish the republic's Whampoa Military Academy. Chiang Kai-shek, the army's commander in chief, has now assumed leadership of the forces after facing opposition from his older leadership challenger, Wang Ching-wei. Chiang has vowed to purge communist dissidents from within the armed forces.

time out

Calvin Coolidge made radio history when the largest audience ever tuned in to the broadcast of his final campaign speech. Americans then heard their newly elected president take the oath of office on the radio for the first time.

Political and Civil Unrest Grip China

Shanghai, China, June 23: China sits poised on the brink of civil war today as regional warlords in the north battle for power against the increasingly polarized National Revolutionary Army led by Chiang Kai-shek, while protests from workers in other parts of the country against unequal treaties have spread to Canton. Strikes and boycotts against British goods and shipping have escalated after British troops killed 12 Chinese demonstrators in Shanghai on May 30. Further unrest has come after 50 Whampoa Military Academy cadets were killed in fights with British and French forces. US Navy South China Patrol ships are standing by to help French and British forces protect their interests in the region.

Stanley Baldwin

Ignoble Effects of Noble Experiment

Philadelphia, USA, December 3: As the USA faces constant increases in charges for drunkenness and prohibition-related crimes, Federal agents brandishing 43 warrants have cracked one of the largest international rum rings yet found in Philadelphia. In a city faced with constantly increasing arrests for drunkenness (55,766 arrests in 1924, rising to 58,617 this year), the fight against liquor seems an increasingly difficult one to win, especially as those politicians who oppose prohibition look unlikely to be voted into office. The humorist Will Rogers recently remarked: "If you think this country ain't dry, just watch 'em vote; if you think this country ain't wet, just watch 'em drink. You see, when they vote, it's counted, but when they drink it ain't."

Some citizens resort to hiding the booze.

The Chinese revolutionary leader Sun Yat-sen on a visit to the Ming tombs.

Oslo, Norway, January 1: Christiania, the capital of the Scandinavian country, is renamed.
Moscow, USSR, January 16: Leon Trotsky is ousted from the Soviet War council. This is a victory for Stalin and his allies, Zinoviev and Kamenev.
Peking, China, March 12: Sun Yat-sen, the "father of the republic," dies, aged 58. His political philosophy, the Three Principles of the People, is highly influential. General Chiang Kai-shek assumes the mantle of Chinese leader.

Great Britain and Australia, April 8: The Australian federal government has promised 34 million dollars in low-interest loans to encourage migration from Britain over the next 10 years.
Germany, April 25: Field Marshal von Hindenburg is elected President in the first popular elections to be held in the country.
Cyprus, May 1: The Mediterranean island becomes a colony of the British Empire.
Tennessee, USA, May 25: Teacher John Scopes is indicted for teaching Darwin's theory of evolution.

Shanghai, China, June 23: China is on the brink of civil war as regional warlords compete for power. Anti-British sentiment is high following the dispersal of student demonstrations by British troops.
South Africa, June 29: The parliament legislates to prohibit non-whites from working in skilled and semi-skilled jobs.
Santa Barbara, USA, June 29: A 6.3 magnitude earthquake destroys Santa Barbara's downtown area.

Washington DC, USA, August 8: More than 40,000 Ku Klux Klan members march through the streets of the Capitol.
Australia, September 23: New legislation allows for refusal of entry to the country of immigrants of any race, class or occupation at the discretion of the governor-general.
Locarno, Switzerland, October 16: Germany and France sign a peace treaty, seven years after hostilities ended, agreeing never to fight each other again and recognizing a demilitarized zone along the Rhine.

Philadelphia, USA, December 3: Federal agents brandishing 43 warrants swoop on an international rum ring in control of millions in liquor, money and ships. Agents label it the "greatest roundup in the history of Prohibition."
Persia, December 13: After deposing the self-exiled Shah, Reza Khan is crowned the new Shah of Persia. He initiates a reform policy.
Moscow, USSR, December: At the 14th Soviet Party Congress, Stalin calls for socialism at home rather than worldwide revolution.

Benito Mussolini

> "Is it possible that my people live in such awful conditions? …I tell you…that if I had to live in conditions like that I would be a revolutionary myself."
>
> KING GEORGE V (1865–1936), ON BEING TOLD THE LIFE STORY OF A MAN CALLED MR WHEATELY

There Is Power in the Union!

UK, May 12: A paralyzing nine-day strike in the United Kingdom, staged in defense of the nation's coalminers, has broken today. The strike, which included railway men, transport workers, printers, dockers, and steel workers, had been called by the General Council of the Trade Union Congress (TUC) on May 1 in order to demand that the government prevent reductions in wages and worsening conditions for miners. Many politicians and unionists hold grave fears about what the revolutionary elements within the unions might be capable of doing to the British economy. The changes to wages and conditions came as a result of depleted coal seams from heavy mining during the Great War, a drop in the price and demand for British coal due to Germany supplying France and Italy with free coal as part of its war reparations, and Churchill's reintroduction of the gold standard for the British currency. This has brought about an increase in the value of the pound, which has made exporting coal impossible.

Mine owners and the government were hopeful that an editorial in the *Daily Mail* damning the strike would bring an end to the industrial action; however, the newspaper refused to run this piece, forcing other avenues of negotiation to open. The strike was finally brought to an end when the Conservative Government led by Prime Minister Stanley Baldwin agreed to the intermediate measure of providing a nine-month subsidy in order for miners to maintain their wages, as well as ordering a royal commission, which is to be chaired by the British High Commissioner, Sir Herbert Samuel, into the conditions and problems facing the British coal industry, and in particular the lives of its miners. These concessions from the government are being hailed as a major triumph for the working class of Britain.

time out

Escapologist Harry Houdini remained underwater in an airtight bronze coffin for an hour and a half. When accused of cheating, he said, "There is no trick, there is no fake; you simply lie down in a coffin and breathe quietly."

"Il Duce" Will Prevail

Rome, Italy, November 2: "I declare…in front of the Italian people…that I alone assume the political, moral, and historic responsibility for everything that has happened. Italy wants peace and quiet, work and calm. I will give these things with love if possible and with force if necessary."

Benito Mussolini, the Italian Prime Minister, has declared himself to be without peer or equal in Italy, banning all political parties but his own and demanding that all journalists be members of the Fascist Party. Il Duce is not without his enemies, however, having survived two assassination attempts this year, the first by an Irish woman, Violet Gibson, the sister of Baron Ashbourne, whose bullet merely grazed Mussolini's nose in April, and another attempt in Rome on September 11. In this attempt, anarchist Gino Lucetti hurled a bomb at the windscreen of the leader's passing car, but the device failed to explode until it had reached the pavement.

Japan's Enlightened New Emperor

Tokyo, Japan, December 25: Upon the death of his father, Emperor Yoshihito, Hirohito has become Emperor of Japan, taking the name of Showa Tenno, and ending the Taisho period. His ascendancy has officially been proclaimed as the Showa ("enlightened peace") era. The new emperor has the distinction of being the first in several hundred years to have his biological mother, Crown Princess Sadako, as the official wife of his predecessor. The 25-year-old Hirohito has traveled extensively throughout Europe, and is the first Japanese crown prince to have done so. He spent considerable time mixing with the British royal family, and was pleased to see how informal their lifestyle is. He is married to Princess Nagako.

Strikers on a march during the General Strike organized by the Trade Union Congress in support of the miners.

Canada, January: Canada joins the Commonwealth of Nations.

Mecca, Hejaz, January 8: Abdel-Aziz ibn Saud takes the title of King of the Hejaz, stating his intention to rename the region Saudi Arabia.

Turkey, February 17: Under the modernizing influence of Kemal Ataturk, new civil, criminal and law codes based on European systems are adopted.

Rome, Italy, April 7: Mussolini survives an assassination attempt by Irishwoman Violet Gibson. He only suffers an injured nose.

Calcutta, India, April: Sectarian riots between Muslims and Hindus erupt, injuring hundreds.

England, May 12: A paralysing general strike, precipitated by the walkout of coal miners on May 1, ends. Transport, press and industry have been at a standstill. Strikes were called following the government withdrawing subsidies from the miners.

Targuist, Morocco, May 26: Under siege from 160,000 French troops, 30,000 riffian rebels, led by Abd el Krim, surrender.

Warsaw, Poland, June 13: Josef Pilsudski is installed as leader following a military coup.

New Jersey, USA, July 10: A lightning strike on a munitions depot causes a massive explosion.

Paris, France, July 23: A new coalition government consisting of former opponents is sworn in. The nation is on the brink of bankruptcy following devaluation of the franc.

Transvaal, South Africa, August 22: Discovery of massive reserves of diamonds brings 50,000 to the region.

Hankou, China, September 6: Nationalist Kuomintang troops, led by General Chiang Kai-shek, capture the strategic treaty port of Hankou. The northern troops have retreated and there is fear that Peking will fall.

Geneva, Switzerland, September 8: Germany is formally admitted to the League of Nations furthering its rehabilitation from pariah status.

Florida, USA, September 18: A tropical hurricane ravages Florida, killing 1,500 and leaving 40,000 homeless.

Rome, Italy, November 2: Mussolini survives another assassination attempt. On October 7, the Fascist party outlawed all opposition and Il Duce became paramount leader.

London, England, November 18: The Imperial Conference concludes with the formation of the British Commonwealth of equal, autonomous nations.

Tokyo, Japan, December 25: Hirohito becomes Emperor following his father Yoshihito's death, ending the Taisho period.

Lindbergh poses next to his airplane *The Spirit of St Louis*.

A Transatlantic Triumph

Paris, France, May 21: Today, American aviator Charles A. Lindbergh has completed the first non-stop flight from New York to Paris in a total of 33.5 hours. Flying his single-engine *The Spirit of St Louis* (a custom-made and significantly modified version of a standard Ryan M-2), Charles Lindbergh is the first solo pilot to have completed the transatlantic flight, having left the Roosevelt Field on Long Island at 8 a.m. on May 20 before flying the 3,610-mile (5,810-km) journey to Le Bourget Field in Paris. The venture was funded by the New York hotelier Raymond Orteig.

Having always been a keen aviator, Lindbergh was even more enthusiastic at the prospect of a $25,000 prize for the first person to make the journey.

On his way, he encountered many of the obstacles he'd expected: rain, sleet, and high winds, though he couldn't have contemplated the crowd of 100,000 Parisians who were waiting at Le Bourget to welcome him when he touched down at 10.22 p.m.: "I saw there was danger of killing people with my propeller, and I quickly came to a stop."

Astoundingly, the pilot was able to carry out conversations throughout the journey with people below: "I have carried on short conversations with people on the ground by flying low with throttled engine, and shouting a question and receiving the answer by some signal. When I saw this fisherman, I decided to try to get him to point towards land. I had no sooner made the decision than the futility of the effort became apparent. In all likelihood, he could not speak English, and even if he could, he would undoubtedly be far too astounded to answer. However, I circled again, and closing the throttle as the plane passed within a few feet of the boat I shouted, 'Which way is Ireland?' Of course the attempt was useless, and I continued on my course."

Charles Lindbergh has become an international hero overnight!

Guilty or Not?

Massachusetts, USA, August 23: Nicola Sacco and Bartolomeo Vanzetti have been found guilty and sentenced to death for the murder of two men in a payroll robbery that took place in the main street of South Braintree, Massachusetts, on April 15, 1920. In the years since the robbery, the case has become a *cause célèbre*, not so much for its nature, but for the racial and political scapegoating that has influenced the trial and the media attention surrounding it. Sacco and Vanzetti, both Italian migrants, anarchists, and social agitators, are widely believed to have been tried and convicted on these aspects of their characters alone, while the murders themselves are in want of further proof. There are a very great number of supporters who see their conviction as a grave failing of the court system and rank this as the most politically charged case in the history of American jurisprudence.

Vanzetti had this to say on the passing of his sentence: "This is what I say: I would not wish to a dog or to a snake, to the most low or misfortunate creature of the earth—I would not wish to any of them what I have had to suffer for things that I am not guilty of. But my conviction is that I have suffered for things that I am guilty of. I am suffering because I am a radical, and indeed I am a radical; I have suffered because I was an Italian, and indeed I am an Italian; I have suffered more for my family and for my beloved than for myself; but I am so convinced to be right that if you could execute me two times, and if I could be reborn two other times, I would live again to do what I have done already."

Emperor Hirohito

Crowds converge to view the Parliament House in Canberra, the new capital of Australia.

Canada, January: The Indian Act prohibits "First Nations" from raising money or hiring a lawyer for the purpose of pursuing land claims.

Shanghai, China, January 31: Following rioting, nationalist sentiment and civil unrest, 12,000 British troops are ordered to protect British interests. The Chinese protest at the deployment.

Lisbon, Portugal, February 9: A revolt against the dictatorship of General Carmona is crushed. Since founding in 1910, Portugal has been wracked by instability.

England, February 27: Up to 1,000 people per week die in a nationwide outbreak of influenza.

Shanghai, China, April 28: Infighting in the Kuomintang between moderates and Communists leads to raids on union strongholds.

Berlin, Germany, May 1: The government lifts its ban on the Nazi party; Adolf Hitler addresses a rally.

Canberra, Australia, May 9: The parliament convenes in the new capital for the first time. Melbourne had held parliamentary sittings since federation.

Paris, France, May 21: American Charles Lindbergh completes the first non-stop flight from New York to Paris in 33 hours, and 100,000 Parisians gather to celebrate the landing.

Xining, China, May 22: An 8.6 magnitude earthquake leaves over 200,000 dead– one of the worst earthquakes in history.

Moscow, USSR, June 9: Twenty alleged British spies are executed without trial, following the UK severing diplomatic ties with the communist state.

Vienna, Austria, July 15: Rioting breaks out following the acquittal of three nationalists on murder charges. The Ministry of Justice is set on fire, 89 people die and 600 are injured.

Massachusetts, USA, August 23: Italian anarchists Sacco and Vanzetti, convicted of murder and robbery six years ago, are executed, continuing to maintain their innocence. Their case became a *cause célèbre*.

St Louis, USA, September 30: A tornado of five minutes duration devastates St Louis, killing 69.

Mexico, October: The leaders of the "Cristero War" are executed. A reaction to government seizure of church property, the rebellion is brutally suppressed by President Calles.

Moscow, USSR, November 15: Stalin expels his main opponents, Trotsky and Zinoviev from the Communist Party. They had led a peaceful demonstration criticizing Stalin by implication last week.

Canton, China, December 19: General Chiang Kai-shek crushes a Communist uprising and expels all Russian citizens.

Chiang Kai-shek

Amelia Takes to the Air

Carmarthenshire, Wales, June 18: Amelia Earhart, who has been playfully nicknamed the "Lady Lindy" because of her uncanny resemblance to Charles Lindbergh, today became the first woman to cross the Atlantic Ocean in an airplane. Piloted by Wilmer "Bill" Stutz with Louis "Slim "Gordon as the co-pilot, the flight was the first of its kind since Lindbergh's non-stop journey from New York to Paris in May last year. The three aviators made the historic crossing from Trepassy Harbor, Newfoundland, to Burry Port in the south of Wales. Earhart took her first ride in an airplane only eight years ago.

> "A COUNTRY GROWS IN HISTORY NOT ONLY BECAUSE OF THE HEROISM OF ITS TROOPS ON THE FIELD OF BATTLE, IT GROWS ALSO WHEN IT TURNS TO JUSTICE AND TO RIGHT FOR THE CONSERVATION OF ITS INTERESTS."
>
> ARISTIDE BRIAND (1862–1932), FRENCH STATESMAN, PRIME MINISTER AND NOBEL PRIZE WINNER

Epic flight for *Southern Cross*

Sydney, Australia, July 10: Today, the acclaimed aviator Charles Kingsford Smith and his crew will arrive in Sydney from Brisbane to a rapturous reception,

having definitively proven that air travel across the Pacific is achievable.

During this pioneering era of flight, as records are continuously being bettered, Charles Kingsford Smith is one of Australia's pre-eminent aviators. Born in Brisbane, Australia, in 1897, Smith enrolled in the Australian military in 1915, serving in the Middle East during the Great War. Joining the Royal Flying Corps as a fighter pilot, he was shot down over France, aged twenty, earning the Military Cross for his bravery.

In 1926, he completed a round-Australia flight in ten days with his co-pilot Charles Ulm. Ulm and Smith then headed to America seeking an aircraft

Amelia Earhart and her pilot Wilmer Stultz and mechanic Louis Gordon pose with dignitaries at Southampton.

to fly across the Pacific. After numerous setbacks, the *Southern Cross*, a Fokker F. VIIb, took off from Oakland, California, on May 31, 1928. With Harry Lyon as navigator and Jim Warner operating the radio, the first stage to Hawaii took 27 hours. The second stage to Fiji was

extremely turbulent, as the *Southern Cross* passed through a massive tropical storm, finally arriving after 33 hours in the air. Twenty-five thousand well-wishers greeted the exhausted aviators upon completion of the final leg to Brisbane on July 9.

China, One at Last

Nanjing, China, November: Chiang Kai-shek, the newly elected president, has completed the unification of China under the Nationalist Nanjing Government, which is under the control of the Kuomintang. After years of political turbulence, all 12 states have signed treaties giving the Nationalist Government absolute tariff autonomy. Having annulled all treaties with western powers that were considered "unequal," Chiang faces an uneasy future. He may have seized control, but he still faces serious dissent from several political factions and vengeful hostility from the remaining vestiges of warlord power.

Stocking Up for Christmas

New York, USA, December: After another turbulent period, the New York Stock Exchange (NYSE) has ended the year with the stock market industrial average up 48 percent. Excessive glee is being tempered by those who believe that many marketplaces are reaching saturation point, and that the dramatic increase in wealth being enjoyed by investors ranging from the traditionally moneyed to the recent, lower income investors must come at a price. Newly elected President, Herbert Hoover, a staunch economic conservative, has become a serious critic of the country's excessive use of borrowed money and overspeculation. Hoover's powers over the stock market are limited, however, and the controlling body, the Federal Reserve Board, appears to be deaf to the words of naysayers. The new Governor of New York, Franklin D. Roosevelt, has dismissed the President's concern.

Moscow, USSR, January 16: Stalin, in attempt to dilute any influence in opposition to his rule, exiles Trotsky, Zinoviev and Kamenev.

Nicaragua, January 26: US President Coolidge sends 1,000 Marines to combat guerrillas led by General Sandino. An ardent nationalist, his troops have been waging a bloody battle against US influence for two years.

Darwin, Australia, February 22: Aviator Bert Hinkler completes the first solo flight from England in 15 days.

California, USA, March 12: The St Francis dam bursts, sending a 40-foot (12-m) wall of water down stream, killing over 400 people.

Turkey, April 29: Premier Mustafa Kemal introduces the English alphabet in preference to the Arabic.

Shantung, China, May 11: Three days of heavy fighting between Japanese and Chinese troops leave 1,000 dead.

Italy, May 12: Universal suffrage is abandoned. The eligible electorate drops to three million as Mussolini's grip on the country tightens.

Carthmarthenshire, Wales, June 18: Aviatrix Amelia Earhart crosses the Atlantic from Boston in 22 hours. On June 10, Charles Kingsford-Smith successfully flew from the USA to Australia in eight days.

Zagreb, Yugoslavia, August 1: Croats set up a separatist parliament and demand a federal system.

Paris, France, August 27: The Kellogg-Briand Pact is signed, renouncing "war as an instrument of national policy." Eleven nations including Germany, USA, France, and UK are signatories.

Lucknow, India, August 30: Dissatisfied with the adoption of the Nehru Plan, the Independence of India League is established under the leadership of Jawaharlal Nehru, son of the author of the plan.

Moscow, USSR, October 1: The beginning of Stalin's first five-year plan. Farms are to made collectives and heavy industry expanded.

Addis Ababa, Ethiopia, October 7: Ras Tafari is crowned King. Sharing power with his aunt, Empress Zauditu, the coronation legitimizes his 10-year rule.

USA, November 6: Republican Herbert Hoover wins a landslide victory in the federal election over Democrat Alfred E. Smith.

Nanking, China, November: The Kuomintang government of Chiang Kai-shek gains international legitimacy, signing treaties with 12 states. Rival warlords eventually recognise the Nanking government, unifying China.

New York, USA, December: The New York stock exchange sees a turbulent year, with a massive depreciation in stock values.

An Old Wound Healed

Rome, Italy, February 11: In a landmark moment for Italy, Catholicism, and the Papacy, the Lateran Treaty was signed today by Benito Mussolini and Cardinal Pietro Gasparri, the Papal Secretary of State, on behalf of Pope Pius XI. The treaty is designed to re-establish the sovereignty of the Pope and fully restore the diplomatic and political power of the Holy See of Rome after 60 years of tension. The treaty formally brings into existence the "Vatican City State."

The conflict between the Church and State first arose in 1871 when the newly formed kingdom of Italy had annexed the Papal states and offered an annual indemnity of 3,250,000 lire for its loss of sovereignty. Pope Pius IX never accepted this edict, nor did he accept the payments, and consequently Popes have lived as virtual prisoners in the Vatican since. The Papacy has continued to demand independence from any political interference over its spiritual jurisdiction, and with this treaty that independence has once again been granted.

Mussolini and Gasparri sign the Lateran Treaty.

Herbert Hoover for President! Republican party candidate Herbert Clark Hoover, born in 1874, helps his United States presidential push with a promotional campaign button.

Black Thursday and the Chips Are Down

New York, USA, October 24: It is a "Black Thursday" indeed following a dramatic fall in share values on the New York Stock Exchange. On a day when many more investors wanted to sell than to buy, stock prices declined by 3.2 percent and brought the Dow Jones Industrial Average down to 372, continuing the decline for the much-beleaguered Dow, which had fallen 8 percent in a ten-day period earlier in the month. These falls follow an even steeper drop of 7.5 percent in the previous afternoon's trading, precipitating the second largest day in trading volume the exchange has ever experienced, with in excess of 16 million shares being sold and average falls in value of more than 11 percent—in all, a total decline in share value of somewhere between $10 and $15 billion.

The crash in share prices follows a series of events including a scandal in which the English financier, Clarence Hatry, recalled British funds invested in the USA, and a more general instability in global markets. Some are even ascribing the sudden drop in investor confidence to a famous New York astrologer, Evangeline Adams, who advises 100,000 investors (counting among them celebrities such as Mary Pickford and financier

time out

In Paris, hundreds of Americans, ruined by the Wall Street crash, tried to sell valuables they had purchased recently. Local jewelers said that over half of their recent customers were trying to return gems for half their original price.

John Pierpont Morgan) with her monthly newsletter. Her forecast of falls on October 22 certainly created an enormous flurry to sell. Many US investors have borrowed money, mortgaged their homes, or sold off government securities such as Liberty Bonds in recent times to capitalize on what they hoped would be an ongoing boom in the US market. It seems that the current levels of debt and the declining US economy have contributed heavily to the selling fever that has overtaken today's markets. Some are so fearful of their financial ruin that reports of suicide in many parts of the country are already being reported.

"Inquilab Zindabad!" (Long Live, Revolution!)

Lahore, India, December: Protests in India have escalated this year from both Muslim and Hindu sectors, leading to an all-out call for independence from the All India Congress. A bomb hurled into the Central Legislative Assembly by the revolutionaries Bhagat Singh and Batukeshwar Dutt, whose cries of "Inquilab Zindabad!" or "Long live Revolution," accompanied the blast in April, was a direct protest against the proposed enactment of controversial new public safety legislation, the Defence of India Act and the Trades Disputes Bill, both designed to give British authorities and the military significantly greater power to arrest citizens who they saw as behaving in a suspicious manner. While the bills have yet failed to be passed by the Assembly, growing civil unrest has meant that the ruling British powers are increasingly eager to find ways to maintain control of the country, even as independence appears increasingly to be inevitable.

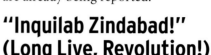

Charles Kingsford Smith

Key Events

Yugoslavia, January 6: Alexander I takes direct control of the Kingdom of the Serbs, Croats and Slovenes, renaming it Yugoslavia.
USSR, January 30: Leon Trotsky is expelled from Russia; he has been Stalin's most vocal critic. Exile to Alma-Ata was insufficient to silence him; he now departs for Turkey.
Rome, Italy, February 11: Mussolini and the Papacy sign the Lateran Treaty, creating the Vatican and re-establishing the sovereignty of the Pope after 60 years of tension.

Chicago, USA, February 14: Gangster Al Capone's mob executes six members of a rival gang in the "St Valentine's Day massacre." Extortion, prostitution and bootleg liquor are the gang's main business.
Mexico, April 6: The USA send in planes equipped for bombing after US citizens are killed in the latest attack by rebels, who want to topple the government of President Gil.
Berlin, Germany, May 3: Communist protestors fight pitched battles with police.

London, England, June 10: Ramsay MacDonald forms a new Labour government after a hung parliament was delivered in the general election. Margaret Bondfield is the first woman member of the Cabinet.
Nelson, New Zealand, June 24: A massive earthquake on the South Island spectacularly rearranges the landscape and kills 20 people.
USSR/China Border, July 22: Tensions are mounting after disputes concerning the Chinese Eastern Railway in Manchuria. Troops are massing along the border.

Jerusalem, Palestine, August 31: Jewish access to the Wailing Wall causes a violent uprising by Arabs, leaving 500 dead. British troops act swiftly to restore the rule of law.
Geneva, Switzerland, September 5: French Premier Aristide Briand puts forward a proposal for European Union at the League of Nations, which is coolly received.
Berlin, Germany, September 22: Armed groups of Communists and Nazis clash in chaotic scenes throughout the city.

Kabul, Afghanistan, October 16: Rebel General Nadir Khan captures Kabul and is proclaimed Shah.
New York, USA, October 24: The "Black Thursday" stock market crash wipes millions off the value of shares.
Lahore, India, December: Escalating violence between Hindus and Muslims leads to the All-India Congress calling for independence from Britain.
Paisley, Scotland, December 31: A fire in a movie theater leaves 69 children dead.

Dr Frederick Banting

New Hope for Diabetics

Toronto, Canada, August, 1921: There is new hope on the horizon for sufferers of diabetes with a new cure discovered by Dr Frederick Banting and science graduate Charles Best, whose laboratory tests on dogs at Toronto University have now revealed a startling new hormone that could be used to treat the fatal disease. The two made the discovery by blocking off the pancreas of laboratory dogs with a ligature tied around the pancreatic duct, effectively rendering the animals diabetic. They then took fluid from healthy dogs' islets of Langerhans (an important, hormone-producing component of the pancreas) and injected it into the diabetic dogs, temporarily returning them to health. They have been able to modify the extraction process and obtain a purer form of insulin from cattle to continue their experiments.

"Insulin," which comes from the Latin *insula* meaning *island*, is produced and secreted by the group of "islet cells" contained within the pancreas, along with many other enzymes. The function of insulin then is to absorb any glucose (sugar) detected in the bloodstream and extract the calories from within it, as well as control the release and storage of fat (triglycerides), the absorption of amino acids, and the uptake of electrolytes. It also contributes considerably to the maintenance of small vessel muscle tone. People with diabetes cease to produce this hormone, and without it, the body is unable to access the calories and nourishment within glucose, and consequently their bodies experience starvation, which in the past has resulted in coma and death. The tests carried out in Toronto this summer have proven that diabetic animals at least can be kept alive for considerable lengths of time when the insulin hormone is administered regularly.

> *"THE OPPOSITE OF A CORRECT STATEMENT IS A FALSE STATEMENT. BUT THE OPPOSITE OF A PROFOUND TRUTH MAY WELL BE ANOTHER PROFOUND TRUTH."*
>
> NIELS BOHR (1885–1962), DANISH PHYSICIST AND NOBEL PRIZE WINNER

The Nobel Prize in Physics

Stockholm, Sweden, December 10 , 1921: Albert Einstein has been awarded the Nobel Prize for his services to Theoretical Physics, and especially for his discovery of the law of the photoelectric effect. The latter (previously called the Hertz effect) relates to the emission of electrons from matter when absorbing electromagnetic radiation and X-rays.

The Chairman of the Nobel Committee for Physics, Svante August Arrhenius, of the Royal Swedish Academy of Sciences, in presenting the award, said: "There is probably no physicist living today whose name has become so widely known as that of Albert Einstein. Most discussion centers on his theory of relativity. This pertains essentially to epistemology (the study of the nature, origin, and scope of knowledge), and has therefore been the subject of lively debate in philosophical circles.

It will be no secret that the famous philosopher Henri Bergson in Paris has challenged Einstein's ground-breaking theory of relativity, while other philosophers have acclaimed it wholeheartedly. The theory in question also has a range of astrophysical implications, which are presently being rigorously examined.

Albert Einstein himself was not able to attend the ceremony in Stockholm.

time out

Lieutenant Lester J. Maitland, who piloted the first non-stop flight from California to Hawaii, put forward that the word "avigation" be used for the directing or operating of aircraft from one place to another. The word would differentiate this skill from simple "navigation."

Albert Einstein shows his mathematical calculations.

Inventor Dies

Baddeck, Nova Scotia, Canada, August 2 , 1922: Alexander Graham Bell, one of the world's foremost telecommunication pioneers and the man traditionally believed to have been the inventor of the telephone, has died aged 75.

Born in Edinburgh, Scotland, in 1847, he settled in Boston to begin his career as an inventor. His professional motivation throughout life had been educating the deaf, which led him to invent the first useful microphone. He invented his electrical speech machine in 1876, which has come to be known around the world as the telephone. News of his discovery spread quickly throughout the world, and in 1878 he established the first telephone exchange in New Haven, Connecticut. By 1884, long-distance calls could be made between Boston, Massachusetts, and New York City. The first phone that Bell used

These telephones are an improvement on Bell's original machine.

Archeologist Howard Carter removes oils from the coffin of Tutankhamen.

was built by Thomas Watson, and it consisted of a wooden stand, some copper wire, a cup of acid, and a funnel. The words of the first phone call were reported to be: "Mr Watson, come here, I want you." Bell was not alone in his quest to invent the device, however, and he filed for a patent just hours before his rival Elisha Gray, whose "notice of invention" outlined some of the science that Bell needed to complete his own project.

The Treasures of Tutankhamen's Tomb

Valley of the Kings, Egypt, November 23, 1922: Howard Carter has successfully opened the tomb of Tutankhamen, revealing the treasures within. In his diary entry, he writes: "In the upper part of this sealed doorway traces of two distinct reopenings and successive reclosings were apparent, and that the seal-impressions first noticed, Nov. 5, of the Royal Necropolis—i.e. 'Anubis over Nine Foes,' had been used for the reclosing. Here was evidence of at least the reign of the tomb, but its true significance was still a puzzle, for in the lower rubbish

that filled the staircase entrance we found masses of broken potsherds, broken boxes, the latter bearing the names and protocol of Akhenaten, Smenkh-Ka-Ra, and Tut.ankh.Amen, and with what was even more upsetting a scarab of Tehutimes III, as well as a fragment bearing the cartouche of Amenhetep III. These conflicting data led us for a time to believe that we were about to open a royal cache of the El Amarna branch of the XVIIIth Dyn. Monarchs, and that from the evidence mentioned above it had been probably opened and used more than once."

Among the treasures discovered in the tomb were cartouches (a symbolic framework surrounding hieroglyphs bearing the Pharaoh's name) and Ancient Egyptian senet games (the equivalent of board games that were popular in ancient Egypt).

Technicolor on the Big Screen

New York, USA, November 26, 1922: The first Technicolor movie to debut on the big screen has been released. *The Toll of the Sea*, an adaptation of Puccini's famous opera story, *Madame Butterfly*, has been branded a critical success by those who know in Hollywood. It has also grabbed the attention of heavyweights D. W. Griffith and Douglas

Rorschach inkblot, used in psychology.

Fairbanks, who are keen to use the medium in their future films. The film was written by Frances Marion, and starred Hollywood's first Asian–American screen goddess, Anna May Wong, whose allure and screen presence steal the show.

The Technicolor Motion Picture Corporation was founded in 1915 by Doctor Herbert T. Kalmus, Doctor Daniel Comstock, and Burton Wescott, setting up their first laboratory in a disused railway car. The color process they employed recorded red and blue-green images simultaneously with a single lens, using a beam splitter and color filters to record the images, stacked one on top of the other. The film is in actual fact black and white, but it runs through a special projector with two apertures and a filter that adds the tints.

While still in need of some fine tuning, the medium seems sure to be a success with cinemagoers everywhere.

New Breakthroughs in Psychoanalysis

Austria, December, 1923: Sigmund Freud, the father of modern psychology, has published his most important work to date, *The Ego and the Id*. The book introduces the structural theory of psychoanalysis. Freud's theory divides the human mind into three distinct agencies or "structures," these being the *id*, the *ego* (from the Latin meaning "I"), and the *superego*. The id is the source of psychological energy experienced from instinctual needs and drives; the ego is the conscious mediator between the internal person and the external identity; and the superego is the internalization of the conscious self extenuated by rules, conflict, morality, and guilt.

Alexander Graham Bell

Austria, March 30, 1925: Rudolf Steiner, philosopher, architect, educator, playwright, dies, aged 64.

USA, June 6, 1925: Walter Chrysler forms the Chrysler Motor Company from the ashes of the Maxwell Motor Company.

Egypt, November 13, 1925: Egyptologists unwrap the mummy of King Tutankhamen; the king was only a youth, dying at the age of 15.

London, England, December 31, 1925: Surgeon Henry Souttar performs a successful operation inside the heart of a young patient, a world first.

New York, USA, January, 1926: Victor introduces the Electrola phonograph.

London, England, January 27, 1926: John Logie Baird demonstrates his invention "television" to the Royal Institute.

Yucatan, Mexico, February 8, 1926: American archaeologists find a complex of Mayan temples in the dense jungle.

Auburn, USA, March 16, 1926: Physicist Robert Goddard's liquid-fuelled rocket launches successfully.

New York, USA, January 5, 1927: Movietone, a new invention synchronizing motion pictures and sound, is unveiled by Fox Studios.

Solo, Central Java, Indonesia, August 31, 1927: Scientists believe that *Pithecanthropus erectus*, "Java Man," may be the earliest human forebear.

USA, October 28, 1927: Pan Am Airlines launch the world's first commercial international flight.

New York/London, December 31, 1927: The first transatlantic telephone service is operational.

USA, May 11, 1928: The first commercial television broadcasts begin with three 90-minute sessions per week.

London, England, September 15, 1928: Bacteriologist Alexander Fleming makes a discovery while studying *Staphylococcus* bacteria; *Penicillium notatum*, a mould growing on some specimens, has killed the bacteria.

Boston, USA, October 12, 1928: The Iron Lung, a machine enabling a person to breathe, is used for the first time on a child with infantile paralysis.

Washington, D.C., USA, January 17, 1929: Edwin Hubble observes that all galaxies are moving away from each other by an analysis of the light spectra emitted changing wavelength (red shift).

Ladenburg, Germany, April 4, 1929: Carl Benz, inventor of the first practical internal combustion engine, dies, aged 84. Collaborating with Otto Daimler, a three-wheeler car was developed in 1885.

New York, USA, December, 1929: This year, biochemist P. Levene identifies the components of DNA.

Rudolf Steiner

A Lost Civilization is Found

Yucatán, Mexico, February 8, 1924: American archeologist Sylvanus Griswold Morley has led an excavation team to a fascinating discovery in Chichen Itza on Mexico's Yucatán Peninsula. Funded by the Carnegie Institution and Harvard University, the team has revealed a sprawling complex of buildings and ruins, many of which are completely concealed beneath earth and dense jungle. While parts of the site had been documented and photographed late last century and in the early years of this century by historical authorities such as Teoberto Maler, Alfred Maudslay, and Eduard Seler, they had done little in the way of excavation themselves. The rather eccentric amateur enthusiast Augustus Le Plongeon, and his wife, Alice Dixon, had attempted a dig, but it had yielded little more than a type of Mayan statue called a *chacmool*, which has come to be the most symbolic image of these particular ruins.

Little has changed, however, since the site was first discovered in 1842 by explorers Frederick Catherwood and John Lloyd Stephens, whose reports of discovery ignited interest in the region. While the site is situated 75 miles (120 km) east of Mérida and is one of the largest Mayan sites on the peninsula, local Maya farmers still work the surrounding land.

Throughout the period of Maya civilization (approximately 1,000 BCE to the early sixteenth century CE), this site had been a place of pilgrimage and

Images of the Toltec god Quetzalcoatl are found at Chichen Itza.

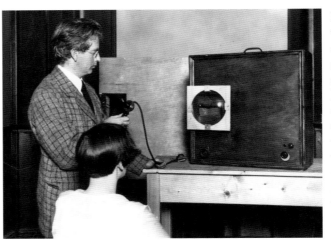

John Logie Baird demonstrates a transmission from his "televisor."

ceremony. The appellation "Chichen Itza" translates as "the mouth of the well of Itza" (there is a sacred well nearby), and Itza was the name of the people who once inhabited this region. It is believed that Chichen Itza was invaded and overthrown during the tenth century by Toltec forces led by the ruler Quetzalcoatl, who was named after a Mesoamerican deity. The invaders came from the west of the continent, and their rule lasted a century or more.

First Television Transmission

London, England, January 27, 1926: John Logie Baird has demonstrated the first television transmission of an image today in front of some 50 scientists in his Soho workshop. Born in Helensburgh, Scotland, in 1888, the inventor studied electrical engineering at the Glasgow and West of Scotland Technical College, but his studies were interrupted by the outbreak of World War I. Chronic poor health rendered him unfit for military service, and he therefore took up the post of superintendent engineer with the Clyde Valley Electrical Company.

Fascinated with the idea of a machine that could transmit images, Baird moved to England in 1922, and worked tirelessly with two dedicated but unpaid helpers, Victor Mills and Norman Loxdale, to create a working television system, which has been the aspiration of many inventors for decades. Mills aided Baird in the refinement of his electronics, while Loxdale built the various components. The prototype is a crude affair supported by a washstand—the motor's base is a tea chest, and a biscuit tin

houses the projection lamp, while scanning disks are cut from cardboard and are supported by hatboxes that are mounted on a coffin lid. He has also used fourpenny cycle lenses, wood scraps, darning needles, and string, while the entire contraption is held together with sealing wax. The very first image transmitted today was the flickering image of a Maltese cross.

The machine, which is capable of transmitting images through transparent rods, has proved an unprecedented example of reflected light being used rather than backlit silhouettes.

Baird has also been involved with experiments on the transmission, reflection, and detection of radio waves, which would enable surveillance systems to determine the distances of objects, an area of potential importance to military forces in the wake of recent wars.

Pan American Goes International

USA, October 28, 1927: Pan American Airlines has become the "chosen instrument" for US Government overseas air transport and the first airline to offer international flights to the public. It has been announced that flights to South America and the Caribbean will now be available, and on October 19 their first commercial flight departed from Key West in Florida for Havana.

The company has come into existence through the merger of several entrepreneurial and aviation interests—namely, airline entrepreneur Juan Trippe, who brought with him the financial backing of Cornelius Vanderbilt Whitney and William A. Rockefeller (with whom he had already established the Aviation Corporation of America), as well as other aviation entrepreneurs.

This merger brings together the components needed to get the business started, whether it be the contracts for mail runs, capital, or landing sites. Trippe, however, provided Pan Am with its first airplane, a Fairchild FC-2 floatplane.

"One sometimes finds what one is not looking for"

London, England, September 15, 1928: Medical science has received a new bolt of hope with the discovery of a mold capable of destroying bacteria. Alexander Fleming, a Scottish scientific researcher who has worked extensively on antiseptics

and the natural bacterial action of the blood, made the discovery upon returning to his small, musty laboratory in London's St Mary's Hospital after a two-week vacation. He noticed a transparent ring of greenish-yellow mold that had accidentally contaminated a dish. A spore of *Penicillium notatum* (a type of mold or fungus) from the nearby mycology lab had drifted in and created the phenomenon, while a cold spell had given this peculiar type of mold a chance to grow. When the temperature increased, the staphylococcus bacterium grew over the entire plate, except for the area directly around the penicillium contaminant. Observing this, Fleming correctly assumed the mold had released a bacteria-inhibiting substance. From there, he was able to isolate the enzyme "lysozyme" (a substance secreted through mucosal membranes that acts as the body's own antibiotic) and extract the substance, which Fleming has called "penicillin."

Born in 1881 on an 800-acre (323-ha) farm in Lochfield, East Ayrshire, in Scotland, Fleming was the seventh of eight children. He attended St Mary's Hospital medical school in London and the Royal College of Surgeons before becoming a pioneer in vaccine therapy. During the Great War, he served as a captain for the Army Medical Corps in battlefield hospitals in France.

Fleming is credited as being the first doctor in Britain to administer Salvarsan, an effective new treatment for the common disease syphilis that was developed by the German scientist Paul Ehrlich in 1909 and is a champion of many types of inoculation for conditions currently plaguing the world.

Hubble's New Law for the Universe

Washington DC, USA, January 17, 1929: The American astronomer Edwin P. Hubble has changed forever the way we think about space with his study of galaxies through both their size and expansion. The lawyer turned astronomer was the first to confirm that the misty patches of illumination visible in the sky called spiral nebula are actually galaxies similar to our own Milky Way. Hubble's more recent research released today has found evidence to support that the universe is in fact expanding, and he has developed a classification system to sort the galaxies

by content, distance, shape, and brightness. He has reported on red shifts in the light that the galaxies emitted, and his observations that they were moving away from each other at a rate constant to the distance between them. From his findings, the 40-year-old astronomer has formulated Hubble's Law, which should

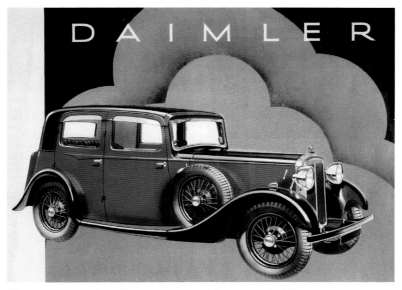

This advertisement shows the elegant lines and dashing red of a Daimler.

prove invaluable to astronomers who have been trying to determine the age of the universe.

Hubble's Law states that any two points moving away from the origin, each along straight lines and with speed proportional to distance from the origin, will be moving away from each other with a speed proportional to their distance apart.

Born in Marshfield, Missouri, in 1889, Hubble received a bachelor's degree in mathematics and astronomy in 1910, before being awarded a Rhodes Scholarship at Oxford University, where he read law. In 1914, he gave up law and took up a position at University of Chicago's Yerkes Observatory, and then after the Great War he took up a post at the Mount Wilson Observatory, where his research into the existence of other galaxies began. These galaxies had previously been believed to be the universe. Even Einstein himself had thought the idea of an expanding universe too far fetched for his theory of relativity, but he is reported to be thankful to Hubble for his discovery.

The Passing of a Mechanical Great

Ladenburg, Germany, April 4, 1929: Karl Friedrich Benz, the inventor of the first practical internal combustion engine, has died. The mechanical engineer was born in Baden Muehlburg, Germany, in 1844, and attended the Karlsruhe Polytechnic University. In 1871, he established a

mechanical workshop with August Ritter, supplying building materials, but the business was a disaster. Benz began working on his design for a two-stroke engine, which he patented in 1879, before going on to found Benz and Company in Mannheim, where he produced industrial engines. His work there led him in 1885 to design a "motor carriage," the Tri-Car, with a four-stroke engine which is based on Nicolaus Otto's patent. Benz designed a 958 cc, 0.75 hp engine for the three-wheeled vehicle, along with electric ignition, differential gears, and water cooling. In 1886, he was granted a patent for his gas-fuelled automobile, which he began selling to the public. By 1893, his Benz Velo had become the world's first relatively inexpensive, mass-produced car. Benz's designs had grown out of date by 1903, when he retired from Benz and Company, but the indefatigable mechanic worked until his death for Gottlieb Daimler, who independently had created a vehicle very similar to the Tri-Car in the 1880s but had failed to patent it before Benz.

Karl Friedrich Benz

Scientific Achievements

Astronomy: Discovery of Cepheids in Andromeda resolved the Shapely-Curtis debate.
Botany: Hortus Bulborum, world's most important bulb garden, established in the Netherlands.
Chemistry: Penicillin is discovered.
Ecology: White lead interior paint banned by the League of Nations.
Geology: Dendrochronology (tree-ring dating) is proposed.
Mathematics: Minimax theorem proven, start made on principles of game theory.
Medicine: First vaccines administered for diphtheria, pertussis, tuberculosis, and tetanus; iron lung invented.
Physics: Liquid-fuelled rocket successfully launched.
Zoology: A new species of fish, the Congo or African blind bard, discovered.

Botanic Gardens
Cluj-Napoca, Romania
Goudhurst, England
Nanjing, China

Observatories
Columbia, USA
Stuttgart, Germany

Universities
University of Aarhus, Denmark
University of Brno, Czechoslovakia
University of Dacca, Bengal
University of Port-au-Prince, Haiti
University of Thessaloniki, Greece

Katherine Mansfield

"Art is Dead"

Berlin, Germany, June 1, 1920: A new post-war arts movement is galvanizing artists and thinkers from Europe to New York. At the first international Dadaist fair this summer, the German painter George Grosz carried a sign proclaiming, "Art is dead: This is the new art machine." The artist, a gifted radical, is one of many creative people keen to turn the art world upside down in the wake of the Great War's carnage and destruction.

The Dada cultural movement began in Switzerland during the war and has been characterized with absurdist and nihilist works spanning all creative mediums, including Cabaret Voltaire, a traveling theater show designed to shock viewers out of their personal and political complacency, protesting, as it does vehemently, against the barbarism of war and the traditionally bourgeois nature of art.

Tristan Tzara, another artist and exponent of the movement, was quoted as saying, "God and my toothbrush are Dada, and New Yorkers can be Dada too,

if they are not already." And indeed they are! Having already attracted such names as Marcel Duchamp, Man Ray, Francis Picabia, and Beatrice Wood to exhibit their works in sympathetic New York galleries, *American Art News* has described the Dada philosophy as "the sickest, most paralyzing and most destructive thing that has ever originated from the brain of man." Dadaists would contend, however, that the Great War would better foot that bill.

The name Dada remains something of a mystery. No one can agree whether it comes from the Romanian *"da, da,"* meaning "yes, yes," or from *"dada,"* a childish French word for "hobbyhorse." It seems that with Dadaism's central themes of anarchy and internationalism that such confusion might be quite appropriate.

The funeral procession of Camille Saint-Saëns travels through Paris.

The Last Note for a French Great

Algiers, Algeria, December 16, 1921: French-born pianist and composer Camille Saint-Saëns has died. The renowned musician was born in Paris in 1835, and from an early age showed himself to be a precocious pianist and composer. He studied at the Paris Conservatoire, where his brilliant talent was quickly noticed by Rossini, Berlioz, and Liszt, who described him as the world's greatest organist. He composed prolifically throughout his career, and was a founder of the Société Nationale de Musique in 1871.

Saint-Saëns wrote 13 operas, of which *Samson et Dalila* is the most popular, and he also penned a witty orchestral romp entitled *Le carnaval des animaux (Carnival of the animals)*. He also wrote four symphonic poems in a style influenced by his mentor, Liszt. Toward the end of the nineteenth century, he developed a more austere style that has been compared to composers such as Fauré and Ravel.

time out

James Joyce's novel *Ulysses* was published in Paris with a print run of 1000. It tells the story of Leopold Bloom's journeys around Dublin. The title "Ulysses" is a Latinized version of "Odyssey" and the novel carries many echoes of Homer's classic.

"How to Keep Young Mentally"

USA, February 5, 1922: It's all in the first issue of *Reader's Digest*, a new type of publication aimed at condensing magazines so that readers can cut to the chase of modern journalism and find out what's happening in a fraction of the time it takes in other wordier journals. The concept has been realized by DeWitt Wallace, who had been publishing a modest agricultural digest for US farmers and decided that if he could edit general magazine articles by up to three-quarters while maintaining all the information they covered, then readers would be able to absorb much more in a short reading.

After returning from the war, the enterprising Wallace set about perfecting his skill and produced a trial magazine with 31 short stories in it, one for each day of the average month, and printed them in a pocket-sized volume.

Zelda and F. Scott Fitzgerald.

Paris, France, January 25, 1920: Italian painter, sculptor and drinker Amadeo Modigliani dies, aged 35.
Berlin, Germany, June 1, 1920: At the first Dadaist art exhibition, George Grosz carries a sign: "Art is dead. This is the new art machine."
Los Angeles, USA, September 5, 1920: Comedian Roscoe "Fatty" Arbuckle is charged with the rape and murder of Virginia Rappe.
Barcelona, Spain, December, 1920: Gaudi's Casa Mila is completed.
Ontario, Canada, 1920 The Group of Seven first exhibit their works.

Naples, Italy, August 2, 1921: One of the world's best-known singers, tenor Enrico Caruso, dies aged 48.
Paris, France, September 19, 1921: Charlie Chaplin, Douglas Fairbanks and Mary Pickford take Europe by storm on a promotional tour.
Montreal, Canada, September 9, 1921: Stephen Leacock helps found the Canadian Authors Association.
USA, October 31, 1921: Dashing Rudolf Valentino stars in The Sheik.
Algiers, Algeria, December 16, 1921: Camille Saint-Saëns, French composer and pianist dies, aged 86.

USA, February 5, 1922: The first issue of The Reader's Digest is published, set up by DeWitt Wallace with capital of $5,000.
Sydney, Australia, September 2, 1922: Henry Lawson, Australia's famous bush poet, dies, aged 55. Thousands attend his state funeral.
Paris, France, November 18, 1922: Marcel Proust, intellectual and novelist, dies, aged 51.
Notable Books, 1922: *Ulysses* by James Joyce, *Siddhartha* by Herman Hesse, short stories by F. Scott Fitzgerald.

Fontainbleau, France, January 9, 1923: New Zealand born writer Katherine Mansfield dies, aged 34.
Paris, France, March 29, 1923: After 50 years in the theater, *grand dame* Sarah Bernhardt dies, aged 79.
Weimar, Germany, August 15, 1923: The Bauhaus design movement exhibits works by Kandinsky, Klee, Gropius, Marcks, and Moholy-Nagy.
Stockholm, Sweden, December 10, 1923: The Nobel Prize for Literature is awarded to Irish poet W.B. Yeats.
New Zealand, December, 1923: Maori is accepted as a subject in universities.

New York City, USA, February 12, 1924: George Gershwin's *Rhapsody in Blue* premières, bringing jazz to the concert hall.
Los Angeles, USA, April 16, 1924: MGM Studios forms with the merger of the Metro and Goldwyn Picture Corporations, and Louis B. Mayer Pictures.
Prague, Czechoslovakia, June 3, 1924: Franz Kafka, author of The Metamorphosis, dies, aged 40.
UK and USA, December, 1924: E.M. Forster's novel *A Passage to India* sells over 70,000 copies this year.

Poster advertising the Bauhaus exhibition in Weimar, Germany.

The Bauhaus Movement

Weimar, Germany, August 15, 1923: In a decade that promises to be full of new frontiers, the Bauhaus design school looks to be at its forefront, with an exhibition showcasing at least five of its emissaries: Paul Klee, Lyonel Feininger, Walter Gropius, Wassily Kandinsky, Gerhard Marcks, and László Moholy-Nagy.

The Bauhaus School, the popular name for *Staatliches Bauhaus* (meaning Architecture House), was established in 1919 by architect Walter Gropius in a merging of the Weimar Academy of Fine Arts and the Weimar School of Arts and Crafts, the intention being to combine architecture with traditional fine arts and crafts. Gropius wanted to create and encourage an innovative modern style of architecture and design that reflected a more progressive post-war era in which consumer items could be inexpensive, functional, and in line with newer mass-market production methods, while still maintaining their artistic merits. The result often gives the impression of industrial modernity to domestic consumer items and architectural design. To emphasize his efforts, he is publishing the magazine *Bauhaus*, which will highlight the achievements of many bold new creators.

Gershwin Swings

New York, USA, February 12, 1924: American music will never be the same again after tonight's "An Experiment in Modern Music" held at New York's Aeolian Hall. George Gershwin, one of Broadway's most popular composers, has premiered his new "jazz concerto," *Rhapsody in Blue*, which he composed in a mere three weeks.

The piece, performed by Paul Whiteman's orchestra, was a triumph, and the audience's applause confirmed what many critics see as the perfect fusion of America's music influences, with praise for "the rich inventiveness of its rhythms, the saliency and vividness of the orchestral color" joining the less kind critics whose comments on "the lifelessness of its melody and harmony, so derivative, so stale, so inexpressive" seem to be falling on deaf ears. No one, it seems, can deny Gershwin's genius—among the audience were such notables as Sergei Rachmaninoff and Efrem Zimbalist, Sr.

Orchestrated by Ferde Grofé, the piece begins with a wailing clarinet and goes on to combine a daring miscellany of influences—from the tuneful piano rags and jazz reminiscent of Harlem's clubs to folksy refrains of Yiddish music hall and the post-Romantic influences of Ravel, Schoenberg, and Stravinsky. *Rhapsody* climaxed with Gershwin himself doing a piano solo, and his piece alone eclipsed all others on this chilly winter's night.

The composer thanks the rhythm and rattle of a train to Boston for the tempo, and claims James McNeill Whistler's painting *Nocturne in Black and Gold* as the inspiration for *Rhapsody*'s title.

William Butler Yeats

George Gershwin, captured on canvas by W. Auerbach Levy.

Hoping to enlist the support of leading magazine publishers, Wallace sent off copies of his trial magazine. However, he received only one reply, from William Randolph Hearst, who believes it could reach a circulation of 300,000, which is not enough for him to consider taking on its distribution.

The first issue of Reader's Digest contains 62 pages of print, no illustrations or advertisements, and is coedited with his wife, Lila Bell Acheson.

Apart from helpful advice on staying young mentally, the edition features articles on a range of topics, including "Watch Your Dog and Be Wise," "Whatever is New for Women is Wrong," and another that poses the question "Is the Stage too Vulgar." To which the answer is a resounding yes!

Key Events

Paris, France, April 30, 1925: The *Arts decoratifs* (Art deco) show opens, showcasing furniture, ceramics, textiles and architecture in this vibrant post-war style.
USA, June 26, 1925: Charlie Chaplin's *The Gold Rush* premières.
Paris, France, November 13, 1925: The first exhibition of surrealist art opens with works by Ernst, Klee, de Chirico, Miro, and Picasso.
USSR, December 21, 1925: Eisenstein's *Battleship Potemkin*, a silent film documenting a Russian naval mutiny, is released.

Barcelona, Spain, June 9, 1926: Architect Antoni Gaudi dies, aged 74, after being run over by a tram.
USA, August 6, 1926: *Don Juan* is the first film to have a pre-recorded soundtrack.
New York, USA, August 23, 1926: Film idol Rudolph Valentino dies of a ruptured appendix, aged 31.
New Zealand, September 9, 1926: The Maori Arts and Crafts Act revives traditional Maori skills.
Germany, 1926: Franz Kafka's reputation grows posthumously with *The Trial* and *The Castle*.

Paris, France, February 6, 1927: Violin virtuoso Yehudi Menuhin debuts to captivated crowds, aged 7.
New York, USA, April 19, 1927: A court finds Mae West guilty of indecency. Her play *Sex* contained numerous lewd impersonations.
Northampton, England, June 14, 1927: Author of *Three Men in a Boat*, Jerome K. Jerome dies, aged 68.
USA, October 6, 1927: *The Jazz Singer* starring Al Jolson, is the first "talkie" to gain widespread success.
Germany, December, 1927: Mies van der Roe designs the Weissenhof Apartments.

Dorchester, England, January 11, 1928: Author Thomas Hardy dies, aged 87. His ashes are interred in Westminster Abbey.
Oxford, England, April, 1928: The final volume of the Oxford English Dictionary is published. The project was initiated in 1879.
Berlin, Germany, August 31, 1928: Bertolt Brecht and Kurt Weil's sardonic theatrical masterpiece *The Three Penny Opera* debuts.
USA, November 18, 1928: Walt Disney's short film *Steamboat Willie* introduces Mickey Mouse.

Belgium and USA, January, 1929: Two comic strip characters make their debut: *Tintin* by Hergé and *Popeye*, drawn by Elzie Segar.
Los Angeles, USA, May 16, 1929: The first Academy Awards is held at the Roosevelt Hotel in Hollywood.
London, England, July 5, 1929: Twelve nude portraits of D.H. Lawrence are seized by police from a Mayfair gallery. *Lady Chatterley's Lover* was published last year.
Stockholm, Sweden, December 10, 1929: German author Thomas Mann wins the Nobel Prize for Literature.

Writer's Life Cut Short by Tuberculosis

Franz Kafka

Germany, June 3, 1924: Franz Kafka, the avant-garde Czech writer, artist, and intellectual, has died. Born on July 3, 1883, Kafka grew up in a middle-class Jewish family whose influences were to dominate most of his life and work. Educated at German schools instead of Czech ones, he mastered the German language early and went on to study law at the Charles-Ferdinand University, believing the profession would provide a financial life without interfering in his mental one. Driven almost to suicide during the Great War when his father forced him to run the family asbestos factory, he developed the tuberculosis that would eventually cut short his life, and by 1920 he was virtually in retirement.

His first published work in 1913 was *Meditation*, a collection of early stories and sketches. This was followed by several short works, including *The Judgment* (1913) and *Metamorphosis* (1915), the latter perhaps his most famous early work concerning a man who turns into a fatally wounded bug. His enigmatic and perplexing short story *A Country Doctor* was published in 1919. Kafka will be remembered for his dark ruminations on human nature and his even more bizarre attitudes toward human sexual behavior.

Kafka requested that the remainder of his unpublished works be destroyed after his death.

Sudden Death for an Architectural Great

Barcelona, Spain, June 9, 1926: Antoni Gaudí, one of the most influential architects of the Art Nouveau movement, has died two days after being run over by a tram in Barcelona. Gaudí, who had long favored ragged attire, was mistaken for a tramp by onlookers, and it consequently took considerable time to find any cab willing to take him to a hospital for medical attention. Eventually he was delivered to a pauper's hospital, where he remained unrecognized until friends tracked him down the following day. They attempted to move him to a better place, but Gaudí insisted he belonged there among the poor of Barcelona, in whose company he died a day later. He will be buried in his unfinished masterpiece, *La Sagrada Familia*.

Born in Reus, Spain, in 1852, Gaudí suffered from serious rheumatism throughout his childhood, often having to travel around on the back of a donkey. He studied at Escola Tècnica Superior d'Arquitectura in Barcelona, and his lifelong fascination with nature led him to incorporate its angles into his work, preferring the curves and arcs of trees and the human form to those of geometric shapes. His irregular visions could easily be realized using reinforced steel rods in the construction of his buildings, magically mimicking the curvature he witnessed in the natural world.

Gaudí was a strict vegetarian and devout Catholic, as well as a militant Catalan nationalist, and was once arrested for speaking Catalan, which had been outlawed by the authorities of the time. In later years he abandoned secular work altogether and devoted himself to the Catholic Church. After the death of his faithful collaborator, Francesc Berenguer Mestres, in 1912, Barcelona fell upon hard economic times, and Gaudí's work came to a halt.

Gaudí's first major commission was for the Casa Vicens, for which he employed a Gothic Revival style that became the trademark of his work. Over the years he developed an entirely original, gracious, and often surreal style to his designs, which put him at the forefront of Spain's Art Nouveau movement and altered completely established forms of contemporary architecture, most particularly in Barcelona where he lived most of his life.

A Classic Departure

Dorchester, England, January 11, 1928: Thomas Hardy, one of Britain's most admired and controversial writers, has died at the age of 87.

Born June 2, 1840, Hardy grew up in Upper Bockhampton, Dorset. He attended Julia Martin's school in Bockhampton from the age of 8 and later studied Latin and French.

He trained as an architect in Dorchester, and for some years in London, before poor health forced him back to Dorset. In 1874, he married Emma Gifford, who encouraged him in his writing, and they had four children. Written in 1867, his first novel, *The Poor Man and the Lady*, was rejected by publishers because it was seen as too hostile toward the upper classes. His second novel, a melodrama entitled *Desperate Remedies* (1871), was published anonymously, followed by *Under the Greenwood Tree* (1872). A number of his works were originally published as serials in magazines.

Success for Hardy really arrived with *Far from the Madding Crowd* (1874), *The Return of the Native* (1878), *The Mayor of Casterbridge* (1886), *The Woodlanders* (1887), and *Tess of the D'Urbervilles* (1891), which have all become classics.

When Hardy's *Jude the Obscure* was published in 1895, the public outcry was so great over his frank treatment of sex that he never wrote another novel, and in his later years turned his attention to poetry, discontinuing his prose writing.

A World of Words From Oxford

Oxford, England, April, 1928: *The Oxford English Dictionary*—the most comprehensive guide to the English language—has finally become a reality with the completion of the 125th fascicle (a contributing section to a reference work). The final section covers "Wise to the end of W." Today, for the first time, the entire dictionary is available in ten volumes or as a set of 20 half-volumes, with two choices of binding. The price is 50 or 55 guineas (£52.50 or £57.75) depending on the format and binding.

The completion of the project has been a triumph of will and perseverance involving a great many contributors and editors dating back as far as 1857, when the Philological Society consisting of Richard

The roofline of apartment building *Casa Ballto* shows Gaudí's surreal design style.

"*You see things; and you say, 'Why?' But I dream things that never were; and I say 'Why not?'*"

GEORGE BERNARD SHAW (1856–1950), IRISH PLAYWRIGHT AND CRITIC AND NOBEL PRIZE WINNER, 1921

"*BULLFIGHTING, BULLSLINGING, AND BULLSH[*]T.*"

ZELDA FITZGERALD (1920–1948), AMERICAN WRITER AND WIFE OF NOVELIST F. SCOTT FITZGERALD, DESCRIBING ERNEST HEMINGWAY'S NOVEL, *THE SUN ALSO RISES*, 1926

Chenevix Trench, Herbert Coleridge, and Frederick Furnivall formed the Unregistered Words Committee, whose goal became the gathering of words not listed and defined in existing dictionaries. They called the project [A study] *On Some Deficiencies in our English Dictionaries*. Their task was by no means a simple one, and at that stage Oxford University had no part in the project.

In 1879, after two years of negotiation, Oxford University Press agreed to publish the dictionary, and James Murray was formally appointed as the editor.

In the years since, editors working on the project have built up its contents in Britain and the USA by requesting the public to send in slips of paper with sentences using words in context, and by 1882 Murray and his assistants had gathered some 3,500,000 of them. These slips were then allocated to their various letters of the alphabet at the Scriptorium, from where they've finally found meaning and posterity.

Spanish artist Pablo Picasso painted *Three Musicians* in 1921.

Rudolph Valentino

The Stars Come Out

Los Angeles, USA, May 16, 1929: A quiet but important event took place this evening to honor the achievements of Hollywood's films and actors. The Academy of Motion Picture Arts and Sciences held their inaugural Academy Awards presentation at a black-tie banquet in the Blossom Room at the Hollywood Roosevelt Hotel. Some 270 people attended the ceremony, and while Academy members were admitted free, their guests were charged $5 each.

To be eligible for the Academy Awards, the films were required to be released between August 1, 1927 and July 31, 1928. Award winners were notified three months prior to the dinner, while newspapers have been advised tonight. Douglas Fairbanks, the Academy's president, gave an after-dinner speech and, aided by William C. De Mille, called the winners up to receive their trophies. The "Academy Award of Merit" statuettes were sculpted by George Stanley from bronze and depict a knight upon a reel of film clutching his sword.

The Best Actor award went to Emil Jannings for *The Way of All Flesh*, while Janet Gaynor took out Best Actress for *Seventh Heaven*.

Other awards presented at today's ceremony included: Best Production to the silent movie *Wings*, Best Director to Frank Borzage for *Seventh Heaven*, the Academy Award for Unique and Artistic Quality of Production to *Sunrise*, and Best Comedy Direction to Lewis Milestone for *Two Arabian Knights*.

David Herbert Lawrence

Obscenity in Our Midst

London, England, July 5, 1929: David Herbert (D. H.) Lawrence, the novelist whose written works have made him one of the most controversial and celebrated writers of his time, has always been of interest to censors with his graphic depictions of human relationships. It seems that his visual artwork has put him under renewed scrutiny, with the seizure of several of his nude paintings from the Warren Gallery in London by police officers today.

Lawrence was born on September 11, 1885, in Eastwood, Nottinghamshire. His father was an uneducated coalminer and his mother a schoolteacher. His early life was spent close to poverty and the working classes, an influence that has profoundly colored his work over the years.

Throughout adulthood, much of his time has been spent in self-imposed exile in France and Italy. Strict censorship laws in Britain have caused his work to be both highly praised and vehemently opposed. He describes his frequent and prolonged departures abroad as "savage pilgrimages," even preferring Mussolini's fascism to England's censoriousness. His most recent novel, *Lady Chatterley's Lover*, is said to be so lurid that it was initially published in private editions in Florence and Paris, and sold at great discretion by booksellers. Since its publication, he has written a number of pieces, both serious and satirical, on the closed-mindedness of contemporary British thought, and his outspokenness has had him branded as a pornographer in some circles, while writers such as E. M. Forster have credited him as being "the greatest imaginative novelist of our generation."

Chronic ill health resulting from tuberculosis has reduced his written works considerably, but has renewed his interest in oil painting. It seems that no matter what medium he chooses, it meets with similar responses in his native country. His most notable novels include *Sons and Lovers*, *Women in Love*, and *Kangaroo*.

Achievements in The Arts

Key Structures
Aalsmeer House, Aalsmeer, Netherlands
Bauhaus, Dessau, Germany
Einstein Tower, Potsdam, Germany
El Pueblo Ribera Court, La Jolla, USA
Goetheanum I, Dornach, Switzerland
H. Lange House, Krefeld, Germany
Het Schip, Amsterdam, Netherlands
Hollyhock House, Los Angeles, USA
I. G. Farben Offices, Frankfurt, Germany
Imperial Hotel, Tokyo, Japan
Manhyia Palace, Kumasi, Ghana
Melnikov House, Moscow, Russia
Opera House, Asmara, Eritrea
Ozenfant House and Studio, Paris, France
Police Headquarters, Copenhagen, Denmark
Reitveld Schroder House, Utrecht, Netherlands
Rufer House, Vienna, Austria
Rusakov Club, Moscow, Russia
St Vitus Cathedral, Prague, Czechoslovakia
Sun Yet-Sen Mausoleum, Nanking, China
Taliesin, Spring Green, USA
Turun Sanomat Building, Turku, Finland
Villa Stein, Garches, France
Weissenhof Seidlung, Stuttgart, Germany

Nobel Prize for Literature
1920 Knut Hamsun; 1921 Anatole France; 1922 Jacinto Benavente; 1923 William Butler Yeats; 1924 Wladyslaw Reymont; 1925 George Bernard Shaw; 1926 Grazia Deledda; 1927 Henri Bergson; 1928 Sigrid Undset; 1929 Thomas Mann.

Academy Awards
Best Film 1928 *Wings*; 1929 *The Broadway Melody*.

Duke Kahanamoku

War's Over—Let the Games Begin

Antwerp, Belgium, August 14–September 12, 1920: Antwerp has triumphantly hosted the Games of the VII Olympiad after an eight-year hiatus caused by war. These post-war Games were originally scheduled for Berlin, a choice that was made impossible by Germany's reparations commitments, and indeed Germany and its allies were not welcomed. Last year, Antwerp outbid its rival cities, Amsterdam and Lyon, and the Belgian city was chosen to commemorate the country's suffering during the Great War.

The Antwerp Games have seen the introduction of the Olympic Oath for athletes, delivered on this occasion by Belgian fencer Victor Boin: "We swear that we will take part in the Olympic Games in a spirit of chivalry, for the honor of our country, and for the glory of sport."

Also unprecedented at these Games was the flying of the Olympic flag, as well as the release of white doves by hundreds of spectators to symbolize peace.

time out

Construction began on Yankee Stadium in the Bronx. The Yankees bought the land from William Waldorf Astor and the project was largely financed by their star player Babe Ruth's drawing power. Thus the stadium was known as "The House That Ruth Built."

Twenty-nine nations competed, with the United States topping the medal score, returning home with a grand total of 41 gold, 27 silver, and 27 bronze medals. Sweden, Great Britain, Finland, and Belgium completed the table of top five nations.

Many of the athletic events were poorly attended due to the prohibitive cost of tickets.

Finland's surprise success was Paavo Nurmi, a long-distance runner who won three gold medals and one silver. Another Finn, Hannes Kolehmainen, who tasted success at the 1912 Games, won the marathon. Hawaiian swimmer Duke Kahanamoku won the 100 meter freestyle, and Italian fencer Nedo Nadi won five titles. American boxer Edward Eagan took out the light-heavyweight title. In tennis, Frenchwoman Suzanne Lenglen, who has won several titles at Wimbledon, was determined to win the gold medal, and lost only four games in ten sets.

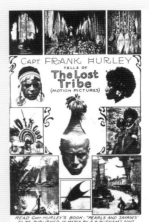

Poster advertising adventurer Frank Hurley's film, *The Lost Tribe*.

These post-war Games have proved an important occasion for the people of Europe to find new hope in the sporting spirit of the Olympic Games.

Shackleton's Fourth Expedition Cut Short

Southern Ocean, January 5, 1922: Sir Ernest Henry Shackleton, the intrepid explorer famed for his leadership abilities and affectionately nicknamed "Boss," has died from a heart attack at the beginning of his fourth polar expedition. The heart attack occurred at Grytviken, on South Georgia Island, where he has been buried.

Shackleton had been determined to explore the poles since childhood: "I seemed to vow to myself that some day I would go to the region of ice and snow, and go on and on till I came to one of the poles of the earth, the end of the axis upon which this great round ball turns." He went to sea at the age of 16, and by 24 was a Master capable of captaining a British ship on any sea.

In 1901, he volunteered for Scott's National Antarctic Expedition, having impressed its members with his personality. Shackleton, however, became very ill on the journey, and had to be sent

Shackleton's monument in South Georgia, with the rugged mountains he crossed to reach Grytviken in May 1916.

London, England, February 17, 1920: Police are to have their horses replaced by cars.

Washington DC, USA, February 20, 1920: Robert Peary, credited with being the first man to the North Pole, dies, aged 64.

Geneva, Switzerland, June 13, 1920: The first International Feminist Conference opens.

Antwerp, Belgium, August 14–September 12, 1920: The Olympic Games held only two years after Belgium's devastation in the Great War are an unqualified success.

Redlands, California, USA, April 23, 1921: US sprinter Charles Paddock runs the 100-meter dash in 10.4 seconds, a new world record.

Paris, France, May, 1921: Gabrielle "Coco" Chanel unveils *Chanel Number 5* perfume.

Berlin, Germany, September 19, 1921: The AVUS experimental highway is completed.

USA, November 23, 1921: Doctors are banned from prescribing beer, closing a loophole in the new prohibition laws.

Southern Ocean, January 5, 1922: Antarctic explorer Sir Ernest Shackleton dies of a heart attack, aged 48, while on his fourth expedition. His renown spread with the miraculous survival of his Endurance expedition (1914-1916).

Mt Everest, June 7, 1922: The expedition led by George Mallory reaches 26,800 ft (8,168 m), 3,200 ft (975 m) below the summit, without the aid of oxygen.

USA, July 9, 1922: Johnny Weissmuller breaks the 100-meter swimming record in 58.6 seconds.

USA, March 2, 1923: The first issue of *Time* magazine hits newsstands.

USA, April 14, 1923: The "dance till you drop" craze is sweeping America. Dancers have been known to exert themselves for up to 52 hours non-stop.

London, England, July 2, 1923: American Philip Rosenbach purchases the Gutenberg Bible at auction for $43,350.

London, England, July 7, 1923: Frenchwoman Suzanne Lenglen wins her fifth consecutive Wimbledon singles championship.

Chamonix, France, January 25–February 5, 1924: The first Winter Olympic Games are held in the French Alps.

Paris, France, May 4–July 27, 1924: Paavo Nurmi of Finland wins five gold medals in athletics at the VIII Olympic Games. Forty-four nations compete in 17 sports.

Mt Everest, June 19, 1924: Mallory and Irvine die within 1,000 ft (305 m) of the summit of Mt Everest.

Croydon, England, December 24, 1924: Eight people die in the country's worst aviation disaster.

back. On his recovery, he was asked to take a ship back and rescue Scott's expedition, and to dissuade him from persevering for another terrible winter in the Antarctic. He decided against this, preferring to undertake an expedition of his own.

This ambition was fulfilled between 1907 and 1909, as commander of the Nimrod Expedition His team made a number of important scientific discoveries, climbing Mt Erebus, and traveling to within 97 miles (155 km) of the South Pole, before being forced to turn back due to low rations. He was knighted in 1909, and in 1915 commanded the Imperial Trans-Antarctic Expedition on the ship *Endurance*, which was crushed by pack ice. Miraculously, Shackleton led all those aboard to safety.

"Simplicity is the Keynote of True Elegance"

Paris, France, May, 1922: Coco Chanel (Gabrielle Bonheur Chanel), France's most famous female couturier, has launched the fragrance Chanel No. 5.

Born in Saumur in 1883 (though she always maintained that she was born in 1893 in Auvergne), Chanel was just a young child when her mother died. Her father abandoned his family, leaving his children to be raised by relatives.

It was during a brief career as a café and cabaret singer between 1905 and 1908, that the designer took the name Coco. After a succession of wealthy suitors, Chanel has been able to successfully establish herself, beginning in 1910 with a small hat shop in a humble district of Paris. Within a year, however, she had moved to the fashionable Rue Cambon,

"Coco" Chanel is known for her grace.

and her business began to grow as the chic and wealthy women of Paris came to buy her expanding array of elegant and classic fashions.

A Fatal Defeat at Altitude

Mt Everest, Nepal, June 19, 1924: Two British mountaineers have perished in an attempt to reach the summit of Mt Everest. Sandy Irvine, only 22 years old, and 38-year-old George Mallory attempted the climb with oxygen, which they believed would ease the climb above 28,185 ft (8,590 m).

Mallory is one of Britain's most famed high altitude rock climbers, having already participated in the Everest expeditions of 1921 and 1922. Irvine, however, had no experience in the Himalayas, but proved very able when it came to utilizing the oxygen apparatus, which had proven fallible in the past. No climbers previously have been successful in climbing beyond 24,600 ft (7,498 m), and it has been assumed in the past that oxygen was the key to the final assault on the peak.

On June 6, the two climbers, who were positioned at their high camp, believed they were in a position to tackle the summit. They set off from their position of 23,100 ft (7,040 m), hoping to reach the summit within three days. The two figures dressed in

black were last seen through the mist as they approached a steep, rocky incline at the base of the summit pyramid on the afternoon of June 8 by Noel Odell, who was following behind for support. Clouds drifted across his view, and the two were lost forever in the mountain mist. Odell retreated to their final camp and kept a watch for the pair, but no other sighting was ever made.

It is not known if Mallory and Irvine reached the summit before they perished.

Teaching of Evolution Banned in Tennessee

Tennessee, USA, March 23, 1925: Governor Austin Peay has signed the Butler Act, prohibiting the teaching of evolution in Tennessee's public schools. He expressed the opinion that the law will never be enforced. The push to abolish Darwin's theory from classrooms has been led by William Jennings Bryan, a three-time Democratic candidate for president. Described as a "Fundamentalist Pope," he has enacted a bill that makes it unlawful "to teach any theory that denies the story of divine creation as taught by the Bible and to teach instead that man was descended from a lower order of animals."

William Jennings Bryan

The British Empire Exhibition was attended by 56 imperial nations at Wembley, England, in 1924.

Tennessee, USA, March 23, 1925: The teaching of Darwin's theory of evolution is banned in favor of creationism.

Charleston, USA, September, 1925: The "Charleston" dance, performed at a frenetic tempo while turning in your toes and kicking out your legs, is increasingly popular throughout the USA and Britain.

Paris, France, October 27, 1925: Nineteen-year-old African-American dancer Josephine Baker is the toast of Paris due to her erotic dancing in La Revue Negre.

London, England, April 21, 1926: Princess Elizabeth, first daughter of George VI and the Duchess of York, is born.

North Pole, May 9, 1926: Americans Richard E. Byrd and Floyd Bennett complete the first successful flight over the pole, launching from Spitzbergen Island. The trip takes 16 hours.

Kent, England, August 6, 1926: US swimmer Gertrude Ederle becomes the first woman to swim the English Channel and sets a new record of 14.5 hours.

Pendine Sands, Carmarthenshire, Wales, February 4, 1927: Malcolm Campbell, driving the *Bluebird*, sets a new land speed record of 174.88 mph (279.81 km/h).

United Kingdom, May 19, 1927: There is an explosion in the number of hairdressers across the nation as women opt for the new shorter shingled look.

New York, USA, September 30, 1927: George Herman "Babe" Ruth hits his sixtieth home run for the New York Yankees this season, a new record.

UK, January 5, 1928: The British government introduces the aged pension of ten shillings per week for people over 65 on a low income.

St Moritz, Switzerland, February 11-19, 1928: The second Winter Olympics are held, taking place in a different country from the summer Games for the first time.

Amsterdam, Netherlands, May 17-August 12, 1928: The IX Olympic Games introduces women's athletics and gymnastics. Almost 3,000 athletes from 46 nations compete.

Florida, USA, March 11, 1929: Harry Segrave reclaims the land speed record at 231.45 mph (370.32 km/h).

London, England, July 22, 1929: Charles Kingsford-Smith flies from Australia to the UK in 13 days.

Lakehurst, New Jersey, USA, August 29, 1929: The *Graf Zeppelin* completes its circumnavigation of the world in 21 days.

New York, USA, November 7, 1929: The Museum of Modern Art opens, confirming the significance of avant-garde artists this century.

Josephine Baker

> "IF A MAN
> CANNOT MAKE
> HIS POINT TO
> KEEN BOYS IN
> TEN MINUTES,
> HE OUGHT TO
> BE SHOT!"
>
> ROBERT BADEN-
> POWELL (1857–1941),
> BRITISH MILITARY
> OFFICER AND FOUNDER
> OF THE BOY SCOUT
> MOVEMENT, 1928

> "THERE ARE NO
> ILLEGITIMATE
> CHILDREN—
> ONLY
> ILLEGITIMATE
> PARENTS."
>
> LEON R. YANKWICH
> (1888–1975), AMERICAN
> LAWYER AND JUDGE, IN
> A CALIFORNIAN
> DECISION, QUOTING
> JOURNALIST O. O.
> MCINTYRE, 1928

The "Monkey Trial"

Dayton, USA, July 21, 1925: In the town of Dayton, Tennessee, a vigorous and sometimes humorous trial has concluded between creationists and evolutionists, in which John Scopes, a 24-year-old general science teacher and football coach, has been convicted of teaching the theory of evolution and fined $100. The teacher, who had been using Hunter's *Civic Biology*, the state-approved textbook, to conduct his classes, had merely been stating the case for both evolution and creationism as set out in the book. The trial came about through a conversation between Scopes and George Rappleyea (a local coal company manager), as much to drum up interest and publicity for the failing town than out of any passion either held for the issues at stake.

As the trial approached, Dayton became a carnival of banners, decorated streets, and lemonade stands. Monkeys were even brought in to perform in the town to testify for the prosecution. Nearly 1,000 people crammed the courthouse on the first day of the trial, which lasted 11 days, and while much lively banter and debate accompanied the trial, Judge John T. Raulston, a Christian conservative, was immune it seems to the skilled company of lawyers whose arguments were debated in his court.

Everybody's Doin' It

Charleston, USA, September, 1925: The vibrations of the Charleston are being felt all over the world, but in Boston they've

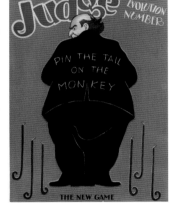

Caricature of a Congressman.

proven fatal. Fifty patrons have been killed at a dancehall called the Pickwick Club, in a down-at-heel Boston suburb, when the building collapsed from the frenetic movements of the dancers.

The energetic new dance has its roots in African–American music traditions, specifically that of the Ashanti peoples of Africa. The dance has become the signature of an entire generation in the Ragtime Jazz era, and has been named after Charleston, South Carolina, where African–Americans have been doing it for years. It seems that waitresses can't get jobs if they don't know the moves. It's so infectious that it's got all the girls flapping; in fact, it has defined a whole generation of women as "flappers" with its bird-like arm gestures.

The Charleston was first seen in the Harlem stage production of *Rubberlegs* in 1913, and Bessie Love premiered it on the big screen in this year's film *King on Main Street*.

American Woman Crosses Channel

Kent, England, August 6, 1926: American swimmer Gertrude Caroline Ederle has become the first woman to swim the English Channel, at the age of 19. Ederle, who was plucked from the icy waters in an unsuccessful attempt at crossing the Channel a year ago, entered the waters of Cap Gris-Nez, France, at 7.04 a.m. coated in layers of lard and petroleum jelly to protect her from the cold. The weather had turned foul by mid-afternoon, and she was fighting wind, rain, and heavy swells. The rough conditions forced her to swim 35 miles (56 km) in order to

Gertrude Ederle prepares to cross the English Channel.

cover what would have been 21 miles (33.8 km) in calmer seas. At 9.35 p.m, Ederle arrived at Kingsdown on the English coast. Her time broke all existing records, at 14 hours and 31 minutes. Ederle already holds 29 records in the USA, and won gold at the 1924 Paris Olympics in the 400 m relay, as well as two bronzes in the 100 m and 400 m freestyle. On her return to her home city of New York, horns blasted from every steamship in New York harbor, flowers dropped from airplanes, and she was showered with tickertape on Broadway.

Babe Ruth Makes Baseball History

New York, USA, September 30, 1927: George Herman Ruth, Jr, the USA's most popular baseball player, has confirmed himself at the very pinnacle of his game when he hit 60 home runs during a 154-game stretch this year, an all-time world record. Affectionately known as Babe Ruth, the star has attracted other nicknames, such as "The Great Bambino" and "The Sultan of Swat," his greatness is already the stuff of sporting legend.

Born on February 6, 1895, in Baltimore, Maryland, Ruth had a troubled childhood; at the age of 7 his parents placed him in a Catholic orphanage and reformatory where he spent many years. Here he received his early baseball training from a Brother Matthias, who took a keen interest in the young boy's swing. At 19, he was signed to the Baltimore Orioles by the team's owner, Jack Dunn. The Orioles were a minor league team, but Dunn was known to be one of the

Dancers kick their heels and flap their arms to the rhythms of the Charleston.

best talent scouts in the business, and he recognized Ruth's talents. After only five months, Ruth made it into Boston's major league when he signed for the Boston Red Sox. Ruth quickly made headlines both on and off the field with his legendary eating habits and relentless accuracy in the game.

While famed as the greatest hitter of all time, Ruth was considered equally adept as a pitcher, and he set a world record in his first World Series game for Boston in 1916. Taking the mound in the fourth game against the National League champions, the Brooklyn Robins, he

Sporting Achievements

Baseball *World Series* 1920 Cleveland (American League); 1921 New York (National League); 1922 New York (NL); 1923 New York (AL); 1924 Washington (AL); 1925 Pittsburgh (NL); 1926 St Louis (NL); 1927 New York (AL); 1928 New York (AL); 1929 Philadelphia (AL). **Cycling** *Tour de France* 1920 P. Thys; 1921 L. Scieur; 1922 F. Lambot; 1923 H. Pelissier; 1924-1925 O. Bottecchia; 1926 L. Buysse; 1927-1928 N. Frantz; 1929 M. De Waele. **Horse Racing** *Epsom Derby* 1920 Spion Kop; 1921 Humorist; 1922 Captain Cuttle; 1923 Papyrus; 1924 Sansovino; 1925 Manna; 1926 Coronach; 1927 Call Boy; 1928 Felstead; 1929 Trigio. *Kentucky Derby* 1920 Paul Jones; 1921 Behave Yourself; 1922 Morvich; 1923 Zev; 1924 Black Gold; 1925 Flying Ebony; 1926 Bubbling Over; 1927 Whiskery; 1928 Reigh Count; 1929 Clyde Van Dusen. *Melbourne Cup* 1920 Poitrel; 1921 Sister Olive; 1922 King Ingoda; 1923 Bitalli; 1924 Blackwood; 1925 Windbag; 1926 Spearfelt; 1927 Trivalve; 1928 Statesman; 1929 Nightmarch. **Ice Hockey** *Stanley Cup* 1920 Ottawa; 1921 Ottawa; 1922 Toronto; 1923 Ottawa; 1924 Montreal; 1925 Victoria; 1926 Montreal; 1927 Ottawa; 1928 New York; 1929 Boston. **Marathon** *Boston, Men's* 1920 P. Trivoulides; 1921 F. Zuna; 1922 C. DeMar; 1923 C. DeMar; 1924 C. DeMar; 1925 C. Mellor; 1926 J. Miles; 1927 C. DeMar; 1928 C. DeMar; 1929 J. Miles. **Sailing** *America's Cup* 1920 *Resolute*. **Tennis** *Australasian Championships, Men's Singles* 1920 P. O'Hara Wood; 1921 R. Gemmell; 1922 J.Anderson; 1923 P. O'Hara Wood; 1924-1925 J. Anderson; 1926 J. Hawkes; *Women's Singles* 1922-1923 M. Molesworth; 1924 S. Lance; 1925-1926 D. Akhurst. *Australian Championships, Men's Singles* 1927 G. Patterson; 1928 J. Borotra; 1929 J. Gregory; *Women's Singles* 1927 E. Boyd 1928-1929 D. Akhurst. *French Championships, Men's Singles* 1920 A. Gobert; 1921 J. Samazeuilh; 1922 H. Cochet; 1923 F. Blanchy; 1924 J. Bototra; 1925 R. Lacoste; 1926 H. Cochet; 1927 R. Lacoste; 1928 H. Cochet; 1929 R. Lacoste; *Women's Singles* 1920-1923 S. Lenglen; 1924 D. Vlasto; 1925-1926 S. Lenglen; 1927 K. Bouman; 1928-1929 H. Wills. *US National Championship, Men's Singles* 1920-1925 B. Tilden; 1926-1927 R. Lacoste; 1928 H. Cochet; 1929 B. Tilden; *Women's Singles* 1920-1922 M. Bjurstedt Mallory; 1923-1925 H. Wills; 1926 M. Bjurstedt Mallory; 1927-1929 H. Wills. *Wimbledon, Gentlemen's Singles* 1920-1921 B. Tilden; 1922 G. Patterson; 1923 B. Johnston; 1924 J. Borotra; 1925 R. Lacoste; 1926 J. Borotra; 1927 H. Cochet; 1928 R. Lacoste; 1929 H. Cochet; *Ladies' Singles* 1920-1923 S. Lenglen; 1924 K. McKane; 1925 S. Lenglen; 1926 K.McKane Godfree; 1927-1929 H. Wills.

pitched 13 scoreless innings in a two to one win. The 14-inning accomplishment stands as the longest complete game in World Series history.

In 1919 Ruth was sold to the Yankees; in him they had a star who would change the course of sporting history. With what has become known as "The Curse of the Bambino," the Yankees began a period of success, which has culminated in Ruth's record-breaking success this year.

Dirigible Circles the Globe in 21 Days

Lakehurst, New Jersey, August 29, 1929: In a feat of great daring, the LZ 127, or *Graf Zeppelin*, a 772 ft (245 m) long, 100 ft (30.48 m) high German dirigible replete with luxurious appointments for its passengers, has successfully completed a round-the-world voyage in 21 days, 5 hours, and 31 minutes. Named after Graf Ferdinand von Zeppelin, the inventor of the airships, this vessel has already won the hearts of wealthy and adventurous air travelers all over the world. With the popularity of these "giants of the air," sponsorship for their travels has not been hard to find for Dr Hugo Eckener, the Zeppelin company chief. One of the most notable sponsors is newspaper tycoon William Randolph Hearst, who took in an official tour prior to the start of the epic journey.

On August 8, the *Graf Zeppelin*, with Eckener at the helm, took off with 40 crew, 20 passengers, and several large bags of mail. It flew from Lakehurst to Friedrichshafen on the 10th, refueled and took off for Tokyo, arriving there on the 19th, then on to San Francisco on the 23rd, making the first non-stop flight across the Pacific Ocean. From there it traveled down to Los Angeles and back across the United States, over Chicago, returning to Lakehurst, New Jersey, on the 29th. The entire trip took 21 days including layovers, and the total distance traveled by the *Graf Zeppelin* on this worldwide voyage was a staggering 19,500 miles (31,400 km).

While zeppelins are taking the northern hemisphere by storm, in the southern hemisphere the pioneer

aviator Charles Kingsford Smith is also making history piloting his own plane, the *Southern Cross* (a Fokker Trimotor aircraft). Kingsford Smith is already the first to have flown across the Australian continent, made a flight to the UK in 13 days, and this year has completed a flight around the world.

Modern Art Set to Shock and Delight

New York, USA, November 7, 1929: Today, three of New York's most progressive patrons of the arts, Lillie Bliss, Mary Sullivan, and Abby Aldrich Rockefeller have founded the Museum of Modern Art (MOMA). The museum is being established to fulfill a need for modern and progressive artwork to be exhibited to the public. Its founding director, Alfred Barr Junior, intends that the museum will enable people to understand and enjoy the visual arts of our time, believing in time it will offer New York "the greatest museum of modern art in the world."

It will initially consist of six rented rooms in the Hecksher Building on the corner of Fifth Avenue and 57th Street, and will exhibit art crossing a wide range of mediums including photography, painting, sculpture, prints, and illustrated books. Already, the museum has received eight gifts of important works.

George Herman (Babe) Ruth

The German dirigible *Graf Zeppelin* can carry 20 passengers in luxurious comfort.

Joseph Stalin

Stalin's Farms of Terror

USSR, March 16: In a bid to increase crop production and exports from the USSR, Joseph Stalin has announced the forced collectivization of all farms. His aim is to control the peasantry, increase output with large-scale mechanized farms, eliminate individually run agricultural concerns, and make tax collection more efficient. His initial target is to see a 200 percent increase in industrial growth and a 50 percent increase in agricultural output.

If kulaks (rich peasants) resist the collectivization of their farms, they will face execution or be transported and imprisoned in remote parts of the country. Not since the abolition of serfdom in 1861 has there been such a change to industrial relations, and the new structures will mean a sharp drop in living standards for workers. Fifty percent of farms are already collectivized and the outcry from workers is being heard far and wide, especially in the Ukraine where collectivization had not previously been established.

On March 2, *Pravda* (the *Truth*), the daily newspaper and the mouthpiece for Stalin's Communist Party, published an article entitled "Dizzy with Success," setting out the changes and offering stern warnings to anyone who might be thinking of sabotaging the new order:

"…That a radical turn of the countryside towards socialism may be considered as already achieved. There is no need to prove that these successes are of supreme importance for the fate of our country, for the whole working class, which is the directing force of our country, and, lastly, for the Party itself. To say nothing of the direct practical results, these successes are of immense value for the internal life of the Party itself, for the education of our Party. They imbue our Party with a spirit of cheerfulness and confidence in the victory of our cause. They bring forward additional millions of reserves for our Party. Hence the Party's task is: To consolidate the successes achieved…"

> "WITH US THE LEADER AND THE IDEA ARE ONE, AND EVERY PARTY MEMBER HAS TO DO WHAT THE LEADER ORDERS."
>
> ADOLF HITLER (1889–1945), GERMAN DICTATOR, TO OTTO STRASSER, 1930

> "THE LOSS OF INDIA WOULD MARK AND CONSUMMATE THE DOWN-FALL OF THE BRITISH EMPIRE."
>
> WINSTON CHURCHILL (1874–1965), ENGLISH STATESMAN AND PRIME MINISTER, 1930

The main thoroughfare of the newly renamed city of Constantinople.

time out

Five hundred farmers stormed London, Arkansas, USA, demanding food. The Red Cross, who farmers said tried to manage relief efforts alone, lobbying against federal aid, bore the brunt of the attack. The riot ended when the Red Cross distributed extra vouchers.

Constantinople No More

Turkey, March 28: Turkish Prime Minister Ismet İnönü has formally changed the name of Turkey's capital, from Constantinople to Istanbul. For centuries Istanbul has been its popular name so far as those who dwell in the city are concerned, and the formal change marks the end of centuries of takeovers and attacks for a city whose strategic position and central trading ports have made it attractive to other expanding empires.

The name Istanbul comes from the Greek phrase *eis ten polin*, meaning "in the city" and it was indeed the Greeks who founded it in 600 BCE. Alexander the Great later seized it from the Persian Empire in 73 CE, dubbing it Byzantium. Finally, the name was changed to Constantinople in honor of Constantine the Great, who took power in 330 CE. It seems at last to have come full circle.

English Aviatrix Arrives in Darwin

Darwin, Australia, May 24: Amy Johnson, Britain's most adventurous aviatrix, has become the first woman to fly solo to Australia. Hoping to break Bert Hinkler's record of 16 days, the young pilot made the flight in 19 days. She set off from Croydon, England, on May 5, flying a used De Havilland Moth with a gypsy engine and extra fuel tanks. The plane cost £600. Her 11,000-mile (17,700-km) adventure was funded partially by Lord C. C. Wakefield and his oil company as well as by her father.

Johnson was born in July 1903 and became the first woman in Britain to receive an Air Ministry's ground engineer's license in 1929. She has only been flying for two years, and prior to her Australian flight had never flown further than between London and her hometown of Hull.

Her flight took her via Karachi and Calcutta. The plane was damaged by bad weather in Jhansi and a crash landing just north of Rangoon. The plane was repaired and she was able to complete the last leg to Darwin, but Hinkler's record stands.

Amy Johnson has flown from England to Australia.

Cairo, Egypt, February 1: The *Science News-Letter* reports one of the largest Egyptian tombs ever found has been discovered at Meidum, near Cairo. The *mastaba*'s unknown inhabitant lived about 2800 BCE.

London, England, March 14: Plans to build a tunnel from England to France are approved by the Channel Tunnel Committee.

USSR, March 16: Joseph Stalin begins a terror campaign to eradicate wealthy farmers.

Turkey, March 28: The name of the city of Constantinople is officially changed to Istanbul.

Dandi, India, April 6: After completing his 100-mile (161 km) Salt March, Mahatma Gandhi boycotts the British salt tax by taking his own salt.

China, April 23: Nationalists and Soviet communists challenge General Chiang Kai Shek's efforts to control China.

Pegu, Burma, May 5: A massive earthquake kills as many as 6,000 people.

Darwin, Australia, May 24: British aviator Amy Johnson arrives in Darwin 19 days after commencing her solo flight from London.

Cairo, Egypt, July 22: Riots in Egypt occur, following the dismissal of the government.

Ariano, Italy, July 22: An earthquake kills 1,500 people.

Brazil, August 13: A giant meteorite lands deep in the River Curuçá region of the Amazon rainforest, producing a massive explosion.

UK, August 14: The Church of England reluctantly accepts the use of contraceptives.

Washington DC, USA, August 16: The government allocates $121.9 million toward the drought, which has cut corn output by 690 million bushels.

Japan, November 14: Prime Minister Hamaguchi Osachi is wounded in an assassination attempt.

New York, USA, December 31: The collapse of the Bank of the United States, which has 60 branches in New York alone, leads to a run on banks throughout the country.

Japan's Once and Future Leader

Tokyo, Japan, April 14: Reijiro Wakatsuki, who served as twenty-fifth prime minister of Japan from January 30, 1926, to April 20, 1927, has returned to his post, becoming the twenty-eighth prime minister.

Osachi Hamaguchi, the departing prime minister, was nicknamed "the lion prime minister" because of his physical attributes. He had held the office since 1929. An assassination attempt against him was carried out on November 14 last year by ultranationalist Tomeo Sagoya, a member of the Aikoku-sha (Love of Country Association). The attack left Osachi badly injured, although he did manage to win the February 11 election this year. However, poor health forced him to resign the office a month later.

Reijiro Wakatsuki became Hamaguchi's replacement, in spite of his reputation for lying. In fact, the opposition gave him the title *Usotsuki Reijiro* (Reijiro the Liar).

Born in 1866, Wakatsuki is the son of a samurai and studied law at Tokyo University. He then went on to the Ministry of Finance, where he ultimately became the Minister for Finance. In 1911 he joined the parliament.

Towering above the Rest

New York, USA, May 1: Amid much hoopla, President Herbert Hoover today turned on the lights in the world's tallest building, the Empire State Building. As the lights went on in every one of its 102 stories, the ultimate New York landmark was proclaimed open. New York now claims a skyline and architectural feat unrivalled anywhere in the world.

The grand structure was built on the former site of the Waldorf-Astoria Hotel at 350 Fifth Avenue, between 33rd Street and 34th street. Designed by Shreeve, Lamb, and Harmon Associates, the Empire State Building became the focus

The Empire State Building is the world's tallest so far.

of the fierce competition between Walter Chrysler of the Chrysler Corporation and John Raskob, a director of General Motors. The Chrysler Building itself opened in May 1930, but with a total of 77 floors, it was soon to be overshadowed by the Empire State's 102 stories.

Raskob attracted some of New York's most prominent investors to participate in his 102-story scheme, and construction began in March 1930, with the cornerstone laid by Alfred E. Smith, former two-time governor of the city. It was completed in only 14 months.

The Art-Deco style building is 1,472 ft (448 m) high at the top of the mast (which will be used for the mooring of dirigibles) and 1,050 ft (320 m) high at the observatory on the 86th floor. The cost, including the land, was $40,948,900. Building costs were $24,718,000, which is only half of what had been projected, due to the current depression.

Al Capone Imprisoned

Chicago, USA, November 24: Chicago's notorious crime boss Al Capone has been indicted for tax evasion during the years 1925 to 1929 and charged with the misdemeanor of failing to file tax returns in 1928 and 1929. The government has charged that he owes $215,080 in taxes from gambling profits. An extra indictment has also been added, charging the famed bootlegger with conspiracy to violate the Prohibition Act of 1922.

Al Capone

Capone pleaded guilty to the charges in the mistaken belief that plea-bargaining and jury bribes would minimize his sentence; however, presiding judge James H. Wilkerson was not inclined to make any deals and changed the jury.

Capone then pleaded not guilty, but was found to be so on 18 of the 23 counts. He was sentenced to 10 years in a federal prison and one year in the county jail. He was also fined $50,000 and ordered to pay prosecution costs of $7,692.

Born January 17, 1899, Capone was baptized Alphonsus Capone and grew up in a rough Brooklyn neighborhood. His violent and murderous career left his face scarred and won him the nickname "Scarface." By the mid-1920s, he controlled many of the speakeasies, bookie joints, gambling houses, brothels, racetracks, nightclubs, and distilleries in Chicago and was believed to have an income of more than $100,000 per year. A 1927 ruling that made illegal profits taxable was the key to ending Capone's reign of corruption.

King Alfonso XIII has left Spain.

Iraq, January 6: Archeologists unearth a 550 BCE royal palace at the ancient city of Ur.

Coolgardie, Australia, January 15: Western Australia's biggest gold nugget, the Golden Eagle, is found, weighing 78 pounds.

Hawke's Bay, New Zealand, February 3: An earthquake measuring 7.8 on the Richter scale kills 256.

Moscow, USSR, February 21: Soviet revolutionary Leon Trotsky is stripped of his citizenship and exiled.

Washington DC, USA, March 3: President Hoover signs an act declaring *The Star-Spangled Banner* to be the US national anthem.

India, March 25: Racial riots in Cawnpore kill hundreds in a throat-slitting bloodbath.

Nicaragua, March 31: An earthquake and subsequent fire in Managua kill between 1,000 and 2,000 people.

Madrid, Spain, April 14: King Alfonso XIII abdicates the throne and flees the country, and the Republic of Spain is proclaimed. Niceto Alcalá Zamora takes over the presidency under a provisional government.

Tokyo, Japan, April 14: Prime Minister Osachi Hamaguchi dies and is succeeded by Reijiro Wakatsuki.

New York, USA, May 1: The Empire State Building is opened.

Germany, August 5: Banks reopen, after closing on July 13 when the German Danatbank went bankrupt.

China, August 31: A Yangtze River flood leaves 23 million homeless, just one month after the Yellow River floods that killed millions.

London, England, September 7: King George V takes a £50,000-a-year pay cut to help deal with the economic crisis.

Manchuria, September 18: Japan invades Manchuria in a surprise attack, violating the Kellogg-Briand pact.

London, England, September 30: Riots protesting pay cuts follow a month of strikes.

Chicago, USA, November 24: Al Capone is sentenced to 11 years in prison and fined.

Washington DC, USA, December: Hundreds of hunger marchers petition for employment at a minimum wage.

Mahatma Gandhi

> *"FASCISM IS NOT AN ARTICLE FOR EXPORT."*
>
> BENITO MUSSOLINI (1883–1945), ITALIAN PRIME MINISTER AND DICTATOR, 1932

> *"I PLEDGE YOU, I PLEDGE MYSELF, TO A NEW DEAL FOR THE AMERICAN PEOPLE."*
>
> FRANKLIN D. ROOSEVELT (1882–1945), AMERICAN PRESIDENT, ACCEPTING HIS NOMINATION FOR THE PRESIDENCY, 1932

Massacre in Shanghai

Shanghai, China, January 29: The Chinese coastal city of Shanghai, already the focal point of much international interest, has become a stepping stone for Japanese troops and the scene of escalating resistance from the Chinese, resulting in mass rioting throughout this month. Japan has concentrated its military presence around the region, with approximately 30 ships, 40 airplanes, and nearly 7,000 troops near the city's shoreline.

Japan's pressure on the Chinese Government has increased after a successful assault on a vast northeastern section of the country. To justify further advances, they are reported to have staged an attack on Japanese monks near the Sanyou Factory and blamed it on the Chinese. The Chinese Government agreed to pay the compensation asked by the Japanese; however, at midnight on January 28, 3,000 Japanese troops proceeded to attack strategic targets around the city as the Battle of Shanghai began.

Other foreign nations with interests in the city have attempted to negotiate a cease-fire with Japan to no avail. The Japanese ordered the Chinese to retreat 12½ miles (20 km) from the city, but the Chinese refused, thus further intensifying hostilities. In their wake, the Japanese torched and bombed Shanghai's commercial and residential districts, resulting in the deaths of between 10,000 and 20,000 civilians.

time out

Following the assault by Berlin storm troopers of American Roland Veiz for failing to salute a Nazi parade, Foreign Minister von Neurath assured the American ambassador that arrests had been made and punishment would be promptly carried out.

"Little It" Found Dead

New Jersey, May 12: A dead body believed to be that of Charles Augustus Lindbergh III, the 20-month-old toddler, son of Charles Lindbergh II and Anne Morrow Lindbergh, has been found by a truck driver in a grove of trees 4½ miles (7 km) from the Lindbergh family's New Jersey estate. The child had died from a blow to the head. The body was missing its left leg and both hands.

In what journalist H. L. Mencken has called the biggest story since the Resurrection, the kidnapping of the Lindbergh heir, nicknamed "Little It" by his parents and "The Little Eagle" by the media, has been one of the most bizarre cases of its type. It has involved bogus ransom notes and two different sets of potential kidnappers, as well as "consultants" from high society, tabloid journalists, and organized crime figures. Even Al Capone promised to help track down the perpetrators from prison if his sentence was reduced.

Charles Lindbergh III celebrating his first birthday.

The case spawned a search from Hopewell, New Jersey, to Brooklyn and Martha's Vineyard. It seems, however, that all the activity has been for nothing and the $50,000 ransom that was finally paid was for a child already murdered.

In light of this kidnapping, President Herbert Hoover has put all such crimes under federal jurisdiction.

Religious Riots Kill Thousands in India

Bombay, India, May 16: In a confrontation drastically undermining India's broader struggle for freedom, thousands have been killed or injured in Bombay today following violent clashes between Muslims and Hindus. The divide comes largely from the proposed new political structure and representation within the congress, with fears that new power structures will favor Hindus and not Muslims.

These events are bound to jeopardize the efforts of Mahatma Gandhi. In a bid to improve the status of the Hindu Untouchables, Gandhi undertook a "fast unto death," which resulted in his party (the Indian National Congress) gaining a foothold as a separate part of the Indian electorate. Gandhi's hunger strikes have proved a powerful tool against the British.

Refugees from the Chapei district of Shanghai, victims of the Sino-Japanese War.

Key Events

India, January 4: Mahatma Gandhi is arrested at 3 am after the Indian National Congress is declared illegal.
El Salvador, January 22: Reprisals begin as the government regains control after a peasant uprising led by socialist Augustín Farabundo Martí. Government retaliation is to massacre 15,000 to 30,000.
Shanghai, China, January 29: A mass bombing levels the city and kills thousands.

Spain, January: Anarchist insurrections break out all over the country.
Japan, February 18: Japan declares Manchuria to be an independent state.
Sydney, Australia, March 19: The Sydney Harbour Bridge opens, bringing road access across the harbor between the city's north and south.
New Jersey, USA, May 12: Baby Charles Augustus Lindbergh III is found dead after his kidnapping on March 1.

Tokyo, Japan, May 15: Prime Minister Tsuyoshi Inukai is assassinated by radical young naval officers. The original plan includes killing Charlie Chaplin, presently in Japan. Known as *go ichi go jiken*, it heralds the end of party political control over national decisions until after World War II.
Bombay, India, May 16: Riots between Hindus and Muslims.
New Zealand, May: Economic depression leads to riots in several major New Zealand cities.

Siam, June 29: The military seizes power, making Siam a constitutional monarchy.
India, September 20: Gandhi begins a hunger strike in prison, protesting the British electorates for the depressed classes.
Saudi Arabia, September 22: King Ibn Saud unites Kingdom Hejaz and Sultanate Nejd as the Kingdom of Saudi Arabia.
Iraq, October 3: Iraq gains independence from its British-imposed rule under a treaty granting the UK certain privileges.

Washington DC, USA, November 8: Franklin Delano Roosevelt becomes the thirty-second president of the USA after winning the election against incumbent Herbert Hoover.
Washington DC, USA, November 24: The Federal Bureau of Investigation (FBI) Scientific Crime Detection Laboratory is officially declared open, after several months in operation.
China, December 25: An earthquake in Gansu province leaves 70,000 dead.

1933

milestones

Franklin Delano Roosevelt

Roosevelt Closes Banks

USA, March 6: In a dramatic economic move to offset a looming bank crisis, President Franklin Delano Roosevelt has used a wartime statute passed in 1917 to order the closure of banks for four days and prohibited the exporting of gold in order to protect US reserves.

Moves are also underway to make illegal the private possession of gold bullion or its use in transactions.

The United States is facing the worst depression in its history, with 25 percent of the workforce unemployed, a 50 percent drop in production since 1929, and 2 million people homeless.

The president believes that the closure will allow the banks to be assessed and audited in the face of panic withdrawals. The move has come in a bid to prevent the hoarding of funds and earmarking of bullion or currency. "There is nothing to fear but fear itself," Roosevelt has stated. "Our first task is to open all sound banks."

More than 19,000 banks have been inspected, of which 4,004 will not reopen.

The Sydney Harbour Bridge was opened last year.

Uncertain Future Ahead

Germany, August 29: Adolf Hitler now has total constitutional power in Germany and changes are under way throughout the nation with the abolition of all other political parties. It has also been confirmed that the Oranienburg concentration camp, which will be used to confine any political opponents and Jews found to be in the way of Hitler's vision for a new Germany, has been opened outside Berlin. Under new laws such citizens may now be imprisoned without a trial or any right of appeal.

Similar camps in Dachau in southern Germany, Buchenwald in central Germany, and Sachsenhausen near Berlin will all serve similar purposes.

New laws allow anyone to inform on any person toward whom they have a grudge, and warrants state only: "In Article One of the Reich President for the Protection of People and State of 28 February 1933, you are taken into protective custody in the interest of public security and order. Reason: Suspicion of activities inimical to the State."

Hitler's appointment as Chancellor of Germany on January 30 this year and the passing of his Enabling Act on March 23 ended democracy in Germany. The act was passed in the Kroll Opera House in Berlin following the burning of the Reichstag building (the traditional seat of the German government).

The only man to oppose Hitler on that evening was Otto Wells, the leader of the Social Democrats, who said, "We German Social Democrats pledge ourselves solemnly in this historic hour to the principles of humanity and justice, of freedom and socialism. No enabling act can give you power to destroy ideas which are eternal and indestructible."

Hitler was enraged and responded with: "You are no longer needed! The star of Germany will rise and yours will sink! Your death knell has sounded!"

US Prohibition Repealed

Washington DC, USA, December 5: The "Noble Experiment" has come to an end. With diminishing support in the electorates, and dramatic increases in criminal activity by those involved in the business of bootlegging, the repeal of prohibition laws has come as a powerful readjustment to the US Constitution.

Woman voters were pivotal in the repeal effort. Ironically, it was women who were the most powerful within the temperance movement that brought about the 18th Amendment, but who now see the illegal supply of alcohol as a corrupting force in families.

Chicago bartenders pour a free round of drinks to celebrate the repeal.

President Franklin D. Roosevelt's own Democratic Party platform supported the repeal, and the president himself vowed to see an end to prohibition upon his inauguration. Three-quarters of Americans and 46 states were in favor of repealing the 18th Amendment, and federal prohibitionary laws have consequently been ratified; however, Prohibition has continued in some states under their own jurisdiction. So powerful is the temperance movement in some states that a scholar has been employed to revise the Bible to remove all references to alcoholic drinks.

Key Events

Spain, January 8: The army quells an uprising in Barcelona of Anarchists and Syndicalists against the government's social reform movement. The violence continues in Catalonia, Levante and Andalusia.
Berlin, Germany, February 28: The German Reichstag burns down. Chancellor Adolf Hitler declares the act to be a communist plot.
China, March 4: Japanese forces occupy the province of Jehol and continue their advance into Manchuria.

USA, March 6: President Roosevelt closes banks for four days in 47 states.
Germany, March 22: The first Nazi concentration camp at Dachau, near Munich, begins operation.
Germany, March 23: Hitler becomes Dictator of Germany after the Reichstag grants him full powers, less than two months after being appointed Chancellor of Germany.

Berlin, Germany, April 1: The Nazi government uses violence to orchestrate its boycott of Jewish businesses, forcing stores to close and barring professionals from their offices.
Berlin, Germany, April 11: The Nazis decree "non-Aryans" to include anyone descended from non-Aryan, particularly Jewish, parents or grandparents.
Scotland, May 2: A sighting of a bizarre creature is reported in Loch Ness.

Paraguay, May 10: Paraguay declares war on Bolivia.
Poona, India, August 23: An emaciated Mahatma Gandhi is released from hospital, five days into a fast protesting his exclusion from working with Untouchables while in prison. Earlier in the year he had been on a three-week hunger strike to protest the treatment of lower castes.
Germany, August 29: Jews and socialists are herded into concentration camps.

New Zealand, September 13: Elizabeth McCombs becomes the first female member of parliament in New Zealand.
South Dakota, USA, November 11: An enormous dust storm strips the dry topsoil from the state's drought-stricken farmlands.
Washington DC, USA, December 5: The prohibition of intoxicating liquor ends. The repeal of the law goes into effect after Utah became the 36th state to ratify the change.

343

Paul von Hindenburg

> "WHAT PROGRESS WE ARE MAKING. IN THE MIDDLE AGES THEY WOULD HAVE BURNED ME. NOW THEY ARE CONTENT WITH BURNING MY BOOKS."

SIGMUND FREUD (1856–1939), AUSTRIAN PSYCHOANALYST, ON THE 1933 BURNING OF HIS BOOKS IN BERLIN

> "EIN REICH, EIN VOLK, EIN FÜHRER." ("ONE REALM, ONE PEOPLE, ONE LEADER.")

NAZI PARTY SLOGAN FIRST USED IN 1934 AT NUREMBERG

Bonnie and Clyde Ambush

Louisiana, USA, May 23: Two of the most wanted criminals in the United States were shot and killed today in an ambush near Black Lake in Louisiana. Clyde Champion Barrow, 25, and Bonnie Parker, 23, have been the focus of one of the country's largest and most extensive manhunts. Wanted for 13 counts of murder including two police officers, automobile theft, several counts of burglary and bank robbery, as well as kidnapping, the pair seemed to foil police at every turn.

The showdown finally came when law enforcement authorities in both Texas and Louisiana were told that the pair would be returning to the place where a party was held the night before. Before dawn, a posse of officers including Frank Harmer, a Texas Ranger, concealed themselves beside the highway outside Sailes, Louisiana. When Bonnie and Clyde's car appeared, the two were surrounded and, as they attempted to escape in the vehicle, the officers opened fire, killing the pair.

Hitler is Führer

Germany, August 2: German President Paul von Hindenburg has died at 86 from lung cancer, leaving a clear route for Adolf Hitler to merge his current position as chancellor and the vacant role of president into one. Hindenburg had continued in his role for as long as possible under pressure from advisers who warned that should he retire, Hitler would gain far too much power.

Following Hitler's *Nacht der langen Messer* (Night of the Long Knives, or blood purge), which occurred over June 30 and July 1 this year, the Nazi leader successfully eliminated the paramilitary SA, or Brown Shirts, from his party. The SA was led by Ernst Röhm, who was a homosexual and employed others like him. The SA was quickly seen as decadent and not part of Hitler's vision.

The leader was also determined to put a stop to any socialist influences the Nazi Party might still be harboring, and it was from the ranks of the SA that Hitler believed those influences would manifest themselves. The exercise was swift and cost between 70 and 400 lives.

About the purge, he said, "If anyone reproaches me and asks why I did not resort to the regular courts of justice, then all I can say is this: In this hour I was responsible for the fate of the German people, and thereby I became the supreme judge of the German people."

Long March Begins

China, October 21: Mao Tse-tung, a Chinese peasant from Shaoshan in the Hunan Province, is leading the Red Army on a 6,000-mile (9,654-km) march from Jiangxi, where they had been besieged by Chiang Kai-shek's National Revolutionary Army, to Yenan to spread the word of communism throughout China.

In what is essentially a massive military retreat by the Chinese Communist Army, 86,000 women and men have undertaken the journey that is expected to take over a year. Among the numbers are Zhou Enlai, and Deng Xiaoping leading the Third Army group with Mao Tse-tung. The marchers can expect to face ongoing hostilities with warlords and further battles with the National Revolutionary Army.

The Communists are armed with more than 33,000 rifles, carbines, pistols, heavy machine guns, and light machine guns, and are carrying almost 2,000,000 cartridges, and 4,000 mortar shells.

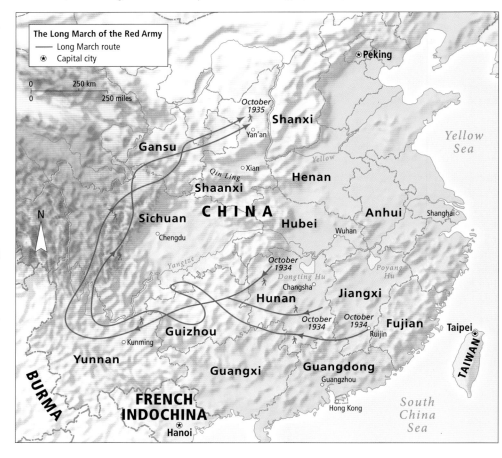

The Long March of the Red Army
— Long March route
⊛ Capital city

Berlin, Germany, January 1: A Nazi law forcing people with genetic defects to be sterilized comes into effect in Germany.
India, January 15: Over 10,000 people are feared dead after an earthquake strikes Bihar.
Berlin, Germany, January 15: Germany and Poland sign a 10-year non-aggression pact following a period of tension.
World, February 11: Friendship treaties are signed between Saudi Arabia and Britain, and between Britain, India, and Yemen.

Hsinking, Manchukuo (China), March 1: Henry Pu-yi becomes emperor of Manchukuo, but is a puppet ruler under Japan.
Washington DC, USA, March 24: The USA declares the Philippines will become independent from 1945.
India, April 7: Attempting to quell mass rioting and violence, Gandhi suspends his civil disobedience campaign against British authorities.

Tokyo, Japan, April 18: Japan's foreign office announces it has a virtual protectorate over Chinese relations with Western powers.
USA, May 11: A violent two-day dust storm in the Great Plains removes massive amounts of topsoil.
Louisiana, USA, May 23: Bank robbers Bonnie Parker and Clyde Barrow are shot dead during an ambush near their hideout.

Germany, August 2: Following the death of President Paul von Hindenburg, Adolf Hitler proclaims himself *Führer* of Germany, making him both Head of State and Chancellor. The armed forces are forced to swear an oath of allegiance.
Honshu, Japan, September 21: A typhoon is believed to have killed up to 4,000 people.
Japan, October 2: A tornado in Osaka and Kyoto kills 1,660, leaves 5,400 injured, and destroys the rice harvest.

Marseilles, France, October 9: Croatian and Macedonian extremists assassinate King Alexander of Yugoslavia and the French Foreign Minister Louis Barthou.
China, October: The communist Red Army commences a 6,000-mile (9,654-kilometer) march, retreating from southeastern China after being encircled by General Chiang Kai-shek's nationalist forces and suffering heavy losses.

...ke and Duchess of Kent (shown with their parents), a son, Edward is born.

Mao Tse-tung

Dust-bowl Heatwave Hits Lakeside City

Chicago, USA, July 24: Temperatures in the city of Chicago, Illinois, today reached a record high of 109°F (44°C), the highest temperature ever recorded here. Even Chicago's famous wind has made itself scarce as the desperate citizens waded into the depths of Lake Michigan in search of relief from the heat.

The Nazi Vision Becomes a Reality

Nuremberg, Germany, September 15: Two new Nazi laws, the Reich Citizenship Law and the Law for the Protection of German Blood and German Honor, have formally revoked German citizenship from all Jews and outlawed marriage between Jews and Germans. The "Nuremberg Laws," as they have been called, have meant that all Jews in government positions have been dismissed, as have Jews working for Germans.

The new laws have employed a pseudo-scientific method to determine who is Jewish and who is not. Anyone with three or more Jewish grandparents is considered a Jew, those with two or more are considered to be of mixed blood.

The Nuremberg Laws have been introduced to ensure the purity of the "German master race," which aims to preserve the purity of Aryan and Nordic genes and political and cultural purity. They also facilitate the persecution of other peoples considered impure, such as gypsies, Mormons, Jehovah's Witnesses, and homosexuals, as well as allowing the development of the T4 Euthanasia Program. This program aims to terminate the lives of the chronically ill and disabled. The new laws also allow compulsory sterilization for anyone who is considered to have hereditary defects ranging from mental illness to alcoholism. So far, 400,000 individuals have been sterilized.

New Leader, But March Continues

China, December 1: Kuomintang leader General Chiang Kai-shek, with the might of his National Revolutionary Army, has been elected president of the Chinese Executive Committee in yet another step in his steady rise to power.

Chiang was born into a middle-class merchant family in Zhejiang province. He studied at the Paoting Military Academy, and continued his education in Japan at the Military State Academy. During this period he became a member of Sun Yat-sen's United Revolutionary League, a precursor of the Kuomintang. From there he went on to serve in the Japanese army from 1909 to 1911. He returned home in 1911 to become an artillery officer in the Wuchang Uprising against the Qing Dynasty. When the imperial government was overthrown, Chiang joined the Kuomintang. The People's Republic of China was established in 1912.

In 1918, Chiang worked with Sun Yat-sen at his headquarters in Guangzhou, and over the next several years earned Sun's trust and support. After Sun Yat-sen's death in 1925, Chiang was appointed Commander in Chief of the National Revolutionary Forces, and attempted to unify the country. As Chairman of the National Government, he implemented business, agricultural, and social reforms. Chiang severed ties between the Kuomintang and the Communists in 1927. For the past five years, much of his military efforts have been focused on suppressing the Communists, led by Mao Tse-tung, who has gathered the support of peasants throughout the country. Mao's Long March from Jiangxi to Yenan ended in October this year, and although the marchers' numbers were severely decimated due to cold, illness, and hunger, they have managed to secure an enclave in the isolated north.

time out

John Dillinger, the most notorious criminal of his time, was shot dead by Federal agents as he left a theater on Chicago's North Side. He had just seen *Manhattan Melodrama*, a mobster movie starring Clark Gable and William Powell.

Chiang Kai-shek, the leader of the Kuomintang army, was a protegé of Sun Yat-sen.

Africa, January 1: The Italian colonies of Kyrenaika and Tripoli are joined as Libya.
Southern Africa, January 14: The Lower Zambezi bridge opens, creating an uninterrupted rail connection between Nyasaland and the Indian Ocean port of Beira.
Florida, USA, January 16: The FBI kills members of the notorious Barker gang, including Ma Barker, during a shootout at a Lake Weir cottage.

Berlin, Germany, March 16: Germany denounces the disarmament clauses of the Versailles Treaty, resuming military conscription.
Iran, March 21: Persia officially changes its name to Iran to gain favor with Germany; "Iran" means "Aryan."
Sydney, Australia, April 25: While on display in a Sydney beach pool, a recently caught shark disgorges the tattooed arm of ex-boxer James Smith, revealing clues to his murder.

India, May 30: An earthquake destroys Quetta, killing 30,000.
Chicago, USA, July 24: The dust bowl heatwave hits its peak, with the temperature in Chicago soaring to a record 109°F (43°C).
Moscow, USSR, August 20: The Seventh World Congress of the Communist International calls for the USSR and all communists to unite with democracies against their common enemy, the fascist dictatorships.

Washington DC, USA, August 31: Congress passes the first of its neutrality Acts designed to keep the USA out of the next world war.
Nuremberg, Germany, September 15: The Nuremberg decree legalizes the Nazi persecution of Jews.
Abyssinia, October 2: Italian forces invade Abyssinia.
China, October 20: Mao Tse-tung concludes the Red Army's Long March, reaching Yenan in the Shensi province of northwestern China.

Philippines, November 15: The Philippine Islands are made a US Commonwealth.
New Zealand, November 27: The first Labour government, with a platform of social and economic reform, is elected in New Zealand.
China, December 1: The nationalist General Chiang Kai-shek is elected President of the Chinese Executive Committee.

Howard Hughes

> "GUNS WILL
> MAKE US
> POWERFUL;
> BUTTER WILL
> ONLY MAKE US
> FAT."
>
> HERMANN GOERING
> (1893–1946), GERMAN
> MILITARY LEADER,
> 1936

> "THIS BERLIN-
> ROME CON-
> NECTION IS...
> AN AXIS,
> AROUND
> WHICH CAN
> REVOLVE ALL
> THOSE STATES
> OF EUROPE
> WITH A WILL
> TOWARDS
> COLLABOR-
> ATION AND
> PEACE."
>
> BENITO MUSSOLINI
> (1883–1945), ITALIAN
> PRIME MINISTER AND
> DICTATOR, 1936

France Fears the Worst

Germany, March 7: German troops have begun to amass near the Rhineland border of France in direct defiance of the conditions of the Versailles Treaty.

German Führer and Chancellor Adolf Hitler has maintained that this move is a ramification of a mutual assistance pact between France and Russia, which he believes is directed against Germany. While the previously demilitarized zone is actually German territory, as a permanent guarantee of French security articles 42 and 43 of the Versailles Treaty decree that no troops or fortifications were ever to be placed there.

The force of the treaty has been considerably weakened since Hitler's rise to power, and has already been defied by his announcement of rearmament and the introduction of the military draft. Even the treaty's guarantors, Britain and France, have done no more than condemn German actions, while Britain has gone as far as concluding a naval pact with Hitler allowing him to build a battle fleet that includes submarines.

Will Spain be the Next Fascist Nation?

Spain, July 17: The ongoing feud between Spain's Republican Nationalists and the opposing socialists has finally erupted into all-out civil war.

The hostilities follow an uprising of the army in Morocco and the murder of antifascist police lieutenant José Castillo on January 12 by four fascist gunmen and the retaliatory murder of Calvo Sotelo a day later. Sotelo was the leader of the right-wing monarchist party and was shot by his own police colleagues, while Castillo had been a member of the UMRA, an antifascist military organization, as well as being a socialist youth worker.

Morocco has already been seized by the rebel forces, and the chances of the

The new Duke and Duchess of Windsor, happily together at last.

conflict being short lived look unlikely, although the Nationalist Party is growing in strength with the support of Italian and German troops whose own fascist leaders are supporting General Franco and his struggle for totalitarian power.

A Divorcee Fit for a King

London, England, December 12: Prince Albert Frederick Arthur George Windsor has today been proclaimed King George VI, succeeding his older brother King Edward VIII after his abdication of the throne. Edward Albert Christian George Andrew Patrick David Windsor, who was king of the United Kingdom of Great Britain and Northern Ireland and the British Dominions beyond the Seas as well as Emperor of India, has

forfeited all these titles in order to marry Bessie Wallis Simpson née Warfield, an American two-time divorcee whom he loves above all other honors. A new honorary title, Duke of Windsor, has been created for him.

Edward's reign, though a popular one, has lasted less than a year due to the establishment's grave concerns about his attachment to Wallis Simpson. They felt that her dubious pedigree and marital instability made her an entirely unsuitable and unacceptable consort for a king. So great was this disapproval that Edward's mother refused to receive her son's mistress at court.

King Edward met with British Prime Minister Stanley Baldwin and the Archbishop of Canterbury Cosmo Lang to see if there was any way he could marry the woman he loved without having to abdicate, but no solution that was acceptable to all parties could be found.

Wallis Simpson has been married twice before, the second husband being Ernest Aldrich Simpson, a shipping executive, from 1928 until their divorce in 1936. It is said that her irreverence for the protocols of royal life is one of the things Edward finds most enchanting about her.

The funeral procession of King George V of England, on January 28.

Sandringham, England, January 20: George V dies, aged 70. He is succeeded by his son, Edward VIII.
Germany, March 7: France decides a large military force will be needed after German troops reoccupy the Rhineland.
Spain, April 10: President Niceto Alcalá Zamora is deposed and flees to France, after his attempts to limit the powers of extremist political parties are rejected.

Abyssinia, May 5: Abyssinia is taken by Italy, crumbling under the weight of the massive offensive as Italy seizes the capital, Addis Ababa.
Tokyo, Japan, May 21: Sada Abe, a former prostitute, is arrested for manslaughter after she asphyxiated Kichizo Ishida during sex, removed his penis, wrapped it in paper and wandered the streets of Tokyo for three days with it in her hand.
Spain, June 9: Over one million workers are now on strike.

Spain, July 17: Civil war breaks out.
Berlin, Germany, August 1: The Games of the XIth Olympiad open. Hitler temporarily abstains from his actions against Jews.
Athens, Greece, August 4: Prime Minister General John Metaxas leads a military coup and establishes a dictatorship.
Hobart, Australia, September 7: The last surviving Thylacine ("Tasmanian tiger") dies in Hobart Zoo in Tasmania.

Spain, October 1: General Franco is appointed commander-in-chief of the rebel forces in the civil war after capturing Toledo.
Washington DC, USA, November 3: Franklin Roosevelt is re-elected president in a landslide victory over Alfred Landon.
Germany, November 25: Germany signs an anti-Comintern pact with Japan to protect the countries' common interests.

London, England, November 30: The Crystal Palace, built in 1851, is destroyed by fire.
London, England, December 12: Prince Albert is proclaimed King George VI after his brother Edward VIII abdicates the British throne.
China, December 12-25: Nationalist General Chiang Kai-shek is kidnapped in Xi'an in an attempt to force him to negotiate with the Communists—his enemies—against their external enemy, Japan.

Airship Meets Fiery End

New Jersey, USA, May 6: The future of the airship as a method of luxury travel looks dim today after the magnificent German airship, the *Hindenburg*, burst into flames 200 ft (60 m) above where it was to land at the Lakehurst Naval Station. Thirty-five people on board the craft and one grounds-man were killed in this dreadful accident.

The *Hindenburg*'s thirty-seventh ocean crossing was its last.

The 803-ft (245 m) long craft was considered the height of luxury, complete with elegant sleeping quarters, a dining room, exquisite lounge, and a library, with a complement of almost two crew members to every passenger. The *Hindenburg* did not make the trip in winter, and this was its first flight to the United States for the season.

On board were 61 crew and 36 passengers, of whom 23 passengers and 39 crew survived. Although poor weather delayed the landing, experts are at a loss to explain what caused the blue flame that appeared shortly before the explosion that ripped through the airship.

Stalin Purges Ranks

Moscow, USSR, June 30: Joseph Stalin, the head of Russia's Politburo and a leader who enjoys almost complete control over his country, has undertaken to purge the Communist Party of those he deems to be "counter revolutionary infiltrators." His justice is swift and often deadly for those falling foul of his leadership; punishments range from party expulsion to exile in gulags (labor camps) and death.

Having already expelled and exiled his most feared rival Leon Trotsky in the late 1920s, Stalin has been able to condemn anyone seen to be following Trotsky's model of Marxist communism. Trotsky-ism is now a crime, and the punishment for its followers is most severe.

Following the mysterious assassination of Sergei Kirov in 1934, Stalin has eliminated most of the old Bolsheviks from the Communist Party, but a series of trials in Moscow are set to eliminate any more potential adversaries from the system.

The Trial of Sixteen in August 1936 and the Trial of Seventeen this January have both involved a number of important party members. Of the 16, all were charged under the Criminal Code of the SFSR (Soviet Federative Socialist Republic) with forming a terrorist organization with the intent to kill Joseph Stalin, and were sentenced to death. Of the 17, all but four were sentenced to death on similar charges. Those not sentenced to death were banished to gulags.

Another secret trial has also taken place which has been dubbed the "Tukhachevsky Affair" after Marshall Tukhachevsky, one of the eight high-ranking military commanders who were tried on June 11 and 12. They were accused of anti-communist conspiracy, sentenced to death, and executed immediately. That trial was the beginning of an enormous purge of the Red Army, which has resulted in 45,000 deaths.

More War for China

Peking, China, July 28: After what is being described by China as the "Luokouchiao Incident" on July 7, the Chinese government in Nanking is determined to resist Japan as that country attempts to begin a second Sino-Japanese war.

The Luokouchiao Incident followed Japanese claims that several of their troops had failed to return from recent Japanese military exercises in the Yuang Peng County near Peking. This ploy follows a long line of similar incidents in which the Japanese have used unsubstantiated grounds for escalating hostilities.

When the Chinese authorities denied a request by the Japanese to enter the county and search the town for the missing men, they launched a full scale attack on the Yuan Peng County over the Luokouchiao Bridge. The Chinese successfully repelled the attack, but the incident has effectively marked the start of another war.

Amelia Earhart

Eire's first Taoiseach, Eamon de Valera (front, third from left), and Cabinet.

New York, USA, January 19: Howard Hughes sets a new flying record: Los Angeles to New York City in seven hours and 28 minutes.

Moscow, USSR, January 23: The trial of 17 leading Communists, accused of participating in Leon Trotsky's plot to overthrow Joseph Stalin's regime and assassinate its leaders, begins.

Moscow, USSR, February 1: Thirteen 'Trotskyists' are executed.

Detroit, USA, February 11: A 44-day sit-down strike ends as General Motors recognizes the United Automobile Workers Union. The strike is one of 477 sit-down strikes in this year.

India, April 1: The British Parliament's Government of India Act, aimed at transforming India's governmental system, goes into effect, giving provincial governments greater autonomy.

New Jersey, USA, May 6: The German airship *Hindenburg* bursts into flame while mooring, killing 35 people on board and one member of the ground crew.

London, England, May 12: The coronation of King George VI and Queen Elizabeth takes place at Westminster Abbey.

South America, May 26: The Chaco War between Bolivia and Paraguay ends.

California, USA, May 28: The Golden Gate Bridge, linking San Francisco and Marin County, opens.

World, June 8: The first total solar eclipse to exceed seven minutes of totality in over 800 years is visible in Peru and the Pacific.

Moscow, USSR, June 12: Eight Russian generals are executed, causing international outrage.

South Pacific Ocean, July 2: Aviatrix Amelia Earhart disappears between New Guinea and Howland Island near the end of an around-the-world flight.

Alabama, USA, July 24: The state drops its rape charges against the "Scottsboro Boys."

Peking, July 28: Japanese forces complete their occupation of the city after an initial strike on July 7 at nearby Lukouchiao.

China, September 29: General Chiang Kai-shek unites forces with his rival, Communist Mao Tse-tung, against the Japanese.

Ireland, December 29: The new Irish Constitution comes into force and the Irish Free State officially becomes Eire.

Black Gold in Arabia

Saudi Arabia, March 3: After five years of oil exploration in Arabia, a well has finally been located in Dahrahan.

The search for oil began with a concessionary agreement between the Saudi Arabian government and the American company Standard Oil of California (SOCAL). The agreement was signed in May 1933 and gave the American company oil exploration rights. They in turn passed the concession on to an associated company called California-Arabian Standard Oil (CASOC). Having no success after three years, they sold half their interest to the Texas Oil Company.

The newly discovered well has been named Dammam Number 7, and American industrialists have hopes that this will be the beginning of a flourishing and profitable industry in the Middle East.

Hitler's Troops Move East

Czechoslovakia, October 5: Hitler's troops have now moved into Czechoslovakia in what the Nazi leader maintains is a necessary measure to deal with the Sudeten German minority problem. This group of ethnic Sudeten Germans numbers about 3 million and represents almost 25 percent of the Czechoslovakian population.

The Sudetenland possesses a number of large chemical production plants as well as strong textile and glass manufacturing enterprises. However, many believe the Germans' real aim is to penetrate eastern central Europe.

Czech Konrad Henlein of the Sudeten-German Party (SDP) offered to let Hitler use the SDP as the vehicle for him to carry out his campaign and, after meeting with Hitler in March, was expected to raise demands to the Czech government that he knew they would not meet.

The SDP demanded total autonomy for the Sudetenland and complete freedom to implement Nazi policy, which if granted would allow the region to align itself with Germany. The new Czech president Edvard Benes opposed the demands and troops were mobilized.

Hitler had in fact already initiated a secret directive in May that a war against Czechoslovakia should begin during October at the latest.

France and Britain do not at this stage wish to engage in a war with Germany on their own and British Prime Minister Neville Chamberlain has become a major spokesman for the western European nations. Chamberlain has attended a conference in Munich with leaders of other European nations who are prepared to believe that Hitler's expansion policies are limited. That conference resulted in the Munich Agreement, signed by Britain, France, Italy, and Germany, which allows Hitler's advance into Czechoslovakia.

Czech representatives were not present at the conference and have called the agreement "The Munich Betrayal," as it sold them out completely and did not take into account existing alliances with Britain or France.

Orson Welles

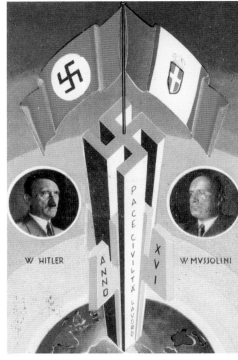

Hitler and Mussolini sign the Munich Pact in September.

"It is the last territorial claim which I have to make in Europe, but it is the claim from which I will not recede."

ADOLF HITLER (1889–1945), GERMAN DICTATOR, ON THE SUDETENLAND (CZECHOSLOVAKIA), 1938

"Every Communist must grasp the truth, 'Political power grows out of the barrel of a gun.'"

MAO TSE-TUNG (1893–1976), CHINESE COMMUNIST LEADER, 1938

China Will Fight, Whatever the Cost

Canton, China, October 21: Japan has succeeded in capturing the southern Chinese city of Canton after months of tireless fighting and bombing.

The seizure of the city, which is a vital entry point to China and the major rail link to the British Crown Colony of Hong Kong via the Canton–Kowloon railway, is a devastating blow to the Chinese, who have been determined to maintain the sovereignty of this most strategic of cities.

Following the massacre of Nanking in the winter of 1937, in which nearly 300,000 people, mostly civilians, were killed by the Japanese, China is now prepared to face the invaders with determination and fight to the bitter end. Already a million new recruits are being trained and the universities have been moved further inland along with the nation's famed art treasures.

China has adopted a scorched earth policy whereby Chinese military forces are torching their own villages prior to enemy invasion rather than having them plundered by the Japanese invaders.

People flee during a Japanese bombing raid on Canton.

Key Events

London, England, January 3: The government plans to provide all schoolchildren with gas masks.
Saudi Arabia, March 3: Oil is discovered in Saudi Arabia.
Austria, March 13: Germany declares *Anschluss* (political union with Austria) after invading Austria on March 12.
Nanking, China, March 13: Japanese troops slaughter up to 300,000 civilians and prisoners of war in a massacre following the city's fall to Japan on December 13, 1937.

London, England, March 17: A report by the Cadogan Committee recommends that flogging be abolished, indicating that no correlation has been found between corporal punishment and levels of criminal activity.
Latvia, June 11: Fire destroys 212 buildings in Ludes.
Pennsylvania, USA, June 28: A 500-ton meteorite breaks up over Butler County; one part lands near Chicora and injures a cow.

China, July: Massive floods follow General Chiang Kai-shek's orders to destroy the dikes on the Yangtze and Yellow Rivers, intended to deter the Japanese. They result in numerous drownings, with countless more made homeless.
Rome, Italy, August 3: Mussolini introduces his anti-Semitic laws into Italy, following the lead of his German allies.

Munich, Germany, September 30: The Munich Agreement, made by Germany, Italy, Britain and France, allows Hitler to take Sudetenland, and Hungary and Poland to take border districts from Czechoslovakia. Another resolution is signed to resolve future disputes between Britain and Germany peacefully.
Czechoslovakia, October 5: Hitler's army marches into Czechoslovakia.

Canton, China, October 21: The Japanese capture the southern city of Canton.
New York, USA, October 30: Panic erupts when a radio drama based on H.G. Wells's *War of the Worlds* and produced by Orson Welles's Mercury Players airs; some listeners believe the world is under Martian attack.
Berlin, Germany, November 9: Jewish shops, homes, and synagogues are looted or destroyed as Hitler's anti-Jewish scheme is unleashed throughout Germany.

Spain's Civil War Has Ended

Spain, April 1: General Francisco Franco has declared today that the civil war between the Second Spanish Republic and other left-wing groups against Franco's own right-wing-backed nationalist movement is at an end at last.

The war has lasted just three years but in that time the lives of between 300,000 and one million people have been taken. The deaths mostly occurred in bloody, non-military-style massacres. Republican radicals saw the Catholic Church, as oppressive and in support of the old order, and it suffered huge reprisals, with the burning of churches, convents and monasteries and the deaths of 12 bishops, 283 nuns, 2,365 monks, and 4,200 priests.

General Franco has ousted the incumbent Republican government and established a personal dictatorship over what the famous Spanish writer Antonio Machado y Ruiz has dubbed "the two Spains," whose differences still remain.

Chamberlain: It's War!

London, England, September 3: Today, shortly after 11 a.m., Prime Minister Neville Chamberlain made the following broadcast to the nation:

"This morning the British Ambassador in Berlin handed the German Government a final note stating that, unless we hear from them by 11 o'clock that they were prepared at once to withdraw their troops from Poland, a state of war would exist between us. I have to tell you now that no such undertaking has been received, and that consequently this country is at war with Germany.

"You can imagine what a bitter blow it is to me that all my long struggle to win

time out

Du Pont in New Jersey released the first nylon products on the market: toothbrushes. Nylon was made from coal, water, and air and was the first commercially successful polymer. It was created as a substitute for silk.

peace has failed. Yet I cannot believe that there is anything more or anything different that I could have done and that would have been more successful.

"Up to the very last it would have been quite possible to have arranged a peaceful and honourable settlement between Germany and Poland, but Hitler would not have it. He had evidently made up his mind to attack Poland, whatever happened, and although he now says he put forward reasonable proposals that were rejected by the Poles, that is not a true statement.

"The proposals were never shown to the Poles, nor to us, and though they were announced in a German broadcast on Thursday night, Hitler did not wait to hear comments on them but ordered his troops to cross the Polish frontier the next morning.

"His action shows convincingly that there is no chance of expecting that this man will ever give up his practice of using force to gain his will. He can only be stopped by force.

"We and France are today, in fulfilment of our obligations, going to the aid of Poland, who is so bravely resisting this wicked and unprovoked attack upon her people. We have a clear conscience—we have done all that any country could do to establish peace.

"The situation in which no word given by Germany's ruler could be trusted, and no people or country could feel itself safe, has become intolerable. And now that we have resolved to finish it I know that you will play your part with calmness and courage.

"At such a moment as this the assurances of support which we have received from the empire are a source of profound encouragement to us.

"When I have finished speaking, certain detailed announcements will be made on behalf of the government. Give these your

closest attention. The government have made plans under which it will be possible to carry on work of the nation in the days of stress and strain that may be ahead…

"Now may God bless you all. May He defend the right. For it is evil things that we shall be fighting against—brute force, bad faith, injustice, oppression and persecution—and against them I am certain that right will prevail."

Thousands Dead in Turkey

Turkey, December 27: An earthquake in Erzincan has claimed the lives of at least 30,000, with more deaths likely to follow as the aftershocks make themselves felt.

The earthquake, which registered 7.9 on the Richter scale, began at 5.36 a.m. and lasted no more than two minutes. It is the worst quake experienced in the country this century, causing surface ruptures, snow avalanches, and landslides, as well as a tsunami in the Black Sea.

Neville Chamberlain

English twins inspect their gas masks as war looks imminent.

Australia, January 13: The day is declared Black Friday after 71 people across Victoria die in the country's worst bushfires.

Chile, January 24: An earthquake strikes south-central Chile, killing 28,000.

Washington DC, USA, February 27: The US Supreme Court outlaws sit-down strikes.

Essex, England, February 27: Borley Rectory, built in 1863 and reputedly England's most haunted house, burns down.

Czechoslovakia, March 16: The German Army occupies Prague and Czechoslovakia becomes a Nazi protectorate.

Spain, April 1: Franco declares the end of the civil war.

Rome, Italy, May 22: Mussolini signs a military pact with Hitler, obligating Italy to fight alongside Germany.

Florida, USA, June 4: The USA denies entry to the *St Louis*, a ship carrying 930 Jewish refugees, after it is turned away by Cuba. It returns to Europe.

Moscow, USSR, August 23: Hitler and Stalin sign a Nazi-Soviet pact of non-aggression that divides Eastern Europe between Germany and USSR.

Poland, September 1: German forces invade Poland from Germany in the west, East Prussia in the north and Czechoslovakia in the south.

Europe, September 3: Britain and France declare war on Germany in accord with treaty obligations to Poland. They are followed by New Zealand, Australia and India.

South Africa, September 6: South Africa declares war on Germany.

Canada, September 10: Canada declares war on Germany.

Poland, September 17: USSR invades Poland from the east.

Poland, September 29: The Nazis and Soviets divide up Poland. Over two million Jews reside in Nazi-controlled areas, and 1.3 million in the Soviet area.

Poland, September 29: Warsaw surrenders; 700,000 Polish troops are taken prisoner.

Germany, October: The Nazis begin a program to euthanize the sick and disabled in Germany.

Finland, November 30: The USSR attacks Finland after their strategic negotiations on November 12 fail.

Turkey, December 27: An earthquake in Erzingan kills 100,000.

Karl Landsteiner

Ninth Planet Discovered

Arizona, USA, May 24, 1930:
The long-sought Planet X, discovered on March 13, was been named "Pluto" today by its discoverer, American astronomer Clyde William Tombaugh. The discovery of the newly named planet and its orbit had been predicted as early as 1910 by astrono- mers Percival Lowell and William Pickering, to explain irregularities in the orbits of Uranus and Neptune. Pluto is named after the Roman god of the underworld, who was able to make himself invisible, but the name also honors Lowell's work—the first two letters are Lowell's initials.

The discovery was made at the Lowell Observatory in Flagstaff using a blink comparator, a device allowing the comparison of similar photographs by placing them in alternation before the viewer's field of vision. Using the device, the observer is able to distinguish stars and planets by noting movements and changes in the image. The planets move, while the stars remain in fixed positions.

Tombaugh painstakingly compared months of images and on February 18 he was able to confirm that the fixed object was in fact the planet now named Pluto.

Nobel for Blood Research

Stockholm, Sweden, December 12, 1930:
One of medicine's most outstanding con- tributors, Karl Landsteiner, has today been honored with the Nobel Prize for Physi- ology or Medicine for his research into the grouping of human blood. His dis- covery was made in 1901 and has been the foundation of many breakthroughs in modern hematology and immunology.

Hydrotherapy is believed to help in the treatment of polio patients.

Born in Vienna in 1868, Landsteiner graduated in medicine in 1891, having published his first paper on the influence of diet on blood composition while still a student. He spent the following five years working in the most prestigious labora- tories of Zurich, Wurzburg, and Munich.

Landsteiner's interest in the nature of immunity and antibodies led him back to the Hygiene Institute in Vienna, where he became an assistant under Max von Gruber. From there, he moved to the University De- partment of Patho- logical Anatomy, and in 1911 he became Pro- fessor of Pathological Anatomy at the Univer- sity of Vienna.

His work on monkeys enabled him to lay the foundations of current knowledge of the cause and immunology of poliomyelitis.

His research came after experiments in which he noted that transfusing blood from one person to another can result in shock, jaundice, and hemoglobinuria. While his beliefs that the make-up of hemoglobin (red blood cells) might vary received little initial attention, he began to categorize hemoglobin into the A, B, AB, and O blood types that are widely used today. He found that problems came only when people were transfused with blood from incompatible groups.

Lights Out for One of Technology's Greats

New Jersey, USA, October 18, 1931: Thomas Alva Edison, the inventor most famously noted for the light bulb, has died in his home. Edison, who was born in 1847, has been responsible for the mass production of many devices that have made life easier in this century. He was the first to establish an industrial research laboratory where he and a team of researchers were able to modify existing patents and develop them into practical consumer products.

Schooled almost entirely at home by his mother, Edison was encouraged from an early age to experiment with things. After working as a newsboy on trains,

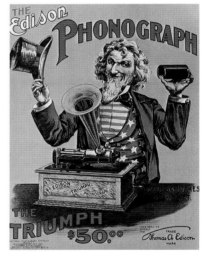

The phonograph, one of Edison's inventions.

he became a telegraph operator and devel- oped the automatic repeater. He first gained fame in 1877 when he invented the phonograph, a device so amazing as to be considered almost miraculous. His first phonograph recorded sounds on cylinders covered with tin foil and could only play the recording once before it was corrupted.

Edison's patents were largely utility

UK, January, 1930: Engineer Frank Whittle submits a patent for the first jet-propelled engine.
Arizona, USA, May 24, 1930: The ninth planet is given the name Pluto.
New Jersey, USA, September 1, 1930: Thomas Edison tests the nation's first electric passenger train.
Sweden, December 12, 1930: Karl Landsteiner wins the Nobel Prize for Medicine.
London, England, January 22, 1931: A vaccine against polio appears to be possible in the near future.

New Jersey, USA, October 18, 1931: Inventor Thomas Alva Edison dies in his home, aged 84.
Alabama, USA, November 8, 1931: A new radioactive halogen is discovered by Frederick Allison.
Germany, December, 1931: Max Knott and Ernst Ruska jointly invent the electron microscope this year.
Cambridge, England, February 27, 1932: In the journal *Nature*, James Chadwick reports the potential existence of a new subatomic particle, the neutron.

Pittsburgh, USA, April 4, 1932: Vitamin C is isolated by scientists.
USA, April 28, 1932: A yellow fever vaccine is created.
USA, December, 1932: This year astronomer Theodore Dunham finds there is carbon dioxide in Venus's atmosphere.
New Jersey, USA, May, 1933: Astronomer Karl Jansky detects radio waves coming from the center of the galaxy.

UK, July 7, 1933: Doctors announced they have been able to isolate the influenza virus.
USA, October 31, 1933: A scientific research vessel, the *Atlantis*, finds clues that life exists in our deepest oceans.
Savoy, France, July 4, 1934: The discoverer of radium, Nobel Prize winner Marie Curie, dies aged 66.
USA, December 10, 1934: Harold Clayton Urey wins the Nobel Prize for Chemistry for his 1931 discovery of deuterium, the heavy form of hydrogen.

Germany, December, 1934: Inventor Semi Joseph Begun builds the first tape recorder for broadcasting.
England, December, 1934: After examining human bones found in 1674 in the Tower of London, Lawrence Tanner and William Wright report that the remains may belong to the sons of King Edward IV who went missing in 1683, but the evidence is inconclusive.
USA, February 28, 1935: Nylon is invented by Wallace Carothers, working for DuPont.

patents, but he did hold at least a dozen design patents. He did not, in fact, invent the light bulb, but bought an existing patent from a syndicate of other inventors. His researchers then set about developing bulbs that lasted, and by 1879 they came up with a model that would last for hundreds of hours.

From there he worked on producing them and, after establishing the Edison Electric Light Company in New York City, developed electricity distribution systems for businesses and homes. He also became involved in the battle to use the safer direct current (DC) power instead of the more dangerous alternating current (AC).

Despite his opposition to capital punishment, Edison went on to develop the electric chair as a vehicle to demonstrate the dangers of AC, which he did by publicly electrocuting cats, dogs, and on one occasion an elephant. His pleas were not successful, however, and AC power became the most widely used.

New Frontiers in Nuclear Science

Cambridge, Massachusetts, USA, February 27, 1932: A fundamental discovery in the realm of nuclear science occurred today when the English physicist James Chadwick proved the existence of neutrons in his research on particle theory.

These particles in the nucleus of the atom are devoid of any electrical charge; they operate in contrast to the alpha rays, which are charged and repelled by the electrical forces that are present within the nuclei of heavy atoms. The discovery paves the way to many potential possibilities for energy extraction, as this newly found particle does not need to overcome electrical barriers to penetrate and split the nuclei of the most heavy elements.

time out

In Indianapolis a new, low-cost car was unveiled capable of a maximum speed of 50 mph (80 km/h) with mileage of 50 mpg (21 km/liter). The retail price was to be $325 or $350, depending on model.

Chadwick, who was born in 1891 and graduated from the Honours School of Physics in 1911, spent several years working for Professor Ernest Rutherford in the Physical Laboratory in Manchester tackling a number of areas of radioactivity research. They succeeded in shattering atoms by bombarding nitrogen with alpha particles and proton emission. They achieved the first-ever artificial nuclear transformation.

Farewell to the Mother of Science

Savoy, France, July 4, 1934: One of science's most determined women, Madame Marie Curie, has died. Curie was born Maria Sklodowska in Warsaw, Poland, in 1867. Curie was a gifted student, but Poland's repressive Tsarist rule forbade women to be educated in the sciences.

Marie Curie's brilliance and drive helped her win the Nobel Prize twice.

Marie and her sister Bronya made a pact that they would help each other obtain professional educations from universities in western Europe. While Bronya studied medicine, Marie worked as a teacher to pay her sister's way. When Bronya completed her degree, she in turn funded Marie's studies in mathematics, physics, and chemistry. Some of her learning had to be undertaken at a "floating university," which was conducted in secret because the Russian authorities forbade the Poles from teaching students laboratory science.

At the age of 24, Marie had saved enough to go to France to study science at the Sorbonne, where she obtained a masters degree in physics and mathematics in just three years.

Marie married Pierre Curie in 1895, completed her research and had her first child in 1897, and began her doctorate in science (an achievement unprecedented by a woman). Two discoveries were made that led her to her life's work: One was Wilhelm Roentgen's discovery that rays could pass through solid wood or flesh; the second was Henri Becquerel's discovery that minerals containing uranium gave off rays.

Curie decided to investigate the uranium rays; she began experimenting and named the rays that emanated from certain minerals "radioactivity." She and her husband discovered two new elements, polonium and radium. Sadly, exposure to radioactivity drastically affected her health and, when she and Pierre were awarded the Nobel Prize for Physics in 1903, she was too ill to attend.

Thomas Edison

Middlesex, England, April, 1935: An aircraft-locating device, "radar," is patented by Scottish physicist Robert Watson-Watt.
New York, USA, June 27, 1935: Wendell Stanley is the first to crystallize a disease virus, showing it is infectious.
California, USA, August 20, 1935: Scientists isolate Vitamin E.
USA, December, 1935: Charles Richter develops a new logarithmic scale to measure earthquake intensity.

St Petersburg, USSR, February 27, 1936: The father of classical conditioning, Russian physiologist Ivan Petrovich Pavlov, dies aged 85.
Germany, February, 1936: Testing begins on a rocket with a 3,300-lb (1,498-kg) thrust.
Durham, North Carolina, USA, December, 1937: Surgeon J. Deryl Hart reduces the number of post-operative infectious deaths this year by using ultraviolet lamps in operating rooms.

Chicago, USA, March, 1937: Cook County Hospital sets up the world's first "blood bank" to store blood taken from living donors, expected to greatly increase survival from major surgery.
England, April 12, 1937: Tests of Frank Whittle's new jet-propelled engine are successfully carried out.
Bremen, Germany, July 4, 1937: Hanna Reitsch makes the first controlled helicopter flight.

USA, April 6, 1938: Working for DuPont, Roy J. Plunkett accidentally creates an extremely slippery new polymer (teflon).
Berlin, Germany, December, 1938: Radiochemists Otto Hahn and Fritz Strassmann unexpectedly discover nuclear fission.
USA, December, 1938: A fourth kingdom, for bacteria, has been added to the three existing kingdoms in the taxonomy of life: plants, animals and protista.

Netherlands, March 17, 1939: Mathematician Johannes van der Corput of the University of Groningen shows that prime numbers can be infinitely progressed.
Long Island, USA, August 2, 1939: Albert Einstein writes a letter to President Roosevelt to recommend the USA develop an atomic bomb.

Better Than Silk

USA, February 28, 1935: A new synthetic fiber is about to change the fabric of our daily lives. Dr Wallace Hume Carothers, the head of organic chemistry at DuPont, one of the largest chemical companies in the world, and his colleagues have been working on polymers for years. They successfully developed neoprene, a synthetic rubber in 1930.

Their synthetic experiments led them to create polyester, the forerunner to what will now be known as nylon.

This spinning machine is used for making nylon, for hosiery.

Carothers, with his colleague Elmer Bolton, experimented widely in the early 1930s to find a fabric that would withstand solvents and would not melt at such low temperatures as the early polyesters. Using synthetic proteins known as polyamides, which are similar in structure to natural fats and oils, they were able to create the polyamide fiber that is set to take on the lucrative silk stocking market.

No More Stealth Attacks for Britain

Middlesex, England, April, 1935: Britain's air defense has been given a boost with the newly patented aircraft detection technology called "radar." Meteorologist Robert Watson-Watt, superintendent of a new radio department at the National Physics Laboratory in Teddington, and his assistant, Arnold Wilkins, have released a report entitled "The Detection of Aircraft by Radio Methods." The report has been presented to the Committee for the Scientific Survey of Air Defence chaired by Sir Henry Tizard.

A successful trial of the theory has already taken place, when the BBC's shortwave radio transmitter was used to detect a Heyford

Bomber on February 26. The success of the trials and the defense applications for radar usage along the coastlines will be an enormous boost to England's security.

Farewell to a Great Man and His Dog

Leningrad, USSR, February 27, 1936: Russian scientist Ivan Petrovich Pavlov has died.

Born in 1849 and the son of a village priest, Pavlov's research into the field of physiology and the mechanisms underlying the digestive systems of mammals has paved the way to a much greater understanding of the links between the brain and other organs.

Awarded with the Nobel Prize in Physiology or Medicine in 1904, his work since then has focused primarily on the laws of conditioned responses, most famously illustrated in the case of "Pavlov's Dog."

As he worked on discovering the mechanisms of the digestive system, Pavlov observed the triggers that also related to it, such as the secretion of saliva. When dogs see food, they begin to salivate and drool from glands in the oral cavity. Saliva is essential in making food easier to swallow, as well as containing important enzymes to break food down.

Pavlov then noticed that dogs in the laboratories often drooled when no food was present. It became apparent that the dogs were drooling when they saw lab coats. It turned out that every time the

dogs were fed it was by someone wearing a lab coat, and the dogs' digestive processes were being activated by the expectation of food they had associated with seeing the lab coats.

In further experiments, Pavlov sounded bells when food was to be served. As predicted, the dogs soon began to salivate at the sound of the bell.

Harold Clayton Urey

> "I DO NOT LIKE IT, AND I AM SORRY I EVER HAD ANYTHING TO DO WITH IT."
>
> ERWIN SCHRÖDINGER (1887–1961), AUSTRIAN PHYSICIST AND NOBEL PRIZE WINNER, OF QUANTUM MECHANICS, 1933

> "THE ETERNAL MYSTERY OF THE WORLD IS ITS COMPREHENSIBILITY… THE FACT THAT IT IS COMPREHENSIBLE IS A MIRACLE."
>
> ALBERT EINSTEIN (1879–1955), GERMAN PHYSICIST AND NOBEL PRIZE WINNER, ON PHYSICS, 1936

Robert Watson-Watt's first experiments detected an aircraft by reflected radio waves at a distance of about 6 miles (10 km).

Pavlov used dogs in his conditioned-reflex experiments.

Pavlov's influence in the study of physiology has been great, helping Russia to become a leader in this field.

Jet Power a Reality

England, April 12, 1937: Turbojet power for aircraft may soon be a reality after today's successful trial of a laboratory test rig comprising a single-stage centrifugal compressor combined with a single-stage turbine. Construction of the engine began in July 1936 and involved pushing the compressor and turbine well beyond the currently perceived technological limits, with heat intensities 20 times normal. While the engine still cannot accelerate beyond 8,500 rpm, the test has proven that the engine could have feasible applications in modern aviation.

The prototype engine has been developed with private money by Englishman Frank Whittle. The son of a mechanic, Whittle was born in 1907. He began as an apprentice in the Royal Air Force in 1928 and became a test pilot by 1931.

Dr Hans von Ohain, a German airplane designer and doctor in physics, worked simultaneously but separately on the same concept. Without knowledge of each other's work, both men came up with a similar model at the same time.

Although Whittle has been the first to lodge a patent application, von Ohain's engine looks set to be the first off the ground. Von Ohain's continuous-cycle combustion engine was developed in 1933, when he was just 22 years old, and while his design produced the same results it was configured differently.

Whittle is working with Power Jets Ltd., who intend to develop the Whittle engine for use in experimental aircraft.

Hitler's Darling of the Sky

Bremen, Germany, July 4, 1937: Germany's most accomplished and daring woman pilot, Hanna Reitsch, has today flown in a new kind of air-beast. In the first test flight of the Focke-Achgelis Fa 61, a fully controlled helicopter, Reitsch has proven that rotary propeller blades may work as well as wings when it comes to staying in the air.

Born in Germany in 1912, her ambition had been to be a missionary doctor. However, following Germany's defeat and consequential debts from the Great War, she became very patriotic and an enthusiastic admirer of Adolf Hitler.

Reitsch's early fame came from her record-making flights across the Alps in a glider and later as a stunt pilot in movies and airshows. Reitsch was also a highly proficient photographer and is responsible for some of the best early aerial photography. She also went on expeditions to South America to study weather patterns and was the first women ever to be made an honorary flight captain by Hitler, who also greatly admires her work and nationalism. She dubbed German warplanes "guardians and the portals of peace."

Power for Good, Power for Evil?

Berlin, Germany, December, 1938: The atom has finally been split, unleashing the potential for unprecedented power output.

University of Berlin radiochemists Otto Hahn and Friedrich Wilhelm (Fritz) Strassberg have communicated results of their experiments bombarding uranium with thermal neutrons to Lise Meitner and Otto Robert Frisch, scientists who had previously been involved with the research but have now fled Nazi Germany. They were able to confirm that what had occurred was, in fact, nuclear fission (a term devised by Frisch).

With the establishment of nuclear fission as a reality, so too comes the possibility of producing vast amounts of energy using this process, energy that could be used for domestic utilities if carefully controlled, or for military weaponry if an uncontrolled chain reaction were allowed to occur.

Ivan Pavlov

An enthusiastic crowd witnesses the first practical demonstration of a helicopter in 1930.

Hooray for Mickey Mouse

New York, USA, January, 1930: America's favorite and most recognizable mouse has now made his newspaper debut in the *New York Mirror*. Walt Disney, the owner-creator of the happy little mouse called Mickey, has been approached by the Hearst empire's King Features Syndicate to license the cartoon to newspapers published all over the country.

The plots are being conceived by Walt Disney himself, while the artwork is done by Ub Iwerks and inking by Win Smith. The first series in print is to be titled "Plane Crazy" and follows Mickey's attempts to imitate Charles Lindbergh while at the same time trying to court Minnie Mouse. Minnie is an entirely new addition to Mickey's entourage and she is set to introduce more than a little romantic interest to Mickey's life.

Mickey Mouse made his debut in November 1928 in film, and has starred in numerous short cartoons. Already he's caused copyright and licensing battles for his creator, but the crazy antics of this character are leading him to tabloid stardom as well. There's no stopping this mouse.

Academy Awards War Story

Hollywood, California, USA, November 5, 1930: In what is considered to be the most powerful movie adaptation of a war story to date, *All Quiet on the Western Front* has tonight won an Academy Award for outstanding production as well as one for best direction for Lewis Milestone.

The story, based on a novel by German writer Erich Maria Remarque and adapted by George Abbott, Maxwell Anderson, and Del Andrews, is unprecedented as an English-language film in that it tells the bitter story of war in English but from the German point of view. The story follows a group of young men, initially inspired by the idea of fighting for their country, through to their bitter disillusionment and misery in the face of war's realities. It has been applauded by many who believe that war should be seen as equally futile from both sides.

The movie's cast includes Louis Wolheim, Lew Ayres, John Wray, Arnold Lucy, Ben Alexander, Scott Kolk, Walter Rogers, Russell Gleason, Richard Alexander, and Beryl Mercer.

Humphrey Bogart

> *"Our American professors like their literature clear and cold and pure and very dead."*
>
> SINCLAIR LEWIS (1885–1951), AMERICAN NOVELIST, ON RECEIVING THE NOBEL PRIZE, 1930

> *"What is a highbrow? It is a man who has found something more interesting than women."*
>
> EDGAR WALLACE (1875–1932), BRITISH CRIME WRITER, 1931

Walt Disney's Mickey Mouse has captured the hearts of Americans.

Ben Alexander and Lew Ayres, in *All Quiet on the Western Front*.

Art, Not Pornography

New York, USA, December 6, 1932: The checkered history of what is already one of the most famous books of the century added another chapter to its catalogue of controversies today when the trial, "United States versus One Book Called Ulysses" came to an end. US District Judge John M. Woolsey ruled that the previously banned book was not pornographic and therefore could not be considered obscene.

The trial followed an elaborate plan by the US publisher Random House, who organized to have an imported edition of the work seized by customs so that it could go to trial to have the ban lifted. They would then be able to publish the book in the United States.

Ulysses, by Irish writer James Joyce, is a vast work of 267,000 words. It is a rambling Irish take on Homer's Greek classic, *The Odyssey*, and tells the story of a day in the life of Dublin resident Leopold bloom, his wife Molly, and Stephen Dedalus. It was written over a period of seven years and originally published in

time out

Architect Frank Lloyd Wright has completed Fallingwater for Edgar J. Kaufmann in Bear Run, Pennsylvania. The house is designed around revolutionary concrete cantilevers that blend with stone to relate the building to its forest site.

In the most dramatic scene of *King Kong*, the ape captures Ann Darrow and takes her to the top of the Empire State Building.

Marlene Dietrich

audiences gasping at how real this great celluloid beast looks on screen as it rampages through New York.

The King and Queen of "Carioca"

New York, November 15, 1934:
Everyone will be dancing the Continental this year as *The Gay Divorcee* takes cinemas by storm. Fred Astaire and Ginger Rogers are an unrivalled dancing duo in this all-singing, all-dancing romantic comedy of the year.

The movie tells the cheeky story of the beautiful Mimi Glossop (Ginger Rogers), who wants a divorce. To establish the grounds for the divorce, she asks her aunt to employ a "professional" to pose as the object of her infidelity. When Mimi meets Guy Holden (Fred Astaire),

Paris in 1922. The novel has been banned at various times in all English-speaking countries, but has been sold and circulated secretly among the intelligentsia, many of whom believe it to be one of the greatest novels of all time.

Ulysses's US battle originated after it was serialized in the *Little Review* in 1920. One of the passages printed dealt with masturbation, which outraged the New York Society for the Suppression of Vice so greatly they took immediate action to have the book banned.

What a Beauty! What a Beast!

Hollywood, California, USA, March, 1933:
Hollywood's most ambitious cinema extravaganza yet is taking moviegoers' breath away. *King Kong*, taglined as "Out-leaping the maddest imaginings!

Out-thrilling the wildest thrills!" and "The Most Awesome Thriller of all Time," arrived in theaters this month. The studio is promoting the movie as "The strangest story ever conceived by man."

King Kong is the story of an expedition to a remote tropical island ruled by a ferocious giant ape, which is captured and brought back to New York to be exhibited as the eighth wonder of the world. However, things go terribly wrong when the huge creature falls in love with a beautiful actress and takes her prisoner on the top of the Empire State Building.

Directed by Merian C. Cooper and Ernest B. Schoedsack, with a screenplay by James Ashmore Creelman and Ruth Rose, the movie stars Fay Wray and Robert Armstrong.

While the actual model ape used in the film was only 18 in (45 cm) high, the movie's cutting-edge special effects have

she thinks he's the one, but she's mistaken and much dancing and mayhem ensues as the plot unravels.

Directed by Mark Sandrich, the movie is adapted from a musical play called *The Gay Divorce* by Dwight Taylor. Other stars include Betty Grable, William Austin as the unwanted husband, Alice Brady as scheming Aunt Hortense, and Lillian Miles singing the movie's signature tune, "The Continental."

Fred and Ginger do the "Continental."

Key Events

New York, USA, October 10, 1935: The Gershwins' musical *Porgy and Bess* opens on Broadway.

USA, December, 1935: This year's hits are Cole Porter's "Begin the Beguine" and George Gershwin's "Summertime."

Hollywood, USA, 1936: Humphrey Bogart repeats his Broadway success in *The Petrified Forest* with the film of the same name.

New York, USA, February 15, 1936: The Cotton Club, Harlem's famous nightclub, closes its doors.

London, England, September 21, 1936: J. R. R. Tolkien's book *The Hobbit* is published.

New Orleans, USA, December, 1936: Roy "Professor Longhair" Byrd invents the beat known as "rock and roll."

Paris, France, 1937: Pablo Picasso takes a stand against General Franco in a cartoon strip, "The Dream and Lie of Franco."

Spain, February, 1937: Author Ernest Hemingway begins working as a war correspondent in Spain.

Los Angeles, USA, December 21, 1937: Walt Disney's first feature-length animation film, *Snow White and the Seven Dwarfs*, is screened.

New York, USA, June, 1938: Glenn Miller's Orchestra tops the charts after recently breaking the city's record for the largest dancing crowd during their performance at the State Fair in Syracuse.

USA, June, 1938: *Action Comics*' first cover features a new action hero, Superman.

USSR, December 27, 1938: Poet Osip Mandelstam dies in Vtoraya Rechka, aged 47. He was arrested twice and exiled from 1936 to 1937 for his anti-Stalinist poetry.

Hollywood, USA, 1939: Marlene Dietrich makes a successful film comeback in *Destry Rides Again*, a western, with James Stewart.

Menton, France, January 28, 1939: Irish poet, playwright and politician William Butler Yeats dies, aged 73.

Wisconsin, USA, August 12, 1939: *The Wizard of Oz*, starring Judy Garland, premieres.

London, England, August 23, 1939: With war looming, staff at the National Gallery pack almost 2,000 artworks to take to safety.

Wellington, New Zealand, November 8, 1939: The New Zealand Centennial exhibition opens, featuring cultural events, memorials and historical re-enactments of white settlement.

Atlanta, USA, December 15, 1939: The epic 4.5-hour long film *Gone With the Wind* premieres, billed as "the most magnificent picture ever!"

Clark Gable

> "POLITICS AND THE FATE OF MANKIND ARE SHAPED BY MEN WITHOUT IDEALS AND WITHOUT GREATNESS. MEN WHO HAVE GREATNESS WITHIN THEM DON'T GO IN FOR POLITICS."

ALBERT CAMUS (1913–1960), FRENCH NOVELIST, 1935

> "MAN HAS ALWAYS SACRIFICED TRUTH TO HIS VANITY, COMFORT, AND ADVANTAGE. HE LIVES BY MAKE-BELIEVE."

W. SOMERSET MAUGHAM (1874–1965), ENGLISH DRAMATIST AND NOVELIST, 1938

We All Loves Porgy

New York, USA, October 10, 1935: George and Ira Gershwin's greatest masterpiece yet, *Porgy and Bess*, opened tonight at the Alvin Theater in New York after a short test run in Boston.

The opera has been a long time in development and is based on the bestselling book *Porgy* by Southern writer DuBose Heyward, which Gershwin read in 1926. He immediately approached the author with the possibility of collaborating on a folk opera. The author agreed, but it was 1934 before they managed to pull it together. George wrote the music, while Ira and Heyward wrote the libretto. In the meantime, the novel was dramatized by Heyward and his wife Dorothy and performed as a play in 1927.

The opera includes some new songs, such as "Summertime," "It Ain't Necessarily So", and "I Got Plenty of Nuttin'," which we all may be humming soon.

The story follows the lives of a group of black residents in a fishing village in South Carolina in 1912. Bess is a woman with a shady past who is trying to break free from Crown, her brute of a lover who is wanted for murder. The only person

Popular composer George Gershwin, at work.

Bess can turn to who will overlook her history is Porgy, a cripple. The pair must overcome great odds, including the disapproval of the other townspeople, Bess's weakness for cocaine, and the return of Crown, if happiness is to ever be theirs.

The show has a cast of nineteen, and stars Todd Duncan as Porgy and Anne Brown as Bess. It is produced and directed by Rouben Mamoulian and is conducted by Alexander Smallens.

"In a Hole in the Ground There Lived a Hobbit…"

London, England, September 21, 1936: Fairy tales have never been stranger than the mythical tale of the Hobbit which has made its way into bookshops and libraries today. The story *The Hobbit* is written by John Ronald Reuel Tolkien, an English scholar born in 1892, and is published by George Allen and Unwin.

The book follows the adventures of a cloven-footed dwarf-like creature called a hobbit on his travels through the perils of Middle-earth. There, he encounters elves, dwarves, trolls, orcs, goblins, and other hobbits like himself while he wrestles with the forces of darkness and makes some interesting new friends.

The idea for the story came as Tolkien, Professor of Anglo-Saxon at Oxford University, was marking a student's essay and noticed an entire blank page in the boy's exercise book. For no reason he could think of he wrote, "In a hole in the ground there lived a hobbit." And from there the idea grew into a story for children that is unlike anything written to date.

Achievements in the Arts

Key Structures
Baoti Pagoda, Hangzhou, China
Brazilian Pavilion, New York World's Fair, USA
Casa del Fascio, Como, Italy
Chermayeff House, Halland, England
Chrysler Building, New York, USA
Empire State Building, New York, USA
Fiat Tagliero Building, Asmara, Eritrea
Finnish Pavilion, Paris World Fair, France
Glass Palace, Heerlen, Netherlands
Golden Gate Bridge, San Francisco, USA
Great Mosque, Asmara, Eritrea
Khuner Villa, Payerback, Austria
Maison de Verre, Paris, France
Salginatobel Bridge, Schiers, Switzerland
Stockholm Exhibition, Stockholm, Sweden
Sun Yet-Sen Memorial, Nanking, China
Sydney Harbour Bridge, Sydney, Australia
Tiger Balm Gardens, Hong Kong
Town Hall, Hilversum, Netherlands
Tugendhat House, Brno, Czechoslovakia
Viipuri Library, Vyborg, Russia
Villa Mairea, Noormaku, Finland

Nobel Prize for Literature
1930 Sinclair Lewis; 1931 Erik Axel Karlfeldt; 1932 John Galsworthy; 1933 Ivan Alekseyevich Bunin; 1934 Luigi Pirandello; 1935 no award; 1936 Eugene O'Neill; 1937 Roger Martin du Gard; 1938 Pearl S. Buck; 1939 Frans Eemil Sillanpaa.

Academy Awards
Best Film 1930 *All Quiet on the Western Front*; 1931 *Cimarron*; 1932 *Grand Hotel*; 1933 *Cavalcade*: 1934 *It Happened One Night*; 1935 *Mutiny on the Bounty*; 1936 *The Great Ziegfeld*; 1937 *The Life of Emile Zola*; 1938 *You Can't Take It With You*; 1939 *Gone With the Wind*.

Australian Robert Helpmann is the principal dancer of London's Vic-Wells ballet company.

Howard Arlen's musical score, particularly the song "Over the Rainbow," adds to the enjoyment of this wonderful film.

Pablo Picasso

Directed by Victor Fleming with a screenplay by Noel Langley, the film stars Judy Garland as Dorothy, with Frank Morgan, Ray Bolger, Bert Lahr, Jack Haley, Billie Burke, and Margaret Hamilton, plus Terry as Toto.

Scarlett's Story

Atlanta, Georgia, USA, December 15, 1939: *Gone With the Wind*, the film being billed as "the most magnificent picture ever," premiered tonight in Atlanta, Georgia.

It stars newcomer Vivien Leigh as the beautiful but treacherous Southern belle, Scarlett O'Hara, and Clark Gable as her suave admirer, Rhett Butler. The four-and-a-half-hour-long epic movie is set against the backdrop of the divisive Civil War in America's Deep South.

Based on the equally epic novel of the same name by Margaret Mitchell, *Gone with the Wind* charts the changing fortunes and romantic calamities of a plantation family and their grand mansion, Tara. The shallow and selfish manipulations of the heiress Scarlett are central to the plot, as is her ultimate realization of true love which, alas comes too late. When Scarlett begs Rhett to stay, "Rhett…if you go, where shall I go, what shall I do?" he replies, "Frankly, my dear, I don't give a damn."

Spain's Cubist Dissents

Paris, France, April, 1937: In a strong protest against Spain's ruling despot, General Francisco Franco, the Spanish cubist artist Pablo Picasso has created a series of sketches entitled *The Dream and Lie of Franco*. One sketch depicts the fascist leader as a grinning monster devouring the innards of his own horse. Several others detail the horrors of war, while two more are of Franco battling with an angry bull symbolizing the war-torn Spain. The last four images in the tableau depict the bombing of Guernica in the Basque region of the country.

Although he is now living in Paris, Picasso's artwork has become a signature for modern art in Spain, and the artist is one of the nation's most outspoken critics against the current fascist regime under which the country struggles. His painting *Guernica*, a huge mural inspired by the battle of the same name, will appear in the Spanish Pavilion at Paris's World Fair later this year.

Detail from *Guernica*, by cubist Pablo Picasso.

Off to See the Wizard!

Oconomowoc, Wisconsin, August 12, 1939: Metro-Goldwyn-Mayer's Technicolor triumph *The Wizard of Oz* promises "Gaiety! Glory! Glamor!" And an audience in this small Wisconsin town viewing the film's premiere have today had the first taste of what the studio has described as the "Greatest picture in the history of entertainment."

The film is an adaptation of L. Frank Baum's classic story of the same name and follows Dorothy Gale and her dog Toto as they are carried on a hurricane from the black-and-white world of Kansas to the technicolored magic of the Land of Oz. There she and Toto travel the yellow brick road, encountering all sorts of characters, including witches both good and bad, and befriends a scarecrow in need of a brain, a tin man who longs for a heart, and a lion who wishes for courage. Together they go on an all-singing, all-dancing adventure in search of the wizard in the hope that he can put all things right.

David O. Selznick auditioned more than 1,000 actresses for the lead role.

357

Adolphe Menjou

Frozen Foods...What Next?

Massachusetts, USA, June 6, 1930: Mass-produced frozen foods are now available for the first time, thanks to businessman Clarence Birdseye whose research into the science of food freezing has been an obsession for many years.

In 1924, he established the General Seafoods Company and set up a shop in Gloucester, Massachusetts, where he developed a number of quick-freezing devices and ultimately the first commercially practical freezer.

What began with a 20-ton (20.3 tonne) "double belt, quick freeze machine" soon developed into the more practical multiplate freezer, which has enabled his vision to have broader applications.

Test marketing began today in 18 stores in Springfield, Massachusetts. Items on sale include fruits, vegetables, fish, and meats. While the depression has rendered many businesses unable to afford freezers, Birdseye has created a range of economical models that can be leased by stores wishing to stock his frozen foods.

> *"They can't collect legal taxes from illegal money."*
>
> AL CAPONE (1899–1947), ITALIAN-BORN AMERICAN GANGSTER, ON BEING REQUIRED TO PAY BACK TAXES, 1930

> *"Civilization is a method of living, an attitude of equal respect for all men."*
>
> JANE ADDAMS (1860–1935), AMERICAN SOCIAL WORKER AND NOBEL PRIZE WINNER, 1933

Goodbye Glue...

St Paul, USA, September 8, 1930: ...and hello transparent Scotch Tape! Richard Drew, a banjo-playing engineer at the 3M Company in Minnesota, who changed the way we think of adhesive in 1925 with his development of a new 2-in (5 cm) wide adhesive paper has developed a transparent version of the tape.

Originally inspired by a colleague's work in a car body-shop, Drew developed a tape to mask of sections of bodywork they didn't want to get paint on. The adhesives used previously had been too strong and would take the paint off when removed.

The name "Scotch Tape" came when the worker tested the tape for the first time and found there wasn't enough adhesive to hold it to the surface. "Take this back to your stingy Scotch bosses and tell them to put more adhesive on it," the worker grumbled, invoking the old ethnic slur that Scottish folk are stingy.

The 1938 Empire Exhibition, held at Bellahouston Park in Glasgow, Scotland, attracted 12.5-13 million visitors.

The new transparent tape will be a hugely valuable advance in these times of unemployment and enforced frugality. Originally designed for industrial use, this new waterproof tape can be used to unobtrusively mend all kinds of materials.

time out

In a discussion entitled "The Home vs. Work for Women" Mrs Franklin D. Roosevelt said that housewives deserved a salary. She also said that women who went out to work to help support their families must have their working day limited to eight hours.

Drivers Get the Big Picture

New Jersey, USA, June 7, 1933: The town of Pennsauken last night played host to the nation's most intriguing new entertainment medium, the cinema that you can drive into! The concept is the inspiration of Richard Hollingshead, Jr., heir to a successful chemical products plant in neighboring Camden. The automobile movie theater is located on 250,000 sq ft (23,225 sq m) of land located opposite the airport and utilizes an outdoor movie-delivery system developed after much trial and error by Hollingshead in his own driveway.

Outdoor cinemas have taken many forms in the past, but Hollingshead's idea is the first to allow people to view movies from their cars. "Inveterate smokers rarely enjoy a movie because of the smoking prohibition," he claimed in an interview. "In drive-in theaters one may smoke without offending others…People may chat or even partake of refreshments brought to their cars without disturbing those who prefer silence. The drive-in virtually transforms an ordinary motor car into a private box."

The first movie to be shown was an edited version of an offbeat Adolphe Menjou comedy, *Wives Beware.* Admission is 25 cents for patrons on foot, 75 cents for two people in a car, or $1 for the entire family in a carload. At least 600 patrons filled the drive-in on a summer night that promises to be just the beginning of a grand new entertainment.

Detail from *Descent from the Cross* by della Rovere in the early seventeenth century shows Christ wrapped in the Holy Shroud.

George Eastman

at making (play) money by real-estate wheeling and dealing.

The game has been around for a while in various makeshift formats, but Charles Darrow, an enterprising but unemployed salesman living in Germantown, Pennsylvania, developed the game while drawing local maps on his kitchen table. With the help of his son, he created early models of the game himself and tried to sell it to Parker Brothers, who rejected it citing "fifty-two fundamental errors" as to why the game would not work, including the fact that the game took too long to play, had too many rules, and had no clear objectives for the winner.

Undeterred, Darrow went on to print 5,000 copies of the game to fill department store orders. One customer went on to sing her praises of the game to Sally Barton, the daughter of Parker Brothers founding director, George Parker. On closer inspection, and with an already growing demand for the game, Parker Brothers bought the game and produced a simplified version of it.

Interestingly, a similar game called "The Landlord's Game" was patented in 1904 by Lizzie Magie, a Quaker woman from Virginia, who created the game to illustrate the injustices of rental properties and the cruelty of capitalism. Unlike Darrow's, her game has never become popular.

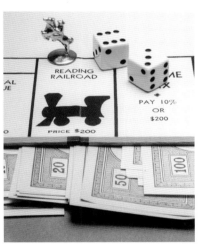

English version of Monopoly, released in 1936.

Holiest Relic or Medieval Fraud?

Turin, Italy, September 24, 1933: A shroud widely believed to be that in which Jesus Christ's body was wrapped after his crucifixion has attracted more than 250,000 viewers to its first public exhibition in years. The Turin Shroud, made from linen, is about 14 ft 4 in (4.4 m) long and 3 ft 8 in (1.1 m) wide, and bears a faded image rather like a photographic negative of a bearded man covered with bloodstains. The stains from the wounds correspond closely to those of Christ, as narrated in the New Testament.

The shroud has been housed in the Cathedral of Turin for four centuries, although its history can be traced back to the sixth century and legends go even further back to the first century. Since 1355, millions of devout Catholics have believed the shroud to be the authentic burial cloth of Christ.

The image on the shroud has no sharp outline and is described as "melting away" the closer the viewer moves to the cloth. While there has always been skepticism and controversy surrounding the relic, experts remain baffled as to how it could have been counterfeited.

Millionaires by the Millions

USA, November 5, 1935: What could prove a better escape during these times of economic hardship than the fantasy of becoming a millionaire?

Monopoly, a new game from Parker Brothers, allows anyone to try their luck

Aussie Cricketer's 1,000 Runs

Joe Louis

Southampton, England, May 27, 1938: The Australian cricketer who simply can't be ignored has made a spectacular comeback, being the first batsman this season to score his thousandth run.

Donald Bradman, who is considered without peer as a batsman, scored 974 runs over the course of the five Ashes Tests in the English summer of 1930, giving him the highest individual score in any Test series. His 254 in the Second Test at Lord's was his personal best, and in the Third Test at Headingley, he achieved 309 runs on one day (only matched by British cricketer Walter Hammond in 1933).

Donald Bradman (right), after scoring his thousandth run in 1938.

Bradman who missed the 1935–1936 season due to an infected appendix, kept himself in shape playing squash and was reluctantly made captain of the team.

Write Away

Paris, France, June 10, 1938: A Hungarian journalist living in Argentina has submitted a patent application for a ballpoint pen that could change forever the way we write. Biro Laszlo Jozsef (Laszlo Biro) had noticed how quick ink was to dry on news-papers, but found the same ink too viscous to use in fountain pens.

With the help of his brother George, he decided to create a new type of pen that would be smudge free, with quick-drying ink, but he needed to develop some sort of point to evenly dispense the ink. He did this by fitting a small tungsten ball bearing at its tip so that the ball rotated and measured out the correct amount of ink from a storage cartridge as the pen moved across the paper.

The idea is not entirely original, and in fact an early patent existed from 1888 when a John Loud created something similar, to mark leather. However, Loud's patent had remained commercially unexploited, and even the patent Biro lodged fails to secure him the North American rights to the invention.

Brown Bomber Wins More Than a Fight

New York, USA, June 22, 1938: Joe Louis has today broken all boxing records, while retaining the heavyweight crown for the third time this year. He also dealt Hitler's Germany a hefty blow with his defeat of German champion Max Schmeling.

Joe Louis Barrow, the son of an Alabama sharecropper, was born in 1914 and raised in poverty with little education. Nevertheless, he has ascended to the top of the boxing world with astounding speed. Known to many as the "Brown Bomber," he had won the National Light Heavyweight Amateur Crown of the Golden Gloves by the time he was 19, and under the guidance of his manager John Roxborough dropped the Barrow from his name.

By 1935, Louis had become a pro, winning his first eight fights but losing to the German Max Schmeling, a key sporting figure in Hitler's plan to assert Aryan superiority. Louis was knocked out by the German in the twelfth round.

In 1937, Louis took the Heavyweight Championship of the World when he beat James Braddock, but was quoted as saying, "I don't want nobody to call me champ until I beat Schmeling."

Sporting Achievements

Baseball *World Series* 1930 Philadelphia (American League); 1931 St Louis (National League); 1932 New York (AL); 1933 New York (NL); 1934 St Louis (NL); 1935 Detroit (AL); 1936 New York (AL); 1937 New York (AL); 1938 New York (AL); 1939 New York (AL).

Cycling *Tour de France* 1930 A. Leducq; 1931 A. Magne; 1932 A. Leducq; 1933 G. Speicher; 1934 A. Magne; 1935 R. Maes; 1936 S. Maes; 1937 R. Lapebie; 1938 G. Bartali; 1939 S. Maes.

Football *World Cup Soccer* 1930 Uruguay; 1934 Italy; 1938 Italy.

Golf *US Masters* 1934 H. Smith; 1935 G. Sarazen; 1936 H. Smith; 1937 B. Nelson; 1938 H. Picard; 1939 R. Guldahl.

Horse racing *Epsom Derby* 1930 Blenheim; 1931 Cameronian; 1932 April the Fifth; 1933 Hyperion; 1934 Windsor Lad; 1935 Bahram; 1936 Mahmoud; 1937 Midday Sun; 1938 Bois Roussel; 1939 Blue Peter. *Kentucky Derby* 1930 Gallant Fox; 1931 Twenty Grand; 1932 Burgoo King; 1933 Brokers Tip; 1934 Cavalcade; 1935 Omaha; 1936 Bold Venture; 1937 War Admiral; 1938 Lawrin; 1939 Johnstown. *Melbourne Cup* 1930 Phar Lap; 1931 White Nose; 1932 Peter Pan; 1933 Hall Mark; 1934 Peter Pan; 1935 Marabou; 1936 Wotan; 1937 The Trump; 1938 Catalogue; 1939 Rivette.

Ice Hockey *Stanley Cup* 1930 Montreal; 1931 Montreal; 1932 Toronto; 1933 New York; 1934 Chicago 1935 Montreal; 1936 Detroit; 1937 Detroit; 1938 Chicago; 1939 Boston.

Marathon *Boston, Men's* 1930 C. DeMar; 1931 J. Henigan; 1932 P. DeBruyn; 1933 L. Pawson; 1934 D. Komonen; 1935 J. Kelley; 1936 E. Brown; 1937 W. Young; 1938 L. Pawson; 1939 E. Brown.

Sailing *America's Cup* 1930 *Enterprise*; 1934 *Rainbow*; 1937 *Ranger*.

Tennis *Australian Championships, Men's Singles* 1930 G. Moon; 1931-1933 J. Crawford; 1934 F. Perry; 1935 J. Crawford; 1936 A. Quist; 1937 V. B. McGrath; 1938 D. Budge; 1939 J. Bromwich; *Women's Singles* 1930 D. Akhurst; 1931-1932 C. Buttsworth; 1933-1934 J. Hartigan; 1935 D. Round; 1936 J. Hartigan; 1937 N. Wynne; 1938 D. Bundy; 1939 E. Westacott. *French Championships, Men's Singles* 1930 H. Cochet; 1931 J. Borotra; 1932 H. Cochet; 1933 J. Crawford; 1934 G. von Cramm; 1935 F. Perry; 1936 G. von Cramm; 1937 H. Henkel; 1938 D. Budge; 1939 D. McNeill; *Women's Singles* 1930 H. Wills Moody; 1931 C. Aussem; 1932 H. Wills Moody; 1933-1934 M. Scriven; 1935-1937 H. Sperling; 1938-1939 S. Mathieu. *US National Championship, Men's Singles* 1930 J. Doeg; 1931-1932 E. Vines; 1933-1934 F. Perry; 1935 W. Allison; 1936 F. Perry; 1937-1938 D. Budge; 1939 B. Riggs; *Women's Singles* 1930 B. Nuhall; 1931 H. Wills Moody; 1932-1935 H. Jacobs; 1936 A. Marble; 1937 A. Lizana; 1938-1939 A. Marble. *Wimbledon, Gentlemen's Singles* 1930 B. Tilden; 1931 S. Wood; 1932 E. Vines; 1933 J. Crawford; 1934-1936 F. Perry; 1937-1938 D. Budge; 1939 B. Riggs; *Ladies' Singles* 1930 H. Wills Moody; 1931 C. Aussem; 1932-1933 H. Wills Moody; 1934 D. Round; 1935 H. Wills Moody; 1936 H. Jacobs; 1937 D. Round; 1938 H. Wills Moody; 1939 A. Marble.

The Graham Supercharger is manufactured by the Graham-Paige automobile company in Detroit, USA.

American boxer James Braddock and his wife, Mae.

Max Schmeling

Louis continued to successfully take on all manner of contenders with his "Bum of the Month" campaign, but could not get over the indignation of his defeat to Max Schmeling—the only opponent ever to defeat him.

The chance for revenge finally arrived today when Louis took on the German again. This time he has been victorious, with Schmeling lasting only two minutes and four seconds. Louis has not just taken the world title; he's thrown down the gauntlet for Hitler's entire regime and its notions of racial supremacy.

Television Becomes a Reality

New York, USA, April 30, 1939: President Franklin D. Roosevelt opened the New York World's Fair today with a television broadcast relayed from the transmitter atop the Empire State Building. The event heralds the beginning of regular broadcasting in the United States via the NBC (National Broadcasting Corporation), which is the broadcasting wing of RCA (Radio Corporation of America).

The ceremony was viewed by several hundred spectators on television receivers in the RCA pavilion at the fairgrounds as well as on several others operating inside Radio City. Viewers' appetites were whetted with the taste of entertainment to come with shows on cooking, travel, fashion, opera, ice skating, and cartoons.

Regular television broadcasts have been under way for 10 years already in the United Kingdom, with BBC transmitters initially using the Baird 30-line mechanical system. While those images were of low resolution, thousands of enthusiastic viewers had tuned in. Those broadcasts were shut down in 1935 when the "405-line EMI-Marconi all-electronic system" was chosen to succeed the 30-line system. By 1936, the BBC was broadcasting high-resolution television programming.

The United States has been slow to fulfill the promise of television, due mainly to a long-winded legal battle between RCA and independent inventor Philo T. Farnsworth, whose camera patents became an issue of contention when RCA wanted to buy them and Farnsworth wanted to license them.

The RCA Pavilion at the World's Fair was designed by modernist architectural firm Skidmore & Owings, and from the air it appears to be just like a radio tube. Inside, the television set is showcased in "the radio living room of tomorrow" with the centerpiece of future home entertainment units also housing radiograms and record players.

Visitors were also invited into the Hall of Television, which contains 13 of RCA's latest TRK-12 receivers, all operating, as well as a large projector screen television. While only the very rich can afford them today, RCA strongly believes we'll all own television sets in the future.

Pan Am Flies New York to London

USA, July 8, 1939: Today marks the first of what Pan American Airways hopes will be many transatlantic passenger flights. One of the company's new Boeing 314 flying boats has successfully made the trip from New York to London, giving hope of dramatically reduced future travel times

Originally a seaplane service out of Key West, Florida, Pan Am—and aircraft technology—has evolved over the past decade to make safe world-wide air travel possible. Pan Am's China Clipper, a Martin M-130 flying boat, made its first transpacific passenger flight last year, but it was the Boeing 314 Clipper in 1938 that was chosen as the long-distance flying boat that could make the long transatlantic passenger flights.

The theme of the 1939 New York World's Fair is "the world of tomorrow"—the fair attracted 25 million visitors.

Winston Churchill

*"NEVER GIVE
IN, NEVER
GIVE IN,
NEVER, NEVER,
NEVER,
NEVER—IN
NOTHING,
GREAT OR
SMALL, LARGE
OR PETTY—
NEVER GIVE IN
EXCEPT TO
CONVICTIONS
OF HONOR
AND GOOD
SENSE."*

SIR WINSTON
SPENCER CHURCHILL
(1874–1965), ENGLISH
STATESMAN AND
PRIME MINISTER, TO
SCHOOLBOYS AT
HARROW, 1940

Germany Overruns Belgium

Belgium, May 28: Just two weeks after Germany's invasion of France and the surrender of the Netherlands, King Leopold III today ordered Belgian troops to cease hostilities. German troops entered Belgium on May 10 and rolled westward, with the Belgians retreating to the Dyle Line. Despite reinforcements from France and Britain, this defensive line was abandoned on May 15. On May 26 Boulogne fell, and the Belgian army was isolated and exhausted. This is the latest in a series of setbacks for the Allies, which began with the occupation of Denmark and the offensive against Norway on April 9. Members of the Belgian government in exile in France have declared Leopold deposed. The Belgian surrender has also exposed the British Expeditionary Forces now on the beaches at Dunkirk to greater risk of attack. As many troops as possible will be evacuated.

Three-Power Pact Signed

Berlin, Germany, September 27: Representatives of Germany, Italy, and the Empire of Japan met in Berlin today to sign an agreement recognizing each other's spheres of interests, as well as promising to come to one another's aid should one of them be attacked by any state "not now a belligerent." This is being seen as a warning to both the United States and the USSR to remain neutral in the current conflict. Article 6 of what is now being referred to as the Three-

time out

An officer on the staff of Commander in Chief Douglas MacArthur suggested that the flag at the US Army's headquarters at Manila might be used as a target by Japanese pilots. The General laughed and ordered that the flag be kept flying.

Power Pact states it will come into effect "immediately upon signature and shall remain in force 10 years" from that day.

London Battered by German Bombers

London, England, December 30: Last night London suffered one of the most devastating bombing raids of the Blitz when thousands of incendiary bombs rained down between St Paul's Cathedral and the Guildhall. The very center of London was targeted, where many of the buildings dating from medieval times huddle close together around narrow alleyways. The area is also home to the press, clothing, and publishing industries. Hundreds of fires were burning along the Thames; thousands of Londoners fled to shelters and underground tube stations, for many their last place of refuge.

Under fire from the Germans, Allied troops withdraw from Dunkirk.

A London street devastated by German bombs.

One hospital was so close to the inferno that when the power failed they took down their blackout curtains and worked by the glow of the fire. Buildings have collapsed all along Shoe Lane, a few paces from St Paul's Cathedral, which was ringed by fire. Prime Minister Winston Churchill ordered that the cathedral be saved at all costs.

Wave upon wave of German aircraft pounded the city for hours. The heat was so intense that timber buildings not on fire were suddenly bursting into flames. A low tide in the Thames reportedly made it difficult to draw water to fight the flames as the pumps clogged with mud.

Many buildings built to replace those lost after the Great Fire of 1666 have now been lost. London was battered for nearly five hours, the first bombers appearing in the skies just after 6 p.m. Between 150 and 200 people have perished, and an entire square mile (2.6 sq km) of central London has been laid waste. Not since concentrated bombing of London's industrial targets and civilian centers began on September 7 has the city witnessed such a sustained onslaught, which is an obvious attempt by Hitler to destroy the morale of the British people before invasion.

By the early hours of this morning, everyone was expecting a follow-up raid designed to hinder the effectiveness of firefighters in fighting the massive blaze. Mercifully, that raid has not come.

Nazi Lands in Scotland

Scotland, May 10: Rudolph Hess has been detained after parachuting out of his Messerschmitt ME-110 over Scotland. Hitler's deputy, Hess is considered to be the third highest-ranking Nazi after Goering. In an encounter with a Scottish farmer, he insisted on seeing the Duke of Hamilton to discuss terms for an end to hostilities.

During interrogation he apparently said that if Britain would allow the Nazis to dominate Europe, Hitler would cease to threaten the British Empire. However, reports also suggest that Hess displayed symptoms of mental instability. Rather than being an official envoy, he has more than likely acted alone, and Prime Minister Churchill has ordered him to be imprisoned for the duration of the war.

US Losses at Pearl Harbor

Honolulu, Hawaii, December 8: Yesterday morning at 7.55 a.m. air and sea forces

from the Japanese Pacific Fleet launched a surprise attack on US military and naval facilities at Pearl Harbor on the Hawaiian island of Oahu. Virtually all the US planes, which were parked wingtip to wingtip at Wheeler Field, were destroyed on the ground. Also hit was the Marine airfield at Ewa and the Army Air Corps fields at Bellows and Hickam. At Ewa the complement of mainly carrier-based bombers and fighters was reduced from more than 50 to less than 20 planes.

The primary targets, however, were the battleships moored along the southeast side of Ford Island. Bombed and torpedoed, they never had a chance. Only the USS *Nevada* managed to get under way, although a second wave of enemy planes appeared as she edged toward the open sea. She was ordered to beach herself at Hospital Point to avoid being sunk and thus block the harbor entrance.

The USS *Oklahoma* and USS *West Virginia* sank quickly, but it was the USS *Arizona* that suffered the greatest loss of

life. Over a thousand men died when an armor-piercing bomb smashed through the forward deck, igniting the magazines and causing a massive explosion. Of the seven battleships moored in "battleship row," all have been put out of action and three have been sunk.

In the two-hour attack, 21 ships in all were either sunk or damaged and 188 aircraft destroyed. Over 2,000 American servicemen were killed. Sixty-eight civilians were also killed, some of them struck by American anti-aircraft shells falling back onto Honolulu.

Amy Johnson

US Declares War on Japan

Washington DC, USA, December 8: President Roosevelt has today signed a declaration of war against Japan, calling December 7 a day that "will live in infamy." The long debate over US neutrality in this conflict that has divided the nation ever since the Nazis marched into Poland has been silenced. Britain, Australia, and New Zealand have also declared war on Japan.

Japanese in Hong Kong

Hong Kong, December 25: Today, units of the Japanese 228th Regiment entered Hong Kong despite all road bridges being destroyed by British troops. Using traditional village trails, the Japanese crossed into Hong Kong from China and have reached the "Gin Drinkers' Line," surprising the island's defenders. Tonight they are pushing toward Needle Hill, from where they will be able to conduct detailed surveillance of the British citadel.

The citadel is vulnerable. Begun in the 1930s, it was never completed and needs the equivalent of six battalions to defend it properly. Only 50 men from the Royal Scots currently occupy it, and with an overall force of some 6,000 Allied soldiers occupying the island it is feared this will prove insufficient against the far more numerous forces of the Japanese Empire.

The US battle fleet suffered terrible losses of life and ships when the Japanese attacked Pearl Harbor.

General Dwight
D. Eisenhower

*"France has
lost a
battle. But
France has
not lost
the war."*

CHARLES DE GAULLE
(1890–1970), FRENCH
MILITARY LEADER
AND PRESIDENT,
DURING WORLD
WAR II

*"I fear we
have only
awakened a
sleeping
giant, and
his reaction
will be
terrible."*

ISOROKU YAMAMOTO
(1884–1943), JAPANESE
ADMIRAL, ON THE
DECEMBER 1941
ATTACK ON PEARL
HARBOR

US Gains Upper Hand in the Pacific

Midway Atoll, USA, June 7: Today one of the most significant engagements in US naval history has been fought off Midway Atoll. US forces surprised a Japanese aircraft-carrier strike force sent to capture the island's airstrip; air attacks against the Japanese carriers were launched by the US aircraft-carriers *Enterprise, Hornet,* and *Yorktown.* The *Yorktown* was hit several times by Japanese dive bombers and was last reported to be listing badly, hit by several torpedoes, one of which opened a huge hole midships in her port side.

According to reports, three squadrons of SBD Dauntless dive bombers, two from *Enterprise* and one from *Hornet,* attacked the carriers *Kaga* and *Akagi,* whose flight decks were laden with fully armed and fueled aircraft. *Yorktown's* aircraft attacked *Soryu.* All three aircraft carriers were reportedly left ablaze and it appears certain they will either be sunk or scuttled. Only the carrier *Hiryu* remained operational, and late in the afternoon air-

SBD Dauntless dive bombers over Midway Atoll.

craft from *Enterprise* and *Hornet* located it and also attacked it, leaving it ablaze.

By nightfall it appeared that US forces had won an overwhelming victory. Japan now has only two remaining operational aircraft carriers—the *Zuikaku* and the *Shokaku.* It would seem the destruction of four of Japan's fleet carriers is an irredeemable loss, giving US forces the advantage at last in the Pacific theater.

Japan to Use POWs to Build Railway

Siam, June: The Japanese are about to begin construction on a single-line meter-gauge railway from Ban Pong in Siam, via the Three Pagoda's Pass on the Siamese–Burmese border, to Thanbyuzayat in Burma. Prisoners of war from Australia, Denmark, Britain, and the United States will be used to build the railway, as well as captured Tamils, Malays, and Burmese. August 1943 is the projected completion date. It is expected that the mortality rate will be high as lengthy sections of the proposed route pass through impenetrable jungle and traverse hazardous mountainous terrain.

The railway is an obvious alternative to the long and exposed sea route to Rangoon via Singapore and the Straits of Malacca amid the constant threat from Allied submarines and aircraft. It will enable further Japanese expansion westward into India, thus solving Japan's supply problems to its forces in the Far East. There is only one road from Siam into southern Burma which runs through Kowkareik to Moulmein, but this has been rejected by the Japanese as being unfit for prolonged heavy traffic.

A rail project was under consideration before the war but abandoned due to the sheer cost of such a massive undertaking. Now, with an estimated 100,000 prisoners

Japanese-Americans before being sent to an internme

of war at its disposal, Japan finally has the manpower to make the project happen.

Representatives of the Japanese government and the prime minister of Siam are expected to sign an official agreement within days to build this railway. It is estimated it will be capable of transporting some 3,000 tons (3,060 tonnes) of supplies each day. Two workforces, one based in Siam and the other in Burma, will work from opposite ends and meet at Nieke, just south of Three Pagoda's Pass.

time out

The head of Japan's board of information, Eiji Amau, told the Japanese that they must win the war this year or they would be fighting it for 100 years. The address was broadcast on Tokyo radio and reported by Federal Communications Commission monitors.

Offensive Against Germany in Africa

Morocco and Algeria, North Africa, November 8: Following the Battle of El Alamein in October, a major Allied invasion of French North Africa that has been codenamed Operation Torch has begun. Three Allied task forces under the command of US General Dwight D. Eisenhower have landed in Morocco and Algeria. They will attempt to open a second front to help reverse the German assaults in the east, and to trap Rommel's Afrika Corps between Operation Torch and the British Eighth Army to the east. This is the first offensive operation the United States has undertaken against Germany in this war.

Decisive Allied Victory in the Pacific

Bismarck Sea (north of New Guinea), March 4: Three Japanese merchant ships were sunk when B-17 "Flying Fortresses" attacked a Japanese convoy comprising eight destroyers, eight troop transports, and associated escort vessels today. At the time of the assault, the convoy was en route to Lae in New Guinea to reinforce troops. Later the same day, attacks by Beaufighters of RAAF Squadron No. 30 and USAAF Mitchells claimed many hits, leaving up to half the transport ships either sunk or sinking.

At day's end all Japanese transport ships in the convoy were reported lost, as well as three of their destroyers—the *Shirayuki*, the *Arashio*, and the *Toki-tsukaze*. A fourth destroyer was sunk later while it was picking up survivors.

The battle was a total disaster for the Japanese, who were able to get only 800 of the almost 7,000 troops through to Lae. The remaining four destroyers rescued what survivors they could, and fled to Rabaul on New Britain Island.

The battle of the Bismarck Sea was the first time the Americans used a new aerial tactic called skip-bombing, where the attacking aircraft drops a bomb close to the surface with a delayed fuse, letting it skip into the side of the target ship.

Italy Signs Armistice with Allies

Cassibile, Sicily, September 8: General Dwight D. Eisenhower today announced that Italy has signed an unconditional armistice with the Allies. It was signed in secret in the town of Cassibile, Sicily, on

Benito Mussolini and Pietro Badoglio.

September 3 by a representative of Italy's prime minister since the fall of Mussolini on July 25, Marshal Pietro Badoglio. He immediately engaged in secret negotiations with the Allies with the aim of ending of hostilities.

Rome has now been occupied by German troops. Marshal Badoglio and other government officials have established a government in exile in the southern city of Brindisi. The Axis and the Tripartite Pact between Germany, Italy, and Japan is now in tatters.

Lieutenant General Maxwell Taylor of the 82nd US Airborne parachuted into Rome in order to begin negotiations with the Italian government in the first few days of September.

In a broadcast on Algiers radio today, General Eisenhower said, "All Italians who now act to help eject the German aggressor from Italian soil will have the assistance and support of the United Nations."

In a simultaneous radio broadcast, Marshal Badoglio was quoted as saying, "The Italian forces will cease all acts of hostilities against the Anglo-American forces wherever they may be. They will, however, oppose attacks from any other forces."

Pietro Badoglio was born in 1871 in Monferrato, Italy. Distinguishing himself in World War I, he emerged from that terrible war with his career intact and then participated in the armistice talks. He was Chief of Staff from 1919 to 1921.

Promoted to Field Marshal in 1926, Badoglio governed Libya for six years and has been Viceroy of Ethiopia.

After becoming Supreme Chief of the General Staff, Badoglio resigned that commission following his opposition to the disastrous campaign in Greece back in October 1940.

Chiang Kai-shek Elected President of China

China, September 13: Chiang Kai-shek was today elected president of the Republic of China. Chiang and his nationals have been fighting a long and bitter war with the Chinese communists, led by arch rival Mao Tse-tung. Chiang's contribution to the war against Japan, however, has been significant. He has forced Japan to commit a large number of troops to China rather than making them available for the Pacific War. This has had the result of elevating Chiang Kai-shek to almost equal status with Roosevelt, Churchill, and Stalin in the war against the Axis.

Marshal Pietro Badoglio

A Japanaese kamikaze pilot dives into a US battleship, October 1943.

Tripoli, Libya, January 23: British forces capture Tripoli.

North Africa, January 24: Churchill and Roosevelt hold a conference in Casablanca to plan an offensive aimed at achieving the "unconditional surrender" of the Axis powers.

Volgograd (Stalingrad), USSR, February 2: Axis troops surrender to the Red Army.

Featherston, New Zealand, February 25: Japanese POWs in Featherston camp riot; 48 POWs and one New Zealand guard are killed.

Bismark Sea, March 4: Allied forces sink 22 Japanese ships.

Moscow, USSR, May 23: The Third International has been dissolved, allowing communist powers in other countries to be autonomous of Soviet rule.

France, July 8: French Resistance leader Jean Moulin is killed while being tortured by the Gestapo.

Italy, July 10: Allied forces enter Sicily.

Italy, July 25: Premier Benito Mussolini is ousted. A new government under Marshal Pietro Badoglio places him under arrest.

Italy, July 28: Badoglio declares Italy is no longer a fascist state. He may have started secretly negotiating with Allied forces.

Italy, August 17: Allies occupy Sicily. With North Africa, this gives them control of the Mediterranean Sea.

Italy, September 11: Germany occupies northern Italy.

Corsica, September 11: Free French troops occupy the island of Corsica.

Italy, September 12: Italy surrenders unconditionally to the Allied forces.

China, September 13: General Chiang Kai-shek is elected President of the Republic of China.

Siam, October: The rail link between Burma and Siam is completed.

Italy, October 13: Badoglio declares war on Germany.

Italy, October 14: Allied forces take control of southern Italy.

Lebanon, November 22: France grants Lebanon independence.

Cairo, Egypt, December 1–4: The USA, Britain, and China sign the Cairo Declaration, a joint plan to force Japan to surrender.

USSR, December 31: Soviet troops force the Axis powers to retreat from the central area of the Eastern Front in Belarus (White Russia).

Bombing Raid Destroys Berlin

General Charles de Gaulle

Berlin, Germany, January 21: Berlin is in ruins today after a massive raid by Britain's Bomber Command that involved 495 Lancasters, 264 Halifaxes, and 10 Mosquitoes. This is the latest in a series of raids on Berlin and other German cities where broad "area bombing" has been preferred to more localized "strategic bombing." This approach has long been advocated by the controversial commander of Bomber Command, Arthur Harris, who believes that an enemy can literally be "bombed into submission" and that the war can be shortened by destroying the will of the civilian population, just as Germany's Hitler tried to do with the London Blitz four years ago.

Berlin Cathedral ablaze after the January 21 air raid by the Allies.

Allied Forces Move into Europe

Normandy, France, June 6: Operation Overlord began today under the command of US General Dwight D. Eisenhower. In the greatest amphibious assault in military history, the Allied forces stormed ashore on the beaches of Normandy in northern France, utilizing nearly 5,000 vessels and over 10,000 aircraft. This is part of the Allies' ambitious attempt to breach Hitler's "Atlantic Wall" and create a second front in Europe.

According to the official sources, more than 7,000 Allied aircraft took to the skies to keep the Luftwaffe at bay.

Before the landings, paratroopers from the 6th, 82nd, and 101st US Airborne Divisions were dropped behind enemy lines to secure bridges and other strategic sites, including the causeways behind the landing beaches, a step that was vital for moving inland from the beach heads. At 5.30 a.m. some 200 ships began a bombardment of the enemy positions along the 50 miles (80 km) of coastline selected for the assault, which ran from Carentan in the west to Caen in the east.

Groups from the French Resistance started by sabotaging rail and communication links. The first assault wave, comprising more than 175,000 men, landed at five designated beaches that had been code-named Sword, Juno, Gold, Omaha, and Utah. The British and Canadian forces met only modest resistance at Gold and Juno beaches, and units of the US VII Corps quickly smashed the defenses at Utah beach and began moving inland.

However, at Omaha beach, where most of the German coastal artillery had not been destroyed by the Allies' high-altitude bombing campaign, a heavy onslaught from the defenders saw an enormous number of casualties among the troops of the US 1st and 29th Infantry Divisions, as well as among the 2nd and 5th Ranger Battalions. The deep beaches backed by very steep hills meant that the US troops were dangerously exposed to the enemy's attack. Warships were even called in to provide direct gunfire support.

time out

Following Japan's surrender to the Allies, Japanese aircraft continued to approach the Pacific Fleet off Tokyo and were shot down by the 3rd Fleet. Admiral Halsey told his fliers to shoot down any enemy planes "in friendly fashion."

By the afternoon of June 6, US troops at Omaha beach had begun moving inland after liberating the town of St Laurent, and troops from Utah beach had cleared the area of enemy forces and linked up with the 101st Airborne. Hermanville, behind Sword beach, has been liberated, and after four years of German occupation "Fortress Europe" has finally been breached.

Japanese Navy Virtually Destroyed

Leyte Gulf, Philippines, October 20–25: What many commentators have been calling the greatest battle in naval history has just been fought. In the course of five days 244 ships were involved in four separate engagements in the waters surrounding the Philippine island of Leyte, with Japan desperate to thwart a planned US 7th Fleet landing in the Philippines. In an attempt to reduce the growing threat to the Japanese home islands, Japan's Imperial Navy decided to commit its remaining surface fleet to a campaign in Leyte Gulf.

The battle eventually cost the Japanese 26 vessels—most of its remaining warships including four aircraft carriers, and three battleships including the giant ship *Musashi*. United States losses amounted to six vessels. The Japanese navy is now finished as an effective fighting force.

Allied troops land on the beaches of Normandy.

Key Events

Berlin, Germany, January 21: Allied bombing leaves the city in ruins.
Italy, January 22: Allied troops make a surprise invasion south of Rome.
St Petersburg (Leningrad), USSR, January 27: The Siege of Leningrad is fully lifted; over 640,000 people died during the 900 days of the siege.
USSR, February 1: A new USSR constitution allows Soviet republics to conduct their own armies and negotiations.

Hungary, March 23: A German puppet government is created in Hungary after German occupation on March 22.
Rome, June 4: Rome is freed by Allied forces.
France, June 6: Allied forces storm Normandy on the French coast.
Japan, June 15: The USA begins heavily bombing Kyushu.
Iceland, June 17: Iceland breaks free of Danish rule, becoming a republic.

France, June 27: Allied forces capture the port of Cherbourg.
East Prussia, July 20: An attempt by a number of German military officers to assassinate Hitler fails.
USSR, July 24: Soviet forces capture the strategic city of Pskov, almost entirely destroying it.
India, August 11: An advance by Allied troops forces the Japanese to retreat to Burma.

Paris, France, August 23: Citizens and underground resistance assist Allied forces in taking Paris.
Bucharest, Romania, August 31: Soviet forces occupy Bucharest, six days after Romania declared war against Germany, taking control of German oil supplies.
France, September: Charles de Gaulle becomes president of the provisional government.
Belgium, September 4: British forces take Brussels.

London, England, September 9: The city is again under German attack, this time from the new silent V-2 bombs.
Greece, October 14: British forces retake Athens, freeing it after four years of German occupation.
Leyte Gulf, Philippines, October 20: Allied forces tackle Japanese forces occupying the Philippines, in what is known as the Battle of Leyte Gulf.
Belgium, December 16: German forces make a surprise attack, known as the Ardennes Offensive, to penetrate the Allied front in Belgium.

Hitler Suicides

Berlin, Germany, April 30: Adolf Hitler today committed suicide inside the Führerbunker as Russian troops engaged in bitter fighting in the streets above. Eva Braun, whom he had married only the day before, reportedly killed herself by ingesting poison. Both bodies were hastily placed inside a crater in the Reich Chancellory garden and burned, with Russian troops as close as two city blocks away.

The prevous night, Hitler had been advised by Field Marshal Keitel that Russian troops were fighting their way into Berlin and that the city would soon be lost. Such news may have convinced Hitler that the end was near.

Jubilation at End of War in Europe

London, England, May 8: Crowds of spectators have jammed London's streets to hear Prime Minister Churchill's broadcast announcing that the war in Europe will end at midnight. Around 50,000 revelers took to the streets singing, dancing, and hugging one another in a spontaneous outpouring of joy and relief that six years of war is at last an end. Huge crowds were outside Buckingham Palace as the king and queen emerged on the balcony. In the broadcast from the Cabinet Room at No. 10, Churchill announced that the cease-fire was signed at 2.41 a.m. yesterday at the American advance headquarters in Reims.

Japan Surrenders

Tokyo, Japan, August 15: Japan has surrendered to the allies today after nearly six years of war. Emperor Hirohito ordered a surrender document be sent through Swiss channels to the United States, accepting the

Japan formally surrenders on September 2, on board USS *Missouri*.

terms of the recent Potsdam Declaration demanding unconditional surrender.

It is understood that since June the Emperor has been urging the government to seek a way out of the conflict. On August 9–10 the Imperial Council was tied 3–3 on a surrender vote. On August 10, the Emperor stepped away from his usual ceremonial role and broke the tie, ordering Japan to surrender. On August 12, the United States announced it would accept the offer, stating the Emperor could remain, but only as a ceremonial figure.

August 15 has been declared Victory in Japan Day. At midnight the recently elected British Prime Minister Clement Attlee confirmed the news in a broadcast,

People celebrate the end of the war, at London's Piccadilly Circus.

stating that "The last of our enemies has been laid low."

Japan's situation at home and abroad had been becoming increasingly desperate. Its economy was in ruins, with its stock of oil and steel all but exhausted. Millions had become refugees. The Japanese merchant navy was unable to leave home waters or sail from the few possessions still under Japanese control. Futhermore, the Japanese navy had all but ceased to exist.

On August 6 the *Enola Gay*, a B-29 Superfortress, dropped a uranium atomic bomb on Hiroshima, wiping out half the city, and killing or maiming an estimated 200,000 people. Of the city's 90,000 buildings, some 60,000 were demolished.

On August 8, Field Order 17 issued from the 20th Air Force Headquarters on Guam called for a second bomb to be used on August 9. Nagasaki was the secondary target, but smoke cover over the primary target of Kokura saved it from destruction. Thirty-nine percent of all buildings in Nagasaki were destroyed by the equivalent of 40 million pounds of TNT. Forty-two thousand people were killed. World War II officially came to an end six days later.

US President Harry Truman authorized deployment of the bombs only after the Japanese initially rejected the terms of the Potsdam Declaration. The use of the atomic bombs was weighed up against the prospect of the loss of thousands of American lives in a possible ground invasion of the Japanese mainland.

Late today the US Army's General Douglas MacArthur and his staff arrived at Tokyo's Atsugi Airfield lightly armed with pistols. They were greeted by thousands of Japanese civilians, who gave MacArthur a warm welcome. The occupation of the Empire of Japan has begun.

Emperor Hirohito

Ho Chi Min

> "VICTORY HAS A HUNDRED FATHERS, BUT DEFEAT IS AN ORPHAN."

COUNT GALEAZZO CIANO (1903–1944), ITALIAN POLITICIAN, DURING WORLD WAR II

> "ALL OF YOU ARE EXHAUSTED. I FIND IT COMFORTING THAT…WE FIND OUR-SELVES IN SUCH COMPLETE UNANIMITY."

PAUL HENRI SPAAK (1899–1972), BELGIAN STATESMAN AND CHAIRMAN OF THE FIRST SESSION OF THE UNITED NATIONS GENERAL ASSEMBLY

United Nations Founded

Geneva, Switzerland, April 18: The League of Nations, the international organization created in the aftermath of World War I, was officially dissolved today because its best efforts failed to remove the obstacles to peace throughout the 1930s. It has been replaced with the United Nations.

Despite the league's political failure, a number of its key principles can be found in the new UN Charter. All properties and assets of the League of Nations have been handed over to the United Nations, including the Palais des Nations in Geneva, even though the headquarters for the new organization will be in New York City.

In 1945 representatives of 50 countries met in San Francisco and drew up the charter which set up the United Nations. Poland, which was not represented at the conference, signed later and became one of the original 51 founding states.

Up to 4,000 Dead in Riots

Calcutta, India, August 19: Three days of rioting between Muslims and Hindus in the Indian city of Calcutta has resulted in the deaths of between three and four thousand people, the newspaper *Calcutta Statesman* was quoted as saying today. By late afternoon two battalions of British military, together with some 10,000 members of the city's police, had regained control. The rioting is a result of a Muslim call to "direct action" in response to the British–Hindu plans for a new government.

Many of the bodies have been mutilated; many victims are women, children, and the elderly. Hundreds were thought to have been burned alive inside their homes as buildings were set alight by rampaging mobs.

Calcutta's population of over 2.5 million is tonight under a 9 a.m. to 5 p.m. curfew; the sound of gunfire can be heard after dark throughout the city.

War Criminals to Die

Nuremberg, Germany, October 1: Hermann Goering, along with eleven other former

time out

Emperor Hirohito of Japan, receiving an American education mission in Tokyo, requested a recommendation for an American tutor for his son, the Crown Prince Akihito. The tutor was sought to supplement the English language tuition of Englishman R. H. Blythe.

high-ranking Nazis who helped Adolf Hitler plunge the world into the terrible abyss that was World War II, were today sentenced to death by the hangman's noose. The likely date for the hangings is October 16 in Nuremberg jail.

Those sentenced to hang are Goering, Field Marshal Wilhelm Keitel, Ernst Kaltenbrunner, Alfred Rosenberg, Hans Frank, the former German foreign minister Joachim von Ribbentrop, Wilhelm Frick, Julius Streicher, Frits Sauckel, Colonel General Alfred Jodl, and Arthur Seyse-Inquart, as well as Martin Bormann, who was tried in absentia. Sentenced to life imprisonment were Hitler's former deputy, Rudolph Hess, and Walther Funk. Baldup von Schirach and Albert Speer received sentences of 20 years in jail, Constantia von Neurath 18 years, and Grand Admiral Karl Dönitz 10 years.

This trial was the only trial of Nazi war criminals to be conducted by an international tribunal. As such, it required the consideration of some legal interpretations and perspectives of the tribunal's representative nations.

As the sentences were being read out, Goering held his head in his hands and appeared to be lost in thought, Keitel stared into space, and Rudolf Hess threw off his headphones, refusing to even listen to the sentence being pronounced.

Hjalmar Schacht, Franz Joseph von Papen, and Hans Fritzsche were acquitted, and smiled broadly as they walked out of prison and straight into a turbulent news conference. Schacht, the bankroller of the Nazi war effort, deplored the absence of "laws and free opinion" in Germany today. Russia's representative on the tribunal, Major General I. T. Nikitchenko, disagreed with the acquittals and also with the "light" sentence of life imprisonment handed down to Rudolf Hess.

A meeting of the United Nations, London. The name "United Nations" was coined by US President Roosevelt.

London, England, January 30: The first meeting of the United Nations General Assembly is held.

Fulton, Missouri, USA, March 5: Winston Churchill makes a speech, "Sinews of Peace," warning the Western powers of the dangers of Soviet expansion and referring for the first time to an "iron curtain" descending across Europe.

Paris, France, March 6: France recognizes the Democratic Republic of Vietnam.

USA, March 20: The last Japanese-American internment camps are closed.

Australia, April 11: The War Crimes Commission reports that Japan routinely committed acts of torture on Australian prisoners of war.

Geneva, Switzerland, April 18: The League of Nations is officially dissolved.

San Francisco, USA, May 2–4: Nine guards are taken hostage by inmates at Alcatraz prison; five people are killed.

Canada, May 14: The Canadian Citizenship Act is passed, recognizing a separate Canadian (rather than British) citizenship for the first time.

Italy, June 3: Italy abolishes its monarchy after a referendum and becomes a republic.

Argentina, June 4: Juan Perón is inaugurated as Argentina's first president.

Germany, June–September: One hundred thousand Jews have left Poland for displaced persons camps in Germany.

Marshall Islands, July 1: The USA tests a 20,000-ton atomic bomb at Bikini Atoll.

Philippines, July 4: The nation gains independence from the USA, and becomes known as the Republic of the Philippines.

India, August 19: Up to 4,000 Muslims and Hindus die during days of religious riots in Calcutta.

Nuremberg, Germany, October 1: The international war crime tribunal finds 22 Nazi leaders guilty of war crimes.

Washington DC, USA, November 5: John F. Kennedy is elected to the House of Representatives.

Indochina, December 19: The Communist leader Ho Chi Minh attacks the French in Hanoi, prompting the beginning of a new war.

USA, December: This year has seen the country's worst work stoppages since 1919. Those suffering the most are the coal, electric, and steel industries.

Ancient Religious Scrolls Discovered

Jerusalem, March–May: A shepherd boy is being credited with one of the most significant archeological discoveries of all time, in a cave in Qumran, a village 20 miles (32 km) east of Jerusalem on the northwestern shores of the Dead Sea.

Chasing a lost goat, the boy threw a rock into a cave and heard a cracking sound. The rock had hit some ceramic pots containing papyrus and leather scrolls that could be up to 20 centuries old. The scrolls seem to be documents written in a mix of Hebrew, Aramaic, and Greek, and they appear to contain many references to books from the Old Testament of the Bible.

The authors may have been a monastic group called the Essenes, an ascetic Jewish religious community who were both contemporaries of, and also pre-dated, John the Baptist. Other scholars have suggested that, rather than a monastic community, the authors may have been a militant nationalistic group, and that Qumran was in fact a fortress.

Teenager's Wartime Diary Published

Amsterdam, Netherlands, June: *The Diary of Anne Frank* was published today. Anne Frank started the diary on her thirteenth birthday, June 12, 1942, just weeks before she went into hiding from the Nazis with her mother, father, sister, and four others in a sealed-off annex above her father's office in Amsterdam.

After they were betrayed to the Nazis, Anne, her family, and all those they were living with were deported to concentration camps. Nine months after the arrest, in March 1945, Anne died of typhus at the Bergen-Belsen concentration camp. She was just 15 years old.

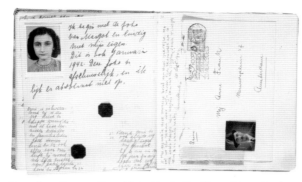

Pages from the recently published book, *The Diary of Anne Frank.*

Europe in Dire Straits– USA to Assist

Paris, France, July 11–13: In March this year President Truman's "Truman Doctrine" contained a pledge to "support free peoples everywhere." It is in that spirit that the European Recovery Program conceived by General George C. Marshall (popularly known as the Marshall Plan) promises US aid to a shattered war-torn Europe, which US leaders see as being vulnerable to the spread of communism.

When Marshall traveled to Europe he was shocked at what he saw. The continent had just suffered one of its worst winters in recorded history. Machinery has fallen into disrepair or is obsolete. Long-standing commercial ties in banking, shipping, and insurance have to be re-established. People in Europe's cities have no food or fuel, which is purchased by their governments using money that is needed for reconstruction.

Returning from Europe, Marshall convinced Truman that all of Europe may turn communist if something is not done to regenerate their economies. In a speech to students at Harvard University in June, General Marshall outlined his detailed plan of reconstruction and promised that America "would do whatever it is able to do to assist in the return of normal economic health in the world."

Yesterday, at a meeting of foreign ministers held in Paris, the British foreign secretary called the Marshall Plan "a lifeline to sinking men." US aid of $22 billion has been requested. The plan will also help the US economy—some of the money will no doubt be used in the purchase of American goods, which will need to be shipped across the Atlantic onboard US merchant vessels.

Marshall also made an offer of assistance to the Soviet Union and its allies, but Stalin has rejected the offer and has forbidden any Comintern nation from participating in the plan.

The situation is very serious. Europe's economy has been destroyed. People in the cities cannot produce enough to afford to buy food from farmers, who in turn are not able to purchase the machinery needed in the production of food. Starvation is rife, and it is hoped Congress will not delay in signing the Bill into law.

General George C. Marshall

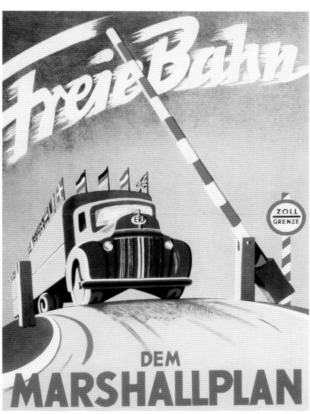

A German poster promoting General Marshall's aid recovery program.

Paris, France, February 10: Peace treaties for Italy, Finland, Hungary, Romania, and Bulgaria are signed.

Germany, February 20: The state of Prussia is abolished to become part of the newly formed Federal Republic of Germany and German Democratic Republic.

USA, March 12: The Truman Doctrine proposes containment of communist expansion and aiding Greece and Turkey in resisting communist forces.

Jerusalem, March–May: A Bedouin shepherd find mysterious religious scrolls in Qumran on the Dead Sea.

London, England, May 23: Britain agrees to the plan proposed by Lord Mountbatten, the Viceroy of India, to divide India into two states—one for Muslims and one for Hindus.

China, July 1: General Chiang Kai-shek mobilizes his troops across the country to fight the communists.

Roswell, New Mexico, USA, July 9: The US military announces that the flying object reported crashing in the desert on July 2 was a weather balloon. The site is cordoned off.

New Zealand, July 10: The government decrees that official correspondence will replace the word "native" with "Maori."

Paris, France, July 11–13: Europe's foreign ministers meet to draw up a plan for European post-war recovery.

Haifa, Palestine, July 18: The *Exodus,* a ship loaded with nearly 4,500 Jewish Holocaust survivors, is refused refugee status by the UK.

India, August 15: The newly formed countries Pakistan and India gain independence after 163 years under British rule.

Amsterdam, Netherlands, June: Newspapers review the published diary of a Jewish girl, Anne Frank.

New Zealand, August 23: The first post-war assisted migrants arrive on New Zealand shores.

Hungary, September 1: The communists win the election.

Amritsar, India, September 24: India's violence explodes when 1,200 Muslim refugees heading for Pakistan are slaughtered.

India, October 22: Tribal forces in Pakistan invade the Indian border state of Kashmir.

London, England, November 20: Princess Elizabeth and Lieutenant Philip Mountbatten marry.

State of Israel Declared

David Ben-Gurion

> *"I LIKE OLD JOE STALIN. HE'S A GOOD FELLOW."*
>
> HARRY S. TRUMAN
> (1884–1972),
> AMERICAN
> PRESIDENT, 1948

Tel Aviv, Israel, May 14: At a festive session of the People's Council comprised of representatives of the Jewish community in Palestine as well as members of the Zionist movement, the Declaration of the Establishment of the State of Israel was approved several hours before the British Mandate was due to expire.

The document asserts the rights of the Jewish people to exercise self-determination in the new sovereign state, as well as to establish self-government institutions and principles of political rule, and to create an elected assembly with the aim of drafting a new constitution. It also calls for peace and cooperation to be pursued with its Arab neighbors.

David Ben-Gurion, chairman of the National Council and first premier of the reborn Israel, delivered the Declaration at 4 p.m. The new government revoked the Palestinian White Paper of 1939, meaning that Jewish immigration and land purchases were no longer forbidden.

This historic event flowed from the United Nations vote last November 29 to divide the area of Palestine and to create a Jewish homeland. Jerusalem has been envisaged as an international region to be administered by the UN.

The United States has been one of the first nations to recognize Israel. President Truman has long favored partition.

Yesterday, the Arab League met and agreed to send troops to Palestine when the British Mandate expires. Abdullah of Transjordan has been named as the commander-in-chief of the combined Arab armies, and it is feared the new state's survival will depend largely upon the continuing support of the United States.

Ben-Gurion reads Israel's Declaration.

Essential Supplies Airlifted

Berlin, Germany, June 26: A Soviet blockade has halted all supplies of food and fuel into West Berlin, in an apparent attempt to gain control of the city. This has prompted the Allied forces to start a massive round-the-clock airlift to fly in supplies.

With US troops in Germany numbering 140,000, while the Soviets still have 17 divisions there and thousands of tanks, taking supplies overland is not seen as a viable option as it could trigger a ground conflict that the US could not possibly win.

So today the first US C-47 transport planes began landing at Berlin's Templehof Airport. Flights are being coordinated between the British and Americans, flying in from two airstrips, with planes landing a mere three minutes apart.

Food and coal are the two most essential supplies, and the US Air Force has brought in C-54s from Alaska, Hawaii, and the Caribbean to Germany to assist. It is calculated that the people would require almost 3,555 tons (3,626 tonnes) of supplies per day. Lieutenant General William H. Tunner has been put in charge of the airlift. He joined the air force from West Point at a time when it possessed no transport aircraft and no airlift strategies. In two years he created the Ferrying Command and developed the Air Transport Command, flying supplies over the Himalayas into China.

Nation of Israel Formed–1948
- Jewish landownership before UN Partition
- Jewish state after UN Partition
- Arab state after UN Partition

LEBANON · Beirut · Damascus · SYRIA · Mediterranean Sea · Haifa · Sea of Galilee · Nazareth · Nablus · Tel Aviv · Jaffa · Amman · Jerusalem · Bethlehem · Hebron · Gaza · Dead Sea · Beersheba · Jordan · N · Negev · EGYPT · TRANSJORDAN (JORDAN) · Elat · Aqaba · Gulf of Aqaba

0 50 km
0 50 miles

Burma, January 4: At 4.20 a.m. Burma is granted independence by Britain. Astrologers choose this auspicious timing.

Indonesia, January 17: The Renville Truce Agreement is signed by UN representatives, proposing a truce between the Netherlands and the Republic of Indonesia along the Van Mook Line.

New Delhi, India, January 30: Mahatma Gandhi is assassinated by Nathuram Godse, a fanatical Hindu.

Sri Lanka (Ceylon), February 4: Ceylon is granted independence.

Prague, Czechoslovakia, February 27: The Communist Party of Czechoslovakia seizes full power in a coup; democratic politicians are taken prisoner.

Bogotá, Colombia, April 30: The Organization of American States Charter is signed by 35 independent American nations.

Tel Aviv, Israel, May 14: Jews proclaim the Nation of Israel.

South Africa, May 26: The election victory of the Afrikaner National Party is quickly followed by new apartheid laws.

London, England, June 10: A surgeon at Guy's Hospital performs the first open-heart surgery.

Berlin, Germany, June 26: A Soviet blockade prompts Allied forces to start a massive airlift of supplies.

USSR, June 28: Yugoslavia's Communist Party is thrown out of the Cominform in retaliation for Marshal Tito's defiance of Stalin's leadership.

Washington DC, USA, July 26: US President Truman signs Executive Order 9981, ending racial segregation in the US military.

London, England, July 29: King George VI today opens the first Olympic Games since 1936.

Korea, August 15: Following an election supervized by the United Nations, the Independent Republic of Korea is proclaimed.

New Zealand, September 6: The British Nationality and New Zealand Citizenship Act is passed; most people born in New Zealand and naturalized immigrants are now New Zealand, rather than British, citizens.

North Korea, September 9: Kim Il-sung proclaims North Korea a republic, and becomes its first president. As head of the Korean Communist Party, Kim Il-sung has close ties with the Soviets, who helped him into power after he led the resistance against the Japanese.

Tokyo, Japan, December 23: The Japanese Prime Minister, General Tojo Hideki, nicknamed "The Razor," is hanged after being found guilty of war crimes on November 12. Six other Japanese wartime leaders are also executed.

Israel and Egypt Reach Agreement

Rhodes, Greece, February 24:
Today, after many grueling weeks of talks, representatives of Israel and Egypt have finally signed an armistice agreement on the Greek island of Rhodes. Israel demanded that Egypt withdraw all its forces from the former area of Palestine, while Egypt insisted Arab forces would withdraw to the positions they held on October 14, 1948.

The main points of the agreement are: The armistice line is to be drawn along the international border, except for a small strip of land along the Mediterranean Sea, over which Egypt will retain control; Egyptian forces trapped in the Faluja Pocket are to be allowed to return to Egypt with weapons intact, and the land is to be returned to Israel; and a zone on both sides of the border around the town of Nitzana is to be demilitarized and will become the seat of a bilateral armistice committee.

This armistice and those to be negotiated with Israel's other neighbors are regarded as only temporary agreements, to be replaced by formal peace treaties at some point in the future.

Egypt's King Farouk I (left).

West Germany Now a Separate State

West Germany, May 23: The western region of Germany has been formally established as the Federal Republic of Germany, with Bonn as its provisional capital. The eastern region remains occupied by the Soviets. Advice on the possible creation of a separate state was discussed at the recent Potsdam Conference, with calls emerging for a convention to draft a constitution

for a German state to be formed from the western occupation zones.

Despite some objections that this would lead to a permanent division of the nation, it was evident to all that this was already a fact. A parliamentary council made up of 65 delegates from the respective *Land* diets, and chaired by Konrad Adenauer, convened in Bavaria in August last year, and then again in autumn to work out the final details. The Basic Law, after some months of debate, was approved by a vote of 53 to 12 on May 8. Following approval by western military governors, the Basic Law was promulgated today.

The intention was to safeguard democracy and so avoid the abuses of the past. The lower house, or Bundestag, was enhanced considerably, with prime consideration given to the rights of the individual. The Basic Law also supports the principles of a free market and a strong social security system. In the end, it bears a striking resemblance to the US model.

Article 146 states that the document will be replaced as soon as all German people are free to determine their own futures. A new state, to be known as the Federal Republic of Germany, now exists.

time out

Three hundred soldiers at Chambery in France slept through reveille, and slept on as officers attempted to wake them. A medical officer discovered that the battalion had been drugged and robbed of wallets and valuables to the tune of 50,000 francs.

Mao Proclaims a People's Republic

China, October 1: Today, Mao Tse-tung said "The Chinese people have stood up!" as he proclaimed the establishment of the People's Republic of China after a near-complete victory against Chiang Kai-shek in the Chinese Civil War. The conflict began in 1927 when forces led by Chiang

purged the communists from an alliance with his own Chinese Nationalist Party.

Since the breakdown of peace talks in 1946, the two sides have been engaged in what the Chinese press has referred to as a "war of liberation." By 1948 rampant corruption within the Nationalist government, economic chaos, hyperinflation, and disillusioned troops proved no match for Mao's highly disciplined People's Liberation Army (PLA).

In January this year the capital, Peking, was captured by the communists and renamed Beijing. Mao's decisive military victory, which paved the way for today's announcement, was of course the Huai Hai Campaign, when 500,000 troops of the old Nationalist Republic were surrounded and destroyed by the PLA.

Mao Tse-tung

A poster produced to celebrate the new People's Republic of China.

Otto Hahn

New Radioisotope Found

California, USA, February 27, 1940: Two young scientists at the University of California at Berkeley—Martin Kamen and Samuel Ruben—have discovered a radioisotope called "carbon 14." Working in the university's Lawrence Radiation Laboratory, they were fascinated by the chemical reactions in photosynthesis, which they hoped to unwind by tracing the behavior of the carbon-based molecules. Most carbon atoms in nature are in the stable form of carbon 12. Their idea was to replace these stable carbon 12 atoms with radioactive versions that could always be located by the radiation they emitted.

The only known radioactive isotope, carbon 11, had too short a life. In search of longer-lived isotopes, the two scientists bombarded graphite in a cyclotron. The result was carbon 14, which has a half-life of 5,730 years. Carbon 14 will enable biochemists to trace the movement of carbon through photosynthesis, metabolism, and a host of other biological processes.

Martin Kamen was born in Toronto, Canada, in 1913 and earned his BS and PhD degrees from the University of Chicago. Samuel Ruben was also born in 1913, his parents having immigrated to the United States from Poland in 1910. He gained his PhD in Chemistry from the University of California in 1938, but included biological experiments with radioactive phosphorus as a tracer. Ruben works as an instructor in the university's Department of Chemistry; Kamen is a research fellow in the Radiation Laboratory, headed by Ernest Lawrence.

time out

Britain revealed a new weapon in the war with Germany: Chemically treated incendiary cards dropped in large numbers. Composed of guncotton and phosphorus, the cards were dropped moist, but burst into flames as they dried and became warmer.

Co-founder of carbon 14, Martin Kamen, works on an experiment.

Nurse Honored for Polio Success

Pittsburgh, USA, September 14, 1942: The American Congress of Physical Therapy has today honored the Australian nurse Sister Elizabeth Kenny for her unconventional but extremely successful treatment of polio victims.

Born in the town of Warialda in New South Wales, in 1880, Kenny trained as an army nurse and for 31 years treated the sick throughout the Australian outback. She was always known as "Sister," a carryover from her time in the Australian Medical Corps in World War I.

Sister Kenny encountered her first polio victim in 1911. Unaware of the prevailing treatment of the day, which was to immobilize the limbs with splints, she started applying moist hotpacks to loosen muscles, relieve pain, and enable limbs to be moved, stretched, and strengthened. She followed the theory that muscles could be "taught" to function as they once had.

In 1940, Kenny and her daughter Mary traveled to the United States. She approached the American Medical Association to seek endorsement of her methods, but was rebuffed. On her way back to the west coast to board a ship home, she decided to stop at the Mayo Clinic in Rochester. Doctors there told her they had no polio patients, but directed her to Minneapolis, one of the cities hardest hit by the disease. Eventually she was permitted to present her unorthodox methods at the University of Minnesota. In the first year after her methods gained widespread use, the incidence of residual paralysis fell from 85 percent to just 15 percent. Earlier this year she went on to establish the Sister Kenny Institute in Minneapolis.

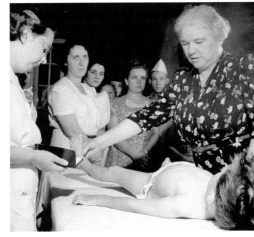

Sister Kenny demonstrates her polio treatment.

Major Breakthrough in Nuclear Physics

Chicago, USA, December 2, 1942: Today, the Manhattan Project on atomic bomb research overcame a major obstacle when Enrico Fermi and his team created the first successful self-sustaining nuclear chain reaction in uranium.

Fermi believed that he could achieve a controlled chain reaction using nuclear uranium. Although fission has been observed on a small scale in many laboratories, no one has, until today, carried out a controlled chain reaction that would provide a continuous production of

California, USA, February 27, 1940: Martin Kamen and Samuel Ruben discover an isotope, called "carbon-14," which decays at a set rate.
Nevada, USA, March–May 1940: Archeologists discover a mummy in a cave. "Spirit Cave Man" had been wrapped in a skin and sewn into some mats.
USA, May 20, 1940: Igor Sikorksky demonstrates his helicopter in a 15-minute flight.
France, August 20, 1940: Radar is used for the first time.

Europe, February 12, 1941: Rhesus negative blood is shipped to Europe as standard supply after it was discovered recently that blood types are negative or positive; wounded soldiers need a matching type when undergoing transfusions.
Oxford, England, November 26, 1941: Howard Florey makes a high-yield penicillin that kills bacteria. It is expected to increase survival rates from surgical infections.
USA, December 1941: Plutonium has been synthesized this year.

Pittsburgh, USA, September 14, 1942: The American Congress of Physical Therapy honors polio nurse Sister Kenny.
Chicago, USA, December 2, 1942: The Manhattan Project creates the first successful self-sustaining nuclear chain reaction in uranium.
France, June 1943: Jacques-Yves Cousteau makes his first dive with the aqualung he and Emile Gagnan invented, reaching a depth of 60 ft (18 m).

Sweden, December 10, 1943: Nobel Prizes for Medicine are awarded to Henrik Carl and Peter Dam for the discovery of, and research into, vitamin K.
New Jersey, USA, December 1943: A cure for tuberculosis and meningitis has been found: the antibiotic streptomycin.
New York, USA, May 9, 1944: New York Hospital establishes the world's first eye bank.

Germany, September 7, 1944: Germany uses ballistic missiles called V-2 rockets as weapons. They are far more advanced than cruise missiles or the V-1 bomb.
Sweden, December 10, 1944: Otto Hahn is awarded the Nobel Prize for Chemistry.
USA, July 16, 1945: Radiation monitoring tests report that radioactive fallout from the atomic bomb test is a major concern. Eyewitnesses 20 miles (32 km) away felt heat from the explosion on their skin.

plutonium for isolation. Work aimed at achieving this goal began with Leo Szilard at Columbia University in New York, but was relocated to the University of Chicago earlier this year.

This first nuclear reactor, called a "pile," was a daring and sophisticated experiment that required nearly 50 tons (51 tonnes) of machined and shaped uranium and uranium oxide pellets along with 385 tons (392 tonnes) of graphite blocks.

The pile was assembled in a squash court at Chicago University, in the shape of a sphere. Neutron-absorbing rods were inserted into the pile. By slowly withdrawing these rods, neutron activity would increase until there would be one neutron produced for each neutron absorbed. Today, with 57 of the anticipated 75 layers in place, Fermi and his colleagues began the first controlled nuclear chain reaction. At 3.20 p.m. the reactor went "critical": That is, it produced one neutron for every neutron absorbed by the uranium nuclei. Fermi allowed the reaction to continue for 27 minutes before inserting neutron-absorbing fuel rods. The energy-releasing chain reaction ceased just as Enrico Fermi predicted it would.

This experiment heralds a new age in nuclear physics and the study of the atom.

New Cure Discovered

New Jersey, USA, December 1943: A cure for tuberculosis and meningitis was found today—the antibiotic streptomycin. The discovery of penicillin in 1928 has spurred the search for new drugs that treat specific illnesses. Streptomycin is being hailed as the next great advance in this effort.

Selman Waksman, a Russian-born scientist working at Rutgers University, New Jersey, is being credited with the discovery. He has long been recognized as one of the world's foremost researchers in the field of soil microbiology, particularly the microorganisms called *Actinomyces*, which exude substances that were seen to

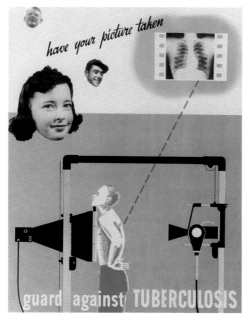

A poster promoting early diagnosis of tuberculosis.

kill certain bacteria. It was one of Waksman's graduate students, Albert Schatz, who was in charge of performing the laboratory work that actually isolated *Streptomyces griseus* on October 19.

Earlier this year, Waksman and his research team discovered two strains of *Actinomyces* called *Streptomyces*, and found they produced substances that are remarkably effective in fighting bacteria that cause tuberculosis, whooping cough, typhoid, and dysentery.

Credited with coining the term "antibiotics," Waksman gained his PhD in biochemistry in 1918 after immigrating to the United States from his native Ukraine.

Hahn's Nobel Prize for Work on Nuclear Fission

Stockholm, Sweden, December 10, 1944: The German-born scientist Otto Hahn has been awarded the Nobel Prize for Chemistry for his discovery of nuclear fission.

Born in 1879, he studied chemistry at Marburg and Munich before spending time at University College, London. From

1905, he worked at the Physical Institute at McGill University in Montreal, Canada. After World War I, Hahns became director of the Kaiser Wilhelm Institute for Chemistry in Germany before migrating to the United States in 1933.

His discovery of the fission of uranium and thorium in medium to heavy atomic nuclei came at the end of 1938, his papers on these subjects appearing on January 6 and February 10, 1939, in *Naturwissenschaften*. Since then he has continued investigations on the proof and separation of atoms that arise through fission.

He has also worked on the discovery of an artificially active uranium isotope, which represents the basic substance of the elements neptunium and plutonium.

Before 1939, it was generally believed that elements with atomic numbers higher than 92 (known as transuranic elements) are formed when uranium is bombarded with neutrons. In 1938, however, Hahn and the German chemist Fritz Strassman found traces of the element barium while looking for transuranic elements in a sample of uranium that had been irradiated with neutrons. This discovery was undeniable evidence that the uranium had undergone fission, splitting into smaller fragments consisting of lighter elements.

Igor Sikorksky

A "Type 16" Fighter Direction radar station, France.

Key Events

Sweden, December 10, 1945: The Nobel Prize for Medicine is awarded jointly to Alexander Fleming, Ernst Boris Chain, and Howard Florey.
Pennsylvania, USA, February 14, 1946: The Electronic Numerical Integrator and Calculator (ENIAC) is unveiled, weighing 30 tons (30.6 tonnes).
San Francisco, USA, May 16, 1946: Jack Mullin demonstrates his prototype hi-fi tape recorder to members of the Institute of Radio Engineers. The quality of the sound reproduction stuns the audience.

USA, May 26, 1946: A patent for the hydrogen bomb is filed.
Buffalo, USA, October 2, 1946: A medical symposium suggests that smoking may cause lung cancer.
Arizona, USA, May 1, 1947: Fossilized remains of a herd of mammoths are unearthed in Tucson.
Raroia, Polynesia, August 7, 1947: Norwegian marine biologist Thor Heyerdahl completes his 101-day journey across the Pacific in a balsawood raft.

USA, August 29, 1947: Scientists find that plutonium fission can be used to produce power.
California, USA, October 14, 1947: Test pilot Chuck Yeager becomes the first person to break the sound barrier in flight, achieving the feat in a rocket-powered XS-1 fighter plane.
USA, April 1, 1948: A letter by George Gamow in *The Physical Review* postulates a theory that the universe was started with a hot "Big Bang."

California, USA, June 3, 1948: The Hale reflecting telescope at the Palomar Mountain Observatory commenced operation.
USA, December, 1948: Alfred Kinsey's book of extensive sexual research, *Sexual Behavior in the Human Male*, stirs up a sensation.
USA, May 1, 1949: Gerard Kuiper discovers a new satellite orbiting Neptune. He also finds the atmosphere of Titan (Saturn's satellite, in 1944) and Mars (1948, carbon dioxide).

UK, May 6, 1949: EDSAC, one of the first British computers, runs its first mathematical programs.
USA, October 4, 1949: US Patent 2483892 is granted to Crooks, Bartz, Rebstock, and Controalis for a new typhoid antibiotic.
USA, December 1949: It is announced that the first crash test dummy, Sierra Sam, is to be delivered to the Air Force to test its ejection seats.

Howard Florey

> "THE ATOM
> BOMB IS A
> PAPER TIGER
> WHICH THE
> UNITED STATES
> REACTIONARIES
> USE TO SCARE
> PEOPLE."
>
> MAO TSE-TUNG
> (1893–1976), CHINESE
> COMMUNIST LEADER,
> 1946

> "TO SAY THAT A
> MAN IS MADE
> UP OF CERTAIN
> CHEMICAL
> ELEMENTS IS A
> SATISFACTORY
> DESCRIPTION
> ONLY FOR
> THOSE WHO
> INTEND TO USE
> HIM AS A
> FERTILIZER."
>
> HERMANN JOSEPH
> MULLER (1890–1967),
> AMERICAN GENETICIST
> AND NOBEL PRIZE
> WINNER

Penicillin Discoverers Awarded Nobel Prize

Stockholm, Sweden, December 10, 1945: The Nobel Prize for Medicine has been awarded jointly to Alexander Fleming, Ernst Boris Chain, and Howard Florey for the discovery of penicillin and its curative effects.

After seeing action in World War I, Fleming returned to his laboratory at St Mary's Hospital in London determined to find a chemical that could stop bacterial infections. First he discovered lysozyme, an enzyme that occurs in many body fluids, including tears. He found that it had a natural antibiotic effect but not against the strongest of the infectious agents.

Then one night, while cleaning up, he discovered some mold growing on some discarded petri dishes. On one of these dishes he noticed that the *Staphylococcus* bacteria growing around the mold had been killed. He took a sample of the mold and discovered it to be from the penicillin family. Since the bacteria could not survive in close proximity to the mold, he deduced that a chemical secreted by the mold was responsible. Fleming named this new chemical penicillin.

Scientific Achievements

Astronomy: Solar radio waves and solar X-rays detected.
Botany: Book published about viruses that affect tulips.
Chemistry: DNA shown to be the hereditary material for most living organisms.
Ecology: World body set up for the conservation of nature and natural resources.
Geology: Development of radiocarbon dating.
Mathematics: First mathematical programs run on British computers.
Medicine: First successful implant of intraocular lens performed.
Physics: ENIAC, first digital computer, came on line; "Big Bang" theory published.
Zoology: *Birds of South Africa* published.

Botanic Gardens
San Francisco, USA

Observatories
Asiago, Italy
Cheshire, England
Mt Aragats, Armenia
Villach, Austria

Universities
University of Bogota, Colombia
University of Legon, Ghana
University of Mona, Jamaica
University of Monterey, Mexico
University of Pyongyang, Korea
University of Ulaanbaatar, Mongolia

Alexander Fleming, joint winner of the 1945 Nobel Prize for Medicine.

When he presented his findings in 1929, they raised little interest. Later, in 1935, the Australian Howard Florey was appointed professor of pathology at Oxford University. He hired a researcher named Ernst Chain to do cancer research, work that overlapped Florey's own interest, and to work on lysozyme. Florey began reading Fleming's papers from the 1920s, and experimenting with penicillin mold.

Rather than simply doing experiments in a petri dish, Florey and Chain injected it into live mice. With controlled experimentation they found that the mold cured bacterial infections in the mice. It was then trialed in several human subjects, with astonishing results.

With another world war raging, the race was on to produce it in large quantities. Florey traveled to America, where an agricultural resource center in Illinois had developed excellent techniques of fermentation. The US government then pressed 21 US chemical companies into producing the new vaccine.

New Electronic Calculator Unveiled

Pennsylvania, USA, February 14, 1946: The Electronic Numerical Integrator and Calculator (ENIAC) was unveiled today. Weighing 30 tons (30.6 tonnes), it was designed at the University of Pennsylvania and is a product of World War II. ENIAC was built by the US Army for its Ballistics Research Laboratory, for the purpose of calculating ballistic firing tables. Its chief designers are John Mauchly and J. Presper Eckert, who began its construction at the behest of the US military in 1942. The original agreement between the government and the University of Pennsylvania, dated June 5, 1943, called for six months of "research and development of an electronic numerical integrator and computer." The work was not completed until the autumn of 1945, two months after the close of the war.

Filling up a 30 × 50 ft (9 × 15 m) room, it contains 17,468 vacuum tubes, 1,500 relays, 70,000 resistors, and 10,000 capacitors. It consumes 200 kilowatts of power. The calculator generates so much heat that it has to be housed in one of the few rooms at the university that has a forced air-cooling system.

ENIAC is 1,000 times faster than any other calculating machine to date. In one second it can perform 5,000 additions, 357 multiplications, or 38 divisions. The increase in speed is achieved by using vacuum tubes instead of switches and relays.

The accumulator is the basic arithmetic unit of ENIAC. It consists of 20 registers, which perform addition and subtraction, and also provide temporary storage. The master programmer component controls the execution of programs. While most of the programming is done manually by setting switches and cable connections, the master programmer unit permits iteration and program alteration. Reprogramming is not quick, however, with changes taking the technicians weeks to complete.

ENIAC is 10 ft (3 m) tall and takes up 1,000 sq ft (92.6 sq m) of floor space. It cost $500,000 to build.

Prehistoric Pacific Crossing Proved Possible

Raroia, Polynesia, August 7, 1947: Thor Heyerdahl, the Norwegian marine biologist with an interest in anthropology, has sailed with a crew of five across the Pacific on a simple raft made of balsawood and other native materials. This 101-day odyssey west from South America to the islands of Polynesia is proof that prehistoric peoples could have made such a trip.

Contrary to the prevailing anthropological viewpoint, Heyerdahl maintained that the islands of Polynesia were not settled by people from Southeast Asia, but

Thor Heyerdahl in his balsawood raft, the *Kon Tiki*.

rather by migrants from the west coast of South America. Though he has spent much time with the peoples of Polynesia and Peru, he knew that simply presenting his theory to his contemporaries would do little to change their views.

Heyerdahl's raft was built solely from materials that would have been available to ancient peoples. Nine balsa logs were lashed together side by side with separate lengths of hemp rope. The bow of the raft featured an organ pipe layout, with the longest log measuring 45 ft (15 m). Nine smaller cross-beams of balsa covered with bamboo helped lift the highest portion of the deck 18 inches (45 cm) above sea level. A plaited bamboo hut with a thatched roof completed the design.

On the voyage sextants were used to plot the raft's location, and plankton was used for food experimentation. Heyerdahl also found that when fresh water is mixed with up to 4 percent of sea water, the water is still drinkable. More than 200 coconuts and Peruvian food plants were also transported on the raft to prove they could be carried across the ocean without loss of germinating power.

Heyerdahl's epic journey has proved that transoceanic travel would have been possible in prehistoric times.

Chuck Yeager, with the XS-1 plane he used to break the sound barrier.

Sound Barrier Broken

California, USA, October 14, 1947: At Muroc Dry Air Field near Edwards Air Force Base in California, test pilot Chuck Yeager flew the Bell XS-1 past the sound barrier at an altitude of 45,000 ft (13,715 m), becoming the world's first supersonic pilot.

With a distinguished war record flying P-51 Mustangs out of England, Yeager returned to the United States to attend a pilot instructor course before going on to fly various test aircraft such as the P-80 Shooting Star and the P-84 Thunderjet. This experience led to his selection as pilot of the nation's first research rocket aircraft, the Bell XS-1.

The XS-1 was air-launched at altitude 23,000 ft (7,000 m) from the underbelly of a B-29 Superfortress and climbed to 43,000 ft (13,110 m), where it reached a speed of 700 mph (1,127 km/h), or Mach 1.06. Yeager named the aircraft *Glamorous Glennis* in a tribute to his wife.

The XS-1 uses some innovative design features. Its wings are thin but exceptionally strong, and its fuselage is in the shape

of a .50-caliber bullet. Even the windscreen is specially flared to retain the bullet shape. On the flight it carried more than 500 lb (227 kg) of flight-test instruments.

Big Bang Brought Universe into Being

USA, April 1, 1948: A new theory, that the universe began with a "Big Bang," has been put forward by George Gamow, a Russian-American theoretical physicist, in a letter to the *Physical Review*. Though over the years others have also postulated an expanding universe, notably Edwin Hubble and Edward Teller, Gamow has modified these earlier theories and named his version the "Big Bang."

In the letter entitled "The Origin of Chemical Elements," in which Gamow tries to explain the presence of chemical elements throughout the universe, he proposes that the universe began with a primeval thermonuclear explosion.

According to his theory, after the Big Bang atomic nuclei were built up by the successive capture of neutrons by the initially formed pairs and triplets. From his earlier work on stellar evolution, Gamow also postulates that the sun's energy results from thermonuclear processes.

Gamow was born Georgy Antonovich Gamov on March 4, 1904, in Odessa in the Soviet Union. He attended Leningrad University before gaining a fellowship to the Copenhagen Institute of Theoretical Physics in 1928. After defecting from the Soviet Union, Gamow was appointed professor of physics at George Washington University, Washington DC, in 1934.

World's Largest Telescope

Edward Teller

California, USA, June 3, 1948: Dedicated to the memory of George Ellery Hale, who died in 1938, the Hale Reflecting Telescope at the Palomar Mountain Observatory commenced operation today. The dome of the observatory is 135 ft (41.1 m) high and 137 ft (41.7 m) in diameter, and is divided into two sections—a fixed lower section and an upper section that allows full rotation of the telescope, enabling any part of the sky to be viewed.

Starting in 1928 Hale, although retired, began raising money to build a reflecting telescope with a large Cassegrain mirror, and assembled a team of the day's leading astronomers, technicians, and engineers. Because even tiny temperature changes can make glass expand and contract, and given the great size of the lens, the team decided to make the lens from Pyrex. Once solidified it doesn't expand and contract as ordinary glass does.

The disk was cast in New York, and transported across the nation at speeds not exceeding 25 mph (40 kph), and only in daylight, taking a route that avoided tunnels, bridges, and overpasses. All the parts, except for the mirror, were ready by 1941, but World War II intervened and work on the disk came to a halt. It wasn't until 1947 that it was transformed into a mirror and placed in the telescope.

Interior of the Hale telescope, which features a 200-inch (508 cm) glass mirror.

Amazing Cave Art Discovered

Vera Lynn

"OF ALL THE GREAT VICTORIAN WRITERS, HE WAS PROBABLY THE MOST ANTAGONISTIC TO THE VICTORIAN AGE ITSELF."

EDMUND WILSON (1895–1972), AMERICAN CRITIC AND WRITER, OF ENGLISH NOVELIST CHARLES DICKENS, 1941

"PAINTING IS A BLIND MAN'S PROFESSION. HE PAINTS NOT WHAT HE SEES, BUT WHAT HE FEELS."

PABLO PICASSO (1881–1973), SPANISH ARTIST, 1946

Lascaux, France, September 26, 1940: Two weeks ago, on September 12, four French schoolboys in the southwest region of the Dordogne discovered astonishingly well-preserved Paleolithic paintings in a cave dating back some 17,000 years.

While playing in the woods not very far from the town of Montignac, Marcel Ravidat, Jacques Marcal, Georges Agnel, and Simon Coencas found a large hole in the ground that had opened up by the fall of a pine tree years before. Crawling through a narrow crevice, the boys made their way into what is now referred to as the Great Hall of the Bulls.

The cave system stretches 300 ft (90 m) north to south and 150 ft (45 m) east to west. In total there are seven decorated chambers and passages.

Some of the depictions are enormous in scale. The first cavern has a continuous fresco 60 ft (18 m) long, which depicts various animals such as bison, stags, and mammoths. The artists would certainly have been hunters and would have had an intimate knowledge of the anatomy of these animals. Horses alone account for a quarter of the images.

There are more than 600 paintings of animals throughout the caves. Fish, bears, reindeer, and even rhinoceros are represented.

More than 100 such sanctuaries dot this region of southern France. Lascaux is situated on the left bank of the Vézère River, somewhat isolated from other prehistoric sites further downstream.

Only one painting of a human can be found. Called "The Scene of the Dead Man," it shows a hunter and a bison, the bison's head lowered as though about to gore its tormentor.

The Main Gallery of the cave is made up of a series of adjoining chambers, some of the art of which is very sophisticated. The panel of "The Back-To-Back Bison" is a typical example of the rendering of three dimensions in this sanctuary. Reserves around the limbs in the background, distortion of shapes, choice of surface, and symmetrical composition are all used to create a three-dimensional impression.

The paintings cover many of the walls and even the ceilings, despite many of these areas appearing to be quite inaccessible. For instance, the entrance to the Painted Gallery is nearly 12 ft (3.5 m) high. It appears that some form of temporary wooden structure may have been used to gain access to these areas. In some instances narrow ledges may run under the friezes, as is the case with "The Great Black Bull" and "The Falling Cow."

The chambers at Lascaux show no sign of human habitation and may have been used for ritual. Engravings on soft stone, bone, and ivory, as well as low-reliefs and a few free-standing sculptures have been found in the vicinity.

The late Virginia Woolf.

Virginia Woolf Dead at 59

Sussex, England, March 28, 1941: After a lifetime of battling mental illness and depression, acclaimed author Virginia Woolf committed suicide today by filling her pockets with stones and throwing herself in the Ouse River.

Born on January 25, 1882, in London, Woolf was educated at home and grew up in the family home at Hyde Park Gate. Her mother died when Woolf was in her early teens. In 1904 her father suffered a slow death from cancer, after which she and her sister Vanessa moved to a house in Bloomsbury. This period coincided with a social change for the family and the famous Bloomsbury Group began to evolve. When her brother Toby died in 1906, Woolf suffered the first of many mental breakdowns.

She began writing for *The Times Literary Supplement* in 1905, and published her first book, *The Voyage Out*, in 1915. With *To the Lighthouse* (1927) and *The Waves* (1931), she was hailed as one of the great writers of modernism. In addition to writing novels, Virginia Woolf was a prodigious essayist, writing more than 500 essays, which appeared in periodicals

One of the cave paintings recently discovered by French schoolboys at Lascaux. It depicts a steer.

and collections from 1905, among them the essay *A Room of One's Own* (1929).

Virginia Woolf was one of the great innovators in the English language, always looking at the underlying psychological motives of her characters and the various possibilities of fractured narratives and chronologies in her works.

Vera Lynn Sings for British Troops

London, England, November 1941: Vera Lynn's BBC radio show, "Sincerely Yours," which started broadcasting this month, has made her the sweetheart of the troops overseas. The half-hour show not only showcases Vera's singing talents, but also provides a welcome link to home for forces personnel stationed overseas, as messages from family and friends are relayed across the airwaves. Some of her hits include "White Cliffs of Dover" and "We'll Meet Again."

Born in London on March 20, 1917, Vera started singing at the age of 7 years. She began appearing in radio broadcasts with the Joe Loss Orchestra in 1935.

Magazine Covers Portray Four Essential Freedoms

USA, February 20–March 13, 1943: The previous four weekly issues of the magazine *Saturday Evening Post* have featured covers on a common theme by the artist Norman Rockwell. Drawing inspiration from the recent State of the Union address by President Franklin D. Roosevelt, in which the president spoke of the four basic freedoms that should be common to all people, Rockwell has set out to interpret those goals in four indelible images.

"Freedom of Speech" (February 20) was inspired by an incident in Rockwell's home town of Arlington, Vermont, when a resident stood up in a town meeting to voice an unpopular point of view. Rather than object, the other residents allowed him to have his say.

In "Freedom to Worship," featured on the February 27 issue, the muted palette softens the various skin tones of the participants, who include one figure with dark skin, suggesting that a person's color is irrelevant in the eyes of God.

"Freedom from Want," on the March 6 issue, is a particularly timely message when much of Europe is at war and food is scarce—it shows a family sitting down to a bountiful Thanksgiving dinner. "Freedom from Fear" (March 13 issue) depicts a mother and father tucking their children into bed at night. The father is holding a newspaper that features a headline on wartime bombings. A light in the outside hallway perhaps dispels the aura of this somber scene.

Born in New York in 1894, Rockwell left high school when he was 16 years old to attend classes at the National Academy of Design and later at the Art Student's League. He sold his first cover to the *Saturday Evening Post* in 1916.

Big Band Leader Lost Over English Channel

English Channel, December 15, 1944: The Big Band legend Glenn Miller has disappeared over the English Channel after his plane tragically went down. He was just 40 years old.

Since joining the US Army Air Corps in 1942, Miller has given more than 800 performances for Allied servicemen overseas. He was on a flight from Twinwoods airfield in Clapham, England, heading to Paris to play at the opening of the new Supreme Headquarters Allied Expeditionary Force (SHAEF) in Versailles, which is moving from London to Paris.

time out

The French fashion designer Christian Dior released his "New Look." In defiance of the conservatism of wartime fashion, the look used luxurious fabrics in widely flared skirts. The style also emphasized narrow shoulders and tight waists.

Alton Glenn Miller was born in Iowa in 1904. He was playing the trombone professionally at the age of 20, and by the mid-1930s he was adept at organizing musical groups, bringing musicians together for the Dorsey Brothers in 1934 and Ray Noble in 1935.

Forming his own band in 1939, he had hit after hit with tunes such as "In the Mood" and "Chattanooga Choo Choo," which featured in the 1941 movie *Sun Valley Serenade* and was the first record ever to be certified a "Gold Disc," selling 1.2 million copies.

Miller's triumphs in the ballroom were based on sweet orchestrations that were meticulously executed.

The Miller reed sound, which sometimes included a lead clarinet playing above the saxophones, was instantly recognizable and a much-copied style.

Bertolt Brecht

A poster advertising the movie *Casablanca*, 1942.

Austria, May 13, 1945: A large cache of missing French art is discovered. Like many European art treasures, it had been stolen by the Nazis during the war.

Italy, September 1, 1945: The singing group Trio Lescano gives its last radio show before leaving for South America. During the war their Jewish ancestry led them to prison; they were accused of spying.

USA, December 1945: Bing Crosby releases his album *Merry Christmas*.

USA, June 19, 1946: The motion picture *Anna and the King of Siam*, starring Irene Dunne and Rex Harrison, opens.

London, England, August 13, 1946: Author H. G. Wells, best known for his book *The Time Machine*, dies aged 78.

France, September 20, 1946: The town of Cannes holds its first international film festival.

Sweden, December 10, 1946: Swiss novelist Herman Hesse wins the Nobel Prize for Literature.

France, January 23, 1947: French painter Pierre Bonnard dies, aged 79.

Hollywood, USA, November 25, 1947: Ten prominent Hollywood film industry figures are accused of communist activity and blacklisted.

New York, USA, December 4, 1947: *A Streetcar Named Desire*, a play by Tennessee Williams, premieres. It follows his highly successful 1945 play, *The Glass Menagerie*.

New York, USA, February 12, 1948: The musical *Annie Get Your Gun* closes today after 1,147 performances. *South Pacific* is the year's newest hit.

USA, June 20, 1948: Television show *The Toast of the Town*, starring Ed Sullivan, begins.

Stockholm, Sweden, December 10, 1948: The poet T. S. Eliot wins the Nobel Prize for Literature.

New York, USA, December 1948: The Museum of Modern Art acquires popular American artist Andrew Wyeth's painting of a girl in summer fields, *Christina's World*.

USA, May 1949: Arthur Miller's play *Death of a Salesman* wins the Pulitzer Prize for drama.

USA, December 1949: This year's music hits include "The Huckle-Buck," "Trouble Blues," "Saturday Night Fish Fry," and "For You My Love."

Hesse Wins Nobel Prize for Literature

Hermann Hesse

Stockholm, Sweden, December 10, 1946: Hermann Hesse, the Swiss novelist, has won the 1946 Nobel Prize for Literature for *The Glass Bead Game*, first published in Germany in 1943. Set in the year 2400 it looks back to the present time, predicting a cultural breakdown in the second half of this century.

Hesse's themes often deal with our need to break out of the established modes of civilization to find our essential "spirit."

Before World War I, Hesse was a freelance writer. During that war he lived in neutral Switzerland, writing denunciations of militarism and nationalism. He achieved fame with *Demian* (1919), an examination of the achievement of self-awareness by a troubled adolescent. His later works show an interest in Jungian concepts of introversion and extroversion, the collective unconscious, idealism, and symbols.

"To be a poet is a condition rather than a profession."

ROBERT GRAVES (1895–1985), BRITISH POET, NOVELIST, AND CRITIC, 1946

"Authors are easy to get on with—if you're fond of children."

MICHAEL JOSEPH (1897–1958), BRITISH PUBLISHER, 1948

Communists Blacklisted by Motion Picture Industry

Hollywood, USA, November 25, 1947: Today, in a meeting of the Association of Motion Picture Producers at the Waldorf-Astoria hotel in New York City, the association's president, Eric Johnston, has issued a press release. It states that the Hollywood Ten will be fired or suspended and not re-hired until they are either acquitted or purged of contempt, and have sworn they are not communists. Expressing support for the House Un-American Activities Committee (HUAC), the association also announced its intent to blacklist any other individuals working in Hollywood thought to have communist associations.

Communism was a popular political movement among young idealists in the thirties. Now, in this post-World War II environment of Soviet expansionism and Cold War, many regard it as a matter of national security that people in positions

Two of the 10 Hollywood communists who have been blacklisted.

of power and influence be investigated should there be suspicion of subversive activity.

The HUAC was formed in 1934 and has looked at Hollywood several times since then. Often making headlines for all the wrong reasons, it famously interrogated the 10-year-old Shirley Temple in 1938 after one "witness" accused her of being a communist dupe!

Recently the HUAC turned its attention to Hollywood again. Launched on October 20, the hearings have at times been high drama, making headlines from coast to coast. "Communists Plot to Run Movies," said the *Minneapolis Star*. "Hollywood Crawling with Reds," screamed the *Des Moines Register*. Even Walt Disney claimed the communists had financed a strike against his studio in 1937. These headlines give some impression of the climate of fear and uncertainty that has led to today's events.

Investigating communist influences in the film industry's labor unions, HUAC last month summoned to appear before it a group of actors, directors, and screenwriters who were either alleged or actual members of the American Communist Party. The 10 who were subpoenaed cited their First Amendment rights (freedom of speech) and refused to give evidence, acting under instructions from the American Communist Party, which was providing their counsel.

The 10 are Alvah Bessie (screenwriter), Herbert Biberman (screenwriter and director), Lester Cole (screenwriter), Edward Dmytryk (director), Ring Lardner Jr (journalist and screenwriter), John Howard Lawson (writer), Albert Maltz (screenwriter and author), Samuel Ornitz (screenwriter), Adrian Scott (screenwriter and film producer), and Dalton Trumbo (screenwriter and novelist).

The aim of HUAC was threefold: It intended to prove that the Screenwriter's Guild had communist members; it hoped to prove these writers had inserted veiled communist propaganda into their work; and J. Parnell Thomas, Head of the Committee, wanted to prove that former president Roosevelt had encouraged pro-Soviet films during World War II.

In a vote of 346 to 17 yesterday, the US House of Representatives approved 10 citations for contempt of Congress.

Popular Broadway Musical Finally Closes

New York, USA, February 12, 1948: Irving Berlin's musical *Annie Get Your Gun*, starring Ethel Merman, finally closed

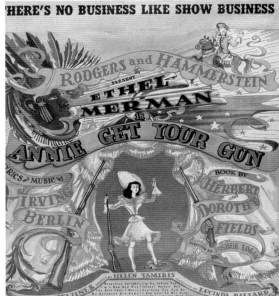

A poster for the long-running musical *Annie Get Your Gun*.

today after 1,147 performances since its opening at the Imperial Theater on May 16, 1946. The most endearing story of a riflewoman who outguns the sharpshooting star of Buffalo Bill's Wild West Show, and then falls in love with him, is set to a wonderful score by prolific composer Irving Berlin and includes such hits as "There's No Business Like Show Business," "The Girl That I Marry," and "Anything You Can Do."

Achievements in the Arts

Key Structures
Capanema Palace, Brazil
Casa Luis Barragan, Tacubaya, Mexico
Church of St Francis of Assisi, Pampulha, Brazil
Eames House, Pacific Palisades, USA
Equitable House, Portland, USA
Exhibition Building, Turin, Italy
Ho Phra Keo, Vientiane, Laos
New Gourna, Luxor, Egypt
Rockefeller Center, New York, USA
The Pentagon, Arlington, USA
Turku Cemetery Chapel, Turku, Finland
Woodland Crematorium, Stockholm, Sweden

Nobel Prize for Literature
1940–1943: no awards; 1944 Johannes Vilhelm Jensen; 1945 Gabriela Mistral: 1946 Hermann Hesse; 1947 Andre Gide; 1948 T. S. Eliot; 1949 William Faulkner.

Pulitzer Prize for Fiction
1948 *Tales of the South Pacific*, James A. Mitchener; 1949 *Guard of Honor*, James Gould Cozzens.

Academy Awards
Best Film 1940 *Rebecca*; 1941 *How Green Was My Valley*; 1942 *Mrs Miniver*; 1943 *Casablanca*; 1944 *Going My Way*; 1945 *The Lost Weekend*; 1946 *The Best Years of Our Lives*; 1947 *Gentleman's Agreement*; 1948 *Hamlet*; 1949 *All The King's Men*.

BAFTAs
Best Film 1947 *The Best Years of Our Lives*; 1948 *Hamlet*; 1949 *Ladri di Bicyclette*.

Eliot is Nobel Laureate

Stockholm, Sweden, December 10, 1948:
Acclaimed US poet T. S. Eliot has been awarded this year's Nobel Prize for Literature for his "outstanding pioneer contribution to present-day poetry."

Before Eliot gave his acceptance speech, Gustaf Hellstrom of the Swedish Academy said: "The position you have long held in modern literature provokes a comparison with that occupied by Sigmund Freud a quarter of a century earlier, within the field of psychic medicine. As a poet you have, Mr Eliot, for decades, exercised a greater influence on your contemporaries and younger fellow writers than perhaps anyone else of our time."

Born in St Louis, Missouri, in 1888, Eliot is one of the most distinguished literary figures in the world today. Educated at Smith Academy in St Louis, he went on to Harvard where he contributed poetry to the *Harvard Advocate*. In 1910, after gaining both bachelor's and master's degrees, he left the United States to study at the Sorbonne in Paris for a year. He then returned to Harvard to pursue a doctorate in philosophy before moving to England in 1914. There he began to transform poetic diction in collaboration with his friend Ezra Pound, often called "the poet's poet" and who immediately recognized Eliot's poetic genius.

Eliot's first book of verse, *Prufrock and Other Observations,* was published in 1917, and from 1919 Eliot was a regular contributor to *The Times Literary Supplement*. In 1922 "The Waste Land" was published and has since become a touchstone of modern literature, often being interpreted as the disillusionment of the post-World War I generation and elevating Eliot to almost mythic proportions.

Eliot also has had an enormous impact on contemporary literary tastes as a critic, propounding views of a rather conservative religious nature. His conversion to orthodox Christianity in the late 1930s is the reason for this.

Over the years Eliot has been open to charges of anti-Semitism. His poem "Gerontion" contains a negative portrayal of a "greedy landlord" known as "the Jew who sits on the window sill." In his poem "Burbank with a Baedeker: Bleistein with a Cigar" he implicates the Jews in the of Venice—"The rats are underneath the piles. The Jew is underneath the lot."

Eliot also wrote a `letter to the *Daily Mail* newspaper in 1932 commending it for a series of positive articles on the rise of the Italian dictator Benito Mussolini.

In 1943 a suite of four poems entitled "Four Quartets" displaced "The Waste Land" for a period as his most celebrated work. Although the British public did respond positively to the frequent topical references in these wartime poems, many of Eliot's longtime readers were not as enthusiastic. His conservative religious convictions are seeming less congenial in the post-war world, and with many reacting with suspicion to its assertions of authority, the standing of this once towering work has seen a progressive downward revision in recent years.

Nobel Laureate T. S. Eliot.

Wyeth Painting Acquired

New York, December 1948:
The Museum of Modern Art has purchased the popular American artist Andrew Wyeth's painting of a girl in summer fields, *Christina's World*. Born in 1917 in Chadds Ford, Pennsylvania, in the Brandywine River Valley, Wyeth had a privileged upbringing as the son of a celebrated illustrator.

The young Wyeth was schooled at home, and never gained a high-school diploma or college degree. His images of country people and rural landscapes have led many to refer to him as a "painter for the people," with much of the spirit of his works coming from the environment that molded his childhood and the special relationship he had with his father.

Ever since his sell-out New York solo exhibition in 1937 at the young age of twenty, many critics have hailed this artist as the successor to Winslow Homer.

Christina's World exemplifies Wyeth's mastery of unusual angles of perspective and his use of light to pinpoint time. The painting was inspired by one of Wyeth's neighbors, who suffered from infantile paralysis. Wyeth was inspired to paint her as she gazed up at her home from the wide field in the foreground.

The house in the painting overlooking the Georges River and the distant ocean was built in the 1700s by the Hathornes, a sea-faring family. Captain Samuel Hathorne IV replaced the old hip roof with a pitched roof in 1871, as well as adding several bedrooms, to give it the appearance it has in Wyeth's painting. A half-century later Hathorne's descendants, the Olsons, invited the young Wyeth to use one of the upstairs bedrooms as a studio on a part-time basis, and he has done so for more than 20 years.

Christina's World is a work in tempera, a medieval term for pigments based on various water-based binders, particularly egg whites, and characterized by tight, carefully placed strokes in an airless shallow space. By the early 1940s Wyeth's palettes grew progressively browner and grayer, his landscapes seeming to be trapped in a perpetual December, with hints of snow in the air.

Ella Fitzgerald

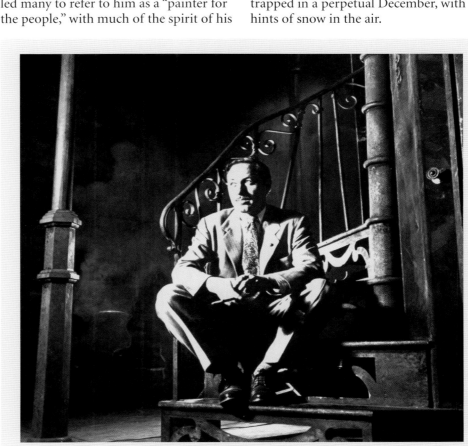
Tennessee Williams, whose play *A Streetcar Named Desire* opened in December 1947.

Superhighway Open!

J. P. Morgan

Pennsylvania, USA, October 1, 1940: The Pennsylvania Turnpike, America's first multi-lane highway, will open today, slashing travel time between Pittsburgh and Harrisburg by three hours.

The genesis of the nation's first "superhighway" lies in William Vanderbilt's project last century to construct a personal railroad from Pittsburgh to Harrisburg that would not be under the control of the Pennsylvania Railroad. Tunnel excavations began in 1884, but were abandoned in 1885 after banker J. P. Morgan won a seat on the board of Vanderbilt's New York City and Hudson River Railroad, and then sold the right-of-way to George Roberts, president of Pennsylvania Railroads. The unfinished project became known as "Vanderbilt's Folly."

The new highway is built along many of the routes selected by Vanderbilt, and the original tunnels, which soon filled with water and "reverted to nature" in the intervening decades, are now a part of this grand superhighway.

Previous highways have been designed with flat curves to discourage speeding. Now long sweeping curves have been incorporated to give ample room for high speeds and safe stopping distances.

Construction began in August 1939, with contracts awarded to 155 companies from 18 states. The first concrete was poured on August 31. By spring this year 15,000 workers were helping shape the future of highway construction.

The massive project called for 160 miles (258 km) of new four-lane concrete highway, seven two-lane tunnels totaling nearly 7 miles (11 km) in length, 11 interchanges with toll booths, and 10 service plazas where travelers can stop for something to eat and fill up with gas.

As today's opening drew nearer, local motorists have been seen sneaking onto the turnpike for their own personal test drives. The Fourth of July was originally

> *"I THINK IF THE PEOPLE OF THIS COUNTRY CAN BE REACHED WITH THE TRUTH, THEIR JUDGMENT WILL BE IN FAVOR OF THE MANY, AS AGAINST THE PRIVILEGED FEW."*
>
> ELEANOR ROOSEVELT (1884–1962), AMERICAN WRITER AND CIVIL RIGHTS SUPPORTER, 1942

The newly opened Pennsylvania Turnpike.

scheduled as the opening date, and President Roosevelt reportedly was to be the guest of honor who would cut the ribbon. Independence Day passed, with inclement weather canceling any plans for an official opening ceremony.

As recently as late August no date had been set. Toll rates had not even been decided. It wasn't until September 11 that a rate of one cent per mile for cars was set, with tolls for trucks based upon weight and vehicle class. Finally, with less than 12 hours' notice for a 6 p.m. opening tonight, the announcement was made.

Breakfast Breakthrough

USA, May 1, 1941: CheeriOats, a new oat-based breakfast cereal that is ready to eat without cooking has been introduced to consumers. Manufactured and marketed by General Mills Inc., the oatmeal, rye, and corn cereal shaped into "little doughnuts" is sold using the slogan "The breakfast food you've always wanted!"

General Mills Inc. was formed in 1928 through a merger of several of the leading milling firms in the United States. After

the merger, General Mills Inc. was the largest flour miller in the world, controlling 27 different milling companies.

When cereal was first developed, it was made up of simple flat flakes. In 1937 General Mills Inc. invented the "puffing gun," which heats grains such as rice until they puff up into crunchy little balls. The first puffed cereal available was "Kix."

Update on Rationing

UK, February 2, 1942: Rose-hip syrup, the richest source of vitamin C, is now available. It is said to be able to cure a number of ailments, from coughs and colds to diarrhea and dysentery. The hip seeds are ground and treated with boiling water to destroy an enzyme that breaks down the vitamin C in the fruit. Even patients with fractures recover more quickly if treated with rose-hip syrup.

Since the beginning of World War II, the government has been encouraging householders to grow their own food to help supplement rations, and rose hips have been recommended as a rich source of vitamin C. Rugosa roses are an excellent choice for quality hips. The flowers have a lovely fragrance, but resist the temptation to cut them—the more you cut, the fewer hips you will have.

Postwar rations: jackets are worth 6 coupons, skirts 4

UK, January 15, 1940: Since blackout started, road fatalities are nearly double the number of deaths due to war.

UK, August 12, 1940: Wasting food is now illegal. Food rationing includes butter, sugar, and meat.

Pennsylvania, USA, October 1, 1940: Pennsylvania Turnpike opens.

UK, June 1, 1941: Clothes rationing begins today.

France, August 5, 1941: Wine is limited to 2 liters (4 pints) weekly per person.

Moscow, USSR, November 13, 1941: The bitterly cold winter sees the temperature near Moscow drop to –80°F (–22.2°C).

USA, December 1941: CheeriOats, a new no-heat breakfast cereal, is popular: General Mills sell 1.8 million cases in this first year.

UK, February 2, 1942: Rose-hip syrup, the richest source of Vitamin C, is now available.

Malta, June 1942: To help all the homeless people prepare food, 42 victory kitchens are set up.

Australia, June 13, 1942: Rationing of clothing begins.

UK, November 6, 1942: Women are allowed into church without hats.

London, England, July 31, 1943: To conserve fuel resources needed for the war effort, pleasure driving is banned throughout the UK.

World, December 1943: With warring nations rationing foods such as butter, tea, sugar, beef, pork, and chocolate, newspapers and magazines are replete with methods to expand butter, grow vegetables, and create meat- or egg-free meals.

UK, April 6, 1944: A new "pay as you earn" income tax system comes into force.

London, England, November 20, 1944: After five years in blackout, locals see the lights of Piccadilly, the Strand, and Fleet Street switch on again.

Washington DC, USA, November 29, 1944: Congress passes the Highway Act to establish a national system to reach 182 of the 199 most populous cities.

Canberra, Australia, February 1, 1945: Prime Minister John Curtin announces that meat rations are to be reduced as a result of the continuing Australian drought.

Tokyo, Japan, March 18, 1945: War work is made mandatory in Japan for anyone aged 6 years and older.

UK, July 15, 1945: The lights of Britain are turned on for the first time in five and a half years.

Food rationing continues across the nation. Before the war, Britain imported 55 million tons (55.5 million tonnes) of food a year. This was reduced after the outbreak of hostilities, particularly when the Germans started targeting the North Atlantic supply convoys. On January 8, 1940, the entire population was issued with ration books, and bacon, butter, and sugar were rationed. As the war drags on, more items have been added to the rationing program— cheese, jam, and eggs in 1941, and then rice, tinned tomatoes, peas, and dried fruit this year.

Of course, rationing does not only apply to foodstuffs. From June 1941, clothing has also been rationed, and people have been encouraged to "make do and mend." A points system allows each individual to purchase one completely new outfit per year. Every item of clothing has its own coupon value, with each person having the equivalent of 48 coupons per year.

Island's Indomitable Spirit Recognized

Malta, July, 1942: On April 15, Britain's King George VI took the unprecedented step of awarding the highest civilian honor, the George Cross, to the island of Malta, for standing firm in the face of a sustained German air assault that began in June 1940, following the Italian declaration of war, and which continues to this day.

Later in June, Malta received its first delivery of eight fighter aircraft, Hawker Hurricanes. The Royal Navy submarines and Allied aircraft operating out of Malta were creating havoc for Axis shipping supplying Rommel's "Afrika Korps" in North Africa. The Germans eventually decided they had to neutralize Malta.

All through this spring Malta has faced the full fury of the German Luftwaffe, and much of this Mediterranean island lies

in ruins. Barely a building is left standing in the cities of Vittoriosa, Cospicua, and Senglea; the capital Valletta has fared little better. Some 7,000 tons (7,140 tonnes) of bombs fell on the isolated island in April alone, nearly half the amount that fell on London during the entire Blitz.

However, the Germans failed to break the spirit of the island. On May 10 this year, 65 Axis aircraft were gunned down by the Royal Air Force (RAF), and this represented a turning point in the air war over the island. Following this, Air Vice Marshal Keith Park arrived there in July, established a "forward interception plan," and virtually eliminated further daylight bombing raids, cause for an increase in local optimism.

The soup kitchens that were established by the government there have been replaced by so-called "victory kitchens," which can cater for more of the population as well as being better equipped to economize on food and kerosene. The first such kitchen was opened on January 3 at Lija. More victory kitchens then began to spread throughout the island.

The staff of the kitchens—including supervisors, sales assistants, laborers, and cooks—are mostly housewives, and the number of people now catered for by these kitchens is nearing 100,000 a day. Subscribers give up a percentage of their rations or pay sixpence in return

time out

In Pennsylvania, requests for an extra gasoline allowance for trips to polls were denied if other means of transportation were available. Those who had no other means of traveling to vote were invited to submit special forms to ration boards.

for one meal a day of stew and vegetables. The kitchens do have some critics, who object to the quality of the meals.

"Pay As You Earn" Income Tax System Introduced

Britain, April 6, 1944: A new "pay as you earn (PAYE)" income tax system is to be introduced to British taxpayers today, replacing the old system of annual or six-monthly collections. At the same time, a "tax code" telling employers the proportion of an employee's income to be deducted and a "P45 form" will also be introduced. This is the beginning of "self-assessment." Now all taxpayers will be required by law to keep a record of all income and capital gains so that they can complete a tax return if required to do so.

Anyone still requiring the Inland Revenue to collect their tax liability on their behalf, must lodge an annual return on or before September 30, after the end of that financial year.

King George VI

Fighter planes take off from Luca's bombed runway, in response to attacks on Malta.

USA, June 3, 1946: Racial separation on public buses is deemed unconstitutional by a Supreme Court ruling.
Paris, France, July 5, 1946: The bikini debuts at a fashion show.
USA, July 14, 1946: Dr Spock's book on how to raise children, *The Common Sense Book of Baby and Child Care*, is published.
New Zealand, December 1946: The Universal Family Benefit is introduced this year for every child under 16.

London, England, March 13, 1947: To boost Britain's productivity, the government bans weekday sport.
Paris, France, March–May 1947: Christian Dior's latest spring fashions include nipped-in waists and billowing skirts. The British government requests women balk the trend for long skirts to avoid wasting material.
London, England, April 1, 1947: The school leaving age is raised to 15.

London, England, May 9, 1947: Britain's first laundrette opens in Queensway for a six-month trial.
Geneva, Switzerland, April 7, 1948: The United Nations' World Health Organization (WHO) is established, to improve the health of the world's population.
Toronto, Canada, June 24, 1948: The Toronto School Board grants female teachers equal pay to their male counterparts.

London, England, July 15, 1948: Alcoholics Anonymous is started in the UK, 13 years after it was founded in the United States.
Boston, USA, November 26, 1948: The first Polaroid camera goes on sale today, retailing for $89.50.
New York, USA, December 10, 1948: The Universal Declaration of Human Rights is adopted.
California, USA, December 12, 1948: The revamped McDonald's Hamburger Restaurant opens.

USA, January 10, 1949: Vinyl records are launched by RCA (45 rpm) and Columbia (33⅓ rpm).
Canada, April 1, 1949: After the extension of the vote to include Japanese-Canadians in 1948, all remaining travel restrictions on Japanese-Canadians are lifted.
London, England, April 2, 1949: Advertising lights illuminate the streets again, after being restricted for the past 10 years.
UK, July 29, 1949: BBC Television begins a regular weather forecast.

Bikini Creates Fashion Sensation

Paris, France, July 5, 1946: A skimpy two-piece bathing suit called the bikini made its debut at a Paris fashion show today, creating far more public interest and outrage than its namesake location in the South Pacific, where French atomic bombs were recently detonated.

Louis Reard is credited with the design of the bikini, although five months before its debut another designer, Jacques Heim, also produced a two-piece bathing suit. Reard's showmanship, however, outdid the quieter Heim, and it is Reard's design that is shaking the fashion world tonight.

Dr Benjamin Spock

Sporting Achievements

Baseball *World Series* 1940 Cincinnati (National League); 1941 New York (American League); 1942 St Louis (NL); 1943 New York (AL); 1944 St Louis (NL); 1945 Detroit (AL); 1946 St Louis (NL); 1947 New York (AL); 1948 Cleveland (AL); 1949 New York (AL).
Cycling *Tour de France* 1940-1946 no competition; 1947 J. Robic; 1948 G. Bartali; 1949 F. Coppi.
Football *World Cup Soccer* no competition.
Golf *US Masters* 1940 J. Demaret; 1941 C. Wood; 1942 B. Nelson; 1943-1945 no competition; 1946 H. Keiser; 1947 J. Demaret; 1948 C. Harmon; 1949 S. Snead.
Horse Racing *Epsom Derby* 1940 Pont l'Eveque; 1941 Owen Tudor; 1942 Watling Street; 1943 Straight Deal; 1944 Ocean Swell; 1945 Dante; 1946 Airborne; 1947 Pearl Diver; 1948 My Love; 1949 Nimbus. *Kentucky Derby* 1940 Gallahadion; 1941 Whirlaway; 1942 Shut Out; 1943 Count Fleet; 1944 Pensive; 1945 Hoop Jr; 1946 Assault; 1947 Jet Pilot; 1948 Citation; 1949 Ponder. *Melbourne Cup* 1940 Old Rowley; 1941 Skipton; 1942 Colonus; 1943 Dark Felt; 1944 Sirius; 1945 Rainbird; 1946 Russia; 1947 Hiraji; 1948 Rimfire; 1949 Foxzami.
Ice Hockey *Stanley Cup* 1940 New York; 1941 Boston; 1942 Toronto; 1943 Detroit; 1944 Montreal; 1945 Toronto; 1946 Montreal; 1947 Toronto; 1948 Toronto; 1949 Toronto.
Marathon *Boston, Men's* 1940 G. Cote; 1941 L. Pawson; 1942 B. Smith; 1943 G. Cote; 1944 G. Cote; 1945 J. Kelley; 1946 S. Kyriakides; 1947 Y. Suh; 1948 G. Cote; 1949 K. Leandersson.
Sailing *America's Cup* no competition.
Tennis *Australian Championships, Men's Singles* 1940 A. Quist; 1941-1945 no competition; 1946 J. Bromwich; 1947 D. Pails; 1948 A. Quist; 1949 F. Sedgman; *Women's Singles* 1940 N. Wynne; 1941-1945 no competition; 1946-1948 N. Wynne Bolton; 1949 D. Hart. *French Championships, Men's Singles* 1940-1945 no competition; 1946 M. Bernard; 1947 J. Asboth; 1948-1949 F. Parker; *Women's Singles* 1940-1945 no competition; 1946 M. Osborne; 1947 P. Todd; 1948 N. Landry; 1949 M. Osborne duPont. *US National Championship, Men's Singles* 1940 D. McNeill; 1941 B. Riggs; 1942 T. Schroeder; 1943 J. Hunt; 1944-1945 F. Parker; 1946-1947 J. Kramer; 1948-1949 P. Gonzales; *Women's Singles* 1940 A. Marble; 1941 S. Palfrey Cooke; 1942-1944 P. Betz; 1945 S. Palfrey Cooke; 1946 P. Betz; 1947 L. Brough; 1948-1949 M. Osborne duPont. *Wimbledon, Gentlemen's Singles* 1940-1945 no competition; 1946 Y. Petra; 1947 J. Kramer; 1948 B. Falkenburg; 1949 T. Schroeder; *Ladies' Singles* 1940-1945 no competition; 1946 P. Betz; 1947 M. Osborne; 1948-1949 L. Brough.

Of course, Heim and Reard didn't invent the idea of the bikini. Drawings of bikini-like bathing suits have been found on wall paintings dating back to 1600 BCE!

Child Care Revolutionized

USA, July 14, 1946: A new book on how to raise children, *The Common Sense Book of Baby and Child Care*, was released today. Written by pediatrician Dr Benjamin Spock, it advocates his basic philosophy on child care—namely "to respect children because they're human beings and they deserve respect, and they'll grow up to be better people. I've always said ask for respect from your children, ask for co-operation, ask for politeness. Give your children firm leadership."

Born in New Haven, Connecticut, in 1903, Spock was the eldest of six children and thus was involved in child care from a very young age, helping to change diapers, baby-sit, and feed. He attended Yale University and the Yale School of Medicine. After specializing in pediatrics, he went on to study psychoanalysis for six years so that he could gain a better understanding of the dynamics and emotional aspects of childhood.

The more he talked with parents, the more he realized the prevailing wisdom of the day was flawed. Parents were told not to kiss their children, or to hug them. They were to feed them on a schedule regardless of how hungry they may be at any one time, to let them cry, to prepare them for a tough world by not becoming too emotionally involved with them. With this book Dr Spock asserts that no parent feels like this naturally. Do what feels right for your own situation and you very likely won't go wrong, is what he proposes.

His new book is a manifesto on the importance of attachment and the emotional relationship between parent and child. The book has been written for women, who Spock correctly assumes will be the primary carers

A bikini designed by Louis Reard.

in most households. These days, the average age for marrying is dropping rapidly, and millions of middle-class women are leaving college and wanting to start a family.

One of Dr Benjamin Spock's lesser-known achievements is that he is an Olympic gold medalist. During his first year at Yale he became a campus figure when James Stillman Rockefeller, Class of 1924, asked the 6 ft 4 in (193 cm) freshman to row. In 1924, with Spock in seat seven, Yale's heavyweight Varsity Eight, won an Olympic gold medal on the River Seine, in a world record time of 5 minutes 51 seconds over a 6,560-ft (2,000-m) course.

Organization Established to Improve World Health

Geneva, Switzerland, April 7, 1948: Today the United Nations announced the creation of a specialized agency for health care—the World Health Organization (WHO). WHO's objective, as set out in its constitution, is the attainment by all peoples of the highest possible standard of health. "Health" is defined in WHO's constitution as a state of complete physical, mental, and social well-being, not merely the absence of disease or infirmity.

In collaboration with national governments and other international agencies, WHO will work to reduce human disease, fund medical research, provide emergency aid during and after natural disasters, and

Britain's first laundrette opened in Queensway, London, on May 9, 1947.

also aim to improve housing, nutrition, sanitation, and working conditions in developing nations.

Instant Photographs a Reality

Boston, USA, November 26, 1948: At the Jordan Marsh department store in Boston today, a new Polaroid Land camera, model 95, the world's first "instant" camera that develops its own pictures in just 60 seconds, went on sale for $89.50.

It weighs 4 lb (1.8 kg), and a battery for powering the camera and its flash lamp is included in the pack. The camera works as follows: A negative is exposed and then brought into contact with a positive print sheet. Both are drawn through two rollers by hand, and a pod of chemicals is ruptured and spread evenly across the positive print sheet. If you want a copy you just take another photograph. As the negative has to be exposed accurately, the camera is supplied with a simple but ingenious light meter.

Its inventor, Edwin Land, said he first thought of manufacturing a camera that took instant pictures when his daughter wanted to see pictures he had just snapped of her.

He conceived and produced the first modern filters to polarize light (patented in 1929) and formed a company to market them in sunglasses, glare-free automobile headlights, and stereoscopic photography.

Land, Chairman of the Polaroid Corporation which he founded in 1937, and previously an undergraduate at Harvard University, has created a one-step method of photography that uses the principle of diffusion transfer to reproduce the image recorded by the camera's lens directly onto a photosensitive surface, which functions as both film and photo.

Land even went to the great length of enlisting the help of famed photographer Ansell Adams as a consultant in the camera's developmental process, to test films and analyze results. Apparently, Land felt that the artist would be able to tell him things from a point of view that would be quite different from that of the company's technical staff.

UN Proclaims Declaration of Human Rights

New York, USA, December 10, 1948: Today the General Assembly of the United Nations adopted and proclaimed the Universal Declaration of Human Rights, and has called upon all member countries to publicize the text of the declaration.

The vote was passed unanimously in the General Assembly with only eight nations abstaining—the entire Soviet bloc and Saudi Arabia.

After all the horrors of World War II, in particular the Holocaust, many in the United Nations felt that the UN Charter did not sufficiently clarify the rights it protected. It was thought that a new universal declaration, detailing each of these rights, was required.

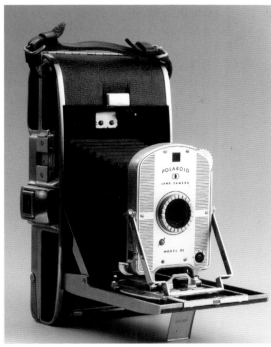

The new instant Polaroid camera, with an $89.50 price tag.

Its principal drafter was John Peters Humphrey, a Canadian legal scholar, jurist, and leading human rights advocate. After graduating from McGill University in Montreal, he practiced law from 1929 to 1936. In 1946 he was appointed the first director of the Human Rights Division in the UN Secretariat.

Nobel laureate René Cassin of France also played a significant role in the document's initial drafting process.

Although the declaration is simply a statement of objectives to be pursued by governments, and therefore not a binding international law, it will nevertheless be a potent instrument to apply moral and diplomatic pressure on any state that violates its principles.

RCA Victor's New Vinyl Record

USA, January 10, 1949: RCA Victor has launched a new vinyl record that spins at 45 rpm. The company is now in direct competition with Columbia, which late last year released the 12-in (30 cm) $33\frac{1}{3}$ rpm microgroove long-playing (LP) vinylite record with 23 minutes playing time per side. There is also a special turntable to play these records on, made by Philco.

The two competing systems both use records made from vinyl plastic, which is flexible and unbreakable in normal use. Columbia's LPs come in a paper sleeve with a color jacket that also provides a list of the tracks included. They possess a far lower level of surface noise than the previous shellac-covered 78s.

This "rivalry" was never intended to be. With the announcement last year by Columbia of its $33\frac{1}{3}$ format, the chairman of CBS (which owns Columbia), William Paley, showed the disk to General David Sarnoff, chairman of NBC (which owns RCA). Paley's hope was that the two companies would join together to ensure the success of the new format. Sarnoff, it is reported, angrily refused to do so.

Columbia was so eager to have its new system accepted that it neglected to patent it, allowing other companies to use the system without having to pay any royalties. Refusing to admit it had been beaten by a competitor, RCA went to work on its own system, clinging to the notion that the recording industry sold songs one at a time. So they took the old 78 rpm 10-in (25 cm) disks and reduced their diameter to 7 in (18 cm) and the speed to 45 rpm.

Columbia's approach was to accept the size of the older 78 format but to put more songs on each side. The $33\frac{1}{3}$ rpm speed was already in use for transcriptions in radio stations, so that seemed to be the obvious choice. One other thing that makes the LP possible is the use of tape recorders for the original masters. These had been perfected by German broadcasters during the war, and a number were brought back to the United States after the armistice.

Record companies and consumers now face uncertainty over which format will ultimately prevail in the marketplace.

Christian Dior

An advertisement for RCA Victor's new vinyl record, featuring their mascot Nipper.

Jawaharlal Nehru

Republic of India Declared

New Delhi, India, January 26: Two and a half years after independence, and nearly a century after British rule began, India has cut its last ties to Britain and declared itself a sovereign republic. Effectively this means replacing King George VI with a president as nominal head of state. To that end Doctor Rajendra Prasad, a key figure in the nationalist movement, has been sworn in as the nation's first president, although Prime Minister Jawaharlal Nehru and the Parliament will remain the seat of executive power.

The occasion was celebrated by millions of people throughout the nation, and the president was cheered by thousands as he drove through the streets. In comparison to the riots, chaos, and communal slaughter that accompanied partition in 1947, the reaction of the public today was peaceful. Many religious and ethnic problems continue to trouble the new state, however, and Kashmir remains a point of hot contention between Hindu India and Muslim Pakistan.

> "'WAR IS THE CONTINU-ATION OF POLITICS.' IN THIS SENSE WAR IS POLITICS AND WAR ITSELF IS A POLITICAL ACTION."
>
> MAO TSE-TUNG (1893–1976), CHINESE COMMUNIST LEADER

> "PERHAPS IT IS BETTER TO BE IRRESPON-SIBLE AND RIGHT THAN TO BE RESPON-SIBLE AND WRONG."
>
> WINSTON CHURCHILL (1874–1965), BRITISH STATESMAN AND PRIME MINISTER

President Commits Forces to "Police Action"

Washington DC, USA, June 30: Today President Truman committed US ground forces to the aid of South Korea. The authorization came after a request from General MacArthur, who will lead the US forces. MacArthur yesterday personally observed the retreat of a devastated South Korean army, half of which has been killed, wounded, or taken prisoner. The capital, Seoul, fell two days ago.

On June 25 North Korean forces swept over the border of South Korea, leading to the present crisis. The next day the United Nations Security Council condemned the

US President Harry S. Truman and General Douglas MacArthur.

invasion, although it must be noted that the Soviet delegate had absented himself in order to protest the exclusion of Communist China from the council and could not, therefore, veto the proposal.

time out

Thought to be extinct since 1615, 18 pairs of cahows, or Bermuda petrels, were rediscovered on rocky islets in Castle Harbor, Bermuda. The cahow nests in natural erosion, limestone crevices and artificial burrows, with a breeding season from January to June.

It is assumed by Washington insiders that it was Stalin's decision to invade South Korea. Some are concerned that it heralds the start of a wider communist assault on the free world and may lead to a third world war. President Truman ordered US air cover and naval support for South Korean forces three days ago, a move that earned him an ovation in Congress. However, leading Republican Robert Taft asserted that the US Administration had "usurped the power of Congress," which, he says, is the only body authorized to declare war, thereby setting a dangerous precedent.

The president stated yesterday that "we are not at war", and called the effort a "police action." The United Nations has ratified the military commitment, calling for the first time on members to resist aggression with force and restore peace in South Korea.

Atomic Bombs Against Korea?

Washington, USA, November 30: Today President Truman affirmed that the USA was giving "active consideration" to the use of atomic bombs in Korea. This comes after the unequivocal entrance of Chinese forces into the war over the last week, thereby extending a war that seemed almost over into an indefinite future.

Warnings have emanated from Peking since early October, when UN forces pressed forward their rout into North Korean territory. Then on November 24, General MacArthur announced a major offensive aimed at sweeping up to the Yalu River, which marks the border with China. The following day the United Nations forces met a massive and devastating counterattack from Chinese forces, which killed an estimated 3,000 men from the 2nd Regiment on one day alone. Some have raised the specter of Dunkirk.

Government sources say MacArthur is responsible for this reversal of fortune, as Washington explicitly ordered him not to advance into the Yalu valley.

American medics at a Mobile Army Surgical Hospital (MASH) in Korea.

Israel, January 23: A resolution is approved by the Israeli Knesset proclaiming Jerusalem the capital of Israel.

India, January 26: India becomes a republic and is no longer under British dominion. Dr Rajendra Prasad, the new president, is sworn in.

USA, January 31: President Truman puts through an order to rapidly develop the hydrogen bomb.

Moscow, USSR, February 15: Joseph Stalin and Mao Tse-tung sign a defense treaty.

USSR, March 8: The Soviets announce they have developed their own atomic bomb.

USA, March 30: President Truman denounces Senator Joseph McCarthy as sabotaging US foreign policy; McCarthy claimed in February he had a list of 205 communists among government employees.

Jordan, April 24: King Abdullah of Jordan annexes the West Bank, offering citizenship to Palestinians.

South Africa, April 27: The *Group Areas Act* comes into effect today, formally segregating blacks from whites.

Korea, June 25: War breaks out after North Korean communists invade South Korea.

USA, June 30: President Truman calls up reserve units to aid South Korea in their fight against the North Koreans.

London, England, July 26: The United Kingdom announces it is sending troops into Korea. Other US allies, Australia and New Zealand, announce that they will do likewise.

Calcutta, October 26: A nun, Mother Theresa, establishes the Missionaries of Charity. This global order of nuns will care for the poorest of the poor in India.

Ethiopia (Eritrea), November 25: The United Nations hands over Eritrea to Ethiopia.

North Korea, November 28: China joins forces with the North Koreans in the Korean War.

USA, November 30: President Truman affirms that the US is giving "active consideration" to the use of atomic bombs in Korea.

New Zealand, December 11: The New Zealand volunteer army unit "Kayforce" embarks for Korea.

Tibet, December 19: The Dalai Lama flees Chinese-occupied Tibet following the invasion of his country on October 21.

Death Sentence for the Rosenbergs for Spying

New York, USA, April 5: Last week, former government employee Julius Rosenberg and his wife Ethel were found guilty of infringing the Espionage Act, which forbids passing of information that relates to national defense to a foreign government.

Today the Rosenbergs were sentenced to death by Judge Irving Kaufman who, in his verdict, blamed the couple for the "communist aggression in Korea," the resultant casualties of more than 50,000, and possibly "millions more of innocent people." He went on to declare that the Rosenbergs had committed a crime "worse than murder" and "altered the course of history to the disadvantage" of the United States.

The Rosenbergs were found to be part of an atomic spy ring that operated out of Los Alamos between 1943 and 1946. The revelations began with the arrest of atomic scientist Klaus Fuchs early last year. He confessed to spying for the Soviet Union and named Harry Gold as his courier. Gold was then arrested in May, and he confessed to also receiving information from a machinist working at Los Alamos named David Greenglass.

Greenglass, in turn, implicated his sister and his brother-in-law, Julius and Ethel Rosenberg. Last year, Fuchs received a jail sentence of 14 years, and Gold and Greenglass were sentenced to 30 years each. All those involved were said to be active members of the Communist Party.

Greenglass claimed that it was the Rosenbergs who asked him to obtain information about the bomb, that Ethel had typed up the relevant material, and that Julius had put him in contact with Harry Gold. He said Julius had torn a Jell-O box in two, giving Greenglass one half and telling him that, when a man knocked on the door and showed him the other half, he would be his contact.

The Rosenbergs maintained their innocence throughout the trial, which has polarized the nation. Mrs Rosenberg will become the first woman executed in the United States since the Civil War. The couple will be survived by their two young sons.

Ethel Rosenberg faces the death penalty.

China and Tibet in "Agreement"

Peking, China, May 27: Today in Peking, the head of the Tibetan Government, the Dalai Lama, signed the Agreement on Measures for the Peaceful Liberation of Tibet with Communist China. The agreement is supposed to guarantee a joint administration, Tibetan autonomy and freedom of religion. It also allows for the establishment of Chinese military and civil headquarters at the Tibetan capital, Lhasa.

The introduction to the 17-point document describes Tibet as belonging "within the boundaries of China" and speaks of the need to free the Tibetan people and "successfully eliminate… the influences of aggressive imperialist forces." In order to achieve this "liberation," 40,000 Communist Chinese forces invaded the region seven months ago, quickly surrounding the small Tibetan army, and forcing it to surrender.

The level of "agreement" between the two sides is suggested by the protest and unsuccessful appeal for assistance made to the United Nations by the Tibetan Government last November, in which it spoke of "armed invasion," "force," and "violation of the weak by the strong."

Segregation of Voters in South Africa

Pretoria, South Africa, June 18: The South African Parliament today passed the Separate Representation of Voters Act, which will remove all non-white voters from the common voting roll. Instead, it will place them on a separate roll, which will permit them to elect a total of four white representatives, although this vote will not occur at general elections.

The act follows on from recent legislation classifying all South Africans as either black, white, or colored (of mixed race), banning mixed marriages and interracial intercourse, creating separate amenities for white and black, and assigning races to specific residential and business sections of urban areas, with forceful removal from the "wrong" area.

The Cape Franchise Action Council has organized protests against the bill, and will fight it in court, arguing that black voting rights are protected by the constitution. The Minister of Native Affairs stated that if the courts overturn the bill, Parliament will find a way to reverse the decision.

The boy Dalai Lama, Tenzin Gyatso

No-man's land between the Jordanian and Israeli sectors of Jerusalem.

Key Events

Bermuda, January 8: An animal believed extinct since 1615, an ocean bird called the cahow, is found alive on an islet.

Washington DC, USA, January 15: The US Supreme Court rules that an incitement to riot is a cause for arrest.

New Guinea, January 17: Over 3,000 people are killed following the volcanic eruption of Mt Lamington.

USSR, February 16: Stalin accuses the United Nations of inciting war.

USA, February 17: The FBI's J. Edgar Hoover begins an unauthorized program to flush out employees suspected of having communist interests.

USA, February 26: A constitutional amendment is enacted that limits a US president to two terms of office.

USA, March 30: General MacArthur, commander of the UN forces in Korea, aims to take the war into China.

New York, USA, April 5: Julius and Ethel Rosenberg are found guilty of espionage and sentenced to death.

USA, April 19: General Douglas MacArthur bids farewell to US Congress after President Truman relieves him of his command.

Tibet, May 23: The Dalai Lama's delegation to Beijing is forced to agree to the incorporation of Tibet into China.

Mozambique, June 11: The country of Mozambique becomes a province overseen by Portugal.

South Africa, June 18: Black people and those of mixed racial heritage are denied the right to vote.

Jerusalem, Israel, July 20: King Abdullah Ibn Hussein of Jordan is assassinated by a Palestinian extremist; his 15-year-old son witnesses the murder.

Manchuria, August 6: Massive floods following a typhoon kill 4,800 people.

San Francisco, USA, September 1: The USA, Australia, and New Zealand make a joint security alliance, the ANZUS Pact.

San Francisco, USA, September 8: Forty-nine nations sign a peace treaty with Japan.

California, USA, October 24: Doctor Albert Bellamy, head of Radiological Services, assures residents that the test explosions of the hydrogen bomb near Las Vegas in May will cause no ill effects.

London, England, October 25: Winston Churchill becomes Prime Minister again after winning the general election against the Labour Party.

Egypt, November 18: British troops occupy Ismailiya.

Argentina Mourns Evita

Eva Perón

Buenos Aires, Argentina, July 26: Eva Perón, the much-loved wife of Argentinian President Juan Perón, has died of cancer today. She was aged only 33. Eva was the illegitimate child of poor parents and received no formal education. Nonetheless she has made a remarkable impression on Argentinian social life and politics.

"Evita," as she became known, won the hearts of the Argentinian masses, whom she referred to as "the shirtless ones." This compassion typified her approach. She had never held an official position but her influence was crucial in gaining the vote for women, legalizing divorce, providing substantial wage increases for unions, and setting up both the Peronista Feminist Party and the Eva Perón Foundation. The latter was responsible for spending millions on the poor, establishing thousands of orphanages, schools, hospitals, and homes for the elderly. Shortly before her death, she gained the nomination for the vice-presidency but was forced to withdraw by the army—a sign of the controversy and disdain she aroused in some sectors of Argentinian society.

Bloodless Coup Ends Foreign Rule in Egypt

Cairo, Egypt, July 26: Three days after a bloodless coup d'état by military officers, King Farouk I has abdicated and fled to Italy. The deposed ruler was a member of the Muhammad Ali dynasty, a family of Albanian origin, which was the most recent in a long line of foreign invaders and rulers, including the Macedonians, Romans, Byzantines, Arabs, French, Turks, and British. The new leadership thus brings to an end nearly 2,300 years of foreign rule in Egypt.

King Farouk came to the throne in 1936 at the age of 16. He fell out of favor during World War II, owing to the contrast of public hardship with his own extraordinarily lavish lifestyle, his shopping sprees to Europe, and his refusal to extinguish the lights in his palace when the city was blacked out during bombing. He had kleptomaniac tendencies, pickpocketing objects from both ordinary people and foreign dignitaries; it is alleged that he even stole a priceless watch from Winston Churchill

The years after World War II have been a time of rising nationalism and radicalism in Egypt, with increasingly strident calls for change. Matters were exacerbated when Egypt, together with Jordan, Syria, and Iraq, launched the Arab–Israeli War of 1948–1949, which was undertaken in support of the Arab cause in Palestine.

The dramatic loss by the Arab forces focused dissatisfaction with Farouk's reign and added to the political instability. This was further worsened by conflict with British forces over the last nine months, reflecting a nationalist desire to be rid of the British, who have dominated Egypt for the last 70 years. The coup of the "Free Officers" was led by Colonel Gamal Abdel Nasser. The coup has left Egypt in the hands of a military council, which will have its hands full resolving the large number of internal political tensions and shaping the country's future.

time out

In the USA, 13 convicted communists were offered the chance to go to Russia to avoid imprisonment for "criminal conspiracy to teach and advocate the overthrow of the United States Government by force and violence." The defendants emphatically rejected the proposal.

Great Smog a Mass Killer

London, England, December 31: December has been a strange month indeed this year, owing to the "great smog" that enshrouded London for four days early in the month. It has become apparent in the ensuing weeks that, on top of the mayhem caused by severe lack of visibility, at least 4,000 people died as a direct consequence of the weather. The casualties were mostly among the very young, the elderly, and those with respiratory problems and weak hearts. It seems the smog was caused by toxic by-products from the burning of coal, which was at high levels owing to the exceptionally cold weather and the absence of ventilating winds.

Road, rail, air, and shipping services were severely disrupted over the four days, with transportation grinding to a virtual halt and in-demand emergency services hindered by icy roads. Sporting events were canceled and so, too, was the opera when the smog infiltrated the auditorium of Sadler's Wells theater.

> "THE ONLY WAY TO WIN AN ATOMIC WAR IS TO MAKE CERTAIN IT NEVER STARTS."
>
> OMAR NELSON BRADLEY (1893–1981), AMERICAN MILITARY LEADER, 1952

> "MY DEFINITION OF A FREE SOCIETY IS A SOCIETY WHERE IT IS SAFE TO BE UNPOPULAR."
>
> ADLAI STEVENSON (1900–1965), AMERICAN STATESMAN

TIME — THE WEEKLY NEWSMAGAZINE

KING FAROUK
When a fellah needs a friend . . .

King Farouk I of Egypt made the cover of *Time* in September 1951.

Cairo, Egypt, January 26: After an attack by British troops on the police barracks at Ismailiya on January 25, riots break out as Egyptian police stage protests at the death of 50 of their colleagues.

Sandringham, England, February 6: George VI dies in his sleep after succumbing to lung cancer. His 25-year-old daughter, on safari in Kenya, accedes the throne as Elizabeth II.

Vietnam, April 26: France decides to ask the United Nations for aid in Vietnam if China becomes involved in its conflict against the Viet Minh.

North Korea, May 8: Allied forces destroy the city of Suan in a massive air raid.

USSR, May 31: The Volga-Don Canal opens, connecting the Black, Azov, and Caspian Seas.

East Germany, June 1: East Germany closes access to West Germany from midnight. Only permit holders may enter.

Argentina, July 26: President Juan Perón's wife, Eva "Evita" Perón, dies aged 33.

Cairo, Egypt, July 26: King Farouk I abdicates following a military coup by General Gamal Abdel Nasser's Free Officers, a nationalist group.

Helsinki, Finland, August 3: The Games of the XVth Olympiad end, with track events dominated by the Czech sprinter Emil Zatopek, who broke several records.

Australia, October 3: The UK's atomic bomb is tested in the remote Monte Bello Islands off the northwest coast of Western Australia.

California, USA, October 11: Researchers announce the discovery of a polio vaccine that is suitable for large-scale manufacture.

Washington DC, USA, November 5: Dwight D. Eisenhower is elected the 34th president of the USA, the first Republican president in 20 years. Richard Nixon is vice-president.

Eniwetok Island, Pacific Ocean, November 6: The USA explodes its first hydrogen bomb on a Pacific island, blasting it apart.

Kenya, November 8: Jomo Kenyatta, a prominent Kenyan nationalist leader, is among hundreds of people rounded up as suspects in the Mau Mau terrorist uprising over the last few weeks in which more than 40 people were murdered.

London, England, December 31: Thousands of people die in the last month from inhaling the fumes of the city's toxic smog.

Queen Elizabeth II at her coronation in Westminster Abbey.

Millions Celebrate as Queen Elizabeth Crowned

London, England, June 2: Today Elizabeth II was officially crowned Queen of England and Defender of the Faith in Westminster Abbey in London. The coronation ceremony was presided over by Doctor Geoffrey Fisher, the Archbishop of Canterbury, who handed Queen Elizabeth the symbols of power—the scepter, the royal ring, the rod of mercy, the orb, and Saint Edward's Crown, which was placed upon her head in front of 8,000 dignitaries from throughout the Commonwealth.

The ceremony's completion was greeted with volleys of official gunfire, cries of "God save the Queen," and roars from the crowd, some of whom had waited up all night in order to obtain a quality view of the Queen Elizabeth's passage in the golden coach of state. Such measures began to seem less extreme as the numbers swelled to three million. The Queen, the Queen Mother, and other members of the royal family waved to the crowd from the balcony at Buckingham Palace.

Those who were not fortunate enough to witness events first-hand gathered around their own or neighbors' television sets to view the coverage, which was broadcast in 44 languages. They also bought commemorative stamps and other souvenirs, and listened to Her Majesty's address on the radio. The RAF undertook a special flyover for the event and a fireworks display lit up the evening skies.

Elizabeth II became queen on February 6, last year when her father, King George VI, died in his sleep.

Everest Conquered

London, England, July 2: News reached civilization today that New Zealand beekeeper Edmund Hillary and Nepalese Sherpa Tenzing Norgay have reached the very peak of the world's tallest formation, Mt Everest, on May 29. The first people ever to reach the summit, they spent a mere 15 minutes atop the 29,028 ft (8,850 m) mountain owing to a shortage of oxygen. While there, Hillary took some photographs of Tenzing Norgay waving the British, Nepalese, Indian, and UN

Heroes of Everest: John Hunt, Tenzing Norgay, and Edmund Hillary.

flags, and Norgay then scattered some sweets and biscuits in a Buddhist offering.

Hillary, who acquired a taste for climbing during a school trip to Mt Ruapehu in his home country, was part of the New Zealand expedition to the Himalayas two years ago that discovered the southern approach to the summit. Tenzing Norgay set a previous record last year when he attained a height of 28,215 ft (8,602 m) with a Swiss party. John Hunt, the leader of the present expedition, attributed their success to careful planning, learning from previous climbers, good weather, and good oxygen supplies.

Queen Elizabeth II

Armistice Ends Carnage

Panmunjeom, North–South Korean border, July 27, 1953: After three years of fighting and two years of truce talks, an armistice agreement has finally been signed in Korea. The long-standing point of disagreement, which has now conceded by the communists, was their refusal to allow prisoners of war to choose whether to return to their native country.

The war's origins date back to World War II, when the USSR accepted the surrender of Japanese prisoners in the north and the USA did so in the south. Unification negotiations failed in 1947, and the USSR refused to cooperate with UN plans to hold general elections. This resulted in the establishment of two separate governments in 1948. North Korea then invaded South Korea in June 1950.

The war has led to an estimated death toll of 2,800,000 people, mostly civilians. Claims of torture and war crimes have been made by both sides. No permanent peace treaty has been signed as yet. The boundary between the two nations is similar to that of June 1950.

Key Events

Yugoslavia, January 14: Josip Tito is elected President of Yugoslavia.

Netherlands, February 3: A massive storm breaches sea dikes in the south; more than 1,800 people are believed dead in the Netherlands and a further 307 in the UK.

USSR, March 5: Soviet dictator Joseph Stalin dies from a brain hemorrhage, aged 73, after ruling for 29 years. His is succeeded by his deputy, Georgy Malenkov.

Kenya, April 8: Jomo Kenyatta and five others are sentenced to jail for seven years for orchestrating the Mau Mau terrorist uprising against white settlers.

Vevey, Switzerland, April 17: Charlie Chaplin vows to never return home to the USA after being banned last year on suspicion of communism.

Nepal, May 29: New Zealander Edmund Hillary and Tenzing Norgay of Nepal reach Mt Everest's summit.

London, England, June 2: Queen Elizabeth II's coronation takes place in Westminster Abbey.

Washington DC, USA, June 8: Restaurants in the capital are not allowed to refuse service to blacks by Supreme Court ruling.

East Berlin, June 17: Tanks were brought in to quell an uprising against Communism.

Cairo, Egypt, June 18: Egypt becomes a military-ruled republic, led by general Muhammad Neguib.

London, England, July 2: It is announced that Edmund Hillary and Sherpa Tenzing Norgay have reached the top of Mt Everest.

Canada, June–November: A severe polio epidemic strikes Canada, with around 9,000 cases and 500 deaths resulting from the disease.

Moncada, Cuba, July 26: The leader of a rebel communist group, Fidel Castro, is jailed.

Panmunjeom, North Korea, July 27: An armistice signed by the United Nations, Korea, and China ends three years of war.

Greece, August 14: A recent earthquake and consequent tsunamis in the Ionian Islands kill 1,000 people and leave at least 100,000 homeless.

Iran, August 22: The exiled Shah is restored to power following General Zahedi's bloody military coup, which ousted Prime Minister Mossadegh and left 300 dead.

Japan, September 27: A massive typhoon destroys a large part of the city of Nagoya.

Tangiwai, New Zealand, December 24: A railway bridge collapses, causing a night express train to plunge into the flooded Whangaehu River. Of the 285 people on board, 151 are killed.

Joseph McCarthy

French War Effort in Vietnam Collapses

Geneva, Switzerland, July 20: The seven-year war in Indo-China formally ended today with the signing of the Geneva Accords. More than 300,000 people have died in the fighting. The French Government, which had been attempting to regain control of its former colony, sought an end to the war after a humiliating military loss in the Battle of Dien Bien Phu on May 7. A French garrison of 16,500 troops was surrounded by 40,000 Vietminh troops, and blockaded and bombarded into surrender. Only 3,000 of the French survived.

The Geneva Accords have prescribed the temporary division of Vietnam into a communist north and a non-communist south, with provisions for a general election in 1956. It is unknown how the United States will respond to the latest events, as it is widely believed the communists will win the election. Neither South Vietnam nor the United States would sign the Final Declaration. It is understood that the US Government contributed hundreds of millions of dollars to the French war effort in an attempt to ensure the defeat of the communists.

Ellis Island Shuts Up Shop

New York, USA, November 12: The Ellis Island immigration center finally closed its doors today, after processing around 20 million immigrants since it was first established in 1892.

Its role was effectively to quarantine migrants while authorities questioned them and examined their persons and papers to weed out the diseased, insane, criminal, infirm, unskilled, and penniless,

Members of the French Foreign Legion at Dien Bien Phu.

in order to ensure the public were not endangered or financially burdened.

About 2 percent of arrivals were deported, while others were hospitalized on the island, where some 3,000 died. Those approved were transported to the mainland after a few hours or a day. At its peak (around 1900) about 5,000 people were arriving daily. Immigrant reception shifted to New York City in 1943 and the island became a detention center for deportees and aliens. Today, nearly all immigrants are admitted without inspection.

time out

Austria's single worst avalanche killed 200 people in Blons, a village with a population of 380. Nine hours later, a second avalanche struck, moving 3,800 ft (1,150 m) downhill in less than 30 seconds, killing 115 rescue workers and inhabitants.

McCarthy Censured for Misconduct

Washington DC, USA, December 2: Today the US Senate voted 67 to 22 that Joseph McCarthy had engaged in conduct unbecoming of a senator and had brought the Senate "into dishonor and disrepute."

This criticism comes nearly five years after the senator from Wisconsin catapulted himself into public prominence by sensationally claiming that there were "205 card-carrying communists" in the State Department. This proved to be merely the first in a string of unsubstantiated accusations against public figures, such as the highly respected George Marshall, whom McCarthy said was part

of a "conspiracy so immense and an infamy so black as to dwarf any previous such venture in the history of man." Nonetheless, the Cold War has created a context of public and political concern that has rendered such accusations plausible.

With the Democrats in Washington, McCarthy's party supported his claims of "20 years of treason," but when the Republicans took office in January 1953 the senator, shielded by his power, his willingness to denounce, and his public support, focused his attacks on Republican, and even Eisenhower, appointees. However, it is evident he had outlived his political usefulness to the GOP and, when he slipped, few were willing to catch him.

His downfall came after his strident attacks on the top echelons of the US Army this year. When the investigations were broadcast on network television, the ugly reality of the senator's bluster, bullying, brutishness, sarcasm, and lack of principle were transmitted into every home, embarrassing Senate colleagues and undermining his crucial public support.

Actor Paul Robeson was a victim of McCarthyism.

Berlin, Germany, January 31: Free elections in a reunited Germany are discussed at the Four Power Foreign Ministers' conference. The proposal is rejected.
UK, February 12: A report by the British Standing Committee on cancer says cigarette smoking is directly linked to lung cancer.
Marshall Islands, March 22: Japanese fishermen have severe radiation sickness after exposure to the fallout from the US hydrogen bomb test at Bikini Atoll on March 1.

USSR, March 25: The Soviet Union grants sovereignty to East Germany.
USA, May 2: Walt Disney announces his plan to build Disneyland, a massive theme park of a type never seen before, in California.
Oxford, England, May 6: A medical student, Roger Bannister, runs a mile in under four minutes at the Iffley Road Sports Ground.
Vietnam, May 8: After 55 days of bloody battle, the French military outpost Dien Bien Phu falls to the Vietminh.

USA, May 17: The Supreme Court deems racial segregation in public schools unlawful in the landmark case of Brown v. Board of Education of Topeka (No. 1).
New Guinea, June 10: A hitherto unknown tribe of 100,000 people has been found.
Geneva, Switzerland, July 20: War in Indo-China ends with the signing of the Geneva Accords.
Christchurch, New Zealand, August 28: Two NZ teenage girls are found guilty of murdering the mother of one of them in a brutal bashing.

Manila, Phillipines, September 8: The Southeast Asia Treaty Organization (SEATO) is established. Signatories to the treaty are France, Australia, New Zealand, Pakistan, Phillipines, Thailand, the UK, and the USA.
Algeria, September 9: A series of earthquakes in Orleansville claims 1,460 lives.
USA, October 7: Marilyn Monroe and Joe DiMaggio are divorced, just nine months after their marriage in San Francisco.

Egypt, October 19: Egypt and Britain agree to terms over the Suez Canal.
Algeria, November 1: NLF guerillas launch a full-scale attack on significant infrastructure in a fight for its independence from France.
New York, USA, November 12: The immigration center on Ellis Island closes today.
Washington DC, USA, December 2: Senator Joseph McCarthy is condemned by the US Congress for misconduct.

Rosa Parks

Terrified Black Community Expelled at Gunpoint

Johannesburg, South Africa, February 9: Today in Johannesburg about 65,000 terrified residents of crowded Sophiatown were awakened by barked orders from 2,000 soldiers and policemen who were armed with truncheons and machine guns. The residents were compelled, at gunpoint, to load their movable possessions into trucks while demolition teams began bulldozing their homes. Sounds of screaming and crying children filled the air as the people were taken to crudely constructed two-room houses in the newly created black township of Meadowlands. Some do not qualify for re-settlement and will have to find their own accommodation elsewhere.

Sophiatown is, or was, a working-class, racially mixed area of Johannesburg. In spite of its poverty and the gang-related violence, it possessed a lively culture, a close-knit but diverse community, and a very active nightlife. However, it is to be completely destroyed to make way for a white community under the Group Areas Act, which is compelling all races to live in separate areas of the city, with the best locations to be reserved for whites.

Communist Military Alliance Signed in Warsaw

Warsaw, Poland, May 14: After a three-day conference in Poland, the USSR and its allies have agreed upon a mutual security pact. It is intended to strengthen the military and other ties between the eight signatories—the USSR, Albania, Bulgaria, Czechoslovakia, East Germany, Hungary, Poland, and Romania. Their armed forces will be placed under one central command

and all have agreed to assist one another if any one of them is attacked.

The pact was signed within two weeks of West Germany's inclusion in NATO. The re-arming of a country that recently invaded Russia is clearly a prospect that makes the USSR uneasy.

The Times in London has noted that the agreement allows the USSR to place

Martin Luther King Jr. outlines bus boycott strategies to his organizers.

its troops in the seven other countries, thereby enhancing its control of those states. Whatever the case, the formalized NATO versus Warsaw Pact alignments further entrench the schism between east and west and ratchet up the tension.

Black Bus Boycott Staged in Montgomery

Montgomery, USA, December 5: A quite remarkable event has occurred in Montgomery, Alabama, this Monday morning. The city's buses, which are usually heavily occupied by black citizens, passed by all day with virtually no colored passengers.

The story started last Thursday evening when a middle-aged Negro woman named Rosa Parks boarded her bus, at the conclusion of her working day as a seamstress at a department store. The segregation laws of the southern states stipulate

separate seating for whites and coloreds, with Negroes at the rear. If the white section is filled, colored passengers must give up their seats and stand, in order that all white passengers may be seated.

Tension arose on the bus when the white section filled and a white man was left standing. The driver demanded that Mrs Parks stand, but she refused. A policeman was duly called and Mrs Parks, a respected member of her community, was placed under arrest. That evening leading figures from the Negro community arranged a boycott of the city buses for this Monday morning and advised the community via leaflets. The unity of the response has been quite remarkable.

At an electrifying meeting of thousands of Negroes at Holt Street Baptist Church this evening, there was a unanimous vote to continue the boycott, which will be led by 26-year-old minister Dr Martin Luther King Jr. The action is bound to affect the bus companies economically. Negro community leaders have a number of requests, including that Negroes be permitted to retain their seats in the colored section if the white section becomes full, greater courtesy to colored passengers, and colored drivers for predominantly black routes.

Mrs Parks appeared in court today and was fined $10 and $4 costs.

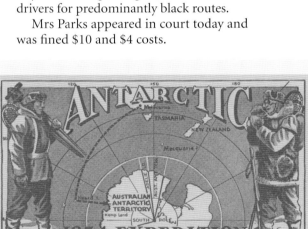

A postcard commemorating the 1954 Australian Antarctic expedition.

Nikita Khrushchev

> "WE ARE NOT AT WAR WITH EGYPT. WE ARE IN AN ARMED CONFLICT."
>
> ANTHONY EDEN (1897–1977), BRITISH STATESMAN AND PRIME MINISTER, ON THE SUEZ CRISIS, 1956

> "RUSSIAN COMMUNISM IS THE ILLEGITIMATE CHILD OF KARL MARX AND CATHERINE THE GREAT."
>
> CLEMENT ATLEE (1883–1967), BRITISH STATESMAN AND PRIME MINISTER, 1956

Soviets Denounce Stalin

Washington DC, USA, March 18: The text of a secret speech by Soviet leader Nikita Khrushchev last month was made public in Washington today. It consisted of an extraordinary denunciation of the former leader Joseph Stalin, who died in 1953. At a closed session, Khrushchev had referred to Lenin's will, in which Lenin had warned that Stalin would use his power corruptly. Krushchev referred to a reign of "suspicion, fear, and terror," and violent nationalism.

Khrushchev said Stalin repeatedly made false accusations, authorized torture to extract confessions, arranged assassinations, and blamed them on others who were, in turn, arrested and shot. He criticized Stalin's conduct of World War II, and the mass deportation of ethnic groups from their homelands. The speech has not been made public in the USSR.

Hungarian Ally Savaged by Russian Bear

Budapest, Hungary, November 4: Soviet troops and about 1,000 tanks poured into the streets of Budapest this morning, accompanied by an air-force bombardment of the Hungarian capital.

Relations between the allies began to deteriorate under the prime ministership of Imre Nagy, who tried to implement reforms, such as an end to peasant collectives and the forced development of heavy industry. Nagy was dismissed from office and expelled from the party last year, and a more "orthodox," but unpopular, communist regime returned.

However, Khrushchev's denunciation of Stalinism earlier this year and the recent challenge to Soviet authority in Poland appear to have fueled the desire for liberalization. On October 23, about

time out

The popular black singer Nat "King" Cole was attacked on stage in Birmingham, Alabama, by a group of white supremacists. He has often been criticized by African Americans for not taking a stronger stance on the issue of civil rights.

100,000 students and workers took to the streets of Budapest, demanding an end to Soviet rule, the withdrawal of Soviet troops, freedom of the press, free elections, and the return of Imre Nagy.

The demonstration turned violent when police began firing on the crowds, and the revolt soon spread to other Hungarian cities. Soviet tanks opened fire on unarmed protesters on October 25, causing hundreds of casualties. By the following day thousands lay dead on the streets but the protests still did not abate. Nagy was reinstated as prime minister, and he pledged reform. The Soviet troops began pulling out of Budapest five days ago. However, it seems that Nagy's announcement of a return to a multi-party state and the withdrawal of Hungary from the Warsaw Pact alliance with the USSR was too much for Moscow.

Nagy has appealed for assistance from the West, but no support seems to be forthcoming. There are rumors he has been captured by Soviet forces, which

have announced that they have "crushed" the "reactionary conspiracy."

Suez Crisis Over

Egypt, November 8: Fighting is at a halt in Egypt. The crisis was precipitated on July 26 when President Nasser of Egypt an-nounced he would nationalize the Suez Canal Company (which was owned mainly by British and French interests), in order to raise the money for the building of the Aswan Dam on the Nile.

When Israel launched a military attack against Egypt 10 days ago, Britain and France demanded that both sides cease hostilities and offered troops to keep the peace. When President Nasser refused, British and French forces began to bomb Egyptian airfields, landed troops around the Suez Canal three days ago, and engaged in heavy fighting.

The Anglo-French effort has met with strong criticism at home and from the USA, the Commonwealth, the UN, and the USSR. Diplomatic and economic pressure, particularly from the USA, has led to a complete cessation of hostilities.

Russian T54/55 tanks in Budapest during the riots that broke out against the communist regime in 1956.

Cyprus, January 12: British troops are sent to quell the rising tension between Greeks and Turks.

Melbourne, Australia, January 12: A survey reveals that the lung disease asbestosis is affecting one-third of all Victoria's miners.

USSR, February 24: Nikita Khrushchev, the First Secretary, speaks out against Stalin's excesses.

Karachi, Pakistan, March 23: Pakistan is declared an Islamic Republic.

Monaco, April 19: Actress Grace Kelly marries Prince Rainier III of Monaco.

Poznan, Poland, June 29: Workers stage an uprising against communist rule, only to be crushed when police open fire; tanks and machine guns are used to control crowds.

London, England, July 5: The Clean Air Bill is passed today in a bid to remove the threat of the city's toxic "pea soup" smogs.

Alexandria, Egypt, July 26: Egypt takes control of the Suez Canal just two weeks after the last British troops leave, nationalizing the Suez Canal Company which controls the canal.

Hungary, October 23: Hungarians begin a nationwide rebellion against communism, demanding freedom from Soviet rule.

Budapest, Hungary, October 25: Armed with 500 tanks, the Soviets open fire with machine guns on men, women and children, with estimates of up to 3,000 killed.

Egypt, October 29: Israel invades Egypt, entering via the Sinai Peninsula and heading toward the Suez Canal.

Cairo, Egypt, October 31: French and British forces bomb military airfields after a 12-hour ultimatum to Egypt and Israel to withdraw is ignored.

Budapest, Hungary, November 4: Soviet troops take Budapest.

Egypt, November 6: The UN Security Council imposes sanctions against the UK, over yesterday's invasion by the UK and France of Port Said in the Suez Canal.

Egypt, November 8: The UN imposes a cease-fire in the Suez Canal which will take effect at midnight.

Melbourne, Australia, November 22: The Games of the XVIth Olympiad begin today.

A New Common Market for Europe

Rome, Italy, March 25: An economic association known as the European Economic Community formally came into being when the Treaty of Rome was signed today by Italy, France, the Netherlands, West Germany, Luxembourg, and Belgium. The treaty is intended to create a kind of common market between the member states.

More specifically, it is intended to further the shared objectives of free trade, joint economic, financial, agricultural, and social policies, coordinated transportation systems, the free movement of capital, entrepreneurship and labor, and the abolition of restrictive trading practices. Underlying political objectives have also been suggested, such as the reconciliation of France and Germany, and the broader development of a political union in Western Europe that can reduce fears of war.

101st Airborne Division Protects Schoolchildren

Little Rock, Arkansas, USA, September 25: The United States awoke this morning to the extraordinary sight of 1,000 US paratroopers in occupation of the town of Little Rock, Arkansas.

The troops are there to protect nine Negro children who successfully applied to attend the local high school. Their application was prompted by a 1954 Supreme Court decision, which ruled that segregated schooling was inherently unequal and therefore unconstitutional.

The story began on September 3, the first day of the school year, when Governor Orval Faubus mobilized 250 National Guardsmen to stand at the perimeter of the school and prevent the entry of the Negro schoolchildren, claiming that, if they should attend, "Blood will run in the

Military escorts guard black students at Little Rock Central High.

streets." The following day, the National Guardsmen were joined by a mob of furious people, chanting anti-integrationist slogans. The children were supposed to be driven to school in police cars.

However, one child, Elizabeth Eckford, did not receive this message and, arriving early and alone, she was barred entry by a bayoneted National Guardsman. The crowd called her unprintable names and the cry "Lynch her!" was heard.

After being spat upon by an older woman, Elizabeth ran to a nearby bench followed by calls to "drag her to a tree." She was frozen on the seat in terror, as guardsmen looked on impassively. She was eventually escorted onto a bus by a white woman. None of the children were admitted to school that day.

President Eisenhower then met with Governor Faubus, who promised that the children would be accommodated. He withdrew the National Guard but made no arrangements to ensure their safety.

Two days ago, the children attended school for the first time. As a police car drove them into the grounds, the crowd outside cursed and shouted, and some women wept hysterically. Journalists, colored and white, were set upon, and the mob outside the school swelled to a thousand during the course of the day. The children were escorted home early.

Yesterday, the mayor of Little Rock requested federal troops, and last night President Eisenhower went on national television calling for law and order to be respected. Today, the paratroopers ringed the school, and escorted the children to school in armed military vehicles. Each student was accompanied by an individual armed guard. It does not appear likely that this extraordinary state of affairs will end in the near future.

Gamal Abdel Nasser

Laika the Cosmic Dog

USSR, November 3: Just one month after the historic launch of the Soviet satellite *Sputnik*, *Sputnik II* is now orbiting Earth. However, this time it is not an unmanned spaceflight. Inside is a dog named Laika.

Monitors are transmitting data to Earth about Laika's vital signs so that scientists can learn about the impact of weightlessness and solar radiation. Laika has been specially trained to cope with the close confinement of the space capsule. There are rumors that she is to be catapulted back to Earth, but the dog's fate is not clear. Protests from animal lovers around the world have been vocal.

Laika's transport is about 13 ft (4 m) high with a diameter of 6 ft (1.8 m), weighs 1,100 lb (500 kg), and is traveling at a rate of 5 miles (8 km) per second.

Laika the dog in her specially designed capsule in *Sputnik II*.

London, England, January 10: Prime Minister Anthony Eden resigns due to ill health. His deputy Harold Macmillan takes his place.
West Africa, March 6: The Gold Coast and Togoland become Ghana, gaining independence from Britain.
Egypt, March 8: Minor ships are allowed entry into the Suez Canal as Israeli troops leave Egypt, but President Nasser bars the UN's toll-sharing plan.

Gaza, March 11: The USA sends a warning to Egypt, reconfirming Gaza is under the control of the United Nations, after President Nasser claimed Gaza on March 10.
Egypt, March 15: President Nasser bars Israeli ships from entering the Suez Canal.
Rome, Italy, March 25: The Treaty of Rome is signed by France, West Germany, Italy, Belgium, the Netherlands and Luxembourg to create the European Economic Community (EEC).

Egypt, April 10: The Suez Canal re-opens to all shipping.
Jordan, April 25: King Hussein declares martial law in the aftermath of a failed coup earlier this month.
Tunisia, July 25: Tunisia abolishes its monarchy to become a republic.

Arkansas, USA, September 24: The president calls in troops to quell mobs preventing integration of black students into Little Rock Central High School.
USSR, October 4: The space age begins as the USSR launches *Sputnik I*, the first satellite to orbit Earth.
Australia, October 13: New South Wales and Queensland are faring worst in the grip of a devastating national drought.

USSR, November 3: The Soviets launch *Sputnik II*, carrying a dog called Laika. It is the first craft to take an animal into space.
Sydney, Australia, December 2: The city is ringed by bushfires, driven by gale-force winds.
Oslo, Norway, December 10: The Nobel Peace Prize is awarded to Canadian politician Lester Bowles Pearson for his role in using peacekeeping forces to resolve the highly volatile Suez Canal crisis.

Scientists Petition for an End to Nuclear Tests

Linus Pauling

"When you're abroad you're a statesman... at home you're just a politician."

HAROLD MACMILLAN (1894–1986), BRITISH STATESMAN AND PRIME MINISTER, 1958

"Don't tell me that man doesn't belong out there. Man belongs wherever he wants to go; and he'll do plenty well when he gets there."

WERNHER VON BRAUN (1912–1977), AMERICAN ROCKET SCIENTIST, ON THE POSSIBILITY OF SPACEFLIGHTS

New York, USA, January 15: Today Nobel Prize-winning scientist Linus Pauling has presented a petition to the United Nations signed by over 11,000 scientists from 49 countries. It calls for an end to the atmospheric testing of nuclear bombs and decries the world's nuclear stockpiles.

By putting the prestige and expertise of science behind the petition, Pauling is trying to draw attention to what he says his studies suggest are the dangers posed by atomic radiation to human health and Earth's environment.

However, clearly Pauling does not have the support of all scientists. Some, such as Edmund Teller, who is known as the "father of the hydrogen bomb," have strongly criticized Pauling and defended the position of the US Government, as have most members of the press.

Some years ago Pauling's activism for peace led the State Department to revoke his passport. However, world opinion led to a reversal of this decision when Pauling was unable to travel to Sweden to collect his Nobel Prize for Chemistry in 1954.

First Successful Trek across Antarctica

Antarctica, March 2: The Commonwealth Transantarctic Expedition represents the first known occasion on which human beings have successfully trekked across the surface of Antarctica. The 12-member British team, led by Dr Vivian Fuchs, set off from the Shackleton Base on the Weddell Sea late last November. Since then the team has successfully traveled 2,158 miles (3,474 km) using specially adapted tractors through uncharted terrain to arrive safely at New Zealand's Scott Base on the Ross Sea today.

The historic journey took 99 days. En route they arrived at the South Pole, to find New Zealand's Edmund Hillary

already waiting for them with a supply support team. In 1953, Hillary and Tenzing Norgay had been the first to successfully climb Mt Everest.

Hillary had set off from Scott Base and arrived at the South Pole on January 3. In the process, Hillary became only the third party to reach the pole, preceded by Roald Amundsen in December 1911 and Robert Scott's party, which arrived 35 days later, only to die of starvation.

Iraqi Coup a Threat to Regional Stability

Middle East, July 17: Two thousand British paratroopers have flown into Amman today after reports that Syrian troops have been gathering on the border with Jordan. Already, 1,700 US marines have arrived in Lebanon.

This crisis in the Arab world was precipitated three days ago when the monarchy of Iraq was overthrown in a military coup, a republic declared, and King Faisal

and several members of the royal family and their associates were murdered.

Iraqis are said to be celebrating in the streets. Suspected coup leader, Major-General Abdul Karim el Qasim, has declared himself Iraq's new prime minister, defense minister, and commander-in-chief. Broadcasts from Baghdad Radio have put forward the point of view of the new regime, declaring that the army had freed the people from a corrupt government which had been installed by imperialist powers.

This and other rhetoric appears to align this coup with the anti-Western, pro-communist Arab nationalism that was the inspiration for the successful military takeover in Egypt in 1952.

Some Middle Eastern and Western powers are concerned about regional stability, links to the Soviet Union, and oil. Specifically, there is concern that Arab nationalist coups may inspire nationalists in other countries to rise up and that pro-Western, oil-supplying states may fall.

President Eisenhower's decision to send troops to Lebanon is in response to a call for assistance from President Camille Chamoun of Lebanon. This came after a Muslim rebellion there and fears of an overthrow aimed at creating stronger ties to the newly created United Arab Republic (UAR) of Egypt and Syria. King Hussein of Jordan has also condemned the Iraqi coup, fearing invasion from the UAR and rebellion within.

Fears of destabilization in the region have escalated further as the Soviet Union has announced major maneuvers near the Turkish and Persian borders.

Iraq was one of the signatories of the 1955 Middle East Treaty Organization, intended to counter the threat of Soviet influence over the oil-producing regions. Fears exist today that it may withdraw and enhance ties with the USSR.

US marines board ship as they withdraw from Lebanon.

Antarctica, January 3: Edmund Hillary reaches the South Pole.

London, England, January 3: The creation of the West Indies Federation, with Lord Hailes as governor-general, is announced. It includes Barbados, Jamaica, Trinidad, Tobago, and the Windward and Leeward Islands.

New York, January 15: Over 11,000 scientists from 49 countries petition to ban nuclear testing.

Middle East, February 1: Syria and Egypt merge to form the United Arab Republic.

Antarctica, March 2: The Commonwealth Transantarctic Expedition is successfully completed.

Yemen, March 2: Yemen announces it will join the United Arab Republic.

USA, March 27: CBS Laboratories today announce the development of stereophonic records, which require two loudspeakers and provide a superior sound.

Algiers, May 13: A mass demonstration of 40,000 French settlers rebelling against the Algerian nationalists creates a political crisis for France.

China, May 23: To update China's economy, Mao Tse-tung begins his "Great Leap Forward."

Algiers, June 4: General de Gaulle, recalled as premier, attempts to convince French rebels that reconciliation is essential to Algeria's future.

Hungary, June 16: Former prime minister Imre Nagy is executed, along with other leaders of a "free" Hungary.

Alaska, July 10: The largest known tsunami rises 1,600 feet (500 meters) up a mountain, caused by an earthquake and rock fall.

Middle East, July 17: Britain sends 2,000 paratroopers to Jordan, two days after the USA dispatches 1,700 marines to Lebanon.

Honshu, Japan, September 27: Typhoon Vera kills almost 5,000 and leaves thousands more injured on the island of Honshu. It is the worst human disaster in Japan since World War II.

Vatican City, Italy, October 28: After 12 ballots, Angelo Giuseppe Roncalli has been elected as Pope John XXIII after the death of Pope Pius XII.

USSR, October 31: Boris Pasternak, the author of *Doctor Zhivago*, refuses his Nobel Prize in Literature after his expulsion from the Union of Soviet Writers.

Africa, November: The French-ruled African countries of Mali, Mauritania, Congo, Chad, and Gabon are made republics this month.

Regime Falls in Cuba

Santiago, Cuba, January 1: Cubans took to the streets this morning, to celebrate the flight of their hated ruler, President Batista, who took power in a coup in 1952.

His departure has been prompted by the approach to Santiago of Fidel Castro's rebel army. Castro was imprisoned for two years in 1953 for acting against the Batista regime. He then left Cuba but returned in 1956 to lead the guerrillas.

The success of the rebels is thought to be due, in part, to popular support, reflecting the hatred of the Cuban people for the Batista regime's ruthless suppression of opposition and dissent, which included torture and summary executions. Hundreds of political prisoners were released from prison today.

Fiftieth State Declared

Hawaii, USA, August 21, 1959: Hawaii is now officially the fiftieth state of the USA. The road to statehood has been a long one, starting with the overthrow of the native monarchy in 1893. The coup was staged by nine Americans, two Britons, and two Germans, and received US military support. A republic was formed in 1894 but sugar planters requested that the US government annex Hawaii in 1898 and, despite some opposition, Hawaii became a US territory in 1900.

In March this year the US Congress passed the legislation necessary for Hawaii to become a state and President Eisenhower signed the bill. A plebiscite in June indicated about 93 percent of Hawaiians supported statehood and the union was declared today.

It is only seven months since the United States welcomed Alaska as its forty-ninth state. Alaska was purchased from Russia in 1867, but local government was largely ignored there until the gold strikes of the late 1890s swelled the population and brought it to national attention. It was declared a territory in 1912. Statehood bills have been many but it was only on June 30 last year that Congress voted to admit Alaska to the union. President Eisenhower issued the statehood proclamation on January 3 of this year.

Fulgencio Batista

Founding Dates of States and Provinces of North America
- United States of America
- Canada

Cuba, January 2: Revolution leader Fidel Castro has seized power as president. Incumbent General Fulgencio Batista resigns and flees to the Dominican Republic.
Alaska, USA, January 3: Alaska is admitted as the 49th state of the USA, with Juneau as its capital.
USSR, January 12: The space race heats up as the USSR's *Lunik* goes into orbit around the moon. It is the first craft to leave Earth's gravitational field.

Cyprus, February 19: Cyprus gains independence in an agreement signed by Britain, Turkey and Greece.
Zimbabwe (Rhodesia), February 27: A state of emergency is declared as violent outbreaks are feared.
Washington DC, USA, March 3: Approval is granted for Hawaii to become the 50th US state.
Tibet, March 31: The Dalai Lama flees to India following a national uprising against China. The Chinese arrest and kill thousands of rebels and install a harsh government.

North America, April 25: The St Lawrence Seaway is completed, enabling ships to sail from the Atlantic Ocean to the Great Lakes.
Rome, Italy, May 10: Italian archeologists find the remnants of Emperor Nero's gardens.
London, England, May 24: The UK and the USSR sign a five-year trade pact.
Atlantic Ocean, May 28: Able and Baker are the first animals to return from space, as the spacecraft with the two live monkeys on board splashes down.

Singapore, June 3: Lee Kuan Yew is sworn in as the first prime minister of Singapore, after winning the national elections. The country becomes a self-governing state in the British Commonwealth.
London, England, June 11: A new kind of vehicle that goes on both land and sea, the hovercraft, is revealed today.
Olduvai Gorge, Tanzania, July 17: Dr Mary Leakey discovers the oldest hominid skull. "Nutcracker Man" dates back at least 1.8 million years.

Colombo, Sri Lanka (Ceylon), September 26: Prime minister Solomon Bandaranaike dies in hospital after being shot at point blank range the previous day. His assassin is a Buddhist monk, Talduwe Somarama.
Aswan, Egypt, October 31: Contracts to build the Aswan Dam, which will be one of the world's largest reservoirs, are signed by the USSR and Egypt.

Dr Francis Crick

Comet's Core Like a Dirty Snowball

New York, USA, March 31, 1950: The latest issue of the *Astrophysical Journal* contains an article by astronomer Fred Whipple that posits a new theory: That the core of a comet is not made solely of dust and sand, as previously thought, but is, in fact, a very solid "icy conglomerate" of dust cemented by ice and other frozen molecules. Whipple suggests that, in the presence of the sun, the outer layers vaporize and solar wind causes massive tails to form, which consist not just of loosened dust but also of volatile gases.

Whipple was born in Iowa in 1906. He wanted to be a tennis professional until thwarted by childhood polio; he became an astronomer instead and has discovered a number of comets and asteroids. He has also been rewarded by President Truman for inventing a wartime device that produced tinfoil fragments that confused enemy radar when released from an aircraft.

UNIVAC a Certified Genius

New York, USA, November 11, 1952: One of the little-publicized stories of last week's election is the role played by the extraordinary UNIVAC computer used by CBS newsman Walter Cronkite. Fed just a tiny fraction of the counted votes, it was able to calculate that General Eisenhower would win. As CBS was wary of the new technology, it withheld the computer's assessment until the vote count was over, but it proved to be accurate.

The UNIVAC (Universal Automatic Computer) was developed in the late 1940s by engineers J. Presper Eckert and John Mauchly, who had previously invented ENIAC, one of the first electronic digital computers that was made for, and delivered to, the army in 1947 for the refinement of its ballistics tests.

The UNIVAC computer was used to tabulate the votes on election night.

Specifically designed to handle business and administrative data, UNIVAC is the first commercial computer to be built in this country, and it is intended to supplant current punch-card accounting machines. The first contract was with the US Census Bureau, which received its system on March 31 last year and dedicated it on June 14. It cost $159,000.

Since then the US Air Force, the Army Map Service, and the Atomic Energy Commission (AEC) have also purchased systems. It was the AEC that made its computer available for the election analysis. Sales to businesses have been retarded by the fact that UNIVAC utilizes magnetic tape and cannot read the punch-cards on which businesses currently have their data stored, although equipment to automatically transfer the data is being developed.

UNIVAC is over 14 ft (4 m) long, nearly 8 ft (2.4 m) wide and 9 ft (2.7 m) high, and the system occupies 350 sq ft (32 sq m). It weighs 29,000 lb (13,182 kg), uses 5,200 vacuum tubes, can perform nearly 2,000 operations per second, and reads 7,200 decimal digits per second. This renders it far and away the fastest business machine in the world.

The Secret of Life Unraveled

Cambridge, England, April 25, 1953: Today two scientists working at Cambridge University, James Watson and Francis Crick, have published an article that details a miraculous breakthrough in our understanding of human reproduction. It concerns an organic chemical known as deoxyribonucleic acid, or DNA. It was deduced 10 years ago that DNA played a role in genetic inheritance, but it was not known until now how it encoded genetic information and conveyed that information to cells so that they might construct a particular organism.

The article describes the structure of DNA as a double helix. This is like a sort of spiral staircase consisting of two vertical strands of sugar-phosphate coiled around each other (the hand-rails). The strands are connected to each other by a

Pioneer geneticist James Watson with a molecular model of DNA.

New York, USA, March 23, 1950: The United Nations sets up the World Meteorological Organization.
USA, March 31, 1950: *Astrophysical Journal* reports new insights into the nature of comets by astronomer Fred Whipple. He proposes comets are "dirty snowballs," consisting of ice mixed with rock particles.
Chicago, USA, June 17, 1950: The world's first kidney transplant operation is performed by Doctor Richard Lawler.

London, England, February 10, 1951: An article in *the Lancet* describes Munchausen's Syndrome, a psychiatric condition in which people feign illnesses to attract medical attention.
Philadelphia, USA, June 15, 1951: Doctor John Mauchly and J. Presper Eckert Jr. demonstrate UNIVAC, the first commercial computer.
Mexico City, Mexico, October 15, 1951: Dr Carl Djerassi develops a synthetic oral contraceptive.

Pennsylvania, USA, March 8, 1952: The first artificial heart is implanted into a patient.
Washington DC, USA, May 7, 1952: Geoffrey Dummer publishes his idea for an integrated circuit chip.
California, USA, November 11, 1952: John Mullin and Wayne Johnson demonstrate their invention of a video recorder.
Cambridge, UK, April 25, 1953: James Watson and Francis Crick solve the mystery of reproduction in their findings of the molecular model of DNA.

UK, May 14, 1953: Scientists report they believe jet planes can damage eardrums and houses.
England, November 21, 1953: The "Piltdown Man," a skull found by Charles Dawson in Sussex in 1912 believed to be of an ancient human, is proven to be a hoax.
Iowa, USA, December, 1953: Frozen sperm is used to impregnate a woman for the first time.
Groton, USA, January 21, 1954: The USS *Nautilus*, the first atomic submarine, is launched today by First Lady Mamie Eisenhower.

USA, June 16, 1954: The first official flight of a vertical take-off and landing plane takes place.
Alabama, USA, November 30, 1954: A woman is struck by an 8.5-pound (4 kilogram) meteorite as she sleeps on her sofa, suffering only bad bruising.
Boston, USA, December 24, 1954: A kidney is transplanted from Ronald Herrick to his brother Richard.
USA, January 11, 1955: Lloyd Conover patents Tetracycline, an effective broad-spectrum antibiotic.

series of horizontal organic bases (the steps). It is argued that this structure splits into two separate halves and that each half then regenerates an exact replica of the missing strand, so that the original single strand becomes two, and so on.

The organic bases in the DNA constitute a code, which is deciphered by a mechanism within a cell. This mechanism uses the information as a blueprint to generate specific proteins. These proteins then determine a particular cell's structure as well as its function. Humans are made up of billions of these cells; each one is specifically built according to the instructions encoded in our DNA.

Piltdown Hoax Clarifies Human Development

London, England, November 24, 1953: A series of articles in *The Times* over the last four days has outlined the findings of scientists who have proven that the famous anthropological artefact, Piltdown Man, is a fake. Recent developments in fluorine testing have allowed experts to date the relic accurately, and they have found that it is an amalgam of elements that have been deliberately combined and tampered with to make them seem harmonious. In fact, the jawbone and canine tooth derive from a modern ape, the jaw has been carefully stained to make it look as one with the skull, and the tooth has been "artificially pared down." The cranium seems to be a genuine relic, perhaps 50,000 years old.

The remains were originally unveiled to headlines by the Natural History Museum in 1912. They were supplied by amateur anthropologist Charles Dawson, who obtained the cranial fragments from a gravel pit in Sussex.

Some experts were skeptical about the find, but doubts were allayed when similar

fragments were located nearly 2 miles (3 km) away. These too were cunningly altered and some were broken off from the artefacts found at the first site so that they may appear to derive from a separate example of the same species.

When it was first unveiled, Piltdown Man was presented as Darwin's Missing Link, an ancient common ancestor of both modern apes and modern humans. It has been suggested that British anthropologists were keen to place their country at the center of human evolution and were thus inclined toward this belief. However, far from being a let-down for modern science, the exposure of this hoax is a great boon to modern anthropology, as Piltdown Man has been a perplexing anomaly that does not fit in with the rest of the fossil record.

Christmas Present for Identical Twin

Boston, USA, December 24, 1954: Yesterday in Boston, Ronald Herrick gave his identical twin brother Richard the greatest gift one human being can give another—life. Richard had been diagnosed with nephritis and was facing complete kidney failure and death. Past attempts at organ transplant had failed, as the body's immune system rejects foreign tissue.

However, Richard was lucky in one respect; he had an identical twin brother whose tissue was identical and who was willing to give one of his healthy kidneys to his brother. The night before the surgery, the ailing Richard tried to cancel the procedure but Ronald stood firm, and doctors are now optimistic that the operation will have positive results.

The first human organ transplant to give a patient more than a moment's reprieve occurred in Illinois on June 17, 1950, when a kidney was taken from the

still-warm body of a recently deceased woman and given to Ruth Tucker of Indiana. The operation was kept secret but the story leaked out and made global headlines. A month later Mrs Tucker was allowed to return to her home. It was subsequently discovered that the kidney failed after only about six weeks, but it gave Mrs Tucker's good kidney a chance to revive and she remains alive today, although her health is in progressive decline.

Experiments with kidney transplants date back to early this century, when a kidney from another species was placed in a human, though it was not successful. Over the intervening years surgeons have learned of the need to match blood and tissue types to avoid organ rejection.

Piltdown Man

time out

In 1953 young Polish pilot Franciczek Jareck defected from behind the Iron Curtain to Denmark, delivering the first Russian-built MIG-15 jet fighter to the West. After a spectacular landing, the pilot gave himself up to Danish authorities and asked for asylum.

An optical projector used to show the motions of heavenly bodies.

Key Events

New York, USA, January 25, 1955: An atomic clock that is accurate to within one second every 300 years is developed.

Michigan, USA, April 12, 1955: The results of the field trials of Jonas Salk's polio vaccine reveal that the vaccine is effective.

New Jersey, USA, April 18, 1955: Albert Einstein dies, aged 76. Dr Thomas Harvey performs the autopsy and takes Einstein's brain home to study.

USA, April 26, 1955: Calvin Fuller and Gerald Pearson at Bell Laboratories develop a solar cell using a tiny sliver of silicon.

USA, July 24, 1956: Ernst Brandl and Hans Margreiter are granted a patent for oral penicillin.

USA, September 25, 1956: The first transatlantic telephone cable commences functioning.

California, USA, December, 1956: The Palomar sky survey, a seven-year project to photograph the entire northern sky, is completed this year.

London, England, February 28, 1957: Cancer experts express concern about the health of Australians exposed to radiation during British atomic tests.

Victoria, Australia, June 4, 1957: Koalas are relocated from Phillip Island to repopulate rural areas.

California, USA, September, 1957: Oceanographers Roger Revelle and Hans Seuss reveal that oceans cannot absorb all carbon dioxide being released, which will lead to global warming.

Switzerland, May 13, 1958: Velcro is trademarked by Georges de Mestral.

New York, USA, August 27, 1958: The *Nautilus* crew celebrates its first voyage under the North Pole in a tickertape parade.

USA, September, 1958: A prototype of an integrated circuit is created on a piece of silicon.

Cleveland, USA, October 29, 1958: Doctor Mason Sones makes the first diagnostic coronary angiogram.

UK, January 24, 1959: John Cockcroft and Lewis Strauss succeed in creating nuclear fusion.

USA, March 9, 1959: Radar contact is made with the planet Venus.

California, USA, March 24, 1959: Charles Townes is granted a patent for the maser, a precursor to the laser, which is used to amplify radio signals.

South Africa, October 17, 1959: De Beers announces the manufacture of synthetic diamonds.

World, December 1, 1959: The Antarctic Treaty is signed by 12 nations, agreeing to keep the continent free from military use and to use it for scientific research.

Dr Jonas Salk

Polio Is on the Run

New York, USA, April 12, 1955: Today was a landmark day in medical history—the poliomyelitis vaccine created by Dr Jonas Salk has been declared both safe and effective, and it will be released for general usage. This announcement follows a successful national test undertaken last year, which involved over one million children aged between 6 and 9.

Polio is an infectious disease caused by a virus that enters through the respiratory system and spreads throughout the body to the central nervous system. Typically, it causes influenza-like symptoms. Most

> "*OUR IGNO-RANCE IS NOT SO VAST AS OUR FAILURE TO USE WHAT WE KNOW.*"
>
> M. KING HUBBERT (1903–1989), AMERICAN GEOPHYSICIST

> "*SCIENCE IS NOT FORMAL LOGIC—IT NEEDS THE FREE PLAY OF THE MIND IN AS GREAT A DEGREE AS ANY OTHER CREATIVE ART. IT IS TRUE THAT THIS IS A GIFT WHICH CAN HARDLY BE TAUGHT, BUT ITS GROWTH CAN BE ENCOURAGED IN THOSE WHO ALREADY POSSESS IT.*"
>
> MAX BORN (1882–1970), GERMAN PHYSICIST AND NOBEL PRIZE WINNER, 1954

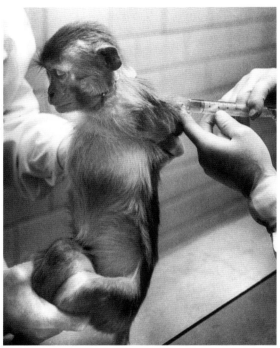

A monkey being administered the Salk vaccine for testing.

patients recover within a few days but, in severe cases, the disease can damage nerve cells in the brain stem and spinal cord, resulting in anything from temporary weakness to total and permanent paralysis. In some cases, the ability to talk and swallow is affected, and victims can suffocate on saliva. It can strike anyone, though young children are more vulnerable.

The disease of polio has been known since ancient Egyptian times. President Roosevelt was permanently paralyzed from the waist down in 1921. The vaccine's arrival is timely, as our country has recorded a very high incidence of the virus since 1942. In 1950 alone over 33,000 cases were recorded. Severe epidemics occurred around the world in 1952.

Doctor Salk's vaccine is based on a recognition that the human body acquires immunity to a virus through contact with a dead but intact sample of that virus. In this form it cannot produce the disease but stimulates human antibodies to recognize the virus, so that they will attack it and destroy it if it invades the body.

World's Greatest Scientist Dies after Long Illness

Princeton, USA, April 19, 1955: The world's most famous scientist, German-born theoretical physicist Albert Einstein, died of an aneurysm yesterday in New Jersey, at the age of 76. Einstein's mustache and shock of white hair have become familiar around the world—no mean feat for a man whose extraordinary contributions to modern science are almost impossible for the layman to properly understand.

In one remarkable year, 1905, when Einsten was just 26 years old, he published papers on the special theory of relativity, Brownian motion (which confirmed the atomic theory of matter), and the photoelectric effect. The latter gave birth to quantum theory, spawned the photoelectric cell, which made television and sound motion pictures possible, and earned him a 1921 Nobel Prize.

However, it is the theory of relativity with which he is most closely identified. A manuscript copy of the original 1905 paper sold for $6 million in 1944 at a Kansas City war bond rally. Einstein's theory introduced new concepts of space, time, gravitation, mass, and motion, and he gained public attention in 1919 when the theoretical predictions he made were exactly confirmed by solar eclipse studies. His famous equation $E = mc^2$ eventually led to the splitting of the atom, and hence to the atomic age. Amazingly, all of these theories were laid out before Einstein even had an academic position; at the time he was working as a clerk in the Swiss Patent Office.

Professor Einstein took up residence and a university position in the United States when Hitler rose to power in Germany in 1933, and he became a US citizen in 1940. In 1939 he prompted the development of the atomic bomb when he wrote a letter to President Roosevelt, warning him that Germany was developing nuclear fission.

Einstein was a lover of classical music, played the violin, had a strong compassion for the downtrodden peoples of the world, was a pacifist (where possible), became a strong advocate of global peace through global laws and government, lived a modest quiet life, was twice married, and was offered the presidency of Israel in 1952, though he turned it down, insisting he was not qualified.

Within hours of Einstein's death, his brain was removed and kept for scientific research. It is expected that in years to come, as techniques develop, it will be found to have some unusual qualities.

TV Goes to the Movies

Chicago, USA, April 15, 1956: Today, at the National Association of Radio and Television Broadcasters Show, the Ampex Corporation demonstrated an exciting new machine, the VR-1000—a videotape recorder that insiders say is set to revolutionize the industry.

Currently, most television goes live to air. Many smaller television stations cannot pick up a live broadcast from major players like CBS, NBC, or ABC, as they are not connected to a network. Stations that are part of a network but that exist in a different time zone can also be prevented from receiving live broadcasts, as this could mean screening the program at an inappropriate time slot. Thus kinescopes are made of broadcasts so that they can be sent to other stations for airing at an opportune moment.

The kines, as they are called, to date have never been of a very high quality. They are created by pointing a 16 mm or 35 mm camera at a TV monitor and

Scientific Achievements

Astronomy: Pictures of the far side of the moon transmitted from *Lunik III*; *Sputnik II* takes dog Laika into orbit.

Botany: It is suggested that a birth control pill could be produced using a drug derived from yams.

Chemistry: Salk polio vaccine developed; double-helix structure of DNA discovered.

Ecology: Antarctic Treaty promotes the continent for scientific research and devoted to peace; United Nations establishes the World Meteorological Organization.

Geology: Great Global Rift discovered in the Mid-Atlantic Ridge.

Mathematics: Radix sort, a computer algorithm used to sort items, is developed.

Medicine: Toposcope invented for brain EEG topography; first successful kidney transplant.

Physics: Nuclear-powered reactor first used to generate electricity.

Zoology: George Schaller began his observation of mountain gorillas.

Botanic Gardens
Brussels, Belgium

Observatories
Boulder, Colorado
Cambridge, England
Daun, Germany
Tucson, USA
Zimmerwald, Switzerland

Universities
University of Beirut, Lebanon
University of Daegu, South Korea
University of Jakarta, Indonesia
University of Riyadh, Saudi Arabia
University of Tehran, Iran

filming the image on the screen. This is not done for all programs, being reserved mostly for news programs and more prestigious shows. Nonetheless, it means that the television industry uses more film than all the Hollywood studios combined, making film a considerable expense to the industry.

The videotape machine used today recorded a picture before a live audience and then played it back. The results, in black and white, were of a very high standard. The machine lays an image on a 2-inch (5-cm) wide reel of magnetic tape, rather than on film, according to the same principles as today's audio recordings. One reel of tape will record about 60 minutes' worth of footage. It is expected this tape will be cheaper than film. This will allow the networks to pre-record many of their programs in the manner of movies, for high-quality reproduction at their own convenience.

Industry insiders are certain the big three networks will bite.

USSR Launches Sputnik

Washington DC, USA, October 4, 1957: The eyes of the world have become riveted on the skies this evening with the launch into space, by the Soviet Union, of a satellite named *Sputnik*. It is the first artificial object to venture beyond Earth's atmosphere and it is currently circling Earth once every 96 minutes, passing over the United States seven times a day.

There is some alarm here in Washington regarding its contents and the potential for launching nuclear weapons into Earth's orbit, although spokespersons for the USSR have given assurances that it is merely transmitting scientific data about its voyage. Concerns have also been expressed about our national priorities, with some decrying a nation gone flabby with self-indulgence in the face of spartan Soviet self-sacrifice. President Eisenhower has been informed but says he will not be speeding up our own satellite program.

According to Soviet sources, *Sputnik* is circling Earth at an approximate height of 560 miles (900 km). It consists of an aluminum sphere 23 in (58 cm) in diameter, weighs about 180 lb (80 kg), and has two radio antennae beaming signals back to Earth, much to the fascination of radio enthusiasts the world over.

J. Allen Hynek (left) and Fred Whipple plotting the orbit of *Sputnik I*.

Hovercraft Opens New Dimension in Travel

Hampshire, England, June 11, 1959: A remarkable sight met the eyes of onlookers as they gathered on a stretch of the Hampshire coast today. They witnessed the launch of a very unusual-looking vehicle, which floated just above the surface of both land and sea, without touching either. A sort of boat-helicopter, the aptly named "hovercraft" travels on a cushion of low-pressure air that is drawn in by propellers atop the vehicle. Steering is achieved by altering the direction of the air-flow.

The outlandish design is the work of Christopher Cockerell, who says he conceived the hovercraft while thinking of ways to improve boat speed by the reduction of friction. Cockerell was prevented from developing his idea on a commercial basis until recently because the government initially insisted on secrecy, owing to the potential military applications of the invention.

The experimental model measures 24 ft (7.3 m) high, 24 ft (7.3 m) wide and 30 ft (9 m) in diameter. The commercial versions are expected to be much larger and capable of crossing the channel. The hovercraft is being developed by aircraft manufacturer Saunders Roe.

Albert Einstein

Moon's Dark Side Revealed

London, England, October 26, 1959: Last night the Soviet Union's national television service revealed a series of 29 photographs taken three weeks ago by the space satellite *Lunik III*, and transmitted via radio to Earth over a distance of 300,000 miles (483,000 km). The snapshots, which were triggered by a remote-control process and recorded on 35 mm film, reveal the hitherto unseen surface of the moon's dark side, permanently hidden from view owing to the moon's orientation.

Lunik III was launched on the second anniversary of *Sputnik*'s launch and was timed to guarantee that the satellite would be between the moon and the sun, thus ensuring the surface would be illuminated for the photo opportunity. *Lunik III* has proven luckier than its two predecessors: One crashed onto the moon's surface and the other missed the moon altogether and continued on an infinite voyage, demonstrating how precise the calculations in such enterprises must be. Nonetheless, the achievement is remarkable.

Features captured in the photographs include a large plain, measuring about 185 miles (298 km) across, a 60-mile (96 km) crater and a mountain range. Some contention has arisen over Soviet-style names given to these features, such as Sovietsky Mountains and Sea of Moscow.

A Saunders Roe hovercraft, with a group of Royal Marines on board, at the Farnborough Airshow in Hampshire.

Ernest Hemingway

"I LOVE MICKEY MOUSE MORE THAN ANY WOMAN I HAVE EVER KNOWN."

WALT DISNEY (1901–1966), AMERICAN FILM PRODUCER AND ANIMATOR AND CREATOR OF MICKEY MOUSE

"A MELODY IS NOT MERELY SOMETHING YOU CAN HUM."

AARON COPLAND (1900–1990), AMERICAN COMPOSER

Crazy British Radio Comedy to Be Aired

London, England, May 27, 1951: Those present at the BBC's Aeolian Hall last night were fortunate. They witnessed the first performance of a very zany new radio comedy aptly called "Crazy People."

The show is performed by a group known as the Goons, consisting of Peter Sellers, Michael Bentine, Harry Secombe, and Spike Milligan. The script was written by Milligan in partnership with Larry Stephens. Each performer plays multiple parts. The plot, if it can be called that, is ludicrous (intentionally so), the characterization absurd in the extreme, the sound effects very silly indeed, and the dialogue surreal and full of ingenious puns. There appears to be a strong element of parody, although it is very broad and indirect, and not narrowly political.

Musical interludes provide a break from the manic pace and style of the comedy and give the advantage of allowing the audience time to digest some of the left-field jokes. The music is performed by the jazzy Ray Ellington Quartet, the harmonica virtuoso Max Geldray, and vocal group the Stargazers.

If this debut is anything to go by, this is a wholly new style of radio comedy. It will be broadcast tomorrow night.

The Goons: Harry Secombe, Michael Bentine, Peter Sellers, and Spike Milligan.

Husband-Wife Duo in Zany New TV Sitcom

New York, USA, October 16, 1951: A new sitcom went to air on CBS television last night. Entitled "I Love Lucy," it is an extension of Lucille Ball's recent successful radio show "My Favorite Husband."

Desi Arnaz and Lucille Ball in a still from the TV sitcom "I Love Lucy."

Her TV debut looks set to follow the comic marital trials and tribulations of Lucy and Ricky Ricardo, the latter played by Lucille Ball's real-life husband, Desi Arnaz, who introduced the conga line to the USA in the 1930s.

This pairing of a real-life couple adds plausibility to the show, particularly as Arnaz plays a Cuban bandleader—his occupation in real life. Rumors have it that, when Lucille Ball insisted Arnaz play the role of her television husband, CBS executives were concerned about how the audience would respond to his Cuban accent and to the mixed marriage, but she made it a precondition of doing the series.

This is a professional production (apparently it is costing sponsor Philip Morris $30,000 a week). Like "Amos 'n' Andy", the show uses three cameras, allowing a more cinematic style. More unusually, it was shot in Los Angeles before a wildly appreciative live studio audience, which may help to explain the dizzy atmosphere and air of spontaneity, something canned laughter does not seem to encourage.

The opening episode, a hyperactive Shakespearian comedy of errors, suggests that the hare-brained but childishly naive and lovable housewife Lucy has a penchant for getting herself into a hilarious mess. Lucille Ball's manic slapstick, superb timing, and expressive face come across better here than in the movies, where she has sometimes been found a little obvious. Some may find this broad humor a little lowbrow but, given the extraordinary popularity of Milton Berle, its exaggerated style seems destined to please.

But Is It Art?

New York, USA, November 10, 1952: There has been much discussion in recent years about a type of art known as "abstract expressionism." The best known painter of this school is Jackson Pollock, an exhibition of whose works opened today.

Life magazine devoted a centerspread to him in 1949, and last year *Time* called him "the greatest living American artist." Others claim that their five-year-old could do the same or, like Congressman Dondero, they feel such art is depraved and communistic. By contrast, the Congress for Cultural Freedom sees Pollock's work as exemplary of American freedom, democracy, and individualism.

For those unfamiliar with his style, Pollock's paintings can be a challenge. Recent footage reveals him walking around a canvas laid flat on the floor, entering into an absorbed state of reverie in which he almost dances about in a trance, flicking, splattering, dribbling,

Abstract expressionist painter Jackson Pollock.

Deborah Kerr

In addition to Best Picture, the film clinched Best Supporting Actress for Donna Reed, who plays a curiously fragile but rigid hostess at a USO club, and Best Director for Fred Zinnemann, who was unsuccessfully nominated for *High Noon* last year, as well as Best Screenplay (Daniel Taradash), Best Cinematography, Best Sound Recording, and Best Film Editing. Perhaps most notable was the Best Supporting Actor Oscar for Frank Sinatra, whose career has recently been on a distinct downhill slide. It is rumored he begged for the role. His screen test was the drunken scene in the bar where he rolls olives as craps. Zinnemann felt it was so well done that he cut the test into the picture.

Deborah Kerr, in the role of the barren estranged wife, lost out to Audrey Hepburn in *Roman Holiday*, while Burt Lancaster and Montgomery Clift were both unsuccessfully nominated for the Best Actor Oscar, which went to William Holden for his performance in *Stalag 17*.

When Jones's novel was released in 1951 it was said to be unfilmable. To gain production approval, the house of prostitution had to be changed to a USO club, the profanity, the savage stockade beatings, and Karen Holmes' gonorrhea had to be cut, and the corrupt Captain Holmes was shown to be drummed out of the army by his superiors rather than promoted. Shot in a mere 41 days for $1 million, the film has made a remarkable profit and has vindicated the risk-taking of all involved.

throwing, and pouring paint—a method said to allow for the direct expression of the subconscious mind. In Pollock's own words, the artist is "expressing his feelings rather than illustrating." No object from the real world is represented and there is no subject or center to these works. The abstractness of the works is also evident in their numeric titles, such as *Number 11*.

And yet, there is nothing of the art dandy about Jackson Pollock, who was born on a sheep ranch in Wyoming and who comes across as a tough blue-collar guy. He was thrown out of school twice for hitting instructors and is known for his hard drinking.

From Here to Eternity: An Instant Classic

Los Angeles, USA, March 25, 1954: This evening, at the 26th Academy Awards, Columbia Pictures' *From Here to Eternity* achieved a level of success not seen since *Gone with the Wind*. Adapted from James Jones' bestselling novel, it took home a remarkable 8 awards from 13 categories, thereby equaling the record set by David Selznick's 1939 Civil War classic.

Nobel Prize for Hemingway

Stockholm, Sweden, November 12, 1954: This year's Nobel Prize in Literature has gone to that adventurous man of letters, Ernest Hemingway. The accompanying citation singles out "his mastery of the art of narrative [and] the influence that he has exerted on contemporary style." The discipline, succinctness, directness, and clarity of his prose were surely influenced by his journalistic apprenticeship in a Kansas City newspaper, while his ability to capture accurately the rhythms and cadences of everyday American speech builds on the innovations of *Huckleberry Finn*. It is characteristic of Hemingway's approach to life and writing that he literally threw himself into the heat of battle by volunteering as an ambulance officer in World War I, in which he was severely wounded by shell splinters. His first-hand observations were distilled in the classic novel *A Farewell to Arms*. Hemingway's fascination with life-and-death struggles and his determination to participate in and write about them are also evident in his involvement with bullfighting, big-game hunting, big-game fishing, and the Civil War in his beloved Spain, where he was a major supporter of the Republicans. For some years now Hemingway has made sunny Cuba his home.

The movie poster for the hit musical comedy *Singin' in the Rain*.

California, USA, September 30, 1955: Film star James Dean crashes his Porsche near Paso Robles and dies, aged 24.

USA, October 3, 1955: A new kids' television program, "The Mickey Mouse Club," starts on ABC TV.

Zürich, Switzerland, January 27, 1956: Austrian conductor Erich Kleiber dies, aged 65.

Sussex, England, January 31, 1956: Creator of Winnie-the-Pooh, A. A. Milne, dies, aged 74.

USA, March 30, 1956: The first printed version of Woody Guthrie's song "This Land is Your Land" is produced.

London, England, August, 1956: *This Is Tomorrow*, an art exhibition featuring the new "Pop Art" style, is put on at Whitechapel Gallery.

London, England, October 3, 1956: The Bolshoi Ballet performs for the first time in the UK, at Covent Garden.

Philadelphia, USA, August 5, 1957: Dick Clark hosts the first episode of *American Bandstand* on ABC TV.

London, England, September 13, 1957: *The Mousetrap* by Agatha Christie becomes Britain's longest running play.

Sweden, October, 1957: The Nobel Prize in Literature is awarded to French writer and philosopher Albert Camus. He is the second-youngest recipient of the prize.

USA, December, 1957: *The Cat in the Hat* by Theodor Geisel (a.k.a. "Dr. Seuss") is released this year.

USA, January 10, 1958: Jerry Lee Lewis' hit "Great Balls of Fire" reaches number one.

Las Vegas, USA, January 29, 1958: Joanne Woodward and Paul Newman are married at the El Rancho Hotel-Casino.

Memphis, USA, March 24, 1958: Elvis Presley enters the army today, having received a draft notice.

New York, USA, August 18, 1958: Putnam publishes the first American edition of Vladimir Nabokov's controversial novel *Lolita*.

USA, January 5, 1959: A live children's television show, *Bozo the Clown*, premières.

Iowa, USA, February 3, 1959: Rock-and-rollers Buddy Holly, Ritchie Valens and J. P. Richardson die in a plane crash.

Arizona, USA, April 9, 1959: Acclaimed architect Frank Lloyd Wright dies, aged 91.

New York, USA, November 16, 1959: Rodgers and Hammerstein's musical *The Sound of Music* opens.

Elvis Presley

"I WAS BORN AT THE AGE OF TWELVE ON A METRO-GOLDWYN-MAYER LOT."

JUDY GARLAND (FRANCES GUMM) (1922–1969), AMERICAN ACTRESS AND SINGER

"THE NOTES I HANDLE NO BETTER THAN MANY PIANISTS. BUT THE PAUSES BETWEEN THE NOTES—AH, THAT IS WHERE THE ART RESIDES."

ARTUR SCHNABEL (1882–1951), AUSTRIAN PIANIST, 1948

No-Action Drama Opens on London Stage

London, England, August 3, 1955: This evening saw the first English performance of a new play by an Irish writer named Samuel Beckett, whose play is perplexing to say the least. It is essentially a drama without drama. The two main characters are tramps who do not go anywhere, do nothing of any note, and engage, for two acts, in some rather pointless, albeit learned, literate, and occasionally amusing, small talk and slapstick tomfoolery. All this while they wait for someone named "Godot" who never arrives. Two other tramps come along in the middle of each act—a master and his slave—though their appearance causes no real development.

The play is unusual in another sense, in that this is no drawing-room play with a missing fourth wall open to the audience. The scenery consists only of a denuded tree. Naturalism this is not.

At one point in this evening's performance, a character in the play remarked, "Nobody comes. Nobody goes. It's awful." "Hear! Hear!" cried someone from the stalls. A portion of the audience cheered, while others dissented.

Beckett has the distinction, or the notoriety, of having served, in the 1930s, as some sort of secretary to his Irish compatriot James Joyce, which may go some way to explaining his perplexing play.

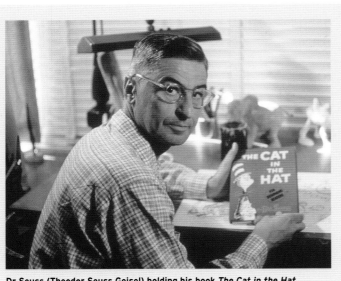

Dr Seuss (Theodor Seuss Geisel) holding his book *The Cat in the Hat*.

"Angry Young Man," Says Press Release for New Play

London, England, May 22, 1956: A startling irreverent new drama, playing to almost empty houses at the Royal Court Theatre, has got critics talking, even if only to say how much they dislike it. The play, *Look Back in Anger,* written by 26-year-old John Osborne, is an assault on both contemporary Britain and on British theater.

Instead of the usual drawing-room play of upper-class manners, Osborne's work is set in a one-bedroom flat. The protagonist is a passionate, idealistic, articulate, but restless and thwarted lower-middle-class man who is trapped in a dead-end job. He rages with frustration and dissatisfaction with his lot, and directs cruel invective at his upper-middle-class wife and at a society which is seen as mediocre, stultifying, and crippled by its seemingly indestructible class structure.

Kenneth Tynan, in the *Observer*, is perhaps the only critic who has become a passionate advocate of this raw drama, seeing it as the first totally original play of a new generation and its protagonist as "the completest young pup in our literature since Hamlet."

A scene from the play *Look Back in Anger*.

Bestseller Hits Raw Nerve

New York, USA, December, 1956: An unlikely bestseller occupied our bookshelves this year. William H. Whyte's *The Organization Man* is not a salacious and page-turning tale but a sometimes dry work of non-fiction (some might wish it were a fiction), and yet its sales suggest that its argument has hit a raw nerve in our seeming utopia.

It documents a fundamental shift in the American way of life from competitive individualism and "inner-directedness," as David Riesman described it in *The Lonely Crowd*, to "other-directedness." This trend parallels the rise of large-scale social organization and the shift away from production to consumption and from blue-collar to white-collar work.

According to Whyte, Americans are losing the independent-mindedness, ambition, and initiative that are the hallmarks of our nation, as their mindset becomes increasingly shaped by the demands of large corporations. In other words, America is becoming a nation of conformists whose focus is on advancement through the firm by fitting in with others and agreeing with established views, rather than innovating. In the process, a fear has developed of difference and originality in thought and lifestyle. His concerns are echoed in the bestselling book and film *The Man in the Gray Flannel Suit.*

Achievements in the Arts

Key Structures
Aalto Studio, Helsinki, Finland
Aalto Summer House, Muuratsalo, Finland
Cao Dai Temple, Tay Nihn, Vietnam
Grand Hotel, Taipei, Taiwan
Guggenheim Museum, New York, USA
Hiroshima Peace Centre, Hiroshima, Japan
House of Culture, Helsinki, Finland
Kingo Houses, Elsinore, Denmark
Los Manantiales, Xochimilco, Mexico
Maisons Jaoul, Paris, France
Maria Konigin, Cologne-Marienburg, Germany
Meiji Shrine, Tokyo, Japan
Munkegaards School, Copenhagen, Denmark
Notre-Dame-du-Haut, Ronchamp, France
One Pillar Pagoda, Ha Noi, Vietnam
Otaniemi Technical University Chapel, Otaniemi, Finland
Philips Pavilion, Brussels, Belgium
Shodan House, Ahmedabad, India
Sidney Myer Music Bowl, Melbourne, Australia
United Nations Headquarters, New York, USA
Unite d'Habitation, Marseilles, France

Nobel Prize in Literature
1950 Bertrand Russell; 1951 Par Lagerkvist; 1952 Francois Mauriac; 1953 Sir Winston Churchill; 1954 Ernest Hemingway; 1955 Halldor Laxness; 1956 Juan Ramon Jimenez; 1957 Albert Camus; 1958 Boris Pasternak (declined prize); 1959 Salvatore Quasimodo.

Pulitzer Prize for Fiction
1950 *The Way West*, A. B. Guthrie, Jr.; 1951 *The Town*, Conrad Richter; 1952 *The Caine Mutiny*, Herman Wouk; 1953 *The Old Man and the Sea*, Ernest Hemingway; 1954 no award given; 1955 *A Fable*, William Faulkner; 1956 *Andersonville*, MacKinlay Kantor; 1957 no award given; 1958 *A Death in the Family*, James Agee; 1959 *The Travels of Jaimie McPheeters*, Robert Lewis Taylor.

Academy Awards
Best Film 1950 *All About Eve;* 1951 *An American in Paris;* 1952 *The Greatest Show on Earth;* 1953 *From Here to Eternity;* 1954 *On the Waterfront;* 1955 *Marty;* 1956 *Around the World in 80 Days;* 1957 *The Bridge Over the River Kwai;* 1958 *Gigi;* 1959 *Ben-Hur.*

BAFTAs
Best Film 1950 *All About Eve;* 1951 *La Ronde;* 1952 *The Sound Barrier;* 1953 *Jeux Interdits;* 1954 *Le Salaire de la Peur;* 1955 *Richard III;* 1956 *Gervaise;* 1957 *The Bridge on the River Kwai;* 1958 *Room at the Top;* 1959 *Ben-Hur.*

Elvis De-pelvised

New York, USA, January 7, 1957: National phenomenon Elvis Presley has made his third appearance on the *Ed Sullivan Show*. After the raging controversy over his wild gyrations, "Elvis the Pelvis" was shown on television last night strictly from the waist up. Sullivan once vowed never to have the singer on his show but relented owing to the ratings success experienced by rivals. Sullivan paid $50,000 for the three appearances, the most ever paid for a performer by a network variety program. Sullivan was duly rewarded with an audience of 60 million (82.6 percent of the television audience).

With his sultry, almost sullen, greasy look, ducktail haircut, informal attire, and his amalgam of hillbilly and black music, the singer topped the Billboard charts for 25 of the 52 weeks last year and had two number-one LPs. Last week the *Wall Street Journal* declared that "Elvis Presley today is a business," noting his impact on the youth market.

Presley merchandising is said to have grossed over $22 million, and includes everything from stuffed hound dogs to colognes. Sales of "rock" records and Presley-style clothing have skyrocketed. He recently starred in his first film, *Love Me Tender*, and is said to have signed a three-picture deal for $450,000.

Presley has been denounced by his own church as a sinful backslider who is playing the devil's music. In August last year a Juvenile Court judge in Florida referred to the singer as a "savage" and declared he would have him arrested if he gyrated while playing in Jacksonville. Presley responded by standing still but wiggling one finger.

Nonetheless, teenagers, especially the young girls, love him. They flock to his concerts and behave in such a hysterical manner that a hundred National Guardsmen had to ring the stage at the Mississippi–Alabama Fair. If his appearances are banned, young people pile into cars and travel to where he is playing.

Today's affluence means that the young have the money to buy their own radios and record players. Radio stations, aware of that spending power, play this music, allowing children to circumvent parental authority. It seems that the more Presley is disdained by the older generation, the more he is beloved by the young. In this way he has become a symbol of the new youth culture and a focus for the older generation's anxieties about the generation gap and juvenile delinquency.

Peyton Place Now a Movie

New York, USA, December 14, 1957: Last night the red carpet was rolled out for the première of the film *Peyton Place*, which is based on a sensational best-seller by Grace Metalious. Few will admit to reading the book, although it has sold three million copies since being released in

The New England town of Gilmanton is fictionalized in the novel *Peyton Place*.

paperback this fall. It has almost single-handedly demonstrated the great profitability of the mass-market paperback.

The novel tears the lid off life in a small New England town. It depicts a community which is driven by lust, incest, infidelity, abortion, murder, social inequality, conformity, hypocrisy, and class privilege. Denounced by the clergy, it was initially expected to sell about 3,000 copies. Instead, it shifted 60,000 within 10 days of its hardback release last year and remained on the bestseller list for 59 weeks. The film rights were sold for $250,000.

Grace Metalious was raised by her grandmother after her father deserted the family and her mother became an alcoholic. She grew up in poverty that was not alleviated by marriage, but drove her to become a writer. She lives in small-town Gilmanton in New England but insists her novel is not autobiographical, even though the incest–murder at the story's heart was based on a real incident in a nearby town and at least one local has filed suit for libel. She is not a popular figure in her home town; she is known for her unladylike style of dressing (jeans, sneakers, flannel shirts) and for the negative publicity she has brought.

Those expecting big-screen sensationalism from the film adaptation may be disappointed, as it is much altered and far tamer than the novel.

Beat Writers Blasted

New York, USA, April 3, 1958: Yesterday, in the *San Francisco Chronicle*, columnist Herb Caen coined the term "beatnik" when he referred to a group of young disaffected writers. Caen's unflattering allusion conjures up a social milieu of bearded complaining malcontents who are eager to avoid work and drink free alcohol.

Caen is not alone in his views. In this season's issue of *Partisan Review*, Norman Podhoretz has delivered a scathing blast in his essay, "The Know-Nothing Bohemians," in which he refers to them as anti-intellectual "barbarians" who, like today's delinquents, are "hostile to civilization" and who worship "primitivism" and "instinct."

One of the group's leading lights, Jack Kerouac, published the novel *On the Road* last September. Despite some good sales, and a positive review in the *New York Times*, Kerouac and the Beats have been criticized in the *Nation*, the *Atlantic Monthly*, the *New York Times Book Review*, *Commentary*, and the *Chicago Tribune*. Most of these reviews have taken exception to the morality (or lack of it) in the novel, which depicts a group of people traveling the country in flight from commitment, steady employment, and "straight" society, listening to jazz, drinking, taking drugs, and engaging in promiscuous behavior. However, in fairness, it must be noted that the protagonist's romanticized attitude to this lifestyle and to his "holy" friend, the ex-con Dean Moriarty, does sour toward the novel's conclusion.

Samuel Beckett

Beat poets Allen Ginsberg (left) and Gregory Corso during a poetry reading party.

Dwight D. Eisenhower

Silly Substance Is the Talk of the Town

New York, USA, September 30, 1950: A recent article in the *New Yorker*'s "Talk of the Town" section has sparked off something of a fad for a gob of goo. Serendipitously created during the last war by scientists searching for a synthetic rubber, it has proved to have intriguing qualities: It is highly elastic when stretched yet it breaks in half when pulled sharply. It is bouncier than a rubber ball yet virtually melts when left undisturbed for a time. It appears to be both solid and liquid and, when it pressed flat against printed materials, it picks up the image, which can then be playfully distorted by stretching the goo.

It is the inherent playfulness of the substance that has ensured its survival, for it was unofficially passed around until it reached marketing expert Peter Hodgson in 1949. Earlier this year Hodgson packaged small balls of what he named "Silly Putty" in egg-shaped containers and convinced Doubleday bookstores and Nieman-Marcus department stores to sell it. In this way it came to the attention of a *New Yorker* reporter with an eye for novelty and an ability to get tongues wagging and wallets opening.

Direct-Dial System Set to Revolutionize Telephony

USA, November 11, 1951: History was made yesterday when Mayor Denning of Englewood, New Jersey, picked up his telephone and spoke to Mayor Osborne in Alameda, California. What was unusual about this transcontinental call was the fact that Mayor Denning did not need or receive the assistance of an operator at any point of the call. He simply dialed 10 digits and waited 18 seconds before his west-coast counterpart picked up the phone and replied.

This contrasts sharply with the first coast-to-coast call, made in 1915, when 5 intermediary operators and 23 minutes were required to connect speakers in San Francisco and New York. It is predicted, as a consequence of this experiment, that long-distance call costs will be reduced, connection will be faster, and the need for operators will be eliminated. The implications for society of such immediacy of communication are harder to guess at.

A child talks on the new telephone.

It seems fitting that this groundbreaking experiment in telephony was conducted by AT&T, otherwise known as the Bell Telephone Company, founded by Alexander Graham Bell in 1877, one year after the Scottish-born inventor was granted a patent on the telephone.

Far from appearing out of the blue, this event has been in the making since the first automatic connection system was introduced in Brooklyn in 1938. AT&T has slowly built up its network of automatic switches and has developed a system of standardized, nationwide, seven-digit telephone numbers and three-digit area codes, which enable dial-up access to distant telephone exchanges.

The telephone has come a long way from the day Alexander Bell first spoke into a crude prototype and summoned his assistant from another room. We can only conjecture as to whether he foresaw the vast scale of direct human interconnection demonstrated yesterday, but then he always was a far-sighted man.

New-Style TV Political Campaigning Gets Results

Washington DC, USA, November 5, 1952: General Eisenhower's successful campaign may have sounded the death knell for the days of presidential candidates making stump speeches, appearing at political rallies, speaking in detail about their party's program, and rendering their party answerable to an audience. This year witnessed an alliance (some say an unholy one) between Madison Avenue's advertising gurus and national politics.

After a rather lackluster and unfocused start to the Eisenhower campaign, and some rather stiff television appearances, a more stage-managed approach was adopted, focusing on the slim notion that the general was a "man of peace."

General Eisenhower speaking to a crowd during the presidential campaign.

In marginal electorates a series of brief television spots, essentially commercials, were sandwiched between popular shows, presenting the general as the returning hero surrounded by cheering grateful crowds and making rather platitudinous statements that were hard to disagree with, perhaps because they lacked any real focus or content.

This new style of electioneering builds on the huge success of the Kefauver hearings into organized crime last year and September's "Checkers" speech by Vice President Nixon. Both events were nationally televised and both demonstrated the new medium's extraordinary reach and its unprecedented ability to focus national attention on a single issue.

They also suggest the potential to transform political issues into entertainment and to reduce party politics to a cult of personality. This new approach to campaigning has been made possible by the growing ubiquity of television, with the number of sets in use sky-rocketing from 500,000 in 1948 to 17 million today.

Presenting candidates as actors or boxes of cereal has the virtue of keeping them clear of any serious or detailed discussion of issues, of unwanted questions, and of spontaneous situations in which their true selves might be revealed. If the Eisenhower campaign is anything to go by, it also has the virtue of success.

The appealing lines and styling of the Austin A95 Westminster make it a popular family car.

Meat's Back on the Menu

London, England, July 4, 1954: Several unusual things happened today: Smithfield Market opened for business at midnight, rather than at 6.00 a.m., the London Housewives' Association could be seen in Trafalgar Square conducting some sort of arcane ritual, and Geoffrey Lloyd, the Minister for Fuel and Power, set fire to an oversized model of a ration book. On such a day, however, a little self-indulgence seems appropriate as British households are released today from 14 years of careful husbandry and self-restraint. Yes, rationing is officially at an end, with all remaining restrictions lifted on the sale and purchase of meat.

During the course of the war many types of food were rationed, essential and unessential, as well as petrol, clothing, soap, and furniture. The system was introduced owing to the difficulties of importing goods in a wartime environment, and to try and ensure fair distribution. The rationing era also developed a memorable, if not always enjoyable, culture of its own, with coupons, private bartering, lengthy and tiresome queues, a black market, and a number of explanatory characters such as Potato Pete and Doctor Carrot. Restrictions were not eased until 1948 and the process of de-rationing has been a very gradual but very welcome one.

time out

Judges at a New York charity horse race announced the placing of the first three horses incorrectly, an error that cost an extra $15,655 in payoffs. The Damon Runyon Fund for Cancer Research was expected to benefit by $10,000 from the mistake.

Equal Pay for Equal Work

Mamie Eisenhower

London, England, January 31, 1955: The campaign to attain equal pay for equal work, regardless of gender, dates back to the late nineteenth century. Despite the fact that Conservative MPs were crucial to the parliamentary defeat of equal pay proposals in 1936 and 1944, the current Conservative government, under Prime Minister Churchill, has given assurances that it will implement these standards within the British civil service, having granted equal pay to female teachers in 1953. It has been suggested that practical politics has played a role in the decision, with the Labour Party announcing last year that it would introduce equal pay if elected. With a tight race expected, the votes of women may prove crucial to the result, possibly prompting this pre-emptive move by the Tories and certainly demonstrating the importance of women attaining the vote.

Women's organizations, such as the Federation of Business and Professional Women, are pleased, but say this is not the time to drop their guard. They stress how long and difficult a struggle it has been to improve women's lives, with earlier gains coming mostly in the fields of legal rights and social conditions. Greater resistance, they suggest, has been met in areas that directly challenge men's positions, such as equal pay and equal access to employment, public positions, and Parliament, thus indicating the importance of this new decision.

London, England, January 31, 1955: The government agrees to give women in the civil service equal pay to men.

San Francisco, USA, March 1, 1955: A report says Americans spend more money on comic books than all schools spend on textbooks.

UK, September 26, 1955: Birdseye frozen fish fingers appear in stores.

USA, October 6, 1955: The drug LSD is made illegal.

UK, January 26, 1956: Heroin imports and exports are made illegal.

Canberra, Australia, March 1, 1956: Taxes on cigarettes, beer, petrol, and spirits rise to combat spiraling inflation. In the USA, the bank rate has risen to 5.5 percent, creating a credit squeeze.

New York, USA, October 9, 1956: The fascination for actor James Dean has exploded after his death on September 30. At the première of *Giant*, his appearance raises cheers from the young audience.

UK, December, 1956: Electric trains replace steam trains between London, Liverpool, and Manchester.

London, England, April 1, 1957: A spoof on the BBC's *Panorama* fools the public into believing that spaghetti is grown on trees in Switzerland.

Chicago, USA, April 15, 1957: Ray Kroc's McDonald's franchise celebrates its second anniversary.

London, England, June 26, 1957: The Medical Research Council releases a report highlighting the link between smoking and lung cancer.

Italy, October 24, 1957: Fashion designer Christian Dior dies. He is succeeded by his favorite assistant, Yves Saint Laurent.

London, England, January 30, 1958: A bill is passed by the House of Lords which allows women to be admitted to the chamber.

London, England, July 10, 1958: The UK's first parking meters appear in Mayfair.

London, England, October 4, 1958: The first transatlantic passenger jetliner service, flying between London and New York, is begun by the British Overseas Airways Corporation.

UK, December, 1958: The ban on portraying homosexuality in the theater is lifted this year.

USA, December, 1958: Popular toys this year include hula hoops and the new Lego bricks.

New York, USA, March 9, 1959: Mattel unveils the Barbie doll.

West Germany, May 1, 1959: Germany introduces the five-day working week.

Toronto, Canada, May 8, 1959: The use of the strap as punishment in Canadian schools is banned.

London, England, July 22, 1959: New figures indicate the crime rate in the last year was 21 percent higher than the year before.

James Dean

"A FAMILY IS A UNIT COMPOSED NOT ONLY OF CHILDREN BUT OF MEN, WOMEN, AN OCCASIONAL ANIMAL, AND THE COMMON COLD."

OGDEN NASH (1902–1971), AMERICAN POET

"THE FRENCH WILL ONLY BE UNITED UNDER THE THREAT OF DANGER. NOBODY CAN SIMPLY BRING TOGETHER A COUNTRY THAT HAS 265 KINDS OF CHEESE."

CHARLES DE GAULLE (1890–1970), FRENCH MILITARY LEADER AND PRESIDENT, 1951

Rebellion without a Cause

New York, USA, October 10, 1956: Last night, at the New York première of the film *Giant*, young audience members cheered whenever James Dean appeared on the screen. The fascination with his persona has exploded to cult status over the last 12 months following his violent death in a chic sports car and owing to the nature of the role he plays in the film *Rebel without a Cause*, also released after his death.

His screen persona has become a symbolic focus for our culture as it grapples with a growing wave of public alarm over juvenile delinquency, which has been on the rise since 1948. High-profile congressional hearings into its causes have reinforced the public's perception that the family is to blame—specifically loosened family ties and declining discipline. *Rebel without a Cause* draws on these anxieties, presenting parents as insensitive and unable to understand their children or to help them.

The film also reflects and reinforces public concern that children from decent homes are living a life that is altogether separate and hidden from their parents, with different clothing, music, rules, rituals, and standards, involving dangerous risk-taking behavior and sometimes violence. In short, it dramatizes a profound generation gap and an absence of admirable role models. Ironically, it is to someone like Dean himself that young people are turning in their search for a figure who represents and understands them.

Dean's on-screen persona is inarticulate, angst-ridden, moody, angry, restless, desperate, confused, and profoundly alone. It is a combination that makes him a troublesome proposition for adults, but a very appealing and romantic figure for young people, as he seems to express their discontent and alienation while projecting sensitivity, profound vulnerability, underlying decency, and a sense of the world's inadequacy. He is reminiscent of that other teen bellwether of our era, Holden Caulfield from *Catcher in the Rye*, with his quest for authenticity in a world of "phoniness." Death has compounded the mythologization of Dean's life and forever wedded his image to youthful rebellion, protecting it for all time from the vicissitudes of ageing.

A poster for the film *Rebel without a Cause*.

Spaghetti Tricks Nation

London, England, April 1, 1957: Normally well-behaved, the BBC has played an April Fool's joke on us. This evening, a spoof documentary has been aired on the *Panorama* program with a straight-faced account of Swiss growers harvesting spaghetti crops. The episode was narrated by no less a figure than the venerable Richard Dimbleby and included footage of women carefully picking limp strands of spaghetti off tree branches and then drying them in the sun.

Dimbleby helpfully explained that a mild winter had produced a bumper crop, although a late frost could "impair the flavor" and reduce its value on the world market. The identical length of all strands was explained as a product of selective breeding. The success of the joke became evident when members of the public began ringing up to ask where they could obtain their own spaghetti bush.

Not everyone found the joke amusing and a few complaints were registered, although some of the irritation arose when patrons were confronted with their own gullibility. In fairness, spaghetti is rarely eaten by much of the general public. We can only speculate whether such uncharacteristic latitude is part of an attempt on the part of the BBC to render itself more appealing to the average viewer, owing to the arrival of competition from the first commercial broadcaster, ITA, two years ago.

Fast Food for Families

Des Plaines, Chicago, April 15, 1957: A fast-food outlet in suburban Chicago is doing a remarkable trade and today celebrated its second anniversary. The outlook of owner/manager Ray Kroc is reflected in his objection to a local reporter's usage of the term "hamburger joint." It is, he says, a family restaurant.

It is evident from the immaculate grounds, neatly and uniformly dressed staff, hygienic kitchen, rapid service, small standardized menu (focusing on hamburgers), low prices, consistent standards, and no-tipping policy, that Kroc's intention is to appeal to busy young suburban families. These pressed-for-time families, he suggests, are seeking a reliable cheap meal that will appeal to children, and a friendly, polite, and safe environment.

Kroc first made a name for himself after the war selling contraptions that allowed busy drugstore owners to mix five milkshakes at a time. When sales began to fall, he recognized that neighborhood drugstores were in decline

Sporting Achievements

Baseball *World Series* 1950 New York (American League); 1951 New York (AL); 1952 New York (AL); 1953 New York (AL); 1954 New York (National League); 1955 Brooklyn (NL); 1956 New York (AL); 1957 Milwaukee (NL); 1958 New York (AL); 1959 Los Angeles (NL).
Cycling *Tour de France* 1950 F. Kubler; 1951 H. Koblet; 1952 F. Coppi; 1953-1955 L. Bobet; 1956 R. Walkowiak; 1957 J. Anquetil; 1958 C. Gaul; 1959 F. Bahamontes. *Football* World Cup Soccer: 1950 Uruguay; 1954 West Germany; 1958 Brazil.
Golf *US Masters* 1950 J. Demaret; 1951 B. Hogan; 1952 S. Snead; 1953 B. Hogan; 1954 S. Snead; 1955 C. Middlecoff; 1956 J. Burke Jr.; 1957 D. Ford; 1958 A. Palmer; 1959 A. Wall Jr.
Horse Racing *Epsom Derby* 1950 Galcador; 1951 Arctic Prince; 1952 Tulyar; 1953 Pinza; 1954 Never Say Die; 1955 Phil Drake; 1956 Lavandin; 1957 Crepello; 1958 Hard Ridden; 1959 Parthia. *Kentucky Derby* 1950 Middleground; 1951 Count Turf; 1952 Hill Gail; 1953 Dark Star; 1954 Determine; 1955 Swaps; 1956 Needles; 1957 Iron Liege; 1958 Tim Tam; 1959 Tomy Lee. *Melbourne Cup* 1950 Comic Court; 1951 Delta; 1952 Dalray; 1953 Wodalla; 1954 Rising Fast; 1955 Toparoa; 1956 Evening Peal; 1957 Straight Draw; 1958 Baystone; 1959 Macdougal.
Ice Hockey *Stanley Cup* 1950 Detroit; 1951 Toronto; 1952 Detroit; 1953 Montreal; 1954 Detroit; 1955 Detroit; 1956 Montreal; 1957 Montreal; 1958 Montreal; 1959 Montreal.
Marathon *Boston, Men's* 1950 K. Ham; 1951 S. Tanaka; 1952 D. Flores; 1953 K. Yamada; 1954 V. Karvonen; 1955 H. Hamamura; 1956 A. Viskari; 1957 J. Kelley; 1958 F. Mihalic; 1959 E. Oksanen.
Sailing *America's Cup* 1958 Columbia.
Tennis *Australian Championships, Men's Singles* 1950 F. Sedgman; 1951 D. Savitt; 1952 K. McGregor; 1953 K. Rosewall; 1954 M. Rose; 1955 K. Rosewall; 1956 L. Hoad; 1957-1958 A. Cooper; 1959 A. Olmedo; *Women's Singles* 1950 L. Brough; 1951 N. Wynne Bolton; 1952 T. Long; 1953 M. Connolly; 1954 T. Long; 1955 B. Penrose; 1956 M. Carter; 1957 S. Fry; 1958 A. Mortimer; 1959 M. Carter Reitano. *French Championships, Men's Singles* 1950 B. Patty; 1951-1952 J. Drobny; 1953 K. Rosewall; 1954-1955 T. Trabert; 1956 L. Hoad; 1957 S. Davidson; 1958 M. Rose; 1959 N. Pietrangeli; *Women's Singles* 1950 D. Hart; 1951 S. Fry; 1952 D. Hart; 1953-1954 M. Connolly; 1955 A. Mortimer; 1956 A. Gibson; 1957 S. Bloomer; 1958 Z. Kormoczy 1959 C. Truman. *US National Championship, Men's Singles* 1950 A. Larsen; 1951-1952 F. Sedgman; 1953 T. Trabert; 1954 V. Seixas; 1955 T. Trabert; 1956 K. Rosewall; 1957 M. Anderson; 1958 A. Cooper; 1959 N. Fraser; *Women's Singles* 1950 M. Osborne DuPont; 1951-1953 M. Connolly; 1954-1955 D. Hart; 1956 S. Fry; 1957-1958 A. Gibson; 1959 M. Bueno. *Wimbledon, Men's Singles* 1950 B. Patty; 1951 D. Savitt; 1952 F. Sedgman; 1953 V. Seixas; 1954 J. Drobny; 1955 T. Trabert; 1956-1957 L. Hoad; 1958 A. Cooper; 1959 A. Olmedo; *Women's Singles* 1950 L. Brough; 1951 D. Hart; 1952-1954 M. Connolly; 1955 L. Brough; 1956 S. Fry; 1957-1958 A. Gibson; 1959 M. Bueno.

However, one hamburger outlet in California, which was called McDonald's, had bought 10 of his "multimixers." Curious, he investigated and was impressed by the business's cleanliness and orderliness, the systematic method, family-friendly atmosphere ("no leather-jacketed guys, jukeboxes or cigarette machines," Kroc says), and remarkable popularity. He convinced the McDonald brothers to make him their franchising agent and soon opened his own McDonald's.

Kroc militantly protects the company's reputation by very carefully considering all potential franchisees and locations, and strictly imposing set menus, prices, standards, and methods on all takers. Twelve McDonald's were opened around the country last year but Kroc envisages hundreds more. With his fierce drive, determination, and competitiveness, he seems sure to succeed.

French fashion designer Yves Saint-Laurent (center) and a group of fashion models at Victoria Station, London.

Ray Kroc

Smoking Linked to Cancer

London, England, June 26, 1957: According to a report released here today by the Medical Research Council, there is a definite causal link between smoking and lung cancer. The research was prompted by a doubling of the incidence of lung cancer over the last decade.

After considering evidence amassed from more than 20 studies and 6 nations, the report concludes that tobacco consumption is the principal cause of lung cancer. Despite this, tobacco companies insist this is merely opinion and, judging from interviews carried out by the BBC in London today, their profits are not under direct threat, as most of the interviewees seem to agree. Tobacco company shares, moreover, remained stable.

Nonetheless, the government has announced that it will mount a campaign to inform the public of the findings, but says that it will then allow people to decide for themselves, rather than banning tobacco or restricting its usage in public spaces. Each year the government currently receives income of around £600 million in taxes from smoking.

Death of Fashion Innovator

Italy, October 24, 1957: There was a changing of the guard today in the world of fashion. Christian Dior, the most influential designer of the postwar era, passed away in Italy, and it is expected that his assistant, Yves Saint-Laurent, will become the chief designer.

Dior was the inventor of the so-called "New Look" that has dominated women's fashion

trends since 1947. Its very feminine quality, highlighting and stylizing the curvaceousness of the female body, was characterized by voluminous padded skirts with hemlines extending halfway down the calf. Dior also designed a stylish and flattering figure-hugging cut. The ideal shape was the hourglass figure, favoring small waists and a large bust. Coiffed hair and full make-up were unofficial but very essential accessories to the style.

The sophisticated womanly look, typified by Grace Kelly and Ava Gardner, contrasted with the austerity of the Depression and war years, the short skirt and the somewhat masculine, shoulder-padded look. Dior's post-war designs invited women to lay aside the world of Rosie the Riveter, embrace their femininity, and return to home life. It is an invitation women decided to accept and one that they have been able to afford in the affluent times we have enjoyed.

Hail the Jet Age

London, England, October 4, 1958: A landmark, not only in air travel, but in global interconnectedness, was attained today when a De Havilland Comet IV took off from Heathrow Airport with 80 people on board. It was the inaugural transatlantic jet-propelled commercial flight.

Passengers spent nearly nine hours in the air, traveling at an average ground

The BOAC De Havilland Comet IV will dramatically reduce flying time.

speed of 404 mph (650 km/h) before landing at New York's Idlewild Airport. The return flight is said to have taken a mere 6 hours and 12 minutes, about half the time it takes a propeller-driven craft.

This is the second time in recent history that the BOAC company has claimed a landmark in air travel, having undertaken the world's first commercial jet service on a De Havilland Comet I between London and Johannesburg on May 2, 1952, dramatically reducing traveling time.

However, some passengers may be wary of taking the leap forward after three disastrous Comet I crashes in 1953–1954. Three years later, BOAC assure the public that lessons learned from the crashes have led to rigorous testing and fundamental changes in materials and design.

A New Concept in Dolls

New York, USA, March 9, 1959: Today at the New York International American Toy Fair, a new concept in children's dolls was on parade, or should that be on the catwalk? Whereas we may have thought of dolls as babies or young children, Mattel's Barbie is a knockout statuesque blonde with an hour-glass figure, tiny feet, and, most unusually of all, a large bust. You might think this is intended for adult men, but Ruth Handler, wife of Mattel co-founder, Elliot Handler, says she noticed that her daughter preferred playing with home-made paper dolls modeled after adults. Mrs Handler's idea for an adult doll was rejected as impractical by Mattel until she spotted a German doll while in Europe that proved them wrong.

Barbie sports blue eyeliner, a top-knot ponytail with tightly-curled bangs, and a black-and-white zebra-style swimsuit. However, because she is a "teenage fashion model," an extensive wardrobe can be purchased separately.

John F. Kennedy

South African Police Fire on Demonstrators

Sharpeville, South Africa, March 21: Today police have opened fire on a crowd of 5,000 unarmed demonstrators in the South African town of Sharpeville.

Eyewitnesses said they saw men, women, and children "fleeing like rabbits," with the bodies of the dead and dying in the streets. More than 80 percent of those killed were shot in the back as they fled.

The demonstrators had been holding a peaceful protest against the "pass laws," which require all black men and women to carry passes containing details such as their name, tax code, and employer details. To be found in a public place without this document means possible detention for up to 30 days.

Ceylon Elects World's First Female PM

Colombo, Ceylon, July 20: Sirimavo Bandaranaike, the widow of the late Prime Minister Solomon Bandaranaike who was assassinated by a Buddhist monk last year, has become the world's first female Prime Minister.

Her Sri Lanka Freedom Party has won 75 out of 150 seats in the national Parliament, and it is expected she will continue with the socialist policies of her late husband, such as the nationalization of the banking, insurance, and other key sectors of the economy.

Her party was elected on a platform promising that government-run distribution would ensure that "goods in everyday use" will be widely available to all Ceylonese citizens at cheap prices.

Sirimavo Bandaranaike.

Doubt Cast on Kennedy Win

USA, November 9: John Fitzgerald Kennedy yesterday won the closest presidential election in US history, defeating a gallant Richard Nixon by 113,000 votes from a total of 68 million votes cast.

Kennedy earned 49.7 percent of the popular vote and his rival Nixon 49.5 percent, representing a margin of just 0.2 percent. Kennedy is the first Roman Catholic to be elected to the Presidency, the first to have been born in the twentieth century, and at 43 years is the youngest President-elect in history.

Despite his inexperience, as compared to Nixon's eight years as Vice President under Eisenhower, and his staunch anti-communism, the Senator from Massachusetts has consistently stressed the importance of character and courage, citing his service during World War II in the South Pacific aboard *PT-109* and his heroic rescuing of crewmates after being rammed by a Japanese destroyer.

In retrospect, however, it may be the first-ever televised Presidential debate that swung the election in Kennedy's favor. The youthful Senator looked well tanned and at ease in front of the cameras, in contrast to Nixon, who was recovering from a recent knee injury and looked tired and drawn. Interestingly, radio listeners gave the debate to Nixon, whereas television viewers, perhaps wooed by the novelty of a televised debate, may have given it to Kennedy in a vote of style over substance.

In a further development, allegations of vote fraud are beginning to surface among Republicans, particularly in Texas, Missouri, and Illinois.

The Republican Party is urging Nixon to demand a recount in Chicago, which is heavily influenced by the political machinery of incumbent Democrat Mayor Daley. Even the nation's most respected newspaper, the *Chicago Tribune*, has editorialized: "The election of November 8 was characterized by such gross and palpable fraud as to justify the conclusion that Nixon was deprived of victory."

In Texas, irregularities in the voting process are surfacing everywhere. Fannin County, which has only 4,895 registered voters, saw 6,138 votes somehow cast, with 75 percent of them going to Kennedy. In another Texas precinct 86 votes were registered, yet the final tally was 147 for Kennedy, 24 for Nixon.

Nixon, to his credit, has refused to pursue a recount, saying it would provoke a constitutional crisis that the country could ill afford.

The Kennedys celebrate John's election victory at home in Massachusetts.

Algiers, Algeria, January 29: France teeters on the brink of civil war as the European inhabitants of Algiers protest the French government's self-determination policy for the North African colony.
Cape Town, South Africa, February 3: British PM Harold Macmillan delivers his "winds of change" speech to the South African parliament, stating "whether we like it or not, this growth of national consciousness is a political fact."

Agadir, Morocco, February 29: 12,000 people die as an earthquake hits the seaside town.
Sharpeville, South Africa, March 21: Police open fire on anti-apartheid protesters, killing 69 and injuring hundreds.
Brasília, Brazil, April 21: The new capital city is inaugurated. The country's administration moves wholesale from Rio de Janeiro.
Seoul, South Korea, April 28: President Syngman Rhee resigns and flees the country following violent protests over recent election results.

Moscow, USSR, May 17: Soviet leader Nikita Khrushchev demands an apology following the downing of an American U-2 spy plane by a Russian missile two weeks ago.
Tel Aviv, Israel, May 21: Nazi war criminal Adolf Eichmann is captured by Mossad agents in Argentina and returned to Israel for trial.
Leopoldville, Congo, June 30: Premier Lumumba declares the Congo's independence from 75 years of Belgian rule. Mali, British Somaliland, and Madagascar have all become self-governing this month.

Congo, July 15: Civil war breaks out as the mineral-rich province of Katanga declares independence.
Colombo, Ceylon, July 20: Sirimavo Bandaranaike becomes the world's first female prime minister.
Cuba, August 7: Fidel Castro nationalizes all American property on the Caribbean island.
Nicosia, Cyprus, August 16: Cyprus gains independence from Britain, ending four years of violence between Turkish, Greek, and British factions.

New York, USA, October 12: Soviet leader Nikita Khrushchev displays undiplomatic behavior at the UN General Assembly, banging his shoe on the desk and interjecting when the Philippines delegate accuses the USSR of implementing imperialist policy in Eastern Europe.
USA, November 9: John F. Kennedy is elected president of the USA, defeating Richard Nixon by a slim margin.

Castro Ends Hopes of Political Freedom in Cuba

Havana, Cuba, May 1: The Cuban President, Fidel Castro, has further tightened his grip on the country today by proclaiming Cuba a socialist country and abolishing further elections.

This follows on from the arrest of over 500 members of the Cuban underground resistance in February. Three other key opposition figures were also arrested at a meeting in Havana earlier this year in March, including Humberto Sori Marin, who was the noted architect of the revolution's Agrarian Reform Law.

Castro's actions today are being interpreted as a response to the failed US-backed "Bay of Pigs" invasion by Cuban rebels. On April 17 this year approximately 1,400 rebels and an undisclosed number of CIA operatives landed about 100 miles (160 km) southeast of Havana at Playa Girón on the Bay of Pigs, with the aim of overthrowing the Cuban dictator and restoring democracy. However, the invasion went terribly wrong when the anticipated popular uprising failed to materialize.

Segregation Ruling Flouted

Montgomery, USA, May, 1961: White residents of the rural Alabama town of Montgomery today attacked a multi-racial group known as the "Freedom Riders" who have been touring the southern states of the USA calling for an end to racial segregation.

Despite Supreme Court rulings in 1952 and 1954 declaring segregation on trains and buses to be unconstitutional, many southern states have persisted with the practice, which meant that, on buses, whites would sit at the front and blacks would sit at the back. Any black would be required to give up his or her seat for a white person if no seats were available. In response to this, a civil rights group, known as the Congress on Racial Equality, formed the Freedom Riders, which is made up of black and white volunteers who travel the Deep South sitting next to one another on public buses and trains.

time out

In the United States' first step toward manned space exploration, Commander Alan B. Shepard Jr rode the capsule *Freedom 7* 115 miles into space, viewing much of the east coast of the USA through a periscope. He declared the mission "very smooth."

Communists Build Wall to Prevent Exodus

Berlin, Germany, August 13: The East German Government is today raising a wall of barbed wire and anti-tank obstacles across Berlin in a bid to prevent an increasing number of refugees fleeing into West Berlin in an attempt to escape from the worsening economic and political conditions in East Germany.

Since January this year some 160,000 people have crossed into West Berlin, and it is estimated that since 1946 over 2.5 million East Germans have fled. The East German Government's pursuit of policies such as the forced collectivization of agriculture and the repression of private trade has been in stark contrast to the hopes for economic prosperity in the west due to the implementation of the post-war Marshall Plan.

The steady loss of skilled workers, professionals, and intellectuals is threatening to destroy the economic viability of the East German state.

Beginning early this morning, entire streets have been cordoned off and many simply torn up. Tanks have been placed at intervals along the wall's length, and subway services linking the two halves of this now divided city have been disrupted.

Inhabitants of East Berlin and the wider German Democratic Republic (GDR) are, as of today, no longer permitted to enter West Berlin, and a process of enforced evacuation of houses along the new line of control has already begun.

The wall's length is estimated to be 200 miles (320 km). It has cut through 192 streets, 97 of which lead to East Berlin and 95 into the GDR. East German propaganda has been referring to the wall as an "anti-fascist protection wall."

East German citizens have been crossing into West Berlin in increasing numbers throughout this year. This response is due to increased tensions stemming from Soviet Premier Nikita Khrushchev's threat to sign a unilateral peace treaty with East Germany that would end existing Four Powers agreements that guarantee access to East Berlin by westerners.

Fidel Castro

Freedom Riders take refuge from police in a Montgomery church.

The Berlin Wall divides East and West.

Katanga, Congo, January 18: After less than one year as prime minister in the newly independent nation, Patrice Lumumba is assassinated. He was arrested in December, indicted over the deaths of 1,000 people.

Laos, March 21: The newly inaugurated US President Kennedy vows to support Laos to overthrow communist rebel forces, the Pathet Lao, sending additional troops to train the Laotian army.

South Vietnam, April 10: Staunch anti-communist President Ngo Dinh Diem is re-elected. His Catholic faith, nepotism, and authoritarian rule have made him unpopular with the mostly Buddhist population.

Cuba, April 19: The Bay of Pigs invasion by 1,400 US-backed Cuban exiles hoping to overthrow the Castro regime is repeled with over 100 killed, sparking a major diplomatic incident with the USA.

Havana, Cuba, May 1: Fidel Castro proclaims Cuba a socialist country.

Dominican Republic, May 30: After a 31-year rule, ruthless dictator General Trujillo is assassinated with the assistance of the CIA.

Montgomery, Alabama, USA, May: White residents supporting segregation attack the "Freedom Riders," a multiracial group touring the southern states.

Vienna, Austria, June 4: Soviet premier Khrushchev and US President Kennedy meet at summit. Despite little agreement, there is progress, following the debacle of the Paris Peace Conference.

Kuwait, July 1: British troops occupy the gulf state to defend against a threatened Iraqi invasion.

Bizerte, Tunisia, July 20: After repeated requests for the French to return the naval base at Bizerte, Tunisian forces lay siege.

Berlin, Germany, August 13: East German troops begin to erect the Berlin wall.

Ndola, Rhodesia, September 18: UN Secretary-General Dag Hammarskjold dies in a plane crash in suspicious circumstances.

Novaya Zemlya, USSR, October 30: Russia explodes the world's largest nuclear bomb, provoking worldwide condemnation. At 58 megatons, the bomb is 4,000 times more powerful than the Hiroshima bomb of 1945.

Saigon, South Vietnam, December 11: Following President Kennedy's pledge to increase military aid to South Vietnam, 400 US troops land in Saigon in two army helicopters.

Jerusalem, Israel, December 15: Former SS commander Adolf Eichmann is sentenced to death.

Martin Luther King Jr

> "A REVOLU-
> TION IS NOT A
> BED OF ROSES.
> A REVOLUTION
> IS A STRUGGLE
> TO THE DEATH
> BETWEEN THE
> FUTURE AND
> THE PAST."
>
> FIDEL CASTRO
> (B. 1926), CUBAN
> STATESMAN, ON THE
> 1959 CUBAN
> REVOLUTION

> "THEY TALK
> ABOUT WHO
> WON AND
> WHO LOST.
> HUMAN
> REASON WON.
> MANKIND
> WON."
>
> NIKITA KHRUSHCHEV
> (1894–1971), SOVIET
> STATESMAN, ON THE
> CUBAN MISSILE
> CRISIS, 1962

Riots Greet Admission of Black Man to "Ole Miss"

Oxford, Mississippi, USA, October 1: Two bystanders died and 50 US marshals were injured (28 from gunfire) as riots broke out today on the campus of the University of Mississippi ("Ole Miss") after James Meredith became the first black student to be admitted to the previously all-white institution.

Marshals were hit by birdshot from snipers during last night's rioting, and were forced to fire tear gas into the mob of demonstrators. The marshals "fought with their backs to the wall," according to eyewitness accounts. US Army soldiers from Fort Bragg arrived prior to daybreak, and only then did the situation begin to come under control.

After two failed attempts at admission earlier this year, Meredith filed a complaint with the District Court on May 31 with the assistance of the NAACP (National Association for the Advancement of Colored People). His claim that he was denied admission to the university because of his color was rejected; however, this judgment was later overturned on appeal to the Fifth Judicial Circuit Court by a 2 to 1 ruling.

The Attorney General, Robert Kennedy, decided to send in the Federal marshals in order to protect Meredith from the very real threat of being lynched.

Second Cuban Missile Crisis

Cuba, October 28: Feeling that a second invasion of Cuba was almost inevitable following the failed US invasion at the Bay of Pigs in April last year, President Fidel Castro has approved a plan by Soviet Premier Nikita Khrushchev to place missiles on the island, only 90 miles

(145 km) from US territory. Recent developments have seen that decision bring the world to the brink of nuclear war.

On October 15 reconnaissance photos revealed Soviet missile bases under construction in Cuba. Within a week the US Kennedy Administration had imposed a naval blockade around the island, to prevent the arrival of further weapons. On October 22 President Kennedy announced the discovery of the missiles to the American public in a televised address.

On October 25 the first Russian ship, the *Bucharest*, was intercepted without incident and allowed to continue when it was determined its cargo consisted only of oil. The following day a freighter was boarded and cleared.

On October 26 Premier Khrushchev sent President Kennedy a long rambling letter in which he stated that the Soviet

time out

In response to the news of President Kennedy's assassination, New York's Times Square was veiled in darkness as theaters, nightclubs and dance halls closed their doors. Immediately after the electric signs lit up automatically at dusk, they were put out one by one.

TIME
MAGAZINE

KHRUSHCHEV

Nikita Khrushchev is famous for his fiery rhetoric.

Union would dismantle the missile installations in return for an assurance that the US would not proceed to invade Cuba.

Yesterday a US U-2 spy plane was shot down, and the Secretary of Defense requested the Air Force to call 24 troop carrier squadrons and their supporting units to active duty, involving some 14,000 Air Force reservists.

The US President received a second letter from Premier Khrushchev yesterday, stating that he would pull the missiles out if the US removed missiles they had stationed in Turkey. The US Administration chose to ignore this second letter, and instead accepted the offer outlined in the letter of October 26.

Today the crisis seems to have finally been brought to a close, with the Soviet Government agreeing to dismantle its offensive weapons in Cuba and return them to the Soviet Union subject to United Nations verification.

UN Resolution 1761 Condemns Apartheid

New York, USA, November 6: The United Nations General Assembly today adopted UN Resolution 1761, condemning South Africa's policy of apartheid and urging all its member states to sever diplomatic relations with South Africa, to cease trade with the country especially in regards to arms exports, and to deny passage to South African ships and aircraft.

The resolution states that apartheid is a violation of South Africa's obligations under the UN Charter and constitutes a threat to international peace and security.

This move by the United Nations reflects a growing call for an international boycott of South Africa by leaders such as Albert Luthuli of the African National Congress and the Reverend Martin Luther King Jr of the United States.

Ranrahirca, Peru, January 11: Whole villages are destroyed and 4,000 people perish in a massive landslide of rocks and ice.
Paris, France, February 8: The Secret Army Organization (OAS), campaigning against Algerian independence, is responsible for a wave of bomb blasts. Anti-OAS demonstrations leave eight dead.
Berlin, Germany, February 10: American U-2 spy plane pilot Gary Powers is released after 21 months in prison, in exchange for Soviet spy Colonel Rudolf Abel.

Algiers, Algeria, April 20: Head of the OAS, General Raoul Salan, is captured, ending the anti-colonial uprising in Algeria and France.
Ramla, Israel, May 31: Former SS commander Adolf Eichmann is executed by hanging.
Laos, May: US troops are deployed to fight the communist group Pathet Lao which captured Nam Tha.
Algeria, July 3: Two days after the Algerian people voted in a referendum on independence, French President de Gaulle severs 132 years of colonial ties.

Jamaica, August 6: Jamaica becomes independent within the British Commonwealth; Alexander Bustamente of the Jamaica Labour Party is the first prime minister.
New York, USA, August 15: The Netherlands signs the New York Agreement, agreeing to cede West New Guinea to Indonesia.
Berlin, Germany, August 17: Eighteen-year-old East German Peter Fechter is the first person to be shot and killed while attempting to cross the Berlin Wall to the West.

Houston, USA, September 12: At Rice University, President Kennedy declares that the US will regain the lead in the "space race" and put a man on the moon by the end of the decade.
Oxford, Mississippi, USA, October 1: Three die and 50 are injured as riots break out at the University of Mississippi after the first African-American is admitted as a student.
India, October 26: Indian and Chinese troops are engaged in heavy fighting over the disputed border region of Arunachal Pradesh.

Cuba, October 28: Seven days of escalating tension bring the world to the brink of nuclear confrontation before the USA and USSR reach a compromise.
New York, USA, November 6: The United Nations officially condemns South Africa's policy of apartheid.
Massawa, Eritrea (Ethiopia), December 19: A group of police desert the Ethiopian force to join the Eritrean Liberation Front, formed in 1961 in response to Ethiopia's annexation (with the UN's blessing) of the strategically important nation.

Amazing "Great Train Robbery"

Cheddington, England, August 8: At 3:03 a.m. today, more than £2.3 million (US$5 million) in untraceable used banknotes were stolen from the Glasgow–London mail train in an audacious and meticulously organized robbery.

Train signals had apparently been rigged, with the result that the Royal Mail Travelling Post Office was brought to a halt between Leighton Buzzard and Cheddington in Bedfordshire. The only reported injury was to the train driver, Jack Mills, who was hit over the head with an iron bar and is recovering in the Royal Buckinghamshire Hospital in Aylesbury tonight.

The train was decoupled and moved a half-mile further along the line to where the robbers' getaway vehicles were waiting. Detective Chief Superintendent Jack Slipper of Scotland Yard has been assigned to the case.

Martin Luther King Jr: "I have a dream…"

Washington DC, USA, August 28: In a massive public demonstration at the Lincoln Memorial in Washington DC today, over 200,000 people gathered in support of civil rights and have heard what is already being called one of the great speeches in the history of the United States, given by the Reverend Martin Luther King Jr.

Referred to as the "March on Washington for Jobs and Freedom," the gathering was organized on the hundredth anniversary of Abraham Lincoln's Emancipation Proclamation. With segregation still a part of the fabric of US society, urban blacks living in tenements, their children attending separate and grossly inferior schools, King chose instead to preach a

Mandy Rice-Davies and Christine Keeler, players in the Profumo affair.

message of hope. His stirring phrase "I have a dream" resonated like a call to arms, encouraging the black community to believe that things can and will change, provided that the civil rights movement maintains its clarity of purpose.

President Kennedy Assassinated in Dallas

Dallas, USA, November 22: Tragedy struck America today when President John F. Kennedy was shot and killed by an unknown assassin this afternoon.

The President was riding in a motorcade through Dealey Plaza in Dallas, Texas. The governor of the state, John Connally, who was seated in the front of the open-topped car, was also injured when a bullet struck him in the back of the head. The First Lady and Mrs Connally, who were traveling in the car along with their husbands, were uninjured.

President Kennedy was shot in the head and collapsed immediately into the arms of his wife, Jacqueline.

The limousine was then driven at speed to Parkland Memorial Hospital, where the President was still alive when admitted. A tracheotomy was performed to relieve his breathing, and blood and

fluids were administered intravenously. Chest tubes were inserted and cardiac massage was attempted, but all to no avail. The thirty-fifth president of the United States of America died at 2 p.m. local time.

Two Roman Catholic priests were present and administered the last rites to him.

The Vice President, Lyndon B. Johnson was sworn in as the nation's president at 2.38 p.m. while he was on board the presidential aircraft *Air Force One*.

Several witnesses to the murder said they saw and heard a number of shots being fired from the nearby Texas School Book Depository. Police and Secret Service agents stormed the seven-story building and were reported to have recovered a weapon with a telescopic sight. No arrests have as yet been made, however.

The Secretary of State, Dean Rusk, and other Cabinet officers had been on their way to Japan when the news came. Their aircraft was immediately ordered to turn round and return to the US.

The New York Stock Exchange has been closed.

The Speaker of the House of Representatives, John McCormack, announced that the President's body would be taken on Sunday to the rotunda of the Capitol, where it will lie in state until Monday.

Adolf Eichmann

The Kennedys arrive in Dallas.

Pope Paul VI

82 Lost in Collision

Tasman Sea, Australia, February 10: Tonight HMAS *Melbourne*, an aircraft carrier engaged in night flying exercises off the coast of New South Wales near Jervis Bay, has been involved in a collision with the Darling-class destroyer HMAS *Voyager*.

In Australia's worst peacetime naval disaster, 82 crewmen from the *Voyager*, including her captain, were lost as the vessel was cut in two by the impact. It is currently understood that HMAS *Voyager* inexplicably maneuvered directly into the path of the RAN flagship and into the carrier's bow. HMAS *Melbourne* suffered no casualties.

RAAF Neptunes have been searching the area where the disaster occurred in the hope of finding survivors, but so far no survivors or bodies of any of *Voyager*'s missing officers and ratings have been located. Seven surface ships are also on their way to the area, including the *Stuart*, and the Royal Navy submarine *Tabard*.

> *"MY GOVERN-MENT WILL PROTECT ALL LIBERTIES BUT ONE—THE LIBERTY TO DO AWAY WITH OTHER LIBERTIES."*
>
> GUSTAVO DIAZ ORDAZ (1911–1979), PRESIDENT OF MEXICO, IN HIS INAUGURAL SPEECH

> *"ONE FIFTH OF THE PEOPLE ARE AGAINST EVERYTHING ALL THE TIME."*
>
> ROBERT KENNEDY (1925–1968), AMERICAN POLITICIAN

Mandela Receives Life Sentence for Sabotage

Pretoria, South Africa, June 12: The anti-apartheid campaigner Nelson Mandela, currently serving a five-year term for incitement to strike, has today been found guilty on four counts of sabotage and given a life sentence, along with seven other members of the African National Congress, the organization that was banned in 1960 immediately following the infamous Sharpeville massacre.

The men will now be taken to Robben Island, 9 miles (14 km) offshore from Cape Town, to serve out their sentences.

Robben Island has long been used as a penal settlement, and has a reputation for brutality and isolation. It became a maximum security prison in 1959.

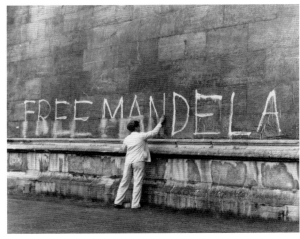

Imprisoned black activist Nelson Mandela has many supporters.

Nehru, Architect of Modern India, Cremated

New Delhi, India, June 13: Jawaharlal Nehru is today being farewelled by more than a million pilgrims who have converged upon the route his funeral train is taking to his cremation at the confluence of the Ganges and Jumna rivers.

Nehru was educated in England at Cambridge University before following his father Motilal into politics. Imprisoned by the British for 32 months after the Quit India Movement was launched in 1942, he went on to become the nation's first Prime Minister when India gained its independence in 1947.

Nehru's friendship with Mohandas Gandhi saw him elected Prime Minister despite nine out of India's fifteen provincial councils having preferred Sardar Patel, one of Gandhi's closest associates. At Gandhi's request, Patel relinquished the post to Nehru.

Nehru was a fervent nationalist, socialist, and visionary who possessed a rare intellect and a personal charisma that endeared him to Indians regardless of caste or socioeconomic background.

He was instrumental in pushing through India's Parliament legal and social reforms for the emancipation of Hindu women. He outlawed the tradition of dowry giving, raised the age for marriage from 12 to 15, and gave women the authority to divorce their husbands.

Nehru's other achievements included inaugurating India's space and nuclear programs, building a strong judicial system, constructing a complex and ambitious national rail network, and steering the nation's foreign policy toward a path of non-alignment.

The 1962 conflict with China, however, revealed India's unpreparedness for war and an embarrassing inability to protect its own borders. The nation's image and self-esteem was left deeply scarred despite the withdrawal of Chinese forces and the establishment of a demilitarized zone.

Nehru was the author of several books, including *Glimpses of World History* (1930–1934) and *The Discovery of India* (1942–1945), both written during periods of incarceration under British rule.

Indians regard his famous "Tryst with Destiny" speech on the eve of Indian independence as significant a moment in their history as the Gettysburg Address is to Americans.

Nehru's ashes will be scattered on the Ganges River.

Key Events

Jerusalem, Israel, January 5: Pope Paul VI makes a visit to the Holy Land, meeting the Patriarch of the Greek Orthodox Church—the first such meeting for over 500 years.

Calcutta, India, January 13: Over 100 people are killed in rioting between Hindus and Muslims.

Tasman Sea, Australia, February 10: HMAS *Melbourne* collides with HMAS *Voyager*, killing 82.

Chattanooga, USA, March 12: Jimmy Hoffa, president of the powerful Teamsters Union, is sentenced to eight years in jail for jury tampering.

Rhodesia, April 13: Ian Smith is elected prime minister, vowing to keep the black majority from participating in elections.

Lima, Peru, May 24: A riot at a soccer match between Peru and Argentina leaves 318 people dead and 500 injured.

Jerusalem, Israel, June 2: The Palestine Liberation Organization (PLO) is founded, after the first Arab League summit in January had laid the groundwork.

Port Moresby, Papua New Guinea, June 8: The first House of Assembly opens. It is a major constitutional step—the country has been administered by Australia since the 1920s.

Pretoria, South Africa, June 12: Nelson Mandela and seven other African National Congress activists are given life sentences for sabotage.

New Delhi, India, June 13: One and a half million people line the route of the funeral of Prime Minister and independence hero Jawaharlal Nehru. He had led the country since independence from Britain in 1947.

Washington DC, USA, July 2: President Lyndon Johnson continues Kennedy's reforming mandate, signing the new Civil Rights Act prohibiting racial discrimination.

Mississippi, USA, August 4: The bodies of three civil rights activists are found six weeks after their disappearance.

Washington DC, USA, August 7: The Senate gives the government increased authority to retaliate against North Vietnamese communists after attacks on the US Navy in the Gulf of Tonkin.

Labis, Malaysia, September 3: Indonesian paratroopers land over the island of Borneo, after two years of conflict between the two countries. New Zealand, Britain, and Australia have pledged assistance to the Malaysians.

Moscow, USSR, October 15: Flamboyant premier Nikita Khrushchev resigns unexpectedly, citing ill health. His replacement is Leonid Brezhnev.

Kenya, November 10: Kenya becomes a republic under the leadership of Jomo Kenyatta.

Britain Says Farewell to Winston Churchill

London, England, January 30: Massive crowds lined the streets of London today to bid farewell to Sir Winston Churchill, Britain's wartime hero and consummate politician who died on January 24, two weeks after suffering a stroke and slipping into a coma. He was 90 years of age.

He will be buried in the family plot at St Martin's Church in Bladon, Oxfordshire, in a private ceremony where only family members will be in attendance. The church lies outside his boyhood home of Blenheim Estate.

Churchill's funeral procession through London.

During the three days that Churchill's body lay in state at Westminster Hall over 300,000 people came to pay their respects.

25,000 March in Alabama to Demand Right to Vote

Montgomery, USA, March 28: Martin Luther King Jr has led a march from the town of Selma, where only a handful of blacks have been permitted to vote, to the Alabama state capital of Montgomery to demonstrate their determination to vote.

The demonstrators walked 12 miles (20 km) a day and slept in fields. They numbered 3,000 on their departure from Selma but the total had increased to well over 25,000 by the time they arrived in Montgomery to present a petition to the recalcitrant Alabama Governor George Wallace.

The march was designed to dramatize the need for a Federal voting-rights law to provide legal support for the enfranchisement of blacks in the southern states.

US Involvement in Vietnam Escalates

Washington DC, USA, July 28: At the conclusion of a what was thought to be a routine press conference today, President Lyndon Johnson has unexpectedly announced the decision to dispatch an additional 50,000 troops to South Vietnam.

This follows on from the earlier decision in March to send 20,000 marines. These two deployments constitute a fundamental shift in US policy and dramatically escalate American involvement in the conflict. The additional deployments also contradict the President's own stated misgivings concerning committing additional US troops, as seen in his recent moment of candor to McGeorge Bundy when he confessed: "I just don't think it's worth fighting for."

It is widely acknowledged though that Johnson requires the support of influential pro-war senators for the passage of civil rights legislation crucial to his vision of building his "Great Society."

This latest commitment of troops comes as a response to increasingly successful Vietcong attacks on US targets. In February, 32 soldiers died and 21 were wounded in separate attacks near Pleiku. This has resulted in the implementation of Operation Rolling Thunder, which is a series of bombing raids on military bases,

time out

A massive power failure brought the northeast of the United States to a standstill, causing huge traffic jams and leaving 800,000 stranded on New York subways. Five thousand off-duty policemen were called upon to help deal with the chaos.

supply depots and infiltration routes through North Vietnam designed to force the Vietcong into negotiations. This action raised US involvement to unprecedented levels, yet still stopped short of a large-scale deployment of troops. However additional forces are now being requested by General Westmoreland to guard US airfields and installations. Many military analysts fear that US troops are ill prepared for the style of warfare they may encounter. The Vietcong isolate their enemy by drawing the troops deep into the countryside away from their bases. The enemy often blends in with the local population, from which they launch guerrilla-style assaults that come with little or no warning.

There have also been five governments in the south since the assassination of Prime Minister Diem last November, with rival military and civilian factions struggling for control.

US strategists hope that a campaign of aerial bombardment will further increase Saigon's political stability, and cause North Vietnamese support for the Vietcong to decline.

In the end, however, President Johnson's decision seems to be influenced by the practical consideration that failure in South Vietnam could seriously derail his ambitious domestic policy agenda. It remains to be seen what price will be paid by US servicemen for the implementation of Johnson's "Great Society."

Ahmed Ben Bella

Malcolm X is assassinated.

London, England, January 30: A state funeral is held for wartime leader Sir Winston Churchill who died six days ago, aged 91.

New York, USA, February 21: Firebrand black nationalist leader Malcolm X is assassinated by two members of his former organization, the Nation of Islam.

Bucharest, Romania, March 19: Nicolae Ceausescu becomes the leader of Romania.

Montgomery, USA, March 21-25: Martin Luther King leads a 54-mile (87 km) march of 25,000 people from Selma.

Danang, South Vietnam, March 31: The first US combat troops are sent to the escalating conflict; 3,000 marines are to protect the US air base at Danang. In February, American bombers began to pound Vietcong positions in the north.

Canberra, Australia, April 29: Prime Minister Menzies commits 1,000 Australian troops to fight in South Vietnam.

Dominican Republic, May: The USA sends 14,000 troops to the Caribbean island after civil war broke out in April following a coup.

Algeria, June 19: Independence hero and Prime Minister Ahmed Ben Bella is deposed in a bloodless coup led by Colonel Boumedienne.

Tokyo, Japan, June 22: Japan and South Korea sign a treaty of basic relations, normalizing relations for the first time since Japan annexed the Korean peninsula in 1910. The Japanese agree to pay $800 million in compensation.

Washington DC, USA, July 28: President Johnson commits a further 50,000 troops to the war in Vietnam.

Singapore, August 9: Serious racial tensions between Malays and Chinese force Singapore to declare independence from Malaysia.

Los Angeles, USA, August 15: Six days of rioting leaves 34 people dead and over 1,000 injured. The trouble began when a black motorist was arrested in the Watts area.

Kashmir, September 6: The Indian army invades West Pakistan in response to earlier incursions by Pakistani soldiers. Both sides have claimed Kashmir since the 1949 war.

New York, USA, October 15: The anti-war movement has gained momentum this year across the USA. The latest protest, in New York, is attended by thousands of concerned Americans.

Rhodesia, November 11: World-wide condemnation greets Prime Minister Ian Smith's decision to sever links with Britain and maintain white-minority rule.

North Sea, December 27: Britain's first offshore oil drilling platform, the Sea Gem, collapses with the loss of 13 lives.

Moshe Dayan

> "I RESPECT
> ONLY THOSE
> WHO RESIST
> ME; BUT I
> CANNOT
> TOLERATE
> THEM."
>
> CHARLES DE GAULLE
> (1890–1970), FRENCH
> MILITARY LEADER
> AND PRESIDENT, 1966

> "A WEEK IS A
> LONG TIME IN
> POLITICS."
>
> HAROLD WILSON
> (1916–1995), BRITISH
> STATESMAN AND
> PRIME MINISTER

The Monsters of the Moors are sentenced

London, England, May 26: Ian Brady, 28, and Myra Hindley, 22, have been sentenced to "never to be released" jail terms, but the evil that they have done lives on.

People cannot comprehend that, for sexual thrills and murderous satisfaction, this Yorkshire pair have brutally done away with Lesley Ann Downey, 10, John Kilbride, 12, and Edward Evans, 17. Police are still searching for the bodies of at least two other children, Keith Bennett, 12, and Pauline Reade, 16.

Brady and Hindley lured the children to their house at Hattersley, in Lancashire, where they were sexually assaulted and killed. The all-male jury heard harrowing tape recordings of Lesley Ann Downey's ordeal and saw nude pictures of her taken by the couple before they strangled her.

The pair buried their victims on Saddleworth Moor, near Manchester, and often spent days there, picnicking and taking photographs of themselves—sometimes on the graves of their victims.

Their killing spree came to light when Brady murdered his final victim, 17-year-old Edward Evans, whom the couple had met in Manchester. Brady murdered the youth with an ax in the front room of his house, while Hindley's brother-in-law, David Smith, was there. Smith fled the house and called police, who found Evans's body in a blanket.

The trial put Brady's personality under the spotlight. It was found that as a child he had tortured children and animals "for fun." When he was sent to Borstal, the boy's reform school, for a petty crime, he vowed to take his revenge on society. The discovery of Hindley as witness and partner to his crimes set the stage for his descent into his psychopathic hell.

Gallic Shrug at Nuclear Protestors

Papeete, Tahiti, July 2: France has exploded an undersea nuclear device at Mururoa Atoll, turning the Pacific Ocean waters a boiling white and sending a radioactive cloud drifting toward South America.

The French Government is making good use of its distant Pacific outposts, avoiding severe criticism in metropolitan France as it carries out its "series of tests." It is playing down international opinion, most vocally expressed by Australia and New Zealand, the USA, and Great Britain. The French say that the protesting nations are being alarmist and that as soon as their scientists are satisfied with the results, the tests will be over. Meanwhile, the furor is doing the French economy little good around the world. Gourmet activists are boycotting French cheese and wine, while motorists are shunning Renaults, Peugeots, and Citroens.

However, the Governor of the French Territory of Tahiti, Renee le Blanc, said in Papeete that he believed the tests would be good for the islands, promoting tourism and development.

time out

Jack Ruby, 55, born Jacob Rubenstein in Poland in 1871, died in a Dallas hospital. Ruby had shot accused presidential assassin Lee Harvey Oswald in the first live broadcast homicide in history. He died awaiting his new trial.

Mao supporters wave the *Little Red Book* at their leader.

Red Guards Rampant in Mao's Cultural Revolution

Beijing, China, August 13: A great ideological upheaval, orchestrated by China's Great Leader Mao Tse-Tung, has targeted the country's "bourgeois" elements and intellectuals, who are being hounded by a revolutionary force of Red Guards who have been ordered to return the country to its pure communist form.

Mao has accused professional workers and intellectuals of creeping capitalist and anti-socialist tendencies. His 1964 Socialist Education Movement includes a work-study program for communes and factories, and advice to intellectuals and scholars to take up manual labor.

Mao retook control of the Party last year and launched his Great Proletarian Cultural Revolution, with the support of Lin Biao and the People's Liberation Army. The force they mobilized, the Red Guards, is made up mostly of student revolutionaries happy to tear down the "capitalist structures" and humiliate Party officials, factory bosses, and professionals.

Professional workers are being paraded through the streets wearing dunce's caps, town officials have been made to kneel before their constituents and confess their faults. These people are all being sent to the fields and the camps, for manual work and re-education, largely through endless quotation from Mao's collection of revolutionary thoughts, which is known in the West as the *Little Red Book*.

Meanwhile, the ordinary machinery of the country—such as the provision of power, food, as well as water supplies, medical treatment and schooling, transportation and law and order—has gone by the board.

Key Events

New Delhi, India, January 19: Indira Gandhi, daughter of former prime minister Pandit Jawaharlal Nehru, is elected prime minister.

Accra, Ghana, February 24: An army coup deposes the prime minister and self-styled redeemer of Ghana, Kwame Nkrumah, while he is on an official visit to China.

Jakarta, Indonesia, March 11: Chaos follows an abortive coup in September last year. General Soeharto receives letter of instruction from Sukarno today, transferring state power to the army.

Rome, Italy, March 27: Pope Paul VI meets Dr Ramsey, Archbishop of Canterbury. It is the first meeting for 400 years between heads of Roman Catholic and Anglican churches.

Sydney, Australia, April 19: Violent scenes erupt in Sydney as Australia's first National Service conscripts fly out for Vietnam.

London, England, May 26: Murderers Ian Brady and Myra Hindley are sentenced to life imprisonment.

Memphis, USA, June 7: James Meredith, the first African-American to brave the color bar in Mississippi, is gunned down in a civil rights march. Martin Luther King takes over as leader of the march.

Mururoa Atoll, French Polynesia, July 2: France explodes a nuclear device.

Washington DC, USA, July 5: During a visit to Washington, Australian Prime Minister Harold Holt vows to go "All the way with L.B.J." as the Vietnam War escalates.

Kuala Lumpur, Malaysia, August 11: Three years of guerrilla warfare between Indonesia and Malaysia come to an end.

Beijing, China, August 13: Mao Tse-tung's cutural revolution targets professionals and intellectuals for re-education.

Vung Tau, South Vietnam, August 18: At Long Tan, Australian troops fight a pitched battle against a Vietcong force about four times its size.

Pretoria, South Africa, September 6: Prime Minister Hendrik Verwoerd, the "Father of Apartheid," is stabbed to death by Demetrio Tsafendas.

Aberfan, Wales, October 21: A sliding slagheap of mine tailings buries a school, killing 116 children and 28 adults.

Moscow, USSR, November 27: The Soviet Communist Party denounces Chinese leadership as the Cultural Revolution gathers speed.

Salisbury, Rhodesia, December 6: The leader of the rebel regime, Ian Smith, rejects proposals by Britain, including bringing black politicians into his cabinet, to end a 13-month dispute since Smith's declaration of independence.

US Forces Assault Iron Triangle

Saigon, South Vietnam, January 28: Increasingly frustrated by its continued inability to engage the Vietcong guerrilla army, the US military has launched a massive offensive—known as Operation Cedar Falls, and involving a 30,000-strong force— on the so-called Iron Triangle, a 60-sq-mile (155-sq-kilometer) jungle area north of Saigon.

The offensive was aimed at rounding up Vietcong soldiers and securing the area against future infiltration. After 19 days of combing the area, the US forces discovered a maze of tunnels containing living quarters, supply depots, and stores and weapons. Only 72 Americans died, while suspected 720 Vietcong were encountered and killed.

All this is occurring against a Stateside background of extreme disenchantment with the war. Veterans from previous wars have staged a protest rally in New York, burning their draft papers.

Israel Triumphant in Six Day War

Tel Aviv, Israel, June 10: Israelis are dancing in the streets after their Six Day War—which saw the amazing triumph of their armed forces against the combined Arab might of Egypt, Jordan, and Syria.

Fighting ended today—the sixth day—with Israel halting an advance into Syria and accepting the UN ceasefire.

Israel now controls vast stretches of Arab territory and faces decisions on handling hostile populations, as well as hundreds of thousands of POWs and refugees. The death toll in the fighting is estimated at over 100,000, with casualties overwhelmingly on the Arab side.

Israel's execution of the war has been overseen by its defense chief, General Moshe Dayan, who is now acclaimed as the hero and spirit of the war.

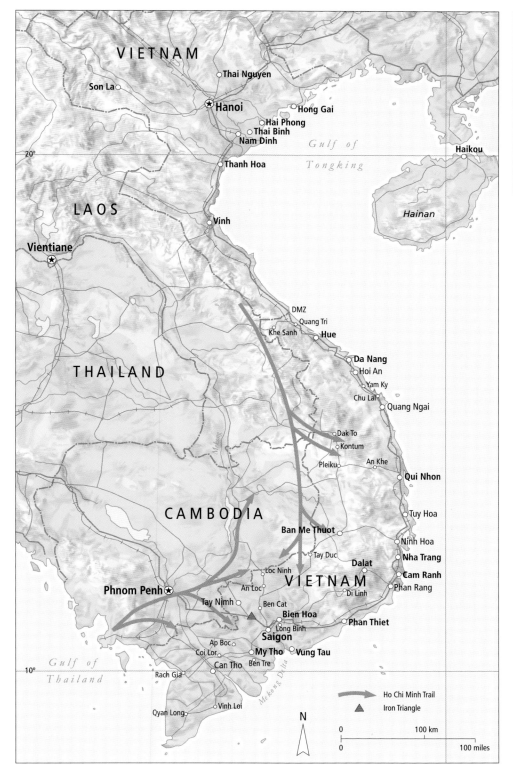

General William Westmoreland

Key Events

Sacramento, USA, January 2: Former film actor Ronald Reagan is sworn in as governor of California.

Cape Kennedy, USA, January 27: Astronauts Virgil "Gus" Grissom, Ed White, and Roger Chaffee die in *Apollo* spacecraft fire.

Saigon, South Vietnam, January 28, 1967: US forces launch Operation Cedar Falls.

Aachen, Germany, March 14: Executives of Chemie Gruementhal are charged over manufacture of the Thalidomide drug, which caused deformities in babies.

Cornwall, England, March 29: Armed forces bomb a stricken oil tanker in an attempt to sink it. The tanker, *Torrey Canyon*, ran aground between Land's End and the Scilly Isles 11 days ago, spreading oil on beaches in France and the UK.

Athens, Greece, April 21: Right-wing army officers under Colonel George Papadopoulos seize power, deposing George Papandreou.

Canberra, Australia, May 27: Australians vote for a proposal to count Aboriginal people in the national census.

Middle East, June 10: The six-day war against Syria and Egypt comes to an end as Israel finally observes a UN ceasefire.

Port Harcourt, Nigeria, July 16: Ibo people of Nigeria set up separate state of Biafra in oil-rich southeast of Nigeria, causing civil war between Nigerian forces and rebels.

Detroit, USA, July 27: Paratroops restore order in Detroit after race riots result in 38 black rioters and looters being shot by police and the National Guard.

Beijing, China, August 30: Red Guards set fire to the British Mission in Beijing and bar all members from leaving without permission.

Villa Grande, Bolivia, October 10: The body of Ernesto "Che" Guevara is put on display after he is shot by troops in Bolivia.

Oakland, California, USA, October 20: The fifth day of anti-war protests sees 4,000 demonstrators battling police. Protests have taken place in 30 US cities in the last week, calling for an end to the Vietnam conflict.

Khe Sanh, South Vietnam, November: Khe Sanh is being heavily fortified by General Westmoreland, ready to carry out reconnaissance attacks on the Ho Chi Minh Trail and other enemy supply lines from the north.

Paris, France, November 27: President Charles de Gaulle states that he will veto British attempts to join the European Economic Union for the second time.

Portsea, Australia, December 22: Australian Prime Minister Harold Holt drowns while swimming in rough seas off Cheviot Beach.

Robert Kennedy

US Forces Struggle to Repel Communist Advance

South Vietnam, January 31: As American forces and their South Vietnamese allies were preparing for Tet holiday festivities today, North Vietnamese and Vietcong troops estimated at over 80,000-strong have launched a massive coordinated attack on South Vietnam's 44 provincial capitals and five of the country's six autonomous cities, including Saigon and the ancient capital of Hue.

This attack represents the first major conventional offensive by the North Vietnamese, and it has caught the US unawares. The fighting around Hue is continuing and is reported as being extremely ferocious. Elements of the US 1st Cavalry and 101st Airborne Division, along with marines and South Vietnamese forces, are engaging in the first urban house-to-house combat of the war.

The US Embassy in Saigon has also been attacked. At least five GIs have been reported killed in the storming of the compound, though US forces ultimately regained control.

The US base at Khe Sanh in the north is also under assault by an estimated 40,000 North Vietnamese and Vietcong forces, although this is seen by intelligence as a deception which is meant to draw the US forces away from the cities.

It has been known for some time that the North Vietnamese forces had been infiltrating arms, ammunition, and men into South Vietnamese towns and cities since late last year. By last November, the traffic heading south along the Ho Chi Minh trail had eight times more than the previous year's monthly average.

On January 5, when a Vietcong was captured near the demilitarized zone with a notebook in his possession giving a broad overview of the offensive to

Coretta King and Harry Belafonte at Martin Luther King Jr's funeral.

come, it was dismissed by military intelligence as a decoy. A CIA analyst, Joseph Hovey, even circulated a memorandum to US leaders predicting a major offensive in the months to come. His analysis was dismissed as unrealistic. This failure of intelligence rivals that of Pearl Harbor, and the "Tet Offensive" is certain to demonstrate to the Johnson Administration that victory in Indochina is likely to require a bigger commitment of troops than the American public is willing to bear.

time out

New Jersey police confiscated 30,000 copies of John Lennon and Yoko Ono's album, *Two Virgins*. A nude photograph of the couple on the cover violated pornography laws in the state. Press and fans also reacted strongly against the cover.

Funeral of Martin Luther King Jr

Atlanta, USA, April 9: More than 150,000 people have attended the funeral of the Reverend Martin Luther King Jr at the Ebenezer Church at Morehouse College in Atlanta, Georgia. King was assassinated in Memphis, Tennessee, five days ago, when he was shot through the head while standing on the balcony of the Lorraine Motel.

King's inspirational speeches and non-violent direct activism have helped alter the fabric of American life, with his concept of "somebodiness" giving blacks and the poor a new sense of worth and dignity. In 1964 King became the youngest ever recipient of the Nobel Peace Prize. His courage and selfless devotion has given direction and momentum to the Civil Rights cause since 1955.

Robert Kennedy Shot in LA Hotel

Los Angeles, USA, June 6: Americans are waking up this morning to the shocking news that the Democratic presidential candidate, Senator Robert Kennedy, has died.

In the early hours of yesterday morning he was shot four times at point-blank range by 24-year-old Palestinian Sirhan Sirhan in the kitchen of the Ambassador Hotel in Los Angeles. Kennedy had just delivered a rousing speech in celebration of his win in the California presidential primary and was greeting some of his supporters working in the kitchen when a series of muffled sounds was heard. Several people were wounded, and Kennedy was shot in the head. The gunman was wrestled to the ground and has been taken away for questioning.

Senator Kennedy has been taken to the Good Samaritan Hospital, where a team of neurosurgeons is working to save the life of our late President's younger brother. The prayers of a nation are with him and his family.

Key Events

Thule, Greenland, January 21: A US B-52 bomber crashes, carrying four hydrogen bombs.

South Vietnam, January 31: North Vietnamese and the Vietcong launch the Tet offensive

UK, February 4: Kenyan Asians flee repressive laws that prevent them from making a living since independence.

My Lai, South Vietnam, March 16: US troops massacre hundreds of unarmed civilians.

Washington DC, USA, March 31: President Lyndon Johnson stuns America by announcing that he will not run for office in the forthcoming elections.

Atlanta, USA, April 9: The funeral of Martin Luther King, who was assassinated in Memphis on April 4, is attended by 150,000 people.

Wellington, New Zealand, April 10: The ferry *Wahine* capsizes in Wellington harbor in a severe storm. Of the 734 passengers and crew on board, 51 lose their lives.

France, May: Ten million workers strike in solidarity with students after leftist student riots earlier this month were brutally suppressed by the police. President de Gaulle issues an ultimatum for the country to back his reforms or sack him.

Los Angeles, USA, June 6: Presidential candidate Robert Kennedy is assassinated by Palestinian militant Sirhan Sirhan.

World, July 1: The Nuclear Non-Proliferation Treaty is signed by 62 nations, including the USA, the USSR, and the UK.

Vatican City, July 29: Pope Paul VI confirms the ban on the use of contraceptives by Catholics, despite calls for change, with the release of the encyclical *Humanae Vitae*.

Addis Ababa, Ethiopia, August 15: Peace talks between Biafran secessionists and Nigeria, aiming to reconcile the two states after Biafra declared itself independent of Nigeria in May, end without progress. The economic blockade of Biafra has led to mass starvation.

Prague, Czechoslovakia, August 21: The "Prague Spring" program of liberalization initiated by Alexander Dubcek comes to an abrupt end when Warsaw Pact countries send in tanks to reinstate hard-line communist policy. Czechoslovaks take to the streets to show their support for the reforms.

China, October: As the whirlwind of Mao Tse-tung's Cultural Revolution continues, the army is given carte blanche to restore order.

USA, November 5: Republican Richard Nixon is elected president.

Man Walks on the Moon

Houston, USA, July 21: Astronaut Neil Alden Armstrong emerged backward from the lunar module *Eagle*, a large figure in a white spacesuit, backpack of breathing apparatus, and helmet. Slowly he descended the steps of the ladder that led to the surface of the moon.

Then came the moment, watched by countless millions around the world on television. Armstrong's foot touched the surface and he said, "That's one small step for man, one giant leap for mankind." US Navy Commander Armstrong was soon joined by USAF Colonel Edwin "Buzz" Aldrin, and they looked like children playing as they experimented with the moon's gravity, taking leaps and jumps that moved them with a floating motion.

Armstrong reported: "The surface is like a fine powder. It has a soft beauty all its own, like some desert of the United States." The astronauts collected samples of rock and dust, planted the Stars and Stripes, and took pictures before returning to the lunar module.

The *Eagle* is scheduled to remain for less than a day, and then must power up and rendezvous with *Apollo 11*, with USAF Colonel Michael Collins on board in his lonely job as pilot. They will transfer to the main spacecraft, taking their samples with them, jettison the *Eagle* and then fire the *Apollo 11* engine to set a course for their return to Earth.

The operation, meticulously planned by NASA, can go badly wrong if anything malfunctions, and NASA engineers cannot relax their concentration until the astronauts are back on Earth.

The landing itself was fraught with tension as the *Apollo* went into orbit around the moon, and Armstrong and Aldrin transferred to the *Eagle*, before firing their engine to begin the descent. There were tense moments as the *Eagle*, on remote control, appeared to be heading for some rocks. Armstrong took manual control of the space vehicle and landed it safely on a flat area. His first words from the moon, again heard by millions, were: "Houston, Tranquility Base here. The Eagle has landed."

Colonel Edwin "Buzz" Aldrin is the second man to walk on the moon's surface.

British Troops Arrive in Ireland to Quell Unrest

Ulster, Northern Ireland, August 14: In response to a dramatic escalation in civil disorder, with thousands of residents forced to leave their homes in the face of riots verging on pogroms, London has dispatched troops to Ulster in Northern Ireland in an attempt to stop the rising unrest between Protestants and Catholics, and their emerging paramilitary arms.

Sectarian divisions in Northern Ireland have been present for well over 300 years. This complex conflict has at its core the centuries-old English sense of superiority over the Irish, and their view of the legitimacy of British colonial rule.

Northern Ireland became a separate state after a nationalist revolt in 1921, effectively partitioning the country.

Okinawa to be Returned Japanese Sovereignty

Okinawa, Japan, November 21: It has been announced today that the Pacific island of Okinawa and other islands in the Ryukyu archipelago will be returned to Japan. The announcement followed a meeting at the White House between President Nixon and the Japanese Prime Minister Eisaku Sato.

Okinawa, an independent kingdom in the fifteenth century, became a Japanese prefecture in 1879. Okinawa was the final island battle fought between the USA and Japan in World War II, and the only battle fought on Japanese soil. Thirteen thousand Americans, 50,000 Japanese, and 150,000 local Okinawans were killed, and US troops have occupied Okinawa and other Ryukyu islands since March 1945. Today's meeting will set in motion a timetable for the return of administrative rights over the islands to the Japanese.

Sato told the Japanese Diet in March that Japan's anti-nuclear policy would apply to the islands after their return.

**Commander
Neil Armstrong**

Key Events

Paris, France, January 18: The Paris peace talks open between the USA, South Vietnam, North Vietnam, and the Vietcong.

Cairo, Egypt, February 3: The leader of the Fatah faction, Yasser Arafat, is the new head of the Palestine Liberation Organization.

Memphis, Tennessee, USA, March 10: The killer of Martin Luther King, James Earl Ray, is sentenced to life imprisonment for the murder of the civil rights leader.

Tel Aviv, Israel, March 17: Seventy-one-year-old Golda Meir comes out of retirement to become Israel's first female prime minister.

Paris, France, April 28: French president Charles de Gaulle resigns, following the defeat of a referendum on sweeping governmental reforms.

USA, May 10: The government signals a crackdown on student protests, with Vice-President Spiro Agnew stating, "The time has come for American colleges under siege to assert themselves."

Midway Island, Pacific Ocean, June 8: US President Nixon meets with South Vietnamese leader Nguyen Van Thieu to discuss the "Vietnamization" of the Vietnam War. Around 25,000 US troops are projected to withdraw by September.

Nigeria, June 30: The Nigerian government bans Red Cross night flights from distributing food aid in disputed Biafra state, jeopardizing the survival of four million people.

The Moon, July 21: Neil Armstrong walks on the Moon, watched by millions of television viewers.

Los Angeles, USA, August 9: Charles Manson and his "family" kill Sharon Tate, wife of director Roman Polanski, and four others, in Polanski's Beverly Hills mansion.

China, August 13: Soviet troops make incursions into Chinese territory; heavy fighting occurs.

Northern Ireland, August 14: British troops are deployed to restore order in Ulster after escalating religious violence.

Libya, September 1: The 18-year rule of King Idris is ended by Colonel Gaddafi's bloodless coup.

Bonn, West Germany, October 21: Social Democrat and former mayor of West Berlin, Willy Brandt, is elected chancellor, ending the Christian Democrats' hold on government since the end of World War II.

Washington DC, USA, November 15: A group of 250,000 people marches to the US capital to demand an end to the Vietnam War.

Okinawa, Japan, November 21: A joint US-Japanese communique announces that Okinawa and the other Ryukyu Islands are to be handed back to the Japanese.

John Rock

Contraceptive Pill Goes on Sale

New York, USA, January 30, 1961: A new contraceptive pill is now available for women. By taking one tablet a night of a progestogen-estrogen mixture, beginning on day five of the menstrual cycle and continuing for 20 days, women can avoid ovulation and therefore pregnancy.

Despite all types of contraceptive preparations and devices, despite the crackpot ideas spanning the ages, despite the condom developed by the vulcanologist Charles Goodyear, it is only now possible for women to have effective birth control, and by their own volition.

Nausea, breast engorgement, premenstrual tension, headaches, and weight gain may occur in the first few months for those taking "the pill," marketed as Enovid in the USA and as Conovid in the UK. There is also talk of an increase in body hair and, most seriously, the possibility of blood clotting.

The pill was developed in the United States. The science is of the last decade, but the ideological battle rings through the century, notably from the publication by New York nurse Margaret Sanger in 1914 of her journal *The Woman Rebel*, in which she advocated birth control. Her cause was the impetus for a Women's Birth Control League.

In 1950, Margaret Sanger met with Gregory Pincus, one of a few scientists already researching birth control through chemicals. John Rock, Frank Colton, and Carl Djerassi were working in this area, and by 1960 research had progressed so far that Enovid was approved for sale by the Federal Drug Administration.

This first birth control pill has been received enthusiastically by many women, although there are religious issues that may affect its acceptance by some.

Million-Year-Old Bones Found in Africa

Dar es Salaam, Tanganyika, February 24, 1961: Dr Louis Leakey, a British anthropologist who has fossicking among old bones in Tanganyika's Olduvai Gorge for decades, has made a discovery that pushes the origins of the human-like species *Australopithecus* back another 400,000 years.

The Olduvai Gorge is an 8-mile-long (13 km) feature of the famous Rift Valley, a split in the Earth's surface that enables researchers to get close to the remnants of earlier life on Earth. Kenyan-born, Cambridge-educated Leakey has been researching there with his wife Mary over four decades. In 1931, he discovered stone tools that led him to believe that hominid fossils would eventually be found at the site.

The Leakeys made a big find in 1959 with the "Nutcracker Man"—a massive skull dominated by a broad concave face and flaring cheekbones. It had teeth four times the size of those of present humans and was declared a new species of the human family. The new find consists of a skull, a collarbone, hands, and feet of a child. The skull has a bigger brain cavity and smaller teeth than those of Nutcracker Man. According to Leakey, the bones are around a million years old, much older than the 600,000-year-old Nutcracker Man.

The penchant of humans for attacking their own kind is apparent in the death of the child. A crack in the skull suggests that the child was killed by a blow.

time out

The Soviet Union claimed a breakthrough in space travel with the orbit in space and safe retrieval of two dogs as well as other small animals and plant life. It was the first successful space travel and re-entry by living creatures.

Soviet Union Sends a Man into Space

Moscow, USSR, April 12, 1961: The Soviet Union has won the first leg of the space race. It has sent 27-year-old Major Yuri Gagarin hurtling skyward in his *Vostok* spacecraft, to orbit the Earth and return safely in a flight lasting 108 minutes.

The flight was conducted in secrecy, and the news was broken by a radio announcer who interrupted a broadcast at 10 a.m. Citizens across Russia have joined each other in celebration. On hearing the amazing news, NASA chief James Webb described it as "a fantastic, fabulous achievement."

The *Vostok* spacecraft was launched from the Tyuratam Space Center in central Asia. Major Gagarin was strapped into a lying position, dressed in heavy protective clothing and with breathing apparatus. Instruments and cameras monitored his responses and stresses. "I feel well. I have no injuries or bruises," he said on landing.

Gagarin did little to fly the spacecraft except to fire braking rockets after the orbit and again at a height of 190 miles (305 km). His spacecraft returned to Earth by parachute.

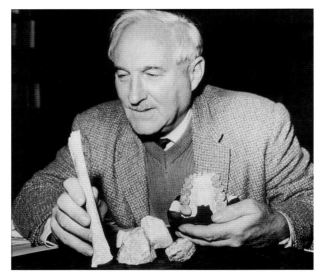

Dr Louis Leakey with some bone remains of early humans.

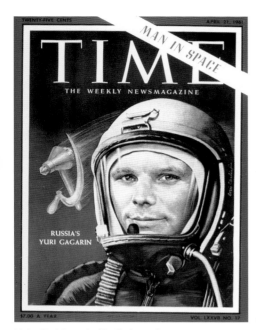
Major Yuri Gagarin, the first man in space.

Willard Libby

The first man to see the view from space said: "The sky looked very, very dark, and the Earth was bluish." He told an ecstatic Soviet Premier Nikita Khrushchev: "I could see seas, mountains, big cities, and forests."

Born in Klushino in 1934, Gagarin joined the Air Force School in Orenburg in 1955. He met his wife Valentina while she was in Orenburg as a medical student, and they have two children.

America has fallen behind in the space race, which intensified in October 1957 when the Soviets launched their first satellite *Sputnik I*, and in the following month they sent a dog, Laika, into space, to orbit the Earth at a height of nearly 1,000 miles (1,600 km). *Sputnik II* supplied Laika with food, water, and air, measured the effects of weightlessness on animals, and gathered data on cosmic rays and other conditions in space.

Since then, various chimps and dogs have been sent into orbit, and Russia has crash-landed onto the moon, discovering its substance of cosmic dust and rocks, and has demystified the legendary "dark side of the moon," revealing it as "monotonous." The big prize—the first man on the moon— remains open.

America has more sophisticated and maneuverable craft than the *Vostok* that carried Gagarin, but it does not yet have the thrust technology to boost such a big craft into orbit. A sub-orbital flight is planned for the near future.

Scientist Sounds Alarm Bells on Pesticide Use

New York, USA, June, 1962: The dangers of the hazardous pesticide DDT have been exposed in a series of articles in *The New Yorker* serializing Rachel Carson's latest book *Silent Spring*.

Carson, America's best-selling science writer, argues persuasively that humankind is fatally tampering with nature in its indiscriminate use of chemical pesticides and in particular DDT (dichloro-diphenyl-trichloroethane), explaining how their use can irrevocably alter the cellular processes of plants, animals, and possibly even humans.

She warns of a time when birdsong may be silenced and spring turned into a barren wilderness unless we reconsider the wisdom of using pesticides.

Early threats of lawsuits and a scare campaign against "this hysterical woman"

Rachel Carson, author of *Silent Spring*.

by the chemical industry have only served to focus national attention upon the issues that Carson has raised. The book is set to become a runaway bestseller.

Ancient Viking Settlement Unearthed

L'Anse aux Meadows, Canada, November, 1963: Archeologists have unearthed a Viking settlement at the northernmost tip of Newfoundland. The settlement is made up of eight houses and a workshop, with remarkably preserved walls and pitched roofs, suggesting that Icelandic explorers reached the shores of North America around 1000 CE.

After surveying the coastlines of Newfoundland and Labrador, archeologists Helge Ingstad and his wife Anne Stine discovered the settlement near Epave Bay and have named it L'Anse aux Meadows, or Meadow Cove. In 1955, Ingstad had followed an old Icelandic map from the 1670s that identified a possible colony called "Promontorium Winlandiae." A local fisherman took him to what was believed to be an old Indian site where there were remains of sod walls, but local Indians never built with sod walls.

Over the next eight summers the site was excavated. Significant finds include a blacksmith shop with forged nails in situ. It is the earliest evidence of iron processing yet found in North America.

The houses are Icelandic in style, with 6 ft (1.8 m) thick walls consisting of two layers of sod with gravel in between for drainage. The roofs are made of turf laid over a sturdy timber frame. Among the over 800 artefacts uncovered so far are spindles, soapstone oil lamps, and pieces of jasper with trace elements that are found only in Iceland.

The work of these archeologists seems to prove that Norsemen visited the shores of North America and established a presence there 500 years before the advent of Christopher Columbus.

André Turcat

Measles Vaccine Now Available

USA, February, 1965: A measles vaccine has been licensed and is now generally available for the first time.

In the USA alone there are three to nine million new cases of measles each year. It is a common cause of pneumonia, blindness, seizures, and brain damage, and despite today's news is nevertheless destined to remain a major worldwide scourge, particularly in the Third World.

It is expected that after just two doses of the vaccine, over 99 percent of recipients will gain immunity. The initial dose for children should be administered at 12 months, with a second dose recommended when the child starts kindergarten at between 4 and 6 years of age.

It was a Scottish physician, Francis Home, who demonstrated in 1757 that measles was caused by an infectious agent in the blood, but it wasn't until 1954 that the virus was isolated in Boston by John F. Enders and Thomas Peebles.

BP Signals Gas Find in North Sea

London, England, December 9, 1965: British Petroleum has announced the discovery of natural gas in the West Sole Field in the North Sea's southern basin by the jack-up drilling rig *Sea Gem*.

It has long being suspected that oil and gas reserves would be found there, but it was felt that such fields would be small and not economically feasible to extract. This view has altered in recent times with the build-up of geological information on the area coupled with BP's recent oil finds in Gainsborough and other areas in Lincolnshire, giving the company the confidence to extend their search to the offshore waters of the North Sea.

The first offshore hole in the North Sea was sunk in May of 1964 in the German sector by the drilling platform *Mr Louie*, striking a pocket of high-pressure nitrogen that was considered too dangerous for commercial exploitation.

The well is the fourth to be spudded in British waters. Drilling to a depth of 10,000 ft (3,000 m), a 40-ft (12-m) flame was ignited at the rig's summit, signaling the beginning of tests to measure the quality and quantity of the find.

Barnard Performs First Heart Transplant

Cape Town, South Africa, December 3, 1967: Dr Christiaan Barnard, a 45-year-old heart surgeon who recently performed the world's first kidney transplant, has today successfully transplanted a heart from a young woman, Denise Darvall, into a Mr Louis Washkansky, a diabetic with incurable heart disease, at the Groot Schurr Hospital in Cape Town.

Washkansky has reportedly recovered well, and has been sitting up in bed eating steak and eggs. Huge doses of azathioprine and hydrocortisone are being used to suppress his immune system in order to prevent rejection of the new heart.

The donor apparently was struck by a car and was declared brain dead. The woman's father did not hesitate when asked permission to donate her organs.

Barnard's team included Marthinus Botha, an immunologist, who made sure the new heart would match Washkansky's body, and Arderne Forder, the bacteriologist who checked everyone for infectious bacteria. Washkansky himself washed several times before the operation, and a germ-free recovery room was prepared.

The son of a poor Afrikaner preacher from Beaufort West, a small town on the edge of South Africa's Great Karroo

Dr Christiaan Barnard with patient Louis Washkansky.

Plateau, the young Christiaan would walk five miles each day to study at Cape Town University, before becoming a family physician on the Western Cape.

Barnard first gained recognition for his work in gastrointestinal pathology, where he proved that the fatal birth defect congenital intestinal atresia (gap in the small intestines) occurred when the unborn fetus did not receive enough blood.

In the late 1950s he studied with Dr Owen Wagensteen at the University of Minnesota where a new heart-lung

Scientific Achievements

Astronomy: Astronauts orbit the Earth; man walks on the moon.
Botany: Term "Green Revolution" used to describe improved wheat and rice productivity in Asia.
Chemistry: Nuclear transplantation used for first cloning of a vertebrate.
Ecology: Hazards of chemical pesticides to the environment exposed; first warnings about global warming.
Geology: Concept of seafloor spreading proposed and basics outlined.
Mathematics: Quicksort, a sorting algorithm that puts lists in order, is developed.
Medicine: First vaccines for polio (oral), measles, mumps administered; first portable defibrillator developed; first heart transplant; first liver transplant.
Physics: First working laser invented.
Zoology: Dian Fossey continues work on gorillas started by Schaller.

Botanic Gardens
Birmingham, England

Observatories
Belogradchik, Bulgaria
Hradec Kralove, Czech Republic
Moletai, Lithuania
Parkes, Australia
San Diego, USA
Tartumaa, Estonia
Tenerife, Spain

Universities
University of Phnom Penh, Cambodia
University of Brasilia, Brazil
University of Guatemala City, Guatemala
University of Joensuu, Finland
University of Veliko Tarnovo, Bulgaria

A dramatic flame of gas is emitted from the oil rig *Sea Gem*, off the coast of East Anglia.

machine had been developed, which included a pump to replace the heart function and an oxygenator to replace the lung function. In 1958, after having been awarded a Master of Science in Surgery, he returned to South Africa and went to work at the Groot Schurr Hospital in their heart unit as a specialist in cardiothoracic surgery.

In 1961 Barnard became Head of the Department of Cardiothoracic Surgery. He soon began experimenting with the transplantation of hearts into dogs and went back to the United States where he studied immunology for three years. "For me the heart has always been an organ without any mystique attached to it… merely a primitive pump…the individual is the brain, not the heart," he has been quoted as saying.

Birth of World's First Sextuplets Stuns Britain

Birmingham, England, October 2, 1968: History was made at the Birmingham Maternity Hospital today when Sheila Thorns gave birth to six babies delivered by cesarean section two months prematurely and with the assistance of a total of 28 medical staff.

The babies—two girls and four boys—were placed in incubators. One of the girls died shortly afterward while being given a blood transfusion.

For the past two years, Mrs Thorns had taken the fertility drug gonadotrophin, which consists of two hormones known as FSH and LH, but she had been unable to conceive until the level of LH was increased, which has resulted in a series of multiple pregnancies.

Prior to 1938 multiple births were registered as separate events, and it's believed around 18 sets of sextuplets have been born in Britain this century, though it's unclear how many have survived.

Sheila's husband Barry told reporters: "We were expecting this multiple birth but were stunned when told Sheila was likely to have five or six babies."

Test Tube Babies Possible

Cambridge, England, February 13, 1969: Human eggs have been fertilized in a test tube outside the body, opening up the possibility test-tube babies some time in the future. This remarkable development has been achieved by Cambridge scientists Robert Edwards and Brian Bavister, collaborating with Patrick Steptoe, a specialist in obstetrics and gynecology at Oldham General Hospital.

The eggs were taken from woman volunteers and were immersed in a nutrient fluid before being brought together with

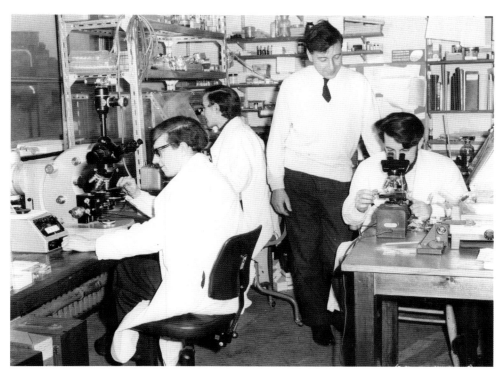

Dr Robert Edwards and his team are researching new technologies and paving the way for "test-tube" babies.

human sperm at body temperature. Of a total of 56 eggs, 18 were fertilized.

The researchers warned that "problems of embryonic development are likely," and that there is a risk that deformed fetuses might be produced. They warned that, although the technique could be used to treat certain types of infertility in older women, a higher incidence of Down syndrome babies or aborted fetuses might be expected.

Supersonic Concorde

Paris, France, May 29, 1969: Concorde, the new wonder of supersonic flight, stopped all Paris as it made a low-level flight over the city on its way to the Paris Air Show. The citizenry will be flocking to have a close-up look at the sleek passenger jet, which will cut Paris–New York flying time to a few luxurious hours.

The Concorde, built by an Anglo-French consortium, had its first test flight on March 2 at Toulouse. Chief Test Pilot André Turcat took Concorde 001, with its four Rolls-Royce Olympus 593 engines, on a 28-minute circle. Concorde 002, the English equivalent, did a similar run last month from Filton, in the hands of the British Aircraft Corporation Chief Test Pilot Brian Trubshaw.

To say there have been political sensitivities involved in the release of this aeronautical symbol of accord between the two countries would be an understatement, but they have been more the concern of politicians. The aircraft has been a triumph of technical cooperation over a decade of planning.

The idea of a joint operation in this huge technical and financial undertaking

was mooted in 1961 in discussions between BAC and France's Sud Aircraft Corporation. The following year France and Britain signed a draft treaty of collaboration, and the specifications for the supersonic airliner were published.

After today's display, and a parade of open checkbooks, the consortium is confident of selling 400 Concordes.

The *Apollo 11* spacecraft

Apollo 8 crew, William Anders, Jim Lovell, and Frank Borman.

Jean-Paul Sartre

"It is not necessary for the public to know whether I am joking or whether I am serious, just as it is not necessary for me to know it myself."

SALVADOR DALI (1904–1989), SPANISH ARTIST

"Is it a book you would wish your wife or your servants to read?"

MERVYN GRIFFITH-JONES (1909–1978) LAWYER, AT THE TRIAL OF *LADY CHATTERLEY'S LOVER*, BY D.H. LAWRENCE, 1960

Lady Chatterley's Lover Sells Out on UK Release

England, November 10, 1960: Penguin Books have sold out of D. H. Lawrence's controversial 1928 novel *Lady Chatterley's Lover* on its first day of release today. A trial for obscenity last month cleared the way for Lawrence's book to be published in the UK for the first time.

The Obscene Publications Act 1959 required Penguin Books to argue convincingly about the literary merit of the work in order to avoid conviction. Ultimately, in answer to the prosecution's question—"Is it a book that you would have lying around in your own house?"— the jury decided that it was, thus clearing the way for greater freedom in the publication of explicit material.

The book's theme is inherently confrontational, with the liberal use of profanities and graphic descriptions of the sexual act, coupled with the radical idea that sexual freedom and sensuality is far more important in life than mere intellectual pursuits.

Rudolf Nureyev Defects to the West

Paris, France, June 16, 1961: Shouting "I want to be free" after dashing through a security barrier at Le Bourget Airport in Paris, Rudolf Nureyev, the principal dancer of the Kirov Ballet, has been granted temporary political asylum in France.

While waiting to board a flight to London with the rest of his troupe, Nureyev was approached by two Russian guards, who informed him that he was required to return to Moscow. He made his dramatic bid for freedom while being escorted to a waiting Russian aircraft.

The Leningrad Kirov Ballet troupe have continued their trip to London where they are to begin a four-week engagement at Covent Garden.

Nureyev's associations with Parisian society have been widespread and include a close friendship with the famed director of the Paris Opéra Ballet, Serge Lifar.

Hemingway Commits Suicide

Ketchum, Idaho, USA, July 2, 1961: The acclaimed American novelist Ernest Hemingway was found dead today in Ketchum, Idaho, killed by a self-inflicted gunshot wound to the head, just three weeks short of his 62nd birthday.

Hemingway was a giant of modern literature whose use of short, concrete, direct prose, with many scenes consisting entirely of pure dialogue, gave his novels and short stories a distinct accessibility. His four major novels—*The Sun Also Rises* (1926), *A Farewell to Arms* (1929), *For Whom the Bell Tolls* (1940), and *The Old Man and the Sea* (1952)—are very simply structured, and yet when added to his body of outstanding short stories they represent a contribution to literature greater than F. Scott Fitzgerald and approximating that of William Faulkner.

After graduating from high school in 1917, Ernest Hemingway became a reporter for the *Kansas City Star*. Unable to join the armed services due to his poor eyesight, he served in World War 1 as an ambulance driver for the American Red Cross. After the war, he became a foreign correspondent for the *Toronto Star*. While living in Paris, Hemingway became part of a community of American expatriates that included literary luminaries Gertrude Stein, Ezra Pound, and F. Scott Fitzgerald.

Hemingway made his American literary debut in 1925 with a collection of short stories, *In Our Time*, and in the following year published his first significant novel, *The Sun Also Rises*.

In 1951, he amazed himself by writing *The Old Man and the Sea* in only eight weeks. It poignantly tells the story of a man who rows out into the Gulf Stream and, after a monumental struggle, catches a great fish and lashes it to his skiff. On the way back to Havana it is eaten by sharks, and he ends up with nothing to show for his efforts. It was the ultimate story of simple "strength of character." Hemingway himself felt it was "the best I can write ever for all of my life."

After its publication his celebrity status skyrocketed. The public appetite for details on his life seemed unquenchable, with periodicals publishing his opinions and personal activities. He was awarded

Peter O'Toole stars in David Lean's 1962 epic film, *Lawrence of Arabia*.

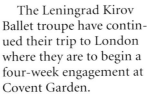

Novelist Ernest Hemingway.

the Pulitzer Prize in 1953 and the Nobel Prize for Literature in 1954, which he was too ill to accept in person.

Hemingway was married four times and had three sons. When his mother died he fell into deep depression. Overwhelmed with loneliness and suffering high blood pressure as well as ongoing physical ailments from an air crash while on safari in Africa, he moved to Ketchum in 1959 with his fourth wife Mary.

After hospitalization for extreme nervous depression and two suicide threats, the great man ended his life today at his home in Ketchum.

Screen Goddess Marilyn Monroe Found Dead

Los Angeles, USA, August 5, 1962: The most glamorous figure of our time, Marilyn Monroe was found dead early today in her Hollywood bungalow. She was found lying naked in her bed, clutching a telephone receiver, with an empty bottle of Nembutal sleeping pills on her bedside table. She was only 36.

So ended the ultimately troubled life of a woman for whom the phrase "sex symbol" was coined. The seductive package of her luminous blonde looks and voluptuous body, combined with pouting lips and air of wide-eyed innocence made her an unforgettable star.

With three failed marriages behind her, dark hints about lovers in the highest of places, and her career in a downward spiral, there might be thoughts that she committed suicide. And yet she had only yesterday consulted her doctor about her sleeping problems, and had wished her housekeeper a cheery "Goodnight, honey" before she went to her suite. Her third husband, playwright Arthur Miller, said: "Her great enemy was sleeplessness."

Marilyn (born Norma Jean Baker) was from the wrong side of the tracks but in the right part of the world, Los Angeles. She married an aircraft worker at 16, but when he shipped out for war in 1944 they divorced, and she became an assembly line worker at a radio factory.

Picked out by a photographer for the cover of *Yank* magazine, she was soon

time out

The Merry Pranksters held a three-day event at the Longshoremen's Hall in San Francisco called the Trips Festival. Celebrating the West Coast counterculture, it involved figures such as writer Ken Kesey, the band The Grateful Dead, and poet Alan Ginsberg.

offered a screen test and became a starlet at 20th Century Fox. After arresting minor roles in films such as *The Asphalt Jungle* and *All About Eve*, she rose to stardom in 22 feature films. In 1954, her marriage to baseball hero Joe DiMaggio was a "tabloid dream," but her high profile troubled him, and they separated after only nine months. He remained a devoted friend.

Marilyn's early roles emphasized her dizzy blonde aspect, but she came to give deeper and more memorable performances in films such as *Niagara, Bus Stop, Something's Gotta Give,* and *Some Like it Hot.*

Arthur Miller wrote her latest film, *The Misfits,* directed by John Huston and co-starring Clark Gable, and noted the signs that Marilyn was troubled. She was quoted in this week's *Life* magazine as saying: "Everybody is always tugging at you. They would all like sort of a chunk of you."

Elizabeth Taylor

Sartre Refuses Nobel Prize for Literature

Paris, France, October 23, 1964: The French existentialist writer Jean-Paul Sartre has refused to accept the Nobel Prize for Literature and the 26 million francs that accompanied it, saying that writers should rely on their words alone, and not any honors bestowed upon them.

Sartre had apparently warned the Swedish Academy of his intentions some weeks ago, advising them that he would refuse to accept the prize because he didn't want to appear to having been "bought off" by the middle-class establishment, and also choosing to remind the Academy that they had never before offered the prize to an avowed Marxist.

Sartre also believes that such honors could interfere with a writer's responsibilities to his readers.

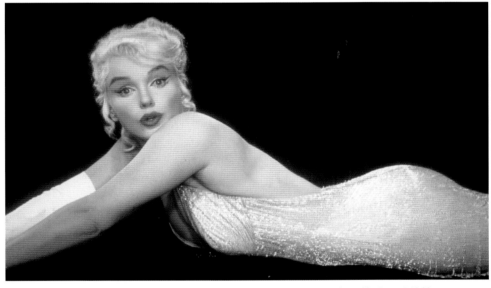

One of Hollywood's most glamorous stars, Marilyn Monroe's life came to a tragic end in August 1962.

Key Events

London, England, January 4, 1965: The poet T. S. Eliot dies, aged 76.

Hollywood, USA, April 6, 1965: Julie Andrews wins the Best Actress Oscar for *Mary Poppins*.

London, England, April 20, 1965: Australian folk group The Seekers top the British charts with "I'll Never Find Another You."

London, England, September 19, 1965: Dusty Springfield, the "white lady of soul," is voted best female singer in Britain.

London, England, December 10, 1965: As Maria Callas gives her last performance in *Tosca* at the Royal Opera, Australian Joan Sutherland takes the mantle as supreme diva.

New York, USA, January, 1966: Truman Capote's *In Cold Blood* is released to widespread acclaim.

Florey, England, April 10, 1966: Novelist Evelyn Waugh dies at 66.

Hollywood, USA, April 18, 1966: *The Sound of Music*, starring Julie Andrews, wins Best Film at the Academy Awards.

New York, USA, February 23, 1967: The raunchy Rolling Stones' songs are banned on TV.

Los Angeles, USA, June 10, 1967: Actor Spencer Tracy dies at 67.

London, England, July 8, 1967: Vivien Leigh, the screen beauty who immortalized Scarlett O'Hara in *Gone with the Wind*, dies at 53.

London, England, August 27, 1967: Beatles' manager Brian Epstein is found dead from an overdose of sleeping pills.

Washington DC, USA, April 2, 1968: Stanley Kubrick's futuristic *2001: A Space Odyssey* premières.

New York, USA, June 3, 1968: Andy Warhol is shot by the founder of the Society for Cutting Up Men (SCUM), Valerie Solanis.

Sydney, Australia, June 24, 1968: Tony Hancock, much-loved English comedian of *Hancock's Half Hour*, suicides in a Sydney hotel.

London, England, August 15, 1968: The hippie musical *Hair* is a hit on both sides of the Atlantic.

Amsterdam, Netherlands, March 20, 1969: Beatle John Lennon and artist Yoko Ono marry.

London, England, June 22, 1969: Singer Judy Garland is found dead in her flat at the age of 47.

Bethel, New York, USA, August 15-17, 1969: The Woodstock Festival of music is attended by over 400,000.

Tallahassee, USA, October 21, 1969: Author Jack Kerouac, whose *On the Road* touched the core of the hippie-beat generation, dies at 47.

Critics Praise Capote's *In Cold Blood*

Sean Connery as James Bond

> "IF BOTTICELLI
> WERE ALIVE
> TODAY HE'D BE
> WORKING FOR
> VOGUE."
>
> PETER USTINOV (1921–
> 2004), BRITISH ACTOR
> AND WRITER, 1962

> "WE'RE MORE
> POPULAR THAN
> JESUS CHRIST
> NOW. *I DON'T
> KNOW WHICH
> WILL GO FIRST.
> ROCK AND
> ROLL OR
> CHRISTIANITY."*
>
> JOHN LENNON (1940–
> 1980), ENGLISH ROCK
> MUSICIAN AND
> MEMBER OF THE
> BEATLES, 1966

New York, USA, January, 1966: The self-styled "Southern Gothic" novelist Truman Capote's latest novel *In Cold Blood*, based upon the true story of the murder of a Kansas family by two drifters, has been released to critical acclaim today.

In 1959, Capote found a 300-word story on the killings tucked away in an edition of the *New York Times* and asked *The New Yorker*'s editor William Shawn to allow him to go to Kansas on assignment. He spent the next six years interviewing the family's friends and neighbors, as well as the killers themselves—Richard Hickock and Perry Edward Smith. At their request, Capote was present at their execution in April last year.

A promising young author, Capote is known for his tight flawless prose and keen insight into human nature. With *In Cold Blood*, Capote claims to have invented a new writing style—the non-fiction novel, a factual retelling of the crime written in the format of a novel. The story is told in the first person, the second person, and in flashbacks.

Capote wanted to experiment with a documentary style of writing, and sought to merge journalism with fiction, enlivening what he saw as stagnant prose conforming to stale, rigid standards.

The author painstakingly details the characters of the four Clutter family members—father Herb, mother Bonnie, and their two children—as well as the planning and motivations of the killers through to the investigation by the Kansas Bureau of Investigation, the killers' capture, trial, and execution.

La Stupenda Overtakes La Divina

London, England, July, 1966: The operatic career of Maria Callas, also known as "La Divina," has reached an impasse after her withdrawal from the Covent Garden season with the Royal Opera earlier this month. Meanwhile, there is a new superstar in the shape of the Australian diva Joan Sutherland, who has come to be known as "La Stupenda."

Callas's troubles seem to be related to health and mood, affecting her soaring voice and dramatic presence that have seen her dominate the world opera stage for a decade. In the 1950s she had the shapely figure expected of a soprano, and her singing was lauded. Record companies clamored for her versions of *Norma* and *Tosca*. Her marriage to the Italian industrialist Giovanni Meneghini back in 1949 brought security and comfort.

In 1954 Callas shed 66 lb (30 kg), and became a glamor society figure as well as a sensational performer at the Metropolitan Opera, Covent Garden, and La Scala.

In Venice in 1957 she met the Greek tycoon Aristotle Onassis. Her behavior gradually became more erratic, with mood swings dominant. She caused an uproar in Rome in 1958 when she walked out after the first act of *Norma*, with the President of Italy among the audience. She refused to appear again unless the management was changed. Soon afterward she was fired by the Director of the Metropolitan Opera, Rudolf Bing, after a contractual disagreement.

In 1959 she and her husband went cruising on Onassis's yacht *Christina*. By the end of the voyage Callas and Onassis were lovers, and the Meneghini marriage was over.

Her performances since have been erratic. Last year Callas acted on medical advice to sing only once in her planned *Tosca* season at Covent Garden. She chose the Royal Gala for what appears to have been a final performance.

Meanwhile, Joan Sutherland's career, after a long apprenticeship as a company soprano at Covent Garden, has blossomed through collaboration with and marriage to conductor Richard Bonynge. Her point of stardom came in the production of *Lucia di Lammermoor* in 1959, staged by Franco Zeffirelli. She began a series of triumphant debuts, singing Lucia at the world's leading opera houses, and is now the most sought-after soprano in the world.

Maria Callas and Tito Gobbi in the London production of Puccini's opera *Tosca*.

Screen Legend Spencer Tracy Dead

Los Angeles, USA, June 10, 1967: Veteran screen actor Spencer Tracy, winner of back-to-back Oscars for *Captains Courageous* (1937) and *Boys' Town* (1938), has died aged 67 years. Stocky and craggy-faced, Tracy was never considered a typical leading man, yet his consistently

Sidney Poitier, Spencer Tracy, and Katharine Hepburn.

fine performances made him a favorite of audiences and critics alike in a career that spanned more than three decades.

Tracy struggled with alcoholism for most of his life. While filming his recent movie *Guess Who's Coming to Dinner*, he suffered from lung congestion, and died of a heart attack today in Beverley Hills, just 17 days after filming was completed.

Mad Woman Takes a Pop at Warhol

New York, USA, June 3, 1968: Pop artist Andy Warhol, 40, better known for his narcissism and general disdain for the mundane than for any acts of kindness, has been brought undone by the act of a crazy woman whom he tried to help.

Valerie Solanas accosted Warhol outside his studio, The Factory, last year and asked him to produce her play *Up Your Ass*. Intrigued by the title he agreed to read it, but Warhol was apparently unimpressed by the work. Today Solanas walked into Warhol's studio with a handgun and shot him three times, causing massive internal damage. She also shot visiting art critic Mario Amaya and then tried to shoot Warhol's manager Fred Hughes. Just then the lift arrived. Hughes suggested she take it, and Solanas left.

The incident is an interesting twist in the life of Warhol, the son of Slovakian immigrants. The former graphic designer had his first solo Pop Art exhibition in 1962, featuring 32 different canvasses of Campbell's soup cans.

A few months later Warhol created his repetitive silkscreens of famous people, with each picture subtly changed by the artist. The first was of actor Troy Donohue, followed by Marilyn Monroe, Elvis Presley, Elizabeth Taylor, Marlon Brando, and the *Mona Lisa*.

Warhol was making news in the art world, but he is not alone in the world of Pop Art. Also in the spotlight are Roy Lichtenstein's comic strip paintings, James Rosenquist's billboard pictures, and the soft sculptures of ice-creams and hamburgers by Claes Oldenburg. Pop has also affected young UK artists such as Peter Phillips, David Hockney, and Peter Blake, and it also features in Ken Russell's film *Pop Goes the Easel*.

John and Yoko Go to Bed

Amsterdam, Netherlands, March 25, 1969: As if to put an emphatic full-stop to the Beatles era, John Lennon has taken his newly wed Japanese wife Yoko Ono to bed in the Hilton Hotel, Amsterdam, decked the room in flowers, invited the press in, and declared that their honeymoon had become a "bed-in" for peace.

The other Beatles never liked Yoko, and her presence became another factor in the imminent break-up of the most successful band in rock music history.

The troubles began when John Lennon and Paul McCartney appeared to grow away from each other, causing tensions within the close-knit four, who recorded their first single "Love Me Do" at EMI's Abbey Road studio, in 1962. From that time on it was a fabulous ride for the four lads from Liverpool, who had a series of hit singles such as "I Want To Hold Your Hand," "She Loves You," "I Should Have Known Better," and many more. They were mobbed at concerts, and made tours to the United States and Australia that had teenage girls out of control at airports and in the streets.

With their mop-top hair, driving music, and lovable personalities, they were number one all the way, as were many of their 39 singles and 221 songs on 19 albums. With time, they developed musically, with beautiful songs such as McCartney's "Yesterday" and "Let it Be," and more complex albums such as *Abbey Road*.

A severe blow to the group came two years ago when their manager, Brian Epstein, was found dead in his flat from an overdose of sleeping pills. Since then there has been more legality than musicality within the group.

Meanwhile, two other musical giants are traveling on—the Rolling Stones, with their raunchy rock'n'roll and Mick Jagger strutting up front, and the US folk-rock poet Bob Dylan, whose "Blowing in the Wind" has captured the essence of the rebellious mood of the times.

Butch Cassidy Leads the Movie Parade

Hollywood, USA, December, 1969: The stay-at-home times of the television bonanza are on the wane, and movies have made a mighty comeback. This year's biggest hit has been *Butch Cassidy and the Sundance Kid*, a stylish bad-boy buddy film with Paul Newman and Robert Redford as a pair of unusually funny villains.

Buddies have been the flavor of the year, with Peter Fonda and Jack Nicholson on the road in *Easy Rider*, and Jon Voigt and Dustin Hoffman as doomed New York hustlers in *Midnight Cowboy*. For the seemingly uncharismatic Hoffman, it was a fine follow-up to his debut role two years ago in *The Graduate*. While there has been much experiment, notably from Stanley Kubrick with *2001: A Space Odyssey* and *Dr. Strangelove*, it has been a time of big budgets and blockbusters.

The musical has held its appeal, with Julie Andrews bringing her English charm to two box-office hits in *Mary Poppins* and *The Sound of Music*. Oddly, she was left out of the film that made her stage name, *My Fair Lady*, for the somewhat miscast Audrey Hepburn.

The most stylish blockbusters have been David Lean's *Lawrence of Arabia*, starring Peter O'Toole as the militaristic Arabist, and *Doctor Zhivago*, a harrowing Russian Revolution story, starring Julie Christie. But the quintessential hero has been James Bond, with deadly charming Sean Connery as licensed-to-kill 007, in the action spectaculars *Dr. No*, *From Russia with Love*, *Goldfinger*, *Thunderball*, and *You Only Live Twice*.

Julie Andrews

Achievements in the Arts

Key Structures
Amsterdam Orphanage, Amsterdam, Netherlands
Bawa House, Colombo, Sri Lanka
Centre Le Corbusier, Zurich, Switzerland
Convent La Tourette, Eveux-sur-Arbresle, France
Enso-Gutzeit Headquarters, Helsinki, Finland
Gateway Arch, St Louis, USA
German Pavilion, Montreal, Canada
Grande Mosquee, Dakar, Senegal
Habitat '67, Montreal, Canada
Helsingborg Library, Helsingborg, Sweden
Independence House, Lagos, Nigeria
Kurashiki City Hall, Kurashiki, Japan
National Palace Museum, Taipei, Taiwan
New National Gallery, Berlin, Germany
Palace of Assembly, Chandigarh, India
Palazzo del Lavoro, Turin, Italy
Paper Mill, Mantua, Italy
Patuxai, Vientiane, Laos
Reuchlinhaus Library, Reuchlinhaus, Germany
Salk Institute, La Jolla, USA
St Antonius Church, Wildegg, Switzerland
St Mary of Zion Church, Aksum, Ethiopia

Nobel Prize for Literature
1960 Saint-John Perse; 1961 Ivo Andric; 1962 John Steinbeck; 1963 Giorgos Seferis; 1964 Jean-Paul Sartre (declined prize); 1965 Michail Sholokhov; 1966 Shmuel Yosef Agnon/Nelly Sachs; 1967 Miguel Angel Asturias; 1968 Yasunari Kawabata; 1969 Samuel Beckett.

Booker Prize for Fiction
1969 *Something to Answer For*, P. H. Newby.

Pulitzer Prize for Fiction
1960 *Advise and Consent*, Allen Drury; 1961 *To Kill a Mockingbird*, Harper Lee; 1962 *The Edge of Sadness*, Edwin O'Connor; 1963 *The Reivers*, William Faulkner; 1964 no award given; 1965 *The Keepers of the House*, Shirley Ann Grau; 1966 *Collected Stories*, Katherine Anne Porter; 1967 *The Fixer*, Bernard Malamud; 1968 *The Confessions of Nat Turner*, William Styron; 1969 *House Made of Dawn*, N. Scott Momaday.

Academy Awards
Best Film 1960 *The Apartment*; 1961 *West Side Story*; 1962 *Lawrence of Arabia*; 1963 *Tom Jones*; 1964 *My Fair Lady*; 1965 *The Sound of Music*; 1966 *A Man For All Seasons*; 1967 *In the Heat of the Night*; 1968 *Oliver!*; 1969 *Midnight Cowboy*.

BAFTAs
Best Film 1960 *The Apartment*; 1961 *Ballada o soldate/ The Hustler*; 1962 *Lawrence of Arabia*; 1963 *Tom Jones*; 1964 *Dr. Strangelove*; 1965 *My Fair Lady*; 1966 *Who's Afraid of Virginia Woolf*; 1967 *A Man For All Seasons*; 1968 *The Graduate*; 1969 *Midnight Cowboy*.

John Lennon and Yoko Ono want to "give peace a chance."

Jacqueline Kennedy

> "EDUCATION
> MUST BE BOTH
> INTELLECTUAL
> AND EMO-
> TIONAL."
>
> ERIC FROMM (1900–
> 1980), AMERICAN
> PSYCHOANALYST, ON
> EDUCATING
> CHILDREN, 1960

> "CHILDREN
> HAVE NEVER
> BEEN VERY
> GOOD AT
> LISTENING TO
> THEIR ELDERS,
> BUT THEY
> HAVE NEVER
> FAILED TO
> IMITATE
> THEM."
>
> JAMES BALDWIN
> (1924–1987),
> AMERICAN NOVELIST,
> 1960

Princess Margaret Weds Photographer

London, England, May 6, 1960: More than 20 million viewers have watched what could be termed the first "modern" royal wedding service, as Princess Margaret's wedding ceremony to Antony Armstrong-Jones in Westminster Abbey was broadcast on TV across the nation.

The younger sister of Queen Elizabeth, Princess Margaret is a glamorous figure on the world stage, and had a reputation as a party girl, who shocked the nation at the age of 19 when she was spotted in public smoking. Her father, King George VI, was a smoker and she embraced the habit with great enthusiasm. She is also an avid supporter of the arts, with a talent for singing and playing the piano.

Margaret further defied convention when she fell in love with a divorced man, Group Captain Peter Townsend. Marriage to Margaret was judged unacceptable by the Church of England and the political establishment. He was also 17 years her senior, and eventually the Princess was forced to make a choice between a life with the man she loved and her royal life, as marriage to a divorcee would have meant the end of her royal privileges.

The Princess soon resumed her social life, and in 1958 at a dinner party in Chelsea she was introduced to a well-connected Cambridge graduate who was starting to make a name for himself as a photographer. Today the unconventional Princess married this photographer, Antony Armstrong-Jones, who, in honor of his Welsh descent, will take the title of the Earl of Snowdon.

Antony Armstrong-Jones found work as a photographer after leaving Cambridge, specializing in the fields of fashion, design, and the theater.

The marriage of Princess Margaret and Antony Armstrong-Jones was broadcast to over two million viewers.

Oil-producing Nations Create Cartel

Baghdad, Iraq, September 14, 1960: Iran, Iraq, Kuwait, Saudi Arabia, and Venezuela have met in Baghdad, Iraq, and have formed the Organization of Petroleum Exporting Countries (OPEC), designed to combat the influence of major western oil companies who up to now have been able to raise and lower the price of oil as they saw fit.

It represents an attempt to regain control over oilfields, which have been under the direct control of multinational conglomerates that purchased the rights to virtually every drop of Middle Eastern oil for next to nothing in the wake of World War I. It is estimated that these large corporations are retaining up to 65 percent of all revenues derived from oil production.

The Baghdad Conference can be traced to actions taken last year by oil companies to lower prices in the face of a huge oversupply, resulting in lower royalties and taxes for the producer nations. Fuad Itayim, the editor of the *Middle East Economic Survey*, commented: "These price cuts will precipitate the establishment of…a cartel to confront the cartel."

OPEC's objectives are firstly to coordinate and unify petroleum prices among member nations in order to secure fair and stable prices, and to facilitate an efficient, economic, and regular supply of petroleum to consumers. At present, however, OPEC has very little real power, as the members are not in control of their own reserves, which still mostly belong to the concessionaries.

OPEC's headquarters will be established in Geneva, Switzerland, and its first Secretary-General is an Iranian, Fuad Rouhani. An international lawyer and musician, he has made clear his determination to keep OPEC out of politics, and to keep its focus solely on oil production and economics. Oil income is necessary for the economic development of all

time out

As James H. Meredith, the first black student to be enroled at the University of Mississippi, spent his first day in attendance, 2000 Army and National Guard troops occupied the campus. He was housed in a male dormitory, next-door to Federal marshals.

USA, February, 1960: African-Americans have been staging sit-ins at restaurants in southern USA in a bid to end segregation.

London, England, May 6, 1960: Princess Margaret weds Anthony Armstrong-Jones in the first televised royal wedding.

New York, USA, July 21, 1960: Francis Chichester wins the first single-handed transatlantic yacht race, shearing 16 days from the previous world record crossing.

Rome, Italy, August 25, 1960: The Games of the XVII Olympiad begin.

Zürich, Switzerland, June 6, 1961: Influential Swiss psychiatrist Carl Jung dies, aged 75.

London, England, July 8, 1961: Australian Rod Laver wins his first Wimbledon singles title after being runner-up for the previous two years.

Baghdad, Iraq, September 14, 1961: Iran, Iraq, Kuwait, Saudi Arabia, and Venezuela form OPEC.

London, England, September 17, 1961: The biggest "ban-the-bomb" protest ever staged ends in violence, with over 1,000 demonstrators arrested.

Paris, France, January, 1962: Algerian-born Yves Saint Laurent displays his new bold take on fashions for his own couture house.

USA, February 14, 1962: Millions of people tune in to watch the US First Lady, Jacqueline Kennedy, lead a televised tour of the White House.

Goodwood, UK, April 23, 1962: Formula One driver Stirling Moss is injured in a dramatic race crash.

Santiago, Chile, June 17, 1962: Brazil wins the FIFA World Cup, despite its star, Pelé, being unable to play in the final due to injury.

Washington DC, USA, March 18, 1963: The Supreme Court hands down a ruling in the Gideon vs. Wainwright, deciding that lawyers are to be provided for defendants who cannot afford representation.

London, England, July 8, 1963: The 20-year-old Australian Margaret Smith wins the Wimbledon singles title at her third attempt.

USA and USSR, August 30, 1963: A "hotline" is established between the White House and the Kremlin in a bid to prevent accidental nuclear annihilation.

New York, USA, February 7, 1964: Beatlemania hits the USA when the band arrives in New York.

Miami, USA, February 25, 1964: Cassius Clay makes good his boasts by beating Sonny Liston to win the world heavyweight boxing title.

Tokyo, Japan, October 10-24, 1964: The Games of the XVIII Olympiad are the first to be held in Asia. The final torchbearer is Yoshinori Sakai, who was born in Hiroshima on the day of the atomic blast in 1945.

OPEC's member nations and to balance their budgets. They see oil as a finite resource, and that fluctuations in the price of oil are no longer acceptable.

Yves Saint-Laurent Leaves Dior

Paris, France, January, 1962: The Algerian-born couturier Yves Saint-Laurent has displayed his bold approach to fashion from his own couture house, following his dramatic departure from the House of Dior, where his turtlenecks and mink-lined alligator jackets proved too "racy" for the conservative Dior clientele.

The couturier has founded the House of Yves Saint-Laurent with his business partner Pierre Bergé. It was Bergé who broke the news that Saint-Laurent had

Yves Saint-Laurent has set up business in Paris.

been dismissed by the House of Dior as the young designer lay in hospital recovering from a nervous breakdown after he was drafted into the French Army to fight against his homeland, Algeria.

Saint-Laurent went to work for Dior in 1954, becoming the company's head designer in 1957 after Christian Dior's untimely death.

Beatlemania Grips America

New York, USA, February 7, 1964: Phenomenally popular British pop group the Beatles arrived at Kennedy Airport in New York today for their first US visit, with a level of police protection usually reserved for kings and presidents.

Thousands of screaming fans jostled to catch a glimpse of the acclaimed "Fab Four"—Paul McCartney, John Lennon, George Harrison, and Ringo Starr—as they emerged from Pan Am Flight 101 from London. The Beatles' first scheduled appearance will be on the top-rating "Ed Sullivan Show" this Sunday night, with more than 5,000 fans applying for tickets to the theater, which only seats 750. Then the young musicians are off to Washington DC to promote their new single "I Want to Hold Your Hand".

Beatles songs are constantly being played on radio stations all across the country, and indeed all over the world, and Beatles wigs have become the latest craze, selling everywhere for $2.99.

Even classical composers are acknowledging the Beatles' musical style. Leonard Bernstein, Aaron Copland, and Leopold Stokowski have all come out in support of the "Fab Four" and their music, and it is that assured tens of millions of Americans will be tuning in to the "Ed Sullivan Show" on Sunday, even if only to see what all the fuss is about.

The Beatles tour is a month-long trek that will take the group to twenty US cities and three in Canada.

Marshall McLuhan Has a Message

Toronto, Canada, February 15, 1964: The Canadian communications savant Professor Marshall McLuhan has coined a colorful phrase that is ringing around the whole western world: "The medium is the message." Professor McLuhan has long anticipated a great speeding up of global communications which are aided by images and messages bouncing off space satellites, and traveling from New York to

Marshall McLuhan

Australian Rod Laver wins the Wimbledon title in 1961.

London, Toronto to Sydney, amazingly, in just a few short seconds.

His thoughts follow the same theme, and see humankind captured by communications and trapped in a web of its own making. "The medium is the message" is his shorthand for saying that the media itself, not the content it carries, is uppermost in importance. He postulates that it would not matter if television showed children's shows or violent programming—the effect would be identical. He is on the cover of *Newsweek* magazine.

New York, USA, April 1, 1965: Cosmetics manufacturer and entrepreneur Helena Rubinstein dies, aged in her nineties.

UK, June 18, 1965: A government plan to introduce a blood alcohol limit for drivers is announced.

Newport, Rhode Island, USA, July 25, 1965: Bob Dylan stuns fans and folk purists alike by "going electric" at the Newport Folk Festival.

Roquebrune-Cap-Martin, France, August 27, 1965: Modernist Swiss architect Charles-Edouard Jeannert, known as "Le Corbusier," dies while swimming on the French Riviera.

Wellington, New Zealand, January 25, 1966: New Zealand's government bans a tour by South Africa's rugby team, the Springboks.

Sydney, Australia, February 28, 1966: The Danish architect who designed the iconic Sydney Opera House, Joern Utzon, resigns from the project.

London, England, July 30, 1966: England wins the FIFA World Cup.

Lake District, England, January 4, 1967: Donald Campbell crashes his boat *Bluebird* and dies in a water-speed record attempt.

Memphis, USA, April 30, 1967: Muhammad Ali, previously Cassius Clay, is stripped of his world heavyweight boxing title after refusing to serve in the US Army.

London, England, June 7, 1967: Queen Elizabeth meets the Duchess of Windsor, healing the 30-year rift caused by Edward VIII's abdication from the throne.

Sweden, September 3, 1967: The changeover from driving on the left to the right side of the road takes place today, bringing Sweden into line with its European neighbours.

Portsmouth, England, July 4, 1968: Alec Rose returns to his home port to a hero's welcome after a 354-day circumnavigation of the globe.

New York, USA, September 9, 1968: Arthur Ashe becomes the first black man to win the US Open tennis tournament.

Mexico City, Mexico, October 12-27, 1968: The Games of the XIX Olympiad are held at 2,300 meters above sea level. Czech gymnast Vera Caslavska wins six medals; she had gone into hiding after the Soviet invasion of her country.

London, England, January 2, 1969: Australian media tycoon Rupert Murdoch beats Robert Maxwell's £34-million offer to win control of the *News of the World* newspaper.

London, England, March 4, 1969: Notorious East End gangsters, the Kray brothers, are found guilty of murder and are facing life in prison.

London, England, March 12, 1969: Beatle Paul McCartney weds Linda Eastman in a civil ceremony.

Bob Dylan

Helena Rubinstein Dies

New York, USA, April 1, 1965: International cosmetics manufacturer Helena Rubinstein has died in New York aged 94.

Born in Cracow, Poland, in 1871, she emigrated to Australia at the age of 18. She noticed Australian women's skin seemed to be affected by their environment and she opened a modest shop in Melbourne, where she began showing women how to care for their skin.

Six years later she traveled to London, to study dermatology. Then she opened beauty salons in London and Paris. Her first US store opened in New York in 1914, and soon she had stores in Chicago, Boston, Los Angeles, and many US cities.

In 1917, she began wider distribution of her products. Her chemists and researchers soon developed the world's first line of medicated skin-care products.

In 1953, she established a foundation to coordinate her gifts to museums, colleges, and institutions for the needy, and she personally directed her enormous empire up until her death.

Folkies Boo Dylan

Newport, Rhode Island, USA, July 25, 1965: Bob Dylan was booed and jeered at this year's Newport Folk Festival. He appeared

"TELEVISION IS A MEDIUM OF ENTERTAINMENT WHICH PERMITS MILLIONS OF PEOPLE TO LISTEN TO THE SAME JOKE AT THE SAME TIME AND YET REMAIN LONESOME."

T. S. ELIOT (1888–1965), AMERICAN POET, 1963

"NEVER IN THE HISTORY OF FASHION HAS SO LITTLE MATERIAL BEEN RAISED SO HIGH TO REVEAL SO MUCH THAT NEEDS TO BE COVERED SO BADLY."

SIR CECIL BEATON (1904–1980), BRITISH PHOTOGRAPHER, ON MINISKIRTS, 1969

Captain Bobby Moore helps England beat Germany in a nail-biting World Cup final.

on stage backed by the Paul Butterfield Blues Band, an electric blues band who use amplified instruments, regarded by folk purists as abandonment of folk tradition.

According to reports, the booing became so loud that, after the first three electric songs, Dylan dismissed the band and finished the set with his acoustic guitar. Unconfirmed accounts say that the Newport board directors were so angry that they struggled unsuccessfully to cut the

electric power. The night is sure to become a part of folk music mythology, although it is not the first instance of "electric music" at the festival. Blues acts have been plugging in for years.

England Wins World Cup

London, England, July 30, 1966: England has defeated West Germany 4–2 in the final of the FIFA World Cup in London.

In extra time in a nail-biting final at Wembley Stadium, Geoff Hurst made history with a hat-trick of goals, including the most controversial goal ever scored in a World Cup final: Did the ball really cross the line after bouncing down from the crossbar? The debate still rages.

After a slow start to the competition, which saw England play out a tame 0–0 draw against Uruguay, they went on to defeat Mexico and France, to advance to the top of their group. This set up a quarter-final against Argentina, which England won 1–0, before defeating Portugal in the semi-final 2–1.

In the final against West Germany, England's controversial second goal was awarded to Hurst by a Russian linesman. Later television replays were unable to conclude whether the ball had in fact crossed the line for a goal.

Germany started the match well with a goal in the twelfth minute to Helmut Haller. Hurst then replied in the eighteenth minute with the first of his three goals. After full-time the score was 2–2. Hurst scored his controversial goal in extra time, and followed this with a third goal at the end of extra time when he took a long ball from Bobby Moore and shot past the German goalkeeper into the roof of the net. Hurst is the toast of England tonight. Never before has an individual scored three goals in a World Cup final.

Sporting Achievements

Baseball *World Series* 1960 Pittsburgh (National League); 1961 New York (American League); 1962 New York (AL); 1963 Los Angeles (NL); 1964 St Louis (NL); 1965 Los Angeles (NL); 1966 Baltimore (AL); 1967 St Louis (NL); 1968 Detroit (AL); 1969 New York (NL).

Cycling *Tour de France* 1960 G. Nencini; 1961-1964 J. Anquetil; 1965 F. Gimondi; 1966 L. Aimar; 1967 R. Pingeon; 1968 J. Janssen; 1969 E. Merckx.

Football *American Super Bowl* 1967 Green Bay; 1968 Green Bay; 1969 NY Jets. *World Cup Soccer* 1962 Brazil; 1966 England.

Golf *US Masters* 1960 A. Palmer; 1961 G. Player; 1962 A. Palmer; 1963 J. Nicklaus; 1964 A. Palmer; 1965-1966 J. Nicklaus; 1967 G. Brewer; 1968 B. Goalby; 1969 G. Archer.

Horse Racing *Epsom Derby* 1960 St Paddy; 1961 Psidium; 1962 Larkspur; 1963 Relko; 1964 Santa Claus; 1965 Sea Bird II; 1966 Charlottown; 1967 Royal Palace; 1968 Sir Ivor; 1969 Blakeney. *Kentucky Derby* 1960 Venetian Way; 1961 Carry Back; 1962 Decidedly; 1963 Chateaugay; 1964 Northern Dancer; 1965 Lucky Debonair; 1966 Kauai King; 1967 Proud Clarion; 1968 Forward Pass; 1969 Majestic Prince. *Melbourne Cup* 1960 Hi Jinx; 1961 Lord Fury; 1962 Even Stevens; 1963 Gatum Gatum; 1964 Polo Prince; 1965 Light Fingers; 1966 Galilee; 1967 Red Handed; 1968 Rain Lover; 1969 Rain Lover.

Ice Hockey *Stanley Cup* 1960 Montreal; 1961 Chicago; 1962 Toronto; 1963 Toronto; 1964 Toronto; 1965 Montreal; 1966 Montreal; 1967 Toronto; 1968; Montreal; 1969 Montreal.

Marathon *Boston, Men's* 1960 P. Kotila; 1961 E. Oksanen; 1962 E. Oksanen; 1963 A. Vandendriessche; 1964 A. Vandendriessche; 1965 M. Shigematsu; 1966

K. Kemihara; 1967 D. McKenzie; 1968 A. Burfoot; 1969 Y. Unetani; *Women's* 1966 R. Gibb; 1967 R. Gibb; 1968 R. Gibb; 1969 S. Berman.

Sailing *America's Cup* 1962 Weatherley; 1964 Constellation; 1967 Intrepid.

Tennis *Australian Championships, Men's Singles* 1960 R. Laver; 1961 R. Emerson; 1962 R. Laver; 1963-1967 R. Emerson; 1968 B. Bowrey; *Women's Singles* 1960-1966 M. Smith; 1967 N. Richey; 1968 B. J. King. *Australian Open, Men's Singles* 1969 R. Laver; *Women's Singles* 1969 M. Court. *French Championships, Men's Singles* 1960 N. Pietrangeli; 1961 M. Santana; 1962 R. Laver; 1963 R. Emerson; 1964 M. Santana; 1965 F. Stolle; 1966 T. Roche; 1967 R. Emerson; *Women's Singles* 1960 D. Hard; 1961 A. Haydon; 1962 M. Smith; 1963 L. Turner; 1964 M. Smith; 1965 L. Turner; 1966 A. Haydon Jones; 1967 F. Durr. *Roland-Garros Tournament (French Open), Men's Singles* 1968 K. Rosewall; 1969 R. Laver; *Women's Singles* 1968 N. Richey; 1969 M. Court. *US National Championship, Men's Singles* 1960 N. Fraser; 1961 R. Emerson; 1962 R. Laver; 1963 R. Osuna; 1964 R. Emerson; 1965 M. Santana; 1966 F. Stolle; 1967 J. Newcombe; *Women's Singles* 1960-1961 D. Hard; 1962 M. Smith; 1963-1964 M. Bueno; 1965 M. Smith; 1966 M. Bueno; 1967 B.J. King. *US Open, Men's Singles* 1968 A. Ashe; 1969 R. Laver; *Women's Singles* 1968 V. Wade; 1969 M. Smith Court. *Wimbledon, Men's Singles* 1960 N. Fraser; 1961-1962 R. Laver; 1963 C. McKinley; 1964-1965 R. Emerson; 1966 M. Santana; 1967 J. Newcombe; 1968-1969 R. Laver; *Women's Singles* 1960 M. Bueno; 1961 A. Mortimer; 1962 K. Susman; 1963 M. Smith; 1964 M. Bueno; 1965 M. Smith; 1966-1968 B. J. King; 1969 A. Jones.

England Swings!

London, England, December, 1966: London has become the swinging capital of the fashion and pop music world, and its heart is a formerly unremarkable lane-way that runs off Regent Street. Carnaby Street has become the mecca for clothes fanatics of both sexes, made famous by Glaswegian John Stephen, who believes that men's clothes should be fun. They cram into Carnaby Street—and emerge wearing kaftans and jewelry for the bearded boys, mini-skirts or pink shorts under long coats and boots for the girls.

The shop windows and signs swirl with the psychedelic color patterns that are a by-product of the hot designer drug LSD (lysergic acid diethylamide). The strobe-light psychedelia of the nightclubs all over London might be enough to cause nausea in itself, but it has been found that the drug can do worse, taking some users from a feeling of raised consciousness and wellbeing to a nightmare of hallucination.

The beat goes on, and the hip young style extends to King's Road in Chelsea, where Mary Quant is Queen at Bazaar Boutique. Quant told the French two years ago that they were out of date and said that young people were tired of "looking the same as their mothers." Her bold designs and short skirts, and her short and angular haircut from Vidal Sassoon soon had a parade of look-alikes—models, actresses, office girls, pop stars, and likely lads—parading along King's Road. They also invade Kensington High Street for Barbara Hulanicki's "total look boutique" at Biba. The rising star of the scene is the model, Twiggy, a stick-thin waif with huge eyes who is earning 10 guineas an hour.

Whether or not those pink hipsters from Carnaby Street gave them the name,

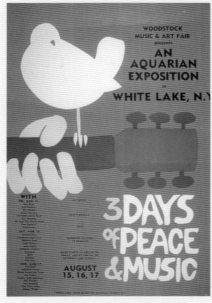
Poster advertising the Woodstock festival.

there seem to be a lot of hippies around, fuelled on pot and rock music, flower power, and a zonked-out style of peace and love. In America they have spread everywhere, but have their headquarters on the corner of Haight and Ashbury Streets, in San Francisco.

On either side of the Atlantic, everybody is dancing to the real swingers of swinging London, the Beatles and the Rolling Stones, and smoking a quiet joint to the cool rebel sounds of Bob Dylan.

Sport and Politics Get Together

Mexico City, Mexico, October 27, 1968: The wholesomeness of sport and the triumphs of staging three Olympiads in this decade were cast suddenly into shadow in the dying moments of this year's Olympic Games in Mexico City. On the podium after coming first and second in the 100 m track event, black American sprinters Tommie Smith and John Carlos raised their clenched fists, affirming their allegiance not to their country but to the radical political movement Black Power that is engaging with black aspirations in America.

The Games did much for black supremacy; every flat race under 800 m was won by a black American, and Bob Beamon advanced the long-jump world record by almost 2 ft (0.6 m) in the thin Mexico City air.

The Tokyo Olympics in 1964 were the first to be held in Asia, and they hummed with efficiency. Two Australian women excelled—swimmer Dawn Fraser in winning her third 100 m gold medal, and sprinter Betty Cuthbert, the Golden Girl of the Melbourne Games in 1956, who won her fourth Olympic gold medal in the 400 m track event.

The Rome Games in 1960 were the first to get saturation TV coverage. The world tuned in to watch fleet-footed Cassius Clay outbox everyone for heavyweight gold, Herb Elliott of Australia shatter the world record and win the 1500 m track event by 18 m, Tennessee beauty Wilma Rudolph win the sprint double, and tiny, barefooted Ethiopian Abebe Bikila win the marathon.

Mary Quant

The Tastes of America

USA, December, 1969: In the 1960s the American family likes to eat out, and its favorite is the ever-reliable restaurant chain Howard Johnson's, with its big steaks and fries, cozy booths, warm atmosphere, and attentive staff. Japanese steakhouses are attracting good custom on the West Coast. Wendy's, a new fast food chain specializing in hamburgers, has been doing good business.

At home the stodgy pot roasts, fried chicken, and casseroles of the 1950s are on the way out, and people are experimenting with the pastry-crusted Beef Wellington and the thinly sliced, heavily sauced Steak Diane, flamed in the frying pan with a dash of brandy. Chicken Kiev (fried chicken breast filled with butter and herbs) is a Saturday night treat, and people are gathering around the fondue pot to try this Swiss-inspired way of eating. The idea is to melt gruyère cheese in the pot, and then to dip morsels of chicken, lamb, mushroom, potato, etc. on skewers into the hot cheese! Another new idea is the smorgasbord, a tradition from Sweden, where all manner of cold meats, seafoods, salads, and so on are assembled on the sideboard, with the guests helping themselves and bringing their (usually heavily laden) plate to the table.

The *New York Times Menu Cook Book* suggests the following. For a small cocktail party, try Camembert amandine, cucumber spread, crackers and toast rounds, mushroom strudels, cocktail croquettes. For a larger cocktail party, serve buttered nuts, chicken liver paté, mushroom-stuffed eggs, tuna-stuffed eggs, toast rounds and crackers, wild rice pancakes, cream cheese pastry turnovers.

New on today's supermarket shelves are Coffee-Mate, Life Cereal, Sprite, Pop Tarts, Shake n'Bake, Doritos, Bac*Os, instant porridge, Gatorade, Pringles, and Tang, among many others.

Pop duo Sonny and Cher, with stick-thin model, Twiggy.

Charles de Gaulle

Nuclear Non-Proliferation Treaty Goes into Effect

Geneva, Switzerland, March 5: After almost a decade since it was first proposed, the Treaty on the Non-Proliferation of Nuclear Weapons went into effect today, having been ratified by 43 nations.

In 1961, Ireland put forth a resolution to the United Nations General Assembly that an agreement be drawn up to ban the procurement and transference of nuclear weapons. Concern was mounting, because by the middle of the 1960s there were five declared nuclear powers—USA, UK, China, France, and the USSR—and many experts believed this number would rise dramatically by the end of the century.

A disarmament conference was held in Geneva in 1965 to consider a draft treaty, and on July 1, 1968, the Non-Proliferation Treaty was completed and signed in Washington, London, and Moscow. It is hoped that the treaty will restrict the growth of nuclear weapons.

Students Killed During Riots

Jackson, Mississippi, USA, May 15: Early this morning, 21-year-old pre-law student Phillip Lafayette Gibbs and 17-year-old passerby James Earl Green were killed when police opened fire during a protest at Jackson State University.

The riot was yet one more in a spate of student demonstrations that have been taking place across the United States in protest against the escalating war in Vietnam, the invasion of Cambodia, and further issues relating to gender and racial politics.

The latest killings occurred 11 days after the tragedy at Kent State University, Ohio, when four students were killed and nine injured by the National Guard. An anti-war rally took place on Friday May 1, and another was planned for the following Monday. Violence on campus gradually escalated over the weekend, reaching the point where the city's mayor called in the Ohio National Guard.

Though Monday's rally was supposedly banned, 2,000 students gathered. The Guard used tear gas, then fired on the crowd. Of the four students killed, two were involved in the demonstration, and two had been walking to class.

time out

In Belfast and Londonderry, Northern Ireland, three women were tarred and feathered for going out with British soldiers. A photo of one of the girls was released, showing her tarred and feathered with her head shaven and tied to a lamppost.

French Statesman Charles de Gaulle Dies Suddenly

Lille, France, November 9: The controversial French military leader and statesman, Charles de Gaulle, died suddenly from a ruptured aneurism today, just two weeks before his eightieth birthday. At the time of his death he was relaxing, taking a break from writing his memoirs, which chronicle a long and illustrious career.

Born in Lille, France, in 1890, De Gaulle was the third child of prosperous, intellectual parents. He studied at the prestigious Ecole Spéciale Militaire de Saint-Cyr, and was injured and imprisoned during World War I. Between the wars he remained in the army, writing books on military theory and management. After World War II broke out, he was appointed commander of the 4th Armoured Division and became leader of the "Free French" resistance movement. He presided over the provisional government from 1944 to 1946, and held the position of president from 1958 until his retirement last year.

De Gaulle's leadership was marked by a number of important achievements. He settled the Algerian conflict in 1962, helped the French economy grow and prosper, and deftly handled the student and labor strikes that could have crippled the country in 1968. But he also made many enemies, both at home and abroad, for his refusal to allow Great Britain to enter the EEC, his push for France to become a nuclear power, and his support of the Arabs in their conflict against Israel. He also alienated the Canadian government by siding with the "Free Quebec" movement.

De Gaulle is survived by Yvonne, his wife of nearly 50 years, and two of their three children, Philippe and Elizabeth. He will be buried next to his daughter Anne (who died at the age of 20 from complications of Down syndrome) in a small private ceremony.

Demonstrators at Kent State experience the horror of seeing their fellow students killed.

Tripoli, Libya, January 16: Colonel Muammar Gaddafi becomes premier of Libya, promoting an Arab nationalist ideology.
London, England, January 23: The first "Jumbo" jet touches down at Heathrow. The airport's infrastructure is overloaded by 362 passengers, twice as many as a Boeing 707 could carry.
Geneva, Switzerland, March 5: The Nuclear Non-Proliferation Treaty, opened for signature in 1968, comes into effect after being ratified by 43 nations.

Hutt River Province, Australia, April 22: An angry Western Australian wheat farmer, Leonard Casley, declares independence for his 18,470-acre (7,474 ha) property, 280 miles (450 km) north of the Western Australian capital, Perth.
Africa, April 24: Gambia becomes a republic. Rhodesia was also declared a republic by Prime Minister Ian Smith seven weeks earlier.
USA, May: Six students engaged in anti-war protests at Ohio and Mississippi university campuses are shot dead.

Indonesia, June 21: Sukarno, the first president of Indonesia, dies of kidney disease, aged 69.
Egypt, July 21: The Aswan High Dam is completed at a cost of $800 million, regulating the flow of the Nile and relieving the threat of flooding downstream.
Jordan, September: After the hijacking of several planes by Palestinian terrorists, the PLO is ejected from their Jordanian stronghold. King Hussein orders his army to attack Palestinians who pose a threat to his leadership.

Melbourne, Australia, October 15: A 394-ft (120 m) section of the half-built West Gate Bridge collapses, killing 35 construction workers. Unions ban all work on the bridge.
Paris, France, November 9: Charles de Gaulle dies, weeks before turning 80 years old.
Canberra, Australia, November 12: The 8th Battalion of the Australian army returns from Vietnam. This marks the beginning of Australian withdrawal from the Vietnam War.

Pakistan, November 12-13: Cyclonic winds, an earthquake, and tidal waves kill in excess of 150,000 people.
Melbourne, Australia, November 25: The Victorian government becomes the first in the world to legislate for the mandatory wearing of seatbelts in cars.
Washington DC, USA, December 2: The US Congress establishes the Environmental Protection Agency (EPA) as the environmental repercussions of human activity become increasingly apparent.

Bill Wilson's Last "Day at a Time"

Miami, Florida, USA, January 24: Bill Wilson, co-founder of Alcoholics Anonymous, has died today of emphysema and pneumonia at the Miami Heart Institute. He was 75 years old.

Wilson was born on November 26, 1895 in East Dorset, Vermont. An intelligent, athletic, but troubled youth, Wilson discovered the elixir of life when he took his first drink of alcohol in 1917, as a soldier in World War I. He attained some success as a Wall Street securities analyst before his drinking reached "rock bottom" in 1934.

Through what he believed was divine intervention, Wilson stopped drinking while he was a patient in Towns Hospital, New York. Together with Dr Bob Smith, whom he met while on a business trip to Akron, Ohio, in 1935, Wilson set about helping fellow sufferers stay sober "one day at a time." Drawing on the spirituality of the Oxford Group, William James, Carl Jung, and others, Wilson and Smith devised the Twelve Step program, which to date has helped close to one million alcoholics in over 80 countries.

Wilson is survived by his wife of more than 50 years, Lois Burnham Wilson.

Charles Manson Convicted of Murder

Los Angeles, California, USA, January 25: Psychopathic cult leader Charles Manson, along with three members of his group, known as "The Family"— Susan Atkins, Leslie Van Houten, and Patricia Krenwinkel—was found guilty in a Los Angeles court today of first-degree murder and conspiring to commit murder. The trial lasted four months, and the jury took nine days to reach a verdict.

Members of the Manson "Family" wait outside the court.

Though he wasn't present at the crime scenes on August 9, 1969, Manson had engineered the gruesome slaying of pregnant actress Sharon Tate and the four unfortunate people who happened to be at her Beverly Hills home that night—Jay Sebring, Steven Parent, Wojciech Frykowski, and Abigail Folger. The following night, the cult members brutally killed Leno and Rosemary LaBianca in the wealthy LA suburb of Los Feliz.

Manson displayed his unstable personality on several occasions during the trial, appearing in court with an "X" carved in his forehead and harassing Judge Charles Older, at one time screaming out "someone should cut your head off!"

The convicted murderers are facing a possible death penalty.

Oz Magazine Editors Found Guilty

London, England, August 5: In the biggest battle of its kind since the trial over the publication of *Lady Chatterley's Lover*, the three editors of counterculture magazine *Oz* were today found guilty of obscenity.

The trial began at the Old Bailey Central Criminal Courts on June 23, and the three men, Richard Neville (29), Jim Anderson (34), and Felix Dennis (24), were charged with "conspiring to corrupt the morals of young children and other young persons." While found guilty of obscenity, the three defendants were deemed not guilty on the more serious conspiracy charges.

Oz began life in Australia in 1963 with Neville at the helm, and by the sixth issue it faced its first obscenity charge. Neville launched an English edition in 1967, and the Australian magazine folded in 1969. Like many underground journals, *Oz* deals with topics such as the Vietnam War, women's liberation, and the environment, but overall its tone is ribald and irreverent. What sets it apart are its stunning psychedelic graphics, some of which have been created by album-cover designer Martin Sharp.

The issue that caused the furore was *Oz*, edition 28 of May 1970, known as "Schoolkids Oz," in which some high school students was invited to participate. A 15-year-old contributor pasted the head of Rupert Bear onto the body of a sexually aroused cartoon character created by underground artist Robert Crumb. In his defense, Neville insisted that the issue was created *by* teenagers, not necessarily *for* them.

The three editors face jail sentences ranging from 9 to 15 months, and Australians Richard Neville and Jim Anderson will most likely be deported.

François Duvalier

Men of *Oz*: Anderson, Neville, and Dennis.

Paris, France, January 10: French fashion designer, Gabrielle "Coco" Chanel, dies aged 87.

Miami, USA, January 24: The co-founder of Alcoholics Anonymous, Bill Wilson, dies.

Los Angeles, USA, January 25: Charles Manson and three female co-defendants are convicted of the murders of seven people.

Kampala, Uganda, January 25: General Idi Amin seizes power while President Obote is abroad.

Middle East, February 3: OPEC decides to set oil prices directly without consulting buyers.

London, England, February 15: The UK introduces the decimal system of currency. The previous system was in place for 1,200 years.

Dacca, East Pakistan, March 26: Following Sheikh Mujibur Rahman's declaration of independence from West Pakistan, civil war erupts in the streets of the new capital.

Port au Prince, Haiti, April 21: The autocratic president of Haiti, François Duvalier or "Papa Doc," dies aged 61. He is succeeded by his 19-year-old son Jean-Claude, or "Baby Doc."

Canberra, Australia, May 24: Neville Bonner becomes the first Aboriginal member of Australian parliament after his selection for a Senate vacancy.

Sydney, Australia, June 13: The Broderick nontuplets are born. This is the first recorded case of nine births.

Kazakhstan, USSR, June 30: Three Russian cosmonauts are found dead in the *Soyuz 11* spacecraft after an apparently normal flight and landing. A new space endurance record had been set by this flight.

London, England, August 5: The three editors of *Oz* magazine are found guilty of obscenity. All three receive jail sentences.

Bahrain, August 15: Britain withdraws from the Persian Gulf islands of Bahrain, and it becomes an independent state.

Australia and New Zealand, August 18: Australia and New Zealand announce they will pull troops out of Vietnam by December.

Ulster, Northern Ireland, September 7: After a draconian crackdown on Loyalists was implemented in August, 100 people have been killed in the violence.

France, December 20: A group of doctors form Médecins Sans Frontières to assist the people of the Biafra region of Nigeria. They formed the group in frustration at the neutrality of the Red Cross.

Stormont Parliament Dissolved

Edward Heath

London, England, March 25: In an attempt to curtail the terrible violence that culminated in the "Bloody Sunday" killings of January 30, the cabinet of Prime Minister Edward Heath has unanimously voted to enforce direct rule in Northern Ireland, thereby making the British government responsible for maintaining law and order. In an impassioned speech last night, Mr Heath announced that as of March 30 the Stormont Parliament in Belfast will be suspended for at least 12 months, and Northern Ireland will be under the leadership of Westminster.

The Stormont Parliament was created in 1921, when 26 Irish counties gained independence and 6 became politically tied to Britain. Stormont has had the power to legislate on local matters but defers to Britain in such areas as foreign policy and defense.

Northern Ireland's prime minister, Brian Faulkner, along with his Unionist colleagues have not supported the transfer of law and order to Westminster, and are less than happy with Mr Heath's announcement.

"WE INTEND TO REMAIN ALIVE. OUR NEIGHBORS WANT TO SEE US DEAD. THIS IS NOT A QUESTION THAT LEAVES MUCH ROOM FOR COMPROMISE."

GOLDA MEIR (1898–1978), ISRAELI STATESWOMAN AND PRIME MINISTER

"NOTHING AND NO ONE CAN DESTROY THE CHINESE PEOPLE."

PEARL BUCK (1892–1973), AMERICAN NOVELIST

Olympics Marred by Terrorist Slaying

Munich, Germany, September 7: In a day-long siege, a total of 17 people—11 Israelis, 5 Palestinian terrorists, and one German policeman—were killed in Munich yesterday.

The atrocities began between 4.30 a.m. and 5 a.m. yesterday when eight members of the Black September Palestinian terrorist organization climbed a 6½-ft (2-m) high fence that surrounded the Olympic Village. Dressed in tracksuits, and with their weapons hidden inside duffel bags, the terrorists aroused no suspicion.

Four of the Israeli athletes murdered at Munich.

Once over the fence, the Palestinians ran toward the Israeli athletes' apartments and pounded on the door. When wrestling coach Moshe Weinberg opened the door, a struggle ensued. Weinberg, along with weightlifter Joseph Romano, was killed; several Israeli team members managed to escape.

The terrorists took nine Israelis hostage and demanded that the Israeli government release the 200-plus Palestinian prisoners being held in jails in Israel. They also wanted transportation from Germany to Egypt. The Israeli government refused to negotiate.

The German government devised a ploy and undertook to have a Lufthansa plane waiting for the Palestinians at Fürstenfeldbruck NATO air base, supposedly to transport them and the hostages to Cairo.

At 10.30 p.m., the terrorists and hostages were airlifted from the Olympic Village to the air base in two helicopters.

time out

The passenger ship and former naval vessel *Queen Elizabeth* was gutted by fire in Hong Kong during a conversion to a floating university for the World Campus Afloat program. The fire was attributed to arson and the *Seawise University* was scrapped.

Five German snipers, ill equipped and poorly trained, were hiding in the control tower roof. At the airfield, a gun battle ensued, in which three terrorists and one German were killed. A terrorist's grenade blew up the hostages in one of the helicopters, and the hostages in the second helicopter were killed by Palestinian bullets.

At 11 p.m., the media misguidedly reported that the hostages were alive. Four hours later, however, ABC's Olympic correspondent, Jim McKay, had to announce to the world: "They're all gone."

Sixteen Survive Andes Plane Crash

Montevideo, Uruguay, December 28: In a press conference at Montevideo today, survivors of the October plane crash over the Andes told of the extreme measures they took to survive their 72-day ordeal.

On October 13, 45 passengers—comprising mainly rugby players and students—boarded a Fairchild FH-227D turboprop at Montevideo, headed for Santiago, Chile. The plane crashed on a mountain peak on the Argentina–Chile border. Twenty-eight passengers were killed almost instantly, and a further nine subsequently died from injury or exposure, or were killed in an avalanche.

All the available food had been eaten within two days, and the survivors had no medical supplies. After 11 days, they heard on a transistor radio that the search had been discontinued. In desperation, they resorted to cannibalizing the dead passengers, in order to survive.

On December 13, two of the healthiest men took off in search of help. Ten days later, they reached the Chilean town of Maitenes, where a rescue mission was set in motion.

Helicopters arrived at the scene of the crash on December 22 and 23 and took the survivors to hospitals in the Chilean capital, Santiago.

Dhaka, Bangladesh, January 12: After being released from nine months' detention, Sheikh Mujibur Rahman returns from West Pakistan to announce the formation of the new state of Bangladesh.
Brussels, Belgium, January 22: Britain, Ireland, Norway, and Denmark join the European Economic Community (EEC).
Londonderry, Northern Ireland, January 30: On "Bloody Sunday," 13 protesters–six under the age of 17–are killed by British troops after a civil rights march became a riot.

USA, February 5: Mandatory inspections of passengers and baggage are introduced into US airports.
Florida, USA, March 2: The *Pioneer 10* space probe is launched, headed for Jupiter and the outer reaches of deep space. It contains a plaque showing some details of human civilization on Earth.
Northern Ireland, March 25: British Prime Minister Edward Heath announces the dissolution of the Stormont Parliament.

Port Moresby, Papua New Guinea, April 20: Michael Somare, leading the National Coalition, wins his first election, becoming the Chief Minister of Papua New Guinea.
Colombo, Sri Lanka, May 22: The ruling United Front party, under Sirimavo Bandaranaike, unveils a new constitution. This proclaims the country as the republic of Sri Lanka, changing its name from Ceylon. "Sri Lanka" means "venerable island."

Moscow, USSR, May 26: President Nixon and Soviet leader Leonid Brezhnev sign the SALT I treaty to limit the number of nuclear missile launchers in each country.
Paris, France, May 28: The Duke of Windsor, formerly known as Edward VIII, dies. He abdicated the throne to marry Wallace Simpson.
Washington DC, USA, June 17: Five men are arrested breaking into the Democratic National Committee offices in the Watergate Hotel. The men have links to the Republican Party and the CIA.

Kampala, Uganda, August 6: Idi Amin orders the expulsion of 50,000 Asians with British passports.
Munich, West Germany, September 5: Palestinian terrorists attack the Israeli delegation at the Olympic Games.
Canberra, Australia, December 3: The Australian Labor Party wins government for the first time in 23 years under the leadership of the charismatic Gough Whitlam.
Uruguay, December 23: Sixteen victims of a plane crash in the Andes are rescued after nearly two months.

30,000 Black Workers Go on Strike

Durban, South Africa, February 6: Approximately 13,000 black municipal workers from the Durban Corporation went on strike today for better wages and conditions, joining the 3,000 employees who stopped work yesterday. The Durban Corporation provides the city with electricity, water, and garbage services, and if the workers stay out indefinitely, Durban could be in chaos.

The strike is part of a wave of industrial disputes that began on January 9, when 2,000 black employees from the Coronation Brick and Tile Works gathered on a nearby football field, demanding a wage increase of 30 South African rand a week. The workers were awarded a much smaller raise, but news of their industrial action spread throughout Durban's factory precinct, and by the end of January a total of 30,000 workers had taken to the streets, demanding a living wage. High inflation and unemployment have contributed to the industrial unrest.

The black workers have received support from many white academics and students and some politicians, and the strikes have attracted international media coverage.

Because the strikes are as much about equality and power as wages and conditions, they have been seen as a positive step for black Africans. It is likely that the union movement will undergo a massive overhaul, with greater black participation.

Watergate Enquiry Begins

Washington DC, USA, May 17: The Senate Select Committee on Presidential Campaign Activities (otherwise known as the Senate Watergate Committee) began its hearings today in the Senate caucus room. The hearings will be broadcast on national television.

In February this year, the Senate voted 70–0 to establish a committee to investigate the events that took place in June 1972 when five people broke into the Democratic National Committee offices in the Watergate Hotel in Washington and attempted to wiretap the telephones. The Senate committee includes three Republicans and four Democrats, and is led by Democrat senator Sam Ervin of North Carolina.

In his opening speech today, Senator Ervin eloquently stated: "The purpose of this committee is to provide full and open public testimony in order that the nation can proceed toward the healing of wounds that now affect the body politic. The nation and history itself are watching us. We cannot fail our mission." Ervin has had an illustrious 19-year career in the senate, and was one of the people instrumental in the downfall of Senator Joseph McCarthy in 1954.

The first witness at the hearings was Robert Odle, administration director for Nixon's re-election committee. Odle struggled to piece together the episodes leading up to the break-in.

Washington's Watergate Hotel, scene of the break-in in June last year.

Papadopoulos Ousted

Athens, Greece, November 25: In a military coup staged by Brigadier Ioannides, the government of George Papadopoulos was overthrown today. Early this morning, tanks entered the city and troops surrounded government buildings.

Today's peaceful coup has taken place just a week after the violent uprising at the National Technical University of Athens, in which students protested against Papadopoulos's repressive dictatorial leadership. At least 13 people were killed and many more injured. Ioannides used the riots as an opportunity to seize control and restore law and order. The main reason for the overthrow, however, was

Richard Nixon

George Papadopoulos (left) had targeted left-wing organizations.

that Ioannides and his followers think that Papadopoulos was steering the country in the wrong direction. Earlier this year, Papadopoulos held a referendum in which the monarchy was abolished and Greece was made a republic, headed by Papadopoulos as president. It is commonly believed that the election was rigged.

Papadopoulos's military junta took effect on April 21, 1967 following a coup d'état. While some Greek citizens, particularly those of the rural religious right, have hailed Papadopoulos as a supporter of the common people, most hate his brutal, heavy-handed tactics, such as mass arrests, censorship, and martial law.

Golda Meir

Golda Meir Resigns as Israeli Prime Minister

Tel Aviv, Israel, April 10: Prime Minister Golda Meir resigned today, five years after taking office. Her resignation comes in the aftermath of last October's Yom Kippur War. Many Israelis believe that Meir should have launched a pre-emptive strike against Syria. Although the fighting ended within a few weeks as a result of UN intervention and Israel could claim a military victory, Meir's decisions caused a schism within her party, which has led to her resignation.

Meir's resignation marks the end of a long and fascinating career. Born in Russia and raised in the United States, Meir emigrated to Palestine in 1921. Her public life began as a kibbutz representative in the General Federation of Labor.

She was one of the signatories to the Declaration of the Establishment of the State of Israel in 1948, and she was appointed as Israel's first ambassador to the USSR.

Meir served as Minister of Labor and then Foreign Minister before succeeding Levi Eshkol as prime minister of Israel on February 26, 1969, following the death of Eshkol.

Kidnap Victim in Bank Robbery

San Francisco, California, USA, April 15: Kidnapped newspaper heiress Patty Hearst accompanied four members of the Symbionese Liberation Army (SLA) as they robbed the Sunset branch of the Hibernia Bank today, leaving with a haul estimated at around $10,000. The bank surveillance camera photographed Hearst brandishing an automatic rifle.

> *"It will be years—and not in my time—before a woman will lead the party or become Prime Minister."*
>
> MARGARET THATCHER (B. 1925), BRITISH STATESWOMAN AND PRIME MINISTER

On February 4 this year, the 19-year-old grand-daughter of media mogul William Randolph Hearst was captured by two men and one woman from the SLA, a left-wing extremist group led by black ex-convict Donald DeFreeze (alias Field Marshall Cinque Mtume.) The urban guerrillas burst into Hearst's Berkeley apartment, where they assaulted her boyfriend, and took the heiress away at gunpoint, bundling her into the trunk of a car.

The SLA offered to free Hearst in exchange for the release of group members who had been jailed for the November 1973 murder of Oakland school superintendent Marcus Foster. When that offer was refused, the Hearsts donated $6 million worth of food to the city's poor, complying with the SLA's demand, but their daughter still remained hostage.

Two weeks ago, Patty Hearst issued a taped message which stated: "I have chosen to stay [with the SLA] and fight." Whether she has elected to stay of her own volition, or has been brainwashed by her captors, remains a mystery.

Kidnapped heiress Patty Hearst.

Surrounded by family members, President Nixon delivers his final address.

President Nixon Resigns

Washington, DC, August 8: A big crowd gathered in front of the White House today as Richard Milhous Nixon announced to the nation that he is resigning as thirty-seventh president of the United States. He is the first US president in history to step down, and he did so under increasing pressure from his few remaining supporters. President Nixon ended his emotional speech by offering a prayer for the American people: "May God's grace be with you in all the days ahead."

Had he not resigned, Nixon would have faced impeachment. In May this year, the House Judiciary Committee began impeachment hearings. Its report stated that: "…President Nixon's conduct posed a threat to our democratic republic."

Nixon was charged with obstruction of justice, abuse of power, and defiance of subpoena in relation to the "Watergate Affair," which began about two years ago when five men were arrested for breaking into the Democratic campaign offices. The burglars were found to be linked to Nixon's Committee to Re-elect the President (CREEP), and over the next two years investigations revealed that Nixon had been aware of the Watergate break-in from the start. Not only had he been covering up the crimes, but he also involved government agencies in his deceit.

Tomorrow, Vice President Gerald Ford will be sworn in as president; he will serve for the rest of Nixon's term. Ford took over as vice president from Spiro Agnew in October 1973, when Agnew resigned after being charged with tax evasion.

Christchurch, New Zealand, January 24: The Commonwealth Games are opened by Prince Philip, the Duke of Edinburgh.

Berkeley, California, USA, February 4: Heiress Patricia Hearst is kidnapped by the Symbionese Liberation Army.

Moscow, USSR, February 13: Nobel Prize-winning author Aleksandr Solzhenitsyn is expelled from the USSR after being arrested. His book, *The Gulag Archipelago*, is a detailed record of the conditions in the infamous Soviet prison camps. He is offered asylum in Switzerland.

Paris, France, March 3: A Turkish Airlines DC-10 crashes, killing all 345 passengers. It is the worst disaster in aviation history.

Middle East, March 13: The oil-producing Arab nations agree to lift the embargo on Western countries.

Tel Aviv, Israel, April 10: Prime Minister Golda Meir resigns following a schism in her party.

Lisbon, Portugal, April 25: Military leaders seize control. Civil liberties are reinstated after 40 years of dictatorship under Antonio Salazar.

West Germany, May 6: Chancellor Willy Brandt resigns after an East German spy is found working as a top aide in his office.

Rajasthan, India, May 18: India becomes the sixth nation to detonate a nuclear device. Prime Minister Gandhi says the test was peaceful.

Northern Ireland, May 29: The Northern Ireland Assembly is dissolved as Westminster brings Northern Ireland under its direct rule once again.

Toronto, Canada, June 30: The leading Russian ballet dancer, Mikhail Baryshnikov, defects and is granted asylum in Canada.

Buenos Aires, Argentina, July 1: Isabel Perón assumes the presidency after the death of her husband, Juan Perón. She was Perón's third wife.

Washington DC, USA, August 8: President Nixon resigns in the aftermath of the Watergate scandal.

Cyprus, August 16: Victorious Turkish invaders divide the island into two following an offensive against Greek Cypriots.

Addis Ababa, Ethiopia, September 12: Emperor Haile Selassie is overthrown in a military coup after ruling for 58 years.

New York, USA, November 12: South Africa is suspended from the UN General Assembly after a 91-22 vote condemns the country's racial policies.

Darwin, Australia, December 24-25: Sixty-six people die and thousands are injured as Cyclone Tracy devastates the Northern Territory on Christmas Eve and Christmas Day.

Saigon Surrenders to Communists

Saigon, Vietnam, April 30: The Vietnam War—which has lasted for 30 years, cost hundreds of billions of dollars, and is responsible for the deaths of around 2.5 million people—is finally over. Today Saigon has fallen, and North and South Vietnam will be united as one nation.

What began in 1945 as a war of independence between the Vietminh and France gradually escalated to a full-scale conflict. The United States stepped up its involvement in 1965 in an attempt stop the North Vietnamese (Vietcong) communists from taking over the part of the country south of the 17th parallel. On January 27, 1973, in Paris, the US signed

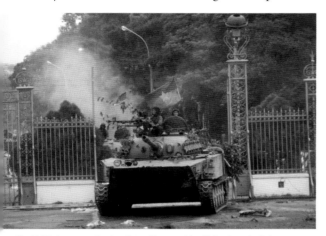
North Vietnamese tanks storm the presidential palace in Saigon.

a peace agreement, and two months later the last American troops pulled out of Vietnam. Only a handful of military personnel remained to guard the US embassy and the Defense Attaché Office.

As American financial aid to South Vietnam dwindled, the Vietcong quietly gathered momentum, culminating in today's dramatic siege of Saigon, in which North Vietnamese tanks smashed through the gates of the presidential palace in the city. Earlier today, South Vietnamese president Duong Van Minh formally

surrendered, agreeing "to hand over to you the power in order to avoid bloodshed."

US President Gerald Ford ordered the Americans to evacuate Saigon, and transportation priority was given to 1,000 US citizens and a select group of 5,500 South Vietnamese. Over the past 24 hours, the city has been in a state of bedlam. Swarms of people gathered at Ton Son Nhut airport and the US embassy, frantically trying to board one of the 81 helicopters that had been dispatched from US Navy carriers in the South China Sea. Two thousand people have lost their lives in a desperate attempt to flee the city.

Sadat Reopens Suez Canal

Port Said, Egypt, June 5: Greeted with cheering and fanfare, Egyptian president Anwar Sadat reopened the Suez Canal today as a token of peace. Egypt had closed the canal exactly eight years ago, in 1967, following the hostilities that became known as the Six Day War. Though the war was brief, 13,500 Arab soldiers were killed. Israel lost 689 lives and emerged victorious, having taken over control of the Sinai Peninsula, the Golan Heights, and East Jerusalem.

First opened on November 17, 1869, the 100-mile (160 km) long canal was an Egyptian–French joint venture. It connects Suez on the Red Sea with Port Said on the Mediterranean, allowing ships to navigate between Europe and Asia without having to go around Africa.

In 1956, Israel, Britain, and France formed an alliance to protest against President Nasser's decision to nationalize

time out

The Greek shipping magnate Aristotle Onassis died near Paris. He made his fortune in tobacco in South America and then with a vast fleet of ships. He was famous outside Greece as Maria Callas' lover and widowed First Lady Jacqueline Kennedy's husband.

the Suez Canal. The USSR offered to support Egypt, and the US intervened, managing to avert a full-scale war.

Juan Carlos is New King

Madrid, Spain, November 22: Two days after the death of General Francisco Franco, Juan Carlos de Borbón has been proclaimed King of Spain. Although the title became official today, Juan Carlos I has virtually been ruling the country since October, when the 82-year-old Franco realized that his death was imminent.

Born on January 5, 1938, Juan Carlos shares blood ties with all the crowned heads of Europe. His grandfather Alfonso XIII, who went into exile in 1931, was the last Spanish king.

Although Franco had earmarked young Juan Carlos as his successor not long after he restored the Spanish monarchy in 1947 (leaving the throne vacant and proclaiming himself de facto monarch), it is unlikely that the new leader's regime will continue the reactionary dictatorship that Spain has endured under Franco. When Franco came to power in 1939, he introduced some right-wing reforms—banning non-government trade unions and the public use of non-Spanish languages, suppressing (and often executing) his political opponents, and enforcing censorship.

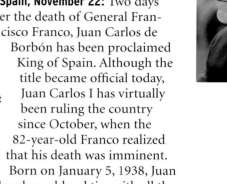
Gerald Ford

General Franco (left) with his replacement, Juan Carlos I.

Hobart, Tasmania, Australia, January 5: The carrier *Lake Illawarra* collides with the Tasman Bridge, demolishing a span. Twelve people, including five drivers, lose their lives.
Kathmandu, Nepal, February 4: King Birendra, heir to the world's only Hindu throne, assumes power, promising to advance Nepal.
London, England, February 11: Margaret Thatcher is elected as the leader of the UK's Conservative Party. She is the first woman to lead the Conservatives.

London, England, February 28: A rush-hour tube crashes into a dead end, killing 34 passengers and the driver.
Riyadh, Saudi Arabia, March 25: King Faysal is assassinated in the palace by his nephew, who has a history of mental illness.
Phnom Penh, Cambodia, April 17: Communist Khmer Rouge forces capture the capital after a three-month siege, following a five-year civil war.
Saigon, Vietnam, April 30: The US presence in Vietnam ends as Saigon falls to the Viet Cong.

Port Said, Egypt, June 5: Anwar Sadat, President of Egypt, reopens the Suez Canal after eight years.
Maputo, Mozambique, June 25: Samora Machel assumes the presidency of the southeast African country, gaining independence from Portugal after nearly five centuries.
New Delhi, India, June 12: Prime Minister Indira Gandhi is found guilty of electoral corruption and barred from holding public office for six years.
Space, July 19: The US *Apollo* and Soviet *Soyuz* spacecrafts undock after two days of stellar détente.

Helsinki, Finland, August 1: Thirty-five countries sign an accord on security and human rights.
Vientiane, Laos, August 23: The Communist Pathet Lao take control of the former French colony. Communists have recently ascended to power throughout Indochina.
Beirut, Lebanon, September 16: Fierce sectarian violence breaks out on the streets of the capital between Muslims and Christians. Prime Minister Karami is reluctant to send in the army, as most soldiers are Christian.

Canberra, Australia, November 11: The Governor-General, Sir John Kerr, sacks the Labor government of Prime Minister Gough Whitlam. This follows weeks of constitutional crisis and political tension. Whitlam is succeeded as prime minister by the Liberal Party's Malcolm Fraser.
Madrid, Spain, November 22: Juan Carlos de Borbón is proclaimed King of Spain following General Franco's death two days ago after leading the country since 1936.

Indira Gandhi

Black Students Riot in Soweto

Soweto, South Africa, June 18: What began as a peaceful demonstration has turned into the worst racial violence seen in South Africa in around 15 years, plunging Soweto and other black Johannesburg townships into anarchy.

The catalyst for the student demonstrations was the government's ruling that at least half of the school curriculum has to be taught in Afrikaans (the language of black oppression and apartheid). Though the demonstrations were precipitated by the language issue, they were really about poor education standards generally—the total budget for black education is a mere fraction of that for whites.

Two days ago, 15,000 black students gathered at appointed meeting places throughout Soweto, planning to march peacefully toward their destination—Orlando West Secondary School—where they would hold a rally. Police tried to stop the demonstration, and when the students failed to comply, the police used dogs, tear gas, and eventually guns. After that all hell broke loose. The students retaliated, setting fire to government vehicles and public buildings.

It is estimated that 100 people have been killed and about 1,000 injured.

Israelis Free Hostages in "Operation Entebbe"

Entebbe, Uganda, July 4: Independence Day took on a new meaning today when more than 100 Israelis and Jews held captive in Uganda by a group of pro-Palestinian terrorists were rescued by the Israeli Defense Force.

One week ago, four skyjackers armed with grenades and guns boarded Air France flight 139 at Athens airport and took control of the plane, reaching their destination, Entebbe, on June 28. There, three more terrorists joined the skyjackers. They agreed to free the hostages in exchange for the release of 53 terrorists imprisoned in Israel, Kenya, and Europe. The deadline was 2 p.m. Israeli time on July 1.

Just hours before the deadline, a team of Israeli commandos in three Hercules cargo planes landed at Entebbe airport. In a feat of brilliance and precision, the commandos destroyed 11 of Uganda's fighting planes, stormed the airport, killed all seven terrorists, and rescued all but three of the hostages, transporting them to safety on IDF planes.

Three hostages were killed, as was Israeli commander, Colonel Y. Netanyahu.

Uganda's murderous dictator, Idi Amin.

Mao Tse-tung Dies at 82

Beijing, China, September 9: One of this century's most prominent leaders, "Chairman" Mao Tse-tung, died today following years of deteriorating health.

Born into a peasant family in Hunan Province in 1893, young Mao was an avid reader. While working at Peking University library he joined a Marxist study group, and in 1921 became an early member of the Chinese Communist Party. Mao believed that in China the revolution would be led by the peasants—not, as Karl Marx proposed, the urban working class.

Throughout the 1920s, Mao gradually assumed more responsibility within the party. During Chiang Kai-shek's purge of communism, Mao led some 100,000 people on his "Long March" north to Yenan in Shaanxi Province. The 8,000-mile (12,900 km) trek took nearly a year, and by the time the tired marchers reached their destination in 1935, 30,000 had perished.

In 1935, Mao was appointed chairman of the Chinese Communist Party. In 1949, after a long period of strife and civil war, he became ruler of the newly formed People's Republic of China, and began to reform the country's rural and industrial economies. The "Great Leap Forward" of 1958, which established huge agricultural communes, was deemed a failure, as was the "Cultural Revolution" of 1966, best known for the publication of *Quotations from Chairman Mao Tse-tung* (*The Little Red Book*).

Mao's body will lie in state in the Great Hall of the People, and a memorial service is being held next week. It is believed that Mao's widow, the extremist Chiang Ching, will be vying for party leadership.

The late "Chairman" Mao Tse-tung.

Uganda's Idi Amin Detains 240 Americans

Kampala, Uganda, February 25: Following US criticism of the Ugandan dictator Idi Amin's brutal regime, Amin has today detained 240 Americans in Kampala. In President Jimmy Carter's words, Amin has "disgusted the entire civilized world." Apparently Amin sent a message back to the US suggesting that Americans should concern themselves with human rights in their own country before they start to interfere elsewhere.

The detainment of Americans gives cause for concern, because only a week ago President Amin personally arranged for the execution of Janani Lwum, the Anglican archbishop of Uganda, and two former cabinet ministers.

Amin came to power in 1971 after ousting Milton Obote in a military coup. In the last six years he has been responsible for the killing of around 300,000 people—mainly professionals such as academics, members of the clergy, doctors, and journalists. He is said to have murdered his wives if he suspected infidelity.

In 1972 he expelled around 70,000 Asians (mainly Indians and Pakistanis) because he believed that they were "sabotaging the economy of the country." However, Uganda went into further economic decline following the expulsion.

Idi Amin is a self-confessed admirer of Adolf Hitler and, as a Muslim, supports the Palestine Liberation Organization.

Indira Gandhi Resigns from Politics

New Delhi, India, March 22: After 11 years as India's third prime minister, Indira Gandhi looks set to resign from political life after her Congress Party's crushing defeat in today's national elections. She lost to Morarji Desai, head of the newly formed Janata Party coalition. Gandhi's son Sanjay failed to hold his seat of Amethi.

Gandhi has had a tenuous hold on her leadership since the June 1975 elections, when she was found guilty of election fraud. Strikes and protests followed, along with demands for her resignation. Gandhi, however, appealed to the Supreme Court and in August that year was cleared of convictions. Due to the widespread chaos caused by the strikes, Gandhi declared a state of emergency. She spent the next 18 months implementing her "Twenty-Point Programme." Although it was relatively successful, many of the program's policies (such as slum clearance and compulsory sterilization) have proved very unpopular.

Oil Slick Threatens the Scottish Coastline

North Sea, Scotland, April 30: The Bravo drilling platform in Norway's Ekofisk field in the North Sea has spewed over 7.5 million gallons (28 million liters) of crude oil into the ocean, creating an oil slick measuring about 45 × 30 miles (72 × 48 km). The oil slick is drifting toward Scotland.

The disaster began eight days ago on April 22, when an oil and gas blowout occurred on the Phillips Petroleum Company's platform, causing a rust-colored fountain of oil and mud to shoot 150 ft (46 m) upward into the air. It is believed that the accident was caused by a technical error—the blow-out prevention mechanism had been installed incorrectly—and crude oil gradually began leaking out through an open pipe. Fortunately, the 112 men working on the platform boarded lifeboats and were taken to safety.

Phillips enlisted the services of legendary specialist firefighter Paul ("Red") Adair, who has previously extinguished such fires as the "Devil's Cigarette Lighter" in the Sahara in 1962 and the offshore blaze at Bay Marchand, Louisiana, in 1970. Despite the unfavorable conditions that prevailed, the geyser of oil was finally staunched today.

The extent of the ecological damage caused by the spill, if any, has not yet been determined. Because about 35 percent of the oil could have evaporated soon after hitting the water and a change of wind direction has also helped the waves break up the oil, authorities are hopeful that the oil slick may not reach the coastline.

Since the severe world oil shortages of 1973, oil production in the North Sea has expanded dramatically, and it is expected that this trend will continue.

Jimmy Carter

Queen Elizabeth II celebrates her silver jubilee in June.

Pope John Paul II

First "Test-tube" Baby is Born

Manchester, England, July 26: In what has been hailed as a medical breakthrough, the first baby fertilized *in vitro* (meaning "in glass") was born just before midnight yesterday at Oldham and District General Hospital near Manchester.

Baby Louise Brown was delivered by cesarean section, and weighed 5 lb 12 oz (2.6 kg). By all accounts, she is healthy and normal. Her mother, Lesley, is doing well, despite having suffered toxemia toward the end of her pregnancy.

Lesley Brown of Bristol had been trying to conceive for nine years without

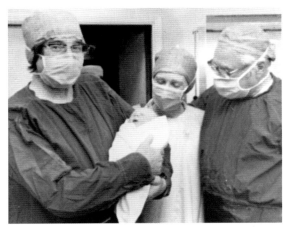

Dr Edwards and Dr Steptoe with Lesley and baby Louise Brown.

success because of blocked fallopian tubes. In desperation, she consulted Dr Patrick Steptoe in 1976. After a number of failed attempts, Dr Steptoe and his colleague Robert Edwards succeeded in implanting an embryo in her uterus, the egg having been fertilized *in vitro* using Mrs Brown's husband's sperm.

Church authorities have expressed concerns, and other critics are predicting a future of surrogate pregnancies, sperm banks, and *Brave New World* and *Frankenstein*-like disasters. But for thousands of infertile couples like John and Lesley Brown, Louise's birth is a miracle.

> *"Much of the world's work, it has been said, is done by men who do not feel quite well. Marx is a case in point."*
>
> JOHN KENNETH GALBRAITH (1908–2006), AMERICAN ECONOMIST

> *"She is trying to wear the trousers of Winston Churchill."*
>
> LEONID BREZHNEV (1906–1982), SOVIET POLITICAL LEADER ON MARGARET THATCHER

First Ever Polish Pope Ordained

The Vatican, Italy, October 16: History was made in the Roman Catholic Church today when Cardinal Karol Wojtyla of Krakow became the first Polish pope—and only the second non-Italian pope since 1522. At 58 years old, Cardinal Wojtyla is also one of the youngest pontiffs ever. What is even more extraordinary is that less than two months ago he was a member of the conclave that elected John Paul I, who died suddenly only 33 days after his appointment. Wojtyla has taken the name John Paul II in deference to his predecessor.

The new pope speaks several languages fluently, and has gained respect as an playwright, actor, and poet. He is anti-communist, and is well known for his rigid stance against artificial contraception.

Cult Leader Orders Mass Suicide

Jonestown, Guyana, November 18: In a remote jungle in Guyana, South America, more than 900 members of the People's Temple cult (at least 270 of them children) have committed mass suicide by drinking a lethal cocktail of cyanide and soft drink. "Jonestown" resembled a battlefield today, with bodies strewn all over the ground. The leader, Reverend Jim Jones, died from a bullet in the head, possibly self-inflicted.

Jones began preaching in Indiana, USA, at 16, and in 1964 he was ordained a minister of the Disciples of Christ, a legitimate denomination. He advocated racial tolerance and social activism, attracting many black converts to his church. In 1965, his "People's Temple" (as his devotees became known) moved to San Francisco, where

Jones was lauded by a number of politicians for his work with the disadvantaged. After allegations of tax evasion and other misdemeanors in 1977, Jones and 1,000 of his most select followers set up operations on his property in the jungle in Guyana, hoping to create a Utopian farm. But the commune was anything but idyllic. Jones became increasingly drug-addled and delusional, and those who were lucky enough to escape reported incidents of brutality and abuse.

Four days ago, US congressman Leo Ryan, accompanied by staff members and journalists, arrived in Jonestown to investigate the claims. When several cult members attempted to escape with the Ryan entourage today, Jones ordered them to be shot at the airstrip; Congressman Ryan and four other people were killed. The mass "revolutionary suicide" (which had been rehearsed many times) took place several hours later.

time out

Sid Vicious, previously of the Sex Pistols, was charged with stabbing his girlfriend Nancy Spungen to death. Vicious told police that he woke from a drug stupor to find her dead in the bathroom of their room in the Hotel Chelsea in New York.

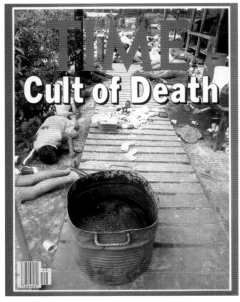

News of the Jonestown massacre shocked the world.

Northern Canada, January 24: A Soviet nuclear-powered spy satellite, *Cosmos 954*, crashes in a shower of radioactive rubble.

Zimbabwe (Rhodesia), March 21: Three black nationalists have been sworn into parliament, sharing executive power with Ian Smith, the prime minister. This ends exclusive white rule of the African country.

Brittany, France, March 24: The supertanker *Amoco Cadiz* sinks off the coast; 230,000 barrels of oil have spilt into the sea. Around 70 miles (112 km) of the French coast have been affected.

Kabul, Afghanistan, April 30: Soviet-backed rebel troops kill President Daoud.

Italy, May 9: The body of Aldo Moro, the Christian Democratic senator who was kidnapped by the Red Brigade eight weeks ago, is recovered.

London, England, May 10: Princess Margaret, Queen Elizabeth's younger sister, seeks a divorce from Lord Snowdon after a volatile relationship, extramarital love affairs by both the princess and her husband, and two years of separation.

Melbourne, Australia, May 15: Sir Robert Menzies, Australia's longest serving prime minister (1939-1941, 1949-1966) dies of heart failure, aged 83.

New Hampshire, USA, June 30: Protestors against the nuclear power plant proposed for Seabrook have a victory after seven years of campaigning as the plan is scrapped.

Spain, July 11: Nearly 200 holidaymakers are killed when a liquid gas tanker rolls over and explodes in a campsite on the Mediterranean coast.

Manchester, England, July 25: The first "test-tube" baby is born.

Nairobi, Kenya, August 22: Kenyan president, Jomo Kenyatta, dies, aged 80.

Camp David, USA, September 18: Israeli Prime Minister Begin and Egyptian president Sadat reach agreement on a framework for peace in the Middle East.

The Vatican, Italy, September 30: The shortest papal reign comes to an end when Pope John Paul I dies of a heart attack after 33 days in office.

The Vatican, Italy, October 16: The first non-Italian pontiff for over four centuries is elected. Karol Wojtyla, from Poland, will be known as John Paul II.

Jonestown, Guyana, November 18: People's Temple cult leader, Reverend Jim Jones, orders his followers to drink poisoned soft drink. A total of 913 people die.

Tehran, Iran, December 29: Supporters of the exiled Ayatollah Khomeini, protesting for the past month, have eroded the power of the Shah of Iran.

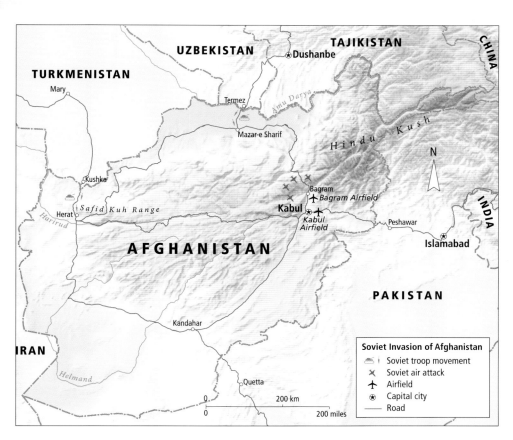

Mountbatten Killed by IRA

Mullaghmore, Ireland, August 27: Louis Mountbatten, first Earl Mountbatten of Burma, died almost instantly today as a bomb exploded on his fishing boat in Donegal Bay. For many years, 79-year-old Mountbatten had spent one month every summer at Classiebawn Castle, near the picturesque village of Mullaghmore, County Sligo, in the northwest of the Republic of Ireland. The Provisional IRA has admitted to the bombing.

One of Mountbatten's 14-year-old twin grandsons, Nicholas, was also killed in the explosion, along with Paul Maxwell, a local lad. Four other relatives of Mountbatten were injured.

Lord Mountbatten had a distinguished military career in both world wars, and served as Viceroy of India. He is respected in Great Britain, India, and Ireland.

Pol Pot

Soviet Troops Invade Afghanistan

Kabul, Afghanistan, December 29: Following several days of chaos, the build-up of Soviet troops in Kabul has become a full-scale invasion today, culminating in the fall of the Afghani government. It is the first time since 1945 that a Soviet military expedition has ventured outside the eastern bloc or Cuba.

China and Pakistan, as well as the US, have condemned the Soviet's actions, saying they are a threat to world peace.

On December 24, three divisions of the Red Army took control of Kabul airport and other airfields around the city. This enabled Soviet troops to send equipment and troops into the area. Yesterday, several more Soviet regiments proceeded south to the border of Afghanistan.

Today, several hundred KGB troops attacked the presidential palace and brutally shot down President Hafizullah Amin, telling the media that he had been executed for crimes against the state.

Soviet Invasion of Afghanistan
- Soviet troop movement
- Soviet air attack
- Airfield
- Capital city
- Road

First Female Prime Minister for Britain

London, England, May 4: The Conservative Party's Margaret Thatcher will take up residence at Number 10 Downing Street, having soundly defeated Labour Prime Minister James Callaghan. There was a 5.2 percent swing to the Conservatives, who won 339 seats (a gain of 62) compared to Labour's 269 seats (a loss of 50).

Thatcher was born in Lincolnshire on October 13, 1925. Her father was a grocer who was also active in the Methodist church and in public life. Having studied science at Oxford University, Thatcher began her professional life as a research chemist, and then became interested in Conservative politics in 1950. She married Denis Thatcher in 1951, and in 1953 she not only gave birth to twins but also became a barrister. She entered the House of Commons in 1959, and after more than 15 years' experience in a variety of portfolios (both in government and in opposition), Thatcher succeeded Edward Heath as leader of the opposition in 1975.

The nickname "Iron Lady" was first applied to Thatcher in 1976 by the Soviet paper *Red Star*, after she harshly and very publicly criticized Soviet policies. Over the next few years, she won the admiration of many people and made just as many enemies for her outspoken views on immigration and trade unions.

It is believed that Labour's loss today is largely due to the "winter of discontent" experienced in England this year, during which massive strikes have nearly crippled the country. With the help of advertizing gurus Saatchi and Saatchi, Thatcher based her campaign on fear of unemployment. She will boost the flagging economy by cutting income tax and public spending.

Cambodia, January 7: Vietnamese troops seize control of Phnom Penh, toppling the pro-Chinese government of Lon Nol.

Tehran, Iran, February 1: The Ayatollah Khomeini returns after 15 years in exile, intending to establish an Islamic state.

Kampala, Uganda, March 29: Idi Amin's murderous regime collapses as Tanzanian-backed troops invade the Ugandan capital.

Pennsylvania, USA, March 31: The Three Mile Island nuclear reactor is shut down after releasing radiation.

Rawalpindi, Pakistan, April 4: Ex-prime minister Zulfikar Ali Bhutto is executed after being convicted of murdering a political opponent.

London, England, May 3: Margaret Thatcher leads the Conservative Party to victory, becoming Europe's first female prime minister.

Vienna, Austria, June 18: US President Carter and Soviet leader Leonid Brezhnev sign the SALT II nuclear arms limitation treaty.

Algiers, Algeria, July 4: Ahmed Ben Bella, former president, is released after 14 years in captivity.

Western Australia, July 11: The US satellite *Skylab* disintegrates on re-entry into Earth's atmosphere, scattering debris over the state.

Managua, Nicaragua, July 17: General Somoza flees into exile. His regime is replaced by a junta representing conservative business interests and communist Sandanistas.

Cambodia, August 19: The leader of the Khmer Rouge, Pol Pot, is sentenced to death in absentia for his murderous regime.

Mullaghmore, Ireland, August 27: The Queen's cousin, Lord Mountbatten, is killed when an IRA bomb destroys his family fishing boat just after it leaves the harbor.

Ireland, September 29: Pope John Paul II flies into Ireland today to be met by over 300,000 people. The new pontiff has been traveling widely, recently visiting the USA.

Tehran, Iran, November 4: Followers of Ayatollah Khomeini storm the US embassy. Nearly 100 embassy staff are taken hostage.

Antarctica, November 28: A New Zealand DC-10 plows into Mt Erebus on a sightseeing flight, killing all 257 on board.

Zimbabwe (Rhodesia), December 21: Robert Mugabe, Joshua Nkomo, and Bishop Abel Muzorewa sign a cease-fire agreement, bringing the seven-year civil war to an end.

Afghanistan, December 29: The build-up of Soviet troops has become an invasion, culminating in the fall of the government in Kabul.

Dr Christiaan Barnard

> "GOD NOT
> ONLY PLAYS
> DICE. HE ALSO
> SOMETIMES
> THROWS THE
> DICE WHERE
> THEY CANNOT
> BE SEEN."
>
> STEPHEN W.
> HAWKING (B. 1942),
> ENGLISH PHYSICIST,
> ON NATURE, 1975

> "IF SUNBEAMS
> WERE
> WEAPONS OF
> WAR, WE
> WOULD HAVE
> HAD SOLAR
> ENERGY
> LONG AGO."
>
> GEORGE PORTER
> (1920–2002), BRITISH
> CHEMIST, 1973

Aswan High Dam Completed

Aswan, Egypt, July 21, 1970: After 10 years of construction, the Aswan High Dam (Saad el-Aali) was completed today, and is being lauded as Egypt's greatest technological feat since the pyramids.

The rock-and-clay embankment dam is 11,811 ft (3,600 m) long and 364 ft (111 m) wide. Its reservoir, Lake Nasser (named in honor of Egyptian president Gamal Abdal-Nasser), is the world's largest artificial lake, measuring 300 miles (480 km) long by 10 miles (16 km) wide.

The Aswan High Dam will increase the amount of arable land available in Egypt by approximately 30 percent, trapping floodwater from the Nile during the wet seasons and releasing it during times of drought. In addition, the electricity generated by the dam will provide power to thousands of households.

In 1902, the Aswan Low Dam was completed. The height of the dam had to be raised twice, and when the dam came close to overflowing in 1946, the decision was made to build a new one 10 miles (16 km) away. The US planned to loan Egypt the sum of $270 million; however, they withdrew the offer for political reasons. Instead, the USSR became the main contributor to the project, in terms of finance, design, and manpower.

The new reservoir started to fill in 1964 just after the first stage of the dam was finished. It is expected to reach capacity in about five years.

Although the Aswan High Dam will be of great benefit to many people, some scientists are concerned about the impact such major changes to the landscape will eventually have on the environment.

Both people and artefacts had to be relocated to build the Aswan High Dam.

First Heart–Lung Transplant Performed

Cape Town, South Africa, July 25, 1971: Nearly four years after making medical history with the world's first human heart transplant, cardiothoracic surgeon Dr Christiaan Barnard has today performed the first combined heart–lung transplant operation at Groote Schuur Hospital in the port city of Cape Town.

Suitable candidates for heart–lung transplants are patients under the age of 50 with the terminal lung disease known as severe pulmonary hypertension. This is a condition in which an increase in pressure in the lung vessels causes the rest of the body to be deprived of oxygen. The donated heart and lungs are taken from a clinically "brain dead" person, and it is essential that there are tissue matches between the recipient and the donor.

On December 3, 1967, Dr Barnard performed his first heart transplant on 55-year-old Louis Washkansky, who died of bilateral pneumonia 18 days after the operation. His second subject was Dr Philip Blaiberg, who received his new heart a month later. Blaiberg fared considerably better, living for 18 months before his body rejected the new heart.

In 1968, one year after Barnard's pioneering efforts, a total of 107 heart transplants were performed in 24 countries, but with low survival rates.

Over the past few years, Barnard has become something of an international superstar, although his origins were very simple. He was born in 1922 in the remote township of Beaufort West, South Africa. His Afrikaans father served as a Dutch Reformed minister. Barnard won a scholarship to the University of Cape Town, where he received his medical degree in 1953. He undertook postgraduate study at the University of Minnesota in the United States, where he became interested in cardiology and heart–lung surgery.

Skylab 4 Crew Returns to Earth

Cape Canaveral, Florida, USA, February 8, 1974: The final manned mission of the Skylab operation, *Skylab 4,* has returned to Earth today. It left Kennedy Space Center on November 16, 1973, and at 84 days' duration it holds the record as

The manned mission *Skylab 4* orbits the Earth.

the longest US space flight. One of the highlights for the crew—William Pogue, Gerald Carr, and Edward Gibson—was observing Comet Kohoutek.

The first US space station–research laboratory, Skylab was developed to fulfil several purposes: to find out if humans can exist in space for long periods, to observe the Earth, and to engage in a detailed study of the sun. The manned crews consisted of scientist–astronauts, who had been training since 1965.

Skylab 1 was an unmanned mission and was launched into orbit from NASA headquarters on May 14, 1973 via a Saturn V booster rocket. The station sustained damages en route, affecting its power supply and temperature control. This delayed the development of *Skylab 2*.

On May 25, 1973, an Apollo spacecraft transported Charles Conrad Jr, Paul Weitz, and Joseph Kerwin to rendezvous with the space station for the 28-day *Skylab 2* mission. The crew fitted a parasol sunshade to make the indoor temperature of the space station cooler and more comfortable, and conducted medical and other scientific experiments. They returned on June 22 the same year.

The second manned mission, *Skylab 3*, lasted 59 days, from July 28 to September 25, 1973, with crew members Alan Bean, Owen Garriott, and Jack Lousma.

Despite the early technical difficulties, the Skylab mission has been deemed an unqualified success. After *Skylab 4*, the space station was placed in a "parking orbit," where it will remain for approximately eight to ten years.

"Lucy" the Skeleton is Found in East Africa

Hadar, Ethiopia, November 24, 1974: While on a research expedition in Hadar, a remote, dusty area of the Great Rift Valley

time out

Huge lightning bolts hit powerlines close to Indian Point Nuclear Power Plant in New York State, hitting feeder lines and causing outages. There was no damage to the plant, but locals reported seeing the sky light up for ten seconds late in the evening.

in East Africa, American anthropologist Donald Johanson and student Tom Gray have today made an amazing discovery. They were just about to head back to camp when they noticed a fragment of what appeared to be an elbow. It didn't take them very long to find other fossilized body fragments distributed along the slope: leg, pelvis, jaw, and skull.

Johanson immediately realized that they had stumbled across about 40 percent of a complete hominid (a member of the primate family that includes humans and our humanlike ancestors). It is rare indeed to find so many associated body parts together.

There was great excitement back at the camp over the discovery. Johanson and his colleagues believe the skeleton is that of a female because of its height (3 ft 6 in [107 cm]). Instead of calling it "the partial *Australopithecus* skeleton from locality 288," they decided to name it "Lucy" after the Beatles' song "Lucy in the Sky with Diamonds," which was playing on the stereo during their celebrations.

It is estimated that Lucy was in her twenties when she died around 3 million years ago. Her pelvis and leg bones indicate that she walked upright, but because her arms are relatively long compared to her legs, she would also have climbed trees.

Finding Lucy may well turn out to be a major breakthrough in the study of human origins.

Major Archeological Discovery in China

Shaanxi Province, China, July 11, 1975: Archeologists in China have today revealed one of the most significant discoveries of this

century—a set of about 6,000 terracotta statues of warriors, together with horses, chariots, and weapons. The figures were uncovered in Shaanxi Province in Northwest China by farm laborers digging a well close to the ancient city of Xian.

The warrior statues are approximately 6 ft (1.8 m) tall and are made from clay and a malleable ocher-colored substance known as "yellow earth." The top part of the statues is hollow and the bottom half is solid. Like the warriors, the horses are life-sized. It appears that they were once colorfully painted, but after 2,000 years most of the paint has worn away.

The "terracotta army" was commissioned by Emperor Q'ing Shih-huang-ti (246–206 BCE), the founder of the Q'ing Dynasty. Among his many achievements are the building of the original Great Wall of China, unification of China, abolition of the feudal system, and the construction of a complex road system. About 700,000 laborers were forced to work on the amazing terracotta statues, which were to be included in the emperor's gigantic mausoleum complex. Apparently, he sought military protection in the afterlife.

It is hoped that one day a museum will be built on the site of the find.

Gerald Carr

A warrior with his horse, part of the enormous "Q'ing's Army."

Boston, USA, January 1975: From his complex computer models, Syukoro Manabe shows how the atmospheric temperature rises when carbon dioxide levels are doubled.

Shaanxi Province, China, July 11, 1975: Archeologists find 6,000 clay figures dating from 221–206 BCE.

USA, November 1975: Bill Gates and Paul Allen form a business partnership called "Micro-Soft."

Venus, October 1975: Soviet space probes land on the surface of Venus and send back the first pictures of the planet's surface.

London and Paris, January 21, 1976: Two Concorde jets take off on their first commercial flights.

California, USA, April 1, 1976: Stephen Wozniak and Steven Jobs form the Apple Computer Company.

San Francisco, USA, April 7, 1976: Genentech, the first commercial company engaged in genetic engineering, is established.

Mars, July 20, 1976: *Viking 1* lands and transmits photographs of the Martian landscape.

California, USA, February 18, 1977: The *Enterprise* space shuttle makes its first flight atop a Boeing 747 jumbo jet.

Washington DC, USA, May 11, 1977: The US Government announces that CFCs will be outlawed as propellants in aerosol cans in two years' time.

South Africa, October 23, 1977: Single-celled fossils that have been dated at 3.4 billion years old are discovered, pushing back the evidence of the first life on earth by 100 million years.

Sweden, January 1978: The Scandinavian nation becomes the first to legislate to ban aerosol sprays.

Ethiopia, February 24, 1978: Mary Leakey finds footprints that have been dated at 3.5 million years old. They are thought to belong to a bipedal hominid.

USA, June 22, 1978: The only moon of Pluto, Charon, is discovered.

New York, USA, November 15, 1978: Renowned anthropologist Margaret Mead dies, aged 76.

London, England, January 1, 1979: Decca releases the first digital recording.

USSR, August 19, 1979: Soviet cosmonauts Lyakhov and Ryumin return from 175 days in space.

Sweden, October 11, 1979: Godfrey Hounsfield is awarded the Nobel Prize for Medicine for the invention of the full body ("CAT") scanner.

Geneva, Switzerland, December 9, 1979: The World Health Organization (WHO) declares that smallpox has been eliminated.

Godfrey Hounsfield

> *"There is no reason for any individual to have a computer in their home."*

KEN OLSON, PRESIDENT AND FOUNDER OF DIGITAL EQUIPMENT CORPORATION, 1977

> *"Truth in science can be defined as the working hypothesis best suited to open the way to the next better one."*

KONRAD (ZACHARIAS) LORENZ (1903–1989), AUSTRIAN ZOOLOGIST AND ETHOLOGIST

Concorde's First Commercial Flights

London and Paris, England, January 21, 1976: After years of preparation, the supersonic transport (SST) known as the Concorde made its first commercial flights today. Two Concordes departed simultaneously at 11.40 a.m. British Airways G-BOAA (206) left from London's Heathrow for Bahrain and arrived at its destination at 2.24 p.m. Air France F-BVFA (205) departed from Paris for Rio de Janeiro, but because of an unexpected lengthy stopover in Dakar, did not arrive in Rio until just after 7 p.m.

The development of the Concorde began as a British and French joint venture in 1962. Britain and France hoped to compete with the US, which up until then had led the world in aircraft technology. The first prototype was manufactured in Toulouse, France, in 1967, and the first flight (Concorde 001) departed from Toulouse in March 1969. One month later, Concorde 002 flew from Filton, Bristol, to Fairford in England, and on September 20, 1973 it made its first visit to the US, landing at Dallas-Fort Worth airport.

The Concorde has a cruising speed of an impressive 1,540 mph (2,480 km/h) and a maximum cruising altitude of 60,000 ft (18,290 m). It accommodates 100 passengers in one class, but does not provide any more head or leg room than economy seats on an ordinary aircraft. It has been reported that turbulence is minimal, and that there is only a slight increase in acceleration when breaking through the sound barrier.

Last month, the United States House of Representatives voted against allowing the Concorde to land in the United States for at least six months. Environmental reasons were cited as highly relevant.

Apple Computer Company is Founded

Palo Alto, California, USA, April 1, 1976: Two college dropouts, 21-year-old Steven Jobs and 25-year-old Stephen Wozniak, have founded a new computer company with

Britain and France have upstaged the US with the supersonic Concorde.

the catchy name of "Apple." Jobs is a visionary entrepreneur and Wozniak is a technical mastermind—they met in 1971 through a shared interest in electronics, and have been collaborating on various projects ever since. One of their endeavors earned them $150 each in 1974: it was a called a Blue Box, and enabled people to make free long-distance telephone calls.

Up until very recently, Wozniak was designing calculator chips for Hewlett-Packard and Jobs worked at video game manufacturing company Atari. Jobs and Wozniak came up with the notion of designing and producing a relatively easy and affordable pre-assembled computer. They raised $1,300 by selling Jobs's Volkswagen van and other personal items, and put together the prototype in Jobs's garage. The machine, which they named

the Apple I, contained an MOS 6502 microprocessor on a single-circuit board. When it is released in a few months, it will sell for between $600 and $700. Already, Wozniak is planning the improved Apple II, which he believes will bring the computer within the reach of the general public.

Over in Albuquerque, New Mexico, another couple of whiz kids are causing a stir in the computer world—Bill Gates and Paul Allen. In November last year they formed a company they named "Micro-Soft" (for microcomputer software). They met as students at a private school in Seattle—at the age of 13, Gates was already studying software and programming computers. After finishing high school, Gates went on to Harvard, and Allen to Washington State University, but they both left before graduation to develop their software program, a new version of the BASIC language for the first microcomputer, the Altair 8800.

Like the Apple team, Gates and Allen are both aged in their twenties.

Viking 1 Lands on Mars

Cape Canaveral, Florida, USA, July 20, 1976: After an 11-month journey from Earth, the NASA *Viking 1* planetary lander has arrived on Mars, touching down today on an area known as Chryse Planitia (Plains of Gold).

The *Viking 1*, comprising an orbiter and a lander, was launched from Kennedy Space Center, Florida, on August 20, 1975. It is the first spacecraft to function on the surface of Mars, and entered the planet's orbit on June 19, 1976. The lander separated from the orbiter, reaching its final destination—the Red Planet—at 11.56 universal time. Originally, the *Viking 1* lander was scheduled to touch down on Mars on 4 July to coincide with the American Bicentennial celebrations, but it was delayed because of problems with the original landing site. Instead, it landed on what is perhaps a more fitting anniversary: July 20 is the seventh anniversary of the Apollo moon landing.

Only 25 seconds after landing, *Viking 1* sent back its first close-up photographic image of Mars. There are two television cameras on board, and it is estimated that several thousand pictures will be taken during the Viking's stay. In addition to cameras, *Viking 1* is equipped with a soil analysis machine, a weather station, and a seismograph. It is capable of taking measurements of soil and weather conditions, digging beneath the planet's surface, and reporting seasonal changes.

It is highly unlikely that *Viking 1* will send back reports of little green Martians, although NASA scientists hope that the

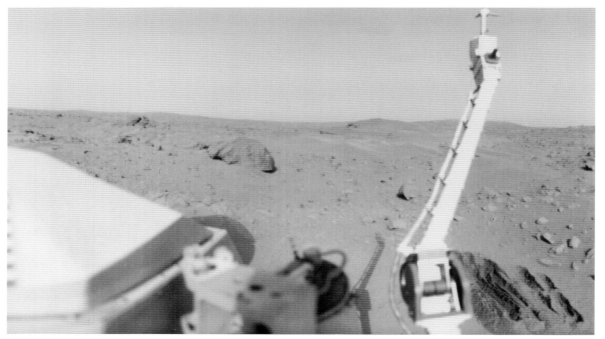

A picture of the planet Mars, taken by the NASA Viking 1 *planetary lander. Will later expeditions find life on Mars?*

Scientific Achievements

Astronomy: Rings of Uranus discovered; Pluto's moon Charon discovered.

Botany: DDT banned in US; aerosol sprays banned in Sweden.

Chemistry: Various foods studied to determine the amounts of dietary fiber they contained.

Ecology: Idea presented that CFCs could damage ozone layer; Greenpeace established in Vancouver, Canada; Greenbelt Movement established in Africa.

Geology: "Lucy," c. 3-million-year-old female hominid fossil, found in Ethiopia.

Mathematics: RSA, an algorithm for public-key encryption, is discovered.

Medicine: First vaccines for rubella, chicken pox, meningitis administered; first test-tube baby delivered.

Physics: Development of the silicon microprocessor.

Zoology: Jane Goodall Institute founded to promote research on and to protect chimpanzees.

Botanic Gardens
Hiroshima, Japan
Palm Desert, USA

Observatories
Almeria, Spain
Coonabarabran, Australia
Mead, USA
Mount Megantic, Canada
Negev, Israel
Shiraz, Iran
Visnjan, Yugoslavia

Universities
University of Famagusta, Cyprus
University of Klagenfurt, Austria
University of Kochi, India
University of Ponta Delgada, Azores
University of Quetta, Pakistan

technology will detect water, which is the best indicator that some sort of life exists.

Anthropologist Margaret Mead Dies at Age 76

New York, USA, November 15, 1978: Margaret Mead, who revolutionized anthropology in 1928 with her subjective observations of Samoan culture, has died of cancer today at the age of seventy-six.

Mead was born on December 16, 1901, into a progressive, intellectually stimulating household in Philadelphia, Pennsylvania. Her father was a professor of economics and her mother a sociologist.

After receiving a psychology degree from Barnard College, New York, in 1920, Mead undertook postgraduate anthropology studies at Columbia University under Professor Franz Boas (considered to be the father of modern American anthropology) and Ruth Benedict. Boas believed that anthropologists should go out and study vanishing cultures, so in 1925 PhD candidate Mead enthusiastically agreed to go to the island of Tau in American Samoa in the Pacific Ocean.

Mead chose to study adolescent girls to find out if they suffered the same emotional difficulties as their American counterparts. She found out that Samoan girls passed through their teens much more smoothly, and published her findings in *Coming of Age in Samoa* (1928). Over the years the book has been criticized for its lack of accuracy but praised for its accessibility. In 1928, her first marriage—to archeologist Luther Cressman—ended, and she married New Zealand anthropologist Reo Fortune. Mead and Fortune collaborated on *Growing Up in New Guinea* (1930). In 1935, she wrote *Sex and Temperament in Three Primitive Societies*, and had by then concluded that human beings are influenced more by nurture than nature.

Margaret Mead married a third time, to English anthropologist Gregory Bateson; they had one child, Catherine, born in 1939. Throughout the remainder of her career Margaret Mead traveled widely and held senior positions at leading universities, as well as becoming curator of ethnology at the American Museum of Natural History. She was president of the American Association for the Advancement of Science.

Cosmonauts Return from 175 Days in Space

Baikonur (Leninsk), USSR, August 19, 1979: Soviet cosmonauts Vladimir Lyakhov and Valery Ryumin have today returned to Earth on the *Soyuz 34* rocket. They had spent a record 175 days aboard the *Salyut 6* space station.

The cosmonauts began their journey on February 25 from the Baikonur Cosmodrome aboard the *Soyuz 32,* linking up with the space station the following day. The *Salyut 6* is a second-generation space station. It is equipped with two docking ports, facilitating the delivery of supplies and equipment and thus making longer stays possible.

While they were in space, commander Lyakhov and flight engineer Ryumin spent their time conducting experiments, using such equipment as a mapping camera, an Earth photography camera, a radio telescope, and an infra-red telescope. Just before returning home, they performed a space walk of one hour and 23 minutes to free the KPT-10 radio telescope antenna, which had become tangled in the external structure.

Both Lyakhov and Ryumin are highly accomplished senior cosmonauts. Lyakhov was born in the Ukraine in 1941 and graduated from the Kharkov Higher Air Force School in 1964, enrolling in the Air Force Cosmonaut Training Center in 1967. Ryumin was born in Khabarovsk, Russia, in 1939, graduating from the Kaliningrad Mechanical Engineering Technical College in 1958. He did further study at the Department of Electronics and Computing Technology at the Moscow Forestry Engineering Institute, majoring in spacecraft control systems. He joined the Energia Engineer Cosmonaut Training Corps in 1973, and has participated in several Soyuz assignments.

Margaret Mead

Smallpox is Eradicated

Geneva, Switzerland, December 9, 1979: After a 21-year campaign by the World Health Organization (WHO), the Global Commission for the Certification of Smallpox Eradication has accepted a report claiming that smallpox has been eliminated.

Smallpox is a highly contagious, often fatal disease caused by the *Variola major* or *Variola minor* viruses. (*Variola major* is the more dangerous form.)

The English physician Edward Jenner developed the smallpox vaccination using cowpox serum in 1796, but it would take many generations before the disease could be totally wiped out. In 1948, smallpox was present in at least 90 countries. Ten years later, the USSR outlined a plan for its eradication that was endorsed by the World Health Assembly. However, it wasn't until 1967, when the Intensified Smallpox Eradication Program began putting various strategies in place, that the incidence of smallpox began to drop worldwide. The last naturally occurring case was in Somalia in 1977.

An announcement will be made at the 33rd World Health Assembly next year.

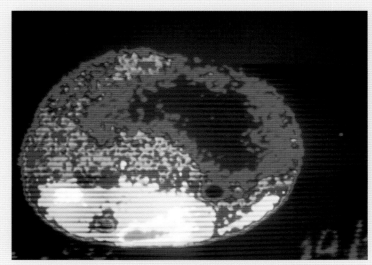

A scan of a brain taken using Godfrey Hounsfield's invention, the "CAT" scan.

Mikhail Baryshnikov

McCartney Files Suit to Dissolve Beatles

London, England, December 31, 1970:
Paul McCartney has today filed a lawsuit against the other three Beatles and their record company, Apple Corps. The writ, issued by the High Court of London, stated that the "partnership and business carried on by the plaintiff and the defendants under the name of The Beatles and Co. ...ought to be dissolved."

On April 10, just days before releasing his first solo album, *McCartney*, Paul hinted that the Beatles would be going their separate ways, and a few months later he began legal proceedings.

The split has been several years in the making. Manager Brian Epstein's death in 1967 left the Beatles without any clear business direction, and Paul took over as self-appointed leader. The band stopped touring at the same time, even though their recording output remained prodigious. Within a week of each other, in March 1969, Paul married American photographer Linda Eastman and John Lennon married Japanese artist Yoko Ono. Both relationships radically altered the group's dynamics. John and George began to resent Paul's control, and George wanted to contribute more of his own songs to the Beatles albums. When Apple Corps began to experience serious financial difficulty, the Beatles decided to hire a new manager. Paul wanted his father-in-law, lawyer Alan Eastman, and the others didn't. Majority ruled, and Rolling Stones manager Allen Klein was hired. For Paul, this was the last straw.

The documentary of the recording of their final album, *Let it Be*, candidly reveals the stresses and personality clashes that contributed to the break-up.

"THE BASIC DIFFERENCE BETWEEN CLASSICAL MUSIC AND JAZZ IS THAT IN THE FORMER THE MUSIC IS ALWAYS GREATER THAN ITS PERFORMANCE— WHEREAS THE WAY JAZZ IS PERFORMED IS ALWAYS MORE IMPORTANT THAN WHAT IS BEING PLAYED."

ANDRÉ PREVIN
(B. 1929), AMERICAN
COMPOSER AND
CONDUCTOR

Marlon Brando, star of *The Godfather*.

Four Oscar Nominations for *A Clockwork Orange*

Hollywood, California, USA, January, 1972:
Stanley Kubrick's disturbing and highly controversial film, *A Clockwork Orange,* has received four Academy Award nominations (for Best Picture, Best Film Editing, Best Director, and Best Adapted Screenplay), and has won the prestigious New York Film Critics Award for Best Picture of 1971.

The film, which was adapted from Anthony Burgess's 1962 futuristic novel of the same title, stars relative newcomer Malcolm McDowell. The 28-year-old British actor plays Alex deLarge, the leader of a gang of thugs who get sadistic pleasure from acts of "ultraviolence"— robbery, bashing, murder, and rape. Alex is imprisoned for his crimes, and while in jail is treated with a new, experimental form of aversion therapy known as the Ludovico Technique. The technique cures him of his violence but turns him into a clockwork robot, incapable of enjoying his beloved "Ludwig van."

For many, the real star of the film is the soundtrack. Original compositions by Wendy Carlos, classical compositions by Beethoven, Rossini, and Elgar, and popular tunes such as "Singin' in the Rain" and "I Want to Marry a Lighthouse Keeper" serve as background music for the horrific acts.

Although *A Clockwork Orange* was released to great critical acclaim, it also has its share of detractors. The Catholic Legion of Decency has given it a "Condemned" rating, and acerbic *New Yorker* critic Pauline Kael said that "one is more likely to feel cold antipathy toward the movie than horror at the violence..." Many authorities are worried that the on-screen brutality will incite hordes of young people to commit copycat crimes. It might. Or it might just turn a whole new generation on to Beethoven.

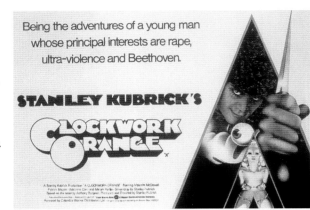

Being the adventures of a young man whose principal interests are rape, ultra-violence and Beethoven.

STANLEY KUBRICK'S CLOCKWORK ORANGE

Kubrick's *A Clockwork Orange* has polarized critics and viewers alike.

Jesus Christ Superstar Opens in West End

London, England, August 10, 1972: After a successful Broadway season, *Jesus Christ Superstar* opened at the Palace Theater in London's West End last night. It stars Paul Nicholas as Jesus, Dana Gillespie as Mary Magdalene, and Stephen Tate as Judas.

Jesus Christ Superstar began life as a record album. Although its creators, 24-year-old, classically trained composer Andrew Lloyd Webber and 28-year-old pop lyricist Tim Rice had conceived it as a rock opera, their managers decided to test

---

London, England, June 15, 1970: Laurence Olivier is the first actor to be awarded a peerage.

London, England, September 18, 1970: Guitarist Jimi Hendrix is found dead at 27. He choked on vomit in his sleep after taking sleeping pills.

Los Angeles, USA, October 4, 1970: Blues and rock singer Janis Joplin dies of an accidental drug overdose, aged 27.

London, England, December 31, 1970: Paul McCartney issues a writ calling for the dissolution of the Beatles.

Trumansburg, USA, 1970: R. A. Moog Inc. releases the MiniMoog, a new portable analog synthesizer.

New York, USA, April 6, 1971: Igor Stravinsky, who revolutionized music with *The Rite of Spring*, dies aged 88.

Paris, France, July 3, 1971: Lead singer of the Doors, Jim Morrison, dies at 27.

New York, USA, August 1, 1971: Ex-Beatle George Harrison organizes a benefit concert for Bangladesh featuring high-profile musical performers such as Eric Clapton.

USA, December 19, 1971: Malcolm McDowell stars in Stanley Kubrik's film *A Clockwork Orange*.

USA, March 24, 1972: *The Godfather*, Francis Ford Coppola's cinematic masterpiece concerning a Mafia family, opens.

London, England, March–December 1972: The British Museum exhibits the treasures of Egyptian pharaoh Tutankhamun.

London, England, August 9, 1972: Andrew Lloyd Webber and Tim Rice's musical *Jesus Christ Superstar* premieres in the West End.

Jamaica, March 26, 1973: Sir Noël Coward—dramatist, songwriter, and performer—dies. His plays included *Private Lives*, *Design for Living*, and *Blithe Spirit*.

Mougins, France, April 8, 1973: Pablo Picasso, the prolific and influential artist, dies aged 91.

Hong Kong, July 20, 1973: Martial artist and film star Bruce Lee dies, aged 32, from a cerebral edema.

New York, USA, September 21, 1973: Jackson Pollock's painting *Blue Poles* is sold for $2 million to the Australian National Gallery.

USA, May 4, 1974: Prolific jazz composer, Duke Ellington, dies of cancer aged 75.

Sweden, 1974: The Nobel Prize for Literature is won, controversially, by two Swedish authors: Eyvind Johnson and Harry Martinson. Both had been on the Nobel panel, and beat nominees Graham Greene and Vladimir Nabokov to the prize.

USA, 1974: Films released this year include Roman Polanski's *Chinatown*, Irwin Allen's *The Towering Inferno*, and Francis Ford Coppola's *The Godfather: Part II*.

the concept by first releasing the music as a double album. (Lloyd Webber and Rice had previously collaborated on the 1968 musical *Joseph and the Amazing Technicolor Dreamcoat*.) The album became a huge hit in the US and to a lesser extent in the UK. The single "I Don't Know How to Love Him" reached number one worldwide, so there was immediate interest once the stage show appeared on both sides of the Atlantic.

Jesus Christ Superstar tells the dramatic story of the last week in the life of Jesus Christ, focusing on his relationships with Judas and Mary Magdalene. The songs are sometimes exuberant, sometimes mournful, but they are always moving.

Many Christians have protested against the musical, saying that it is theologically inaccurate and condemning the somewhat romantic nature of the relationship it portrays between Mary Magdalene and Jesus. They don't like the fact that it ends with the Crucifixion rather than the Resurrection. Other religious leaders, however, have welcomed both *Jesus Christ Superstar* and *Godspell* because the shows have rekindled an interest in the Gospels and the life of Jesus Christ.

Pablo Picasso Dies at 91

Mougins, France, April 8, 1973: Prolific and innovative painter and sculptor Pablo Picasso died today of a heart attack at his home in the south of France.

Picasso was born on October 25, 1881 in Malaga, Spain. His father was an art teacher. After studying at La Lonja, the academy of fine arts in Barcelona, Picasso moved to Paris in 1900; he would live in France for the greater part of his life.

His early years in Paris produced the melancholy art of the "Blue" period. The more optimistic "Rose" period followed,

time out

Photographer Daniel Meadows toured England in a double-decker bus that functioned as a mobile home, darkroom, and gallery. He offered free photographs to anyone who would have their picture taken. He took almost a thousand photos of ordinary people.

inspired by the circus and carnivals. Around this time he formed a friendship with wealthy, eccentric writer and art patron Gertrude Stein. His 1906 portrait of Stein captures her essence. In 1908, Picasso met artist Georges Braque, and together they developed the radical style that became known as Cubism.

Throughout the 1920s and 1930s, Picasso's art was dominated by the female nude—many consider these paintings to be violent, frightening, and deeply disturbing.

Picasso's most celebrated painting is *Guernica* (1937). It was inspired by his outrage at news of the bombing of the undefended town of that name in Spain, and condemns the ruthlessness of modern warfare. One of his most exciting works is the 65-ft (20 m) abstract sheet-metal sculpture he created for the Civic Center in Chicago in 1966.

A lifelong member of the Communist Party, Picasso considered himself a pacifist. His personal life, in contrast, was anything but peaceful. It is thought that the death of his sister when he was 14, along with the complex nature of his relationship with his adoring yet formidable mother, had a profound effect on him. Picasso's lust was legendary, and for him sex and art were inextricably entwined: his two wives and his many mistresses served as both his muses and models.

Picasso is survived by four children and his wife, Jacqueline. Because he died intestate, some of his works went to the French government in lieu of payment of death duties.

Bolshoi Star Defects

Toronto, Canada, June 30, 1974: Last night, after performing with the Soviet Bolshoi Ballet in Toronto, the young star Mikhail Baryshnikov separated from his group and ran to a waiting car. Another vehicle, believed to be driven by KGB agents, followed Baryshnikov's car, but the dancer seems to have escaped to safety. Like dancers Rudolf Nureyev and Natalia Makarova, who defected from the USSR in 1961 and 1970 respectively, Baryshnikov is seeking a better life in the west.

Born in Riga, Latvia, on January 27, 1948, Baryshnikov studied at the Vaganova School in Leningrad under Aleksander Pushkin. On joining the Kirov Ballet in 1967, Baryshnikov was given the principal role in *Giselle*, followed by *Vestris* in 1969. Dance critic Clive Barnes said he was "the most perfect dancer I have ever seen."

Janis Joplin

Jesus Christ Superstar wowed audiences on Broadway then in London's West End.

USA, March 1975: A relative unknown, Sylvester Stallone, sells the script of *Rocky*, insisting that he play the lead role in the film.

USA, April 1975: The second film by Steven Spielberg, *Jaws*, opens.

Moscow, USSR, August 9, 1975: Celebrated Soviet composer Dimitri Shostakovich dies, aged 68.

UK, September 19, 1975: The first season of John Cleese's *Fawlty Towers* television series is shown on British television.

UK, October 1975: Rock group Queen release their innovative song "Bohemian Rhapsody."

UK, January 12, 1976: Novelist Agatha Christie dies, aged 85.

London, England, February 1976: The Tate Gallery withdraws a sculpture consisting of 120 bricks by Carl Andre, after a disgruntled viewer poured blue dye over them.

London, England, December 1, 1976: The punk band Sex Pistols cause a furore by swearing on live TV. Punk is the latest youth culture in fashion, music, and lifestyle.

Paris, France, February 2, 1977: The modernist Le Centre Georges Pompidou, serving as a museum of modern art and a public library, opens to controversy.

USA, May 1977: George Lucas's film *Star Wars* opens.

Montreux, Switzerland, July 2, 1977: Russian author Vladimir Nabokov dies at 78.

Memphis, Tennessee, USA, August 16, 1977: Elvis Presley, the "King" of rock 'n' roll, dies aged 42.

Switzerland, December 25, 1977: Sir Charles Chaplin dies, aged 88.

New York, USA, April 7, 1978: The *Gutenberg Bible* is sold at auction for $2 million. It is the most expensive book on record.

New York, USA, October 12, 1978: The Sex Pistols' Sid Vicious is arrested for the murder of his girlfriend, Nancy Spungen.

Massachusetts, USA, November 8, 1978: Norman Rockwell, illustrator for the *Saturday Evening Post*, dies aged 84. He produced 317 covers for the publication.

USA, June 16, 1978: The nostalgic rock 'n' roll-era film *Grease* opens.

New York, USA, February 2, 1979: Sid Vicious of the Sex Pistols dies of a heroin overdose.

Los Angeles, USA, March 10, 1979: Michelle Marvin, ex-partner of actor Lee Marvin, is suing him for "palimony." The case has garnered publicity due to other celebrities' similar situations.

Los Angeles, USA, June 11, 1979: John Wayne, born Marion Morrison, dies aged 72 from lung cancer.

USA, 1979: This year's films include *Apocalypse Now*, *Mad Max*, *Alien*, and *Nosferatu*.

Agatha Christie

Crime Queen Agatha Christie Dies at 85

Oxfordshire, England, January 12, 1976: The biggest-selling British novelist of all time, Dame Agatha Christie, has died peacefully at her home at Wallingford, Oxfordshire, after a brief illness. She has published more than 80 titles in a number of genres, and it is estimated that she has sold a total of 300 million books during her 56-year career. As a mark of respect, the lights were dimmed at St Martin's Theater and The Savoy, where two of her plays are being performed.

Agatha May Clarissa Miller was born in Devon in 1890. An awkward, socially inept child, Christie took refuge in music and her imagination. In 1914, she married World War I pilot Archie Christie. During the war Christie worked in a hospital, and the knowledge she gained there about drugs and poisons was to prove invaluable in her literary work.

Christie's first whodunit, *The Mysterious Affair at Styles*, was published in 1920 and featured the Belgian detective who would become one of the best-loved characters in fiction, Hercule Poirot. He appears in 33 novels and 54 short stories. Fittingly, the main character of her last novel, to be published later this year, is the much-loved Miss Marple, who was first created for *Murder at the Vicarage* (1930).

Christie mysteriously disappeared in 1926 after learning of her husband's infidelity. It became a case as baffling as any in her novels. Her car was found in a chalkpit in Surrey, and Christie turned out to have been staying at a hotel in Harrogate. Her recent emotional stresses had apparently caused a memory lapse. Four years later, she married renowned archeologist Sir Max Mallowan.

Several of her books have been adapted for film, the most recent of which was *Murder on the Orient Express,* in 1974, starring Albert Finney as Hercule Poirot.

Agatha Christie is survived by her second husband, her daughter, Rosalind, and her grandson, Matthew.

Star Wars a Hit for Lucas

Hollywood, California, USA, May 30, 1977: George Lucas's outer-space fantasy *Star Wars* opened on May 25, and on the first weekend it has grossed over $1.5 million.

Set "a long time ago in a galaxy far, far away," the story owes much to the ideas of mythology expert Joseph Campbell, and echoes such heroes' journeys as *The Wizard of Oz*. The plot is simple: Luke Skywalker and his robot pals, R2-D2 and C-3PO, aided by Han Solo and wise Obi-Wan Kenobi, set out to rescue Princess Leia, and bring justice to the Empire.

Sylvester Stallone and Talia Shire in *Rocky*.

Written and directed by 33-year-old George Lucas (of *American Graffiti* fame), *Star Wars* features Mark Hamill as Skywalker, Harrison Ford as Solo, Carrie Fisher as Princess Leia, Alec Guiness as Obi-Wan Kenobi, and James Earl Jones as the voice of the villainous Darth Vader.

The two-hour long epic movie is well paced, and is enhanced by the stirring music of John Williams. The costumes, sets, make-up, and special effects are indeed out of this world.

In a decade that has been dominated by angst-ridden, violent, and realistic films, *Star Wars* returns to the innocence of a bygone era. It is an escapist treat for adults, teenagers, and children alike. The movie will surely receive a few Academy Awards, and fans will be happy to know that sequels are being planned. Enjoy! And "may the force be with you."

Eminent Writer Vladimir Nabokov Dies at Age 78

Montreux, Switzerland, July 2, 1977: The Russian-born writer and lepidopterist Vladimir Nabokov has died at Montreux Palace Hotel in Switzerland. He was the author of nine English-language novels, as well as several Russian novels and numerous short stories, plays, poems, and critical and scientific works.

Following the 1917 Russian Revolution, Nabokov and his family moved to the Crimea and later emigrated to England. He graduated from Trinity College, Cambridge, in 1923. After living in Berlin and Paris for some years, in 1940 he emigrated to the US with his wife and son, Dmitri. He taught Russian literature at Wellesley College and Cornell University, becoming a US citizen in 1945.

Nabokov had published two novels in English (*The Real Life of Sebastian Knight* and *Bend Sinister*) before achieving worldwide notoriety with *Lolita* in 1955.

Lolita is the story of a middle-aged man who becomes obsessed with "nymphets" in general and twelve-year-old Lolita Haze in particular. Nabokov wrote the screenplay for the 1962 film of the same name, directed by Stanley Kubrick and starring James Mason, Shelley Winters, Peter Sellers, and Sue Lyon.

By 1960, following the success of *Lolita*, Nabokov was able to support himself solely through his writing, and he returned to Europe, living at the Montreux Palace Hotel in Switzerland until his death. He was to write five more novels, including the highly acclaimed *Pale Fire* (1962) and *Ada or Ardor: A Family Chronicle* (1969).

Nabokov's works have stimulated a great deal of debate in the literary world, but he is widely considered to be one of the leading novelists of this century.

Elvis is Dead

Memphis, Tennessee, USA, August 16, 1977: Millions of fans around the world are shocked at the news that Elvis Presley is dead. He was 42 years old. Elvis's girlfriend found him unconscious early this morning at his Memphis mansion, Graceland, and rushed him to the Baptist Memorial Hospital, but it was too late.

At this stage, the cause of death is thought to be heart attack, but because Elvis had been a heavy user of prescription medication for many years, an autopsy will be performed. His general health had been poor for some time;

Fans across the globe are mourning the death of Elvis.

Olivia Newton-John and John Travolta take to the dance floor in *Grease*.

two years ago he was hospitalized for glaucoma and gastrointestinal problems.

Elvis was born in Tupelo, Mississippi, in 1935 and burst onto the music scene in 1954 with his first single, "That's All Right." After appearing on the *Louisiana Hayride* radio program—and in particular on television's "Ed Sullivan Show" in 1956—Elvis became a rock 'n' roll sensation. His humble Southern charm and raunchy sexuality were a magical combination, and being a mixture of R&B, country, and gospel, his music appealed to a wide audience.

His movie career began in 1956 with *Love Me Tender*—in total, Elvis would make 33 films. He was drafted into the US Army in 1958, and while stationed in Germany met fourteen-year-old Priscilla Beaulieu. They were married from 1967 until 1973 and had one daughter, Lisa Marie, born in 1968.

Elvis loved nothing more than performing for his fans. His Las Vegas concert in 1969 and his Aloha Concert in 1973 in Hawaii (broadcast to the world via satellite) were high points of his career. Even after he became fat and bloated, he could still enthrall an audience.

Many believe that Elvis never reached his full creative potential, especially as an actor, because of the control exerted by his manager, Colonel Tom Parker.

Grease is the Word!

Hollywood, California, USA, June 16, 1978: Following on the wave of 1950s nostalgia in movies such as *American Graffiti* and television's *Happy Days* and *Laverne and Shirley*, the romantic musical comedy movie *Grease* has opened to an enthusiastic audience. With an all-star cast including Olivia Newton-John as Sandy, John Travolta as Danny, and Stockard Channing as Rizzo, supported by veterans Eve Arden, Frankie Avalon, Joan Blondell, Edd Byrnes, and Sid Caesar, the movie is sure to be a hit this summer.

Grease tells the story of innocent Sandy, who has a vacation romance with wild child Danny Zuko. When they both return to Rydell High School in the autumn, true love doesn't run smoothly, and Sandy decides that she must shed her good-girl image if she is going to win the boy of her dreams.

The songs are upbeat and catchy, capturing the spirit of the era: "Summer Nights," "Hopelessly Devoted to You," "Greased Lightning," and the title tune, "Grease," written by Bee Gees' Barry Gibb and sung by Frankie Valli.

Sid Vicious Dies of a Drug Overdose

New York, USA, February 2, 1979: The 1970s began with the deaths of hippie icons Janis Joplin, Jimi Hendrix, and Jim

Sid Vicious and Nancy, who he murdered in 1978.

Morrison. All were still in their twenties. Joplin and Hendrix overdosed on heroin, and Morrison succumbed to drug-and-alcohol-related heart failure. Now, one more star has met an untimely and tragic end: 21-year-old punk rocker Sid Vicious.

The former Sex Pistols bass player died in the early hours of this morning in the Greenwich Village apartment of friend Michelle Robinson. Police found a syringe and spoon close to his body. The couple, along with Vicious's mother, had been celebrating because Virgin Records had put up $50,000 bail to secure Vicious's release from New York's Rikers Island prison, where he had been awaiting trial on the charge of murdering his girlfriend, Nancy Spungen. Arrested on October 12, 1978, he claimed that because he was so stoned, he didn't remember doing it.

Sid Vicious was born John Simon Ritchie in London on May 10, 1957. He had a difficult childhood—his mother, Anne, was a heroin addict—and by the

time he was 17 they were sharing drugs. At Hackney Technical College, he befriended a boy named John Lydon (who became the Sex Pistols' Johnny Rotten).

After being a member of several different bands, Vicious joined the Sex Pistols in February 1977. His musical skills were limited, but manager Malcolm McLaren wanted Vicious not so much for his sound as for his look: thin, pale, angry, and anguished. Later that year, a punk groupie from Philadelphia, Nancy Spungen, met Vicious in London, where they began their destructive and in the end ill-fated love affair.

Vladimir Nabokov

Achievements in the Arts

Key Structures
Brion-Vega Cemetery, San Vito d'Altivole, Italy
Central Beheer, Apeldoorn, Netherlands
CN Tower, Toronto, Canada
Ho Chi Minh Mausoleum, Ha Noi, Vietnam
Hotel Camino Real, Cancun, Mexico
Karuizawa House, Karuizawa, Japan
Le Centre Georges Pompidou, Paris, France
National Assembly Building, Dacca, Bangladesh
Sydney Opera House, Sydney, Australia
Teatro Guaira, Curitiba, Brazil
World Trade Center, Dubai, United Arab Emirates
World Trade Center, New York, USA

Nobel Prize for Literature
1970 Aleksandr Solzhenitsyn; 1971 Pablo Neruda; 1972 Heinrich Boll; 1973 Patrick White; 1974 Eyvind Johnson/Harry Martinson; 1975 Eugenio Montale; 1976 Saul Bellow; 1977 Vicente Aleixandre; 1978 Isaac Bashevis Singer; 1979 Odysseas Elytis.

Booker Prize for Fiction
1970 *The Elected Member*, Bernice Rubens; 1971 *In a Free State*, V. S. Naipaul; 1972: *A Novel*, John Berger; 1973 *The Siege of Krishnapur*, J. G. Farrell; 1974 *The Conservationist*, Nadine Gordimer/*Holiday*, Stanley Middleton; 1975 *Heat and Dust*, Ruth Prawer Jhabvala; 1976 *Saville*, David Storey; 1977 *Staying On*, Paul Scott; 1978 *The Sea, The Sea*, Iris Murdoch; 1979 *Offshore*, Penelope Fitzgerald.

Pulitzer Prize for Fiction
1970 *Collected Stories*, Jean Stafford; 1971 no award given; 1972 *Angle of Repose*, Wallace Stegner; 1973 *The Optimist's Daughter*, Eudora Welty; 1974 no award given; 1975 *The Killer Angels*, Michael Shaara; 1976 *Humboldt's Gift*, Saul Bellow; 1977 no award given; 1978 *Elbow Room*, James Alan McPherson; 1979 *The Stories of John Cheever*, John Cheever.

Academy Awards
Best Film 1970 *Patton*; 1971 *The French Connection*; 1972 *The Godfather*; 1973 *The Sting*; 1974 *The Godfather Part II*; 1975 *One Flew Over the Cuckoo's Nest*; 1976 *Rocky*; 1977 *Annie Hall*; 1978 *The Deer Hunter*; 1979 *Kramer vs. Kramer*.

BAFTAs
Best Film 1970 *Butch Cassidy and the Sundance Kid*; 1971 *Sunday Bloody Sunday*; 1972 *Cabaret*; 1973 *La Nuit Americaine*; 1974 *Lacombe Lucien*; 1975 *Alice Doesn't Live Here Anymore*; 1976 *One Flew Over the Cuckoo's Nest*; 1977 *Annie Hall*; 1978 *Julia*; 1979 *Manhattan*.

Pelé

Brazil Wins World Cup for Third Time

Mexico City, Mexico, June 21, 1970: In what has been deemed the best soccer World Cup tournament ever, Brazil has beaten Italy 4–1 in the final match today, in front of a crowd of 107,000 spectators.

The victory is even sweeter because this is the third time that Brazil has won the competition. According to the rules set down by FIFA (Fédération Internationale de Football Association) when the tournament was established in 1930, the first team to win three times would be awarded the Jules Rimet Cup in perpetuity. Named after the first World Cup organizer, the trophy is an art deco-style gold statue of Winged Victory.

The opening ceremony was a spectacle on a scale never before seen at the World

Members of the English soccer team, with mascot.

Cup, and despite the high altitude and heatwave conditions in Estadio Azteca (Aztec Stadium), the tournament was characterized by good sportsmanship.

In the semi-finals, Italy had defeated West Germany 4–3, and Brazil had defeated Uruguay 3–1.

Brazil has qualified for every World Cup since 1930, but had never won until 1958, when seventeen-year-old Edson Arantes do Nascimento (otherwise known as Pelé) participated in the tournament for the first time. Today he proved he is at his peak, scoring one and assisting two in a more attack-oriented game than has been seen in previous Cup matches. Brazil's manager, Mario Zagallo, is ecstatic. He is the first person to have won the World Cup as both a coach and a player.

Evonne Goolagong Wins Wimbledon

Wimbledon, England, July 2, 1971: Fleet-footed nineteen-year-old Evonne Goolagong today beat fellow Australian Margaret Court 6–4, 6–1 in the women's final at Wimbledon. It is the first time that two Australian women have vied for the title, and the first time an Aboriginal woman has achieved international standing in any sport. Goolagong was not expected to win, even though she took out the French Open earlier in the year.

Goolagong has endeared herself to tennis fans around the world with her agility, grace, and humility. She's come a long way since she first attempted Wimbledon last year and got knocked out in the first round. And she's come a very long way from the little New South Wales country town of Barellan, where she grew up one of eight children. Her father is a sheep shearer. Goolagong started hitting tennis balls around when she was just five years old, and two years later she became the youngest member of the local tennis club.

Evonne Goolagong receives her trophy from Princess Alexandra.

Although she clearly has incredible natural talent, Goolagong attributes much of her success to her coach, Vic Edwards, who has been her mentor for the last eight years.

Gay Pride in Oxford Street

London, England, July 1, 1972: Two thousand courageous, jubilant gays and lesbians today marched down Oxford Street to Hyde Park in London's first Gay Pride parade, staged by the Gay Liberation Front (GLF). The gay rights movement gained momentum after the 1969 Stonewall riots in New York, in which police clashed with gay demonstrators. It is believed that today's crowd would have been greater but that many gays did not attend for fear of being arrested. The police presence was aggressive.

Although the march had a serious purpose—that is, to combat homophobia and to raise public awareness of gay issues—the atmosphere was anything but somber. There were music and dancing, lavish costumes, and humorous banners. Most of the participants remained in Hyde Park to eat, drink, and be merry.

time out

Spiro T. Agnew resigned as Vice President of the United States in 1973, admitting tax evasion in 1967 and avoiding jail in an agreement with the Department of Justice. He was sentenced to three years' probation and fined $10,000.

Key Events

USA, April 22, 1970: "Earth Day" focuses attention on environmental problems throughout the USA.

Mexico City, Mexico, June 21, 1970: Brazil beats Italy 4–1 in the FIFA World Cup final, winning the Cup for the third time.

Geneva, Switzerland, July 17, 1970: African countries demand mandatory enforcement of the 1963 embargo on arms sales to South Africa.

London, England, November 27, 1970: The Gay Liberation Front holds a protest rally in Hyde Park.

Melbourne, Australia, January 5, 1971: The first limited-overs cricket match is played between England and Australia to a receptive crowd.

Berlin, Germany, January 31, 1971: Telephone services between East and West Berlin are re-established after 19 years.

USA, May 9, 1971: The Friends of the Earth organization returns 1,500 non-returnable bottles to Schweppes.

Hamble, England, August 6, 1971: Yachtsman Chay Blithe returns after his non-stop circumnavigation from east to west. It took 292 days.

USA, March 23, 1972: The daredevil stuntman Evil Knieval breaks 93 bones after successfully jumping 35 cars on his motorcycle.

Reykjavik, Iceland, September 1, 1972: American Bobby Fischer becomes the first American to be world chess champion. He defeats the USSR's Boris Spassky and wins $160,000.

Munich, Germany, September 1972: US swimmer Mark Spitz wins a record seventh gold medal in the pool at the 20th Olympiad.

Los Angeles, USA, February 19, 1973: Daredevil stuntman Evil Knieval jumps 52 cars on his motorcycle at a demolition derby.

New York, USA, April 4, 1973: The two 110-story towers of the World Trade Center are completed.

Atlantic Ocean and Africa, June 30, 1973: A total eclipse of the sun occurs, lasting seven minutes—the longest in modern times.

Moscow, USSR, August 16, 1973: The US children's TV series Sesame Street is denounced as "veiled neo-colonialism" by the Kremlin.

Philippines, March 9, 1974: A Japanese soldier surrenders after emerging from the jungle, 29 years after the end of World War II.

Arnhem Land, Australia, July 5, 1974: The traditional Aboriginal owners of a site wanted for uranium mining refuse AUD$3.3 million in compensation.

London, England, July 6, 1974: The USA's Chris Evert, aged 19, and Jimmy Connors, aged 21, win the singles titles at Wimbledon.

The first known gay march took place in New York on June 28, 1970—the first anniversary of the Stonewall rebellion. The London GLF was founded on October 13, 1970, and one month later, on November 27, 1970, the group organized Britain's first gay public protest. A torchlight demonstration was held in Highbury Fields, Islington, a popular gay gathering place, where Louis Eaks, a Young Liberal, had been arrested for indecent behavior. Eighty people turned up for this demonstration. Another Islington march was arranged the following year.

In 1971, the London GLF issued an 11-page *Manifesto*. It outlines the ways in which social institutions (family, school, church, media, law, business, medicine, and so on) discriminate against gays, proposes positive suggestions for a new liberated lifestyle, and sets out a list of immediate demands.

Mark Spitz Wins Seven Gold Medals at Munich

Munich, Germany, September 1972: The "Happy Games" were certainly happy for 22-year-old US swimmer Mark Spitz, who has won an unprecedented seven gold medals at the Munich Olympics—and broken seven world records.

Spitz, disappointed with his performance in the 1968 Games in Mexico City, astonished everyone when he won gold in the 100 m and 200 m butterfly, and the 100 m and 200 m freestyle, as well as in three relay events. It was the fulfillment of a lifelong dream for both Spitz and his father, Arnold, who taught Mark to swim as soon as he could walk, and made great personal sacrifices to further his son's swimming career. A graduate of the University of Indiana, Mark Spitz held the title of World Swimmer of the Year in 1969, 1971, and 1972.

What would have been a time of great celebration was marred by the senseless acts of violence that took place on September 5, when Palestinian terrorists killed 11 members of the Israeli team. Because of Spitz's Jewish heritage, he

New York's twin towers are the tallest buildings in the world.

was rushed out of Munich before the closing ceremony. Before he left, he said at a press conference, "I think the murders in the village are very tragic."

Other bright stars of the 20th Olympiad include the 15-year-old Australian swimmer, Shane Gould, who won three gold and two silver medals, and 16-year-old USSR gymnast Olga Korbut, who won three gold and one silver.

The USSR has led the medal tally, followed by the United States, East Germany, West Germany, Japan, and Australia.

World's Tallest Building is Completed

New York, USA, April 4, 1973: The ground was broken on August 5, 1966, and eight years and $1.5 billion later, the 110-story twin towers of the World Trade Center were finally opened today in an official ribbon-cutting ceremony.

At 1,368 ft (417 m) and 1,362 ft (415 m), the twin towers have been classified as the world's tallest buildings, 100 ft (30 m) higher than the previous record-holder, the Empire State Building. The World Trade Center complex occupies 16 acres (6.5 ha) of land and, with the new twin towers, comprises seven buildings set around a central plaza. The Center is located in the financial district, three blocks north of the New York and American Stock Exchanges.

Occupancy of Tower One began in December 1970, and Tower Two in January 1972.

It was David Rockefeller, then President of the Chase Manhattan Bank, who came up with the idea of the World Trade Center in 1964. He was supported by his brother, New York governor Nelson Rockefeller. The buildings were constructed by the Port Authority of New York and New Jersey. Many architects competed for the chance to design the complex, and Minoru Yamasaki won the contract. He worked in conjunction with architects Emery Roth and Sons, and engineers Worthington, Skilling, Helle, and Jackson.

One of many innovative features is the "sky lobby," a space where passengers can go from one local elevator to another.

Yamasaki hopes that the World Trade Center will become "a living representation of man's belief in humanity…and his belief in the cooperation of men."

Mark Spitz

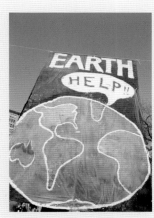
A banner for "Earth Day," 1970.

UK, January 17, 1975: Imperial Typewriters, Britain's last major manufacturer, announces its closure.
Pacific Ocean, March 18, 1975: The CIA manages to salvage the wreckage of a Soviet submarine that sank in 1968.
Mt Everest, Nepal, May 16, 1975: Junko Tabei of Japan becomes the first woman to climb Everest.
Europe, December 1975: A wave of terrorism has hit London (December 12), Amsterdam (December 19), and Austria (December 22).

World, February 29, 1976: Military spending is worth $300 billion throughout the world, growing 45 percent in the last 15 years. The USA and USSR are responsible for 60 percent.
London, England, June 6, 1976: J. Paul Getty, oil billionaire, dies aged 83.
USA, July 4, 1976: The nation celebrates its bicentenary of independence from Britain.
Montreal, Canada, July 18, 1976: Romanian gymnast Nadia Comaneci scores the first perfect gymnastics score in Olympic history.

New York, USA, January 7, 1977: Australian Rupert Murdoch purchases the *New York Post*.
New York, USA, May 26, 1977: George Willig scales the World Trade Center's 110 stories using homemade climbing equipment. He is arrested upon reaching the top.
USA, December 3, 1977: After admitting 165,000 refugees since the end of the Vietnam War in 1975, the US State Department proposes an emergency admission of a further 10,000 Vietnamese "boat people."

USA, February 15, 1978: Muhammad Ali loses the world heavyweight boxing title to Leon Spinks.
Argentina, June 25, 1978: Argentina defeats the Netherlands 3–1 to win the World Cup in front of an enthusiastic home crowd.
Atlantic Ocean, August 19, 1978: Three Americans make the first successful crossing of the Atlantic by balloon, taking 138 hours.
Turin, Italy, October 13, 1978: The Shroud of Turin is subjected to rigorous scientific analysis.

Sydney, Australia, January 16, 1979: Ukrainian Lillian Gasinskaya, 18, jumps overboard from a Russian ship in Sydney Harbour wearing only a red bikini. She is hoping to be granted asylum.
UK, August 14, 1979: The Fastnet yacht race is hit by a fierce storm; 19 lives and 23 yachts are lost.
Zurich, Switzerland, August 15, 1979: Englishman Sebastian Coe now holds three world records for middle distance running, having added the 1,500 meter record to his 800 meter and the mile records.

Nadia Comaneci

First Woman to Climb Mount Everest

Mount Everest, Nepal, May 16, 1975: Thirty-six year-old Junko Tabei, has today become the first woman to climb to the peak of Mt Everest.

Tabei's love of climbing dates from a school excursion to Mt Nasu when she was 10 years old. A rather delicate child, she was thrilled to find a physical activity that she could do at her own pace. Although Tabei is only 4 ft 9 in (145 cm) tall, she has proved emphatically that she is anything but delicate.

In 1969, Tabei formed the Ladies Climbing Club of Japan, whose motto is translated as "Let's go on an expedition abroad all by ourselves." In 1972, she was one of hundreds who applied to be part of an Everest expedition sponsored by a Japanese media company. She was selected as the leader of a group of 15 women, and they trained for three years before attempting the arduous climb, traveling the same route as Edmund Hillary and Tenzing Norgay did in 1953.

When the group was about two-thirds of the way up the mountain, an enormous avalanche hit their camp. All were snowed under, but under Tabei's leadership they pulled themselves out and eventually made it to the top.

America Celebrates Bicentennial

USA, July 4, 1976: From coast to coast, the United States is awash in red, white, and blue today as the country celebrates its Bicentennial. Two hundred years ago, the Declaration of Independence was signed in Philadelphia. President Gerald Ford opened his speech at Philadelphia's Independence Hall by stating: "I am filled

Americans celebrate their Bicentennial in 1976.

with deep emotion at finding myself standing here in the place where collected together the wisdom, the patriotism, the devotion to principle, from which sprang the institutions under which we live."

Over the past year, Bicentennial fever has been sweeping the entire nation, culminating in today's festivities. Special commemorative coins, postage stamps, and car license plates have been issued, and you can't walk into any store without finding red-white-and-blue Bicentennial-themed items such as coffee cups, t-shirts, soft drink bottles, and candy bars.

One of the highlights has been the "American Freedom Train," which began its journey on April 1 and will continue to traverse the country until the end of this year. The train features a wealth of American memorabilia as diverse as a moon rock and the costume Judy Garland wore in *The Wizard of Oz*. Another successful project was the CBS series *Bicentennial Minutes*, short programs featuring historical events, narrated by popular celebrities. Disneyland has been delighting visitors with "America on Parade," a spectacular parade featuring 8-ft-tall (2.4 m) characters, including Uncle Sam and Benjamin Franklin, performing to America's most popular tunes.

Today, a fleet of 16 tall ships and 50 warships from around the globe converged in New York harbor, and tonight the world's biggest-ever fireworks display will take place in Washington, DC.

Although many people have criticized the commercial nature of the Bicentennial, overall the reaction has been positive. In the aftermath of Vietnam and Watergate, Americans have come together and are feeling good about themselves again.

Nadia, Star of Montreal

Montreal, Canada, August 1, 1976: Today, the closing ceremony of the Games of the 21st Olympiad was held. The undisputed star of the spectacle is the pint-sized Romanian gymnast, Nadia Comaneci.

On July 18, for the first time in the history of Olympic gymnastics, 14-year-old Comaneci scored a perfect "10" on the uneven parallel bars, and by the end of the competition she had achieved the perfect score a further six times. She will take home three gold medals (uneven bars, balance beam, and all-around); one silver medal (team all-around); and one bronze medal (floor exercises), helping to bring her country to ninth place. A highlight of the gymnastics events was Nadia performing her floor exercises to "Yes Sir, That's My Baby" with great confidence and poise.

Comaneci started learning gymnastics at age six, and was handpicked by leading Romanian coach Bela Karolyi. At the European championships, held in

Sporting Achievements

Baseball *World Series* 1970 Baltimore (American League); 1971 Pittsburgh (National League); 1972 Oakland (AL); 1973 Oakland (AL); 1974 Oakland (AL); 1975 Cincinnati (NL); 1976 Cincinnati (NL); 1977 New York (AL); 1978 New York (AL); 1979 Pittsburgh (NL).
Cycling *Tour de France* 1970-1972 E. Merckx; 1973 L. Ocana; 1974 E. Merckx; 1975 B. Thevenet; 1976 L. Van Impe; 1977 B. Thevenet; 1978-1979 B. Hinault.
Football *American Super Bowl* 1970 Kansas City; 1971 Baltimore; 1972 Dallas; 1973 Miami; 1974 Miami; 1975 Pittsburgh; 1976 Pittsburgh; 1977 Oakland; 1978 Dallas; 1979 Pittsburgh. *World Cup Soccer* 1970 Brazil; 1974 West Germany; 1978 Argentina.
Golf *US Masters* 1970 B. Casper; 1971 C. Coody; 1972 J. Nicklaus; 1973 T. Aaron; 1974 G. Player; 1975 J. Nicklaus; 1976 R. Floyd; 1977 T. Watson; 1978 G. Player; 1979 F. Zoeller.
Horse Racing *Epsom Derby* 1970 Nijinsky II; 1971 Mill Reef; 1972 Roberto; 1973 Morston; 1974 Snow Knight; 1975 Grundy; 1976 Empery; 1977 The Minstrel; 1978 Shirley Heights; 1979 Troy. *Kentucky Derby* 1970 Dust Commander; 1971 Canonero II; 1972 Riva Ridge; 1973 Secretariat; 1974 Cannonade; 1975 Foolish Pleasure; 1976 Bold Forbes; 1977 Seattle Slew; 1978 Affirmed; 1979 Spectacular Bid. *Melbourne Cup* 1970 Baghdad Note; 1971 Silver Knight; 1972 Piping Lane; 1973 Gala Supreme; 1974 Think Big; 1975 Think Big; 1976 Van Der Hum; 1977 Gold and Black; 1978 Arwon; 1979 Hyperno.
Ice Hockey *Stanley Cup* 1970 Boston; 1971 Montreal; 1972 Boston; 1973 Montreal; 1974 Philadelphia; 1975 Philadelphia; 1976 Montreal; 1977 Montreal; 1978 Montreal; 1979 Montreal.
Marathon *Boston, Men's* 1970 R. Hill; 1971 A. Mejia; 1972 O. Suomalainen; 1973 J. Anderson; 1974 N. Cusack; 1975 B. Rodgers; 1976 J. Fultz; 1977 J. Drayton; 1978 B. Rodgers; 1979 B. Rodgers; *Women's* 1970 S. Berman; 1971 S. Berman; 1972 N. Kuscsik; 1973 J. Hansen; 1974 M. Gorman; 1975 L. Winter; 1976 K. Merritt; 1977 M. Gorman; 1978 G. Barron; 1979 J. Benoit.
Sailing *America's Cup* 1970 *Intrepid*; 1974 *Courageous*; 1977 *Courageous*.
Tennis *Australian Open, Men's Singles* 1970 A. Ashe; 1971-1972 K. Rosewall; 1973 J. Newcombe; 1974 J. Connors; 1975 J. Newcombe; 1976 M. Edmondson; 1977 R. Tanner (January); V. Gerulaitis (December); 1978-1979 G. Vilas; *Women's Singles* 1970-1971 M. Smith Court; 1972 V. Wade; 1973 M. Smith Court; 1974-1976 E. Goolagong; 1977 K. Reid (January); E. Goolagong Cawley (December); 1978 C. O'Neill; 1979 B. Jordan. *Roland-Garros Tournament (French Open), Men's Singles* 1970-1971 J. Kodes; 1972 A. Gimeno; 1973 I. Nastase; 1974-1975 B. Borg; 1976 A. Panatta; 1977 G. Vilas; 1978-1979 B. Borg; *Women's Singles* 1970 M. Smith Court; 1971 E. Goolagong; 1972 B. J. King; 1973 M. Smith Court; 1974-1975 C. Evert; 1976 S. Barker; 1977 M. Jausovec; 1978 V. Ruzici; 1979 C. Evert. *US Open, Men's Singles* 1970 K. Rosewall; 1971 S. Smith; 1972 I. Nastase 1973 J. Newcombe; 1974 J. Connors; 1975 M. Orantes; 1976 J. Connors; 1977 G. Vilas; 1978 J. Connors; 1979 J. McEnroe; *Women's Singles* 1970 M. Smith Court; 1971-1972 B. J. King; 1973 M. Smith Court; 1974 B. J. King; 1975-1978 C. Evert; 1979 T. Austin. *Wimbledon, Men's Singles* 1970-1971 J. Newcombe; 1972 S. Smith; 1973 J. Kodes; 1974 J. Connors; 1975 A. Ashe; 1976-1979 B. Borg; *Ladies' Singles* 1970 M. Smith Court; 1971 E. Goolagong; 1972-1973 B. J. King; 1974 C. Evert; 1975 B. J. King; 1976 C. Evert; 1977 V. Wade; 1978-1979 M. Navratilova.

American Hostages Freed after 444 Days

Tehran, Iran, January 20: Just 20 minutes after President Ronald Reagan completed his inaugural address, the Ayatollah Khomeini has today released the remaining 52 American hostages held captive since November 4, 1979.

Shortly after Ayatollah Khomeini assumed political and spiritual leadership in Iran, several hundred fanatical students responded to his anti-Western rhetoric by storming the US Embassy in Tehran and seizing 66 diplomats and government employees.

President Jimmy Carter immediately stopped American oil imports from Iran, deported many Iranian citizens from the USA, and froze Iranian assets. Then, in 1980, he authorized two unsuccessful rescue missions to free the hostages.

The death of the Shah of Iran in July last year and Jimmy Carter's election loss in November made Iran more amenable to negotiations. The Iranian Government agreed to send the hostages home if the USA released their billions of dollars worth of frozen assets.

The hostages are being flown to Algiers and then to the US Air Force base in Frankfurt, Germany, where they will be met by former President Carter.

Space Shuttle *Columbia* Lands Safely in Desert

California, USA, April 14: *Columbia*, the first reusable spacecraft, has landed safely today at Edwards Air Force Base on the edge of the Mojave Desert. The spacecraft successfully orbited the Earth 36 times in 54 hours and 21 minutes in what was described as a textbook-perfect first mission.

Before lift-off on April 12, President Ronald Reagan sent an encouraging message to astronauts John Young and Bob Crippen: "Once again, we feel the surge of pride that comes from knowing we are the first and we are the best…" Just seconds after the main engine was switched on, the solid rocket boosters ignited, sending the shuttle on its journey.

Commander John Young, an experienced astronaut from the Gemini and Apollo missions, thoroughly enjoyed flying the spacecraft. While he and Crippen were in space, they sent back pictures to Mission Control in Houston, which were then televised.

The success of the mission is most encouraging, because there are several more in the pipeline—the next one is planned for later this year.

Charles and Diana Wed

London, England, July 29: Romantics of the world were thrilled at today's wedding between the 32-year-old heir to the British throne, Prince Charles, and 20-year-old Diana Spencer. It is estimated that some 700 million people watched the spectacle on television, while a crowd of 600,000 packed the streets and sidewalks of London in the hope of sighting the royal couple. The British people have been given a public holiday in honor of the royal occasion, which they have been eagerly awaiting ever since Charles gave Diana an 18-carat sapphire and diamond engagement ring in February this year.

Lady Diana made the journey from Clarence House (the Queen Mother's residence) to St Paul's Cathedral in the Glass Coach, accompanied by her father, Earl Spencer. The bride looked as if she had stepped out of the pages of a fairy tale as she walked up the red-carpeted aisle in her stunning ivory taffeta gown to meet her prince, who was resplendent in his naval commander's dress uniform. Prince Charles was attended by his brothers, Prince Andrew and Prince Edward.

The hour-long Anglican ceremony was conducted by Dr Robert Runcie, the Archbishop of Canterbury. After the signing of the register, the Prince and Princess of Wales joyfully walked down the aisle together to *Pomp and Circumstance* by Edward Elgar. A horse-drawn carriage was waiting in front of the cathedral to take the royal couple to Buckingham Palace, where they shared a kiss on the balcony, much to the enjoyment of the crowd.

After a small, select reception, Charles and Diana left for their honeymoon in Hampshire. They will continue their honeymoon cruising the Mediterranean on the Royal yacht *Britannia*.

For many Britons, the wedding was a much-needed antidote to the unemployment, inflation, and racial violence that had been creating an atmosphere of gloom in the country.

Ayatollah Khomeini

Prince Charles kisses Princess Diana on the balcony of Buckingham Palace after their marriage.

Leonid Brezhnev

> *"THE BRITISH WON'T FIGHT."*
>
> LEOPOLDO GALTIERI
> (1926–2003),
> ARGENTINIAN
> MILITARY LEADER
> AND PRESIDENT, ON
> THE FALKLAND
> ISLANDS CRISIS, 1982

> *"LET NO ONE EXPECT US TO DISARM UNILATERALLY. WE ARE NOT A NAIVE PEOPLE."*
>
> YURI ANDROPOV
> (1914–1983), SOVIET
> STATESMAN, 1982

Falklands War Ends

Port Stanley, Falkland Islands, June 14: After less than two months, the brief but intense Falklands War has come to an end today. British troops have defeated the Argentine garrison at Port Stanley after emerging victorious in a succession of battles. A general ceasefire has taken place, and General Mario Menendez is expected to sign a surrender document within 24 hours.

Prime Minister Margaret Thatcher has managed the crisis assertively and efficiently, thus cementing her status as the "Iron Lady" and boosting her popularity rating. She told the celebrating crowd outside No. 10 Downing Street, "We had to do what we had to do. Great Britain is great again."

Up until recently, many Britons were not even aware of the remote and desolate islands 300 miles (480 km) off the coast of Argentina, which have been under British control since 1833.

The Falkland Islands (Islas Malvinas) are home to some 1,800 people, mostly of British descent. Ownership has long been disputed, and on April 2 the Argentine military junta led by Lieutenant-General Leopoldo Galtieri invaded the islands and raised the Argentine flag. Britain severed diplomatic ties with Argentina, and a British naval task force arrived in Falklands waters on April 22.

A total of 655 Argentine and 255 British servicemen were killed during the dispute.

IRA Bombs Kill 8 British Soldiers

London, England, July 20: The IRA are active again after a long hiatus, admitting to two separate bombings in central London parks, resulting in the deaths of eight soldiers and injuring close to 50 people. Both British and Irish leaders have condemned the IRA's senseless violence as acts of terrorism.

The first explosion occurred when a car bomb operated by remote control exploded in Hyde Park, killing two Household Cavalry soldiers riding along South Carriage Road, about to participate in the changing of the guard. Sadly, seven cavalry horses also died—either from the explosion, or by euthanasia.

A few hours later, six Royal Green Jackets were killed in Regents Park. A bomb had been planted under the bandstand, exploding while the Green Jackets were performing in a lunchtime concert.

Striking employees at Westminster Hospital went back to work to help treat the victims who were lucky enough to survive the blasts.

The frigate HMS *Antelope* explodes in San Carlos Bay during the Falklands War.

Soviet Leader Leonid Brezhnev Dies

Moscow, USSR, November 10: Soviet President Leonid Brezhnev has died today of a heart attack at the age of 75. He had been in poor health for some time, especially since he suffered a stroke in March this year.

Brezhnev was born in 1906 in the Ukrainian mining town of Kamenskoye. After graduating from technical college, he worked as a land surveyor and engineer. At age 16 he joined the Communist youth organization, and became a member of the Communist Party in 1931. A Stalin devotee, Brezhnev transferred his loyalties to Nikita Khrushchev after Stalin's death, and served the party in both Kazakhstan and Moldavia.

In 1956, Brezhnev became a senior party member, and was given the management of the space program, defense, and industry. Although he was Khrushchev's assistant in 1964, Brezhnev sided with the group who ousted Khrushchev. He became First Secretary, then General Secretary of the Communist Party.

Under Brezhnev's 18-year leadership, the economy stagnated and living standards deteriorated because he was more inclined to spend money on military and space programs rather than on agriculture, health, and education. People stood in line for food and other necessities, while Brezhnev enjoyed the trappings of Western society.

In matters of foreign policy, Brezhnev was committed to supporting and promoting global Communism—this policy became known as the "Brezhnev Doctrine." He invaded Czechoslovakia in 1968, supported North Vietnam, and sanctioned the Soviet invasion of Afghanistan.

Brezhnev will be buried beside the Kremlin wall. Yuri Andropov has been appointed as the new General Secretary.

Key Events

Washington DC, USA, January 13: A twin-engine jet crashes in a snowstorm after takeoff, plowing into a bridge on the Potomac River, opposite the White House, 78 die.

Northern Territory, Australia, February 2: The mother of baby Azaria Chamberlain, allegedly taken by a dingo at Ayers Rock, is committed to stand trial for her murder.

Salisbury, Zimbabwe, February 17: The coalition government is dissolved with PM Robert Mugabe taking control. His partner, Joshua Nkomo, is accused of plotting a coup.

Managua, Nicaragua, March 25: The Marxist Sandinista government has declared a state of emergency, curtailing human rights, in fear of an attack by the USA.

Falkland Islands, April 2: Argentina invades the islands, overrunning 84 marines stationed there.

Ottawa, Canada, April 17: The Canada Act receives royal assent, ending British legislative jurisdiction over Canada. The Canadian Charter of Rights and Freedoms, the constitutional guarantee of collective and individual rights, is now in effect.

Sinai, Egypt, April 25: The Sinai peninsula is handed back to Egypt.

Falkland Islands, June 14: The British rout Argentine forces.

London, England, June 22: Prince William is born to Princess Diana and the Prince of Wales. He is second in line for the throne.

London, England, July 20: The IRA claim responsibility for two bombs in Hyde and Regent's parks.

Beirut, Lebanon, August 31: The PLO flee their stronghold, driven out by Israel, which invaded last month.

Monte Carlo, Monaco, September 10: Princess Grace of Monaco dies after her car plunges off a mountain road due to brake failure.

Beirut, Lebanon, September 18: Christian militia massacre hundreds of Palestinian refugees.

West Germany, October 1: Helmut Kohl is elected Chancellor after his predecessor Helmut Schmidt resigned due to a no confidence vote.

Moscow, USSR, November 10: President Leonid Brezhnev dies, aged 75.

Poland, November 12: Lech Walesa, leader of the Solidarity Union is released from detention, 11 months after the union was outlawed.

Tasmania, Australia, December: Hundreds of environmentalists blockade work on the proposed hydroelectric plant on the Gordon River. More than 90 are arrested.

New Zealand and Australia, December 14: New Zealand and Australia sign the Closer Economic Relations Agreement.

The "Butcher of Lyons" Captured in Bolivia

La Paz, Bolivia, February 6: Klaus Barbie, known as the "Butcher of Lyons" for his Nazi war crimes, was captured on January 25 and today has been extradited to France to face trial.

German-born Barbie joined the SS at the age of 21, and a few years later became a member of the NSDAP. In 1941, he was appointed as Intelligence Officer in the Bureau of Jewish Affairs and was posted first to Amsterdam and then to Lyons.

From 1942 to 1944, Barbie served as head of the Gestapo in Lyons. During that time he was responsible for the deportation, torture, and killing of thousands of people, most of them Jews. He became famous for capturing and deporting 44 Jewish children to Auschwitz, as well as arresting and brutally torturing high-ranking French Resistance leader Jean Moulin. For his services, Barbie was honored by Hitler.

After World War II, Barbie worked for British Intelligence until 1947, then for the American Counter-intelligence Corps in Germany. After his services were no longer required, they arranged for him and his family to settle in Bolivia. He changed his name to Klaus Altmann and became a businessman—more than likely involved in the South American drug trade.

Korean Airlines Jet Shot Down by Soviet Planes

Sakhalin Island, USSR, September 1: Relations between the USA and the USSR have taken a backward step today after Korean Airlines Flight KAL 007 disappeared off the east coast of Russia. The US Government believes that the passenger craft was shot down by Soviet interceptors when it strayed off course over the island of Sakhalin, invading Soviet airspace. A similar incident occurred in 1978 when a Soviet plane

US soldiers with a body bag, reportedly containing Maurice Bishop.

shot at a Korean Airlines jet after it had flown over a military base at Murmansk. Several people were killed.

A total of 269 people (240 passengers and 29 crew members) from 13 different countries are thought to have died in this latest incident, including US Congressman Larry McDonald of Georgia. KAL 007 left John F. Kennedy Airport in New York yesterday. It stopped to refuel at Anchorage, Alaska before heading for its destination, Seoul-Kimpo International Airport.

The US Government has demanded an explanation from Moscow, and no doubt full investigations will be carried out.

US Forces Invade Grenada

Grenada, West Indies, October 27: President Ronald Reagan has addressed the nation tonight to explain the US invasion of Grenada that took place two days ago. It is the first major US military invasion since Vietnam, and already people have taken to the streets in protest—a crowd of close to 10,000 marched peacefully through New York yesterday.

About 2,000 US soldiers and marines have stormed the tiny island. Until 1974 Grenada was a British colony, and five years later the socialist New Jewel Movement, led by Maurice Bishop, overthrew

the existing government. The American military operation was precipitated by a recent military coup in which Prime Minister Bishop was seized and assassinated. The more extreme Marxist factions (led by General Hudson Austin and former Deputy Prime Minister Bernard Coard) had been concerned when Bishop expressed a desire for improved relations with the United States.

President Reagan's decision to invade Grenada was in response to a request for aid by the Organization of Eastern Caribbean States, along with Jamaica and Barbados. Reagan also feared for the safety of 1,000 US citizens in Grenada, including 800 medical students at St George's University. He explained, "These small, peaceful nations need our help. I believe our government has a responsibility to go to the aid of its citizens, if their right to life and liberty is threatened."

The UN Security Council, however, is not happy with Reagan's action. Neither is British Prime Minister Margaret Thatcher, who has expressed deep concern that the United States has meddled in the affairs of a Commonwealth country.

Princess Grace of Monaco

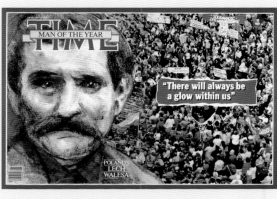

Time's Man of the Year for 1982, Solidarity leader Lech Walesa.

La Paz, Bolivia, January 25: Klaus Barbie, "The Butcher of Lyons," is captured in South America.

Tel Aviv, Israel, February 11: Israeli defence minister Ariel Sharon is implicated in the 1982 massacre of Palestinian refugees in Lebanon. He resigns, but remains a member of the cabinet.

Assam State, India, February 21: Riots protesting the immigration of Muslim refugees from Bangladesh take place. More than 600 people are killed.

Australia, March 6: Bob Hawke leads the Labor Party to a landslide victory, after only a month as opposition leader and less than three years in Parliament.

London, England, March 14: The Organization of the Petroleum Exporting Countries (OPEC) agrees to cut oil prices for the first time in the group's 25-year history.

Beirut, Lebanon, April 18: Forty-eight people die following a car bombing at the US Embassy. Extremist Islamic groups claim responsibility.

USA, May 4: President Ronald Reagan admits that Contra rebels in Nicaragua are being supported by the USA.

UK, June 9: The Conservative government of Margaret Thatcher is returned for a second term.

Manila, Philippines, August 21: Benigno Aquino, returning from a three-year exile in the USA to contest an election, is shot on the tarmac upon arrival.

Sakhalin Island, USSR, September 1: A Korean Airlines jet is shot down by a Soviet fighter.

Africa, October 18: The United Nations warns that 22 African nations are facing famine. A drought has ravaged even wet tropical countries.

Grenada, October 25: US troops invade the small Caribbean island in an effort to restore democracy. The invasion is condemned by the United Nations and some US allies.

The Hague, Netherlands, October 29: A crowd of 500,000 people protest against US missiles.

South Africa, November 2: A whites-only referendum approves a new constitution giving limited political rights to non-whites.

Cyprus, November 15: Turkish Cypriots declare the northern third of the Mediterranean island independent.

Argentina, December 10: Eight years of military rule are brought to an end with the election of a civilian president.

Prime Minister Pierre Trudeau Resigns

Pierre Trudeau

Ottawa, Canada, February 29: Charismatic Canadian Prime Minister Pierre Trudeau has announced his resignation today. He came to his decision after taking a long walk in a heavy snowstorm, saying that now it was "time for someone else to assume this challenge."

Others agree that it is time for a change. Trudeau has served as Liberal Prime Minister for a total of 15 years; serving from April 1968 to June 1979 and again from March 1980 until now.

Trudeau won his first election in 1968 by a landslide. Often compared to John F. Kennedy, he was young (47), flamboyant, privileged, and athletic. Unlike Kennedy, Trudeau was a bachelor, and at age 51 he married Margaret Sinclair, 29 years his junior, and they had three sons. Their 1977 separation was due, in part, to Margaret's public indiscretions and her incompatibility with political life. Trudeau was granted custody of the children.

Although the later years of his leadership were marked by political instability, high unemployment, and massive national debt, Trudeau will be remembered for several notable achievements that helped redefine Canada. His administration passed the Biculturalism/Bilingualism Act of 1969, brought in the metric system and a national health scheme, and was committed to keeping the province of Quebec within the Confederation. In 1982, Constitutional reforms were put in place that cut Canada's ties with Great Britain.

"I CANNOT AND WILL NOT GIVE ANY UNDERTAKING AT A TIME WHEN I, AND YOU, THE PEOPLE, ARE NOT FREE. YOUR FREEDOM AND MINE CANNOT BE SEPARATED."

NELSON MANDELA (B. 1918), SOUTH AFRICAN POLITICAL ACTIVIST, AND FIRST PRESIDENT TO BE ELECTED IN FULLY-REPRESENTATIVE DEMOCRATIC ELECTIONS

IRA Bomb Explodes During Tory Conference

Brighton, England, October 12: British Prime Minister Margaret Thatcher and her husband Denis are lucky to be alive today after an IRA bomb exploded in the Grand Hotel, a 200-room Victorian hotel on the Brighton seafront.

The bomb was planted in a bathroom on the sixth floor, and was intended to destroy Thatcher and members of her Conservative Party who have been attending their annual conference. It tore open the top floors at the front of the hotel, causing a number of guests to plummet down several floors as the central section collapsed. So far, three people are confirmed dead, including Anthony Berry MP and Roberta Wakeham, wife of the Chief Government Whip. Among the 34 people injured are John Wakeham, Trade and Industry Secretary Norman Tebbit, and his wife Margaret.

Shortly after the blast, the hotel was evacuated and rescue workers began searching for victims trapped in the debris. Mrs Thatcher had been writing a speech when the bomb exploded, and disciplined as always, she insisted that the conference go ahead as scheduled at 9.30 that morning. In addressing her party, she stated that, "All attempts to destroy democracy by terrorism will fail."

Security measures in Brighton have been stepped up, and investigators are working to catch the person or persons responsible.

time out

The former Beatle, Paul McCartney, and his wife Linda were arrested in Barbados on possession of cannabis. Four years earlier to the day, Paul had been arrested in Tokyo for the same offense, serving a few days' prison time before being deported.

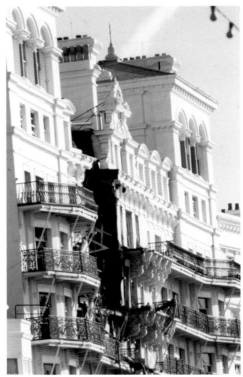

The Grand Hotel, Brighton, after the IRA bomb blast.

Union Carbide Gas Leak Kills 2,000 People

Bhopal, India, December 3: In what is believed to be the worst industrial accident in history, at least 2,000 people have died and tens of thousands have been injured from a toxic gas leak that spread across Bhopal early this morning.

Forty-two tons of the lethal gas methyl isocyanate (MIC) escaped from an underground storage tank at the Union Carbide plant in Bhopal, Central India. The gas traveled from the factory out into the atmosphere of Bhopal, an impoverished city of nearly one million people.

Pandemonium erupted in the streets as thousands tried to get out of the city, which was enveloped in a cloud of toxic fog. Local hospitals couldn't cope with the volume of patients, and they were not even sure how to treat them. The victims suffered from a range of symptoms including eye inflammation, vomiting, respiratory disorders, and dizziness. Some may be permanently blinded, and many could be left with long-term effects such as liver and kidney damage, cancer, and reproductive and genetic disorders.

Union Carbide India Limited (UCIL) is an American-owned company with Indian investors. The Bhopal plant produced pesticides for the cotton-growing industry. It is possible that the disaster was caused by corporate negligence and could have been avoided.

Brunei, January 1: The sultanate achieves independence after 95 years of British rule.

Moscow, USSR, February 13: After ruling for only 15 months, Communist Party chief Yury Andropov dies. Konstantin Chernenko, also in poor health, assumes the top job.

Ottawa, Canada, February 29: Prime Minister Pierre Trudeau resigns.

UK, March 12: A nationwide miner's strike, affecting over 100 pits, begins. It is led by the militant unionist Arthur Scargill.

London, England, April 17: During a protest against Muammar Gaddafi outside the Libyan Embassy, a policewoman is shot and killed. The shots are fired from within the embassy, sparking a major diplomatic incident.

Persian Gulf, May 24: A Saudi Arabian oil tanker is destroyed by Iranian fighters, following criticism of Iran by the Arab League.

Amritsar, India, June 7: Troops storm the Sikh Golden Temple after a four-day siege at the complex—400 people are killed.

New Zealand, July 14: Election of a fourth Labour government begins a period of major economic and social change; restructuring of government services leads to many job losses.

Manila, Philippines, August 21: Over 900,000 Filipinos protest against the repressive Marcos regime.

Beijing, China, September 26: An agreement between China and the UK shall see Hong Kong revert to communist rule in 1997. The island shall be able to preserve its economy.

Brighton, England, October 12: An IRA bomb devastates the Grand Hotel during the Conservative Party annual conference.

New Delhi, India, October 31: PM Indira Gandhi is assassinated by her Sikh bodyguards. Her son Rajiv takes over the leadership.

Oslo, Norway, October: The Nobel Peace Prize is awarded to Bishop Desmond Tutu, for his role against apartheid in South Africa.

Ethiopia, November 1: Bureaucracy is thwarting relief efforts for a famine that has claimed 900,000 lives and threatens 6 million.

USA, November 6: Ronald Reagan is re-elected for a second term with a decisive victory throughout the 50 states.

Bhopal, India, December 3: A toxic gas leak claims over 2,000 lives and affects tens of thousands of others.

A vocal group of demonstraters call for a general strike in support of the British National Union of Mineworkers.

Margaret Thatcher

Striking British Miners Return to Work

England, March 3: The longest and most violent industrial dispute in British history came to an end today when the National Union of Mineworkers (NUM) national executive voted to end the crippling strike that began on March 12 last year. The strike ended up becoming a bitter class struggle, with Prime Minister Margaret Thatcher representing the ruling class and NUM leader Arthur Scargill emblematic of the working man.

In 1983, Mrs Thatcher appointed Ian MacGregor as Chairman of the National Coal Board. One year later, MacGregor announced plans to close up to 20 pits, at a cost of some 20,000 jobs. Employees from the Cortonwood Colliery in Yorkshire stopped work on March 5, 1984, and a week later more than half the miners in the UK followed suit.

Had the miners remained united, a better outcome could have been achieved. However, there was dissent within the union movement itself, with the Nottinghamshire miners breaking away to form the Union of Democratic Mineworkers.

Over the past year, outbreaks of violence have taken place between police and miners, and between miners and "scabs," with about 10,000 arrests taking place during the dispute. It is estimated that the strike has cost the country upward of £1.5 billion (US$1.6 billion).

Terrorist Bomb Destroys Air India Jet

Atlantic Ocean, June 23: At 8.15 (BST) this morning, an Air India 747 jet crashed into the Atlantic Ocean 100 miles (160 km) off the southwest coast of Ireland. It is believed that a bomb planted by Sikh fundamentalists caused the aircraft to blow apart in mid-air.

Air India Flight 182 originated in Toronto, stopping in Montreal before heading for London, Delhi, and Bombay. The flight was delayed in Montreal, where police confiscated three suspicious parcels. It had left London's Heathrow Airport only 45 minutes before the crash, and all 307 passengers and 22 crew members are feared dead. The plane had been cruising at an altitude of 31,000 feet (9,450 m) when it disappeared from radar screens.

It is thought that whoever is responsible for this atrocity had also planted a bomb in a suitcase that exploded earlier today at Narita Airport in Japan. The suitcase was destined for another Air India flight. Two baggage handlers were killed.

Rainbow Warrior Bombers Jailed for Ten Years

Auckland, New Zealand, November 21: On November 3, French secret agents Alain Mafart and Dominique Prieur pleaded guilty in the High Court to manslaughter and arson. Today the couple has been sentenced to 10 years' jail for the bombing and sinking of the Greenpeace ship *Rainbow Warrior* on July 10.

Since 1978 the converted fishing trawler had traveled the world in an attempt to protect whales and seals, and to stop environmental calamities such as the dumping of chemical and nuclear waste. The colorful ship was in Auckland Harbor to support Prime Minister David Lange's anti-nuclear policies and ban on US nuclear warships (which caused the US to exclude New Zealand from the ANZUS alliance in February this year). The *Rainbow Warrior* was also planning to lead a flotilla of seven ships to Mururoa Atoll to protest against French nuclear testing in the area. The non-violent protest, which would have taken the ship into a prohibited zone, was to have taken place on July 14—Bastille Day.

Mafart and Prieur attached two limpet mines to the hull of the ship, which exploded at 11.45 p.m., creating a 6 ft × 8 ft (1.8 m × 2.4 m) hole in the bottom of the boat. Within minutes, the *Rainbow Warrior* had sunk. Of the 11 crew, some managed to evacuate, while others were blown into the water as they were escaping, but survived. The only casualty was Greenpeace photographer Fernando Pereiro, a 33-year-old Portuguese man who was killed when he tried to get his equipment out of his cabin.

Ethiopia, January 13: A train bound for Addis Ababa derails and plunges into a ravine. This is Africa's worst rail disaster, with 392 people dead.
New Zealand, February 9: Labour PM David Lange, adhering to the government's anti-nuclear stance, has refused to allow a US nuclear warship to dock. The US retaliates by excluding NZ from the ANZUS alliance.
UK, March 3: Coalminers call off their strike after nearly a year.

Moscow, USSR, March 13: The new Soviet leader, Mikhail Gorbachev, leads the funeral for Konstantin Chernenko, whom he replaced. At 54, Gorbachev is perceived to be a potential reformer.
Tirana, Albania, April 11: Enver Hoxha, leader of the insular Communist state for 40 years, dies.
Bangladesh, May 27: Up to 10,000 people are killed by a cyclone and tidal wave that has devastated the low-lying country.

Ottawa, Canada, June 13: Manitoba laws are ruled unacceptable by the Supreme Court of Canada as they are written only in English.
Ireland, June 23: An Air India jet is destroyed by a terrorist bomb over the Atlantic.
Auckland, New Zealand, July 10: The Greenpeace ship *Rainbow Warrior* is sunk after explosions rip through her in Auckland harbor. One life is lost.

UK, Japan, USA, August 22: Three major air disasters this month have killed 711 people.
South Africa, August 28: The country has descended into a state of anarchy after President P. W. Botha refused to make concessions to the black majority.
Atlantic Ocean, September 1: A team led by Robert Ballard has located the wreck of the *Titanic*.
Mexico City, Mexico, September 20: A massive earthquake, measuring 7.8 on the Richter scale, has killed approximately 20,000 people.

Auckland, New Zealand, November 3: French secret agents plead guilty to the sinking of the *Rainbow Warrior*.
Geneva, Switzerland, November 21: US President Ronald Reagan and Soviet leader Mikhail Gorbachev hold 6-hour talks at the 14th US-Soviet Summit, stirring optimism.
Rome, Italy, and Vienna, Austria, December 30: Palestinian terrorists attack two El Al Israel Airline check-in counters in coordinated attacks that leave 12 holidaymakers dead and hundreds injured.

Oliver Tambo

Soviets Admit to Nuclear Accident at Chernobyl

Ukraine, USSR, April 30: After several days of silence and secrecy, the Soviet news agency TASS has finally admitted to an explosion at the Chernobyl nuclear power plant, 80 miles (129 km) north of Kiev in the Ukraine. Some 15,000 people from the town of Prypyat, 10 miles (16 km) from Chernobyl, have been evacuated.

On April 28, a Moscow television announcer relayed a brief message from the Council of Ministers, stating: "An accident has taken place at the Chernobyl power station, and one of the reactors was damaged. Measures are being taken to eliminate the consequences of the accident. Those affected by it are being given assistance. A government commission has been set up."

Full details are still unknown, but it seems that following a series of tests and experiments on Chernobyl Nuclear Reactor 4, a massive explosion occurred during the early hours of April 26. The lid blew off the reactor's container, causing radioactive particles to be released into the atmosphere. Abnormal levels of radioactivity have been recorded in countries as far away as Sweden, Norway, and Finland, since the particles would have been carried by the wind.

It is uncertain whether equipment failure or human error is to blame for the tragedy. The sad fact is that it could have been prevented. At Three Mile Island in the United States, the site of a 1979 nuclear accident, a containment unit prevented most of the dangerous material from escaping the plant. The Chernobyl reactor did not have a containment unit. A few months ago, an article in the Kiev journal *Literaturna Ukraina* expressed concern about the poor level of safety at the power station.

"WE DON'T WANT APART-HEID LIBERAL-IZED. WE WANT IT DISMANTLED. YOU CAN'T IMPROVE SOMETHING THAT IS INTRINSICALLY EVIL."

DESMOND TUTU (B. 1931), SOUTH AFRICAN CLERIC AND HUMAN RIGHTS ACTIVIST

"NO PARTY HAS A MONOPOLY OVER WHAT IS RIGHT."

MIKHAIL GOR-BACHEV (B. 1931), SOVIET STATESMAN, 1986

John M. Poindexter was implicated in the "Irangate" scandal.

At this stage, the number of casualties has not been released. The full extent of the damage caused to the environment and the long-term health effects on humans will not be known for a long time.

Tenth Anniversary of the Soweto Uprising

Johannesburg, South Africa, June 16: Today marks the tenth anniversary of the Soweto uprising, in which 100 people were killed when some 15,000 black students took to the streets to protest against education policies.

In his commemorative statement, Oliver Tambo, president of the African National Congress, said, "On this truly historic occasion the nation will pay fitting tribute to the young heroes and martyrs, including 8-year-olds, who fell in that titanic battle against the forces of apartheid repression."

Four days ago, South African President P. W. Botha declared a national state of emergency to prevent any demonstrations taking place to mark the anniversary of the tragedy. On the

time out

Yul Brynner appeared in an anti-smoking television advertisement, after his death from lung cancer. Before his death, he said in a television interview that he wanted to make an anti-smoking commercial. The American Cancer Society made the commercial from a clip from that interview.

first day of the ruling, over 1,000 people were detained.

Tambo responded to Botha's heavy-handed measures by stating, "With the state of emergency, the enemy is there for all to see. The lines are clearly drawn—the fighters for a nonracial, democratic and united South Africa on one side, and on the other the armed defenders of the apartheid crime."

"Irangate" Rocks the White House

Washington DC, USA, November 25: Attorney General Edwin Meese announced today that millions of dollars from the sale of US arms to Iran had been channeled into Swiss bank accounts. These funds had been used to support the Contra rebels in Nicaragua in their campaign to overthrow the Marxist Sandinista regime.

The Iran-Contra deal (already dubbed "Irangate" by the media) was brought to light on November 3 when the Lebanese magazine *Al-Shiraa* reported that the US had sold arms to Iran in exchange for the freedom of US hostages. The government of Iran confirmed the magazine's story. President Ronald Reagan admitted to sending some military equipment to Iran, but emphatically stated that "we did not…trade weapons or anything else for hostages, nor will we."

By giving financial aid to the Contras, Reagan violated the 1982 Boland Amendment, but he craftily used the National Security Council (who were outside the jurisdiction of the amendment) to facilitate the secret operation.

Today, National Security Adviser John M. Poindexter has resigned, and Assistant Deputy Director for Political-Military Affairs Lieutenant-Colonel Oliver North was dismissed by President Reagan.

Port-au-Prince, Haiti, February 7: President-for-life Jean-Claude "Baby Doc" Duvalier flees to France amid widespread unrest. Duvalier and his father, "Papa Doc," ruled the country brutally for 28 years.
Manila, Philippines, February 25: Ferdinand Marcos, president for 20 years, is marginalized by the military and the USA and is forced to resign. Political widow María Corazón Aquino takes power.
Stockholm, Sweden, February 28: Walking unprotected, Swedish PM Olof Palme is assassinated.

Canberra, Australia, March 2: Queen Elizabeth formally severs Australia's constitutional ties with the UK, signing the Australia Act with PM Bob Hawke.
Tripoli, Libya, April 15: US aircraft, with British cooperation, strike terrorist targets, killing dozens of civilians in the Libyan capital.
Ukraine, USSR, April 30: The Chernobyl nuclear reactor melts down, releasing massive amounts of deadly radiation.

Vienna, Austria, June 8: Former Secretary-General of the UN, Kurt Waldheim, is elected president, amid accusations of involvement in Nazi war crimes.
South Africa, June 16: Millions of blacks strike on the tenth anniversary of the Soweto uprising.
Washington DC, USA, June 25: Nicaraguan Contras are paid by US Congress to overthrow the Sandinista government.
New Zealand, July 11: Homosexual Law Reform Act legalizes consensual adult same-sex relationships.

Edinburgh, Scotland, July 24–August 7: The Commonwealth Games are boycotted by 32 countries in protest at Britain's refusal to implement more sanctions against South Africa.
Karachi, Pakistan, August 14: Benazir Bhutto is arrested while leading demonstrations against the government of President Zia.
Cameroon, August 25: Toxic gas is released from a volcanic lake, resulting in 1,700 deaths.
Iceland, October 12: Ronald Reagan and Mikhail Gorbachev attend a summit on arms control.

Basle, Switzerland, November 10: A fire at a chemical plant leads to more than 1,000 tons of toxic chemicals washing into the Rhine.
Washington DC, USA, November 25: The "Irangate" affair comes to light; Ronald Reagan admits secret arms deals with Nicaraguan Contras. Lieutenant-Colonel Oliver North and Vice Admiral John Poindexter resign.
Shanghai, China, December 21: Fifty thousand students hold demonstrations urging democratic reforms, including freedom of the media.

Belgian Ferry Capsizes in Icy Waters

Zeebrugge, Belgium, March 6: The Belgian car and passenger ferry *Herald of Free Enterprise* capsized today, just moments after it left the port of Zeebrugge for Dover. The death toll is uncertain, but it is expected to reach into the hundreds. Most of the casualties would have died of hypothermia in the near-freezing water.

The *Herald of Free Enterprise* is owned by Townsend Thoreson, and was carrying between 500 and 600 passengers, along with a large number of cars and trucks.

The capsized wreck of the *Herald of Free Enterprise*.

Many of the British passengers had gone to the continent on a discount day trip offered by *The Sun* newspaper.

It is not clear how the disaster happened. Survivors say the boat went over in seconds and began filling rapidly with water. The captain had no time to send out an SOS. However, rescue boats and helicopters promptly arrived on the scene. The accident was a terrifying experience for the survivors—the only way out for some was to break windows and cling to the side of the ship while waiting for assistance. Many others were trapped in the hull and had to be rescued by divers.

Full investigations will be conducted, but at this stage it is believed that the bow doors hadn't been shut properly, allowing water to rush into the boat.

India and Sri Lanka Sign Peace Accord

Colombo, Sri Lanka, July 29: Indian Prime Minister Rajiv Gandhi and Sri Lankan President J. R. Jayewardene have today signed a peace accord, hopefully ending years of bloodshed between separatist Tamil Tigers (Liberation Tigers of Tamil Eelam, or LTTE) and Sinhalese government troops in Sri Lanka.

According to the Indo–Sri Lanka Peace Accord, the Sri Lankan Government has agreed to the devolution of power to the provinces, and officially acknowledges the Tamil language. The Indian Government has promised to set up a peacekeeping force to establish order in the northeast.

The Sinhalese and the Tamils are the two main ethnic groups in Sri Lanka, an island nation southeast of India. The Tamils comprise less than 20 percent of the population. Sri Lanka gained independence from Britain in 1948, and the Tamils believe they have been discriminated against ever since.

Since 1983, Tamil separatists have been fighting to create an independent homeland in the northeast of Sri Lanka. Thousands of people have lost their lives in the fighting, most recently on April 27 this year when a car bomb exploded in a Colombo bus station, killing over 110 civilians and 2 policemen.

Reagan and Gorbachev Sign Anti-Nuclear Treaty

Washington DC, USA, December 8: Soviet General Secretary Mikhail Gorbachev has been visiting the USA for the first time. At the end of a three-day summit, Gorbachev and President Reagan have today signed the Intermediate-Range Nuclear Forces (INF) treaty, taking US–Soviet relations to a new level.

The treaty makes provision for the destruction, within the next three years, of more than 1,500 deployed Soviet warheads, as well as all ground-launched intermediate-range missiles. It has also stipulated that all American Pershing II and ground-launched cruise missiles and 400 deployed warheads will be destroyed.

In addition, the treaty allows for stringent on-site inspections of Soviet and American nuclear bases to make sure that the missiles and launchers have, in fact, been destroyed.

During the pre-signing ceremony, President Reagan jovially quoted Russian proverbs, and said, "We can only hope that this history-making agreement will not be an end in itself, but the beginning of a working relationship that will enable us to tackle the other urgent issues before us…" Gorbachev responded by stating, "What we are going to do, the signing of the first-ever agreement eliminating nuclear weapons, has a universal significance for mankind, both from the standpoint of world politics and the standpoint of humanism." The treaty is yet another example of Gorbachev's desire to improve Soviet–Western relations, as well as modernize his own country. His policies are known as *glasnost* (openness) and *perestroika* (restructuring).

Coincidentally, the signing of the treaty took place on the seventh anniversary of the death of John Lennon, who urged the world to "give peace a chance."

Rajiv Gandhi

Mikhail Gorbachev and Ronald Reagan sign the anti-nuclear agreement.

Beirut, Lebanon, February 22: At the request of Lebanese leaders, 7,000 Syrian troops enter West Beirut in an attempt to end fighting between Shia Muslims and Christians.

Rome, Italy, March 1: Bettino Craxi's socialist government, the longest serving since World War II, resigns.

Zeebrugge, Belgium, March 6: A car ferry en route to the UK capsizes; 188 people die.

New Zealand, April 1: State-owned enterprises replace government trading departments.

Suva, Fiji, May 14: Lt-Col Sitiveni Rabuka enters parliament and arrests the PM and 27 members of the Indian-dominated government.

Moscow, USSR, May 28: Matthias Rust, 19, an inexperienced pilot from West Germany, lands in Red Square.

UK, June 11: Margaret Thatcher's Conservative Party is re-elected for a third term.

Seoul, South Korea, June 20: Massive protests throughout South Korea over ten days climax with widespread riots in the capital. Rioters demand democratic reform.

Mecca, Saudi Arabia, July 30: Saudi police shoot 400 pilgrims, mostly Iranians, during the annual hajj.

Colombo, Sri Lanka, July 29: India and Sri Lanka sign a peace accord.

Guatemala City, Guatemala, August 7: The presidents of Costa Rica, Nicaragua, Honduras, Guatemala, and El Salvador sign a peace agreement.

Manila, Philippines, August 29: The fifth coup attempt against President Corazón Aquino's government fails, leaving 40 people dead and hundreds injured.

Ethiopia, September 10: A new civilian constitution is drafted, ending 13 years of military rule. Colonel Mengistu Haile Mariam is elected president.

USA, September 17: The country celebrates the 200th anniversary of the US Constitution, the longest serving in the world. It has been amended 26 times.

UK, October 16: Hurricane force winds batter the British Isles, leaving a £300 million damage bill. It is the worst storm to hit the UK in 300 years; 17 people die.

Worldwide, October 19: Stock markets slump dramatically following the lead of Wall Street; around 25 percent of share values have been wiped out.

Washington DC, USA, December 8: Ronald Reagan and Mikhail Gorbachev sign a treaty to diminish the size of their nuclear arsenals.

Archbishop
Desmond Tutu

"IT SEEMS THAT THE HISTORIC INABILITY IN BRITAIN TO COMPREHEND IRISH FEELINGS AND SENSITIVITIES STILL REMAINS."

CHARLES HAUGHEY
(B. 1925), IRISH
STATESMAN AND
PRIME MINISTER, 1988

"THE UNITED STATES IS THE BEST AND FAIREST AND MOST DECENT NATION ON THE FACE OF THE EARTH."

GEORGE BUSH
(B. 1924), AMERICAN
PRESIDENT, 1988

Australian Bicentennial: Celebration and Survival

Sydney, Australia, January 26: Up to two million people gathered around the foreshores of Sydney Harbor to remember this day 200 years ago, when the First Fleet arrived in Sydney, and Captain Arthur Phillip raised the British flag on Australian soil. Boats filled the harbor on this picture-perfect summer's day, sharing in the spectacle of the tall ship re-enactment, while 150 RAAF aircraft flew overhead.

The crowds stayed to watch the magnificent fireworks display, with the Sydney Harbor Bridge erupting in light and color. A select group of 4,000 people attended a formal gathering inside the Sydney Opera House. The guests of honor were the Prince and Princess of Wales. Also in attendance were the Governor General, Sir Ninian Stephen, and Prime Minister Bob Hawke. In an inspiring speech, Mr Hawke said, "In Australia there is no hierarchy of descent, there must be no privilege of origin…the commitment to Australia is the one thing needful to be a true Australian."

For indigenous Australians, however, it was a somber day of reflection—"Invasion Day" or "Survival Day." Thousands of Aborigines and their supporters marched peacefully from inner-city Redfern to Hyde Park, carrying banners with such slogans as "white Australia has a black history", and "40,000 years doesn't make a bicentennial." They used the march to call attention to serious contemporary issues such as Aboriginal deaths in custody. While white Australians were enjoying the First Fleet re-enactment, Koori activist Burnum Burnum raised the Aboriginal flag on British soil, in Dover.

General Noriega Survives US-led Coup Attempt

Panama City, Panama, March 16: The de facto military leader of Panama, General Manuel Noriega, has survived a coup attempt led by enemies in the Panama Defense Forces (PDF) and supported by the USA. The coup was suppressed by PDF loyalists.

Just last month, US Federal grand juries in Miami and Tampa, Florida, issued an indictment against Noriega and his accomplices for money laundering, and for covertly bringing marijuana into the USA. In addition, Noriega was indicted for his involvement in cocaine trafficking from Colombia to the USA. Noriega pleaded innocent, and threatened to

time out

In his fifth season, basketball player Michael Jordan scored his 10,000th NBA point. At 32.5 points per game, he was the league's top scorer. Postseason honors included membership on the All-NBA First Team and being named Player of the Year by *The Sporting News*.

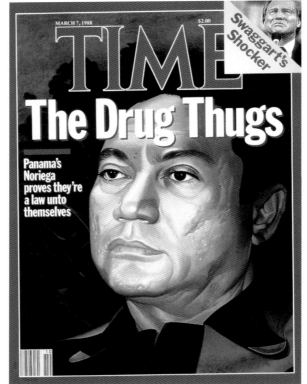

Time magazine's March 7, 1988 cover profile of Manuel Noriega.

expel the thousands of US military personnel from the Panama Canal area. Noriega came to prominence in 1969 when General Omar Torrijos, in gratitude for his loyalty, appointed him Lieutenant-Colonel and Chief of Military Intelligence. The following year, Noriega was hired by the CIA to get information on Cuba and spy on South American drug cartels, all the while trafficking drugs himself. When the CIA became aware of his drug involvement they fired him, but engaged his services again—at a cost of $200,000 a year—to provide information about the Marxist Sandinista regime in Nicaragua. The USA again severed ties with Noriega in 1986 when they discovered he was working as a double agent for Nicaragua and Cuba.

50,000 Die in Massive Armenian Earthquake

Armenia, USSR, December 10: A national day of mourning was declared for the victims of the massive earthquake that hit northern Armenia at 11.41 a.m. on December 7. It is estimated that the earthquake, measuring 6.9 on the Richter scale, has killed between 25,000 to 50,000 people and made 500,000 homeless.

The earthquake ripped through an area roughly 50 miles (80 km) in diameter. Hardest hit was Spitak, a town of around 30,000 people who all live in high-rise apartment buildings—the town has been completely flattened. Leninakan, a city of some 300,000 citizens, has also been badly affected, as have the towns of Kirovakan, and Stepanavan.

Soviet President Mikhail Gorbachev is inspecting the devastation today. Many countries have responded to his request for aid, including the USA, Great Britain, India, and France.

Key Events

Canada and USA, January 2: Canada and the USA sign a Free Trade Agreement.

East Jerusalem, Israel, January 15: Israeli police open fire on Muslim protestors at the Dome of the Rock Mosque, one of Islam's holiest sites.

Cape Town, South Africa, February 29: As part of the latest crackdown on anti-apartheid protests, Archbishop Desmond Tutu and 100 clergy are arrested.

Panama City, Panama, March 16: General Manuel Noriega survives a US-led coup attempt.

Islamabad, Pakistan, April 10: The Ohjri ammunition depot explodes, killing 100 and injuring 1,000 others. Afghan agents are suspected of involvement.

Afghanistan, May 16: Soviet troops begin to withdraw, after over eight years bogged down against US-backed Islamic militants. The unpopular war has been described as "Russia's Vietnam."

Moscow, USSR, May 31: President Reagan, who described the USSR as an "evil empire," makes the first visit by a US president in 14 years.

Cambodia, June 4: Vietnamese forces, who have occupied Cambodia for ten years, begin to withdraw 50,000 troops.

Arabian Gulf, July 3: US Navy warship *Vincennes* mistakenly shoots down an Iranian passenger plane, killing 290 people.

North Sea, July 6: An oil-rig explodes.

Tehran, Iran, July 20: Ayatollah Khomeini declares an end to the eight-year holy war with Iraq, accepting the cease-fire conditions drafted by the UN.

Rangoon, Burma, July 23: Rioting students destroy police stations in the worst violence seen in the past quarter century. Premier Bo Ne Win is ousted from office after 26 years.

Bahawalpur, Pakistan, August 17: President Zia and 30 officials, including the US ambassador, die when their plane is engulfed in flames. Sabotage is suspected.

Ramstein, West Germany, August 28: Three Italian jets collide at an air show, sending the debris into the crowds; hundreds are severely burnt, 46 die.

Burma, September 19: The flirtation with freedom of speech is short-lived in the socialist country. The Army takes control of the civilian government, banning all public demonstrations.

Santiago, Chile, October 6: A referendum ousts General Augusto Pinochet; voters refuse to install the army strongman for another eight years.

Armenia, USSR, December 10: A massive earthquake levels urban areas.

Emperor Hirohito Dies

Tokyo, Japan, January 7: Hirohito, the 124th Emperor of Japan, has died of cancer today at the age of 87. Hirohito was born on April 29, 1901.

As Crown Prince, he visited Europe in 1922—the first Japanese royal to ever travel in the West. His father died on December 25, 1926, and Hirohito was officially crowned emperor on November 10, 1928, proclaiming his reign as *Shōwa*, meaning "Enlightened Peace."

However, an extremely militaristic Japanese Government went to war against China and Manchuria in the 1930s, and became part of the Rome-Berlin-Tokyo axis during World War II. On December 6, 1941, Japan bombed Pearl Harbor, which led to four years of war in the Pacific. Japan surrendered on August 15, 1945, after the United States dropped atomic bombs on Hiroshima and Nagasaki. When Hirohito's surrender speech came over the airwaves, it was the first time the Japanese people had ever heard his voice.

Several Allied leaders, including President Truman, believed that Hirohito should have been placed on trial for war crimes. General Douglas MacArthur, head of the Occupation Forces, did not agree. After World War II, Japan's new Constitution eliminated the emperor's divine right, and instituted democratic and social reforms.

Emperor Hirohito will be succeeded by his son, Crown Prince Akihito, and after a state funeral will be buried in the imperial mausoleum in Hachioji.

Violence and Bloodshed in Tiananmen Square

Beijing, China, June 4: The people's revolt that has been gaining momentum over the past few months has been brutally put down in Tiananmen Square. Up to 2,600 people are thought to have died and 10,000 to have been injured.

Youths celebrate the opening atop the graffiti-covered Berlin wall.

The rebellion was precipitated by the death in April of former General Secretary Hu Yaobang, a liberal anti-Maoist. It was started seven weeks ago by students and intellectuals seeking democratic reforms and protesting against the current reactionary and corrupt regime. Then workers became involved, concerned about high unemployment and inflation. On May 30, protestors erected a Statue of Liberty look-alike, named the Goddess of Democracy, defiantly facing Chairman Mao's picture.

Despite warnings, the demonstrators refused to leave their posts. Units from the People's Liberation Army moved into the square with machine guns, firing into the crowds, many of them innocent passers-by. Then tanks came in, virtually crushing people to death. The demonstrators angrily retaliated, burning army vehicles and turning Tiananmen Square into a battlefield.

World leaders, including US President Bush and Britain's Prime Minister Thatcher, have condemned the Chinese Army's brutality.

Berlin Wall Opens to East and West

Berlin, Germany, November 10: After the defeat of the hardline government of Erich Honecker on October 18, the Berlin Wall (*Die Berliner Mauer*), long a potent symbol of Communist oppression, has opened after a period of 28 years.

Yesterday, East German Minister of Propaganda Gunter Schabowski announced that, as of midnight, East Germans would be able to cross the boundary without permission. Crowds of people had gathered, and at the designated time, cheering mobs of East Berliners poured through the checkpoints, and were welcomed by equally jubilant West Berliners. The more energetic and athletic among them climbed on top of the 28-mile (45-km) edifice.

The wall was the brainchild of East German leader Walter Ulbricht. It was erected at the height of the Cold War in 1961, with the approval of Soviet leader Nikita Khrushchev, to prevent people from East Berlin defecting to the West. Millions of people had defected since 1949, causing a drain on the East German economy. What began as a simple wire fence in 1961 ended up a sophisticated 12 ft (3.5 m) high concrete wall topped with barbed wire in 1965, which was renewed ten years later.

Over the past three decades, over 4,500 people managed to escape. Approximately 200 people were killed in the attempt.

Demolition of the wall will take place over the next few weeks.

Emperor Hirohito

Tokyo, Japan, January 7: Emperor Hirohito, dies, aged 82.

Washington DC, USA, January 20: Republican George H. W. Bush is inaugurated as the 41st president.

Asuncion, Paraguay, February 3: Alfredo Stroessner, Paraguay's president for 35 years, is overthrown in a military coup.

Prince William Sound, Alaska, March 24: The *Exxon Valdez* oil tanker runs aground, spilling over 11 million gallons (42 million liters) of oil. The captain is alleged to be intoxicated.

USSR, March 26: The first democratic elections take place to elect the Congress of People's Deputies. Boris Yeltsin comes out ahead because of his criticism of Mikhail Gorbachev.

Sheffield, England, April 15: The UK's worst sporting disaster occurs when supporters of Liverpool rush onto an already overcrowded stand–94 are killed and 170 are injured.

Poland, June 5: Voters deliver a resounding mandate to the Solidarity Party, led by Lech Walesa, in the first free elections.

Beijing, China, June 5: A student revolt is brutally put down in Tiananmen Square.

Tehran, Iran, June 6: Hysterical mourning greets the death of spiritual leader Ayatollah Seyyed Ruhollah Khomeini, aged 86.

Pretoria, South Africa, August 15: P. W. Botha resigns as PM to be replaced by Frederik Willem de Klerk.

Austria, September 10: Twenty-five thousand East Germans, seeking a new life in the West, flee to Austria via Hungary when the Hungarian Government opens its borders. The travel documents of many are invalid but they are automatically entitled to West German citizenship.

San Francisco, USA, October 21: A massive earthquake rocks the Bay area, measuring 6.9 on the Richter scale. Eighty-three deaths are reported, damage is widespread.

New Zealand, November 1: Major local government and ports reforms come into effect, overturning a post-1876 system and drastically reducing the number of local authorities.

Berlin, West/East Germany, November 10: The Berlin Wall is opened after 28 years.

Panama, December 20: US troops invade. General Manuel Noriega flees and is replaced by Guillermo Endara.

Bucharest, Romania, December 25: Following two weeks of social unrest, brutal dictator, Nicolae Ceausescu and his wife are executed.

Dr Alec Jeffreys

Deadly New Infectious Disease Identified

USA, December, 1981: Doctors have discovered a new, highly infectious, fatal disease, caused by a puzzling and previously unknown virus. Named Acquired Immune Deficiency Syndrome (AIDS), the disorder devastates the victim's immune system, leaving them vulnerable to acute infections from opportunistic diseases, which most people are generally able to shrug off.

The mysterious condition, which consists of two separate diseases—a form of pneumonia, and skin cancer—has been found in almost 200 patients in 15 states since last July. Homosexuals who have contracted either of the two conditions have shown a low resistance to standard tests on their immune system.

AIDS has claimed around 75 lives so far in America, with up to 70 of the victims being homosexual men. One case also involved an intravenous drug user, which implies that the disease could be spread by sharing needles, and, even more importantly, by blood transfusions. Four victims also had rare skin ulcers usually caused by the herpes simplex virus.

Dr James Curran, of the Centers for Disease Control in Atlanta where the epidemic is being investigated, said: "It is a very serious problem and it does not seem to be on the wane." An investigation at the University of California indicates that homosexuals may be recurrently infected with the virus. Researchers claim that their discoveries are "part of a nationwide epidemic of immuno-deficiency among male homosexuals."

Although doctors have identified AIDS, they are yet to devise a cure, and warn that its highly infectious nature raises the real risk of a lethal global epidemic.

Ship Rises from Watery Grave

Portsmouth, England, October 11, 1982: The wreck of the *Mary Rose*, once the pride of the English war fleet and the flagship of King Henry VIII, has been raised to the surface after 437 years at the bottom of the Solent River in Portsmouth.

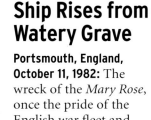

Fragments of the flagship *Mary Rose*.

Salvage of the wreck from its location 50 ft (15 m) below sea level began at 7 a.m., and within two hours the first pieces of the timber skeleton had broken the surface. Just before midday, one of the pins holding the lifting frame sheared, causing a thick steel line to snap, and sending part of the 80-ton (81.3-tonne) frame smashing down onto the hull of the salvage ship.

Speaking afterward, Prince Charles, President of the Mary Rose Trust, said: "I was horrified, but I thought the best thing to do was to be British and not panic."

By 3 p.m. the ship was successfully refloated, and experts can now begin the process of restoring the *Mary Rose* in dry dock.

Since the rediscovery of the ship in 1966, more than 10,000 well-preserved items have been excavated, including weapons, furniture, clothes, and a backgammon set.

IBM Unveils Its New Personal Computer

USA, March 8, 1983: Computer company International Business Machines (IBM) has unveiled the "hard disk drive" in its new personal computer (PC). The PC-XT 5160 is an improved version of the revolutionary IBM 5150 personal computer, released in August 1981.

The PC-XT is based on the same architecture as the 5150 but has greater capacity and speed. Up to now, computers have only contained removable, or "floppy," disk drives. The PC-XT's new hard disk drive, consisting of a series of layered disks that can "read" each other, is much faster than a floppy disk, and can store almost a hundred times as much information in its memory.

The hard drive is permanently sealed within the computer, while the floppy drive may be detached and its information transferred to another computer.

Although PCs have been around for about 10 years, these IBM computers are the first to enable "networking" or serial connection with other computers by means of sockets and electrical leads. This has already proved a huge advantage in business, both within and between

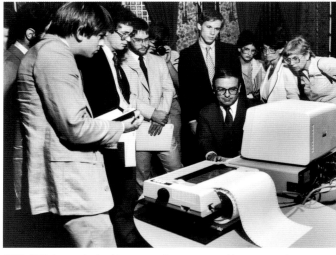

IBM's CEO demonstrates his company's new personal home computer.

An artist's concept of a design for an experimental space-based interceptor system against incoming missiles.

Steve Jobs

The President stressed that SDI does not entail the actual development of a defensive shield, but is merely a "long-term research and development program." However, many commentators have poured scorn on this remark, asking in effect: "If that is the case, then what is the research for, and where will the development lead?"

A laser-beam firing satellite was featured in the 1971 James Bond film *Diamonds Are Forever*, and it has been suggested that the movie had some influence on President Reagan.

Breakthrough in DNA Fingerprinting

Leicester, England, September 15, 1984: In a scientific breakthrough at the University of Leicester, British genetic scientist Alec Jeffreys has discovered that human genetic material (deoxyribonucleic acid, or DNA) contains certain sequences that are unique to each individual.

Though human beings differ genetically from each other by only 0.1 percent, Jeffreys has discovered that certain regions of the DNA molecule are unique to each individual.

The discovery will be of great use in paternity testing, forensic medicine, and studies of inbreeding. It is also another step toward the cloning of identical human beings, and the ability to combine one or more different species into a single organism.

It is now finally possible to accurately distinguish one human being from another with greater than 99.9 percent accuracy (with the exception of identical siblings from multiple births).

By comparison, fingerprinting is only about 96 percent accurate. Already there are moves to allow DNA evidence to be submitted in courts of law.

companies. More than 200,000 units of the 5150 were sold in its first year of release.

The PC-XT contains 128 kilobytes (128,000 pieces, or "bytes") of memory to enable calculations, word-processing, and other functions. The 5¼ in (13 cm) floppy disk has a 360-kilobyte capacity, while the new hard disk has a whopping 10-megabyte (10 million bytes) storage capacity.

The PC-XT costs $7,545 and is tipped to be even more popular than the 5150.

Reagan Plans Space Age Nuclear Defense Shield

Washington DC, USA, March 23, 1983: In a televised address from the White House, President Reagan has unveiled plans to combat nuclear war in space. His Strategic Defense Initiative (SDI) proposes a defensive shield, using laser or particle beam technology to "intercept and destroy" incoming missiles.

Defense analysts have described it as the first major attempt to move away

from the Cold War strategy of Mutually Assured Destruction (MAD)—where the threat of nuclear retaliation acts as a deterrent to attack.

President Reagan said: "We seek neither military superiority nor political advantage. Our only purpose—one all people share—is to search for ways to avert the danger of nuclear war." Dr Carol Rosin, a spokesperson for ballistic missile pioneer Werner von Braun, has dubbed SDI "Star Wars," implying that it lies in the realm of science fiction fantasy. Other critics have opposed—even ridiculed—the staggeringly expensive plan on practical, economic, strategic, or ethical grounds. Many argue that the SDI contravenes the Soviet–American Anti-Ballistic Missile Treaty of 1972, which states: "Each party undertakes not to develop, test or deploy anti-ballistic missile systems or components."

time out

The *Solar Challenger* was the first solar-powered airplane to cross the English Channel. The trip took 5½ hours and was powered by 16,000 photovoltaic cells on the wings. Unlike other solar-powered airplanes, the *Solar Challenger* did not use storage batteries.

High-tech Plans to Raise the *Titanic*

Christa McAuliffe

"IT IS, OF COURSE, A BIT OF A DRAWBACK THAT SCIENCE WAS INVENTED AFTER I LEFT SCHOOL."

LORD CARRINGTON (B. 1919), BRITISH STATESMAN, 1983

"SHOULD WE FORCE SCIENCE DOWN THE THROATS OF THOSE THAT HAVE NO TASTE FOR IT? IS IT OUR DUTY TO DRAG THEM KICKING AND SCREAMING INTO THE TWENTY-FIRST CENTURY? I AM AFRAID THAT IT IS."

GEORGE PORTER (B. 1920), BRITISH CHEMIST

Atlantic Ocean, September 1, 1985: The wreck of the liner *Titanic* has been discovered in the North Atlantic Ocean by a joint US–French team led by Robert Ballard. The "unsinkable" *Titanic* sank in 1915, with the loss of 1,522 lives, after hitting an iceberg on its maiden voyage to the United States.

Ballard's long-held ambition of finding the wreck of the *Titanic* began in 1977. He sailed aboard the *Alcoa Seaprobe*, a converted oil-derrick, expecting that the search would take 10 to 12 days. Disastrously, the whole venture ended suddenly when an error in the rigging sent the exploratory device to the bottom of the ocean. No one was injured, but the attempt was abandoned.

In 1979, Texan millionaire, Jack Grimm, announced that he would try to find the *Titanic*, but the expeditions he made in 1980, 1981, and 1983 were fruitless.

Ballard decided on a high-tech strategy for his next attempt. Leading a team of experts from the Woods Hole Oceanographic Institute in Massachusetts, and a French team from the Research Institute for Exploitation of the Sea, he set off with fiber optic technology, robotic equipment, sonar, and links to Earth-orbiting satellites. To do the actual exploration, they used strobe lights, video cameras linked to the mother ship's computers by cable, and a submersible, highly maneuverable photographic sled.

On September 1 they observed telltale disturbances on the seabed, which led to their historic discovery.

A debate now rages over who owns the wreck, and whether salvage operations should be undertaken.

Robert Ballard adamantly opposes disturbing the remains of the ill-fated liner, saying, "I am opposed to the desecration of this memorial to 1,500 souls."

Space shuttle *Challenger* takes off from the Kennedy Space Center.

Seven Die in *Challenger* Space Shuttle Disaster

Cape Canaveral, USA, January 28, 1986: The space shuttle *Challenger* has blown up, killing all seven astronauts on board. The five men and two women were just over a minute into the flight from Cape Canaveral, Florida, when the shuttle exploded.

Falling debris prevented rescue boats from reaching the scene for more than an hour. In 25 years of space exploration 7 people have died—and now that total has been doubled. President Ronald Reagan described the tragedy as "a national loss."

High winds, and then icicles, had caused the launch to be delayed last week. But National Aeronautical and Space Administration officials insisted that safety remains their highest priority, and there was no pressure to launch today.

The *Challenger* shuttle crew was captained by Commander Dick Scobee. Crew member Christa McAuliffe, a 37-year-old mother of two children selected from over 10,000 competition entries, was to have been the first schoolteacher in space. Speaking before the lift-off, McAuliffe said: "One of the things I hope to bring back into the classroom is to make that connection with the students that they too are part of history, the space program belongs to them…"

The astronauts' families were watching from the airbase, while millions of Americans witnessed the tragedy live on television. TV replays appeared to show a small flame, seeping out from the join between the shuttle cabin and the booster rocket, just before the explosion.

Dinosaur Detectives Find Rare Fossils in Canada

Alberta, Canada, May, 1987: A huge, fossilized duckbill dinosaur nesting site has been discovered near Warner, Alberta, by paleontologist Kevin Aulenback. The site, at Devil's Coulee, contains dozens of unbroken spherical eggs about 4 in (100 mm) in diameter, and also—most amazingly—some partly broken eggs revealing intact fetuses.

The first fossils found in the area were discovered a few weeks ago by local girl, Wendy Sloboda. She found what she believed to be dinosaur eggshells along the Milk River Ridge, and sent them to Dr Philip Currie of the Royal Tyrrell Museum of Paleontology in Drumheller, who confirmed that the pieces were indeed dinosaur eggs, and immediately sent a crew of prospectors to Warner.

After several fruitless days searching, expedition member Aulenback sat down one evening on Devil's Coulee for a snack. Looking down at the ground on his right he saw an eggshell, and on his other side, an embryonic femur sticking out of the ground. Excited, he called for his colleagues, whereupon further exploration uncovered the huge nest.

Scientific Achievements

Astronomy: Discovery of the Great Wall, a sheet of galaxies measuring more than 500 million × 200 million × 15 million light years.

Botany: Development of the first genetically engineered crop.

Chemistry: Cigarette smoking found to be a risk factor for strokes; method found for genetic fingerprinting.

Ecology: World's worst nuclear power accident at Chernobyl, USSR; hole in ozone layer discovered.

Geology: Chengjiang Cambrian fossil site is discovered.

Mathematics: Simulated annealing, used to address the optimization problem, is developed.

Medicine: AIDS recognized; first operation to separate occipital craniopagus twins; first heart-lung transplant.

Zoology: *Gorillas in the Mist* published.

Botanic Gardens
Jerusalem, Israel

Observatories
Baxter, USA
Florence, USA
Itajuba, Brazil
Kamioka-cho, Japan
Mount Suhora, Poland
Narrabri, Australia
Taejon, South Korea

Universities
University of Hong Kong
University of Kathmandu, Nepal
University of Nicosia, Cyprus
University of Noumea, New Caledonia
University of Papeete, Tahiti

Mother ship *Atlantis II* returns home from an expedition to the wreck site of the *Titanic*.

Duckbill dinosaurs, or hadrosaurs, were common 70 million years ago, when this part of southeastern Alberta was sub-tropical. They have been nicknamed "cows of the Cretaceous period" because they were docile herbivores.

In general, hatching and scavenging did damage to dinosaur nests, but occasionally, some eggs survived predators and the elements, and eventually became fossils. Eggs that have retained their original shape and eggshell are the rarest dinosaur fossils in the world.

Agreement to Reduce Greenhouse Gases

Montreal, Canada, September 16, 1987: An agreement to control the production of ozone-destroying chlorofluorocarbons (CFCs) has been signed in Canada by 24 countries, with more due to sign soon.

After years of intense negotiation, the "Montreal Protocol on Substances That Deplete the Ozone Layer" has been designed to reduce the destructive effects of man-made CFCs and related substances upon the ozone layer, which forms a shell around Earth at an altitude of 15 miles (24 km).

Ozone is a pollutant at ground level, causing asthma, stunted growth in plants, and corrosion of certain substances. At lower levels in the stratosphere, it contributes to the greenhouse effect, whereby heat and moisture are trapped in the atmosphere, causing rises in temperature and the phenomenon of global warming. The ozone layer is vital for our survival on Earth, protecting us from cancer-causing ultraviolet rays.

Action to reduce CFCs has already been undertaken by some governments, including the United States, Canada, and the Scandinavian countries. These initiatives banned CFCs as aerosol propellants in non-essential uses such as hairsprays and deodorants. Other initiatives continued through the 1980s, but consensus has been difficult because of a lack of agreement about the extent of the threat.

However, recent research has verified that, over the past 15 years, the ozone layer has diminished by 4–8 percent in the northern hemisphere, and by 6–10 percent in the southern hemisphere, almost entirely attributable to CFCs. The British Antarctic Survey reported the most obvious indicator of ozone depletion in 1985, when they discovered a huge hole over Antarctica, which is steadily growing in size, and is currently almost as large as the continent of North America.

The Montreal Protocol will come into force on January 1, 1989, with signatories agreeing to freeze production of CFCs within seven months, and to reduce consumption by 50 percent over ten years.

Carbon Dating Reveals Shroud's True Age

Oxford, England, October 13, 1988: The Shroud of Turin, which many people believed was used to wrap Christ's body after the crucifixion, has been dated to 1320, give or take 50 years.

Samples from the shroud have been dated by accelerator-mass-spectrometry (AMS) in laboratories at Arizona, Oxford, and Zurich. As controls, three samples, whose ages are known, were also dated.

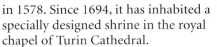

Mir cosmonaut Yuri Romanenko.

The results provide conclusive evidence that the linen of the Shroud is, in fact, medieval.

The shroud bears front and back images of a man who has suffered lashing and crucifixion. It was first displayed at Lirey in France in the 1350s and later passed into the hands of the Dukes of Savoy. After several journeys it was brought to Turin, northern Italy, in 1578. Since 1694, it has inhabited a specially designed shrine in the royal chapel of Turin Cathedral.

Accurate dating has not been possible until now, because previous radiocarbon-dating methods required an unacceptably large piece of the cloth to be removed. However, the recent development of AMS techniques meant that samples of only a few square centimeters were required in this case. In October 1987, tenders from the three laboratories were selected by the Archbishop of Turin, acting on orders from the Pope. The procedures for sampling and treating the results were agreed by representatives of the laboratories at a meeting last January.

The results have been approved by the Archbishop of Turin, and the shroud has been returned to Turin Cathedral.

Mission Over for *Voyagers 1* and *2*

Cape Canaveral, USA, August 25, 1989: The unmanned *Voyager 2* spacecraft has sent back the first sensational close-up pictures of Neptune and its satellite moons. *Voyager* has already sent back pictures and information from Jupiter, Saturn, and Uranus, but its trip past Neptune, more than 2,750 million miles (4,425 million km) from Earth, has proved far and away the most spectacular and revealing.

The capsule flew at 10.5 miles (17 km) per second over Neptune's darkened north pole, at a height of 2,980 miles (4,800 km). Neptune's blue hue, caused by the planet's methane atmosphere, is clearly visible, as are huge, 930 mph (1,500 km/h) windstorms. We have also discovered that Neptune emits radio waves and auroras, and is surrounded by a five-ring system similar to Saturn's, although much smaller. Six new moons have been identified, where only two, Triton and Nereid, were previously known. Triton is covered in rugged ridges, canyons, craters, and huge explosive nitrogen geysers.

Voyager 2 was launched from Cape Canaveral, Florida, in August 1977. It is a twin to *Voyager 1*, which blasted off the following month, but took a more direct course and has now overtaken *Voyager 2*. Originally, their journeys were designed to take in only Jupiter and Saturn, but scientists later decided to extend the "greatest journey of exploration this century," and reprogrammed the spacecraft by remote control.

The *Voyagers* will now pass out of the solar system forever, and we will never know their fate. Though it seems unlikely they will ever be discovered, the *Voyagers* contain messages, including maps of the Milky Way, a diagram of the hydrogen atom, and a long-playing record called *Sounds of Earth*, for the benefit of any civilizations that may discover them. The record includes music by Beethoven, Mozart, and Chuck Berry.

Bill Gates

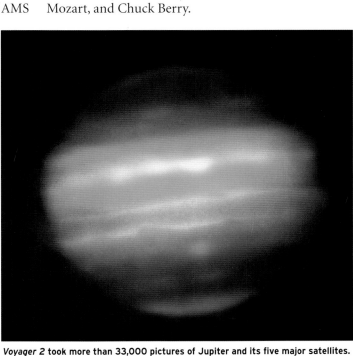

Voyager 2 took more than 33,000 pictures of Jupiter and its five major satellites.

"Master of Suspense" Dies of Kidney Failure

Alfred Hitchcock

Los Angeles, USA, April 29, 1980: One of the world's most prolific and greatly admired directors, the "Master of Suspense" Alfred Hitchcock, has died of kidney failure today, aged 80.

Hitchcock was born and raised in working-class London. He attended St Ignatius College, and from there he went on to study technical subjects at the School of Engineering and Navigation, and art at the University of London.

Fascinated with motion pictures from his teenage years, Hitchcock became a title designer at the Famous Players-Lasky Studio in London, gradually acquiring more skills and responsibilities. His breakthrough film as a director was *The Lodger* (1926), and over the next 13 years he made his mark on British cinema with such classics as *The Man Who Knew Too Much* (1934), and *The 39 Steps* (1935).

His first Hollywood film was *Rebecca* (1940), and for the next several decades he thrilled moviegoers with one great film after another, including *Spellbound* (1945), *Strangers on a Train* (1951), *Rear Window* (1954), *To Catch a Thief* (1955), *Vertigo* (1958), *Psycho* (1960), and *The Birds* (1963). Hitchcock's final film was *Family Plot* (1976). There are several common threads in Hitchcock movies: the beautiful ice-blonde heroine, the theme of mistaken identity, and the director himself making brief cameo appearances.

Alfred Hitchcock Presents was a popular TV series from 1955 to 1962, best remembered for Hitchcock's rotund silhouette, his witty chats with the audience, and the suitably spooky theme music.

Hitchcock is highly regarded for his innovative editing and camera techniques, and he has influenced a number of directors including Brian De Palma and François Truffaut. He is a recipient of many honors and awards, including Knight Commander of the Order of the British Empire. Hitchcock is survived by his wife of 54 years, Alma Reville, and their daughter Patricia.

John Lennon Murdered

New York, USA, December 9, 1980: At the height of Beatlemania, John Lennon was quoted as saying, "I'll probably be popped off by a loony." Tragically, that casual, almost flippant prediction has come true.

At 11.00 p.m. last night, as Lennon and his wife Yoko Ono were walking from their limousine to the entrance of their apartment building on the Upper West Side, Lennon was shot five times in the back. He was rushed by police car to Roosevelt Hospital, but died shortly afterward.

The murderer has been identified as 25-year-old Mark David Chapman, who had been stalking Lennon for some time and had even asked him for his autograph earlier that day—Lennon had graciously obliged. After the shooting, Chapman sat down in front of the building and read the novel *The Catcher in the Rye*.

John Winston Lennon was born in Liverpool, England, on October 9, 1940. After attending Liverpool College of Art, he realized his great love was rock 'n' roll, and eventually joined forces with fellow Liverpudlians Paul McCartney, Ringo Starr, and George Harrison to form The Beatles. They became a pop-culture phenomenon, and in 1966 Lennon caused a huge stir when he claimed The Beatles were more popular than Jesus Christ.

Due to creative and personal differences, The Beatles split up in 1970. By this time Lennon had married his second wife, Japanese artist Yoko Ono, and the pair had become famous for their "Bed-ins for Peace." As a solo artist, Lennon recorded many memorable songs including "Give Peace a Chance," "Imagine," and "Instant Karma." Lennon's son Sean was born on October 9, 1975, and Lennon devoted the next five years to his care. (Lennon also has a 17-year-old son, Julian, from his first marriage to Cynthia Powell.) He emerged from his creative hiatus with a new album, *Double Fantasy*, released just last month. It is a beautiful record, and a bittersweet ending to his life and career.

John Lennon signs an autograph for a fan.

Brideshead Revisited Premieres on ITV

London, England, October 12, 1981: For the next 11 weeks, British television viewers will be in for a real treat. The 12-hour costume epic *Brideshead Revisited*, produced by Granada Television and directed by Charles Sturridge and Michael Lindsay-Hogg, is one of the finest-quality productions ever created for the small screen.

Brideshead Revisited stars Jeremy Irons and Diana Quick.

> *"THE BEST ROCK AND ROLL MUSIC ENCAPSULATES A CERTAIN HIGH ENERGY, AN ANGRINESS, WHETHER ON RECORD OR ONSTAGE. ROCK 'N' ROLL IS ONLY ROCK 'N' ROLL IF IT'S NOT SAFE."*
>
> MICK JAGGER (B. 1943), ENGLISH SINGER, MEMBER OF THE ROLLING STONES, C. 1981

Key Events

Los Angeles, USA, April 29, 1980: Alfred Hitchcock dies, aged 80.

Mexico, November 7, 1980: Screen tough guy Steve McQueen, best known for his roles in *The Great Escape* and *Bullitt*, dies aged 50.

USA, November 21, 1980: Soap opera "Dallas" breaks viewing records as the question "Who shot JR?" is answered.

New York, USA, December 8, 1980: John Lennon is shot dead outside his home.

Miami, USA, May 11, 1981: Bob Marley, Jamaican reggae star, dies of cancer, aged 36.

USA, June 12, 1981: *Raiders of the Lost Ark* starring Harrison Ford is released.

USA, August 1, 1981: The first music video shown on MTV is "Video Killed the Radio Star" by The Buggles.

UK, October 12, 1981: *Brideshead Revisited* starring Jeremy Irons and Phoebe Nicholls premières.

New York, USA, February 17, 1982: Jazz pianist Thelonious Monk dies.

Hollywood, USA, March 5, 1982: John Belushi, star of *The Blues Brothers*, dies of a drug overdose.

USA, June 11, 1982: Steven Spielberg's *ET The Extra Terrestrial* is released.

London, England, October 11, 1982: Author Thomas Keneally wins the Booker Prize for *Schindler's Ark*.

Sweden, December 10, 1982: Colombian magic realist author Gabriel García Márquez receives the Nobel Prize for Literature.

Odense, Denmark, February 5, 1983: A musical manuscript found in a cellar 40 years ago is authenticated as Mozart's First Symphony, written when he was nine.

West Germany, May 11, 1983: The *Hitler Diaries* published in *Stern* are revealed to be fraudulent.

USA, May 25, 1983: George Lucas' *Star Wars* sequel *Return of the Jedi* opens, grossing $6.2 million.

London, England, December 6, 1983: £8.14 million is paid for a twelfth-century German Gospel. The most ever paid at auction for a single item.

New York, USA, February, 1984: Te Maori exhibition opens to acclaim at the Metropolitan Museum of Art—first time traditional Maori art has had such international exposure.

Los Angeles, USA, April 1, 1984: Soul singer Marvin Gaye is shot dead by his father, a priest, after a fight.

Los Angeles, USA, August 25, 1984: Truman Capote dies, aged 59.

UK, December 14, 1984: Britain's top pop stars record "Do They Know it's Christmas" to raise funds for Ethiopia.

The screenplay was adapted by John Mortimer from Evelyn Waugh's 1945 novel, and it opens with world-weary army officer Charles Ryder (Jeremy Irons) returning to the Brideshead mansion after a long absence. He recounts the story of his relationship with the home, and how he came to be gradually enthralled and seduced by its owners, the aristocratic Marchmain family: decadent Sebastian (Anthony Andrews), beautiful Julia (Diana Quick), earnest Cordelia (Phoebe Nicholls), and the pious Lady Marchmain (Claire Bloom). John Gielgud has a small but humorous role as Charles's acid-tongued father, Edward Ryder, and Laurence Olivier portrays the Marchmain's reprobate patriarch.

With a production cost of close to £10 million (US$18 million), no expense was spared in making *Brideshead Revisited* a lavish feast for the senses. The costumes from the 1920s–1940s are exquisite, as are the glorious settings in Oxford, London, aboard the *QEII*, Venice, Malta, and especially Castle Howard in Yorkshire. The musical score, composed by Geoffrey Burgon, complements the romantic, passionate, sometimes light-hearted, sometimes melancholy story.

Brideshead Revisited may rekindle an interest in the works of Evelyn Waugh, and will no doubt endure as a great television classic.

Truman Capote Dies

Los Angeles, USA, August 25, 1984: Truman Capote, the flamboyant author of the bestselling 1966 "non-fiction novel" *In Cold Blood*, has died of phlebitis and liver failure, brought on by years of drug and alcohol abuse.

Capote was born on September 30, 1924, in New Orleans. His wandering mother often left him to stay with

Author of *Breakfast at Tiffany's*, Truman Capote.

relatives in Monroeville, Alabama, where he befriended the future author of the classic *To Kill a Mockingbird*, Harper Lee (who later modeled the character of Dill on the young Truman).

At 17, Capote began work as a copy boy at the *New Yorker* magazine. His first published short story, "Miriam," won an O. Henry Award. In 1948, his first novel, *Other Voices, Other Rooms*, which dealt with homosexual themes, was published. He reached a wider audience with *Breakfast at Tiffany's* in 1958, subsequently adapted to the much-loved film starring Audrey Hepburn.

Tiffany's gave Capote a foot into the door of New York society, which he temporarily abandoned while researching *In Cold Blood*. He spent a couple of years in the small town of Holcomb, Kansas investigating the brutal murder of an entire family. The book took several more years to write, and when published in 1966 was met with both critical and popular acclaim, earning Capote a great deal of fame and fortune.

After the critical success of *In Cold Blood*, Capote's personal and professional

time out

The French designer Philippe Starck designed an apartment in the Palais de l'Elysée for Madame Mitterand. He established his first design firm in 1968, specializing in inflatable objects, and in 1969 became the art director of his firm along with Pierre Cardin.

life went on a downward spiral, but his major works have earned him an important place in American literature.

Band Aid Concert Raises Money for Famine Victims

London, England, December 14, 1984: Just one week after its release, "Do They Know It's Christmas," recorded by the cream of pop music talent in Britain, has reached Number One on the British charts.

Irish rocker Bob Geldof, lead singer of the Boomtown Rats, was inspired to make a record to raise money for famine victims in Ethiopia after seeing a news report on the BBC. Geldof penned the lyrics, and Midge Ure from Ultravox wrote the music.

On November 25, the supergroup that Geldof dubbed "Band Aid" gathered in a London studio, recording the song in just one day. As well as Geldof and Ure, the group included Phil Collins, Paul Young, George Michael, Sting, David Bowie, Paul McCartney, members of Bananarama, U2, Culture Club, Spandau Ballet, and Duran Duran, among others.

The record was produced by Trevor Horn, and the cover art by Peter Blake illustrates the disparity between the "haves" and the "have-nots" of the world.

Bob Marley

Steven Spielberg directs Henry Thomas on the set of the film *ET*.

Saint-Paul, France, March 28, 1985: Marc Chagall, Jewish Belarussian painter often associated with the surrealist movement, dies, aged 97.
London, England, and Philadelphia, USA, July 13, 1985: Bob Geldof has raised $40 million to help the starving in Africa with two *Live Aid* concerts.
USA, October 12, 1985: Orson Wells dies aged 70. This follows Rock Hudson's death from AIDS on October 2 and Yul Brynner from lung cancer, aged 65.

Paris, France, April 14, 1986: Simone de Beauvoir dies, aged 78.
Australia, April 30, 1986: Paul Hogan's *Crocodile Dundee* is a worldwide box office smash, exporting an Aussie larrikin to the world.
UK, August 31, 1986: Modernist sculptor Henry Moore dies, leaving behind a rich (and heavy) body of work.
Stockholm, Sweden, October, 1986: Nigerian Wole Soyinka, poet, dramatist, and author, is awarded the Nobel Prize for Literature, the first African to be honored.

New York, USA, February 22, 1987: The multimedia artist Andy Warhol dies following gall bladder surgery, aged 59.
Rhode Island, USA, August 28, 1987: Actor and film director John Huston dies from emphysema, aged 81. His directorial debut was *The Maltese Falcon*.
New York, USA, November 11, 1987: Vincent Van Gogh's *Irises* sells for $53.9 million at Sotheby's.

USA, March 14, 1988: Clark Kent, alias Superman, celebrates 50 years of superhero adventures in comics, TV, and film.
Wembley, England, July 18, 1988: Eric Clapton, Stevie Wonder, and Dire Straits join with others to commemorate the 70th birthday of Nelson Mandela.
UK, September 26, 1988: Penguin publishes Salman Rushdie's *The Satanic Verses*.
UK, October, 1988: *Oscar and Lucinda* by Australian author Peter Carey wins the Booker Prize.

Figueras, Spain, January 23, 1989: Iconic surrealist artist Salvador Dali dies aged 84.
Tehran, Iran, February 14, 1989: A *fatwa* (death sentence) is issued against Salman Rushdie for *The Satanic Verses*.
London, England, May 9, 1989: Pablo Picasso's self portrait sells for $47.9 million at auction.
London, England, July 11, 1989: Sir Laurence Olivier dies, aged 82.
Paris, France, December 22, 1989: Irish playwright, novelist, and poet Samuel Beckett dies, aged 83.

Andy Warhol

Adieux: Farewell to Simone de Beauvoir

Paris, France, April 14, 1986: French author, existentialist philosopher, and feminist Simone de Beauvoir has died in Paris, the city of her birth, at 78 years of age.

Despite being brought up in a bourgeois Catholic household, de Beauvoir's father encouraged her intellectual development. In adolescence, she became convinced of two things: that there was no God, and that she would never marry or have children. She remained an unmarried atheist until her death.

After studying mathematics, literature, and languages, de Beauvoir obtained a philosophy degree from the Sorbonne in 1929. While at the Sorbonne she met fellow philosopher Jean-Paul Sartre—a student at the prestigious Ecole Normale Supérieure. Her relationship with Sartre, while not an exclusive one, lasted until his death in 1980.

De Beauvoir taught literature and philosophy until 1943, when she devoted herself to writing. Her works spanned many genres: fiction, philosophical treatises, essays, autobiography, and drama. Her novels include *She Came to Stay* (1943), *The Blood of Others* (1945), *All Men Are Mortal* (1946), and *The Mandarins* (1954), which earned her the prestigious French literary award, the Prix Goncourt. In the 1940s, she contributed as both editor and writer to the left-wing periodical *Les Temps Modernes*. *The Second Sex* (1949) is considered to be de Beauvoir's definitive work, and is now a classic feminist text. One of its basic premises is that women have been more affected by social conditioning than biology.

In many areas, de Beauvoir was ahead of her time. This is evident in her travel writing—*America Day by Day* (1954) and *The Long March* (1957), a fascinating account of her trip to China. Her later works focus on ageing and dying: *A Very Easy Death* (1964), which documents her mother's final illness; *The Coming of Age* (1970); and *A Farewell to Sartre* (1981).

Celebrated Pop Artist Andy Warhol Dies

New York, USA, February 22, 1987: The influential multimedia artist Andy Warhol has died today after undergoing routine gall bladder surgery. He was a contradictory and complicated human being—a detached introvert who courted fame and society, openly gay yet devoutly Catholic.

Warhol was born Andrew Warhola in Pittsburgh, Pennsylvania, on August 6, 1928. His parents were Slovakian immigrants. After high school, he obtained a fine arts degree from the Carnegie

> "SOMEBODY SAID TO ME, 'BUT THE BEATLES WERE ANTI-MATERIALISTIC.' THAT'S A HUGE MYTH. JOHN AND I USED TO SIT DOWN AND SAY, 'NOW, LET'S WRITE A SWIMMING POOL.'"
>
> PAUL McCARTNEY (B. 1942), ENGLISH MUSICIAN, MEMBER OF THE BEATLES, 1983

Institute of Technology in Pittsburgh. Throughout the 1950s, Warhol achieved a good deal of success as a commercial artist, his work appearing in top fashion magazines such as *Harper's Bazaar*, *Vogue*, and *Glamour*. He also began exhibiting in New York galleries.

In the early 1960s, the boundaries between "commercial art" and "art" began to blur when Warhol created his now-famous images of Campbell's Soup cans and Coca-Cola bottles. He set up a studio known as The Factory, which was literally a workshop that churned out hundreds of products. His favorite method was silkscreen. As well as pictures of consumer items, Warhol produced fascinating portraits of celebrities such as Marilyn Monroe, Mick Jagger, Elvis Presley, Elizabeth Taylor, Liza Minnelli, and Dennis Hopper.

Warhol was a producer of many avant-garde films, including *Chelsea Girls*, *Sleep*, *Empire*, *My Hustler*, and *Lonesome Cowboys*. He was also the author of several books and founded *Interview* magazine.

In 1968, Valerie Solanas shot Warhol in the chest because he rejected one of her screenplays. Warhol nearly died and was never quite the same afterward, physically or emotionally.

Van Gogh's *Starry Night over the Rhone* reflects the night sky over Arles.

Van Gogh's *Irises* Sells for Art Auction Record

New York, USA, July 11, 1987: *Irises* by Dutch painter Vincent Van Gogh went to auction at Sotheby's today, fetching the astonishing price of US$53 million (including commission), making it the world's most expensive painting to date.

It went for twice the amount expected, and broke the record achieved in March this year by another Van Gogh painting, *Sunflowers*, which was sold to a Japanese businessman for US$39.9 million.

Van Gogh is considered one of the greatest European painters, but he was little appreciated during his lifetime. He often could barely make ends meet, and

Achievements in the Arts

Key Structures
Abteiburg Museum, Monchen-Gladbach, Germany
Asian Games Village, New Delhi, India
Cathedral St Paul, Abidjan, Ivory Coast
Chiang Kai-Shek Memorial Hall, Taipei, Taiwan
Gandhi Labour Institute, Ahmedabad, India
Hajj Jeddah Terminal, Jeddah, Saudi Arabia
Hotel Il Palazzo, Fukuoka, Japan
Hysolar Research Building, Stuttgart, Germany
King Faisal Mosque, Islamabad, Pakistan
L'Institut du Monde Arabe, Paris, France
Lloyds Building, London, England
National Commercial Bank HQ, Jeddah, Saudi Arabia
National Gallery of Canada, Ottawa, Canada
Netherlands Dance Theater, The Hague, Netherlands
Pyramide du Louvre, Paris, France
Santa Monica Place, Santa Monica, USA
Sri Lanka Parliament, Colombo, Sri Lanka
Yaama Mosque, Tahoua, Nigeria

Nobel Prize for Literature
1980 Czeslaw Milosz; 1981 Elias Canetti; 1982 Gabriel Garcia Marquez; 1983 William Golding; 1984 Jaroslav Seifert; 1985 Claude Simon; 1986 Akinwande Oluwole Soyinka; 1987 Joseph Brodsky; 1988 Naguib Mahfouz; 1989 Camilo Jose Cela.

Booker Prize for Fiction
1980 *Rites of Passage*, William Golding; 1981 *Midnight's Children*, Salman Rushdie; 1982 *Schindler's Ark*, Thomas Keneally; 1983 *Life & Times of Michael K*, J. M. Coetzee; 1984 *Hotel du Lac*, Anita Brookner; 1985 *The Bone People*, Keri Hulme; 1986 *The Old Devils*, Kingsley Amis; 1987 *Moon Tiger*, Penelope Lively; 1988 *Oscar and Lucinda*, Peter Carey; 1989 *The Remains of the Day*, Kazuo Ishiguro.

Pulitzer Prize for Fiction
1980 *The Executioner's Song*, Norman Mailer; 1981 *A Confederacy of Dunces*, John Kennedy Toole; 1982 *Rabbit is Rich*, John Updike; 1983 *The Color Purple*, Alice Walker; 1984 *Ironweed*, William Kennedy; 1985 *Foreign Affairs*, Alison Lurie; 1986 *Lonesome Dove*, Larry McMurtry; 1987 *A Summons to Memphis*, Peter Taylor; 1988 *Beloved*, Toni Morrison; 1989 *Breathing Lessons*, Anne Tyler.

Academy Awards
Best Film 1980 *Ordinary People*; 1981 *Chariots of Fire*; 1982 *Gandhi*; 1983 *Terms of Endearment*; 1984 *Amadeus*; 1985 *Out of Africa*; 1986 *Platoon*; 1987 *The Last Emperor*; 1988 *Rain Man*; 1989 *Driving Miss Daisy*.

BAFTAs
Best Film 1980 *The Elephant Man*; 1981 *Chariots of Fire*; 1982 *Gandhi*; 1983 *Educating Rita*; 1984 *The Killing Fields*; 1985 *The Purple Rose of Cairo*; 1986 *A Room with a View*; 1987 *Jean de Florette*; 1988 *The Last Emperor*; 1989 *Dead Poets' Society*.

suffered from a number of nervous maladies. Despite his afflictions, he managed to produce 900 paintings and over 1,000 drawings in the ten years prior to his suicide at age 37. *Irises* was one of Van Gogh's last works. Along with his famous *Starry Night*, Van Gogh painted *Irises* while he was a patient in a psychiatric institution in Saint Rémy de Provence in France.

Ayatollah Condemns Rushdie for Blasphemy

Tehran, Iran, February 14, 1989: Iran's Muslim spiritual leader, the Ayatollah Khomeini, has today issued a *fatwa* (religious edict) against Salman Rushdie, the author of *The Satanic Verses*. The Ayatollah claims that the book is a blasphemy against Islam and announced on Tehran Radio: "I inform the proud Muslim people of the world that the author of *The Satanic Verses* book, which is against Islam, the Prophet and the Koran, and all those involved in its publication who are aware of its content, are sentenced to death."

The author argues that he had no intention of blaspheming Islam, and that the offending passages were taken completely out of context. *The Satanic Verses*, published in September last year, is Rushdie's fourth novel. It won the Whitbread Novel Award and was short-listed for the Booker Prize.

Even before the Ayatollah's edict, the novel has provoked hostility from Muslims around the world and has been banned in several countries. The novel is part political satire, part magic realism, written in an innovative imaginative style. The character

Indian-born writer Salman Rushdie at his London home.

allegedly based on the prophet Muhammad is depicted in a humorous, somewhat irreverent way. What disturbed the Muslims even more was that in the brothel scene, the prostitutes were given the names of some of Muhammad's wives.

Salman Rushdie was born a Muslim in Bombay, India, was educated at Rugby and Cambridge, and is now a British citizen. Because he no longer practices the Muslim faith, he is considered an "apostate," an offense punishable by death. Now that the *fatwa* has been issued, Rushdie will be forced to go into hiding. Because of the controversy *The Satanic Verses* has generated, sales will probably soar.

English actor and director Laurence Olivier, and his wife, actress Joan Plowright.

Good Night, Sweet Prince

West Sussex, England, July 11, 1989: Arguably the greatest actor of the twentieth century, Sir Laurence Olivier has died today in Steyning, West Sussex, after a long illness. He was 82 years old.

Olivier was born in Dorking, Surrey, on May 22, 1907. Encouraged by his father, who was a clergyman, he studied at the Central School of Speech and Drama in London. After serving his apprenticeship with the Birmingham Repertory Company, he embarked on a career in the West End. He received critical acclaim for his roles in *Private Lives* (1930) and *Romeo and Juliet* (1935), and in between he made several movies. It was during the filming of *Fire over England* (1937) that he fell in love with co-star Vivien Leigh—they both left their respective partners and married three years later. He achieved Hollywood sex-symbol status in *Wuthering Heights* (1939) and *Rebecca* (1940).

Throughout the 1940s, Olivier established himself as a Shakespearean hero on both the London and New York stages. One of the highlights of his career, and there were many, was his film version of *Hamlet* (1948), for which he received an

Academy Award for Best Actor. He was also nominated for Best Director.

Olivier has been the recipient of every acting award available on both sides of the Atlantic (except for the Tony), became a Knight Bachelor in 1947, a Life Peer in 1970, and was given the Order of Merit in 1981. Even toward the end of his life, his volume of work was strong and steady. A new generation saw him in such movies as *Sleuth* (1972), *Marathon Man* (1976), *The Boys from Brazil* (1978), and *Brideshead Revisited* (1981) on television.

Sir Laurence is survived by his wife, actress Joan Plowright, and their three children, and a son by his first marriage to Jill Esmond.

Samuel Beckett Dies in Paris

Paris, France, December 22, 1989: Nobel Prize-winning Irish playwright, novelist, and poet Samuel Beckett has died in Paris of a lung condition, aged 83.

Beckett was born into a well-off Protestant family in Dublin in 1906. He was educated at Earlsford House School, the Portora Royal School in Enniskillen, and Trinity College. Upon receiving a BA in French and Italian in 1927, Beckett took up a teaching post at the Ecole Normale Supérieure in Paris, and became a friend and assistant to James Joyce. Throughout his life, Beckett would move between the cities of Dublin, Paris and London, but would spend most of his life in Paris.

His early works include a poem entitled *Whoroscope* (1930), and the novels *Dream of Fair to Middling Women* (1932), and *Murphy* (1938).

Beckett met his life partner Suzanne Descheveaux-Dumesnil in 1938, and worked for the French Resistance during World War II. After the war, he wrote mainly in French, including the novels *Molloy* (1951), *Malone Dies* (1951), and *The Unnamable* (1953).

Beckett's most acclaimed work is the absurdist play *Waiting for Godot*, first performed in Paris in 1953. It features two tramps—Vladimir and Estragon (inspired by Charlie Chaplin and Buster Keaton)—and depicts the despair and meaninglessness of modern life. Other important plays include *Endgame* (1957) and *Happy Days* (1960).

Beckett was awarded the Nobel Prize for Literature in 1969, but he refused to attend the presentation ceremony. He continued to produce quality work until the end of his life.

Simone de Beauvoir

Björn Borg

Cool Swede Björn Borg Retires from Tennis

Stockholm, Sweden, January 23, 1983: Regarded as the world's greatest tennis player, 26-year-old Björn Borg has today announced that he is retiring from the sport, although he had earlier stated that he would be playing at Wimbledon and the US Open this year.

Borg is leaving the competition at the peak of his career, but he told a Swedish newspaper that, "Tennis has to be fun if you are to get to the top, and I don't feel that way anymore. That is why I quit."

Borg has reached the point of burnout, and his is a classic case of "too much, too soon." Born in Södertälje, Sweden, on June 6, 1956, Borg began playing professionally at 17. Since then he has won a total of 11 Grand Slam singles titles: The

"ONE OF THE MANY PLEASURES OF OLD AGE IS GIVING THINGS UP."

MALCOLM MUGGERIDGE (1903–1990), AMERICAN JOURNALIST AND CRITIC, ON AGEING

"FOOTBALL ISN'T A MATTER OF LIFE AND DEATH—IT'S MUCH MORE IMPORTANT THAN THAT."

BILL SHANKY (1914–1981), BRITISH FOOTBALL COACH AND MANAGER, 1981

French Open from 1974 to 1975 and 1978 to 1981, and Wimbledon for five consecutive years from 1976 to 1980, defeating the likes of Ilie Nastase, Jimmy Connors, and John McEnroe. Between 1977 and 1981, Borg periodically held the ranking of World Number 1 player for a total of 109 weeks.

Famed for his heavy top-spin, two-handed backhand, and strong baseline game, Borg kept his cool while some of his opponents lost theirs, earning him the nickname "Ice Borg." He was never able to crack the US Open, and blames it on the electric lights because the games are televised at night.

During his career, Borg earned over US$3,500,000 in prize money.

Torvill and Dean Shine at Olympics

Sarajevo, Yugoslavia, February 19, 1984: The closing ceremony of the XIVth Winter Olympics was held today in Sarajevo. It was the first time the Winter Games have been held in a Communist country, and everyone has praised the citizens of Sarajevo for their friendliness and hospitality.

The East German team led the final medal tally, followed by the USSR, the USA, Finland, and Sweden.

The undisputed stars of the Games were the British figure-skating duo Jayne Torvill and Christopher Dean. Their graceful and sensitive ice-dancing to Ravel's *Bolero* on Valentine's Day—February 14—gave them a total of twelve scores of 6.0 for free dance and nine scores of 6.0 for artistic

Jayne Torvill and Christopher Dean performing at Wembley Arena.

time out

Traffic congestion in the suburbs surrounding New York was attributed by planners to the dispersal of corporate headquarters, soaring housing costs pushing people further from metropolitan centers, and the increase in families with two income earners, both making car journeys to work.

impression, earning them an uproarious standing ovation as well as a gold medal. When interviewed, Dean said, "It's what we've been working for I don't know how many years. Tonight we reached the pinnacle."

Torvill, a former secretary, and Dean, a former policeman, are both from Nottingham, and have been skating together since 1975. Their first Olympic competition was at Lake Placid in 1980, when they reached fifth place, and in the same year they came fourth in the World Championships. Since then, they have come first in every competition they have entered. Their blending of showmanship, innovation, and technical prowess has enabled them take the sport to an entirely new and exciting level.

The silver medal in their event went to Natalya Bestemyanova and Andrei Bukin from the Soviet Union, and the bronze medal went to Judy Blumberg and Michael Seibert from the USA.

Nearly 100 Die in Two Football Tragedies

Brussels, Belgium, May 29, 1985: At today's European Cup final between Liverpool and Juventus (of Italy) at Heysel Stadium near Brussels, 39 Juventus fans were killed and 350 injured when rioting broke out.

Shortly before the match was scheduled to start, a gang of Liverpool fans, fueled by copious amounts of alcohol, pushed their way into the neutral section of the ground, occupied mainly by Italians and Belgians, and separated only by a weak fence. When the Juventus fans tried to get out of the way, blind panic ensued. A wall collapsed, and people were trampled in the stampede. Riot police and the Red Cross were summoned to deal with the chaos and mass injuries.

Key Events

A crowd of 58,000 people had attended the match, which went ahead despite objections. Juventus beat Liverpool 1-0.

BBC reporter Peter Jones said, "This has nothing to do with sport. This is violence. This is death."

Inadequate security systems and police protection, as well as the availability of alcohol, are partly to blame for the tragedy. What makes today's incident appear even more catastrophic is that just a few weeks ago, on May 11, 56 people died and hundreds were injured when a fire broke out at the Valley Parade Stadium at Bradford in Yorkshire. It was the last match of the season, and a crowd of 11,000 had gathered to watch Bradford City play Lincoln City.

Just before half-time, the fire began as just a small flame, and within minutes it had engulfed the roof and the main stands. The intense heat could be felt on the opposite side of the ground.

Pandemonium erupted as spectators rushed for the nearest exit, which was secured by a padlock. Most of the victims

Bradford City's Valley Parade Stadium after the main stand caught fire.

were either very old or very young. It is believed that a burning cigarette may have caused the deadly inferno.

Tragic Death of Influential Fashion Designer

Coventry, England, September 17, 1985: Highly influential fashion and interior designer Laura Ashley has died today. A long-time resident of France, Ashley had been visiting her daughter in the Cotswolds when she fell down the stairs on September 7, on her sixtieth birthday. Rushed to hospital, she remained in a coma for ten days before passing away.

Ashley was born Laura Mountney in Merthyr Tydfil, in South Wales in 1925. Later, her family moved to London, and in 1948 she married stockbroker Bernard Ashley, who became both her collaborator and business partner. The couple started their fashion empire at the kitchen table of their small Pimlico flat, producing silk-screened tea towels, mats, and scarves, and selling them to boutiques and shops in London.

The couple's decision to set up a design and manufacturing business came about when Laura was unable to find Victorian-style

Fabrics being stacked for display in a Laura Ashley retail store.

printed fabrics for her patchworks. They moved from London to Kent, and then set up their business enterprise at the Old Railway House in Carno, Wales.

In the mid-1970s, a "Laura Ashley dress" was considered the epitome of nostalgia and femininity, and Bernard Ashley joked, "It was amazing when Laura had the whole world dressed as milkmaids." Enjoying phenomenal success, retail shops quickly opened all across the UK and Europe, and her products were sold in department stores in Japan, Australia, and Canada. The first US store opened in San Francisco in 1974.

During the past decade, Laura Ashley had expanded her lines to include perfumes and home furnishings. At the time of her death, her company employed 4,000 people worldwide. She is survived by her husband and four children.

Jane Fonda

Fonda Gets Physical

Los Angeles, USA, December, 1985: Jane Fonda has already enjoyed a number of incarnations in one lifetime: daughter of Hollywood royalty, actress, political activist, and now exercise guru. For the last few years she has been at the vanguard of America's interest in health and fitness, and its obsession with the body beautiful.

Fonda's new career began in 1981 with *Jane Fonda's Workout Book*, which was then adapted for video. The original *Workout* (1982) has been the biggest-selling home video of the past two years. This was followed by the more strenuous *Workout Challenge* (1983)—definitely not for the fainthearted—and the *Pregnancy, Birth, and Recovery Workout* (1983).

Her latest video, released this month, is an update of the original and is called *The New Workout*. It is 90 minutes long, consisting of two parts: 35 minutes for beginners and 55 minutes for the more experienced, and includes the latest scientifically approved stretching, toning, aerobic, and strengthening exercises.

Key Events

Brussels, Belgium, May 29, 1985: Rioting at Heysel Stadium leaves 39 soccer fans dead.

London, England, July 7, 1985: German tennis star Boris Becker, 17, becomes the youngest Wimbledon singles winner.

UK, September 17, 1985: Laura Ashley dies after a fall in her home.

Australia, UK, USA, December 31, 1985: Compact discs (CDs) are gaining in popularity.

Darwin, Australia, February 7, 1986: Lindy Chamberlain is released from jail.

UK/France, February 20, 1986: Plans to build a rail tunnel beneath the English Channel are unveiled.

Surrey, England, March 31, 1986: Fire destroys a portion of Henry VIII's palace, Hampton Court, leaving one dead and priceless relics destroyed.

Mexico, June 29, 1986: Argentina wins the World Cup.

Fremantle, Australia, February 4, 1987: *Stars and Stripes* reclaims the America's Cup for the USA.

Geneva, Switzerland, April 2, 1987: The Duchess of Windsor's jewelry collection is auctioned.

London, England, July 5, 1987: Pat Cash beats Ivan Lendl, 7-6, 6-2, 7-5, becoming the first Australian to win the men's singles at Wimbledon since John Newcombe.

New Zealand, August 1, 1987: Maori becomes an official language. The Maori Language Commission is established.

Australia, January 26, 1988: Australia celebrates its bicentenary, the anniversary of the arrival of the First Fleet.

Calgary, Canada, February 27, 1988: The 25th Winter Olympics draw to a close.

USA, March, 1988: A potent new form of cocaine, called "crack," is sweeping through urban areas around the country.

Seoul, South Korea, October 2, 1988: The 24th Olympic Games end.

Moscow, USSR, January 30, 1989: Communism, long trumpeted to remove disparities between rich and poor, has 43 million people living in poverty, as finally acknowledged by the government.

Altamira, Brazil, February 21, 1989: Indian tribal leaders and ecologists gather to stop a proposed hydroelectric dam that will flood their traditional lands.

Eastern Europe, December, 1989: Poland, East Germany, Hungary, Czechoslovakia, and Romania all move toward democratic processes.

Diego Maradona

"IF MEN HAD TO HAVE BABIES THEY WOULD ONLY EVER HAVE ONE EACH."

DIANA, PRINCESS OF WALES (1961–1997), WIFE OF PRINCE CHARLES OF ENGLAND, 1984

"IF SOMEONE ASKS FOR A SOFT DRINK AT A PARTY, WE NO LONGER THINK HE IS A WIMP."

EDWINA CURRIE (B. 1946), ENGLISH POLITICIAN, 1988

Lindy Chamberlain Released from Jail

Darwin, Australia, February 7, 1986: After spending over three years behind bars, 38-year-old Lindy Chamberlain has been released today from a Darwin prison. Five days ago, a matinee jacket, worn by her baby Azaria on the night that she disappeared, was discovered close to a dingo's habitat at Ayers Rock (Uluru). This finding corroborates Mrs Chamberlain's statement of August 16, 1980, that a dingo had indeed taken her baby.

Lindy Chamberlain and her husband, Michael, a Seventh Day Adventist pastor, made international headlines in August 1980 when their two-month-old baby vanished, presumably taken by a dingo. After an intensive search of the area, the baby's body was never found. The first judicial inquiry agreed with Chamberlain's statement, but further investigations found possible traces of blood in the Chamberlains' car. There was no indication that the baby's jumpsuit had been in a dingo's mouth.

Theories abounded as to why Lindy Chamberlain would have murdered her child. Possible motives ranged from post-natal depression to religious ritual killing.

At the end of the trial, which lasted from September 13 to October 29, 1982, the jury found Chamberlain guilty of murdering her daughter and sentenced her to life imprisonment. Her husband was found guilty as an accessory. Less than a month later, on November 17, 1982, Lindy Chamberlain gave birth to her fourth child, Kahlia. She was released on bail, but after an unsuccessful appeal to the Federal Court in April 1983, she returned to prison. The Chamberlains' appeal to the High Court in early 1984 also proved fruitless.

In November 1985, barrister John Bryson's book *Evil Angels* was published, in which he proposed that the Chamberlains were innocent.

Millions of supporters around the world are rejoicing with Lindy Chamberlain as she returns home to her husband Michael, sons Aidan (12), Reagan (10), and daughter Kahlia (3). However, it will be a long time before the Chamberlains' lives return to normal.

Argentina Defeats West Germany in World Cup

Mexico City, Mexico, June 29, 1986: Watched by a capacity crowd of 115,000 at Estadio Azteca (Aztec Stadium), Argentina today defeated West Germany 3–2 in the final of the Thirteenth FIFA World Cup.

Originally, Colombia had been selected to host the Cup, but they pulled out in 1983 due to financial difficulties. Although the United States was especially keen to host the event, Mexico City was chosen, making it the first city to host the World Cup twice (the first time was in 1970). Mexico City is still recovering from the devastating effects of the earthquake of September 1985 that killed thousands of people, but the Cup still went ahead.

A total of 121 teams participated, and 24 teams went to the finals. Making their World Cup debut were Canada and Iraq.

In the gripping quarter-finals, France beat Brazil, West Germany beat Mexico, Belgium beat Spain, and in what was undeniably the most exciting match of the entire competition, Argentina beat England 2–1. The undisputed star of this match was Argentina's Diego Maradona, who scored a goal using his fist instead of his head. The match referees missed this controversial goal, which has already been dubbed the "Hand of God." Later in the second half, Maradona scored another impressive goal to seal the victory.

In the semi-finals of the Cup, West Germany defeated a valiant France 2–0, and Argentina beat Belgium 2–0, Maradona again showing his brilliance. This was an important win for Argentina, because they had lost to Belgium in 1982.

Maradona was awarded the Golden Ball for Best Player, and England's Gary Lineker got the Golden Boot for Top Scorer (six goals). This year's Cup has also become famous for the popularization of the "Mexican wave."

Stars and Stripes Reclaims America's Cup

Fremantle, Australia, February 4, 1987: Jubilant San Diego yachtsman Dennis Conner has won back the America's Cup for the USA, with a 1 minute and 59 second victory over Australia's *Kookaburra III*. "It's a great moment for

Dennis Conner at the helm of *Stars and Stripes*.

Baseball *World Series* 1980 Philadelphia (National League); 1981 Los Angeles (NL); 1982 St Louis (NL); 1983 Baltimore (American League); 1984 Detroit (AL); 1985 Kansas City (AL); 1986 New York (NL); 1987 Minnesota (AL); 1988 Los Angeles (NL); 1989 Oakland (AL).

Cycling *Tour de France* 1980 J. Zoetemelk; 1981–1982 B. Hinault; 1983–1984 L. Fignon; 1985 B. Hinault; 1986 G. LeMond; 1987 S. Roche; 1988 P. Delgado; 1989 G. LeMond.

Football *American Super Bowl* 1980 Pittsburgh; 1981 Oakland; 1982 San Francisco; 1983 Washington; 1984 LA Raiders; 1985 San Francisco; 1986 Chicago; 1987 NY Giants; 1988 Washington; 1989 San Francisco. *World Cup Soccer* 1982 Italy; 1986 Argentina.

Golf *US Masters* 1980 S. Ballesteros; 1981 T. Watson; 1982 C. Stadler; 1983 S. Ballesteros; 1984 B. Crenshaw; 1985 B. Langer; 1986 J. Nicklaus; 1987 L. Mize; 1988 S. Lyle; 1989 N. Faldo.

Horse Racing *Epsom Derby* 1980 Henbit; 1981 Shergar; 1982 Golden Fleece; 1983 Teenoso; 1984 Secreto; 1985 Slip Anchor; 1986 Shahrastani; 1987 Reference Point; 1988 Kahyasi; 1989 Nashwan. *Kentucky Derby* 1980 Genuine Risk; 1981 Pleasant Colony; 1982 Gato Del Sol; 1983 Sunny's Halo; 1984 Swale; 1985 Spend A Buck; 1986 Ferdinand; 1987 Alysheba; 1988 Winning Colors; 1989 Sunday Silence. *Melbourne Cup* 1980 Beldale Ball; 1981 Just A Dash; 1982 Gurner's Lane; 1983 Kiwi; 1984 Black Knight; 1985 What A Nuisance; 1986 At Talaq; 1987 Kensei; 1988 Empire Rose; 1989 Tawriffic.

Ice Hockey *Stanley Cup* 1980 New York; 1981 New York; 1982 New York; 1983 New York; 1984 Edmonton; 1985 Edmonton; 1986 Montreal; 1987 Edmonton; 1988 Edmonton; 1989 Calgary.

Marathon *Boston, Men's* 1980 B. Rodgers; 1981 T. Seko; 1982 A. Salazar; 1983 G. Meyer; 1984 G. Smith; 1985 G. Smith; 1986 R. de Castella; 1987 T. Seko; 1988 I. Hussein; 1989 A. Mekonnen; *Women's* 1980 J. Gareau; 1981 A. Roe; 1982 C. Teske; 1983 J. Benoit; 1984 L. Moller; 1985 L. Larsen-Weidenbach; 1986 I. Kristiansen; 1987 R. Mota; 1988 R. Mota; 1989 I. Kristiansen.

Sailing *America's Cup* 1980 *Freedom*; 1983 *Australia II*; 1987 *Stars and Stripes*; 1988 *Stars and Stripes*.

Tennis *Australian Open, Men's Singles* 1980 B. Teacher; 1981–1982 J. Kriek; 1983–1984 M. Wilander; 1985 S. Edberg; 1986 no competition; 1987 S. Edberg; 1988 M. Wilander; 1989 I. Lendl; *Women's Singles* 1980 H. Mandlikova; 1981 M. Navratilova; 1982 C. Evert-Lloyd; 1983 M. Navratilova; 1984 C. Evert-Lloyd; 1985 M. Navratilova; 1986 no competition; 1987 H. Mandlikova; 1988–1989 S. Graf. *Roland-Garros Tournament (French Open), Men's Singles* 1980–1981 B. Borg; 1982 M. Wilander; 1983 Y. Noah; 1984 I. Lendl; 1985 M. Wilander; 1986–1987 I. Lendl; 1988 M. Wilander; 1989 M. Chang; *Women's Singles* 1980 C. Evert-Lloyd; 1981 H. Mandlikova; 1982 M. Navratilova; 1983 C. Evert Lloyd; 1984 M. Navratilova; 1985–1986 C. Evert-Lloyd; 1987–1988 S. Graf; 1989 A. Sanchez Vicario. *US Open, Men's Singles* 1980–1981 J. McEnroe; 1982–1983 J. Connors; 1984 J. McEnroe; 1985–1987 I. Lendl; 1988 M. Wilander; 1989 B. Becker; *Women's Singles* 1980 C. Evert-Lloyd; 1981 T. Austin; 1982 C. Evert-Lloyd; 1983–1984 M. Navratilova; 1985 H. Mandlikova; 1986–1987 M. Navratilova; 1988–1989 S. Graf. *Wimbledon, Gentlemen's Singles* 1980 B. Borg; 1981 J. McEnroe; 1982 J. Connors; 1983–1984 J. McEnroe; 1985–1986 B. Becker; 1987 P. Cash; 1988 S. Edberg; 1989 B. Becker, *Ladies' Singles* 1980 E. Goolagong Cawley; 1981 C. Evert-Lloyd; 1982–1987 M. Navratilova; 1988–1989 S. Graf.

America and a great moment for the *Stars and Stripes* crew, and a great moment for Dennis Conner," he exclaimed.

Conner had won the Auld Mug in 1980, but was stunned, along with millions of others, when as skipper of the *Liberty* in 1983 he lost to challenger *Australia II*, breaking the USA's 132-year winning streak. It was the longest winning streak in the history of any sport.

Most Australians will fondly remember September 26, 1983, when *Australia II*, representing the Royal Perth Yacht Club and skippered by John Bertrand, won the Cup. It was a day of celebration, and the Prime Minister Bob Hawke famously said, "Anyone who sacks a bloke because he doesn't turn up for work today is a bum." Syndicate owner Alan Bond had been trying to win the Cup for years. For the 1983 challenge, he enlisted the services of designer Ben Lexcen, who came up with the innovative and controversial "winged keel." At first Bertrand was skeptical about the new design, until he saw how well it performed.

The late Duchess of Windsor.

Duchess of Windsor's Jewels Fetch Millions

Geneva, Switzerland, April 2, 1987: At a Sotheby's auction on the shores of Lake Geneva, the jewelry collection belonging to the late Duchess of Windsor has sold for £31 million (US$50 million). It was originally estimated that the jewels would fetch about £5 million (US$8 million). More than 1,000 people attended the two-day event, and several hundred gathered at Sotheby's rooms in New York to bid from a distance.

As well as her beloved pug dogs, the Duchess of Windsor's trademarks were her jewels, especially her favorite Cartier panther necklace and brooch set and her flamingo brooch. However, the highest priced item at the auction was a stunning 31-carat diamond ring that sold for close to £2 million (US$3.15 million). Actress Elizabeth Taylor purchased a diamond brooch for £400,000 (US$560,000). Another well-known actress is believed to have bought a sapphire pendant.

The proceeds of the auction will be donated to the Pasteur Institute in Paris to be used for medical research.

The Duchess of Windsor died almost a year ago on April 24, 1986. She was 90 years old, and for many years had lived in isolation and infirmity in Paris, cared for

by nurses and servants. At her request, the funeral was very simple. It was attended by members of the Royal Family, with the exception of the Queen Mother, with whom she had a problematic relationship. The Duchess of Windsor is buried at the Royal Mausoleum at Frogmore in Windsor, next to her husband, the Duke of Windsor, who died in 1972. The couple had no children.

Half a century ago, the Duchess of Windsor (then Mrs Wallis Simpson, an American divorcee) and the Duke (then King Edward VIII) captured the interest and imagination of the world when they decided to marry. In order to do so, the King was forced to abdicate the throne to his younger brother, George VI.

Surprise Packages Feature at Winter Olympics

Calgary, Canada, February 28, 1988: The 15th Winter Olympics came to an end today, and they will be best remembered for two unusual competitors: Eddie "the Eagle" Edwards from Great Britain, and the Jamaican bobsled team.

Edwards, a plasterer from Cheltenham, had never done ski-jumping until the 1987 World Championships, in which he placed at number 55. He qualified for the Olympics because he was the only person from his country to try out. Although he came in last place in both the 70 m and 90 m jumps, the Mr Magoo look-alike thoroughly enjoyed himself and entertained spectators with his comical style.

The other novelty of the Games was the debut of the Jamaican bobsled team. The members of the team had never attempted bobsledding before preparing for the Games, let alone even seen snow, but they were all accomplished athletes. Even though they came last, they won admiration for their good sportsmanship and adventurous spirit.

Other highlights of these Games included the sensational East German figure skater Katarina Witt, and Matti Nykänen of Finland who took home three gold medals for ski-jumping.

The USSR led the final medal tally, followed by East Germany, Switzerland, Finland, and Sweden.

Ben Johnson Stripped of Gold Medal at Olympics

Seoul, South Korea, October 2, 1988: The closing ceremony of the 24th Olympic Games was held today in Seoul.

Before competition began, politics reared its ugly head when North Korea boycotted the Games because Seoul was unwilling for them to co-host. Cuba and Ethiopia followed suit. On a brighter note, it was the first time since 1976 that teams from both the USA and the USSR participated simultaneously (the USA boycotted in 1980, the USSR in 1984).

However, it was drugs that tarnished this year's events, most notably the disqualification of 26-year-old Canadian sprinter Ben Johnson. Jamaican-born Johnson had won bronze in Los Angeles in 1984, and was looking forward to beating his arch-rival, American sprinter Carl Lewis, in the 100 m. He defeated Lewis in world-record time, but was forced to give up his gold medal when he tested positive for performance-enhancing drugs. Nine other athletes were also disqualified for drug use.

The other name on everyone's lips was American female sprinter Florence Griffith Joyner ("Flo Jo"), who won an impressive three gold medals and one silver. East German cyclist Christa Rothenburger also performed an exceptional feat—she is the first person to have won medals for both summer and winter Olympics in the same year. Grand Slam winner Steffi Graf defeated Gabriella Sabatini in the women's tennis final—it was the first time in 64 years that tennis was included as an Olympic sport.

The USSR led the final medal count, followed by East Germany, the USA, South Korea, and West Germany.

Florence Griffith Joyner

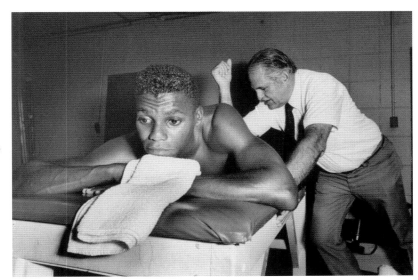

Olympic runner Carl Lewis receiving a massage during training for the Seoul Olympics.

John Major

Nation Celebrates as Mandela is Freed

Cape Town, South Africa, February 11: All over South Africa today the people are celebrating. In Soweto, a few minutes after 4 p.m., the cry went up *"Buya Mandela!"* ("Come Mandela!"), which can only mean one thing: the era of apartheid is finally coming to an end after 42 years.

It was 27 years and 7 months ago that Nelson Mandela, the central symbol of the country's anti-apartheid movement and a man who would become the most famous political prisoner of the twentieth century, was convicted of treason and sabotage, and sent to the isolated maximum security prison on Robben Island off the coast from Cape Town. Mandela, who is now 71, walked to freedom accompanied by his wife, Winnie. He raised his fist in a triumphant gesture, but it was clear that the 27 years had taken their toll. He is no longer a young man.

At a rally today in Cape Town, he told an excited and happy crowd that he had always been a "humble servant" of the people and that he would continue to serve them. He added with passion: "We have waited too long for our freedom. We can no longer wait."

It seems likely now that apartheid in South Africa will be dismantled and that the country's huge black majority will, within a few years, gain effective political control. It is widely anticipated that Mandela, who has given so much to the cause, will become the country's first black African president.

Only nine days ago President F. W. de Klerk suspended executions, removed censorship from the press and the media,

> *"I HAVE CHERISHED THE IDEAL OF A DEMOCRATIC AND FREE SOCIETY IN WHICH ALL PERSONS LIVE TOGETHER IN HARMONY AND WITH EQUAL OPPORTUNITIES …IF NEEDS BE, IT IS AN IDEAL FOR WHICH I AM PREPARED TO DIE."*
>
> NELSON MANDELA (b. 1918), SOUTH AFRICAN POLITICAL ACTIVIST, AND FIRST PRESIDENT TO BE ELECTED IN FULLY-REPRESENTATIVE DEMOCRATIC ELECTIONS, ON HIS RELEASE FROM PRISON, 1990

With his wife, Winnie, Nelson Mandela walks in freedom.

lifted a long-term ban on the African National Congress, and announced a range of reforms to many of the country's overt racist laws. A new South Africa is emerging.

Invasion of Kuwait May Lead to War in the Gulf

Kuwait City, Kuwait, August 8, 1990: Iraq's President Saddam Hussein has today installed a provisional governor in Kuwait and has officially annexed the tiny country.

Saddam described the Iraqi invasion six days ago as a genuine "liberation" from the Kuwaiti Emir, claiming that Kuwait historically was an Iraqi province that had been unreasonably cut off from the home country by British imperialism, and also accusing the tiny Gulf state of engaging in "economic warfare" by drilling at an angle (the technical term is "slant drilling") so that Kuwaiti oilfields were actually drawing their oil from the Iraqi side of the border.

World leaders immediately condemned Saddam's act of aggression, while both

time out

Zsa Zsa Gabor spent a weekend in jail for slapping a Beverly Hills police officer in 1989. She earned the sentence by failing to perform the terms of her probation: 120 hours of community service at a shelter for homeless women.

the Arab League and the United Nations Security Council have rejected Iraq's claims and have demanded that the Iraqis withdraw from Kuwait. Two days ago the Security Council ramped up its criticism by passing Resolution 661, which imposes economic sanctions on Iraq. While intense efforts are being made to negotiate a diplomatic solution to the crisis, many fear that war now looks inevitable.

Germany Celebrates Reunification

Bonn, Germany, October 3: Following the first and only free elections in East Germany (the German Democratic Republic) on March 18 this year, it was decided that both East and West Germany, and the divided city of Berlin, should reunite to form a Greater Germany. This was achieved when the former East German states of Brandenburg, Saxony, Thuringia, and Pomerania formally joined West Germany (the Federal Republic of Germany).

Today the nation celebrates its "reunification" (the term was chosen because the initial unification of the German states occurred in 1871), and the new enlarged country will continue to be part of both NATO and the European Union. Germany is now the largest and potentially the most powerful nation in Europe. This move is the culmination of a process that started with the collapse of Communism in Eastern Europe and saw the Berlin Wall torn down in November 1989.

West German Chancellor Helmut Kohl plans to hold elections later this year.

Chancellor Helmut Kohl.

Western Europe, January 25: Hurricane force winds cause havoc. Forty-seven die in the UK and up to three million trees are uprooted.

Cape Town, South Africa, February 11: Nelson Mandela is released from jail after 27 years.

Managua, Nicaragua, February 25: Violeta Chamorro defeats Sandinista leader Daniel Ortega in the first free elections since 1979.

Canada, March 11–September 26: Disagreement regarding land between the Mohawk Natives and Quebec results in the Oka Crisis.

Vilnius, Lithuania, March 11: The tiny Baltic republic declares itself independent, after half a century of Soviet rule.

Australia, March 26: The Labor government of Bob Hawke wins a record 4th term.

Kathmandu, Nepal, April 8: King Birendra lifts a 30-year ban on political parties and agrees to end the country's feudal-style rule.

Moscow, May 29: "Radical" Boris Yeltsin is elected president of the Russian republic, challenging the power of Mikhail Gorbachev.

Iran, June 22: A massive earthquake in the northwest of the country leaves 40,000 dead and 100,000 injured.

Mecca, Saudi Arabia, July 2: One thousand four hundred pilgrims are crushed to death in a tunnel leading to the Islamic world's holiest site.

Kuwait, August 2: Iraqi troops invade, meeting with little resistance.

South Africa, August 24: Following two weeks of violence that has left 500 dead, a state of emergency is imposed on 27 townships.

Germany, October 3: East and West Germany reunify.

Jerusalem, Israel, October 8: Israeli police shoot dead 21 Arabs during a riot at the Western Wall and the Dome of the Rock.

New Zealand, November 2: National party wins election; Ruth Richardson becomes first woman Minister of Finance; widespread cuts to welfare benefits are soon announced.

Paris, France, November 19: The Cold War officially ends with 22 heads of state agreeing to dismantle their arsenals. There is to be a significant reduction in conventional weaponry.

London, England, November 27: John Major becomes leader of the Conservatives following Margaret Thatcher's resignation five days ago.

Poland, December 9: The founder of the Solidarity union Lech Walesa is elected president, winning 74.4 percent of the vote.

Gulf War Ceasefire

Kuwait City, Kuwait, February 28: Scenes of wild celebration erupted in Kuwait City today with the formal announcement of an end to the war with Iraq. The forces of Iraqi dictator Saddam Hussein have been forced to retreat, and the independence of the tiny Gulf state has been re-established.

Shortly after the Iraqi forces overran Kuwait back on August 2, 1990, it was met with strong condemnation by world leaders, and the UN Security Council demanded the immediate withdrawal of Iraqi troops. In a rare show of agreement, the Arab League also demanded withdrawal. At the time it was seen by many commentators as a decision to protect the West's vital oil interests in Saudi Arabia from a bellicose Iraq.

By August 7, 1990, in an action called Operation Desert Shield, US troops had been moved to Saudi Arabia, and the following day both the USS *Dwight D. Eisenhower* and USS *Independence* were stationed in the Gulf and ready for action. United Nations Resolution 678, which was passed on November 29, gave Iraq until January 15, 1991 to withdraw from the region, and a coalition of 660,000 troops (of whom some 74 percent were American) was formed. After diplomatic attempts at a peaceful settlement failed, the coalition launched a massive air campaign on January 17, using a completely new generation of weapons such as smart bombs, cluster bombs, and daisy cutters to decimate the Iraqi forces. By February 22, Iraq had agreed to a ceasefire, and by February 24 Kuwait City had been re-captured by coalition forces, although the Iraqi troops set the Kuwaiti oil fields alight as they made their retreat.

The actual war between the coalition and the Iraqi forces lasted a total of six weeks. It was a triumph for both the US Chief of Staff General Colin Powell and for General Stormin' Norman Schwarzkopf, who led the coalition forces. Today President George Bush officially declared a ceasefire and announced to the world that Kuwait had been liberated.

George Bush and Mikhail Gorbachev in conference.

Norman Schwarzkopf

USSR Dissolved

Moscow, Russia, December 25: Mikhail Sergeyevich Gorbachev, arguably Russia's greatest post-war leader, gave his people an unusual and surprising Christmas present today when he announced that he was resigning as leader and that the USSR was now officially dissolved.

Mikhail Gorbachev's resignation marks the culmination of a remarkable political career. He graduated from Moscow State University with a degree in Law, and joined the Communist Party in 1952. In 1985, he was appointed as General Secretary of the Party and during his period of office he introduced innovative programs of *perestroika* (reconstruction) and *glasnost* (openness), radically alter the USSR and prepare it for the collapse of communism, be hailed as the *Time* magazine Man of the Year (1988), win a Nobel Prize for Peace (1990), and effectively end the Cold War.

Gorbachev is a rare man of vision who initiated events that are transforming Europe and will lead, hopefully, to an era of peace and harmony between East and West. His resignation demonstrates that the forces unleashed in Eastern Europe—of democracy and independence—are likely to change the face of the region.

New Independent States after Dissolution of the USSR
☐ Independent state

Kuwait, January 16: A US-led coalition launches an offensive to liberate Kuwait following Iraq's failure to comply with UN deadline for withdrawal.
Mogadishu, Somalia, January 27: General Mohammed Siad Barre flees the capital after 21 years of brutal rule over the East African country.
Bangkok, Thailand, February 23: With King Bhumibol's support, the military overthrows the government. Martial law is declared. This is the 19th coup attempt since 1932.

Kuwait, February 28: US President Bush announces the end of the war to liberate Kuwait.
Los Angeles, USA, March 15: Four police officers are indicted for the beating of Rodney King. The event was captured on video, sparking an outcry throughout the country.
Tbilisi, Georgia, April 9: Independence from Moscow is declared after 70 years of Soviet rule. 90 percent of voters support the change.

Bangladesh, April 30: A massive cyclone hits from the Bay of Bengal.
India, May 21: Former PM Rajiv Gandhi is assassinated. Tamil separatists are suspected.
Ethiopia, May 25: After Stalinist dictator Mengistu Haile Mariam flees, Israeli forces airlift 15,000 black Jews, known as Falashas, out of the country in 21 hours.
South Africa, June 17: The law classifying citizens by race is repealed.

Ljubljana, Slovenia, June 29: Yugoslavia is headed toward civil war. Slovenia declares independence.
Moscow, USSR, August 21: An attempted coup by hardliners opposed to reforms fails in the face of popular opposition. Mikhail Gorbachev is released from house arrest in the Crimea after 60 hours; Boris Yeltsin consolidates his position.
USSR, September 5: The Congress of People's Deputies votes for the dissolution of The Union of Soviet Socialist Republics.

Madrid, Spain, October 4: The Madrid protocol governing Antarctica comes into effect, designating the continent as a natural reserve, devoted to peace and science.
Phnom Penh, Cambodia, November 14: Prince Norodom Sihanouk returns after 13 years in exile, following the signing of a peace treaty in Paris on October 23.
Moscow, Russia, December 25: Mikhail Gorbachev resigns the presidency of the USSR.

William Jefferson (Bill) Clinton

"TODAY WE HAVE CLOSED THE BOOK ON APARTHEID."

F. W. DE KLERK (B. 1936), SOUTH AFRICAN PRESIDENT, ON A SUCCESSFUL REFERENDUM TO IMPLEMENT GOVERNMENT REFORM, 1992

"THE REGION IS UNDERGOING ETHNIC CLEANSING."

BROADCAST FROM SERBIAN RADIO, ON BOSNIA-HERZOGOVINA, 1992

Rodney King Trial Verdict Sparks Outrage

Los Angeles, USA, May 2: More than 40 people have died and thousands have been injured in three days of rioting in the predominantly African-American areas of the city of Los Angeles following the trial verdict in the Rodney King case.

On April 29 a jury comprising ten whites, one Asian, and one Hispanic found four Los Angeles Police Department officers (three Caucasian, one Hispanic) innocent of "assault by force likely to produce great bodily injury," assault "under color of authority," and filing false police reports in relation to the high-profile judicial hearing that is known as the Rodney King Trial.

The case was widely publicized after a bystander, George Holliday, videotaped the officers viciously beating King while they were arresting him for speeding through a residential neighborhood in March 1991. The videotape, which lasted only 1 minute 43 seconds, showed the officers and an LAPD sergeant hitting King repeatedly with batons.

UN Condemns Ethnic Cleansing in Bosnia

Bosnia, August 31: The horrific images of Serbia's policy of so-called "ethnic

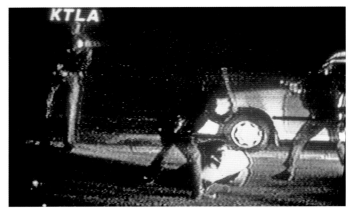

A amateur videotape shows Los Angeles police beating Rodney King.

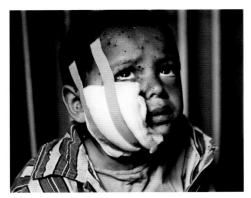

A wounded boy waits at Sarajevo hospital.

cleansing" have this month finally been broadcast for the world to see. Not since the mass extermination of Jews during World War II has a European country so consciously set out to rid itself of unwanted racial minorities.

The images of emaciated men with sunken cheeks and signs of starvation, looking disturbingly like images of victims from Auschwitz at the end of World War II, have been released, and the United Nations and the European Union are now confronted with genocide and concentration camps in the Balkans.

As far as can be determined this policy, practiced by the Yugoslav People's Army, under instructions from their leaders Radovan Karadzic, Slobodan Milosevic, and Ratko Mladic, is specifically designed to remove male Bosnian Muslims from Bosnia-Herzegovina. It has already led to the deaths of hundreds of thousands of Bosnian Muslims, while even greater numbers have fled the advancing

Yugoslav Army. The program has only been active for a few months, but already the consequences are obvious for the international community to see.

In May this year, Karadzic declared six so-called "strategic objectives" for the Serbian people in Bosnia-Herzegovina. Most of these objectives dealt with establishing corridors and redefining borders, but the two critical objectives were "separating the Serbian people from the other two ethnic communities" and dividing the city of Sarajevo into separate Serbian and Bosnian Muslim regions.

In May, Karadzic declared, with cold brutality, that "Muslims can't defend themselves if there is war," while Mladic declared that Serbs "must have their own separate existence." These twin policies have resulted in the indiscriminate rounding up of Muslim men and the establishment of concentration camps. Now, with these frightening images, the world knows the full consequences of the term "ethnic cleansing."

time out

For the first time, the British public are allowed inside Buckingham Palace. Proceeds from ticket sales were to go toward the £40 million restoration of the fire-damaged Windsor Castle. The Palace would be open for July and August, while the Queen was at Balmoral.

Clinton Claims White House Victory

Washington DC, USA, November 3: After 12 years in the political wilderness, the Democratic Party, with their candidate William Jefferson Clinton, Governor of Arkansas, have claimed the White House. The Republican years of Ronald Reagan and George H. W. Bush are over, and a new, young president (the first US president to be born after World War II) has won a stunning election victory.

Born on August 19, 1946, Clinton was educated at Georgetown University in Washington DC, won a Rhodes scholarship to Oxford University, and studied Law at Yale. His victory is a triumph for the Democrats. Clinton attracted 43.01 percent of the vote.

Somalia, January 3: Violent factional conflicts have crippled the East African country; 20,000 people have died, according to UN estimates.
Europe, January 15: The European Commission recognize Croatia and Slovenia as independent states.
South Africa, March 17: White voters give a resounding yes to plans for constitutional reforms giving equality to their black countrymen.
New Zealand, April 1: The Student Loan Scheme Act assists students to borrow money to fund tertiary education.

Miami, USA, April 9: Former Panamanian dictator General Manuel Noriega is found guilty of drug trafficking.
Los Angeles, USA, May 2: The jury's decision to acquit four police indicted in the beating of Rodney King leads to rioting.
Rio de Janeiro, Brazil, June 3-14: Treaties are signed at the UN Earth Summit to avert climate change.
Johannesburg, South Africa, June 18: Supporters of the Inkatha Freedom Party rampage through an outlying township, killing 39 people.

Sarajevo, Bosnia, July 2: UN peacekeeping forces move into position around the airport so that humanitarian aid can commence. Heavy resistance is encountered from Serbian troops.
Bosnia, August 15: Images of emaciated Bosnians in concentration style camps are broadcast around the world.
Rostock, Germany, August 29: Fifteen thousand left-wing protesters clash with police at a rally against racist attacks on refugees.

Lima, Peru, September 12: Responsible for 25,000 deaths, leader of the "Shining Path" guerrillas Abimael Guzmán is arrested after 12 years on the run.
Hanoi, Vietnam, September 23: General Le Duc Anh is elected as president, being the only candidate running for the position.
Amsterdam, Netherlands, October 4: A fully laden Boeing 747 cargo plane crashes into a tower block shortly after take off, killing more than 70 people and injuring hundreds.

USA, November 4: Bill Clinton is elected president of the USA.
London, England, November 24: Queen Elizabeth II refers to 1992 as an "annus horribilis." Bad luck has plagued the Royals this year, with scandals, income tax demands, divorce, and a fire at Windsor Palace four days ago.
Mogadishu, Somalia, December 9: The USA sends in Marines to neutralize gunmen loyal to local warlords and to deliver humanitarian aid.

Terrorist Bombs Rock Mumbai

Mumbai, India, March 12: Terrorism came to Mumbai today when 13 bomb blasts rocked the city, leaving 257 people dead and over 1,400 others injured. It is widely believed that the bombs, many of which were delivered in cars and on motor scooters, were a Muslim response to the attack on the Babri Mosque in Ayodhya by Hindu fundamentalists last December.

The attack on the mosque had been part of a concerted attack on Muslims by Hindu fundamentalists (probably the Shiv Sena and the Vishva Hindu Parishad organizations) who, throughout December 1992 and January 1993, have rioted and rampaged through the city, killing an estimated 1,788 people, many of whom are believed to be Muslims.

The bombings attacked a range of targets, starting with the Mumbai Stock Exchange and moving on to hotels, an airline office, a shopping complex, and the regional passport office. The most serious attack, however, was the bombing of a double-decker bus, which killed nearly 90 people.

Waco Siege Ends in Tragedy

Waco, Texas, USA, April 19: A 51-day siege of the Branch Davidian cult headquarters by the Bureau of Alcohol, Tobacco and Firearms (ATF) and the FBI came to a bloody end today when the entire complex was consumed by fire, causing an estimated loss of life of 76 people including the Branch Davidian leader, David Koresh.

The siege started on February 28 when the ATF raided the Davidian complex at Mt Carmel outside Waco and in the subsequent "battle" four agents of the Bureau and six Davidians were killed.

This "attack" on the complex had been prompted by a group of disgruntled former Davidians who claimed that Koresh and his followers were engaged in highly dubious, near-Satanic practices including polygamy, marriage of older men to underage brides, the physical abuse of children, and the storage of illegal firearms and weapons.

It is clear that David Koresh, who had changed his name from Vernon Howell and formed a splinter group of Davidians in 1984, had some kind of apocalyptic vision fuelled by his interpretation of the Bible's Book of Revelations. He was also determined not to be taken alive by the government agencies.

The FBI tried to force the Davidians out of the complex, but their efforts, which included breaking down walls and using CS gas, met with no success. Around noon, three fires started in the complex (it is thought the Davidians lit these), and it was as a result of these fires that the people died. The incident was broadcast around the world as TV crews and the press were positioned to record the FBI attack on the buildings.

Benazir Bhutto

Treaty Leads to Creation of European Union

Maastricht, Netherlands, November 1: The Maastricht Treaty, which was signed at Maastricht in the Netherlands on February 7, 1992, comes into force today, and so the dream of a united Europe becomes a reality. The old European Community will now become known as the European Union and, in practical terms, this means that for the first time in the continent's long history there will be a common currency (the euro), a common Foreign and Security Policy, a common Economic and Social Policy, and a common Justice and Home Affairs Policy.

It is a truly remarkable change for a continent that less than 50 years ago was wracked by a bloody world war.

Founding Members of the European Union
- Member nations
- ⊛ Capital city

NORWAY · SWEDEN · FINLAND · ESTONIA · RUSSIAN FEDERATION · LATVIA · LITHUANIA · Baltic Sea · North Sea · DENMARK ⊛ Copenhagen · RUSSIAN FEDERATION · BELARUS · Dublin ⊛ IRELAND · UNITED KINGDOM · Amsterdam · NETHERLANDS · Berlin ⊛ · POLAND · London ⊛ · Brussels ⊛ · GERMANY · BELGIUM · Luxembourg · CZECH REPUBLIC · UKRAINE · ATLANTIC OCEAN · Paris ⊛ LUXEMBOURG · SLOVAKIA · LIECHTENSTEIN · MOLDOVA · FRANCE · AUSTRIA · HUNGARY · SWITZERLAND · SLOVENIA · ROMANIA · CROATIA · YUGOSLAVIA · PORTUGAL · MONACO · BOSNIA & HERZEGOVINA · Black Sea · ANDORRA · BULGARIA · Madrid ⊛ · ITALY · ALBANIA · MACEDONIA · SPAIN · Rome ⊛ · TURKEY · Lisbon ⊛ · GREECE · Athens ⊛ · Mediterranean Sea · MOROCCO · ALGERIA · TUNISIA

500 km / 500 miles

Yasser Arafat

Military Junta Extends Suu Kyi's House Arrest

Yangon, Myanmar, January 21: In an attempt to further punish an irritant who has been annoying them since she was democratically elected as Prime Minister in 1990, the military junta in Myanmar have added another year to the house arrest of Nobel Peace Prize winner and democracy advocate Aung San Suu Kyi.

Citing an obscure law, the junta said that a year can be added to Suu Kyi's five-year house arrest simply on the decision of a three-member committee comprising the Ministers of Foreign Affairs, Home Affairs, and Defense. Numerous attempts have been made to expel her from the country. In December 1990, the junta announced that "should she wish to stay together with her husband and children, she would be allowed to leave Burma on humanitarian grounds."

Fearing that she would be denied re-entry if she left the country, Suu Kyi chose to stay in Myanmar and to draw attention to the abuses of civil rights. In 1991, he won the Nobel Peace Prize, and last year seven Nobel laureates tried to visit her but were refused entry to Myanmar. She is due to meet UN and US representatives next month.

> "A SUCCESS-FUL INDUS-TRIAL NATION, THAT IS A NATION WITH FUTURE, CAN NOT BE ORGANIZED AS A COLLECTIVE HOLIDAY RESORT."
>
> HELMUT KOHL (B. 1930), GERMAN STATESMAN AND CHANCELLOR

> "THE ART OF LEADERSHIP IS SAYING NO, NOT YES. IT IS VERY EASY TO SAY YES."
>
> TONY BLAIR (B. 1953), BRITISH PRIME MINISTER, 1994

Mandela is South Africa's First Black President

Pretoria, South Africa, May 10: Nelson Rolihlahla Mandela, born on July 18, 1918, and incarcerated for 27 years by South Africa's white apartheid regime, was sworn in today as the nation's first fully representative, democratically elected president. He was elected to the office on April 27 and took up the position today.

Nelson Mandela's appointment, while a powerful symbol of the changing nature of South African society, is a triumph for all those who, through sanctions, protests, and quiet diplomacy, have managed to persuade South Africa's ruling white elite that their system of government was untenable.

Mandela will be assisted by two Deputy Presidents—his African National Congress ally and colleague Thabo Mbeki and the outgoing President Frederick Willem de Klerk. Mandela will preside over a Government of National Unity whose aims are to heal the wounds created by apartheid and to create a multicultural society so that the problems of the past will not have an adverse effect on the country's dynamic future.

The new South African flag flies over Johannesburg.

time out

A deal between the Ukraine and an American company to sell $70 million of corn seeds and farm equipment caused embarrassment as it emerged that poor quality seeds had been offloaded for large profits at a cost that might ultimately be borne by American taxpayers.

PLO Leader Ends 27-year Exile

Gaza, Israel, July 1: Events that commenced in 1993 culminated today when, after 27 years in exile, Palestinian leader and chairman of the Palestine Liberation Organization political movement, Yasser Arafat, returned in triumph to his beloved homeland. As usual he was a striking figure in his military uniform and with his distinctive keffiyeh headdress.

Leaving Cairo and then traveling by helicopter across the Sinai Desert to the border town of Rafah in the Gaza strip, Arafat said: "Now I am returning to the first free Palestinian lands. You have to imagine how it is moving my heart, my feelings." He was transported quickly to Gaza City in a bulletproof black Mercedes.

His return has already elicited angry responses from Israelis who see Arafat as a terrorist and are eager to assassinate him. It was therefore not surprising that Israeli security forces mounted their largest security operation since the visit to Israel of Egypt's President Sadat in 1979. Upon arrival in Gaza City, Arafat spoke to an enthusiastic crowd of some 200,000 Palestinians.

His return is a triumph for American diplomacy. For a number of years Arafat has been engaged in secret talks with the Israelis, and last year these led to the historic Oslo Accords, which gave Palestine effective self-rule over most of the West Bank and the Gaza Strip.

The key to these major developments was Arafat's preparedness to recognize the legitimacy of the state of Israel and to renounce violence against the Israeli people. He did this on September 9, 1993, and in return Prime Minister Yitzhak Rabin, on behalf of Israel, officially recognized the Palestine Liberation Organization.

Devastating Earthquake Rocks Kobe

Kobe, Japan, January 17: An earthquake measuring 7.2 on the Richter scale occurred today at 5.46 am in the southern section of the Kobe prefecture. It lasted for 20 seconds. It has been estimated that the epicenter was only 12.5 miles (20 km) from Kobe—a city with a population of 1.5 million—and was centered on the northern end of Awajishima Island.

The earthquake, believed to be the largest in Japan since 1923, has also damaged the cities of Osaka and Kyoto, but the greatest damage has been to Kobe, where it is feared thousands of people have been killed and it is known that entire apartment blocks and buildings have been destroyed. Roads and bridges have been seriously damaged and many areas of the city are ablaze with fires caused by the quake. People, many still in their nightclothes and covered only by blankets, are wandering the streets afraid to return to their homes for fear of the dangers produced by aftershocks.

Rwandan Army Closes Down Refugee Camps

Kibeho, Rwanda, April 22: During last year's horrific Rwandan genocide, the small township of Kibeho was central to some of the most violent atrocities and murders committed by the Interahamwe and Impuzamugambi militia groups. It is now estimated that a total of 937,000 people—mostly from the Tutsi tribal group, but also including a large number of moderate Hutus—were slaughtered in a bloody 100-day orgy of violence that lasted from April 6 until mid-July in 1994.

During this period, Hutu militias rampaged throughout the country in one of the worst acts of genocide ever recorded. It is one of the cruelest ironies that, after this intense period of genocide, a camp was set up near Kibeho which, at its peak, was home to between 165,000–200,000 Rwandan refugees, many of whom had been involved in the massacres. It was a

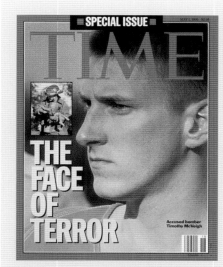
Timothy McVeigh is the Oklahoma bomber.

camp full of tensions, with both killers and victims forced to live side by side.

Today, as if there can be no end to this killing, the Tutsi-dominated Rwandan Army arrived in Kibeho and, following government orders, has forcibly closed down the camp, forcing the refugees to return to their homes, which in many cases are places where neighbors, under government instructions, indiscriminately killed each other.

It remains a blot on Western governments, particularly the administration of US President Bill Clinton, and the United Nations that the events in Rwanda, and what happened again today, have been largely ignored, and that the genocide was not halted by outside forces.

Jury Acquits O. J. Simpson in Murder Trial

Los Angeles, USA, October 3: A jury in Los Angeles today acquitted Orethal James Simpson, known variously as "The Juice" and O. J. Simpson, of the murder of his ex-wife Nicole Brown Simpson and her companion Ronald Goldman on the night of June 12, 1994.

Simpson, a successful professional football player who had enjoyed some success as an actor (his most famous roles had been in the TV mini-series *Roots* and *The Naked Gun* comedy trilogy), had been charged with the murders outside his former wife's condominium. Because of Simpson's high public profile, the trial generated huge publicity, with literally hundreds of members of the media camped outside the Los Angeles Superior Court reporting every twist and turn of the case. The trial, which has been presided over by Judge Lance Ito, lasted for 133 days and the testimony was televised. It is estimated that over 150 million viewers throughout the United States have watched today's acquittal.

Aung San Suu Kyi

O. J. Simpson listens to testimony during his double murder trial.

Manila, Philippines, January 15: Over 1 million people gather to welcome Pope John Paul II at the start of the World Youth Day celebrations.
Kobe, Japan, January 17: Over 6,000 people die in Japan's largest quake in nearly 50 years.
Frankfurt, Germany, March 2: Trader Nick Leeson, 28, responsible for a $1.4 billion loss to Barings Bank, is arrested.

Tokyo, Japan, March 20: Sarin, a deadly nerve gas is released in the subway system, killing eight and affecting 4,000. The Aum Supreme Truth religious sect is linked to the attacks.
Iraq, March 20: Thirty-five thousand Turkish troops cross into north Iraq to crush the PKK, Kurdish separatist rebels who have been waging a guerrilla war since 1984 that has claimed 15,000 lives.
Europe, March 26: Seven of the 15 EU states abolish border controls.

Oklahoma City, USA, April 19: A massive car bomb explodes in front of a federal building, killing 168 and injuring over 800. Main suspect Timothy McVeigh is arrested less than one hour after the blast.
Kibeho, Rwanda, April 22: Government troops massacre Hutu refugees.
San Diego, USA, May: Team New Zealand wins the America's Cup.
Zaire (Congo), May 28: The deadly Ebola hemorrhagic fever kills 256 of the 315 people infected in the second largest outbreak recorded.

Bosnia, May 28: Bosnian Serbs seize more than 350 UN peacekeepers from the "safe haven" of Gorazde. They have been used as human shields to guard against NATO attacks.
Srebrenica, Bosnia, July 15: Poorly armed Dutch peacekeepers are unable to prevent up to 40,000 Muslims being rounded up by Serbian forces in the largest incident of "ethnic cleansing" since WWII.
Washington, DC, USA, September 28: The PLO and the Israelis sign a deal handing over control of the West Bank to the Palestinians.

Los Angeles, USA, October 3: O. J. Simpson is found not guilty of killing his ex-wife.
Tel Aviv, Israel, November 4: Israeli PM Yitzhak Rabin is assassinated by a right wing Jewish extremist at a peace rally.
Port Harcourt, Nigeria, November 10: Authorities execute nine activists, opposed to unfair oil revenue distribution, charged with murder.
Paris, France, December 14: Croatian, Bosnian, and Serbian leaders sign a peace accord ending three years of bloody conflict.

Mother Teresa

"THE ROAD TO TYRANNY, WE MUST NEVER FORGET, BEGINS WITH THE DESTRUCTION OF THE TRUTH."

BILL CLINTON
(B. 1946), AMERICAN
PRESIDENT

90 Dead in Colombo Suicide Bombing

Colombo, Sri Lanka, January 31: Sri Lankan separatist group, Tamil Tigers, wreaked their most deadly attack on the center of Colombo's financial district today when a truck laden with explosives crashed into the city's Central Bank, killing an estimated 90 people and injuring at least 1,400 others. The attack had been carefully and meticulously planned.

At around 10.45 a.m. the truck stopped outside the bank, and a gunfight broke out between the bank's security guards and three people in the vehicle. Two bombs were detonated, and then the driver of the vehicle backed it into the bank and blew it up. The driver was killed in the blast, and the first two floors of the ten-story building collapsed.

Authorities claim that it was clearly the work of the Tamil Tigers, who have been attempting to establish an independent Tamil state in the northeast region of Sri Lanka since the 1970s. This is the deadliest attack in the history of the organization, which is regarded by many countries as a terrorist, rather than an independence, organization.

Spread of Mad Cow Disease Worsens

London, England, April 16: The British Government today announced that all cattle over the age of 30 months in the British Isles are to be slaughtered in an attempt to halt the spread of bovine spongiform encephalopathy (BSE), or Mad Cow Disease.

This ongoing problem has caused havoc in the British cattle industry since BSE was first formally identified by the Central Veterinary Laboratory in November 1986. As early as July 1988, the Chief Veterinary Officer announced a ban on the type of cattle feed being used, which was thought to be connected with the disease. This was then followed in August that year by a government decision to slaughter all BSE-affected cattle. The following year, fearing outbreaks of BSE, the European Commission banned all exports of British cattle born after July 1988.

By July 14, 1993, Great Britain had reported its 100,000th case of BSE.

time out

O. J. Simpson was ordered by a civil court jury to pay $25 million in punitive damages to the families of murder victims Nicole Brown Simpson and Ronald L. Goldman. In 1995 a criminal court had found Simpson not guilty of the murders.

On March 20 this year, the British Government announced that scientists had established a link between BSE and CJD, making the issue much more serious and the control of the disease a matter of the highest priority. Five days later, in an action likely to seriously damage the British beef industry, the European Commission decided to place a worldwide export ban on all British beef.

The British Government has been left with few options. Its decision today to slaughter all cattle over the age of 30 months is an attempt to reassure the world, at least in years to come, that British beef is safe to eat and that eating a British steak will not lead inevitably to Creutzfeldt-Jacob Disease.

Gunman Goes on Shooting Rampage in Port Arthur

Port Arthur, Australia, April 28: The worst mass killing in Australian history took place today in Port Arthur, Tasmania, when a lone gunman, Martin Bryant, went on a killing spree that resulted in the deaths of 35 people and the wounding of a further 37.

Bryant, a 29-year-old Tasmanian, started his murderous rampage at the Seascape Guesthouse near Port Arthur, where he shot and killed two elderly occupants. He then proceeded to the historic convict ruins at Port Arthur, where he entered the Broad Arrow Café, ordered and ate a meal, and then took out an AR15 auto-loading Armalite rifle and fired 29 shots, which killed 22 people, 19 of those people dying from head wounds. Bryant then moved to the nearby car park, where he continued shooting indiscriminately. He then drove toward the exit of the site. Along the way he shot a mother and her two small children, before returning to the Seascape Guesthouse.

Sri Lankan government army soldiers depart for home after serving in Jaffna in the war against the Tamil Tigers.

Key Events

Bosnia, January 2: US combat troops enter northern Bosnia to keep the peace between Bosnian Serbs and Muslims following the Dayton peace agreement signed last month.
Paris, France, January 8: François Mitterrand, socialist PM who led the country for 14 years, dies, aged 79.
Colombo, Sri Lanka, January 31: A truck laden with explosives crashes into the Central Bank, killing 57 and injuring over 1,000.

London, England, February 9: An explosion in the Docklands marks the end of a 17-month cease-fire by the IRA. The bomb causes widespread damage with one fatality and 39 injured.
Cuba, February 24: Cuban fighter jets shoot down two US civilian aircraft. The planes were chartered by an anti-Castro organization to search for refugees.
Australia, March 2: The Liberal party, led by John Howard, is victorious after 13 years in opposition.

Dunblane, Scotland, March 13: Gunman Thomas Hamilton goes on a shooting spree in the local primary school, killing 16 students and a teacher before taking his own life.
Cairo, Egypt, April 18: Islamic militants open fire on Greek tourists outside a Cairo hotel, killing 17.
Tasmania, Australia, April 28: Martin Bryant kills 35 people at Port Arthur.
Iraq, May 20: Iraq and the UN agree on the oil-for-food program allowing Iraq to sell oil for humanitarian necessities.

Bosnia, July 19: Bosnian Serb President Radovan Karadzic resigns from office and withdraws from public life after being indicted for war crimes. His initial refusal to resign was destabilizing the country.
Atlanta, USA, July 27: A bomb explodes at a concert during the Olympic Games, injuring 200 and killing two.
Chechnya, Russia, August: After two years of fierce fighting between separatist rebels and the Russian Army, a peace accord is signed allowing for limited autonomy.

Kabul, Afghanistan, September 27: Taliban militia take the capital, their aim to establish the "purest" Islamic regime in the world. Ousted President Rabbani flees, fearing for his life.
Washington, DC, USA, November 6: Bill Clinton, re-elected, is only the second Democrat to win a second term in office.
Canada, November 21: The Royal Commission for Native Groups recommends that they prepare for self-government.
UK, December: The government culls 100,000 cows in a bid to stop the spread of Mad Cow Disease.

Ceremony Marks British Handover of Hong Kong

Hong Kong, July 1: Another small part of the once-mighty British Empire disappeared today when Hong Kong, which the British had controlled since 1842, was handed back to the Chinese authorities. The official ceremony, held at the Hong Kong Convention Centre, was attended by Prince Charles, British Prime Minister Tony Blair, Foreign Secretary Robin Cook, and the last British Governor of Hong Kong, Chris Patten, as well as representatives from China including President Jiang Zemin and the territory's new Chief Executive Tung

Chinese and Hong Kong flags.

Chee-hwa. The ceremony began at midnight last night when the British flag was lowered for the final time over Government House. At 8.00 o'clock this evening there was a huge fireworks display on the harbor, and the handover was made complete when 509 Chinese troops crossed into Hong Kong.

The British, determined to depart with their sense of Empire intact, left on the Royal yacht *Britannia*, with both "Rule Britannia" and "Land of Hope and Glory" being played, while Prince Charles and the last governor waved the former colony farewell.

World Mourns Death of a Living Saint

Calcutta, India, September 5: The death today of Mother Teresa, the revered Catholic nun who devoted her life to helping the sick and the poor from the slums of Calcutta, has been met with widespread sadness and grief. Mother Teresa, otherwise known as Agnes

Bojaxhui of Skopje in Macedonia, was 87 years old and had been suffering from ill health for a number of years. She eventually succumbed to a heart attack.

At the time she was at the headquarters of her famous Missionaries of Charity order that she founded in 1950. Her tireless work and high profile had resulted in many seeing her as a symbol of goodness and compassion, with some even declaring that she was a living saint. Certainly, it is expected that Pope John Paul II will move quickly to have her recognized as a saint. It is expected that the work she started in Calcutta in 1948 will continue and that she will be remembered as one of the great figures of the twentieth century.

Outpouring of Grief at Princess Diana's Funeral

London, England, September 6: In decades to come it will be almost impossible to explain the mass adulation and hysteria that has occurred in London, and around the world, over the past week following the death of Princess Diana. Her funeral today has created an outpouring of emotion that has taken the British people by surprise and created unprecedented scenes, with literally tons of flowers placed at the gates of Kensington Palace and tens of thousands of people visibly weeping at the death of someone they never knew, but felt they knew.

Diana was fatally injured on the evening of August 31 when a car she was traveling in with her lover, Dodi al-Fayed, crashed in the Pont d'Alma Tunnel in Paris. She was taken to hospital where surgeons tried to save her life, but she

died the following morning. Although Diana had divorced Prince Charles in August 1996, this did not stop the public from seeing her as part of the British royal family, and while they laid flowers at Kensington Palace there was widespread criticism that Queen Elizabeth II had not lowered the flag at Buckingham Palace to half-mast and had not spoken publicly about the tragedy.

Today's funeral procession stretched over 4 miles (6.4 km), with Prince Charles and Diana's two sons, Prince Harry and Prince William, walking behind the cortege with Diana's brother, Earl Spencer. The service was broadcast across the world and included a rewritten version of "Candle in the Wind" performed by Sir Elton John, along with a passionate denunciation of the British royal family by Earl Spencer, who described his sister as "the very essence of compassion, of duty, of style, of beauty."

It has been estimated that more than 1 million wreaths of flowers were thrown or strewn in front of the funeral cortege as Princess Diana's body was driven to her family estate at Althorp, where she was buried on an island.

Princess Diana

Prince Charles and his sons view the floral tributes to Princess Diana.

Southern Ocean, January 9: British yachtsman Tony Bullimore is rescued from his yacht five days after it capsized in the frigid waters southwest of Western Australia.

Hebron, West Bank, Israel, January 19: Greeted by 60,000 Palestinians, Yasser Arafat returns to Hebron after 30 years of Israeli occupation.

Beijing, China, February 19: Paramount leader Deng Xiaoping dies, aged 92. A hardliner, he ruled the country from 1978, allowing some strategic reforms, including limited private enterprise.

Sarajevo, Bosnia, April 12: A plot to assassinate the Pope is unearthed. Twenty anti-tank mines are found under a bridge along the pontiff's route.

Lima, Peru, April 22: A four-month siege at the Japanese embassy ends with the death of 14 Tupac Amaru guerrillas. Seventy-one captives are rescued, with only one civilian casualty.

UK, May 1: In a 10.3 percent swing against the Conservatives, the Labour Party, led by Tony Blair wins the general election. Labour has been in opposition for 18 years.

Kinshasa, Congo, May 20: One day after President Mobutu Sese Seko flees, Laurent Kabila's troops enter the capital, ending a civil war raging since late 1996.

Hong Kong, July 1: The former British colony is handed back to China.

Thredbo, Australia, August 2: Three days after a landslide, sole survivor Stuart Diver is found in the ruins of the destroyed lodges. Eighteen people died.

Jerusalem, Israel, September 4: Three Palestinian suicide bombers kill 7 and injure 170 in a crowded pedestrian area.

Calcutta, India, September 5: Mother Teresa dies, aged 87.

Westminster, England, September 6: Princess Diana is laid to rest.

Assisi, Italy, September 26: Two earthquakes in central Italy kill 10 and severely damage priceless works of art, including important frescos.

Luxor, Egypt, November 17: Sixty-two tourists are slain at the Deir al-Bahri temple complex.

New Zealand, December 8: Jenny Shipley becomes New Zealand's first woman prime minister.

Relizane, Algeria, December 30: About 350 people are massacred by Islamic extremists on the first day of Ramadan. The countryside descends into anarchy, thousands die.

Gerry Adams

Referendum Raises Hopes for Peace

Belfast, Ireland, May 23: There is jubilation today in the cities of London, Dublin, and Belfast as, at last, there has been a convincing "Yes" vote to the Good Friday Agreement after 30 years of fighting and bloodshed. The result is unambiguous—94 percent of voters in the Irish Republic and 71 percent of voters in Northern Ireland supported the peace proposals.

The Good Friday Agreement, signed on April 10, 1998, is a successful attempt to resolve the conflicts that exist between Northern Ireland and the Republic of Ireland, and between the rest of Britain (England, Scotland, Wales) and Northern Ireland. It is a personal triumph for the Northern Ireland Secretary Mo Mowlam, British Prime Minister Tony Blair, Irish Prime Minister Bertie Ahearn, Sinn Fein leader Gerry Adams, and nationalist SDLP leader John Hume, and hopefully will usher in a new era of peace in the troubled province.

With this endorsement, it is now possible for the citizens of Northern Ireland to look forward and ahead to a new Northern Ireland Assembly and genuine devolution from the British Government in Westminster.

US Embassy Bombings in Africa Result in Carnage

Kenya and Tanzania, August 7, 1998: "Is this the beginning of a new age of terrorism?" is the question being asked by terrorism experts in Washington tonight as the administration of President Bill Clinton tries to comprehend one of the worst attacks on American lives and property since World War II.

time out

President Clinton admitted to a sexual relationship with Monica Lewinsky, after previously stating: 'I did not have sexual relations with that woman'. He now said: 'I did have a relationship with Miss Lewinsky that was not appropriate. In fact, it was wrong.'

In the space of a few minutes, at around 10.30 a.m. local time, two huge bombs exploded at the US embassies in Kenya and Tanzania. The first explosion occurred in the Tanzanian capital of Dar es Salaam, and five minutes later another bomb went off in Nairobi, the capital of Kenya. The devastation has been enormous, with an estimated 200 people being killed and another 4,000 people injured. The blasts were so powerful that they brought the city centers to a standstill and the sound could be heard up to 15 km away. Immediately volunteers were on the scenes of the explosions, working frantically to free people buried by the rubble. By mid-morning cranes were lifting large pieces of concrete from the sites.

Although the United States has been on alert for such attacks, these explosions were so powerful that they made any kind of conventional protection irrelevant. Even bombproof front doors were destroyed. It is not known which anti-American group is responsible for the attacks, but already terrorism experts are looking at a shadowy Saudi Arabian businessman and Islamic fundamentalist named Osama bin Laden and his organization which is known as al-Qaeda. This organization has been talking for some time about conducting a series of attacks on America and American citizens.

President Clinton has declared: "These acts of terrorist violence are abhorrent. They are inhumane. We will use all the means at our disposal to bring those responsible to justice."

America's most wanted.

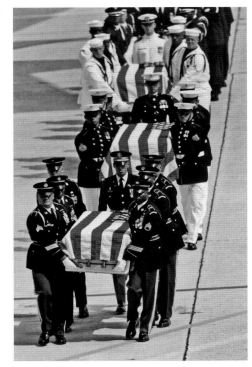

Flag-draped coffins of Americans killed in Kenya.

Terrorists Suspected in Swissair Explosion

Halifax, Canada, September 3, 1998: With the bombings of the US embassies in Dar es Salaam and Nairobi still fresh in people's minds, it is not surprising that the crash today of a Swissair flight SR-111 from New York to Geneva has raised the possibility of another terrorist attack.

The plane, a McDonnell Douglas MD-11 with 229 people on board, was an hour out from New York when it exploded and crashed into the sea off Nova Scotia. Terrorist fears have been heightened by reports that the pilot reported smoke in the cabin and was attempting to make an emergency landing when the plane disappeared off radar screens.

Witnesses on the ground at Halifax also report hearing a huge explosion. There are still many questions to be answered about this explosion, which was the first crash Swissair have had since 1979.

Rostaq, Afghanistan, February 4: An earthquake in the mountainous north of the country leaves 4,000 dead and 15,000 homeless. Fighting between the Taliban and the Northern Alliance continues.

Auckland, New Zealand, April: Power has finally been restored to the central business district after five weeks of blackouts.

Belfast, Northern Ireland, April 10: The "Good Friday" agreement for peace is signed by the British and Irish governments and endorsed by most Northern Ireland political parties.

Cambodia, April 15: Former Khmer Rouge leader Pol Pot dies, aged 72.

USA, May 18: Twenty US states and the Department of Justice submit that Microsoft has abused its monopoly.

Ireland, May 23: A referendum on the Good Friday peace agreement receives a resounding yes.

Pakistan, May 28: In response to Indian nuclear tests two weeks ago, Pakistan explodes five warheads underground.

Sudan, June 11: Up to one million people are at risk of starvation from a famine affecting the south of the country.

Lagos, Nigeria, July 11: Four days of rioting leave 60 dead. The riots were sparked by the death of opposition figure Chief Abiola.

Dar es Salaam, Tanzania and Nairobi, Kenya, August 7: Bombs explode at two US embassies.

Central China, August 13: The Yangtze River, which has risen to its highest level since 1954, threatens Wuhan, a city of seven million people. About 2,500 people perish and millions are left homeless.

Washington DC, USA, August 17: After categorically denying a sexual relationship with White House intern Monica Lewinsky in January, President Clinton publicly admits his deceit.

Halifax, Canada, September 3: A Swissair DC-11 crashes, killing all 229 on board.

Kosovo, September 22: Serbian forces bombard the breakaway region in attempt to crush the Kosovo Liberation Army (KLA). Widespread civilian casualties are reported.

South Africa, October 29: The Truth and Reconciliation Commission hands down its findings on political crimes conducted under the apartheid regime.

Iraq, November 15: Saddam Hussein's regime readmits UN weapons inspectors at the eleventh hour, averting US and British air strikes.

Mont Blanc Tunnel Inferno Rages out of Control

Mont Blanc, France, March 24: One of the worst disasters in the history of both France and Italy occurred today when a Volvo transport truck caught fire in the Mont Blanc Tunnel, which runs through the Alps for 7.2 miles (11.6 km), connecting France and Italy. The truck was carrying a load of flour and margarine when it caught fire at 10.53 a.m. local time.

It is believed that around 40 vehicles were passing through the tunnel at the time, and authorities fear that the chances of survival of the people trapped inside are slim because the fire has produced a poisonous and dense cloud of smoke containing both carbon monoxide and cyanide. It is estimated that the number of casualties could be anywhere between 30 and 40. Not surprisingly, fire and rescue crews have been unable to enter the tunnel to try and save lives because of the intensity of the heat and the thick smoke—temperatures inside the tunnel, exacerbated by the tunnel's air conditioning, which is fueling the fire, have risen to over 1,832°F (1000°C).

Columbine High School Massacre Shocks Nation

Denver, USA, April 20: Wearing balaclavas and looking like characters out of a violent video game, two students, Eric Harris (18) and Dylan Klebold (17) rampaged through Columbine High School near the middle-class suburb of Littleton, half a mile south of Denver, Colorado. They had brought a range of automatic weapons and a large number of homemade bombs to the high school and had made plans to kill some hundreds of students.

They arrived at 11.10 a.m. in separate vehicles and, as a first act, placed a 20 lb (9 kg) bomb, hidden in duffel bags, inside the school cafeteria. This bomb was set to explode at 11.14 a.m., but fortunately it did not go off. At 11.19 a.m. they took two sawn-off shotguns, a TEC-9 semi-automatic pistol and a 9 mm semi-automatic carbine and walked back to

Columbine High School students after the shooting.

the cafeteria. It was at this point that they both started shooting, apparently indiscriminately and with almost clinical disregard for life, at any students who came into their line of fire.

The pair worked their way progressively from the cafeteria along the school corridors to the library. It was in the library that they killed 10 students and wounded another 10, some of them seriously. In total it appears that 15 people have been killed and another 19 injured. By noon the killings were over and, while the two killers still wandered the corridors, a SWAT team surrounded the school and ambulances ferried the wounded to nearby hospitals.

At around 2.00 p.m. they both put guns to their heads and shot themselves. This is the worst high school massacre in American history and is bound to raise complex questions about violent videos (the boys were both known to be enthusiasts of *Doom* and *Wolfenstein 3D*), the ease of access to firearms, and the right to bear arms, which is seen by many as one of the country's inalienable rights.

Rioters Protest Against Third World Debts

London, England, June 18: Protests against capitalism, the gathering of the G8 (Group of Eight) leaders in Cologne, and a belief that the first world is constantly punishing and maltreating the third world led to some of the most violent riots seen in London since the race riots of 1995. The demonstration, billed as a "Carnival Against Capitalism," attracted an estimated crowd of 4,000 who gathered in the city's financial district to protest specifically about the debt burden that the world's poorest countries owe to the world's richest nations.

The protesters were joined, in a novel variation of standard protest, by some 300 banner-carrying cyclists, who rode slowly through the city disrupting traffic. The protest was peaceful until a small group of demonstrators, armed with stones and bottles according to police reports, started attacking the building that houses the London Stock Exchange.

Monica Lewinsky

A child waits for food at Ajiep in southern Sudan.

Colombia, January 25: An earthquake measuring 6 on the Richter scale leaves 1,000 dead and many more homeless. Landslides and poor building standards contributed.

Nigeria, February 27: Former military ruler Olusegun Obasanjo wins the first free elections in 15 years.

France/Italy, March 24: A fire kills 39 people in the Mont Blanc tunnel.

Canada, April 1: The new territory of Nunavut is established, with its capital located at Iqaluit.

Scotland, April 5: The UN lifts sanctions against Libya as the two key suspects in the 1988 Lockerbie bombing of Pan-Am flight 103 are handed over to Scottish authorities.

Denver, Colorado, USA, April 20: Two heavily armed teenagers killing 13 students then commit suicide.

London, England, April 30: A nail bomb explodes in a Soho pub, killing three people. This follows attacks in Brick Lane and Brixton earlier in the month.

Belgrade, Yugoslavia, May 7: NATO bombers mistakenly target the Chinese embassy in a bombing raid in response to the atrocities occurring in Kosovo. Four diplomats die, massive demonstrations follow in China.

Kashmir, India/Pakistan, May 26: India launches air strikes in the disputed region following incursions by Pakistani forces.

Kosovo, Yugoslavia, June 10: NATO forces call off bombing raids as Serbian forces begin to withdraw from the disputed province.

London, England, June 18: Protests against the G8 summit turn violent.

Interlaken, Switzerland, July 28: Twenty-one international tourists die as a flash flood hits a canyoning group.

Izmit, Turkey, August 17: A massive 7.4 magnitude earthquake kills thousands.

East Timor, September 20: UN peacekeepers enter to control violence by pro-Indonesian militia since elections in early September.

Islamabad, Pakistan, October 12: General Pervez Musharraf ousts Prime Minister Nawaz Sharif in a bloodless coup.

Orissa, India, October 29: A massive tidal surge caused by a cyclone with 155 mph (250 km/h) winds hits eastern India, killing 10,000 and leaving 1.5 million homeless.

Worldwide, December 31: Millennium celebrations occur world-wide after a year where panic about the potentially debilitating effects of the Y2K computer glitch ran high.

Sir Ranulph Fiennes

"How to separate dice from design— that is the major question facing evolutionary biology today."

TYLER VOLK (B. 1950),
AMERICAN
BIOLOGIST, 1990

Crater Linked to Dinosaur Extinction

Yucatán Peninsula, Mexico, July, 1991: The age-old question of what killed the dinosaurs has moved toward substantiation of the theory of destruction by a cataclysmic event, with the announcement of important recent discoveries across Mexico's Yucatán Peninsula.

Scientists have discovered a arc-shaped series of lakes that have been measured at 125 miles (200 km) in diameter. The lakes extend across the entire Yucatán Peninsula and appear to be the outline of a gigantic scar on the Earth's surface left by some catastrophic event that occurred about 65 million years ago. There is evidence that this huge depression in the Earth's surface (known as the Chicxulub crater) has, over the past 65 million years, been buried under layers of limestone— in one section up to 3,510 ft (1,070 m) deep. Scientists have searched beyond the area for other clues to the "catastrophic

The Tyrol region, typical of where Otzi was discovered.

event" and have found evidence of fossilized wood and huge boulders 500 miles (800 km) away near Tampico, Mexico. It has been claimed that these deposits, in an otherwise stable area, may have been transported there by huge sea waves caused by an extraterrestrial body such as an asteroid or comet crashing into the Earth. Some scientists are now tentatively arguing that this may have been a great event that, like massive volcanic eruptions, caused the Earth's temperature to lower and filled the atmosphere with poisonous gases, resulting in the mass extinction of many life forms.

Further research may finally solve the riddle of why dinosaurs suddenly became extinct after dominating the planet for over 160 million years.

Otzi the Iceman Frozen in Time

South Tyrol, Austria, October 19, 1991: While hiking through the mountainous South Tyrol region between Austria and Italy last month, two German tourists, Helmut and Erica Simon, stumbled upon a frozen corpse in a glacier. Scientists believe that the corpse may be the oldest human remains ever uncovered.

Early scientific analysis appears to indicate that the corpse, which had been remarkably well preserved by the ice and snow that cover this region, could be anywhere from 3,500 to over 5,000 years old. Some experts believe that the body is that of a hunter who was attempting to cross the mountains.

The hunter, who has been nicknamed Otzi the Iceman after the Otztal area where he was discovered, is about 5 ft 3 in (160 cm) tall and is estimated to be about 40–50 years old. He is extensively tattooed

time out

British scientists successfully cloned an adult sheep to create a lamb: Dolly. In theory, this meant that an adult human could be cloned to create a genetically-identical being, but the major application of the procedure was medical research, the researchers said.

and was wearing a leather vest, leather shoes (made from bear and deer skins, and lined with grass, which operated like socks), and a woven grass cloak. Otzi was carrying an ax, a flint knife, a quiver of arrows, and a huge longbow taller than him.

It will be many years before scientists are able to unravel all the secrets of this remarkable discovery, but it offers an unprecedented intimate look at the personal lives of our interesting early ancestors.

Satellite Helps Locate Fabled Lost City of Ubar

Ubar, Oman, February, 1992: Has Iram of the Pillars, otherwise variously known as the City of a Thousand Pillars, Ubar or Wabar, finally been found? According to ancient records, this legendary lost city was known as one of the great trading cities and was located somewhere in the Rub al Khali Desert in modern-day Oman, on the southern Arabian Peninsula. Archeologists believe the city existed from around 3000 BCE until the first century CE.

Supposedly built by the great-grandchildren of Noah, it was believed to be a city of great sinfulness and decadence that was wiped from the face of the planet by the hand of God. Its decline was probably more prosaic, with the city running out of water and people abandoning it. However, it is mentioned in both the Koran and *The Arabian Nights*.

Now, using satellite images of the region taken in 1984 by the space shuttle *Challenger*, an amateur American archeologist, Nicholas Clapp (sometimes known as "the real Indiana Jones"), claims he has identified exactly where the ancient city once prospered.

Two expeditions to Oman have been mounted; one in 1990 and one in 1991.

Workers celebrate the opening of the Channel Tunnel.

The expedition team included Nicholas Clapp, Dr Ronald Blom, archeologist Dr Juris Zarins, and British explorer Sir Ranulph Fiennes, who had been on previous searches for Ubar.

The team investigated the area around Ash Shisr, and then an archeological excavation began.

Historic Opening of the Channel Tunnel

English Channel, May 6, 1994: A long-held dream became a reality today. For the first time since the last ice age, the peoples of Great Britain and France have a connection by land. The truly remarkable engineering feat known as the Channel Tunnel (sometimes called the Chunnel or the Eurotunnel) was officially opened today by Queen Elizabeth II and President François Mitterand.

The ceremony was heavy on symbolism: Queen Elizabeth traveled from London's Waterloo Station on the high-speed Eurostar passenger train and passed through the tunnel to arrive at Calais at precisely the same time that President Mitterand's train, which had departed earlier from Gare du Nord in Paris, reached the French coastal port. The two heads of state alighted, and then together they cut red and blue ribbons

while the national anthems were played as the French and British prime ministers looked on. After lunch on French soil, Queen Elizabeth and President Mitterand climbed aboard the royal Rolls Royce and enjoyed the experience of the Le Shuttle passenger-vehicle train journey back across the English Channel to Folkestone, where more ribbons were cut and more speeches were made.

The total length of the new tunnel is 31 miles (50 km), of which 23 miles (37 km) are under water. The tunnel has cost a staggering £10 billion (US$15 billion) to build, and some business analysts are skeptical as to whether it will ever make a profit. The tunnel itself is an average of 150 ft (45 m) under the seabed, and the crossing time on the Eurostar is a mere 20 minutes. It is now possible to travel direct from London to Paris by train in just three hours.

Joint Space Mission Heralds New Era

Cape Canaveral, USA, February 6, 1995: Back in the 1960s, when the term "space race" was on everyone's lips and the Cold War saw a desperate, and very masculine, battle between the USA and the USSR, it was hard to imagine that there would ever be any friendship and cooperation between the two countries or that a woman would one day pilot a spacecraft. Yet, today, both of these historic firsts were achieved when Eileen Marie Collins piloted the US space shuttle *Discovery* STS-63 to successfully complete a rendezvous with the Russian space station *Mir*.

It was a triumph for women, and it was also the realization of a personal ambition for Collins, who dreamed of being a pilot growing up in Elmira, New York. She graduated from Syracuse University in 1978, and then earned a Master of

Science degree in operations research from Stanford University in 1986 and a Master of Arts degree in space systems management from Webster University in 1989, at the same time gaining extensive experience as a US Air Force test pilot and military instructor.

The joint mission is also an acknowledgment that the tensions of the Cold War are becoming distant memories for the astronauts and cosmonauts now involved in the exploration of space and the wide range of scientific experiments that are being carried out. This new era of international cooperation was announced back in September 1993 when US Vice President Al Gore and Russian Prime Minister Viktor Chernomyrdin agreed to build a new space station and to share the knowledge and technology of *Mir*. At this meeting it was agreed that the US space shuttles would transport both personnel and supplies to *Mir*.

It is planned that, starting next month, US astronauts will spend time on the space station with their Russian counterparts.

Eileen Collins

time out

Archeologists dated the first human presence in the Americas to 12,500 years ago, a thousand years earlier than was previously thought. Over two decades, findings at Monte Verde in Chile were analyzed and eventually found to support the earlier date.

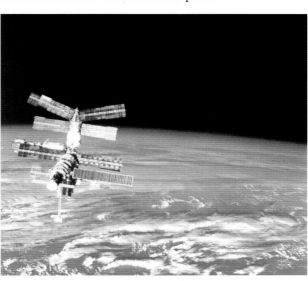
The Russian *Mir* Space Station as seen from US Space Shuttle *Atlantis*.

Renowned Pioneer of Polio Research Dies

Ian Wilmut

"*Trying to capture the physicists' precise mathematical description of the quantum world with our crude words and mental images is like playing Chopin with a boxing glove on one hand and a catcher's mitt on the other.*"

GEORGE JOHNSON,
AMERICAN WRITER
AND JOURNALIST, 1996.

La Jolla, USA, June 23, 1995: The great American medical researcher and physician Jonas Salk died today in La Jolla, California, at the age of 80.

Salk will be remembered as the man who discovered a vaccine for the dreaded infant paralysis commonly known as polio (from poliomyelitis).

Salk was a tireless researcher all his life. As early as the 1930s, when he was still a medical student at New York University, he carried out research into influenza, and in the 1940s he joined a team at the University of Michigan that developed a flu vaccine. In 1947, he moved to the University of Pittsburgh, where he started his research into polio, which at the time was affecting hundreds of thousands of children around the world each year. In 1952, some 58,000 cases had been reported in the USA alone.

Salk was convinced that a cure could be found in an inactivated vaccine. He conducted trials on 1.8 million American schoolchildren, and by 1955 he was able to declare that the vaccine not only worked but that it was also safe. Such was the level of the problem that nationwide vaccination programs were instituted around the world. The results were remarkable, and by the early 1960s the number of new cases had been reduced to around 1,000.

This was greatly assisted in 1988 when the World Health Organization passed a resolution pledging to eradicate polio completely by the year 2000.

At the time of his death, Salk was attempting to produce a vaccine to cure HIV in AIDS sufferers.

History Unearthed: The Legacy of the Leakeys

Nairobi, Kenya, December 9, 1996: Noted British paleoanthropologist and archeologist Mary Leakey has died today in Nairobi, Kenya, at the age of 83. Few people have had such a profound impact on our understanding of the early history of humanity, and Leakey will be remembered with great affection by all those who now accept that early humans emerged from Africa.

So profoundly did Leakey, and her husband Louis, change the perception of early human history that it is now hard to imagine that, when she was a young woman in the 1920s, it was still believed that modern human beings had evolved from creatures living in Asia.

Shortly after the couple were married in 1936, they headed for East Africa, where, over a period of nearly 50 years,

Akashi Kaikyo Bridge, the world's longest suspension bridge, connects Awaji Island to Kobe city.

they made a series of hugely important discoveries. The Leakeys formed a near-perfect team, with Mary as the meticulous researcher, and Louis as the interpreter and popularizer.

The discoveries started in 1948 when Mary unearthed the skull of an 18 million-year-old ape (*Proconsul africanus*) on Rusinga Island, in Lake Victoria. This find was followed in 1959 by the jaw of the 1.75 million-year-old *Australopithecus*, a very early hominid, which she found in the now-famous Olduvai Gorge in Tanzania. At that time, this specimen was thought to be "the missing link," but that claim has subsequently been discredited. Perhaps her most important discovery came some years later in 1965 when, back in the Olduvai Gorge again, she found fragments of a skull that looked remarkably like the skull of a human being, which was dated as being approximately 1 million years old.

Louis died in 1972, but Mary continued her work. In 1978, south of the Olduvai Gorge, she found 3.5 million-year-old footprints, suggesting that humans were standing and walking erect at that time.

Cloning of Sheep Marks Scientific Breakthrough

Edinburgh, Scotland, February 22, 1997: Until today it was the stuff of science fiction and, in the minds of many people, also of science nightmare. The idea of

cloning animals, which was a central part of Aldous Huxley's *Brave New World*, is now a reality as scientists at the Roslin Institute in Scotland announced that Dolly the Sheep, a Finn Dorset ewe, had been successfully cloned. The importance of the breakthrough is that Dolly is the first mammal to be cloned.

The scientific team, led by Dr Ian Wilmut, used a technique known as somatic cell nuclear transfer. The process, explained simply, involves inserting the nucleus of a somatic cell into a denucleated ovum. The two cells fuse, and then they slowly develop into an embryo.

It has been revealed that Dolly was actually born on July 5, 1996, but her birth was kept quiet because there had been a high incidence of failure with previous attempts. Previously identified by the unromantic name of 6LL3, the young sheep was named Dolly by her carers for the famous, and buxom, country music singer Dolly Parton, because Dolly the Sheep had been cloned from an adult mammary cell.

It is hoped that this breakthrough, rather than heralding a "brave new world" of random cloning, will be used for important scientific breakthroughs. Already scientists are talking about the possibility of being able to preserve some endangered species in this way, and researchers are looking into the possibility of cloning human cells.

A double photo of cloned sheep Dolly.

World's Longest Suspension Bridge Opens

Kobe, Japan, April 5, 1998: The desire to extend engineering techniques to new limits found perfect expression when the Akashi-Kaikyo Bridge, which links Maiko in Kobe with Iwaya on Awaji Island, was officially opened to traffic today.

It is a triumph of the bridge engineer's skills. The total length of the new bridge is 12,831 ft (3,911 m), and it has three spans. The main section is the longest bridge span in the world—a distance of 6,529 ft (1,990 m). The two other sections are both exactly 3,150 ft (960 m).

The perfect symmetry of the bridge was altered when (at the time uncompleted) it was "stretched" an extra meter by the Kobe earthquake of 1995. The total cost of the bridge has been estimated at 500 billion yen (US$5 billion), though it is expected that a hefty toll will eventually defray this cost.

Given the often difficult geological and climatic conditions prevailing in the Kobe region, the bridge was designed to withstand an earthquake measuring 8.5 on the Richter scale and cyclonic winds of 178 mph (286 km/h). This is not an overreaction, since the region is known for its wild storms and devastating earthquakes.

Scientific Achievements

Astronomy: Discovery of the accelerating expansion of the universe.
Botany: New genus and species of coniferous tree, *Wollemia nobilis*, discovered in Australia.
Chemistry: Sheep, goats, and pigs successfully cloned.
Ecology: Kyoto Protocol established with defined targets for reducing greenhouse gas emissions.
Geology: NASA uses *Sojourner* to analyse Earth's geology and atmosphere from Mars.
Mathematics: Development of *Shor's algorithm* for quantum computers.
Medicine: First vaccines available for hepatitis A, Lyme disease, and rotavirus.
Physics: Existence of top quark, the most massive of quarks, is established.
Zoology: World Bank and World Wildlife Fund establish a partnership for forest conservation and sustainable use.

Botanic Gardens
Alaska, USA

Observatories
Benson, USA
Kearney, USA
Mount Evans, USA
St Davids, USA

Universities
University of Ankara, Turkey
University of Iringa, Tanzania
University of Gaza City, Palestine
University of Ifrane, Morocco
University of Maseno, Kenya

There had been plans to make the bridge a combined rail and road link between the city and the island, but it is now exclusively a six-lane bridge for road transport. It is believed that the bridge's span will stand as a record for a number of years as it is near the practical engineering limit for a suspension bridge.

Outspoken Genetics Scientist Sacked

London, England, August 12, 1998: Dr Arpád Pusztai, a world authority on food safety and an expert on genetic engineering, went on ITV's *World in Action* program two nights ago and declared that he would not eat genetically engineered food because the testing procedures, so far, have been incomplete and unsatisfactory.

Dr Pusztai, who has a chemistry degree from the University of Budapest and a PhD in biochemistry from the University of London, was articulating a widespread concern about the safety of GE (genetically engineered) foods. At the time he was working for one of the leading food safety laboratories in the United Kingdom—the Rowett Research Institute—and his comments were portrayed as being scientifically incorrect.

However, it should be noted that one of the world's leading GE companies, Monsanto, had provided Rowett with a US$224,000 grant and, at the time, the biotech industry was engaged in a multi-million-pound campaign to persuade the British public that GE foods were safe.

As a result of his comments, Dr Pusztai has been suspended from the Rowett Institute.

Oldest Astronaut Sets New Space Record

Cape Canaveral, USA, November 7, 1998: He was the first American to orbit the Earth, the third American to fly into space, and now, aged 77, he has become the oldest person to fly into space. It is a record unlikely to be matched or beaten for decades. And the remarkable man with all these achievements to his name is John Herschel Glenn Jr, who can also claim to have been a US Marine Corps fighter pilot and a successful US Senator.

John Glenn

Not surprisingly, when Glenn returned today, after spending nine days in space, he was promised a ticker-tape parade. Glenn's second space flight, which commenced on October 29, was more than an ego mission or, as some of his critics claimed, "an easy junket for a politician." He boarded the Space Shuttle *Discovery* specifically to study the effects of space travel on the elderly.

The nine-day journey was a rare opportunity to compare the differing effects of space travel over time. Glenn's flights were separated by 35 years. He had been assigned to NASA in 1959 as one of the original members of Project Mercury, and his famous flight occurred on February 20, 1962, when he took *Friendship 7* three times around the Earth. At this time Glenn was one of the most famous people on the planet.

John Glenn retired from the space program in 1964 and later became a Democratic Senator for Ohio, serving from 1974 to 1998. Now, among his historic firsts, he can also include the "First Politician in Space."

Eight members of the space shuttle *Discovery* crew during pre-flight at Kennedy Space Center.

Jessica Tandy

> *"You can now see the Female Eunuch the world over... Wherever you see nail varnish, lipstick, brassieres, and high heels, the Eunuch sets up her camp."*
>
> GERMAINE GREER (B. 1939), AUSTRALIAN WRITER AND FEMINIST, IN THE TWENTIETH ANNIVERSARY EDITION OF *THE FEMALE EUNUCH*, 1990

Van Gogh Painting Sets New Art Auction Record

New York, USA, May 15, 1990: In 1897, Vincent Van Gogh's sister-in-law sold her brother's painting, *Portrait of Doctor Gachet,* for the sum of 300 francs. Today at Christie's auction house in New York, that same painting broke all the records when it was sold for US$82.5 million to Ryoei Saito, a Japanese businessman.

It was the end of a remarkable journey that had seen the painting travel an extraordinary distance in the 93 years since its first sale. From 1911 to 1933 it was hung in the Städel Museum in Frankfurt. It was removed from public view and locked in a hidden room from 1933 to 1937, when it was confiscated by the Nazis because it was seen as "degenerate art."

Hermann Goering sold it to a dealer in Amsterdam, who in turn sold it to art collector Siegfried Kramarsky. When the Kramarsky family fled from Holland to escape the Nazis, they took the painting with them to the United States. It was often exhibited after the war, and then recently the Kramarsky family decided to sell it. Today it has become a symbol of the current value of great works of art.

World Mourns Death of Great Puppeteer

New York, USA, May 16, 1990: Few modern artists have left an impression quite as deep and enduring as the great puppeteer Jim Henson, who died today from bacterial pneumonia, aged only 53. It was through his memorable Muppets, and the international cultural and educational importance of the popular children's TV show "Sesame Street," that Henson will be remembered and loved.

James Maury Henson was born in Greenville, Mississippi, in 1936. By 1954,

when he was still at high school, he was already experimenting with puppets and performing in segments on a local Saturday morning children's TV show. The first of his novel puppets (which he called Muppets) to appear regularly on television was Rowlf, the cute piano-playing dog. Henson got his big break in 1968 when the Children's Television Network started working on the public television children's program "Sesame Street."

It was on this program that Henson peopled the imaginary street with his wonderful, larger-than-life puppets. These characters became part of the childhood experience of millions of children across North America and, eventually, because of the global success of the show, they became known and loved by the children across the rest of the world.

Such was their success that they moved on to the hit series "The Muppet Show," which they later morphed into a number of highly successful movies, including the 1979 classic *The Muppet Movie.*

Spare a thought tonight for his lovable creations, Kermit the Frog, Miss Piggy, Oscar the Grouch, Bert and Ernie, the Cookie Monster, Big Bird, Gonzo the Great, and Fozzie Bear. Their creator has died, and they will be missing him.

The Three Tenors Make Triumphant Debut

Rome, Italy, July 7, 1990: The idea of not one, not two, but three great tenors singing together has never been tried before. Opera singers traditionally sing solo arias or duets.

So it is an inspired creative decision that sees three of the world's greatest tenors—Placido Domingo, José Carreras, and Luciano Pavarotti—collaborating and lifting their voices in harmonies designed to send fans and music lovers into raptures of hyperbole.

What an inspired idea! It is widely accepted that the Italian impresario Mario Dradi has been the inspiration

Television director and puppeteer Jim Henson poses with several of his Fraggle Rock muppets.

Domingo, Carreras, and Pavarotti are The Three Tenors.

Tom Hanks

The Blue Angel Sings No More

Paris, France, May 6, 1992: Few entertainers can claim to be genuine legends in their own lifetime, but the compellingly beautiful and enigmatic German actress Marlene Dietrich, who died today aged 90, was the authentic goods. Born in Berlin in 1901, she was one of the greatest of all the "femmes fatales" from the golden era of films.

Dietrich got her first movie role when she was still a teenager, but it was her role as the cabaret singer Lola, in Josef von Sternberg's *The Blue Angel* (1930), that established her reputation. It was in this role that she made the song "Falling in Love Again" one of her signature tunes. She moved to Hollywood and there she featured in a number of significant films including *Witness for the Prosecution, Touch of Evil,* and *Judgment at Nuremberg.*

At the same time she enjoyed a successful singing career, recording for the Decca, EMI, and Columbia labels. This combination of talents meant that she could move seamlessly from film to stage and cabaret. During World War II she regularly entertained Allied troops. She had no admiration for the Nazis and, in spite of constant pleas from Hitler, refused to return to Germany.

After the war, Dietrich continued to work as a cabaret artist until 1974, when she fell and broke her leg. She was largely bed-ridden in her declining years, living in isolation in Paris, although it is known that she was a keen letter-writer and regularly phoned world leaders, including Ronald Reagan and Mikhail Gorbachev.

Ballet Legend Tragically Dies of AIDS

Paris, France, January 6, 1993: HIV/AIDS took another victim from the world's arts community today when Rudolf Nureyev died in Paris aged only 54.

Nureyev was born in Irkutsk, Siberia, in 1938, and enrolled in ballet school in 1955. By 1957, his prodigious talent had been recognized, and he was hailed as one of Russia's greatest ballet dancers. In 1961, when the Kirov Ballet Company was on tour in Paris, the lead dancer was injured. Nureyev replaced him, and the audiences and critics were entranced.

In the same year, Nureyev defected. He did not return to Russia until 1989, when he was allowed to visit his dying mother.

In 1962, he met Margot Fonteyn, and they danced together in *Giselle*. She took him to England and integrated him into the Royal Ballet Company. It was then that Fonteyn and Nureyev cemented their status with breathtaking performances in both *Swan Lake* and *Giselle.*

Throughout the 1960s and 1970s, Nureyev elevated the role of a lead ballet dancer to that of a rock star. He loved celebrity and mixed with international icons such as Andy Warhol and Mick Jagger. As he moved into his forties, he refused to acknowledge that he could no longer dance the demanding roles upon which his fame had been built.

Nureyev was an iconic performer who, with Dame Margot Fonteyn, formed one of the most potent and memorable ballet partnerships ever.

Ballet star Rudolf Hametovich Nureyev.

behind the idea. His plan was remarkably simple. He knew the singers might not naturally want to sing with each other, and so he devised the idea that the singers should join together for a worthy cause. The chosen cause was the Carreras Foundation, a charity that was set up to raise funds for leukemia research.

Carreras only recently has recovered from successful treatment for leukemia, and this was to be a welcome back concert for one of this generation's most charismatic tenors. And so it was, with all three singers committed, that this sublime combination of voices performed last night at the Baths of Caracalla in Rome, accompanied by the Orchestra de Maggio Musicale Fiorentino and the Orchestra del Teatro dell'Opera di Roma conducted by Zubin Mehta. Highlights of the program included a sublime version of "Nessun Dorma" from Puccini's *Turandot.*

It is expected the recording of the concert will enjoy huge sales and attract non-opera lovers to the musical form. Today, with the voices ringing in their ears, football fans will gather for the World Cup final in Rome.

Ralph Fiennes

Success for the Coen Brothers

Hollywood, USA, May 8, 1996: The output of Joel and Ethan Coen has been patchy since they exploded onto the film scene 12 years ago with the remarkable *Blood Simple*. Since then they have made the amusing *Raising Arizona* (1987), the exceptional *Miller's Crossing* (1990), the quirky *Barton Fink* (1991), and *The Hudsucker Proxy* (1994)— and now, with their latest theatrical release, *Fargo*, they have made their best film to date. Their canon of films has contained many creations of great and original imagination. However *Fargo* is the first film in which all the elements that the Coen Brothers (as they are commonly referred to) are known for have combined to produce something so popular, compelling, and entertaining as this.

It is the amusing story of a grossly inept crime, which is solved by a hugely pregnant policewoman, Marge Gunderson (played by Frances McDormand, who is married to Joel Coen). Set in the icy wastes of North Dakota and Minnesota, it should establish the Coen Brothers with more mainstream audiences. It also demonstrates that quality and popularity are not mutually exclusive concepts in mainstream American cinema.

The English Patient Picks Up Nine Oscars

Hollywood, USA, March 24, 1997: Nominated for 12 Oscars, *The English Patient*, a complex love story set during World War II, and starring Ralph Fiennes as Count László de Almásy and Juliette Binoche as the nurse Hana, has won nine awards.

Frances McDormand with Joel Coen.

The film is about a doomed love affair, which is revealed slowly as the nurse tends to the badly burned "English patient." It collected awards for Best Supporting Actress (Binoche), Best Art Direction, Best Cinematography, Best Costume Design, Best Director (Anthony Minghella), Best Film Editing, Best Music, Best Picture, and Best Sound. It missed out on Best Actor (Fiennes), Best Actress (Kristen Scott Thomas), and Best Writing, Screenplay Based on Material from Another Medium. This last category nomination resulted because Anthony Minghella wrote the screenplay based on the hugely admired novel by the Sri Lankan-born, Canadian writer Michael Ondaatje, who won the 1992 Booker Prize.

At a time when many critics regard the Academy Awards as lightweight awards for blockbusters (*Braveheart* won last year), this has been a year when a challenging film has beaten movies as populist as *Jerry Maguire*. *The English Patient* is also a triumph for independent film making. The film had been shot entirely around the Mediterranean (in Italy and Tunisia) and the producer, Saul Zaentz (who won the Academy Award for Best Picture), has a long history of turning important literary works into movies. He has previously purchased the rights to *One Flew over the Cuckoo's Nest*, *Amadeus*, and *The Unbearable Lightness of Being* and turned them all into box office successes.

Guggenheim Museum Bilbao Opens to the Public

Bilbao, Spain, October 19, 1997: There are a small number of buildings in the world that are so individualistic and iconic that, even on the day of their official opening, it can be predicted that they will be admired and revered for centuries to come. One such building is the extraordinary Guggenheim Museum in Bilbao, Spain, which has opened its doors to the public today. It is one of a number of museums constructed by the Solomon R. Guggenheim Foundation.

Designed by Frank Gehry, the building looks more like a sculpture than an ordinary museum. It is said that it does not have a single flat surface. Instead, it looks like a beautiful collection of sculptured forms, all carefully organized so they form a harmonious whole that looks vaguely like a ship. This was quite

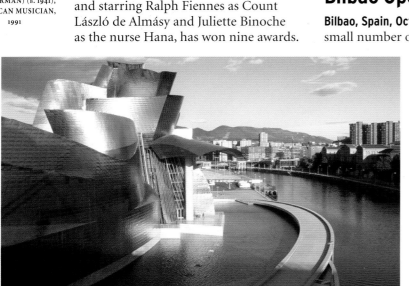

The sculptural forms of Frank Gehry's Guggenheim Museum are silhouetted in the night sky.

Achievements in the Arts

Key Structures
Arch 22, Banjul, Gambia
Basel Signal Box, Basle, Switzerland
Burj Al Arab, Dubai, United Arab Emirates
Campo Volantin Footbridge, Bilbao, Spain
Chek Lap Kok airport, Hong Kong, China
Glyndebourne Opera House, Glyndebourne, England
Guggenheim Museum Bilbao, Bilbao, Spain
Haas Haus, Vienna, Austria
Hotel du Departement, Marseille, France
Ibibio Village, Cameroon
Kiasma Museum of Contemporary Art, Helsinki, Finland
King Hassan II Mosque, Casablanca, Morocco
Niteroi Contemporary Art Museum, Niteroi, Brazil
Petronas Towers, Kuala Lumpur, Malaysia
St Ignatius Chapel, Seattle, USA
Umeda Sky Building, Osaka, Japan
Vitra Design Museum, Weil-am-Rhein, Germany

Nobel Prize for Literature
1990 Octavio Paz; 1991 Nadine Gordimer; 1992 Derek Walcott; 1993 Toni Morrison; 1994 Kenzaburo Oe; 1995 Seamus Heaney; 1996 Wislawa Szymborska; 1997 Dario Fo; 1998 Jose Saramago; 1999 Gunter Grass.

Booker Prize for Fiction
1990 *Possession: A Romance*, A. S. Byatt; 1991 *Famished Road*, Ben Okri; 1992 *The English Patient*, Michael Ondaatje/ *Sacred Hunger*, Barry Unsworth; 1993 *Paddy Clarke Ha Ha Ha*, Roddy Doyle; 1994 *How Late It Was, How Late*, James Kelman; 1995 *The Ghost Road*, Pat Barker; 1996 *Last Orders*, Graham Swift; 1997 *The God of Small Things*, Arundhati Roy; 1998 *Amsterdam*, Ian McEwan; 1999 *Disgrace*, by J. M. Coetzee.

Pulitzer Prize for Fiction
1990 *The Mambo Kings Play Songs of Love*, Oscar Hijuelos; 1991 *Rabbit at Rest*, John Updike; 1992 *A Thousand Acres*, Jane Smiley; 1993 *A Good Scent from a Strange Mountain*, Robert Olen Butler; 1994 *The Shipping News*, E. Annie Proulx; 1995 *The Stone Diaries*, Carol Shields; 1996 *Independence Day*, Richard Ford; 1997 *Martin Dressler: The Tale of an American Dreamer*, Steven Millhauser; 1998 *American Pastoral*, Philip Roth; 1999 *The Hours*, Michael Cunningham.

Academy Awards
Best Film 1990 *Dances With Wolves*; 1991 *The Silence of the Lambs*; 1992 *Unforgiven*; 1993 *Schindler's List*; 1994 *Forrest Gump*; 1995 *Braveheart*; 1996 *The English Patient*; 1997 *Titanic*; 1998 *Shakespeare in Love*; 1999 *American Beauty*.

BAFTAs
Best Film 1990 *Goodfellas*; 1991 *The Commitments*; 1992 *Howard's End*; 1993 *Schindler's List*; 1994 *Four Weddings and a Funeral*; 1995 *Sense and Sensibility*/ *The Usual Suspects*; 1996 *The English Patient*; 1997 *The Full Monty*; 1998 *Shakespeare in Love*; 1999 *American Beauty*.

intentional. The building is located on the foreshore of the Nervión River in Bilbao, and forms part of the city's plan to revitalize its old center.

It is likely that the building will stand as a monument to the technology and enthusiasms of the late twentieth century. It is a fine example of the currently fashionable deconstructionist school of architecture. It glows at all hours of the day and night because large sections of the building have been covered with thin layers of gleaming titanium plate, and it was constructed with the aid of computerized design programs. The titanium plates serve a number of functions. They can appear to be like the scales of a fish. They reflect the nearby Nervión River—and, because they are not straight and simply angular, they can give the impression that the building is actually changing shape as the sunlight shifts across the surface.

It is anticipated that the building will attract tourists, particularly lovers of modern art, to Bilbao. The museum is committed to a program of housing modern works of art. It will be interesting to see whether in years to come it will be patronized by people who come primarily to admire the building rather than its contents, or whether they will come for both.

Ol' Blue Eyes Plays His Final Show

Los Angeles, USA, May 14, 1998: Teen idols really do grow old and die. This is the great lesson all his fans have to accept today when they try to grasp the enormity of the death of one of the greatest popular singers of the twentieth century, Frank Sinatra. Sinatra, who died today from a heart attack, was much more than a smooth crooner.

He was a great vocal stylist (almost certainly the greatest vocal stylist in the pre-rock era), who had a deep emotional commitment to his material. And he was also the first genuine teen idol.

Born in Hoboken, New Jersey, on December 12, 1915, Sinatra was from Sicilian-American stock. He was inspired to sing when he first heard Bing Crosby, and he started his career with the Harry James and Tommy Dorsey bands. It was around 1940, during World War II, that teenage girls, known at the time as "bobby soxers," started screaming at this handsome, thin, young man.

By the 1950s, Sinatra's pop idol career seemed to be over, but he very successfully embraced movies (his performance in *From Here to Eternity* in 1953 won him a Best Supporting Actor Oscar), and he successfully revitalized his singing career by signing with Capitol Records. With this label he made his finest recordings with the brilliant conductors Billy May and Nelson Riddle.

It is hard to imagine the 1950s without *Songs for Swingin' Lovers*. It was a soundtrack for the times. From that time on, Sinatra became a true legend in his own

Renowned violinist Yehudi Menuhin with French jazz musician Stephane Grappelli.

lifetime. He was the center of the infamous "Rat Pack" (with Dean Martin, Sammy Davis Jr, Peter Lawford, and Joey Bishop), he entertained at Las Vegas, and he became friends with President John F. Kennedy. And apparently he was also linked with the Mafia.

All of this, however, was irrelevant to his fans, who loved him for his perfect phrasing, his beautiful crooning style, and his total mastery of microphone singing. He was a true legend and one of the century's great entertainers.

Master Violinist Takes His Last Bow

Berlin, Germany, March 12, 1999: One of the world's most admired and revered musicians, the great Jewish-American violinist, Yehudi Menuhin, died today in Berlin at the age of 82.

Menuhin was born in New York City on April 22, 1916. He was a child prodigy, giving his first public performance of Mendelssohn's *Violin Concerto* at the age of seven, accompanied by the San Francisco Symphony Orchestra. He performed over 500 concerts for Allied servicemen during World War II. Then Menuhin and the composer Benjamin Britten traveled to Germany to perform for the liberated prisoners of Bergen-Belsen immediately after the war.

Although he was proud of his Jewish heritage (his first name, Yehudi, means "Jew" in Hebrew), he was also a great peacemaker. As early as 1947, he went to Germany where he performed with the Berlin Philharmonic under the great conductor Wilhelm Furtwängler. Menuhin was the first Jewish musician to play in German concert halls after the war. After the war he became one of the most widely recognized and admired classical musicians. He was passionate about the disciplines of both yoga and meditation, and is credited with helping to introduce them as alternative therapies to Western audiences.

Frank Sinatra

Menuhin's taste in music was eclectic. At various times he worked with the great French jazz musician Stephane Grappelli, and with the Indian sitar virtuoso Ravi Shankar. He was also a teacher and educator; in 1963 he established the Yehudi Menuhin School in Surrey, where his pupils included the British violinist Nigel Kennedy. Although he was born in New York, Menuhin was essentially a European and spent most of his life in Surrey. In 1993, he became a British life peer and was known as Baron Menuhin of Stoke D'Abernon.

Film Wild Man Dies

Valletta, Malta, May 2, 1999: The death today of the larger-than-life, roistering, wild man Oliver Reed brings to an end an era when movie stars were genuine legends. Reed did everything to excess. He married three times. He was expelled from numerous expensive private schools. And he acted not because he was well trained (he never trained) or because it was an enduring passion, but because it provided the money required to sustain his riotous lifestyle.

Reed, who was a nephew of the great British film director Sir Carol Reed, was a child of the 1960s. He was born in London in 1938, and enjoyed his greatest period of fame with major roles in *Women in Love* (1969), *The Devils* (1971), *Oliver!* (1968), *Tommy* (1975), and *The Three Musketeers* (1973). His reputation was as a ferocious drinker.

He died while filming *Gladiator*. The story is that he drank three bottles of rum and had just beaten three sailors at arm wrestling when he died.

Oliver Reed lived life to the full.

Oprah Winfrey

> "MARRIAGE IN
> MODERN
> TIMES IS
> REGARDED AS
> A PARTNER-
> SHIP OF
> EQUALS AND
> NO LONGER
> ONE IN WHICH
> THE WIFE
> MUST BE THE
> SUBSERVIENT
> CHATTEL
> OF THE
> HUSBAND."
>
> LORD KEITH OF
> KINKEL (B. 1922),
> BRITISH JUDGE,
> RULING THAT RAPE
> CAN OCCUR WITHIN
> MARRIAGE, 1991

Navratilova Makes Tennis History

London, England, July 7, 1990: It seems that all records are meant to be broken, but it is hard to imagine that the record set today by Czech-born tennis sensation Martina Navratilova is likely to be broken in the near future. Today Navratilova won the Wimbledon women's singles title for a record ninth time.

Navratilova won her first Wimbledon Grand Slam title in 1978, when, at the age of 21, she defeated Chris Evert in three sets. She also won the title in 1979 and 1982 (against Evert), in 1983 (against Andrea Jaeger), in 1984 and 1985 (against Evert), in 1986 (against Hana Mandlikova), in 1987 (against Steffi Graf), and today she beat Zina Garrison 6–4, 6–1 to take her ninth title.

Navratilova turned professional in 1973 at the age of 16, and since then has been recognized as one of the greatest serve-and-volley female players in the history of the game. Realizing at the time that Czechoslovakia held limited scope for her, she defected to the USA in 1975 and became a US citizen in 1981.

Navratilova's career has been an extraordinary one. Her best years were 1982, 1983 (when she won three of the four major Grand Slam events), and 1984. During this time she won an extraordinary 86 games while recording only one loss. At one time she held all four of the Grand Slam titles, although she did not win them all in a single year.

Today's triumph is an amazing and remarkable demonstration of the tennis genius of Navratilova.

At 33-years-old, she is still one of the finest tennis players in the world.

Martina Navratilova has won the Wimbledon women's singles title for a record ninth time.

time out

Soviet smokers demonstrated in protest at the severe tobacco shortages forcing them to join long queues or go without cigarettes altogether. Two thousand chanted and waved banners at City Hall in Perm, and angry smokers smashed windows of tobacco kiosks.

Unified Team Surprises the Summer Olympics

Barcelona, Spain, August 9, 1992: With the dissolution of the USSR last year and the decision made by its former Baltic states of Latvia, Lithuania, and Estonia to compete as independent countries at this year's Olympics, it was widely anticipated that the Soviet Union, which participated at these Games as the Unified Team, would not be able to sustain their former high achievements.

So it came as a surprise when the final medal tally was announced to find that the Unified Team, which was comprised of the republics of Armenia, Azerbaijan, Belarus, Georgia, Kazakhstan, Kyrgyzstan, Moldova, Russia, Tajikistan, Turkmenistan, Ukraine, and Uzbekistan, had beaten all other countries on every count. Displayed in the results listings as EUN, or Equipe Unifiée, the Unified Team won a total of 112 medals, including 45 gold, 38 silver, and 29 bronze. The USA came second with 37 gold, 34 silver, and 37 bronze, for a total of 108 medals, and Germany third with 33 gold, 21 silver, and 28 bronze, for a tally of 82 medals.

Particularly impressive for the Unified Team was the performance in the swimming pool of the men's team, which won five gold and three silver medals, with the great Alexander Popov winning both the 50 m and 100 m freestyle, while his teammate Yevgeny Sadovyi won the 200 m and 400 m freestyle events.

These Games were notable as this was the first time that all IOC member countries had sent teams to the Summer Olympics since 1972, and the first time since 1960 that South Africa had competed. The Barcelona Games also saw the debuts of teams from the former Yugoslavian states of Croatia, Slovenia, and Bosnia and Herzegovina.

Key Events

Worldwide, February 14, 1990: Perrier withdraws its entire stock of 160 million bottles after traces of benzine are found in the carbonated water.

London, England, July 7, 1990: Martina Navratilova wins the Wimbledon singles title.

Venezuela, July 27, 1990: OPEC agrees to raise the price of oil for the first time in ten years due to instability in the Middle East.

English Channel, December 1, 1990: The French and British sides of the Channel Tunnel link up.

South Africa, March 27, 1991: The International Olympic Committee re-admits South Africa to the Olympics after a 30-year absence.

Beirut, Lebanon, August 8, 1991: British hostage John McCarthy is released after 1,943 days in captivity.

Los Angeles, USA, November 8, 1991: Top basketball player "Magic" Johnson is diagnosed with AIDS, contracted through heterosexual intercourse.

Washington State, USA, November 21, 1991: Gerard d'Aboville rows 6,000 miles (9,656 km) across the North Pacific alone in 134 days.

New York, USA, 1991: Television celebrity Oprah Winfrey begins a campaign to introduce national register of convicted child abusers.

Albertville, France, February 8-23, 1992: France hosts Winter Olympics: its third Olympiad; a united Germany takes home 26 medals.

Indianapolis, USA, March 26, 1992: Mike Tyson, the world's youngest heavyweight boxing champion is sentenced to 10 years for rape.

Barcelona, Spain, July 25–August 8, 1992: The Unified Team walks away with record haul of medals from Olympics.

Minneapolis-St Paul, USA, August 11, 1992: America's biggest mall opens, covering 4.2 million square feet

Tokyo, Japan, June 9, 1993: Crown Prince Naruhito marries Masako Owado, the first career woman in the Imperial dynasty.

Stockholm, Sweden, October 15, 1993: The Nobel Peace Prize is jointly awarded to President Frederik Willem de Clerk and Nelson Mandela of South Africa for their work toward the peaceful dismantling of apartheid.

Manassas, Virginia, USA, January 21, 1994: Lorena Bobbit, who severed her husband's penis, is found not guilty of malicious wounding due to insanity.

USA, May 5, 1994: *Playboy* magazine celebrates 40 years of centerfolds.

Los Angeles, USA, June 17, 1994: A low-speed car chase in a traffic jam begins the public downfall of O. J. Simpson.

Saugerties, New York State, USA, August 14, 1994: Some 350,000 people gather for Woodstock '94.

The world's largest Snoopy smiles down on the Mall of America.

America's Largest Shopping Mall Opens

Minneapolis-St Paul, USA, August 11, 1992: America's love affair with the shopping mall reached new heights in Bloomington today with the opening of the "megamall" known as the Mall of America. This extraordinary homage to shopping cost US$625 million and was built by the Jerde Partnership of Venice Beach, California.

With a gross area of 4.2 million sq ft (390,000 sq meters), Mall of America is now the USA's largest shopping mall in terms of total area. While it is not the largest in terms of shopping area, this remarkable mall still boasts 2.5 million sq ft (230,000 sq m) of retail space. It has a staggering 13,000 parking spaces spread over 7 levels, 281 retail stores, 48 food stores, 21 restaurants, and 9 nightclubs.

Located in the center of the mall is Camp Snoopy, the world's largest indoor amusement park with the world's largest Snoopy dog, as well as other characters from the ever-popular *Peanuts* cartoon strip. This marriage of a comic strip and a shopping mall is a tribute to one of Minnesota's famous sons, Charles M. Schultz, the creator of *Peanuts*. Schultz was born in St Paul.

Work started on the mall in 1989, and during its construction locals dubbed it "The Megamess" and "The Sprawl of America." The designing architect, Jon Jerde, is famous for his mall designs. He has already completed the Horton Plaza Center in San Diego, which was so successful that it attracted 25 million shoppers in its first year of operation. It is hoped that the Mall of America, will attract up to 40 million visitors each year, both to shop and to enjoy the other attractions.

Crown Prince Naruhito of Japan Weds

Tokyo, Japan, June 9, 1993: There was widespread joy across Japan today as 33-year-old Crown Prince Naruhito, who many royalists had feared might never marry and produce an heir to the throne, married Masako Owada. The traditional ceremony, held in the Imperial Shinto Hall in front of 2,500 invited guests including representatives from all of Europe's royal families, was televised to an estimated audience of 500 million people worldwide.

The bride is a 28-year-old career diplomat who has been working in the Foreign Ministry. She is the daughter of Hisashi Owada, the former Japanese ambassador to the United Nations. A commoner, she will take on a huge responsibility as there will be a national expectation to produce an heir, and the demands of the way of life within the Japanese imperial family will be far removed from the modern lifestyle she is used to.

The couple will live in the Kuyojo Palace, which is located in the imperial compound in Tokyo.

Woodstock '94 Re-creates the Legend

Saugerties, New York, USA, August 14, 1994: Twenty-five years ago, at Max Yasgur's 600-acre (242-ha) farm in New York State, an estimated 500,000 people gathered for the first Woodstock Festival. Over the years it has become a legendary event symbolizing the "peace and love" philosophy of the "hippie era" and launching the careers of a number of hugely successful rock bands. It belonged to the times and expressed the youth culture of the 1960s.

Now, 25 years later, a different generation has organized their own Woodstock believing that they can recapture the original magic. The slogan used to entice music lovers was "Three more days of peace, love and music," and it seems to have worked because, by best estimates, over the past three days between 235,000 and 350,000 people.

The lineup, like the original, has been a veritable "Who's Who" of the music industry, ranging from Bob Dylan and Todd Rundgren, Peter Gabriel, Cypress Hill, Traffic, Arrested Development, and Sheryl Crow, to Primus, the Red Hot Chili Peppers, Metallica, the Neville Brothers, Nine Inch Nails, Green Day, the Violent Femmes, the Cranberries, and African great Youssou N'Dour.

From the original Woodstock list, only The Band, Country Joe McDonald, Joe Cocker, Santana, and Crosby, Stills and Nash were able to make return appearances.

Magic Johnson

Carlos Santana's guitar evokes the hippie era.

Michael Johnson

"IT IS ESPECIALLY IMPORTANT TO ENCOURAGE UNORTHODOX THINKING WHEN THE SITUATION IS CRITICAL. AT SUCH MOMENTS EVERY NEW WORD AND FRESH THOUGHT IS MORE PRECIOUS THAN GOLD. INDEED, PEOPLE MUST NOT BE DEPRIVED OF THE RIGHT TO THINK THEIR OWN THOUGHTS."

BORIS YELTSIN (B. 1931), PRESIDENT OF RUSSIA

First Solo Hot Air Balloon Flight Across the Pacific

Saskatchewan, Canada, February 21, 1995: A modern-day adventurer needs either a rich backer or a personal fortune—and such a man is Steve Fossett, who today has become the first person to fly across the Pacific Ocean in a hot air balloon. Fossett made his fortune on the volatile American financial markets, but he is certainly more than just a rich adventurer.

Born in Tennessee in 1944, Fossett was an Eagle Scout by the age of 13. He is still committed to the ideals of the scouting movement. As a young man he was always adventurous, but he did manage to graduate from Stanford University in 1966 with a Bachelor of Arts degree and then gained a Master of Business Administration degree at Washington University in 1968.

Fossett is a man obsessed with breaking records. In August last year, in what now appears to have been a dummy run for this amazing exploit, he made a transatlantic balloon flight with Tim Cole as his co-pilot, in which they successfully flew from the Canadian city of St John's, Newfoundland, to Hamburg, Germany.

Fossett's latest solo record attempt started in Seoul, Korea, on February 17. After traveling a distance of 5,435 miles (8,748 km), he landed at Mendam in Saskatchewan. Not only is this the first time that someone has successfully crossed the Pacific in a hot air balloon, but it is also recognized as the absolute world distance record for a hot air balloon flight. It is unlikely that this will be the end of Fossett's record-breaking ambitions. Already he is talking about the holy grail of ballooning, a successful circumnavigation of the globe.

Fossett is not only a ballooning enthusiast and a skilled airplane pilot, but he is also an accomplished sailor who in 1993 set yet another record when he sailed around the coastline of Ireland in 44 hours and 42 minutes—the range of possible achievements that lies in front of him is tantalizing.

Michael Johnson Enters Olympic Hall of Fame

Atlanta, USA, July 19–August 4, 1996: There are few great athletes who have genuinely stood out far above the world's best. The legendary Jim Thorpe and the grace and beauty of Jesse Owens will probably spring to most readers' minds. Now, with his extraordinary victories at the Atlanta Olympics, the name of Michael Johnson has to be added to that elite list.

Johnson is the first male athlete in history to win gold medals in both the 200 m and 400 m sprint events at the Olympics. On the 29th of July, he convincingly won the 400 m final in a new Olympic record time of 43.49 seconds, almost a full second ahead of Roger Black from Great Britain, who came in second. Then three days later he set a remarkable new world record of 19.32 seconds in the 200 m final, which shattered his own previous record of 19.66 seconds. As commentators have pointed out, this extraordinary achievement marks the largest improvement ever recorded in a 200 m world record.

The Atlanta Games have been a great triumph for the athletes of the host country. At today's closing ceremony, the announcement of the final medal tally saw the United States top the table with a total of 101 medals (44 gold, 32 silver, and 25 bronze). The nearest competitor was Russia with 63 medals (26 gold, 21 silver, and 16 bronze).

While many observers have criticized these Games as over-commercialized, it is generally accepted that, with the exception of the tragic bomb blast in Centennial Olympic Park on July 27, these have been an exceptional Olympics. The most memorable moment for many people would no doubt have been when Muhammad Ali, crippled by Parkinson's disease, was met with roars of admiration as he lit the main Olympic torch during the opening ceremony.

Stamps commemorate the Olympics in Atlanta.

Tiger Woods Demolishes the Field in US Masters

Augusta, Georgia, USA, April 13, 1997: It has been known for some years in golfing circles that Eldrick T. ("Tiger") Woods is no ordinary golfer, but after his stunning victory in the US Masters today many commentators now rate him as one of the greatest golfers in history.

Woods started playing at the age of three, won the Junior World Golf Championships at the age of eight, won three consecutive US Junior Amateur Championships from 1991–1993 (the youngest player to ever win the event), and then won the US Amateur title three years in succession from 1994–1996.

Woods turned professional in August 1996, and was an instant star, winning two events before the year was out and being named *Sports Illustrated*'s "Sportsman of the Year." In a way this was all a foretaste of the resounding victory he has just achieved at Augusta. This was more than a victory—it was an annihilation of a superb field of professional golfers.

The US Masters, one of the four major championships in men's golf, is held each year at the Augusta National Golf Club in Georgia. Augusta is a challenging course, and the previous record was 17 under par held by the great Jack Nicklaus (1965) and Ray Floyd (1976). When Nicklaus won the US Masters with 17 under par, he was a record-breaking nine strokes ahead of his nearest rival.

Tiger Woods' mother Tida and father Earl have reason to smile with their champion son.

Woods has broken both those records today. He has carded 18 under par, and when he putted out on the last hole he was a clear 12 strokes ahead of his nearest rival. This was the kind of game that people will talk about for decades. A truly inspiring game of golf by a man who may well be the greatest golfer of all time.

Google's Internet Search Engine Launched

Silicon Valley, USA, September 7, 1998: The world of computer and internet technology is moving so fast that it is difficult to predict winners and losers, but the launch today of a new internet search engine named Google seems to be headed for success, although it will have to achieve miracles to beat Yahoo! and AltaVista.

Google is the brainchild of two young computer geeks, Sergei Brin and Larry Page, who named their search engine after the coined mathematical term "googol", representing the number one followed by 100 zeros. Brin was born in the Soviet Union in 1973 and moved to the USA in 1979. He has Bachelor of Science degrees in Computer Science and Mathematics from the University of Maryland. Larry Page was born in Michigan in 1972 and has a Bachelor of Science degree in Computer Engineering from the University of Michigan. They met when studying in a graduate program at Stanford University.

Fascinated by the exponential growth of information available on the world wide web, they devised a search engine program that they initially nicknamed "BackRub." Most of their work was done in Page's dormitory room. Their methodology involves checking web pages for the number of times other pages link to them, whereas previously search engines have simply ordered their results by the frequency of repeated words and phrases.

The company they have established is truly idealistic. They have a 10-point philosophy that includes: "You can make money without doing evil," "Fast is better than slow," and "Focus on the user and all else will follow." It will be interesting to see whether these idealistic philosophies make Page and Brin rich young men.

Tragedy Strikes at Sydney to Hobart Yacht Race

Pacific Ocean, Australia, December 29, 1998: The annual Sydney to Hobart yacht race, which attracts some of the world's most talented sailors and finest sailing boats, has in the past, like all ocean-going races, been fraught with danger, particularly from storms known as "southerly busters." Most years it has been smooth sailing.

This year, however, tragedy has hit the fleet. A freak low depression that produced winds of up to 70 knots (effectively it was the equivalent of a hurricane) rushed across the state of Victoria and hit the fleet, causing massive damage, loss of life, and leading to some truly heroic acts by other sailors and members of the Australian Navy's helicopter fleet.

Commenting today on the experience, US computer billionaire Larry Ellison, who was sailing *Sayonara* in the race, described the experience as: "…just awful. I've never experienced anything remotely like this. This is not what this is supposed to be about."

So far, it appears that six people have died and five boats have been lost. British sailor Glyn Charles was washed off *Sword of Orion*, three appear to be lost from the cutter *Winston Churchill*, and two Australians are missing after their boat capsized.

In one of the largest peacetime rescue operations undertaken in Australian history, a total of 35 military and civilian aircraft and 27 Australian Navy ships were involved in the rescue operation. The scenes recorded for television were a nightmare vision of huge waves and sailors adrift in yachts that had lost their steering or worse in life rafts. Fifty-nine boats were forced to seek shelter.

New euro banknotes will be introduced across Europe.

European Union Adopts Single Currency

Western Europe, January 1, 1999: When the countries of the European Community decided, as part of the famous 1992 Maastricht Treaty of European Union, to become an economic and monetary union, one of the elements of the change was the establishment of a single currency—the euro. It was a radical step because it involved the disappearance of such famous and ancient national currencies as the Spanish peseta, the Dutch guilder, the German mark, the Italian lire, the French franc, and the Greek drachma, among others.

Today, the common currency is launched onto the world's financial markets. In three years' time the process

set in motion today will be converted into reality when the new currency is launched and becomes commonplace in the twelve countries of the European Union.

Larry Page

Sporting Achievements

Baseball *World Series* 1990 Cincinnati (National League); 1991 Minnesota (American League); 1992 Toronto (AL); 1993 Toronto (AL); 1994 series cancelled; 1995 Atlanta (NL); 1996 New York (AL); 1997 Florida (NL); 1998 New York (AL); 1999 New York (AL).

Cycling *Tour de France* 1990 G. LeMond; 1991-1995 M. Indurain; 1996 B. Riis; 1997 J. Ullrich; 1998 M. Pantani; 1999 L. Armstrong.

Football *American Super Bowl* 1990 San Francisco; 1991 NY Giants; 1992 Washington; 1993 Dallas; 1994 Dallas; 1995 San Francisco; 1996 Dallas; 1997 Green Bay; 1998 Denver; 1999 Denver. *World Cup Soccer* 1990; West Germany; 1994 Brazil; 1998 France.

Golf *US Masters* 1990 N. Faldo 1991 I. Woosnam; 1992 F. Couples; 1993 B. Langer; 1994 J. M. Olazabal; 1995 B. Crenshaw; 1996 N. Faldo; 1997 T. Woods; 1998 M. O'Meara; 1999 J. M. Olazabal.

Horse Racing *Epsom Derby* 1990 Quest for Fame; 1991 Generous; 1992 Dr Devious; 1993 Coomaner in Chief; 1994 Erhaab; 1995 Lammtarra; 1996 Shaamit; 1997 Benny the Dip; 1998 High-Rise; 1999 Oath. *Kentucky Derby* 1990 Unbridled; 1991 Strike The Gold; 1992 Lil E. Tee; 1993 Sea Hero; 1994 Go For Gin; 1995 Thunder Gulch; 1996 Grindstone; 1997 Silver Charm; 1998 Real Quiet; 1999 Charismatic. *Melbourne Cup* 1990 Kingston Rule; 1991 Let's Elope; 1992 Subzero; 1993 Vintage Crop; 1994 Jeune; 1995 Doriemus; 1996 Saintly; 1997 Might and Power; 1998 Jezabeel; 1999 Rogan Josh.

Ice Hockey *Stanley Cup* 1990 Edmonton; 1991 Pittsburgh; 1992 Pittsburgh; 1993 Montreal; 1994 New York; 1995 New Jersey; 1996 Colorado; 1997 Detroit 1998 Detroit; 1999 Dallas.

Marathon *Boston, Men's* 1990 G. Bordin; 1991 I. Hussein; 1992 I. Hussein; 1993 C. N'Deti; 1994 C. N'Deti; 1995 C. N'Deti; 1996 M. Tanui; 1997 L. Aguta; 1998 M. Tanui; 1999 J. Chebet; *Women's* 1990 R. Mota; 1991 W. Panfil; 1992 O. Markova; 1993 O. Markova; 1994 U. Pippig; 1995 U. Pippig; 1996 U. Pippig; 1997 F. Roba; 1998 F. Roba; 1999 F. Roba.

Sailing *America's Cup* 1992 *America 3*; 1995 *Black Magic*.

Tennis *Australian Open, Men's Singles* 1990 I. Lendl; 1991 B. Becker 1992-1993 J. Courier; 1994 P. Sampras; 1995 A. Agassi; 1996 B. Becker; 1997 P. Sampras; 1998 P. Korda; 1999 Y. Kafelnikov; *Women's Singles* 1990 S. Graf; 1991-1993 M. Seles; 1994 S. Graf; 1995 M. Pierce; 1996 M. Seles; 1997-1999 M. Hingis. *Roland-Garros Tournament (French Open), Men's Singles* 1990 A. Gomez; 1991-1992 J. Courier; 1993-1994 S. Bruguera; 1995 T. Muster; 1996 Y. Kafelnikov; 1997 G. Kuerten; 1998 C. Moya; 1999 A. Agassi; *Women's Singles* 1990-1992 M. Seles; 1993 S. Graf; 1994 A. Sanchez Vicario; 1995-1996 S. Graf; 1997 I. Majoli; 1998 A. Sanchez Vicario; 1999 S. Graf. *US Open, Men's Singles* 1990 P. Sampras; 1991-1992 S. Edberg; 1993 P. Sampras; 1994 A. Agassi; 1995-1996 P. Sampras; 1997-1998 P. Rafter; 1999 A. Agassi; *Women's Singles* 1990 G. Sabatini; 1991-1992 M. Seles; 1993 S. Graf; 1994 A. Sanchez Vicario; 1995-1996 S. Graf; 1997 M. Hingis; 1998 L. Davenport; 1999 S. Williams. *Wimbledon, Gentlemen's Singles* 1990 S. Edberg; 1991 M. Stich; 1992 A. Agassi; 1993-1995 P. Sampras; 1996 R. Krajicek; 1997-1999 P. Sampras; *Ladies' Singles* 1990 M. Navratilova; 1991-1993 S. Graf; 1994 C. Martinez; 1995-1996 S. Graf; 1997 M. Hingis; 1998 J. Novotna; 1999 L. Davenport.

George W. Bush

"As we look ahead into the next century, leaders will be those who empower others."

BILL GATES (B. 1955), AMERICAN BUSINESSMAN AND PHILANTHROPIST

"...America's military power must be secure because the United States is the only guarantor of global peace and stability."

CONDOLEEZZA RICE (B. 1954), AMERICAN SECRETARY OF STATE, 2000

Concorde Crash Kills 113

Gonesse, France, July 25: An Air France Concorde has crashed just minutes after taking off from Charles de Gaulle airport in Paris, killing all 109 on board and four on the ground as it slammed into a hotel in the town of Gonesse.

Eyewitnesses have said flames were clearly visible trailing behind the left engine and the aircraft seemed unable to gain altitude. The nose was seen to raise higher and higher until the aircraft stalled, rolled to the left, and simply dropped from the sky.

The passengers are all believed to have been German tourists, en route to New York to connect with a luxury cruise liner.

Concorde has long been one of the world's safest planes and can make the journey from Paris to New York in just three and a half hours. Tonight, however, the future of the supersonic aircraft remains uncertain.

Russian Submarine Sinks

Barents Sea, Arctic Circle, August 14: The Russian nuclear submarine *Kursk* has sunk during naval exercises in the Barents Sea yesterday with 118 crew aboard.

Two explosions were heard by Norwegian and US officials who were independently monitoring the exercise, but the cause of the explosions is unclear. A torpedo in one of the forward compartments may have detonated, but it is thought a highly combustible liquid-fuel system may be the cause. Questions also persist as to why the *Kursk* was operating in such shallow waters when it was designed for the open ocean. Whatever the cause of the tragedy, the damage was massive and there was little if no time for its captain to respond.

The ship was located this morning, but strong winds and currents have so far prevented upward of 20 rescue vessels from assisting the stricken submarine.

The *Kursk* was one of the largest submarines in the Russian navy.

Attempts to lower a rescue capsule have repeatedly failed. It is estimated that the vessel will run out of air by Friday.

The *Kursk* has a double-layered hull, and entered service with the Russian Northern Fleet in 1995. It is an Oscar II class cruise-missile attack submarine, designed primarily to attack American aircraft carrier battle groups.

Rescue efforts are still continuing, and are centering on providing the submarine with electricity and oxygen.

Supreme Court Gives Victory to Bush

Florida, USA, December 13: In the closest election in US history, a dispute over how-to-vote papers in Palm Beach County, Florida, saw the Supreme Court halt the recounting of ballots, thus giving the election to George W. Bush, who will be sworn in as the 43rd President of the United States.

Vice President Al Gore became only the third candidate ever to fail to win the Presidency after garnering a majority of the popular vote. Gore received 50,999,897 votes to Bush's 50,456,002—a margin of 543,895.

However, it is the number of Electoral College votes (based on the spread of votes cast) that determines the election, and of these Bush received 271 votes to Gore's 266. George W. Bush will be sworn in on January 20 next year.

Bush has taken a conciliatory tone in his acceptance speech, saying, "I know how difficult this must be for him."

Al Gore (upper right) and wife Tipper greet their loyal supporters.

Moscow, Russian Federation, January 1: After Boris Yeltsin's resignation, Prime Minister Vladimir Putin is named acting President until elections are held in 90 days time.

Baia Mare, Romania, January 30: A breach of a mine tailings dump pollutes the Sassar River with cyanide. Within a month, the spill flows from the Danube to the Black Sea.

Preston, England, January 31: Family GP Howard Shipman is sentenced to life imprisonment for murdering 15 patients. It is estimated that he may have killed as many as 250 patients in 23 years.

New York, USA, April 3: A federal judge rules that Microsoft violated antitrust laws, using its monopoly power in the computer market to stifle competition.

Zimbabwe, April 15: President Mugabe's plans for agricultural land reform claim the first victim when white farmer David Stevens is killed.

Taipei, Taiwan, May 19: Chen Shuibian is inaugurated President after the first democratic elections.

Pyongyang, North Korea, June 14: Kim Jong Il hosts South Korea's President Kim Dae Jung for the first summit between the two countries.

Cuba, June 28: Elian Gonzalez, the Cuban child found floating on an inner tube off Florida in November last year—and the focus of an international tug-of-war—returns to Cuba with his father.

Gonesse, France, July 25: An Air France Concorde crashes, killing all 109 people on board and four people on the ground.

Barents Sea, Arctic Circle, August 14: The Russian submarine *Kursk* is flooded following an explosion, with the loss of 118 crew.

England, September 15: Protesting truck drivers end their seven-day blockade on fuel refineries that has brought the nation to a standstill.

Jerusalem, Israel, September 28: Opposition Leader Ariel Sharon visits Temple Mount, known as Haram al Sharif by Muslims. This action precipitates the second Palestinian intifada, or uprising.

Belgrade, Yugoslavia, October 6: Indicted for war crimes in Kosovo in 1999, President Slobodan Milosevic finally concedes defeat to Vojislav.

Aden, Yemen, October 12: US Navy destroyer USS *Cole* is attacked by two suicide bombers, killing 17 and injuring more than 40 personnel.

New York, USA, November 7: Democrat Hillary Rodham Clinton is elected US Senator.

Kaprun, Austria, November 11: A fire aboard a funicular railway car inside a tunnel kills 155 skiers.

USA, December 13: George W. Bush becomes the 43rd President of the US, with Democrat Al Gore conceding defeat. The vote in Florida came down to a decision in the Supreme Court.

Crown Prince Kills Family

Kathmandu, Nepal, June 1: Crown Prince Dipendra has killed nine members of the Nepalese royal family, including his parents, the King and Queen, before turning the gun on himself.

The massacre occurred following a heated argument over Dipendra's choice of bride, which had reportedly been opposed by the Queen. Apparently intoxicated, Dipendra went back to his room, later returning dressed in army fatigues and armed with an automatic weapon.

Others killed in the attack included the King's sisters, Princess Sharda and Princess Shanti, his brother-in-law Kumar Khadga, and Dipendra's brother Niranjan and his sister Shruti.

Dipendra has been taken to a Kathmandu hospital suffering self-inflicted gunshot wounds to the head, and is not expected to survive.

Nepal's King Barendra and Queen Aiswarya.

Terrorist Attack on US Landmarks

New York and Washington DC, USA, September 11: On an horrific morning that Americans, and indeed the world, will never forget, com-mercial airliners have been hijacked and flown into the Twin Towers of the World Trade Center, both of which later collapsed, with a third plane flown into the Pentagon in Washington DC. A fourth plane later crashed into a field in Somerset County, western Pennsylvania, after the passengers apparently intervened and turned on their hijackers.

The south tower of the World Trade Center was hit at 9.03 a.m. and it was the first to collapse, at 10.00 a.m., covering much of lower Manhattan in a very thick blanket of dust and smoke. A half hour later the north tower, the first to be hit at 8.46 a.m, also collapsed.

Meanwhile, eyewitnesses in Washington have confirmed that the Pentagon was hit and is currently ablaze.

Across America skyscrapers have been evacuated, including the Sears Tower in Chicago and the Space Needle in Seattle. All military bases have been put on the highest possible alert status—Threatcon Alpha—and the Federal Aviation Administration (FAA) has shut down all air traffic, ordering any planes still in the air to land immediately at the nearest available airports. There are currently no aircraft in the skies of North America.

President Bush was visiting an elementary school in Florida when told of the news. He has been taken aboard Air Force

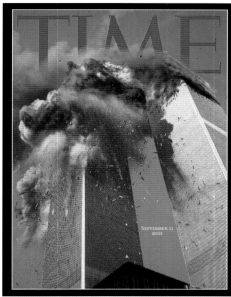

New York's World Trade Center is destroyed.

One to an undisclosed location. In the meantime the White House, the US Capitol, and other Federal buildings in the nation's capital have been evacuated.

The President has vowed to hunt down the perpetrators and bring them to justice. The aircraft that hit the World Trade Center were American Airlines Flight 11, which was carrying 81 people en route from Boston to Los Angeles, and United Airlines Flight 175, which was also heading from Boston to Los Angeles, with 65 people on board.

The aeroplane that crashed in Pennsylvania was United Airlines Flight 93, en route from Newark to San Francisco, and the one that hit the Pentagon was American Airlines Flight 77 from Washington to Los Angeles.

It is unclear how many people on the ground have been killed and injured, but the figure will surely be in the thousands.

China Joins World Trade Organization

Doha, Qatar, November 10: After 15 years of intense diplomatic lobbying, the 142 members of the World Trade Organization have at last ratified China's application for membership.

China had a long battle convincing member nations, particularly the European Union and the US, that it was very serious about opening up its economy to foreign competition. The Chinese government has indicated it will accelerate economic reforms and continue to liberalize foreign investment guidelines, particularly in the finance, trade, and communications sectors.

There were hugs among the Chinese delegation when the announcement was made, and China is hoping that increased integration will assist its transition to a market economy.

Hillary Rodham Clinton

Key Events

Gujarat, India, January 26: A massive earthquake in western India leaves 25,000 people dead and over one million homeless.
Camp Zeist, Netherlands, January 31: At a special Scottish court set up to try the bombers of Pan Am flight 103, which crashed at Lockerbie in 1988, one of the two Libyan suspects is found guilty and sentenced to life imprisonment.
Israel, February 6: Ariel Sharon, leader of the right-wing Likud party, becomes Prime Minister in a decisive election result.

Kalimantan, Indonesia, February: Ethnic violence erupts between the indigenous Dayaks and the Madurese minority, killing over 500.
Belgrade, Yugoslavia, April 1: Wanted by the UN, and facing charges of corruption at home, former President Slobodan Milosevic is arrested.
Hainan Island, China, April 11: The crew of a US surveillance plane are released after the US apologizes for the death of a Chinese pilot, who collided with the US plane over the South China Sea on March 31.

England, May: A foot-and-mouth outbreak has shut down large parts of the countryside since February.
Palawan, Philippines, May 27: The Muslim terrorist group Abu Sayyaf seizes 20 people from a tourist resort.
Kathmandu, Nepal, June 1: Crown Prince Dipendra shoots dead nine members of the royal family, before shooting himself.
Genoa, Italy, July 18-21: Anti-globalization protests turn violent at the G8 Summit as more than 100,000 protestors descend on the conference.

Canberra, Australia, August 29: In response to the *MV Tampa* crisis, the Border Protection Bill is rushed through. The Norwegian ship had rescued 460 Afghan asylum seekers from a sinking boat on August 26; and the Australian government initially refused asylum for them.
New York and Washington DC, USA, September 11: The World Trade Center is destroyed when two hijacked aircraft smash into the twin towers. A third plane hits the Pentagon; the death toll is estimated to be approximately 3,000.

Afghanistan, October 7: The US launches a retaliatory campaign for the September 11 attacks; the Taliban regime and al-Qaeda are the targets of the operation, which began with 50 cruise missiles being launched at Kandahar & Kabul.
USA, September 18-November: 22 people have been infected with anthrax, resulting in five deaths, from exposure to the deadly disease contained within letters.
Doha, Qatar, November 10: China is admitted to the World Trade Organization.

**Queen Elizabeth,
the Queen Mother**

The Euro Enters Circulation

Europe, January 1: The common currency of the European Union (EU), the euro, becomes legal tender today as circulation of euro banknotes and coins begins in 12 countries including France, Germany, Italy, and Portugal. All existing currencies in these countries will be replaced by the euro within six months.

An EU Commissioner, Pedro Solbes, has urged people to be wary of forged banknotes as forgers have been working overtime discarding their stocks of old national currencies.

Most retailers have euro currencies on hand, and there are already over six billion euro notes and 37 billion euro coins in circulation.

Many former colonial outposts outside Europe will also be making the change to the euro, including Guyana in South America, islands along the Mozambique Channel in Africa, and territories off the Canadian province of Newfoundland.

In Ireland, ATMs will be switched off at 1.30 a.m local time as bank staff race to stock them with the new currency. Pubs and convenience stores are avoiding midnight confusion by leaving the local currency, the punt, in their tills.

In Belgium alone, the change-over to the new currency has involved the production of over 2 billion coins weighing 9,000 tons (9,144 tonnes).

Meanwhile the President of the European Central Bank, Wim Duisenberg, has urged the three remaining nations who have abstained from the monetary union—the UK, Sweden, and Denmark—to adopt the euro. "My message is…come and join us," Duisenberg said.

Skepticism is particularly high in the UK however, with deputy Tory leader in the European Parliament Theresa Villiers seeming to sum up the average Briton's point of view: "Do we want to retain democratic control over the UK economy or not…or do we want a one-size-fits-all euro-economic policy set in Frankfurt?"

Theater Siege Ends– 750 Rescued

Moscow, Russian Federation, October 26: Russian troops have stormed the Moscow theater where Chechen terrorists have been holding 800 people hostage for three days. A sedative gas was deployed in the hope it would render the gunmen unconscious, and so avoid the need for a military confrontation. This failed, and a gun battle has seen 80 hostages and 50 Chechens killed.

Over 750 hostages were rescued, including 25 children. Many of the hostages were suffering kidney and liver complications from the gas used by Russian Special Forces, and those affected have been taken to various hospitals in the area around Moscow for treatment.

Many of the terrorists were Chechen women who apparently had strapped explosives around their waists, with their fingers on the detonators.

Television footage of the interior of the theater taken after the siege shows the bodies of several Chechen women slumped dead in their chairs, their explosive devices still intact. All the terrorists inside the building died in the gun battle.

UN Resolution Paves Ways for Weapons Inspections

New York, USA, November 8: The United Nations Security Council has unanimously adopted resolution 1441, demanding access into Iraq for weapons inspections and setting out possibilities for war if the conditions are not met.

The specifics of UN 1441 state that Saddam Hussein must permit access by UN International Atomic Energy Agency inspectors, and must declare all details pertaining to weapons of mass destruction held by Iraq within 30 days.

The United Nations inspectors, who will be accompanied by security guards, will report any cases of obstruction to the Security Council. The inspectors will return an interim report to the council by January 7. There are serious consequences for Iraq if they fail to comply with any of these conditions.

There is no new authorization for the use of force contained within the resolution, which affirms that any breach of the conditions will initially result in a meeting of the Security Council. Economic sanctions currently in place will remain until the inspectors have certified that the country is free of weapons of mass destruction. Economic sanctions in various forms have been in place since 1990.

East Timorese people celebrate their independence, in D

Europe, January 1: The common currency of the European Union, the euro, is legal tender in 12 countries.

Washington DC, USA, January 29: George W. Bush delivers his first State of the Union address to Congress, labelling North Korea, Iran, and Iraq an "axis of evil" for seeking weapons of mass destruction.

The Hague, Netherlands, February 12: Slobodan Milosevic's war crime trial begins, with the former Yugoslav president representing himself in a fiery rebuttal of the legitimacy of the tribunal.

Godhra, India, February 27: A train fire kills 57 Hindu pilgrims, sparking off days of rioting between Hindus and Muslims in Gujarat state.

Afghanistan, March: Coalition forces mount "Operation Anaconda"–a massive push to rout the Taliban and al-Qaeda in the rugged mountains south of Gardez.

Zimbabwe, March 9: Robert Mugabe returns to power in an election characterized by violence and intimidation.

Windsor, England, March 30: The Queen Mother dies, aged 101.

Ramallah, Israel, April 1: After a suicide bombing campaign that has left over 100 Israelis dead, Israel launches a massive military operation in the Palestinian territory. Yasser Arafat's compound is besieged, and a battle rages in the Jenin refugee camp.

The Vatican, April 23: Sexual abuse claims engulf the US Catholic Church. The Pope meets with 12 American cardinals, issuing an apology to victims of pedophile priests.

East Timor, May 20: East Timor finally achieves independence.

Kabul, Afghanistan, June 19: Hamid Karzai is endorsed as President at the loya jirga, or grand assembly. The process took over a week, with intense factional lobbying.

Kuta, Bali, October 12: Bombs explode in two tourist bars, killing more than 180 people. Australia suffers the biggest loss of life, with 88 citizens killed.

Hagerston, Maryland, USA, October 24: John Muhammad and Lee Malvo, responsible for 10 deaths carried out from the trunk of a car, sniper style, are arrested.

Moscow, Russian Federation, October 26: Russian forces storm the theater where Chechen separatists have been holding 800 hostages for three days.

New York, USA, November 8: The UN Security Council adopts resolution 1441, requiring Iraq to submit to weapons inspections.

Nigeria, November 23: The Miss World pageant is forced to relocate to London after riots by Muslims opposed to the show leave more than 100 dead.

Shuttle Breaks Up on Re-entry

Texas, USA, February 1: The space shuttle *Columbia*, the oldest in NASA's fleet, has disintegrated on re-entry into the earth's atmosphere 40 miles (65 km) over Texas—just minutes before it was due to land after its 16-day mission—killing all seven astronauts on board.

The astronauts who died were Michael Anderson, David Brown, Kalpana Chawla, Laurel Clark, Rick Husband, William McCool, and Ilan Ramon.

Residents of northeastern Texas said they heard a rumbling sound, like thunder, at 9.00 a.m local time and looked up to see flames streaking across the sky.

The debris from *Columbia* has been scattered over four states and will be taken to the Kennedy Space Center for analysis and eventual burial.

It is the first time since man ventured into space that an accident has occurred during re-entry. Soon after *Columbia* lifted off on January 16, a small piece of insulating foam from the main fuel tank was seen to have come off, striking the left wing of the shuttle. It is not known if this was a contributing factor in this morning's tragic accident, however NASA has confirmed that the first indication of trouble came with a loss of temperature sensors in the left wing's hydraulic system.

There has been one report of human remains recovered. A hospital employee in Hemphill, Texas, located a charred torso on a country road, in an area where shuttle debris had been reported.

All shuttle fights have been suspended uuntil the reason for the crash is known.

Five male and two female astronauts died when the *Columbia* exploded.

SARS Virus a Threat to World Health

Geneva, Switzerland, March 15: The World Health Organization (WHO) has issued an emergency travel advisory following the outbreak of Severe Acute Respiratory Syndrome (SARS), an atypical pneumonia originating in southern China.

SARS was first identified by Dr Carlo Urbani, a WHO specialist based in Hanoi, Vietnam. An epidemiologist, Urbani was asked to examine a visiting Chinese-American businessman who showed pneumonia-like symptoms but also had a high fever and shortness of breath. Not only did the patient die, he also infected 33 hospital staff including Urbani himself, who died a month later.

In the week prior to today's announcement, WHO had received reports of 150 cases of SARS from Canada, China, Hong Kong, Indonesia, the Philippines, Singapore, Thailand, and Vietnam.

Acknowledging that the virus is now a worldwide health threat, Dr Gro Brundtland, the Director General of WHO, has told the press: "The world needs to work together to find its cause, cure the sick, and stop its spread."

time out

Clonaid, a company associated with the Raëlian Movement, claimed to have produced its second human clone. Scientists received the news with skepticism as no proof was provided of the DNA status of either child. The project was condemned by religious groups.

Symptoms include high fever and either shortness of breath, coughing, or difficulty breathing. Anyone displaying these symptoms, who has traveled to a SARS region recently or had contact with someone who has been diagnosed with SARS, should seek medical attention as soon as possible.

SARS appears to spread primarily by close person-to-person contact, either by touching the skin of other persons, or objects that are contaminated with infectious droplets.

Slobodan Milosevic

Toppling of Saddam Statue High in Symbolism

Baghdad, Iraq, April 9: In a moment full of symbolism and promise, a statue of deposed Iraqi dictator Saddam Hussein has been toppled in Baghdad's Paradise Square, its head broken off and dragged through the streets by jubilant Iraqis.

Earlier in the day groups of Iraqis pelted the statue with shoes and slippers—a major insult for Muslims. The crowd then assaulted the statue erected to celebrate Saddam's sixty-fifth birthday with ropes and a sledgehammer. A group of marines then brought in a recovery vehicle, attached a chain to the statue, and completed the job.

President Bush, who watched the event on television, said the toppling of the statue "demonstrates the power of freedom." Defence Secretary Donald Rumsfeld declared: "Saddam Hussein is now taking his rightful place alongside Hitler, Stalin, Lenin, and Ceausescu in the pantheon of failed brutal dictators…"

Hussein's statue was broken into pieces.

Boston, USA, January 30: After admitting his guilt, and admiration for Osama bin Laden, "shoe bomber" Richard Reid is sentenced to life imprisonment for attempting to down an aircraft in December.

Texas, USA, February 1: Seven astronauts die when the space shuttle *Columbia* disintegrates.

Worldwide, February 15: Massive anti-war protests occur around the world as the threat of war in Iraq grows. 750,000 people gathered in London; New York, Paris, and many other cities saw people gather to express their objections.

Geneva, Switzerland, March 15: The World Health Organization issues an emergency travel advisory following the outbreak of Severe Acute Respiratory Syndrome (SARS).

Iraq, March 20: Coalition land troops enter Iraq, one day after the first American bombs are dropped on Baghdad. Air strikes on military targets are to be carried out as part of the "shock and awe" campaign.

Baghdad, Iraq, April 9: A statue of Saddam Hussein is toppled, as US tanks roll into the capital.

Persian Gulf, May 2: US President George W. Bush proclaims that the fighting in Iraq is now over, but stops short of declaring victory over Saddam Hussein.

Aceh, Indonesia, May 19: Martial law is declared in the oil-rich province as Indonesian troops take the fight to the Free Aceh Movement rebels.

Hong Kong, July 1: 500,000 people demonstrate against proposed anti-subversion laws.

Quetta, Pakistan, July 5: 44 Shia worshippers are killed at a mosque. Terror attacks have been widespread this year, with bombings in Morocco on May 16, Chechnya on May 14, and Saudi Arabia on May 12.

USA and Canada, August 14: Up to 60 million homes lose electricity, from Ohio to New York and Ontario.

Gaza, Israel, September 6: Prime Minister of the Palestinian Authority Mahmoud Abbas resigns after Yasser Arafat hamstrings his reforms.

Kuala Lumpur, Malaysia, October 31: Prime Minister Mohamad Mahathir steps down from office after 22 years. He has presided over a dramatic modernization of the country.

Santa Barbara, USA, November 20: Pop star Michael Jackson is charged with child molestation and is being urged to surrender by authorities.

Tikrit, Iraq, December 14: A disheveled Saddam Hussein is captured; he was found in a tiny underground bunker south of his hometown of Tikrit by US troops.

Pope John Paul II

Madrid Terror Attack

Madrid, Spain, March 11: Three days before Spain is due to go to the polls, 191 people have been killed and more than 500 injured as bomb blasts tore through three Madrid railway stations during the morning rush hour.

It is still too early to say if the attacks were the work of al-Qaeda or just another violent chapter in Spain's long-running battle with Basque separatists.

If indeed it is the work of an Islamic group, their motives would almost certainly stem from the fact that Spain has aligned itself closely with the US in its war on terror, and currently has 1,300 Spanish troops on the ground in Iraq.

The blasts occurred between 7.35 a.m and 7.55 a.m. A total of ten explosions tore apart three commuter trains: three on a train as it entered the busy Atocha station, four more on a train just south of Atocha, one device on a train entering Santa Eugenia station, and two on a double-decker train at El Pozo station.

Survivors have described scenes of pandemonium and panic, with people screaming for help inside the trains. People were seen walking away from Atocha station in tears as rescue workers carried bodies away from the scene.

The worst loss of life occurred at El Pozo where twin blasts killed 70 people.

Tens of Thousands Killed in Sudanese Genocide

Darfur, Sudan, July 24: Government-backed Arab militias have killed up to 70,000 Sudanese in the country's southern region of Darfur. One and a half million people have been displaced since the genocidal attacks began in March.

The tragedy of Darfur is that it's occurring in a world that stood by and watched similar tragedies unfold in Rwanda, Bosnia, and Kosovo. If no intervention occurs, US officials predict as many as 375,000 people could perish by the end of the year.

Crops and livestock have been destroyed by the militia groups. Stocks of food are already low due to five years of drought and poor harvest, with many families reduced to eating wild foods.

It is up to other nations to exert pressure on the Sudanese government to control the Janjaweed militias before the situation spirals into the worst humanitarian crisis since the slaughter in Rwanda.

time out

The Barcelona City Council passed a resolution to ban bullfighting in response to an animal rights campaign against the centuries-old sport. A petition demanding the end of bull-fighting received 250,000 signatures.

Tsunami Devastates 11 Nations

Indian Ocean, December 26: A massive tidal wave, triggered by an undersea earthquake off the coast of Sumatra that registered 9 on the Richter scale, has devastated huge swathes of coastline in Sri Lanka, Thailand, and Indonesia. Initial estimates have put the death toll at over 100,000.

It was the largest earthquake in 40 years, causing the earth to wobble on its axis.

The tsunami traveled some 3,000 miles (4,830 km), as far as the African coastline, and its effects were felt in 11 countries.

The town of Banda Aceh on the Indonesian island of Sumatra has been completely destroyed. Due to the isolation of much of Indonesia's western coastline, it could be weeks before a final death toll is known. Officials say the total figure could even be as high as 200,000.

More than 5,000 people perished when the tsunami smashed into Thailand's southern coastline, and upward of 30,000 people have died along Sri Lanka's southern coast. India's official death toll is already approaching 10,000.

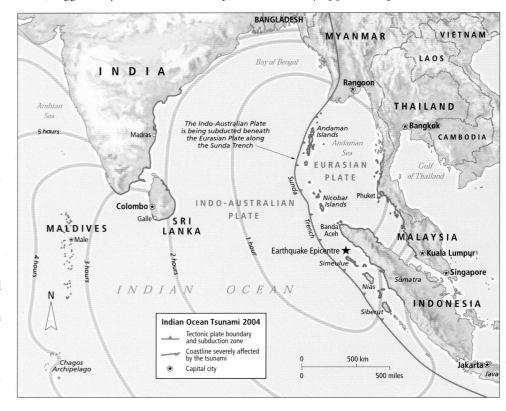

Port-au-Prince, Haiti, February 29: Beleaguered President Jean-Bertrand Aristide resigns and flees the country.
Madrid, Spain, March 11: Bomb blasts tear through three train stations during the morning rush hour. Hundreds are killed and many more are injured.
Gaza, Israel, March 22: Spiritual leader of the Palestinian militant group Hamas, Sheikh Ahmed Yassin is killed by an Israeli air strike, triggering angry scenes and calls for revenge.

Baghdad, Iraq, April 29: Damning photographs emerge of US forces abusing Iraqi prisoners at Abu Ghraib.
Europe, May 1: Cyprus, the Czech Republic, Estonia, Hungary, Latvia, Lithuania, Malta, Poland, Slovakia, and Slovenia join the European Union.
Arlon, Belgium, June 22: Pedophile child killer Marc Dutroux is sentenced to life in prison for his appalling crimes in the mid-90s.
Baghdad, Iraq, June 28: US administrator Paul Berner transfers sovereignty to interim Prime Minister Iyad Allawi.

Darfur, Sudan, July 24: Since March, government-backed Arab militias have killed up to 70,000 Sudanese in the southern region of Darfur; 1.5 million people have been displaced.
Najaf, Iraq, August: Gunmen loyal to Shia cleric Moqtada Sadr besiege the holy city of Najaf. US-led coalition forces have been engaged in fierce house-to-house fighting.
Kuala Lumpur, Malaysia, September 2: Supporters of former Deputy Prime Minister Anwar Ibrahim celebrate, as he is released from jail after the High Court overturned his sodomy conviction.

Beslan, Russia, September 3: More than 300 adults and children die when a siege by Chechen separatists at a school draws to a bloody conclusion.
Afghanistan, October 9: Hamid Karzai, who has been leading the country since the fall of the Taliban, wins the first parliamentary elections held in the country.
USA, November 2: George W. Bush secures a strong mandate, winning his second term in office, over Democrat challenger John Kerry.

Paris, France, November 11: Leader of the Palestinian people for over 40 years, Yasser Arafat dies, after slipping into a coma on November 3. He was 75.
Indian Ocean, December 26: A tsunami leaves coastal communities from Sri Lanka to Indonesia devastated; more than 100,000 people perish.
Ukraine, December 26: Victor Yushchenko is declared the winner of re-run parliamentary elections held after weeks of demonstrations in Kiev.

Hariri Assassinated

Beirut, Lebanon, February 14: Rafik Hariri, the former prime minister, has been killed by a car bomb as his convoy of heavily armed Mercedes drove past the St George Hotel in Beirut. Seventeen people died in the blast and 134 were wounded.

It is suspected that Hariri was killed by a device planted underneath the roadway at a spot that just ten days ago was dug up to repair part of the city's sewerage system.

Bystanders emerged from shop fronts covered in blood after thousands of windows shattered in the massive blast, sending glass fragments flying.

Hariri was elected prime minister of Lebanon in three successive elections from 1992 to 1996 and is generally credited to doing more than any other individual to pull Lebanon out of the mire of civil war and lead it on the path to prosperity.

While he was in government, Hariri launched the largest construction program in the nation's history in 1994, virtually re-building the entire central business district of the city of Beirut.

The assassination has outraged the Lebanese people who believe Syria to be behind the killing.

IRA Units Ordered to Dump Arms

Dublin, Ireland, July 27: The Irish Republican Army has formally announced an end to its 30-year armed struggle against the devisive British rule of Northern Ireland.

Prime Minister Tony Blair called the announcement "a step of unparalleled magnitude." The President of Sinn Fein, Gerry Adams, called it a "courageous and confident initiative" and "a defining point in the search for a lasting peace."

All IRA units have been ordered to dump their arms caches, and independent witnesses from both Protestant and Catholic communities have been invited to witness the decommissioning process.

Sinn Fein negotiator Martin McGuinness (center) reveals the peace plan.

It is felt that in this post-September 11 world the IRA and the republican movement's leaders no longer believe there is a legitimate role for a paramilitary organization to play in pursuit of their goals.

Kashmir Quake Leaves Thousands Homeless

Kashmir, October 8: An earthquake measuring 7.6 on the Richter scale has devastated many areas of Kashmir, with an estimated 50,000 deaths in the region and some 2.5 million people left homeless. The death toll is expected to rise as remote areas are accessed by rescue services and more information is available.

The earthquake could well be the most devastating ever recorded on the sub-continent. In some regions rescuers have been forced to dig for survivors with their bare hands, hampered by up to 144 aftershocks and the constant threat of landslides, which have already cut communications and transport links to dozens of communities.

Though it was centered in the rugged Hindu Kush mountains, the earthquake has had far-reaching effects, also causing the collapse of multi-storied buildings in the Pakistani capital of Islamabad, and it was felt as far away as Kabul in Afghanistan and New Delhi, India. The priority now is to locate those who are still missing and to provide blankets and food to those who have been displaced from their homes, before the coming of winter.

General Farooq Ahmed has been given command of Pakistan's relief operation, and has warned that 260,000 specially designed winter tents are urgently needed to prevent a second wave of deaths, with many people already spending nights in sub-zero conditions and much colder weather to come with the onset of a Himalayan winter.

Medical supplies are also needed, as are doctors and helicopters for ferrying supplies to isolated areas.

Jan Egeland, UN undersecretary for humanitarian affairs and in charge of UN emergency relief, has said that another "Berlin airlift" is needed to access the many remote areas and get people out before winter sets in. The complexity of coordinating relief operations into these areas is a "logistical nightmare" he said.

Rafik Hariri

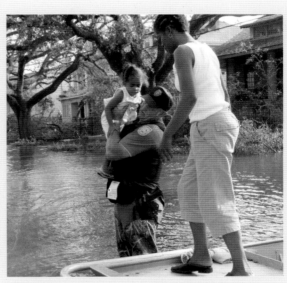
New Orleans residents evacuate after Hurricane Katrina.

Key Events

Washington DC, USA, January 12: Chief investigator Charles Duelfer confirms that the US has stopped searching for weapons of mass destruction in Iraq. One of the chief justifications for the war, the non-existence of WMDs has been suspected since May 2003.
Iraq, January 30: The first democratic parliamentary elections since Saddam Hussein's departure take place, with a better than expected turnout of voters, despite threats of violence from insurgents.

Beirut, Lebanon, February 14: Former Prime Minister Rafik Hariri dies when a car bomb explodes near his motorcade. Syria, which has great influence in the country, is thought to be involved.
The Vatican, April 19: German cardinal Joseph Ratzinger becomes the new pontiff, Benedict XVI. Pope John Paul II died on April 2 after leading the world's one billion Catholics for 26 years.

Iraq, May: Insurgent attacks have escalated since the formation of the new government in April; over 800 Iraqis and 80 foreigners are killed in one month.
France, May 31: Prime Minister Jean-Pierre Raffarin resigns after the French public deliver a resounding *"Non!"* in the referendum on the EU constitution two days ago.
Iran, June 24: Hard-line mayor of Tehran Mahmoud Ahmadinejad wins the run-off (second-round) poll for president by a resounding margin.

London, England, July 7: Four coordinated terrorist attacks on the underground and bus systems during the morning rush hour kill 52 people and injure 700, bringing chaos to the capital.
Harare, Zimbabwe, July 22: President Mugabe's policy of slum clearance that has left up to 700,000 people homeless is condemned by the UN.
Dublin, Ireland, July 27: The IRA brings an end to its 30-year armed campaign and shall pursue its objectives by political means.

New Orleans, USA, September 1: In the aftermath of Hurricane Katrina, which hit the Gulf Coast on August 29, anarchy descends after levees fail and the city is flooded. Thousands die in the disaster.
Kashmir, October 8: An earthquake devastates Kashmir, with approximately 54,000 deaths. Some 2.5 million people are left homeless.
Paris, France, October 27–November 8: After two teenagers are electrocuted as they hide from police, widespread rioting grips Paris, and the government declares a state of emergency.

Jack Kilby

"WE HAVE RECEIVED NO SINGLE ARGUMENT IN FAVOR OF THIS DOCUMENT EXCEPT POLITICAL PRESSURE. NO LINK HAS BEEN ESTABLISHED BETWEEN CARBON DIOXIDE AND CLIMATE CHANGE. NO OTHER OBJECTIVE FACTS HAVE BEEN PRESENTED IN RECENT TIMES."

ANDREY ILLARIONOV (B. 1961), RUSSIAN ECONOMIST, ON THE KYOTO PROTOCOL, 2004

Rare Meteor Fragments Recovered

Western Canada, January 18, 2000: A meteor has crashed into the Canadian arctic, exploding with the force of 5,000–10,000 tons (5,080–10,160 tonnes) of TNT. It created a sonic explosion and fireball that was clearly visible to people on both sides of the US/Canadian border.

The precise location of the impact has not been released in order to discourage treasure hunters. Several dozen fragments of the meteor have been found by a local resident who placed them in plastic bags. They have been identified as carbonaceous chondrites, some of the most organically rich and pristine meteorites known to exist. They are also extremely rare because they are fragile and easily break down passing through the earth's atmosphere.

Being the only meteorite fragments ever recovered in a near-frozen state, keeping them frozen minimizes the potential loss of organic materials and other potentially volatile compounds.

Scientists from the University of Western Ontario are now attempting to reconstruct the meteorite's orbit so they can determine its origin.

NASDAQ's Bull Run is Over

USA, March 10, 2000: The "dot com" bubble has burst, with the technology index—the NASDAQ—peaking at yet another record prior to beginning a spectacular decline in a market that has long been over-inflated.

The equity valuations of many dot com companies have recently been pushed to ridiculous heights, driven by the economic boom of the late nineties, which drove unprecedented amounts of venture capital into the industry. These venture capitalists promised far greater returns on investments than could be had in the traditional stock market and from other methods of investments.

After an unexpected series of liquidity crises, suddenly some companies that have received equity investments of $100 million and more are in danger of bankruptcy, whilst others may be sold for as little as five cents in the dollar.

time out

Thailand planned to release a three-in-one AIDS drug at virtually no cost to assist in the treatment of its 750,000 HIV-infected citizens. Three companies hold the patents in other countries, making the drugs much more expensive elsewhere.

Decision Made on Stem Cells

Crawford, Texas, USA, August 10, 2001: President George W. Bush announces continued Federal funding for stem cell research, but only from stem cells that have already been collected.

When researchers isolate stem cells from a human embryo, these cells can sometimes continue to replicate, creating a "cell line." The decision permits the continuance of research on cell lines already in existence because the destruction of the embryo has already taken place.

The key to Bush's decision was the announcement by the National Institute of Health that there are 64 cell lines currently existing in the world, a much higher number than previously thought.

The institute with the largest number is the Goteborg University in Sweden with 19 cell lines. Twenty cell lines are in the possession of laboratories in the United States, and Monash University in Melbourne, Australia, has six.

The decision has outraged many in the scientific community who have called it an attack on democratic rights and even a violation of the constitutional separation of church and state. They say to limit stem cell research to existing cells will slow progress on many fronts, particularly for victims of spinal cord injuries.

Many scientists also suggest the claim of there being some 64 cell lines to be an exaggeration, and that in any case 64 would prove inadequate considering the demands on research across the world.

Bush, advised by counselor Karen Hughes, spent months agonizing over the decision, in the end seeing it as the best compromise between the demands of science and the concerns of bio-ethicists.

Ice Shelf Collapses

Antarctic Peninsula, January 31–March 7, 2002: Since January 31 some 1,264 sq miles (3,275 sq km) of the Larsen B Ice Shelf in the northern Antarctic Peninsula—over 720 billion tons (732 billion tonnes) of ice—has collapsed into the sea and begun to disintegrate.

The area south of Chile and Argentina has seen an increase in temperatures over the last 60 years of 2.5°C (4.5°F), and the Larsen Ice Shelf system, at 65°S latitude, has been subject

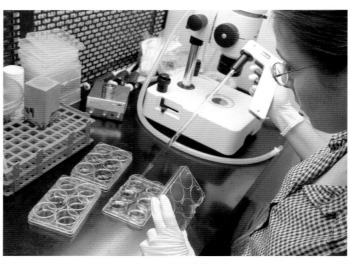

Scientist working with stem cells in an Israeli laboratory.

Key Events

The Ross Ice Shelf in western Antarctica is as large as France and is fed by seven ice streams.

Its inventor, Dean Kamen, is an engineer who invented the first portable insulin pump and a prototype wheelchair that allows its occupant to climb stairs and raise themselves upright to be able to see things at eye-level—activities that were once regarded as unthinkable for wheelchair-bound persons.

Kamen has worked on the development of the Segway for 10 years and at a cost of more than $100 million. It has no brakes, engine, or steering wheel but can transport its owner for a full day on only a few cents worth of electricity.

At the heart of the Segway is a gyroscope, a kind of "inner ear," which allows the user to change direction by simply turning their wrist. If you want to move forward, you just lean forward. If you want to go back, you just lean back. The Segway will mimic your sense of balance and do the rest for you.

To make this high degree of sophistication seem so effortless, the Segway contains 10 microprocessors and a large degree of software.

Karen Hughes

to warming summers for more than half a century. Satellite imaging has shown that glaciers held back by the Larsen B Ice Shelf are now flowing up to eight times faster than before, proving a long-held theory that ice shelves hold back glaciers.

A week after the separation, an iceberg twice the size of Dallas broke off Larsen B as the ice mass continues to deteriorate after having endured several millennia without any evidence of major change.

An ice shelf is a platform of ice that descends from mountain glaciers where ice sheets flow directly from land into the ocean, continuing into the ocean horizontally from its landward boundary.

Larsen B is the largest collapse event of the past 30 years, and brings the total loss of ice extent from seven ice shelves to 6,760 sq miles (17,508 sq km) since 1974.

With scientific modeling predicting that warming trends will be greater in the Arctic and Antarctic rather than in

equatorial regions, increasing instability can be expected with the associated devastation of the region's ecosystems, as coastal species are no longer able to survive in the altered environment.

Ice shelves cover more than 50 percent of the Antarctic coastline, representing more than 10 percent of the total land area of Antarctica. The Ross Ice Shelf in Western Antarctica is as large as France and is fed by seven ice streams.

Once these ice shelves break off they alter the coastline forever. James Ross Island was once encircled by Larsen but is now free of ice and can be circumnavigated for the first time.

From Subway to Segway

USA, November, 2002: The Segway Human transporter, an ingenious two-wheeled self-balancing device with a top speed of 12 mph (19.3 km/h) has been released.

Its inventor hopes that as cities become increasingly congested, his Segways will begin to be seen as genuine alternatives to the automobile for short trips through our central business districts.

On April 23 this year in San Francisco, Kamen was awarded the Lemelson-MIT Prize—which, at $500,000, is the largest single award for invention—for his pioneering of medical technologies and for being a leading advocate for both science and invention.

Dean Kamen and his invention.

Ceduna, Australia, December 4, 2002: Thousands descend on this tiny town to view a total solar eclipse.

Melbourne, Australia, February 19, 2003: Australia's oldest human remains are definitively dated to 40,000 years before present.

Bristol, England and Brisbane, Australia, May 29, 2003: Scientists discover an entirely new class of galaxy named ultra-compact dwarfs.

Ethiopia, June 12, 2003: The oldest remains of *Homo sapiens* are found, dating to back 160,000 years.

Gobi Desert, China, October 15, 2003: China launches its first manned space flight.

Worldwide, November 19, 2003: The World Conservation Union releases its Red List cataloguing endangered species.

Mars, January 25, 2004: The second of two NASA probes lands on the planet after the first, which landed three weeks ago, stops working.

Worldwide, June, 2004: The Census of Marine Life is initiated to explore the mid-water and deep-sea regions.

Mojave Desert, California, USA, October 4, 2004: SpaceShipOne reaches a peak altitude of 70 miles (112 km) to win the Ansari X prize, set up to initiate private space travel.

Stockholm, Sweden, October 4, 2004: Americans Richard Axel and Linda Buck are awarded the Nobel Prize in Physiology for clarification of how the olfactory system works.

Flores, Indonesia, October 27, 2004: Australian archeologists publish their discovery of *Homo floresiensis*, thought to have lived until 12,000 years ago.

Toulouse, France, January 18, 2005: Airbus unveil the world's largest passenger plane, the A380, designed to carry a minimum of 550 people.

Salt Lake City, USA, February 16, 2005: The Omo skulls, discovered by Richard Leakey in Ethiopia in 1967 are re-dated, pushing back the dawn of *Homo sapiens* to 195,000 years.

Florida, USA, July 27, 2005: NASA grounds its space shuttle fleet until it works out why insulation foam broke away from the shuttle *Discovery* yesterday.

Seoul, South Korea, August 3, 2005: Scientists successfully produce the first cloned dog, named Snuppy.

New York, USA, December, 2005: NASA's Goddard Institute for Space Studies estimates that 2005 is the warmest year on record.

Richard Leakey

Extinction Rate Intensifies

Worldwide, November 19, 2003: The World Conservation Union (IUCN) has released its Red List today, cataloguing the world's endangered species.

The IUCN Red List is the world's most authoritative inventory of the future of the planet's plants and animals. This year 12,259 species are listed as threatened, 2,000 more entries than last year. Almost 6,800 plant species are in danger, repre-senting 2 percent of the world's plants and includes 303 species of cycads, the oldest seed-bearing plants in the world.

Extinction is threatening one in eight birds and one in four mammals, and scientists estimate the rate of extinction is anywhere from 1,000 to 10,000 times faster than it would be if it were not for human encroachment and pollution.

Invasive species are causing havoc with fragile island ecosystems. The Galapagos Islands, Hawaii, and the Seychelles are ecological hotspots where loss of habitat could well make them ecologically barren.

China, India, Brazil, and Peru are the countries that have the highest number of threatened birds and mammals, while plants are most under threat in Ecuador, Brazil, Sri Lanka, and Malaysia.

The world's biodiversity is decreasing at an alarming rate. The IUCN is the world's largest forum, working at setting priorities for conservation efforts as well as bringing to public awareness the grow-ing crisis in our world's biodiversity.

Each year the earth's forest cover shrinks by an estimated 40 million acres (16.2 million hectares), mostly in tropical areas where biodiversity is greatest. The past 100 years have seen the earth's wet-lands decrease by 50 percent, while deserts have expanded due to the over-grazing of domesticated animals.

There have been five mass extinctions in the earth's history due to volcanic erup-tions, climate change, and meteorite impact. After each event the return to a world of biological richness has taken tens of millions of years. The World Conservation's Red List represents our best chance to raise awareness of the damage we are doing to our planet be-fore it is too late.

Marine Life Census Initiated

Worldwide, June, 2004: A Census of Marine Life has been initiated to explore the mid-water and deep-sea regions of the world's oceans and to catalogue the life forms inhabiting these waters. It is a massive collaboration involving hundreds of scientists in more than 70 countries.

Burt Rutan, designer of SpaceShipOne, receives the Ansari X Prize.

Researchers estimate there may be as many as 5,000 species of fish and untold hundreds of thousands of other marine organisms still to be found.

The project had its beginnings in March 1997 with a gathering of ichthyologists in La Jolla, California. They concluded that the age of discovery is far from over, and that an effort was needed to assess what is known about life in the world's oceans.

It is envisaged such a census could take up to ten years to complete. The Alfred P. Sloan Foundation, a philanthropic institu-tion, has been assisting the oceanographic community in its ongoing assessment of the feasibility of the project.

New Era in Space Tourism Draws Closer

Mojave Desert, California, USA, October 4, 2004: A privately funded, reusable, suborbital spacecraft—SpaceShipOne—has twice in the past week reached a height of more than 62 miles (100 km) above the earth's surface and into the very outskirts of space, claiming the $10 million Ansari X Prize for private space flight and breaking the altitude record of the X-15.

SpaceShipOne met all the require-ments, and the for-mal ceremony will be held in St Louis, Missouri, on Satur-day, November 6. SpaceShipOne has achieved what the founders of the Ansari X prize wanted: to demonstrate that a vehicle for space tourism can emerge from the private sector at a modest cost, and can be turned round and reused for another flight in a matter of days.

The pilot of today's historic flight, Mike Melvill, had to contend with a flight systems error that threw SpaceShipOne off course by 22 miles (35 km). The G force on descent was greater than that experienced by space shuttle astronauts.

Ape or Human?

Flores, Indonesia, October 27, 2004: Austral-ian archeologists have published their discovery of the remains of a 3-ft (1-m) tall hominid with a small cranial capacity. Called *Homo floresiensis*, he is thought to have lived as recently as 12,000 years ago.

Mike Morwood and Peter Brown of the University of New England in Aust-ralia, along with R. P. Soejono of the

The loggerhead sea turtle (*Caretta caretta*) is classified as endangered by the IUCN.

Scientific Achievements

Astronomy: AbeII1835IR1916, the most distant galaxy viewed to date, discovered.
Botany: Fungus *Beauveria bassiana* found to kill malarial mosquitoes.
Chemistry: The Human Genome Project, a study of genes in human DNA, completed.
Ecology: Kyoto Protocol came into force; EU banned leaded petrol; NZ banned rainforest logging.
Geology: 450 million-year-old fish fossils discovered in Africa.
Mathematics: LZMA, a data compression algorithm, is developed.
Medicine: SARS identified by DNA sequence information as a strain of coronavirus.
Physics: Existence of the neutrino oscillation confirmed.
Zoology: Increased birth rate for pandas in reserves—risk of extinction decreasing.

Botanic Gardens
Eureka, USA

Observatories
Hanle, India

Universities
University of Darwin, Australia
University of Durban, South Africa
University of Port Elizabeth, South Africa

Indonesian Center of Archeology in Jakarta, found the remains of the species of dwarf humans in the Liang Bua cave on the Indonesian island of Flores.

Scientists say that it is not uncommon for dwarf forms of large mammals to evolve in an isolated island environment.

Nicknamed "hobbits" after the characters in J. R. R. Tolkein's *Lord of the Rings*, the bones of seven people were located in an area where anthropologists had been excavating since 1965. The most significant find was an entire skeleton of an adult female who stood just 3 ft (1 m) in height and was fully bipedal, with a very small brain (417cc) approximately the size of a chimpanzee's.

The first humans arrived on Flores some 40,000 years ago, and stories can be found in Indonesian folklore that tell of a race of small humans who possessed a distinctive walk and were inarticulate. DNA testing should go some way toward solving the evolutionary mystery of *Homo floresiensis*, but the tropical climate and high temperatures of Indonesia may make this difficult as DNA is degraded in high temperatures.

Whether or not to classify the find as human remains controversial. University of Pittsburgh Professor of Anthropology Jeffery Schwartz believes the find should be classified as an ape.

However, the concept of "dwarfing" amongst large mammals is a fairly common response on islands where a small body mass is seen as an aid to survival. Is it possible that *Homo erectus* "de-evolved" into *Homo floresiensis*? To quote your typical paleo-anthropologist, "Only time will tell."

Airbus A380 Unveiled

Toulouse, France, January 18, 2005: Airbus has at last shown the world its A380 "Superjumbo" at a ceremony in Toulouse attended by leaders from France, England, Germany, and Spain.

The evening was akin to an opening night in the West End. Staged inside a massive hanger its unveiling was accompanied by dancers, fake fog, acrobats, and an array of water fountains.

The aircraft has a range of 8,000 nautical miles, has a 261 ft (79.5 m) wing span and stands 79 ft (24 m) high, 15 ft (4.5 m) higher than a 747. The plane is so large that some international airports are having to reconfigure their terminals to accommodate the aircraft. If two A380s parked side by side at Los Angeles International airport today, their wings would hit each other. Chicago's O'Hare airport will be widening their taxiways.

London's Heathrow airport is spending more than $800 million on such things as double-decker passenger ramps and larger baggage conveyors capable of processing 555 passengers.

The joint venture between BAE Systems and the European Aeronautic Defence and Space Company has secured over 140 confirmed orders from nearly a dozen airlines. The British Prime Minister Tony Blair has called it "a symbol of European cooperation at its best."

The A380 will be sold in two versions, one able to carry 555 passengers in a three-class configuration, and the other able to carry up to 853 passengers in a single-class economy configuration.

Airbus is predicting sales in excess of 700 aircraft; 250 sales are required to recoup the enormous investment costs, which have totaled close to $11 billion.

The environmental benefits of the aircraft are obvious: by transporting more people the plane's fuel-burn per passenger will be significantly lower than present 747s, making it more environmentally friendly than most cars, according to Airbus. Noise emissions from its giant Rolls-Royce engines will be about half that of Boeing's 747-400s.

With international air passenger numbers doubling every 15 years, Airbus say their aircraft is the logical answer to meeting the future needs of aviation.

Re-Dating Pushes Mankind Back 200,000 Years

Salt Lake City, USA, February 16, 2005: The two Omo skulls discovered by Richard Leakey at Kibish in Ethiopia in 1967 have been re-dated.

Omo I was a skull minus the face and included fragments of the pelvis, arms, feet, and legs, and Omo II was the back of a skull. A team of researchers have recently returned to the site, and using a new technique called "radiometric dating" have pushed the dates for both finds back to 195,000 years old, which tells us that although the skeletons of modern man existed 200,000 years ago, it would be another 150,000 years before humans would begin to display evidence of modern behavioral traits.

The re-dating represents an important advancement in our understanding of the process of human evolution.

Dr Han Woo-Suk
and Snuppy

Richard Axel (second from left) and Linda Black receive the Nobel Prize for their work on the olfactory system.

Nicole Kidman

"WRITING DOES COME A LOT FROM A PLACE OF SADNESS. IT'S SADNESS RELIEF ON A CERTAIN LEVEL. EXPRESSING IT THROUGH MUSIC GIVES YOU HOPE, AND I GUESS THAT'S WHAT ART IS—KIND OF FINDING HOPE IN THE HORROR THAT LIFE IS AND RENDERING IT SOMEHOW."

MATTHEW SWEET
(B. 1964), AMERICAN
MUSICIAN, 2001

Tate Modern Opens to a Mixed Reception

London, England, May 11, 2000: Queen Elizabeth has today opened the world's largest modern art gallery, the Tate Modern, now housed in the converted Bankside Power Station on the River Thames. It will be open to the public from 10 am tomorrow, with admission free.

The museum's North Entrance is on either side of the famous chimney and is reached via a walkway by the river, with the West Entrance being off Holland Street.

The western entrance leads into the Turbine Hall, which runs the length of the building and where escalators take patrons up past glass walls to the exhibition areas above, where works from Warhol and Picasso await, alongside pieces such as a metal ironing board converted into a North American Indian headdress, fashioned by American artist Bill Woodrow. All the exhibits here are illuminated by the translucent roof above.

Instead of hanging art chronologically, the curators have taken a thematic approach, mixing eras and ages in order to trace themes.

Jacques Herzog and Pierre de Meuron, the two Swiss architects responsible for the four-year conversion, have been awarded the prestigious Pritzker Prize in Architecture for their "talent, vision, and commitment."

Celebrities and art lovers have flocked to the opening, but the museum has had its critics. *The New Statesman* has criticized the small number of works of art under its roof—700—as compared to its contemporaries. *The Boston Globe* has commented that contemporary art cannot thrive in such demure surroundings, called it the most hyped building of the year, and has criticized the architects for missing an opportunity to merge art with architecture. *The London Evening Standard* even went so far as to laud the city's new home of modernism as "Britain's best example of fascist architecture."

The Tate Modern continues the recent trend of merging new museums with the concept of urban renewal, for example, the Georges Pompidou Center in Paris, and the Guggenheim Museum in Bilbao—a derelict power station is now Britain's home to modern art that the country has been craving for nearly 50 years.

time out

The Irish city of Cork became the European capital of culture for 2005 with a program of theater, music, art, and literature as well as sporting and other major events. One hundred thousand people took to the streets to celebrate the event.

Goblet of Fire Sets Publishing Record

UK and USA, July 8, 2000: J. K. Rowling's latest installment in the Harry Potter saga, *Harry Potter and the Goblet of Fire*, has broken all publishing records upon its release. Booksellers around the world have staged midnight Harry Potter sit-ins, sleepovers, and reading parties.

For the first time, the book was scheduled for simultaneous release in the US and Britain, and over 370,000 copies have been sold today in bookstores across Britain and on internet sites, dwarfing all previous sales records. It has already almost equaled the 399,000 copies the third installment sold in its first full year.

Amazon.com, the US book retailer, has already pre-sold over 400,000 copies over the internet, making it easily the most successful "e-tailing" book in history.

At over 750 pages it is twice the length of the previous book, *The Prisoner of Azkaban*, which sold a comparatively paltry 64,000 copies in its first three days.

Barnes & Noble in New York says it has ten times the number of pre-orders than for any other previous book.

Goblet of Fire is the darkest installment yet, with a tragic turn of events that will involve the death of one of the saga's major characters.

"If it is done right, I think it will be upsetting, but it is not going to be damaging," Rowling has been quoted as saying.

George Harrison, the "quiet Beatle," was a committed humanitarian.

Author and Cultural Icon Dies

Eugene, Oregon, USA, November 10, 2001: Ken Kesey, author of *One Flew Over The Cuckoo's Nest* and counterculture figurehead, has died aged 67 of complications following surgery for liver cancer.

Born on September 17, 1935, in La Junta, Colorado, as a young man Kesey spent much of his time outdoors, hunting, fishing, and swimming.

He studied at the University of Oregon where he acted in college

Oxford, England, January 1, 2000: On New Year's Eve the Cezanne painting *Auvers-sur-Oise*, valued at £3 million is stolen from the Ashmolean Museum.

Santa Rosa, California, USA, February 12, 2000: Creator of the "Peanuts" comic strip, Charles Schulz, dies aged 77.

London, England, May 11, 2000: The world's largest modern art gallery, the Tate Modern, opens in a former power station on the Thames.

England and USA, July 8, 2000: J. K. Rowling's new book *Harry Potter and the Goblet of Fire* breaks all publishing records upon release.

USA, April 22, 2001: The animated fairytale *Shrek* is released, introducing a reclusive ogre and a talking donkey to the world.

New York, USA, May 2, 2001: A federal jury has indicted the former chairmen of Sotheby's and Christie's auction houses, charging that the world's two largest art auctioneers overcharged clients for commissions during the 1990s.

Santa Barbara, USA, May 11, 2001: Briton Douglas Adams, author of the *Hitchhiker's Guide to the Galaxy*, dies of a heart attack, aged 49.

Canberra, Australia, June 25, 2001: Judith Wright, one of the country's greatest poets, dies aged 85. She also campaigned for Aboriginal peoples' rights and on conservation issues.

Los Angeles, USA, August 8, 2001: Nicole Kidman and Tom Cruise divorce, after separating in February. All attention now turns to the terms of the settlement.

Eugene, Oregon, USA, November 10, 2001: Ken Kesey, author of *One Flew over the Cuckoo's Nest*, dies aged 67.

Los Angeles, USA, November 29, 2001: Former Beatle George Harrison dies of lung cancer, aged 58.

Los Angeles, USA, March 23, 2002: Irish actor Peter O'Toole receives an honorary award at the Oscars, after being nominated seven times.

London, England, July, 2002: The Norman Foster-designed City Hall opens.

Stockholm, Sweden, October 10, 2002: Hungarian Jewish author Imre Kertész is awarded the Nobel Prize in Literature for his writing exploring the experience of the individual in a barbaric society.

New York, USA, December 5, 2002: The second part of the fantastic battle between good and evil *The Lord of the Rings: The Two Towers*, premieres.

USA, December, 2002: Primitive garage rock is the popular sound in the charts, with The White Stripes, The Strokes, and The Vines.

Norman Foster designed the cupola of the Reichstag building in Berlin.

typical air-conditioned office building, its envelope shape minimizes heat gain, while ventilation enters offices through grilles in the floor.

With the aid of computers it has been possible to know precisely how the sun will strike the building on each day of the year, and to adapt the design accordingly. The symmetry of the building is purely esthetic, and the ever-changing views of London, provided as the ramp ascends, are a visual delight.

J. K. Rowling

Nobel Prize Awarded to Holocaust Author

Stockholm, Sweden, October 10, 2002: Imre Kertész has become the first Hungarian Jew to be awarded the Nobel Prize in Literature. He was given the prize for his writing exploring the experience of the individual in a barbaric society.

Born in Budapest in 1929, during World War II, he was sent to Auschwitz at just 15 years of age and was later moved to Buchenwald, where he was liberated in 1945.

Kertész wrote a trilogy of novels about the Holocaust, the first being *Fateless* (1975) which recounted his experiences in the Nazi death camps. His second novel in the series, *Fiasco* (1988), was a commentary on the unsettling compact silence that had greeted the release of *Fateless*. The third novel, published in 1990, is titled *Kaddish For A Child Not Born*. Its story centers around a man who refuses to beget a child in a world that stood by and permitted Auschwitz to exist.

Nobel Prize winner, Imre Kertész.

plays before managing to winning a scholarship to Stanford University.

Kesey joined the counterculture movement after dropping out of Stanford University, began experimenting with drugs, and wrote an unpublished novel about the lifestyle of the San Francisco beatniks titled *Zoo*.

Kesey formed a group called The Merry Pranksters. They traveled the country in a brightly colored bus, using hallucinogens and serving Kool-aid laced with LSD at their many parties.

He gained notoriety, however, for his novel *One Flew Over The Cuckoo's Nest*, based on the author's own experiences as a volunteer patient taking mind-altering drugs and reporting their effects.

In the novel, Kesey took a state psychiatric ward and used it as a metaphor for what he saw as the oppressive society that America had become. A battle of wills develops between the central character, the patient Randall McMurphy, and Head Nurse Ratched, with the suggestion being made by the author that the really dangerous mental patients are those who are in positions of authority.

Foster Masterpiece is All Glass

London, England, July 23, 2002: Looking not unlike a full-faced motorcycle helmet of glass and steel, the distorted glass sphere of the Norman Foster-designed City Hall building in London was opened by the Queen today.

A contest was held to find the best site and design for the Greater London Authority building. An area in need of regeneration near Tower Bridge was finally chosen and the contract was won by the firm of Foster and Partners whose recent design for the Reichstag building in Berlin also involves an innovative and acutely modernist use of glass. Designed to utilize 75 percent less energy than a

Miami, USA, January 12, 2003: Maurice Gibb of the Bee Gees dies, aged 53.

USA, March 18, 2003: Dan Brown's controversial novel *The Da Vinci Code* is published.

Toulca Lake, California, USA, July 27, 2003: American comedian Bob Hope dies aged 100.

Nashville, USA, September 12, 2003: Country music icon Johnny Cash dies, aged 71.

London, England, October 14, 2003: D. B. C. Pierre wins Booker Prize for *Vernon God Little*.

London, England, December 17, 2003: The Merce Cunningham Dance Company celebrates 50 years of productions at the Tate Modern Gallery, under the watchful eye of choreographer Merce Cunningham.

Los Angeles, USA, February 29, 2004: *The Lord of the Rings: The Return of the King* wins 11 Oscars, equaling the record for one film.

Los Angeles, USA, July 3, 2004: Reclusive actor Marlon Brando, star of *The Godfather* and *Last Tango In Paris*, dies aged 80.

Oslo, Norway, August 22, 2004: Masked gunmen escape with the Munch paintings *The Scream* and *Madonna*—valued at $19 million—in broad daylight in front of stunned patrons.

Stockholm, Sweden, October 7, 2004: Austrian author Elfriede Jelinek is awarded the Nobel Prize for Literature.

New York, USA, October 11, 2004: Christopher Reeve, star of the *Superman* movies, who was paralyzed in a horse riding accident in 1995, dies aged 52.

Roxbury, Connecticut, USA, February 10, 2005: Playwright Arthur Miller dies aged 89. Miller was best known for his play *Death of a Salesman* and for being the one-time husband of Marilyn Monroe.

Cannes, France, May 15, 2005: The Star Wars saga is complete; *Star Wars Episode III–Revenge of the Sith* premieres at the Cannes Film Festival.

Santa Maria, California, USA, June 13, 2005: Michael Jackson is found not guilty of child abuse after a four-month trial that descended into a media circus.

Worldwide, July 2, 2005: Bob Geldof's Live 8 concert series takes place in London, Paris, Berlin, Tokyo, and Moscow, hoping to "make poverty history."

Dan Brown

Nothing New for Conspiracy Theorists

USA, March 18, 2003: Dan Brown's purely fictional work *The Da Vinci Code* has been published, with its premise that Leonardo da Vinci was a member of a secret society charged with protecting the true nature of Christianity, which can itself be discerned through oblique references to the occult found in his paintings and other works.

It is a pity that this competent though formulaic "whodunit" has had the argument over the virtues or lack thereof of its prose hijacked, ironically by none other than the author himself, by mixing fact with fiction to the point where the story becomes forgotten amid the mire of its own controversies.

An example is the character of British Royal Historian Leigh Teabing, who asserts without contradiction that the fourth-century Roman Emperor Constantine falsified the New Testament, when historically Constantine had nothing to do with the formation of the canon of scripture.

The conspiracy themes of the book have all been explored in detail before, most notably in *Holy Blood Holy Grail* (1982) and *The Messianic Legacy* (1987). Conspiracy addicts are finding nothing new in this latest offering.

Smart publishers and canny authors, however, are well aware that the best way to sell a book is to spark controversy. One way to do this is by starting a war of words with the followers of a powerful and universally recognized figure—it's good for business.

> *"We're blues people. And blues never lets tragedy have the last word."*
>
> WYNTON MARSALIS (b. 1961), AMERICAN MUSICIAN, 2005

> *"To me, the appeal of opera lies in the fact that a myriad of singers and instruments, each possessed of different qualities of voice and sound, against the backdrop of a grand stage and beautiful costumes, come together in one complete and impressive drama."*
>
> JUNICHIRO KOIZUMI (b. 1942), JAPANESE POLITICIAN AND PRIME MINISTER

Achievements in the Arts

Key Structures
Bahn Tower, Berlin, Germany
Corinthia Bab Africa, Tripoli, Libya
Edificio Neruda, Santiago, Chile
e-Tower, Sao Paulo, Brazil
Grand Gateway Shanghai I and II, Shanghai, China
Hyatt Center, Chicago, USA
I & M Bank Tower, Nairobi, Kenya
Minto Metropole, Ottawa, Canada
Nile City South Tower, Cairo, Egypt
Qatar Telecom Headquarters, Doha, Qatar
Q I Tower, Gold Coast City, Australia
Rakan Office Tower, Kuwait City, Kuwait
Rappongi Hills Mori Tower, Tokyo, Japan
Sultan Qaboos Grand Mosque, Muscat, Oman
Time Warner Center, New York, USA
Torre Banco Plaza, Caracas, Venezuela
Torre Mayor, Mexico City, Mexico
Tower Palace Three, Tower G, Seoul, South Korea
Turning Torso, Malmo, Sweden
Vorobiovy Gory Tower II, Moscow, Russia

Nobel Prize for Literature
2000 Gao Xingjian; 2001 Vidiadhar Surajprasad Naipaul; 2002 Imre Kertesz; 2003 John Maxwell Coetzee; 2004 Elfriede Jelinek; 2005 Harold Pinter.

Booker Prize for Fiction
2000 *The Blind Assassin*, Margaret Atwood; 2001 *The True History of the Kelly Gang*, Peter Carey; 2002 *Life of Pi*, Yann Martel; 2003 *Vernon God Little*, D. B. C. Pierre; 2004 *The Line of Beauty*, Alan Hollinghurst; 2005 *The Sea*, John Banville.

Pulitzer Prize for Fiction
2000 *Interpreter of Maladies: Stories*, Jhumpa Lahiri; 2001 *The Amazing Adventures of Kavalier and Clay: A Novel*, Michael Chabon; 2002 *Empire Falls*, Richard Russo; 2003 *Middlesex*, Jeffrey Eugenides; 2004 *The Known World*, Edward P. Jones; 2005 *Gilead*, Marilynne Robinson.

Academy Awards
Best Movie 2000 *Gladiator*; 2001 *A Beautiful Mind*; 2002 *Chicago*; 2003 *The Lord of the Rings: The Return of the King*; 2004 *Million Dollar Baby*; 2005 *Crash*.

BAFTAs
Best Movie 2000 *Gladiator*; 2001 *The Lord of the Rings: Fellowship of the Rings*; 2002 *The Pianist*; 2003 *The Lord of the Rings: The Return of the King*; 2004 *The Aviator*; 2005 *Brokeback Mountain*.

Lord of the Rings Oscars for Fran Walsh and Peter Jacks[on]

Country Music Legend Dies

Nashville, USA, September 12, 2003: Country music icon Johnny Cash, known as "The Man In Black" and one of the most imposing and influential figures in post-World War II country and western music, has died aged 71 years.

The son of southern Baptist sharecroppers, Cash was born in Kingsland, Arkansas. By the age of 12, young Johnny was writing his own songs. His family used to sit on the front porch and sing hymns while his mother played guitar.

The Great Depression devastated the agricultural communities of Arkansas, with his parents barely able to feed their seven children. In 1935 the family moved to the northeastern region of the state and began growing cotton.

In 1950 he graduated high school and moved to Detroit. He bought his first guitar after joining the air force and taught himself how to play while on active service in Germany. His band The Barbarians played in various bars on air bases. Then Cash returned to the US and settled in Memphis.

At a Sun Records audition, he sang gospel music. Sun's Sam Phillips told him to return with something more commercial. He returned with "Hey Porter."

Johnny Cash and June Carter Cash.

In 1956 he had a national hit with "Folsom Prison Blues," which reached the country Top 5. "I Walk The Line" followed and was number 1 for 6 weeks, as well as breaking into the pop Top 20.

He signed with Columbia in 1958 after having sold more than 6,000,000 records under the Sun label, and toured Europe, Asia, and Australia. By 1959 he was doing over 300 shows a year and began taking amphetamines. His music began to suffer and he left his family behind in California in 1963 and returned to New York. An association with June Carter of the country music Carter family saw him return to the top of the charts with "Ring of Fire." He married June Carter in 1968 and together they sold out Carnegie Hall. His 1975 autobiography *The Man In Black* sold 1.3 million copies, and in 1985 Cash, Kris Kristofferson, Waylon Jennings, and Willie Nelson formed The Highwaymen.

In 1994 Cash's popularity was again revived with American Recordings, a Grammy award-winning collection of stark acoustic recordings ranging from his own compositions to folk and even to songs by such contemporary artists as U2. Though not a commercial success, it brought him much critical acclaim.

June Carter passed away last May following complications from heart surgery, and Johnny Cash followed her today, succumbing to respiratory failure after a long battle with diabetes.

Artwork Stolen in Brazen Daylight Raid

Oslo, Norway, August 22, 2004: *The Scream*, painted by Norway's most influential artist Edvard Munch in 1893 and one of the world's most recognizable paintings, has been stolen by masked gunmen from the Munch Museum in Oslo today, along with his work *Madonna*.

The thieves escaped in a black Audi A6, which was later found abandoned—along with the pictures frames—less than a half mile (0.8 km) away.

Eyewitnesses report that the thieves took the paintings off the wall at gunpoint and walked out. There were 50 people, mostly tourists, in the museum at the time. No shots were fired. Gunnar Soerensen, head of the Munch Museum has denied that security was inadequate, stating that installing devices that would automatically lock down the museum's doors when paintings are removed could endanger the safety of museum patrons.

Munch painted four versions of *The Scream*. This is the second time one has been stolen, the other taken from the National Gallery in 1994 with a note left behind by the thieves that read: "Thanks for the poor security." *The Scream* alone is estimated to be worth $74 million dollars.

It is one of the twentieth century's most potent symbols of psychic agony, enhanced by the artist's bold use of color and perspective. The lonely figure, wide-eyed with hands clasped over the ears and mouth open in a scream of despair, has become a banner for existential dread.

Police spokesmen have refused to speculate whether any particular group is involved. The Director of the National Art Museum, Sune Nordgren, however believes an international group is behind the robbery and is expecting a ransom to be demanded for its safe return.

The other stolen painting, *Madonna*, is part of a series of works the artist painted along with *The Scream* from 1893–94. It depicts a nude woman who is swooning beneath a red halo.

The Scream and other works such as *The Sick Child* are reflections of Munch's traumatic childhood in which his mother and sister both died of tuberculosis. Melancholy and various sexual anxieties suffuse many of his early works. In them women are depicted as lurid, frail, and even as life-devouring vampires. Threateningly shaped trees and brooding houses crowd in around angst-ridden, limp, and featureless figures.

The latter half of Munch's life was spent in relative tranquility, and he has left behind a considerably legacy of etchings, lithographs, and woodcuts. He died in 1944 aged 81.

Christopher Reeve set up a foundation that has raised $50 million for research.

Superman Dead at 52

New York, USA, October 11, 2004: Christopher Reeve, star of the *Superman* movies who became paralyzed in a horse riding accident in 1995, has died at his home in Pound Ridge, New York State. He was 52.

Reeve proved to be a real-life hero as an untiring advocate for spinal cord and stem cell research. He slipped into a coma yesterday after developing an infection during treatment for bedsores.

Vowing to walk again, he combined a strict regimen with rigorous therapies and had regained sensation in various parts of his body, including moving an index finger in 2000.

"To be able to feel the lightest touch really is a gift," Reeve once said.

Origin of Movie Villain Revealed

Cannes, France, May 15, 2005: After 28 visionary years, George Lucas's *Star Wars* saga is finally complete with *Star Wars Episode III—Revenge of the Sith* premiering at the 58th Cannes Film Festival today.

Stormtroopers paraded up and down the red carpet as Lucas and other cast members arrived, receiving two standing ovations from the capacity black-tie audience. Lucas was also awarded the Festival Trophy aboard the luxury liner *Queen Mary 2*.

The movie's theme of democracy in decline and of a leader preaching war in order to preserve the peace has many observers drawing parallels between the film and the current War on Terror being pursued by the West in response to the September 11 attacks.

Michael Jackson

Live 8 Concerts Attract Huge TV Audience

Worldwide, July 2, 2005: Bob Geldof's worldwide Live 8 concert series sees more than one million people crowd venues in London, Paris, Berlin, Tokyo, and cities the world over, with the laudable aim of "making poverty history."

The concerts aim is to raise awareness of global poverty and have been timed to exert the maximum pressure upon the leaders of the world's wealthiest nations at next week's G8 meeting in Scotland.

Over one million people are expected in Philadelphia, with another 259 acts at 10 venues spread across four continents expected to garner the world's biggest ever global television audience of over 2 billion people.

George Lucas (fourth from left) with the cast of *Star Wars Episode III–Revenge of the Sith*.

New Millennium Arrives in Triumph

Ian Thorpe

Worldwide, January 1, 2000: The new millenium is being celebrated around the world in spectacular style today, with the forecast widespread computer viruses and malfunctions attributed to the Y2K bug not having materialized.

The year 2000 is, of course, the last year of the current millennium and not the start of the next one. The entire world, however, seems transfixed upon all those zeros. The controversy over just when the new millennium begins goes back to the calendar makers in ancient Rome who had no concept of the number zero, and jumped from 1 BCE to 1 CE.

The world, however, didn't allow that to get in the way of the greatest mass celebration in history.

"Terrorist attacks can shake the foundations of our biggest buildings, but they cannot touch the foundation of America. These acts shatter steel, but they cannot dent the steel of American resolve."

GEORGE W. BUSH, ADDRESS TO THE US AFTER HIJACK ATTACKS ON THE US WORLD TRADE CENTERS AND PENTAGON, SEPTEMBER 11, 2001

Sydney Olympic Games "The Best Ever"

Sydney, Australia, September 15–October 1, 2000: Outgoing IOC Chairman Juan Antonio Samaranch has declared the Sydney Olympic Games to be "the best ever" in his traditional closing address.

The Sydney Games were the largest ever with 10,651 athletes competing in 300 events. Highlights included Steven Redgrave becoming the first rower to win gold at five consecutive Olympic Games, and kayaker Birgit Fischer becoming the first woman in any sport to win medals 20 years apart.

time out

The Mattel toy company said that Barbie was to have a new boyfriend called Blaine, an Australian boogie boarder. In spite of reports that Barbie and Ken had now broken up, the Ken doll was still being manufactured.

The games began in spectacular fashion for the host nation when Ian Thorpe won two gold medals in the pool on day one.

The 46,967 volunteers that came to Sydney from all over Australia were invaluable in making these Olympics the best organized in modern games history.

The honor of lighting the Olympic flame went to Australian sprinter Cathy Freeman, who went on to win gold in the final of the 400 meters ten days later.

Australia's final medal tally saw the host nation win 16 gold, 25 silver, and 17 bronze medals for a total of 58, finishing fourth on the tally board behind the USA, Russia, and China. These games also saw the emergence of Asia as a serious force in athletics with China and Japan both finishing in the top five places.

Sports making their debuts included synchronized diving, trampoline, tae kwon do, women's pole vault, women's water polo, and women's weight-lifting.

After the perceived disorganization of the 1996 Atlanta Games, Sydney's stunning

The London Eye Ferris Wheel (Millennium Wheel) opened in March, 2000.

Sprinter Cathy Freeman carries the Olympic torch.

scenery and state-of-the-art facilities gave the world two amazing weeks of competition, with a party atmosphere prevailing from start to finish.

Donald Campbell's Remains Found

Coniston Water, England, March 11, 2001: The remains of Donald Campbell have been found just days after his boat *Bluebird K7* is raised from the depths of Coniston Water in England's Lakes District where it had lain since 1967.

After years of breaking water speed records with his father Malcolm in a series of speedboats named *Blue Bird* (later *Bluebird*), Donald Campbell was traveling at 328 mph (528 km/h) in another attempt when *Bluebird's* bow lifted from the water, somersaulted, and plunged into the lake, killing him instantly. "I'm going, I'm on my back, I'm gone" were his last words to his crew.

Key Events

Worldwide, January 1, 2000: The millennium is celebrated around the world in spectacular fashion.
USA, January 10, 2000: The largest company merger in history; AOL (America On Line) agrees to buy Time Warner.
Auckland, New Zealand, March 2, 2000: New Zealand successfully defends the America's Cup beating *Prada* 5–0.
UK, August 4, 2000: Throughout the UK, celebrations are held to commemorate the 100th birthday of The Queen Mother.

Sydney, Australia, September 15–October 1, 2000: The 2000 Olympic Games are a resounding success, with 10,651 athletes competing in 300 events.
San Cristobal, Galapagos Islands, January 16, 2001: A fuel supply tanker runs aground, leaking about 180,000 gallons (680,000 liters) of fuel into the pristine environment.
Coniston Water, England, March 11, 2001: The remains of Donald Campbell are found, days after his boat *Bluebird* is raised from the depths, where it had lain since 1967.

Amsterdam, Netherlands, April 1, 2001: Four couples wed in the world's first same-sex marriages after the Dutch government approved legislation earlier today.
Rhyl, Wales, May 16, 2001: Deputy Prime Minister John Prescott punches a protester who had thrown an egg at him.
Oslo, Norway, December 10, 2001: The UN and Secretary-General Kofi Annan are the recipients of the Nobel Peace Prize for their work toward a better-organized and more peaceful world.

Salt Lake City, USA, February 8–24, 2002: The XIX Olympic Winter Games are held. Ole Einar Bjoerndalen wins four gold medals for biathlon events.
Switzerland, March 3, 2002: Swiss voters narrowly approve joining the United Nations after five decades of neutrality.
London, England, June 3, 2002: Queen Elizabeth II celebrates 50 years on the throne with a rock concert in the grounds of Buckingham Palace.

USA, June 27, 2002: Following on from the Enron scandal of last year, communications company WorldCom collapses after inflating its cash flows by $4 billion; 17,000 people lose their jobs.
Yokohama, Japan, June 30, 2002: Brazil wins their fifth FIFA World Cup, defeating Germany 2–0. Ronaldo scored both goals, and won the Golden Boot for scoring eight goals in the tournament.
Johannesburg, South Africa, March 23, 2003: The Cricket World Cup final is won by Australia from India by 125 runs.

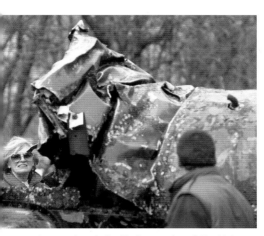

Tonia Bern-Campbell with the remains of *Bluebird*.

A new water brake fitted to the craft had stirred up the water more than anticipated in a crossing of the lake minutes earlier. Campbell took off on another attempt before the rippling effect from the new brake had subsided. *Bluebird* sank in 150 ft (46 m) of water and Campbell's body was never recovered.

Their first boat, registered as *K3*, was a single step hydroplane built in 1937 with a mahogany hull. The same year, on September 1, Malcolm created a new world record on Lake Maggiore in Switzerland of 126.33 mph (203 km/h).

Queen Elizabeth II Celebrates Golden Jubilee

London, England, June 4, 2002: Queen Elizabeth II celebrated 50 years on the throne yesterday with a rock concert in the grounds of Buckingham Palace.

All the icons of British music were there: Paul McCartney, Rod Stewart, Sir Cliff Richard, Sir Elton John, and many more, in what certainly was the greatest night of music in this country since Live Aid. A day of great pageantry ended with a spectacular fly past of 27 aircraft including Concorde and the Red Arrows.

Forty-seven members of the Royal Family, one of the largest gatherings of Royals in recent times, took part in the day's festivities. It is estimated over one million people filled The Mall outside Buckingham Palace in celebration. Council workers have been working feverishly throughout the night to clean up the city in readiness for business as usual today.

Prime Minister Tony Blair spoke of the huge affection the British public have for the Queen, and the Archbishop of Canterbury said the relationship between the people and their monarch has only grown closer with the passage of time.

The Queen herself has been overwhelmed by the response. Even New York's Empire State Building, in a rare tribute to a non-American, was lit in the royal colors of regal purple and gold.

Brazil Wins Fifth FIFA World Cup

Yokohama, Japan, June 30, 2002: Brazil, the nation that claims to have taken the game of soccer and transformed it into an art form, has won its fifth FIFA World Cup, defeating Germany 2–0.

Ronaldo, erasing his nightmare of the 1998 3–0 drubbing by France, scored both goals in the second half, and was awarded the Golden Boot for scoring eight goals during the course of the month-long tournament, equaling the legendary Pele's Brazilian record of 12 in World Cup finals.

Germany harassed Brazil early in the game and nearly took the lead in the second half when the German striker Neuville hit the woodwork with a vicious free kick from 40 yards (36 m) out that had the Brazilian keeper Marcos saving desperately at full stretch.

Brazil has now joined Uruguay (1930) and Italy (1938) as the only nations to have won all of their games in a FIFA World Cup tournament.

The entire team gathered on the field prior to collecting the trophy for a collective prayer of thanks as Brazilian players took off their tournament shirts to reveal t-shirts worn beneath adorned with colorful tributes to Jesus Christ. Many of Brazil's players are part of a growing evangelical movement in Brazil, and in a touching moment players wrote a religious message on captain Cafu's top as he was thrust upon the podium to receive the famous trophy.

Elizabeth II

The proud Brazilian team defeated Germany to win the World Cup for the fifth time.

Key Events

Nebraska, USA, June 22, 2003: The largest hailstone ever recorded in the USA is deposited in Aurora, measuring 7 in (18 cm) in diameter.

South Atlantic, August 28, 2003: The *Viarsa*, a Uruguayan vessel suspected of illegally fishing for the rare Patagonian toothfish in Australian waters, is boarded by fishery officers after a 21-day chase.

London, England, October 19, 2003: US illusionist David Blaine ends 44 days in a glass box suspended above the Thames with no food.

London, England, December 1, 2003: New laws are introduced making it illegal to use a hand-held mobile phone whilst driving.

Madrid, Spain, March 15, 2004: Prime Minister-elect Zapatero vows to bring home the 1,300 Spanish troops stationed in Iraq.

Arromanches, France, June 6, 2004: The 60th anniversary of the D-Day landings of World War II are commemorated by Queen Elizabeth II and 16 other world leaders alongside the surviving veterans.

Athens, Greece, August 13–29, 2004: The modern Olympic Games return to Greece, with 201 nations competing. US swimmer Michael Phelps wins six gold medals and eight in total, a games record.

New York, USA, September 27, 2004: Light crude oil reaches $50 per barrel for the first time, sending prices at the fuel pump ever upward.

Oslo, Norway, December 10, 2004: Wangari Maathai is awarded the Nobel Peace Prize for her contribution to sustainable development. She is the first African woman to be so honored.

Worldwide, February 16, 2005: The Kyoto Protocol climate change treaty on greenhouse gases comes into effect.

West Virginia, USA, March 4, 2005: Homemaking guru Martha Stewart is released from prison. She was sentenced last year for insider trading.

Windsor, England, April 9, 2005: Prince Charles and Camilla Parker-Bowles wed in a civil ceremony.

Washington DC, USA, May 31, 2005: Former FBI agent W. Mark Felt is identified as "Deep Throat" of the 1970s Watergate scandal.

Canada, June 28, 2005: Legislation is passed legalizing same-sex marriages.

Paris, France, July 24, 2005: Lance Armstrong wins a record seventh consecutive Tour de France.

London, England, September 12, 2005: England draw the Fifth Test match to claim victory in the Ashes.

W. Mark Felt
("Deep Throat")

Illusionist Spends 44 Days Suspended Over Thames

London, England, October 19, 2003: The American illusionist David Blaine has ended a 44-day fast in a glass box suspended above the River Thames near Tower Bridge in London.

The doctors responsible for treating the magician say he had lost almost a quarter of his body weight.

The world-renowned performance artist last year sat atop a pole in New York for 35 hours. His "Frozen In Time" stunt saw him encased in 6 tons (6.09 tonnes) of ice for three days.

Some onlookers have done what they can to make the experience a difficult one, including cooking food beneath

Illusionist David Blaine has spent 44 days in a glass box.

him, pelting eggs, and even stripping off. One man has been charged with criminal damage after having thrown pink paint at the magician–performer.

Blaine's behavior is being closely monitored. Doctors say that he is showing increasing signs of withdrawal, folding and re-folding his blanket up to 20 times a day and tapping on the glass.

Spain to Pull Out of Iraq

Madrid, Spain, March 15, 2004: Spain's new Socialist Prime Minister-elect Zapatero has promised to bring home the 1,300 troops currently stationed in Iraq.

In a victory seen as unlikely had it not been for last week's train bombings in Madrid, Zapatero's socialist party has won 164 seats in the 350-member Chamber of Deputies.

The outgoing conservative party headed by Prime Minister Jose Maria Aznar suffered a voter backlash due to his government's support of US policies in Iraq, with over 85 percent of the Spanish people opposed to the conflict there.

In the wake of the bombings the government too quickly blamed the Basque separatist group ETA, without possessing real proof. When an al-Qaeda spokesman later claimed responsibility, it was felt by the electorate that the Spanish government had not been honest with its citizens in the run-up to an election in which being an ally of the United States was suddenly a massive liability.

Zapatero has promised to bring all Spanish troops in Iraq home by June 30

Greenpeace activists in Beijing, China.

unless the United Nations wrests control militarily and politically from the US.

Protocol Gets Green Light

Worldwide, February 16, 2005: The Kyoto Protocol climate change treaty on greenhouse gases comes into effect today.

The protocol's first phase will require signatory nations to reduce greenhouse emissions by 5.2 percent of 1990 levels by 2012. The protocol will not come into force until 55 nations ratify it by making it part of their domestic law, and until the emissions of ratifying countries totals at least 55 percent of developed country's 1990 levels.

So far 126 nations have ratified or approved the treaty, although the United States and Australia have not signed. US co-operation is vital. With only 4 percent of the world's population it emits 25 percent of its carbon dioxide, with Australia emitting even more carbon dioxide per person than the US.

Each year 7 billion tons (7.1 billion tonnes) of carbon is released into the atmosphere. Kyoto only allows for relatively modest cuts in emissions, with no emissions at all required by developing countries.

Watergate's Deep Throat Revealed At Last

Washington DC, USA, May 31, 2005: Former FBI agent W. Mark Felt has been identified as the mysterious "Deep Throat," the insider whose meetings with *Washington Post* reporters Bob Woodward and Carl Bernstein led to the Watergate scandal, and subsequently to President Nixon's resignation in 1974.

Felt joined the FBI in 1942 and moved up to become the bureau's acting associate director when Nixon was President. Felt always denied being Deep Throat, telling reporters as early as 1974: "It was not I, and it is not I." He resigned from

Sporting Achievements

Baseball *World Series* 2000 New York (American League); 2001 Arizona (National League); 2002 Anaheim (AL); 2003 Florida (NL); 2004 Boston (AL); 2005 Chicago (AL).
Cycling *Tour de France* 2000–2005 L. Armstrong.
Football *American Super Bowl* 2000 St Louis; 2001 Baltimore; 2002 New England; 2003 Tampa Bay; 2004 New England; 2005 New England. *World Cup Soccer* 2002 Brazil.
Golf *US Masters* 2000 V. Singh; 2001–2002 T. Woods; 2003 M. Weir; 2004 P. Mickelson; 2005 T. Woods.
Horse Racing *Epsom Derby* 2000 Sinndar; 2001 Galileo; 2002 High Chaparral; 2003 Kris Kin; 2004 North Light; 2005 Motivator. *Kentucky Derby* 2000 Fusaichi Pegasus; 2001 Monarchos; 2002 War Emblem; 2003 Funny Cide; 2004 Smarty Jones; 2005 Giacomo. *Melbourne Cup* 2000 Brew; 2001 Etheral; 2002 Media Puzzle; 2003 Makybe Diva; 2004 Makybe Diva; 2005 Makybe Diva.
Ice Hockey *Stanley Cup* 2000 New Jersey; 2001 Colorado; 2002 Detroit; 2003 New Jersey; 2004 Tampa Bay; 2005 not awarded.
Marathon *Boston, Men's* 2000 E. Lagat; 2001 L. Bong-Ju; 2002 R. Rop; 2003 R. Cheruiyot; 2004 T. Cherigat; 2005 H. Negussie; *Women's* 2000 C. Ndereba; 2001 C. Ndereba; 2002 M. Okayo; 2003 S. Zakharova; 2004 C. Ndereba; 2005 C. Ndereba.
Sailing *America's Cup* 2000 Team New Zealand; 2003 Alinghi.
Tennis *Australian Open, Men's Singles* 2000–2001 A. Agassi; 2002 T. Johansson; 2003 A. Agassi; 2004 R. Federer; 2005 M. Safin; *Women's Singles* 2000 L. Davenport; 2001–2002 J. Capriati; 2003 S. Williams; 2004 J. Henin-Hardenne; 2005 S. Williams. *Roland-Garros Tournament (French Open), Men's Singles* 2000–2001 G. Kuerten; 2002 A. Costa; 2003 J. Ferrero; 2004 G. Gaudio; 2005 R. Nadal; *Women's Singles* 2000 M. Pierce; 2001 J. Capriati; 2002 S. Williams; 2003 J. Henin-Hardenne; 2004 A. Myskina; 2005 J. Henin-Hardenne. *US Open, Men's Singles* 2000 M.Safin; 2001 L. Hewitt; 2002 P. Sampras; 2003 A. Roddick; 2004–2005 R. Federer; *Women's Singles* 2000–2001 V. Williams; 2002 S. Williams; 2003 J. Henin-Hardenne; 2004 S. Kuznetsova; 2005 K. Clijsters. *Wimbledon, Gentlemen's Singles* 2000 P. Sampras; 2001 G. Ivanisevic; 2002 L. Hewitt; 2003–2005 R. Federer; *Ladies' Singles* 2000–2001 V. Williams; 2002–2003 S. Williams; 2004 M. Sharapova; 2005 V. Williams.

Lance Armstrong wins his seventh consecutive Tour de France.

the FBI in 1973. In his 1979 book *The FBI Pyramid from the Inside*, he again denied he was Deep Throat.

Ironically, as the bureau's associate director in 1972 he was put in charge of finding the source of the leaks, putting him in charge of investigating himself in a twist worthy of a John Le Carré novel.

Up until today many Washington insiders had believed that Deep Throat, rather than one individual, was a composite of several informants given a persona for the sake of Woodward and Bernstein's best-selling book *All The President's Men*. Richard Nixon himself, however, always privately suspected Felt as the man who ultimately brought about his dramatic downfall.

Woodward and Bernstein have always maintained they wouldn't disclose Deep Throat's identity until after he was dead, however the magazine pre-empted that with an article posted on their web site last Tuesday. The magazine reported that Felt himself had confessed to family friend and Californian attorney John D. O'Connor: "I'm the guy they called Deep Throat." O'Connor has told ABC news that Felt had thought of himself for years as a dishonorable man for talking to the two young *Washington Post* reporters. "Mark wants the public's respect and wants to be known as a good man," O'Connor went on to say. "He's very proud of the bureau, he's very proud of the FBI. He now knows he is a hero."

On Tuesday, Felt answered the door of his daughter's home in Santa Rosa where he is staying, greeting the media. "Thanks for coming," he told reporters.

Late today on the *Washington Post* website, Woodward, Bernstein, and Ben Bradlee the newspaper's then-editor, confirmed the identity of the man who surely now is the most "famous anonymous" person in history.

Felt was always under suspicion by the Nixon White House. In a meeting in the White House on October 19, 1972, between Nixon and his Chief-of-Staff Bob Haldeman, the President complained that Acting FBI Director L. Patrick Gray seemed unable to prevent the constant leaks to the press. Haldeman told Nixon that Felt had been identified as the primary source of the leaks but "if we move on him, he'll go out and unload everything. He knows everything that's to be known in the FBI."

Despite Felt being a known whistleblower, however, Haldeman always believed Deep Throat to be a Justice Department man named Fred Fielding.

Armstrong Wins Tour de France Again

Paris, France, July 24, 2005: "The Star-Spangled Banner" has again played over the Champs-Elysées in honor of Lance Armstrong, the 33-year-old American cyclist who has won the Tour de France for a record seventh consecutive time.

As his twin three-year-old daughters Grace and Isabelle, five-year-old son Luke, and girlfriend Sheryl Crow looked on, Armstrong announced his retirement from competitive cycling. He won a Tour total of 83 yellow jerseys—one for each stage victory. Only the Belgian rider Eddy Merckx—with 111—has won more.

Armstrong insists that the secret to his success is that he simply trains and prepares harder than anyone else. His time for the 2,233 miles (3,594 km) of the tour was 86 hours, 15 minutes, and two seconds riding at an average speed of 26.8 mph (43.13 km/h).

Stricken with testicular cancer in 1996—which spread to his brain and lungs—Armstrong began his remarkable comeback in 1998, winning his first Tour the following year.

England Regain Ashes in "Greatest Series Ever"

London, England, September 12, 2005: The English cricket team has drawn the Fifth Test match against Australia to win the series 2–1, their first series win against their tormentors since 1987.

With England again regarded as underdogs at the start of the summer, it looked as though it would all go to script for the Australians after they convincingly won the First Test at Lords by 239 runs.

However, things began to go wrong for the visitors when strike bowler Glenn McGrath rolled his ankle on a stray ball prior to the start of play in the Second Test at Edgbaston. With their other strike bowler Jason Gillespie in a form slump, the momentum finally swung England's way. They won the Second Test by just 2 runs and drew the Third Test at Old Trafford, which they would likely have won if bad weather had not intervened.

The English then took a 2–1 series lead with a victory in the Fourth Test at Trent Bridge by three wickets in yet another thriller. The Australians had to win the Fifth and final Test at The Oval to retain the Ashes, and may well have done so had Shane Warne not dropped Kevin Pieterson twice before he reached 16 on his way to his maiden Test century. But the heroic efforts of Warne in this series makes any criticism of his performance nigh on impossible. In a losing side he captured an astonishing 40 wickets at the miserly average of 19.9. Not content with that, he also contributing with the bat, scoring 249 runs at an average of 27.6 runs.

Martha Stewart

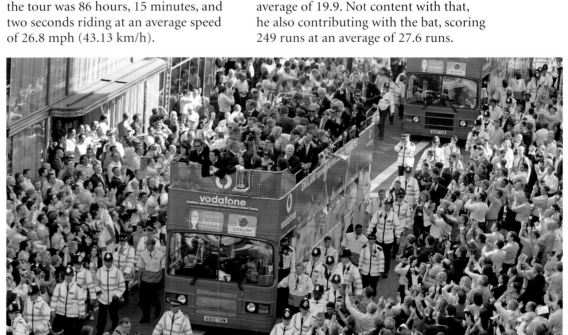

The English cricket team (in open-top bus) are honored in a victory parade through London, after regaining The Ashes.

North America, 1000: Leif Eriksson reputedly discovers North America.

Norway, 1000: The forces of King Olaf I of Norway are defeated by the Danes at the Battle of Svolder.

Islip, England, 1003: Edward, son of Ethelred II, is born.

Peshawar, India, 1004: Mahmud of Ghazna defeats the armies of a Hindu confederacy. He annexes the Punjab and introduces Islam there.

Jerusalem, 1009: Caliph al-Hakim sacks the Church of the Holy Sepulchre and the tomb believed to be Christ's is hacked down to bedrock.

Hanoi, Vietnam, 1009: Ly Cong Uan founds the Ly Dynasty, and establishes Vietnam as an independent state

Khmer Empire (Cambodia), 1010: Suryavarman I takes the throne, eventually defeating rival claimant Jayaviravarman.

England, 1012: Ethelred II pays 48,000 lbs (about 21,770 kg) of silver to the Danes, after paying 36,000 lbs (about 16,330 kg) two years previously to prevent attacks.

England, December 1013: The Danes overrun England and Ethelred II flees.

Denmark, February, 1014: Harald becomes King of Denmark, upon the death of his father, Sweyn.

Dublin, Ireland, April 23, 1014: Brian Boru, the High King of Ireland, is killed at the Battle of Clontarf.

England, October 18, 1016: Canute's Danish forces defeat the English under Edmund Ironside at the Battle of Ashingdon and Canute becomes king of England.

Java, Indonesia, 1016: Airlangga becomes the founding ruler of the Kingdom of Mataram, greatest of the medieval Southeast Asian island empires.

Denmark, 1019: Harald II, King of Denmark dies, and Canute becomes King of England and Denmark.

Cairo, Egypt, February 13, 1021: Caliph al-Hakim—variously described as compassionate, cruel, or raving mad, depending on the source—mysteriously disappears.

Norway, 1028: Already king of England and Denmark, Canute ousts King Olaf II of Norway.

Stiklestad, Norway, July, 1030: Former king, Olaf II, attempts to regain the throne of Norway, but is defeated in battle.

Ghazna, Afghanistan, April 30, 1030: Emperor Mahmud of Ghazna dies, aged about 59. He is succeeded by his son, Mas'ud.

Hampshire, England, August 2, 1100: King William II (William Rufus) dies on a hunting trip, aged about 44. He is succeeded by his brother, Henry I.

Tinchebrai, France, September 28, 1106: The Battle of Tinchebrai is fought between the forces of Henry I of England and his brother, Robert Curthose, Duke of Normandy. Robert is defeated and imprisoned.

Tripoli, Middle East, July 12, 1109: After surviving a number of years under siege, the city of Tripoli finally falls to the Crusaders.

Beirut, Middle East, May, 1110: The city capitulates to the Crusaders.

Sidon, Middle East, December 4, 1110: The Crusaders capture the city of Sidon.

Beijing, China, 1115: Jurchen warriors from Manchuria defeat the Khitan Liao dynasty, and establish the Jin dynasty in northern China.

Jerusalem, Middle East, c. 1118: The religious military order of the Knights Templars is founded by French nobleman Hughes de Payens.

English Channel, November 25, 1120: The heir to the English throne—William the Aethling—drowns after the event known as the "Wreck of the White Ship." Henry I resorts to naming his daughter Mathilda as his heir. This proves unpopular, as the realm is reluctant to accept the possibility of a female monarch.

China, 1127: The Jin army drives the Song dynasty from its capital at Kaifeng. The Southern Song dynasty is later established in southern China.

Guimarães, Portugal, June 24, 1128: The Battle of Sao Mamede is fought out between the forces of Afonso Henriques (the victor, who will go on to become Afonso I of Portugal), and his mother, Teresa.

France, 1131: Louis VII is anointed as successor to his father Louis VI.

Cardiff, Wales, February 10, 1134: Robert Curthose, Duke of Normandy, dies in prison, aged about 80.

China, 1135: Huizong, former Song Dynasty emperor, dies a prisoner, aged 52.

Northallerton, England, August 22, 1138: The Battle of the Standards takes place between local English forces supporting King Stephen and the forces of King David of Scotland.

Tikrit, Iraq, 1138: Birth of Saladin.

Ghazni, Afghanistan, 1140: Ghorid forces of central Afghanistan capture the city of Ghazni.

Uzbekistan, September 8, 1141: The Battle of Samarkand sees Seljuk Sultan Sanjar defeated by the Qara-Khitai forces.

Middle East, 1202-04: The Fourth Crusade is undertaken.

Constantinople, Turkey, April 12, 1204: The city is sacked by the combined forces of the Venetians and the Crusaders.

Fontevrault, France, April 1, 1204: Eleanor of Aquitaine, a powerful and influential women of her time, dies, aged about 82.

Karakorum, Mongolia, 1206: Temüjin takes title Genghis Khan, and becomes the supreme ruler of all the Mongol tribes.

Delhi, India, 1206: Qutb-ud-din Aybak founds the Sultanate of Delhi, establishing Islamic rule in northern India.

Winchester, England, October 1, 1207: Henry III is born.

Spain, July 16, 1212: The Christians' victory at the Battle of Las Navas de Tolosa marks the beginning of the end of the Almohad grip on Spain.

Jersey, 1213: The French, who had lost control of the Channel Islands in 1204, attack Jersey.

Flanders, 30/31 May, 1213: An English fleet defeats the French in the Battle of Damme.

Poissy, France, April 25, 1214: Louis IX is born.

Europe, July 27, 1214: The plan of Otto IV, Holy Roman Emperor, and King John of England to attack and seize France comes horribly undone—John retreats, Otto is defeated at the Battle of Bouvines, and Philip II emerges victorious.

Central Asia, 1215: Kublai Khan, grandson of Genghis Khan, is born.

Central Asia, 1215: Renowned Mongol leader Genghis Khan finally adds China to his conquests.

Runnymede, England, June 15, 1215: King John signs the Magna Carta.

Newark, England, October 9, 1216: King John I dies, aged about 49. He is succeeded by his son, Henry III.

Middle East, 1217-21: The Fifth Crusade is undertaken.

Mantes, France, July 14, 1223: King Philip II dies, aged 67. He is succeeded by his son, Louis VIII.

Central Asia, August 18, 1227: After building an extensive empire and a reputation as a fearless warrior and an astute leader, Genghis Khan dies, leaving control of his vast realm to his son, Ogedei.

Middle East, 1228-29: In response to Jerusalem falling into the hands of the Muslims once more in 1224, the Sixth Crusade is undertaken.

Mali, West Africa, 1235: Sundiata Keita emerges victorious from the Battle of Kirina, and establishes the Mali Empire.

Caltabellota, Sicily, 1302: The Peace Treaty of Caltabellota brokered between the Angevins and the Aragonese ends the 20-year-long War of the Sicilian Vespers.

Kortrijk, Belgium, July 11, 1302: Following the massacre of French residents at Bruges (Brugge Metten), Philip IV of France sends troops to regain the region. However, these crack troops are defeated by the local forces at the Battle of the Golden Spurs.

London, England, August 23, 1305: Sir William Wallace, who had been betrayed and captured earlier in the month, is executed.

Avignon, France, 1305-1378: The pope resides in Avignon, rather than the traditional papal seat of Rome. This is known as the Avignon Papacy, or Babylonian Captivity.

Burgh-by-Sands, England, July 7, 1307: Edward I dies, aged 68. He is succeeded by his son Edward II.

Mali, West Africa, 1312: Mansa Musa becomes king of the formidable Mali Empire.

Avignon, France, March 22, 1312: Pope Clement V issues a papal bull demanding the dissolution of the Knights Templar movement.

Bannockburn, Scotland, June 23-24, 1314: The Scottish forces of Robert I (Robert the Bruce) defeat the English troops of Edward II.

Fontainebleau, France, November 29, 1314: Philip IV dies, aged 46. He is succeeded by his son Louis X.

Vincennes, France, June 5, 1316: Louis X dies, aged 26. His brother Philip becomes regent for Louis' unborn child.

Bursa, Turkey, 1326: Ottoman forces take Bursa, and make it the capital of their empire. The founder of the empire, Osman I, dies, and is succeeded by his son, Orhan.

India, 1326: The Hindu kingdom of Vijayanagara is established in southern India by brothers Harihara and Bukka Sangama.

London, England, January 25, 1327: Edward II is forced to abdicate and is imprisoned. His son, Edward III, claims the throne.

Vincennes, France, February 1, 1328: Charles IV dies, aged about 33. He has no male heirs, and is the last of the Capetian Dynasty. His cousin Philip is finally chosen as successor to the throne, but England's Edward III believes he has a claim to the French throne.

London, England, 1330: Edward III takes full control of the English throne.

Mali Empire, West Africa, 1332: Mansa Musa dies. He is succeeded by his son, Maghan I.

1000 – 1099

Shaftesbury, England, November 12, 1035: King Canute dies, aged about 40. He is succeeded by his son Harald.

Wales, 1039: Prince Gruffydd ap Llewelyn of Gwynedd and Powys defeats the English.

Scotland, 1040: King Duncan dies in battle and Macbeth claims the throne.

Pagan, Burma, 1044: Burmese King Anawratha fortifies the capital at Pagan.

Europe, 1054: The Roman Catholic Church and Eastern Orthodox Church go their separate ways.

Lumphanan, Scotland, August 15, 1057: King Macbeth dies, aged about 52. He is succeeded by his stepson, Lulach.

Sicily, 1059: Norman forces, fighting on behalf of the pope, begin their campaign to regain the region from Arab control.

London, England, January 5, 1066: Edward III (Edward the Confessor) dies, aged about 62. He is succeeded by Harold II.

Stamford Bridge, Yorkshire, England, September 25, 1066: Harold II successfully defends his realm, defeating the Norwegians.

Hastings, England, October 14, 1066: The English forces of Harold II are defeated by the Normans under the leadership of William of Normandy. Harold falls in battle.

London, England, December 25, 1066: William the Conqueror is crowned King William I of England.

Isle of Ely, Norfolk, England, 1071: Hereward the Wake leads a rebellion against William I.

Algiers, Africa, 1082: The Almoravids, led by Youssef bin Tachfin, capture the city of Algiers.

Rome, Italy, 1084: Robert Guiscard of Normandy storms the city as he rescues Pope Gregory VII from Holy Roman Emperor Henry IV.

Spain, 1085: The Almoravids begin their quest to control Spain.

Rouen, France, September 9, 1087: William I (William the Conqueror) dies, aged about 59. He is succeeded by his son, William II (William Rufus).

Persia, 1092: Malik Shah, Sultan of the Seljuk Empire, dies, aged 37. He is succeeded by his son, Mahmud I.

Clermont, France, 1095: Pope Urban II appeals to the Christian princes to wrest control of the Holy Land from the grip of the Turks.

Valencia, Spain, July 10, 1099: Rodrigo Diaz de Vivar (El Cid), heroic soldier, dies, aged about 56.

Jerusalem, Middle East, July 15, 1099: The Crusaders seize Jerusalem.

1100 – 1199

Portugal, October 5, 1143: Portugal becomes an independent kingdom.

Europe, 1147: Following the fall of the County of Edessa in 1144, the Second Crusade begins.

Angkor, Cambodia, 1150: Suryavarman II, one of the greatest leaders of the Khmer Empire, dies in battle.

Bordeaux, France, 1152: Henry II marries Eleanor of Aquitaine, consolidating her extensive holdings in France into his realm.

Scotland, May 23, 1153: King David I of Scotland dies, aged about 68. He is succeeded by his grandson, Malcolm IV.

Dover, England, October 25, 1154: King Stephen dies, aged about 57, and is succeeded by Henry II.

Rome, Italy, 1155: Frederick Barbarossa, King of Germany, is proclaimed Holy Roman Emperor.

Oxford, England, September 8, 1157: Birth of Richard I, who will later become better known as Richard the Lionheart.

Lake Baikal, Russia, c. 1167: Birth of Genghis Khan.

Canterbury, England, December 29, 1170: The Archbishop Thomas Becket is murdered in Canterbury Cathedral, aged about 50.

Khandahar, Afghanistan, 1173: Mohammad Ghori becomes the Sultan of Afghanistan and plans the conquest of India.

Angkor, Cambodia, 1181: King Jayavarman VII takes the throne of the Khmer Empire. The empire will expand and be at its most powerful during his reign.

Italy, 1182: Birth of Francis of Assisi.

Dan-no-Ura, Japan, April 25, 1185: Minamoto samurai warriors win the civil war by defeating the Taira clan in a great naval battle.

Tiberias, Middle East, 1187: The Battle of Hattin sees a resounding victory for Saladin's forces over the Crusaders. Over the next few years, the Crusader strongholds will fall to Saladin's forces, with the city of Tyre proving the only exception.

Europe, 1189: In an attempt to regain control of the Holy Land from Saladin, the Third Crusade begins.

France, July 6, 1189: Henry II of England, dies at Chinon, aged about 66. He is succeeded by his son, Richard I (Richard the Lionheart).

Japan, 1192: Minamoto no Yoritomo becomes the first Shogun of the Kamakura dynasty, unifying Japan.

Damascus, Middle East, March 4, 1193: Saladin, Muslim sultan and warrior, dies after a brief illness, aged about 55.

Chalus, France, April 6, 1199: Death of Richard I of England. He is succeeded by his brother, King John.

1200 – 1299

Russia, 1237: The Mongol forces, under the leadership of Batu Khan, invade Russia.

Karakorum, Mongolia, 1241: Death of Ogedei Khan. He is succeeded by his son, Guyuk.

Liegnitz, Poland, April 5, 1241: The Mongol army overcome the combined forces of the Polish army and the Teutonic knights.

Russia, 1242: Batu Khan establishes the Kipchak Khanate, which is known in Russia as the "Golden Horde."

Middle East, 1248-54: France's Louis IX leads the Seventh Crusade.

Fiorentino, Italy, December 13, 1250: Frederick II, Holy Roman Emperor and King of Germany, dies, aged 55.

New Zealand, c. 1250: Settlers from eastern Polynesia arrive in New Zealand by voyaging canoe.

Venice, Italy, 1254: Marco Polo is born.

Karakorum, Mongolia, May 6, 1260: Kublai Khan becomes ruler of the Mongol Empire.

Evesham, England, August 4, 1265: Simon de Montford dies at the Battle of Evesham.

Middle East, 1270: French king Louis IX leads the Eighth Crusade.

Beijing, China, 1271: Niccolò and Maffeo Polo travel to the court of Kublai Khan, accompanied by Niccolò's son, Marco.

London, England, November 16, 1272: Henry III dies, aged 65. He is succeeded by his son, Edward I.

Germany, 1273: Rudolf I, founder of the Habsburg Dynasty, becomes King of Germany.

Kyushu, Japan, November, 1274: Mongol forces invade Japan but are repelled by samurai aided by a typhoon or *kamikaze* (divine wind).

Beijing, China, 1279: Kublai Khan proclaims himself emperor of China and founds the Yuan Dynasty.

Perpignan, France, October 5, 1285: Philip III dies, aged 40. He is succeeded by his son, Philip IV.

Acre, Middle East, 1291: The Christian-held city of Acre falls to the Mamelukes, who had risen to power in Egypt in 1250.

China, February 12, 1294: Kublai Khan, Mongol leader, dies, aged about 78.

Scotland, 1296: The Battle of Dunbar is won by the English.

Stirling Bridge, Scotland, September 11, 1297: William Wallace is victorious over the English forces.

Falkirk, Scotland, July 22, 1298: Sir William Wallace escapes after defeat of the Scottish forces at the Battle of Falkirk.

Turkey, c. 1299: Osman I establishes the Ottoman Empire.

1300 – 1399

Japan, 1333: Emperor Go-Daigo re-establishes imperial rule as the Kamakura Shogunate comes to an end.

Paterno, Sicily, 1337: Frederick III, king of Aragon and Sicily, dies, aged 64. He is succeeded by his son Peter III, despite the Peace Treaty of Caltabellota.

France, 1338: In his quest for the French throne, which he believes is rightfully his, England's Edward III invades France. This event marks the beginning of the Hundred Years' War.

Bruges, Belgium, June 24, 1340: The English fleet record a solid victory over the French at the Battle of Sluys.

Crécy, France, August 26, 1346: The English longbowmen bring England victory at the Battle of Crécy.

Calais, France, August 4, 1347: After almost 12 months of siege, the city of Calais falls to the English.

Laos, Southeast Asia, 1352: Fa Ngum establishes the Kingdom of Lan Xang (Kingdom of a Million Elephants) and founds his capital of Luang Prabang.

Gallipoli, 1354: The Ottoman Turks capture the peninsula, formerly a Byzantine possession.

Prague, Hungary, 1355: Charles of Luxembourg becomes the Holy Roman Emperor.

Poitiers, France, September, 1356: The English forces, under the leadership of Edward, the Black Prince, score a resounding victory over the French, and capture the French king, John II, his son, and a number of high-ranking nobles.

Turkey, 1361: The Ottoman forces take the city of Adrianople, renaming it Edirne and making it a second capital in the Ottoman Empire.

Nanjing, China, 1368: Rebel Zhu Yuanzhang defeats the Mongols in China and becomes the founding emperor of the Ming Dynasty

London, England, 1377: The acts introduced in the previous year by the "Good Parliament" are rescinded by the "Bad Parliament." This sitting of Parliament introduces unpopular measures such as the poll tax.

France, September 16, 1380: Charles V dies, aged 42. He is succeeded by his son, 11-year-old Charles VI.

Seoul, Korea, 1392: General Yi Songgye overthrows the Koryo Dynasty and establishes the Kingdom of Choson.

Sarai, Asia, 1398: Timur attacks Delhi and brings about the downfall of the Delhi Sultanate.

London, England, 1399: Richard II returns from Ireland, and is forced to abdicate by Henry of Bolingbroke.

1400 — 1499

Baghdad, Iraq, June, 1401: After his success in taking the city of Damascus earlier in the year, Timur and his forces capture Baghdad.

Northumberland, England, 1402: The Battle of Homildon Hill takes place. Loyal to the English king, the Duke of Northumberland and his son Henry "Hotspur" Percy intercept Scottish rebels during a foray into northern England.

Ankara, Turkey, July 28, 1402: Timur attacks the Ottoman forces at Ankara, conquering the city and capturing the ruler, Bayezid I.

Nanjing, China, 1402: Zhu Di, son of the Ming founder, wins civil war with his nephew and takes the throne as Yongle, the third emperor of the Ming dynasty.

Shrewsbury, England, July 21, 1403: The Battle of Shrewsbury takes place between the forces of King Henry IV and his former ally, Henry "Hotspur" Percy.

Samarkand, Central Asia, February, 1405: Timur, the great Mongol leader, dies, aged about 68. He is succeeded by his son, Shah Rukh.

Domrémy, France, January 6, 1412: Joan of Arc is born.

London, England, March 20, 1413: Henry IV dies, aged 45. He is succeeded by his son, Henry V.

Ottoman Empire, Asia, 1413: Mehmet I eliminates his opposition and takes control of the Ottoman Empire.

Agincourt, France, October 25, 1415: The English troops of Henry V overcome the French at the Battle of Agincourt.

Bohemia, Europe, 1420-1434: The power of the Church is challenged as the Hussite Wars are waged.

Ottoman Empire, Asia, 1421: Mehmet I dies, aged about 32. He is succeeded by his son, Murad II.

Bois de Vincennes, France, August 31, 1422: Henry V of England dies, aged about 35. He is succeeded by his son, Henry VI.

Paris, France, October 21, 1422: Charles VI dies, aged about 35. He is succeeded by his nephew, Henry VI of England, as laid down in the Treaty of Troyes.

Scotland, May, 1424: James I claims the Scottish throne.

Orleans, France, April, 1429: Joan of Arc leads the French troops at Orléans, and the English abandon their siege of the city.

Reims, France, July 17, 1429: Charles VII is crowned King of France.

Rouen, France, May 30, 1431: Joan of Arc, known as the Maid of Orléans, is burned at the stake.

Paris, France, December 16, 1431: The English conduct a French coronation for Henry VI.

1500 — 1549

Eastern Europe, 1500: War breaks out again between Lithuania and Russia, as Russia's Ivan III invades the neighboring country.

Brazil, April, 1500: Portuguese explorer Pedro Alvares Cabral discovers Brazil.

Madagascar, August, 1500: Portuguese explorer Diego Diaz discovers the island of Madagascar.

Tabriz, Persia, 1502: Shah Ismail I, having defeated his rival Alwand of the White Sheep, founds Persia's Safavid Dynasty.

Mexico, 1502: Montezuma II becomes leader of the Aztecs.

London, England, April, 1502: Prince Arthur, heir to the Tudor Dynasty, dies, aged 16.

Eastern Europe, March, 1503: War between Russia and Lithuania ends when a truce is brokered.

Afghanistan, 1504: Mogul leader Babur conquers Kabul and remains in power there for 15 years.

Rome, Italy, January, 1506: The Swiss Guard is formed to protect the pope.

Valladolid, Spain, May 20, 1506: Christopher Columbus, explorer, dies, aged 55.

London, England, 1509: Henry VIII is crowned then marries his brother Arthur's widow, Catherine of Aragon.

Constantinople, Turkey, September 14, 1509: An earthquake destroys the city.

Goa, India, 1510: The Portuguese establish a trading colony at Goa, the first permanent European settlement in Asia.

Branxton, England, September, 1513: The forces of James IV of Scotland are defeated at the Battle of Flodden; James dies in battle.

Panama, September 25, 1513: Vasco Nuñez de Balboa discovers the Pacific Ocean.

North America, April, 1513: Ponce de Leon discovers Florida.

Wittenberg, Germany, October 31, 1517: Martin Luther, leader of the reformation, nails his 95 theses to a church door.

Seville, Spain, September 20, 1519: Magellan sets sail to circumnavigate the world.

Mexico, June 30, 1520: Montezuma II is killed by his own people.

Turkey, September, 1520: Suleiman I becomes the Ottoman sultan and the Ottoman empire enters its most powerful period.

Sweden, November, 1520: The Danish forces of Christian II conquer Sweden.

Rome, Italy, January, 1521: Martin Luther is excommunicated from the Catholic Church by Pope Leo X.

1550 — 1599

Libya, Africa, 1551: Ottoman forces invade and conquer Tripoli.

Devon, England, 1552: Walter Raleigh is born.

London, England, July, 1553: Edward VI dies, and 4 days later Lady Jane Grey takes the throne. She reigns for just 9 days before being ousted.

London, England, July 19, 1553: Mary I, daughter of Henry VIII and Catherine Aragon, takes the throne and sets about re-establishing the Catholic religion into English life.

Arctic region, 1554: Hugh Willoughby, the British explorer who discovered Novaya Zemlya, perishes in the Arctic weather.

London, England, July 25, 1554: Mary I of England marries Prince Philip of Spain, but the British Parliament do not recognize him as king.

India, 1556: Humayun, Mogul of India, dies, aged 48. He is succeeded by his son Akbar.

Macau, China, 1557: Portuguese traders found the port city of Macau, the first European trading enclave in China.

France, 1558: The French retake the port of Calais, formerly an English possession.

London, England, November 17, 1558: Elizabeth I succeeds to the English throne, following the death of her half-sister, Mary I.

Amboise, France, 1560: The Huguenots fail in their attempt to capture Charles IX. This act sparks fresh religious fighting.

Spain, 1560: Madrid becomes the Spanish capital.

Spain, 1561: Philip II ends colonizing activities in Florida in the New World after a number of failed attempts.

England, 1563: Witchcraft is declared an offence punishable by death.

Manila, Philippines, 1565: First Manila galleon laden with Mexican silver arrives in the Philippines from Acapulco, inaugurating Spanish trans-Pacific trade.

Edinburgh, Scotland, June 19, 1566: James VI of Scotland is born.

Constantinople, Turkey, September, 1566: Suleiman I, Ottoman leader, dies, aged about 71. He is succeeded by his son, Selim II.

Edinburgh, Scotland, May 1567: Mary, Queen of Scots marries the Earl of Bothwell at the Palace of Holyroodhouse. Bothwell had been implicated in the murder of her second husband, Lord Darnley.

Carberry Hill, Edinburgh, Scotland, June 15, 1567: The forces of Mary, Queen of Scots, are defeated by the Protestant lords.

1600 — 1649

Sekigahara, Japan, October 21, 1600: Tokugawa Ieyasu defeats forces loyal to Toyotomi Hideyoshi, and establishes the Tokugawa (Edo) Shogunate.

London, England, 1600: The British East India Company is founded.

Fife, Scotland, November 19, 1600: Charles, son of James I of Scotland, is born.

Netherlands, 1602: The Dutch East India Company is founded.

Turkey, 1603: Mehmet III, Ottoman ruler, dies, aged about 36. He is succeeded by his son, Ahmed I.

Richmond, Surrey, England, March 24, 1603: Elizabeth I dies, aged 69. She is succeeded by James VI of Scotland, who becomes James I of England.

Agra, India, October 17, 1605: Akbar the Great, Mogul ruler, dies, aged about 63. He is succeeded by his son, Jahangir.

North America, 1610: After several previous voyages, Henry Hudson once more sails for an English trading company, and discovers the bay and the strait that will bear his name.

Paris, France, May 14, 1610: The assassination of Henry IV, aged 57, cuts short a peaceful reign. He is succeeded by his son, Louis XIII.

Northern Europe, 1611-1613: Disputed seafaring trade routes see Denmark and Sweden engage in the Kalmar War.

Russia, 1613: Mikhail Romanov comes to the Russian throne, ending the "Time of Troubles."

Jamestown, North America, April 5, 1614: Pocahontas, an Algonquin princess, marries John Rolfe, English tobacco farmer.

Canada, 1616: William Baffin, English maritime explorer, arrives at the bay named for him—Baffin Bay.

Constantinople, Turkey, November 22, 1617: Ahmed I, Ottoman ruler, dies, aged 27. He is succeeded by his brother Mustafa I.

Prague, Eastern Europe, 1618: The Bohemian nobility oppose the Austrian (Habsburg) overlords, beginning with an incident known as "the Defenestration at Prague."

London, England, 1618: Sir Walter Raleigh, adventurer, courtier, and poet, is beheaded, aged about 64.

Europe, 1619: Ferdinand II becomes the Holy Roman Emperor.

Provincetown, North America, November 21, 1620: A group of English Puritans known as the Pilgrims land in North America after a 65-day voyage from Portsmouth, England in the *Mayflower*.

Netherlands, 1621: The Dutch West India Company is founded.

New Plymouth, Massachusetts, North America, 1621: After the death of their first elected Governor, John Carver, William Bradford is elected Governor of the Pilgrims' colony.

1400–1499

Arboga, Sweden, 1435: A group of nobles from all over the country meet in the nation's first "parliament" as part of the rebellion against King Erik.

Mexico, 1440: The Aztec emperor, Itzcoatl, dies. He is succeeded by his nephew, Montezuma (Moctezuma) I. Itzcoatl first came to power as a member of the Triple Alliance that defeated the Tepanecs.

Ottoman Empire, Asia, 1451: Murad II dies, aged about 46. He is succeeded by his son, Mehmet II.

Constantinople, Turkey, 1453: The fall of Constantinople signals the end of the Byzantine era, and the rise of the Ottoman Empire.

France, 1453: The English have been all but driven from France.

St Albans, England, 1455: The Battle of St Albans between Lancaster and York marks the beginning of the Wars of the Roses.

Belgrade, Hungary, July 14, 1456: The invading Ottomans are defeated by an undermanned but determined Hungarian force under the leadership of János Hunyadi.

England, 1461: York defeats Lancaster at the Battle of Mortimers Cross. King Henry VI is ousted, replaced by Edward IV.

Kyoto, Japan, 1467: Rival daimyo vying for power spark the breakout of the Onin Wars.

South America, 1471: Topa Inca (also known as Tupac Yupanqui) succeeds his father Pachacuti and continues the expansion of the Inca Empire.

London, England, April 9, 1483: Edward IV dies, aged 40, leaving the throne to his son, Edward V, with Richard of Gloucester as regent.

London, England, July 6, 1483: Richard, Duke of Gloucester, is crowned King Richard III.

Bosworth, England, August 22, 1485: The Battle of Bosworth Field sees Richard III killed in battle when his allies switch their allegiance to Henry Tudor. Henry claims the throne as Henry VII.

Stoke, England, June 16, 1487: Victory for Henry VII at the Battle of Stoke Field marks the end of the Wars of the Roses.

Cadiz, Spain, September 25, 1493: Columbus embarks on his second voyage to the New World.

Canada, June 24, 1497: Italian explorer John Cabot (Giovanni Caboto) explores the Atlantic coast of Canada in his English-sponsored search for a northwest passage to India.

Calicut, India, May 22, 1498: Portuguese navigator Vasco da Gama becomes the first European to reach India by sea.

Japan, September 20, 1498: A tsunami kills over 30,000 people.

1500–1549

Philippines, April 27, 1521: Ferdinand Magellan, explorer, dies, aged about 48.

Caribbean, 1523: Hernán Cortés conquers New Spain and is made governor of the region.

Cochin, India, December 24, 1524: Vasco da Gama, famed Portuguese explorer, dies, aged about 74.

Panipat, India, April, 1526: Babur, founder of the Mogul Dynasty, defeats his rivals at the Battle of Panipat.

China, January 10, 1529: Wang Yang-ming, statesman and philosopher, dies, aged 56.

Agra, India, December 26, 1530: Babur, Mogul leader, dies, aged 47. He is succeeded by his son, Humayun.

London, England, September 7, 1533: Elizabeth I born to Henry VIII and his second wife Anne Boleyn.

London, England, 1534: An Act of Parliament recognizes Henry VIII as Supreme Head of the Church of England.

North America, May, 1534: French explorer Jacques Cartier arrives in Newfoundland.

London, England, October 24, 1537: Jane Seymour, third wife of Henry VIII, dies 12 days after giving birth to Henry's son, Edward.

North America, May 8, 1541: Spanish explorer Hernando de Soto discovers the Mississippi River.

Lima, Peru, June 26, 1541: Francisco Pizarro, Spanish explorer, dies, aged about 69.

Rome, Italy, July, 1542: Pope Paul III establishes the inquisition into Prostestantism.

Linlithgow, Scotland, December 8, 1542: Mary, daughter of James V, is born.

China, 1542: A landslide into the Yangtze River makes navigation of the waterway impossible.

Japan, 1542: A Portuguese ship lands in Japan.

Peking, China, 1542: Ming Dynasty forces repel an attempted invasion of China by Mongol leader Altan Khan.

London, England, July 12, 1543: Henry VIII takes his sixth wife, Katherine Parr, after Catherine Howard was executed in 1542 for indiscretions committed prior to her marriage.

Portsmouth, England, July 19, 1545: The *Mary Rose* capsizes in Portsmouth harbor.

Russia, January 16, 1547: Ivan IV is crowned the first Tsar of Russia.

Seville, Spain, December 2, 1547: Hernán Cortés, Spanish conquerer of Mexico, dies, aged about 62.

1550–1599

Japan, 1570: Nagasaki becomes the first Japanese port open to overseas trade.

Ionian Sea, October 7, 1571: Don John of Austria's combined Holy League naval forces defeat the Turkish fleet commanded by Ali Pasha

France, August 24, 1572: The St Bartholomew's Day Massacre sees more than 8,000 Huguenots killed in Paris.

Poland, May 11, 1573: Henry of Anjou becomes the first elected king of Poland, with limited power.

Kyoto, Japan, 1576: After more than a century of civil war, Oda Nobunaga completes his campaign for military reunification of Japan.

Canada, 1576: British explorer Martin Frobisher discovers Frobisher Bay.

Plymouth, England, December 1577: Sir Francis Drake sets sail in search of Terra Australis. He has five ships in his fleet, including *The Golden Hind*.

Kyoto, Japan, June, 1582: Oda Nobunaga, warlord, dies, aged about 48.

Canada, 1583: Newfoundland is claimed by Sir Humphrey Gilbert for the Queen of England.

Fotheringhay, England, February 8, 1587: Mary, Queen of Scots is executed, aged 44.

Tabriz, Persia (Iran), 1587: Safavid dynasty ruler Shah Mohammed Khodabanda is forced to abdicate and is succeeded by his son, Shah Abbas I.

English Channel, August, 1589: The Spanish Armada is defeated in the English Channel.

France, April, 1589: Huguenot Henry of Navarre succeeds to the French throne.

Japan, 1590: Toyotomi Hideyoshi, successor to Nobunaga, successfully unites Japan.

West Africa, 1591: Timbuktu is taken by the Moroccans.

Italy, 1592: The ruins of the Roman city of Pompeii are discovered.

Pusan, Korea, 1592: Samurai forces dispatched by Japanese Shogun Hideyoshi invade Korea.

India, January 5, 1592: Shah Jahan is born.

Panama, January 28, 1596: Sir Francis Drake, explorer and privateer, dies, aged 56.

Arctic region, June 20, 1597: Willem Barents, Dutch explorer, dies, aged about 39.

Nantes, France, April, 1598: The Edict of Nantes is issued, allowing religious freedom to French Huguenots after years of persecution.

Madrid, Spain, September 13, 1598: Philip II dies, aged about 71.

Huntingdon, England, April 25, 1599: Oliver Cromwell is born.

1600–1649

Paris, France, 1624: Cardinal Richelieu becomes the Prime Minister of France.

London, England, March 27, 1625: James I dies, aged 58. He is succeeded by his son, Charles I.

Agra, India, 1628: Jahangir, Mogul ruler, dies, aged 59. He is succeeded by his son, Shah Jahan.

Persia, 1629: Shah Abbas I (known as Abbas the Great), Safavid ruler, dies, aged about 72. He is succeeded by his son Safi I.

London, England, 1629: Constant conflict sees Charles I dissolve the Houses of Parliament.

Asia, 1634: Ligdan Khan, the last great Mongol ruler, dies, after a reign of 30 years.

Quebec, Canada, 1635: Samuel de Champlain, explorer, dies, aged about 68.

Shimabara, Japan, 1636: The rebellion of Christians ends in the slaughter of over 30,000 rebels.

Japan, 1638: Japan embarks on a period of isolation from the rest of the world.

Ireland, 1641: Dissatisfied with years of English control, the Irish nobility band together and launch a rebellion to regain control of the country and oust the English administration.

England, 1642: England is plunged into civil war, as the parliamentarian "Roundhead" forces and the royal "Cavalier" forces engage in battle.

Tasmania, Australia, 1642: Dutch explorer Abel Tasman discovers Van Diemen's Land (Tasmania).

New Zealand, 1642: Abel Tasman sights New Zealand.

Persia, 1642: Shah Safi, Safavid ruler, dies. He is succeeded by his son, Shah Abbas II.

Paris, France, May 14, 1643: Louis XIII dies aged 41. He is succeeded by his four-year-old son, Louis XIV, with his wife, Anne of Austria, taking on the role of regent.

Peking, China, April 25, 1644: Zhu Youjian, the last Ming emperor, hangs himself as Manchu forces enter the Forbidden City.

Tainan, Taiwan, 1645: Pirate-patriot Zheng Chenggong establishes the Ming loyalist regime on Taiwan, and resists the newly-established Qing (Manchu) Dynasty.

Europe, 1648: The Peace of Westphalia brings about the end of the Thirty Years War.

London, England, 1649: Charles I of England is found guilty of treason and executed on January 30. His son and heir, Charles, is forced into exile in Europe. Oliver Cromwell becomes Lord Protector of England.

1650 – 1699

Japan, 1651: Tokugawa Iemitsu, Shogun, dies, aged 47. He is succeeded by his 10-year-old son, Ietsuna, under five regents.

London, England, December, 1653: The collapse of Parliament, a protectorate is established, with Oliver Cromwell as Lord Protector.

Europe, April, 1654: The signing of the Peace of Westminster brings to an end two years of naval battles and standoffs between England and the Netherlands, as each nation fights for trade opportunities.

Agra, India, 1658: Shah Jahan is imprisoned by his son, Aurangzeb, who now assumes rule over the Mogul Empire.

London, England, September 3, 1658: Lord Protector Oliver Cromwell dies, aged 59. In the previous year, the "Humble Petition" had been bestowed upon Cromwell, allowing him power almost equaling that of a monarch. He is succeeded by his son, Richard.

London, England, May, 1659: Richard Cromwell is ousted from his position of Lord Protector.

Batavia, Indonesia, c. 1659: Abel Janszoon Tasman, Dutch explorer, dies, aged 56. Tasman is remembered as the first European to discover New Zealand and Tasmania, Australia.

London, England, May 29, 1660: The monarchy is restored as Charles II takes back the throne left vacant since his father's execution in 1649.

China, 1661: Emperor Shunzhi dies, aged 23. He is succeeded by his son, Kangxi as the next Qing Emperor, under four regents.

Paris, France, 1661: Cardinal Jules Mazarin, prime minister, dies, aged about 58.

New York, North America, 1664: Known as New Amsterdam to the Dutch settlers, the English seize the area and rename it New York.

London, England, 1665: Black Death–bubonic plague–strikes. Known as the "Great Plague," it causes many deaths.

Congo, Africa, 1665: The King of the Kongo Empire, António I, is killed by the Portuguese at the Battle of Mbwila.

Europe, 1665-1667: The naval fleets of England and the Netherlands lock horns again in an effort to control the seas.

London, England, September 2, 1666: The Great Fire of London consumes much of the city.

North America, July, 1667: A peace treaty is signed between the Iroquois people and the French.

Sault Ste Marie, North America, June 4, 1671: At a ceremony held in Sault Ste Marie, the French lay claim to all land lying west of Montreal.

1700 – 1749

London, England, March 19, 1702: William III of Orange dies, aged 51. Anne, his wife's sister, succeeds the throne.

Turkey, August 22, 1703: Sultan Mustafa II is deposed.

Blenheim, Bavaria, August 13, 1705: The Battle of Blenheim is won by English, Austrian and Dutch forces.

Ahmadnagar, India, March 3, 1707: Aurangzeb Alamgir, Mogul emperor, dies aged 88.

Great Britain, May 1, 1707: England and Scotland unite under one ruler and one Parliament.

Poltava, Russia, July 8, 1709: Charles XII of Sweden is defeated by Peter I of Russia at the Battle of Poltava.

Malplaquet, France, September 11, 1709: Great Britain, Netherlands and Austria defeat France, with enormous loss of life on both sides.

London, England, 1710: The *Post Office Act* is passed, regulating the passage of mail between England and North America.

Pruth River, Ukraine, July 21, 1711: The Treaty of Pruth is signed by Russia and Turkey, restoring lost territory to the Turks.

North Carolina, North America, September 22, 1711: The Tuscarora Indians attack, killing settlers and destroying farms.

Utrecht, Netherlands, 1713: The War of the Spanish Succession is ended by the Treaty of Utrecht. Philip V remains King of Spain, but Spanish territories in other parts of Europe are given up. The American colonies see fighting too (known as Queen Anne's War).

Hanover, Germany, June 8, 1714: Sophia, Electress of Hanover and heir to Great Britain, dies, aged 84.

London, England, March, 1715: William Dampier, English explorer and privateer dies, aged about 63.

Versailles, France, September 1, 1715: Louis XIV dies of gangrene, aged 76.

Belgrade, Serbia, August 22, 1717: Prince Eugene of Savoy defeats the Turks at the Battle of Belgrade.

Fredriksten, Norway, November 30, 1718: Charles XII, King of Sweden, dies, aged 36.

Louisiana, North America, 1718: French rulers establish a trading post named New Orleans.

Liechtenstein, September 23, 1719: The newly-established principality declares its independence.

Delhi, India, 1720: Mohammed Ibrahim, Mogul emperor, dies after a short reign, the fourth emperor in two years.

Easter Island, South Pacific, April 5, 1722: Discovered by Dutch explorer Jacob Roggeveen.

Berkshire, England, June 16, 1722: John Churchill, Duke of Marlborough, dies, aged 72.

Peking, China, December 20, 1722: Emperor Kangxi dies, aged 68.

1750 – 1799

Paris, France, 1751: Charles-Marie de la Condamine publishes the journal of his voyage down the Amazon River.

Europe and Africa, November 1, 1755: An earthquake shakes Italy, Switzerland, France, North Africa, and Portugal. Lisbon is destroyed.

London, England, May 15, 1756: Great Britain declares war on France, formalizing the existing conflict in the American colonies and starting the Seven Years' War.

Calcutta, India, June 20, 1756: Indian troops confine British prisoners to a room so small and hot that many deaths occur. It is later dubbed the "Black Hole of Calcutta."

Plassey, India, June 22, 1757: Robert Clive's victory over French forces ensures British domination of India.

Quebec, Canada, September 13, 1759: James Wolfe and the British and American forces defeat Louis-Joseph, Marquis de Montcalm, and the French and Canadian forces. Wolfe dies in the battle and Montcalm is fatally wounded.

St Petersburg, Russia, January 5, 1762: Elisabeth, Empress of Russia, dies, aged 52.

Moscow, Russia, September 22, 1762: Catherine II is crowned Empress of All Russia.

Paris, France, February 10, 1763: The Treaty of Paris ends wars in both Europe and North America.

Great Lakes, North America, 1763: Chief Pontiac, Ottawa tribal leader, organizes a series of raids against British forts to reclaim tribal lands.

Brazil, 1763: Rio de Janeiro replaces Salvador as the nation's capital.

Benares, India, August 12, 1765: The Treaty of Allahabad gives the East India Company control of much of India.

North America, 1765: Great Britain imposes the unpopular *Stamp Act* on the American colonies. The tax covers just about everything produced by the Americans, which leads to civil unrest.

Kathmandu, Nepal, September 25, 1768: Gorkha King Prithvi Narayan Shah becomes first king of Nepal.

New Zealand, October, 1769: The *Endeavour*'s crew become the first Europeans to land on New Zealand.

New Holland (Australia), August 22, 1770: Captain James Cook claims the east coast for Great Britain.

Java, Dutch East Indies, August 12, 1772: An avalanche caused by the eruption of Papandayan volcano destroys about 40 villages and leads to almost 3,000 deaths.

Afghanistan, April, 1773: Ahmad Shah Durrani dies, aged about 50.

Boston, North America, December 16, 1773: Chests of tea are thrown overboard by local colonists disguised as Indians.

1800 – 1824

United Kingdom, January 1, 1801: The Act of Union between Ireland and Great Britain comes into effect.

Washington DC, USA, March 4, 1801: Thomas Jefferson becomes the new president.

St Petersburg, Russia, March 23, 1801: Paul I, Tzar of Russia, is assassinated and succeeded by his son Alexander.

London, England, 1802: The *Health and Morals of Apprentices Act* limits the working hours of children in textile mills to 12 hours a day.

Hue, Vietnam, 1802: The country is reunited after about 30 years of internal conflict.

Paris, France, April 30, 1803: The French government sells its Louisiana Territory to the USA.

Haiti, January 1, 1804: Jean-Jacques Dessalines declares Haiti a free republic after slaves mount a successful revolution against France.

Paris, France, December 2, 1804: Napoleon Bonaparte crowns himself Emperor of France at Notre Dame Cathedral.

Cape Trafalgar, Spain, October 21, 1805: Admiral Horatio Nelson leads the British Royal Navy to victory against France and Spain at the Battle of Trafalgar. He is fatally wounded.

Liechtenstein, July, 1806: The tiny nation joins the Rhine Confederation as an independent sovereign state.

London, England, March 25, 1807: The Abolition of the Slave Trade Act is passed, outlawing the transport of slaves by British ships.

USA, January 1, 1808: Congress bans the importation of slaves.

South America, 1810: South American Wars of Independence begin. Columbia and Mexico gain independence.

Paris, France, 1810: The Napoleonic Code prohibits abortion unless the mother's life is at risk.

London, England, February 5, 1811: The Prince of Wales takes office as regent for King George III after his father becomes insane.

Batavia, Dutch East Indies, August 6, 1811: The British fleet captures Batavia, and wrests control of Java from the Dutch.

England, 1811-1812: Textile workers destroy new machines.

Mississippi Valley, USA, February 7, 1812: The country's most powerful earthquake strikes.

Fort William, Canada, 1812: English-born David Thompson, explorer for the North West Company, retires, after mapping much of Canada.

Wyoming, USA, 1812: Robert Stuart and his party find an easy crossing through the Rocky Mountains.

Washington DC, USA, 1812: America declares war on British North America.

1650 - 1699

Europe, 1672-1674: The Third Anglo-Dutch War takes place as the maritime rivals take up the contest again for control of the high seas, and trade.

North America, 1673: Louis Joliet and Father Marquette travel down the Mississippi by canoe to determine the river's path and the opportunities it may offer.

Carolina, North America, 1677: John Culpepper and George Durant lead a rebellion against the British restriction of the colonies' trade.

Louisiana, North America, April 9, 1682: René-Robert Cavelier, Sieur de la Salle, claims the Mississippi area for France, naming the area Louisiana in honor of the king.

Russia, 1682: Brothers Ivan IV and Peter I take the Russian throne after the death of Fyodor III, with Peter's half-sister Sofia as regent.

Pescadores Islands, China, 1683: The Qing Dynasty fleet defeats Ming loyalist forces based on the island of Taiwan; Taiwan surrenders three months later.

Africa, 1684: Changamire Dombo resists the Portuguese traders and starts to establish his Rozvi Empire.

Bombay (Mumbai), India, 1685: British forces take Bombay, which becomes a base for expansion of East India Company control.

Australia, 1688: Englishman William Dampier and other crew members land on the west coast.

London, England, February, 1689: William III and Mary II accept the throne as co-rulers, after James II has been forced into exile following the "Glorious Revolution."

Scotland, July 27, 1689: Supporters of James VII of Scotland (former James II of England) take on the English forces of the new royals at the Battle of Killiecrankie. Among the Jacobite force is Rob Roy.

Ireland, July 1, 1690: Ousted English King James II is defeated by the English and Dutch forces of the Parliament-appointed William III.

Scotland, February 13, 1692: The Massacre at Glencoe sees clan leader Maclain and his kinfolk murdered in their homes by their guests.

Sweden, October 13, 1694: German historian, Baron Samuel von Pufendorf, dies aged 62.

Quebec, North America, 1694: The intrepid Louis Joliet sets off to explore the Labrador region.

Australia, 1698: William Dampier, a former English pirate, sails to the west coast of Australia to investigate the region.

Eastern Europe, 1699: Defeat at the Battle of Zenta brings an end to the Great Turkish War, made official with the signing of the Treaty of Karlowitz by the Ottomans.

1700 - 1749

Peking, China, 1723: Prince Yin-zhen, outwitting his brothers and executing or imprisoning some of them, takes the throne as Emperor Yongzheng.

England, November, 1724: Henry Kelsey, Canadian explorer, dies, aged 57.

Madrid, Spain, August, 1724: King Philip V returns to the throne, after the death of his son Louis I.

St Petersburg, Russia, February 8, 1725: Peter the Great dies, aged 52.

Montevideo, South America, 1726: The city of Montevideo (later the capital of Uruguay) is founded.

Kiakhta, Russia, 1727: The Treaty of Kiakhta defines the boundary between the Chinese and the Russian empires.

St Petersburg, Russia, May 17, 1727: Catherine I, Empress of Russia, dies, aged 43.

Hanover, Germany, October 11, 1727: George I, King of Great Britain, dies, aged 67. He is succeeded by his son, George II.

Bering Strait, August 13, 1728: Vitus Bering discovers the passage between Russia and Alaska.

Dublin, Ireland, 1728: Irish Catholics lose the right to vote.

Moscow, January 29, 1730: Peter II, Emperor of Russia, dies of smallpox, aged 14.

Turkey, September, 1730: Ottoman Sultan Ahmed III is deposed by janissaries, as was his predecessor.

Tupelo, Mississippi, North America, May 26, 1736: The French governor of Louisiana attacks the Chickasaw Indian town of Ackia in an attempt to control traffic along the Mississippi.

Peking, China, 1736: Emperor Qianlong ascends the throne, inaugurating the golden age of the Qing Dynasty.

Kandahar, Afghanistan, 1738: The Persian army of Nadir Shah takes Kandahar, making way for invasion of India in the following year.

Vienna, Austria, October 20, 1740: Charles VI of Austria, Holy Roman Emperor, dies, aged 55, leaving no male heirs. This sparks the War of the Austrian Succession.

Russia, October 28, 1740: Empress Anna Ivanova dies, aged 47.

St Petersburg, Russia, September 25, 1741: The reign of the one-year-old Ivan VI, with his mother as regent, is overthrown.

Russia, May 2, 1742: Russian explorer Semyon Chelyuskin reaches the most northern point in Eurasia.

North America, February, 1743: Louis and François La Vérendrye, reach the base of the Rocky Mountains.

Culloden, Scotland, April 16, 1746: The British Army defeat Scottish Highlander clansmen at the Battle of Culloden.

Fathabad, Persia, June, 1747: Nadir Shah is assassinated, aged 58.

Aachen, Germany, October 18, 1748: The Treaty of Aix-la-Chapelle ends the War of the Austrian Succession.

1750 - 1799

Lexington, Massachusetts, North America, April 19, 1775: British troops fire on local militiamen who are alerted by Paul Revere. The American Revolution begins.

Philadelphia, North America, July 4, 1776: Continental Congress adopts the Declaration of Independence.

Hawaii, February 14, 1779: Captain James Cook, explorer, dies, aged 50.

Austria, September, 1781: Emperor Joseph II abolishes serfdom, giving all subjects freedom to marry, own property, migrate, and work.

Cape Colony, southern Africa, 1781: The First Cape Frontier War begins.

Glaris, Switzerland, June 17, 1782: Anna Goeldi dies. She is the last known person executed for witchcraft in Europe.

Bangkok, Siam, 1782: Rama I founds a new royal dynasty, and moves the Thai capital from Thonburi to Bangkok.

Paris, France, September 3, 1783: Great Britain and America sign the Treaty of Paris, ending the American Revolutionary War.

Potsdam, Germany, August 17, 1786: Frederick the Great dies, aged 74.

Port Jackson (Sydney), New South Wales, Australia, January 26, 1788: The 11 ships of the First Fleet arrive.

Rome, Italy, January 31, 1788: Charles Edward Stuart ("Bonnie Prince Charlie"), claimant to the English throne, dies, aged 67.

London, England, May 12, 1789: William Wilberforce speaks against the slave trade in Parliament.

Paris, France, July 14, 1789: Parisians storm the Bastille, releasing the prisoners and killing Governor de Launey.

Pitcairn Island, January 15, 1790: Fletcher Christian leads the *Bounty* mutineers and some Tahitians. They settle the uninhabited island.

San Domingue (Haiti), August 22, 1791: Slaves in this French colony revolt against harsh conditions, burn plantations, and murder the owners.

Kyushu Island, Japan, 1792: The eruption of Unzen volcano causes an avalanche and tsunami. More than 14,000 people die.

Fiordland, New Zealand, 1792: First sealing parties arrive; thus begins its integration with the global economy.

Paris, France, January 21, 26, 1793: King Louis XVI and Queen Marie Antoinette are guillotined.

Canada, July 22, 1793: Alexander Mackenzie is the first European to cross Canada from the Atlantic Ocean to the Pacific.

Paris, France, December 24, 1799: The Consulate, led by Napoleon Bonaparte, becomes France's governing body.

Mount Vernon, Virginia, USA, December 14, 1799: George Washington dies, aged 67.

1800 - 1824

New South Wales, Australia, June, 1813: Explorers Gregory Blaxland, William Wentworth, and William Lawson return from their crossing of the Blue Mountains, enabling access to fertile land that will help feed the fast-growing colony.

Gulistan, Persia, October 12, 1813: Persia signs the Treaty of Gulistan, ceding Baku, Karabagh, and other territories to the Russian Empire.

Ghent, Belgium, December 24, 1814: The Treaty of Ghent marks the end of the War of 1812 between the UK and USA.

Sumbawa, Indonesia, April 11, 1815: The Tambora Volcano eruption, the most powerful ever recorded, causes local devastation and affects northern hemisphere temperatures.

Waterloo, Belgium, June 18, 1815: The French forces are defeated at the Battle of Waterloo.

Vienna, Austria, 1815: The Congress of Vienna reshapes Europe after Napoleon's defeat. It establishes the German Confederation, guarantees the neutrality of Switzerland, and bans the trading of slaves by its signatories.

New York, USA, March 8, 1817: The New York Stock and Exchange Board is established.

Valley of the Kings, Egypt, 1817: Giovanni Battista Belzoni discovers a number of ancient tombs, including the sepulchre of Seti I.

Canada, October 20, 1818: USA and Britain establish the boundary between Canada and the USA.

Singapore, February 1819: A port is established at Singapore.

Manchester, England, August 16, 1819: Eleven people die at the Peterloo Massacre.

Africa, 1819: Shaka, king of the Zulus, defeats the Ndwandwe and destroys their lands.

New Zealand, 1820: Ngapuhi chief, Hongi Hika, trades food for muskets in Australia and attacks rival tribes, starting the "musket wars."

Liberia, 1821: The American Colonization Society purchases land around Cape Mesurado in West Africa to enable "free people of color" from the USA to settle there.

South America, 1821: El Salvador, Guatemala, Honduras, Nicaragua, and Peru all gain independence from Spain.

Chios, Greece, April 2, 1822: Thousands are slaughtered in the Agios Minas monastery.

Spain, October 1, 1823: After French troops free Ferdinand VII and restore him to the throne, he revokes the Constitution.

Washington, USA, December 2, 1823: President Monroe states that "the American continents...are henceforth not to be considered as subjects for future colonization by European powers."

Lima, Peru, February 10, 1824: Simón Bolívar is named as dictator of the new republic of Peru.

1825 – 1849

South America, 1825: Bolivia declares separation from Peru, and Uruguay from Brazil.

Istanbul, Turkey, June 14, 1825: The Janissaries' revolt fails with the Sipahis (Ottoman cavalry) killing thousands.

Southeast Asia, 1825: Indonesians revolt against the Dutch colonists in the Java War.

Yandaboo, Burma, February 24, 1826: Following British victory in the First Anglo-Burmese War, the Treaty of Yandaboo secures British control of Assam.

USA, July 4, 1826: Thomas Jefferson dies, aged 83, on the 50th anniversary of the Declaration of Independence.

Mediterranean, October 20, 1827: Russia, France, and Britain unite to destroy the Turkish and Egyptian armada at the Battle of Navarino.

South Africa, 1828: Shaka, founder and dictator of the Zulu empire is murdered by his half-brothers.

Italy, March 31, 1829: Pius VIII becomes pope.

Australia, 1829: Western Australia becomes a free colony.

Paris, France, July, 1830: Charles X abdicates and flees to England. His cousin Louis Philippe is crowned the "citizen king."

Algeria, July, 1830: France invades after Algeria threatens to withdraw French trading rights.

Europe, 1830: Revolutionary unrest in France, Italy, Germany, and Poland.

Belgium, October 3, 1830: Belgium wins independence from the Netherlands.

Colombia, December 17, 1830: Simón Bolívar, national hero and liberator, dies, aged 47.

Anatolia, 1832: Egyptian viceroy Mehemet Ali defeats the Ottomans at the Battle of Konya.

Falklands, 1832: Britain occupies the Falklands.

India, 1833: Hindu social reformer Ram Mohan Roy dies, aged 60.

1835: Haley's Comet reappears.

Southern Africa, 1835: More than 10,000 Boers leave Cape Colony to found the republics of Natal, Transvaal, and Orange Free State. This mass migration becomes known as "The Great Trek."

USA, 1836: Texas gains independence from Mexico.

UK, 1837: Victoria becomes Queen of the United Kingdom of Great Britain and Ireland.

Canada, 1837: Constitutional revolts occur in upper and lower Canada.

New York, USA, May 10, 1837: Inflated land values and paper speculation cause financial panic; banks stop payment in gold and silver coinage.

Quetta, Afghanistan, 1838: The first Anglo-Afghan War erupts when the British governor of India attacks.

1850 – 1874

London, England, 1850: Australian Colonies Government Act grants the colonies self-government.

Australia, 1851: Goldrush in New South Wales and Victoria.

Nigeria, 1851: Slave trade ends when the British occupy Lagos.

Thistle Mountain, Guangxi, China, January 11, 1851–1864: Taiping Rebellion begun by Hong Xiuquan, self-proclaimed younger brother of Jesus Christ, causes 20–30 million deaths.

New Zealand, 1852: Constitution is granted.

Africa, 1852: Transvaal becomes an independent Boer Republic.

France, 1852: Louis Napoleon III becomes emperor with fall of the Republic.

Uraga, Japan, July 8, 1853: American Commodore Mathew Perry arrives with squadron of warships, demanding treaty talks with Japanese government.

New Zealand, July 14, 1853: First general election is held; the sole candidate, Hugh Carleton, is elected.

Balkans, 1853–1856: Crimean War. The Ottomans and their allies fight Russia to control the Middle East.

Africa, 1854: Britain returns Orange Free State to the Boers.

Japan, 1854: The Treaty of Kanagawa opens trade between USA and Japan.

Balkans, 1855: Florence Nightingale reforms British military hospitals.

China, 1856–1860: Second Opium War; French forces join the British.

Afghanistan, 1856–1857: Persia is at war with Britain after invasion.

France, 1856: Treaty of Paris ends Crimean War.

Meerut, India, May 10, 1857: Native Indian troops begin uprising (Sepoy Mutiny).

Ireland, 1858: A Republican Brotherhood is established to work towards gaining an independent Irish Republic.

China, June, 1858: Treaty of Tientsin allows further ports to open for foreign trade.

Italy, 1859: France and Piedmont Sardinia declare war on Austria.

Vladivostok, Russia, 1860: A port is founded on the Sea of Japan.

Italy, 1860: Guerrilla leader Giuseppe Garibaldi leads an invasion to Sicily and then on to Naples to drive out the Bourbon king.

Peking, China, 1860: China and Russia sign the Treaty of Peking.

Hong Kong, 1860: Second Opium War ends after four years, with mainland Kowloon handed to the British.

Taranaki, New Zealand, March 17, 1860: War breaks out between Maori and settlers, starting over a decade of fighting over land and sovereignty (known as the "New Zealand Wars").

Australia, 1861: Women are given the right to vote.

Russia, 1861: Serfs are emancipated.

Italy, 1861: The War of National Unification breaks out.

1875 – 1899

Washington DC, USA, March 1, 1875: The Civil Rights Act implements equal rights in public accommodations regardless of race.

Little Big Horn, Dakota, USA, June 25, 1876: The 7th Cavalry, commanded by General George Custer is obliterated; 265 troopers face 3,500 Indian warriors led by chiefs Sitting Bull and Crazy Horse.

Mexico City, Mexico, November 29, 1876: Porfirio Díaz, war hero, appoints himself president after overthrowing the government of Sebastián Lerdo de Tejada.

Transvaal, South Africa, April 12, 1877: Britain annexes Boer Republics.

Russia, April 24, 1877: Russia declares war on the Ottoman Empire in order to liberate the Balkans.

Chicago, USA, July 25, 1877: Nineteen striking railwaymen are killed when police open fire.

Kumamoto, Japan, September 24, 1877: Satsuma Rebellion of samurai is quashed by government troops.

New Zealand, November 29, 1877: Education Act provides free and secular primary education, compulsory for ages 7–13.

Berlin, Germany, July 13, 1878: The Treaty of Berlin divides the Balkans, following the Russo-Turkish War.

Isandhlwana, southern Africa, January 22, 1879: Zulu warriors slaughter around 1,600 British imperial troops, in response to British demands for cultural change.

Afghanistan, May 26, 1879: The Treaty of Gandamak is signed between the Afghans and British, ceding the strategic Khyber Pass to the British.

China, 1879: Millions die in the north as famine and drought stretch into a third year.

Melbourne, Australia, November 11, 1880: The colony's most notorious bushranger Edward (Ned) Kelly is hanged, aged 25.

St Petersburg, Russia, March 13, 1881: Reforming tsar, Alexander II is assassinated by the People's Will (a revolutionary organization).

Transvaal, South Africa, March 23, 1881: The Boers are given self-government following numerous victories in bloody battles.

Vienna, Austria, May 20, 1882: Italy enters into the triple alliance treaty with Germany and Austria-Hungary.

London, England, March 13, 1883: Karl Marx, co-author of the *Communist Manifesto*, dies aged 64.

Sunda Strait, Dutch East Indies, August 27, 1883: The Krakatoa volcano erupts, destroying two-thirds of the island and killing 36,000 people.

Hue, Vietnam, June 6, 1884: Treaty of Hue gives France effective control of Vietnam.

Berlin, Germany, February 26, 1885: Three months of negotiations by 15 nations divides Africa among the colonial powers.

1900

London, England, February 27: Various socialist organizations and trade unions unite as the Labour Representation Committee, hoping to elect candidates to Westminster.

Ladysmith, South Africa, February 28: Ending a four-month siege by Boer forces, General Sir Redvers Buller liberates Ladysmith in a decisive victory for the British.

India, March 27: Famine is affecting at least five million people throughout the subcontinent as Viceroy Lord Curzon pledges 8.5 million pounds in famine relief.

Brussels, Belgium, April 4: The Prince of Wales (Albert Edward) survives an assassination attempt by a 16 year-old anarchist in retaliation for the British role in the Boer War.

Coomassie, Gold Coast, April 6: West African Ashanti tribesmen, incensed by British imperial demands to hand over important icons, attack British troops.

Paris, France, April 14: The World Exposition opens in Paris. More opulent than any previous World's Fair, monumental exhibits cover a large area of the French capital.

Mafeking, South Africa, May 20: British troops are relieved after a seven-month siege, causing ecstatic celebrations throughout the Empire.

China, May 31: The Boxer Rebellion begins. Known as I-ho ch'uan, the Boxers are a secret nationalistic society hostile to foreign interests.

Berlin, Germany, June 12: The Reichstag passes legislation continuing Germany's naval expansion. It is projected that 38 battleships will be built in the next 20 years.

Australia, July 9: The British parliament and Queen Victoria accept the Commonwealth of Australia Act, uniting the colonies under a federal government.

Monza, Italy, July 20: An anarchist assassinates Umberto I, aged 56.

Peking, China, August 14: Allied troops break the Boxers' siege.

Gulf of Mexico, September 8: Cyclonic winds cause a massive tidal wave, inundating Galveston—over 6,000 perish; $10 million damage results on the Gulf Coast.

Philippines, October: The Philippine Insurrection descends into bloody guerrilla warfare as nationalists battle US troops. The USA has colonized the country following Spain's withdrawal in 1898.

USA, November 6: Republican William McKinley wins a second term with Theodore Roosevelt as his running mate.

Italy and France, December 16: A Franco-Italian agreement allows France free reign in Morocco and Italy likewise in Libya.

1825 – 1849

USA, 1838-1839: Cherokee Native Americans are forced to relocate; they move westward on the brutal "Trail of Tears."

Canton, China, November, 1839: Imperial commissioner Lin Zexu seizes opium from British warehouses.

Spain, 1839: The Carlist War, ends with the Convention of Vergara.

Bay of Islands, New Zealand, February 6, 1840: The Treaty of Waitangi is signed between Maori chiefs and Captain William Hobson, granting British sovereignty.

London, England, 1840: Queen Victoria marries a German, Prince Albert.

Canada, 1840: Act of Union unites upper and lower Canada.

London, England, July 13, 1841: The Straits Convention is signed by Britain, France, Russia, Austria, and Prussia.

Nanking, China, August 29, 1842: Treaty of Nanking signed, signalling China's defeat in First Opium War. British demands such as opening of ports, monetary compensation, fixed tariffs, ceding of Hong Kong granted.

USA, 1842: The border dispute between America and Canada is settled with the signing of the Webster-Ashburton Treaty.

Tahiti, 1842: The French begin their occupation of Tahiti.

Sindh, India (Pakistan), 1843: British troops conquer the Sindh region.

New Zealand, 1843: The Maoris revolt against the British.

Morocco, 1844: The Treaty of Tangiers, recognizing French sovereignty over Algeria, ends the conflict.

Ireland, 1845-1850: Potato blight causes famine, and begins mass migration to Britain and the USA.

Sabraon, India, 1845: The Sikhs are defeated by the British, resulting in the signing of the Treaty of Lahore, giving Jalandhar and Kashmir to the British.

UK, 1846: The Corn Laws are repealed to move toward complete free trade.

Poland, 1846: The Poles revolt against Russian rule.

Mexico, 1846: The USA declares war on Mexico.

Canada, 1847: British naval officer Sir John Franklin and all crew die in their ice-bound ship only miles short of completing their voyage through the Northwest Passage.

London, England, 1848: Karl Marx and Freidrich Engels publish the *Communist Manifesto*, attacking capitalism.

Europe, 1848: Revolutions are staged in Italy, France, Hungary, Austria, Germany, Switzerland, and Denmark.

Germany, March 28, 1849: The first German *Reichsverfassung* (Constitution) is passed.

1850 – 1874

USA, 1861-1865: American Civil War.

Prussia (Germany), 1862: Otto von Bismark becomes Minister-President of Prussia.

Williams Creek, British Columbia, Canada, 1862: Gold miners hit vast deposits of gold.

USA, April 9, 1863: President Abraham Lincoln issues his *Emancipation Proclamation*, declaring that all slavery must end.

USA, April 14, 1865: President Abraham Lincoln is assassinated.

USA, 1865: An estimated 4 million slaves are freed upon defeat of the south in the American Civil War.

China, 1866: Sun Yixian, considered founder of modern China, is born.

England, 1866: First petition for women's suffrage is presented to parliament.

Sitka, Alaska, October 18, 1867: Russia sells Alaska to USA for $7.2 million.

Canada, 1867: The Dominion of Canada is created by the British North America Act.

Kimberley, South Africa, 1867: Diamonds are discovered.

Spain, 1868: The Spanish Revolution begins.

Kyoto, Japan, 1868: Emperor Meiji assumes full governmental powers, ending military rule and ushering in Japan's modern era.

Egypt, 1869: Suez Canal opens.

USA, 1869: Fifteenth Amendment is passed, which requires all Southern States to allow Negroes to vote.

India, 1869: Mohandas Karamchand Ghandi, statesman and religious leader, is born.

Paraguay, 1870: Fighting ends bringing the War of the Triple Alliance to a close.

France, 1870: Emperor Napoleon III is deposed and Third Republic is declared.

Russia, 1870: Vladimir Ilyich Lenin, statesman, is born.

France, 1870: Franco-Prussian War begins.

USA, 1871: The National Rifle Association is granted a charter by the State of New York.

UK, 1871: The Trade Union Act legalizes the trade union movement.

Germany, 1871: Wilhelm I becomes kaiser.

Paris, France, 1871: The Paris Commune uprising begins.

Germany, 1871: Proclamation of German Empire.

UK, 1872: The Ballot Act is passed, which allows for secret ballots at elections.

Spain, February, 1873: The First Spanish Republic is proclaimed when Cortes deposes King Amadeus.

Hanoi, Vietnam, 1874: French occupation.

West Africa, March 14, 1874: The Anglo-Ashanti War is ended with the signing of the Treaty of Fomena.

1875 – 1899

Bombay, India, December, 1885: The Indian National Congress forms after lobbying by British civil servant Allan Hume.

London, England, June 8, 1886: The Irish Home Rule Bill, tabled by William Ewart Gladstone, leading his third cabinet, is defeated and an election is called.

London, England, June 21, 1887: Queen Victoria celebrates 50 years on the throne with lavish golden jubilee celebrations attended by 50 heads of state.

Potsdam, Germany, June 15, 1888: Emperor Frederick III dies after a 3-month reign; his son, Wilhelm II ascends to power.

Brazil, November 16, 1889: A republic is proclaimed after a coup. Pedro II abolished slavery in 1888, despite resistance from plantation owners; thus signing the monarchy's death warrant.

Salisbury, Mashonaland, southern Africa, September 12, 1890: British South Africa Company founds Fort Salisbury.

Wounded Knee, South Dakota, December 29, 1890: The cavalry massacres hundreds of Sioux.

London, England, August 3, 1892: Independent MP James Kier proposes to form a Labour party.

Ontario, Canada, 1892: Women permitted to study and practice law.

Paris, France, June, 1893: Investors lose over 1 billion francs in the Panama Canal scandal.

Onehunga, New Zealand, November 29, 1893: Elizabeth Yates is elected mayor; she is the first woman mayor in the British Empire.

Paris, France, December 22, 1894: Captain Alfred Dreyfus is sentenced to life imprisonment. Found guilty of spying for Germany, his case has been extremely divisive, splitting France into factions.

Shimonoseki, Japan, April 17, 1895: Japan defeats China in the Sino-Japanese War. Japan now controls Taiwan and Korea.

Adwa, Ethiopia, March 2, 1896: The Ethiopian army routs Italian troops bent on a foreign conquest.

Turkey, August 29, 1896: More than 3,000 Armenians are massacred by Ottoman authorities, three days after Armenians seized an Ottoman bank in Istanbul.

Paris, France, December 10, 1898: Spain cedes Cuba, Puerto Rico, Guam, and the Philippines to the USA for $20 million.

Peking, China, 1899: Boxer Uprising rebels besiege foreign legations in Peking for 100 days before being defeated.

1901

Australia, January 1: The separate British colonies unite to form the Commonwealth of Australia. Edmund Barton is the first prime minister.

New Zealand, January 1: New Zealand fails to join the federation of Australian colonies.

Cowes, England, January 22: After a 64-year reign Queen Victoria dies, aged 82. Edward VII ascends the throne.

Japan, February 3: Influential thinker and author Fukuzawa Yukichi dies, aged 66. He promoted western ideas during the Meiji era.

St Petersburg, Russia, March 17: Anti-Tsarist students riot at Kazan Cathedral in response to repressive laws and the excommunication of Leo Tolstoy.

Philippines, March 27: Rebel leader Emilio Aguinaldo is captured by US forces. The nationalist rebel has been leading resistance against colonial powers since 1896—first Spain, and then the USA from 1898.

South Africa, April 22: The British government pledges to improve conditions of Boer women and children interred in camps.

Cuba, June 12: The Caribbean island is to become a US protectorate following the adoption of the Platt Amendment.

Brussels, Belgium, July 17: King Leopold announces that he shall not formally annexe the Congo, but continues to exploit the region for his own personal gain.

London, England, July 22: In Taff Vale Company v Amalgamated Society of Railway Servants, the House of Lords rules that trade unions can be sued for the actions of members.

Oklahoma, USA, August 9: Over two million acres (810,000 ha) are acquired from Indian tribes for $2 million.

China, September 7: The end of the Boxer Rebellion is negotiated with 12 foreign powers and China signing a peace protocol.

Buffalo, USA, September 14: After being shot by a Polish anarchist, President William McKinley dies, aged 58. Roosevelt is sworn in.

Gold Coast, September 25: Britain annexes the Ashanti kingdom following strong resistance from tribesmen.

New Orleans, USA, October 28: Thirty-four people die in race riots sparked by Booker T. Washington's visit to the White House, the first by an African-American.

USA and UK, November 18: The Hay-Pauncefote Treaty is signed, allowing the USA to build and maintain a canal in Central America, but it must remain neutral.

UK and Canada, December 12: Italian Guglielmo Marconi transmits wireless telegraphic signals from Cornwall to Newfoundland, a distance of 2,232 miles (3,593 km).

1902

UK and Japan, January 30: Interests in China and Korea are safeguarded with the signing of the Anglo-Japanese Treaty. Japan has been resolutely isolationist prior to this treaty.
Russia, February 4: Thirty thousand students strike in response to laws aimed at controlling student organizations.
Barcelona, Spain, February 20: Five hundred strikers die as tensions rise between industrialists and workers. A state of siege is declared and 80,000 workers stop work.

Cape Town, South Africa, March 26: Cecil Rhodes, former prime minister of the Cape Colony, founder of the DeBeers Mining Company and in honor of whom Rhodesia was named, dies, aged 48.
Texas, USA, April 7: The Texas Company (Texaco) is founded after discoveries at Spindletop and other Texan oil fields.
Russia and China, April 8: The Sino-Russian conflict over Manchuria comes to an end with the signing of a treaty committing to the withdrawal of Russian troops.

Dublin, Ireland, April 20: Twenty thousand people gather to protest draconian British laws aimed at stifling dissent among nationalists.
Saint-Pierre, Martinique, May 8: Mt Pelée, a volcano in the French West Indies, erupts destroying the town of Saint-Pierre. Only three people survive out of 30,000.
Pretoria, South Africa, May 31: The Treaty of Vereeniging is signed.
New Zealand, June 4: Lieutenant Robert McKeich is the last New Zealander to be killed in the Boer War, after the treaty was signed.

Madrid, Spain, May 31: Alphonso XIII suspends the Cortes (parliament) and imposes martial law following widespread strikes.
Australia, July: A restrictive immigration policy is established aiming to keep the number of non-white immigrants low. This follows similar legislation in the USA, where the Chinese Exclusion Act was passed in April.
Russia, July 3: The Tsar agrees to talk to 200 citizens following riots among peasants who are suffering from starvation and unemployment.

Agram, Croatia, September 1: The Austro-Hungarian rulers impose martial law as violence erupts between Croats and Serbs.
Finland, September 22: Tsar Nicholas II of Russia abolishes Finnish autonomy.
Aswan, Egypt, December 10: The first dam to tame the Nile River is completed.
Venezuela, December 19: The government agrees to honor its debts after Britain, Germany, and France blockade five ports and seize the Venezuelan fleet of four boats.

1904

Okahandja, southwest Africa, January 11: Over 100 German settlers are massacred by Herero warriors in retaliation for a lack of compensation for dispossessed tribesmen.
Havana, Cuba, February 5: US troops withdraw from the Caribbean island. Tomas Palma is the first prime minister of the new republic.
Port Arthur, Manchuria, February 8: The beginning of the Russo-Japanese War. Japan launches a surprise attack on the Russian fleet stationed at Port Arthur.

Tibet, March 31: British forces kill over 300 of the Dalai Lama's men on a mission in central Asia.
Aceh, Dutch East Indies, April 3: Dutch colonial forces kill over 500 Achinese in 30-year Sumatran War.
UK and France, April 8: An Anglo-French treaty, "Entente Cordiale," is signed between the two colonial powers, settling a number of disputes.
Port Arthur, Manchuria, April 13: Russian forces suffer a major blow in the Russo-Japanese War, losing a battleship with 600 men.

New York, USA, June 15: Over 1000 people perish as the steamer *General Slocum* catches fire on the East River.
London, England, July 12: The British government pledges to resolve disputes with Germany through arbitration. The border dispute between Brazil and the UK over British Guiana was resolved in June in a similar manner.
The Vatican, July 29: The French Ambassador to the Holy See is recalled as tension between church and state in France escalates.

Lhasa, Tibet, September 7: A treaty is reached between the UK and the Dalai Lama, giving the British trading posts.
Belgium, September 15: King Leopold agrees to investigate claims of atrocities in the Congo.
North Sea, October 22: The Russian Navy sinks British fishing trawlers at Dogger Bank, mistaking them for Japanese warships.
New York, USA, October 27: The New York subway opens, and some 100,000 citizens take a ride on the new convenience.

St Louis, USA, October 28: St Louis Police Department try a new investigation method—fingerprints.
Panama, November 16: The USA buys the concession for building the waterway from French interests.
Washington DC, USA, December 6: Theodore Roosevelt's corollary to the Monroe Doctrine, invoked to force the Dominican Republic to pay its debts, sees the USA take on the role of international police.
Moscow, Russia, December 26: The Tsar promises reforms in an effort to quell peasant unrest.

1906

London, England, January 31: Suffragette leader Emmeline Pankhurst warns that women are impatient with waiting for the right to vote and are prepared to take radical action to advance their cause.
England, February 7: The Liberals are swept to power in a landslide victory over the Conservatives after 10 years in opposition. The Labour Party increased its representation significantly.
Tahiti, February 8: A fierce typhoon inundates the Pacific kingdom, killing 10,000 people.

England, March 8: The "Census of the British Empire" of 1901 is released.
San Francisco, USA, April 19: Over 1,000 people are killed and the city is devastated in the aftermath of an earthquake.
Lhasa, Tibet, April 27: China reluctantly cedes control of Tibet to Britain. In an attempt to forestall Russian ambitions, no foreign power may occupy Tibetan territory without British permission.
St Petersburg, Russia, May 10: The Tsar inaugurates the Duma, elected by universal suffrage.

Chicago, USA, May 10: At a government commission into unfair practices, the Standard Oil Company is charged with stifling competition.
Switzerland and Italy, May 19: The Simplon Tunnel is opened to traffic. It is the longest tunnel in the world, at 12.3 miles (20 km).
Auckland, New Zealand, June 12: Longest-serving prime minister Richard Seddon dies, aged 61.
Central America, July 20: Guatemala signs peace treaty with El Salvador and Honduras after war breaks out in May.

Tehran, Persia, August 5: Mozafaredin Shah is forced to decree a constitution and create a parliament (the majlis), limiting royal power after revolutionary agitation.
Valparaiso, Chile, August 18: A massive earthquake, measuring 8.6 on the Richter scale, kills 5,000 people and destroys the port.
Cuba, September 28: US War Secretary William Taft is installed as provisional governor. President Palma resigned after fierce fighting between liberal forces and government troops.

Russia, November 2: Bolshevik Leon Trotsky is exiled to Siberia for revolutionary activities. Anti-Tsarist feelings are running high after Nicholas II suspended the Duma in July.
Transvaal, Southern Africa, December 12: Limited autonomy is granted, with white males gaining the right to vote.
Dacca, India, December 31: Aga Khan is elected president of the All-India Muslim League, set up to advance the cause of Muslims in the Hindu-dominated society.

1908

Transvaal, Southern Africa, January 30: Mohandas Gandhi is released from jail, after a two-month sentence for refusing to register under the "Asiatic Law."
Lisbon, Portugal, February 3: Following the assassination of King Carlos and the Crown Prince on February 1, dictator Premier Franco and his cabinet resign. Prince Manuel is proclaimed King.
London, England, April 12: Liberal Herbert Asquith takes over as prime minister from Campbell-Bannerman, who has been ill for some time.

Muzaffarpur, India, April 30: Colonial forces crack down on extremist nationalists after a bomb meant for a British magistrate kills two English women by mistake.
Washington DC, USA, May 22: The Wright brothers apply for a patent for their "flying machine."
Baltic Sea, Russia, June 9: Britain's monarch Edward VII and Tsar Nicholas II meet, signalling closer relations.
London, England, June 21: Over 200,000 turn out for a demonstration in support of women's suffrage.

Tehran, Persia, June 26: Shah Muhammad Ali leads a successful counter-revolution, ousting the government and abolishing the liberal constitution.
Ottoman Empire, July 24: The Young Turk movement, supported by the army, forces the Sultan to reinstall the constitution of 1876.
Detroit, USA, August 12: The Model T Ford begins production.
The Congo, August 20: Belgium officially annexes the Congo, formally the fiefdom of King Leopold, who ruthlessly exploited it.

St Petersburg, Russia, September: The city suffers the most devastating cholera outbreak since 1892; over 7,000 die.
Lucerne, Switzerland, September 29: The International Conference for the Protection of Labor legislates against night time work for children. In the USA, some 1.75 million children under 16 work in factories.
Bosnia and Herzegovina, October 6: Widespread condemnation greets Austria-Hungary's annexation of the Balkan provinces. Russia, Turkey, Serbia and Montenegro all had similar designs and protest.

North Island, New Zealand, November 9: The first scheduled passenger trains run between Wellington and Auckland. The trip takes two days.
Peking, China, December 2: Three year-old Pu Yi is crowned Emperor of China. Dowager Empress Tsu-Hsi, who wielded true power, died last month, one day after Emperor Kuang-Hsu.
Sicily, Italy, December 28: Over 100,000 people die in a massive earthquake centered on the Straits of Messina.

1903

Delhi, India, January 1: At a vast ceremony unattended by the primary participant, Edward VII is proclaimed Emperor of India.

Cuba, February 23: The government accepts the Platt Amendment at the insistence of the USA. Cuba agrees to US intervention if deemed necessary and leases two naval bases.

Washington DC, USA, March 3: An anti-immigration law is ratified, seeking to keep out "undesirables," a significant change from the "open door" policy of last century.

Kishinev, Russia, April 16: Peasants' anti-Semitic feelings are encouraged by officials under Tsar Nicholas II. A bloody pogrom results in the deaths of hundreds of Jews.

France, April 29: Nine years of conflict between church and state leads to the government of President Combes closing monasteries.

Belgrade, Serbia, June 11: Serbian Army officers assassinate King Alexander and Queen Draga. The army installs Prince Kara-georgevitch as leader.

The Vatican, July 20: Pope Leo XIII dies, aged 93, after a 25-year pontificate that has seen him work toward unifying Christendom.

Paris, France, August 10: A fire started by an electrical fault in the Paris Metro leaves 84 dead.

Bogotá, Colombia, August 12: The Colombian government fails to ratify the Hay-Herran Treaty on US construction of a canal in Panama.

Basle, Switzerland, August 19: At the sixth Zionist Conference, Theodor Herzl declares Palestine the best site for a Jewish state.

Monastir, Bulgaria, September 8: Turkish troops massacre 50,000 Bulgarians after Macedonian revolutionaries urge uprising.

Vienna, Austro-Hungarian Empire, September 16: Facing widespread dissatisfaction from Hungarian Magyars, Emperor Franz Josef declares his intention to maintain a unified and common army and empire.

Alaska, USA, October 16: Conflict between the USA and Canada over the southeastern Alaskan border is resolved in favor of the USA.

London, England, November 17: Russian Social Democratic Party splits into Mensheviks (minority party), led by Martov, and Bolsheviks (extremists, majority party), led by Lenin.

Panama, November 18: Following Panama's secession from Colombia, the USA signs a treaty with the new state, which opens the way to a canal being built under US control.

Kitty Hawk, USA, December 17: The first heavier-than-air powered flight is achieved by the Wright Brothers.

1905

Port Arthur, Manchuria, January 2: Japanese troops take Port Arthur after seven months of fierce fighting, both sides sustaining heavy casualties. The Tsar anticipated that victory would quell internal unrest.

St Petersburg, Russia, January 22: One hundred thousand workers march to the Tsar's Winter Palace to present a petition. Cossack troops open fire, killing 100.

Moscow, Russia, February 17: One of the Tsar's most senior advisors, Grand Duke Aleksandrovich, is assassinated.

Tangier, Morocco, March 31: German Kaiser Wilhelm's visit to Morocco causes tension among the other colonial interests in North Africa. Britain's and France's faith in the Entente Cordiale is vindicated.

Lahore, India, April 4: An earthquake, with magnitude 8.6, devastates the northern province, killing over 10,000 people.

Warsaw, Poland, May 1: At the annual demonstration of workers' solidarity, Russian troops open fire on protestors, killing 100 and injuring thousands.

Tsushima Strait, Sea of Japan, May 28: Russia's Baltic fleet is destroyed by Admiral Togo's navy.

Norway, June 7: The Storting (parliament) dissolves union with Sweden, asserting independence.

Odessa, Russia, June 27: The crew of the battleship *Potemkin* mutineer. Odessa is paralysed by a strike.

Paris, France, July 3: Parliament passes the bill separating church and state.

Basle, Switzerland, July 30: The Zionist Conference rejects British offer of Jewish homeland in Uganda.

St Petersburg, Russia, August 19: Nicholas II establishes the Duma, a representative assembly, taking an unwilling step toward constitutional monarchy.

Portsmouth, USA, September 5: Japan and Russia sign a treaty to end the Russo-Japanese War. Japan has achieved most of its aims in going to war.

Bengal, India, October 16: Lord Curzon divides the eastern province into Bengal and Assam. Muslims are favored in the partition; Hindus are dissatisfied with the outcome.

New Zealand, October 30: The Workers' Dwellings Act initiates a state housing scheme.

St Petersburg, Russia, October 30: After a year of intense unrest, Nicholas II initiates genuine constitutional reforms.

Dublin, Ireland, November 28: Arthur Griffith forms Sinn Fein, a loose collection of nationalists aiming to unite Ireland.

Guyana, November 28–December 5: Riots ensue as sugar workers go on strike for better wages.

1907

Kingston, Jamaica, January 14: Kingston is devastated by an earthquake followed by a fire.

Dutch East Indies, January 22: 1,500 people die when a tsunami hits the East Indies.

London, England, February 13: Police repel suffragettes attempting to storm Westminster. Sixty women are arrested in fierce struggles.

Washington DC, USA, February 26: President Roosevelt puts the US Army in charge of the construction of the Panama Canal.

Transvaal, Southern Africa, March 22: The Indian population of the newly independent state, led by Mohandas Gandhi, vows a campaign of passive resistance if restrictive racial legislation is introduced.

Manchuria, April 15: Russian and Japanese troops complete their withdrawal, ceding the territory to China, under the terms of the Treaty of Portsmouth, negotiated to end the Russo-Japanese War.

Russia, April 20: Up to 20 million people are starving in the worst famine ever experienced in Russia.

Boise, Idaho, USA, May 9: Labor relations are strained as angry workers march in support of union leader Bill Haywood, who is on trial for commissioning a 1905 murder.

Cartagena, Spain, May 16: The UK, France and Spain sign the Pact of Cartagena in an effort to quell German expansionist aspirations in the Mediterranean.

St Petersburg, Russia, June 16: Tsar Nicholas II dissolves the second Duma (parliament), charging that socialists have been plotting against the monarchy.

Korea, July 25: Emperor Kojong abdicates as the country is placed under Japanese control.

Philippines, July 30: The first parliament is elected and victorious nationalists press for independence from the USA.

Casablanca, Morocco, August 4: French troops enter Casablanca after two days of intense shelling leaves the town devastated.

China, September 8: Sun Yat-sen founds the Kuomintang Party.

New Zealand, September 26: The colony is granted dominion status.

India, October 11: A nationwide ban on public meetings is imposed. Rioting has been rife since May—not helped by the British government's stance that under no circumstances would they withdraw.

The Hague, Netherlands, October 18: The Second Peace Conference closes with a commitment to the establishment of an International Court of Justice. The Conventions of War have been extended.

Russia, December 31: Of the 169 delegates from the first Duma, 167 are found guilty of treason.

1909

USA, February: The temperance movement is gaining momentum throughout the country with individual states and counties adopting laws banning the sale of alcohol.

Morocco, February 8: A new Franco-German agreement is reached recognizing France's pre-eminent position and Germany's interests in North Africa.

London, England, March 12: Britain's Naval fleet is to be strengthened, as parliament legislates to regain naval pre-eminence over Germany.

Serbia, March 31: The war crisis in the Balkans is resolved with Serbia agreeing to recognize the Austrian annexation of Bosnia and Herzegovina.

Constantinople, Turkey, April 26: Sultan Abdul Hamid II is deposed, as parliament votes to end his rule.

Sofia, Bulgaria, April 27: Austria-Hungary, Germany, and Italy recognize the Black Sea country, after it declared independence from the Ottoman Empire the previous year.

Georgia, USA, May 17: In protest at the hiring of African-American workers, white firemen strike. Racial tensions rise as African-Americans strive to achieve equal rights.

India, May 25: The Indian Councils Act (Morley-Minto Reforms) is introduced to end nationalist terrorism. The Act allows Indians to be elected to the legislative councils.

Paris, France, July 21: The Clemenceau cabinet resigns after a violent altercation concerning the navy's capability. Aristide Briand succeeds as premier.

Dover, England, July 25: French aviator Louis Blériot crosses the English Channel, flying a monoplane.

Crete, August 8: Forty years of ethnic tension is resolved as Greece seeks to acquire the Mediterranean island.

Pittsburgh, USA, August 22: Striking for better conditions, five steelworkers are killed in a violent confrontation with police.

Catalonia, Spain, September 26: Alfonso XIII brutally suppresses a Catalan uprising over military service.

Harbin, Manchuria, October 26: First Prime Minister of Japan, Prince Ito, is assassinated by a Korean nationalist.

South Africa, December 7: By royal decree, the Union of South Africa is formed from the colonies of the Cape of Good Hope, Natal, Transvaal and Orange River.

Nicaragua, December 17: A two-month civil war ends as anti-US President Zelaya resigns under pressure from US Marines. José Madriz replaces him.

1910

Paris, France, January: Floods inundate Paris; the Seine threatens the art collections at the Louvre.

India, February 4: A new press censorship bill restricts nationalist sentiment. In January, five provinces banned "seditious" gatherings in a bid to quell unrest.

UK, February 14: The general election results in a tie between the Liberals and the Conservatives.

Egypt, February 21: Prime Minister Butros Ghali is assassinated, leading to severe repression of nationalists by the British administration.

Lhasa, Tibet, February 23: The Dalai Lama flees, as Lhasa is occupied by Chinese troops.

London, England, May 20: Over half a million gather for the funeral of Edward VII, who died of bronchitis, aged 68. His successor, George V, leads the ceremony, attended by kings from nine European countries.

Kiev, Russia, May: Around 12,000 Jews flee Kiev as anti-Semitism, encouraged by the Tsar, leads police to conduct searches. The USA is unwilling to grant sanctuary to large numbers of these refugees.

South Africa, July 1: The Union of South Africa becomes a British dominion. Boer War hero Louis Botha is prime minister. Perceived by many Boers as too pro-British, Botha faces challengers already.

USA, July 4: Race riots break out throughout the country as African-American boxer Jack Johnson wins his world title defense against Jim Jeffries.

Canada, July 31: Doctor Crippen, suspected of murdering his wife in London, is apprehended on a ship off the east coast of Canada.

Korea, August 24: Japan announces that it will annexe Korea, formalizing a situation that began in 1904.

Lancashire, England, October 2: As 700 mills close, 150,000 mill workers lose their jobs. In September, 50,000 dockworkers were sacked after striking for better pay and improved conditions.

Portugal, October 3–7: Soldiers of the Portuguese Royal Army revolt. King Manuel II flees to England. The monarchy is abolished and all nuns and monks are expelled.

Greece, October 18: Eleftherios Venizelos becomes prime minister of Greece, implementing a program of constitutional, administrative, and financial reform.

Astopovo, Russia, November 20: Leo Tolstoy, author of *War and Peace* and *Anna Karenina* dies, aged 82. Born into nobility, he abandoned his possessions and turned ascetic in his later years.

Palestine, December 14: Turkish troops are sent to Palestine to suppress an uprising of 200,000 Bedouin Arabs.

1912

Peking, China, February 15: The Manchu dynasty ends as Emperor Pu Yi abdicates. Yat-sen resigns and Yuan Shikai is elected president.

Berlin, Germany, March 8: Anglo-German discussions on naval power end abruptly when the Reichstag passes a bill enlarging the navy.

Belfast, Ireland, April 11: The Asquith government introduces the Third Home Rule Bill. Thousands of Protestants in Ulster protest against the bill, which they believe is against their interests.

Atlantic Ocean, near Newfoundland, April 15: The White Star liner *Titanic*, on its maiden voyage, strikes an iceberg and sinks. Almost 1,600 people perish.

Dardenelles, Turkey, April 18–May 4: In the Tripolitan War, attempting to wrest control of Libya from the Ottomans, Italian ships bomb the Dardanelles and Beirut. The Turks close the straits, blockading Russian trade.

Havana, Cuba, May 31: US Marines land in Cuba in order to protect US interests.

Alaskan Peninsula, USA, June 6–8: The Novarupta volcano forms, rising to 2,759 feet (841 m), in the largest eruption since Krakatoa in 1883.

London, England, June 22: Lord of the Admiralty, Winston Churchill, recalls the British Navy's Malta fleet and redeploys it to the North Sea to combat the growing threat from the strengthened German Navy.

Tokyo, Japan, July 30: Emperor Mutsuhito, known also as Meiji, who oversaw the modernization of Japan, dies, aged 60. His son Yoshihito succeeds him.

Chicago, USA, August 5: The Progressive or "Bull Moose" Party formed by Theodore Roosevelt meets, nominating Roosevelt as its candidate in the forthcoming election.

Morocco, August 11: Sultan Mulai Abd al-Hafiz abdicates, as internal dissent follows the signing of the Treaty of Fez, making the country a French protectorate.

Ulster, Ireland, September 28: Unionists and loyalists are both opposing Home Rule for Ulster, although for different reasons.

The Balkans, October 18: Following Montenegro's lead, Bulgaria, Serbia and Greece declare war on Turkey.

Lausanne, Switzerland, October 18: Italy and Turkey sign a treaty, bringing the Tripolitan War to a close.

USA, November 5: Democrat Woodrow Wilson wins the presidency with a minority vote.

Albania, November 28: Albania declares independence from the Ottoman Empire, after 500 years of external rule.

1914

South Africa, January 28: Following a month of intense unrest, with miners striking over poor conditions and pay, the government exiles 10 strike leaders to England.

Ulster, Ireland, February 25: The Ulster Volunteer Force, set up in opposition to Home Rule for Ireland as a whole, has over 100,000 men prepared for a civil war.

Europe, March 17: An arms race fuels fears of a war. The UK unveils a massive new navy budget, while Germany's and Russia's largest expenditure is on the military.

Vera Cruz, Mexico, April 21: US Marines seize the Gulf port in retaliation for the arrest of Marines at Tampico, as the Mexican revolution continues.

London, England, June 26: A black South African delegation visits the Colonial Secretary to protest the Native Titles Act, which gave all but 7 percent of land to whites the previous year.

Sarajevo, Bosnia, June 28: The heir to the Austrian throne, Archduke Franz Ferdinand, is assassinated by a 19 year-old Serbian nationalist.

Belgrade, Serbia, July 29: Following a month of increasing tensions, Austria-Hungary declares war on Serbia and bombs Belgrade.

Germany, August 1: In support of Austria-Hungary, Germany declares war on Russia as Russian troops mobilize to protect Serbia.

Europe, August 2: Germany invades France, Switzerland, and Luxembourg as Russia pushes into Germany, capturing Eydtkuhnen.

London, England, August 3–4: Britain declares war on Germany as German troops invade Belgium.

Togoland, Africa, August 26: Four days after Japan declares war on Germany and begins capturing German interests in the Far East, British colonial troops capture the first of Germany's colonies.

Samoa, August 29: New Zealand military administration takes over Samoa, ousting previous German administration without conflict.

East Prussia, Germany, August/September: At the battles of Tannenberg and Masurian Lakes, 225,000 Russian troops are captured as Russia's advance is halted.

France, September 8–12: German advance across Western Europe is halted 30 miles (48 km) from Paris, as Allied troops hold their ground at the Battle of the Marne.

Turkey, November 5: England, France and Russia declare war on supposedly neutral Turkey, after German ships were allowed through the Dardanelles, then bombarded Russian Black Sea ports.

Ypres, Belgium, November 22: The Battle of Ypres bogs down at the onset of winter; German and Allied troops face off in the trenches.

1916

London, England, January 6: Compulsory military service is introduced as voluntary conscripts are falling short of the number of men required on the frontline.

Netherlands, January 14: Extensive flooding, caused by a storm surge, leads to reappraisal of plans to reclaim the Zuyderzee.

Verdun, France, February 21: Germany switches its focus from the Eastern to the Western Front, launching into battle at Verdun. One million German troops are pitted against 200,000 French defenders.

Haiti, February 28: Following the murder of President Guilliaume Sam and the subsequent occupation by US Marines, Haiti becomes a US protectorate.

Guerrero, Mexico, March 31: US troops attack Pancho Villa's rebels.

Maungapohatu, New Zealand, April 2: The violent arrest of Maori leader Rua Kenana confirms the end of no-go areas for law enforcement.

Kut-al-Amara, Persia, April 29: After a siege lasting 196 days, 8,000 sick and emaciated Anglo-Indian troops surrender to Turkish forces.

Dublin, Ireland, May 1: The Easter Uprising of republicans is put down by British forces. An Irish Republic is declared.

North Sea, May 31: The Battle of Jutland is fought between Germany's High Seas Fleet and the Royal Navy. Both sides suffer great losses, but the British have a strategic victory as their dominance of the North Sea is assured.

Hejaz, Arabia, June 5: Grand sheriff of Mecca, Hussein, leads an Arab revolt against the Turkish with the assistance of the British.

The Somme, France, July 1: Over 58,000 British casualties are sustained, one-third fatalities, in the first day of the new Western Front offensive.

London, England, July 7: Lloyd George becomes Secretary of State for War one month after Lord Kitchener's death aboard *HMS Hampshire*, exploded by a mine.

Berlin, Germany, August 27: General von Falkenhayn is replaced by Field Marshall von Hindenburg as Chief of Staff.

Transylvania, August 27: Romania enters the war on the side of the Allies.

Philippines, August 29: The USA announces its intention to withdraw sovereignty from the Philippines.

Ontario, Canada, September 1: The city of Berlin changes its name to Kitchener due to anti-German sentiment.

Vienna, Austria, November 21: After a 68-year reign, Austrian Emperor Franz Josef dies, aged 86.

London, England, December 7: David Lloyd George replaces Herbert Asquith as Prime Minister.

Petrograd, Russia, December 30: "Mad monk" Rasputin is murdered.

1911

London, England, January 3: Winston Churchill joins police at the siege of Sidney Street. Three anarchists holed up in a house keep 1,000 police at bay for 10 hours. Fire in the building ends the drama; two suspects die.
Mexico, April 15: USA troops fight rebels led by Francisco Madero, on the Mexican frontier.
Fez, Morocco, April 23: French troops arrive to end a revolt at the Sultan's request. Germany objects, citing that the Algeciras Agreement of 1906 has been breached.

Canada, May 11: The introduction of section 49A of the Indian Act further diminishes Native rights.
Mexico City, Mexico, May 25: Ending a 35-year rule, Porfirio Diaz departs for France, after the revolution instigated by Madero achieves its aims.
Washington DC, USA, June 12: The Senate amends the Constitution to provide election of representatives by popular vote.
London, England, June 22: The coronation of George V is held at Westminster Abbey.

Agadir, Morocco, July 2: Germany sends a warship to southern Morocco in a show of force.
Machu Picchu, Peru, July 24: American explorer Hiram Bingham re-discovers the ancient Inca city.
London, England, August 10: The House of Lords agrees to surrender its veto power. Asquith had threatened to force the bill through by creating hundreds of peers to vote for it.
Lisbon, Portugal, August 24: Manuel de Arriaga is elected first president and adopts a liberal constitution.

China, September: Up to 100,000 people perish in flooding on the Yangtze River. Plague and famine kill thousands more.
Kiev, Russia, September 14: Premier Piotr Stolypin is shot while attending the opera.
Tripoli, Libya, September 30: Italy declares war on the Turkish Empire after entry into Tripoli by Italians is rejected.
China, October 30: Revolution comes to China, as boy Emperor Pu Yi of the Manchu dynasty is forced to grant a constitution.

Morocco, November 4: France and Germany sign a treaty recognizing France's right to establish a protectorate in Morocco. France cedes land in the French Congo to Germany.
South Pole, December 14: Norwegian Roald Amundsen reaches the South Pole. Both poles have been conquered in just three years.
Nanking, China, December 30: Leader of the revolutionary forces, Sun Yat-sen, is elected president of a provisional government.

1913

Istanbul, Turkey, January 23: The Young Turks overthrow the Ottoman government in a coup.
Antarctica, February 12: News of the discovery of the remains of the Scott polar expedition reaches the world. The three remaining men perished in a blizzard in March 1912.
Mexico City, Mexico, February 23: Deposed President Madero is shot dead. A coup led by General Huerta on February 9 overthrew Madero, who had come to power in a similar fashion in 1910.

Auburn, New York, USA, March 10: Harriet Tubman dies, aged 93. She led more than 300 slaves into freedom from the South on the Underground Railroad in the 1860s.
Canberra, Australia, March 12: The foundation stone for the new Australian capital is laid.
Salonika, Greece, March 18: George I is assassinated. Born a Danish prince, he was elected monarch of Greece in 1863.
Peking, China, April 8: Chinese parliament convenes for the first time.

London, England, May 30: Turkey signs a treaty with the Balkan League members, ending the eight-month war. Turkey is compelled to cede large amounts of territory in the Balkan Peninsula.
Epsom, England, June 4: Emily Davison is struck by a horse when she runs onto the Derby track to gain publicity for the suffragette cause.
Salonika, Greece, June 30: Greek and Serbian troops rout Bulgarian forces as the Second Balkan War begins, with dispute over Macedonia.

Bucharest, Romania, August 10: A peace treaty is signed by Bulgaria and the Balkan states, ending one theater of the Second Balkan War.
Michigan, USA, October 7: Henry Ford establishes an assembly line at his automobile plant. Production time for a Model T Ford is scheduled to decrease from 14 hours to two.
Panama, October 10: After a construction phase of 10 years, the link between the Pacific and Atlantic oceans is completed.

New Zealand, November: Much of the country is brought to a standstill in a major waterfront strike.
Juarez, Mexico, November 15: Rebel leader "Pancho" Villa captures Juarez, with plans to move on Mexico City and oust dictator Huerta's troops.
Natal, South Africa, November 25: Widespread rioting follows the jailing of Mohandas Ghandi.
Paris, France, December 31: The *Mona Lisa* is returned to the Louvre. It was discovered in Florence two years after Vincenzo Perugia stole it.

1915

Avezzano, Italy, January 13: A massive earthquake, measuring 6.8, completely obliterates the city, leaving over 30,000 dead.
Norfolk, England, January 19: German Zeppelins bomb Great Yarmouth and King's Lynn, killing 20.
Dogger Bank, North Sea, January 24: The British navy sinks the German battleship *Blucher*.
North Sea, February 4: Germany declares blockade; U-boats attack Allied and neutral shipping. Britain retaliates with the seizure of all goods bound for Germany.

Gallipoli Peninsula, Turkey, February 19: Churchill orders a bombardment of Turkish positions in an effort to divert the Turks from Caucasian objectives. Russia is uneasy as capture of Constantinople (Istanbul) is its prerogative.
East Prussia, Germany, February 21: In the second Battle of Masurian Lakes, begun in a blizzard, Russia suffers heavy losses—over 50,000 casualties and 100,000 captured.
Ypres, Belgium, April 22: Poison gas is used by Germany in desperate trench warfare on the Western Front.

Gallipoli Peninsula, Turkey, April 25: Allied troops land at Gallipoli.
Atlantic Ocean, May 7: German U-boats torpedo the *Lusitania*.
Peking, China, May 8: President Yuan Shikai acquiesces to 21 restrictive Japanese demands that threaten Chinese sovereignty.
Italy, May 23: Italy joins the Allies, having quit the Triple Alliance.
Turkey, June: The Turkish Government murders and displaces thousands of Armenians, using the pretext of the war to carry out domestic objectives.

Warsaw, Poland, August 4: The Polish capital falls to Germany as Russian troops withdraw on the Eastern Front.
Gallipoli, Turkey, August 8: The Wellington Battalion seizes the summit of Chunuk Gair in a campaign which cost the lives of over 2,500 New Zealand soldiers.
Western Front, France, September 28: Allied troops make initial gains at Loos and Artois in the major Allied offensive of 1915, but no significant result is achieved.

Serbia, October: Germany-Austria and Bulgaria overrun Serbia. Allied forces landing at Salonika in Greece render little assistance.
London, England, November 12: First Lord of the Admiralty Winston Churchill resigns as dissent within the Asquith government grows.
Gallipoli Peninsula, Turkey, December 20: Allied troops withdraw from Gallipoli in the wake of the failure to take Turkish positions and indifference from London. The evacuation is carried out with minimal losses.

1917

USA, February 3: The USA severs diplomatic ties with Germany in response to Germany's resumption of unrestricted submarine warfare.
Mexico, February 5: A new constitution is adopted, the most progressive socialist constitution in the world to date. It provides for universal suffrage, separation of church and state, and a bill of rights.
Puerto Rico, March 2: Puerto Rico becomes a US protectorate, with all citizens awarded American citizenship.

Russia, March 16: A provisional government is formed as months of turmoil force Nicholas II to abdicate.
Victoria, Canada, April 5: Women in British Columbia win provincial voting rights. The Prairie Provinces were granted similar rights last year.
Washington DC, USA, April 6: The USA declares war against Germany. The discovery of the "Zimmerman Note," outlining German designs on the Americas, was a deciding factor.
Petrograd, Russia, April 10: Vladimir Ilyich Lenin arrives in Russia after 11 years in exile.

France, April 20: The Nivelle Offensive, including the second Battle of Aisne and third Battle of Champagne, is unsuccessful. Germany inflicts massive losses on the infantry, resulting in widespread disillusionment in the French troops.
Athens, Greece, June 12: Pro-German King Constantine abdicates under pressure from the Allies.
France, June 27: US soldiers, under the command of General Pershing, land in France to a rapturous reception from the beleaguered populace.

Moscow, Russia, July 20: Aleksandr Kerensky, Minister of War, assumes the leadership of the provisional government after a failed Eastern Front offensive and an attempt to seize power by the Bolsheviks.
Corfu, Greece, July 20: Croatian, Montenegrin, Serbian, and Slovenian politicians sign the Corfu Declaration, providing for the establishment of a new nation, Yugoslavia, at the end of the war.
Verdun, France, August 20: The Allies gain several key positions at the second Battle of Verdun.

Vincennes, France, October 15: Dutch exotic dancer Mata Hari is executed by the French for spying.
Passchendaele, Belgium, November 6: Sir Douglas Haig calls off the third Battle of Ypres as Allied forces capture Passchendaele.
Petrograd, Russia, November 7: Lenin's Bolsheviks revolt, seizing power in the year's second coup.
Jerusalem, Palestine, December 9: British troops capture Jerusalem from the Turks. Britain announced its support of a Zionist homeland with the Balfour Declaration.

1918

Washington DC, USA, January 8: President Wilson presents his 14-point plan for a post-war settlement. Disarmament, reparations, and a League of Nations are key facets.

Finland, January 28: Following its declaration of independence, Finland descends into a bloody civil war between the socialist Reds, who control the south, and the Whites, supported by the new senate.

Brest-Litovsk, Belarus, March 3: Hostilities on the Eastern Front cease with the signing of the Treaty of Brest-Litovsk.

Moscow, Russia, March 7: The Bolsheviks are renamed the Russian Communist Party. Moscow becomes the permanent seat of power.

Western Front, March 31: A new German offensive gains 40 miles (64 km) of territory in 10 days, the most dramatic advance on this front.

New Zealand, April 10: National prohibition is avoided due to strong opposition from servicemen abroad.

The Somme, France, April 21: German flying ace, Baron von Richthofen, "The Red Baron," is shot down and killed, aged 26.

Ireland, May 17: Eamon de Valera, leader of Sinn Féin, and 500 nationalists are imprisoned on grounds of colluding with Germany.

Canada, May 24: All female citizens of Canada over the age of 21 are allowed to vote in federal elections.

Russia, May: Peace is short lived, as the Czechoslovak Corps, followed by the White Russians, rebel against the Red Guard, launching civil war.

Ekaterinburg, Russia, July 16: The Romanov dynasty is eliminated with the execution of Tsar Nicholas and his family by Bolsheviks.

Amiens, France, August 8: In a black day for Germany, Allied forces push German troops back to the Hindenburg Line. Both sides sustain heavy losses.

Europe, September: The Central powers are on the back foot, with the Hindenburg Line breached, the British offensive in Palestine taking its toll and Bulgaria's surrender.

Western Front, October 4: Successful military campaigns at Ypres and Argonne by the Allies force the German government to begin negotiations for an armistice.

Worldwide, October: The "Spanish Flu" virus is spreading rapidly, killing more people worldwide than the war.

Vienna, Austria, October 31: Revolution breaks out in Austria and Hungary after Emperor proclaims reorganization of the monarchy. The Habsburg dynasty comes to an end.

Worldwide, November 11: The Great War comes to an end at 11:01 a.m. as Germany surrenders.

Iceland, December 1: Iceland proclaims independence from, but retains ties with, Denmark.

1920

Canada, January: Native people are given the right to vote, but must give up their Indian status to do so.

USA, January 16: The 18th Amendment officially bans beer, wine, and liquor.

London, England, February 11: The first session of the League of Nations is held. Delegates from Britain, France, Belgium, Japan, Spain, Greece, Italy, and Brazil attend.

Russia, February 22: Ninety thousand Allied troops are on the verge of defeat against Bolshevik forces.

Germany, March 19: The country is beset by socialist unrest. Strikes bring industry to a standstill. A monarchist coup led by Doctor Kapp in Berlin failed a week ago.

Frankfurt, Germany, April 7: French troops occupy the Ruhr region following German forces violating the Treaty of Versailles. Colonial troops open fire on German civilians, killing seven.

San Remo, Italy, April 25: The League of Nations gives the British mandate over Mesopotamia and Palestine.

Ireland, May 14: Tensions run high as 94 police stations are attacked. The British government released 40 Irish hunger strikers from jail in London last week.

Versailles, France, June 4: The Treaty of Trianon redefines Hungary's borders. The German, Austrian, Russian, and Turkish empires have all been radically redrawn since the end of the war.

Northern Mexico, July 28: Pancho Villa, one of the leaders of the Mexican Revolution, surrenders to the government.

Warsaw, Poland, August 23: The Polish Army bravely turns back the Bolsheviks from the capital's gates.

USA, August 26: American women gain the right to vote.

India, September 10: The Indian Congress adopts Gandhi's proposals for self-determination (Hind Swaraj) including non-cooperation.

New York, USA, September 16: A bomb explodes in Wall Street, killing 39 and injuring 300. The bomb was detonated from a horse-drawn carriage outside the J. P. Morgan building.

UK, October 18: Over a million miners strike in support of a pay rise. A demonstration in London turns violent when police restrain 5,000 miners.

USA, November 2: Republicans sweep to victory in the general election. Warren Harding is elected president with Calvin Coolidge as vice-president.

Ireland, December 14: The British government partitions Ireland into two separate territories, following Bloody Sunday (November 21), when 26 people were killed.

1922

Dublin, Ireland, January 10: The Dáil Éireann (Irish parliament) approves the formation of the Irish Free State. Eamon de Valera resigns to be replaced by Michael Collins.

The Vatican, February 12: The Archbishop of Milan becomes Pope Pius XI, succeeding Benedict XV. The new Pope is anxious to succeed in his role as international peacemaker.

Egypt, February 28: Egypt becomes independent from Britain. Britain has safeguarded its defense and communications infrastructure.

Ahmedabad, India, March 18: Mahatma Ghandi is sentenced to six years in prison for civil disobedience.

Rapallo, Italy, April 16: The Treaty of Rapollo is signed by the Soviet Union and Russia, establishing closer economic and political ties.

Peking, China, May 5: The civil war between the south, led by General Wu Pei-fu, and General Chang Tso-lin's northern forces ends with General Wu taking Beijing. He hopes to unify China.

Northern Iraq, June 18: Led by Sheikh Mahmud, Iraqi Kurds revolt demanding independence or autonomy from Baghdad.

Cork, Ireland, August 22: A political vacuum is left as Michael Collins, head of the provisional government of the Irish Free State, is assassinated. Arthur Griffith, head of the Dáil Éireann, died of a heart attack on August 12.

USA, September 13: Striking railroad workers return to work. Strikes have crippled the country and have been marked by violence.

Changchun, China, September 24: Japanese forces continue to occupy the strategic Sakhalin Islands after talks between Japan and Russia fail.

Dardanelles, Turkey, September 27: Turkish troops oust Greek military forces.

London, England, October 22: PM David Lloyd George resigns and an election is called for November.

Rome, Italy, October 30: Mussolini's fascists march on Rome, threatening to attack. The King hands power to him and dissolves the government.

Angora (Ankara), Turkey, November 4: Ottoman rule in Turkey comes to an end as the republican assembly declares the Sultanate invalid.

Valley of the Kings, Egypt, November 26: Lord Carnarvon and Howard Carter open the tomb of Tutankhamen. Finding untold wealth contained inside, the imagination of the world is piqued.

Moscow, USSR, December 30: The Union of Soviet Socialist Republics is proclaimed, tying together Russia, White Russia, the Ukraine, and Transcaucasia.

1924

Gorky, USSR, January 21: Vladimir Ilyich Lenin, the architect of the Russian revolution, dies following a fourth stroke, aged 54.

London, England, January 23: Ramsey MacDonald becomes the first Labour Prime Minister, forming a minority government.

Bombay, India, February 4: Mohandas Ghandi's deteriorating health lead authorities to release him from jail unconditionally.

Luxor, Egypt, February 12: Howard Carter opens King Tutankhamen's sarcophagus.

Ankara, Turkey, March 3: President Kemal Ataturk declares a new constitution. In an effort to modernize the country, the caliphate (Islamic spiritual leadership) is abolished and a secular state is established.

Greece, March 25: In a peaceful uprising, George II abdicates in favor of a civilian government.

Munich, Germany, April 1: Adolf Hitler is sentenced to five years jail for his role in the 'beer hall' putsch. He shall be eligible for parole in six months.

India, April: Plague decimates the Punjab region, claiming over 25,000 lives.

Moscow, USSR, May 26: Joseph Stalin is elected General Secretary of the Communist Party. He survives an attempted censure by Lenin in his testament, recommending Leon Trotsky for the top job.

Rome, Italy, June 10: Socialist leader Giacomo Matteotti is kidnapped and murdered by fascists. Mussolini's party was swept to power in elections in April, gaining 64 percent of the vote.

Germany, August 30: In an effort to stabilize the economy, the Reichsbank is made independent. This follows on from the Dawes plan for war reparations, including a loan for eight million reichsmarks.

Geneva, Switzerland, October 2: The Geneva protocol is put forward at the League of Nations, providing for compulsory arbitration of disputes.

Shanghai, China, October 13: The northern factions' headquarters is captured after three years of civil war. Their leader flees to Japan.

USA, November 4: Republican Calvin Coolidge wins a second term in office in a decisive victory over Democratic hopeful John W. Davis.

London, England, November 6: A conservative government under Prime Minister Stanley Baldwin replaces the Labour leadership, in power for just 11 months. Winston Churchill has been promoted to Chancellor of the Exchequer.

Munich, Germany, December 20: Hitler is freed after eight months in prison. He completed his book *Mein Kampf* during his incarceration.

1 9 1 9

Berlin, Germany, January 15: Communist Spartacists revolt against the government; the army quells the insurrection, killing hundreds. Spartacist leaders Karl Liebknecht and Rosa Luxemburg are murdered while in custody.
Dublin, Ireland, January 21: The first unofficial Dáil Éireann (Irish parliament) is convened. Sinn Féin MPs refuse to attend Westminster.
Weimar, Germany, February 6: The first session of the new German parliament is held, electing Friedrich Ebert president of the new republic.

Paris, France, February 14: At the Paris Peace Conference, 27 nations vote for the establishment of a League of Nations. The brainchild of US President Wilson, the league is to be formed as an international peacekeeper and mediator.
Moscow, Russia, March 4: Lenin convenes The Third International, with the goal of international communist revolution.
Chinameca, Mexico, April 10: Rebel leader Emiliano Zapata is killed in an ambush set up as a meeting.

Amritsar, India, April 13: At the Jallianwala Bagh, British troops open fire on a peaceful gathering, killing at least 379 and injuring thousands.
Korea, April: Occupied by Japan since 1910, rioting and open rebellion breaks out. Japan agrees to install a civil government and introduce self-rule in an effort to quash the unrest.
Kelut, Java, Dutch East Indies, May 19: A massive volcanic eruption claims up to 16,000 lives.

Scapa Flow, Orkney Islands, Scotland, June 21: Interned at the end of the war, 51 German ships are scuttled to prevent them falling into the possession of the Allies.
Versailles, France, June 28: Germany signs the Treaty of Versailles, officially ending the war. German officials are resentful at the terms of the treaty and the manner in which they are treated.
Budapest, Hungary, August 4: Romanian troops enter the Hungarian capital, ending the short rule of Bela Kun's communist party.

Rawalpindi, India, August 8: The end of the third Anglo-Afghan War is negotiated. The war was sparked by Afghan nationalist Amanullah Khan's attack on British forces.
South Africa, August 31: General Jan Smuts becomes prime minister after the death of Louis Botha.
London, England, November 28: US-born Lady Astor becomes the first woman in parliament.
Russia, November: The advantage has been gained by Trotsky's Red Army in the Russian Civil War; the White Army now seems worn out.

1 9 2 1

Paris, France, January 24: The Allies, without German input, have decreed a figure of $56 billion in war reparations that Germany shall be paying over the next 42 years.
Ireland, February 18: Eamon de Valera, leader of the Irish independence movement, heads a violent rebellion against British troops.
Germany, March 8: Allied troops occupy Dusseldorf, Mulheim, and other cities in response to Germany's rejection of reparation demands.

Russia, March 12: In an attempt to win over peasants, Lenin announces that state planning of the economy is to be ended.
Mongolia, March 13: With the help of White Russian troops, Mongolia expels the Chinese after 200 years.
Panama, April 20: Colombian treaty grants Colombia free access to the Panama Canal and $25 million in exchange for US possession of the strategic waterway.
Berlin, Germany, May 11: The German government finally agrees to war reparations.

Tulsa, Oklahoma, USA, June 1: In the worst race riots ever seen in America, 85 people are killed, hundreds are injured and thousands made homeless.
Shanghai, China, June 30: The Chinese Communist Party holds its first meeting.
London, England, July 22: Peace talks are held between British Prime Minister David Lloyd George and Eamon de Valera, the Irish Republican leader. A truce is declared.

Russia, August 4: Lenin appeals to the West for aid to combat a famine that is sweeping the country. Over 18 million people are thought to be suffering a shortage of food.
Rif, Northern Morocco, September 19: Abd el-Krim, leader of the Rif tribes, declares the Rif Republic. His forces have had a number of military victories over the Spanish colonial troops this year.
Ludwigshafen, Germany, September 21: An explosion at the BASF factory kills 574 workers and injures over 1,000.

Budapest, Hungary, October 21: The former leader of Austria, Emperor Charles, marches on Budapest with 12,000 troops. After making initial gains, they are routed by the Allied armies.
Milan, Italy, November 7: Benito Mussolini, head of the National Fascist Party, names himself *Il Duce*, or leader of the party.
Ireland, December 6: Southern Ireland becomes a free state under the dominion of Britain. The eight counties forming Ulster in the North shall remain part of the United Kingdom.

1 9 2 3

Ruhr region, Germany, January 11: French and Belgium troops occupy the Ruhr district as Germany defaults on war reparations. Civilians are encouraged to passively resist occupying forces.
Moscow, USSR, March 9: Ill health forces Vladimir Lenin to step down following his third stroke.
Kabul, Afghanistan, April 9: A new constitution aimed at modernizing the country is enacted.
Sofia, Bulgaria, June 9: A bloodless coup overthrows the regime of Stambuliski.

Germany, June 22: The decline of the Deutsch mark is becoming increasingly desperate, losing more than half its value in the last month. The war contributed to the present crisis, which is being exacerbated by the French occupation of the Ruhr.
USA, June 30: Membership of the Ku Klux Klan passes one million. Their anti-minority stance has proven popular throughout the USA.
Lausanne, Switzerland, July 24: The Near East Treaty establishes peace between Greece and Turkey.

Washington DC, USA, August 3: Calvin Coolidge is sworn in as President after the sudden death of President Harding from a stroke, aged 58.
Tokyo, Japan, September 1: The Great Kanto Earthquake (magnitude 8.3 on the Richter scale) levels Tokyo and Yokohama, killing 150,000 and leaving 2.5 million people homeless.
Southern Rhodesia, September 1: The British Crown takes control of the southern African colony from the British South Africa Company.

Madrid, Spain, September 13: Miguel Primo de Rivera leads a coup with the blessing of the King. The parliament is abolished and there is no guarantee of civil liberties.
India, September 25: The Swaraj Party, advocates of self-determination, win control of the Indian National Congress.
Persia, October 28: Reza Khan, commander-in-chief since 1921, becomes premier. The Shah of Persia, in response to a near-dictatorship, goes into exile.

Angora (Ankara), Turkey, October 29: Leader of the nationalist movement that brought an end to the Ottoman Empire, Mustafa Kemal has been elected President of the new Turkish republic.
Munich, Germany, November 12: Disaffection and conflict throughout Germany is exploited by Adolf Hitler to gain popular support in Bavaria. The Beer Hall Putsch fails and Hitler and other key figures are arrested.
Germany, November 15: Chronic inflation has devalued the mark. One US dollar is now worth 4 trillion marks.

1 9 2 5

Oslo, Norway, January 1: Christiania, the capital of the Scandinavian country, is renamed.
Moscow, USSR, January 16: Leon Trotsky is ousted from the Soviet War council. This is a victory for Stalin and his allies, Zinoviev and Kamenev.
Peking, China, March 12: Sun Yat-sen, the "father of the republic," dies, aged 58. His political philosophy, the Three Principles of the People, is highly influential. General Chiang Kai-shek assumes the mantle of Chinese leader.

Great Britain and Australia, April 8: The Australian federal government has promised 34 million dollars in low-interest loans to encourage migration from Britain over the next 10 years.
Germany, April 25: Field Marshal von Hindenburg is elected President in the first popular elections to be held in the country.
Cyprus, May 1: The Mediterranean island becomes a colony of the British Empire.
Tennessee, USA, May 25: Teacher John Scopes is indicted for teaching Darwin's theory of evolution.

Shanghai, China, June 23: China is on the brink of civil war as regional warlords compete for power. Anti-British sentiment is high following the dispersal of student demonstrations by British troops.
South Africa, June 29: The parliament legislates to prohibit non-whites from working in skilled and semi-skilled jobs.
Santa Barbara, USA, June 29: A 6.3 magnitude earthquake destroys Santa Barbara's downtown area.

Washington DC, USA, August 8: More than 40,000 Ku Klux Klan members march through the streets of the Capitol.
Australia, September 23: New legislation allows for refusal of entry to the country of immigrants of any race, class or occupation at the discretion of the governor-general.
Locarno, Switzerland, October 16: Germany and France sign a peace treaty, seven years after hostilities ended, agreeing never to fight each other again and recognizing a demilitarized zone along the Rhine.

Philadelphia, USA, December 3: Federal agents brandishing 43 warrants swoop on an international rum ring in control of millions in liquor, money and ships. Agents label it the "greatest roundup in the history of Prohibition."
Persia, December 13: After deposing the self-exiled Shah, Reza Khan is crowned the new Shah of Persia. He initiates a reform policy.
Moscow, USSR, December: At the 14th Soviet Party Congress, Stalin calls for socialism at home rather than worldwide revolution.

1926

Canada, January: Canada joins the Commonwealth of Nations.

Mecca, Hejaz, January 8: Abdel-Aziz ibn Saud takes the title of King of the Hejaz, stating his intention to rename the region Saudi Arabia.

Turkey, February 17: Under the modernizing influence of Kemal Ataturk, new civil, criminal and law codes based on European systems are adopted.

Rome, Italy, April 7: Mussolini survives an assassination attempt by Irishwoman Violet Gibson. He only suffers an injured nose.

Calcutta, India, April: Sectarian riots between Muslims and Hindus erupt, injuring hundreds.

England, May 12: A paralysing general strike, precipitated by the walkout of coal miners on May 1, ends. Transport, press and industry have been at a standstill. Strikes were called following the government withdrawing subsidies from the miners.

Targuist, Morocco, May 26: Under siege from 160,000 French troops, 30,000 riffian rebels, led by Abd el Krim, surrender.

Warsaw, Poland, June 13: Josef Pilsudski is installed as leader following a military coup.

New Jersey, USA, July 10: A lightning strike on a munitions depot causes a massive explosion.

Paris, France, July 23: A new coalition government consisting of former opponents is sworn in. The nation is on the brink of bankruptcy following devaluation of the franc.

Transvaal, South Africa, August 22: Discovery of massive reserves of diamonds brings 50,000 to the region.

Hankou, China, September 6: Nationalist Kuomintang troops, led by General Chiang Kai-shek, capture the strategic treaty port of Hankou. The northern troops have retreated and there is fear that Peking will fall.

Geneva, Switzerland, September 8: Germany is formally admitted to the League of Nations furthering its rehabilitation from pariah status.

Florida, USA, September 18: A tropical hurricane ravages Florida, killing 1,500 and leaving 40,000 homeless.

Rome, Italy, November 2: Mussolini survives another assassination attempt. On October 7, the Fascist party outlawed all opposition and Il Duce became paramount leader.

London, England, November 18: The Imperial Conference concludes with the formation of the British Commonwealth of equal, autonomous nations.

Tokyo, Japan, December 25: Hirohito becomes Emperor following his father Yoshihito's death, ending the Taisho period.

1928

Moscow, USSR, January 16: Stalin, in attempt to dilute any influence in opposition to his rule, exiles Trotsky, Zinoviev and Kamenev.

Nicaragua, January 26: US President Coolidge sends 1,000 Marines to combat guerrillas led by General Sandino. An ardent nationalist, his troops have been waging a bloody battle against US influence for two years.

Darwin, Australia, February 22: Aviator Bert Hinkler completes the first solo flight from England in 15 days.

California, USA, March 12: The St Francis dam bursts, sending a 40-foot (12-m) wall of water downstream, killing over 400 people.

Turkey, April 29: Premier Mustafa Kemal introduces the English alphabet in preference to the Arabic.

Shantung, China, May 11: Three days of heavy fighting between Japanese and Chinese troops leave 1,000 dead.

Italy, May 12: Universal suffrage is abandoned. The eligible electorate drops to three million as Mussolini's grip on the country tightens.

Carthmarthenshire, Wales, June 18: Aviatrix Amelia Earhart crosses the Atlantic from Boston in 22 hours. On June 10, Charles Kingsford-Smith successfully flew from the USA to Australia in eight days.

Zagreb, Yugoslavia, August 1: Croats set up a separatist parliament and demand a federal system.

Paris, France, August 27: The Kellogg-Briand Pact is signed, renouncing "war as an instrument of national policy." Eleven nations including Germany, USA, France, and UK are signatories.

Lucknow, India, August 30: Dissatisfied with the adoption of the Nehru Plan, the Independence of India League is established under the leadership of Jawaharlal Nehru, son of the author of the plan.

Moscow, USSR, October 1: The beginning of Stalin's first five-year plan. Farms are to be made collectives and heavy industry expanded.

Addis Ababa, Ethiopia, October 7: Ras Tafari is crowned King. Sharing power with his aunt, Empress Zauditu, the coronation legitimizes his 10-year rule.

USA, November 6: Republican Herbert Hoover wins a landslide victory in the federal election over Democrat Alfred E. Smith.

Nanking, China, November: The Kuomintang government of Chiang Kai-shek gains international legitimacy, signing treaties with 12 states. Rival warlords eventually recognise the Nanking government, unifying China.

New York, USA, December: The New York stock exchange sees a turbulent year, with a massive depreciation in stock values.

1930

Cairo, Egypt, February 1: The *Science News-Letter* reports one of the largest Egyptian tombs ever found has been discovered at Meidum, near Cairo. The *mastaba*'s unknown inhabitant lived about 2800 BCE.

London, England, March 14: Plans to build a tunnel from England to France are approved by the Channel Tunnel Committee.

USSR, March 16: Joseph Stalin begins a terror campaign to eradicate wealthy farmers.

Turkey, March 28: The name of the city of Constantinople is officially changed to Istanbul.

Dandi, India, April 6: After completing his 100-mile (161 km) Salt March, Mahatma Gandhi boycotts the British salt tax by taking his own salt.

China, April 23: Nationalists and Soviet communists challenge General Chiang Kai Shek's efforts to control China.

Pegu, Burma, May 5: A massive earthquake kills as many as 6,000 people.

Darwin, Australia, May 24: British aviator Amy Johnson arrives in Darwin 19 days after commencing her solo flight from London.

Cairo, Egypt, July 22: Riots in Egypt occur, following the dismissal of the government.

Ariano, Italy, July 22: An earthquake kills 1,500 people.

Brazil, August 13: A giant meteorite lands deep in the River Curuçá region of the Amazon rainforest, producing a massive explosion.

UK, August 14: The Church of England reluctantly accepts the use of contraceptives.

Washington DC, USA, August 16: The government allocates $121.9 million toward the drought, which has cut corn output by 690 million bushels.

Japan, November 14: Prime Minister Hamaguchi Osachi is wounded in an assassination attempt.

New York, USA, December 31: The collapse of the Bank of the United States, which has 60 branches in New York alone, leads to a run on banks throughout the country.

1932

India, January 4: Mahatma Gandhi is arrested at 3 am after the Indian National Congress is declared illegal.

El Salvador, January 22: Reprisals begin as the government regains control after a peasant uprising led by socialist Augustín Farabundo Martí. Government retaliation is to massacre 15,000 to 30,000.

Shanghai, China, January 29: A mass bombing levels the city and kills thousands.

Spain, January: Anarchist insurrections break out all over the country.

Japan, February 18: Japan declares Manchuria to be an independent state.

Sydney, Australia, March 19: The Sydney Harbour Bridge opens, bringing road access across the harbor between the city's north and south.

New Jersey, USA, May 12: Baby Charles Augustus Lindbergh III is found dead after his kidnapping on March 1.

Tokyo, Japan, May 15: Prime Minister Tsuyoshi Inukai is assassinated by radical young naval officers. The original plan includes killing Charlie Chaplin, presently in Japan. Known as *go ichi go jiken*, it heralds the end of party political control over national decisions until after World War II.

Bombay, India, May 16: Riots between Hindus and Muslims.

New Zealand, May: Economic depression leads to riots in several major New Zealand cities.

Siam, June 29: The military seizes power, making Siam a constitutional monarchy.

India, September 20: Gandhi begins a hunger strike in prison, protesting the British electorates for the depressed classes.

Saudi Arabia, September 22: King Ibn Saud unites Kingdom Hejaz and Sultanate Nejd as the Kingdom of Saudi Arabia.

Iraq, October 3: Iraq gains independence from its British-imposed rule under a treaty granting the UK certain privileges.

Washington DC, USA, November 8: Franklin Delano Roosevelt becomes the thirty-second president of the USA after winning the election against incumbent Herbert Hoover.

Washington DC, USA, November 24: The Federal Bureau of Investigation (FBI) Scientific Crime Detection Laboratory is officially declared open, after several months in operation.

China, December 25: An earthquake in Gansu province leaves 70,000 dead.

1 9 2 7

Canada, January: The Indian Act prohibits "First Nations" from raising money or hiring a lawyer for the purpose of pursuing land claims.
Shanghai, China, January 31: Following rioting, nationalist sentiment and civil unrest, 12,000 British troops are ordered to protect British interests. The Chinese protest at the deployment.
Lisbon, Portugal, February 9: A revolt against the dictatorship of General Carmona is crushed. Since founding in 1910, Portugal has been wracked by instability.

England, February 27: Up to 1,000 people per week die in a nationwide outbreak of influenza.
Shanghai, China, April 28: Infighting in the Kuomintang between moderates and Communists leads to raids on union strongholds.
Berlin, Germany, May 1: The government lifts its ban on the Nazi party; Adolf Hitler addresses a rally.
Canberra, Australia, May 9: The parliament convenes in the new capital for the first time. Melbourne had held parliamentary sittings since federation.

Paris, France, May 21: American Charles Lindbergh completes the first non-stop flight from New York to Paris in 33 hours, and 100,000 Parisians gather to celebrate the landing.
Xining, China, May 22: An 8.6 magnitude earthquake leaves over 200,000 dead— one of the worst earthquakes in history.
Moscow, USSR, June 9: Twenty alleged British spies are executed without trial, following the UK severing diplomatic ties with the communist state.

Vienna, Austria, July 15: Rioting breaks out following the acquittal of three nationalists on murder charges. The Ministry of Justice is set on fire, 89 people die and 600 are injured.
Massachusetts, USA, August 23: Italian anarchists Sacco and Vanzetti, convicted of murder and robbery six years ago, are executed, continuing to maintain their innocence. Their case became a *cause célèbre*.
St Louis, USA, September 30: A tornado of five minutes duration devastates St Louis, killing 69.

Mexico, October: The leaders of the "Cristero War" are executed. A reaction to government seizure of church property, the rebellion is brutally suppressed by President Calles.
Moscow, USSR, November 15: Stalin expels his main opponents, Trotsky and Zinoviev from the Communist Party. They had led a peaceful demonstration criticizing Stalin by implication last week.
Canton, China, December 19: General Chiang Kai-shek crushes a Communist uprising and expels all Russian citizens.

1 9 2 9

Yugoslavia, January 6: Alexander I takes direct control of the Kingdom of the Serbs, Croats and Slovenes, renaming it Yugoslavia.
USSR, January 30: Leon Trotsky is expelled from Russia; he has been Stalin's most vocal critic. Exile to Alma-Ata was insufficient to silence him; he now departs for Turkey.
Rome, Italy, February 11: Mussolini and the Papacy sign the Lateran Treaty, creating the Vatican and re-establishing the sovereignty of the Pope after 60 years of tension.

Chicago, USA, February 14: Gangster Al Capone's mob executes six members of a rival gang in the "St Valentine's Day massacre." Extortion, prostitution and bootleg liquor are the gang's main business.
Mexico, April 6: The USA send in planes equipped for bombing after US citizens are killed in the latest attack by rebels, who want to topple the government of President Gil.
Berlin, Germany, May 3: Communist protestors fight pitched battles with police.

London, England, June 10: Ramsay MacDonald forms a new Labour government after a hung parliament was delivered in the general election. Margaret Bondfield is the first woman member of the Cabinet.
Nelson, New Zealand, June 24: A massive earthquake on the South Island spectacularly rearranges the landscape and kills 20 people.
USSR/China Border, July 22: Tensions are mounting after disputes concerning the Chinese Eastern Railway in Manchuria. Troops are massing along the border.

Jerusalem, Palestine, August 31: Jewish access to the Wailing Wall causes a violent uprising by Arabs, leaving 500 dead. British troops act swiftly to restore the rule of law.
Geneva, Switzerland, September 5: French Premier Aristide Briand puts forward a proposal for European Union at the League of Nations, which is coolly received.
Berlin, Germany, September 22: Armed groups of Communists and Nazis clash in chaotic scenes throughout the city.

Kabul, Afghanistan, October 16: Rebel General Nadir Khan captures Kabul and is proclaimed Shah.
New York, USA, October 24: The "Black Thursday" stock market crash wipes millions off the value of shares.
Lahore, India, December: Escalating violence between Hindus and Muslims leads to the All-India Congress calling for independence from Britain.
Paisley, Scotland, December 31: A fire in a movie theater leaves 69 children dead.

1 9 3 1

Iraq, January 6: Archeologists unearth a 550 BCE royal palace at the ancient city of Ur.
Coolgardie, Australia, January 15: Western Australia's biggest gold nugget, the Golden Eagle, is found, weighing 78 pounds.
Hawke's Bay, New Zealand, February 3: An earthquake measuring 7.8 on the Richter scale kills 256.
Moscow, USSR, February 21: Soviet revolutionary Leon Trotsky is stripped of his citizenship and exiled.

Washington DC, USA, March 3: President Hoover signs an act declaring *The Star-Spangled Banner* to be the US national anthem.
India, March 25: Racial riots in Cawnpore kill hundreds in a throat-slitting bloodbath.
Nicaragua, March 31: An earthquake and subsequent fire in Managua kill between 1,000 and 2,000 people.

Madrid, Spain, April 14: King Alfonso XIII abdicates the throne and flees the country, and the Republic of Spain is proclaimed. Niceto Alcalá Zamora takes over the presidency under a provisional government.
Tokyo, Japan, April 14: Prime Minister Osachi Hamaguchi dies and is succeeded by Reijiro Wakatsuki.
New York, USA, May 1: The Empire State Building is opened.

Germany, August 5: Banks reopen, after closing on July 13 when the German Danatbank went bankrupt.
China, August 31: A Yangtze River flood leaves 23 million homeless, just one month after the Yellow River floods that killed millions.
London, England, September 7: King George V takes a £50,000-a-year pay cut to help deal with the economic crisis.

Manchuria, September 18: Japan invades Manchuria in a surprise attack, violating the Kellogg-Briand pact.
London, England, September 30: Riots protesting pay cuts follow a month of strikes.
Chicago, USA, November 24: Al Capone is sentenced to 11 years in prison and fined.
Washington DC, USA, December: Hundreds of hunger marchers petition for employment at a minimum wage.

1 9 3 3

Spain, January 8: The army quells an uprising in Barcelona of Anarchists and Syndicalists against the government's social reform movement. The violence continues in Catalonia, Levante and Andaulusia.
Berlin, Germany, February 28: The German Reichstag burns down. Chancellor Adolf Hitler declares the act to be a communist plot.
China, March 4: Japanese forces occupy the province of Jehol and continue their advance into Manchuria.

USA, March 6: President Roosevelt closes banks for four days in 47 states.
Germany, March 22: The first Nazi concentration camp at Dachau, near Munich, begins operation.
Germany, March 23: Hitler becomes Dictator of Germany after the Reichstag grants him full powers, less than two months after being appointed Chancellor of Germany.

Berlin, Germany, April 1: The Nazi government uses violence to orchestrate its boycott of Jewish businesses, forcing stores to close and barring professionals from their offices.
Berlin, Germany, April 11: The Nazis decree "non-Aryans" to include anyone descended from non-Aryan, particularly Jewish, parents or grandparents.
Scotland, May 2: A sighting of a bizarre creature is reported in Loch Ness.

Paraguay, May 10: Paraguay declares war on Bolivia.
Poona, India, August 23: An emaciated Mahatma Gandhi is released from hospital, five days into a fast protesting his exclusion from working with Untouchables while in prison. Earlier in the year he had been on a three-week hunger strike to protest the treatment of lower castes.
Germany, August 29: Jews and socialists are herded into concentration camps.

New Zealand, September 13: Elizabeth McCombs becomes the first female member of parliament in New Zealand.
South Dakota, USA, November 11: An enormous dust storm strips the dry topsoil from the state's drought-stricken farmlands.
Washington DC, USA, December 5: The prohibition of intoxicating liquor ends. The repeal of the law goes into effect after Utah became the 36th state to ratify the change.

1934

Berlin, Germany, January 1: A Nazi law forcing people with genetic defects to be sterilized comes into effect in Germany.

India, January 15: Over 10,000 people are feared dead after an earthquake strikes Bihar.

Berlin, Germany, January 15: Germany and Poland sign a 10-year non-aggression pact following a period of tension.

World, February 11: Friendship treaties are signed between Saudi Arabia and Britain, and between Britain, India, and Yemen.

Hsinking, Manchukuo (China), March 1: Henry Pu-yi becomes emperor of Manchukuo, but is a puppet ruler under Japan.

Washington DC, USA, March 24: The USA declares the Philippines will become independent from 1945.

India, April 7: Attempting to quell mass rioting and violence, Gandhi suspends his civil disobedience campaign against British authorities.

Tokyo, Japan, April 18: Japan's foreign office announces it has a virtual protectorate over Chinese relations with Western powers.

USA, May 11: A violent two-day dust storm in the Great Plains removes massive amounts of topsoil.

Louisiana, USA, May 23: Bank robbers Bonnie Parker and Clyde Barrow are shot dead during an ambush near their hideout.

Germany, August 2: Following the death of President Paul von Hindenburg, Adolf Hitler proclaims himself *Führer* of Germany, making him both Head of State and Chancellor. The armed forces are forced to swear an oath of allegiance.

Honshu, Japan, September 21: A typhoon is believed to have killed up to 4,000 people.

Japan, October 2: A tornado in Osaka and Kyoto kills 1,660, leaves 5,400 injured, and destroys the rice harvest.

Marseilles, France, October 9: Croatian and Macedonian extremists assassinate King Alexander of Yugoslavia and the French Foreign Minister Louis Barthou.

China, October: The communist Red Army commences a 6,000-mile (9,654-kilometer) march, retreating from southeastern China after being encircled by General Chiang Kai-shek's nationalist forces and suffering heavy losses.

1936

Sandringham, England, January 20: George V dies, aged 70. He is succeeded by his son, Edward VIII.

Germany, March 7: France decides a large military force will be needed after German troops reoccupy the Rhineland.

Spain, April 10: President Niceto Alcalá Zamora is deposed and flees to France, after his attempts to limit the powers of extremist political parties are rejected.

Abyssinia, May 5: Abyssinia is taken by Italy, crumbling under the weight of the massive offensive as Italy seizes the capital, Addis Ababa.

Tokyo, Japan, May 21: Sada Abe, a former prostitute, is arrested for manslaughter after she asphyxiated Kichizo Ishida during sex, removed his penis, wrapped it in paper and wandered the streets of Tokyo for three days with it in her hand.

Spain, June 9: Over one million workers are now on strike.

Spain, July 17: Civil war breaks out.

Berlin, Germany, August 1: The Games of the XIth Olympiad open. Hitler temporarily abstains from his actions against Jews.

Athens, Greece, August 4: Prime Minister General John Metaxas leads a military coup and establishes a dictatorship.

Hobart, Australia, September 7: The last surviving Thylacine ("Tasmanian tiger") dies in Hobart Zoo in Tasmania.

Spain, October 1: General Franco is appointed commander-in-chief of the rebel forces in the civil war after capturing Toledo.

Washington DC, USA, November 3: Franklin Roosevelt is re-elected president in a landslide victory over Alfred Landon.

Germany, November 25: Germany signs an anti-Comintern pact with Japan to protect the countries' common interests.

London, England, November 30: The Crystal Palace, built in 1851, is destroyed by fire.

London, England, December 12: Prince Albert is proclaimed King George VI after his brother Edward VIII abdicates the British throne.

China, December 12-25: Nationalist General Chiang Kai-shek is kidnapped in Xi'an in an attempt to force him to negotiate with the Communists—his enemies—against their external enemy, Japan.

1938

London, England, January 3: The government plans to provide all schoolchildren with gas masks.

Saudi Arabia, March 3: Oil is discovered in Saudi Arabia.

Austria, March 13: Germany declares *Anschluss* (political union with Austria) after invading Austria on March 12.

Nanking, China, March 13: Japanese troops slaughter up to 300,000 civilians and prisoners of war in a massacre following the city's fall to Japan on December 13, 1937.

London, England, March 17: A report by the Cadogan Committee recommends that flogging be abolished, indicating that no correlation has been found between corporal punishment and levels of criminal activity.

Latvia, June 11: Fire destroys 212 buildings in Ludes.

Pennsylvania, USA, June 28: A 500-ton meteorite breaks up over Butler County; one part lands near Chicora and injures a cow.

China, July: Massive floods follow General Chiang Kai-shek's orders to destroy the dikes on the Yangtze and Yellow Rivers, intended to deter the Japanese. They result in numerous drownings, with countless more made homeless.

Rome, Italy, August 3: Mussolini introduces his anti-Semitic laws into Italy, following the lead of his German allies.

Munich, Germany, September 30: The Munich Agreement, made by Germany, Italy, Britain and France, allows Hitler to take Sudetenland, and Hungary and Poland to take border districts from Czechoslovakia. Another resolution is signed to resolve future disputes between Britain and Germany peacefully.

Czechoslovakia, October 5: Hitler's army marches into Czechoslovakia.

Canton, China, October 21: The Japanese capture the southern city of Canton.

New York, USA, October 30: Panic erupts when a radio drama based on H.G. Wells's *War of the Worlds* and produced by Orson Welles's Mercury Players airs; some listeners believe the world is under Martian attack.

Berlin, Germany, November 9: Jewish shops, homes, and synagogues are looted or destroyed as Hitler's anti-Jewish scheme is unleashed throughout Germany.

1940

UK, January 27: The worst storm of the century so far concludes a month of freezing temperatures and heavy snowfalls, which saw the Thames River freeze over on January 17.

Norway, February 16: A raid on the German tanker *Altmark* frees over 300 British POWs.

Europe, February 20: Hitler orders his U-boat captains to attack all shipping, Allied vessels and neutral ships alike.

Southport, England, February 28: The camouflaged *Queen Elizabeth* sets sail on a secret voyage to New York.

Moscow, USSR, March 13: Russia defeats Finland following its 200,000-strong invasion on January 2; a peace treaty is signed in which Finland loses territory.

London, England, May 10: Winston Churchill becomes prime minister after Neville Chamberlain resigns.

Europe, May 10: After invading Norway and Denmark on April 9, Germany now invades Luxembourg, Belgium, Netherlands, and France.

Netherlands, May 15: Netherlands surrenders to Germany after Rotterdam falls.

Belgium, May 28: Belgium surrenders to Germany.

Rome, Italy, June 10: Under an agreement made with Germany on May 30, Italy declares war on Britain and France.

Estonia, August: Lithuania, Estonia, and Latvia are annexed to the USSR.

Coyoacán, Mexico, August 21: Leon Trotsky is assassinated.

Berlin, Germany, September 27: Japan, Germany, and Italy sign a 10-year pact.

London, England, September 30: The city has been continually "blitzed" by German war planes since September 7.

London, England, October 13: Princess Elizabeth makes a radio broadcast to evacuated children.

Germany, October 25: The RAF carries out four days of raids on Berlin and Hamburg.

Washington DC, USA, November 5: Roosevelt wins a record third term as president, defeating Wendell L. Wilkie.

UK, November 30: Germany is mass bombing regional cities: Glasgow, Birmingham, Coventry, Manchester, and Sheffield have been hit.

London, England, December 29: The city burns from more than 10,000 German fire bombs.

1935

Africa, January 1: The Italian colonies of Kyrenaika and Tripoli are joined as Libya.

Southern Africa, January 14: The Lower Zambezi bridge opens, creating an uninterrupted rail connection between Nyasaland and the Indian Ocean port of Beira.

Florida, USA, January 16: The FBI kills members of the notorious Barker gang, including Ma Barker, during a shootout at a Lake Weir cottage.

Berlin, Germany, March 16: Germany denounces the disarmament clauses of the Versailles Treaty, resuming military conscription.

Iran, March 21: Persia officially changes its name to Iran to gain favor with Germany; "Iran" means "Aryan."

Sydney, Australia, April 25: While on display in a Sydney beach pool, a recently caught shark disgorges the tattooed arm of ex-boxer James Smith, revealing clues to his murder.

India, May 30: An earthquake destroys Quetta, killing 30,000.

Chicago, USA, July 24: The dust bowl heatwave hits its peak, with the temperature in Chicago soaring to a record 109°F (43°C).

Moscow, USSR, August 20: The Seventh World Congress of the Communist International calls for the USSR and all communists to unite with democracies against their common enemy, the fascist dictatorships.

Washington DC, USA, August 31: Congress passes the first of its neutrality Acts designed to keep the USA out of the next world war.

Nuremberg, Germany, September 15: The Nuremberg decree legalizes the Nazi persecution of Jews.

Abyssinia, October 2: Italian forces invade Abyssinia.

China, October 20: Mao Tse-tung concludes the Red Army's Long March, reaching Yenan in the Shensi province of northwestern China.

Philippines, November 15: The Philippine Islands are made a US Commonwealth.

New Zealand, November 27: The first Labour government, with a platform of social and economic reform, is elected in New Zealand.

China, December 1: The nationalist General Chiang Kai-shek is elected President of the Chinese Executive Committee.

1937

New York, USA, January 19: Howard Hughes sets a new flying record: Los Angeles to New York City in seven hours and 28 minutes.

Moscow, USSR, January 23: The trial of 17 leading Communists, accused of participating in Leon Trotsky's plot to overthrow Joseph Stalin's regime and assassinate its leaders, begins.

Moscow, USSR, February 1: Thirteen 'Trotskyists' are executed.

Detroit, USA, February 11: A 44-day sit-down strike ends as General Motors recognizes the United Automobile Workers Union. The strike is one of 477 sit-down strikes in this year.

India, April 1: The British Parliament's Government of India Act, aimed at transforming India's governmental system, goes into effect, giving provincial governments greater autonomy.

New Jersey, USA, May 6: The German airship *Hindenburg* bursts into flame while mooring, killing 35 people on board and one member of the ground crew.

London, England, May 12: The coronation of King George VI and Queen Elizabeth takes place at Westminster Abbey.

South America, May 26: The Chaco War between Bolivia and Paraguay ends.

California, USA, May 28: The Golden Gate Bridge, linking San Francisco and Marin County, opens.

World, June 8: The first total solar eclipse to exceed seven minutes of totality in over 800 years is visible in Peru and the Pacific.

Moscow, USSR, June 12: Eight Russian generals are executed, causing international outrage.

South Pacific Ocean, July 2: Aviatrix Amelia Earhart disappears between New Guinea and Howland Island near the end of an around-the-world flight.

Alabama, USA, July 24: The state drops its rape charges against the "Scottsboro Boys."

Peking, July 28: Japanese forces complete their occupation of the city after an initial strike on July 7 at nearby Lukouchiao.

China, September 29: General Chiang Kai-shek unites forces with his rival, Communist Mao Tse-tung, against the Japanese.

Ireland, December 29: The new Irish Constitution comes into force and the Irish Free State officially becomes Eire.

1939

Australia, January 13: The day is declared Black Friday after 71 people across Victoria die in the country's worst bushfires.

Chile, January 24: An earthquake strikes south-central Chile, killing 28,000.

Washington DC, USA, February 27: The US Supreme Court outlaws sit-down strikes.

Essex, England, February 27: Borley Rectory, built in 1863 and reputedly England's most haunted house, burns down.

Czechoslovakia, March 16: The German Army occupies Prague and Czechoslovakia becomes a Nazi protectorate.

Spain, April 1: Franco declares the end of the civil war.

Rome, Italy, May 22: Mussolini signs a military pact with Hitler, obligating Italy to fight alongside Germany.

Florida, USA, June 4: The USA denies entry to the *St Louis*, a ship carrying 930 Jewish refugees, after it is turned away by Cuba. It returns to Europe.

Moscow, USSR, August 23: Hitler and Stalin sign a Nazi–Soviet pact of non-aggression that divides Eastern Europe between Germany and USSR.

Poland, September 1: German forces invade Poland from Germany in the west, East Prussia in the north and Czechoslovakia in the south.

Europe, September 3: Britain and France declare war on Germany in accord with treaty obligations to Poland. They are followed by New Zealand, Australia and India.

South Africa, September 6: South Africa declares war on Germany.

Canada, September 10: Canada declares war on Germany.

Poland, September 17: USSR invades Poland from the east.

Poland, September 29: The Nazis and Soviets divide up Poland. Over two million Jews reside in Nazi-controlled areas, and 1.3 million in the Soviet area.

Poland, September 29: Warsaw surrenders; 700,000 Polish troops are taken prisoner.

Germany, October: The Nazis begin a program to euthanize the sick and disabled in Germany.

Finland, November 30: The USSR attacks Finland after their strategic negotiations on November 12 fail.

Turkey, December 27: An earthquake in Erzingan kills 100,000.

1941

London, England, January 5: Aviator Amy Johnson is believed drowned after her airplane goes down in the Thames Estuary.

Washington DC, USA, March 11: The *Lease-Lend Act* will enable the USA to sell, lend, or lease supplies to other nations.

Yugoslavia, April 17: The country surrenders after Germany occupies Sarajevo.

Greece, April 18: Prime Minister Alexandros Korizis, who took over after Metaxas's death on January 29, suicides.

Greece, April 30: Most of Greece is under German and Italian occupation; German forces took Athens on April 26.

Scotland, May 10: Rudolf Hess, Hitler's deputy, is detained in the United Kingdom.

London, England, May 10: A mass bombing raid is carried out by Germany in the city's worst terror raid yet.

North Atlantic Ocean, May 27: Germany's battleship *Bismark* is destroyed by British forces.

Crete, Greece, June 1: German forces take the island of Crete in a bloody battle. Allied troops are evacuated to Egypt.

USSR, June 22: Germany invades the USSR, breaking the Nazi-Soviet pact.

Syria, June 28: Allied troops take Damascus.

Albania, June 28: Albania declares war on the USSR.

French Indochina, July 27: Japanese troops take Saigon.

Honolulu, Hawaii, December 7: Japanese planes make a surprise attack on the US fleet at Pearl Harbor.

Washington DC, USA, December 8: The USA, Britain, Australia, and New Zealand declare war on Japan.

Europe, December 8: Hungary and Romania declare war on Britain. Britain reciprocates.

USA, December 11: The USA reciprocates Germany's and Italy's declarations of war.

Central America, December 11: Cuba, Costa Rica, Nicaragua, and the Dominican Republic declare war on Germany and Italy.

Europe, December 12: Hungary, Romania, and Bulgaria declare war on the USA.

Hong Kong, December 25: Japan seizes Hong Kong.

St Petersburg (Leningrad), USSR, December 25: Over 3,000 people have starved to death since the German siege on the city began in September.

1942

Washington DC, USA, January 1: The Declaration of United Nations to pledge support for the Atlantic Charter is signed by 26 countries.

Philippines, January 2: Japan takes Manila.

Berlin, Germany, January 20: Nazi leaders at the Wannsee Conference structure the "final solution of the Jewish question," aiming to exterminate over 11 million European Jews.

London, England, January 29: Winston Churchill is re-elected.

Singapore, February 15: The city surrenders to Japan.

Darwin, Australia, February 19: Australia's northernmost city has become a ghost town following Japanese air strikes.

Washington DC, USA, February 19: President Roosevelt signs executive order 9066 to inter 120,000 citizens of Japanese ancestry in camps.

Canada, February 25: Men of Japanese descent living in Canada are removed from their homes and interned in camps.

Germany, March 28: Allied forces drop thousands of bombs on Lübeck, near Berlin.

London, England, May 26: A 20-year alliance treaty is signed by the USSR and Britain.

Sydney, Australia, May 31: Three midget Japanese submarines enter Sydney Harbour; one manages to fire two torpedoes and sink the barracks ship *Kuttabul*.

Midway Atoll, June 7: Following an attck by US naval forces, the Japanese navy withdraws from the Pacific atoll.

New Zealand, June 14: A garrison of US troops arrives in New Zealand to train for Pacific "island-hopping" campaigns.

Siam, June: Japan begins forcing 60,000 Allied POWs to construct a crucial 260-mile (418 km) rail link between Burma and Siam.

Dieppe, France, August 19: A nine-day Allied offensive takes out key German infrastructure.

Volgograd (Stalingrad), USSR, October: German aerial attacks kill thousands of civilians and destroy 80 per cent of the city's livable area.

Papua New Guinea, November 2: Australian troops take Kokoda after surviving horrific conditions of steep inclines, mud, and malaria while fighting on the Kokoda Trail.

Morocco and Algeria, North Africa, November 8: A major Allied invasion of North Africa, Operation Torch, is launched.

Guadalcanal, Solomon Islands, November 15: US Marines make important gains in securing the strategicaly important island of Guadalcanal from Japan.

1944

Berlin, Germany, January 21: Allied bombing leaves the city in ruins.

Italy, January 22: Allied troops make a surprise invasion south of Rome.

St Petersburg (Leningrad), USSR, January 27: The Siege of Leningrad is fully lifted; over 640,000 people died during the 900 days of the siege.

USSR, February 1: A new USSR constitution allows Soviet republics to conduct their own armies and negotiations.

Hungary, March 23: A German puppet government is created in Hungary after German occupation on March 22.

Rome, June 4: Rome is freed by Allied forces.

France, June 6: Allied forces storm Normandy on the French coast.

Japan, June 15: The USA begins heavily bombing Kyushu.

Iceland, June 17: Iceland breaks free of Danish rule, becoming a republic.

France, June 27: Allied forces capture the port of Cherbourg.

East Prussia, July 20: An attempt by a number of German military officers to assassinate Hitler fails.

USSR, July 24: Soviet forces capture the strategic city of Pskov, almost entirely destroying it.

India, August 11: An advance by Allied troops forces the Japanese to retreat to Burma.

Paris, France, August 23: Citizens and underground resistance assist Allied forces in taking Paris.

Bucharest, Romania, August 31: Soviet forces occupy Bucharest, six days after Romania declared war against Germany, taking control of German oil supplies.

France, September: Charles de Gaulle becomes president of the provisional government.

Belgium, September 4: British forces take Brussels.

London, England, September 9: The city is again under German attack, this time from the new silent V-2 bombs.

Greece, October 14: British forces retake Athens, freeing it after four years of German occupation.

Leyte Gulf, Philippines, October 20: Allied forces tackle Japanese forces occupying the Philippines, in what is known as the Battle of Leyte Gulf.

Belgium, December 16: German forces make a surprise attack, known as the Ardennes Offensive, to penetrate the Allied front in Belgium.

1946

London, England, January 30: The first meeting of the United Nations General Assembly is held.

Fulton, Missouri, USA, March 5: Winston Churchill makes a speech, "Sinews of Peace," warning the Western powers of the dangers of Soviet expansion and referring for the first time to an "iron curtain" descending across Europe.

Paris, France, March 6: France recognizes the Democratic Republic of Vietnam.

USA, March 20: The last Japanese-American internment camps are closed.

Australia, April 11: The War Crimes Commission reports that Japan routinely committed acts of torture on Australian prisoners of war.

Geneva, Switzerland, April 18: The League of Nations is officially dissolved.

San Francisco, USA, May 2–4: Nine guards are taken hostage by inmates at Alcatraz prison; five people are killed.

Canada, May 14: The Canadian Citizenship Act is passed, recognizing a separate Canadian (rather than British) citizenship for the first time.

Italy, June 3: Italy abolishes its monarchy after a referendum and becomes a republic.

Argentina, June 4: Juan Perón is inaugurated as Argentina's first president.

Germany, June–September: One hundred thousand Jews have left Poland for displaced persons camps in Germany.

Marshall Islands, July 1: The USA tests a 20,000-ton atomic bomb at Bikini Atoll.

Philippines, July 4: The nation gains independence from the USA, and becomes known as the Republic of the Philippines.

India, August 19: Up to 4,000 Muslims and Hindus die during days of religious riots in Calcutta.

Nuremberg, Germany, October 1: The international war crime tribunal finds 22 Nazi leaders guilty of war crimes.

Washington DC, USA, November 5: John F. Kennedy is elected to the House of Representatives.

Indochina, December 19: The Communist leader Ho Chi Minh attacks the French in Hanoi, prompting the beginning of a new war.

USA, December: This year has seen the country's worst work stoppages since 1919. Those suffering the most are the coal, electric, and steel industries.

1948

Burma, January 4: At 4.20 a.m. Burma is granted independence by Britain. Astrologers choose this auspicious timing.

Indonesia, January 17: The Renville Truce Agreement is signed by UN representatives, proposing a truce between the Netherlands and the Republic of Indonesia along the Van Mook Line.

New Delhi, India, January 30: Mahatma Gandhi is assassinated by Nathuram Godse, a fanatical Hindu.

Sri Lanka (Ceylon), February 4: Ceylon is granted independence.

Prague, Czechoslovakia, February 27: The Communist Party of Czechoslovakia seizes full power in a coup; democratic politicians are taken prisoner.

Bogotá, Colombia, April 30: The Organization of American States Charter is signed by 35 independent American nations.

Tel Aviv, Israel, May 14: Jews proclaim the Nation of Israel.

South Africa, May 26: The election victory of the Afrikaner National Party is quickly followed by new apartheid laws.

London, England, June 10: A surgeon at Guy's Hospital performs the first open-heart surgery.

Berlin, Germany, June 26: A Soviet blockade prompts Allied forces to start a massive airlift of supplies.

USSR, June 28: Yugoslavia's Communist Party is thrown out of the Cominform in retaliation for Marshal Tito's defiance of Stalin's leadership.

Washington DC, USA, July 26: US President Truman signs Executive Order 9981, ending racial segregation in the US military.

London, England, July 29: King George VI today opens the first Olympic Games since 1936.

Korea, August 15: Following an election supervized by the United Nations, the Independent Republic of Korea is proclaimed.

New Zealand, September 6: The British Nationality and New Zealand Citizenship Act is passed; most people born in New Zealand and naturalized immigrants are now New Zealand, rather than British, citizens.

North Korea, September 9: Kim Il-sung proclaims North Korea a republic, and becomes its first president. As head of the Korean Communist Party, Kim Il-sung has close ties with the Soviets, who helped him into power after he led the resistance against the Japanese.

Tokyo, Japan, December 23: The Japanese Prime Minister, General Tojo Hideki, nicknamed "The Razor," is hanged after being found guilty of war crimes on November 12. Six other Japanese wartime leaders are also executed.

1943

Tripoli, Libya, January 23: British forces capture Tripoli.

North Africa, January 24: Churchill and Roosevelt hold a conference in Casablanca to plan an offensive aimed at achieving the "unconditional surrender" of the Axis powers.

Volgograd (Stalingrad), USSR, February 2: Axis troops surrender to the Red Army.

Featherston, New Zealand, February 25: Japanese POWs in Featherston camp riot; 48 POWs and one New Zealand guard are killed.

Bismark Sea, March 4: Allied forces sink 22 Japanese ships.

Moscow, USSR, May 23: The Third International has been dissolved, allowing communist powers in other countries to be autonomous of Soviet rule.

France, July 8: French Resistance leader Jean Moulin is killed while being tortured by the Gestapo.

Italy, July 10: Allied forces enter Sicily.

Italy, July 25: Premier Benito Mussolini is ousted. A new government under Marshal Pietro Badoglio places him under arrest.

Italy, July 28: Badoglio declares Italy is no longer a fascist state. He may have started secretly negotiating with Allied forces.

Italy, August 17: Allies occupy Sicily. With North Africa, this gives them control of the Mediterranean Sea.

Italy, September 11: Germany occupies northern Italy.

Corsica, September 11: Free French troops occupy the island of Corsica.

Italy, September 12: Italy surrenders unconditionally to the Allied forces.

China, September 13: General Chiang Kai-shek is elected President of the Republic of China.

Siam, October: The rail link between Burma and Siam is completed.

Italy, October 13: Badoglio declares war on Germany.

Italy, October 14: Allied forces take control of southern Italy.

Lebanon, November 22: France grants Lebanon independence.

Cairo, Egypt, December 1-4: The USA, Britain, and China sign the Cairo Declaration, a joint plan to force Japan to surrender.

USSR, December 31: Soviet troops force the Axis powers to retreat from the central area of the Eastern Front in Belarus (White Russia).

1945

Poland, January 27: Soviet forces seize a concentration camp at Auschwitz to find 5,000 starving prisoners left near death, the remainder having already been herded out.

USSR, February 12: At a conference in Yalta, Roosevelt, Churchill, and Stalin finalize their plans for the defeat of Germany.

Germany, February 14: The city of Dresden lies in ruins after massive bombing by Allied forces.

Warm Springs, Georgia, USA, April 12: President Roosevelt dies. Harold S. Truman is sworn in as US President.

San Francisco, USA, April 25: Heads of government meet to establish the United Nations, the organization that is to replace the League of Nations.

Milan, Italy, April 28: Mussolini and his mistress Clara Petacci are strung up for public display after being shot dead.

Germany, April: Allied forces discover dens of horror in the Nazi concentration camps, finding starved, critically ill captives and grounds piled with rotting corpses.

Berlin, April 30: Hitler suicides in his bunker by shooting himself. His newly wed wife, Eva Braun, poisons herself and dies.

Reims, France, May 7: Germany signs its surrender after the foreign minister gives notice in a radio broadcast.

London, England, May 8: Crowds of spectators jam London's streets to hear Churchill's broadcast announcing the war in Europe will end at midnight. Around 50,000 gleeful revellers take to the streets, singing, dancing, and embracing.

Japan, June 21: American troops take Okinawa after two months of intense fighting.

New Mexico, USA, July 16: The first atomic bomb is tested in the desert near Alamogordo.

London, England, July 26: Churchill loses the British election to Clement Attlee, who wins a massive landslide victory.

Japan, August 6-9: The United States drops atomic bombs on Hiroshima and Nagasaki.

Japan, August 15: Japan signs an unconditional surrender to the Allied powers.

Nuremberg, Germany, November 20: Hitler's collaborators stand trial for war crimes.

1947

Paris, France, February 10: Peace treaties for Italy, Finland, Hungary, Romania, and Bulgaria are signed.

Germany, February 20: The state of Prussia is abolished to become part of the newly formed Federal Republic of Germany and German Democratic Republic.

USA, March 12: The Truman Doctrine proposes containment of communist expansion and aiding Greece and Turkey in resisting communist forces.

Jerusalem, March-May: A Bedouin shepherd find mysterious religious scrolls in Qumran on the Dead Sea.

London, England, May 23: Britain agrees to the plan proposed by Lord Mountbatten, the Viceroy of India, to divide India into two states—one for Muslims and one for Hindus.

China, July 1: General Chiang Kai-shek mobilizes his troops across the country to fight the communists.

Roswell, New Mexico, USA, July 9: The US military announces that the flying object reported crashing in the desert on July 2 was a weather balloon. The site is cordoned off.

New Zealand, July 10: The government decrees that official correspondence will replace the word "native" with "Maori."

Paris, France, July 11-13: Europe's foreign ministers meet to draw up a plan for European post-war recovery.

Haifa, Palestine, July 18: The *Exodus*, a ship loaded with nearly 4,500 Jewish Holocaust survivors, is refused refugee status by the UK.

India, August 15: The newly formed countries Pakistan and India gain independence after 163 years under British rule.

Amsterdam, Netherlands, June: Newspapers review the published diary of a Jewish girl, Anne Frank.

New Zealand, August 23: The first post-war assisted migrants arrive on New Zealand shores.

Hungary, September 1: The communists win the election.

Amritsar, India, September 24: India's violence explodes when 1,200 Muslim refugees heading for Pakistan are slaughtered.

India, October 22: Tribal forces in Pakistan invade the Indian border state of Kashmir.

London, England, November 20: Princess Elizabeth and Lieutenant Philip Mountbatten marry.

1949

Rhodes, Greece, January 13: Negotiations on armistice agreements between Israel and Egypt, Jordan, Lebanon, and Syria have commenced.

USA, January 20: President Truman proposes the Point Four program, a plan to help the world's developing nations.

China, January 22: Chiang Kai-shek announces his retirement after the communist takeover of Peking.

Rhodes, Greece, February 24: Israel finally signs an armistice with Egypt after many weeks of difficult talks.

Washington DC, USA, April 4: The North Atlantic Treaty Organization treaty was signed today by 12 nations, forging a new peace alliance designed to deter aggressors.

Ireland, April 18: The Republic of Ireland Bill comes into force today, officially making Eire a republic.

Israel, May 11: Israel has become the 59th member of the United Nations.

Berlin, Germany, May 12: The blockade has ended after successful United Nations negotiations; cheered on by large crowds, cars are finally making their way into the city.

Germany, May 23: The western part of Germany has been formally established as the Federal Republic of Germany. The eastern zone remains occupied by Soviets.

Ecuador, August 5: An earthquake measuring 6.75 on the Richter scale has killed more than 6,000 people and destroyed at least 50 towns.

USSR, August 29: The Soviets have successfully tested their first atomic bomb at Semipalatinsk.

New Jersey, USA, September 5: A war veteran kills 13 neighbors in a single shooting.

London, England, September 18: The pound sterling has been devalued by a massive 30 percent.

China, October 1: Mao Tse-tung officially proclaims the establishment of the Communist People's Republic of China. The USSR officially recognizes the regime.

Germany, October 7: The eastern part of Germany has become the German Democratic Republic under Soviet rule.

Greece, October 16: The civil war ends after communist troops surrender.

Korea, December 15: A typhoon strikes the coast, leaving several thousand dead.

Indonesia, December 27: Indonesia becomes a united country after settling its conflict with the Dutch.

1950

Israel, January 23: A resolution is approved by the Israeli Knesset proclaiming Jerusalem the capital of Israel.

India, January 26: India becomes a republic and is no longer under British dominion. Dr Rajendra Prasad, the new president, is sworn in.

USA, January 31: President Truman puts through an order to rapidly develop the hydrogen bomb.

Moscow, USSR, February 15: Joseph Stalin and Mao Tse-tung sign a defense treaty.

USSR, March 8: The Soviets announce they have developed their own atomic bomb.

USA, March 30: President Truman denounces Senator Joseph McCarthy as sabotaging US foreign policy; McCarthy claimed in February he had a list of 205 communists among government employees.

Jordan, April 24: King Abdullah of Jordan annexes the West Bank, offering citizenship to Palestinians.

South Africa, April 27: The *Group Areas Act* comes into effect today, formally segregating blacks from whites.

Korea, June 25: War breaks out after North Korean communists invade South Korea.

USA, June 30: President Truman calls up reserve units to aid South Korea in their fight against the North Koreans.

London, England, July 26: The United Kingdom announces it is sending troops into Korea. Other US allies, Australia and New Zealand, announce that they will do likewise.

Calcutta, October 26: A nun, Mother Theresa, establishes the Missionaries of Charity. This global order of nuns will care for the poorest of the poor in India.

Ethiopia (Eritrea), November 25: The United Nations hands over Eritrea to Ethiopia.

North Korea, November 28: China joins forces with the North Koreans in the Korean War.

USA, November 30: President Truman affirms that the US is giving "active consideration" to the use of atomic bombs in Korea.

New Zealand, December 11: The New Zealand volunteer army unit "Kayforce" embarks for Korea.

Tibet, December 19: The Dalai Lama flees Chinese-occupied Tibet following the invasion of his country on October 21.

1952

Cairo, Egypt, January 26: After an attack by British troops on the police barracks at Ismailiya on January 25, riots break out as Egyptian police stage protests at the death of 50 of their colleagues.

Sandringham, England, February 6: George VI dies in his sleep after succumbing to lung cancer. His 25-year-old daughter, on safari in Kenya, accedes the throne as Elizabeth II.

Vietnam, April 26: France decides to ask the United Nations for aid in Vietnam if China becomes involved in its conflict against the Viet Minh.

North Korea, May 8: Allied forces destroy the city of Suan in a massive air raid.

USSR, May 31: The Volga-Don Canal opens, connecting the Black, Azov, and Caspian Seas.

East Germany, June 1: East Germany closes access to West Germany from midnight. Only permit holders may enter.

Argentina, July 26: President Juan Perón's wife, Eva "Evita" Perón, dies aged 33.

Cairo, Egypt, July 26: King Farouk I abdicates following a military coup by General Gamal Abdel Nasser's Free Officers, a nationalist group.

Helsinki, Finland, August 3: The Games of the XVth Olympiad end, with track events dominated by the Czech sprinter Emil Zatopek, who broke several records.

Australia, October 3: The UK's atomic bomb is tested in the remote Monte Bello Islands off the northwest coast of Western Australia.

California, USA, October 11: Researchers announce the discovery of a polio vaccine that is suitable for large-scale manufacture.

Washington DC, USA, November 5: Dwight D. Eisenhower is elected the 34th president of the USA, the first Republican president in 20 years. Richard Nixon is vice-president.

Eniwetok Island, Pacific Ocean, November 6: The USA explodes its first hydrogen bomb on a Pacific island, blasting it apart.

Kenya, November 8: Jomo Kenyatta, a prominent Kenyan nationalist leader, is among hundreds of people rounded up as suspects in the Mau Mau terrorist uprising over the last few weeks in which more than 40 people were murdered.

London, England, December 31: Thousands of people die in the last month from inhaling the fumes of the city's toxic smog.

1954

Berlin, Germany, January 31: Free elections in a reunited Germany are discussed at the Four Power Foreign Ministers' conference. The proposal is rejected.

UK, February 12: A report by the British Standing Committee on cancer says cigarette smoking is directly linked to lung cancer.

Marshall Islands, March 22: Japanese fishermen have severe radiation sickness after exposure to the fallout from the US hydrogen bomb test at Bikini Atoll on March 1.

USSR, March 25: The Soviet Union grants sovereignty to East Germany.

USA, May 2: Walt Disney announces his plan to build Disneyland, a massive theme park of a type never seen before, in California.

Oxford, England, May 6: A medical student, Roger Bannister, runs a mile in under four minutes at the Iffley Road Sports Ground.

Vietnam, May 8: After 55 days of bloody battle, the French military outpost Dien Bien Phu falls to the Vietminh.

USA, May 17: The Supreme Court deems racial segregation in public schools unlawful in the landmark case of Brown v. Board of Education of Topeka (No. 1).

New Guinea, June 10: A hitherto unknown tribe of 100,000 people has been found.

Geneva, Switzerland, July 20: War in Indo-China ends with the signing of the Geneva Accords.

Christchurch, New Zealand, August 28: Two NZ teenage girls are found guilty of murdering the mother of one of them in a brutal bashing.

Manila, Phillipines, September 8: The Southeast Asia Treaty Organization (SEATO) is established. Signatories to the treaty are France, Australia, New Zealand, Pakistan, Phillipines, Thailand, the UK, and the USA.

Algeria, September 9: A series of earthquakes in Orleansville claims 1,460 lives.

USA, October 7: Marilyn Monroe and Joe DiMaggio are divorced, just nine months after their marriage in San Francisco.

Egypt, October 19: Egypt and Britain agree to terms over the Suez Canal.

Algeria, November 1: NLF guerillas launch a full-scale attack on significant infrastructure in a fight for its independence from France.

New York, USA, November 12: The immigration center on Ellis Island closes today.

Washington DC, USA, December 2: Senator Joseph McCarthy is condemned by the US Congress for misconduct.

1956

Cyprus, January 12: British troops are sent to quell the rising tension between Greeks and Turks.

Melbourne, Australia, January 12: A survey reveals that the lung disease asbestosis is affecting one-third of all Victoria's miners.

USSR, February 24: Nikita Khrushchev, the First Secretary, speaks out against Stalin's excesses.

Karachi, Pakistan, March 23: Pakistan is declared an Islamic Republic.

Monaco, April 19: Actress Grace Kelly marries Prince Rainier III of Monaco.

Poznan, Poland, June 29: Workers stage an uprising against communist rule, only to be crushed when police open fire; tanks and machine guns are used to control crowds.

London, England, July 5: The Clean Air Bill is passed today in a bid to remove the threat of the city's toxic "pea soup" smogs.

Alexandria, Egypt, July 26: Egypt takes control of the Suez Canal just two weeks after the last British troops leave, nationalizing the Suez Canal Company which controls the canal.

Hungary, October 23: Hungarians begin a nationwide rebellion against communism, demanding freedom from Soviet rule.

Budapest, Hungary, October 25: Armed with 500 tanks, the Soviets open fire with machine guns on men, women and children, with estimates of up to 3,000 killed.

Egypt, October 29: Israel invades Egypt, entering via the Sinai Peninsula and heading toward the Suez Canal.

Cairo, Egypt, October 31: French and British forces bomb military airfields after a 12-hour ultimatum to Egypt and Israel to withdraw is ignored.

Budapest, Hungary, November 4: Soviet troops take Budapest.

Egypt, November 6: The UN Security Council imposes sanctions against the UK, over yesterday's invasion by the UK and France of Port Said in the Suez Canal.

Egypt, November 8: The UN imposes a cease-fire in the Suez Canal which will take effect at midnight.

Melbourne, Australia, November 22: The Games of the XVIth Olympiad begin today.

1951

Bermuda, January 8: An animal believed extinct since 1615, an ocean bird called the cahow, is found alive on an islet.
Washington DC, USA, January 15: The US Supreme Court rules that an incitement to riot is a cause for arrest.
New Guinea, January 17: Over 3,000 people are killed following the volcanic eruption of Mt Lamington.
USSR, February 16: Stalin accuses the United Nations of inciting war.

USA, February 17: The FBI's J. Edgar Hoover begins an unauthorized program to flush out employees suspected of having communist interests.
USA, February 26: A constitutional amendment is enacted that limits a US president to two terms of office.
USA, March 30: General MacArthur, commander of the UN forces in Korea, aims to take the war into China.
New York, USA, April 5: Julius and Ethel Rosenberg are found guilty of espionage and sentenced to death.

USA, April 19: General Douglas MacArthur bids farewell to US Congress after President Truman relieves him of his command.
Tibet, May 23: The Dalai Lama's delegation to Beijing is forced to agree to the incorporation of Tibet into China.
Mozambique, June 11: The country of Mozambique becomes a province overseen by Portugal.
South Africa, June 18: Black people and those of mixed racial heritage are denied the right to vote.

Jerusalem, Israel, July 20: King Abdullah Ibn Hussein of Jordan is assassinated by a Palestinian extremist; his 15-year-old son witnesses the murder.
Manchuria, August 6: Massive floods following a typhoon kill 4,800 people.
San Francisco, USA, September 1: The USA, Australia, and New Zealand make a joint security alliance, the ANZUS Pact.
San Francisco, USA, September 8: Forty-nine nations sign a peace treaty with Japan.

California, USA, October 24: Doctor Albert Bellamy, head of Radiological Services, assures residents that the test explosions of the hydrogen bomb near Las Vegas in May will cause no ill effects.
London, England, October 25: Winston Churchill becomes Prime Minister again after winning the general election against the Labour Party.
Egypt, November 18: British troops occupy Ismailiya.

1953

Yugoslavia, January 14: Josip Tito is elected President of Yugoslavia.
Netherlands, February 3: A massive storm breaches sea dikes in the south; more than 1,800 people are believed dead in the Netherlands and a further 307 in the UK.
USSR, March 5: Soviet dictator Joseph Stalin dies from a brain hemorrhage, aged 73, after ruling for 29 years. His is succeeded by his deputy, Georgy Malenkov.

Kenya, April 8: Jomo Kenyatta and five others are sentenced to jail for seven years for orchestrating the Mau Mau terrorist uprising against white settlers.
Vevey, Switzerland, April 17: Charlie Chaplin vows to never return home to the USA after being banned last year on suspicion of communism.
Nepal, May 29: New Zealander Edmund Hillary and Tenzing Norgay of Nepal reach Mt Everest's summit.
London, England, June 2: Queen Elizabeth II's coronation takes place in Westminster Abbey.

Washington DC, USA, June 8: Restaurants in the capital are not allowed to refuse service to blacks by Supreme Court ruling.
East Berlin, June 17: Tanks were brought in to quell an uprising against Communism.
Cairo, Egypt, June 18: Egypt becomes a military-ruled republic, led by general Muhammad Neguib.
London, England, July 2: It is announced that Edmund Hillary and Sherpa Tenzing Norgay have reached the top of Mt Everest.

Canada, June-November: A severe polio epidemic strikes Canada, with around 9,000 cases and 500 deaths resulting from the disease.
Moncada, Cuba, July 26: The leader of a rebel communist group, Fidel Castro, is jailed.
Panmunjeom, North Korea, July 27: An armistice signed by the United Nations, Korea, and China ends three years of war.
Greece, August 14: A recent earthquake and consequent tsunamis in the Ionian Islands kill 1,000 people and leave at least 100,000 homeless.

Iran, August 22: The exiled Shah is restored to power following General Zahedi's bloody military coup, which ousted Prime Minister Mossadegh and left 300 dead.
Japan, September 27: A massive typhoon destroys a large part of the city of Nagoya.
Tangiwai, New Zealand, December 24: A railway bridge collapses, causing a night express train to plunge into the flooded Whangaehu River. Of the 285 people on board, 151 are killed.

1955

Alice Springs, Australia, January 15: Renowned Aboriginal artist Albert Namatjira is refused permission to build a house on his own land among whites.
USA, January 17: The first nuclear-powered submarine, USS *Nautilus*, embarks on its maiden voyage to Puerto Rico.
Johannesburg, South Africa, February 9: Police forcibly evict 65,000 black Africans, razing their homes and forcibly resettling them in new black townships.

London, England, April 5: Aged 80, the frail Prime Minister Winston Churchill today announces his resignation, with Anthony Eden to succeed him.
West Germany, May 5: West Germany reverts to its pre-war sovereign state.
Warsaw, Poland, May 14: The Warsaw Pact, a mutual defense agreement between Eastern European nations, is signed.

USA, July 15: Led by Bertrand Russell, 11 eminent scientists and thinkers send world leaders a plea to renounce war as nuclear weapons threaten the existence of human-kind. The so-called "Russell–Einstein Manifesto" is signed by Albert Einstein, who had died on April 18.
New Zealand, August 2: All publications containing sex or violence are burned by publishers following raids.

Argentina, September 19: President Juan Perón is ousted and hides out in a gunboat in Buenos Aires Harbor.
Austria, October 25: Austria regains its sovereignty after the last Allied forces depart.
South Vietnam, October 26: Ngo Dinh Diem proclaims South Vietnam a republic with himself as president.
USA, October-November: Jesse Owens tours India, Singapore, Malaya, and the Phillipines after President Eisenhower names him "Ambassador of Sports."

Israel, November 2: David Ben-Gurion forms a new government and becomes prime minister of Israel, having returned to politics earlier this year.
Alabama, USA, December 1: Rosa Parks is arrested in Montgomery for refusing a bus driver's order to give up her seat to a white man.
Alabama, USA, December 5: Martin Luther King Jr leads a boycott of Montgomery buses to protest racial segregation on public transport.

1957

London, England, January 10: Prime Minister Anthony Eden resigns due to ill health. His deputy Harold Macmillan takes his place.
West Africa, March 6: The Gold Coast and Togoland become Ghana, gaining independence from Britain.
Egypt, March 8: Minor ships are allowed entry into the Suez Canal as Israeli troops leave Egypt, but President Nasser bars the UN's toll-sharing plan.

Gaza, March 11: The USA sends a warning to Egypt, reconfirming Gaza is under the control of the United Nations, after President Nasser claimed Gaza on March 10.
Egypt, March 15: President Nasser bars Israeli ships from entering the Suez Canal.
Rome, Italy, March 25: The Treaty of Rome is signed by France, West Germany, Italy, Belgium, the Netherlands and Luxembourg to create the European Economic Community (EEC).

Egypt, April 10: The Suez Canal re-opens to all shipping.
Jordan, April 25: King Hussein declares martial law in the aftermath of a failed coup earlier this month.
Tunisia, July 25: Tunisia abolishes its monarchy to become a republic.

Arkansas, USA, September 24: The president calls in troops to quell mobs preventing integration of black students into Little Rock Central High School.
USSR, October 4: The space age begins as the USSR launches *Sputnik I*, the first satellite to orbit Earth.
Australia, October 13: New South Wales and Queensland are faring worst in the grip of a devastating national drought.

USSR, November 3: The Soviets launch *Sputnik II*, carrying a dog called Laika. It is the first craft to take an animal into space.
Sydney, Australia, December 2: The city is ringed by bushfires, driven by gale-force winds.
Oslo, Norway, December 10: The Nobel Peace Prize is awarded to Canadian politician Lester Bowles Pearson for his role in using peacekeeping forces to resolve the highly volatile Suez Canal crisis.

1958

Antarctica, January 3: Edmund Hillary reaches the South Pole.

London, England, January 3: The creation of the West Indies Federation, with Lord Hailes as governor-general, is announced. It includes Barbados, Jamaica, Trinidad, Tobago, and the Windward and Leeward Islands.

New York, January 15: Over 11,000 scientists from 49 countries petition to ban nuclear testing.

Middle East, February 1: Syria and Egypt merge to form the United Arab Republic.

Antarctica, March 2: The Commonwealth Transantarctic Expedition is successfully completed.

Yemen, March 2: Yemen announces it will join the United Arab Republic.

USA, March 27: CBS Laboratories today announce the development of stereophonic records, which require two loudspeakers and provide a superior sound.

Algiers, May 13: A mass demonstration of 40,000 French settlers rebelling against the Algerian nationalists creates a political crisis for France.

China, May 23: To update China's economy, Mao Tse-tung begins his "Great Leap Forward."

Algiers, June 4: General de Gaulle, recalled as premier, attempts to convince French rebels that reconciliation is essential to Algeria's future.

Hungary, June 16: Former prime minister Imre Nagy is executed, along with other leaders of a "free" Hungary.

Alaska, July 10: The largest known tsunami rises 1,600 feet (500 meters) up a mountain, caused by an earthquake and rock fall.

Middle East, July 17: Britain sends 2,000 paratroopers to Jordan, two days after the USA dispatches 1,700 marines to Lebanon.

Honshu, Japan, September 27: Typhoon Vera kills almost 5,000 and leaves thousands more injured on the island of Honshu. It is the worst human disaster in Japan since World War II.

Vatican City, Italy, October 28: After 12 ballots, Angelo Giuseppe Roncalli has been elected as Pope John XXIII after the death of Pope Pius XII.

USSR, October 31: Boris Pasternak, the author of *Doctor Zhivago*, refuses his Nobel Prize in Literature after his expulsion from the Union of Soviet Writers.

Africa, November: The French-ruled African countries of Mali, Mauritania, Congo, Chad, and Gabon are made republics this month.

1960

Algiers, Algeria, January 29: France teeters on the brink of civil war as the European inhabitants of Algiers protest the French government's self-determination policy for the North African colony.

Cape Town, South Africa, February 3: British PM Harold Macmillan delivers his "winds of change" speech to the South African parliament, stating "whether we like it or not, this growth of national consciousness is a political fact."

Agadir, Morocco, February 29: 12,000 people die as an earthquake hits the seaside town.

Sharpeville, South Africa, March 21: Police open fire on anti-apartheid protesters, killing 69 and injuring hundreds.

Brasília, Brazil, April 21: The new capital city is inaugurated. The country's administration moves wholesale from Rio de Janeiro.

Seoul, South Korea, April 28: President Syngman Rhee resigns and flees the country following violent protests over recent election results.

Moscow, USSR, May 17: Soviet leader Nikita Khrushchev demands an apology following the downing of an American U-2 spy plane by a Russian missile two weeks ago.

Tel Aviv, Israel, May 21: Nazi war criminal Adolf Eichmann is captured by Mossad agents in Argentina and returned to Israel for trial.

Leopoldville, Congo, June 30: Premier Lumumba declares the Congo's independence from 75 years of Belgian rule. Mali, British Somaliland, and Madagascar have all become self-governing this month.

Congo, July 15: Civil war breaks out as the mineral-rich province of Katanga declares independence.

Colombo, Ceylon, July 20: Sirimavo Bandaranaike becomes the world's first female prime minister.

Cuba, August 7: Fidel Castro nationalizes all American property on the Caribbean island.

Nicosia, Cyprus, August 16: Cyprus gains independence from Britain, ending four years of violence between Turkish, Greek, and British factions.

New York, USA, October 12: Soviet leader Nikita Khrushchev displays undiplomatic behavior at the UN General Assembly, banging his shoe on the desk and interjecting when the Philippines delegate accuses the USSR of implementing imperialist policy in Eastern Europe.

USA, November 9: John F. Kennedy is elected president of the USA, defeating Richard Nixon by a slim margin.

1962

Ranrahirca, Peru, January 11: Whole villages are destroyed and 4,000 people perish in a massive landslide of rocks and ice.

Paris, France, February 8: The Secret Army Organization (OAS), campaigning against Algerian independence, is responsible for a wave of bomb blasts. Anti-OAS demonstrations leave eight dead.

Berlin, Germany, February 10: American U-2 spy plane pilot Gary Powers is released after 21 months in prison, in exchange for Soviet spy Colonel Rudolf Abel.

Algiers, Algeria, April 20: Head of the OAS, General Raoul Salan, is captured, ending the anti-colonial uprising in Algeria and France.

Ramla, Israel, May 31: Former SS commander Adolf Eichmann is executed by hanging.

Laos, May: US troops are deployed to fight the communist group Pathet Lao which captured Nam Tha.

Algeria, July 3: Two days after the Algerian people voted in a referendum on independence, French President de Gaulle severs 132 years of colonial ties.

Jamaica, August 6: Jamaica becomes independent within the British Commonwealth; Alexander Bustamente of the Jamaica Labour Party is the first prime minister.

New York, USA, August 15: The Netherlands signs the New York Agreement, agreeing to cede West New Guinea to Indonesia.

Berlin, Germany, August 17: Eighteen-year-old East German Peter Fechter is the first person to be shot and killed while attempting to cross the Berlin Wall to the West.

Houston, USA, September 12: At Rice University, President Kennedy declares that the US will regain the lead in the "space race" and put a man on the moon by the end of the decade.

Oxford, Mississippi, USA, October 1: Three die and 50 are injured as riots break out at the University of Mississippi after the first African-American is admitted as a student.

India, October 26: Indian and Chinese troops are engaged in heavy fighting over the disputed border region of Arunachal Pradesh.

Cuba, October 28: Seven days of escalating tension bring the world to the brink of nuclear confrontation before the USA and USSR reach a compromise.

New York, USA, November 6: The United Nations officially condemns South Africa's policy of apartheid.

Massawa, Eritrea (Ethiopia), December 19: A group of police desert the Ethiopian force to join the Eritrean Liberation Front, formed in 1961 in response to Ethiopia's annexation (with the UN's blessing) of the strategically important nation.

1964

Jerusalem, Israel, January 5: Pope Paul VI makes a visit to the Holy Land, meeting the Patriarch of the Greek Orthodox Church—the first such meeting for over 500 years.

Calcutta, India, January 13: Over 100 people are killed in rioting between Hindus and Muslims.

Tasman Sea, Australia, February 10: HMAS *Melbourne* collides with HMAS *Voyager*, killing 82.

Chattanooga, USA, March 12: Jimmy Hoffa, president of the powerful Teamsters Union, is sentenced to eight years in jail for jury tampering.

Rhodesia, April 13: Ian Smith is elected prime minister, vowing to keep the black majority from participating in elections.

Lima, Peru, May 24: A riot at a soccer match between Peru and Argentina leaves 318 people dead and 500 injured.

Jerusalem, Israel, June 2: The Palestine Liberation Organization (PLO) is founded, after the first Arab League summit in January had laid the groundwork.

Port Moresby, Papua New Guinea, June 8: The first House of Assembly opens. It is a major constitutional step—the country has been administered by Australia since the 1920s.

Pretoria, South Africa, June 12: Nelson Mandela and seven other African National Congress activists are given life sentences for sabotage.

New Delhi, India, June 13: One and a half million people line the route of the funeral of Prime Minister and independence hero Jawaharlal Nehru. He had led the country since independence from Britain in 1947.

Washington DC, USA, July 2: President Lyndon Johnson continues Kennedy's reforming mandate, signing the new Civil Rights Act prohibiting racial discrimination.

Mississippi, USA, August 4: The bodies of three civil rights activists are found six weeks after their disappearance.

Washington DC, USA, August 7: The Senate gives the government increased authority to retaliate against North Vietnamese communists after attacks on the US Navy in the Gulf of Tonkin.

Labis, Malaysia, September 3: Indonesian paratroopers land over the island of Borneo, after two years of conflict between the two countries. New Zealand, Britain, and Australia have pledged assistance to the Malaysians.

Moscow, USSR, October 15: Flamboyant premier Nikita Khrushchev resigns unexpectedly, citing ill health. His replacement is Leonid Brezhnev.

Kenya, November 10: Kenya becomes a republic under the leadership of Jomo Kenyatta.

1959

Cuba, January 2: Revolution leader Fidel Castro has seized power as president. Incumbent General Fulgencio Batista resigns and flees to the Dominican Republic.

Alaska, USA, January 3: Alaska is admitted as the 49th state of the USA, with Juneau as its capital.

USSR, January 12: The space race heats up as the USSR's *Lunik* goes into orbit around the moon. It is the first craft to leave Earth's gravitational field.

Cyprus, February 19: Cyprus gains independence in an agreement signed by Britain, Turkey and Greece.

Zimbabwe (Rhodesia), February 27: A state of emergency is declared as violent outbreaks are feared.

Washington DC, USA, March 3: Approval is granted for Hawaii to become the 50th US state.

Tibet, March 31: The Dalai Lama flees to India following a national uprising against China. The Chinese arrest and kill thousands of rebels and install a harsh government.

North America, April 25: The St Lawrence Seaway is completed, enabling ships to sail from the Atlantic Ocean to the Great Lakes.

Rome, Italy, May 10: Italian archeologists find the remnants of Emperor Nero's gardens.

London, England, May 24: The UK and the USSR sign a five-year trade pact.

Atlantic Ocean, May 28: Able and Baker are the first animals to return from space, as the spacecraft with the two live monkeys on board splashes down.

Singapore, June 3: Lee Kuan Yew is sworn in as the first prime minister of Singapore, after winning the national elections. The country becomes a self-governing state in the British Commonwealth.

London, England, June 11: A new kind of vehicle that goes on both land and sea, the hovercraft, is revealed today.

Olduvai Gorge, Tanzania, July 17: Dr Mary Leakey discovers the oldest hominid skull. "Nutcracker Man" dates back at least 1.8 million years.

Colombo, Sri Lanka (Ceylon), September 26: Prime minister Solomon Bandaranaike dies in hospital after being shot at point blank range the previous day. His assassin is a Buddhist monk, Talduwe Somarama.

Aswan, Egypt, October 31: Contracts to build the Aswan Dam, which will be one of the world's largest reservoirs, are signed by the USSR and Egypt.

1961

Katanga, Congo, January 18: After less than one year as prime minister in the newly independent nation, Patrice Lumumba is assassinated. He was arrested in December, indicted over the deaths of 1,000 people.

Laos, March 21: The newly inaugurated US President Kennedy vows to support Laos to overthrow communist rebel forces, the Pathet Lao, sending additional troops to train the Laotian army.

South Vietnam, April 10: Staunch anti-communist President Ngo Dinh Diem is re-elected. His Catholic faith, nepotism, and authoritarian rule have made him unpopular with the mostly Buddhist population.

Cuba, April 19: The Bay of Pigs invasion by 1,400 US-backed Cuban exiles hoping to overthrow the Castro regime is repeled with over 100 killed, sparking a major diplomatic incident with the USA.

Havana, Cuba, May 1: Fidel Castro proclaims Cuba a socialist country.

Dominican Republic, May 30: After a 31-year rule, ruthless dictator General Trujillo is assassinated with the assistance of the CIA.

Montgomery, Alabama, USA, May: White residents supporting segregation attack the "Freedom Riders," a multiracial group touring the southern states.

Vienna, Austria, June 4: Soviet premier Khrushchev and US President Kennedy meet at summit. Despite little agreement, there is progress, following the debacle of the Paris Peace Conference.

Kuwait, July 1: British troops occupy the gulf state to defend against a threatened Iraqi invasion.

Bizerte, Tunisia, July 20: After repeated requests for the French to return the naval base at Bizerte, Tunisian forces lay siege.

Berlin, Germany, August 13: East German troops begin to erect the Berlin wall.

Ndola, Rhodesia, September 18: UN Secretary-General Dag Hammarskjold dies in a plane crash in suspicious circumstances.

Novaya Zemlya, USSR, October 30: Russia explodes the world's largest nuclear bomb, provoking worldwide condemnation. At 58 megatons, the bomb is 4,000 times more powerful than the Hiroshima bomb of 1945.

Saigon, South Vietnam, December 11: Following President Kennedy's pledge to increase military aid to South Vietnam, 400 US troops land in Saigon in two army helicopters.

Jerusalem, Israel, December 15: Former SS commander Adolf Eichmann is sentenced to death.

1963

Congo, January 15: Secessionist leader of breakaway Katanga province, Moise Tshombe, is forced to reunite with the Congo under intense pressure from the UN and other African states.

Paris, France, January 29: French President de Gaulle vetoes Britain's entry into the European Economic Community (EEC) and is supported by Germany's Chancellor Adenauer.

Paris, France, February 15: A plot is uncovered to assassinate President de Gaulle, one of numerous attempts on his life in the past year.

Atlantic Ocean, April 10: The nuclear-powered submarine USS *Thresher* is lost off Cape Cod, with 129 men on board.

Birmingham, USA, April 12: Black activist Martin Luther King is arrested for leading a peaceful demonstration.

Alabama, USA, April 25: Alabama governor George Wallace refuses to end school segregation.

Jakarta, Indonesia, May 18: Sukarno, hero of the struggle against the Dutch in the 1940s, declares himself president for life.

London, England, June 5: Harold Macmillan's Tories are suffering as Secretary of War John Profumo resigns when it is revealed that he had misled parliament over his affair with prostitute Christine Keeler, who was also seeing Eugene Ivanov, a Soviet naval attaché.

Berlin, Germany, June 26: West Berliners gather to hear US President Kennedy's speech denouncing communism. "Ich bin ein Berliner," he states.

Skopje, Macedonia, July 26: The Macedonian capital is devastated when a massive earthquake levels 80 percent of the town.

Cheddington, England, August 8: More than $5 million in cash and jewellery is seized in a daring train robbery.

Washington DC, USA, August 28: Martin Luther King delivers his "I have a dream..." speech.

Malaysia, September 16: Malaysia is formed by unifying Singapore, Malaya, North Borneo, and Sarawak.

London, England, October 10: Prime Minister Howard Macmillan resigns.

Cho Lon, South Vietnam, November 2: Despotic leader Ngo Dinh Diem is assassinated, with the US complicit in the murder. Diem's suppression of Buddhists had led numerous monks to commit suicide in protest this year.

Dallas, USA, November 22: President Kennedy is assassinated; Lyndon B. Johnson is sworn in less than two hours after the tragedy.

Nicosia, Cyprus, December 21: Violence erupts between Greek and Turkish Cypriots.

1965

London, England, January 30: A state funeral is held for wartime leader Sir Winston Churchill who died six days ago, aged 91.

New York, USA, February 21: Firebrand black nationalist leader Malcolm X is assassinated by two members of his former organization, the Nation of Islam.

Bucharest, Romania, March 19: Nicolae Ceausescu becomes the leader of Romania.

Montgomery, USA, March 21-25: Martin Luther King leads a 54-mile (87 km) march of 25,000 people from Selma.

Danang, South Vietnam, March 31: The first US combat troops are sent to the escalating conflict; 3,000 marines are to protect the US air base at Danang. In February, American bombers began to pound Vietcong positions in the north.

Canberra, Australia, April 29: Prime Minister Menzies commits 1,000 Australian troops to fight in South Vietnam.

Dominican Republic, May: The USA sends 14,000 troops to the Caribbean island after civil war broke out in April following a coup.

Algeria, June 19: Independence hero and Prime Minister Ahmed Ben Bella is deposed in a bloodless coup led by Colonel Boumedienne.

Tokyo, Japan, June 22: Japan and South Korea sign a treaty of basic relations, normalizing relations for the first time since Japan annexed the Korean peninsula in 1910. The Japanese agree to pay $800 million in compensation.

Washington DC, USA, July 28: President Johnson commits a further 50,000 troops to the war in Vietnam.

Singapore, August 9: Serious racial tensions between Malays and Chinese force Singapore to declare independence from Malaysia.

Los Angeles, USA, August 15: Six days of rioting leaves 34 people dead and over 1,000 injured. The trouble began when a black motorist was arrested in the Watts area.

Kashmir, September 6: The Indian army invades West Pakistan in response to earlier incursions by Pakistani soldiers. Both sides have claimed Kashmir since the 1949 war.

New York, USA, October 15: The anti-war movement has gained momentum this year across the USA. The latest protest, in New York, is attended by thousands of concerned Americans.

Rhodesia, November 11: World-wide condemnation greets Prime Minister Ian Smith's decision to sever links with Britain and maintain white-minority rule.

North Sea, December 27: Britain's first offshore oil drilling platform, the Sea Gem, collapses with the loss of 13 lives.

1966

New Delhi, India, January 19: Indira Gandhi, daughter of former prime minister Pandit Jawaharlal Nehru, is elected prime minister.

Accra, Ghana, February 24: An army coup deposes the prime minister and self-styled redeemer of Ghana, Kwame Nkrumah, while he is on an official visit to China.

Jakarta, Indonesia, March 11: Chaos follows an abortive coup in September last year. General Soeharto receives letter of instruction from Sukarno today, transferring state power to the army.

Rome, Italy, March 27: Pope Paul VI meets Dr Ramsey, Archbishop of Canterbury. It is the first meeting for 400 years between heads of Roman Catholic and Anglican churches.

Sydney, Australia, April 19: Violent scenes erupt in Sydney as Australia's first National Service conscripts fly out for Vietnam.

London, England, May 26: Murderers Ian Brady and Myra Hindley are sentenced to life imprisonment.

Memphis, USA, June 7: James Meredith, the first African-American to brave the color bar in Mississippi, is gunned down in a civil rights march. Martin Luther King takes over as leader of the march.

Mururoa Atoll, French Polynesia, July 2: France explodes a nuclear device.

Washington DC, USA, July 5: During a visit to Washington, Australian Prime Minister Harold Holt vows to go "All the way with L.B.J." as the Vietnam War escalates.

Kuala Lumpur, Malaysia, August 11: Three years of guerrilla warfare between Indonesia and Malaysia come to an end.

Beijing, China, August 13: Mao Tse-tung's cultural revolution targets professionals and intellectuals for re-education.

Vung Tau, South Vietnam, August 18: At Long Tan, Australian troops fight a pitched battle against a Vietcong force about four times its size.

Pretoria, South Africa, September 6: Prime Minister Hendrik Verwoerd, the "Father of Apartheid," is stabbed to death by Demetrio Tsafendas.

Aberfan, Wales, October 21: A sliding slagheap of mine tailings buries a school, killing 116 children and 28 adults.

Moscow, USSR, November 27: The Soviet Communist Party denounces Chinese leadership as the Cultural Revolution gathers speed.

Salisbury, Rhodesia, December 6: The leader of the rebel regime, Ian Smith, rejects proposals by Britain, including bringing black politicians into his cabinet, to end a 13-month dispute since Smith's declaration of independence.

1968

Thule, Greenland, January 21: A US B-52 bomber crashes, carrying four hydrogen bombs.

South Vietnam, January 31: North Vietnamese and the Vietcong launch the Tet offensive.

UK, February 4: Kenyan Asians flee repressive laws that prevent them from making a living since independence.

My Lai, South Vietnam, March 16: US troops massacre hundreds of unarmed civilians.

Washington DC, USA, March 31: President Lyndon Johnson stuns America by announcing that he will not run for office in the forthcoming elections.

Atlanta, USA, April 9: The funeral of Martin Luther King, who was assassinated in Memphis on April 4, is attended by 150,000 people.

Wellington, New Zealand, April 10: The ferry *Wahine* capsizes in Wellington harbor in a severe storm. Of the 734 passengers and crew on board, 51 lose their lives.

France, May: Ten million workers strike in solidarity with students after leftist student riots earlier this month were brutally suppressed by the police. President de Gaulle issues an ultimatum for the country to back his reforms or sack him.

Los Angeles, USA, June 6: Presidential candidate Robert Kennedy is assassinated by Palestinian militant Sirhan Sirhan.

World, July 1: The Nuclear Non-Proliferation Treaty is signed by 62 nations, including the USA, the USSR, and the UK.

Vatican City, July 29: Pope Paul VI confirms the ban on the use of contraceptives by Catholics, despite calls for change, with the release of the encyclical *Humanae Vitae*.

Addis Ababa, Ethiopia, August 15: Peace talks between Biafran secessionists and Nigeria, aiming to reconcile the two states after Biafra declared itself independent of Nigeria in May, end without progress. The economic blockade of Biafra has led to mass starvation.

Prague, Czechoslovakia, August 21: The "Prague Spring" program of liberalization initiated by Alexander Dubcek comes to an abrupt end when Warsaw Pact countries send in tanks to reinstate hard-line communist policy. Czechoslovaks take to the streets to show their support for the reforms.

China, October: As the whirlwind of Mao Tse-tung's Cultural Revolution continues, the army is given carte blanche to restore order.

USA, November 5: Republican Richard Nixon is elected president.

1970

Tripoli, Libya, January 16: Colonel Muammar Gaddafi becomes premier of Libya, promoting an Arab nationalist ideology.

London, England, January 23: The first "Jumbo" jet touches down at Heathrow. The airport's infrastructure is overloaded by 362 passengers, twice as many as a Boeing 707 could carry.

Geneva, Switzerland, March 5: The Nuclear Non-Proliferation Treaty, opened for signature in 1968, comes into effect after being ratified by 43 nations.

Hutt River Province, Australia, April 22: An angry Western Australian wheat farmer, Leonard Casley, declares independence for his 18,470-acre (7,474 ha) property, 280 miles (450 km) north of the Western Australian capital, Perth.

Africa, April 24: Gambia becomes a republic. Rhodesia was also declared a republic by Prime Minister Ian Smith seven weeks earlier.

USA, May: Six students engaged in anti-war protests at Ohio and Mississippi university campuses are shot dead.

Indonesia, June 21: Sukarno, the first president of Indonesia, dies of kidney disease, aged 69.

Egypt, July 21: The Aswan High Dam is completed at a cost of $800 million, regulating the flow of the Nile and relieving the threat of flooding downstream.

Jordan, September: After the hijacking of several planes by Palestinian terrorists, the PLO is ejected from their Jordanian stronghold. King Hussein orders his army to attack Palestinians who pose a threat to his leadership.

Melbourne, Australia, October 15: A 394-ft (120 m) section of the half-built West Gate Bridge collapses, killing 35 construction workers. Unions ban all work on the bridge.

Paris, France, November 9: Charles de Gaulle dies, weeks before turning 80 years old.

Canberra, Australia, November 12: The 8th Battalion of the Australian army returns from Vietnam. This marks the beginning of Australian withdrawal from the Vietnam War.

Pakistan, November 12-13: Cyclonic winds, an earthquake, and tidal waves kill in excess of 150,000 people.

Melbourne, Australia, November 25: The Victorian government becomes the first in the world to legislate for the mandatory wearing of seatbelts in cars.

Washington DC, USA, December 2: The US Congress establishes the Environmental Protection Agency (EPA) as the environmental repercussions of human activity become increasingly apparent.

1972

Dhaka, Bangladesh, January 12: After being released from nine months' detention, Sheikh Mujibur Rahman returns from West Pakistan to announce the formation of the new state of Bangladesh.

Brussels, Belgium, January 22: Britain, Ireland, Norway, and Denmark join the European Economic Community (EEC).

Londonderry, Northern Ireland, January 30: On "Bloody Sunday," 13 protesters—six under the age of 17—are killed by British troops after a civil rights march became a riot.

USA, February 5: Mandatory inspections of passengers and baggage are introduced into US airports.

Florida, USA, March 2: The *Pioneer 10* space probe is launched, headed for Jupiter and the outer reaches of deep space. It contains a plaque showing some details of human civilization on Earth.

Northern Ireland, March 25: British Prime Minister Edward Heath announces the dissolution of the Stormont Parliament.

Port Moresby, Papua New Guinea, April 20: Michael Somare, leading the National Coalition, wins his first election, becoming the Chief Minister of Papua New Guinea.

Colombo, Sri Lanka, May 22: The ruling United Front party, under Sirimavo Bandaranaike, unveils a new constitution. This proclaims the country as the republic of Sri Lanka, changing its name from Ceylon. "Sri Lanka" means "venerable island."

Moscow, USSR, May 26: President Nixon and Soviet leader Leonid Brezhnev sign the SALT I treaty to limit the number of nuclear missile launchers in each country.

Paris, France, May 28: The Duke of Windsor, formerly known as Edward VIII, dies. He abdicated the throne to marry Wallace Simpson.

Washington DC, USA, June 17: Five men are arrested breaking into the Democratic National Committee offices in the Watergate Hotel. The men have links to the Republican Party and the CIA.

Kampala, Uganda, August 6: Idi Amin orders the expulsion of 50,000 Asians with British passports.

Munich, West Germany, September 5: Palestinian terrorists attack the Israeli delegation at the Olympic Games.

Canberra, Australia, December 3: The Australian Labor Party wins government for the first time in 23 years under the leadership of the charismatic Gough Whitlam.

Uruguay, December 23: Sixteen victims of a plane crash in the Andes are rescued after nearly two months.

key milestones

1967

Sacramento, USA, January 2: Former film actor Ronald Reagan is sworn in as governor of California.

Cape Kennedy, USA, January 27: Astronauts Virgil "Gus" Grissom, Ed White, and Roger Chaffee die in *Apollo* spacecraft fire.

Saigon, South Vietnam, January 28, 1967: US forces launch Operation Cedar Falls.

Aachen, Germany, March 14: Executives of Chemie Gruementhal are charged over manufacture of the Thalidomide drug, which caused deformities in babies.

Cornwall, England, March 29: Armed forces bomb a stricken oil tanker in an attempt to sink it. The tanker, *Torrey Canyon*, ran aground between Land's End and the Scilly Isles 11 days ago, spreading oil on beaches in France and the UK.

Athens, Greece, April 21: Right-wing army officers under Colonel George Papadopoulos seize power, deposing George Papandreou.

Canberra, Australia, May 27: Australians vote for a proposal to count Aboriginal people in the national census.

Middle East, June 10: The six-day war against Syria and Egypt comes to an end as Israel finally observes a UN ceasefire.

Port Harcourt, Nigeria, July 16: Ibo people of Nigeria set up separate state of Biafra in oil-rich southeast of Nigeria, causing civil war between Nigerian forces and rebels.

Detroit, USA, July 27: Paratroops restore order in Detroit after race riots result in 38 black rioters and looters being shot by police and the National Guard.

Beijing, China, August 30: Red Guards set fire to the British Mission in Beijing and bar all members from leaving without permission.

Villa Grande, Bolivia, October 10: The body of Ernesto "Che" Guevara is put on display after he is shot by troops in Bolivia.

Oakland, California, USA, October 20: The fifth day of anti-war protests sees 4,000 demonstrators battling police. Protests have taken place in 30 US cities in the last week, calling for an end to the Vietnam conflict.

Khe Sanh, South Vietnam, November: Khe Sanh is being heavily fortified by General Westmoreland, ready to carry out reconnaissance attacks on the Ho Chi Minh Trail and other enemy supply lines from the north.

Paris, France, November 27: President Charles de Gaulle states that he will veto British attempts to join the European Economic Union for the second time.

Portsea, Australia, December 22: Australian Prime Minister Harold Holt drowns while swimming in rough seas off Cheviot Beach.

1969

Paris, France, January 18: The Paris peace talks open between the USA, South Vietnam, North Vietnam, and the Vietcong.

Cairo, Egypt, February 3: The leader of the Fatah faction, Yasser Arafat, is the new head of the Palestine Liberation Organization.

Memphis, Tennessee, USA, March 10: The killer of Martin Luther King, James Earl Ray, is sentenced to life imprisonment for the murder of the civil rights leader.

Tel Aviv, Israel, March 17: Seventy-one-year-old Golda Meir comes out of retirement to become Israel's first female prime minister.

Paris, France, April 28: French president Charles de Gaulle resigns, following the defeat of a referendum on sweeping governmental reforms.

USA, May 10: The government signals a crackdown on student protests, with Vice-President Spiro Agnew stating, "The time has come for American colleges under siege to assert themselves."

Midway Island, Pacific Ocean, June 8: US President Nixon meets with South Vietnamese leader Nguyen Van Thieu to discuss the "Vietnamization" of the Vietnam War. Around 25,000 US troops are projected to withdraw by September.

Nigeria, June 30: The Nigerian government bans Red Cross night flights from distributing food aid in disputed Biafra state, jeopardizing the survival of four million people.

The Moon, July 21: Neil Armstrong walks on the Moon, watched by millions of television viewers.

Los Angeles, USA, August 9: Charles Manson and his "family" kill Sharon Tate, wife of director Roman Polanski, and four others, in Polanski's Beverly Hills mansion.

China, August 13: Soviet troops make incursions into Chinese territory; heavy fighting occurs.

Northern Ireland, August 14: British troops are deployed to restore order in Ulster after escalating religious violence.

Libya, September 1: The 18-year rule of King Idris is ended by Colonel Gaddafi's bloodless coup.

Bonn, West Germany, October 21: Social Democrat and former mayor of West Berlin, Willy Brandt, is elected chancellor, ending the Christian Democrats' hold on government since the end of World War II.

Washington DC, USA, November 15: A group of 250,000 people marches to the US capital to demand an end to the Vietnam War.

Okinawa, Japan, November 21: A joint US-Japanese communique announces that Okinawa and the other Ryukyu Islands are to be handed back to the Japanese.

1971

Paris, France, January 10: French fashion designer, Gabrielle "Coco" Chanel, dies aged 87.

Miami, USA, January 24: The co-founder of Alcoholics Anonymous, Bill Wilson, dies.

Los Angeles, USA, January 25: Charles Manson and three female co-defendants are convicted of the murders of seven people.

Kampala, Uganda, January 25: General Idi Amin seizes power while President Obote is abroad.

Middle East, February 3: OPEC decides to set oil prices directly without consulting buyers.

London, England, February 15: The UK introduces the decimal system of currency. The previous system was in place for 1,200 years.

Dacca, East Pakistan, March 26: Following Sheikh Mujibur Rahman's declaration of independence from West Pakistan, civil war erupts in the streets of the new capital.

Port au Prince, Haiti, April 21: The autocratic president of Haiti, François Duvalier or "Papa Doc," dies aged 61. He is succeeded by his 19-year-old son Jean-Claude, or "Baby Doc."

Canberra, Australia, May 24: Neville Bonner becomes the first Aboriginal member of Australian parliament after his selection for a Senate vacancy.

Sydney, Australia, June 13: The Broderick nontuplets are born. This is the first recorded case of nine births.

Kazakhstan, USSR, June 30: Three Russian cosmonauts are found dead in the *Soyuz 11* spacecraft after an apparently normal flight and landing. A new space endurance record had been set by this flight.

London, England, August 5: The three editors of *Oz* magazine are found guilty of obscenity. All three receive jail sentences.

Bahrain, August 15: Britain withdraws from the Persian Gulf islands of Bahrain, and it becomes an independent state.

Australia and New Zealand, August 18: Australia and New Zealand announce they will pull troops out of Vietnam by December.

Ulster, Northern Ireland, September 7: After a draconian crackdown on Loyalists was implemented in August, 100 people have been killed in the violence.

France, December 20: A group of doctors form Médecins Sans Frontières to assist the people of the Biafra region of Nigeria. They formed the group in frustration at the neutrality of the Red Cross.

1973

Washington DC, USA, January 21: The Supreme Court overturns state laws prohibiting abortion. The statute is made law by a majority of 7 to 2.

Paris, France, January 27: The US and Vietnamese combatants in the Vietnam War sign a peace accord.

South Africa, February 6: A strike of 30,000 black workers begins.

Sinai Desert, Israel, February 21: Israeli jets shoot down a Libyan passenger plane, which was off-course and disregarded all signals.

Brisbane, Australia, March 8: A firebomb attack at the Whisky Au Go Go Nightclub leaves 15 dead.

Washington DC, USA, May 17: The enquiry into the Watergate affair begins.

Athens, Greece, June 1: President Papadopoulos abolishes the monarchy and proclaims a republic.

Kabul, Afghanistan, July 17: The Communist Party, led by Daoud Khan, leads a successful coup, overthrowing the monarchy and declaring a republic.

Mururoa Atoll, French Polynesia, July 22: France commences nuclear testing despite the presence of a New Zealand protest vessel.

Santiago, Chile, September 11: A bloody military coup led by General Pinochet results in the death of Marxist president Salvador Allende.

Washington DC, USA, October 12: Vice-President Spiro Agnew resigns following his indictment for tax evasion.

Middle East, October 17: OPEC countries place an embargo on the export of oil to countries who supported Israel in the Arab-Israeli conflict. The price of oil rises.

Sydney, Australia, October 20: Queen Elizabeth II opens the Sydney Opera House, declaring it "one of the wonders of the world." It cost 14 times the original estimate.

Israel, October 22: A cease-fire between Egypt, Syria, and Israel goes into effect after two weeks of fierce fighting.

London, England, November 14: Queen Elizabeth's only daughter, Princess Anne, marries Captain Mark Phillips at Westminster Abbey.

Athens, Greece, November 25: A military coup ousts the president.

Paris, France, December: The first part of Aleksandr Solzhenitsyn's book *The Gulag Archipelago* is published in the West. Solzhenitsyn comes under immediate attack from the Soviet press and government.

World, December: The oil crisis has caused acute economic distress in the Western world and Japan.

1974

Christchurch, New Zealand, January 24: The Commonwealth Games are opened by Prince Philip, the Duke of Edinburgh.

Berkeley, California, USA, February 4: Heiress Patricia Hearst is kidnapped by the Symbionese Liberation Army.

Moscow, USSR, February 13: Nobel Prize-winning author Aleksandr Solzhenitsyn is expelled from the USSR after being arrested. His book, *The Gulag Archipelago*, is a detailed record of the conditions in the infamous Soviet prison camps. He is offered asylum in Switzerland.

Paris, France, March 3: A Turkish Airlines DC-10 crashes, killing all 345 passengers. It is the worst disaster in aviation history.

Middle East, March 13: The oil-producing Arab nations agree to lift the embargo on Western countries.

Tel Aviv, Israel, April 10: Prime Minister Golda Meir resigns following a schism in her party.

Lisbon, Portugal, April 25: Military leaders seize control. Civil liberties are reinstated after 40 years of dictatorship under Antonio Salazar.

West Germany, May 6: Chancellor Willy Brandt resigns after an East German spy is found working as a top aide in his office.

Rajasthan, India, May 18: India becomes the sixth nation to detonate a nuclear device. Prime Minister Gandhi says the test was peaceful.

Northern Ireland, May 29: The Northern Ireland Assembly is dissolved as Westminster brings Northern Ireland under its direct rule once again.

Toronto, Canada, June 30: The leading Russian ballet dancer, Mikhail Baryshnikov, defects and is granted asylum in Canada.

Buenos Aires, Argentina, July 1: Isabel Perón assumes the presidency after the death of her husband Juan Perón. She was Perón's third wife.

Washington DC, USA, August 3: President Nixon resigns in the aftermath of the Watergate scandal.

Cyprus, August 16: Victorious Turkish invaders divide the island into two following an offensive against Greek Cypriots.

Addis Ababa, Ethiopia, September 12: Emperor Haile Selassie is overthrown in a military coup after ruling for 58 years.

New York, USA, November 12: South Africa is suspended from the UN General Assembly after a 91-22 vote condemns the country's racial policies.

Darwin, Australia, December 24-25: Sixty-six people die and thousands are injured as Cyclone Tracy devastates the Northern Territory on Christmas Eve and Christmas Day.

1976

Beijing, China, January 8: Premier Chou En-lai, second in command to Mao, dies after 50 years of pragmatic and ruthless revolutionary service.

Guatemala and Honduras, February 4: A 7.9 magnitude earthquake leaves 23,000 people dead and some 60,000 homeless.

San Francisco, USA, March 20: Patty Hearst, former hostage and heiress, is found guilty of armed robbery. Her lawyer's argument of coercion fell on deaf ears.

Buenos Aires, Argentina, March 24: President Isabel Perón is overthrown by a military junta. She is to be charged with corruption.

London, England, April 5: James Callaghan became prime minister after the unexpected resignation of Harold Wilson last month.

Messkirch, West Germany, May 26: Martin Heidegger, philosopher, dies aged 86. He was a principal influence on the Existentialist movement.

Soweto, South Africa, June 18: The worst racial violence in 15 years has plunged the black townships outside Johannesburg into anarchy.

Lebanon, June 20: Syrian troops begin an assault on Palestinian guerrilla strongholds after initially entering Lebanon as peace negotiators.

Seychelles, June 28: The Indian Ocean republic gains independence from Britain after 162 years.

Entebbe, Uganda, July 4: Israeli commandos storm the airport to free 105 hostages held by terrorists.

Montreal, Canada, July 8: The Games of the 21st Olympiad open. Twenty-four nations, mostly from Africa, have boycotted the games in protest of the apartheid regime in South Africa.

Tangshan, China, July 29: Officials estimate that up to 242,000 people have been killed in an earthquake registering 8.2 on the Richter scale.

Belfast, Northern Ireland, August 14: Approximately 20,000 Protestant and Roman Catholic women rally for peace after the deaths of three children hit by a car.

Beijing, China, September 9: Mao Tse-tung, father of the Chinese revolution, dies aged 82.

Washington DC, USA, November 2: Jimmy Carter defeats the incumbent Republican president, Gerald Ford, 297 votes to 240.

Geneva, Switzerland, December 7: Kurt Waldheim, an Austrian diplomat, has been backed by the UN Security Council to serve another five-year term as Secretary-General.

1978

Northern Canada, January 24: A Soviet nuclear-powered spy satellite, *Cosmos 954*, crashes in a shower of radioactive rubble.

Zimbabwe (Rhodesia), March 21: Three black nationalists have been sworn into parliament, sharing executive power with Ian Smith, the prime minister. This ends exclusive white rule of the African country.

Brittany, France, March 24: The supertanker *Amoco Cadiz* sinks off the coast; 230,000 barrels of oil have spilt into the sea. Around 70 miles (112 km) of the French coast have been affected.

Kabul, Afghanistan, April 30: Soviet-backed rebel troops kill President Daoud.

Italy, May 9: The body of Aldo Moro, the Christian Democratic senator who was kidnapped by the Red Brigade eight weeks ago, is recovered.

London, England, May 10: Princess Margaret, Queen Elizabeth's younger sister, seeks a divorce from Lord Snowdon after a volatile relationship, extramarital love affairs by both the princess and her husband, and two years of separation.

Melbourne, Australia, May 15: Sir Robert Menzies, Australia's longest serving prime minister (1939-1941, 1949-1966) dies of heart failure, aged 83.

New Hampshire, USA, June 30: Protestors against the nuclear power plant proposed for Seabrook have a victory after seven years of campaigning as the plan is scrapped.

Spain, July 11: Nearly 200 holidaymakers are killed when a liquid gas tanker rolls over and explodes in a campsite on the Mediterranean coast.

Manchester, England, July 25: The first "test-tube" baby is born.

Nairobi, Kenya, August 22: Kenyan president, Jomo Kenyatta, dies, aged 80.

Camp David, USA, September 18: Israeli Prime Minister Begin and Egyptian president Sadat reach agreement on a framework for peace in the Middle East.

The Vatican, Italy, September 30: The shortest papal reign comes to an end when Pope John Paul I dies of a heart attack after 33 days in office.

The Vatican, Italy, October 16: The first non-Italian pontiff for over four centuries is elected. Karol Wojtyla, from Poland, will be known as John Paul II.

Jonestown, Guyana, November 18: People's Temple cult leader, Reverend Jim Jones, orders his followers to drink poisoned soft drink. A total of 913 people die.

Tehran, Iran, December 29: Supporters of the exiled Ayatollah Khomeini, protesting for the past month, have eroded the power of the Shah of Iran.

1980

Moscow, USSR, January 22: Prominent dissident, Dr Andrei Sakharov is exiled to Gorky after speaking out on the Soviet role in Afghanistan. Sakharov and his wife are given two hours to depart.

North Sea, March 27: A wild storm with gale-force winds overturns the Alexander Kielland oil platform.

Salisbury, Zimbabwe, April 18: The last British colony in Africa becomes independent under the leadership of ex-freedom fighter Robert Mugabe.

Iran, April 28: Eight American soldiers, engaged in a covert operation to free US hostages in Tehran, die when their helicopter collides with a transport plane.

London, England, May 5: SAS forces storm the Iranian Embassy, killing four terrorists and releasing 19 hostages.

Belgrade, Yugoslavia, May 8: One hundred and fifteen world leaders gather to honor President-for-life Josip Tito, who died aged 87.

Washington State, USA, May 19: Mt St Helens catastrophically erupts.

East Africa, June 12: Over 10 million people are threatened with famine following two years of drought and various civil wars.

Canada, July 1: "Oh Canada" becomes the official anthem of Canada. Robert Stanley Weir translated the original French version into English in 1908.

Moscow, USSR, July 19: The Olympic Games open. USA, West Germany, and Japan boycott in protest against the Soviet invasion of Afghanistan.

Gdansk, Poland, August 30: Two months of crippling strikes in the shipyards have led the Communist regime to agree to sweeping concessions to the workers led by Lech Walesa.

Abadan, Iran, September 24: The simmering hostilities between Iraq and Iran explode into a full-scale war, with the Iraqis attacking the oil refinery at Abadan.

Amazon, Brazil, October 2: A gold rush in the Amazonian jungles has seen more than $50 million worth of nuggets found since February.

El Asnam, Algeria, October 11: A 7.3 magnitude earthquake has left up to 20,000 people dead.

Detroit, USA, October 28: The Ford Motor Co. has reported the biggest loss for one quarter by a US company, of $595 million.

USA, November 4: Ronald Reagan becomes 40th president of the United States.

1975

Hobart, Tasmania, Australia, January 5: The carrier *Lake Illawarra* collides with the Tasman Bridge, demolishing a span. Twelve people, including five drivers, lose their lives.
Kathmandu, Nepal, February 4: King Birendra, heir to the world's only Hindu throne, assumes power, promising to advance Nepal.
London, England, February 11: Margaret Thatcher is elected as the leader of the UK's Conservative Party. She is the first woman to lead the Conservatives.

London, England, February 28: A rush-hour tube crashes into a dead end, killing 34 passengers and the driver.
Riyadh, Saudi Arabia, March 25: King Faysal is assassinated in the palace by his nephew, who has a history of mental illness.
Phnom Penh, Cambodia, April 17: Communist Khmer Rouge forces capture the capital after a three-month siege, following a five-year civil war.
Saigon, Vietnam, April 30: The US presence in Vietnam ends as Saigon falls to the Viet Cong.

Port Said, Egypt, June 5: Anwar Sadat, President of Egypt, reopens the Suez Canal after eight years.
Maputo, Mozambique, June 25: Samora Machel assumes the presidency of the southeast African country, gaining independence from Portugal after nearly five centuries.
New Delhi, India, June 12: Prime Minister Indira Gandhi is found guilty of electoral corruption and barred from holding public office for six years.
Space, July 19: The US *Apollo* and Soviet *Soyuz* spacecrafts undock after two days of stellar détente.

Helsinki, Finland, August 1: Thirty-five countries sign an accord on security and human rights.
Vientiane, Laos, August 23: The Communist Pathet Lao take control of the former French colony. Communists have recently ascended to power throughout Indochina.
Beirut, Lebanon, September 16: Fierce sectarian violence breaks out on the streets of the capital between Muslims and Christians. Prime Minister Karami is reluctant to send in the army, as most soldiers are Christian.

Canberra, Australia, November 11: The Governor-General, Sir John Kerr, sacks the Labor government of Prime Minister Gough Whitlam. This follows weeks of constitutional crisis and political tension. Whitlam is succeeded as prime minister by the Liberal Party's Malcolm Fraser.
Madrid, Spain, November 22: Juan Carlos de Borbón is proclaimed King of Spain following General Franco's death two days ago after leading the country since 1936.

1977

Sydney, Australia, January 18: A train derails and crashes into bridge supports in Granville, causing the bridge to collapse on the train carriages. Eighty-three people are killed, and more than 200 injured.
Washington DC, USA, January 20: Democrat Jimmy Carter is inaugurated as US president.
Kampala, Uganda, February 25: Following the USA's condemnation of the escalating political violence under Idi Amin, 240 Americans are detained in Kampala.

New Delhi, India, March 22: Indira Gandhi quits politics following a crushing defeat in the elections.
Tenerife, Canary Islands, March 28: Two Boeing 747s collide in thick fog while taxiing for takeoff. There are 574 fatalities, making it the worst aviation disaster in history.
North Sea, Scotland, April 30: A massive oil spill at the Bravo drilling platform spews over 7.5 million gallons (34 million liters) of crude oil into the ocean.

London, England, May 13: The Australian media mogul Kerry Packer signs up 35 of the world's leading cricketers to play in the first-ever series of one-day cricket matches.
Israel, May 18: The Likud Party, led by Menachem Begin and standing on a right-wing platform, wins power after 29 years in opposition.
UK, June 7: Week-long celebrations commemorating Queen Elizabeth's 25 years on the throne commence.
Djibouti, June 27: France's last African colony gains independence.

Pakistan, July 5: Prime Minister Zulfikar Ali Bhutto is deposed in a coup led by the head of the army, General Zia ul-Haq. Bhutto has been charged with fraud and corruption.
Beijing, China, September 28: Pol Pot, the leader of Cambodia's Khmer Rouge, arrives for talks concerning aid from China.
Mogadishu, Somalia, October 18: West German commandos storm a hijacked Lufthansa jet and free 86 hostages. A German communist terrorist group, the Baader-Meinhof, is responsible for the hijack.

Tel-Aviv, Israel, November 21: Egyptian Prime Minister Anwar Sadat addresses the Knesset, the Israeli Parliament, acknowledging the existence of the Jewish state and making overtures toward peace.
South Africa, December 2: A magistrate rules that police cannot be held responsible for the death of black activist Steve Biko.
Vietnam, December: Refugees are fleeing the communist regime in increasing numbers. Up to 1,500 per month are taking to dangerously unseaworthy boats to escape.

1979

Cambodia, January 7: Vietnamese troops seize control of Phnom Penh, toppling the pro-Chinese government of Lon Nol.
Tehran, Iran, February 1: The Ayatollah Khomeini returns after 15 years in exile, intending to establish an Islamic state.
Kampala, Uganda, March 29: Idi Amin's murderous regime collapses as Tanzanian-backed troops invade the Ugandan capital.
Pennsylvania, USA, March 31: The Three Mile Island nuclear reactor is shut down after releasing radiation.

Rawalpindi, Pakistan, April 4: Ex-prime minister Zulfikar Ali Bhutto is executed after being convicted of murdering a political opponent.
London, England, May 3: Margaret Thatcher leads the Conservative Party to victory, becoming Europe's first female prime minister.
Vienna, Austria, June 18: US President Carter and Soviet leader Leonid Brezhnev sign the SALT II nuclear arms limitation treaty.
Algiers, Algeria, July 4: Ahmed Ben Bella, former president, is released after 14 years in captivity.

Western Australia, July 11: The US satellite *Skylab* disintegrates on re-entry into Earth's atmosphere, scattering debris over the state.
Managua, Nicaragua, July 17: General Somoza flees into exile. His regime is replaced by a junta representing conservative business interests and communist Sandanistas.
Cambodia, August 19: The leader of the Khmer Rouge, Pol Pot, is sentenced to death in absentia for his murderous regime.

Mullaghmore, Ireland, August 27: The Queen's cousin, Lord Mountbatten, is killed when an IRA bomb destroys his family fishing boat just after it leaves the harbor.
Ireland, September 29: Pope John Paul II flies into Ireland today to be met by over 300,000 people. The new pontiff has been traveling widely, recently visiting the USA.
Tehran, Iran, November 4: Followers of Ayatollah Khomeini storm the US embassy. Nearly 100 embassy staff are taken hostage.

Antarctica, November 28: A New Zealand DC-10 plows into Mt Erebus on a sightseeing flight, killing all 257 on board.
Zimbabwe (Rhodesia), December 21: Robert Mugabe, Joshua Nkomo, and Bishop Abel Muzorewa sign a cease-fire agreement, bringing the seven-year civil war to an end.
Afghanistan, December 29: The build-up of Soviet troops has become an invasion, culminating in the fall of the government in Kabul.

1981

Dewsbury, England, January 5: Peter Sutcliffe, believed to be the "Yorkshire Ripper," is arrested after the murders of 13 women.
Tehran, Iran, January 20: Fifty-two US Embassy hostages are released.
Beijing, China, January 25: Chiang Ching, the widow of Mao Zedong is sentenced to death.

London, England, January 27: Australian media tycoon, Rupert Murdoch purchases *The Times* and *The Sunday Times*, raising concerns about a media monopoly.
Washington DC, USA, March 30: President Ronald Reagan is shot in the chest by a 25-year-old from Colorado. Three others are wounded.
Brixton, England, April 12: Racial tensions reach boiling point and explode into the largest riots in London this century.

California, USA, April 14: The space shuttle *Columbia* completes its first flight, orbiting the Earth 36 times.
Northern Ireland, May 12: Fierce rioting for eight days follows the deaths of jailed IRA hunger strikers Bobby Sands and Francis Hughes.
Vatican, May 13: Pope John Paul II survives an assassination attempt.
Israel, June 24: After attacking a nuclear reactor near Baghdad on June 7 to stop Iraq gaining nuclear weapons, the Israelis reveal they have nuclear capacity.

New Zealand, July 22: The first match of the South African Springbok rugby tour generates sometimes violent public opposition.
London, England, July 29: Lady Diana Spencer marries Prince Charles at St Paul's Cathedral.
Poland, September 18: The Soviet Union warns Polish leaders to quell the anti-Soviet feeling being encouraged by the Solidarity Union.
Cairo, Egypt, October 6: The Egyptian leader, Anwar Sadat, is assassinated by members of the army with extremist Islamic links.

Antigua and Barbuda, Caribbean, November 1: The island nations become independent from the UK.
Sweden, November 5: A Soviet submarine suspected to have a nuclear capability and charged with spying on a sensitive naval base has been released after a week.
Poland, December 17: Martial law is imposed in this Soviet bloc country in an attempt to crack down on the union movement following recent political unrest.

1982

Washington DC, USA, January 13: A twin-engine jet crashes in a snowstorm after takeoff, plowing into a bridge on the Potomac River, opposite the White House, 78 die.

Northern Territory, Australia, February 2: The mother of baby Azaria Chamberlain, allegedly taken by a dingo at Ayers Rock, is committed to stand trial for her murder.

Salisbury, Zimbabwe, February 17: The coalition government is dissolved with PM Robert Mugabe taking control. His partner, Joshua Nkomo, is accused of plotting a coup.

Managua, Nicaragua, March 25: The Marxist Sandinista government has declared a state of emergency, curtailing human rights, in fear of an attack by the USA.

Falkland Islands, April 2: Argentina invades the islands, overrunning 84 marines stationed there.

Ottawa, Canada, April 17: The Canada Act receives royal assent, ending British legislative jurisdiction over Canada. The Canadian Charter of Rights and Freedoms, the constitutional guarantee of collective and individual rights, is now in effect.

Sinai, Egypt, April 25: The Sinai peninsula is handed back to Egypt.

Falkland Islands, June 14: The British rout Argentine forces.

London, England, June 22: Prince William is born to Princess Diana and the Prince of Wales. He is second in line for the throne.

London, England, July 20: The IRA claim responsibility for two bombs in Hyde and Regent's parks.

Beirut, Lebanon, August 31: The PLO flee their stronghold, driven out by Israel, which invaded last month.

Monte Carlo, Monaco, September 10: Princess Grace of Monaco dies after her car plunges off a mountain road due to brake failure.

Beirut, Lebanon, September 18: Christian militia massacre hundreds of Palestinian refugees.

West Germany, October 1: Helmut Kohl is elected Chancellor after his predecessor Helmut Schmidt resigned due to a no confidence vote.

Moscow, USSR, November 10: President Leonid Brezhnev dies, aged 75.

Poland, November 12: Lech Walesa, leader of the Solidarity Union is released from detention, 11 months after the union was outlawed.

Tasmania, Australia, December: Hundreds of environmentalists blockade work on the proposed hydroelectric plant on the Gordon River. More than 90 are arrested.

New Zealand and Australia, December 14: New Zealand and Australia sign the Closer Economic Relations Agreement.

1984

Brunei, January 1: The sultanate achieves independence after 95 years of British rule.

Moscow, USSR, February 13: After ruling for only 15 months, Communist Party chief Yury Andropov dies. Konstantin Chernenko, also in poor health, assumes the top job.

Ottawa, Canada, February 29: Prime Minister Pierre Trudeau resigns.

UK, March 12: A nationwide miner's strike, affecting over 100 pits, begins. It is led by the militant unionist Arthur Scargill.

London, England, April 17: During a protest against Muammar Gaddafi outside the Libyan Embassy, a policewoman is shot and killed. The shots are fired from within the embassy, sparking a major diplomatic incident.

Persian Gulf, May 24: A Saudi Arabian oil tanker is destroyed by Iranian fighters, following criticism of Iran by the Arab League.

Amritsar, India, June 7: Troops storm the Sikh Golden Temple after a four-day siege at the complex—400 people are killed.

New Zealand, July 14: Election of a fourth Labour government begins a period of major economic and social change; restructuring of government services leads to many job losses.

Manila, Philippines, August 21: Over 900,000 Filipinos protest against the repressive Marcos regime.

Beijing, China, September 26: An agreement between China and the UK shall see Hong Kong revert to communist rule in 1997. The island shall be able to preserve its economy.

Brighton, England, October 12: An IRA bomb devastates the Grand Hotel during the Conservative Party annual conference.

New Delhi, India, October 31: PM Indira Gandhi is assassinated by her Sikh bodyguards. Her son Rajiv takes over the leadership.

Oslo, Norway, October: The Nobel Peace Prize is awarded to Bishop Desmond Tutu, for his role against apartheid in South Africa.

Ethiopia, November 1: Bureaucracy is thwarting relief efforts for a famine that has claimed 900,000 lives and threatens 6 million.

USA, November 6: Ronald Reagan is re-elected for a second term with a decisive victory throughout the 50 states.

Bhopal, India, December 3: A toxic gas leak claims over 2,000 lives and affects tens of thousands of others.

1986

Port-au-Prince, Haiti, February 7: President-for-life Jean-Claude "Baby Doc" Duvalier flees to France amid widespread unrest. Duvalier and his father, "Papa Doc," ruled the country brutally for 28 years.

Manila, Philippines, February 25: Ferdinand Marcos, president for 20 years, is marginalized by the military and the USA and is forced to resign. Political widow María Corazón Aquino takes power.

Stockholm, Sweden, February 28: Walking unprotected, Swedish PM Olof Palme is assassinated.

Canberra, Australia, March 2: Queen Elizabeth formally severs Australia's constitutional ties with the UK, signing the Australia Act with PM Bob Hawke.

Tripoli, Libya, April 15: US aircraft, with British cooperation, strike terrorist targets, killing dozens of civilians in the Libyan capital.

Ukraine, USSR, April 30: The Chernobyl nuclear reactor melts down, releasing massive amounts of deadly radiation.

Vienna, Austria, June 8: Former Secretary-General of the UN, Kurt Waldheim, is elected president, amid accusations of involvement in Nazi war crimes.

South Africa, June 16: Millions of blacks strike on the tenth anniversary of the Soweto uprising.

Washington DC, USA, June 25: Nicaraguan Contras are paid by US Congress to overthrow the Sandinista government.

New Zealand, July 11: Homosexual Law Reform Act legalizes consensual adult same-sex relationships.

Edinburgh, Scotland, July 24–August 7: The Commonwealth Games are boycotted by 32 countries in protest at Britain's refusal to implement more sanctions against South Africa.

Karachi, Pakistan, August 14: Benazir Bhutto is arrested while leading demonstrations against the government of President Zia.

Cameroon, August 25: Toxic gas is released from a volcanic lake, resulting in 1,700 deaths.

Iceland, October 12: Ronald Reagan and Mikhail Gorbachev attend a summit on arms control.

Basle, Switzerland, November 10: A fire at a chemical plant leads to more than 1,000 tons of toxic chemicals washing into the Rhine.

Washington DC, USA, November 25: The "Irangate" affair comes to light; Ronald Reagan admits secret arms deals with Nicaraguan Contras. Lieutenant-Colonel Oliver North and Vice Admiral John Poindexter resign.

Shanghai, China, December 21: Fifty thousand students hold demonstrations urging democratic reforms, including freedom of the media.

1988

Canada and USA, January 2: Canada and the USA sign a Free Trade Agreement.

East Jerusalem, Israel, January 15: Israeli police open fire on Muslim protestors at the Dome of the Rock Mosque, one of Islam's holiest sites.

Cape Town, South Africa, February 29: As part of the latest crackdown on anti-apartheid protests, Archbishop Desmond Tutu and 100 clergy are arrested.

Panama City, Panama, March 16: General Manuel Noriega survives a US-led coup attempt.

Islamabad, Pakistan, April 10: The Ohjri ammunition depot explodes, killing 100 and injuring 1,000 others. Afghan agents are suspected of involvement.

Afghanistan, May 16: Soviet troops begin to withdraw, after over eight years bogged down against US-backed Islamic militants. The unpopular war has been described as "Russia's Vietnam."

Moscow, USSR, May 31: President Reagan, who described the USSR as an "evil empire," makes the first visit by a US president in 14 years.

Cambodia, June 4: Vietnamese forces, who have occupied Cambodia for ten years, begin to withdraw 50,000 troops.

Arabian Gulf, July 3: US Navy warship Vincennes mistakenly shoots down an Iranian passenger plane, killing 290 people.

North Sea, July 6: An oil-rig explodes.

Tehran, Iran, July 20: Ayatollah Khomeini declares an end to the eight-year holy war with Iraq, accepting the cease-fire conditions drafted by the UN.

Rangoon, Burma, July 23: Rioting students destroy police stations in the worst violence seen in the past quarter century. Premier Bo Ne Win is ousted from office after 26 years.

Bahawalpur, Pakistan, August 17: President Zia and 30 officials, including the US ambassador, die when their plane is engulfed in flames. Sabotage is suspected.

Ramstein, West Germany, August 28: Three Italian jets collide at an air show, sending the debris into the crowds; hundreds are severely burnt, 46 die.

Burma, September 19: The flirtation with freedom of speech is short-lived in the socialist country. The Army takes control of the civilian government, banning all public demonstrations.

Santiago, Chile, October 6: A referendum ousts General Augusto Pinochet; voters refuse to install the army strongman for another eight years.

Armenia, USSR, December 10: A massive earthquake levels urban areas.

1983

La Paz, Bolivia, January 25: Klaus Barbie, "The Butcher of Lyons," is captured in South America.

Tel Aviv, Israel, February 11: Israeli defence minister Ariel Sharon is implicated in the 1982 massacre of Palestinian refugees in Lebanon. He resigns, but remains a member of the cabinet.

Assam State, India, February 21: Riots protesting the immigration of Muslim refugees from Bangladesh take place. More than 600 people are killed.

Australia, March 6: Bob Hawke leads the Labor Party to a landslide victory, after only a month as opposition leader and less than three years in Parliament.

London, England, March 14: The Organization of the Petroleum Exporting Countries (OPEC) agrees to cut oil prices for the first time in the group's 25-year history.

Beirut, Lebanon, April 18: Forty-eight people die following a car bombing at the US Embassy. Extremist Islamic groups claim responsibility.

USA, May 4: President Ronald Reagan admits that Contra rebels in Nicaragua are being supported by the USA.

UK, June 9: The Conservative government of Margaret Thatcher is returned for a second term.

Manila, Philippines, August 21: Benigno Aquino, returning from a three-year exile in the USA to contest an election, is shot on the tarmac upon arrival.

Sakhalin Island, USSR, September 1: A Korean Airlines jet is shot down by a Soviet fighter.

Africa, October 18: The United Nations warns that 22 African nations are facing famine. A drought has ravaged even wet tropical countries.

Grenada, October 25: US troops invade the small Caribbean island in an effort to restore democracy. The invasion is condemned by the United Nations and some US allies.

The Hague, Netherlands, October 29: A crowd of 500,000 people protest against US missiles.

South Africa, November 2: A whites-only referendum approves a new constitution giving limited political rights to non-whites.

Cyprus, November 15: Turkish Cypriots declare the northern third of the Mediterranean island independent.

Argentina, December 10: Eight years of military rule are brought to an end with the election of a civilian president.

1985

Ethiopia, January 13: A train bound for Addis Ababa derails and plunges into a ravine. This is Africa's worst rail disaster, with 392 people dead.

New Zealand, February 9: Labour PM David Lange, adhering to the government's anti-nuclear stance, has refused to allow a US nuclear warship to dock. The US retaliates by excluding NZ from the ANZUS alliance.

UK, March 3: Coalminers call off their strike after nearly a year.

Moscow, USSR, March 13: The new Soviet leader, Mikhail Gorbachev, leads the funeral for Konstantin Chernenko, whom he replaced. At 54, Gorbachev is perceived to be a potential reformer.

Tirana, Albania, April 11: Enver Hoxha, leader of the insular Communist state for 40 years, dies.

Bangladesh, May 27: Up to 10,000 people are killed by a cyclone and tidal wave that has devastated the low-lying country.

Ottawa, Canada, June 13: Manitoba laws are ruled unacceptable by the Supreme Court of Canada as they are written only in English.

Ireland, June 23: An Air India jet is destroyed by a terrorist bomb over the Atlantic.

Auckland, New Zealand, July 10: The Greenpeace ship *Rainbow Warrior* is sunk after explosions rip through her in Auckland harbor. One life is lost.

UK, Japan, USA, August 22: Three major air disasters this month have killed 711 people.

South Africa, August 28: The country has descended into a state of anarchy after President P. W. Botha refused to make concessions to the black majority.

Atlantic Ocean, September 1: A team led by Robert Ballard has located the wreck of the *Titanic*.

Mexico City, Mexico, September 20: A massive earthquake, measuring 7.8 on the Richter scale, has killed approximately 20,000 people.

Auckland, New Zealand, November 3: French secret agents plead guilty to the sinking of the *Rainbow Warrior*.

Geneva, Switzerland, November 21: US President Ronald Reagan and Soviet leader Mikhail Gorbachev hold 6-hour talks at the 14th US–Soviet Summit, stirring optimism.

Rome, Italy, and Vienna, Austria, December 30: Palestinian terrorists attack two El Al Israel Airline check-in counters in coordinated attacks that leave 12 holidaymakers dead and hundreds injured.

1987

Beirut, Lebanon, February 22: At the request of Lebanese leaders, 7,000 Syrian troops enter West Beirut in an attempt to end fighting between Shia Muslims and Christians.

Rome, Italy, March 1: Bettino Craxi's socialist government, the longest serving since World War II, resigns.

Zeebrugge, Belgium, March 6: A car ferry en route to the UK capsizes; 188 people die.

New Zealand, April 1: State-owned enterprises replace government trading departments.

Suva, Fiji, May 14: Lt-Col Sitiveni Rabuka enters parliament and arrests the PM and 27 members of the Indian-dominated government.

Moscow, USSR, May 28: Matthias Rust, 19, an inexperienced pilot from West Germany, lands in Red Square.

UK, June 11: Margaret Thatcher's Conservative Party is re-elected for a third term.

Seoul, South Korea, June 20: Massive protests throughout South Korea over ten days climax with widespread riots in the capital. Rioters demand democratic reform.

Mecca, Saudi Arabia, July 30: Saudi police shoot 400 pilgrims, mostly Iranians, during the annual hajj.

Colombo, Sri Lanka, July 29: India and Sri Lanka sign a peace accord.

Guatemala City, Guatemala, August 7: The presidents of Costa Rica, Nicaragua, Honduras, Guatemala, and El Salvador sign a peace agreement.

Manila, Philippines, August 29: The fifth coup attempt against President Corazón Aquino's government fails, leaving 40 people dead and hundreds injured.

Ethiopia, September 10: A new civilian constitution is drafted, ending 13 years of military rule. Colonel Mengistu Haile Mariam is elected president.

USA, September 17: The country celebrates the 200th anniversary of the US Constitution, the longest serving in the world. It has been amended 26 times.

UK, October 16: Hurricane force winds batter the British Isles, leaving a £300 million damage bill. It is the worst storm to hit the UK in 300 years; 17 people die.

Worldwide, October 19: Stock markets slump dramatically following the lead of Wall Street; around 25 percent of share values have been wiped out.

Washington DC, USA, December 8: Ronald Reagan and Mikhail Gorbachev sign a treaty to diminish the size of their nuclear arsenals.

1989

Tokyo, Japan, January 7: Emperor Hirohito, dies, aged 82.

Washington DC, USA, January 20: Republican George H. W. Bush is inaugurated as the 41st president.

Asuncion, Paraguay, February 3: Alfredo Stroessner, Paraguay's president for 35 years, is overthrown in a military coup.

Prince William Sound, Alaska, March 24: The *Exxon Valdez* oil tanker runs aground, spilling over 11 million gallons (42 million liters) of oil. The captain is alleged to be intoxicated.

USSR, March 26: The first democratic elections take place to elect the Congress of People's Deputies. Boris Yeltsin comes out ahead because of his criticism of Mikhail Gorbachev.

Sheffield, England, April 15: The UK's worst sporting disaster occurs when supporters of Liverpool rush onto an already overcrowded stand— 94 are killed and 170 are injured.

Poland, June 5: Voters deliver a resounding mandate to the Solidarity Party, led by Lech Walesa, in the first free elections.

Beijing, China, June 5: A student revolt is brutally put down in Tiananmen Square.

Tehran, Iran, June 6: Hysterical mourning greets the death of spiritual leader Ayatollah Seyyed Ruhollah Khomeini, aged 86.

Pretoria, South Africa, August 15: P. W. Botha resigns as PM to be replaced by Frederik Willem de Klerk.

Austria, September 10: Twenty-five thousand East Germans, seeking a new life in the West, flee to Austria via Hungary when the Hungarian Government opens its borders. The travel documents of many are invalid but they are automatically entitled to West German citizenship.

San Francisco, USA, October 21: A massive earthquake rocks the Bay area, measuring 6.9 on the Richter scale. Eighty-three deaths are reported, damage is widespread.

New Zealand, November 1: Major local government and ports reforms come into effect, overturning a post-1876 system and drastically reducing the number of local authorities.

Berlin, West/East Germany, November 10: The Berlin Wall is opened after 28 years.

Panama, December 20: US troops invade. General Manuel Noriega flees and is replaced by Guillermo Endara.

Bucharest, Romania, December 25: Following two weeks of social unrest, brutal dictator, Nicolae Ceausescu and his wife are executed.

1990

Western Europe, January 25: Hurricane force winds cause havoc. Forty-seven die in the UK and up to three million trees are uprooted.

Cape Town, South Africa, February 11: Nelson Mandela is released from jail after 27 years.

Managua, Nicaragua, February 25: Violeta Chamorro defeats Sandinista leader Daniel Ortega in the first free elections since 1979.

Canada, March 11-September 26: Disagreement regarding land between the Mohawk Natives and Quebec results in the Oka Crisis.

Vilnius, Lithuania, March 11: The tiny Baltic republic declares itself independent, after half a century of Soviet rule.

Australia, March 26: The Labor government of Bob Hawke wins a record 4th term.

Kathmandu, Nepal, April 8: King Birendra lifts a 30-year ban on political parties and agrees to end the country's feudal-style rule.

Moscow, May 29: "Radical" Boris Yeltsin is elected president of the Russian republic, challenging the power of Mikhail Gorbachev.

Iran, June 22: A massive earthquake in the northwest of the country leaves 40,000 dead and 100,000 injured.

Mecca, Saudi Arabia, July 2: One thousand four hundred pilgrims are crushed to death in a tunnel leading to the Islamic world's holiest site.

Kuwait, August 2: Iraqi troops invade, meeting with little resistance.

South Africa, August 24: Following two weeks of violence that has left 500 dead, a state of emergency is imposed on 27 townships.

Germany, October 3: East and West Germany reunify.

Jerusalem, Israel, October 8: Israeli police shoot dead 21 Arabs during a riot at the Western Wall and the Dome of the Rock.

New Zealand, November 2: National party wins election; Ruth Richardson becomes first woman Minister of Finance; widespread cuts to welfare benefits are soon announced.

Paris, France, November 19: The Cold War officially ends with 22 heads of state agreeing to dismantle their arsenals. There is to be a significant reduction in conventional weaponry.

London, England, November 27: John Major becomes leader of the Conservatives following Margaret Thatcher's resignation five days ago.

Poland, December 9: The founder of the Solidarity union Lech Walesa is elected president, winning 74.4 percent of the vote.

1992

Somalia, January 3: Violent factional conflicts have crippled the East African country; 20,000 people have died, according to UN estimates.

Europe, January 15: The European Commission recognize Croatia and Slovenia as independent states.

South Africa, March 17: White voters give a resounding yes to plans for constitutional reforms giving equality to their black countrymen.

New Zealand, April 1: The Student Loan Scheme Act assists students to borrow money to fund tertiary education.

Miami, USA, April 9: Former Panamanian dictator General Manuel Noriega is found guilty of drug trafficking.

Los Angeles, USA, May 2: The jury's decision to acquit four police indicted in the beating of Rodney King leads to rioting.

Rio de Janeiro, Brazil, June 3-14: Treaties are signed at the UN Earth Summit to avert climate change.

Johannesburg, South Africa, June 18: Supporters of the Inkatha Freedom Party rampage through an outlying township, killing 39 people.

Sarajevo, Bosnia, July 2: UN peacekeeping forces move into position around the airport so that humanitarian aid can commence. Heavy resistance is encountered from Serbian troops.

Bosnia, August 15: Images of emaciated Bosnians in concentration style camps are broadcast around the world.

Rostock, Germany, August 29: Fifteen thousand left-wing protesters clash with police at a rally against racist attacks on refugees.

Lima, Peru, September 12: Responsible for 25,000 deaths, leader of the "Shining Path" guerrillas Abimael Guzmán is arrested after 12 years on the run.

Hanoi, Vietnam, September 23: General Le Duc Anh is elected as president, being the only candidate running for the position.

Amsterdam, Netherlands, October 4: A fully laden Boeing 747 cargo plane crashes into a tower block shortly after take off, killing more than 70 people and injuring hundreds.

USA, November 4: Bill Clinton is elected president of the USA.

London, England, November 24: Queen Elizabeth II refers to 1992 as an "annus horribilis." Bad luck has plagued the Royals this year, with scandals, income tax demands, divorce, and a fire at Windsor Palace four days ago.

Mogadishu, Somalia, December 9: The USA sends in Marines to neutralize gunmen loyal to local warlords and to deliver humanitarian aid.

1994

Los Angeles, USA, January 18: An earthquake measuring 6.6 on the Richter scale hits the densely urbanized area in the early morning; 34 people die.

Yangon, Burma, February 15: Aung San Suu Kyi refuses to leave the country.

Hebron, Israel, February 25: A Jewish extremist kills 30 Muslim worshippers kneeling for prayer. Riots erupt throughout the occupied territories.

Bosnia, February 28: Four Bosnian Serb warplanes are shot down over the UN no-fly zone by NATO forces. This is the first offensive action by NATO forces in its 45-year history.

Rwanda, April 21: The Red Cross estimate 100,000 people have been killed in two weeks of ethnic bloodshed since the president's death.

New Zealand, April: Official opening of Clyde power station.

Pretoria, South Africa, May 10: Nelson Mandela is made head-of-state.

Algiers, Algeria, June 29: Fifteen thousand Algerians peacefully demonstrate against violence between the government and Islamic extremists. Two explosions and gunfire leave 64 wounded.

Gaza, Israel, July 1: Yasser Arafat returns after 27 years in exile.

Pyongyang, North Korea, July 8: Kim Il Sung, dictator since World War II dies, aged 82.

Pasadena, USA, July 17: Brazil wins its fourth World Cup title, beating the Italian team.

Northern Ireland, August 31: After a quarter century of armed resistance, the IRA announces a "complete cessation of military operations."

Haiti, September 19: US troops invade the Caribbean island. Bloodshed is spared after 11th hour negotiations ensure the removal of the military junta.

Baltic Sea, September 28: An Estonian passenger ferry sinks rapidly in heavy weather off the Finnish coast; 912 people lose their lives in the freezing waters.

Iraq, October 13: Saddam Hussein pulls back 60,000 troops and 700 tanks from the Kuwaiti border after the USA rushes troops back to the region.

Sri Lanka, November 10: Chandrika Kumaratunga is swept to power in a landslide election result. Her father and husband, both politicians, were assassinated.

Chechnya, December 11: After two weeks of bombing the breakaway republic, Russian tanks cross the border in an attempt to "re-establish Constitutional order."

1996

Bosnia, January 2: US combat troops enter northern Bosnia to keep the peace between Bosnian Serbs and Muslims following the Dayton peace agreement signed last month.

Paris, France, January 8: François Mitterrand, socialist PM who led the country for 14 years, dies, aged 79.

Colombo, Sri Lanka, January 31: A truck laden with explosives crashes into the Central Bank, killing 57 and injuring over 1,000.

London, England, February 9: An explosion in the Docklands marks the end of a 17-month cease-fire by the IRA. The bomb causes widespread damage with one fatality and 39 injured.

Cuba, February 24: Cuban fighter jets shoot down two US civilian aircraft. The planes were chartered by an anti-Castro organization to search for refugees.

Australia, March 2: The Liberal party, led by John Howard, is victorious after 13 years in opposition.

Dunblane, Scotland, March 13: Gunman Thomas Hamilton goes on a shooting spree in the local primary school, killing 16 students and a teacher before taking his own life.

Cairo, Egypt, April 18: Islamic militants open fire on Greek tourists outside a Cairo hotel, killing 17.

Tasmania, Australia, April 28: Martin Bryant kills 35 people at Port Arthur.

Iraq, May 20: Iraq and the UN agree on the oil-for-food program allowing Iraq to sell oil for humanitarian necessities.

Bosnia, July 19: Bosnian Serb President Radovan Karadzic resigns from office and withdraws from public life after being indicted for war crimes. His initial refusal to resign was destabilizing the country.

Atlanta, USA, July 27: A bomb explodes at a concert during the Olympic Games, injuring 200 and killing two.

Chechnya, Russia, August: After two years of fierce fighting between separatist rebels and the Russian Army, a peace accord is signed allowing for limited autonomy.

Kabul, Afghanistan, September 27: Taliban militia take the capital, their aim to establish the "purest" Islamic regime in the world. Ousted President Rabbani flees, fearing for his life.

Washington, DC, USA, November 6: Bill Clinton, re-elected, is only the second Democrat to win a second term in office.

Canada, November 21: The Royal Commission for Native Groups recommends that they prepare for self-government.

UK, December: The government culls 100,000 cows in a bid to stop disease.

1991

Kuwait, January 16: A US-led coalition launches an offensive to liberate Kuwait following Iraq's failure to comply with UN deadline for withdrawal.

Mogadishu, Somalia, January 27: General Mohammed Siad Barre flees the capital after 21 years of brutal rule over the East African country.

Bangkok, Thailand, February 23: With King Bhumibol's support, the military overthrows the government. Martial law is declared. This is the 19th coup attempt since 1932.

Kuwait, February 28: US President Bush announces the end of the war to liberate Kuwait.

Los Angeles, USA, March 15: Four police officers are indicted for the beating of Rodney King. The event was captured on video, sparking an outcry throughout the country.

Tbilisi, Georgia, April 9: Independence from Moscow is declared after 70 years of Soviet rule. 90 percent of voters support the change.

Bangladesh, April 30: A massive cyclone hits from the Bay of Bengal.

India, May 21: Former PM Rajiv Gandhi is assassinated. Tamil separatists are suspected.

Ethiopia, May 25: After Stalinist dictator Mengistu Haile Mariam flees, Israeli forces airlift 15,000 black Jews, known as Falashas, out of the country in 21 hours.

South Africa, June 17: The law classifying citizens by race is repealed.

Ljubljana, Slovenia, June 29: Yugoslavia is headed toward civil war. Slovenia declares independence.

Moscow, USSR, August 21: An attempted coup by hardliners opposed to reforms fails in the face of popular opposition. Mikhail Gorbachev is released from house arrest in the Crimea after 60 hours; Boris Yeltsin consolidates his position.

USSR, September 5: The Congress of People's Deputies votes for the dissolution of The Union of Soviet Socialist Republics.

Madrid, Spain, October 4: The Madrid protocol governing Antarctica comes into effect, designating the continent as a natural reserve, devoted to peace and science.

Phnom Penh, Cambodia, November 14: Prince Norodom Sihanouk returns after 13 years in exile, following the signing of a peace treaty in Paris on October 23.

Moscow, Russia, December 25: Mikhail Gorbachev resigns the presidency of the USSR.

1993

Czech Republic and Slovakia, January 1: In direct contrast to the strife in the former Yugoslavia, Czechoslovakia splits into two separate entities in what has been termed a "velvet divorce."

New York, USA, February 26: A bomb blast in a garage under the World Trade Center leaves five people dead and hundreds injured.

Bombay, India, March 12: Car bomb blasts kill 300 people.

Waco, Texas, USA, April 19: Fires lit by Branch Davidian cult members rage through their compound.

Eritrea, April 27: Succession looks likely after voters ask to become independent from Ethiopia.

Agrigento, Sicily, May 9: Following the recent spate of assassinations of the judiciary linked to the mafia, the Pope calls for an end to the violence.

Canada, June: Nunavut Inuit and the Canadian government sign a land claim for 135,000 sq miles (350,000 sq km) of the Arctic Region. Inuit are given title.

Georgia, July 6: Georgian PM and former Soviet foreign minister Eduard Shevardnadze is given sweeping powers to deal with Abkhazi rebels, who are seeking their own state.

Midwest, USA, August 1: The Mississippi has finally receded after months in flood, leaving at least 50 dead and a massive clean-up bill.

Washington DC, USA, September 13: Palestinians gain a modicum of self-rule in Israeli-occupied territory with the signing of an accord between the PLO and Israel brokered by US President Bill Clinton.

Phnom Penh, Cambodia, September 24: Prince Sihanouk is returned to power after a 30-year absence.

Moscow, Russia, October 4: A rebellion against Boris Yeltsin by hardliners is crushed with the assistance of the military.

Islamabad, Pakistan, October 20: Benazir Bhutto is reinstalled as PM three years after being ousted.

Maastricht, Netherlands, November 1: A treaty signed by the members of the European community comes into force.

Mostar, Bosnia, November 9: The sixteenth-century Ottoman bridge, in a city renowned for its heritage value, is destroyed by Croat shells.

Canberra, Australia, December 22: The Native Title Bill passes through parliament, confirming Aboriginal rights to claim land lost upon European colonization.

Pretoria, South Africa: Parliament votes for the first all-race election to take place next year. It shall inevitably lead to black majority rule.

1995

Manila, Philippines, January 15: Over 1 million people gather to welcome Pope John Paul II at the start of the World Youth Day celebrations.

Kobe, Japan, January 17: Over 6,000 people die in Japan's largest quake in nearly 50 years.

Frankfurt, Germany, March 2: Trader Nick Leeson, 28, responsible for a $1.4 billion loss to Barings Bank, is arrested.

Tokyo, Japan, March 20: Sarin, a deadly nerve gas is released in the subway system, killing eight and affecting 4,000. The Aum Supreme Truth religious sect is linked to the attacks.

Iraq, March 20: Thirty-five thousand Turkish troops cross into north Iraq to crush the PKK, Kurdish separatist rebels who have been waging a guerrilla war since 1984 that has claimed 15,000 lives.

Europe, March 26: Seven of the 15 EU states abolish border controls.

Oklahoma City, USA, April 19: A massive car bomb explodes in front of a federal building, killing 168 and injuring over 800. Main suspect Timothy McVeigh is arrested less than one hour after the blast.

Kibeho, Rwanda, April 22: Government troops massacre Hutu refugees.

San Diego, USA, May: Team New Zealand wins the America's Cup.

Zaire (Congo), May 28: The deadly Ebola hemorrhagic fever kills 256 of the 315 people infected in the second largest outbreak recorded.

Bosnia, May 28: Bosnian Serbs seize more than 350 UN peacekeepers from the "safe haven" of Gorazde. They have been used as human shields to guard against NATO attacks.

Srebrenica, Bosnia, July 15: Poorly armed Dutch peacekeepers are unable to prevent up to 40,000 Muslims being rounded up by Serbian forces in the largest incident of "ethnic cleansing" since WWII.

Washington, DC, USA, September 28: The PLO and the Israelis sign a deal handing over control of the West Bank to the Palestinians.

Los Angeles, USA, October 3: O. J. Simpson is found not guilty of killing his ex-wife.

Tel Aviv, Israel, November 4: Israeli PM Yitzhak Rabin is assassinated by a right wing Jewish extremist at a peace rally.

Port Harcourt, Nigeria, November 10: Authorities execute nine activists, opposed to unfair oil revenue distribution, charged with murder.

Paris, France, December 14: Croatian, Bosnian, and Serbian leaders sign a peace accord ending three years of bloody conflict.

1997

Southern Ocean, January 9: British yachtsman Tony Bullimore is rescued from his yacht five days after it capsized in the frigid waters southwest of Western Australia.

Hebron, West Bank, Israel, January 19: Greeted by 60,000 Palestinians, Yasser Arafat returns to Hebron after 30 years of Israeli occupation.

Beijing, China, February 19: Paramount leader Deng Xiaoping dies, aged 92. A hardliner, he ruled the country from 1978, allowing some strategic reforms, including limited private enterprise.

Sarajevo, Bosnia, April 12: A plot to assassinate the Pope is unearthed. Twenty anti-tank mines are found under a bridge along the pontiff's route.

Lima, Peru, April 22: A four-month siege at the Japanese embassy ends with the death of 14 Tupac Amaru guerrillas. Seventy-one captives are rescued, with only one civilian casualty.

UK, May 1: In a 10.3 percent swing against the Conservatives, the Labour Party, led by Tony Blair wins the general election. Labour has been in opposition for 18 years.

Kinshasa, Congo, May 20: One day after President Mobutu Sese Seko flees, Laurent Kabila's troops enter the capital, ending a civil war raging since late 1996.

Hong Kong, July 1: The former British colony is handed back to China.

Thredbo, Australia, August 2: Three days after a landslide, sole survivor Stuart Diver is found in the ruins of the destroyed lodges. Eighteen people died.

Jerusalem, Israel, September 4: Three Palestinian suicide bombers kill 7 and injure 170 in a crowded pedestrian area.

Calcutta, India, September 5: Mother Teresa dies, aged 87.

Westminster, England, September 6: Princess Diana is laid to rest.

Assisi, Italy, September 26: Two earthquakes in central Italy kill 10 and severely damage priceless works of art, including important frescos.

Luxor, Egypt, November 17: Sixty-two tourists are slain at the Deir al-Bahri temple complex.

New Zealand, December 8: Jenny Shipley becomes New Zealand's first woman prime minister.

Relizane, Algeria, December 30: About 350 people are massacred by Islamic extremists on the first day of Ramadan. The countryside descends into anarchy, thousands die.

1998

Rostaq, Afghanistan, February 4: An earthquake in the mountainous north of the country leaves 4,000 dead and 15,000 homeless. Fighting between the Taliban and the Northern Alliance continues.

Auckland, New Zealand, April: Power has finally been restored to the central business district after five weeks of blackouts.

Belfast, Northern Ireland, April 10: The "Good Friday" agreement for peace is signed by the British and Irish governments and endorsed by most Northern Ireland political parties.

Cambodia, April 15: Former Khmer Rouge leader Pol Pot dies, aged 72.

USA, May 18: Twenty US states and the Department of Justice submit that Microsoft has abused its monopoly.

Ireland, May 23: A referendum on the Good Friday peace agreement receives a resounding yes.

Pakistan, May 28: In response to Indian nuclear tests two weeks ago, Pakistan explodes five warheads underground.

Sudan, June 11: Up to one million people are at risk of starvation from a famine affecting the south of the country.

Lagos, Nigeria, July 11: Four days of rioting leave 60 dead. The riots were sparked by the death of opposition figure Chief Abiola.

Dar es Salaam, Tanzania and Nairobi, Kenya, August 7: Bombs explode at two US embassies.

Central China, August 13: The Yangtze River, which has risen to its highest level since 1954, threatens Wuhan, a city of seven million people. About 2,500 people perish and millions are left homeless.

Washington DC, USA, August 17: After categorically denying a sexual relationship with White House intern Monica Lewinsky in January, President Clinton publicly admits his deceit.

Halifax, Canada, September 3: A Swissair DC-11 crashes, killing all 229 on board.

Kosovo, September 22: Serbian forces bombard the breakaway region in attempt to crush the Kosovo Liberation Army (KLA). Widespread civilian casualties are reported.

South Africa, October 29: The Truth and Reconciliation Commission hands down its findings on political crimes conducted under the apartheid regime.

Iraq, November 15: Saddam Hussein's regime readmits UN weapons inspectors at the eleventh hour, averting US and British air strikes.

2000

Moscow, Russian Federation, January 1: After Boris Yeltsin's resignation, Prime Minister Vladimir Putin is named acting President until elections are held in 90 days time.

Baia Mare, Romania, January 30: A breach of a mine tailings dump pollutes the Sassar River with cyanide. Within a month, the spill flows from the Danube to the Black Sea.

Preston, England, January 31: Family GP Howard Shipman is sentenced to life imprisonment for murdering 15 patients. It is estimated that he may have killed as many as 250 patients in 23 years.

New York, USA, April 3: A federal judge rules that Microsoft violated antitrust laws, using its monopoly power in the computer market to stifle competition.

Zimbabwe, April 15: President Mugabe's plans for agricultural land reform claim the first victim when white farmer David Stevens is killed.

Taipei, Taiwan, May 19: Chen Shui-bian is inaugurated President after the first democratic elections.

Pyongyang, North Korea, June 14: Kim Jong Il hosts South Korea's President Kim Dae Jung for the first summit between the two countries.

Cuba, June 28: Elian Gonzalez, the Cuban child found floating on an inner tube off Florida in November last year—and the focus of an international tug-of-war—returns to Cuba with his father.

Gonesse, France, July 25: An Air France Concorde crashes, killing all 109 people on board and four people on the ground.

Barents Sea, Arctic Circle, August 14: The Russian submarine *Kursk* is flooded following an explosion, with the loss of 118 crew.

England, September 15: Protesting truck drivers end their seven-day blockade on fuel refineries that has brought the nation to a standstill.

Jerusalem, Israel, September 28: Opposition Leader Ariel Sharon visits Temple Mount, known as Haram al Sharif by Muslims. This action precipitates the second Palestinian intifada, or uprising.

Belgrade, Yugoslavia, October 6: Indicted for war crimes in Kosovo in 1999, President Slobodan Milosevic finally concedes defeat to Vojislav.

Aden, Yemen, October 12: US Navy destroyer USS *Cole* is attacked by two suicide bombers, killing 17 and injuring more than 40 personnel.

New York, USA, November 7: Democrat Hillary Rodham Clinton is elected US Senator.

Kaprun, Austria, November 11: A fire aboard a funicular railway car inside a tunnel kills 155 skiers.

USA, December 13: George W. Bush becomes the 43rd President of the US, with Democrat Al Gore conceding defeat. The vote in Florida came down to a decision in the Supreme Court.

2002

Europe, January 1: The common currency of the European Union, the euro, is legal tender in 12 countries.

Washington DC, USA, January 29: George W. Bush delivers his first State of the Union address to Congress, labelling North Korea, Iran, and Iraq an "axis of evil" for seeking weapons of mass destruction.

The Hague, Netherlands, February 12: Slobodan Milosevic's war crime trial begins, with the former Yugoslav president representing himself in a fiery rebuttal of the legitimacy of the tribunal.

Godhra, India, February 27: A train fire kills 57 Hindu pilgrims, sparking off days of rioting between Hindus and Muslims in Gujarat state.

Afghanistan, March: Coalition forces mount "Operation Anaconda"—a massive push to rout the Taliban and al-Qaeda in the rugged mountains south of Gardez.

Zimbabwe, March 9: Robert Mugabe returns to power in an election characterized by violence and intimidation.

Windsor, England, March 30: The Queen Mother dies, aged 101.

Ramallah, Israel, April 1: After a suicide bombing campaign that has left over 100 Israelis dead, Israel launches a massive military operation in the Palestinian territory. Yasser Arafat's compound is besieged, and a battle rages in the Jenin refugee camp.

The Vatican, April 23: Sexual abuse claims engulf the US Catholic Church. The Pope meets with 12 American cardinals, issuing an apology to victims of pedophile priests.

East Timor, May 20: East Timor finally achieves independence.

Kabul, Afghanistan, June 19: Hamid Karzai is endorsed as President at the loya jirga, or grand assembly. The process took over a week, with intense factional lobbying.

Kuta, Bali, October 12: Bombs explode in two tourist bars, killing more than 180 people. Australia suffers the biggest loss of life, with 88 citizens killed.

Hagerston, Maryland, USA, October 24: John Muhammad and Lee Malvo, responsible for 10 deaths carried out from the trunk of a car, sniper style, are arrested.

Moscow, Russian Federation, October 26: Russian forces storm the theater where Chechen separatists have been holding 800 hostages for three days.

New York, USA, November 8: The UN Security Council adopts resolution 1441, requiring Iraq to submit to weapons inspections.

Nigeria, November 23: The Miss World pageant is forced to relocate to London after riots by Muslims opposed to the show leave more than 100 dead.

2004

Port-au-Prince, Haiti, February 29: Beleaguered President Jean-Bertrand Aristide resigns and flees the country.

Madrid, Spain, March 11: Bomb blasts tear through three train stations during the morning rush hour. Hundreds are killed and many more are injured.

Gaza, Israel, March 22: Spiritual leader of the Palestinian militant group Hamas, Sheikh Ahmed Yassin is killed by an Israeli air strike, triggering angry scenes and calls for revenge.

Baghdad, Iraq, April 29: Damning photographs emerge of US forces abusing Iraqi prisoners at Abu Ghraib.

Europe, May 1: Cyprus, the Czech Republic, Estonia, Hungary, Latvia, Lithuania, Malta, Poland, Slovakia, and Slovenia join the European Union.

Arlon, Belgium, June 22: Pedophile child killer Marc Dutroux is sentenced to life in prison for his appalling crimes in the mid-90s.

Baghdad, Iraq, June 28: US administrator Paul Berner transfers sovereignty to interim Prime Minister Iyad Allawi.

Darfur, Sudan, July 24: Since March, government-backed Arab militias have killed up to 70,000 Sudanese in the southern region of Darfur; 1.5 million people have been displaced.

Najaf, Iraq, August: Gunmen loyal to Shia cleric Moqtada Sadr besiege the holy city of Najaf. US-led coalition forces have been engaged in fierce house-to-house fighting.

Kuala Lumpur, Malaysia, September 2: Supporters of former Deputy Prime Minister Anwar Ibrahim celebrate, as he is released from jail after the High Court overturned his sodomy conviction.

Beslan, Russia, September 3: More than 300 adults and children die when a siege by Chechen separatists at a school draws to a bloody conclusion.

Afghanistan, October 9: Hamid Karzai, who has been leading the country since the fall of the Taliban, wins the first parliamentary elections held in the country.

USA, November 2: George W. Bush secures a strong mandate, winning his second term in office, over Democrat challenger John Kerry.

Paris, France, November 11: Leader of the Palestinian people for over 40 years, Yasser Arafat dies, after slipping into a coma on November 3. He was 75.

Indian Ocean, December 26: A tsunami leaves coastal communities from Sri Lanka to Indonesia devastated; more than 100,000 people perish.

Ukraine, December 26: Victor Yushchenko is declared the winner of re-run parliamentary elections held after weeks of demonstrations in Kiev.

1999

Colombia, January 25: An earthquake measuring 6 on the Richter scale leaves 1,000 dead and many more homeless. Landslides and poor building standards contributed.

Nigeria, February 27: Former military ruler Olusegun Obasanjo wins the first free elections in 15 years.

France/Italy, March 24: A fire kills 39 people in the Mont Blanc tunnel.

Canada, April 1: The new territory of Nunavut is established, with its capital located at Iqaluit.

Scotland, April 5: The UN lifts sanctions against Libya as the two key suspects in the 1988 Lockerbie bombing of Pan-Am flight 103 are handed over to Scottish authorities.

Denver, Colorado, USA, April 20: Two heavily armed teenagers killing 13 students then commit suicide.

London, England, April 30: A nail bomb explodes in a Soho pub, killing three people. This follows attacks in Brick Lane and Brixton earlier in the month.

Belgrade, Yugoslavia, May 7: NATO bombers mistakenly target the Chinese embassy in a bombing raid in response to the atrocities occurring in Kosovo. Four diplomats die, massive demonstrations follow in China.

Kashmir, India/Pakistan, May 26: India launches air strikes in the disputed region following incursions by Pakistani forces.

Kosovo, Yugoslavia, June 10: NATO forces call off bombing raids as Serbian forces begin to withdraw from the disputed province.

London, England, June 18: Protests against the G8 summit turn violent.

Interlaken, Switzerland, July 28: Twenty-one international tourists die as a flash flood hits a canyoning group.

Izmit, Turkey, August 17: A massive 7.4 magnitude earthquake kills thousands.

East Timor, September 20: UN peacekeepers enter to control violence by pro-Indonesian militia since elections in early September.

Islamabad, Pakistan, October 12: General Pervez Musharraf ousts Prime Minister Nawaz Sharif in a bloodless coup.

Orissa, India, October 29: A massive tidal surge caused by a cyclone with 155 mph (250 km/h) winds hits eastern India, killing 10,000 and leaving 1.5 million homeless.

Worldwide, December 31: Millennium celebrations occur world-wide after a year where panic about the potentially debilitating effects of the Y2K computer glitch ran high.

2001

Gujarat, India, January 26: A massive earthquake in western India leaves 25,000 people dead and over one million homeless.

Camp Zeist, Netherlands, January 31: At a special Scottish court set up to try the bombers of Pan Am flight 103, which crashed at Lockerbie in 1988, one of the two Libyan suspects is found guilty and sentenced to life imprisonment.

Israel, February 6: Ariel Sharon, leader of the right-wing Likud party, becomes Prime Minister in a decisive election result.

Kalimantan, Indonesia, February: Ethnic violence erupts between the indigenous Dayaks and the Madurese minority, killing over 500.

Belgrade, Yugoslavia, April 1: Wanted by the UN, and facing charges of corruption at home, former President Slobodan Milosevic is arrested.

Hainan Island, China, April 11: The crew of a US surveillance plane are released after the US apologizes for the death of a Chinese pilot, who collided with the US plane over the South China Sea on March 31.

England, May: A foot-and-mouth outbreak has shut down large parts of the countryside since February.

Palawan, Philippines, May 27: The Muslim terrorist group Abu Sayyaf seizes 20 people from a tourist resort.

Kathmandu, Nepal, June 1: Crown Prince Dipendra shoots dead nine members of the royal family, before shooting himself.

Genoa, Italy, July 18-21: Anti-globalization protests turn violent at the G8 Summit as more than 100,000 protestors descend on the conference.

Canberra, Australia, August 29: In response to the MV Tampa crisis, the Border Protection Bill is rushed through. The Norwegian ship had rescued 460 Afghan asylum seekers from a sinking boat on August 26; and the Australian government initially refused asylum for them.

New York and Washington DC, USA, September 11: The World Trade Center is destroyed when two hijacked aircraft smash into the twin towers. A third plane hits the Pentagon; the death toll is estimated to be approximately 3,000.

Afghanistan, October 7: The US launches a retaliatory campaign for the September 11 attacks; the Taliban regime and al-Qaeda are the targets of the operation, which began with 50 cruise missiles being launched at Kandahar & Kabul.

USA, September 18-November: 22 people have been infected with anthrax, resulting in five deaths, from exposure to the deadly disease contained within letters.

Doha, Qatar, November 10: China is admitted to the World Trade Organization.

2003

Boston, USA, January 30: After admitting his guilt, and admiration for Osama bin Laden, "shoe bomber" Richard Reid is sentenced to life imprisonment for attempting to down an aircraft in December.

Texas, USA, February 1: Seven astronauts die when the space shuttle Columbia disintegrates.

Worldwide, February 15: Massive anti-war protests occur around the world as the threat of war in Iraq grows. 750,000 people gathered in London; New York, Paris, and many other cities saw people gather to express their objections.

Geneva, Switzerland, March 15: The World Health Organization issues an emergency travel advisory following the outbreak of Severe Acute Respiratory Syndrome (SARS).

Iraq, March 20: Coalition land troops enter Iraq, one day after the first American bombs are dropped on Baghdad. Air strikes on military targets are to be carried out as part of the "shock and awe" campaign.

Baghdad, Iraq, April 9: A statue of Saddam Hussein is toppled, as US tanks roll into the capital.

Persian Gulf, May 2: US President George W. Bush proclaims that the fighting in Iraq is now over, but stops short of declaring victory over Saddam Hussein.

Aceh, Indonesia, May 19: Martial law is declared in the oil-rich province as Indonesian troops take the fight to the Free Aceh Movement rebels.

Hong Kong, July 1: 500,000 people demonstrate against proposed anti-subversion laws.

Quetta, Pakistan, July 5: 44 Shia worshippers are killed at a mosque. Terror attacks have been widespread this year, with bombings in Morocco on May 16, Chechnya on May 14, and Saudi Arabia on May 12.

USA and Canada, August 14: Up to 60 million homes lose electricity, from Ohio to New York and Ontario.

Gaza, Israel, September 6: Prime Minister of the Palestinian Authority Mahmoud Abbas resigns after Yasser Arafat hamstrings his reforms.

Kuala Lumpur, Malaysia, October 31: Prime Minister Mohamad Mahathir steps down from office after 22 years. He has presided over a dramatic modernization of the country.

Santa Barbara, USA, November 20: Pop star Michael Jackson is charged with child molestation and is being urged to surrender by authorities.

Tikrit, Iraq, December 14: A disheveled Saddam Hussein is captured; he was found in a tiny underground bunker south of his hometown of Tikrit by US troops.

2005

Washington DC, USA, January 12: Chief investigator Charles Duelfer confirms that the US has stopped searching for weapons of mass destruction in Iraq. One of the chief justifications for the war, the non-existence of WMDs has been suspected since May 2003.

Iraq, January 30: The first democratic parliamentary elections since Saddam Hussein's departure take place, with a better than expected turnout of voters, despite threats of violence from insurgents.

Beirut, Lebanon, February 14: Former Prime Minister Rafik Hariri dies when a car bomb explodes near his motorcade. Syria, which has great influence in the country, is thought to be involved.

The Vatican, April 19: German cardinal Joseph Ratzinger becomes the new pontiff, Benedict XVI. Pope John Paul II died on April 2 after leading the world's one billion Catholics for 26 years.

Iraq, May: Insurgent attacks have escalated since the formation of the new government in April; over 800 Iraqis and 80 foreigners are killed in one month.

France, May 31: Prime Minister Jean-Pierre Raffarin resigns after the French public deliver a resounding "Non!" in the referendum on the EU constitution two days ago.

Iran, June 24: Hard-line mayor of Tehran Mahmoud Ahmadinejad wins the run-off (second-round) poll for president by a resounding margin.

London, England, July 7: Four coordinated terrorist attacks on the underground and bus systems during the morning rush hour kill 52 people and injure 700, bringing chaos to the capital.

Harare, Zimbabwe, July 22: President Mugabe's policy of slum clearance that has left up to 700,000 people homeless is condemned by the UN.

Dublin, Ireland, July 27: The IRA brings an end to its 30-year armed campaign and shall pursue its objectives by political means.

New Orleans, USA, September 1: In the aftermath of Hurricane Katrina, which hit the Gulf Coast on August 29, anarchy descends after levees fail and the city is flooded. Thousands die in the disaster.

Kashmir, October 8: An earthquake devastates Kashmir, with approximately 54,000 deaths. Some 2.5 million people are left homeless.

Paris, France, October 27-November 8: After two teenagers are electrocuted as they hide from police, widespread rioting grips Paris, and the government declares a state of emergency.

index

index

index

electric lighting 262
electric telegraph 231
electromagnetic induction 230
   Franklin investigates 185
   light bulbs 351
   neon lights 306
   photoelectric effect 328, 396
   term first used 150
   Treatise on Electricity and Magnetism 249
Electronic Numeric Integrator and Calculator
   374, 394
elements
   atomic theory 214
   newly discovered 351, 373
   table of 249
elevators 232, 247, 287
Eliot, Thomas Stearns 379
Elisabeth, Tsarina of Russia 203
Elizabeth I, Queen of England 130–132, 145
Elizabeth II, Queen of England 387, 483, 509
Elizabethan style 145
Elliott, Herb 427
Ellis, Havelock 316
Ellis Island 388
Ellison, Larry 493
embryology 198
Emerson, Ralph Waldo 236
Emin Pasha 270–271
Emma 220
Empire State building 341
Encyclopedia Britannica 207
Enders, John F 418
Endurance 316
England *see also* British Empire; Great
   Britain; London, England; *names of*
   kings and queens
   Act of Uniformity 129
   Acts of Union 178
   agriculture 182
   anti-Semitism 65, 81
   architecture 187
   Arthur legends 58
   Assize of Arms 80
   Assize of Bread and Ale 80
   Assize of Northampton 64–65
   Barnardos homes 294
   Battle of Crécy 84
   Battle of Hastings 36, 44–45
   beer bottling 143
   billiards 144
   Black Death 96
   Boke of Husbandrie 126–127
   Boldon Book 65
   Book of Winchester 48–49
   Civil War 149
   Copyright Bill 188
   corn law riots 213
   cricket in 270, 511
   dancing in 224–225

dissection ban lifted 134
Elizabethan style 145
Eton College 111
first woman member of Parliament 305
food canning 215
football in 257, 426
garden design 208
harrying of the north 48
Hearth tax 177
Historia rerum Anglicarum 61
Hundred Years War 100
invades France 98–99
Lord Protectorate 149
Luddites 211
Mary Rose 117, 460
Methodists 192
naval weaponry 120
New Testament 127
Oxford English Dictionary 334–335
Parliaments of 78, 83
Peasant's Revolt 97
Peterloo Massacre 213
Pre-Raphaelite Brotherhood 237
prepaid postage stamps 240
Protectorate 162
Qur'an translated 192–193
Royal Observatory 168
Royal Society 166
soccer banned in 94
Spanish Armada 132
steam locomotives 214–216
War of the Spanish Succession 179
Wimbledon tennis tournament 294
window tax 177
English Channel 313, 338
English Patient 488
ENIAC 374, 394
Enola Gay 367
Entebbe operation 434
epigenesis theory 198
Epistola de magnete 72
Epsom, England 299
Equipe Unifiée 454
Erasmus, Desiderius 125
Erebus, Mt 437
Ervin, Senator Sam 431
Erzberger, Matthias 304–305
Erzincan earthquake 349
Esmond, James 242
Espionage Act 385
Essay on the Antiquity of the
   Hindoo Medicine 231
Essay on the Principle of Population 201
Essenes 369
Esterhazy, Ferdinand 261
Ethelred II "the Unready," King of England 34
ether as anasthetic 241
Eton College 111
EUN 454

Euro 493, 496
Europe *see also names of countries*
   Beowulf 42
   Black Death 95–96
   Channel tunnel 483
   climate change 94
   European Econonomic Community 391
   European Union 475
   firearms 120
   Great Schism 36
   Marshall Plan 369
   opium use 120
   revolutions of 1848 229
   single currency 493, 496
   tobacco introduced to 143
   Warsaw pact 389–390
   World War I 300–305
Eustachian tubes 134
Eustachio, Bartolommeo 134
euthanasia 345
Eva Perón Foundation 386
Everest, Mount 337, 387, 448
evolution *see* creationism
evolutionary theory 248, 337–338
Expositions Universelle 246–247, 274, 292
Expressionism 310, 398–399
extinctions 502

F

Fabricius, Hieronymus 150
Fairbanks, Douglas 313, 335
Faisal II, King of Iraq 392
Fakhri sextant 103
falconry 79
Falkenhayn, Erich von 302
Falkirk, Scotland 69
Family, The (cult) 428
famines 94–95, 209
Fannin County, Texas 406
Faraday, Michael 230, 249
Fargo 488
Farnsworth, Philo T 361
Farooq Ahmed 499
Farouk I, King of Egypt 386
farthingale underskirt 128
Farynor, Thomas 164
fascism 324, *see also* Nazi Germany
fast food 404–405, 427
Fastnet Yacht Race disaster 449
Fatehpur Sikri, India 140
Faubus, Orval 391
Faulkner, Brian 430
Faust: der tragödie erster teil 218–219, 235–236
fauvism 290
Fawkes, Guy 158
Federal Republic of Germany *see* Germany
Ferdinand, Archduke of Austria 300
Fermi, Enrico 372–373

The Publisher would like to thank the following picture libraries and other copyright owners for permission to reproduce their images. Every attempt has been made to obtain permission for use of all images from the copyright owners, however, if any errors or omissions have occurred Millennium House would be pleased to hear from copyright owners.

KEY: (t) top of page; (b) bottom of page; (l) left side of page; (r) right side of page; (c) center of page.

Bridgeman Art Library, London:

Bibliotheque de la Faculte de Medecine, Paris, Archives Charmet: 38(l); Bibliotheque Nationale, Paris: 86(b); British Library, London: 103(c); British Museum, London: 41(r), 55(b), 58(c), 75(b), 130(r); Dinodia: 113(t); Fitzwilliam Museum, University of Cambridge: 70(c), 74(b); Giraudon: 124(r), 160(l); Jagiellonian Library, Cracow, Poland/ Giraudon: 41(c); Kunsthistorisches Museum, Vienna: 154(l); Louvre, Paris: 122(r); Mauritshuis, The Hague: 156(b); Museo Bardini, Florence: 97(r); Private Collection, © Philip Mould, Historical Portraits Ltd, London: 130(l); Santa Maria della Grazie, Milan: 109(b); School of African and Oriental Studies, London: 41(b); © Wallace Collection, London: 156(t).

Cathedral of Santiago de Compostela:

58(l); Cathedral of Santiago de Compostela / Dagli Orti; 57(l), 71(r), 71(c), 81(r); Cava dei Tirreni Abbey, Salerno / Dagli Orti: 61(b); Centre Jeanne d'Arc Orléans / Dagli Orti: 111(t); Chateau de Compiegne / Dagli Orti: 245(b); City of Manchester: 184(b); Courage Breweries / Eileen Tweedy: 204(b); Culver Pictures: 146(l), 175(t), 177(l), 177(b), 246(b), 256(b), 257(r), 259(b), 281(t), 283(b), 338(c), 371(t), 380(l), 383(b); Dagli Orti (A): 41(b), 50(c), 59(c), 81(b), 133(b), 145(t), 209(c), 228(t), 299(b), 327(l), 353(b), 362(b), 383(c); Dagli Orti: 56(l), 59(b), 62(l), 66(l), 74(c), 96(b), 109(c), 261(c), 333(l), 438(t), 439(b); Domenica del Corriere / Dagli Orti: 365(r), 365(b); Domenica del Corriere / Dagli Orti (A): 274(b), 277(l), 280(b), 283(t), 318(r); Eileen Tweedy: 128(t), 181(t), 183(r), 198(c), 199(b), 217(c), 229(b), 240(b), 254(b), 374(t); Eglise de Saint Germain, Saint Germain-en-Laye / Dagli Orti: 174(r); Egyptian Museum, Cairo / Dagli Orti: 320(c); Galleria d'Arte Moderna, Rome / Dagli Orti (A): 87(r); Galleria degli Uffizi, Florence / Dagli Orti: 151(r), 156(l); Galleria degli Uffizi, Florence / Dagli Orti (A): 90(c), 104(b), 108(b), 131(r), 171(b), 176(l); Galleria dell'Accademia, Florence / Dagli Orti: 122(b); Galleria Sabauda, Turin / Dagli Orti: 359(t); Genius of China Exhibition: 61(r); Geographical Society, Paris / Dagli Orti: 196(r); Gift of Boris Laver-Leonard / Museum of the City of New York / 57.317.1: 215(b); Gift of L.D. Levy / Museum of the City of New York / 67.109: 333(b); Gift of William F Davidson / Buffalo Bill Historical Center, Cody, Wyoming /

18.60: 180(c); Global Book Publishing: 207(c); Gripsholm Castle, Sweden / Dagli Orti (A): 180(l); Guildhall Library / Eileen Tweedy: 225(b); Harper Collins Publishers: 164(t), 206(t), 265(b); Historiska Muséet, Stockholm / Dagli Orti: 47(r); Imperial War Museum: 316(b), 348(t), 373(b), 381(b); J.A.Brooks/Jarrold / Jarrold Publishing: 165(b); Jarrold Publishing: 48(t); JFB: 93(t); John Meek: 201(l); John Webb: 115(b); Kandinsky Collection, Neuilly / Dagli Orti: 310(t); Kew Gardens Library / Eileen Tweedy: 145(c); Kobal Collection: 422(l); Kodaiji Temple, Kyoto / Laurie Platt Winfrey: 146(b); Kunsthistorisches Museum, Vienna: 138(b); Kunstmuseum, Bern / Dagli Orti: 245(r); Laurie Platt Winfrey: 53(r); Lucien Biton Collection, Paris / Dagli Orti: 190(b); Lund Cathedral, Sweden / Dagli Orti (A): 88(r); Marc Charmet: 217(b)

Getty Images, Sydney: Creative:

31(r), 117(r), 119(l), 124(b), 134(r), 139(b), 178(l), 181(r), 185(t), 186(l), 186(b), 187(r), 220(c), 224(l), 225(r); Creative/Ashmolean Museum, University of Oxford: 234(r); Creative/Bridgeman Art Library: 27(r), 234(b), 237(c), 237(b), 252(b), 265(l), 268(l), 270(l), 274(l), 291(t); Editorial: 25(r), 29(l), 30(b), 398(c), 405(r), 418(r), 419(l), 494(l), 494(t), 494(b), 495(l), 496(b), 497(t), 498(r), 499(t), 500(b), 502(l), 502(t), 503(r), 504(l), 505(t), 506(l), 507(b), 508(l), 508(b), 509(l), 510(l), 510(t), 510(b), 511(r); AFP: 25(l), 28(b), 292(l), 484(l), 493(r), 495(r), 497(r), 497(b), 499(r), 499(b), 500(l), 501(t), 501(r), 501(b), 502(b), 503(b), 505(r), 505(b), 506(r), 507(r), 508(r), 509(r), 509(b), 511(l), 511(b); Don Klumpp: 45(r); Hulton Archive: 1(c), 11(r), 24(l), 25(b), 27(b), 28(l), 29(r), 30(l), 31(b), 31(l), 34(l), 34(b), 35(c), 35(r), 35(b), 36(l), 37(r), 40(b), 44(l), 48(l), 49(r), 49(c), 49(b), 54(l), 57(r), 69(r), 69(c), 70(l), 73(r), 76(r), 77(c), 77(r), 79(r), 79(b), 87(t), 88(l), 89(r), 89(c), 90(l), 91(t), 92(l), 94(l), 95(r), 96(l), 98(t), 99(b), 101(r), 104(c), 105(r), 105(t), 105(b), 106(l), 109(r), 110(l), 113(c), 116(l), 116(b), 118(l), 119(r), 120(l), 121(r), 122(l), 123(r), 124(l), 125(b), 126(l), 127(r), 127(c), 128(l), 129(l), 134(l), 135(r), 137(r), 138(l), 139(l), 140(l), 142(l), 145(r), 149(r), 152(l), 152(b), 153(r), 155(r), 158(b), 160(b), 161(t), 163(b), 164(l), 164(b), 165(r), 166(l), 166(r), 166(b), 167(t), 167(r), 168(l), 168(t), 168(b), 169(r), 169(c), 172(b), 177(r), 182(l), 184(l), 184(c), 185(r), 185(b), 188(l), 188(b), 189(l), 190(l), 191(t), 191(r), 191(b), 192(l), 193(t), 193(r), 193(b), 194(l), 195(r), 195(b), 196(l), 197(r), 198(b), 199(l), 199(r), 200(l), 200(c), 200(b), 201(r), 202(l), 202(b), 203(r), 204(l), 205(t), 205(r), 206(l), 208(l), 210(t), 211(r), 212(t), 213(t), 213(r), 214(b), 215(r), 216(l), 216(r), 216(b), 217(r), 219(t), 219(r), 219(b), 220(b), 221(r), 222(l), 222(t), 223(r), 224(t), 228(l), 230(l), 231(l), 231(r), 231(c), 232(l), 233(t), 233(r), 233(b), 237(r), 238(l), 238(b), 239(b), 240(l), 240(c), 241(r), 242(l), 242(b), 243(r), 246(l), 247(b), 248(l), 248(b),

250(l), 252(l), 253(r), 254(l), 254(r), 255(r), 257(c), 258(l), 258(b), 259(t), 260(r), 261(b), 262(l), 262(t), 264(l), 264(b), 265(r), 266(t), 267(b), 272(l), 272(t), 272(b), 273(r), 273(b), 275(l), 278(l), 279(r), 280(l), 280(t), 281(r), 283(r), 284(l), 284(c), 285(r), 285(t), 286(b), 288(l), 290(l), 290(c), 290(b), 293(c), 294(l), 294(c), 295(l), 295(r), 296(t), 297(r), 297(c), 298(l), 299(r), 299(t), 300(l), 302(l), 302(t), 304(l), 304(b), 305(l), 306(r), 306(b), 307(r), 308(l), 308(r), 309(r), 309(t), 310(l), 312(l), 312(b), 313(r), 314(l), 314(b), 315(t), 315(r), 315(b), 316(t), 317(r), 317(t), 317(b), 318(l), 318(b), 319(r), 320(l), 320(b), 321(t), 321(r), 322(b), 323(r), 323(c), 323(l), 324(l), 324(b), 325(l), 326(l), 326(c), 327(r), 327(t), 328(l), 328(r), 329(r), 329(b), 330(l), 330(t), 331(r), 332(l), 332(b), 333(r), 334(l), 334(b), 335(t), 335(b), 336(l), 336(b), 337(r), 337(c), 338(l), 338(r), 338(b), 339(r), 340(l), 340(t), 340(b), 341(r), 341(b), 342(r), 342(b), 343(r), 343(c), 343(l), 344(l), 345(r), 346(l), 347(r), 347(t), 347(b), 349(r), 348(b), 348(l), 349(b), 350(l), 351(r), 351(b), 352(c), 352(b), 354(r), 354(b), 355(t), 355(b), 356(t), 357(r), 357(t), 357(l), 357(b), 358(l), 359(r), 360(l), 360(c), 361(l), 361(b), 362(l), 362(r), 363(r), 363(b), 366(t), 367(r), 367(b), 368(b), 369(t), 371(r), 372(l), 374(l), 374(b), 375(r), 376(c), 377(r), 377(b), 378(l), 378(r), 378(b), 379(r), 379(c), 380(b), 381(r), 382(l), 382(t), 382(b), 384(l), 384(t), 384(b), 385(r), 385(c), 385(b), 386(l), 387(l), 387(b), 388(t), 390(l), 390(b), 391(t), 391(b), 392(l), 394(l), 397(r), 397(b), 398(b), 399(r), 399(b), 400(l), 400(c), 400(b), 401(r), 402(l), 402(c), 404(l), 404(c), 405(t), 405(b), 406(b), 407(r), 407(c), 409(r), 409(t), 410(t), 411(r), 411(l), 412(b), 414(l), 414(t), 415(r), 415(b), 416(b), 418(l), 418(b), 419(t), 420(l), 420(r), 421(r), 421(b), 422(r), 422(b), 423(r), 423(b), 424(t), 425(c), 425(b), 426(l), 426(t), 427(r), 427(t), 427(b), 428(l), 428(b), 429(r), 429(b), 430(l), 430(t), 431(c), 431(b), 432(r), 432(b), 432(l), 433(b), 434(l), 434(t), 434(b), 435(b), 436(l), 436(c), 438(l), 438(b), 439(r), 440(l), 440(c), 441(r), 442(l), 442(t), 442(b), 443(r), 444(t), 444(b), 445(r), 445(l), 445(c), 446(l), 446(r), 446(b), 447(b), 448(l), 448(c), 449(r), 449(t), 449(b), 450(l), 451(r), 451(b), 452(l), 452(b), 454(l), 454(b), 455(r), 457(l), 459(r), 461(r), 462(t), 463(r), 463(c), 464(l), 464(b), 465(r), 465(t), 465(b), 466(l), 467(b), 467(c), 468(l), 468(b), 469(t), 470(l), 471(c), 473(r), 474(l), 474(t), 477(b), 480(l), 481(b), 481(c), 482(l), 482(b), 483(l), 487(r), 487(b), 489(c), 489(b), 490(b), 491(b), 504(b); National Geographic: 24(c), 29(c), 46(c); Philip Craven: 45(b); Roger Viollet: 26(l), 27(t), 43(b), 87(b), 104(l), 114(b), 144(l), 163(r), 218(b), 261(r), 287(r), 288(b), 308(b), 332(t), 352(l), 368(l), 395(r), 433(l), 478(l); Time & Life Pictures: 24(b), 26(t), 26(b), 30(r), 43(r), 46(l), 47(b), 55(l), 79(c), 135(t), 136(l), 140(b), 141(c), 157(r), 162(b), 174(c), 182(b), 192(r), 214(l), 223(b), 235(r), 238(t), 239(r), 256(c), 262(b), 263(r), 263(c), 267(t), 269(c), 271(r), 275(r), 276(l), 282(l), 282(b), 285(b), 288(r), 289(r), 293(r), 303(t), 303(r), 305(b), 306(l), 311(r),